THE ROUTLEDGE COMPANION TO PHILOSOPHY OF PSYCHOLOGY

The Routledge Companion to Philosophy of Psychology, Second Edition is an invaluable guide and major reference source to the key topics, problems, concepts, and debates in philosophy of psychology and is the first companion of its kind. A team of renowned international contributors provide forty-eight chapters, organized into six clear parts:

- Historical background to philosophy of psychology
- Psychological explanation
- Cognition and representation
- The biological basis of psychology
- Perceptual experience
- Personhood.

The Companion covers key topics, such as the origins of experimental psychology; folk psychology; behaviorism and functionalism; philosophy, psychology and neuroscience; the language of thought, modularity, nativism, and representational theories of mind; consciousness and the senses; dreams, emotion, and temporality; personal identity; and the philosophy of psychopathology.

For the second edition, six new chapters have been added to address the following important topics: belief and representation in nonhuman animals; prediction error minimization; contemporary neuroscience; plant neurobiology; epistemic judgment; and group cognition.

Essential reading for all students of philosophy of mind, science, and psychology, *The Routledge Companion to Philosophy of Psychology* will also be of interest to anyone studying psychology and its related disciplines.

Sarah Robins is Associate Professor of Philosophy and Director of Graduate Studies in the Department of Philosophy at the University of Kansas, USA.

John Symons is Professor of Philosophy in the Department of Philosophy at the University of Kansas, USA.

Paco Calvo is Professor of Logic and Philosophy of Science at the University of Murcia, Spain, and Principal Investigator of the Minimal Intelligence Lab (MINT Lab).

Routledge Philosophy Companions

Routledge Philosophy Companions offer thorough, high quality surveys and assessments of the major topics and periods in philosophy. Covering key problems, themes and thinkers, all entries are specially commissioned for each volume and written by leading scholars in the field. Clear, accessible and carefully edited and organised, *Routledge Philosophy Companions* are indispensable for anyone coming to a major topic or period in philosophy, as well as for the more advanced reader.

Also available:

The Routledge Companion to the Philosophy of Race
Edited by Paul C Taylor, Linda Martín Alcoff, Luvell Anderson

The Routledge Companion to Bioethics
Edited by John Arras, Rebecca Kukla, and Elizabeth Fenton

The Routledge Companion to Islamic Philosophy
Edited by Richard C. Taylor and Luis Xavier López-Farjeat

The Routledge Companion to Ancient Philosophy
Edited by Frisbee Sheffield and James Warren

The Routledge Companion to Virtue Ethics
Edited by Lorraine Besser-Jones and Michael Slote

The Routledge Companion to Shakespeare and Philosophy
Edited by Craig Bourne, Emily Caddick Bourne

The Routledge Companion to the Frankfurt School
Edited by Peter E. Gordon, Espen Hammer, Axel Honneth

The Routledge Companion to Feminist Philosophy
Edited by Ann Garry, Serene J. Khader, and Alison Stone

The Routledge Companion to Philosophy of Psychology, Second Edition
Edited by Sarah Robins, John Symons, and Paco Calvo

For more information about this series, please visit:
www.routledge.com/Routledge-Philosophy-Companions/book-series/PHILCOMP

Praise for the first edition:

"This work should serve as the standard reference for those interested in gaining a reliable overview of the burgeoning field of philosophical psychology. Summing Up: Essential."

– *CHOICE*

"If someone were to ask me to select a book to be placed in a cornerstone or time capsule to be opened 100 years hence, this book would be on my short list, for it will offer the intellectual historian working in 2110 a clear view of how the mind of our time is understood."

– *Contemporary Psychology: APA Review of Books*

"In sum, *The Routledge Companion to Philosophy of Psychology* provides a helpful survey of the issues that define one of today's hottest areas of philosophical research. . . . The entries are clear, engaging, and balanced, and the companion is, on the whole, a welcome research tool for graduate students and professionals seeking to enrich their understanding of foundational issues in cognitive science."

– *David Pereplyotchik, Metapsychology Online Reviews*

"The essays here, by outstanding scholars in philosophy of psychology, are exemplary for their theoretical sophistication, informative explanations of empirical work, and balanced overviews of relevant research areas. Nobody interested in philosophy of psychology will want to be without this excellent volume."

– *David Rosenthal, City University, New York, USA*

"This collection provides an exceptionally wide-ranging review of recent advances and theoretical disputes in psychology, and closely related issues in evolutionary biology and neuroscience. It reflects philosophical sophistication, scientific expertise, and historical sensitivity."

– *Margaret Boden, University of Sussex, UK*

"This is a highly useful and timely collection of essays by philosophers who consider advances in cognitive neuroscience and their relevance for the philosophy of mind. This is a compendium that will help connect the two cultures and I enthusiastically endorse this volume to both communities."

– *Howard Eichenbaum, Boston University, USA*

"An excellent collection of new essays, many by major contributors to the literature. No library or individual interested in current work in the philosophy of psychology should wish to be without it."

– *George Graham, Georgia State University, USA*

THE ROUTLEDGE COMPANION TO PHILOSOPHY OF PSYCHOLOGY

Second Edition

Edited by
Sarah Robins, John Symons, and Paco Calvo

LONDON AND NEW YORK

Second edition published 2020
by Routledge
2 Park Square, Milton Park, Abingdon, Oxon OX14 4RN

and by Routledge
52 Vanderbilt Avenue, New York, NY 10017

Routledge is an imprint of the Taylor & Francis Group, an informa business

First edition published by Routledge 2009

British Library Cataloguing-in-Publication Data
A catalogue record for this book is available from the British Library

Library of Congress Cataloging-in-Publication Data
Names: Robins, Sarah, editor. | Symons, John (John Francis), editor. | Calvo, Paco, editor.
Title: The Routledge companion to philosophy of psychology / edited by Sarah Robins, John Symons, and Paco Calvo.
Description: Second edition. | Abingdon, Oxon ; New York, NY : Routledge, Taylor & Francis Group, 2020. | Includes bibliographical references and index.
Identifiers: LCCN 2019015260 | ISBN 9781138855410 (hardback : alk. paper) | ISBN 9780367336790 (pbk. : alk. paper) | ISBN 9780429244629 (e-book)
Subjects: LCSH: Psychology—Philosophy. | MESH: Psychological Theory. | Philosophy.
Classification: LCC BF38 .R68 2020 | DDC 150.1—dc23
LC record available at https://lccn.loc.gov/2019015260

ISBN: 978-1-138-85541-0 (hbk)
ISBN: 978-0-367-33679-0 (pbk)
ISBN: 978-0-429-24462-9 (ebk)

Typeset in Goudy
by Apex CoVantage, LLC

CONTENTS

CONTRIBUTORS

Fred Adams is Professor of Linguistics and Cognitive Science at the University of Delaware. He publishes in the areas of epistemology, philosophy of mind, philosophy of language, and philosophy of science.

Ken Aizawa is Professor of Philosophy at Rutgers University. He is the author of *The Systematicity Arguments* and, with Fred Adams, *The Bounds of Cognition*. He has co-edited with Carl Gillett *Scientific Composition and Metaphysical Ground*.

Kristin Andrews is York Research Chair in Animal Minds and Professor of Philosophy at York University. She is currently working on problems in folk psychology and theory of mind, the evolution of morality, and animal ethics.

Anthony P. Atkinson (DPhil) is Associate Professor of Psychology at Durham University. He previously held a lectureship in psychology at King Alfred's College Winchester (now the University of Winchester). Originally from New Zealand, Dr. Atkinson completed his doctorate in psychological sciences at the University of Oxford. While maintaining his more philosophical interests, his research efforts are now principally devoted to experimental investigations of the psychological and neural processes underlying social perception, including the perception of emotion from faces and from body postures and movement.

Valtteri Arstila is Collegium Researcher at the Turku Institute for Advanced Studies and the Department of Philosophy and a member of the Consciousness Research Group in the Department of Psychology, University of Turku. His research interests are mainly in philosophy of psychology and philosophy of mind. Currently, his research focuses on issues concerning the philosophy and psychology of subjective time, the theories of time consciousness, cognitive penetration of perceptual experiences, and the prerequisites of strong artificial intelligence.

Tim Bayne completed an undergraduate degree in philosophy at the University of Otago and a PhD in philosophy at the University of Arizona. He has taught at Macquarie University, the University of Western Ontario, the University of Manchester, and the University of Oxford. He is currently Professor of Philosophy at Monash University. He is an editor of *The Oxford Companion to Consciousness* and the author of *The Unity of Consciousness* (Oxford University Press, 2010), *Thought:*

A Very Short Introduction (Oxford University Press, 2013), and *Philosophy of Religion: A Very Short Introduction* (Oxford University Press, 2018).

William Bechtel is Professor of Philosophy and a faculty member in the Center for Circadian Biology and the Interdisciplinary Program in Cognitive Science at the University of California, San Diego. His research explores issues in the philosophy of the life sciences. Among his published books are *Discovering Complexity: Decomposition and Localization as Strategies in Scientific Research* (coauthor Robert Richardson, 1993/2010); *Mental Mechanisms: Philosophical Perspectives on Cognitive Neuroscience* (2008); *Discovering Cell Mechanisms: The Creation of Modern Cell Biology* (2006); and *Connectionism and the Mind: Parallel Processing, Dynamics, and Evolution in Networks* (coauthor Adele Abrahamsen, 1991/2002).

Mark H. Bickhard received his BS in mathematics, MS in statistics, and PhD in human development from the University of Chicago. He taught at the University of Texas at Austin for eighteen years before joining Lehigh University in 1990 as Henry R. Luce Professor in Cognitive Robotics and the Philosophy of Knowledge. He is affiliated with the Departments of Philosophy and Psychology and is Director of the Institute for Interactivist Studies. He was Director of Cognitive Science from 1992 through 2003 and of the Complex Systems Research Group from 1999 through 2005. His work focuses on the nature and development of persons as biological, psychological, and social beings. This work has generated an integrated organization of models encompassing "the whole person," which is the tentative title for a book in preparation.

John Bickle is Professor of Philosophy and Adjunct Professor of Psychology at Mississippi State University. He is also Affiliated Faculty in the Department of Neurobiology and Anatomical Sciences at the University of Mississippi Medical Center. He is the author of *Psychoneural Reduction: The New Wave* (1998), *Philosophy and Neuroscience: A Ruthlessly Reductive Account* (2003), *Understanding Scientific Reasoning*, 5th edition (coauthors Ronald Giere and Robert Mauldin, 2005), and *Engineering the Next Revolution in Neuroscience* (coauthors Alcino J. Silva and Anthony Landreth), and he edited the *Oxford Handbook for Philosophy and Neuroscience* (2009, 2012). He is also the author of more than eighty articles and book chapters in philosophy and neuroscience journals, volumes, and collections. His research interests include philosophy of neuroscience, scientific reductionism, and cellular and molecular mechanisms of cognition and consciousness. Most recently he has begun to study the development of experiment tools in neurobiology and implications these practices hold for the role of theory in wet-lab sciences.

David Braddon-Mitchell is Professor of Philosophy at the University of Sydney. He was previously at the University of Auckland and Research Fellow at the Australian National University. He is the author of articles in leading philosophy journals, including *The Journal of Philosophy*, *Nous*, *Mind*, *The British Journal for Philosophy* *of Science*, *Philosophical Studies*, *Philosophy and Phenomenological Review*, *Synthese*, *Erkenntnis*, *Analysis*, *The Monist*, *Ration*, *The Journal of Political Philosophy*, and the *Australasian Journal of Philosophy*. He is the author, with Frank Jackson, of *The Philosophy of Mind and Cognition*. He works in philosophy of mind, metaphysics, and philosophy of psychology and occasionally crosses borders into philosophy of science, philosophy of biology, metaethics, and political philosophy.

Paco Calvo is Professor of Logic and Philosophy of Science at the University of Murcia, where he is Primary Investigator of the Minimal Intelligence Lab (MINT Lab). He publishes in the areas of philosophy of cognitive science and philosophy of plant neurobiology.

Jonathan Cohen is Professor of Philosophy and faculty member of the Interdisciplinary Cognitive Science Program at the University of California, San Diego. Before coming to UC San Diego, he was a Killam Postdoctoral Fellow in the Department of Philosophy at the University of British Columbia. He earned his PhD in philosophy at Rutgers University. He has published extensively in philosophy of perception (particularly on color and on informational interactions within and between perceptual modalities) and philosophy of language (especially on issues about context sensitivity and the semantics/pragmatics interface). He is the author of *The Red and the Real: An Essay on Color Ontology* (Oxford University Press, 2009) and co-editor of *Color Ontology and Color Science* (with Mohan Matthen, MIT Press, 2010) and *Contemporary Debates in the Philosophy of Mind* (with Brian McLaughlin, Wiley-Blackwell, 2007).

Carl F. Craver is Professor of Philosophy in the Department of Philosophy and the Philosophy-Neuroscience-Psychology (PNP) Program at Washington University in St. Louis. He is the author of *Explaining the Brain: Mechanisms and the Mosaic Unity of Neuroscience* (Clarenden Press) and (with Lindley Darden) of *The Search for Mechanisms: Discoveries across the Biomedical Sciences*, as well as several articles on the philosophy and history of neuroscience.

David Danks is L. L. Thurstone Professor of Philosophy and Psychology and Head of the Department of Philosophy at Carnegie Mellon University. He is also an adjunct member of the Heinz College of Information Systems and Public Policy and the Center for the Neural Basis of Cognition. His research interests are at the intersection of philosophy, cognitive science, and machine learning, using ideas, methods, and frameworks from each to advance our understanding of complex, interdisciplinary problems. Danks has done significant research in computational cognitive science, including his book *Unifying the Mind: Cognitive Representations as Graphical Models* (2014, The MIT Press). Danks received a McDonnell Foundation Scholar Award and an Andrew Carnegie Fellowship.

Frederick Eberhardt is Professor of Philosophy at California Institute of Technology (Caltech). Before coming to Caltech he was Assistant Professor in the PNP

Program and the Department of Philosophy at Washington University in St. Louis. He holds a PhD in philosophy from Carnegie Mellon University and was a James S. McDonnell Postdoctoral Fellow with Alison Gopnik in the Institute of Cognitive and Brain Science at the University of California, Berkeley. His research interests are in causal learning and the foundations of probability.

Edward Erwin was educated at the City College of New York and at Johns Hopkins University, where he received his PhD. He joined the University of Miami Philosophy Department in 1974 after teaching at the State University of New York at Stony Brook. He is the author of four books: *The Concept of Meaninglessness* (1971), *Behavior Therapy: Scientific, Philosophical and Moral Foundations* (1978), *A Final Accounting: Philosophical and Empirical Issues in Freudian Psychology* (1996), and *Philosophy and Psychotherapy: Razing the Troubles of the Brain* (1997), as well as articles in the philosophy of science, epistemology, philosophy of language, and philosophy of psychology. He is also a co-editor of *Ethical Issues in Scientific Research* (1994). He was recipient of the Excellence in Teaching Award from the State University of New York at Stony Brook; is the 1998 Matchette Lecturer, Loras Collage; and is editor-in-chief of *The Freud Encyclopedia: Theories, Therapy, and Culture* (2002).

Jordi Fernández is Associate Professor in Philosophy at the University of Adelaide. His research interests include epistemology, metaphysics, and the philosophy of mind. He is the author of *Transparent Minds: A Study of Self-Knowledge* (2013) and *Memory: A Self-Referential Account* (in press).

Owen Flanagan is James B. Duke Professor of Philosophy, Professor of Psychology and Neuroscience, and Professor of Neurobiology at Duke University, where he is also codirector of the Center for Comparative Philosophy. His most recent book is *The Geography of Morals* (Oxford 2017).

Alan Garnham studied psychology and philosophy at Oxford University, before completing a DPhil in experimental psycholinguistics at the University of Sussex, in which he developed the notion of mental models of discourse. Since completing his DPhil he has worked mainly at the University of Sussex, where he became Professor of Experimental Psychology in 1999. He has a continuing interest in cognitive science in general and psycholinguistics in particular.

Verena Gottschling is Associate Professor in the Department of Philosophy, York University. She works in the philosophy of cognitive science and the philosophy of mind and psychology, with special interest in cognitive architecture, emotions and affective states, non-linguistic elements in cognitive processes and reasoning, and central cognitive capacities.

Rick Grush is Full Professor of Philosophy at University of California, San Diego, and is the founder and former director of the UCSD Summer Program for

Women in Philosophy. His research focuses on the nature of perception and mental representation.

Valerie Gray Hardcastle is Vice-President for Health Innovation and St. Elizabeth Healthcare Executive Director of the Institute for Health Innovation at Northern Kentucky University. Currently the editor-in-chief for the *Journal of Consciousness Studies* and the author of five books and more than 170 essays, she studies the nature and structure of interdisciplinary theories in cognitive science and has focused primarily on developing a philosophical framework for understanding conscious phenomena responsive to neuroscientific and psychological data. In addition to more traditional issues in philosophy of mind, she is also interest in how (and whether) psychological phenomena (such as consciousness, memory, perception) relate to underlying neurophysiology, what these relations tell us about the mind, ourselves as cognitive creatures, and what this should mean for public policy and law.

Gary Hatfield teaches philosophy at the University of Pennsylvania. He has published *The Natural and the Normative: Theories of Spatial Perception from Kant to Helmholtz* (1990) and *Descartes' Meditations* (2014), as well as many articles and chapters on seventeenth-century philosophy and on the philosophy and history of psychology. He translated Kant's *Prolegomena* (second edition, 2004). Some of his essays have been collected in *Perception and Cognition: Essays in the Philosophy of Psychology* (2009). He edited, with Sarah Allred, *Visual Experience: Sensation, Cognition, and Constancy* (2012) and, with Holly Pittman, *The Evolution of Mind, Brain, and Culture* (2013).

Manuel Heras-Escribano is a Juan de la Cierva-Formación Research Fellow at the University of the Basque Country. He has been a postdoctoral researcher at the University of Granada, Spain, and the Alberto Hurtado University, Chile. His work focuses on the philosophy of the embodied and situated cognitive sciences.

William Hirstein is Professor of Philosophy at Elmhurst College. He is the author of several books, including *Brain Fiction: Self-Deception and the Riddle of Confabulation* (2005), *Mindmelding: Consciousness, Neuroscience, and the Mind's Privacy* (2012), and, with Katrina Sifferd and Tyler Fagan, *Responsible Brains: Neuroscience, Law, and Human Culpability* (2018).

Jakob Hohwy is Professor of Philosophy at Monash University. He leads the Cognition & Philosophy Lab, which conducts research in philosophy of neuroscience and experimental cognitive science. The focus of his research is theoretical neurobiology, predictive processing, and consciousness. He has published widely in philosophy, psychology, and neuroscience and is the author of *The Predictive Mind* (OUP, 2013).

Brian L. Keeley is Professor of Philosophy at Pitzer College. He works at the intersection of philosophy of science and neurobiology. He is the editor of *Paul Churchland*

(Contemporary Philosophy in Focus) (2005). He has published a number of papers, including two in *The Journal of Philosophy*: "Making Sense of the Senses: Individuating Modalities in Humans and Other Animals" and "Of Conspiracy Theories."

Daniel Kelly is Associate Professor in the Philosophy Department at Purdue University. He received his BA in philosophy and English literature from Illinois Wesleyan University, an MA from Tufts University, and his PhD from Rutgers University. His research focuses on issues at the intersection of philosophy of mind and cognitive science, moral theory, and evolution. His book *Yuck! The Nature and Moral Significance of Disgust* (MIT Press, 2011) brings together evolutionary and ethical perspectives on disgust, and he has published on moral judgment, norms, racial cognition, implicit bias, cross-cultural diversity, and David Foster Wallace and free will. He has been a Mellon Fellow at the Center for Advanced Study in the Behavioral Sciences at Stanford University and is a founding member of the Moral Psychology Research Group. He is also is a member of the Cultural Evolution Society and the Building Sustainable Communities group at Purdue's Center for the Environment. He likes a good argument.

Alex Kiefer is a PhD in philosophy from the CUNY Graduate Center. His research is mainly in the philosophy of mind, with heavy influence from machine learning and cognitive psychology.

Alan Kim teaches philosophy at the State University of New York at Stony Brook. His publications on philosophical psychology include articles on Paul Natorp in the *Internationale Zeitschrift für Philosophie* and the *Stanford Encyclopedia of Philosophy*, as well as entries on Wilhelm Wundt and J. F. Herbart in the *Stanford Encyclopedia*. He is the author of *Plato in Germany: Kant – Natorp – Heidegger* (2010) and the editor of *Brill's Companion to German Platonism* (2019).

Aarre Laakso earned his PhD in cognitive science and philosophy at the University of California, San Diego, with Pat Churchland and Gary Cottrell. He subsequently did postdoctoral work with Linda Smith in the Department of Psychological and Brain Sciences at Indiana University and served as Adjunct Professor in the Department of Behavioral Sciences at the University of Michigan – Dearborn. While he has broad interest in questions at the intersections of philosophy, psychology, linguistics, and computer science, his research focuses on first-language acquisition and the structure of semantic memory.

Sarah Beth Lesson is a philosophy instructor at Santa Rosa Junior College. When not in the classroom, she works on puzzles related to self-knowledge and self-deception.

Arthur B. Markman is Annabel Irion Worsham Centennial Professor of Psychology and Marketing at the University of Texas at Austin and director of the IC2 Institute. He has written over 150 scholarly papers on topics including reasoning, decision-making, motivation, and knowledge representation. He is the author of several books, including *Knowledge Representation*, *Smart Thinking*, and *Bring Your Brain to Work*.

Raymond Martin (PhD, University of Rochester, 1968) is Research Professor of Philosophy at Union College. He is also Professor Emeritus, University of Maryland, College Park, where he taught for thirty years. His main areas of research have been on the philosophy of historical methodology and on issues having to do with the self, personal identity, and what matters in survival. His books, some coauthored or coedited, include *The Rise and Fall of Soul and Self* (2006), *Personal Identity* (2003), *Naturalization of the Soul* (2000), *Self-Concern* (1998), *Self and Identity* (1991), and *The Past Within Us* (1989).

Alfred R. Mele is William H. and Lucyle T. Werkmeister Professor of Philosophy at Florida State University. He is the author of twelve books and over two hundred articles and an editor of six books. He is past director of two multi-million dollar interdisciplinary projects: the Big Questions in Free Will project (2010–13) and the Philosophy and Science of Self-Control project (2014–17).

Christopher Mole is Professor of Philosophy and Chair of the Programme in Cognitive Systems at the University of British Columbia. He is the author of *Attention is Cognitive Unison* (Oxford University Press, 2010) and of *The Unexplained Intellect* (Routledge, 2016) and coauthor, with Daniel Lafleur and Holly Onclin, of *Understanding Mental Disorders* (Routledge, 2019).

Jennifer Nado is Assistant Professor of Philosophy at the University of Hong Kong. She works on issues surrounding experimental philosophy, intuition, and philosophical methodology. She has published on these topics in journals such as *Philosophy and Phenomenological Research*, *Philosophical Studies*, the *Australasian Journal of Philosophy*, and the *British Journal for the Philosophy of Science*.

Jennifer Nagel is Professor of Philosophy at the University of Toronto. Her research focuses on the distinction between knowledge and belief and on what we can learn about these states by studying the ways in which they are instinctively and reflectively attributed.

Shaun Nichols is Professor of Philosophy at the University of Arizona. He has published widely at the intersection of philosophy and psychology. He is the author of *Sentimental Rules: On the Natural Foundations of Moral Judgment* and the coauthor (with Stephen Stich) of *Mindreading: An Integrated Account of Pretence, Self-awareness, and Understanding Other Minds*.

Casey O'Callaghan is Professor of Philosophy at Washington University in St. Louis. He is the author of *Sounds: A Philosophical Theory* (2007), *Beyond Vision: Philosophical Essays* (2017), and *A Multisensory Philosophy of Perception* (2019).

Thomas W. Polger is Professor of Philosophy at the University of Cincinnati. His work focuses on the ontology of mental states and processes and spans philosophy of mind, philosophy of science, and metaphysics. He is the author of numerous articles and *Natural Minds* (2004) and coauthor with Lawrence A. Shapiro of *The Multiple Realization Book* (2016).

Ian Ravenscroft is Associate Professor of Philosophy at Flinders University. He is coauthor (with Gregory Currie) of *Recreative Minds: Imagination in Philosophy and Psychology* (2002), author of *Philosophy of Mind: A Beginner's Guide* (2005), and editor of *Minds, Ethics, and Conditionals: The Philosophy of Frank Jackson* (2008). He is presently working on a project that applies current research in the philosophy of psychology to understanding the beliefs and motivations of terrorists.

Hendrik Reimann is currently a post-doc in the CoBal Lab in the Kinesiology and Applied Physiology Department at the University of Delaware. Hendrik studies how humans maintain balance during walking. He induces artificial sensations of falls in people by electrically stimulating the vestibular system or moving a projected visual scene. Hendrik started in academia as a mathematician; got a PhD in theoretical neuroscience at Ruhr-University Bochum, Germany; and became an experimental neuroscientist with a focus on neural control of movement. Hendrik is currently combining experimental and computational modeling approaches to study how the brain regulates balance during human walking.

Mark Rowlands (DPhil, Oxford University) is Professor of Philosophy at the University of Miami. He is the author of nineteen books, translated into more than twenty languages, and over a hundred journal articles, book chapters, and reviews. His work in the philosophy of mind comprises several books, including *The Body in Mind* (Cambridge Uuniversity Press, 1999), *The Nature of Consciousness* (Cambridge University Press, 1999), *Externalism* (Acumen 2003), *Body Language* (MIT Press 2006), *The New Science of the Mind* (MIT Press 2010), *Memory and the Self* (Oxford University Press 2016), and *Can Animals Be Persons?* (Oxford University Press 2019). His work in ethics and moral psychology includes *Animal Rights* (Macmillan 1998), *The Environmental Crisis* (Macmillan, 2000), *Animals Like Us* (Verso, 2002), *Can Animals Be Moral?* (Oxford University Press 2012), *Animal Rights: All That Matters* (Hodder 2013), and *A Good Life* (Granta 2015). His memoir, *The Philosopher and the Wolf* (Granta, 2008), became an international bestseller.

Kevin Ryan is a philosophy PhD student at the University of Memphis. His primary research interests are in philosophy of mind, philosophy of cognitive science, and aesthetics, particularly music. He was the action editor for a special issue of *Empirical Musicology Review* (2014; Vol. 9, No.3) on music and embodied cognition.

Dan Ryder is Associate Professor of Philosophy at the Barber School of Arts and Sciences, University of British Columbia. His areas of research range broadly within analytic philosophy, with special emphasis on philosophy of mind, metaphysics, and philosophy of science. He has also collaborated with Oleg Favorov on some work in theoretical neuroscience and has a book forthcoming titled *Models in the Brain*.

Richard Samuels is Professor of Philosophy at The Ohio State University. His primary area of research is the philosophy of psychology, and he has published extensively on various topics in the foundations of cognitive science, including the modularity of mind, computational theories of mind, the notion of innateness, and the philosophical implications of empirical research on reasoning. He is currently writing a book on number concepts.

Marya Schechtman is Professor of Philosophy at the University of Illinois at Chicago, where she is also a member of the Laboratory of Integrative Neuroscience. She is the author of *The Constitution of Selves* (1996) and *Staying Alive: Personal Identity, Practical Concerns, and the Unity of a Life* (2014), as well as numerous articles on personal identity. Her current research is on the connection between practical and metaphysical questions of personal identity.

Susan Schneider is Associate Professor of Philosophy and Cognitive Science at the University of Connecticut, a Distinguished Scholar at the Library of Congress, a fellow at the Institute for Advanced Study at Princeton University, and a member of the Ethics and Technology Group at the Yale Interdisciplinary Center for Bioethics. She writes about the fundamental nature of the self and mind, especially from the vantage point of issues in philosophy, artificial intelligence, and astrobiology. The topics she has written about most recently include radical brain enhancement, spacetime emergence, superintelligence, the nature of life, whether minds are in some sense programs, panpsychism, and the nature of the self. She has been featured in *The New York Times*,*Science*, *Nautilus*, *Smithsonian*, *Discover*, PBS, *National Geographic TV*, *The History Channel* and more.

Gregor Schöner is Director of the Institute for Neural Computation and Chair for Theory of Cognitive Systems at the Ruhr-University Bochum. For the last thirty years, Gregor Schöner has brought to bear his background in nonlinear dynamics on problems in motor control, perception, embodied cognition, and motor and cognitive development. He has held academic positions in the US, France, and Germany and has published over 250 scientific articles.

Amanda J. C. Sharkey completed her PhD in psycholinguistics in 1989 at University of Essex. Since then she conducted research in neural computing at University of Exeter, before moving to University of Sheffield, where she has been Senior Lecturer in the Department of Computer Science. She has investigated methods of combining neural nets and other estimators, and her current research interests are robot ethics and the issues raised by robot care of older people and children. She has over one hundred publications. She was a founding member of the scientific committee for the international series of workshops on multiple classifier systems and is an associate editor of the journal *Connection Science* and a member of the executive advisory board of the *Foundation for Responsible Robotics*.

Noel Sharkey is Emeritus Professor of Artificial Intelligence and Robotics and Professor of Public Engagement in the Department of Computer Science at the University of Sheffield; Chair of the International Committee for Robot Arms Control; and codirector of the Foundation for Responsible Robotics. He has held a number of research and teaching positions in the United Kingdom (Essex, Exeter, Sheffield) and the United States (Yale, Stanford, Berkeley). He has published more than two hundred academic articles and books in addition to editing several journal special issues on modern robotics. His main research interests are now in biologically inspired robotics, cognitive processes, history of automata (from ancient times to present), human-robot interaction and communication, representations of emotion, and machine learning. Now he is an advocate, campaigner, and writer focusing on the ethical/legal and societal impact of technology and the use of AI and robotics in warfare.

Stephen Stich is Professor of Philosophy at Rutgers University. His philosophical interests are in the philosophy of mind, cognitive science, epistemology, experimental philosophy, and moral psychology. His books include *From Folk Psychology to Cognitive Science* (1983), *The Fragmentation of Reason* (1990), and *Deconstructing the Mind* (1996), *Mindreading* (coauthored with Shaun Nichols) (2003), *Mind and Language: Collected Papers, Vol* 1(2011), and *Knowledge, Rationality and Morality: Collected Papers, Vol. 2*, (2012).

John Sutton is Professor of Cognitive Science at Macquarie University. He is author of *Philosophy and Memory Traces: Descartes to Connectionism* and co-editor most recently of *Embodied Cognition and Shakespeare's Theatre: the early modern body-mind* (2014) and *Collaborative Remembering: theories, research, and applications* (2018). His recent publications address skilled movement, distributed cognition, and social memory. He was first President of ASPP, the Australasian Society for Philosophy and Psychology, which held its first conference in 2018.

Brandon Tinklenberg is a Phd candidate in philosophy at York University. He is currently working on issues relating to folk psychology and the evolution of cognition.

Deborah Tollefsen is Professor of Philosophy at the University of Memphis. Her research and teaching interests include the philosophy of mind, epistemology, and collective intentionality. Her book *Groups as Agents* was published in 2015.

Michael Wheeler is Professor of Philosophy at the University of Stirling. Before this he held teaching and research posts at the Universities of Dundee, Oxford, and Stirling. His doctoral work was carried out at the University of Sussex. His primary research interests are in philosophy of science (especially cognitive science, psychology and artificial intelligence) and philosophy of mind, with his recent work focusing on the nature of, and the prospects for, 4E (embodied-embedded-extended-enactive) cognition. His book, *Reconstructing the Cognitive World: the Next Step*, was published in 2005.

Cory D. Wright is Professor of Philosophy at California State University, Long Beach, and is the Director of Graduate Studies for the College of Liberal Arts. Among recent publications is *Recipes for Science* (coauthored with Matteo Colombo and Angela Potochnik).

Jessica Wright is a doctoral student in philosophy at the University of Toronto. Her thesis examines the question of how mental states reflect upon the person who has them, with a particular focus on beliefs and implicit attitudes.

INTRODUCTION TO THE SECOND EDITION

Sarah Robins, John Symons, and Paco Calvo

In this introduction, we describe some of the prominent characteristics of the second edition of *The Routledge Companion to Philosophy of Psychology* and explain how it reflects the current state of the field. The editors of the first edition observed in their introduction that philosophy of psychology had changed significantly since its origins in the late 1970s and early 1980s. Specifically, they noted that the *Routledge Companion* stood in sharp contrast with Ned Block's classic anthology *Readings in Philosophy of Psychology* of thirty years earlier. The differences between these two books signaled the changed character, as well as the dramatic expansion, of the sub-discipline. A decade has now passed between the first and second editions of this Companion. Philosophy of psychology continues to change, with perhaps the most significant development in the intervening years being the blending of work from other sub-disciplines in productive ways.

Ten years ago it was necessary to provide some justification for the shift away from solely focusing on questions of rationality, modularity, nativism, and intentionality. The editors argued that this focus was not exhaustive of topics in this area. A decade later it no longer seems necessary to justify the increased attention to the broad range of topics that fall under the purview of philosophy of psychology. In this second edition we continue to expand the range of topics under consideration and also hope to reflect the increased sophistication of contemporary research. For example, today we find an increasingly nuanced understanding of nonhuman cognitive capacities and a richer appreciation of nonhuman mental lives. Even ten years ago it would have been necessary to argue that animals had mental life, and whether that argument could extend to plants was rarely considered. Today, we see active research programs into the cognitive capacities of a range of nonhuman animals – plants, microorganisms, and even parts of the brain. Similarly, the recent work on group cognition points in directions that would have been alien to traditional philosophy of psychology. Other forms of expansion in the field are reflected in the addition of chapters on predictive processing, group cognition, and the psychology of epistemic judgment. We have also added a substantial review of recent philosophy of neuroscience.

We continue to believe that appreciation of the major positions that frame current debates is improved by attending to the historical development of the relevant concepts and methods, as we do in Part I of this *Companion*. Ten years ago the editors received some pushback for giving such prominence to historical research. Today, it seems much more natural for philosophers of psychology to be attentive to the history of their enterprise. In this spirit, Part I remains unchanged, presenting the necessary historical background for the discussions that follow. It provides a selective tour of the relevant history of psychology and philosophy, moving from the origins of psychology in early-modern philosophy to twentieth-century debates between behaviorists and cognitivists. As the field continues to expand, we can confidently predict deeper engagement with the historical roots of the topics covered in this volume and possible interest in expanding the historical content included.

Part II explores the nature of psychological explanation and its relationship to various models of mental life. In the early 1980s, philosophers of psychology had settled into a consensus with respect to the demise of behaviorism and the centrality of cognitivist architectures. This model assumed a functionalist metaphysical framework, a computationalist approach to explanation, and a central role for representation. Part II reflects developments in the intervening years, by presenting the more critical contemporary approach to psychological explanation, folk psychology, and functionalism. Alternative explanatory frameworks to cognitivism are explained and defended in detail. Connectionism and the embodied/embedded framework not only represent novel approaches to cognitive architecture but also present fundamental challenges to the cognitivist views of psychological explanation. This plurality of explanatory frameworks is one of the hallmarks of contemporary philosophy of psychology.

Part III reviews the well-known cluster of questions related to the nature of cognition and representation. The problems addressed here relate to both the architecture within which representational states are couched and the possibility of naturalizing content. For the most part, these essays fall close to the subject matter of mainstream debates in the philosophy of mind. However, as described in Part III, philosophers of psychology have also challenged the foundational assumptions that govern these debates. One of the central concerns in the recent philosophy has been the difficulty of accounting for intentionality. Despite a variety of new metaphors and scientific developments, many of the traditional problems continue to be relevant. So, for example, whether psychological inquiry converges on a theory where minds are understood as symbol-manipulating machines, as statistically driven networks, or as embodied-embedded systems, it still faces the philosophical problem of accounting for the role of representation in psychology. Whether one denies the reality of representation along behaviorist lines or rests one's account on some variant of cognitivism or its alternatives, the difficulty of explaining (or explaining away) the role of representation remains. A central venue for debates of this kind involves reflection on the behavior and capacities of nonhuman agents. To reflect this, we have added a chapter on comparative cognition and representation, by Sarah Beth Lesson, Brandon Tinklenberg, and Kristin Andrews. We have also included a chapter on predictive processing, from Alex Kiefer and Jakob Hohwy, which reflects the increased interest in this alternative framework for characterizing cognition and representation.

Part IV reviews the principal problems that emerge from consideration of the relationship between psychology and its biological basis. The early days of computational functionalism encouraged philosophers to consider the choice of theories independently of the details of implementation. For philosophers of psychology the biological facts of cognition were more difficult to ignore. In recent decades, philosophy of psychology has moved away from a view that downplayed the significance of biological structures and constraints in the development of psychological theories. Techniques and insights from neuroscience have moved to the heart of psychological investigation. Philosophers have taken note of the import of the neurosciences. So, for example, modern theories concerning cognitive architecture and the nature of representation generally take a stand with respect to the relevance of constraints that result from the properties of the neural substrate. Our understanding of the neural substrate continues to develop along with the development of the relevant empirical sciences. William Bechtel's new chapter reflects these developments, reviewing the conceptual implications of recent neuroscience in detail. While neuroscience has loomed large in recent psychology, biology has figured in a range of other important ways in psychological inquiry. For decades, ontogenetic and evolutionary biological considerations have influenced psychological theorizing. These factors continue to shape discussions in philosophy of psychology. Thus, developmental and evolutionary considerations feature prominently in many of the chapters in this *Companion*. One important change has been the idea that psychological explanation can also influence our interpretation of biological phenomena. For example, the newly added chapter from Manuel Heras-Escribano and Paco Calvo covers the emerging field of plant neurobiology.

The scientific study of consciousness has also matured considerably over the past decade. This research has productively broken the problem of explaining conscious experience into its component parts. Part V surveys some of the ways that philosophers of psychology have pursued the divide-and-conquer approach to consciousness. Attention, introspection, and the temporal components of experience are distinguished from the emotions. These, in turn, are distinguished from perceptual experience in the sensory modalities and in dream states. By taking an incremental approach to the problem of consciousness, philosophers of psychology can attend more carefully to distinctions obscured by blanket terms like "consciousness."

The concerns that bring philosophers to the study of psychology often involve problems of personhood, moral agency, and the nature of the good life. As the field continues to mature, the connections between philosophers of psychology and broader issues in philosophy continue to expand. Over the past decade the interplay between moral philosophy, epistemology, and philosophy of psychology have deepened considerably. The contributions to Part VI demonstrate the relevance of philosophy of psychology to vital normative and epistemic questions. In this edition we have included a chapter on group cognition, from Deborah Tollefsen and Kevin Ryan, and a chapter on the psychology of epistemic judgment, from Jennifer Nagel and Jessica Wright, which exemplify some of these developments.

We are very grateful to the contributors and referees for this volume. We would also like to thank Tony Bruce for encouraging us to develop this second edition and for all his practical support during its production.

Part I

Historical background to the philosophy of psychology

1

RATIONALIST ROOTS OF MODERN PSYCHOLOGY

Gary Hatfield

The philosophers René Descartes (1596–1650), Nicolas Malebranche (1638–1715), Benedict Spinoza (1632–77), and Gottfried Wilhelm Leibniz (1646–1716) are grouped together as *rationalists* because they held that human beings possess a faculty of reason that produces knowledge independently of the senses. In this regard, they contrast with *empiricist* philosophers, such as John Locke and David Hume, who believed that all knowledge arises from the senses. The rationalists contended that proper use of reason would yield the first principles of metaphysics, the most basic science of all. Metaphysics was also called "first philosophy," and it took as its subject matter nothing less than the basic properties and principles of everything. For our purposes, it is important to note that the rationalists believed that metaphysics could provide foundations for specialized disciplines, including ethics and physics, and also medicine and other applied subjects.

The rationalists and their followers developed theoretical positions of ambitious intellectual scope, ranging from metaphysical conclusions about the existence and nature of God to detailed theories of physical and physiological processes. Although they put great store in the faculty of reason for establishing overarching principles, they looked to observation and experience to provide data and evidence for their detailed theories. They took special interest in the metaphysics and physics of the human organism, and this led them to psychological topics concerning the characteristics and principles of animal behavior, the process of sense perception, the passions, emotions, and appetites, the cognitive operations of the mind (including attention and understanding), and the relation between mental phenomena and bodily processes in the brain and sense organs. The various rationalists, but especially Descartes, made original contributions to these topics. After considering the character of psychology as a discipline in the seventeenth century, we will examine these contributions in turn.

Psychology in the seventeenth century

The term "psychology" was first used in print in the sixteenth century (Lapointe 1972). The discipline is much older. As a subject taught in school (a root meaning of the word "discipline"), psychology was well-established in Aristotle's Lyceum. He taught the subject matter under the Greek name *Peri psyches* ("On the Soul"), which is the title of one of his major written works. Although Aristotle was Greek and taught and wrote in Greek, through an historical oddity his works are known under their Latin names, so that today we refer to this work as *De anima* ("On the Soul").

Aristotle understood the soul to be a vivifying and animating principle: it was an agent of life, sense, motion, and thought. To account for the range of living things and their capacities, Aristotelian thinkers ascribed various powers to the soul: nutritive, growth-directing, and reproductive (*vegetative* powers possessed by plants and all other living things); sensory and motor (*sensitive* powers possessed by nonhuman animals and human beings); and *rational* (possessed by human beings alone). In this scheme, the sensory capacities of animals include simple cognitive abilities to guide animal behavior, such as the ability to perceive danger or to recognize food by sight from afar; human beings share such abilities with other animals and additionally are endowed with the faculty of reason. Because Aristotle conceived of the soul as the animating force in all living things, the topics covered in Aristotelian psychology extended to subject areas that today are divided between biology, physiology, and sensory and cognitive psychology.

When the term "psychology" came into use in the sixteenth century, it named this Aristotelian discipline. Literally, the term means "rational discourse concerning the soul" (*logon peri tes psyches*). In the early seventeenth century, then, "psychology" as the science of the soul covered vivifying as well as sensory and cognitive processes. In European thought, the notion of the soul was also interpreted in a religious and theological context. The first book with the title *Psychologia*, by Goclenius (1590), focused on the theological question of whether the human soul is transferred to the fetus by the semen of the father (as in standard Aristotelian theory) or is directly infused by God (at an appropriate moment). The other standard topics concerning the sensory and cognitive powers of the soul were, however, also included. Moreover, in the wider *De anima* literature (leaving aside whether the Greek root *psyche* was used in the title), the larger part of discussion concerned the sensory and cognitive powers of the soul, with comparatively little space devoted to the nutritive, growth-directing, and reproductive powers. Discussion of these latter powers did not in fact follow a strictly Aristotelian line, but was strongly influenced by the medical tradition stemming from the second century Egyptian, Claudius Galen (whose work nonetheless showed the influence of Aristotelian physics, despite going beyond Aristotelian physiology).

Aristotle's works provided the framework for university instruction in both Protestant and Catholic lands into the seventeenth century (and into the eighteenth in Spain, Italy, France, and Austria). The curricular structure reflected an Aristotelian division of knowledge. Accordingly, the study of the soul fell under the rubric of physics (or natural philosophy). "Physics" comes from the Greek *physis*, meaning nature; "physics" or "natural philosophy" is then the "science of nature." It was not restricted to inorganic nature, but included all topics starting from the basic elements of things (earth, air, fire, and water) and working through the various kinds of natural bodies and their characteristic activities up to animals and human beings.

Sixteenth- and seventeenth-century physics books, then, contained discussions of the soul, including its sensory and cognitive functions. That these powers were classified as "physical" bore no connotation, in the Aristotelian scheme, that they were reducible to matter in a modern materialistic sense; rather, Aristotelians posited that all natural bodies possess an active principle, its "form," that serves to explain the characteristic properties and motions of every type of substance, from elemental substances to complex bodies such as plants, animals, and the human body. The human soul was the form of the human body, animating everything from growth to intellectual thought. The rational power of the soul, or the "intellect" (*nous*) as it was known in technical discussions, was granted a special status. Some questions about the rational soul, such as its immortality or whether the human intellect directly communicates with a single world-intellect, were reserved for the discipline of metaphysics, or were treated in appendixes to the usual "physical" discussion of the soul's powers. By contrast with the sensitive powers, which required material organs for their operation, the intellect was assigned no special organ. This point is somewhat tricky. Aristotelians believed that the intellect requires the assistance of a material organ (the brain, in late medieval Aristotelian anatomy) to provide it with objects of thought (as explained below); but they deemed the operations that the intellect performed in relation to such objects to be immaterial. This meant that these operations did not involve changes in a material organ.

Within the Aristotelian scheme, the rational power of the soul was studied in more than one disciplinary locus. It was studied as a natural power within physics. It was also studied as a knowing power within logic, which catalogued the proper operations of intellect and reason in obtaining and organizing knowledge. In the seventeenth century, this division between studying the sensory and cognitive powers as natural powers, in physics and physiology, and as knowing powers, in logic or methodology, was maintained and developed by rationalist writers (even as empiricists such as Thomas Hobbes chipped away at it, seeking to fully naturalize logic and reason). Modern philosophers showed disdain for the old Aristotelian logic, so they tended to discuss the scope and limits of knowledge under the title of "method." The modern philosophical field of epistemology arose from the study of the mind's powers as instruments for knowing. By contrast with study of the natural circumstances of the operations of the mind (in physics and physiology), methodology or epistemology examined the conditions for arriving at truth.

In this context, a word is needed about the notion of the intellect or reason as a faculty of knowing. Later psychologists, especially in the latter eighteenth and nineteenth centuries, reacted unfavorably to the "faculty psychology" of the seventeenth and eighteenth centuries. Their criticisms were summarized in allusions to a play by the French playwright Molière, in which a doctor explains the ability of opiates to make a person sleepy, by saying that opium has a *virtus dormitiva*, or "dormitive power." Clearly, the designation of such a power does not explain the operation of that power: it redescribes the phenomena with more abstraction and generality, by adding the notion of a "power" or "ability" that operates with regularity (opiates make this person sleepy because *they generally are able* to make people sleepy). In the Aristotelian and early-modern contexts, the assignment of "faculties" or "powers" to the mind, such as the sensitive and intellectual powers, was not an attempt to *explain* the ability to sense or to understand; it was part of an effort to *catalogue* and *describe* the general cognitive capacities of nonhuman animals and human beings. More specific factors were then introduced in explanatory contexts, including detailed analyses of the sensory processes that underlie the perception of distance, or the attribution of innate ideas to explain some cognitive abilities. Thus, the mere mention of "faculties" or "powers" is not inherently vacuous, but may be part of a taxonomic effort that catalogues and describes the variety of psychological abilities to be examined within psychology.

Over the course of the seventeenth century, the content and boundaries of Aristotelian psychology were challenged in various ways. Starting in the sixteenth century and continuing into the seventeenth, a debate raged about whether nonhuman animals possess sufficient cognitive ability to be deemed "rational" and to be described as possessing "knowledge," characteristics that would place them in the same category as human beings. These debates raised questions about the empirically determined behavioral capacities of animals and about the theoretical resources needed to explain such capacities. Larger philosophical changes also had implications for psychological topics. The seventeenth century saw the pronouncement of a "new science" of nature, in which Aristotelian forms (as active principles) were banished from nature and matter was reconceived as passive, spatially extended stuff. If nonhuman animals are constituted of this matter and possess no souls, then even supposing that their cognitive capacities are quite simple, those capacities nonetheless must be explained through purely material mechanisms of the sort permitted by this new science.

The rationalists favored this new science of matter, but they were also committed to finding a place for human mentality within the new science. Starting with Descartes, they reconceived mind and matter as mutually distinct entities, or at least as mutually distinct conceptual and explanatory domains. This new way of thinking generated a revised problem of mind-body interaction and relation. These changes entailed a further question concerning whether all the psychological capacities of human beings and nonhuman animals must be assigned to the mental domain, or whether some psychological capacities can instead be explained through material processes alone. If psychology is the science of the soul, then the answer is clear: the psychological belongs with the mental, period. But if psychology is identified by the domain of phenomena covered in Aristotelian psychology – or perhaps by a subset of that domain, the sensory, motor, and cognitive phenomena – then the equation of the psychological with the mental is not so clear. Thus, one of our tasks is to consider the various conceptual loci of the discipline of psychology in the seventeenth and into the eighteenth centuries.

Descartes and psychology

Descartes started his intellectual career in 1618–19, working on problems in mathematics and in "mathematical physics" (hydrostatics and falling bodies, 1974–6: Vol. 11, 67–78). His early results included the mathematical techniques that later made analytic geometry possible, and that underlay the introduction of Cartesian coordinates in the nineteenth century. During the 1620s, he sought to create a general method – for solving all types of problems, including philosophical ones – based on the kind of thinking found in mathematics. In the late 1620s he abandoned this project and the book he was writing, the *Rules for the Direction of the Mind*, to begin an ambitious project for a comprehensive new physics. This new physics involved the fundamental reconception of matter as nothing but bare geometrical extension, devoid of the active principles and "real qualities" of Aristotelian physics. Descartes' aim (1991: 7, 40) was to explain all of the phenomena of material nature by appeal to matter and motion alone. His new physics was to cover the topics found in Aristotelian physics and more, including the formation of the solar system and the Earth, the properties of minerals and other inorganic natural kinds, the origin and properties of plants and animals, and the human body, the human soul, and their relation (1985: 131–41). Descartes did not publish this treatise in his lifetime, and when he died only two portions were extant: the *Treatise on Light*, his general physics of inorganic nature, and the *Treatise on Man*, his treatise on human and animal physiology and behavior. The original French manuscripts were first published in 1664.

At about the same time as he started work on his new physics, Descartes also reported some metaphysical insights concerning God and the soul (1991: 22). We may therefore believe that in 1629–30 he elaborated revolutionary new conceptions of both matter and mind. These radical new conceptions – which he adumbrated in the *Discourse on the Method* of 1637, revealed in the *Meditations on First Philosophy* of 1641, and used to develop his new physics in the *Principles of Philosophy* of 1644 and the *Passions of the Soul* of 1649 – had implications not only for physics conceived as the science of nature in general, but also for the subfields of physiology and psychology, as well as for the metaphysics of mind and the theory of knowledge. Let us consider these new conceptions of matter and mind in turn.

The new conception of matter as bare extension was the more radical of the two, for it denied activity or agency to material bodies. This idea had some precedent in the work of the ancient atomists Democritus, Epicurus, and Lucretius; however, at least the latter two allowed weight as a natural property that would propel bodies downward (whereas Descartes felt obliged to explain weight as arising from interactions between particles in motion). Nonetheless, Descartes' new conception of matter went contrary to nearly every previous physics, whether Aristotelian, Platonic, or Stoic; for, in denying activity to matter, it allowed only motion conceived as change of place (and governed by laws of motion established by God). Descartes extended the new conception to living matter, which meant that he had to explain physiological processes without invoking the vital and sentient powers that pervaded the dominant Galenic physiological tradition of his day. He set himself the task of explaining all features of nonhuman animals by appeal to purely material mechanisms, that is, to organized matter in motion.

Descartes' conception of soul or mind also departed from accepted theory. In Aristotelian theory, the soul, as the form of the human body, cannot exist on its own, any more than the human body could be a unified "human body" without the informing presence of the soul (according to the Aristotelianism of Thomas Aquinas). Further, the various powers of the soul are immediately involved in directing the characteristic activities of all bodily organs: the vital organs; the senses, including the direct presence of the sensory power in the sense organs and nerves; and the brain, which was the locus of the common sense and the cognitive powers (in late medieval Aristotelian physiology). Descartes envisioned mind and body as distinct substances, which meant that each was a substance capable of existing on its own, without the other. He granted only two basic powers to the mind: intellect and will. He explained the bodily operation of the sense organs in a purely mechanical manner. In sense perception, the brain affects the mind (or the intellectual power) in a way that produces a conscious experience. (Descartes preferred the term "mind" over "soul" in philosophical contexts, 1984: 114, 246.)

Descartes also broke with the Aristotelian theory of cognition, according to which the intellect depends for its content (its objects of thought) on materials provided by the senses. Accordingly, for an Aristotelian there is no thought without an image (immaterial things, such as God or angels, are dimly understood by analogy with material things that can be imaged). By contrast, Descartes (1984: 50–1) held that the highest acts of intellect, the "clear and distinct" perception of the essences of things, occur through an intellectual act that does not require or involve images. In place of the empirical basis for fundamental knowledge envisioned by the Aristotelians, Descartes posited that the human intellect comes provisioned with a stock of innate ideas that have been attuned (by God) to the real essences of the basic kinds of stuff in the world. We have innate ideas of mind (as immaterial), of matter (as extended), and of God (as infinite being). In this way, his theory of intellectual cognition bears similarity with the Platonic tradition, but with some differences. Platonists held that the mind grasps extramental Forms when it knows the essences of things, whereas Descartes held that the fundamental contents of intellectual cognition are innate to the individual mind. Platonists also despised sensory knowledge, whereas Descartes supposed that the senses could provide important data for scientific knowledge, if the content of such data were properly interpreted using metaphysical knowledge gained by use of the intellect alone.

Descartes' new conceptions of mind and matter required that he redistribute the functions of the Aristotelian soul across the mind-body divide. Restricting ourselves to the sensory and cognitive functions, Descartes was required to explain the capacities of nonhuman animals – including simple cognitive abilities such as when a sheep detects danger in the presence of a wolf – by brain mechanisms alone, without appealing to the mind or any properly mental operations. Indeed, Descartes welcomed this challenge, and he extended it to human beings, claiming that he could explain many human behaviors without invoking the mind (1984: 161). In this way, he developed a mindless mechanistic psychology to replace portions of the Aristotelian psychology. At the same time, he reserved to the mind some psychologically important functions, including consciousness, will, general reasoning, and meaningful language use. He believed that these functions could not be explained through matter in motion.

In the ensuing sections we will examine these and other themes from Descartes' psychology, with attention to their reception and development by his followers and also the other major rationalists.

Animal machines

Nonhuman animals exhibit a variety of behaviors. Their sense organs and motor apparatus allow them to seek nutrients, navigate the local terrain, and avoid bodily harms. These phenomena were acknowledged in the Aristotelian and Galenic traditions, and had to be accommodated in any new account of animal behavior. Debates about what was needed to explain the abilities of nonhuman animals were a stimulus to psychological theorizing in the seventeenth century and beyond.

During the seventeenth century, scholars debated whether animals possess only the lower cognitive powers as described in the Aristotelian tradition, such as the ability to perceive harms and goods, or should in fact be granted a limited form of reason. Marin Cureau de La Chambre (La Chambre 1989) contended that animals have a limited form of reasoning, restricted to particulars and not rising to truly universal notions. He allowed, as usual, that an animal such as a dog can perceive by sight that honey is white, can perceive its sweet taste, and is drawn by natural appetite to eat it. But he contended that when a dog subsequently sees honey from a distance, without being able to smell or taste it, the animal exhibits reasoning in recognizing it as a good. According to La Chambre, the dog combines previous sensory images to achieve the equivalent of a syllogism: the white thing is sweet, sweet is good to eat, the white thing is good to eat. The animal generalizes to the extent that it responds to similarities among separate instances of the white quality, the sweetness, and its own appetitive response; but, according to La Chambre, it does not thereby achieve true cognitive grasp of a universal, which would involve understanding the essence of honey (an achievement he restricted to human reason). In other cases, La Chambre ascribed means-ends reasoning to animals, as when a dog realizes that it must run after the hare if it is to catch and eat it.

In opposition to La Chambre, Pierre Chanet (1646) maintained that any behavioral capacities of animals going beyond the direct perception of good and bad through sensory qualities and giving the appearance of reasoning must be explained either through habit and memory or through instinct. In the case of the sweet honey, the animal might simply remember that the white appearance and good taste go together, and the memory of the taste would arouse its appetite. As for the dog running after its prey, Chanet disallowed means-end reasoning. He ascribed such behavior to instinct, which induces an animal to behave in ways that yield benefits or avoid harms, without the animal foreseeing those outcomes.

Descartes was greatly interested in developing physiological hypotheses to account for animal and human behavior. During the 1630s, he dissected animal parts obtained from butchers, and may even have performed vivisections (1991: 40, 81–2, 134). Throughout the 1630s and 1640s he revised his *Treatise on Man* and worked on a separate work, the *Description of the Human Body*. During his lifetime, he published portions of his physiological theories in the *Dioptrics* of 1637 and in the *Passions of the Soul*. He considered his theories of human physiology to apply also to nonhuman animals, or to the "animal in general" (1991: 134–5; 1985: 134). In these works he developed mechanistic accounts of the operation of the nerves, muscles, sense organs, and brain, in order to be able to explain the basic phenomena of animal behavior, including avoidance of things harmful to the body and approach to things beneficial (1998: 163). The *Treatise* offers the fullest description of animal physiology, by describing a human body and its behavioral capacities in the absence of a soul or mind (a counterfactual thought experiment, since Descartes considered human beings to be essentially composed of both mind and body).

Descartes developed detailed mechanistic accounts of psychological functions that occur in nonhuman and human animals. These included the reception of sensory stimulation, the conveyance of stimulus patterns to the brain, the effects of such patterns on the motor nerves, and resultant behavior. In these descriptions, he considered both instinctual responses and responses mediated by "memory" – here interpreted as a purely corporeal (brain) function. As an example of instinct, he described the mechanisms by which a mindless human body would withdraw its hand from a fire (1998: 163). As an example of the effects of memory, he observed (1991: 20) that "if you whipped a dog five or six times to the sound of a violin, it would begin to howl and run away as soon as it heard that music again" (where "hearing" the sound, for a dog, amounts to the effects of sound waves on the nerves and brain, without consciousness or feeling). As he explained them, the mechanisms of a purely corporeal memory effect associative connections between brain structures, so that if an image is frequently repeated, say, an image of a face, then, if part of the pattern occurs later, say, eyes and a nose, the brain mechanisms fill out the rest of the pattern, supplying the forehead and mouth (1998: 151–2).

Because Descartes believed that immaterial minds essentially have intellectual capacity and that animals lack such capacity, he denied minds, and therefore sentience and feeling, to animals. (Recall that sentient feeling is a form of intellection for Descartes.) This animal-machine hypothesis was adopted by his major followers, including Malebranche (1997: 324), Pierre Regis (1970: Vol. 2, 506), who accepted it on theological grounds, and Antoine Le Grand (2003: Vol. 1, 230, Vol. 2, 228–9). Spinoza (1985: 494–7) and Leibniz (1969: 578, 650–1) affirmed that all animal behavior can be explained mechanistically and extended this thesis to all human behavior. Because their respective metaphysical views on the mind-body relation (discussed below) differed from those of Descartes and his followers, Spinoza and Leibniz were able to allow a mental aspect to animal life without granting reason to animals, and to allow a mechanical counterpart to human mental life without diminishing the status of the mental. Other adherents to the new science found it implausible to deny sentient feeling to animals, even though they denied them immaterial souls; the English physician Thomas Willis (1971) solved this problem by supposing that animal nerves and brains contain a fine, subtle matter that is capable of sentience (echoing a Galenic position).

Sense perception

The study of visual perception is the first area in which mathematical models were applied to psychological phenomena. The second-century Egyptian, Claudius Ptolemy, developed models of the perception of size and shape, and the eleventh-century Arab, Ibn al-Haytham, produced a comprehensive treatise on vision that including perception of size, distance, shape, color, and other visible properties. This literature went under the title of "optics," considered as the science of vision in general (and so covering physical, physiological, and psychological aspects). In the Aristotelian catalogue of disciplines, optics was a "mixed mathematical" science, which meant that it applied mathematics to a physical subject matter (in the broad sense of "physical," as pertaining to nature in general, and so including biology and psychology). This optical literature provided the background to Johannes Kepler's discovery of the retinal image. Natural philosophers also studied the other senses, including especially hearing, but they focused mainly on vision.

The rationalist philosophers, as was typical of those promulgating the new science of nature, were deeply interested in the theory of the senses and the status of sensory qualities. The theory of sensory qualities such as color, sound, or odor was bound up with the new mechanistic vision of matter as constituted of bare extension.

In the previously dominant Aristotelian philosophy, the basic properties of material things were qualitative: the elements of earth, air, fire, and water were formed by adjoining pairs of the qualities hot, cold, wet, and dry to an underlying substrate. The visible quality of color existed in the object as a "real quality"; the perception of color involved the transmission of the form of color through the air to the eye and into the brain, where this sample of color provided the content for a conscious experience. The metaphysics of the transmission process was subtle, for it had to account for the fact that the air is not rendered colored by the transmitted form (Simmons 1994). Because the new mechanistic science banished real qualities along with the substance-making forms of the Aristotelians, it had to provide a replacement account of the physics and physiology of color vision (as well as the other sensory qualities).

Descartes offered this replacement conception of color in his *Dioptrics* and in his description of the rainbow in the *Meteorology* of 1637, and then again in the *Principles*. According to this theory, color as it exists in objects is a surface property that affects the way light is reflected from objects. Light is made up of corpuscles, which take on various amounts of spin depending on the surface color of the object: red things cause the particles to rotate more quickly, blue things less quickly (1998: 88–91). The rotating corpuscles of light then affect the nerves in the retina, causing them to respond in characteristic ways (more vigorously for red, less for blue). This nervous response is transmitted mechanically into the brain, where it affects the pineal gland (the seat of mind-body interaction) and consequently causes a sensation of red or blue (1984: 295, 1985: 165–8, 1998: 148–9). In this account, color in bodies is what Locke would later call a "secondary quality": it is a dispositional property of the surfaces of things to cause sensations of color in the mind of a perceiver. Descartes' followers, as also Spinoza (1985: 170) and Leibniz (1969: 547), accepted this account of the status of color in bodies. This acceptance did not mean that these philosophers held the experience of color to be illusory or uninformative: we can tell objects apart by their color, even if we are ignorant of the physical properties of color in bodies. Nonetheless, they cautioned that we should not be fooled by the experience of color into accepting the Aristotelian theory that there is something in objects that is "similar to" or "resembles" our experiences of colors (Descartes 1985: 167, 216). Rather, we should accept the account of the new, mechanistic physics concerning what colors are in bodies.

We are able, by sight, to perceive the size, shape, and distance of objects. Theorists since al-Haytham had conceived this process as beginning with a two-dimensional projection of the field of vision into the eye, which Kepler correctly understood to be a projection onto the surface of the retina (Lindberg 1976: Ch. 9). Descartes (1998: 146–55) described the transmission of this two-dimensional image into the brain by means of the optic nerves, which he believed consisted of threads ensleeved by tubules. According to this conception, the pattern of light activity on the retina causes the sensory nerve threads to tug open the mouths of the tubules, which are topographically ordered in the brain so that the image structure from the retina is preserved in the pattern of open tubules. In his physiology, "animal spirits" (a subtle, ethereal fluid) then flow out from the pineal gland into the open tubules, in a manner that corresponds to the image structure, as in Figure 1.1. The pineal gland is the seat of mind-body interaction, and the two-dimensional pattern of out-flowing spirits causes a sensation in the mind exhibiting the same pattern, which then enters into further processes that lead to the perception of size, shape, and distance. As Descartes explains, the image size together with perception of the distance yields a perception of the actual size of the object. In Figure 1.1, visual angle 1–5 (or pineal image a–c)

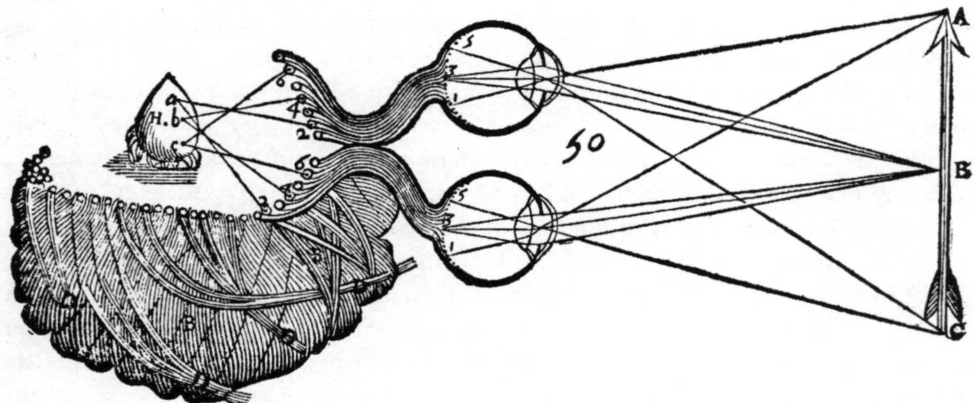

Figure 1.1 The geometry of sight and the physiology of nervous transmission according to Descartes. Object ABC reflects light rays focused on the retina at 1-3-5, jiggling the nerve fibrils and leading to tubule openings 2-4-6, which induce spirit flows *a*2, *b*4, and *c*6, resulting in pineal image abc. Source: Reproduced from Descartes (1677). Note: The inversion of the spirit flow is not required by Descartes' text and presumably was introduced by Gerard van Gutschoven (professor of medicine at Leiden), who produced the drawing at the request of Claude Clerselier, who prepared *L'Homme* for publication after Descartes' death.

would be combined with perceived distance to yield the perception of object size A–C. Descartes in fact provided an early description of the phenomenon of size constancy; but not the first, as al-Haytham had an even earlier description (Hatfield and Epstein 1979).

Descartes (1985: 170–2) described several ways in which distance might be perceived. For objects of known size, the distance could be determined by comparing visual angle (as conveyed in the initial sensation) with known size: for an object of a given size, the smaller the visual angle, the further away it is. In this case, the distance of the object is derived by rapid and unnoticed judgments (1984: 295), based on past experience (an *empiristic* account of distance perception). In other cases, we directly perceive distance through an innate physiological mechanism (a *nativistic* account) that depends on the fact that changes in the ocular musculature directly reflect distance, at least for relatively near objects. Muscles in the eye cause the lens to accommodate, and the eyes to converge, for nearer or farther distances; the central nervous state in the brain that regulates these muscles then co-varies with the distance of objects. This nervous state causes the idea of distance in the mind (1998: 155). Finally, as to shape, if we perceive the direction and distance of all the points of an object, as object ABC in Figure 1.1, we thereby perceive its shape.

In addition to these points about the psychology of size and distance perception, Descartes is responsible for an early statement of a principle that is similar to Johannes Müller's law of specific nerve energies. Descartes held that the various sensory nerves operate according to similar mechanical principles: by the motion of nerve threads, which cause an opening of the nerve tubules, causing a flow of animal spirits, causing a sensation in the mind (Hatfield 2000). The intensity of the sensation co-varies with the intensity of the stimulus as reflected in the motion of the nerve threads and the resultant pineal outflow. The character of the sensation depends on which nerve is affected: optical, auditory, olfactory, and so on, each of which terminates in a specific region of the brain. In this way, Descartes (1985: 280–4) introduced the conceptual framework according to which the characteristics of changes in a brain state are directly correlated with characteristics of the resulting sensations (and vice versa for motor volitions, motor nerve tubules, and muscle actions). His followers embraced this point, and spoke of "laws" of mind-body interaction (Regis 1970: Vol. 1, 126–7) or of the conditional "dependency" of brain and mental states (Le Grand 2003: Vol. 1, 325). Malebranche, Spinoza, and Leibniz each recognized this conditional dependency and accounted for it metaphysically in ways that we will consider under mind-body relations.

Passions and emotions

The passions and emotions had been an important philosophical topic from antiquity and were studied in natural philosophical, medical, moral, and theological contexts (Knuuttila 2004). In the middle ages, Thomas Aquinas articulated a detailed theory of the passions as responses of the sensitive soul to present or future goods or evils; more specifically, passions are passive responses of the sensitive appetite to the sensory perception or the imagination of a good or evil. (Aquinas also recognized active intellectual emotions unique to humans, such as intellectual love, as did Descartes and other theorists.)

Interest in the passions grew throughout the sixteenth and into the seventeenth centuries (James 1997). Descartes' *Passions* presented the passions as perceptions of the general characteristics of a current or future situation, as regards what is good, bad, or simply "important" for the body. The passions arise as passive responses of the mind to a brain state. The brain states are produced through neural mechanisms that yield distinctive states depending on whether the current situation is of a type that is usually good or bad for the body, or that is novel and deserving of sensory attention. Descartes contended that bodily mechanisms mediate the initial behavioral response to such situations, "without any contribution from the soul" (1985: 343). Thus, in the presence of a "strange and terrifying" animal, neural mechanisms cause the legs to run. These mechanisms produce brain states that affect the body (especially the heart), and these same brain states cause a passion in the mind, which is fear in the case of a terrifying animal. The feeling of this passion serves the function of making the mind want to do what the body is already doing: the passion induces the mind to want to keep running, by presenting the present situation as evil or dangerous. Descartes thus proposed a cognitive theory of the passions: they are perceptions of the situation that have motivational import. Like sensory perceptions, they cannot be willed away. The mind can countermand the impulse to run, but it cannot simply will the fear to go away. Malebranche (1997: 338) and the other Cartesians (Le Grand 2003: Vol. 1, 338) adopted a similar view of the passions, while Leibniz's (1981: 188–95) few remarks on the passions indicate that he viewed them as motivating us toward good and away from evil.

Spinoza developed an intricate theory of the passions and the active emotions in his *Ethics* (1985). According to Spinoza, every being strives toward its own preservation. This *conatus*, or striving, is the basis for his psychology of the passions. Spinoza identified three basic passions: desire, joy, and sadness. Desire is the appetite toward self preservation. It drives us toward things that increase our strength and vitality, and away from things that decrease it. Joy is the passion (or passive response) that we feel when our body's vitality is increased, while sadness is what we feel when that vitality decreases. Spinoza believed that such passions, when uncontrolled, lead to unhappiness. He therefore proposed that each of us, insofar as we are able, should seek to replace these passions with active emotions. This can occur by our understanding the causes of our desire, sadness, or happiness, and seeking to replace the passion with this understanding. The ultimate aim is to achieve a contented mind that is rationally at peace with its place in world. The active process of understanding our place in the world produces an active emotion of love or contentment.

Attention, the intellect, and apperception

If one compares the major divisions of seventeenth-century *De anima* textbooks, or the corresponding sections of Cartesian textbooks, with textbooks of the "new" psychology of the latter nineteenth century, most of the categories line up. There is coverage of the external senses, of neural structures and processes, of memory and imagination, and of higher cognition, including judgment and reasoning, the guidance of bodily motion, and appetite and will (motivation). However, the later textbooks contain two new categories: attention, and the laws of association. The psychology of association, although noted by Aristotle and implicitly mentioned by Descartes (in the memory example above), belongs to the history of empiricist contributions to psychology. The phenomena of attention, by contrast, were brought into prominence by the rationalists.

Many of the phenomena of attention had been noted in the ancient world, by Aristotle, Lucretius, and Augustine. These included the narrowing aspect, or attentional bottleneck; the active directing of attention, whether in preparation for a coming event or to select among current objects; involuntary shifts by which attention is drawn to a novel or otherwise salient object; clarity of representation through heightened attention; and the drawing of attention to preferred objects (Hatfield 1998). Malebranche covered all these phenomena in his extensive discussion of attention (1997: 79–81, 411–39).

The rationalists were especially interested in using attention to focus on cognitively important thought content that might otherwise be masked by the salience of sensory content. Descartes wrote his *Meditations* as a cognitive exercise to train thinkers to attend to their own innate intellectual ideas of the essences of things, including the essence of matter as bare extension, by contrast with categories of description suggested by uncritical reliance on sensory experience (such as Aristotelian "real qualities"). Descartes (1985: 355) added a new entry to the catalogue of attentional phenomena: the voluntary or involuntary fixation of attention on sensory objects or other mental contents over time. Malebranche (1997) recognized the importance of attentiveness in intellectual thought, and he sought psychologically effective aids to attention, enlisting the passions and the imagination in this cause, including the use of diagrams to help fix attention when considering mathematical subject matter.

Spinoza (1985: 28) and Leibniz (1969: 388) also highlighted the importance of being able to focus the attention in intellectual matters. The rationalist focus on attention continued in the eighteenth-century psychology textbooks of Christian Wolff, who was heir to the rationalist tradition through his connection with Leibniz. Wolff (1738) described the main phenomena of attention in systematic order. He also speculated that quantitative (proportional) relations obtain within those phenomena, postulating an inverse relation between the extensity of attention and its intensity (1740: §360).

The intellect took pride of place in rationalist theories of cognition, as the faculty that most effectively represents truth. Seventeenth-century Aristotelian logic divided the acts of intellect and reason into three: conceptualization or categorization of objects and properties; the representation of subject-predicate content and its affirmation or denial in judgments; and discursive reasoning, deriving one judgment to another. Descartes was skeptical of logical analysis, but these three logical acts were represented in Cartesian textbooks (Le Grand 2003: Vol. 1, 1–2). Descartes was more interested in the fourth act included in some textbooks, the act of "ordering," which was treated under "method." He offered some rules for reasoning in the *Discourse* (1985: 120, 150), which counted as his replacement for traditional logic. Theoretically, he analyzed judgments into two factors: the content to be judged, as represented by the intellect, and the affirmation or denial of that content by the will (1984: 39). The rational control of judgment lay at the core of his epistemology. Among the rationalists, Leibniz was greatly interested in logic, and in his unpublished writings developed the beginnings of predicate logic (1969: 240–6).

Leibniz was responsible for a further rationalist contribution to the phenomenology of cognition. He distinguished *petites perceptions* ("small perceptions") that fall below a threshold of open consciousness from *apperception*, or reflective awareness (1969: 557, 644). Thus, in hearing the roar of the waves at the seashore, many individual sounds that do not enter singly into our awareness constitute *petites perceptions* that, when conjoined, produce the overwhelming sound of the surf. These *petites perceptions* have the qualities of conscious perceptions and are in fact perceptions, even though we do not notice them. Descartes, the Cartesians, Malebranche, and Spinoza had all posited unnoticed and unremembered sensations – and even unnoticed complex psychological processes such as judgments underlying size and distance perception (Hatfield 2005) – but Leibniz's contribution is better known because he developed terminology for this distinction between bare consciousness and reflective awareness.

Mind-body relations

As metaphysicians, the rationalists sought to discern the *ontology*, or the basic categories of being, of all existing things. Descartes proposed a theory according to which there is an infinite being (God) who creates two kinds of stuff: mind and matter. His *mind-body dualism* marked a conceptual divide between mind and matter, since he contended that mind, which has the essence *thought*, shares no properties (save existence and temporal duration) with matter, which has the essence *extension*. In regarding mind and matter as separate substances, he was proposing that each can exist without the other (1984: 54).

Because Descartes held that mind and matter share no properties, subsequent philosophers wondered how, or whether, such really distinct substances would be able to interact, as apparently happens in sense perception (external objects cause neural activity that causes mental sensation) and voluntary motion (the mind decides to walk, and the body's limbs move). In the face of this problem, the other rationalists each proposed their own mind-body ontologies. Malebranche (1997) accepted Descartes' substance dualism, but proposed *occasionalism* as the solution to mind-body causation: God causes appropriate sensations in the mind when a specific brain state occurs, and he causes the body's motor nerves to become active when the mind wills a bodily motion. Mind and body do not themselves interact.

Spinoza rejected substance dualism. He held that only one substance exists – an infinite substance that he called "God or nature" – and that this substance has distinct attributes of thought and extension (1985: 451). His position is called *dual-aspect monism*, because he proposed one substance with two aspects (although in fact he allowed that there might be additional attributes besides thought and extension, without naming or describing them). Accordingly, for each material state in the world there is a corresponding mental state (panpsychism). In the case of human beings, the mental and bodily domains form closed causal systems that are in one-to-one correspondence but that do not interact (parallelism). For every mental state or process, there is a corresponding bodily process; all human behavior has a purely mechanical explanation, and all human thoughts follow one another by mental causation. There is no mind-body causation.

Leibniz adopted a third system. He maintained that God creates an infinity of individual substances ("monads"), all of which are mind-like. All monads have perception and appetite (1969: 644). Their perceptions unfold deterministically according to appetite. Each monad perceptually represents a distinct point of view in the universe. Some monads have the point of view of rocks or wood; their perceptions are obscure, and they lack apperceptive awareness. Other monads have the point of view of human bodily organs; their sequence of perceptions is closely related to those of the soul-monad for that person. Monads do not causally interact, but the states of all the monads in the world are put in correspondence through a *pre-established harmony*, set up by God at the beginning but unfolding now through intramonadic perception and appetite. Within the perceptions of the monads, the events of the world, from microphysical events to human perception and volition, unfold just as if there were mechanical laws governing bodies and just as if mind and body interacted (although in reality they do not).

Regarding the disciplinary locus of mind-body relations, among the Cartesians Regis (1970: Vol. 1, 120–1) examined the substantial nature of mind within metaphysics, and Le Grand (2003: Vol. 1, 77) spoke of *pneumatica* or the science of spirits in general (which also covered God and angels), of which "psychology" (the "doctrine of the soul" which considers "the mind of man") was a subdivision. Most Cartesians, even if they placed study of the mind qua spirit into metaphysics, put mind-body interaction into physics or natural philosophy. The Cartesian conception of regular natural laws governing mind-brain relations is the deep background to Gustav Fechner's "inner psychophysics" of the nineteenth century (Scheerer 1987).

Rationalist legacy

The most fundamental legacy of rationalism is the division of mental and material into separate domains. Despite their separate views on the ontology of the mental and the material, the major rationalists agreed that matter should be thought of as extension. As regards the mental, they agreed that sense perception, imagination, remembrances, the passions and emotions, appetites and volitions, and acts of intellection belong to a single domain. The property that unified these mental states is less clear. Some scholars have proposed that Descartes made consciousness the unifying element. Others argue that representation was the key feature, a proposal that would also encompass the conceptions of the mental in Spinoza and Leibniz.

The identification of the mental and the material as distinct domains provided the framework for the notion that psychophysical or psychophysiological laws obtain between these domains. The search for such regularities was undertaken within the empirical psychology of the eighteenth century and in the psychophysics of the nineteenth century. The proper relation of the mental to the physical (where "physical" is used in its narrow sense, as referring to matter) remains an open question today. There has been no reduction of mental to physical. Nonetheless, using new methods of physiological recording and brain imaging, there have been further investigations of the correlations or regularities holding between psychological processes and brain processes.

A second rationalist contribution arose from Descartes' animal machine hypothesis, as adopted and extended by Spinoza and Leibniz. Descartes inspired later work with his view that situationally appropriate behavior can be explained by mechanistically conceived brain and nerve processes. His thesis of animal automatism was extended to human beings in the materialism of Julien Offray de La Mettrie, and was hailed as a model by the nineteenth-century Darwinist Thomas H. Huxley (1884) and so formed part of the intellectual context for John B. Watson's early behaviorist theories. The dual-aspect monism of Spinoza and the pre-established harmony of Leibniz allowed them to maintain that all human thoughts and actions have a mechanical explanation, without endorsing materialism or reducing the importance of the mental.

The employment of mechanistic explanations for psychological phenomena meant that the psychological did not neatly fall on the mental side of the divide between mind and body. When Descartes used his mechanistic physiology to explain the phenomena of the Aristotelian sensitive soul (or at least some of them, leaving conscious sensation aside), he introduced into modern thought the possibility of two different definitions of a science of psychology: the definition of Wilhelm Wundt and others of psychology as the science of mental life, and the definition of Watson and others of psychology as the science of adaptive behavior.

The term "psychology" was used with low frequency during the seventeenth century. It meant the "science of the soul," and as such it did not conform to the later definitions. Either it applied to the full range of *De anima* topics, including the biological topics of reproduction and growth, or it applied exclusively to souls and so left out Cartesian mechanistic psychology. It was left to Wolff (1738, 1740) in the eighteenth century to firmly entrench the meaning of psychology as the science of sensory, motor, and cognitive phenomena (excluding purely biological topics). His follower Michael Hanov (1766) clarified this division by introducing the term "biology" (Latin *biologia*) for the science of life, reserving the term *anima*, and by implication the connate term "psychology," for the science of the mental.

Despite their extension of mechanical modes of explanation to much or all of human behavior, the rationalists did not envision a reduction of reasoning and knowledge to purely physical or physiological categories (as in more recent "naturalisms"). They maintained a conception of the intellect as a power of perceiving truth. As such, they continued the Aristotelian distinction between the *De anima* topics in physics and the study of the proper use of *nous* or intellect in logic. This division between *psyche* and *nous* later became the division between psychology and epistemology: between the study of the mind as a natural power and study of the mind as a noetic or epistemic power. It was left to empiricist philosophers such as Hume to attempt to reduce human belief formation to sense and imagination, that is, to those psychological capacities that human beings were thought to share with animals. Subsequent empiricist attempts to effect this reduction raise the question of whether the normative elements of human thought can be reduced or even reduced away. This is the question of whether epistemology can be reduced to or replaced by either behaviorist or cognitive psychology. It is not the question of whether psychology is *relevant* to epistemology (for it surely is), but of whether the concepts of epistemology, concepts such as *warranted belief*, or *justification*, are really psychological concepts, or are illusory concepts, or are legitimate concepts within a separate domain of epistemology. This question, to which authors in the seventeenth and eighteenth centuries had their own implicit or explicit answers, remains open today.

References

Chanet, Pierre (1646) *De L'Instinct et de la connoissance des animaux* [On instinct and the knowledge of animals], La Rochelle: Toussaincts de Gouy.

Descartes, René (1677) *Traité de l'homme* [Treatise on man], 2nd edn, Paris: Girard.

—— (1974–6) *Oeuvres*, new edn, ed. Charles Adam and Paul Tannery, CNRS, Paris: Vrin.

—— (1984) *Philosophical Writings of Descartes*, vol. 2, trans. J. Cottingham, R. Stoothoff, and D. Murdoch, Cambridge: Cambridge University Press. (Includes the *Meditations* with Objections and Replies, originally published in 1641.)

—— (1985) *Philosophical Writings of Descartes*, vol. 1, trans. J. Cottingham, R. Stoothoff, and D. Murdoch, Cambridge: Cambridge University Press. (Contains the *Rules*, *Discourse*, *Passions*, and selections from the *Principles*, *Dioptrics*, and other scientific works.)

—— (1991) *Philosophical Writings of Descartes*, vol. 3: *The Correspondence*, trans. J. Cottingham, R. Stoothoff, D. Murdoch, and A. Kenny, Cambridge: Cambridge University Press.

—— (1998) *Descartes: The World and Other Writings*, trans. S. Gaukroger, Cambridge: Cambridge University Press. (Contains the *Treatise on Light*, *Treatise on Man*, *Description of the Human Body*, and selections from the *Dioptrics* and *Meteorology*.)

Goclenius, Rudolph (1590) *Psychologia: Hoc Est, de Hominis Perfectione, Animo*, Marburgh: Egenolphi.

Hanov, Michael Christoph (1766) *Philosophiae Naturalis sive Physicae Dogmaticae*, vol. 3: *Geologiam, Biologiam, Phytologiam Generalem*, Halle: Renger.

Hatfield, Gary (1998) "Attention in early scientific psychology," in R. D. Wright (ed.), *Visual Attention*, New York: Oxford University Press, pp. 3–25.

—— (2000) "Descartes' Naturalism about the Mental," in Stephen Gaukroger, John Schuster, and John Sutton (eds), *Descartes' Natural Philosophy*, London: Routledge, pp. 630–58.

—— (2005) "Rationalist Theories of Sense Perception and Mind-Body Relation," in Alan Nelson (ed.), *Companion to Rationalism*, Oxford: Blackwell, pp. 31–60.

Hatfield, Gary, and Epstein, William (1979) "The Sensory Core and the Medieval Foundations of Early Modern Perceptual Theory," *Isis* 70: 363–84.

Huxley, Thomas Henry (1884) "On the Hypothesis That Animals Are Automata and Its History," in T. H. Huxley, *Science and Culture*, New York: Appleton, pp. 206–54.

James, Susan (1997) *Passion and Action: The Emotions in Seventeenth-Century Philosophy*, Oxford: Clarendon Press.

Knuuttila, Simo (2004) *Emotions in Ancient and Medieval Philosophy*, Oxford: Clarendon Press.

La Chambre, Marin Cureau de (1989) *Traité de la connaissance des animaux* [Treatise on the knowledge of animals], Paris: Fayard; original work published 1648.

Lapointe, Francois H. (1972) "Who originated the term 'psychology'?" *Journal of the History of the Behavioral Sciences* 8: 328–35.

Le Grand, Antoine (2003) *An Entire Body of Philosophy, according to the Principles of the Famous Renate des Cartes*, trans. R. Blome, Bristol: Thoemmes Press; repr. of 1694 trans.; original work first published in Latin in 1672–5.

Leibniz, Gottfried Wilhelm (1969) *Philosophical Papers and Letters*, trans. L. E. Loemker, Dordrecht: Reidel; original works written in Latin and French in the seventeenth and early eighteenth centuries.

—— (1981) *New Essays on Human Understanding*, trans. Peter Remnant and Jonathan Bennett, Cambridge: Cambridge University Press; original work published in 1765.

Lindberg, David C. (1976) *Theories of Vision from Al-Kindi to Kepler*, Chicago: University of Chicago Press.

Malebranche, Nicolas (1997) *Search after Truth*, trans. Thomas M. Lennon and Paul J. Olscamp, Cambridge: Cambridge University Press; original work published in 1674–5.

Regis, Pierre (1970) *Cours entier de philosophie, ou systeme general selon les principes de M. Descartes* [Entire Course of Philosophy, or General System according to the Principles of M. Descartes], New York: Johnson Reprint; repr. of 1691 edn.

Scheerer, Eckart (1987) "The unknown Fechner," *Psychological Research* 49: 197–202.

Simmons, Alison (1994) "Explaining sense perception: a scholastic challenge," *Philosophical Studies* 73: 257–75.

Spinoza, Benedict (1985) *Collected Works of Spinoza*, trans. E. Curley, Princeton: Princeton University Press.

Willis, Thomas (1971) *Two Discourses Concerning the Soul of Brutes, Which Is That of the Vital and Sensitive in Man*, Gainesville: Scholars' Facsimiles & Reprints; original work published 1683.

Wolff, Christian (1738) *Psychologia empirica*, new edn, Frankfurt and Leipzig: Renger.

—— (1740) *Psychologia rationalis*, new edn, Frankfurt and Leipzig: Renger.

2
EMPIRICIST ROOTS OF MODERN PSYCHOLOGY

Raymond Martin

From the thirteenth through the sixteenth centuries, European philosophers were preoccupied with using their newfound access to Aristotle's metaphysics and natural philosophy to develop an integrated account, hospitable to Christianity, of everything that was thought to exist, including God, pure finite spirits (angels), the immaterial souls of humans, the natural world of organic objects (plants, animals, and human bodies), and inorganic objects. This account included a theory of human mentality. In the sixteenth and early seventeenth centuries, first in astronomy and then, later, in physics, the tightly knit fabric of this comprehensive medieval worldview began to unravel.

The transition from the old to the new was gradual, but by 1687, with the publication by Isaac Newton (1642–1727) of his *Principia Mathematica*, the replacement was all but complete. Modern physical science had fully arrived, and it was secular. God and angels were still acknowledged. But they had been marginalized. Yet, there was a glaring omission. Theorists had yet to expand the reach of the new science to incorporate human mentality. This venture, which initially was called "moral philosophy" and came to be called "the science of human nature," became compelling to progressive eighteenth-century thinkers, just as British empiricism began to seriously challenge an entrenched Cartesian rationalism.

Rationalism and empiricism

The dispute between rationalists and empiricists was primarily over concepts and knowledge. In response to such questions as, where does the mind get its stock of concepts?, how do humans justify what they take to be their knowledge?, and how far does human knowledge extend?, rationalists maintained that some concepts are innate, and hence not derived from experience, and that reason, or intuition, by itself, independently of experience, is an important source of knowledge, including of existing things. They also maintained that one could have a priori knowledge of the existence of God. Empiricists, on the other hand, denied that any concepts are innate, claiming instead that all of them are derived from experience. They also tended to claim that all knowledge of existing things is derived from experience. And, as time went on, empiricists became increasingly skeptical, first, that one could have a priori knowledge of God and, later, that one could have knowledge of God at all.

Rene Descartes (1596–1650), who, along with Galileo Galilei (1564–1642), was one of the founders of modern physical science, was the most influential rationalist of the seventeenth century. Even though, when it came to the study of animal biology, Descartes was an avid experimentalist, in his abstract philosophy he elevated rational intuition over sense experience as a source of knowledge. He also claimed that humans have innate ideas, such as an idea of God, which do not come from experience. And he claimed that through reason alone, independently of appeal to experience, one could demonstrate the existence of God and the existence of immaterial souls – one such soul, intimately conjoined with a body, for each human person.

During the time that Descartes was making his major philosophical and scientific contributions, he had predecessors and contemporaries who were well known and highly influential empiricists. Chief among these were Francis Bacon (1561–1626), Pierre Gassendi (1592–1655), and Thomas Hobbes (1588–1679). However, Descartes' rationalism overshadowed the empiricism of his day – providing the framework for the most influential philosophy of the seventeenth century. It was not until close to the dawn of the eighteenth century, when John Locke (1632–1704) published his *Essay Concerning Human Understanding* (1975 [1690–94]) that the tide began to turn against rationalism and toward empiricism.

In 1690, Aristotelean science was still firmly entrenched in the universities. Even so, in his *Essay* Locke not only expressed contempt for it, but generally dismissed it without much argument, taking it as obvious that it was on the wrong track. His main target, against which he argued at length, was Cartesian rationalism. In Britain especially, but also in France, Locke found an eager audience. He quickly became the most influential empiricist of the modern era.

Concepts

One of Locke's central ideas was that the human mind at birth is a *tabula rasa* (blank tablet) on which experience subsequently writes. He allowed that the mind might have innate capacities, such as the capacity to reason and to learn from experience, but he vehemently denied that it has any innate ideas (concepts). In trying to make this point, he taunted rationalists with the perhaps irrelevant observation that children, the mentally impaired, and "savages" lack many of the ideas that were said by rationalists to be innate. But his main thrust was to try to explain how humans *could have* acquired all of their concepts from experience, thereby making the appeal to innate ideas superfluous.

Throughout the eighteenth century many empiricists enthusiastically embraced Locke's tabula-rasa thesis, in whole or in part. These included George Berkeley (1685–1753), who allowed that humans have a *notion* (as opposed to an idea) of the self that is not derived from experience, and David Hume (1711–76), who defended Locke's view by refashioning a central component of the way Locke had supported it. Some other philosophers simply ran with Locke's idea, including the French philosopher Étienne Bonnot de Condillac (1715–80), who in his *Treatise on Sensations* (of 1754) claimed that external sensations by themselves could account not only for all human concepts, but for all mental operations as well. Using the example of a statue endowed with only the sense of smell, Condillac tried to explain how from this bare beginning attention, memory, judgment, and imagination – indeed, one's entire mental life – might have developed. His views thus embodied a more extreme version of the tabula-rasa perspective than can be found even in Locke.

In contrast to Condillac, many British empiricists after Locke had doubts about Locke's explanations of the experiential origins of several of the concepts that he examined, including especially those of causation and of the self. Over time these more austere empiricists – Hume is the premier example – tended increasingly to agree that ideas as robust as the ones Locke assumed that we have could not have been derived from experience. But then, rather than rejecting Locke's tabula-rasa thesis, they concluded that our ideas are not as robust as Locke had imagined. Thus, Hume developed his "bundle theory of the self" and his "regularity theory of causation" in order to fashion concepts of these notions thin enough that they actually could have been derived from experience. A question, then, was whether these thinner concepts were nevertheless thick enough to account for the ways humans meaningfully think about the world, especially in science.

The tabula-rasa thesis played an important role in encouraging thinkers to speculate about how the mind becomes stocked with its simple ideas, how it then combines and augments these to form more complex ideas, and finally what the laws might be – the so-called *principles of association* – that govern how one idea leads to another in human thought. The tabula-rasa thesis also put great pressure on the assumption that humans understand what it might even mean to have, or be, an immaterial self, let alone to know that one has, or is, one.

Effectively doing away with the idea that to understand human nature one must understand the role of an immaterial self in human mentality was crucial to the emergence of a scientific psychology. In the eighteenth century, empiricism, and the tabula-rasa thesis in particular, was at the forefront of this important initiative. More generally, the tabula-rasa thesis encouraged an austere empiricist epistemology and metaphysics that inhibited acceptance of many common sense and even scientific assumptions about the reality of the external world and our epistemological access to it, as well as about the meaning of the concepts in terms of which we think about ourselves and the world. Not all empiricists embraced this entire program, but for those who did, which included most notably Hume, empiricism tended to lead to skepticism. This encouraged other thinkers – Immanuel Kant (1724–1804) is the premier example – to explore radically alternative ways to account for human knowledge, including new proposals about how the human mind might have come to be stocked with its concepts.

Today something like the doctrine of innate ideas, under the guise of what is called *nativism*, has become the prevailing orthodoxy among philosophers and psychologists. However, it was not until the second half of the twentieth century that nativism gained this sort of ascendancy, at which time nativism's rise was due initially, and perhaps primarily, to widespread acceptance of the approach to language acquisition championed by Noam Chomsky.[1] Once nativism had made this inroad the way was open for others to advance a variety of nativist theses – for instance, for Jerry Fodor to argue that since there is no viable empiricist theory of concept acquisition it is *prima facie* reasonable to believe that all concepts are innate.[2]

Knowledge

In addition to Locke's making subsequent empiricists uncomfortable by conceding too much to common sense about the content of our ideas, he also muddied his empiricist credentials by agreeing with Descartes that we have a demonstrative knowledge of God's existence and an intuitive knowledge of our own existence. Locke even claimed to believe that the self is an immaterial substance. However, he coupled these agreements with the wildly controversial observation that matter might think.[3] And, even more threatening to the idea of the self as immaterial substance, he gave an empirical account of personal identity that made no appeal to anything immaterial.

Subsequently Berkeley and Hume denied that we have a demonstrative knowledge of God's existence. Berkeley, however, claimed that we can know on empirical grounds that God exists. And he claimed that we have an intuitive knowledge of our own existence as an immaterial substance (privately he expressed doubt on the point). Hume, in the work that he published during his lifetime, eschewed any concession to the idea that God exists and even denied that we intuit our own existence, at least if it is conceived as robustly as Locke conceived it. In addition, Hume famously gave more empirically austere analyses of several of Locke's key notions. Other empiricists, as we shall see, did not become so preoccupied with Locke's tabula-rasa thesis that they allowed their commitment to an austere empiricist epistemology to interfere with their contributions to the newly emerging science of human nature. Instead, they allowed themselves realistic assumptions about the material world and our epistemological access to it. David Hartley (1705–57), Adam Smith (1723–90), and Joseph Priestley (1733–1804) were in this group.

There was, thus, a major divide within the empiricist camp, not so much over whether Locke's tabula-rasa thesis is true, since few empiricists questioned it, but over the role that it and the austere empiricist epistemology that it encouraged should play in science, particularly in an empirical investigation of the human mind. But, due to the high visibility and persuasiveness of those empiricists who were preoccupied with the more austere approach, empiricism quickly became linked with skepticism, a reputation that it retained into our own times. As late as 1945, Bertrand Russell (1872–1970), himself a latter-day empiricist, wrote that Hume "developed to its logical conclusion the empirical philosophy of Locke and Berkeley, and by making it self-consistent made it incredible." Hume, thus, represents, Russell continued, "a dead end"; in his direction "it is impossible to go further." And, although "to refute him has been, ever since he wrote, a favourite pastime among metaphysicians," Russell could "find none of their refutations convincing." Russell concluded, "I cannot but hope that something less sceptical than Hume's system may be discoverable."[4]

Such was the influence of the austere epistemology spawned by empiricism. But what Russell expressed is a philosopher's worry. Whether it has much to do with how science should be conducted, and a science of psychology in particular, is a separate question. Hume, though, thought that it had a lot to do with how a science of human nature should be conducted. In his view, austere empiricism and science are inextricably linked. Hence, in his strictures about how a science of human nature should be pursued, psychology never escapes from the clutches of epistemology. That, as it turns out, was not the way forward.

The self

Although Locke's official view was that the self is an immaterial substance, he saw that for the purpose of developing a science of human nature, that idea was a nonstarter. However, rather than challenge the immaterial-self thesis directly, Locke turned to the topic of personal identity, where he had two main ideas, one negative and one positive. His negative idea was that the persistence of persons *cannot* be understood empirically as parasitic upon the persistence of any underlying substance, or substances, out of which humans or persons might be composed. His positive idea was that the persistence of persons *can* be understood empirically in terms of the unifying role of consciousness.

Most of the time when Locke talked about consciousness in the context of talking about personal identity he meant *remembers*. His eighteenth-century critics invariably attributed to him the view that a person at one time and one at another have the same consciousness, and hence are the same person, just in case the person at the later time *remembers*, from the inside, the person at the earlier time. Whether or not this is what Locke had in mind, his eighteenth-century critics were right in thinking that the memory interpretation of personal identity that they attributed to him is vulnerable to decisive objections.[5] However, almost all of them wanted to defeat what they took to be Locke's memory view to retain the view that personal identity depends on the persistence of an immaterial soul.

For his part, Locke pointed out correctly that one can determine empirically whether someone retains the same consciousness over time, but not whether someone retains the same immaterial soul. As a consequence, he thought, the soul view is not only a wrong account of personal identity, but the wrong *kind* of account, whereas his own view, by contrast, is at least the right kind of account. As it happened, Locke was right: the *kind* of account he offered was riding the crest of a wave of naturalization that was about to engulf his critics.

An early indication of what was about to happen occurred soon after Locke's death. Between 1706 and 1709 Samuel Clarke (1675–1729) and Anthony Collins (1676–1729) confronted each other in a six-part written debate.[6] At the time, Clarke, who was Newton's right hand man, was an enemy of empiricism and one of the most highly respected philosophers of the time, a status that he retained throughout the century. Collins, who in the last years of Locke's life had been one of his most beloved and devoted disciples, was a relative unknown.

Clarke and Collins' point of departure was the question of whether souls are naturally immortal, where by "soul," they agreed to mean "Substance with a Power of Thinking" or "Individual Consciousness."[7] Clarke, who had a sophisticated understanding of Newtonian science and was revered throughout the century for his opposition to empiricism, defended the traditional Platonic idea that souls are immaterial. Collins countered that the soul is material.

Both men agreed that individual atoms are not conscious. Their dispute, thus, turned on the question of whether it is possible that a *system* of matter might think. Clarke argued that it is not possible, Collins that matter does think. Throughout their debate Clarke played the part of the traditional metaphysician. He argued largely on *a priori* grounds. Collins, though not always consistently, played the part of the empirical psychologist. His faltering, but often successful, attempts to reformulate traditional metaphysical issues empirically embodied the birth pangs of a new approach, one that grew steadily throughout the century. The Clarke-Collins debate is, thus, a poignant record of two thinkers' struggles to cope with a rapidly changing intellectual climate, Clarke by hanging onto the old, Collins by groping for the new.

Although Collins' approach was the progressive side of Locke's, he went beyond Locke, first, in espousing materialism, and second, in replacing Locke's metaphysically awkward same-consciousness view of personal identity with a more defensible connected-consciousness view. Throughout Collins said that he sought, and that Clarke should have been seeking, an empirical account of consciousness. Collins repeatedly criticized Clarke for trying to settle by verbal fiat what could only be settled empirically.[8]

Clarke countered by reiterating a priori dogma. For instance, he claimed that strictly speaking, consciousness is neither a capacity for thinking nor actual thinking, "but the Reflex Act by which I know that I think, and that my Thoughts and Actions are my own and not Another's." He also claimed that "it would necessarily imply a plain and direct Contradiction, for any power which is really One and not Many ... to inhere in or result from a divisible Substance."[9] However, he conceded that his own "affirming Consciousness to be an individual Power" was neither "giving an Account of Consciousness" nor "intended to be so." It is enough, he concluded, that "every Man feels and knows by Experience what Consciousness is, better than any Man can explain it."[10] As it turned out, however, this was not enough.

It soon became clear to subsequent thinkers that while intuition might be a sufficient basis to resist the reduction of the mental to the material, it was impotent as a source of explanations of mental phenomena. Collins returned to this point again and again, even claiming to be able to explain how consciousness could be transferred from a material system of the brain initially composed of certain particles to one subsequently composed of other particles, without changing the individual subject of consciousness whose brain is involved.[11] By our current standards, his explanation is crude, but it was a genuine scientific explanation, and Clarke had nothing comparable to offer.

Throughout the eighteenth century the Clarke-Collins debate was well known to subsequent theorists. Yet even though Collins' orientation was directly toward the development of a science of psychology of a sort that would be familiar to psychologists in our own times, the extent of his influence is unclear. However, even among those who sided with Clarke there was a gradual awakening to the idea that at least for scientific purposes the self had to be understood empirically. Thus, Clarke's bravado in his debate with Collins contrasts with the subsequent defensiveness of Berkeley and Joseph Butler (1692–1752), a few decades later, as well as with the reluctance of most immaterial-soul theorists after Hume even to do battle on the issue. And whereas toward the beginning of the century, it was enough simply to defend the immateriality of the soul and related *a priori* doctrines, such as the reflexivity of consciousness (the view that necessarily if one is conscious, then one knows that one is conscious), without also contributing to the emerging science of human nature, eventually soul theorists tended to bracket their commitment to the immaterial soul to conduct meaningful empirical research. Thus, while the immateriality of the soul is crucial to Berkeley's metaphysics, it is almost irrelevant to his inquiries into vision; and although Hartley, Thomas Reid (1710–96), and Abraham Tucker (1705–74) remained committed to the existence of the immaterial soul, each of them segregated that commitment from their empirical inquiries.

As a consequence, in debates among theorists about the nature of the mind, it tended to matter less and less as the century wore on what one's view was of the immaterial soul. Toward the end of the century, Hartley, the dualist, was regarded as an ally by Priestley, the materialist, while Reid, the dualist, attacked both. And while the main influences on Tucker, the dualist, were Locke, Clarke, and Hartley, it was not Locke and Hartley's dualism that most impressed Tucker, but their more scientific pursuits. It is only a slight exaggeration to suggest that Priestley could have put forth the very same views he did, even if, like Hartley, he had been a dualist; and Reid could have put forth most of his views, even if he had been a materialist.

This bracketing of commitment to the immaterial soul, which was reinforced later in a different context by the methodological strictures of Kant, arguably was one of empiricism's two greatest contribution to the eventual emergence of a science of psychology. The other was their contributions to formulating the principles of association. In both cases the basic message was that from the point of view of developing a science of human nature, the only ontological commitments that matter are those that can be tracked empirically; and the only theories that matter, those that can be confirmed or refuted empirically. Rationalists never quite got this, but it was central to the approach of empiricists. Unfortunately empiricists, for their part, tended not to get that for the purpose of doing science, it was more productive to make realistic assumptions about the world than to ground every claim in an empirically austere epistemology and metaphysics.

Self-constitution

In empiricist traditions, it was not only the *immaterial* self that came under a cloud of suspicion, but even the *empirical* self. To see how this happened, one has to go back again to Locke, who in the *Essay* sometimes used the words *person* and *self* interchangeably, but more often used *self* to refer to a momentary entity and *person* to refer to a temporally extended one. Locke even defined the two terms differently.[12] His definition of *person* highlighted that persons are *thinkers* and, as such, have reason, reflection, intelligence, and whatever else may be required for trans-temporal self-reference. His definition of *self* highlighted that selves are *sensors* and as such feel pleasure and pain, and are capable of happiness, misery, and self-concern.

We know how, in Locke's view, humans come into being. It is a biological process. How do selves (or persons) come into being? His answer was that is a psychological process that begins with an organism's experience of pleasure and pain, which gives rise, first, to the idea of a self – its own self – that is the experiencer of pleasure and pain, and then to concern with the quality of that self's experience (each of us wants more pleasure, less pain). Then the momentary self thus constituted (or perhaps the organism) thinks of itself (or its self) as extended over brief periods of time (say, the specious present); finally, through memory and the appropriation ingredient in self-consciousness, it thinks of itself as extended over longer periods of time.[13] Locke, thus, thought of the constitution of the self as at least being capable of being analyzed into an ordered, multi-step process. He may or may not have thought that the prior phases of this process temporally precede the subsequent phases.

Whatever Locke's view on this question of timing, he clearly thought that self-constitution involves appropriation – a kind of self-declaration of ownership – and that appropriation and accountability go hand in hand. A person, he said, is "justly accountable for any Action" just if it is appropriated to him by his self-consciousness.[14] He regarded the appropriation ingredient in self-consciousness as a natural relation between the organism and its present and past, which then is the basis for a non-natural relation of moral ownership.[15]

Joseph Butler, more than any other eighteenth-century critic of Locke, took Locke's observations about the role of appropriation in self-constitution seriously. It is "easy to conceive," Butler said, "how matter, which is no part of ourselves, may be appropriated to us in the manner which our present bodies are."[16] But, he continued, where there is appropriation, there must be an appropriator. Locke had an appropriator in "man," which he distinguished from "person" and allowed might be merely a material organism. Butler thought that he (Butler) had already shown that the appropriator must be something simple and indivisible, and, hence, could not possibly be a material organism. This simple, indivisible appropriator, he assumed, is who we truly are. But what this being appropriates, he went on to explain, is not thereby part of itself, but, rather, something it owns. Butler had learned from Locke that, for all we know, the thinking principle in us may be material. So, he astutely conceded that the appropriator might be a simple material entity.[17] In his view, it is our simplicity, not our immateriality, that ensures our survival. He thereby adapted the Platonic argument for immortality to the purposes of an age in which materialism was on the rise, recasting the a priori in an empirical mold.

When Butler turned to the topic of personal identity per se, he argued that on a relational view such as that of Locke or Collins, people would have no reason to be concerned for the future life of the person who they nominally regard as themselves, for if our being were just to consist in successive acts of consciousness, then it would be a mistake "to charge our present selves with anything we did, or to imagine our present selves interested in anything which befell us yesterday" or will befall us tomorrow "since our present self is not, in reality, the same with the self of yesterday, but another like self or person coming in its room, and mistaken for it: to which another self will succeed tomorrow."[18]

In response to what Butler saw as the dangers of empirical analysis, he proposed that we take as primitive the idea of personal identity, which he said defies analysis. Like Clarke, he maintained that we can determine intuitively that we have persisted, not just in "a loose and popular sense" such as we might employ in saying of a mature oak that it is the same tree as one that stood in its spot fifty years previously, even though it and that former tree have not one atom in common, but in "the strict and philosophical sense" which requires sameness of substance.[19] On Locke's view, he claimed, we would have to consider ourselves to be selves and persons not really, but only in a fictitious sense. He thought that such a consequence refutes Locke's view. And, like Clarke, he admitted that he thought this not because he thought that he could show Locke's view to be false (he admitted that he could not), but rather because "the bare unfolding this notion [that selves are merely fictitious entities] and laying it thus naked and open, seems the best confutation of it."[20] Empiricists continued to struggle with this issue throughout the nineteenth century.

One who did so was John Stuart Mill (1806–73), who claimed that the self-knowledge that humans unquestionably have must be based on an intuitive belief in our own continued existence that comes with our ability to remember past states of mind as our own. Self and memory, Mill said, are "merely two sides of the same fact, or two different modes of viewing the same fact."[21] He explained that when a person – I – remembers something, "in addition" to the belief that I have "that the idea I now have was derived from a previous sensation" there is "the further conviction that this sensation" was "my own; that it happened to my self." He continued,

> I am aware of a long and uninterrupted succession of past feelings, going back as far as memory reaches, and terminating with the sensations I have at the present moment, all of which are connected by an inexplicable tie, that distinguishes them not only from any succession or combination in mere thought, but also from the parallel succession of feelings

which are had by others.

> This succession of feelings, which I call my memory of the past, is that by which I distinguish my Self. Myself is the person who had that series of feelings, and I know nothing of myself, by direct knowledge, except that I had them. But there is a bond of some sort among all the parts of the series, which makes me say that they were feelings of a person who was the same person throughout and a different person from those who had any of the parallel successions of feelings; and this bond, to me, constitutes my Ego.[22]

William James (1842–1910) later criticized Mill for having fallen back "upon something perilously near to the Soul," quoting as evidence Mill's remark that it is "indubitable" that "there is something real" in the tie which is revealed in memory when one recognizes a sensation's having been felt before, and thereby "connects the present consciousness with the past one of which it reminds me." This tie, Mill said, "is the Ego, or Self." Mill continued, "I ascribe a reality to the Ego – to my own mind – different from that real existence as a Permanent Possibility, which is the only reality I acknowledge in Matter." This Ego, he concluded, "is a permanent element." James remarked that

> this "something in common" by which they [remembered feelings] are linked and which is not the passing feelings themselves, but something "permanent," of which we can "affirm nothing" save its attributes and its permanence, what is it but metaphysical Substance come again to life?[23]

James concluded that Mill here makes "the same blunder" that Hume had earlier made:

> the sensations per se, he thinks, have no "tie." The tie of resemblance and continuity which the remembering Thought finds among them is not a "real tie" but "a mere product of the laws of thought"; and the fact that the present Thought "appropriates" them is also no real tie.

But, James continued, whereas Hume was content "to say that there might after all be no 'real tie', Mill, unwilling to admit this possibility, is driven, like any scholastic, to place it in a non-phenomenal world."

In James' own approach to the self, the spirit of traditional empiricism burned brightly, but was now linked with a newfound interest both in physiology and in social interaction. From this perspective James claimed that the core of personhood is "the incessant presence of two elements, an objective person, known by a passing subjective Thought and recognized as continuing in time."[24] He resolved to use the word *me* for "the empirical person" and *I* for "the judging Thought." Since the "me" is constantly changing: "the identity found by the I in its me is only a loosely construed thing, an identity 'on the whole', just like that which any outside observer might find in the same assemblage of facts."[25] The I of any given moment is a temporal slice of "a stream of thought," each part of which, as "I," can "remember those which went before, and know the things they knew" and "emphasize and care paramountly for certain ones among them as 'me', and appropriate to these the rest." The core of what is thought to be the "me" "is always the bodily existence felt to be present at the time."[26]

Remembered-past-feelings that "resemble this present feeling are deemed to belong to the same me with it." And "whatever other things are perceived to be associated with this feeling are deemed to form part of that me's experience; and of them certain ones (which fluctuate more or less) are reckoned to be themselves constituents of the me in a larger sense," such as one's clothes, material possessions, friends, honors, and so on. But while the "me" is "an empirical aggregate of things objectively known," the "I" which "knows them cannot itself be an aggregate." Rather, "it is a Thought, at each moment different from that of the last moment, but appropriative of the latter, together with all that the latter called its own."[27] In other words, what one calls "the I" is constantly changing. The *I* as a persisting thing is a fiction.

Closely related to the questions of how the self is constituted and whether anything so constituted could be a real thing was the question of how humans acquire a self-concept. Descartes had maintained that for anyone to be conscious one would have to know (or be conscious) that oneself is conscious. But to know that *oneself* is conscious, one would have to already be in possession of a self-concept. Thus, in such a view there is no room for conscious beings to gradually develop a self-concept; they must already have one in order to be conscious in the first place. Eighteenth-century rationalists, such as Clarke, continued to accept this view, and even Locke accepted it. It was not until the end of the eighteenth century that empiricists *explicitly* abandoned it.

The moment came in William Hazlitt's (1778–1830) first work, *An Essay on the Principles of Human Action* (1969 [1805]), which was the culmination of a kind of perspective on human mentality that had begun with Locke and been developed by Collins, Hume, and Priestley. According to Hazlitt, people are naturally concerned about whether someone is pleased or suffers as a consequence of their actions. This is because "there is something in the very idea of good, or evil, which naturally excites desire or aversion." But, he wrote, before the acquisition of self-concepts, people are indifferent about whether those who may be pleased or suffer are themselves or others: "a child first distinctly wills or pursues his own good," he said, "not because it is his but because it is good." As a consequence, he claimed, "what is personal or selfish in our affections" is due to "time and habit," the rest to "the principle of a disinterested love of good as such, or for its own sake, without any regard to personal distinctions."[28]

Hazlitt asked why, if people connect to the future through imagination, which does not respect the difference between self and other, the force of habit is almost invariably on the side of selfish feelings. His answer involved his trying to account for the growth of selfish motives in humans by appeal to their acquisition of self-concepts. In his view, when very young children behave selfishly it is not because they like themselves better, but because they know their own wants and pleasures better. In older children and adults, he thought, it is because they have come under the control of their self-concepts, which is something that happens in three stages. First, young children acquire an idea of themselves as beings capable of experiencing pleasure and pain. Second, and almost "mechanically" (since physiology insures that children remember only their own pasts) children include their own pasts in their notions of themselves. Finally, imaginatively, they include their own futures.[29]

In the first half of the eighteenth century, the possibility of a developmental account of the acquisition of self-concepts that Locke may have seen dimly was invisible to most of his readers. As commonsensical as the idea of this possibility may seem to us today, it did not begin to emerge in the views of eighteenth-century thinkers until mid-century. Hartley had formulated a developmental, associational account of the mind, but he focused on the development of the passions and did not consider the acquisition of self-concepts. Jean Jacques Rousseau (1712–78), especially in *Emile*, was sensitive to developmental concerns, but not particularly with respect to the acquisition of self-concepts. Reid, late in the century, had a developmental psychology, but because of his commitment to the immateriality of the soul and the reflexive nature of consciousness, he may actually have made an exception in the case of the idea of self. Priestley, largely under the influence of Hartley, accepted the possibility of a developmental account of the acquisition of self-concepts, but did not elaborate.

Hazlitt thought that to progress through all three of the development stages that he distinguished in the acquisition of self-concepts, a child has to differentiate its own mental activities from those of others. In his view, this involves "perceiving that you are and what you are from the immediate reflection of the mind on its own operations, sensations or ideas." He then raised the question of how a child's formation of self-concepts is related to its development of empathy and sympathy. No one previously had asked this question.

In Hume's emotional contagion model of human sympathy, humans infer from external behavior, facial expressions, and the like that others are in some particular mental state. Then, the resulting idea that humans form of another's state becomes converted in their own minds into an impression, so that now they too are in the same state, though perhaps less vivaciously. In explaining how this conversion from idea to impression occurs, Hume appealed to the idea's "proximity" in one's mind to the impression one has of oneself, which he said is "so lively" that "it is not possible to imagine that any thing can in this particular go beyond it."[30] But, then, he added not a word of explanation about how people acquire their super-lively self-impressions.

Two decades later, Adam Smith gave an unusually thorough account of the role, in sympathy, of shifts from one's own to another's point of view. Yet Smith never attempted to explain how people acquire their ideas of the distinction between self and other. Aside from the applications of his ideas to ethical theory, Smith's gaze was fixed on the importance of point of view as a feature of adult minds, not on the psycho-genetics of point of view in our mental development. In explaining how sympathy is possible, it did not occur to him to explain how the conceptual apparatus that makes it possible came to be acquired in the first place.

Hazlitt speculated that young children imaginatively include only their own futures and not the futures of others in their ideas of self because the "greater liveliness and force" with which they can enter into their future feelings "in a manner identifies them" with those feelings. He added that once the notion of one's own personal identity is formed, "the mind makes use of it to strengthen its habitual propensity, by giving to personal motives a reality and absolute truth which they can never have." This happens, he thought, because "we have an indistinct idea of extended consciousness and a community of feelings as essential to the same thinking being," as a consequence of which we assume that whatever "interests [us] at one time must interest [us] or be capable of interesting [us] at other times."[31]

Hazlitt claimed that a bias in favor of ourselves in the future could never "have gained the assent of thinking men" but for "the force" with which a future-oriented idea of self "habitually clings to the mind of every man, binding it as with a spell, deadening its discriminating powers, and spreading the confused associations which belong only to past and present impressions over the whole of our imaginary existence."

However, whereas a host of previous thinkers – Descartes, Locke, Berkeley, Butler, and others – thought that people have intuitive knowledge of their own identities, Hazlitt rejected as "wild and absurd" the idea that people have any sort of identity that could be available to be intuited. We have been misled, he claimed, by language: by "a mere play of words." In his view, both children and adults fail to look beyond the common idioms of personal identity and as a consequence routinely mistake linguistic fictions for metaphysical realities. To say that someone has a "general interest" in whatever concerns his own future welfare "is no more," he insisted, "than affirming that [he] shall have an interest in that welfare, or that [he is] nominally and in certain other respects the same being who will hereafter have a real interest in it." No amount of mere telling "me that I have the same interest in my future sensations as if they were present, because I am the same individual," he claimed, can bridge the gulf between the "real" mechanical connections I have to myself in the past and present and the merely verbal and imaginary connections that I have to myself in the future.[32]

Toward a science of human nature

When Locke published his *Essay*, he was eager to launch a science of human nature. Four decades later, when Hume published *A Treatise of Human Nature* (1888 [1739]), he assumed that a science of human nature had not only been launched, but had already taken a wrong turn. He was intent on setting things right, which he thought involved having the science of human nature assume its rightful position among the sciences. In his view, that position was at the *foundation* of a mighty edifice of human knowledge. Whereas today we tend to think of physics as the most fundamental science, Hume thought of the science of human nature as the most fundamental since only it would build an account based on experience (rather than things), which for Hume was our ultimate source both of evidence and meaning. "There is no question of importance," Hume said, "whose decision is not comprised in the science of man; and there is none, which can be decided with any certainty, before we become acquainted with that science." In explaining "the principles of human nature," he continued, "we in effect propose a complete system of the sciences, built on a foundation almost entirely new, and the only one upon which they can stand with any security."[33]

How, then, to proceed? The first step, Hume thought, was to reveal the basis on which any genuine science of human nature must be built. That, he said, is "experience and observation," by which he meant the ultimate *impressions* (what twentieth-century philosophical empiricists would call *sense-data*) on the basis of which all of a human's more complex *ideas* (concepts) would have to be wholly constructed. As it happened, however, for psychology to find its feet as a science it had to abandon such epistemological and metaphysical pretensions. Its practitioners had to realize that it was not their job, qua psychologists, to get to the absolute bottom of things. Happily, that task could be left to philosophers. Rather, it was their job, as psychologists, to explain human behavior. To do that, they had to take certain things for granted that in a more philosophical frame of mind could be seen to be deeply questionable. This was the approach that Hartley followed and that Hume's friend and confidant Adam Smith followed in his early work on "the moral sentiments" (mainly human sympathy). It is also the approach that Hume himself often followed, in spite of his methodological manifesto.

This contrast between an austere empirical philosophical approach and a more realistic scientific approach is especially poignant in Hume's account of self and personal identity. In Book I of the *Treatise*, the heart of his account is his argument that belief in a substantial, persisting self is an illusion. More generally, he was intent on showing that belief in the persistence of anything is an illusion. This is what today we would call *philosophy*, rather than *psychology*. However, in the remainder of Book I, Hume addressed the task of explaining why people are so susceptible to the illusion of self. And in Book II he explained how certain dynamic mentalistic systems in which we represent ourselves and others actually work, such as those systems in us that generate sympathetic responses to others. In these more psychological projects, Hume often seems to have taken for granted things that in Book I he had subjected to withering skeptical criticism.

In Hume's view, since all ideas arise from impressions and there is no impression of a "simple and continu'd" self, there is no idea of such a self. This critique of traditional views led him to formulate his alternative "bundle" conception of the self and also to compare the mind to a kind of theatre in which none of the actors – the "perceptions [that] successively make their appearance" – is either "simple" at a time or, strictly speaking, identical over time. Hence, none is the traditional self. Beyond that, Hume claimed, humans do not even have minds, except as fictional constructions. Thus, in his view, a crucial respect in which minds are not analogous to real theatres is that there is no site for the mental performance, or at least none of which we have knowledge; rather, there "are the successive perceptions only, that constitute the mind; nor have we the most distant notion of the place, where these scenes are represented, or of the materials, of which it is compos'd."[34]

With these *philosophical* preliminaries out of the way, Hume turned to the *psychological* task of explaining how objects that are constantly changing, including the materials out of which we ourselves are constructed, nevertheless seem to persist. His answer, in one word, was: resemblance. When successive perceptions resemble each other, he said, it is easy to imagine that the first simply persists. In fact, "our propensity to this mistake" is so ubiquitous and strong "that we fall into it before we are aware." And even when we become aware of our error "we cannot long sustain our philosophy, or take off this biass from the imagination."[35]

Hume may have thought that a crucial difference between Locke and himself on the question of personal identity is that whereas Locke thought that there is a fact of the matter about whether a person persists, Hume thought that there is a fact of the matter only about the circumstances under which the illusion of persistence is nourished. In his capacity as a psychologist, Hume tried to explain what those circumstances were. But he did not stop there. As soon as he moved on to the largely psychological concerns that dominate Book II of the *Treatise*, he became deeply involved in what today we would call social psychology of the self. He, thus, completed a transition from skeptical philosophy to the most general sorts of associational issues, and then to specific psychological hypotheses about how self-representations function in our mental economy, as for instance in his explanation of how sympathy works.

Subsequently Reid, who in spite of his own empirical investigations was a virulent opponent of empiricist epistemology, criticized Hume for denying that there is anything more to mind than a "succession of related ideas and impressions, of which we have an intimate memory and consciousness." Reid asked,

> to be farther instructed, whether the impressions remember and are conscious of the ideas, or the ideas remember and are conscious of the impressions, or if both remember and are conscious of both? and whether the ideas remember those that come after them, as well as those that were before them?

His point was that since ideas and impressions are passive, they cannot do anything, whereas Hume implied that the "succession of ideas and impressions not only remembers and is conscious" but also "judges, reasons, affirms, denies," even "eats and drinks, and is sometimes merry and sometimes sad." Reid concluded, "If these things can be ascribed to a succession of ideas and impressions in a consistency of common sense, I should be very glad to know what is nonsense." In Reid's view, if in accounting for the mind substance were to have no place, then agency would have no place either.[36] Since Reid thought it would be absurd to deny agency, substance had to be retained.

But what Reid might instead have concluded from his criticism is that in order to conduct a science of human nature one has to make realistic assumptions about the mind.

Associationism

The theory that complex ideas in the human mind are constructed out of simple components and that the succession in the mind of (mostly) complex ideas can be explained by appeal to their similarity with each other and their repeated juxtaposition had been around since classical times.[37] However, this theory not only resurfaced in the modern era, but became a preoccupation of empiricists. In the seventeenth century, Hobbes used it to explain the succession and coherence of ideas:

> The *cause* of the *coherence* or consequence of one conception to another, is their first *coherence* or consequence at that time when they are produced by sense; as for example, from St. Andrew the mind runneth to St. Peter, because their names are read together; from St. Peter to a *stone*, for the same cause; from *stone* to *foundation*, because we see them together; and for the same cause from foundation to *church*, and from church to *people* ... [and thus] the mind may run almost from anything to anything.[38]

In the eighteenth century, such appeals to association acquired renewed vitality, due primarily to the influence of Locke, Hume, and Hartley, all of whom gave association a central role in their accounts of experiential phenomena. But neither Locke nor Hume appealed to association to speculate on the physiological underpinnings of empirical phenomena. That task was left to Hartley.

Philosophically Hartley was a dualist, but methodologically he was a materialist. Differing in this respect from Collins before him and Priestley after, Hartley believed that "man consists of two parts, body and mind," where the mind "is that substance, agent, principle, &c. to which we refer the sensation, ideas, pleasures, pains, and voluntary motions." But Hartley accepted Locke's concession that it is possible, for all we know, that matter thinks. And he doubted that either problems with materialism or pre-scientific intuitions we may have about the so-called unity of consciousness could be used to prove that the soul is immaterial, confessing that "it is difficult to know [even] what is meant by the Unity of Consciousness." He claimed that there is a problem with materialism in that "Matter and Motion, however subtly divided, or reasoned upon, yield nothing more than Matter and Motion still." But it was, he said, "foreign to [his] Purpose" to pursue the issue.

In addition to being a dualist, Hartley was a theist. But he never allowed his metaphysical and theological views to interfere with his attempt to establish a deterministic associationist psychology. Inspired by Newton's suggestion in *Principia Mathematica* that vibrations of corpuscles of light might cause vibrations in the retina of the eye, which would then be transmitted to the brain where they would produce the sensation of sight, and by some intimations of associationism in John Gay's (1699–1745) *Dissertation Concerning the Fundamental Principles of Virtue or Morality* (of 1731), Hartley proposed a "physics of the soul" in which physical vibrations in the brain, spinal cord, and nerves are the basis of all sensations, ideas, and motions of men and animals.[39] In his view, the "higher" the mental function – images and ideas, for instance, are higher than sensations – the more delicate the vibrations with which it is associated. And when mental functions are similar, as in the case of images and ideas that faithfully replicate sensations, it is due to a correspondence in the vibrations.

All learning, Hartley claimed, including that involved in perception, memory, imagination, emotion, and language, is the consequence of repetitive juxtapositions of corpuscular vibrations and mental associations that produce habits in accordance with a pleasure-pain principle, a view that he illustrated especially by appeal to the study of how children learn languages. Hartley thereby produced the first truly general account of human and animal psychology, which was an association based, mechanistic, deterministic, physiological psychology.

In France, the physician Julien Offray de la Mettrie (1709–1751), in his *Natural History of the Soul* (of 1745) and his *Man a Machine* (of 1748) developed Hartley's approach by arguing that human beings are merely physiological machines. Subsequently, Condillac laid the groundwork for an association-based psychophysiological account of human nature that became influential on the continent in the nineteenth century. Meanwhile, in Britain, Priestley encouraged the acceptance of Hartley's ideas in his *Theory of the Human Mind, on the Principle of Association of Ideas* (of 1775). Priestley thought that the sentient and thinking principle in man must be "a property of the nervous system or rather of the brain," insisting that it is scientifically useless to postulate an immaterial substance to account for *any* aspect of human mentality or behavior.[40] Priestley saw the differences between humans and other animals as differences of degree, rather than kind, and held that human infants begin like other animals and only gradually learn adult human modes of thinking, including the ability to conceptualize themselves.

In British philosophy, where empiricism still held sway in the nineteenth century, interest in associationism gathered strength. Thomas Brown (1778–1820), in his three volume, *Lectures on the Philosophy of the Human Mind* (of 1820), importantly elaborated associationist theory by distinguishing primary and secondary laws of suggestion (his word for *association*). And James Mill (1773–1836), in his *Analysis of the Human Mind* (of 1829), sketched a general view of the mind in which it was little more than mere machinery for the association process, a view that many psychologists came to regard as an important advance on Hartley's approach.

John Stuart Mill, James Mill's son, became an enthusiastic follower of the Positivism of Auguste Comte (1798–1857), but criticized Comte's negative attitude toward psychology: Comte "rejects totally, as an invalid process, psychological observation properly so called, or in other words, internal consciousness, at least as regards our intellectual operations."[41] To fill this gap, Mill made detailed comments on and refinements to his father's thoughts, ultimately arguing for his own associationist system of "mental chemistry." However, J. S. Mill's own contributions to psychology, while extremely attentive to internal consciousness, were primarily epistemological. Like Hume, he thought that his own phenomenalism, which he called *the psychological theory*, was a kind of foundational psychology. In Mill's view, material objects are "permanent possibilities of sensation," and other minds are inferred to exist based on an analogy with one's own case, which he presumed one knows directly. He claimed that like objects in the external world, minds too are just actual and possible sensations. Subsequent psychologists tended to regard his psychology as too philosophical to be responsive to their own interests.

Meanwhile Alexander Bain (1818–1903) revived and greatly developed Hartley's interest in a physiological approach to the understanding of human mentality. In *The Senses and the Intellect* (of 1855) and *The Emotions and the Will* (1876 [1859]), Bain drew upon Hartley and others to work out a sensory-motor associationism that marked a turning point in the history of associationist psychology. Before his work associationists like Hume and J. S. Mill were committed to experience as the primary source of knowledge. Bain, in a more realist mode, accepted movement and social interaction as primary, which he then used to explain higher mental functions, including self-attributions. He claimed, for instance, that when attention is turned inward upon oneself as a personality "we are putting forth towards ourselves the kind of exercise that properly accompanies our contemplation of other persons."[42]

Bain's more sophisticated psychophysiology was distinctive, first, for its realism, in that he began by assuming the existence of the physical world, including as items in it other people and himself; second, by the primacy he gave to social observation, in that we first make judgments about others, and only later think of ourselves as one "other" among many; and, third, by his suggestion that this progression from others to self not only explains the origin of the notion of self, but also our ability to feel toward the self emotions that originally we felt toward others. Ultimately J. S. Mill would praise Bain's account as the highest point yet reached by the empiricist tradition.

Concurrent with such philosophical and psychological developments there was in the nineteenth century a growing spirit of naturalized science, typified by the work of Charles Darwin (1809–82), but independently including inquiry into the development of self concepts and the physiology of the brain. In 1855, the same year in which Bain published *The Senses and the Intellect*, Herbert Spencer (1820–1903) published *The Principles of Psychology*, which grounded psychology in evolutionary biology. Subsequently William James would build on both of these contributions.

James followed Bain, who had defined belief as a rule or habit of action, and Charles Sanders Pierce (1839–1914), who had claimed that the point of theory is not to represent reality, but to enable us to act more effectively, in turning partly away from empiricism toward what came to be known as pragmatism.[43] In some ways, James was the last philosopher/psychologist and arguably the last psychologist of importance in whom a sort of empiricism that could be traced back directly to Locke and Hume still resonated strongly. Increasingly, in the twentieth century, philosophy and psychology tended to go their separate ways. Throughout the first half of the century empiricism, particularly in its incarnation in epistemology, continued to be a potent force in philosophy, but was much less so in psychology. There the influence of empiricism tended to be supplanted by a newfound preoccupation with behavior and with the social dimensions of mental development.

Notes

1. See, for instance, Samet (1998).
2. See, for instance, Cowie (1998).
3. Locke (1694 [1690]: Bk 4, sec. 3, pp. 540–1).
4. Russell (1945: 659).
5. See Marya Schechtman's contribution to the present volume.
6. Clarke (1828 [1738]: Vol. 3, pp. 720–913).
7. *Ibid.*: Vol. 3, p. 750.
8. *Ibid.*: Vol. 3, pp. 769–73.
9. *Ibid.*: Vol. 3, pp. 784–7.
10. *Ibid.*: Vol. 3, p. 790.
11. *Ibid.*: Vol. 3, pp. 809, 870.
12. Locke (1975 [1690–4]: Bk 2, sec. 27, pp. 335, 341).
13. *Ibid.*: Bk 2, sec. 27, p. 346.
14. *Ibid.*: Bk 2, sec. 27, p. 341.
15. For a competing view, see Ayers (1991: Vol. 2, pp. 266–7).
16. Butler (1852 [1736]: 86).
17. *Ibid.*: 87–8.
18. *Ibid.*: 328, 331–2.
19. *Ibid.*: 330.
20. *Ibid.*: 322, 325.
21. Mill (1869: Vol. 2, p. 174).
22. *Ibid.*: Vol. 2, pp. 174–5.
23. Mill (1878 [1865]: 262–3); James (1890: Vol. 1, p. 358).

24. *Ibid.*: Vol. 1, p. 371.
25. *Ibid.*: Vol. 1, p. 373.
26. *Ibid.*: Vol. 1, p. 400.
27. *Ibid.*: Vol. 1, pp. 400–1.
28. *Ibid.*: 33–4.
29. *Ibid.*: 34–5.
30. Hume (1888 [1739]: 317).
31. Hazlitt (1969 [1805]: 10–1, 140).
32. *Ibid.*: 6, 10–1, 27–9.
33. *Ibid.*: Introduction.
34. *Ibid*: 253.
35. In and of itself, Hume suggested, our supposing that objects persist is not so bad. But "in order to justify to ourselves this absurdity," we make up a story, often one in which the principle character is the notion of substance; that is, we invent the fictions of "soul, and self, and substance to disguise the variation" in our perceptions. When, as in the case of "plants and vegetables," we cannot fool ourselves into believing that the persistence of an underlying substance accounts for the persistence of the organism, we invent an equally "unknown and mysterious" surrogate – presumably, "life" – to connect the successive and different perceptions, *ibid.*: 254–5.
36. Reid (1967 [1785]: 444).
37. See, for instance, Plato's *Phaedo* (73d) and Aristotle's *On Memory and Reminiscence* (*passim*). Throughout this section of my paper, I am indebted to the account of associationism in Sahakian (1975).
38. Hobbes (1969 [1640]: Ch. 4, "Of the Several Kinds of Discursion of the Mind").
39. Hartley's formulation of associationism states that "Any sensation A, B, C, etc. by being associated with one another a sufficient number of times, gets such a power over the corresponding ideas *a*, *b*, *c*, etc. that one of the sensations A, when impressed alone shall be able to excite in the mind *b*, *c*, etc. the ideas of the rest." In (1749: Vol. 1, prop. 10).
40. Priestley's rootedness in science, together with the matter of factness of his materialistic approach and his unproblematic commitment to realism, differed radically from the epistemologically oriented versions of empiricism championed by Locke, Berkeley, and Hume. Because of it Priestley did not think that his style of empiricist epistemology led to skepticism about the external world, as Reid had claimed, or indeed to skepticism about anything, and he more cleanly separated philosophy from science than Hume, in particular, had been able to do (Priestley 1976 [1777]: 163).
41. Mill (1968: 64).
42. Bain (1876: 203–4).
43. Richard (2004 [1998]).

Acknowledgements

Throughout the present paper I have drawn freely from two books that I co-authored with John Barresi: *Naturalization of the Soul: Personal Identity in the Eighteenth Century* (2000) and *The Rise and Fall of Soul and Self: An Intellectual History of Personal Identity* (2006). I am grateful to John for allowing me to draw upon work that is as much his as mine. I am also grateful to him, Marya Schechtman, and Michael Mathias for comments on an earlier draft.

References

Ayers, Michael (1991) *Locke*, 2 vols, London: Routledge.

Bain, Alexander (1876) *The Emotions and the Will*, 3rd edn, New York: Appleton & Co.

Butler, Joseph (1852 [1736]) *The Analogies of Religion, Natural and Revealed*, London: Henry G. Bohn.

Clarke, Samuel (1928 [1738]) *The Works of Samuel Clarke*, 4 vols, New York: Garland Publishing.

Cowie, Fiona (1998) "Language, Innateness of," in E. Craig (ed.) *Routledge Encyclopedia of Philosophy*, London: Routledge; available: http://www.rep.routledge.com/article/U014SECT1 (accessed 12 December 2006).

Hartley, David (1749) *Observations on Man*, repr., with intro. T. L. Huguelet, Gainesville, FL: Scholars' Facsimiles & Reprints

Hazlitt, William (1969 [1805]) *An Essay on the Principles of Human Action and some Remarks on the Systems of Hartley and Helvetius*, repr., with intro. J. R. Nabholtz, Gainesville, FL: Scholars' Facsimiles & Reprints.

Hobbes, Thomas (1969 [1640]) *The Elements of Law, Natural and Political*, London; New York: Routledge.

Hume, David (1888 [1739]) *A Treatise of Human Nature*, ed. L. A. Selby-Bigge, Oxford: Clarendon Press.

James, William (1890) *Principles of Psychology*, 2 vols, New York: Henry Holt & Co.

Locke, John (1975 [1690–4]) *An Essay Concerning Human Understanding*, ed. P. H. Nidditch, Oxford: Clarendon Press.

Martin, Raymond, and Barresi, John (2000) *Naturalization of the Soul: Personal Identity in the Eighteenth Century*, London: Routledge

—— (2006) *The Rise and Fall of Soul and Self: An Intellectual History of Personal Identity*, New York: Columbia University Press.

Mill, J. S. (1869) Notes to James Mill, *Analysis of the Human Mind*, 2 vols, ed. A. Bain, A. Findlater, and G. Grote, London: Longman's Green Reader & Dyer.

—— (1878 [1865]) *An Examination of Sir William Hamilton's Philosophy*, London: Longman's, Green, Reader, & Dyer.

—— (1968) *Auguste Comte and Positivism*, Ann Arbor: University of Michigan Press.

Priestley, Joseph (1976 [1777]) *Disquisitions Relating to Matter and Spirit and the Doctrine of Philosophical Necessity Illustrated*, repr. New York: Garland Publishing.

Reid, Thomas (1967 [1785]) *Essay on the Intellectual Powers of Man*, in W. Hamilton (ed.), *Philosophical Works of Thomas Reid*, vol. 1, repr. Hildesheim: George Olms, 213–508.

Rorty, Richard (2004 [1998]) "Pragmatism," in E. Craig (ed.), *Routledge Encyclopedia of Philosophy*, London: Routledge; available: http://www.rep.routledge.com/article/N046 (accessed 18 December 2006).

Russell, Bertrand (1945) *A History of Western Philosophy*, New York: Simon & Schuster.

Sahakian, William S. (1975) *History and Systems of Psychology*, New York: Schenkman Publishing [John Wiley & Sons].

Samet, Jerry (1998) "Nativism," in E. Craig (ed.), *Routledge Encyclopedia of Philosophy*, London: Routledge; available: http://www.rep.routledge.com/article/W028 (accessed 12 December 2006).

Further reading

For further reading on this topic, see Ludy T. Benjamin Jr., *A Brief History of Modern Psychology* (Oxford: Blackwell, 2007); Edwin G. Boring, *A History of Experimental Psychology*, 2nd edn (New York: Appleton-Century-Crofts, 1950); B. R. Hergenhahn, *An Introduction to the History of Psychology*, 5th edn (Belmont, CA: Wadsworth, 2004); Raymond Martin and John Barresi, *Naturalization of the Soul: Self and Personal Identity in the Eighteenth Century* (London: Routledge, 2000), and *The Rise and Fall of Soul and Self: An Intellectual History of Personal Identity* (New York: Columbia University Press, 2006); Henry K. Misiak and Virginia S. Sexton, *History of Psychology: An Overview* (New York: Grune & Stratton, 1966); David J. Murray, *A History of Western Psychology*, 2nd edn (1983; Englewood Cliffs, NJ: Prentice-Hall, 1988); William S. Sahakian, *History and Systems of Psychology* (New York: Schenkman; John Wiley & Sons, 1975), and *History of Psychology: A Source Book in Systematic Psychology* (Itasca, IL: F. E. Peacock, 1968); and Roger Smith, *The Norton History of the Human Sciences* (New York: W. W. Norton & Co., 1997).

3
EARLY EXPERIMENTAL PSYCHOLOGY

Alan Kim

Introduction

"The physiology of the senses is a border land in which the two great divisions of human knowledge, natural and mental science, encroach on one another's domain; in which problems arise which are important for both, and which only the combined labour of both can solve."[1] It was some forty years before Hermann von Helmholtz wrote these words that Johannes Müller and Ernst Heinrich Weber first forayed into the philosophers' realm of the mental with tactics and tools devised in the fields of natural science. For many decades thereafter, philosophers, particularly of an idealist stripe, readjusted the borderline between psychology and philosophy as they tried to preserve a "pure" domain of research, one untouchable by empirical (and this came more and more to mean "experimental") psychology.[2] The early history of experimental psychology is instructive for philosophers today because it was at this stage that the question of the very possibility of a science of mind was first addressed. Moreover, the *way* in which psychology asserted itself as a discipline holds lessons for those concerned with the form that contemporary debates regarding mind and brain have taken.

Psychology, or inquiry into the nature of mental phenomena such as sensation, perception, thought, feeling, and willing – indeed, the nature of "soul" itself – had long been the domain of philosophers whose general approach was speculative, and whose aim was, as James Sully wrote in the inaugural issue of *Mind* (1876), "to determine the substance of mind with the view of embodying this idea in an ultimate ontological theory."[3] Sully took a dim view of these thinkers. He complained that they had "little patience in the observation and classification of mental phenomena, little penetrative insight into the causal relations of these phenomena [, while] on the other hand we see abundant metaphysical ingenuity in building new hypotheses on arbitrarily selected groups of facts."[4] Yet, as we will also see, it is not the case, at least in Germany, that with the new rigor of experiment, psychology abruptly broke with philosophy and its alleged speculative excess. Maybe this happens later; but for the founding fathers, especially Fechner and Wundt, psychology was *still* a part of philosophy, indeed its foundation. Experimental methodology merely gives this foundation a scientific rigor – a necessity insofar as (German) philosophers continued to consider philosophy the science of sciences. For them, the notion of a "philosophy *of* psychology" would have sounded very obscure.

I will limit myself in this chapter to the following questions: How can experiment aid us in observing, classifying and understanding the causal relations among mental phenomena? Conversely, how must the mental be construed so as to be susceptible to experiment? Proceeding historically, I examine four founding figures of experimental psychology – E. H. Weber, G. T. Fechner, H. von Helmholtz, and W. Wundt – to determine how and to what extent they recognized and dealt with these *philosophical* questions. What if anything remains of the mental as of "purely" philosophical interest lies beyond our scope.

Background

In the eighteenth century, Kant raised several objections against any form of psychology other than his own "transcendental" variety.[5] He argued against the very possibility of both rational and empirical psychology, i.e., psychology based, respectively, on metaphysical first principles or on introspective observation of subjective phenomena;[6] the latter is especially germane here. Introspection, according to Kant, necessarily distorts, by participating in, the very phenomena it seeks to observe.[7] Moreover, Kant held that psychology could never be a science inasmuch as the "exactness" of mathematics necessarily eluded it.[8] What does this mean? A science is exact just when it can express its propositions mathematically. But for this to be possible, its objects must be capable of measurement; measurement in turn requires the fixing of units. Physics can operate "exactly" because it possesses various exact units of measurement, such as joules or meters. But how could psychic phenomena (the "manifold of inner observation," as Kant calls it)[9] be measured? What unit of measurement could a psychologist employ in determining (mathematically) the ebb and flow of consciousness?

These philosophical obstacles – introspection, exactness, psychic units, and psychic measurement – turn out, as we will see, to be evaded or ignored by the pioneers of experimental psychology: it does not begin as a self-conscious effort to reply to Kant. Rather, it is in the course of other scientific projects that problems of subjectivity ineluctably arise, e.g., in astronomy the discrepancy between observers' reaction times in marking the movement of stars across a meridian, expressed in the so-called personal equation;[10] and, more obviously, the phenomenology connected with the function of the nervous system. It was in fact a set of ingenious physiological experiments conducted by Weber that opened up the possibility, behind Kant's back, as it were, of developing an experimental psychology; but it was only exploited in a philosophically, that is, psychologically self-conscious way by Fechner and his successors.[11]

Ernst Heinrich Weber (1795–1878)

It is in the work of the Leipzig physicist and physiologist, E. H. Weber, that a subjective or "psychological" element enters into the sensory physiology pioneered by his contemporary, Johannes Müller. We can see this in the way Weber phrases the issue of his classic studies of cutaneous and muscular sensation of temperature and touch. His *De Tactu* (1834) and *Tastsinn und Gemeingefühl* (1846) concern the human *experience* of warmth and cold; our power of *discerning* locations on the surface of the skin; of *judging* differences in weight[12] – all phenomena on the psychological side of the mind-body divide. For our purposes, Weber's work is important for two reasons. First, his innovative experimental approach to sensation revealed the possibility of psychological experimentation, later developed by Fechner.[13] Second, Weber's experiments led him to postulate an active subjective contribution to the formation of "sense-perceptions," a notion that would prove fundamental to Helmholtz and Wundt's work some decades later. Let us briefly consider these two contributions.

Let us begin with a précis of Weber's experimental work. In *De Tactu* and *Tastsinn*, he describes his experiments on the sense of touch. He discovered that when the points of a compass close together on the skin, they are sensed as a single point, yet as they are moved apart, we become conscious of being touched at two points. Weber called this moment at which we become aware of feeling two contacts instead of one the two-point threshold or *limen*.[14] This threshold, he found through exhaustive tests, varies on different regions of the body's surface, a phenomenon he explained by postulating *Empfindungskreise* or "sensory regions,"[15] tiny fields of sensitivity associated with a single nerve ending;[16] the more such regions lie between the compass points, the further apart they appear to us to be, and vice versa.[17]

Weber also studied the sense of temperature, which, unlike the sense of brightness and dimness, is relative and mutable. Whereas the zero-point (*Nullpunkt*) of illumination is absolute darkness, and thus the various degrees of illumination are necessarily positive magnitudes, the zero-point of the temperature sense, Weber says, is an internal thermal source.[18] Weber hypothesized that "the experience of warmth and cold is not dependent directly on the temperature of the stimulating object, but on the *increase* and *decrease* of the temperature of the skin,"[19] since any body that upon contact with the skin raises or lowers its "zero-point" temperature will appear warm or cold, respectively.[20] Thus what is sensed is not temperature as such, but the contrast between the temperature of the skin and the stimulating object.

These examples show that Weber's chief interest lay not so much in the qualitative phenomenology of sensation as in the difference between sensations, specifically, in the moment at which one sensation ends and another begins. Difference of sensations is philosophically significant for two reasons. First, it suggests a criterion of separating mental events, namely noticeability; if, moreover, a regular relationship between two just noticeably different sensations can be established, then we might come into possession of a method by which mental events more generally could be manipulated in a controlled fashion, that is, an experimental method for psychology.

In fact, Weber discovered just such a law-like regularity between changes in stimulatory intensity, on the one hand, and differentiation of sensations, on the other, a regularity that Fechner would later codify and name Weber's law. It was Weber's work on the sensation of just noticeable differences in weight or pressure (*Drucksinn*), in lengths of lines, and in changes in tone that proved most important for establishing this functional rule relating stimulus and sensation.[21] On the basis of numerous documented trials, Weber concludes in *De Tactu* that "when noting a difference between things that have been compared, we do not perceive the difference between the things [i.e., the absolute weight difference], but the ratio of the difference to their magnitude."[22] His point is quite simple. If a weight of half an ounce is placed in our hand, we can easily perceive it; however, if "two weights of 33 and 34 half-ounces are compared by touch, we do not perceive the difference" between the two weights, even though they differ by the previously perceptible weight, namely half an ounce.[23] The reason for our not perceiving the difference in this case is that "the ratio of the difference between the two weights is only a 34th part of the heavier weight," and this ratio (rather than the difference in absolute weight) is too small to be discerned. Similarly, when comparing the length of lines, Weber found his subjects to be unable to discern differences less than one percent, regardless whether the lines were, say, 100 and 101 mm, or 50 and 50.5 mm in length, respectively: "The disparity is recognized as easily in the latter case, even though it is twice as small, because in both cases the difference between the two lines is equal to 1/100 of the longer line."[24]

Weber's law, both in its more pragmatic formulation by Weber himself and in Fechner's formalizations of it (see below), proved immensely controversial and fruitful for decades after. From a strictly philosophical point of view, it seems most interesting for the mathematical regularity it reveals in certain psychological, that is, subjective phenomena. Moreover, Weber recognized, on the one hand, that "tactile acuity depends partly on the structure of the organ, and partly on movements of the organ made *deliberately* and *consciously*,"[25] and on the other hand, that his experimental subjects may become more "practised," that is, may improve their tactile acuity. Although he did not himself draw any psychological or philosophical conclusions from these facts, they clearly indicate a regular connection between measurable stimuli and subjective activity of conscious deliberation and will – a connection more explicitly and deeply worked out by Helmholtz and Wundt.

Gustav Theodor Fechner (1801–87)

Fechner for the first time clearly states the problem of a scientific psychology: how can the subjective realm be made the object of an exact *and* experimental science?[26] In other words, how is psychology as an exact science possible?[27] Fechner's answer is, only by becoming psychophysics. Fechner's method and practice of psychophysics, as laid out in his groundbreaking *Elemente der Psychophysik* (1860) and defended against objections in his *In Sachen der Psychophysik* (1877), cannot be treated in detail here.[28] What interest us, rather, are his philosophical conception of psychology as psychophysics, and his justification of an experimental approach to the subjective realm.[29]

Fechner was an idealist, a panpsychist, a satirical mystic who wrote a comparative anatomy of angels and argued in print that plants have souls. At the same time, he was a champion of atomism and mentor to Mach, an influence on Schlick and Carnap, and an untiring experimenter, whose visual trials even led to temporary blindness and nervous collapse. As philosophically riven as he may strike us today, Fechner saw his work as coherent: on the one hand, it describes the world as it gives itself to us, appearing from the "outside" as material and mechanistic, while, on the other, it penetrates that same world from the "inside," from the point of view of life and soul.

Fechner defines psychophysics as the "exact theory of the functionally dependent relations of body and soul, or, more generally, of the material and the mental, of the physical and the psychological worlds."[30] What metaphysical presupposition would make such a theory of "functionally dependent relations of body and soul" possible? Fechner, like Wundt after him, subscribes to psychophysical parallelism, i.e., the theory that mental and physical events run on rigorously corresponding but irreducible tracks. However, as I have argued elsewhere regarding Wundt,[31] this label is misleading insofar as it suggests the existence of two ontologically independent, if parallel, realms. Instead, I call Fechner and Wundt's view "perspectival monism":[32] there is just *one* line, one "track," not two, with the left and right "sides" of this line representing, respectively, its mental and physical *appearances*.

Now instead of "right" and "left," Fechner himself speaks of the "inner" and "outer": the natural sciences take the external standpoint towards reality, whereas the humanities take the inner, though it is one and the same reality in both cases. The two approaches can be compared to observers of a circle: to an observer inside the circle, it appears concave, and its convex appearance is hidden, whereas for the observer outside the circle, it appears convex while its concavity is concealed. "It is just as impossible, standing in the plane of a circle, to see both sides of the circle simultaneously, as it is to see both sides of man from the plane of human existence."[33] Again, the "inner" and "outer" are Fechner's criterion for determining the psychological and the material.[34] The psychological includes "all that can be grasped by introspective observation or that can be abstracted from it," while the material is "all that can be grasped by observation from the outside or abstracted from it."[35] It is just the exact sciences that combine measurement, experiment, and mathematics that deal with external phenomena, for it is only among these that units and instruments of measurement have traction; the soul's inner realm by contrast is immeasurable and intractable. If, however, Fechner is correct that these two realms are only different aspects of one reality, related to each other as the convex and concave, then it could be possible to find a functional relationship between the two, such that if the one were mathematically determinable, the other could be found as a function of it.

In his preface to the *Elements*, Fechner writes, "Since the measure of physical magnitudes is already known, the first and main task of [psychophysics] will be to establish the as yet nonexistent measure of psychic magnitudes."[36] A *science* of subjectivity is possible only if the manifest differences in subjective intensities (more or less bright, long, heavy, loud) can be associated with a metric – which is what he believes to have done. He considers Weber's discovery of a constant ratio between (external) stimulus intensity and (internal) sensation to provide an empirical basis for such an "exact" mapping of the inner realm, a transformation code, as it were, and so, too, an indirect way of establishing units of psychic magnitude. Weber had experimentally discovered that the ratio of a given stimulus (*Reiz*, R) to another stimulus required to elicit a just noticeable difference in sensation is constant (k), a fact that can be expressed as follows:

$$\Delta R/R = k.$$

Fechner elaborates this simple equation to read

$$\Delta S = k\,(\Delta R/R).$$

In other words, for any difference in sensation, whether just noticeable or not, the proportion of stimulus-increase to original stimulus will remain constant.[37] This new formula, which Fechner calls the "basic formula [*Fundamentalformel*],"[38] is made possible by his assumption that the JNDs (i.e., ΔS) are constant (since they are always *equally* "just" noticeably different).[39] In this way he tries to satisfy the scientific requirement for a psychic unit of measurement.

After further elaboration,[40] Fechner finally arrives at

$$S = k \log R,$$

which he calls Weber's law.[41] This equation expresses the notion that sensation (S) stands in a constant logarithmic relationship to stimulus (R), such that as the S increases arithmetically, R increases geometrically.[42] In other words, for every addition of one sensation-unit (JND), the stimulus increases by some constant factor (which, of course, must be discovered by empirical trial). Fechner thus took Weber's law to represent the functional relation between the external stimulus and the internal sensation, interpreting Weber's original finding in a "fresh" way "as psychological measurement," rather than in its former, merely physiological sense.[43]

Fechner's claims for his Weber's law were immediately criticized, both for taking the JND as a constant unit,[44] as well as for the very notion of a "magnitude" of sensation.[45] While such criticisms exposed obscurities in psychophysics' theoretical foundations, they did not lessen the experimental fecundity of Fechner's formulae.[46] His philosophical relevance, however, lies mainly in his perspectival monism, expressive of the impulse towards ontological unification mentioned by Sully. Yet, in Fechner's defense, he makes every effort to keep distinct the empirical and cosmological senses of his psychophysical parallelism. Psychophysics as a science is based on the empirical postulate that there obtains a functional relationship between mental and physical phenomena, "without referring back in any way to the nature of the body or of the soul beyond the phenomenal in the metaphysical sense."[47]

Hermann von Helmholtz (1821–94)

Helmholtz was a giant of nineteenth-century physics and physiology. His work in physiological optics and acoustics led him across the border, as he put it, into the realm of psychology.[48] Our interest in this section remains with the theoretical problems that arise on this frontier, especially in the area of spatial perception. Helmholtz writes that although physiology concentrates only on "material changes in material organs, and that of the special physiology of the senses [on] the nerves and their sensation, so far as these are excitations of the nerves," science cannot "avoid also considering the apprehension of external objects, which is the result of these excitations of the nerves."[49] Yet this takes us from the somatic or material domain into the mental, since "apprehension of external objects must always be an *act* of our power of realization, and must therefore be accompanied by consciousness."[50] Thus Helmholtz goes beyond Fechner's achievement, fulfilling the latter's goal of psychophysics:[51] at first, experiment can illuminate mental processes

> only so far as we are able by experiment to determine the particular sensible impressions which call up one or another conception in our consciousness. But from this first step will follow *numerous deductions* as to the nature of the mental processes which contribute to the result,

namely the apprehended perception.[52] Whereas in Fechner we see the problem of a scientific psychology framed in terms of a functional relationship between the physical and the mental, in Helmholtz, the mind-body problem is conceived differently, the question posed at a higher level: what is the *active* contribution of mind to its appearances, even when these are perceived as being of an external (physical) object?

The reason for this divergence may be found in the differing nature of Fechner and Helmholtz's physiological research, Fechner concerning himself primarily with sensual intensity, Helmholtz with perception of objects.[53] As I discuss more closely below, Helmholtz's work in optics leads him to conclude that our conscious perceptions of spatial location result not from our native sensory apparatus, but from a process of active, interpretive "experiments" by which sensations are construed as spatial and spatially located objects. He thus goes beyond Fechner, as Fechner went beyond Weber. Where Weber's ratio had simply expressed an experimental fact, Fechner gave it a psychophysical interpretation, that there obtains a lawful relation between the mental and the material, thanks to which measurement of the mental is possible. Helmholtz now asks: what is the origin of such a relation? This deeper, genetic concern arises from the fact that depth perception cannot be explained by a simple correspondence relation between what is sensed by the eye and what we are aware of seeing. Hence Helmholtz is forced to consider an active, synthetic power on the side of the mind. Fechner, by contrast, mainly occupied himself with the measurement of *intensities* of tactile pressure, temperature, and tone, all of which appear "in" the sensing body itself. He would therefore not have been as vividly concerned with phenomena of external objectivity, such as depth, location, dimension, etc.[54] Since these intensities are passively felt or "noted" by the mind, the question of its active contribution does not arise.

Helmholtz's theory of perception is epitomized by his theory of vision. There were in his day two conflicting views of how external objects come to be perceived as extended and located in space. According to nativism, the optic apparatus suffices to represent the external world. In Helmholtz's words, Müller held that

> the retina or skin, being itself an organ which is extended in space, *receives* impressions which carry with them this quality of extension in space; that this conception of locality is innate; and that impressions derived from external objects are transmitted of themselves to corresponding local positions in the image produced in the sensitive organ.[55]

Against this view, empiricists like Helmholtz hold that visual perception[56] requires experience[57] on the basis of which we learn to construe and construct sensible objects. Both terms, "nativism" and "empiricism," can lead to misunderstanding. In our context "nativism" does not mean a commitment to ideal *a priori* structures or faculties of mind, but rather to hypothetical *neural* – i.e., material – mechanisms and their innate capacities and functions.[58] Similarly, Helmholtz's empiricism does not imply a rejection of a subjective contribution to the construction of experience; with respect to the problem of visual perception of objects in space, the empiricist holds that these percepts are not given to us *as* spatial through the receptive function of our visual apparatus (the nativist view) but that they are learned constructions or interpretations of our visual sensations.

In other words, Helmholtz rejects the notion that space and the "quality of extension" of spatial objects is given directly through sensation, with the visual apparatus simply serving to transmit this quality – he rejects, in short, the notion that sensation equals perception, that sensing equals perceiving. Instead, "none of our sensations give us anything more than 'signs' for external objects and movements, and that we can only learn how to *interpret* these signs by means of experience and practice."[59] Again, the qualities of visual sensations "can only be regarded as signs of certain different qualities, which belong sometimes to light itself, sometimes to the bodies it illuminates," "but there is not a single actual quality of the objects seen which precisely corresponds to our sensations of sight."[60]

Perhaps the most important of these signs is the so-called local sign (*Lokalzeichen*), a color sensation making it possible to "distinguish local differences in the field of vision."[61] Now both nativists and empiricists may accept the theory of local signs, but where the nativist "supposes that the local signs are nothing else than *direct* conceptions of differences in space as such, both in their nature and their magnitude," the empiricist regards them "as signs the signification of which must be learnt, and is actually learnt, in order to arrive at a knowledge of the external world;" and for this, "it is not at all necessary to suppose any kind of correspondence between these local signs and the actual differences of locality which they signify."[62] Thus Helmholtz distinguishes between sensations and perceptions, i.e., between "bare sensory patterns ...

directly dependent upon the stimulus-object" and our consciousness of an (external) object itself.[63] We do not directly sense the "immediate action of the external exciting cause upon the ends of our nerves, but only the changed condition of the nervous fibres which we call the state of *excitation* or functional activity."[64] Excitation, in turn, requires interpretation, Helmholtz argues, in order to enter consciousness as "of" an object.[65] Under normal circumstances, we are of course unaware of any such interpretive activity. Helmholtz therefore speaks of "unconscious inferences": when we interpret certain local signs to indicate, "that there in front of us at a certain place there is a certain object of a certain character," these inferences are "generally not conscious activities, but unconscious ones," equivalent "in their result ... to a conclusion."[66] His use of the word "sign" suggests an analogy with learned conventional signs, such as letters. Before we learned them, letters appeared to us as mere sensations or, at most, shapes, but their (functional) meaning remained obscure. After learning our letters and words, their signific function now overwhelms their qualities as mere sensa. If you are reading this, it is scarcely possible, except by an act of great concentration, *not* to see "through" their sensory shape directly to their significance; Q, or "catacomb," e.g., will forever more *appear*, that is, be perceived as a letter or word, respectively, and not as whatever we took them before we learned to read.

Helmholtz explains the phenomenon of visual illusions in a similar way. Precisely because perceptual inferences are unconscious, they are also involuntary and thus "irresistible," by which he means that their effects "cannot be overcome by a better understanding of the real relations."[67] Through experience, over time, we come to prefer using our sensory organs in ways that "we recognize as enabling us to reach the most certain and consistent judgment with regard to ... the form, spatial relationships and composition" of external objects.[68] We are thus led automatically to interpret certain sensory patterns as indicating a certain external state of affairs in the world, what Helmholtz calls normal, veridical perception.[69] An illusion occurs when a sensory pattern contains certain cues that trigger the automatic inference, even though in this abnormal case the pattern in fact does not reflect the objective state of affairs (e.g., cues indicating distance distorting our perception of the size of the moon on the horizon).[70]

We now can see interesting relations between Helmholtz's empiricism and Kantianism. Where a (neo-) Kantian might find Helmholtz's theory congenial insofar as it involves an active "imposition" of categories upon intuitively given "sense-data," thereby making experience "possible," Helmholtz diverges in his *genetic* interpretation of what we may call the "categories" of interpretation. For while Helmholtz, like the Kantians, thinks that the mind "assigns meaning to our sensations," this activity crucially "depends upon experiment, and not upon mere observation of what takes place around us."[71] We constantly perform "experiments" by moving our bodies, thereby subjecting our perceptions of space to continual verification.[72] Interpretation of the local signs takes place over time by "comparing them with the result of our own movements, with the changes which we thus produce in the outer world."[73] Thus our interpretive (loosely: "categorial") framework as well as our conception of space are not *a priori* at all, but "experimental," empirical. Helmholtz's doctrine thus stands in a peculiar relation to Kant's transcendental aesthetic and transcendental analytic in the first *Critique*. On the one hand, Helmholtz seems to reject the transcendental aesthetic's doctrine of space as a native "form" of intuition, whereas, on the other hand, his theory of unconscious inference seems in accord with the doctrine of categorial structuring of the perceptual "matter" provided by the senses.

There is some confusion on this in the literature. Boring, e.g., writes that Helmholtz opposed a German philosophical psychology that "had stressed intuitionism – that is to say, the doctrine of innate ides, of *a priori* judgments, of native categories of the understanding."[74] No doubt Kant (and Helmholtz)[75] would have been surprised to hear that his doctrine of "native categories of the understanding" (or even of innate ideas, if by this Boring means the Ideas of reason) made him an "intuitionist,"[76] since for Kant the categories are radically opposed to intuition: they are the basic concepts by which the understanding makes sense of sensible intuition, that is, in Helmholtzian terms, interprets sensibility so as to *construct* experience.[77]

Helmholtz's empiricism has two important philosophical consequences for the next psychologist in our survey, Wilhelm Wundt, who studied and worked under him at Heidelberg from 1858 until 1871.[78] In the first place, it retains the decisive quasi-Kantian element of spontaneity, for these sense-making experiments depend on an active, voluntary factor. As Helmholtz says, we "learn by experiment that the correspondence between two processes takes place at any moment that we *choose*."[79] This point reappears in Wundt's psychological voluntarism. Secondly, Helmholtz accepts introspection as basic to psychological study. For example, the common phenomenon of double vision that ineluctably and constantly accompanies the vast majority of our visual perceptions can only be recognized when, as he says, we learn "to pay heed to our individual sensations."[80] The problem with introspection in his view is not, as Kant said, its tendency to distort or change the very things it seeks to observe, but rather that they – our *pure* sensations – so easily elude observation. For it is our natural habit, as discussed above, to interpret them unconsciously as external objects, a habit that through constant exercise is honed to a fine skill. But "we are completely unskilled in observing the sensations *per se* … [so that] the practice of associating them with things outside of us actually prevents us from being distinctly conscious of the pure sensations."[81]

Wilhelm Wundt (1832–1920)

We end our overview of early experimental psychology with Wundt, the "father" of a discipline, which, as we have seen, also had several grandfathers. He makes a fitting (if temporary) stopping-point, since it is in his vast œuvre that we find the philosophical issues latent in Weber, Fechner, and Helmholtz brought to the surface and dealt with explicitly. In particular, Wundt synthesizes the voluntaristic and introspective elements of Helmholtz with the psychophysical parallelism of Fechner.

For Wundt, experimental psychology just meant physiological psychology. But unlike Weber, Fechner, or Helmholtz, Wundt for the first time sees psychology as an independent discipline, with physiology as its methodological basis, rather than as a subdiscipline of the physiology of sensation. Although Fechner announced in the *Elements* that the "psychophysical experiment, which has so far found only an incidental place in either the physical or the physiological laboratory now demands its own laboratory, its own apparatus, its own methods,"[82] it was left to Wundt to take this decisive step. Much of Wundt's work, therefore, consists in testing, clarifying, and codifying of the theories of Weber, Fechner, and Helmholtz. Let us consider how he does this.[83]

Wundt finds Weber's law, the cornerstone of experimental psychology, to be theoretically unstable: what is it a law *of*? It can be taken as a physiological law of the "excitation of neural matter," or as a psychophysical (Fechnerian) law governing the relation of matter and mind.[84] Against these, Wundt favors a purely *psychological* interpretation, that is, one that takes into account the phenomenon of "apperception." Wundt argues that the estimation of sensory intensity involves not just excitation but also apperceptive concentration. We see here Helmholtz's influence: since we can *say* nothing immediate about how sensations would be sensed independently of the latter, Weber's law only ever concerns *apperceived* sensations; hence it could just as well have its origin in the (active) apperceptive comparison of sensation as in the our (passive) neural receptors.[85] But apperception is a purely psychological act of consciousness; hence Wundt takes Weber's law to apply not to "sensations in and for themselves, but to processes of apperception, without which a quantitative estimation of sensations could never take place."[86] Since Weber's law simply expresses a ratio between noticeably different mental conditions,[87] Wundt interprets it as an instance of a more general "law" of consciousness: we have "no absolute, but merely a relative measure of the intensity of its conditions," in a word, all our inner conditions are relative to each other.[88] Wundt thus adapts Fechner's view, that the psychic and physical phenomena do not conflict, but are simply separate spheres of explanation. But his reading of Weber's law goes beyond Fechner, in that Fechner sees it as expressing the relation between these spheres, whereas for Wundt it expresses the relativity within the psychic realm alone – and yet these purely psychological relationships are revealed by physiological experiment. Thus his "psychological interpretation [of Weber's law] offers the advantage of not excluding a simultaneous [parallel] physiological explanation," while the two rival readings "only permit a one-sided explanation."[89]

For Wundt, the possibility of an experimental psychology depends on the possibility of introspection, or better, self-observation (*Selbstbeobachtung*). Yet self-observation is useful only if the sequence of inner phenomena is assumed to obey an independent principle of psychic causality. For if it does not, then these phenomena would be chaotic and intractable to knowledge. However, if they were governed by physical causality, a special psychological approach such as self-observation would be superfluous. In fact, however, Wundt thinks a system of psychic causality can be determined that is at no point reducible to physical causality: "no connection of physical processes can ever teach us anything about the manner of connection between psychological elements."[90] This fact leads him to his so-called principle of psychophysical parallelism.

Commentators continue to misconstrue this principle as a metaphysical doctrine. Wundt himself clearly states that it names only an "empirical postulate" necessary to explain the phenomenal "fact" of consciousness of which we are immediately and incontrovertibly aware.[91] Thus, he insists that the physical and psychic do not name two ontologically separate realms whose events unfold on separate yet parallel tracks.[92] Instead, the physical and psychic represent two mutually irreducible *perspectives* from which one reality may be observed: "Nothing occurs in our consciousness that does not find its sensible foundation in certain physical processes," and all psychological acts of association, apperception, willing, "are accompanied by physiological nerve-actions."[93] The psychologist must therefore assume for heuristic reasons two "parallel" and mutually irreducible causal chains by which two distinct types of phenomena may be accounted for.[94] Just as Fechner compared the convex and concave "views" of one and the same circle, Wundt draws an analogy from science: the distinct psychological and physiological explanatory schemes are like chemical and physical accounts of a single object, a crystal. Just as chemistry and physics describe or explain the same crystal from two distinct points of view, so too physiology and psychology describe the same process seen from the outside and inside, respectively. "'Inner' and 'outer' experience merely designate distinct *perspectives* that we can apply in our grasp and scientific investigation of what is, in itself, a unitary experience."[95] Like Fechner and Kant, Wundt rejects any metaphysical psychology, that is, any speculation on what the circle or crystal is "in itself." Fechner and Wundt both continually stress that they are concerned only with appearances, but that these themselves dictate distinct treatment for the mental and the material, the "internal" and the "external."

By the principle of psychophysical parallelism, then, Wundt commits himself to an ontological monism while also justifying a separate, that is, nonphysical approach to the study of psychological phenomena. I have described his theory of consciousness in detail elsewhere,[96] and want here briefly to highlight the so-called voluntarism that is its most peculiar characteristic. Wundt views consciousness as a continuous flow of representational acts. The sensations that lie at the root of all consciousness always enter awareness as compounds he calls "representations [*Vorstellungen*]," the synthetic products of the representational acts.[97] So far, Wundt's view seems firmly rooted in Helmholtz's theory of mental synthesis of a sensible manifold. But Wundt presses forward into a purely psychological dimension. Consciousness is not merely a parade of representations; it is also, crucially, *attention to* our representations.[98] He likens consciousness to the field of vision (*Blickfeld*); when we attend to something in this field, it becomes our "visual focal point [*Blickpunkt*]." When a representation enters the *Blickpunkt*, it is no longer a "perception," but an "apperception."[99] Apperception admits of degrees of intensity that vary as we pay more or less close attention to a given representation. Thus, regardless of the "strength of the external impression" upon the sensorium, the degree of apperception is to be measured "solely according to the subjective activity through which consciousness turns to a particular sense-stimulus."[100] Thus, as subjective activity, apperception is an activity of will[101] that operates according to its own laws of collection and division (*Verbindung* and *Zerlegung*), independent of any physiological or psychophysical laws.[102] While the details lie outside our scope, these laws govern apperception's tendency to "agglutinate" or fuse disparate sensory representations, synthesizing them in successive stages into a single, ultimately symbolic representation.[103]

Conclusion

Returning to the guiding question of this survey – how experiment can aid the observation, classification, and grasping of the causal relations among mental phenomena – the result is surprising. None of our four founders speak of physical *causation* of psychological appearances; indeed, they scrupulously avoid such statements as unscientific, metaphysical speculation. Further, despite being firmly grounded in physiology and physics, Weber, Helmholtz, and Wundt all avoid reductionism, recognizing an element of spontaneity that radically distinguishes the inner flow of subjective phenomena from the train of outer events. They point instead to an *association* between the physical and mental, which they consider a sufficient foundation for experimental inquiry. Fechner, Helmholtz, and Wundt thus take a broadly Kantian attitude, seeing both physical and psychological science as the determination of relations among *appearances*: the former, of outer appearances; the latter, of inner. This perspectival phenomenalism justifies, in Wundt and Fechner's view, the linkage of experimental manipulation of outer stimuli with the introspective registration of their corresponding (if not caused) inner phenomena. The Kantian objection to introspection is, ultimately, ignored as irrelevant: introspection allows us to attend and observe psychological phenomena, and one can frankly admit that it is just *these* phenomena – the ones introspected – that are the objects of experimental psychology. This is no different than saying that the chemicals studied in the lab under highly artificial conditions are the proper objects of experimental chemistry, and that if you wish to believe that they behave differently "in the wild," then you are free to do so. Indeed Helmholtz seems to consider introspection a special cathartic form of attention, very much akin to the focused, controlled, and artificial observations conducted in a physical laboratory. Finally, regarding the second question posed at the outset – how the mental must be construed so as to be susceptible to experiment – it too turns out to be answered in a nonmetaphysical way: psychic ontology is simply avoided; subjectivity is instead determined phenomenologically by its quality of "interiority" and flux. Again, as much as its flowing nature would seem to thwart its scientific examination, the early experimentalists take this in stride: psychology must simply be a hydrodynamics rather than a chemistry of the soul.

Notes

1. Helmholtz (1868: 61).
2. Some philosophers deserving special mention in this regard are the neo-Kantian Paul Natorp; Gottlob Frege; and the founder of Phenomenology, Edmund Husserl. Natorp, in two books devoted to what he calls "psychology according to the critical method," indeed continued to argue Kant's point, albeit with newer and more extravagant arguments, that psychology could never be a true, i.e., "objective," science. See below; see also Macnamara (1986) and Kusch (1995).
3. Sully (1876: 21).

4. Sully (1876: 21).
5. On transcendental psychology, see Kitcher (1990) and Hatfield (1992). For an attempt at working out a transcendental or "critical" psychology, see Natorp (1888 and 1912).
6. For Kant's flurry of objections to the possibility of an "empirical doctrine of the soul" see Kant (2004: 7). See also, Hatfield (1992: 200–1, *et passim*).
7. Kant (2004: 7).
8. Kant (2004: 5, 7).
9. Kant (2004: 7).
10. Boring (1950: 134–53).
11. Nevertheless, it would be wrong to suggest that the early physiological psychologists deliberately turned away from philosophy as overly speculative, as Sully suggests (see above). On the contrary, both Weber and Fechner were influenced by the *Naturphilosophie* of German idealism, Fechner decisively so (see Murphy 1949: 79, 84–5; Adler 1966: xx; Ross and Murray, at Weber 1978b). Helmholtz had a personal connection to Fichte through his father, and Wundt saw his psychological work as foundational to philosophy. Historians of nineteenth-century German philosophy such as Herbert Schnädelbach perhaps have exaggerated the divorce of science and philosophy in the aftermath of German idealism's collapse.
12. Weber (1905: 46).
13. See Ross and Murray, at Weber (1978b: 8).
14. This notion of threshold goes back to Herbart (and, according to Boring, Leibniz) (see Boring 1950: 284).
15. The common translation of "sensory" or "sensation circle" is misleading, since, as Weber says, these *Kreise* have various shapes; I therefore translate the word, *Kreis*, as "region."
16. Weber (1905: 68–9, 1978b: 19–54), Murphy (1949: 81), see Ross and Murray, at Weber (1978b: 9–10), Boring (1950: 28, ch. 6).
17. Weber (1905: 70).
18. Weber (1905: 101).
19. Murphy (1949: 80).
20. Weber (1905: 101).
21. Weber distinguishes two types of pressure-sensation, namely, that arising from an object pressing down on a bodily part (the hand, e.g.) (Weber 1905: 94) and that involving the voluntary muscular action of lifting (Weber 1905: 96, 115). The latter is more sensitive to weight or pressure differences than the former (Weber 1905: 115, 1978a: 61, 120). He writes: "The smallest difference between two weights that we can distinguish by means of the sense of exerting our muscles seems, according to my trials, to obtain between weights that stand in a proportion of 39 to 40, i.e., when the one is about 1/40 heavier than the other. [On the other hand,] by sensing the pressure that the two weights exert on our skin, we can only notice a weight-difference of 1/30, so that the weights are related as 29 is to 30." These two means of weight-sensation are "almost always used together" (Weber 1978a: 120).
22. Weber (1978a: 131).
23. Weber (1978a: 131).
24. Weber (1978a: 131, see 220–3, 1905: 115–18). According to Boring, "Weber's experimental finding may be expressed: $\delta R/R$ = constant, for the jnd [just noticeable difference]" (where R stands for the magnitude of the stimulus [*Reiz*]) (Boring 1950: 287).
25. Weber (1978a: 108).
26. I specify "experimental" psychology here in order to distinguish Fechner's project from Herbart's earlier efforts to create a scientific, but purely mathematical and non-experimental psychology. See Boring (1950: 286) and Fechner (1966: xxx).
27. See Fechner (1966: xxvii).
28. For a standard overview, see Boring (1950); the most recent major study of Fechner, and especially his relation to recent philosophy of science and of psychology, is Heidelberger (2004). I refer the reader to these two sources for detailed discussions, especially of Fechner's mathematical permutations of Weber's law.
29. For the significance to the philosophy of *science* (as opposed to the philosophy of psychology) of

certain problems in Fechner's formulations, such as the *Fundamentalformel* and the *Maßformel*, as well as of his statistical methods, see esp. Boring (1950: 284–5) and Heidelberger (2004: 191–207, 309ff.).

30. Fechner (1966: 7).
31. See my 2006.
32. While I agree with Boring that "Fechner's view of the relation of *mind and body* was not that of psychophysical parallelism," Boring's claim that Fechner's view was instead "what has been called the *identity hypothesis* and also *panpsychism*" is equally misleading. The material and the mental are *not* "identical" for Fechner. Rather, they are irreducible perspectives on a metaphysical reality that must be *postulated* as self-identical, though it can never appear to us as such.
33. Fechner (1966: 2).
34. Fechner's talk of inner and outer aspects of reality should not be confused with his notion of "inner" and "outer" psychophysics. In the latter, "the [external] stimulus rather than the bodily response is compared with subjective intensities" and "was accepted only because it was more immediately practicable" (Murphy 1949: 89); "inner psychophysics," by contrast, relates the subjective intensity of sensation to the intensities of the somatic activities mediating between the external stimulation and the sensation itself (see Murphy 1949: 88; Adler 1966: xxiii).
35. Fechner (1966: 7).
36. Fechner (1966: xxvii).
37. See Boring (1950: 287–8) and Heidelberger (2004: 201ff.).
38. For Fechner's notation, see Fechner (1877: 10).
39. See Boring (1950: 287–8) and Heidelberger (2004: 201–2). For troubles with this assumption, see Boring (1950: 289ff.) and Heidelberger (2004: 204ff.).
40. Beyond our scope here; see Fechner (1877: 9–12), Boring (1950: 288–9), and Heidelberger (2004: 202–3).
41. See Boring (1950: 289).
42. See Murphy (1949: 86). See Wundt (1893, vol. 1: 359).
43. Fechner (1966: xxviii). Wundt will reject both the physiological and psychophysical interpretations of Weber's law, as I discuss below.
44. See esp. Stevens (1960).
45. See especially Heidelberger (2004: 207ff.).
46. As Boring nicely puts it, "the experimentalists went on measuring sensation while the objectors complained, or at least they went on measuring whatever Fechner's S is" (Boring 1950: 291).
47. Fechner (1966: 7). See Heidelberger (2004: 169ff.).
48. Helmholtz (1868: 61–2).
49. Helmholtz (1868: 61).
50. Helmholtz (1868: 61).
51. See Fechner's preface to Fechner (1966: xxvii).
52. Helmholtz (1868: 62).
53. It is also true that despite their both being physicists, they had fundamentally different approaches to psychology. Although Fechner denies his metaphysics any explanatory role in psychophysics, he clearly wants to harmonize the fact of physics with the truth, as he saw it, of *Naturphilosophie* à la Schelling and Oken: mind and matter are ultimately identical. Against this top-down approach, by contrast, Helmholtz confronts psychological issues in the course of his research into the physics and physiology of sensation, without any prior commitments as to their metaphysical status.
54. Even in such optical experiments on vision as Fechner does address, he confines himself to *two*-dimensional acuity, e.g., distinguishing longer and shorter lines, or, again, the magnitude of light-intensities. See Fechner (1966: 223ff.) and Helmholtz (1868: 111–14).
55. Helmholtz (1868: 110; emphasis added).
56. I.e., of objects, as opposed to mere subjective sensations. See below.
57. A view traceable to Berkeley's *An Essay Towards a New Theory of Vision* (1709: see, e.g., §41).
58. See Warren and Warren (1968: 17).
59. Helmholtz (1868: 110; emphasis added).
60. Helmholtz (1868: 106).

61. Helmholtz (1868: 110); Helmholtz borrows the notion of "local signs [*Lokalzeichen*]" from Lotze; the details are beyond our scope here. See Helmholtz (1868: 110), Sully (1878b: 182), and Boring (1950: 267ff.), whose discussion of Lotzean *Lokalzeichen* is rather different from Helmholtz's, depending as it does on tactual intensities and motions of the ocular muscles.
62. Helmholtz (1868: 111).
63. Terminological note: what I call "sensation" here, and is usually called *Empfindung* in German, Helmholtz calls *Perzeption*; and what I call "perception" here, namely, the conscious synthesis of sensations, Helmholtz calls *Anschauung* (see Boring, 1950: 311–12). This can lead to all sorts of confusion, especially since Kant's *Anschauung* is always translated as the sensible "intuition" prior to being worked over by the categories, i.e., prior to becoming a Helmholtzian *Anschauung*. (One encounters a similar problem in Wundt's use of the term, *Apperzeption*, which also departs from Kant's.)
64. Helmholtz (1868: 82).
65. One of his several arguments to this conclusion has to do with our binocular vision. "Two distinct sensations are transmitted from the two eyes, [and] reach the consciousness at the same time and without coalescing," something everyone has noticed when alternately closing one eye and seeing the image slightly shift (Helmholtz, 1868: 125). It follows, that "the combination of these two sensations into the *single* picture of the external world of which we are conscious in ordinary vision is not produced by an anatomical mechanism of sensation, *but by a mental act*" (Helmholtz 1868: 125; emphasis added).
66. Helmholtz (1866: 174, 1878: 220); see Natorp's theory of objectivation in my 2003.
67. Helmholtz (1866: 175).
68. Helmholtz (1866: 256).
69. Helmholtz (1866: 130); Warren and Warren (1968: 21–2).
70. Helmholtz (1868: 129).
71. Helmholtz (1868: 128; see 135).
72. Helmholtz (1868: 135).
73. Helmholtz (1868: 127); see Berkeley (1709).
74. Boring (1950: 304).
75. See Helmholtz's praise of Kant's "correct" analysis of mental activity in generating sense-perception at Helmholtz (1866: 172).
76. Helmholtz himself calls nativism the "Innate or Intuitive Theory" (Helmholtz 1868: 110).
77. It would be of great philosophical interest to examine the relation between Helmholtz's rejection of Kant's theory of space and his empirical constructivism with the reinterpretation of Kant by the Marburg school of neo-Kantians, such as Hermann Cohen and Paul Natorp (see Patton 2004).
78. See Boring (1950: 319).
79. Helmholtz (1868: 128).
80. Helmholtz (1866: 177).
81. Helmholtz (1866: 179). Again, it would be of great philosophical interest to contrast Helmholtzian introspection with Husserl's phenomenological reduction, insofar as both seek to neutralize our natural tendency to understand our sensations as of a "world," rather than in their purely subjective phenomenality.
82. Fechner (1966: xxix).
83. For a detailed study of Wundt from a philosophical point of view, see my 2006.
84. Wundt (1893, vol. 1: 390–1).
85. Wundt (1893, vol. 1; 391–2).
86. Wundt (1893, vol. 1: 393, see vol. 2: 269).
87. *Zustände* is Wundt's rather noncommittal word.
88. Wundt (1893, vol. 1: 393).
89. Wundt (1893, vol. 1: 393).
90. Wundt (1894: 43, quoted in Kusch, 1995: 134).
91. Wundt (1911: 22).
92. He is therefore not an epiphenomenalist.
93. Wundt (1893, vol. 2: 644).

94. Wundt (1911: 44–5).
95. Wundt (1896, quoted at Natorp, 1912: 264).
96. In my 2006.
97. Wundt (1893, vol. 2: 1).
98. It would be useful to contrast Wundt's theory of attention with Brentano's theory of intentionality.
99. Wundt (1893, vol. 2: 267).
100. Wundt (1893, vol. 2: 269).
101. Wundt (1919: 34).
102. Wundt (1893, vol. 2: 470).
103. Wundt gives the simple example of a representation of "church-tower" arising out of elementary representations, "church" and "tower" (Wundt 1919: 38f.).

References

Adler, H. E. (1966) Translator's foreword. In Fechner (1966), pp. xix–xxvi.

Berkeley, G. (1709) "An Essay Towards a New Theory of Vision," in Berkeley (1963), pp. 7–102.

—— (1963) *Works on Vision*, ed. C. M. Turbayne, Indianapolis: Bobbs-Merrill.

Boring, E. G. (1950) *A History of Experimental Psychology*, New York: Appleton-Century-Crofts.

—— (1966) "Gustav Theodor Fechner." Introduction to Fechner (1966), pp. ix–xvii.

Dennis, W. (ed.) (1948) *Readings in the History of Psychology*, New York: Appleton-Century-Crofts.

Fechner, G. T. (1860) *Elemente der Psychophysik*, Leipzig: Breitkopf und Härtel.

—— (1877) *In Sachen der Psychophysik*, Leipzig: Breitkopf und Härtel; reissued as a facsimile by Verlag Dr Müller, Saarbrücken, 2006.

—— (1966) *Elements of Psychophysics*, trans. H. E. Adler, New York: Holt, Rinehart & Winston.

Guyer, P. (ed.) (1992) *The Cambridge Companion to Kant*, Cambridge: Cambridge University Press.

Hatfield, G. (1992) "Empirical, Rational, and Transcendental Psychology: Psychology as Science and as Philosophy," in Guyer (1992), pp. 200–27.

Heidelberger, M. (2004) *Nature from Within: Gustav Theodor Fechner and His Psychophysical Worldview*, trans. C. Klohr, Pittsburgh: University of Pittsburgh Press; originally published as *Die innere Seite der Natur: Gustav Theodor Fechners wissenschaftlich-philosophische Weltauffassung*, Frankfurt am Maine, 1993: Klostermann.

Helmholtz, H. von (1866) "Concerning the Perceptions in General," trans. J. P. C. Southall, in Warren and Warren (1968), pp. 171–203; also in Dennis (1948), pp. 214–30.

—— (1867) *Handbuch der physiologischen Optik*, Hamburg: Leopold Voss.

—— (1868) "The Recent Progress of the Theory of Vision," in Warren and Warren (1968), pp. 61–138; also in Dennis (1948), pp. 144–222.

—— (1878) "The Facts of Perception," in Warren and Warren (1968), pp. 207–46.

—— (1894) "The Origin of the Correct Interpretation of our Sensory Impressions," in Warren and Warren (1968), pp. 249–60.

—— (1909) *Handbuch der physiologischen Optik*, Hamburg: Leopold Voss.

—— (1962) *Helmholtz's Treatise on Physiological Optics*, ed. J. P. C. Southall, New York: Dover.

—— (1971) *Selected Writings of Hermann von Helmholtz*, ed. R. Kahl, Middletown, CT: Wesleyan University Press.

Kant, I. (2004) *The Metaphysical Foundations of Natural Science*, trans., ed. M. Friedman, Cambridge: Cambridge University Press.

Kim, A. (2006) "Wilhelm Maximilian Wundt," in Edward N. Zalta (ed.), *The Stanford Encyclopedia of Philosophy*; available: http://plato.stanford.edu/entries/wilhelm-wundt/

—— (2003) "Paul Natorp," in Edward N. Zalta (ed.), *The Stanford Encyclopedia of Philosophy*; available: http://plato.stanford.edu/entries/natorp/

Kitcher, P. (1990) *Kant's Transcendental Psychology*, New York: Oxford University Press.

Kusch, M. (1995) *Psychologism: A Case Study in the Sociology of Philosophical Knowledge*, London: Routledge.

Macnamara, J. (1986) *A Border Dispute: The Place of Logic in Psychology*, Cambridge, Mass.: MIT Press.

Murphy, G. (1949) *Historical Introduction to Modern Psychology*, New York: Harcourt, Brace & World.
Natorp, P. (1888) *Einleitung in die Psychologie*. Freiburg: J. C. B. Mohr.
—— (1912) *Allgemeine Psychologie nach kritischer Methode*. Tübingen: J. C. B. Mohr (Paul Siebeck); Amsterdam: E. J. Bonset, 1965.
Patton, L. (2004) "Hermann Cohen's History and Philosophy of Science," PhD thesis, McGill University, Montreal.
Robertson, G. C. (1876) "Prefatory Words." *Mind* 1, no. 1: 1–6.
—— (1877) Review of *The Physiology of Mind*, by Henry Maudsley, *Mind* 2, no. 6: 235–9.
Stevens, S. S. (1960) "The Psychophysics of Sensory Function." *American Scientist* 48: 226–53.
Sully, J. (1876) "Physiological Psychology in Germany," *Mind* o.s. 1, no. 1: 20–43.
—— (1878a) "The Question of Visual Perception in Germany," pt 1, *Mind* o.s. 3, no. 9 (January): 1–23.
—— (1878b) "The Question of Visual Perception in Germany," pt 2, *Mind* o.s. 3, no. 10 (April): 167–95.
Warren, R. M., and Warren, R. P. (1968) *Helmholtz on Perception: Its Physiology and Development*. New York: John Wiley.
Weber, E. H. (1834) *De Pulsu, Resorptione, Auditu et Tactu: Annotationes Anatomicae et Physiologicae*. Leipzig: C. F. Koehler.
—— (1846) "Tastsinn und Gemeingefühl," in R. Wagner (ed.), *Handwörterbuch der Physiologie*, Braunschweig: Vieweg.
—— (1905) *Tastsinn und Gemeingefühl*, vol. 149 of *Ostwalds Klassiker*, ed. E. Hering, Leipzig: Wilhelm Engelmann; repr. Weber, 2006.
—— (1978a) *De Tactu*, in *The Sense of Touch:* De Tactu [De Subtilitate Tactus] *and* Der [*sic*] Tastsinn, trans. H. E. Ross and D. J. Murray, London: Academic. (Ross and Murray nowhere indicate that *De Tactu* is in fact a section of Weber's more comprehensive work [1834].)
—— (1978b) *The Sense of Touch:* De Tactu [De Subtilitate Tactus] *and* Der [*sic*] Tastsinn, trans. H. E. Ross and D. J. Murray, London: Academic.
—— (2006) *Tastsinn und Gemeingefühl*, Saarbrücken: Verlag Dr Müller; repr. Weber, 1905. (The publisher wrongly indicates that this is a facsimile of the original 1846 edn; it is a reprint of Hering's 1905 edn.)
Wundt, W. (1893) *Grundzüge der physiologischen Psychologie*, vols 1 and 2, Leipzig: Wilhelm Engelmann.
—— (1894) "Über psychische Kausalität und das Prinzip des psychophysischen Parallelismus," *Philosophische Studien* 10: 1–124.
—— (1896) *Grundriss der Psychologie*, Leipzig: Engelmann.
—— (1911) *Kleine Schriften*, vol. 2, Leipzig: Engelmann.
—— (1919) *Logik*, vol. 1, Stuttgart: Enke.

4
FREUD AND THE UNCONSCIOUS

Edward Erwin

How do I know that the man I am conversing with has a conscious mind? Well, he acts as if he is conscious of what I am saying, and when he puts out his cigarette and places it in a nearby ashtray, he acts as if he is conscious of his immediate surroundings. Yet all that I observe is his behavior, not what lies behind it. If my belief that the man is conscious were challenged, I could argue as follows: When I act in ways similar to the way the man acts, I really do understand and perceive; so, it is likely that he does too, and so he must be conscious. Although this sort of argument by analogy has often been challenged, it appears to give *a* reason for thinking that others are conscious even if the reason is only a weak one.

How do I know that this same man has an unconscious mind? I cannot reason as before; I cannot reason from my own case to his because I am not conscious of my unconscious mind. How, then, can I determine whether he or I or anyone else has an unconscious mind? Some philosophers and psychologists have argued that we cannot, but many others, including Sigmund Freud, have disagreed.

Pre-Freudian debates about the unconscious

In the nineteenth century, leading psychologists and philosophers split on the issue of the existence of the unconscious. Those who argued in support of the unconscious include the psychologist Hermann von Helmholtz (1821–94) and the philosophers Arthur Schopenhauer (1788–1860), Friedrich Nietzsche (1844–1900), Eduard von Hartmann (1842–1906), and J. F. Herbart (1776–1841).

Herbart, one of the first nineteenth-century theorists to postulate an unconscious, introduced into psychology the idea of a "threshold of consciousness" and the suppression of conscious ideas (1895 [1816]). A concept (or idea) is in consciousness in so far as it is not suppressed, according to Herbart's theory; concepts that are suppressed fall below the threshold of conscious, but do not disappear altogether. They remain in the unconscious mind where they continue to exert an effect on conscious ideas. Herbart's theory of the suppression of ideas and their continuing effects is strikingly similar to Freud's theory of the dynamic unconscious. His argument for postulating an unconscious also anticipates one of Freud's key arguments for the unconscious. Herbart argued that because there are gaps in consciousness, we need to account for them by inferring unconscious mental ideas (Sand 2002; Zentner 2002).

Not all nineteenth-century philosophers agreed with Herbart or others who believed in the unconscious. One of the opponents of the unconscious was the philosopher Franz Brentano (1838–1917); another was the philosopher-psychologist William James (1842–1910).

Brentano, in his seminal work, *Psychology from an Empirical Standpoint* (1995 [1874]), points out that even if there are unconscious ideas, they cannot be in the domain of our conscious experience; if they were, they would not be unconscious. Yet he agrees that even if we cannot directly perceive unconscious ideas, it might still be possible to infer their existence from known empirical facts. The question is: How is this to be done? There are exactly four ways one might proceed, Brentano contends, but most proponents of the unconscious use just two.

First, some argue that effects we are conscious of demand the hypothesis of an unconscious mental phenomenon as their *cause*; second, some argue that events we are conscious of must bring about an unconscious mental state as its *effect*.

After setting forth his classification of arguments for the unconscious, Brentano develops criteria for evaluating these arguments. One criterion requires that any proof arguing from an effect to an unconscious mental cause must first establish that the effect really does occur or has occurred. Some of Hartmann's (1931 [1868]) arguments for unconscious ideas, which appeal to such dubious phenomena as clairvoyance and premonition, violate Brentano's first requirement.

Even if an effect has been firmly established, the appeal to hypotheses postulating unconscious mentality is justified, Brentano points out, only if proof is provided that no rival hypothesis can just as plausibly explain the effect. Many arguments for the unconscious, he argues, fail this test.

One example of neglecting rival hypotheses is the common argument that we can possess a store of knowledge without consciously thinking about it; so, it is argued, the knowledge must be stored in our unconscious mind. Brentano replies that we can conceive of this sort of knowledge – or more precisely the beliefs associated with it – as dispositions toward certain acts of thinking rather than mental states existing in the unconscious. There is no basis for inferring, then, that the beliefs we are not aware of exist as unconscious mental states.

Helmholtz and others who postulate unconscious inferences in perception are also guilty, Brentano contends, of violating his requirement that known plausible rival hypotheses must be ruled out: They never take into account, he says, the means which psychology already offers for doing justice to the facts without postulating unconscious mental events.

Brentano appears to make his criteria for justifying inferences about the unconscious even more demanding by insisting that ruling out competing theories that we have thought of is not enough; we also need to provide evidence that no unformulated theory would explain the phenomena unless it talked about unconscious mental causes: "For the present, it is sufficient to have pointed out that the alleged consequences from unconscious inference cannot furnish any proof for the existence of unconscious mental activity, as long as the impossibility or extreme improbability of any other conception has not been established, and that so far no one has fulfilled this condition" (Brentano 1995 [1874]: 111).

It might appear that Brentano has gone too far here in raising the evidential bar. Why is it not enough to say that inferring from the most likely of known explanations to a claim of evidential support is illicit unless there is independent evidence that the set of potential explanations we are aware of contains the true one? Why insist that we have to take the extra step of obtaining evidence that it is unlikely that some explanation outside the set is the correct one?

There is only an illusion here, however, of extra and unnecessary rigor on Brentano's part. If we require independent evidence that the set of available explanatory hypotheses contains the true one, then we are logically committed to Brentano's criterion. In every case where we lack such evidence, the inference will be unwarranted, as his criterion insures; in any case where we possess such evidence, his criterion will automatically be satisfied. Evidence that one of the currently considered explanations is correct is necessarily evidence that any competing explanation outside the set is improbable.

After carefully criticizing most of the major arguments for there being unconscious mental activity, Brentano concludes with a positive argument for saying that no such activity occurs. Here, however, he writes with less clarity than before.

The argument appears to be as follows. When we are conscious of something, there is an act of presentation of the thing we are conscious of and this act has a certain intensity. This intensity is always equal to the intensity with which the object that is presented appears to us. That the two intensities are always equal Brentano takes to be self-evident (1995 [1874]: 120). Starting with these assumptions, Brentano reasons that there are no unconscious mental acts. For, he continues, wherever there exists a mental act of greater or lesser intensity, it is necessary to attribute an equal intensity to the presentation which accompanies it and of which this act is the object (*ibid.*: 121).

Brentano's positive argument for the nonexistence of the unconscious is unconvincing if for no other reason than he assumes without argument that every mental act, whether it be conscious or unconscious, has an accompanying presentation. Someone who believes that there are unconscious mental acts can rightly challenge this assumption.

William James, in *The Principles of Psychology* (1950 [1890]), does something similar to what Brentano does. He sets up 10 proofs that have been offered for an unconscious mind and tries to refute them all. Some of these so-called "proofs" are marred by obvious fallacies, but others are more interesting. In what James designates "the Third Proof," it is pointed out that after thinking of A we immediately find ourselves thinking of C; *B* is the natural logical link between A and C, but we are not conscious of having thought of *B*. So, it is reasoned, it must have been in our mind unconsciously and in that state affected the sequence of our ideas. James' reply to this argument is that we have a choice between this explanation and either of two more plausible ones.

Either B was consciously there but in the next instant forgotten or its *brain tract* alone was adequate to do the whole work of coupling A and C, without the idea of B being in the mind at all either consciously or unconsciously. On either alternative, there is no need to speak of unconscious mental events.

According to the Fourth Proof, problems unsolved when we go to bed are sometimes solved when we wake up, and sometimes we awake the next morning, without the aid of an alarm clock, at an hour predetermined the night before. Unconscious thinking, volition, or time registration, etc., must be responsible for these acts, it is claimed. James replies rather tersely: Consciousness forgotten, as in the hypnotic trance. What he means, presumably, is that the mental events responsible for the problem solving or awakening at a certain time were present in consciousness but we quickly forgot them.

In the Ninth Proof, James discusses cases of perceptual inference of the sort talked about by Helmholtz, as when we see a man in the distance who appears tiny but we infer that he is of normal size or when a certain grey-appearing patch is inferred to be a white object seen in a dim light. In such cases, it is argued, we are not conscious of any inference; so, it must be unconscious. James replies, in part, as Brentano does, to this argument. He points out that we need not postulate any inference at all; rapid judgments of size, shape, distance, and the like are best explained as processes of simple cerebral associations.

Although James carefully examines most of the arguments known to him for there being unconscious mental states, he says very little about those given by von Hartmann and Schopenhauer, claiming that it would, on the whole, be a waste of time to consider their arguments in detail. For this reason, his critique is incomplete. In addition, some of Freud's arguments, which were published after James' book was published, and which may be more powerful than the arguments James examines, are not affected by his criticisms.

James, like Brentano, also appears to offer a positive argument for concluding that there are no unconscious mental states, but if that is his intention, he begs the question at the outset by assuming "There is only one 'phase' in which an idea can be, and that is a fully conscious condition" (James 1950 [1890]: 173). Freud and others who argue for unconscious ideas would surely challenge this assumption and they would be right to do so.

General lessons: The nineteenth-century debates about the unconscious leave us with unresolved issues but also some general positive suggestions. First, as Brentano indicates, the debates were generally about the existence of unconscious mental events, states, or processes, not about a "thing" or "entity" existing in the human mind beneath the level of consciousness, and certainly not about something that could in principle survive the destruction of the body. When nineteenth-century philosophers or psychologists did speak of an unconscious mind, they generally meant unconscious mental phenomena of some kind or other, but not necessarily a mental entity.

Second, there is a general warning to be found in the writings of Brentano, James, and others about facile invocations of the unconscious. When we cannot otherwise explain some mental occurrence or behavior, it is tempting, but often unwarranted, to postulate some unconscious mental event.

Third, there are at least three general sources of hypotheses that are rivals to ones that speak of the unconscious. Even if none of these rivals singly or all together will suffice to discredit the entire case for unconscious mental activity, they at least need to be kept in mind when evaluating specific hypotheses postulating unconscious phenomena.

The first, discussed by both Brentano and James, is the hypothesis of a mechanical association of ideas. If I conclude that a man is wealthy once I hear that he drives a Rolls-Royce, a logician may insist that I am implicitly presupposing that most people who drive such a car have a great deal of money, but such a thought may never have entered my mind either at the conscious or unconscious level. I might, instead, just automatically associate the two thoughts, so that when I entertain the one, I quickly move to the other.

A second source of rival hypotheses is that of dispositions. Just because I immediately answer "4004" to the question "What is the sum of 2001 and 2003?" does not mean that I did some mental arithmetic unconsciously. I may have, but then again I may have been disposed to give this answer and what disposes me need not have been an unconscious idea.

A third, and perhaps most troubling, source of rival hypotheses comes from neuroscience. We may not know what causes some conscious act of thinking, but that may be because we do not know enough about brain activity. As Brentano nicely puts the point when discussing the possibility of demonstrating the existence of unconscious mental activity, "The possibility of proof ends only at the point where the field of brain-physiology, which is so far inaccessible, begins" (1995 [1874]: 116).

Freud on the unconscious

Freud developed his ideas about the unconscious in many of his works, but two in particular were devoted to this topic: a brief paper, "A Note on the Unconscious in Psychoanalysis" (1912) and a longer paper "The Unconscious" (1915b). In the briefer paper, Freud is mainly concerned with proving that the unconscious exists and in explaining the different senses in which the term "unconscious" is used in psychoanalytic theorizing. In the longer paper, Freud's concerns are the same, but he also gives a much more detailed theory about the nature of the unconscious.

Freud's proofs of the unconscious

In the opening pages of his "Note" (1912), Freud gives a commonly used argument for saying that at least something is unconscious (at this stage, Freud is not distinguishing the unconscious and the preconscious). A conception is present to my consciousness, but then may become absent, and later may become present again when I remember it. To illustrate, I am conscious of putting change in a coin holder in my car, but then I cease thinking about what I have done until I remember that I need to place coins in the parking meter. When I was not conscious of the thought of where I had placed the coins in my car, what happened to that thought? Freud says of such thoughts that they are present in the mind even when outside of consciousness, but they are *latent* in consciousness. He takes this to be a satisfactory common-sense proof of the existence of an unconscious, but not before he disposes of "the philosophical objection" that what we are calling unconscious mental ideas in these sorts of cases are not in the mind at all; what exists rather are dispositions to think or behave in a certain sort of way. Freud replies that this reply begs the question in asserting "conscious" to be a term identical with "mental."

Freud is not being fair here to his critics, at least not all of them. Although Brentano believed that everything mental was conscious, this assumption played no role in his reply that instead of postulating unconscious thoughts in the sort of case Freud is talking about, it is at least as plausible to postulate dispositions instead.

Freud places more weight on his next argument which appeals to the phenomenon of hypnosis. He points out that in the sort of experiment performed by Bernheim a subject is put into a hypnotic state and while in this state is ordered to execute a certain action at a specified time when he awakens. After waking up, the subject has no memory of his hypnotic state, but at the appointed time has an impulse to perform the assigned task and does so. It seems impossible, Freud says, to give any other account than to say that the experimenter's order had been present in the unconscious of the subject. But a further idea is also suggested by this case, Freud says: the idea of a dynamic unconscious. What later emerged into consciousness was only part of what the person had experienced, the conception of the task. At the time of awakening, the subject was not conscious of the original order to perform the task: It remained unconscious, and so it was *active* and *unconscious* at the same time.

Freud's appeal to hypnotic states to prove unconscious mentality has been criticized by many commentators including some sympathetic to many of his theoretical views (see Levy 1996: 57–64). William James, as noted earlier, had rather quickly dismissed arguments appealing to hypnosis with the remark "Consciousness forgotten, as in the hypnotic trance."

To make his reply credible, James would have had to develop it further, but here is what he could have said. Hypnosis works by suggestion. The hypnotist suggests to someone, for example, that he do something at a certain time and not remember the original order. The act of suggestion creates in the subject a disposition to perform the act and a disposition to forget the origin of the order. There is no need in such cases to speak of any unconscious mental states or processes.

We can, of course, press the issue further and inquire about the basis of the disposition. James would presumably say: It may well have an underlying neural basis. This neural state or event, of which we know nothing at present, may well be the real cause of the person's behavior in cases of hypnosis. Without some basis for preferring Freud's explanation to a neural one, hypnotic phenomena fail to be a sound basis for introducing talk of unconscious ideas.

In his later (1915b) paper, Freud seems to downgrade the importance of his hypnosis argument. He devotes but one sentence to it (*ibid.*: 169). His main argument in this second paper, the one that most Freudians have traditionally relied on, is the "unintelligible gaps" argument. The data of consciousness, Freud says (*ibid.*: 166), have a very large number of gaps in them. Both in sick and healthy people, psychical acts often occur which can be explained only by presupposing other acts of which the subjects are not conscious. These psychic acts (some are behavioral) include parapraxes, such as forgetting and slips of the tongue, and dreams in healthy people, and neurotic symptoms in the sick; in addition, our most personal experience acquaints us with ideas that come into our head from we know not where and with intellectual conclusions arrived at we do not know how. All these conscious acts, Freud argues, remain unconnected and unintelligible if we insist that all mental acts be conscious. They fall into a demonstrable connection, however, if we interpolate between them the unconscious acts we have inferred (1915b: 166–7).

An example of the sort of gap that Freud is talking about is the odd behavior of one of his patients who was prone to perform seemingly pointless actions such as running from room to room and ringing a bell to fetch her maid when she had no need to see the maid. The whole pattern of behavior falls into place and becomes intelligible, Freud claims, when we understand that the woman had an unconscious desire to restore her husband's honor after the maid had discovered evidence that he had been unable to perform sexually on the woman's wedding night.

Another example is Freud's "Irma dream." Freud dreamt of a junior colleague, Otto, using an unclean syringe in injecting Irma, who was Freud's patient. What is the meaning of this event in the dream? Freud answers that Otto had the day before reproached him because Freud was only partly successful in treating Irma. In the dream, Irma's problems are attributed not to Freud's incompetence but to the unclean syringe. Freud comments "It occurred to me, in fact, that I was actually *wishing* that there had been a wrong diagnosis; for if so, the blame for my lack of success would have been got rid of" (1900: 109). The wish, according to Freud, was something that he had not been conscious of. If we postulate an unconscious wish, we can make sense of the dream; if we restrict the mental to the conscious, we cannot.

Although Freud takes his "unintelligible gaps" argument to be proof enough for an unconscious, he adds an additional argument. He argues that when the assumption of there being an unconscious enables us to construct a successful procedure – he means psychoanalytic therapy – by which we can exert an effective influence upon the course of conscious processes, this success will have given us an "incontrovertible proof" of the existence of what we assumed (1915a: 167).

Various meanings of "the unconscious"

Freud distinguishes three senses of the expression "the unconscious": the descriptive, the dynamic, and the systems sense. In fact, however, his use of the term in the first two cases introduces no ambiguity; rather, what he adds is a bit of theorizing.

If we say that an idea of which we are unaware is unconscious, but support this claim only by appeal to cases of memory or association, and make no claim about the effects of the unconscious idea, then we are applying the concept of the descriptive unconscious (1912: 23). That is, we are only describing the unconscious. Facts about hypnotism, however, warrant our going further, Freud claims, and postulating ideas that are both active and unconscious at the same time. Here we need to introduce the concept of the dynamic unconscious (1912: 24).

As a result of psychoanalytic research, Freud claims, we need to go beyond the descriptive unconscious and the postulation of individual dynamic unconscious mental acts. Unconscious mental acts are systematically related to each other: Each act is part of a larger system of unconscious acts. Freud introduces the term "the Unconscious" to refer to this system and, also refers to it, when writing in German, by the letters *Ubw*, which is an abbreviation of the German word *Unbewußt* (1912: 29). In English translations, the system unconscious is referred to by *Ucs* rather than *Ubw*. Here the term "unconscious" is used in a different sense: It refers to a system, not to individual unconscious ideas.

Besides postulating the system Unconscious (*Ucs*), Freud postulates two other systems: the system Consciousness (*Cs*) and the system Preconscious (*Pcs*). Here a second change of meaning occurs. In ordinary speech, any mental state outside of consciousness might be said to be unconscious, but on Freud's usage, ideas outside of consciousness that can easily return to consciousness are not "unconscious." If I believe that my coins are in the coin holder and I am not presently thinking of this but can easily recall the thought, then the idea is preconscious, or as Freud puts it, is "in my preconscious." If I have a motive I am unaware of but can easily become aware of if someone points it out to me, Freud would say that it existed in my preconscious. It was not unconscious.

What distinguishes for Freud the unconscious and the preconscious is, partly, the ease with which such mental items can enter consciousness, although this is not the sole distinguishing mark of the unconscious. A further characteristic is that unconscious ideas are typically unconscious because they have been and continue to be repressed; it is this feature which accounts for their inaccessibility. Some Freudians take the central mark of unconscious ideas to be their inability to enter consciousness without the overcoming of the accompanying resistances that people experience when in the grips of repression. To overcome the resistances and lift the repression, it is necessary that the subject undergo psychoanalytic treatment. On this view, we can distinguish the unconscious from the preconscious as follows. Unconscious ideas have a dynamic quality in that they have effects; they are also typically prevented from entering consciousness due to the operation of repression; and they can enter consciousness only when the repression is "lifted," which requires overcoming the person's resistances through the use of psychoanalysis. Preconscious ideas may also have effects but they lack the other features of unconscious ideas.

What sorts of things are unconscious?

Freud often speaks of unconscious ideas, but the German word he uses for "idea" applies not only to what in English is termed an idea, but also to images and presentations (Strachey 1915b: 174n1). In addition to ideas, images, and presentations, Freud also speaks of wishes and motives as being unconscious. Sometimes, he also speaks of unconscious instincts and emotions, but this latter usage needs to be clarified.

As Strachey explains in his Editor's note to Freud's "Instincts and Their Vicissitudes" (1915a: 111), the editors of the English translation of Freud's works had to make a decision as to how to translate his use of the German word *Trieb*. One choice was "drive" and another, the one they fixed on, was "instinct." In asking whether, on Freudian theory, instincts can be unconscious, we are also inquiring about what some scholars call drives.

Freud is quite clear on the issue of whether instincts (or drives) can be unconscious. They are outside of consciousness, but this is not enough to make them unconscious *mental* states. Because they cannot become an object of consciousness even with the aid of psychoanalytic treatment, Freud says (1915b: 177) that the idea of the unconscious does not apply to them. What is unconscious with respect to instincts is the idea that represents them. Freud says that when he speaks of an unconscious instinctual urge, this should be interpreted as a harmless but loose use of words. What is meant is that the ideational representative of the urge is unconscious; the instinctual urge is not.

Other items that are often classified as mental include sensations, feelings, affects, and emotions, such as love, hate, and anger. Freud does not apply "unconscious" to sensations but, with an important qualification, he does apply the concept to the other items. He notes (1915b: 177–8) that an affective or emotional impulse can be misconstrued due to the operation of repression. It becomes connected to another idea and is regarded by consciousness as the manifestation of this other idea. If we restore the true connection, Freud points out, he calls the original affective impulse an unconscious one. Yet the original affect was never unconscious. All that has happened was that its idea had undergone repression. Affects can also be transformed into anxiety or prevented from being developed at all. When the latter occurs, Freud terms such emotions and affects as "unconscious," but there is a significant difference between them and unconscious ideas. Unconscious ideas continue to exist after repression as actual structures in the unconscious, whereas all that corresponds in the unconscious to unconscious affects is a potential beginning which is prevented from developing.

An assessment

Assessing Freud's theory of the unconscious is difficult partly because of disagreements as to the distinctive content of his theory. Freud clearly believed that there are unconscious mental states, but proving this single proposition would not be sufficient to establish any *distinctively* Freudian thesis, i.e. one unique to Freud's theories. As pointed out earlier, Freud's predecessors, such as Herbart, Schopenhauer, Nietzsche, and von Hartmann also believed in the existence of unconscious mental states, as do most of Freud's critics. Disagreements about Freudian theory are rarely, if ever, disagreements about the mere existence of unconscious mentality.

According to some of Freud's supporters, his distinctive contribution was his development of the theory of the *dynamic* unconscious. He clearly did develop this theory, but what does it claim? If talk of a dynamic unconscious means, as some scholars say, merely that unconscious mental events have effects, then the theory is not distinctively Freudian. Herbart and others who preceded Freud, and many of Freud's critics, share a belief in a dynamic unconscious if all that is meant is that unconscious mental events are sometimes causally efficacious. More needs to be added besides causal efficacy. One idea is to add to Freud's theory of the unconscious his theory of repression.

Up until approximately 1923, the theory of the dynamic unconscious was closely linked to the theory of repression, and even with the post-1923 changes, there is still an important linkage, though a modified one.

On Freud's early account, there is a reason why unconscious ideas cannot enter consciousness. The reason is that a certain force opposes them, namely repression. What is repressed, Freud held, is unconscious and what is unconscious is repressed. It is for this reason that he says, "Thus we obtain our concept of the unconscious from the theory of repression. The repressed is the prototype of the unconscious for us" (Freud 1923: 15).

On 26 September 1922, however, Freud read a short unpublished paper at the Seventh International Psycho-Analytical Congress, "Some Remarks on the Unconscious," in which he indicated dissatisfaction with his earlier theory. In an abstract of the paper, which Freud's editor says may have been written by Freud himself, it is noted that the speaker, i.e. Freud, repeated the history of the development of the concept "unconscious" in psychoanalysis. The dynamic view of the process of repression, the abstract points out, made it necessary to give the unconscious a systematic sense, so that the unconscious had to be equated with the repressed. "It has turned out, however" – the abstract continues – "that it is not practicable to regard the repressed as coinciding with the unconscious and the ego with the preconscious and conscious. The speaker [Freud] discussed the two facts which show that in the ego too there is an unconscious, which behaves dynamically like the repressed unconscious ..." (Strachey 1923: 4). The two facts are resistance proceeding from the ego during analysis and an unconscious sense of guilt.

Freud's short talk and its abstract anticipated the publication of "The Ego and the Id" (1923) in which he makes an important modification of his earlier views. On his new theory, the structural theory, which postulates an Id, Ego, and Superego, the unconscious is not equated with the repressed. All that is repressed is unconscious, but some of what is unconscious is not repressed. Some of what is in the id and, consequently, is unconscious is repressed, but some of it is not. In addition, Freud now holds that part of the ego too is unconscious, but not as the result of repression.

It would be incorrect, then, to say of Freud's post-1923 theory that the unconscious for Freud just is the repressed; nevertheless, even in the post-1923 phase, the repression theory remains an important part of the theory of the dynamic unconscious. On Freud's account of the unconscious, it is repression that explains how most of what is in the unconscious got there and why it remains there; the repressed cannot enter consciousness until the repression is lifted through psychoanalytic therapy.

The repression theory is important for another reason. As discussed earlier, Freud's main argument in defense of the unconscious is his "unintelligible gaps" argument. The data of consciousness, Freud says (1915b: 166), have a very large number of gaps which appear in slips of the tongue, dreams, and neurotic symptoms.

Pointing out that there are these unexplained mental gaps, however, does not by itself support the postulation of unconscious mental events. To complete the argument, Freud needs to argue that the phenomena have unconscious mental causes as opposed, for example, to having conscious causes we have not thought of or neurological or conditioning causes. He does try to meet this challenge, but not merely by postulating unconscious mental events. It is his theory of repression that is supposed to explain the content of dreams, slips of the tongue, and the origin and maintenance of neurotic symptoms. As Freud notes, "The theory of repression is the corner-stone on which the whole structure of psycho-analysis rests" (1914: 16).

If Freud's theory of repression, then, is false or is not supported by credible empirical evidence, then two things result. His main argument for saying that there are unconscious mental phenomena fails, and his distinctive theory of the unconscious, the theory of the dynamic unconscious, is either false or unsupported. Much depends, therefore, on the empirical status of the repression theory.

Freud argued for his repression theory primarily by appealing to observations he made when treating his patients plus various arguments he gave about the correct interpretation of these observations. Largely because of the detailed rebuttals provided by the philosopher Adolf Grünbaum (1984, 2002), the cogency of Freud's arguments for the repression theory and the entire project of trying to support the repression theory by appealing to nonexperimental clinical data has been rendered doubtful. Some who support Freud argue that the failure of the clinical evidence is not decisive: There is Freudian experimental evidence, they argue, that firms up central parts of Freud's repression theory. Some who take this latter position fail to pay enough attention to the question of whether the theories being defended are distinctively Freudian. For example, see Baumeister, Dale, and Sommer (Baumeister et al. 1998) on experimental studies of defensive behavior and Westen's (1998) defense of five allegedly Freudian hypotheses, not one of which is distinctively Freudian (see Erwin 2003: 880, for a discussion of both papers).

Erwin (1996) concludes that neither the Freudian clinical evidence nor the experimental evidence provides any credible support for Freud's repression theory or for his claims of therapeutic effectiveness. For a more favorable assessment of the Freudian experimental evidence, see Kline (1981) and Fisher and Greenberg (2002).

Whatever the status of Freud's arguments, there is other evidence for the existence of unconscious mental phenomena. Some of this evidence has been unearthed in experimental studies of the so-called "cognitive unconscious" (see, for example, Marcel 1983; Eagle 1987). The issue of the causal role of unconscious mental events in explaining behavior and the occurrence of other mental events remains a thriving part of the enterprise of psychology.

References

Baumeister, R., Dale, K., and Sommer, K. (1998) "Freudian Defense Mechanisms and Empirical Findings in Modern Social Psychology: Reaction Formation, Projection, Displacement, Undoing, Isolation, Sublimation, and Denial," *Journal of Personality* 66: 1081–1124.

Brentano, F. (1995 [1874]) *Psychology from an Empirical Standpoint*, New York: Routledge.

Eagle, M. (1987) "The Psychoanalytic and Cognitive Unconscious," in S. Stern (ed.), *Theories of the Unconscious and Theories of the Self*, Hillsdale, NJ: Analytic Press.

Erwin, E. (1996) *A Final Accounting: Philosophical and Empirical Issues in Freudian Psychology*, Cambridge, MA: MIT Press.

—— (2003) "Did the boy come to nothing?" A review of *The Annual of Psychoanalysis*, vol. 24: *Sigmund Freud and His Impact on the Modern World*, *APA Review of Books* 48: 878–81.

Fisher, S., and Greenberg, R. (2002) "Scientific Tests of Freud's Theories and Therapy," in E. Erwin (ed.) *The Freud Encyclopedia: Theory, Therapy, and Culture*, New York: Routledge.

Freud, S. (1900) *The Interpretation of Dreams*, in Strachey (1953–74) 4 and 5: 1–627.

—— (1912) "A Note on the Unconscious in Psycho-Analysis," in J. Riviere (ed.), *Sigmund Freud: Collected Papers*, vol. 4, New York: Basic Books.

—— (1914) "On the History of the Psycho-Analytic Movement," in Strachey (1953–74) 14: 7–66.

—— (1915a) "Instincts and Their Vicissitudes" in Strachey (1953–74) 14: 117–40.

—— (1915b) "The Unconscious," in Strachey (1953–74) 14: 166–215.

—— (1923) *The Ego and the Id*, in Strachey (1953–74) 19: 12–63.

Grünbaum, A. (1984) *The Foundations of Psychoanalysis: A Philosophical Critique*, Berkeley, CA: University of California Press.

—— (2002) "Critique of Psychoanalysis," in E. Erwin (ed.) *The Freud Encyclopedia: Theory, Therapy, and Culture*, New York: Routledge.

Herbart, J. F. (1895 [1816]) *A Text-Book in Psychology: An Attempt to Found the Science of Psychology on Experience, Metaphysics, and Mathematics*, New York: D. Appleton and Company.

James, W. (1950 [1890]) *The Principles of Psychology*, New York: Dover.

Kline, P. (1981 [1972]) *Fact and Fantasy in Freudian Theory*, 2nd edn, London: Methuen.

Levy, D. (1996) *Freud among the Philosophers: The Psychoanalytic Unconscious and Its Philosophic Critics*, New Haven: Yale University Press.

Marcel, A. (1983) "Conscious and Unconscious Perception: Experiments on Visual Masking and Word Recognition." *Cognitive Psychology* 15: 197–237.

Sand, R. (2002) "Herbart, Johann Friedrich," in E. Erwin (ed.) *The Freud Encyclopedia: Theory, Therapy, and Culture*, New York: Routledge.

von Hartmann, E. (1931 [1868]) *Philosophy of the Unconscious: Speculative Results according to the Inductive Method of Physical Science*, New York: Harcourt Brace and Company.

Strachey, James (ed., trans.) (1953–74) *The Standard Edition of the Complete Psychological Works of Sigmund Freud*, 24 vols, London: Hogarth Press.

—— (1923) Editor's note, in Strachey (1953–74) 19: 3–11.

—— (1915a) Editor's note, in Strachey (1953–74) 14: 111–116.

—— (1915b) Editor's note, in Strachey (1953–74) 14: 161–165.

Westen, D. (1998) "The Scientific Legacy of Sigmund Freud: Toward a Psychodynamically Informed Psychological Science," *Psychological Bulletin* 124: 333–71.

Zentner, M. (2002) "Nineteenth Century Precursors of Freud," in E. Erwin (ed.), *The Freud Encyclopedia: Theory, Therapy, and Culture*, New York: Routledge.

5

THE EARLY HISTORY OF THE *QUALE* AND ITS RELATION TO THE SENSES

Brian L. Keeley

Introduction

In philosophy of psychology and philosophy of mind these days, qualia are all the rage. Like them or doubt their very existence, it seems impossible to develop a contemporary philosophy of psychology that does not reckon with them. For a term that has such a strong foothold in the contemporary literature, it is striking how little of its history is discussed. Given the current lack of agreement over how to think about qualia, it would behoove us to explore how this concept came into current discussions. This sentiment has recently been voiced by Tim Crane (2001), one of the few philosophers to have explored the history of qualia in order to understand contemporary debates:

> To have a clear understanding of [the mind-body problem], we have to have a clear understanding of the notion of qualia. But despite the centrality of this notion [...], it seems to me that there is not a clear consensus about how the term 'qualia' should be understood, and to this extent the contemporary problem of consciousness is not well-posed.
>
> (170)

This is a disturbing possibility, especially if John Searle (1998) is correct in claiming that, "[t]he problem of consciousness is identical with the problem of qualia" (28). Searle's sentiment here might be an overly strong one – or perhaps not; it depends on who is writing – but there can be no denying the centrality of this notion in contemporary philosophical discussions of the mind, as indicated by attempts to define it in reference works (Blackburn 1994; Nagel 1995; Shoemaker 1999; Colman 2001) to even the shallowest survey of recent works (Jackson 1982; Dennett 1988; Shoemaker 1991; Tye 1994; Chalmers 1995; Kind 2001; Graham and Horgan, 2008).

My modest goal here is to explore the history of this term in an attempt to throw some light on contemporary concerns. I suspect that the history explored here might prove useful to anybody currently engaged in debates over the nature, reality, etc., of qualia. However, my own entrée into qualia talk stems from their alleged role in differentiating sensory modalities from one another. One tempting – and on my view, misguided – proposal is that differences in the special introspectable character of sensory experiences – that is, *qualia* – should ground our differentiation of the senses. For example, it has been proposed that what makes smelling different from hearing, say, is that the conscious experience of smelling just *feels different* from that of hearing. Or put yet another way: that the qualia of smelling are clearly different from those of smelling.[1] Engaging this proposal led me to wonder about the early history of the philosophical character of the qualia concept and its relationship to the senses. One upshot of that historical exploration, presented here, is that the close connection between the senses and qualia currently assumed has not always been the case. In fact, early uses of the term often specifically reserved talk of qualia for *nonsensory* conscious experiences.

It's a curious tale of how the two came to be so closely associated with one another, and it has to do with the interaction between the concept of qualia and the short-lived philosophical interest in "sense-data." As it happens, I propose that after philosophy's dalliance with sense-data, our understanding of qualia changed significantly, and this is when qualia picked up the close association it has now with sensory modalities. The responsibility for this shift, I believe, falls largely on C. I. Lewis, and was cemented, in part by his student, Nelson Goodman. The shift they brought about plays on an ambiguity in the use of the term, between a quality itself and the entity that carries or possesses that quality.

In the course of this short investigation, I want to propose some answers to the following questions: (1) Why, despite the apparent similarity between the two terms, has one term (quale) persisted while the other (sense-datum) has largely been left on the dust heap of history? (*Short answer*: Contrary to the received version of the history of these terms, "qualia" had a rich, prior history in the metaphysics of mind that "sense-data" lacked.) (2) Is the current understanding of qualia synonymous with its use in this rich, prior history and, if not, how did it differ? (*Short answer:* No; whereas ***today's*** paradigm cases of qualia are specifically *sense* qualities – the redness of red, the distinct smell of a rose – ***then*** these were *not* generally considered cases of qualia. In the prior usage, the term was reserved for exactly those cases in which a phenomenal experience was not a unimodal, sense perception. Sometimes, they looked more like *primary* – not *secondary* – qualities. (That is to say, sometimes they looked more like qualities shared by multiple senses, rather than like those unique to single senses. At other times, they aren't sensory qualities at all.) As a result of these two differences, qualia as then understood were poorly situated to play an important – much less a *necessary* – role in differentiating the sensory modalities from one another. To the extent that current confusions over the nature of qualia have carried over from this historical shift in the meaning of the term, it goes some ways towards explaining why qualia cannot do the philosophical work in psychology that some would like them to do.

In the section that follows, I will present the history of the qualia concept, as we typically encounter it. It is a history in which C. I. Lewis is the key figure, therefore in the third section, I will précis his use of the concept. In the rest of the paper, I will present an earlier sense of the term, starting with its nineteenth-century origin in English (fourth section), continuing with Charles Sanders Peirce's use of it (fifth), and finishing with the varied uses of the term between the time of Peirce and Lewis (sixth section). The result of this historical investigation is the delineation of two related, but importantly different, senses of the quale concept.

The received history of an unhappy word

What are qualia? Here's an answer from Bill Lycan (1996) one of the few who answers the question with an eye to the term's history:

> Take phenomenal color as a paradigm case of a quale, and let us be unusually careful about our use of this unhappy word. The sense I have in mind is roughly C.I. Lewis's (1929) original sense, in which a *quale* is the introspectable monadic qualitative property of what seems to be a phenomenal individual, such as the color of what Russell called a visual sense datum.
>
> (69)

This association of qualia with sense-data makes sense, given the received understanding of the etymology of the term "quale." When attention is given to the historical source of the term, the story told is that to which Lycan alludes. According to this story, the term "quale" comes from C. I. Lewis's 1929 *Mind and the World Order*. Lycan (1996) goes on to give us a slightly fuller account: "Actually the term 'quale' predates Lewis; it was used, though less precisely, by [Charles Sanders] Peirce" (175). Crane (2001) gives us some more detail:

> While sense-data are largely a British invention, it is American philosophy which can lay claim to the invention of qualia. The first philosopher to use terms "quale" and "qualia" in something like its modern sense was C. S. Peirce. When Peirce wrote in 1866 that "there is a distinctive *quale* to every combination of sensation . . . a peculiar *quale* to every day and every week – a peculiar *quale* to my whole personal consciousness," he was talking about what experience is like, in a general sense, not restricted to the qualia of experience in the sense in which it is normally meant today. William James occasionally used the term specifically to discuss sensation, but as far as I can see the term had no special technical significance in his philosophy or psychology.
>
> (177–8) [2, 3]

So, according to the received story, "quale" is a hand-me-down term. It wasn't much used before Lewis, and when it was, it was not used in any clear, technical sense. It was Lewis who gave the term rigor and clarity, cleaning up the term's sense and reference and generally making it respectable for future philosophical use.

I do not believe this received understanding of the history is quite true to what happened, but it *does* reflect our current understanding of how the concept comes into the contemporary dialogue. Rewriting that history requires going back to the beginning of the story. However, before doing that, it would be useful to explore in some detail Lewis's use of the term, even if that means starting our story in the middle.

In medias res: the foundationalist epistemology of C. I. Lewis leading to *The Structure of Appearance*

How does Lewis (1929) use the term? The not surprising answer: In ways that sound very familiar to the contemporary philosopher of psychology. He writes, "In any presentation [that is, the "given element in a single experience of an object"], this content is either a specific quale (such as the immediacy of redness or loudness) or something analyzable into a complex of such. The presentation as an event is, of course, unique, but the qualia which make it up are not. They are recognisable from one to another experience" (60).

We have here the idea that qualia are the fundamental ontological elements that constitute sensory experience. Just as the physical universe can ultimately be reduced to fundamental, atomic (in its original, literal sense) *quanta*, which are themselves both irreducible and interchangeable, the psychic universe of phenomenal, sensory experience can ultimately be reduced to fundamental, atomic *qualia*, which are themselves irreducible and interchangeable.[4] The term "quale" is our way of giving a name to this mental "something" of which it is not easy to speak. As Lewis (1929) says,

> Qualia are subjective; they have no names in ordinary discourse but are indicated by some circumlocution such as "looks like"; they are ineffable, since they might be different in two minds with no possibility of discovering that fact and no necessary inconvenience to our knowledge of objects or their properties. All that can be done to designate a quale is, so to speak, to locate it in experience, that is, to designate the conditions of its recurrence or other relations of it. Such location does not touch the quale itself; if one such could be lifted out of the network of its relations, in the total experience of the individual, and replaced by another, no social interest or interest of action would be affected by such substitution.
>
> (124–5)[5]

So what? What philosophical advantage does Lewis hope to gain by invoking this term of his intellectual forebears? According to Crane, for Lewis, the quale plays the same role as does the sense datum for Moore, Austin and the British sense-data philosophers: it provides us with an epistemic foundation upon which the rest of knowledge can be built. The quale is offered as an epistemic given. This is the core commonality between Lewis and the sense-data theorists, as Crane puts it:

> The heart of the matter, it seems to me, is this. Lewis' qualia-theory and the sense-datum theory resemble each other in their central claim: that in experience, something is given. They differ in that Lewis thinks that the qualitative properties of experience are in a sense ineffable, and can only be indirectly described; but in the context of their common commitment to the given, this is a relatively unimportant disagreement. As far as the core commitments of the two theories go, it would not mislead to say that the given is a sense-datum, and qualia are its properties.
>
> (181)

We now come to the upshot of this discussion of Lewis on qualia. Let me highlight two features of Lewis's account of qualia that we will see set his use of the term apart from his predecessors, and which mark the significant ways in which he changed how those who followed him thought of the term. First, the epistemic role of the quale/sense-datum goes some way towards explaining Lewis's emphasis upon the *sensational* aspect of phenomenal experience. If it is true that Lewis makes use of the term as a ground for epistemology, then of course he is going to focus on *sensory* experience, for those experiences are, in some way or another, *about* the external world to which the senses are responding. And when we want to provide an epistemic foundation for knowledge, what that means is knowledge about that very same external world.

Second, and again related to the role the term plays in a foundationalist epistemology, for Lewis, it is important that qualia are *reductionist* in nature. They are, in a robust sense, the "building blocks" of conscious experience. When Lewis claims that all experience "is either a specific quale (such as the immediacy of redness or loudness) or something analyzable into a complex of such," this is in part required by the role qualia play in his epistemology. All of our knowledge as we experience it, on his account, can ultimately be boiled down to the data of our senses, thereby tying our entire epistemic lives to the given products of our sensory experience.

This second, reductionist, element of Lewis's sense of qualia was picked up by his graduate student, Nelson Goodman, and features as one of the key ideas of his important 1951 book, *The Structure of Appearance* (Goodman [1966] is the more oft-cited second edition). Goodman's book lays out a philosophical framework for understanding the phenomenology of perception through the naturalistic lens of the psychological science of psychophysics. What the perceptual science of psychophysics does is give us the empirical tools for identifying individuals' sensory qualia: "If we divide the stream of experience into its smallest concrete parts and then go on to divide these concreta into sense qualia, we arrive at entities suitable as atoms for a realistic system. A visual concretum might be divided, for example, into three constituent parts: a time, a visual-field place, and a color [...] Just as the atoms for a particularistic system may be chosen from among the various sorts of concrete parts of experience, so the atoms for a realistic system may be chosen from among various sorts of qualitative parts" (Goodman 1966: 189).

One useful byproduct of Goodman's account of the phenomenology of experience is that it provides us with a systematic way of differentiating the senses. Goodman (179ff.) points out that once one starts to divide the stream of experience into its parts, you'll find that they fall into empirically distinct sensory classes, which in turn map on to what we think of as the distinct sensory modalities.[6] Voilà! From qualia, we get a means of differentiating the sensory modalities; a line of argument that still has its proponents, e.g., Austen Clark (1993, 2000).[7]

Early English appearances of the term

Although one finds references to "quale" in Latin texts going back to at least the medieval period, there are some early English language examples that are informative. For instance, one of the earliest uses cited in the *Oxford English Dictionary* is to an 1834 edition of Abraham Tucker's seven-volume *Light of nature pursued*, originally published 1768–78. This work is a collection of philosophical musings on natural philosophy and Christian theology, and in a chapter entitled "Word, or Logos," he discusses the relationship between existence and essence:

> Existence belongs solely to substances, and essence solely to qualities. Even if I were asked for the essence of a substance, I could not describe it otherwise than by the confused idea of a quality of possessing qualities, and of existing independently of them; wherein it differs from all qualities, which cannot actually subsist, though they may be thought of, without a quale to possess them.
>
> (Tucker 1834: 462)

This is the only reference to "quale" and its cognates in this work, and Tucker is apparently trying to capture the concept of a substantial embodiment (or possession) of an abstract quality. That the term comes up in a context that is confused or difficult to articulate is echoed in Lewis. This is a recurring theme here.

Another *OED*-cited early use of the term in an English context is in Benjamin Jowett's 1875 translation of Plato's *Meno*. In the opening exchange of this dialogue, Meno asks Socrates whether virtue is innate or is acquired by teaching or practice. As Socrates is perennially wont to do, he pleads ignorance; he notes that were any Athenian asked this question, that Athenian,

> would laugh in your face, and say: "Stranger, you have far too good an opinion of me, if you think that I can answer your question. For I literally do not know what virtue is, and much less whether it is acquired by teaching or not." And I myself, Meno, living as I do in this region of poverty [of wisdom], am as poor as the rest of the world; and I confess with shame that I know literally nothing about virtue; and when I do not know the "quid" of anything how can I know the "quale"? How, if I knew nothing at all of Meno, could I tell if he was fair, or the opposite of fair; rich and noble, or the reverse of rich and noble? Do you think that I could?
>
> (Plato 1875: 469–70)

In the Jowett translation, "quale" is distinguished from "quid." The Latin term "quid" is defined by the *Oxford English Dictionary* as "That which a thing is." "Quale," on the other hand, is listed as deriving from the Latin *qualis* ("Of what kind") and the term means "The quality of a thing; a thing having certain qualities."[8] So, according to Jowett, Socrates is asking how one can know the qualities of something – or, perhaps what sort of thing it is or what it is like – if one does not know what that thing is, what its nature is. Intellectual historian of psychology Daniel Robinson (1976) helps us see what is going on in this passage: "In the *Theaetetus* and in the *Meno*, Socrates distinguished between perception of particular instances and general ideas, which themselves cannot be received through perception. The [word][9] 'cat' is illustrative. We can see a particular cat but we can only know (perceptually) that it is *a* cat because it answers to the description given by our general idea of *the* cat" (80; emphases in original). "Quale" then is being used by Jowett to refer to the qualities possessed by a thing.

However, during this period, rather than Plato, it is more common to find this term and its cognates in English translations of Aristotle – specifically in translations and elucidations of his *Categories* (one element of the collection of Aristotelian logical texts known as the *Organon*). See, for example, Aristotle (1878). Thomas Taylor, in the early nineteenth century, offers us an early example of how the term is used in glosses on Aristotle's category of "Quality":

> Aristotle, says Simplicius, has delivered the division of qualities through four members ... Of qualities, therefore, it must be said, that some are natural, but others adventitious ... [O]f natural qualities, some are according to capacity, and others according to energy. And the qualities according to capacity are those by which we are said to be adapted to effect any thing. But of those qualities which are according to energy, one kind is that which operates profoundly, which also is predicated in a twofold respect according to passive qualities. For either by the assistance of passion something is inserted in the senses, or because qualities accede from passion, such as sweetness, heat, whiteness, and the like. For these are qualities, and their possessors are very properly called *qualia*. But they are also called passive, so far as they insert passion in the senses, or so far as they accede according to passion.
>
> (Aristotle 1812: 103; italics in original)

What we have in all of these early appearances of the term is a sense that fits the *OED* definition: "The quality of a thing; a thing having certain qualities," perhaps with an emphasis on the second part of this definition; although, as we'll see the use of the term plays on the ambiguity between referring to the quality itself and what it is that possesses that quality. Goodman (1966) notes that when we talk of the qualities of things that we perceive, in ordinary language we mix up two different senses that a more nuanced consideration ought to distinguish, namely something taken to be a mind-independent property of the object itself and something which is a property of our experience of that object. So, in ordinary speech, when we talk of a red sunset we make reference both to some objective property of the interaction of the earth's atmosphere and the sunlight, as well as the quality of visual perception of that scene.

Goodman, following Lewis, wishes to reserve the term "quale" for the second of these and use "property" for the first. However, these early uses of the term do not make this distinction. These early appearances of the term are apparently metaphysical in nature, although it does not obviously have the *mental* connotations it has in its modern guise.

Nonetheless, it is useful to the current historical investigation to note a number of things about the choice of translation here. First, the dates of these translations (1812–78) overlap and predate Peirce's putative coining of the modern sense of the term (1866). Next – and this is important – notice that it was these translators' choice to use the term *quale* in the context of an *English translation*.[10] This would be an odd choice indeed, if it were the case that the term had some technical sense or if were not a term that their English-understanding readers would recognize. Their use of the term suggests that "quale," while a foreign term – it is often italicized – was nonetheless in common use in the English-speaking intellectual world. This hypothesis has only been reinforced by my survey of its use in the half century of philosophical and psychological use prior to its appearance in *Mind and the World Order*, to which I will soon be turning. In all the references to the term discussed below, no attempt is made to explain the term to the reader, which is what one would expect if the writer believed that the term needed no special introduction. The term is exclusively *used* and never *mentioned*. Further, in this early literature, no originator is ever cited with any of the term's instances; that is, nobody explicitly notes that this is a term of art introduced by Peirce or anybody else.[11] My reading of this situation is that "quale" is a word that was once in relatively common use among philosophers, scientists and other intellectuals, but has now become archaic in everyday speech; it now lives on solely as a technical term in academic philosophy and perceptual psychology.

"In the beginning ..." Peirce says some obscure things about qualia

Where this prior use suggests a nontechnical origin, Charles Sanders Peirce is the first philosopher to make use of it within a novel philosophical framework. As best as I can tell, this much the received history gets right. What did Peirce have in mind by his use of the term? The earliest reference that I have been able to find is from lecture 9 of his 1866 Lowell lectures on "The Logic of Science; or, Induction and Hypothesis." In this particular lecture, he is trying to spell out the proper taxonomy of the components of the process by which we move to a full understanding of things. He is presenting his own set of logical and metaphysical categories, much as Aristotle and Kant do before him.

He begins by noting that, "Our first impressions are entirely unknown in themselves and the matter of cognition is the matter of fact and what is not a question of a possible experience is not a question of fact. The impressions are grasped into the unity which the mind requires ... by conceptions and sensations" (Peirce 1982 [1866]: 471). According to Peirce, impressions are the data with which the mind uses sensations and conceptions in order to create a coherent understanding of what it is experiencing. He continues by noting that,

> both sensations and conceptions are hypothetic [sic] predicates. They are, however, hypotheses of widely different kinds. A sensation is a sort of mental name. To assign a name to a thing is to make a hypothesis. It is plainly a predicate which is not in the *data*. But it is given on account of a logical necessity; namely the necessity of reducing the manifold of the predicates given to unity. We give the name *man* because it is needed to convey at once rationality, animality, being two-legged, being mortal, &c. To give a name is therefore to make a hypothesis ... Sensation is, as it were, the writing on the page of consciousness. Conception is the meaning of the sensation.
>
> (472–3; emphasis in original)

What Peirce is here calling "impressions" or "data" sounds very reminiscent of Lewis's "given element" in experience, what Lewis calls *qualia*. There is clearly a connection here because, in his lecture, Peirce soon coins the term "Quale" in the context of this discussion. Peirce's discussion here is an early statement of his semiotic theory, in which the key concept in understanding how the mind creates meaning is the "symbol," and symbols can be evaluated into three divisions: Term, Proposition and Representation (*ibid.*: 478). The theory here is quite convoluted and involves a lot of nomenclature unique to Peirce (or worse, the terminology is familiar, but he uses it in his own proprietary way). However, the Quale is a foundational concept in Peirce's categories, so I hope I can present this notion without getting much into the larger theory in which it plays a role.

The first element in his tripartite taxonomy of the understanding is what he calls a term: "a *term* is a symbol which is intended only to refer to a Ground or what is the same thing, to stand instead of a Quale or what is again the same, to have *meaning* without *truth*" (*ibid.*: 477). A term simply *refers* to some ground. Further, "Reference to a ground is the possession of a Quality" (475). One can talk of two terms resembling one another, or not, but nothing more involved can be invoked. This is what Peirce means by speaking of "meaning without truth." Terms have meanings by virtue of their reference, but we cannot speak of any "true" or "false" terms. This relation to a ground is what Lewis transforms in his own theory into talk of the given. And to specify the taxonomy of his discussion, Peirce speaks of a "*Term* intended to refer to a ground – whose object is formally a Quale" (478). In other words, "Quale" is the name his theory gives to the otherwise impossible-to-describe data of the mind's understanding. This in-principle resistance to description is what Lewis develops later in terms of "ineffability."

The second division of symbols is "Proposition." Whereas terms simply refer to a ground, a Proposition relates that ground to something further, generally more terms. A proposition is a claim, and hence has a truth value (which derives ultimately from the meanings of the components that make up the proposition): The terms either stand in the relationship claimed, or they do not.

The third division of symbols – "Argument" – adds a third component to the previous two (grounds and relations): an interpretant. This results in a full-blown *representation*, in Peirce's taxonomy. Crudely put, one only has genuine representation on Peirce's account, when one has a triune of grounded reference with claimed relationship for an interpretant.

The Peircean metaphysics and semiotic theory here is convoluted and involved, and my sketch above does not come close to doing it justice. However, my goal here is not to leave the reader with a full understanding of Peirce's theory, but rather to give some idea of what role the concept of a quale was playing in Peirce's overall theory. I believe I have presented enough of his account to begin to piece this together.

What Peirce is doing is taking the understood notion of a quale, as it was used in the translations of Plato and Aristotle at the time, and applying it to his own account of the categories. This is not such a long stretch, as he is doing this in the context of coming up with a set of taxonomic categories with which to understand how the mind arrives at coherence, just as Aristotle and Kant do before him (and both of whose work greatly influenced the young Peirce). Indeed, in the year following the writing of the Lowell Lectures, he presents a paper entitled, "On a new list of categories" which opens, "This paper is based upon the theory already established, that the function of conceptions is to reduce the manifold of sensuous impressions to unity, and that the validity of a conception consists in the impossibility of reducing the content of consciousness to unity without the introduction of it" (Peirce 1984 [1867]: 49).

The Aristotelian and Kantian themes of Peirce's philosophy discussed above mesh well with the Lewisian use of the qualia concept discussed in the third section. Invoking qualia in the context of presenting the very logical and metaphysical categories required to explain the unity of experience is not a million miles away from the foundationalist project of grounding the entirety of our epistemology. So far, Lewis is giving the impression of being a good student of Peircean ideas (which would be no surprise coming from a student of Josiah Royce, himself a very sympathetic student of Peirce). However, Peirce's later development of the concept points to some important differences between his use of the term and those who followed him. This difference is well-illustrated by considering the 1898 passage that Crane excerpted from above. Let us turn to a more full rendition of that difficult discussion, together with my gloss:[12]

> 6.222 If a man is blind to the *red* and *violet* elements of light and only sees the *green* element, then all things appear of one color to him, and that color is a green of colorific intensity beyond anything that we with normal eyes can see or imagine. Such is the color that all things look to him. Yet since all things look alike in this respect, it never attracts his attention in the least. He may be said to be dead to it. If the man is at the same time deaf, without smell and taste, and devoid of skin sensations, then it is probable the green will be still more chromatic; for I suppose colors are for us somewhat diluted by skin sensations. But for the very reason that it is his own kind of sensation, he will only be the more completely oblivious of its *quale*. Yet for all that, that *is* the way things look to him, more intensely green than any scarlet or magenta is red to us.

> This illustration puts into a high light the distinction between two kinds of consciousness, the *quale*-consciousness and that kind of consciousness which is intensified by attention, which objectively considered, I call *vividness*, and as a faculty we may call *liveliness*.

Peirce's use of the term here seems to expand on the sense intended by Jowett. Here, it quite clearly refers to the qualities of conscious experience; he says his example is intended to illustrate a "distinction between two kinds of consciousness." *Quale*-consciousness refers to a dimension of qualitative difference *other* than a difference in intensity. Attending to a sensation – or being forced to do so by a relative lack of other in-principle conflicting sensations, as in the case of Peirce's colorblind individual – may change the intensity of the sensation, but this change is not the kind of change of quality marked by the term "quale." Although the details of what he has in mind here are admittedly obscure – particularly his idea of the relationship between visual and tactile experience – it is clear at least that he is claiming that one can only notice the *quale* of given experience if it stands out from the background of other qualities in some sense.

Let's continue with the passage:

> 223. The *quale*-consciousness is not confined to simple sensations. There is a peculiar *quale* to *purple*, though it be only a mixture of red and blue. There is a distinctive *quale* to every combination of sensations so far as it is really synthetized – a distinctive *quale* to every work of art – a distinctive *quale* to this moment as it is to me – a distinctive *quale* to every day and every week – a peculiar *quale* to my whole personal consciousness. I appeal to your introspection to bear me out in this.

We find here that the concept of a *quale* is quite a general one with respect to conscious experience. It is not restricted to "simple sensations"; it also refers to more complex sensations (such as admixtures of colors; Peirce was no doubt familiar with what came to be known as the Young-Helmholtz theory of trichromatic color vision). But more than that, *qualia* referred to nonsensory conscious experience, as when we note the *quale* of a Monday morning versus that of a Friday afternoon at 4:45. As we will return to below, this nonsimple aspect of Peircean qualia represents an important difference from Lewisian qualia.

> 224. Each *quale* is in itself what it is for itself, without reference to any other. It is absurd to say that one *quale* in itself considered is like one or unlike another. Nevertheless, comparing consciousness does pronounce them to be alike. They are alike to the comparing consciousness, though neither alike nor unlike in themselves.
>
> 225. And now I enunciate a truth. It is this. In so far as *qualia* can be said to have anything in common, that which belongs to one and all is *unity*; and the

> various synthetical unities which Kant attributes to the different operations of the mind, as well as the unity of logical consistency, or *specific* unity, and also the unity of the individual object, all these unities originate, not in the operations of the intellect, but in the *quale*-consciousness upon which the intellect operates.

Ignoring the difficult Peircean metaphysics at play here,[13] we should note a number of things about Peirce's discussion of qualia here. First, it is clearly a phenomenological term; when applied to a visual phenomenon, it describes a way of looking – a way of appearing – to a perceiver. Second, while Peirce begins the passage by reference to a simple, sensational example, he goes on to stress that this is only part of the story. It refers to whatever makes a given conscious experience its particular feeling. Finally, it is largely ineffable.

The upshot of considering this later discussion of qualia is that we can now more clearly identify where Peirce and Lewis agree and disagree in their respective uses of the qualia concept. On the agreement side of things, the two philosophical positions concur concerning the ineffability of qualia. On both accounts, the nature of qualia as either a "ground" (Peirce) or a "given" (Lewis) positions qualia as a brute starting point about which not much can be said. In both systems, quale acts as a label for that nonarticulable starting point. That qualia are some kind of brute starting point (the flipside to their being ineffable) is an additional important point of agreement between the two systems.

On the disagreement side of things, where Lewis sees qualia as the simple, sensory, building blocks of experience, for Peirce they are often anything but sensory and anything but simple. For Peirce they often have a sum-is-greater-than-the-sum-of-its-parts quality, as when he speaks of the distinctive qualia of a work of art.[14] This nonreductionist take on qualia runs against what Lewis needs them to do in his own account: serve as part of a foundationalist epistemology. Peirce's own epistemic goals are more transcendental than reductionist, if anything, so his system does not require this feature; but this reductionism is a linchpin in Lewis's account.

Of course, any philosopher can define her terms however she wishes. However, what is striking is that a survey of the use qualia were put to in the years between Peirce and Lewis reveals that if there was a consensus concerning whose view is the better one, it was Peirce and not Lewis whose account comes out the victor. What's more, the received history of the term completely erases this intervening history of ideas. In the penultimate section that follows, I will rehabilitate that history somewhat by considering the ways in which "quale" and its cognates appear in the philosophical and psychological literature of the intervening years. My hope is that this history will lend some credence to the view that Peirce's use of the term is not simply the idiosyncratic eccentricities of a single theorist.

A motley menagerie of early qualia

After Peirce's invocation of the concept, "quale," "qualia" and "quales" appear regularly in the literature of philosophy and psychology from the 1870s through the early twentieth century.[15] What is striking about how the term is used during this period is that while it is clearly used at least some of the time to refer to sensational experiences, more often, it is used to describe experiences that, today, we would find odd to think of in straightforward sensational or perceptual terms. Here is a list of how the term was used, roughly in descending order of commonality:

Feelings of pleasure and pain

There is much discussion of the *quale* of feeling, where "feeling" here refers to the experience of pleasure (approbation) or pain (disapprobation).[16] This seems connected to Peirce's mention of the quale of a work of art or of a particular day: one strong element of such a quale would be how pleasing such a thing is. This sense of the term is sometimes referred to as the "emotional" quality of experience. Examples of qualia being discussed in the context of feelings are numerous: Ward (1883), Whittaker (1890) and Stanley (1892).

One early example of the use of quale in this sense, Stout (1888) points to the fusion of sensations (as in the sound of a chord), and continues, "Purely sensuous pleasures and pains are explained on the same lines. Only in their case the presentations between which fusion takes place are not separately discernible. They are merged in a single distinctionless *quale*, which defies all attempts to resolve it into its component parts" (489).

Nichols (1892) also discusses qualia in the context of feelings of pleasure and pain. He does so in a revealing fashion, in that he explicitly distinguishes talk of senses from talk of qualia. His paper explores the question of whether pain should be a separate sense (on par with vision, hearing, etc.) or whether it should be considered a phenomenal aspect of one of the other senses. This latter view he terms the "doctrine *of qualia*" (431). He thinks the then recent findings of Goldsheider – that there is a peripheral nerve system for pain that is separate from other cutaneous senses – is evidence that pain is a separate sense, not a quality of other senses: "Thus pain sometimes stays while all the other senses go, and sometimes goes when the other senses stay, which surely looks as if it were not a *quale* inseparable from the other sense" (406).

Extensity

In addition to the context of pleasure and pain, the other main context for discussing qualia comes up in terms of the experience of *space*. For example, Hyslop (1891) makes use of the term in his critical examination of Helmholtz's concept of "unconscious inference" as a means of explaining how the mind constructs its perception of the visual world; that is, how the mind comes to experience a three-dimensional world as a result of the two-dimensional input to our retinas, on the one hand; and our tactile experience of the world, on the other. As he puts it, "I have desired to indicate the existence in vision of a *quale* distinct from differences of shade and colour, which may as well be called extension as not; because it is capable of being identified with a tactual *quale* of the same meaning, while the sensations proper are not so connected" (78–9).

Further, the most famous discussion of qualia during this early period comes from William James. His two 1879 papers on the "spatial qualia" (1879a), (1879b) are the ancestors of his chapter "The Perception of Space" in his 1890 *Principles of Psychology*.[17] (See also James [1887a, b].) Here is how James (1981 [1890]) describes this phenomenon:

> THE FEELING OF CRUDE EXTENSITY: In the sensations of hearing, touch, sight, and pain we are accustomed to distinguish from among the other elements the element of voluminousness. We call the reverberations of a thunderstorm more voluminous than the squeaking of a slate-pencil; the entrance into a warm bath gives our skin a more massive feeling than the prick of a pin; a little neuralgic pain, fine as a cobweb, in the face seems less extensive than the heavy soreness of a boil or the vast discomfort of a colic or a lumbago.
>
> (776)

Non-sensorial thought

Yet another case is that of non-sensorial thought; that is, cognition that is not sensation-based in its phenomenology. For example, Woodworth (1906) describes a number of situations in which we have a distinct phenomenology in the absence of any particular sense-modality-specific experience:

> It seems impossible to describe these facts without admitting the existence of other than sensorial contents of consciousness. I would suggest that in addition to sensorial elements, thought contains elements which are wholly irreducible to sensory terms. [. . .] There is a specific and unanalyzable conscious quale for every individual and general notion, for every judgment and supposition. These qualities recur in the same sense as red and other sensory qualities recur.
>
> (705–6)

Shand (1898) covers very similar ground while discussing what he calls the "*quale* of thought," concluding that it "defies analysis and remains absolutely unique" (500).[18]

Emotion

The phenomenal quality of emotion is yet another context for the early discussion of qualia, as found in Irons (1897b), who speaks of "the true emotional *quale*" (489) (see also Irons [1897a]). Similarly, Rogers (1904) concludes, "That the emotion is not wholly identical with organic sensations, seems to be the conclusion toward which psychology is tending. To me it appears that there is a special *quale*, which cannot be reduced to anything more simple and elementary" (41).

Effort

A final context in which early philosophers discuss qualia involves the "sense of effort," for example the phenomenal feeling of effort one experiences while trying to concentrate on a symphony or trying to solve a math problem (known as "moral" effort) or in trying to hold one's hand in a flame ("muscular" effort). Dewey (1897) wants to defend a "sensational" account of this phenomenon that reduces this phenomenal quality to sensory experience; that is, effort is explained in such terms as the feeling of holding one's breath or furrowing one's brow: "There are three distinguishable views regarding the psychical quales experienced in cases of effort. [... One] view declines to accept the distinction made between moral and physical effort as a distinction of genesis, and holds that all sense of effort is sensationally (peripherally) determined" (43).

It isn't easy to figure out a unified characterization of qualia that makes sense of all these different uses of the term (and, in all honesty, I have not mentioned other uses of which I cannot make sense). However, there are strains that flow through all of them. All are aspects of experienced phenomenology. They all recognize that not everything we experience is systematically correlated with our classic Aristotelian five senses – sight, hearing, smell, taste and touch – in a one-to-one fashion. Some, such as the feeling of extensity or feelings of pleasure, are associated with more than one sensory modality. Others, such as emotion or non-sensorial thought, do not seem to be associated with any sense whatsoever.

(Incidentally, this is part of why I argue that phenomenology is not a good guide for differentiating the senses from one another. When Stout (1888: 489) observes that experiences of pleasure or pain "are merged in a single distinctionless *quale*, which defies all attempts to resolve it into its component parts" one worries about the utility of such qualia to separate out pleasures of different senses.)

Strikingly, at several points in these early discussions, a "qualia account" is presented as in opposition to a "sensational account." This points to one way of understanding these odd qualia that aren't associated with a single modality: Perhaps these early theorists thought of "qualia" as defining a catch-all or otherwise-non-definable category. In other words, membership in the qualia-category is defined by the inability to place a given experience within one of the other categories, which are defined in terms of the senses.[19]

Conclusion

With luck, this paper has fleshed out an historical development in the philosophy of perceptual psychology that has largely been ignored. Instead of the commonplace belief that the first philosophically sensible discussion of qualia starts with Lewis, instead, the historical picture presented here demonstrates that prior to Lewis's use of the term, there was another, related but different sense of the concept in the literature, exemplified most clearly in the work of Peirce.

The question of how to differentiate the sensory modalities is one (but probably not the only) philosophical issue where the differences in the meaning of qualia make a difference. Because of the important philosophical work they do in grounding a foundationalist epistemology, Lewis qualia are tightly coupled to the senses. On Lewis's account, qualia truly are the data of the senses. As such, Goodman and more recently, Austen Clark, have been able to further develop the implications of a Lewisian account of qualia to propose a means of differentiating the senses from one another, giving us an account of how to distinguish sight from smell from touch and so on. In fact, when the extant history of qualia only makes reference to Lewis qualia, such an account seems inevitable.

But the existence of a rich, prior, alternative account of qualia – an account that does not relate qualia necessarily with sensation – removes the air of inevitability from qualia-based accounts of modality differentiation. Indeed, on this alternative account, qualia are often invoked precisely when attempts to understand experience in terms of sensation fail. At the very least, the alternative Peirce-qualia account emphasizes the importance of those elements of conscious experience that do not fall neatly under the heading of "*sensory* experience."

As I discussed in the introduction, this concern with the differentiation of sensory modalities is merely my own bailiwick, and reflects my own entrée into this odd, pre-Lewis history of the quale concept. However, I feel certain that this history will be of interest to others who are currently struggling over this central concept in the philosophy of psychology. My hope is that by pulling back the curtain on this unexplored history of ideas – if only to the tiny degree I have been able to here – others will be stimulated to explore it more fully and more clearly situate current debates over what Lycan rightly calls "this unhappy word."

Notes

1. The reference to "special introspectable character" comes from (Grice 1989 [1962]), although to be fair, Grice himself avoids reference to the term "qualia." For some of the debate over the relationship between the senses and qualia, see Dretske (2000) and Lopes (2000). For my own initial foray into these issues, see Keeley (2002).
2. There is some confusion in Crane's citation of the 1866 date here. The quoted passage is from Peirce's *Collected Papers* and is from his notes for a series of lectures in 1898. (I will quote the passage more fully below.) However, according to the *Writings of Charles S. Peirce: A Chronological Edition*, Peirce did indeed first use the term in 1866; however, *this* is not that early passage. (Again, I will consider this earlier passage below, as well.)
3. As we will see below, somewhat contrary to what Crane says here, James does not use the term in the context of "sensation" *per se*, but only when discussing a *particular instance* of sensation, namely the perception of space (or "voluminousness" or "crude extensity"). Further, in the fourth section, I will present some evidence that "quale" *does* play a significant role in Peirce's philosophy of psychology.
4. Later, Goodman (1966: 189ff.) explicitly endorses this way of thinking about qualia.
5. It's interesting to note that this sort of "inverted spectrum" situation – supposing that qualia in two different people might well be different, for all we know – and Lewis's talk of "lifting" a quale out of

"the network of its relations" mirrors closely what Peirce wrote about the concept exactly a century earlier (see, e.g., Peirce 1982 [1866]: 472).

6. Although Goodman makes it clear that his notion of qualia is taken from Lewis, he notes that he draws the sensory modality argument from Carnap's 1928 discussion of "sense classes" in the *Aufbau* (§§ 85, 114, 115).
7. See my (2002: 15–16) for a discussion and critique of this line of argument.
8. Perhaps it is also worth noting that this is the second definition of "quale" given in the *OED*; the first being to "torment, torture" with references to "**quale-house**, house of torture" and "**quale-sithe**, death from pestilence." There's a joke in here somewhere.
9. The original text reads "world." I believe this is in error.
10. Further, the choice of a *Latin* term in translating a Greek passage for an English-speaking audience is even more striking.
11. Neither does Lewis credit anybody else with using the term when he makes use of it. Goodman (1966: 130n3) credits Lewis (1929).
12. The numbering system refers to the once canonical eight-volume *Collected Papers of Charles Sanders Peirce* (Peirce 1931–58), in this case, paragraph 222 of volume 6. This edition is slowly being superseded by the much more thorough *Writings of Charles S. Peirce: A Chronological Edition*, from which I have been quoting above. The chronological edition has only made it to 1890, to date, so after this date we must fall back on the *Collected Papers*.
13. My guess, for the Peirce scholars out there, is that though it is not explicit in Peirce's work, the sense of quale at play in this passage is a representative of "Firstness" in his tripartite metaphysics. Compare what Rosensohn (Rosensohn 1974: 80–1) says about the place of experiential qualities within Peirce's metaphysical system. Consider also this from Peirce, which although it does not explicitly mention qualia, seems to be on the same track: "What the world was to Adam on the day he opened his eyes, before he had drawn any distinctions, or had become conscious of his own existence – that is first ... fresh, new, initiative, original, spontaneous, free, vivid, conscious, and evanescent. Only, remember that every description of it must be false to it" (1.357).
14. In a passage I didn't quote before, Peirce (1982 [1866]) speaks of beauty in the same way: "when we hear a sonata of Beethoven's the predicate of beautiful is affixed to it as a single representation of the complicated phenomena presented to the ear. The beauty does not belong to each note or chord but to the whole" (472).
15. "Quale" is consistently used as the singular form of the term. It appears in the plural as either "qualia" or "quales" at roughly an equal rate.
16. Nichols (1892) well captures the sense of the term at play in these discussions:

    > From Plato and Aristotle down through Descartes, Leibnitz, Hobbes, Sulzer, Kant, Herbart, Bain, Spencer, Dumont, and Allen – down to the latest articles of Mr. Marshall in *Mind*, the idea, at base, has ever been the same: The experience, the judgment, the attainment of a perfect or imperfect life; the perfect or imperfect exercise of a faculty; the furtherance or hindrance of some activity; the rise or fall of some vital function, force, or energy. Everywhere pleasure and pain have been looked upon as complementary terms of a single phenomenon, and as the very essence of expression of the rise and fall of our inmost existence.
    >
    > (403)

17. Note a few unrelated things: First, the 1879a paper is the earliest reference to be found in the JSTOR ("Journal Storage") catalogue of archived philosophy journal publications (as of June 2007). However, it should be taken as a cautionary note that the *other* (1879b) paper is not to be found in JSTOR, because the journal in which it appears is not included in that archive. Finally, the chapter on space perception in James' *Principles* is the only place in that entire, voluminous work where the term "quale" and its cognates makes an appearance, including those chapters discussing other aspects of sensory perception.
18. I can't pass without noting that this view – that there exists a unique experience of non-sensorial thought – has recently been rediscovered. See Pitt's (2004) "The Phenomenology of Cognition or *What Is It Like To Think That P?*"
19. Thanks for Charles Young (per. commun.) for suggesting this possibility.

Acknowledgements

Like too many of my papers, this one has had a long gestation period – a fact that leaves me with a lot of folks to thank. An early version, under the title "The Hunt for the Wily Quale," was presented at the 2005 annual meeting of the Society for Philosophy and Psychology at Wake Forest University, where Bill Lycan presented a helpful commentary. The same paper was presented as an invited talk at the Claremont Graduate University (thanks to James Griffith), where Peter Ross gave his view of things. My philosophical colleagues at the Claremont Colleges also helped shape my early thoughts about the history of qualia. George Graham gave me valuable feedback at a crucial point in this paper's development. Both Hugh Clapin and Chuck Young gave me valuable feedback at significant points in the paper's development.

References

Aristotle (1812) *The Works of Aristotle, Translated from the Greek, with Copious Elucidations from the Best of his Greek Commentators*, London: Robert Wilkins, Co.

—— (1878) The Organon, *or Logical Treatises, of Aristotle, with the Introduction of Porphyry*, London: George Bell & Sons.

Blackburn, S. (1994) "Qualia," in S. Blackburn (ed.), *The Oxford Dictionary of Philosophy*, Oxford: Oxford University Press, p. 313.

Chalmers, D. J. (1995) "Absent Qualia, Fading Qualia, Dancing Qualia," in T. Metzinger (ed.), *Conscious Experience*, Paderborn, Germany: Ferdinand-Schöningh, pp. 309–27.

Clark, A. (1993) *Sensory Qualities*, Oxford: Oxford University Press.

—— (2000) *A Theory of Sentience*, New York: Oxford University Press.

Colman, A. M. (2001) "Qualia," in A. M. Colman (ed.), *A Dictionary of Psychology*, Oxford: Oxford University Press, p. 609.

Crane, T. (2001) "The Origins of Qualia," in T. Crane and S. Patterson (eds), *History of the Mind-Body Problem*, London: Routledge, pp. 169–94.

Dennett, D. C. (1988) "Quining qualia," in A. J. Marcel and E. Bisiach (eds), *Consciousness in Contemporary Science*, Oxford, Oxford University Press, pp. 42–77.

Dewey, J. (1897) "The psychology of effort," *The Philosophical Review* 6, no. 1: 43–56.

Dretske, F. (2000) "Reply to Lopes," *Philosophy and Phenomenological Research* 60, no. 2: 455–9.

Goodman, N. (1966) *The Structure of Appearance*, Indianapolis: Bobbs-Merrill.

Graham, G., and Horgan, T. (2008) "Qualia Realism: Its Phenomenal Contents and Discontents" in E. Wright (ed.), *The case for qualia* Cambridge, MA: MIT Press.

Grice, H. P. (1989 [1962]) "Some Remarks about the Senses," in I. R. J. Butler (ed.), *Analytical Philosophy*, 1st series, Oxford: Oxford University Press.

Hyslop, J. H. (1891) "Helmholtz's theory of space-perception," *Mind* o.s. 16, no. 61: 54–79.

Irons, D. (1897a) "The Nature of Emotion," pt 1, *Philosophical Review* 6, no. 3: 242–56.

—— (1897b) "The Nature of Emotion," pt 2, *Philosophical Review* 6, no. 5: 471–96.

Jackson, F. (1982) "Epiphenomenal Qualia," *Philosophical Quarterly* 32: 127–36.

James, W. (1879a) "The Sentiment of Rationality," *Mind* o.s. 4, no. 15: 317–46.

—— (1879b) "The spatial quale," *Journal of Speculative Philosophy* 13, no. 1: 64–87.

—— (1887a) "The Perception of Space," pt 1, *Mind* o.s. 12, no. 45: 1–30.

—— (1887b) "The Perception of Space," pt 2, *Mind* o.s. 12, no. 46: 183–211.

—— (1890–81) *The Principles of Psychology*, Cambridge, MA: Harvard University Press.

Keeley, B. L. (2002) "Making Sense of the Senses: Individuating Modalities in Humans and Other Animals," *Journal of Philosophy* 99: 5–28.

Kind, A. (2001) "Qualia Realism," *Philosophical Studies* 104: 143–62.

Lewis, C. I. (1929) *Mind and the World-Order*, New York: Charles Scribner's Sons.

Lopes, D. M. M. (2000) "What Is It Like to See with Your Ears? The Representational Theory of Mind," *Philosophy and Phenomenological Research* 60: 439–53.

Lycan, W. G. (1996) *Consciousness and Experience*, Cambridge, MA: MIT Press-Bradford.

Nagel, T. (1995) "Qualia," in. T. Honderich (ed.), *The Oxford Companion to Philosophy*, Oxford: Oxford University Press, p. 736.

Nichols, H. (1892) "The Origin of Pleasure and Pain," pt 1, *Philosophical Review* 1, no. 4: 403–32.

Peirce, C. S. (1931–58) *Collected Papers of Charles Sanders Peirce*, ed. C. Hartshorne, P. Weiss, and A. W. Burks, Cambridge, MA: Harvard University Press.

—— (1982 [1866]) "Lowell Lecture, ix," in M. H. Fisch (ed.), *Writings of Charles S. Peirce: A Chronological Edition*, vol. 1: 1857–66, Bloomington, IN: Indiana University Press, 471–86.

—— (1984 [1867]) "On a New List of Categories," in E. C. Moore (ed.), *Writings of Charles S. Peirce: A Chronological Edition*, Bloomington, IN: Indiana University Press, vol. 2: 49–59.

Pitt, D. (2004) "The Phenomenology of Cognition or *What Is It Like to Think That P?*," *Philosophy and Phenomenological Research* 69, no. 1: 1–36.

Plato (1875) Meno, in B. Jowett (ed.), *The Dialogues of Plato*, vol. 1, Oxford: Clarendon Press.

Robinson, D. N. (1976) *An Intellectual History of Psychology*, New York: Macmillan.

Rogers, A. K. (1904) "Rationality and Belief," *Philosophical Review* 13, no. 1: 30–50.

Rosensohn, W. L. (1974) *The Phenomenology of Charles S. Peirce: From the Doctrine of Categories to Phaneroscopy*, Amsterdam: B. R. Grüner B.V.

Searle, J. R. (1998) "How to Study Consciousness Scientifically," in J. Cornwell (ed.), *Consciousness and Human Identity*, New York: Oxford University Press, pp. 21–37.

Shand, A. F. (1898) "Feeling and Thought," *Mind* o.s. 7, no. 28: 477–505.

Shoemaker, S. (1991) "Qualia and Consciousness," *Mind* 100, no. 4: 507–24.

—— (1999) "Qualia," in R. Audi (ed.), *The Cambridge Dictionary of Philosophy*, Cambridge: Cambridge University Press, p. 762.

Stanley, H. M. (1892) "On Primitive Consciousness," *Philosophical Review* 1, no. 4: 433–42.

Stout, G. F. (1888) "The Herbartian Psychology," pt 2, *Mind* o.s. 13, no. 52: 473–98.

Tucker, A. (1834) *The Light of Nature Pursued*, London: Thomas Tegg & Son.

Tye, M. (1994) "Qualia, Content, and the Inverted Spectrum," *Noûs* 28, no. 2: 159–83.

Ward, J. (1883) "Psychological Principles," Mind o.s. 8, no. 32: 465–86.

Whittaker, T. (1890) "Volkmann's Psychology," pt 2, *Mind* o.s. 15, no. 60: 489–513.

Woodworth, R. S. (1906) "Imageless Thought," *Journal of Philosophy, Psychology and Scientific Methods* 3, no. 26: 701–8.

6
BEHAVIOURISM

David Braddon-Mitchell

All forms of behaviourism identify mental states with behaviours or behavioural dispositions. Thus it might be that the desire to eat ice cream is identified with ice-cream-eating behaviour, or a disposition to eat ice cream. The basic distinction between varieties of behaviourism is over what domain this identification is made, or on what basis.

Varieties of behaviourism

Methodological behaviourism is the doctrine that was most prevalent in empirical psychology. It is the idea that for the purposes of doing scientific psychology, one ought to study only behaviours or behavioural dispositions, rather than attempting to study internal states or via phenomenological introspection. Thus one studies colour blindness, not by asking subjects to introspect about their colour experience, but rather by testing the behaviours which revealed capacities to discriminate colour. This view quite likely transformed psychology for the better in the first half of the twentieth century, but also arguably outlived its usefulness as better methods of studying internal states led to cognitivism as a methodological practice. In any case, what is distinctive about the methodological version of behaviourism is that it is silent on whether there are mental states or properties other than those identified for scientific purposes. The doctrine had enormous impact on research practices in psychology, but less impact in the philosophy of psychology.

Eliminative behaviourism is the doctrine that there are no mental states. Mental language should be retained, however, because it does not refer to nonexistent mental states, but instead refers to behaviours or tendencies to behave. The difference between this view and revisionary behaviourism is more verbal than real. On both ways of describing behaviourism it is agreed that (a) mental states are not inner, *categorical* states of persons; and (b) what makes psychological claims true are subjects' behavioural dispositions. They disagree about whether some analysis in terms of behaviours and behavioural dispositions does justice to the preexisting psychological concepts.

Revisionary behaviourism is a name that might be used for another doctrine that is often mistaken for methodological behaviourism. The revisionary behaviourist accepts that there can be no successful analysis of mental states as behaviours, given the meanings of existing language, but rather advocates terminological and conceptual reform so as to henceforth use mental language to refer only to behaviours or behavioural dispositions. Perhaps the revisionary behaviourist advocates this because she would be attracted to *eliminativism* were the language to be unreformed. A revisionary behaviourist might often be a methodological behaviourist who thinks that in reality there is nothing of interest about the mind other than what she is studying qua behaviourist, and so we would all be best to use the operationalizations of scientific psychology in every day life. Perhaps Skinner (1974) and Watson (1925) are the paradigms of this view. It too has had little influence in the philosophy of psychology, and this article will concentrate on the third variety of behaviourism, *analytical behaviourism*, according to which it is a matter of philosophical analysis that mental states are behaviours or dispositions to behave. Many of the arguments for and against analytical behaviourism, however, apply equally to these two other varieties.

The appeal of analytical behaviourism

According to analytical behaviourism, careful analysis of mental language reveals that mental state terms must refer to behaviours or behavioural dispositions. Although their views were in many ways different Ryle (1949), Hempel (1949) and Wittgenstein (1953) and perhaps Quine (1960) were very influential in making analytical behaviourism a widespread view.

The initial appeal of behaviourism depends on what appear to be conceptual connexions between claims about psychological states and behaviours. Suppose John claims that he wants to marry Mary. He says it is what he all things considered wants, and he has no special phobias or disabilities. Mary is more than willing, the budget is flush with money, time is on their hands, the relatives of all parties want the union to go ahead, and both John and Mary enjoy pleasing their relatives. Yet somehow John never does marry Mary. It seems that he can't really want to marry her. He was lying, or misunderstood his own desires. And this discovery seems to be based on a kind of conceptual truth: if there is an action that you all things considered desire to perform, and there is no impediment to performing it and no competing desire, then you do perform it. The tension is even more obvious in the case of intention. Someone who says "I intend to eat ice cream, but I won't" seems to be saying something absurd (unless this is because they expect to be prevented from carrying out their intention). Perception is in the same boat: the connexion between poor vision and poor capacities to perform behavioural discriminations is not accidental.

The person who desires to eat ice cream will, or course, only succeed in exhibiting behaviours that would be rational attempts to eat ice cream if their beliefs are true. Thus the would be ice cream eater who believes that ice cream is available only at Gelato Massi in their local area is likely to exhibit the behaviour of heading in the direction of that shop, regardless of the truth of their belief. This is an example of a principle of *belief-desire psychology*: the idea that it is a conceptual truth that people will behave in ways that will satisfy their desires if their beliefs are true. This principle seems to tell us that it is an essential feature of mental states that they must be displayed in behaviour. Someone in pain tries to relieve the pain, intelligent people perform certain tasks better than others, those who desire food greatly eat lots of it. A good chess player is likely to beat a bad chess player on average. These are not mere empirical generalizations, the thought goes, rather they reveal essential features of psychological states. Someone who does not grasp these claims doesn't understand the concepts of the relevant psychological states.

The most straightforward way to explain how this is a conceptual truth, is to claim that the concept of a certain mental state just is the concept of a certain kind of behaviour or behavioural disposition. Thus just as it is no empirical discovery that fragile things often break if dropped – that fragility just is the disposition to break if dropped is an analytical truth – it is equally no empirical discovery that those that desire ice cream eat it when it is available. It too will be an analytical truth, which is why this kind of behaviourism is known as analytical behaviourism.

The point can be made in terms of a supervenience claim. If the examples we have discussed generalize, then difference in psychological state implies difference in behavioural disposition. But then *sameness* in behavioural dispositions implies sameness in psychological state. This of course is equivalent to saying that mental states supervene on behavioural dispositions. If the supervenience claim is right, then what makes psychological claims about an agent true is the behavioural dispositions. This alone is a kind of behaviourism, and it seems to have been obtained only from conceptual resources – so it is analytical behaviourism.

Behaviourism and positivism

Another source of behaviourism lies in verificationism and other positivist doctrines. The positivists of the early twentieth century were notoriously hostile to unobservable entities in science. That alone made them loath to quantify over internal states that could not (at that time) be directly observed. This distaste certainly may have influenced the identification of mental states with the observable behaviours that might otherwise have been thought to be mere evidence for mental states. But more than that, their views about meaning led them to behaviourism. The logical positivists were concerned that there were large chunks of discourse that was neither true nor false, because they were meaningless. Much of nineteenth-century philosophy was thought to literally mean nothing. But this required a criterion of meaningfulness. When faced with sentences like "the apple weighs 100 g" and "being is present for itself" they wanted a way to mark them out as either meaningful or not. One intuition, shared in part by the current author, is that it has something to do with the thought that one has a direct or indirect grasp of what you would have to find out to tell if either of them is true. Taking direct grasp very literally, you might think that what you needed to know is what observation would confirm each claim. It's easy to list observations that confirm the first claim. It's very unclear what observations would confirm the second. If for a sentence to have a meaning to a language user is for the user to know what observations would confirm it, the first sentence in meaningful and the second (plausibly) not.

So far we have a criterion of meaningfulness. We can go further and ask what the meanings of sentences are. If grasping the observational conditions that would confirm a sentence is what it takes to grasp its meaning, then it would be very neat to claim that its meaning just is the states that we would observe and which would confirm it – the sentence's verification conditions. What are the observations that confirm mental state sentences? Well, at least in the early twentieth century these observations were observations of behaviour. Telepathy does not work, and PET scans had not been invented (though no doubt hard line behaviourists would have doubted their relevance). So if the meaning of mental state talk is the states that we would observe to verify it, what does "Jane desires gelato" mean? It means "Jane walks to the gelato shop, pays her money, and eats it," etc. If that's what "Jane desires gelato" means, then what is this desire for gelato? It is the very behaviours or dispositions that give the sentence its meaning.

Behaviourism and physicalism

It was surely part of the appeal of behaviourism that it is consistent with physicalism. If behaviours and tendencies to behave just are complicated physical states, then mental states are physical states. But it should be noted that while behaviourism is compatible with physicalism, it does not entail it. Thus behaviourists could be physicalists, but need not be *a priori* physicalists – it all comes down to whether the behaviours and dispositions to behave were physical states. This has the advantage that a behaviourist could say what the psychological states are in worlds that contain non-physical ghosts, or ectoplasmic minds or any other beings of the sort we might imagine. Just so long as the non-physical beings exhibited behaviour of the right sort, they count as having mental states.

Problems for behaviourism

Failure of supervenience

One of the earliest lines of objection to behaviourism was that not all mental states do show up in behaviour. Perhaps the most well-known version of this objection is Putnam (1963). It is certainly possible to imagine someone who greatly values keeping their beliefs and desires unknown. Putnam's example is of a society in which everyone is suffused by pain but never exhibits its behaviour. Thus they have mental features – the pain – but there is no behavioural correlate. What this line of objection illustrates is that a crude behaviourism that concentrates on individual mental states and actual behaviours is not even going to get off the ground. In fact such an example simply shows that the strongest desire (the desire to be stoical in this case) is the one that is manifested in behaviour. But then of course we need behavioural criteria for the existence of desires that are trumped by stronger ones. This is where behavioural dispositions are essential. The actual behaviour may be one that exhibits no pain behaviour, but the behaviourist will insist that there are nonetheless behavioural dispositions that make true the claims about the agent's pain. The agent will be disposed to pain behaviour if they were to lose their desire to be stoical, for example. It might be hard to see why this objection seemed to have so much force, but the explanation is simple: counterfactual conditionals have only fairly recently (perhaps since Lewis) been rehabilitated as acceptable parts of austere philosophy.

Failure of analysis

The reply to the failure of supervenience objection, however, leads us straight to a stronger one. Behaviourism simply failed in its analytical task – the promised analyses were never delivered, even for a single mental state. The mature version of behaviourism that can cope with the failure-of-supervenience objection holds that psychological claims can be analysed in terms of behavioural dispositions. The obvious models are the ones that concerned the positivists: things like solubility and fragility. To be soluble in water is to have the dispositions to dissolve in water (in a range of temperatures and pressures). To be fragile is to be disposed to break if dropped (in a range of gravitational fields, from a certain height and so on).

We do seem to have acceptable though rough analyses of these properties, though even in these cases the qualifications in brackets need to be spelt out in rather more detail. In the case of psychological claims, though, the brackets do all of the work. Consider the case of the desire for ice cream we mentioned earlier. What behaviour is it identical with? That depends entirely on the other desires and beliefs of the agent. If the agent desires to be thin more than he desires ice cream, it may lead to ice-cream-avoiding behaviour (thinking that temptation must be avoided at all costs). If the agent desires other things that require his money more than ice cream, there may be no discernible behaviour. It also depends crucially on beliefs. If the agent believes ice cream can be found only in Florence, she may take a flight to Italy. If the agent believes ice cream is contaminated locally, she may either travel far or else exhibit no ice-cream-related behaviour, or perhaps she will start to lobby for clean ice-cream standards. Thus the behavioural dispositions involved are immensely complicated and exhibit a wide range of behaviours (I leave it as an exercise for the reader to see how all possible behaviours can be made to be the appropriate ones for the desire for ice cream when suitably combined with other beliefs and desires). Crucially, they need to mention the complete belief and desire state of the agent. So to spell out the analysis we would need to list each possible belief-desire profile, and for each one add the behaviour appropriate if we add the desire for ice cream. This is of course an impossible task.

Causal impotence

A powerful objection to all forms of behaviourism with the possible exception of eliminative behaviourism is that it denies that mental states actually cause behaviour.

If there is one intuition that seems to be central to taking psychology seriously, it's that desires cause behaviours. Our desire for ice cream causes our bodies to move towards it in certain conditions. Our pains cause us to flinch. To deny all of that is to eliminate psychology – which is why perhaps eliminative behaviourism could live with this consequence.

Truisms of this kind abound. My scratching is caused by my itch; Mary's cleverness causes her to be good at Philosophy exams. My belief that it never rains in Sydney is what causes me to never carry an umbrella, and thus get soaked from time to time.

But the behaviourist must deny all of this. For according to her, my itch is my scratching; Mary's cleverness is the fact that she is good at exams (inter alia); and my belief that it never rains in Sydney is my umbrella carrying behaviour. Nothing causes itself, so these psychological states do not cause behaviour.

The retreat to dispositions doesn't help either. My disposition to scratch is simply the fact that I do scratch from time to time. So that can hardly be the cause of the scratching. My disposition to not carry umbrellas unless it is actually pouring is not what causes me to go out unprotected into a gloomy day: it is simply the fact that that's what I tend to do. It is important not to confuse the disposition to behave in a certain way, with the categorical state inside an agent that is responsible for the disposition. The disposition to break if dropped is just the fact that something will break if dropped – the categorical state in the glass is the structural state responsible for the disposition obtaining, and will vary from one fragile thing to the other. Behaviourists who retreated to dispositions never intended to retreat to categorical states. To do so would be to give up on behaviourism and identify psychological states with internal states of the very kind that they wanted to avoid.

Conceptual connexions and causal connexions

At this point the reader may be wondering how behaviourists talked themselves into denying something so central as the idea that psychological states cause behaviour. In fact there was what seemed like a very plausible argument – and seeing how this argument can be defeated helps explain the connexion between behaviourism and contemporary views in the philosophy of psychology that have a behaviourist element without actually being behaviourism.

One way of putting the idea was that, as we have seen, it may seem as though there is a conceptual connexion between psychological states and behaviours. But the causes of behaviour, whatever they are, are surely physical states of a certain kind. But there is no *conceptual* connexion between these physical states and behaviour. The connexion is, at best, a nomological one, and at worst contingent in every way. Thus, by Leibniz law, psychological states cannot be mental states.

A way of trying to make clear what this argument was supposed to be is to see it as drawing our attention to an apparently inconsistent triad of independently very plausible principles.

1 Causal connections are essentially contingent.
2 Psychological states cause behaviour.
3 There is a conceptual connection between being in a psychological state and behaviour.

Each of these is plausible enough. Causal connexions are surely contingent. That a certain match lit the fire is a contingent fact; it may not have. Had things been different it may not even have had the capacity to do so, despite being intrinsically exactly the same. The best case that can be made for necessity is that if all of the physical facts within the light cone are kept the same, then the match might have to cause the fire: though even that might be wrong given indeterminacy. But even if it is right it gives only a kind of nomological necessity in extreme circumstances – it gives neither logical necessity, nor conceptual connexion.

That mental states cause behaviour is certainly independently very plausible. They seem to precede behaviour in many cases, and it is certainly embedded in folk psychology that what brings about the movements of others is underlying psychological states.

And the final claim is one that there is little need to labour further, since it formed the background to the earlier discussion of what makes behaviourism plausible. Suffice to say that you simply wouldn't understand psychological concepts unless you knew some of their connexions to behaviour, and this is perhaps enough to make the claim of conceptual connexion plausible.

Suppose then that all these are true. There is then a problem. If psychological states cause behaviour, then the connexion between psychological states and behaviour is essentially contingent. This then seems to be incompatible with (3), since there cannot it seems be a conceptual connexion between things whose connexions are entirely contingent.

It should be easy to see now how if any two of these are true, it might seem plausible that the third must be false. So the behaviourist has the option of denying any one of these. It would seem very unpromising for a school of thought which takes empirical science seriously to deny (1) – that would be to reduce causation to logic, which would make science, at least ideally, an *a priori* discipline. Denying (3) would be to deny the very principles that seemed to give us a grip on the meaning of psychological terms. So in the absence of better alternatives, it's easy to see how you might be driven to deny that psychological states cause behaviour – or at least not flinch too much when it is pointed out that your position entails it.

Showing the triad to be consistent

In fact, however, the triad is consistent. We can see that something is wrong with the argument by considering a substitution instance of the underlying schema.

1 Causal connections are essentially contingent.
2 Poisons cause death.

3 There is a conceptual connection between ingesting a poison and dying.

Clearly, at least sometimes, poisons cause death. And (1) is just the same obvious principle that is given in the previous version of the argument. And in this case the conceptual connexion is even more obvious. It really is part of the meaning of 'poison' that it is connected to death or milder harm. Indeed the formal definition of 'poison' usually involves a substance's LD_{50}: i.e. the dose that will kill 50 percent of a population that is administered it.

So all three seem unassailable, yet the very same argument applies.

But the way out in this case is fairly clear. The conceptual connexion in this case is between being a poison and being a *cause* of death; not directly between poison and dying. The LD_{50} definition says that a certain dose has to actually kill – i.e. be a cause of death – 50 percent of the sample.

So (2) and (3) are preserved. Does this mean that we have to deny (1)? No; because it is entirely contingent that a certain substance is a poison. Suppose arsenic in a certain dose will kill 50 percent of a sample size of rats. This is no necessary truth. Rats might evolve immunity; there might be a substance that becomes ubiquitous in the environment that confers immunity. There are certainly possible states of affairs in which arsenic kills nothing. But of course these are possible states of affairs in which arsenic is not a poison. The conceptual connexion tells you that arsenic must kill to be a poison, but not that it must kill. It's only contingently a poison – there are circumstances in which the very same substance is not a poison.

The very same move can be applied to psychology – indeed this is what Armstrong's (1968) causal theory of the mind does. We can accept that there is a conceptual connexion between psychology and behaviour, but that the connexion is between psychology and the *causing* behaviour. Indeed this would explain not only the strength of our intuition that there is a conceptual connexion between psychological concepts and behaviour, but also our firm conviction that psychological states cause behaviour. After all, until recently no one ever demonstrated the existence of internal states that cause complex behaviours, so the strong conviction evidenced even then that psychological states do cause behaviour suggests that these states were always (at least in part) theoretical posits whose role was to causally explain behaviour.

This would then give us an account of psychological states in which it is a conceptual truth that psychological states cause behaviour. But by analogy with the poison case above, this means that the physical states that cause behaviour must only contingently be psychological. This is because if they cause behaviour they do so contingently, in which case there is a possible circumstance in which they do not cause behaviour. But in that circumstance, the very same state does not count as psychological. This is an outcome that many are happy to live with. It just shows that psychology is a relatively relational matter. One brain state may get to be a psychological state because of its connexions to the rest of the system. Isolate it in a test tube, and you may have in some sense the same state, but not the same psychological state.

The influence of behaviourism on contemporary philosophy of psychology

Perhaps the greatest influence that behaviourism has had on philosophy of psychology is that it is in a sense the progenitor of analytical functionalism. When you change the conceptual connexion to one between psychology and the causes of behaviour, and thus define psychological states in terms of their causal roles, what you have is analytical functionalism (Lewis 1966; Armstrong 1968; Braddon-Mitchell and Jackson 2007). Such a view still exhibits its behaviourist inheritance. Indeed some of the classic arguments against functionalism (Block 1981) were promulgated originally as arguments for psychologism as against behaviourism. It is striking that arguments against behaviourism find as their contemporary target analytical functionalism – this is because of their shared view that there are conceptual connexions between behaviour and psychology. These conceptual connexions have been the target of much fairly contemporary debate, such as in Galen Strawson's (1994) attack. Finally the line between behaviourism and varieties of contemporary eliminativism (Stich 1983; Churchland 1989) might seem to be blurred, inasmuch as some terms for behavioural patterns must survive the elimination, but of course these views emphasize the importance of internal causal processes in an un-behaviouristic way, while denying they are sufficiently isomorphic to our psychological concepts to be their referents. Contemporary instrumentalism/pattern realism, such as we find in (Dennett 1991), comes much closer to analytical behaviourism. Hempel would certainly have accepted that there were real patterns in behaviour. So this final distinction may in the end come down to mere terminological differences.

References

Armstrong, David (1968) *A Materialist Theory of the Mind*, London: Routledge & Kegan Paul.

Block, N. (1981) "Psychologism and Behaviorism," *Philosophical Review* 90: 5–43.

Braddon-Mitchell, D., and Jackson, F. (2007) *The Philosophy of Mind and Cognition*, Oxford, UK; Cambridge, MA: Blackwell.

Churchland, P. M. (1989) *The Neurocomputational Perspective*, Cambridge, MA: MIT Press.

Dennett, D. (1991) "True Believers," in D. Rosenthal (ed.), *The Nature of Mind*, Oxford: Oxford University Press, pp. 339–53.

Hempel, C. G. (1949) "The Logical Analysis of Psychology," in H. Feigl and W. Sellars (eds), *Readings in Philosophical Analysis*, New York: Appleton-Century-Crofts.

Lewis, D. K. (1966) "An Argument for the Identity Theory," *Journal of Philosophy* 63, no. 1: 17–25.

Putnam, H. (1963) "Brains and Behavior," *Mind, Language and Reality: Philosophical Papers*, vol. 2, Cambridge: Cambridge University Press.

Quine, W. V. (1960) *Word and Object*, Cambridge, MA: MIT Press.

Ryle, G. (1949) *The Concept of Mind*, London: Hutchinson.

Skinner, B. (1974) *About Behaviourism*, London: Jonathan Cape.

Stich, S. (1983) *From Folk Psychology to Cognitive Science*, Cambridge, MA: MIT Press.

Strawson, G. (1994) *Mental Reality*, New York: Oxford University Press.

Watson, J. (1925) *Behaviourism*, London: Kegan Paul.

Wittgenstein, L. (1953) *Philosophical Investigations*, Oxford: Basil Blackwell.

7
COGNITIVISM

Alan Garnham

Cognitivism is an approach to the mind and behaviour that, on the one hand, espouses an experimental, or more generally an empirical approach to understanding psychological functioning, and, on the other hand, claims that mental activity should be modelled as the processing of information using an internal symbol system, with discrete abstract symbols. Cognitivism, as a term, does not have the currency of, say, behaviourism or connectionism. However, as an approach to much of psychology, it is equally if not more important than those movements with more familiar names. The heyday of cognitivism was from the mid-1950s to the early 1980s. So, when I was a student (of psychology in the United Kingdom) in the 1970s it seemed that almost all of psychology, except perhaps psychophysics, was cognitive psychology. And anything that wasn't, wasn't worth talking about. Cognition is the act of acquiring knowledge, and requires such ancillary skills as perception, language use, memory, thinking and reasoning, hence its ubiquity. Even the other two faculties of the human mind with which cognition is traditionally contrasted, conation and affection, cannot be easily separated from cognition. Both can have cognitive components, and both can impinge on the acquisition of knowledge. The cognitive approach was supposed to apply to these aspects of behaviour as well. By the 1970s the cognitive revolution of the 1950s had borne fruit. Behaviourism had been routed, and even theories of learning, the former bastion of radical behaviourism, were becoming cognitive (though there had been cognitively oriented theories in other branches of behaviourism – the concept of a cognitive map originated with Tolman in the 1930s). Developmental psychology was seen as being primarily about cognitive development, perhaps not surprisingly given the legacy of Piaget. Even social psychologists were turning to issues in what they called social cognition.

I was only partly aware that I was steeped in an Anglo-Saxon tradition, according to which behaviourism had swept aside introspective approaches that led to irreconcilably different conclusions in the 1910s. It had then dominated North American psychology, in particular, up to the 1950s, when it adopted what was in some ways its most radical form, under the influence of B. F. Skinner. Skinner's refusal to model internal processes was characterised by cognitivists as intellectually bankrupt, and Chomsky was widely regarded as having shown Skinner's approach to be incapable of providing a satisfactory account of how people acquire and use language, an ability central to cognition. Karl Lashley's analysis of structure in what he called the serial order of behaviour also suggested that the associationist principles underlying behaviourism were not sufficient to explain action, language and other aspects of human activity.

Cognitivism as a major force in psychology has its roots in a computational (information processing) metaphor for the mental processes and behaviour of people and other animals. So, just as there had been an interest in, broadly speaking, computational metaphors before the twentieth century, there had been approaches to mind and behaviour that might be classed as cognitive (e.g., in the work of Leibniz, Pascal, and Babbage). However, with the advent of computers and other systems for the transmission of information, and the concomitant interest in related mathematical analyses, such as information theory and the (abstract) theory of computation, the metaphor finally took hold. These analyses showed that it was possible, pace Skinner, to describe in detail what happened inside a device that transformed inputs into outputs.

Psychological background

Psychology emerged as an independent discipline in the newly independent (or at least semi-independent) departments of German Universities in the second half of the nineteenth century. The founding of Wilhelm Wundt's laboratory in Leipzig in the 1870s is traditionally seen as the beginning of psychology as an independent empirical discipline, though William James began working in Harvard at about the same time. Both Wundt and James might be classified as cognitive psychologists. James claimed to have founded the first laboratory of experimental psychology in 1875, though he himself did not really engage in experimental work. Nevertheless, he developed a precursor of the modern modal model of memory, and one version of the James-Lange theory of emotion, which clearly has a cognitive component to it. Briefly, the theory claims that emotion arises from the mind's perception of the bodily changes that are part of the reaction to an emotion-arousing stimulus; not, as is usually assumed, that the emotional response to the stimulus produces the bodily changes.

Wundt saw psychology as having consciousness as its object and advocated a version of introspection as an experimental technique, though he also wished to relate inner experiences to physiological processes. Wundt's ideas were exported, by Edward Tichener and others, to the United States, where problems with the introspective method led to behaviourism, which, in its various forms, dominated much of experimental psychology into the 1950s. Many cognitivists identify behaviourism with its radical version, espoused by Skinner, because that was the dominant version of behaviourism at the time of the cognitive revolution. J. B. Watson, usually regarded as the founder of behaviourism, had rejected mental states as part of a scientific psychology. Skinner held a related view that such states could only be studied in experimental psychology in so far as they were treated as behaviour. It was Skinner's version of behaviourism, and in particular his treatment of language, that was rejected by Chomsky as part of the cognitive revolution.

For cognitivism, and probably more generally, a more important contribution of behaviourism was Edward C. Tolman's work on cognitive maps. Tolman showed that rats could learn mazes just by exploring them, and when there was no overt reinforcement for this exploratory behaviour. Within behaviourism this approach is often referred to as S-S (stimulus-stimulus) learning (as opposed to the S-R [stimulus-response] approach of Clark Hull and Skinner).

As already mentioned, another cognitive strand in pre-1950s psychology was Jean Piaget's work on cognitive development. Piaget was influenced by James Baldwin and by the European structuralist tradition (and ultimately by Kant). On Piaget's view, developing structures within the child's mind underpin cognitive development, and these structures represent in much the way that the mental structures of modern cognitive psychology do.

The cognitive revolution of the 1950s

Cognitive psychology, in its modern form, underpinned by cognitivism as an implicit and sometimes explicit philosophy, came into being in the 1950s. Its antecedents were many. As has already been indicated, many of those precedents come from within psychology itself. Despite the attempted redefinition by behaviourists, psychology has always had both behaviour and the mind as its objects of study. What was, perhaps, lacking in earlier approaches to the mental side of this equation (except, perhaps, Piaget's) was a set of systematic ideas about how to describe and explain the mind and its mental processes.

One of the most important underpinnings of the cognitive revolution was the emergence of new technologies in the mid-twentieth century and of the mathematics needed to analyse their operation. Some of these developments were hastened by demands placed on governments in the Second World War. Of these developments, the two most important were information theory and electronic digital computing. Crucial in both is the notion of information.

Information theory, as formalised by Claude Shannon in 1948, came to psychologists as a way of thinking about the transmission of information on a noisy channel, though Alan Turing had used some of its ideas in his World War II code breaking activities at Bletchley Park. Information theory had a specific impact on work on attention and vigilance, particularly in the work of Colin Cherry and Donald Broadbent. It was also used in the study of language processing, by George Miller among others. Information theory also strongly influenced Norbert Wiener's Cybernetics, a discipline that has had a somewhat peculiar relation with psychology, given their overlapping subject matters.

Particularly in the psychology of language, the specific impact of information theory was short-lived. George Miller quickly became acquainted with the linguistic work of Noam Chomsky, and went on to develop a psychology of language that was influenced by Chomsky's syntactic theory, and the notion of information in a broader sense. This broader sense was closely related to the notion of information processing, which developed in part out of work with digital computers. The notion that intelligent behaviour might be modelled in what we would now call computational terms was put forward in a general sense by the seventeenth-century French mathematician and philosopher Blaise Pascal, among others. Charles Babbage's Difference Engine of the 1820s and his later project for the Analytical Engine began to make these ideas more concrete, though realistic digital computation had to wait for electronic components to be developed in the twentieth century. Interestingly, the Analytic Engine was to be programmed by punch cards of the kind used to define patterns for jacquard weaving looms and also to program early electronic computers.

Relatively early in the history of electronic computers, surprisingly early given the limitations on those early machines, people began to think about programming them to perform tasks such as proving logic theorems, playing draughts (checkers) or chess, or solving puzzle book problems. Allen Newell, Herb Simon and J. C. Shaw invented a programming language (IPL – information-processing language) in which the information (or knowledge) needed to perform such tasks could be written in a way that was both (reasonably) accessible to people and specific enough to be interpreted as a precise instruction to a computer. Pieces of information could be linked to each other ("associated in memory") and changed during the course of processing. These so-called list-processing features of IPL were incorporated into its successor, LISP (for LISt Processing) invented by John McCarthy and for many years the most important programming language in artificial intelligence (AI).

McCarthy was instrumental (with Marvin Minksy, Nathaniel Rochester, and Claude Shannon) in organising an extended research conference on AI at Dartmouth College, New Hampshire, in the summer of 1956. The Dartmouth conference was attended both by people engaged in symbolic AI and by people interested in using computers to model the properties of nerve cells (the research programme that eventually led through perceptrons to connectionism). Marvin Minsky, who had done some of the earliest work on computer modelling of neural networks went on to champion symbolic AI (after demonstrating, with Seymour Papert, some important limitations on perceptrons). Not everyone at the Dartmouth Conference was convinced that this was the correct direction to take. Nevertheless, symbolic AI was, sometimes explicitly sometimes implicitly, a major formative influence on cognitivism.

Newell and Simon (with Shaw in their earlier work on the Logic Theory Machine, the Chess Player, and the General Problem Solver) and later Minsky and his colleagues at the Massachusetts Institute of Technology (whose AI laboratory was founded by Minsky and McCarthy) were the early champions of symbolic AI. Other influential work included Arthur Samuel's checker (draughts) player and Herbert Gerlernter's geometry theorem prover.

Two of the crucial aspects of these early AI programs were the explicit symbolic representations (and the manipulation of them) made possible by list processing languages such as IPL and LISP, and the purely functional perspective that was taken in this research (later underpinned by ideas from philosophers such as Putnam and Fodor). Symbolic AI (and early cognitivism more generally) recognised that intelligent (and even stupid!) human behaviour was mediated by the brain. However, programs such as the Logic Theory Machine were regarded as descriptions/explanations of cognitive processes at a level above that at which particular brain mechanisms could be identified. So, unlike in neural network modelling, no attempt was made to model specific brain processes. Solving logic problems, for example, was described at a functional level (a mapping from input to output) that could equally well be implemented on a digital computer or a human brain (with the same description/explanation applying despite the differences in hardware). This idea relates to David Marr's distinction between algorithmic and implementational levels of explanation, discussed below.

The heyday of the symbolic approach in AI was the 1960s and 1970s. The work that had the most impact on cognitive psychology came mainly from the AI lab at MIT. Much of it was summarised in Minsky's 1968 edited book *Semantic Information Processing*. Terry Winograd's program for understanding natural language (called SHRDLU), a later product of the same lab, was also hugely influential, despite Winograd's disagreements with Chomsky. SHRDLU interacted with a version of the MIT Blocksworld, analysed by some of the early AI vision programs, and encountered some of the same problems of generalisation from that limited domain. Winograd himself became disillusioned with symbolic AI research, and later played a(n indirect) role in the founding of Google. Other work included early attempts to study machine learning, though this area of research became more important within AI at a later date. Similarly early work on expert systems, such as MYCIN for the diagnosis and prescription of treatment for bacteriological infections and DENDRAL for the analysis of mass spectrograms of organic molecules, had its impact on investigations into expertise in cognitive psychology at a later date.

Linguistics

Another major influence on cognitivism was Chomskyan linguistics. Chomsky was a key anti-behaviourist for two main reasons. First, he set himself against the structuralism of mid-twentieth-century North American linguistics. Bloomfield, by the time he published *Language* in 1933, was behaviourist in orientation, having repudiated his earlier Wundtian leanings, which manifested themselves in his 1914 book *An Introduction to the Study of Language*. For Bloomfield, language was behaviour and mentalistic constructs were not needed in linguistic theory. Not surprisingly, given its relatively unsophisticated approach to language, Bloomfield was not directly influenced by behaviourist work in psychology. The second major anti-behaviourist element in Chomsky's work was his attack on B. F. Skinner's attempt to provide a (psychologically) behaviourist account of language, which he characterised as *Verbal Behavior*, in his 1957 book. Importantly, Chomsky argued that language (specifically grammar) could not be learned by the principles of Skinnerian learning theory, and that much of what we know about our languages must be innate. He further argued that the underlying principles of grammar are the same in all languages – the universal grammar that is innate and allows us to learn any human language.

Most of cognitive psychology and AI was not particularly concerned with learning. Functionalist analyses of adult behaviour did not address the question of where that behaviour came from. So issues about innateness were not central to cognitivism, though many psychologists paid lip service to Chomsky's claims, in the domain of language at least. More important was Chomsky's notion that grammar was generative. And although the notion of generation in generative grammar is an abstract one, an abstract mechanism for generating sentences readily suggests the form (or forms) that psychological mechanisms might take. Thus, Chomsky's approach to syntax, and particularly his early approach (in *Syntactic Structures*, and *Aspects of the Theory of Syntax*) led directly to ideas in both psychology and AI about how people or computers could generate and understand sentences.

Chomsky's anti-behaviourist approach and his collaboration with cognitive psychologists, in particular George Miller, led to a brief flirtation with the idea that genuinely psychological data (i.e. data generated by the methods of the discipline of psychology) might impact on linguistic theory. The flirtation was indeed brief, and Chomsky developed his distinction between competence and performance into a form in which his linguistic insights could be fully protected from the intrusion of psychological results. Nevertheless, Chomsky has always maintained that language is properly studied as a psychological (or biological) faculty of the mind. Interestingly, the anti-Chomskyan modern movement of cognitive linguistics shares with Chomsky the claim that language is cognitive together with a deep fear of incorporating genuinely psychological techniques into its investigations.

The relationship between grammatical descriptions and processing accounts was, even in the early days, somewhat complex in the Chomskyan framework. The importance of deep structure (particularly in the *Aspects of the Theory of Syntax* version of Chomsky's theory, in which deep structure determined all aspects of meaning) meant that a comprehension theory was inevitably forced to claim that deep structure had to be recovered from surface structure. This recovery process was initially characterised as an "undoing" of the transformations that (abstractly) generated the surface structure, and transformations acted on whole clauses. This led to George Miller's idea that the difficulty of comprehending a clause or sentence should be related to the number of transformations that had to be undone – an idea later dubbed the derivational theory of complexity. This theory was always problematic, not least because it finessed the question of how surface structure was computed. This question was put on the psycholinguistic map in John Kimball's seminal 1973 paper "Seven Principles of Surface Structure Parsing in Natural Language." The importance of surface structure parsing was reinforced in the late 1970s and early 1980s with a re-examination of Chomsky's arguments for transformations (which all turned out to be invalid, even if there were other valid arguments against a purely phrase structure analysis of natural languages). Many of the people who developed phrase structure grammars, such as Stuart Shieber and Aravind Joshi, were highly versed in computation algorithms for phrase structure parsing, such as the Cocke-Younger-Kasami algorithm (or a variant thereof) used for parsing many programming languages.

Phrase structure analyses also readily allied themselves, in conjunction with Emmon Bach's rule-to-rule hypothesis, to compositional semantics. Neither Bloomfield's nor Skinner's attempts to analyse semantics in a behaviourist framework had been successful. And Chomsky focused on syntax, using arguments for the autonomy of syntax (from semantics) to justify studying syntax in and for itself. However, Richard Montague, somewhat ironically from this perspective a Platonist by inclination, had shown how to develop a mechanistic but sophisticated formal semantics for a language (a bit) like English. His student, Hans Kamp extended this work, in his discourse representation theory, both by making it apply more directly to natural languages and by modelling in more detail the dependence of semantic interpretation in a natural language on the context of the particular discourse in which an utterance occurs. All this linguistic work gave strong hints about how cognitivist models of psychological processes might be constructed.

Psychology

As previously mentioned, information theory had a direct influence on work on attention and, for a short while, on language processing. The models of attention developed, initially, by Cherry and by Broadbent incorporated the notion of information channels and of limitations on what would now be called bandwidth. These models also incorporated the notion of stages of processing, thus postulating complex internal processes mediating between stimuli and the responses they evoked. Other psychological research influenced by ideas from the foundations of digital computing included signal detection theory, which was based on statistical decision theory. The development of signal detection theory was also influenced by attempts to analyse vigilance in human observers, which had been a crucial issue in radar operators in the Second World War.

The idea of limitations on the amount of information that could be processed was also emphasised in George Miller's work on short-term memory, with the idea that people could hold seven plus or minus two chunks of information in short-term memory – with the implication that chunking processes could influence the total amount of information stored. This work marked a transition in Miller's ideas from the use of information theoretic concepts (a narrow definition of information) to a broader notion of information processing, derived in part from an analysis of what digital computers, programmed in languages such as IPL or LISP, do. The twenty years or so following the publication of Miller's "magical number seven" paper marked the flowering of Cognitive Psychology in its strict cognitivist sense. Processes (such as sentence comprehension) and functions (such as memory) were divided and subdivided and represented in models containing interconnected sets of boxes representing subprocesses or subfunctions. Later, because of its limitations this approach was disparagingly referred to as "boxology". Miller's own work provided a conception of short-term memory as a subcomponent of memory in the so-called modal model of Atkinson and Shiffrin and Waugh and Norman, whose other components were sensory stores and long-term memory. Short-term memory was itself later subdivided in the working memory model of Baddeley and Hitch. Various divisions of long-term memory were also proposed. Furthermore, at least in the first instance, these divisions were made in purely functional terms, with no direct implications about which particular parts of the brain were involved. In 1960, with Eugene Galanter and Karl Pribram, Miller sketched a generalisation of the information processing approach to all aspects of psychology in the book *Plans and the Structure of Behaviour*.

Another major line of work within the cognitive tradition in psychology was on language processing. Again George Miller was a major player. As we have already seen, he was initially influenced by information theory, but later by Chomsky. And although Chomsky quickly rejected the idea that psychological results might inform linguistic theory, the broad philosophy underlying Chomsky's linguistics, including those aspects, such as nativism, that were peripheral to cognitivism more generally, continued to be broadly influential in psychological research.

Perhaps surprisingly, however, another important line of research – on word identification (both written and spoken) – was located much more within mainstream cognitive psychology than in psycholinguistics. John Morton's logogen model was a classic of box and arrow research, as were the dual route models of identifying written words, which derived at least in part from the logogen model. Later these models were both pitted against connectionist accounts and combined with them to form hybrid models. A great deal of work on visual cognition was also carried out in the same tradition.

Jerry Bruner's work on concepts and concept formation provided a second line of research in the broad area of thinking within the cognitive tradition – the first being Newell and Simon's work on problem solving, which went hand in hand with their computer modelling efforts. Bruner's work was also particularly influential on later symbolic AI work on the representation of concepts. Peter Wason's work on thinking and reasoning was a third strand of research in this general area. Wason's approach was strongly influenced by Karl Popper's falsificationist philosophy of science.

Dysfunction

Within the cognitivist tradition, both psychology and AI aimed primarily at modelling and explaining the behaviour of normal adults. There was some interest in developmental questions, though, for various reasons, and despite his clearly cognitive intentions, Piaget's work was viewed with some suspicion. In the later days of cognitivism, information-processing models of Piagetian tasks were proposed by researchers such as Siegler and Case, and contrasted with the original Piagetian accounts.

Partly because of the influence of notions derived from the consideration of complex machinery (e.g., digital computers and radios,) many cognitivists were, at least initially, reluctant to use data from dysfunctional adults (e.g., amnesics or aphasics) to inform their modelling activities. You can take one valve (or transistor) out of a radio, say, and completely impair its functioning. Trying to infer the function of that valve by observing the behaviour of the radio when it is removed is likely to be a fruitless activity. Similarly, trying to work out how a properly functioning radio works from the behaviour of a damaged radio is also near impossible.

Nevertheless, there is a certain fascination about the behaviour of brain damaged individuals, and some very striking patterns of behaviour that are at least potentially more informative than the whine (or failure to work at all) of a damaged radio. Particularly in the UK, in the work of Young and Ellis, and others, the cognitivist subdiscipline of cognitive neuropsychology was founded. In cognitive neuropsychology the focus was on individuals as individuals, since virtually every patient showed a different pattern of symptoms. And the behaviour of the individuals was typically interpreted in relation to functional (box and arrow) models, rather than to brain function. Of course it was recognised that, for example, damage to Broca's and Wernicke's areas is associated with particular language deficits. However, the correlations between lesion area and deficit were so coarse and variable as to be relatively uninformative. Cognitive neuropsychology studied deficits in functional terms.

More recently, brain imaging techniques, and in particular functional magnetic resonance imaging, have provided more detailed information about brain activity during the performance of cognitive tasks in normal people. This work, usually dubbed cognitive neuroscience, has produced a wealth of information about brain functioning. But a diehard cognitivist would argue that it does not necessarily advance our understanding of how complex functions are performed, and that this task can only be properly achieved by a (good old-fashioned) functionalist analysis.

The "decline" of cognitivism

The late 1960s and the 1970s were the heyday of cognitivism. The cognitive approach permeated most branches of psychology. And apart from a vague feeling that in practice, if not necessarily in principle, cognitivism tended to ignore individual differences, all seemed well. Indeed, the cognitive science movement of the 1970s, primed partly by money from the Alfred P. Sloan foundation in the United States, tried to make a more systematic connection between cognitive psychology, the key disciplines that had influenced its formation – AI and linguistics – and other cognate disciplines such as anthropology, education, neuroscience, and philosophy. It is not really clear that this movement forged relationships that did not already exist. However, one piece of work, on the edges of the cognitive science movement, signalled a new way of thinking about the relation between psychological, neurological and computational approaches to behaviour – David Marr's study of vision and particularly low-level vision.

Marr originally studied neurophysiology and neuroanatomy, and developed an important and still current theory of cerebellar functioning in the late 1960s. He became interested in AI and moved to the AI laboratory at the Massachusetts Institute of Technology in the early 1970s. However, he was critical of the semantic information processing/Blocksworld approach to computer vision that was current at MIT in the late 1960s and early 1970s. Apart from problems that he identified with the details of the analyses developed, Marr felt that, at least if it were to be regarded as providing a theory of human psychological function, AI research suffered from a confounding of science and engineering (the production of working computer programs). Marr proposed that psychological functioning should be analysed at three levels, which he called computational, algorithmic and implementational.

The computational level is somewhat misleadingly labelled. It refers to an abstract analysis of the task or tasks that a psychological system performs. This is the level of analysis that Marr found missing, or largely missing, in the standard AI approach to vision (and in much psychological work, too). The algorithmic level is, more or less, the standard abstract functional level of analysis of cognitivism, and the implementational level relates the algorithmic analysis to specific neuronal functioning. In much of Marr's work, the algorithmic analysis uses neural network type computations, similar to those found in connectionist models. Particularly at the lower levels of vision, this type of analysis is informed by what is known about the underlying neuronal architecture (for example in the retina).

Marr's approach to the relation between neuroanatomy and neurophysiology reflects standard thinking about, for example, the relation between sciences such as physics and chemistry. Chemical laws and principles are discovered and supported in their own terms (by chemists doing chemistry). But it is also necessary to show, at least in principle, how they relate to the more fundamental physical mechanisms and processes that underlie them.

In his study of higher level visual processes (object recognition) Marr's work became both more speculative and less tied to theories of implementation. In Marr's approach, identifying gross brain areas that support certain functions is relatively uninformative. Real understanding comes when a detailed algorithmic analysis can be related to the details of the underlying hardware. So although Marr is described (for example in his Wikipedia entry) as the founder of cognitive neuroscience, it is not clear that the lessons of his work have properly been absorbed in any of the core disciplines that his research relates to (psychology, neuroscience, and AI), nor that it fully informs current research in cognitive neuroscience.

The cognitive science movement failed to entrench cognitivism's position as the dominant movement in the study of psychological functioning. Indeed, cognitivism has suffered a number of setbacks since the early 1980s. The connectionist approach, which as has been mentioned was related to some of the algorithmic analyses developed by Marr, became influential following the publication in 1986 of McClelland and Rumelhart's two volume edited book on *Parallel Distributed Processing*. Connectionism gained some kudos from being the revival of an approach that had been (allegedly wrongly) rejected in the 1960s, particularly following Minsky and Papert's analysis of the failings of perceptrons. It formed the basis of some interesting psychological models, particularly in the field of word processing, and related methods of computation found widespread application in the real world. Connectionism is often seen as rejecting some of the fundamental tenets of cognitivism, such as discrete symbolic representations, and the need for structured relations (other than association) between them. Pure (functionalist) cognitivism is also sometimes seen as being undermined by the results of imaging techniques, which, it might be thought, make it foolish to propose theories of cognitive functioning that are completely abstracted from brain mechanisms.

Another line of work that is sometimes seems as antipathetic to cognitivism in its original form is that based on the related ideas of embodied cognition, situated cognition, and distributed cognition (including the use of external representations). Traditional AI and cognitive psychology focus on processes taking place in individual minds, which they characterise as the manipulation of symbols that are usually, at least implicitly, conceived of as abstract. Embodied cognition suggests that our concept of a chair, for example, is defined in part by the ways in which beings of a certain size and configuration (humans) interact with other objects (chairs) to perform such activities as working, eating, and resting. Brain imaging techniques confirm that some of the same brain areas are active when we talk or read about chairs as when we use them. Once stated, the basic facts of embodiment seem uncontroversial, and embodied cognition is best viewed as a development of cognitivism that calls on us to think carefully about the nature of our (internal) symbol systems and the mechanisms by which our symbols are grounded. Likewise with situated and distributed cognition, it is hard to deny that some of our cognitive activities involve other agents and external representations. We do not usually play chess on mental chessboards, for example, but on real ones. And those boards store some of the information that we use in playing games of chess.

There are hard problems in correctly explaining both the embodiment and the distribution of cognition. However, neither set of issues poses a general challenge to the basis tenets of cognitivism. More radical challenges to cognitivism come from anti-representationalists, including some dynamicists and connectionists, and anti-empiricists, such as phenomenologists. In addition, John Searle and some other philosophers argue that cognition is an essentially biological phenomenon, and that an abstract computational analysis is inevitably inadequate. Whether these challenges to cognitivism are decisive remains to be seen. Intellectual fashion aside, most, if not all, of the arguments for cognitivism remain valid.

Further reading

A detailed report of Bruner's work on concept formation is J. S. Bruner, J. J. Goodnow, and G. A. Austin, *A Study of Thinking* (New York: Wiley & Sons, 1956). N. Chomsky, *Syntactic Structures* (The Hague: Mouton, 1957) gives detailed exposition of an early version of Chomsky's syntactic theory. Chomsky's classic attack on the application of behaviourist ideas to language learning and language use his review of *Verbal Behavior*, by B. F. Skinner, *Language* 35 (1959): 26–58. Chomsky's *Aspects of the Theory of Syntax* (Cambridge, MA: MIT Press, 1965) describes what came to be referred to as the "standard theory" of syntactic structure within the Chomskyan framework. A. W. Ellis and A. W. Young, *Human Cognitive Neuropsychology* (Hove, UK: Psychology Press, 1988) is a textbook providing an overview of the cognitive neuropsychological approach. H. Kamp and U. Reyle, *From Discourse to Logic: Introduction to Model-Theoretic Semantics of Natural Language, Formal Logic and Discourse Representation Theory* (Dordrecht: Kluwer Academic, 1993) is the standard text on the discourse representation theory; and J. Kimball, "Seven Principles of Surface Structure Parsing in Natural Language," *Cognition* 2 (1973): 15–47, constitutes an early, highly influential paper on the issue of how surface structure is computed in language comprehension. G. A. Miller, "The Magical Number Seven, Plus or Minus Two: Some Limits on Our Capacity for Processing Information," *Psychological Review*, 63 (1956): 81–97, constitutes the classic paper applying information theoretic notions to analysing the capacity of short-term memory, and G. A. Miller, E. Galanter, and K. H. Pribram, *Plans and the Structure of Behavior* (New York: Holt, Rinehart & Winston, 1960) sketches a generalisation of the information-processing approach to all aspects of psychology. M. Minsky, ed., *Semantic Information Processing* (Cambridge, MA:

MIT Press, 1968) is a classic collection of papers on semantic information processing from the MIT AI Lab; A. Newell and H. Simon, *Human Problem Solving* (Englewood Cliffs, NJ: Prentice-Hall, 1972), an in-depth presentation of Newell and Simon's information-processing approach to human problem-solving; U. Neisser, *Cognitive Psychology* (New York: Appleton-Century-Crofts, 1967), the first important cognitive psychology textbook. C. E. Shannon, "A Mathematical Theory of Communication," *Bell System Technical Journal* 27 (1948): 379–423, 623–56, would have to be considered the classic presentation of information theory; and B. F. Skinner, *Verbal Behavior* (New York: Appleton-Century-Crofts, 1957), Skinner's attempt to apply behaviourist ideas to language learning and language use (as criticised by Chomsky). The original presentation of cybernetics is N. Wiener, *Cybernetics: On Control and Communication in the Animal and the Machine* (Cambridge, MA: MIT Press, 1948).

Part II

Psychological explanation

8
WHAT IS PSYCHOLOGICAL EXPLANATION?

William Bechtel and Cory D. Wright

What does psychological explanation refer to?

Frequently the expression *psychological explanation* is used as a catch-all term denoting any attempt to understand phenomena related to intelligent behavior. The philosophy of psychology would benefit from a more precise analytical conception of what constitutes explanation in psychology. The approach we take in this chapter focuses on what sort of explanatory practices are distinctive of experimental or scientific psychology. By noting three prototypical examples from diverse subfields of experimental psychology, we hope to provide a context for further analytical discussion. These examples point toward two very different models of explanation, which have also been discussed in the broader context of philosophy of science – namely, nomological explanation and mechanistic explanation. Two initial questions are therefore pertinent:

- To what extent are laws needed in explanations in psychology?
- What do psychologists have in mind when they appeal to mechanisms in explanation?

In some subfields of psychology, the mechanisms appealed to are characterized as *information-processing* mechanisms, which raises an additional question:

- Are information-processing mechanisms interestingly different from other mechanisms, and are there special challenges psychologists confront in advancing explanations in terms of information processing mechanisms?

To understand better what is involved in mechanistic explanation in psychology, we will specifically focus on how the decomposition and localization of psychological processes figure in psychological explanation. This will, in part, require us to examine the role that understanding the brain plays. We will then turn to a set of general questions about explanation that are answered differently in terms of nomological and mechanistic accounts:

- What are the tools employed in representing and reasoning about psychological phenomena?
- Can philosophy say anything constructive about the discovery and development of explanations?
- What sort of scope or generality applies to psychological explanation?

Lastly, we will consider the extent to which the framework of mechanistic explanation might actually provide a unifying perspective within which the role of laws can be accommodated, and whether there are forms of explanation in psychology that lie beyond the mechanistic perspective.

Three examples of explanation in psychology

A cursory look at the history of the discipline – particularly, in the nineteenth and twentieth centuries – reveals a rich collage of explanatory forms and strategies that have been invoked to render intelligible our mental lives and behavioral repertoires. We will begin by giving brief sketches of three in particular, drawn respectively from psychophysics, physiological psychology, and information-processing psychology.

Psychophysics

Some of the earliest roots of the experimental tradition in psychology are found in *psychophysics*, which is the subfield that attempts to identify the relation between physical features of sensory stimuli and the psychological experience of them. For example, Ernst Weber (1834) investigated the relationship between features such as the weight of an object and its perceived heaviness, and concluded that "we perceive not the difference between the things, but the ratio of this difference to the magnitude of the thing compared" (172). This conclusion was later expressed as *Weber's law*, ($\Delta I / I = k$), where I is the intensity of a stimulus; ΔI is the minimum increment over I that is detectable (i.e., *just noticeable difference*); and the value of k is constant (≈ 0.15 for loudness), except at extreme values for a given perceptual modality. Gustav Fechner (1860) extended Weber's research, adding an assumption of cumulativity so as to obtain a logarithmic function: $\Psi = c \log (I / I_0)$. On Fechner's account, the intensity of a sensation (Ψ) is proportional to the logarithm of the intensity of the stimulus (I), relative to threshold intensity (I_0). The accomplishments of Weber and Fechner were extremely important in demonstrating how to bring the same formal rigor achieved with purely physical phenomena to the domain of mental experience. They directly inspired the pioneering studies of memory by Hermann Ebbinghaus, who revealed mathematical relationships that characterize forgetting, and their efforts were perpetuated with the emergence of mathematical psychology in the 1960s.

In the mid-twentieth century, S. S. Stevens (1957) proposed a power function rather than a logarithmic function that made stronger – and occasionally more accurate – predictions than Fechner's law. Psychophysical laws such as Stevens are often viewed as providing explanations of individual percepts, insofar as they show that those percepts are instances of a more general regularity. Subsequently, the discovery of such laws has been viewed as an important theoretical contribution to psychology because they describe elegant and often amazingly simple and regular relations between physical and psychological phenomena. Unfortunately, the nomic regularities described by such laws are themselves left unexplained – e.g., while the relation described by Stevens' power law is regarded as ubiquitous, there have been no accounts of why it occurs.[1]

Information-processing psychology

Technological developments (e.g., telephone, computer) led theorists such as Claude Shannon and Warren Weaver to provide a mathematical characterization of information, and others such as Alan Turing and Emil Post to explore how it might be manipulated formally in mechanical systems. These and other developments (e.g., Chomsky's characterization of the requirements on any automaton that could process the syntax of a natural language) fostered psychologists' attempts to characterize mental activity as involving the processing of information (e.g., Miller 1956). In attempting to characterize information-processing operations, psychologists reintroduced a procedure that was initially developed by Frans Cornelis Donders (1868) for measuring the time required for particular mental activities. In Donder's use of the technique, a shock was applied to either a person's left or right foot, and the person had to respond expeditiously by pressing a telegraph key with the corresponding hand. He determined that when subjects were uninformed about which hand would be shocked, they required an additional 0.067 seconds to respond.

A particularly elegant use of reaction times to assess mental operations occurs in an early study in which Saul Sternberg investigated the retrieval of information from short-term memory (retention of information over a period of seconds to minutes during which there is no interruption). He required subjects to study a list of digits (e.g., 6, 9, 2, 4), and afterwards asked them to determine whether a particular digit (e.g., 5) was on the list, measuring the time it took them to respond. Sternberg evaluated three hypotheses: (a) subjects mentally examine all the items in memory simultaneously; (b) subjects examine them serially, stopping when they encounter the target item; and (c) subjects examine them serially, but complete the list regardless of whether they encounter the target. These hypotheses predicted different reaction times. If all items were examined simultaneously, the length of time required to answer should remain constant regardless of the length of the list. If subjects examined items serially and stopped when they reached the target, then the times should be longer for longer lists, but the times for positive responses should be shorter than for negative responses (as the target item would typically be encountered before the list was completed). Finally, if subjects examined items serially but completed the list before responding, then the reaction times should be the same for both positive and negative responses, and longer the longer the list. Sternberg discovered that it was the last prediction that was true, providing positive evidence for hypothesis (c). More specifically, it took subjects on average 392.7 + 37.9 *s* milliseconds to respond (where *s* was the number of items on the list to be remembered).

Physiological psychology

A third main type of psychological explanation involves characterizing the physiological processes governing psychological phenomena. There are many examples of physiologically based explanations, from the opponent-processing of visual input to the neural oscillatory patterns involved in sleep and wakefulness. One of the more intriguing is the electrophysiological explanation of pleasure and reward, which was inaugurated by James Olds and Peter Milner's (1954) serendipitous discovery that electrical stimulation of certain anatomical sites of rats' brains causes them to work extremely hard, suggesting they found the stimulation rewarding. Electrophysiological self-stimulation studies were immediately performed on a variety of animals, from snails to monkeys, and within 10 years it had become entirely clear just how rewarding the stimulation was: Olds (1955) found that rats would self-stimulate more than 50,000 times in a 26-hour period, and Valenstein and Beer (1964) reported that rats averaged 29.2 self-stimulating responses per minute for three weeks without respite. In human studies, subjects were found to self-stimulate various midbrain structures in 0.5-second trains up to 400 times per hour (Bishop et al. 1963; Heath 1963). Olds and Milner quickly discovered that self-stimulation behavior can be elicited from stimulation spanning the full length of the medial forebrain bundle (MFB), and so suggested that the activation patterns of this pathway directly mediate both the hedonic effects of, and complex behavioral responses to, all pleasures and rewarding stimuli. The MFB is a major neuronal band traversing the brain ventrally from the brainstem to numerous sets of limbic and cortical structures across the cerebrum – most notably, the ventral tegmental area (VTA), lateral hypothalamus, nucleus accumbens (NAc), and the frontal and prefrontal cortex (pFC) – and has also been proposed as a major structure in the final common pathway of reinforcement and approach behavior (Wise 1989: 410).

Eventually, Olds and Milner's initial explanation that reward is governed by the activity of this neuronal band did not do justice to the complexity found in this band, or to the mesocorticolimbic system more generally. Valenstein and Campbell (1966) showed that self-stimulation behavior was not disrupted even when virtually all of the MFB was ablated. So, although these fibers are clearly involved in producing self-stimulation behavior governing animals' experience of reward, the initial one-to-one identification of reward function with MFB activity was a vast oversimplification. This suggested the need for more complex localizations in contiguous neural systems and subsystems. For example, the initial localization to the MFB was made much more precise with the advent of dopamine-selective (DA) neurotoxins such as 6-hydroxy-dopamine HBr, which can be used to lesion particular MFB substructures and thus cause the animal to become oblivious to the hedonic valence of most rewards. Better explanations also require increasingly complex decompositions of a given mechanistic activity into component operations and suboperations, followed by an assessment of the extent of their interaction and integration. Complex localization usually evolves from a better understanding of the organization of those systems, taking into account the fact that mechanistic systems are not always serial, but employ nonlinear cycles, parallel processing, positive and negative feedback loops, etc. As a result of increasingly precise complex decompositions and localizations, explanations of reward have converged on several highly interconnected anatomical structures constituted, in part, by the long and fast myelinated DA axons projecting afferently from the VTA to the NAc.[2]

From laws to information-processing mechanisms

Traditionally, accounts of explanation in philosophy of science have given pride of place to laws and lawlike generalizations. On the deductive-nomological account of explanation, a given phenomenon is explained by showing that a statement of it can be derived from one or more laws and specification of initial conditions. For example, to explain the period (time required to complete a swing, e.g., from the far left back to the far left) of a given pendulum, a physicist would derive the value from the pendulum's length (l) and the law discovered by Galileo:

$$T = 2\pi\sqrt{\frac{l}{g}},$$

where g is gravitational force. There has been a great deal of philosophical discussion of just what is required of a law, what laws actually describe, and how they explain. Most accounts hold that a law is at least a universally qualified conditional statement which specifies what *must* happen when the initial conditions are satisfied. Psychophysics exemplifies this strategy by appealing to laws such as those advanced by Weber, Fechner, or Stevens to explain the percepts that people experience as a result of experiencing stimuli with specific features.

Beyond psychophysics, however, there are few subfields of psychology in which researchers have established relations between variables that are referred to as *laws*. Psychologists appeal to and discuss laws relatively infrequently. A recent bibliometric study of abstracts from the PsycLit database from 1900 to 1999 ($>$1.4 million) revealed an average of only 0.0022 citations for the term *law*; as Figure 8.1 shows, that number has continuously dwindled over the last few decades – down to 0.001 from 1990 to 1999 (Teigen 2002).

As Robert Cummins (2000) pointed out, such relations tend to be called *effects*, not *laws*. Indeed, there are numerous examples of such effects discussed throughout psychological literature. One well-known example is the Garcia effect, which is the tendency of animals to avoid foods eaten prior to experiencing nausea, even if the proximal cause of nausea was something other than the food. The difference between referring to *laws* and *effects* is not merely terminological. As Cummins argued – and

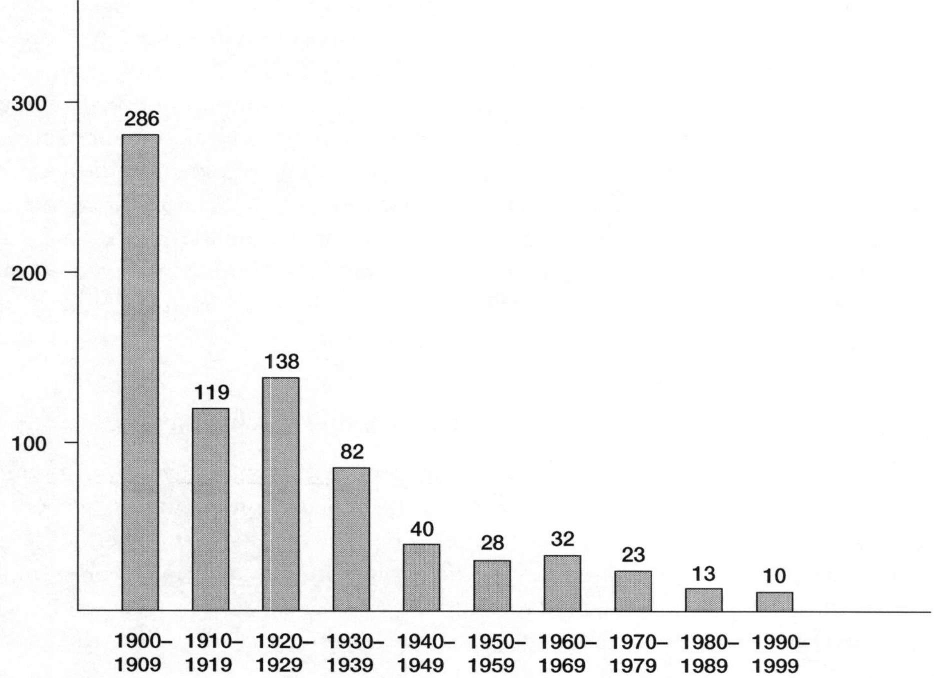

Figure 8.1 Occurrence of law in PsychLit abstracts per 10,000 entries (redrawn from Teigen 2002).

as we noted in the case of psychophysical laws – appeals to effects are typically not explanatory. Instead, they serve to describe phenomena that in turn require explanation and elucidation – i.e., the explanandum.

Within accounts of explanation, philosophers of science often distinguish between *empirical* (or *observational*) and *theoretical* laws. Since effects are descriptions of the relations between empirically measured variables, they do seem to correspond to empirical laws. How, then, can psychologists explain these empirical laws? The strategy described in many philosophical accounts is to explain empirical laws by deriving them from theoretical laws. In classical physics, for example, Newton's theoretical laws concerning forces can be invoked to explain the empirical law describing the pendulum stated above. The challenge in applying this strategy to psychology is that it is unclear what the theoretical laws are to which one might appeal in explanations. An alternative is to appeal to the laws of more basic sciences (e.g., neurophysiology). Unfortunately, this approach is likewise problematic, as there are even fewer examples of relations called *laws* in physiology or biology.

Marcel Weber (2005) has argued compellingly that the laws invoked in explaining physiological phenomena are drawn from physics and chemistry. The laws of physics and chemistry are certainly not irrelevant to psychological phenomena. Psychological phenomena are realized in brains comprised of neurons that generate action potentials, and the electrical currents that constitute the action potential are governed by principles such as Ohm's law. However, psychologists seldom allude or explicitly appeal to such basic physical laws in their explanations (for reasons addressed below). Rather, when psychologists (as well as physiologists and many other investigators in the life sciences) offer explanations that go beyond the empirical laws or effects they identify, they frequently suggest that such explanations model a *mechanism* – i.e., a composite system whose activity is responsible for the target phenomenon (Wright and Bechtel 2006; Bechtel 2007). Thus, in the example from physiological psychology, after Olds and Milner seemingly found a neural locus for reward, other investigators began to identify other components of the brain's reward system and develop accounts of their role in reward function. Information-processing psychology is also engaged in a quest to identify mechanisms, as in the example from Sternberg, although the mechanisms are of a special kind – namely, those that process information.

The appeal to mechanisms in explanation, despite being a staple of both biology and psychology, has received little attention in philosophy until the last two decades. Recently, a variety of philosophers turned their attention to the conceptual analysis of what is meant by *mechanism* and *mechanistic explanation*. A mechanism is simply a composite system organized in such a way that the coordinated operations of the component parts constitute the mechanistic activity identified with the explanandum. Hence, a central feature of mechanisms is that they are mereological: the mechanism as a whole is comprised of component parts, the orchestrated operation of which constitute its function(s). Not infrequently, the parts of a mechanism are themselves mechanisms consisting of component parts at lower levels, which implies that mechanisms are intrinsically hierarchical. We will return to this issue later.

The primary challenge confronting researchers advancing a mechanistic explanation is how to model the appropriate decomposition of that composite system into its component parts and their operations, and to determine how those parts and operations are organized. In giving a mechanistic explanation, investigators must represent the system (either in their heads or in terms of external symbols such as diagrams or physical models) and make inferences about how the parts' operations suffice to account for the mechanism's activity, and how that activity thereby is the phenomenon to be explained. Often these inferences result from simulating the mechanism (whether mentally, or by invoking computer programs or computer models, etc.).

We will return shortly to the strategies by which psychologists develop mechanistic explanations; in the meantime, note that the mechanisms appealed to by many psychologists are of a distinctive kind. Rather than serving to transform chemical substances as in basic physiology (e.g., the process of synthesizing proteins from free amino acids), many of the mechanisms appealed to in psychology are those that serve to regulate behavior or process information. Reward mechanisms, for example, figure in control systems responsible for the information relevant to approach and consummatory behavior. Other psychological mechanisms, especially in primates, are a stage removed from the actual regulation of behavior, and are instead involved in tasks like planning future behaviors or securing information about the world. The advent of digital computers provided a model for understanding how mechanisms process information. Some of the physical processes within the mechanism serve as representations for other entities and processes (i.e., they have as their content these other entities or processes) and the manner in which these states are operated on is appropriate to their content. Specifying how representations have content has been a major concern for philosophers of psychology (Dretske 1981; Millikan 1984); but, for the purposes of characterizing information-processing mechanisms, the key point is that those mechanisms use the representations to coordinate the organism's behavior with respect to or in light of the represented features of its environment.[3]

Decomposing the mind into operations and localizing them in the brain

The major tasks in developing mechanistic explanations in psychology are to identify the parts of a mechanism, determine their operations, discern their organization, and finally, represent how these things constitute the system's relationship to the target explanandum. There are many ways of decomposing a mechanism into parts; but the explanatorily interesting parts are those that figure in the operations – i.e., *operative parts*. These are the parts that either perform the operations or are operated on in an operation. Both identifying the parts and determining the operations involved in a mechanism can be challenging activities. Many ways of decomposing a mechanism into parts fail to identify operative ones. Neuroanatomists in the nineteenth century put considerable effort into identifying and naming the gyri of the cortex; but sulci and gyri turned out to be the indirect result of folding the sheet of cortex, and not to be operative parts. The areas identified via cytoarchitecture by Korbinian Brodmann and numerous other investigators at the beginning of the twentieth century more closely approximated functional areas, although they often turned out to contain distinct component parts within them.

If anything, identifying operations is even more difficult. Smoothly functioning mechanisms are organized such that the various operations engage each other in a coordinated manner. Behaviorists eschewed such projects, arguing that psychologists' attempts to identify operations inside the head would invariably invoke the same imprecise mentalistic vocabulary that was used to label the overall activity. Where behaviorists and others declined to tread, researchers in the newly emergent tradition of cognitive psychology in the mid-1950s pushed forward in the attempt to reverse engineer the mind. They approached their task by hypothesizing types of operations that transformed representations so as to produce the overall information-processing activity. As the example from Sternberg reveals, they often drew inspiration from the then-new field of computer engineering, and postulated activities of storing, retrieving, and operating on representations. (These operations in computers were in turn inspired by the activities of humans who were employed to compute functions and did so by repeatedly reading and writing symbols from a page, performing simple computational operations on these symbols, and then writing the results on the page. The representations appealed to by psychologists when they adapted this account to explain human activities were themselves hypothetical constructs postulated to account for the overall performance.)

From the 1950s until the 1990s, researchers in cognitive psychology had to pursue their efforts to identify mental operations with little guidance from neuroscience, primarily because there were few tools for characterizing brain regions that realize psychological phenomena. An oft-invoked resource was the analysis of patients with brain damage. From their deficits in overall performance, researchers advanced inferences as to what the damaged area contributed to normal function. For example, on the basis of deficits in articulate speech resulting from a damaged area in the left pFC, Paul Broca (1861) famously proposed that this area was responsible for articulate speech. Broca's studies, and most studies within the field known as *neuropsychology*, have relied on damage occurring either from accidents, tumors, or strokes, which typically do not respect the boundaries of operative parts in the brain. An influential case of a cognitive deficit in the early development of cognitive psychology involved William Scoville's removal of the hippocampus and surrounding areas of the medial temporal lobe in an epileptic patient H.M. (Scoville and Milner 1957). The surgery successful reduced H.M.'s seizures, but left him with severe amnesia for post-surgical events (anterograde amnesia) and – in a more graded fashion – for events in the years prior to surgery (graded retrograde amnesia). Although H.M. exhibited profound amnesia for events in his life and was unable to learn new facts, he could learn new skills (albeit not remembering, and therefore denying, that he had learned new skills). This case provided powerful support for a distinction between declarative or explicit memory and procedural or implicit memory, and also initiated a program of research directed at determining hippocampal contributions to the acquisition of new declarative memories. That H.M. retained memories from much earlier in his life indicated that the hippocampus was not the locus of long-term storage and the graded retrograde amnesia further indicated that the consolidation of long-term memories was protracted, lasting several years.

Broca's case and that of H.M. reflect attempts to relate operative parts in the brain to the operations they perform – what is often called *localization*. Naturally or even surgically induced lesions in humans typically do not involve a precisely delineated brain area, rendering localization claims difficult. When cognitive psychologists began advancing decompositions of mental function, neuroscientists working with other species (especially cats and monkeys) were developing more precise tools for localizing operations in the brain. In addition to increasingly precise surgically induced lesions, neuroscientists developed techniques either to record from or induce electrical activity into individual neurons. This strategy proved especially effective in the case of visual processing. By systematically varying visual stimuli so as to determine what features of a stimulus would generate action potentials in a given cell, investigators have identified brain regions in which cells seemingly process particular features of visual stimuli such as motion, shape, etc. It is possible, for example, to identify cells that respond to the perceived color or motion of the stimulus, not the wavelength or actual motion of the stimulus. Importantly, this research enabled researchers to determine both the brain regions and perceptual operations involved. Although many details remain to be resolved, this research has generated detailed models of the mechanisms involved in visual processing (van Essen and Gallant 1994).

Research on nonhuman animals, however, provided little insight into the mental activities of greatest interest to cognitive psychologists (e.g., reasoning, problem-solving, language processing, memory). Cognitive psychologists therefore had to proceed by first hypothesizing how a mechanism might perform the requisite activity, and then test the hypothesis with predictions using more indirect measures such as reaction times and errors made in normal performance. Although their explanatory aim was to identify the task-relevant mental operations, cognitive psychologists more often succeeded in establishing differences between psychological phenomena and showing that they rely on different mental operations without thereby specifying them. For example, in addition to the distinction between declarative and procedural memory, Endel Tulving (1983) advanced a distinction within declarative memory between memory for factual information, including facts about oneself (*semantic memory*) and memory that involves reliving episodes in one's own life (*episodic memory*). Tulving proposed that episodic and semantic memory (plus other types of memory) are due to separate memory systems (Schacter and Tulving 1994). Others psychologists (Roediger et al. 1999) have questioned whether some of the operations involved in performing different memory tasks are actually the same; unfortunately, little progress has been made in further articulating the nature of these operations.

In the 1990s, cognitive psychologists gained access to a new research technique that altered their potential to use information from the brain in understanding mental operations. Functional neuroimaging, either via positron emission tomography or functional magnetic resonance imaging, provided a means to identify the brain areas in which increased blood flow accompanied a particular psychological phenomenon. Although the actual relationship between neural processing and blood flow has not been established, increased blood flow is commonly assumed to indicate increased metabolism, which in turn indicates increased neural processing in the region.[4]

Neuroimaging has provided a means to localize component operations involved in performing cognitive tasks with brain regions in which they are performed, and so has elicited much interest (both popular and academic). However, it is important to consider exactly how neuroimaging figures in psychological explanation. It often seems that the goal of neuroimaging is simply to establish where in the brain cognitive activities are occurring; but this does little to advance the explanatory charge of psychology. It is useful to consider again what neuroscientists accomplished using single-cell recording in the case of visual processing. Their goal was not simply to determine what areas of the brain are involved in vision (though it is suggestive that over ⅓ of the primate brain is involved in visual processing); rather, the functional decomposition of the brain was advanced by determining what operations individual brain areas performed. Recent neuroimaging, for instance showing how the same brain areas are involved in both mnemonic and perceptual tasks, suggests that the areas are performing operations required for both, which directs inquiry to questions about what common operations may be involved in perceiving and remembering.

Consequently, learning the various areas involved in task performance plays a heuristic role in investigating the nature of the operations performed. The heuristic also works in the opposite direction: ideas about the operations to be performed can guide inquiry toward the brain areas that perform them. Moreover, the heuristic benefit is often achieved by playing the proposed decompositions into parts and operations off one another, providing grist for revising each account. Accordingly, Bechtel and McCauley (1999) characterize localization in terms of a *heuristic identity theory*. Whereas the classical identity theory in philosophy of mind treated the identification of a mental operation with a particular brain area as an end in itself, the heuristic identity theory treats the goal of identity claims instrumentally – i.e., as advancing the project of discovering mechanisms by helping to understand how component parts and operations are involved in psychological phenomena.

Producing and generalizing psychological explanations

The dominant account in twentieth-century epistemology represented knowledge linguaformally, with propositions reporting sensory experiences justifying, by their logical relations, those propositions that do not. A similar account was adopted in philosophy of science, whereby statements about events are derived from – and thus putatively explained by – knowledge of laws and initial conditions. Moreover, success in deriving not just what had happened but what would happen (*prediction*) was taken as providing evidence that one had fixed upon the correct laws. On this account, which was exemplified in explanations in psychophysics, understanding a scientific explanation required understanding the laws and reasoning appropriate to derive or subsume consequences. Hence, the challenge in discovery was to formulate laws, and this – many philosophers contended – was not a matter of logic and hence not something for which philosophy could provide an account. A few philosophers and artificial intelligence researchers dissented from this pessimistic assessment, and attempted to develop procedures for discovering laws (see, e.g., Holland et al. 1986; Langley et al. 1987; Thagard 1988).

Insofar as laws are taken to have the form of universal generalizations, this perspective offered a straightforward way of generalizing from one case to additional cases – i.e., additional cases were simply instances covered by the same generalization. As we noted, for nomological accounts of explanation, laws provide the basic explanatory resource; in turn, explaining a law then amounts to the ability to derive it from more fundamental laws. These more fundamental laws involved generalizations of greater scope, and hence the gradual process of axiomatizing theories so that specific laws were seen to be instances of more general and fundamental laws could be envisaged as leading to grand unification in science (Nagel 1961).

Mechanistic accounts of explanation provide a very different understanding of what producing and generalizing explanations involves. At the core of mechanistic accounts are models that represent the nature of the component parts and the operations they perform, plus how these are organized such that the phenomenon of interest can be understood as the overall mechanistic activity. Operative parts are spatially

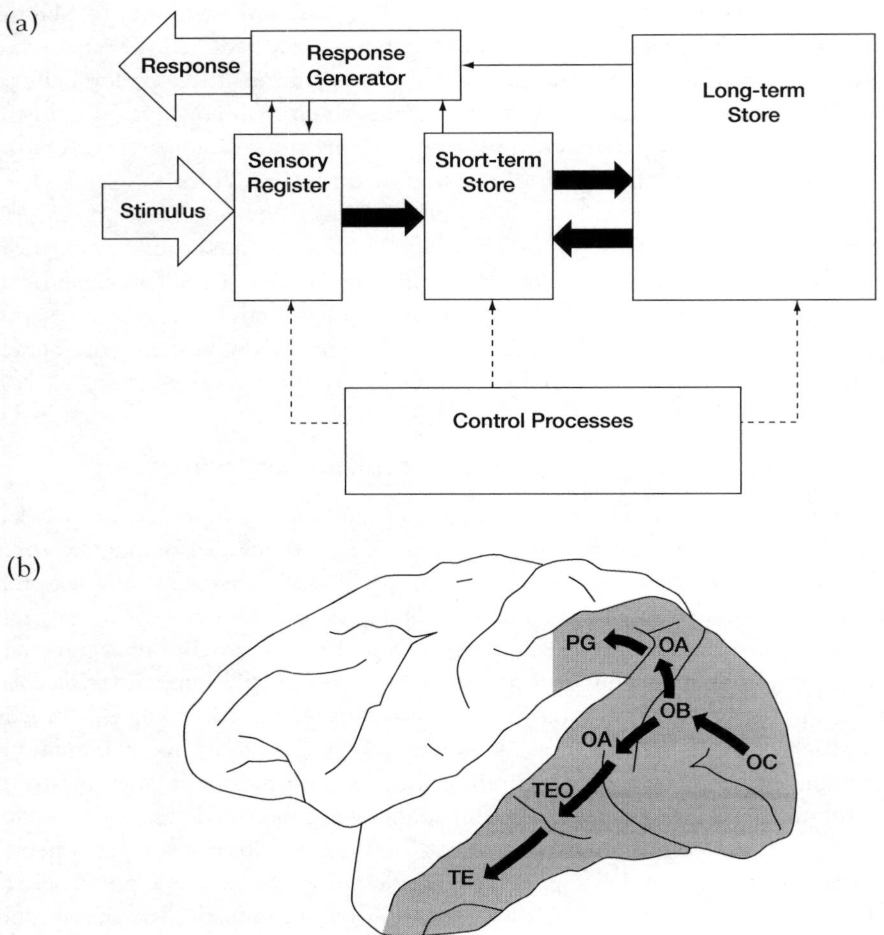

Figure 8.2 (a) Box and arrow diagram of the Atkinson and Shiffrin (1968) model of memory processes; and (b) arrows overlaid on brain areas in Mishkin et al.'s (1983) identification of two visual systems in primate brains.

situated, and their spatial relation to other operative parts often figures critically in how they behave. While it is possible to describe such spatial layouts propositionally, the use of diagrams, maps and other visual displays often facilitates problem-solving and is easier to process. Operations involve component parts interacting with other parts; and while these too can be described propositionally, it is often easier to portray the changes, e.g., with video. Even a static diagram that uses arrows to indicate what part is acting on another often provides superior understanding. Accordingly, early cognitive theories were often presented in box-and-arrow diagrams, with boxes representing mental operations; arrows designating operations were sometimes overlaid on pictures of the brain to indicate both the neural components and their operations (Figure 8.2).

While there is little direct evidence about what occurs inside people as they reason about mechanisms, it seems likely that they often create visual or tactile models of mechanisms, which they then transform to simulate the mechanism's activity (see Waskan 2006). By emphasizing the role of visual representation, we note that linguistic representations often function somewhat differently without thereby negating their contributions to explanation. Consider, e.g., figure captions in journal articles, which provide interpretations of aspects of the visual representation and help focus attention. Insofar as people understand how a mechanism works through simulation (whether mentally or orthographically), it is the ability to model mechanisms that provides the dynamics of understanding – not traditional logic.

Whereas philosophers focused on nomological explanation had little to say about the discovery of laws, there is much to say about the discovery of mechanisms. Insofar as decomposing mechanisms into operative parts and organization is crucial to eventually understanding them, one can examine the ways in which scientists generate such decompositions. Experimental techniques play a crucial role in decomposition, and various techniques both provide important types of information (but also are potentially misleading). Scientists also face challenges in developing appropriate concepts for operative parts, and here they often reason by analogy from a domain where decomposition has been successful to a novel domain.

In the nomological tradition, generalization was straightforward: the law generalized to all cases that satisfied its antecedent. Models of mechanisms, in contrast, are developed to account for specific cases chosen for study. In biology, researchers often employ model organisms or preparations, and work out detailed explanations of the mechanisms active in that organism or preparation. For example, the giant squid axon provided the basis for much of the research in electrophysiology that led to understanding the action potential of neurons. The giant squid axon was chosen not because it was typical, but because it was possible to conduct experiments on it given its size and the crudeness of the available electrodes. Other neurons will differ, and it is never clear in advance of conducting experiments on them how much the model of the mechanism will have to be revised to be applicable, much less whether a very different sort of account will be required. Cognitive psychologists, for the most part, limit their investigations to one species – namely, humans, and particularly college students – as their model system. They face questions about whether mechanistic models developed for this population will apply to others differing in age, education, cultural heritage, etc. So, generalization with mechanisms does not involve simply applying a law to other instances of the specified natural kind, but engaging in inquiry to determine what modifications are required to characterize the similar yet somewhat different mechanism active in another person or in different circumstances in the same person.

Mechanism as a unifying framework for understanding psychological explanation

There is perhaps no greater disciplinary crucible than psychology for working out the issues and problems of scientific explanation, if only because of the sheer range of explanatory practices and strategies that figure in research on psychological phenomena. We have indicated some examples of psychological explanation in which individual phenomena were putatively explained by showing them to be instances of general laws, as well as examples that involved representing target phenomena as mechanistic activities. In the previous section, we identified a number of contrasts between these two kinds of cases; in this final section, we conclude by showing that appeals to laws and appeals to mechanisms are quite compatible, and that the mechanistic framework allows for both. Consequently, it provides a unifying framework for answering the question, "What is psychological explanation?"

We have already alluded to one strategy for incorporating laws into the mechanistic framework; laws (*effects* in psychology) often provide precise descriptions of the phenomenon to be explained. A great deal of research goes into establishing psychological phenomena – e.g., identifying variables and specifying as precisely as possible (ideally, mathematically) the relations between these variables that characterize the phenomena. But description and explanation can certainly diverge. Explanation requires developing a model of the mechanism in terms of parts, operations, and organization. Stuart Glennan (1996) proposed a second role for laws in mechanistic explanations: mechanistic explanations both explain lawlike regularities and appeal to other lawlike regularities to characterize the operations (he speaks of *interactions*) constituting the mechanistic activity. It is occasionally possible to describe the operations in mathematical detail, but operations in psychological explanations are rarely characterized in terms of laws. Yet, appropriately modified, Glennan's proposal may be acceptable; after what may be several iterations of decomposing a mechanism's component parts and operations, investigators may reach processes that fall under the scope of physical or chemical laws (e.g., Ohm's law and the Nernst equations in the case of the action potential of neurons).

This iterative nature of decomposition and its role in the refinement of mechanistic models deserves further elucidation. The discovery of operative parts often inspires further investigation into how those operations are performed. This practice of taking mechanisms apart into their components, and, in turn, the components into their components, is clearly reductionistic; yet, reduction in the context of mechanism has a rather different flavor than philosophical accounts of reduction emphasizing derivation of laws from more fundamental laws. Eventually, such accounts envisage deriving all laws of the special sciences from fundamental laws of physics. Such derivations can only go through, though, with the specification of boundary conditions, whose source is seldom identified. Given that lawful regularities are often explained by models of mechanisms, we can see that descriptions of boundary conditions provide a specification of the components and organization of the mechanism. At best, lower level laws describe some operative parts – not their presence or configuration. Accordingly, lower level laws fall far short of providing all the information needed to derive the higher level regularities, which are better explained using mechanistic models. For example, the organization of components parts and operations, both spatially and temporally, are crucial to a mechanism's activities, and this is not provided simply by lower level laws or even knowledge of the component parts and operations themselves.

Additionally, a given mechanistic activity is always constrained by its environmental conditions. And because mechanisms are composite hierarchical systems with myriad mereological part-whole relations, their component parts operate at a lower level than – and are organized differently from – the level at which the mechanism as a whole produces the target phenomenon (e.g., as a final common pathway). Again, mechanisms are often themselves a component part in yet a higher level mechanism, and the regularities resulting from the organization and situatedness of that higher level mechanism constrain the activities of the initial component mechanism. Hence, the process of both decomposing *and* composing systemic structures and functions across various levels is a fundamental part of the mechanistic framework. Accordingly, while mechanistic explanations are in part reductionistic, they also accommodate the emergence of higher levels of organization and the need for autonomous inquiry into the regularities found amongst the denizens of these higher levels. So, as mechanists have consistently pointed out, the inherently reductionistic elements of mechanistic explanation need not threaten the explanatory autonomy of higher level psychological explanations – indeed, it depends on them to situate the mechanism in context (Wright and Bechtel 2006; Wright 2007).

By accommodating both a reductionist and an emergentist perspective, mechanistic explanation provides a unifying framework that integrates a variety of explanatory projects in psychology. Many psychological explanations focus on particular aspects of the behavior of whole agents. To explain these, psychologists try to identify the operations involved and increasingly localize these to brain regions where they are performed. In other subfields of psychology, e.g., social psychology, the focus is not just on the behavioral propensities of agents but also the social situations in which these are realized; and increasingly, investigators interested in cognitive capacities are also concerned with the embodied and situated context of the agent performing these activities. As noted, environmental contexts often figure centrally in determining the activities of mental mechanisms, and therefore have a nontrivial role in being represented in the explanans of a mechanistic explanation. Turning downwards, researchers are increasingly discovering the importance of the chemical milieu in the brain to aspects of behavior and mood. To understand how, e.g., the chemistry of an individual's brain affects the person's performance on memory and problem-solving tasks, researchers need to understand how the particular chemistry affects the component operations (or the components of the components) of the responsible mechanism. Besides neurochemistry, other subfields of neuroscience are increasing understanding of how component mechanisms operate in psychological agents. Findings in both neuroscience and the social sciences are highly pertinent to the development of psychological explanations. Nonetheless, for phenomena falling within the purview of psychology, the relevant mechanisms are those that scientific psychology investigates. Psychological explanation is integrated into the explanations offered in related sciences, but retains its own identity.

Having suggested how mechanistic accounts of explanation can incorporate the insights of their nomological counterparts, there remains the question of whether mechanistic explanation exhausts psychological explanation. Two endeavors in contemporary psychology suggest alternatives to mechanistic explanation or the need to expand the characterization of mechanistic explanation. The first involves the application of tools of dynamical systems theory to psychological phenomena (Thelen and Smith 1994; Kelso 1995; Port and van Gelder 1995). Much in the spirit of nomological explanation, advocates of dynamical models appeal to equations relating variables that characterize the behavior of mental systems, and – at times – seem to deny the utility or even possibility of decomposing systems into component parts, operations, and organization (van Gelder 1995; van Orden et al. 2001). Whether such explanations are a genuine alternative primarily turns on the nature of the variables in dynamical accounts. If these variables characterize operative parts, then dynamical models may be subsumed under mechanistic accounts of explanation, although they rightly refocus attention on the complex dynamics resulting from components that interact in complex ways over time. The second endeavor involves appeals to evolution – especially natural selection – to explain psychological phenomena. As with biological explanation, there appears to be a tension between providing mechanistic explanations of a current system (what Mayr termed *proximal explanation*) and an evolutionary explanation (*ultimate explanation*) (Mayr 1982). The very terms *proximal* and *ultimate* imply some prioritization, but many in evolutionary biology have come to recognize the critical constraints that understanding specific mechanisms, especially mechanisms of development, places on processes such as natural selection. Natural selection is often itself characterized as a mechanism of evolution, but there is currently active discussion as to whether explanation in terms of natural selection fits extant philosophical accounts of mechanisms (Skipper and Millstein 2005) or requires a different account of explanation altogether.

Notes

1. Interestingly, Weber himself, in applying the relation he discovered to line length, noted that it was inconsistent with a possible perceptual process in which the mind counts the nerve endings touched in the retina to assess length; but he offered no alternative procedure that would give rise to the relation he discovered.
2. Other catacholaminergic neurotransmitter systems were explored early on – particularly, norepinephrine (NE) fibers in substructures of the MFB (which is also a major point of convergence for NE systems). Yet, by showing that lesions to the dorsolateral noradrenergic bundle and other NE sites did not abolish self-stimulation behavior from the locus coeruleus, Clavier et al. (1976) showed that NE was not as significant in mediating reward function as previously thought. Later reinterpretations of NE data (e.g., Wise 1978) confirmed that this transmitter system responsible for playing the role attributed to NE was actually DA.
3. See Newell (1980) for a developed account of such mechanisms as physical symbol systems.
4. See Raichle and Minton (2006) for discussion and a proposal for the causal relation.

References

Atkinson, R. C., and Shiffrin, R. M. (1968) "Human Memory: A Proposed System and Its Control Processes," in K. W. Spence and J. T. Spence (eds), *The Psychology of Learning and Motivation: Advances in Research and Theory*, vol. 2, New York: Academic, pp. 89–195.

Bechtel, W. (2007) *Mental Mechanisms: Philosophical Perspectives on the Sciences of Cognition and the Brain*, Mahwah, NJ: Erlbaum.

Bechtel, W., and McCauley, R. N. (1999) "Heuristic Identity Theory (or Back to the Future): The Mind-Body Problem against the Background of Research Strategies in Cognitive Neuroscience," in M. Hahn and S. C. Stoness (eds), *Proceedings of the 21st Annual Meeting of the Cognitive Science Society*, Mahwah, NJ: Lawrence Erlbaum Associates, pp. 67–72.

Bishop, M. P., Elder, S. T., and Heath, R. G. (1963) "Intracranial Self-Stimulation in Man," *Science* 140: 394–6.

Broca, P. (1861) "Remarques sur le siége de la faculté du langage articulé, suivies d'une observation d'aphemie (perte de la parole)," *Bulletin de la Société Anatomique* 6: 343–57.

Clavier, R. M., Fibiger, H. C., and Phillips, A. G. (1976) "Evidence That Self-Stimulation of the Region of the Locus Coeruleus in Rats Does Not Depend upon Noradrenergic Projections to Telencephalon," *Brain Research* 113: 71–81.

Cummins, R. (2000) "'How Does It Work?' versus 'What Are the Laws?': Two Conceptions of Psychological Explanation," in F. Keil and R. Wilson (eds), *Explanation and Cognition*, Cambridge, MA: MIT Press, pp. 117–44.

Donders, F. C. (1868) "Over de Snelheid van psychische Processen: Onderzoekingen Gedaan in het Physiologisch Laboratorium der Utrechtsche Hoogeschool: 1868–1869," *Tweede Reeks* 2: 92–120.

Dretske, F. I. (1981) *Knowledge and the Flow of Information*, Cambridge, MA: MIT Press-Bradford Books.

Fechner, G. T. (1860) *Elemente der Psychophysik*, Leipzig: Breitkopf und Härtel.

Glennan, S. (1996) "Mechanisms and the Nature of Causation," *Erkenntnis* 44: 50–71.

Heath, R. G. (1963) "Electrical Self-Stimulation of the Brain in Man," *American Journal of Psychiatry* 120: 571–7.

Holland, J. H., Holyoak, K. J., Nisbett, R. E., and Thagard, P. R. (1986) *Induction: Processes of Inference, Learning and Discovery*, Cambridge, MA: MIT Press.

Kelso, J. A. S. (1995) *Dynamic Patterns: The Self Organization of Brain and Behavior*, Cambridge, MA: MIT Press.

Langley, P., Simon, H. A., Bradshaw, G. L., and Zytkow, J. M. (1987) *Scientific Discovery: Computational Explorations of the Creative Process*, Cambridge: MIT Press.

Mayr, E. (1982) *The Growth of Biological Thought*, Cambridge, MA: Belknap.

Miller, G. A. (1956) "The Magical Number Seven, Plus or Minus Two: Some Limits on Our Capacity for Processing Information," *Psychological Review* 63: 81–97.

Millikan, R. G. (1984) *Language, Thought, and Other Biological Categories*, Cambridge, MA: MIT Press.

Mishkin, M., Ungerleider, L. G., and Macko, K. A. (1983) "Object Vision and Spatial Vision: Two Cortical Pathways," *Trends in Neurosciences* 6: 414–17.

Nagel, E. (1961) *The Structure of Science*, New York: Harcourt, Brace.

Newell, A. (1980) "Physical Symbol Systems," *Cognitive Science* 4: 135–83.

Olds, J. (1955) "A Physiological Study of Reward," in D. McClelland (ed.), *Studies of Motivation*, New York: Appleton, pp. 134–43.

Olds, J., and Milner, P. (1954) "Positive Reinforcement Produced by Electrical Stimulation of Septal Area and Other Regions of Rat Brain," *Journal of Comparative and Physiological Psychology* 47: 419–29.

Port, R., and van Gelder, T. (1995) *It's About Time*, Cambridge, MA: MIT Press.

Raichle, M. E., and Minton, M. A. (2006) "Brain Work and Brain Imaging," *Annual Review of Neuroscience* 29: 449–76.

Roediger, H. L., Buckner, R. L., and McDermott, K. B. (1999) "Components of Processing," in J. K. Foster and M. Jelicic (eds), *Memory: Systems, Process, or Function*, Oxford: Oxford University Press, pp. 32–65.

Schacter, D. L., and Tulving, E. (1994) "What Are the Memory Systems of 1994?," in D. L. Schacter and E. Tulving (eds), *Memory Systems 1994*, Cambridge, MA: MIT Press, pp. 1–38.

Scoville, W. B., and Milner, B. (1957) "Loss of recent memory after bilateral hippocampal lesions," *Journal of Neurology, Neurosurgery, and Psychiatry* 20: 11–21.

Skipper, R. A., and Millstein, R. L. (2005) "Thinking about Evolutionary Mechanisms: Natural Selection," *Studies in History and Philosophy of Biological and Biomedical Sciences* 36: 327–47.

Stevens, S. S. (1957) "On the Psychophysical Law," *Psychological Review* 64: 153–81.

Teigen, K. H. (2002) "One Hundred Years of Laws in Psychology," *American Journal of Psychology* 115: 103–18.

Thagard, P. (1988) *Computational Philosophy of Science*, Cambridge, MA: MIT Press-Bradford Books.

Thelen, E., and Smith, L. (1994) *A Dynamical Systems Approach to the Development of Cognition and Action*, Cambridge, MA: MIT Press.

Tulving, E. (1983) *Elements of Episodic Memory*, New York: Oxford University Press.

Valenstein, E. S., and Beer, B. (1964) "Continuous Opportunity for Reinforcing Brain Stimulation," *Journal of the Experimental Analysis of Behavior* 7: 183–4.

Valenstein, E. S., and Campbell, J. F. (1966) "Medial Forebrain Bundle-Lateral Hypothalamic Area and Reinforcing Brain Stimulation," *American Journal of Physiology* 210: 270–4.

van Essen, D. C., and Gallant, J. L. (1994) "Neural Mechanisms of Form and Motion Processing in the Primate Visual System," *Neuron* 13: 1–10.

van Gelder, T. (1995) "What Might Cognition Be, If Not Computation," *Journal of Philosophy* 92: 345–81.

van Orden, G. C., Pennington, B. F., and Stone, G. O. (2001) "What Do Double Dissociations Prove? Inductive Methods and Isolable Systems," *Cognitive Science*, 25, 111–72.

Waskan, J. (2006) *Models and Cognition*, Cambridge, MA: MIT Press.

Weber, E. H. (1834) *De Pulsu, Resorpitione, Auditu et Tactu: Annotationes Anatomicae et Physiologicae*, Leipzig: Koehlor.

Weber, M. (2005) *Philosophy of Experimental Biology*, Cambridge: Cambridge University Press.

Wise, R. A. (1978) "Catecholamine Theories of Reward: A Critical Review," *Brain Research* 152: 215–47.

—— (1989) "The Brain and Reward," in J. M. Liebman and S. J. Cooper (eds), *The Neuropharmacological Basis of Reward*, Oxford: Oxford University Press, pp. 377–424.

Wright, C. D. (2007) "Is Psychological Explanation Going Extinct?," in M. Schouten and H. Looren de Jong (eds), *The Matter of the Mind: Philosophical Essays on Psychology, Neuroscience, and Reduction*, Oxford: Blackwell, pp. 249–74.

Wright, C. D., and Bechtel, W. (2006) "Mechanisms and Psychological Explanation," in P. Thagard (ed.), *Philosophy of Psychology and Cognitive Science*, Amsterdam: Elsevier, pp. 31–77.

9
IS FOLK PSYCHOLOGY A THEORY?

Ian Ravenscroft

Introduction

The concept of folk psychology has played a central role in the philosophy of psychology in recent decades. The term "folk psychology" is deliberately used to mark a contrast with what we might call "scientific psychology." Whilst the latter is a body of theory developed and articulated by researchers within a scientific specialization, the former is said to be common to nearly all human beings. Given the centrality of folk psychology in contemporary philosophical thought about the mind, it is surprising that there is little consensus on either its nature or its status. Many philosophers and cognitive scientists insist that folk psychology is a *theory of mind*, but this claim is by no means universally accepted. Moreover, there are marked disagreements even amongst those philosophers who understand folk psychology to be a theory. In the second and third sections, I explore two ways in which folk psychology has been taken to be a theory. Following Stich and Nichols (2003) I call these the *platitude* approach and the *mindreading* approach.[1] Then, in the fourth section, I briefly discuss eliminativism – the doctrine that the mental states over which folk psychology quantifies simply don't exist. The final two sections of this chapter are devoted to theorists who deny that folk psychology is a theory. In the fifth section, I briefly sketch the claim that folk psychology is best understood in terms of mental simulation, and in the sixth section, I discuss the claim that folk psychology is a *stance* or *attitude* that we take to a range of systems.

The platitude approach

In the early 1970s David Lewis (1970, 1972) suggested that we can think of our everyday talk about mental states as constituting a theory of the mind. In particular, he suggested that we can think of it as a *term-introducing* theory. Some of the terms used in science refer to entities or properties with which we can be fairly directly acquainted. The terms "mammal" and "fluid" are examples. However, some of the terms used in science refer to entities with which we are not directly acquainted –

and perhaps cannot become directly acquainted. Examples include "electron" and "atomic number." Lewis proposed that the latter sorts of terms get their meaning from the theories in which they are introduced. For example, the term "electron" gets its meaning from the theory of atomic structure. Of course, terms like "electron" are rarely explicitly defined in scientific theories. Lewis held, though, that such terms are *implicitly* defined by the theories which introduce them, and he showed how, using the machinery of modern logic, it is possible to extract explicit definitions from the theory.

Lewis construed our everyday talk about the mind as a term-introducing theory which implicitly defines the items of our mental vocabulary – terms like "belief," "desire," "pain," "hunger" and "hope." He began by imagining that we had collected all the everyday "platitudes" which link either sensory stimuli with mental states, mental states with other mental states, or mental states with behaviour. Examples include "bodily damage typically causes pain," "pain sometimes causes anxiety," and "pain sometimes causes us to cry out." Other kinds of platitudes may also be relevant to Lewis's project. For example, he suggests that we also imagine collecting platitudes which group one kind of mental state under a more general kind (for example, "toothache is a kind of pain"). Lewis then treated the collection of platitudes as a theory of mind. Since the platitudes are everyday remarks to which we would all assent, the theory of mind has been dubbed "folk psychology" (or, sometimes, "commonsense psychology"). Explicit definitions of the terms of folk psychology can then be obtained by the same logical manipulations as were applied in the case of scientific theories.

The explicit definitions of mental states which Lewis obtains are *functional* or *causal role* definitions. The typical functional definition has three clauses.

(1) An *input* clause, which specifies the sorts of environmental impacts which bring about the mental state. In the case of pain, for example, the input clause will mention (and perhaps be exhausted by) the fact that pain is caused by bodily damage.
(2) An *internal* clause, which specifies the causal relations between the mental state in question and other mental states. In the case of pain the internal clause will mention the way pain sometimes causes anxiety.
(3) An *output* clause, which specifies the behavioural effects of the mental state. For example, pain often causes us to cry out.

It is important to note that the output condition may mention other mental states. For example, I may not cry out after dropping the hammer on my toe because I *believe* that it is important not to make a fuss.

Understood this way, folk psychology is a kind of *functionalism* with which is associated a metaphysical doctrine and a semantic doctrine.

The metaphysical doctrine

As a metaphysical doctrine, functionalism claims that mental states are states which occupy certain kinds of functional roles, that is, they are states which are caused by sensory stimuli, have causal relations with other mental states, and cause certain kinds of behaviour. One considerable advantage of this doctrine is that it allows that mental states can be *multiply realized*. Let me explain.

In the 1950s, U. T. Place (1956), H. Feigl (1958) and J.J.C. Smart (1959) proposed the *identity theory of mind*, viz, that each type of mental state was identical to a type of neurological state. To use an old example, the mental state of pain is identical to c-fibre firing.[2] Whilst many scientifically orientated philosophers were impressed by the bold conjecture that mental states *simply were* neurological states, the identity theory was soon rejected. The problem was that, following Putnam (1967), it became widely accepted that mental states can be multiply realized: whilst in humans pain is c-fibre firing, in dolphins it might be some distinct neurological states (say d-fibre firing). Indeed, in aliens it may not be a neurological kind at all.

Functionalism gives us a way to respond to this problem. According to functionalism, mental states are identical to *whatever state it is that plays the relevant functional role*. This leaves open the possibility that in humans the functional role of pain is played by c-fibre firing, in dolphins by d-fibre firing, and in aliens by a state which is not even neurological. In short, functionalism is compatible with the multiple realization of mental states.

Another attractive feature of functionalism is that, with the addition of suitable premises, it entails physicalism (Lewis 1966; Armstrong 1968). For say it was discovered that, as a matter of contingent fact, the states which play the relevant functional roles are physical states. Then it would have been shown that mental states are physical states. However, whilst it is plausible – some would say overwhelmingly plausible – that the states which *actually* play the relevant functional roles are physical states, it might not have turned out that way. Perhaps in distant possible worlds the states which play the roles are nonphysical, "ectoplasmic" states. That is, the platitude version of folk psychology is compatible with dualism. (To put this point another way, our actual mental tokens are only contingently identical with physical tokens.) This is an endorsement of Smart's view that our everyday talk about mental states is "topic neutral" (Smart 1959). As he observes, the atheist and the vicar can share the common language of folk psychology because folk psychology itself carries relatively few metaphysical commitments.

Notice that functionalism is also compatible with *eliminativism* – the doctrine that the mental states with which folk psychology is concerned simply don't exist. For it may turn out that *no states* actually play the relevant functional roles, in which case there are no folk psychological mental states. I will discuss eliminativism in more detail in the fourth section.

As we have seen, functionalism identifies mental states with the occupants of the relevant functional roles. However, many philosophers have wondered whether all mental states and properties can be understood in these terms. In particular, it has seemed implausible to many that *qualia* can be identified purely in terms of their functional role (see especially Block [1978]). Qualia are the subjective properties of our conscious experiences – the property of redness when we attend to a red surface in good light, the property of hurtfulness when we suffer bodily damage, the property of thirstiness when we urgently need a drink, and so forth. It seems possible that a creature could have states which occupy the functional roles *typically associated* with redness, hurtfulness, etc., and yet not have the qualia of redness, hurtfulness, etc. Such a creature would react to bodily damage exactly as would an ordinary person, but there would be no associated feeling of pain. (The term *zombie* is often used to pick out creatures which are functionally identical to ordinary human beings but have no conscious life.) If such creatures are indeed possible, then functionalism does not give a complete metaphysical story of mental states and properties. We can put the point this way: if zombies are indeed possible, then after God had made sure that all the relevant functional roles were occupied, She still had work to do. Ensuring that some state or other occupies the functional role is insufficient for the instantiation of qualia.

Since Lewis's platitude version of folk psychology is committed to functionalism, and since metaphysics appears to clash with our (folk) intuitions about the possibility of zombies, we have reason to be cautious about the platitude version of folk psychology. It must be stressed, though, that functionalists have made a variety of replies to zombie-style objections. See for example Shoemaker (1975) and Braddon-Mitchell and Jackson (1996: chapter 8).

The semantic doctrine

We have seen that, according to Lewis, explicit definitions of the mentalistic terms can be obtained from the folk psychological platitudes. This is a version of the descriptive theory of reference, according to which referring terms are shorthand for a description which picks out the item to which the term refers. To take a well-worn example, "Aristotle" might abbreviate "the student of Plato and the teacher of Alexander." "Aristotle" then picks out the person who fits that description.[3] The description theory has, though, fallen on hard times (see in particular Putnam [1975] and Kripke [1980]). The core observation behind objections to the description theory is that we can discover that everything included in the description associated with a term is false. To take one of Saul Kripke's examples, say that we associate with the name "Gödel" the description "the man who discovered the incompleteness of arithmetic." It could turn out, though, that someone else – Schmidt – actually discovered the incompleteness of arithmetic, and that Gödel stole it from Schmidt. In that case we would, very naturally, say that Gödel did not discover the incompleteness of arithmetic. However, if the description theory of reference is correct, "Gödel did not discover the incompleteness of arithmetic" means "The man who discovered the incompleteness of arithmetic did not discover the incompleteness of arithmetic." And surely that isn't right (see Kripke 1980: 83–4).

Philosophers unimpressed with the description theory of reference sometimes prefer to give an account of meaning in terms of causal relations between the referring term and the object to which it refers. On this view, "Gödel" refers to Gödel because tokens of "Gödel" are appropriately causally connected to Gödel. In virtue of these causal connections, we can succeed in referring to Gödel even if everything we currently believe about Gödel is false (he did not discover the incompleteness of arithmetic, he did not work at the Institute for Advanced Study for many years, etc.). Similarly, it has been urged that "belief" refers to beliefs because tokens of the term are appropriately causally connected to beliefs. And, once more, reference can succeed even if our folk conception of belief turns out to be false.

Needless to say, champions of the platitude approach to folk psychology are aware of these issues, and have defended versions of the description theory of reference.[4] This is not the place to further pursue issues in the theory of meaning. Enough has been said, though, to make us cautious about the description theory of reference, and since the platitude version of folk psychology is committed to that approach, we have a further reason to be cautious about the platitude version.

The mindreading approach

With the demise of behaviourism in the late 1950s and early 1960s, psychologists once again felt free to postulate rich representational structures in the minds of their subjects. One of the key proponents of this new cognitive approach to psychology was Noam Chomsky (1959), whose review of B. F. Skinner's *Verbal Behavior* (1957) played a major role in bringing the behaviourist paradigm to an end. Chomsky argued that encoded in the brains of normal human beings are representations of the grammars of the natural languages which they speak. Those representations underpin our everyday capacity to understand and produce grammatical sentences. Following Chomsky, a number of other cognitive capacities were explained by positing detailed representations (or "theories") of the relevant domains, stored in the heads of normal human beings.[5] I will call this explanatory strategy the *cognitive strategy*.

One cognitive capacity which humans typically possess is the capacity to predict and explain the behaviour of others. Very often the explanations we offer of each other's behaviour involve attributing to the target a variety of mental states. For example, we might explain the presidential candidate's antiabortion stance by saying he *believes* that by opposing abortion he will attract the conservative vote. The label "mindreading" has been used to pick out this capacity. A number of researchers have adopted the cognitive strategy towards mindreading, arguing that humans typically possess a rich theory of human mental states which specifies the relations those mental states have to environmental stimuli, behaviour and each other. The theory of mental states postulated by these researchers is often called "folk psychology" (sometimes "theory of mind").

Intriguingly, mindreading research had its origins in primatology. In the 1970s, primatologists David Premack and Guy Woodruff (1978) asked whether chimpanzees have a theory of mind. Chimpanzees live in troops with complex social structures. Other things being equal, those individuals capable of grasping that other troop members are motivated by particular beliefs and desires would enjoy a considerable advantage.

Premack and Woodruff tentatively applied the cognitive strategy to chimpanzee social behaviour, and speculated that chimpanzees possess folk psychology. Of course, obtaining behavioural evidence in support of the hypothesis that chimpanzees possess folk psychology is very difficult. In particular, it is very hard to judge whether the animal is responding to the target's mental states or merely to an observed behavioural regularity. (Does chimpanzee *X* recognize that chimpanzee *Y* wants the banana and thinks that the best way to get the banana is to reach for the stick, or has *X* simply learnt that when the banana is over there, *Y* reaches for the stick?)

Commenting on the Premack and Woodruff paper, Daniel Dennett suggested that the crucial test would be whether chimpanzees can understand that their conspecifics' behaviour can be directed by *false* beliefs – by states which *misrepresent* the world (Dennett 1978b). Subsequently, child psychologists Heinz Wimmer and Josef Perner (1983) embraced the cognitive strategy with respect to the human capacity to mindread, and tested young children to determine at what age they can successfully predict the behaviour of someone labouring under a (relevant) false belief. In a classic experiment, they introduce their subjects to a puppet called "Maxi" who is holding a chocolate. Maxi hides her chocolate in location A and then goes out to play. Whilst Maxi is off the stage, her mother enters, finds the chocolate, and moves it to location *B*. After mother leaves, Maxi returns and announces that she is going to get her chocolate. The puppet action stops and the subjects are asked where Maxi will look for her chocolate: location A or location *B*? Children less than about four typically predict that Maxi will look in location *B*; children older than four typically predict that Maxi will look in location A. That is, it is not until children are about four years old that they appreciate that behaviour can be motivated by false representations. Wimmer and Perner's study has been replicated in various ways, and the term "false belief task" is now commonly used for both their Maxi experiment and other similar experiments.

Working within the cognitive strategy, Wimmer and Perner concluded that somewhere around the age of four, children's capacity to deploy folk psychology undergoes a marked development. There are in fact at least two hypotheses available to the cognitive strategist at this point. (1) It could be that the theory of mind possessed by the young child goes through a marked maturation around the age of four. (2) It could be that the changes observed in young children around the age of four are due not to the maturation of their theory of mind, but to a maturation of the cognitive capacities needed to successfully utilize their theory of mind. It is fair to say that the former is the more popular hypothesis, although Jerry Fodor (1992) has defended the latter. (To make matters more complicated, it could be that the development of the mindreading capacity involves *both* maturation of folk psychology *and* maturation of those cognitive capacities needed to fully utilize folk psychology.)

Famously, Chomsky (1988) hypothesized that the theory of grammar possessed by native speakers is innate – that its development is to an important extent under the control of certain genes. Other theorists have argued that the individual's theory of grammar is largely the outcome of processes of learning. Of course, the learning mechanisms are themselves innate; however, the claim is that the *content* acquired by those mechanisms is dependent on the child's environment, not on its genetic endowment.[6] A parallel debate exists in the case of mindreading. Some theorists, for example Fodor (1992) and Peter Carruthers (1996, section 1.7), defend the view that folk psychology is largely innate; others, for example Alison Gopnik and Andrew Meltzoff (1997), defend the view that folk psychology is largely learnt. Gopnik and Meltzoff argue that the mechanisms involved in acquiring folk psychology are precisely those deployed by adult scientists in developing theories about the natural world. This view is sometimes called the "child as little scientist" view, although Gopnik and Meltzoff have suggested that it would be better called the "scientist as big child" view. They seek support for their position in the history and philosophy of science, arguing that the pattern of theory development exhibited in the small child is repeated in the history of science. Assessing this theory is not easy, for our understanding of both the development of scientific theories and the development of cognitive capacities in children is incomplete.[7]

Another important debate concerns the extent to which the mechanism that deploys folk psychology is *modular*. Fodor (1983) argues that many key cognitive mechanisms – in particular those underpinning perception and language – are modular. Whilst Fodor identifies a range of characteristics of modular mechanisms, for our purposes, we can focus on the idea of *informational encapsulation*. A mechanism is informationally encapsulated if it has little or no access to information which lies outside it. Thus Fodor argues that the visual system is informationally encapsulated, for whilst visual processing utilizes important information and is thus cognitive, it only has access to its own, proprietary, store of information. It cannot access, for example, scientific theories possessed by the perceiver.

More recently, some cognitive scientists have argued that the mechanism which deploys folk psychology is informationally encapsulated. Fodor defends the informational encapsulation of visual processing on the grounds that the visual illusions persist even when we understand that they are just that – illusions. Our knowledge of visual illusions does not "penetrate" visual processing. Similarly, Gabriel Segal (1996) has pointed out that our knowledge that we are watching a play does not penetrate our folk psychological processing. Unless the play is especially poor, we automatically attribute mental states to the characters on the stage; our knowledge that the actors do not really have the beliefs and desires they portray does not impact upon our folk psychological mechanism. Segal's argument is not, though, especially convincing. For whilst it is true that our knowledge that we are watching a play does not seem to readily penetrate our folk psychological mechanism, other kinds of information do seem to penetrate. Information about how the agent is situated in their environment, their inclination to exaggeration or dishonesty, and so forth, influences the beliefs and desires we ascribe to them. There are good reasons to doubt, therefore, that the folk psychology mechanism is informationally encapsulated (see Sterelny 2003: 218–21).

We have seen that, in the early 1980s, Wimmer and Perner discovered that children's mindreading capacity undergoes an important development around four years of age. Soon after Wimmer and Perner's groundbreaking research, Simon Baron-Cohen et al.

(1985) tested autistic children on the false belief task. They discovered that autistic children quite a bit older than four typically perform considerably worse than normal children on the false belief task. (Since autistic children are often mentally retarded, Baron-Cohen et al. were careful to control for mental age.) To use a phrase of Baron-Cohen's (1995), it would seem that such children are "mindblind." As with the child development case mentioned earlier, there has been discussion of whether the autistic child lacks folk psychology or, whilst possessing folk psychology, lacks the capacity to utilize it successfully. In addition, there has been discussion of whether the failure to mindread is the fundamental deficit in autism, or whether the mindreading deficit is itself due to an earlier, more basic, deficit. For example, the executive functions, which include planning and abstract reasoning, are often impaired in people with autism (Rumsey 1985), and it has been suggested that deficits of executive function in turn give rise to difficulties with mindreading. Finally, it is worth noting that difficulties with the false belief task are also found in people suffering from schizophrenia (Frith 1992). This raises important issues as autism and schizophrenia are quite distinct disorders.

The cognitive strategy is not the only explanatory approach which has been taken to the capacity to mindread. Simulation theorists deny that mindreading is underpinned by a theory of mental states; indeed, they go as far as to deny that there is such a thing as folk psychology understood to be a theory of mind represented in people's brains. I discuss simulation theory in the fifth section.

Eliminativism

The history of science is littered with theories which have turned out to be false, including Aristotle's astronomy, Newton's mechanics and Lamark's theory of evolution. Indeed, many philosophers of science have argued that it is a hallmark of a scientific theory that it could, at least in principle, be shown to be mistaken (Popper 1968). Moreover, once a theory has been shown to be false, the grounds for accepting the states which it postulates are often taken away. For example, once we rejected Aristotle's astronomy, we no longer had grounds for believing in the heavenly spheres postulated by that theory.

If we accept that folk psychology is a theory of mind akin, in important ways, to scientific theories, it seems that we have to accept that we might discover it to be false. Moreover, if folk psychology were shown to be false, we would have grounds for thinking that the mental states postulated by folk psychology don't exist. So it *could* turn out that there are no beliefs and no desires, no hungers and no pains, no hopes and no fears.

Eliminativists argue that we have good reasons for doubting that folk psychology is true and consequently that we have good reasons for doubting the existence of the mental states postulated by folk psychology. That is, they think that we have good reasons for *eliminating* folk psychological mental states from our ontology. The point is often illustrated by reference to other folk theories which have turned out to be false. It was once widely believed, for example, that catastrophic events like tsunamis were caused by supernatural agents. We now reject both the agent-based theory of tsunamis and the agents it postulates.

What reasons are offered for denying the truth of folk psychology? In what follows I will focus on the arguments offered by Paul Churchland whose 1981 paper remains the most widely discussed articulation of eliminativism. Churchland offers three considerations in favour of the claim that folk psychology is false. (1) Folk psychology is a stagnant research programme which has not appreciably advanced in thousands of years. (2) There is a wide range of mental phenomena about which folk psychology has nothing to say, including mental illness, sleep, learning, vision, memory and creativity. (3) Folk psychology lacks extensive evidential connections with other sciences.

In assessing these considerations, it is important to distinguish between folk psychology itself and scientific extensions of folk psychology – scientific accounts of some aspect of the mind which quantify over mental states originally postulated by folk psychology. A good example of a scientific extension of folk psychology is cognitive behavioural therapy (sometimes called "cognitive therapy"). Cognitive behavioural therapy quantifies over states which are readily recognizable as folk psychological beliefs. Much work in cognitive behavioural therapy has focused on depression, with theorists in the field arguing that self-denigrating beliefs ("I can't cope," "I will never be happy") play a major causal role in many cases of depression.[8] The scientific credentials of cognitive behavioural therapy are not in serious dispute: it has been shown to be approximately as successful as medication in treating depression.[9]

With the distinction between scientific theories which refine or extend folk psychology and folk psychology itself in place, we can consider Churchland's anti-folk-psychology arguments, beginning with Churchland's claim that folk psychology is a stagnant theory. It may be true that the psychological theory held by the "folk" has not changed much in centuries; however, scientific extensions of folk psychology have certainly advanced. Since scientific extensions of folk psychology share folk psychology's basic ontology, the progressiveness of the former provides support for the ontology of the latter. Similarly, whilst folk psychology has little to say about mental illness, sleep, learning and so forth, some scientific extensions of folk psychology have something to say about at least some of the items on Churchland's list. Cognitive behavioural therapy serves as an example here, as it has shed light on at least one mental illness – depression.

What of the claim that folk psychology lacks extensive evidential connections with other scientific theories? There seems little reason to doubt that evidential relations are emerging between neuroscience and folk psychology (including what I have been calling "scientific extensions of folk psychology"). To give but one example, Brian Knutson and co-workers (2007) have explored the neural mechanisms involved in, of all things, shopping behaviour. Subjects were given credit with which to purchase items like chocolates and DVDs. Pictures of the sale items were flashed on a screen, followed by the item's price. The part of the brain which responded to the sale item was distinct from that which responded to price. Intriguingly, excessively high prices caused activation in the insula, a part of the brain involved with processing painful and upsetting stimuli. Activity in the insula was especially high when the subject decided not to purchase the item. This kind of experiment strongly supports the idea that evidential relations will be found between neuroscientific and (broadly speaking) folk psychological theories.[10]

We saw earlier in this chapter that there are two ways of approaching the claim that folk psychology is a theory: the platitude approach and the mindreading approach. Consequently there are two ways of understanding the eliminativist claim that folk psychology is false: as a claim about a theory implicit in our everyday talk about mental states, and as a claim about a theory represented in the human brain (Stich and Ravenscroft 1994). Eliminativists are rarely explicit about which of these theories is their target, yet it maybe turn out to be important. For example, it may be that whilst the theory of mind explicit in our everyday talk about mental states is largely false, the theory of mind represented in the human brain is largely true.

Folk psychology as mental simulation

In its purest form, simulation theory denies that folk psychology involves a theory of human psychology. Rather, mindreading is achieved by simulating the causal processes giving rise to the target behaviour. Stephen Stich and Shaun Nichols (1992) have provided a useful analogy. There are two ways to predict the behaviour of a prototype airplane. (1) Obtain an accurate description of the plane and the conditions under which it will be operating, and then use a theory of aerodynamics to work out how the plane will behave under those conditions. (2) Make an accurate scale model of the plane and observe its behaviour in a wind tunnel under a variety of conditions. In an obvious sense the former is a theory-based approach to prediction; the latter, a simulation-based approach. The mindreading approach to folk psychology is akin to the first strategy, simulation theory akin to the second.

Simulation theory begins with the model of human action offered by intentional psychology. On this model, agents make decisions on the basis of their beliefs and desires, and (*ceteris paribus*) act on those decisions. For example, say that Fred desires to learn more about the Australian megafauna and believes that the best way to learn more about the megafauna is to visit the famous caves at Naracoorte. Other things being equal, his decision-making processes will generate an intention to visit the Naracoorte caves and, again other things being equal, he will visit the caves. According to simulation theory, we predict Fred's behaviour by adopting states which are akin to his beliefs and desires, and then observing what intentions those states lead us to have. The states are "akin" to beliefs and desires in that they impact on decision-making in the same way as do the corresponding beliefs and desires. However, we do not act on the intentions formed on the basis of these states; rather, the intention is recorded as a prediction of Fred's behaviour. The states which I have described as "akin" to beliefs and desires are known, respectively, as "pretend beliefs" and "pretend desires." This terminology is unfortunate because the use of "pretend" suggests that these states are not real. However, if simulation theory is correct, these are *bona fide* cognitive states found in the brains of all folk psychologists. According to simulation theory, if I were to predict Fred's behaviour I would form the pretend desire to learn more about the megafauna and the pretend belief that the best way to learn about the megafauna is to visit the Naracoorte caves. These states would lead me to form the intention to visit the caves. However, I would not actually visit the caves; rather, my intention would form the basis of my prediction: Fred will visit the Naracoorte caves (see Goldman 1989; Stich and Nichols 1992).

So far we have only considered the simulationist account of the prediction of behaviour. What about our capacity to explain behaviour in terms of intentional states like beliefs and desires? Let us return to the example of Fred's visit to the Naracoorte caves. Fred's behaviour is correctly explained by attributing to him the desire to learn more about the megafauna and the belief that the best way to learn more about the megafauna is to visit the Naracoorte caves. Simulation theory suggests that we obtain such explanations by generating and testing pairs of pretend beliefs and desires, stopping when we locate a pair which would lead to the intention to go to the caves. We might try, for example, the pretend desire to sample lots of Australian wine and the pretend belief that the best place to sample lots of Australian wine is the Barossa Valley. But that pair of pretend beliefs and desires would not lead us to form the intention to visit the Naracoorte caves, and so the corresponding beliefs and desires are not plausible candidates for the states which motivated Fred. Eventually we strike upon the pretend desire to learn more about the megafauna and the pretend belief that the best place to learn more about the megafauna is the Naracoorte caves. Those states lead us to form the intention to visit the caves, and so the corresponding beliefs and desires are attributed to Fred.

This account of our capacity to form intentional explanations is not especially plausible. There are an infinite number of pairs of pretend beliefs and desires to generate and test. Worse still, there are an infinite number of pairs of pretend beliefs and desires which would lead to the decision to visit the Naracoorte caves. (The pretend desire for an ice cream and the pretend belief that the Naracoorte caves is the best place to get an ice cream lead to the intention to go to the Naracoorte caves.) Robert Gordon (1986) and Alvin Goldman (1989) have attempted to address this problem by appealing to a principle of humanity: assume that the target has the beliefs and desires which you would have if you were "in their shoes." But this hardly suffices. How do I determine which beliefs and desires I would have if I were in Fred's shoes? By a further act of simulation? Moreover, we sometimes successfully predict the behaviour of people whose beliefs and values are quite different from our own. I might work out why Fred went to the Naracoorte caves even though I have no interest in the Australian megafauna and a profound fear of caves.

Much of the debate between advocates of the mindreading approach and advocates of simulation theory has concerned cases in which we *mispredict* another's behaviour. Stich and Nichols (1992) have argued that some examples of misprediction cannot be explained by simulation theory. Consider, for example, the so-called "position effect." When asked to choose an item from a range of identical items presented on a table, subjects typically select an item on their right. Intriguingly, subjects universally deny that position had any bearing on their choice. Notice that the subject's choice is surprising: few of us would have predicted the subject's behaviour. The mindreading approach to folk psychology can seek to explain our inability to predict the subject's behaviour by insisting that the theory of human psychology which drives behaviour prediction is limited: whatever its virtues, folk psychology is ignorant about the position effect. What about simulation theory? How can it explain the common failure to predict the subject's behaviour in the position effect experiment? Stich and Nichols suggest that simulationists seem to have two possible ways of accounting for misprediction: (i) failure to generate the right pretend beliefs and desires; and (ii) divergence between the simulator's decision-maker and the target's. They argue, however, that neither option is attractive in the position effect case. Option (i) is unattractive because it seems *ad hoc:* What is it about these particular circumstances that make pretend belief and desire generation so difficult? Why is it so hard to correctly interpret the output of mental simulation in the position effect case but not in other cases? Option (ii) is unattractive because the subjects in the position effect experiment were selected at random, and so there is no reason to think that their decision-making processes diverge from those of us who did not anticipate their behaviour. I think that there is a range of replies open to the simulationist at this point (see my 1999), but I will not pursue the issue any further here.

Finally, it is worth noting that the debate about simulation theory no longer takes the form of a straightforward choice between simulation and theory. Rather, a number of possible hybrid positions have been articulated. For example, it may be that some aspects of mindreading are achieved by simulation, others by theory (Stich and Nichols 2003). Again, it may be that any plausible simulation model must postulate a large element of theory involved in, for example, the generation of pretend beliefs and desires (Ravenscroft 1999).

Folk psychology as a stance

There is another important group of theorists who insist that folk psychology is not a theory. On this view, sometimes called *interpretationalism,* folk psychology is best seen as the taking of a particular *attitude* or *stance* to a wide range of systems. This view originates in the work of W. V. O. Quine (1960) and Donald Davidson (1985); however, it has received its most extensive articulation in the work of Daniel Dennett (see especially 1971 and 1981a).

I'll begin with the case of attributing beliefs and desires to our fellow human beings. (Later we will see that Dennett does not restrict the attribution of beliefs and desires to members of our species.) According to Dennett, we attribute beliefs and desires to our fellow human beings by taking the *intentional stance* towards them. Central to the intentional stance is the assumption that the person to whom we are attributing beliefs and desires is *rational.* Rationality is a normative notion: a rational agent has the beliefs and desires it *ought* to have. Which beliefs and desires are those? Dennett suggests that, given time, a rational agent will come to believe most of the facts about her environment which (i) can be ascertained by simple observation and (ii) are of sufficient relevance to her projects to warrant her attention. In addition, a rational agent will, given time, come to know many of the more obvious, and more pertinent, logical consequences of her beliefs. Similarly, Dennett suggests that a rational agent will desire food, mates, the absence of pain, and so forth, and will also (instrumentally) desire those states of affairs which are likely to ensure the consumption of food, the having of mates, the absence of pain, and so forth (see Dennett 1981a).

It is important to note that the intentional stance is not merely a device for making attributions which could, in principle, be made some other way. Rather, being attributable from the intentional stance is constitutive of what beliefs and desires *are*. In short, Dennett is advancing a metaphysical claim as well as an epistemological one, that is, he is advancing a claim about what beliefs and desires are as well as a claim about how we gain knowledge of who has what beliefs and desires. Dennett's position is sometimes called "fictionalist" to stress that he doubts that beliefs and desires are entities in the head which could, in principle, be recognized without recourse to the intentional stance. It may be, he asserts, that there is no subcomponent or pattern of activation of the brain which can be identified as, say, the belief that snow is white. However, it is important to stress that, according to Dennett, the attributions made from the intentional stance are objective (see especially Dennett [1987b]). It is possible to get them wrong, just as it is possible to incorrectly measure the mass of the hydrogen nucleus. I might, for example, quite incorrectly attribute to my wife the desire to dine out tonight because I have not attended closely enough to what she is saying and doing. Moreover, the attributions are objective in that they typically yield accurate predictions of behaviour.

Of course, not all humans are rational, and even the best of us have lapses. Dennett is aware of this (although some of his critics have written as if he were not). Small lapses of observation, memory, reason and so forth can, Dennett argues, be handled by temporarily moving away from the intentional stance. On the basis of common knowledge and life experience, we can sometimes identify the relevant errors of observation, reasoning or memory, and adjust accordingly. For example, in a poorly lit cafe I receive the wrong change and hypothesize that the barista has mistaken a five dollar bill for a twenty. I cannot have arrived at this hypothesis via the intentional stance since the barista is clearly not forming the beliefs he ought to. Rather, I rely on my extensive experience of varied lighting conditions, baristas and five dollar bills. Once I have concluded that the barista believes my five dollar bill is a twenty, I can return to the intentional stance taking, as it were, my conclusion with me.

What about more radical cases of irrationality? Consider the following description of a schizophrenic patient at the height of her florid, delusional state:

> She repeatedly removed her dressing gown and made highly inappropriate sexual advances to the male staff, and then tore bits off a picture of a swan. … She said that God talked to her, saying "Shut up and get out of here." When replying to an enquiry as to interference with her thinking the patient said "The thoughts go back to the swan. I want the cross to keep it for ever and ever. It depends on the soldier Marcus the nurse."
>
> (Frith 1992: 3)

It is apparent that this patient lacks many of the beliefs and desires she ought to have, and has a good number she ought not to have. Consequently, the intentional stance is unavailable in this instance. This is not, however, a strike against Dennett. For surely we *are* at a loss in cases like this. Does this patient really believe that the swan in the picture is interfering with her thoughts and that God told her to shut up and get out? Is it appropriate to say that she believes that something (the cross? the interference?) depends on the soldier Marcus the nurse? Intentional idioms seem unduly strained in cases like this.

So far I have only considered the application of the intentional stance to human beings. Dennett proposes that it can be applied to a vast range of systems. For example, he thinks that we can – and do – apply the intentional stance to thermostats (see, for example, Dennett 1981a). I know that the thermostat in my office is supposed to maintain room temperature within a certain range because that is what it was designed to do. Consequently, if I assume that the thermostat is rational I can attribute to it certain beliefs and desires. For example, when the room is too hot it will believe that the room is too hot and desire that the room be cooler. Given those beliefs and desires, the assumption of rationality leads me to predict that the thermostat will turn off the heater. Such attributions are sometimes dismissed as "anthropomorphizing"; however, Dennett regards them as literally – and objectively – true.

Any system whose behaviour can be predicted from the intentional stance is called an *intentional system*. We have seen that the class of intentional systems includes both thermostats and human beings. Is there any general way of characterizing the set of intentional systems? Dennett includes amongst the intentional systems those which have been naturally selected and those which have been designed by rational agents such as ourselves. It may, though, include other kinds of systems. For example, the behaviour of the planets can be accurately predicted by assuming them to be rational agents which overwhelmingly desire to follow paths described by Kepler's laws.

Realists about mental states claim that beliefs and desires are *bona fide* states of the human organism (and perhaps of other systems as well). They can, in principle, be located and measured by appropriate anatomical and physiological procedures. *Antirealists* deny that there are any such states. We have seen that, according to Dennett, a system has beliefs and desires if, and only if, we can successfully predict its behaviour from the intentional stance. There may be structures within the system which can be identified as beliefs and desires; there may not. Dennett is strongly inclined to the view that there are unlikely to be such structures, at least in the human case. He is, consequently, strongly inclined to a form of antirealism about beliefs and desires. However, his antirealism is more moderate than other antirealist positions. This is because, as mentioned above, the attribution of beliefs and desires from the intentional stance is objective.

It is not clear, though, that Dennett can both insist that the intentional stance yields, in a wide range of circumstances, accurate behavioural predictions *and* deny that beliefs and desires are real internal states of intentional systems. We are entitled to ask why the intentional stance works so well, and one plausible answer is that the beliefs and desires identified from the intentional stance are real, causally efficacious states inside the human brain (Fodor 1985). By way of analogy, consider Mendelian genetics. The very considerable explanatory success of Mendelian genetics supports the claim that genes are real, causally efficacious states inside organisms. It is important to note that, once again, Dennett is alert to this objection, drawing attention to cases where we don't accept the inference from predictive success to realism. An example he offers is the attribution of centres of gravity to objects with mass. Such attributions are predictively successful and yet we don't conclude that all the mass of an object really is located at the centre of gravity. Should we think of beliefs and desires as analogous to Mendelian genes, or think of them as more like centres of gravity? I doubt that this question can be satisfactorily answered from the armchair; rather, settling the realism-antirealism debate about mental states will involve extensive empirical research in psychology and neuroscience. From psychology we might hope to learn more about the nature of beliefs and desires; from neuroscience, we might hope to learn more about the causally efficacious structures of the brain. The realist bets that these inquiries will allow us to identify mental state tokens with neurological tokens; the antirealist bets that even when all the science is in no such identifications will be forthcoming. As indicated in the fourth section, my own view is that the existing evidence supports some version of realism.

I remarked that we are entitled to ask why the intentional stance works so well. So far we have considered what might be called a *proximal* answer to that question: an answer in terms of the internal states of the agent. Dennett offers what we might call a *distal* answer to that question. He suggests that natural selection will, over time, give rise to agents which typically form true beliefs and typically desire food, mates, the absence of pain, etc. (1983). That is, natural selection will tend to favour organisms which closely approximate the assumptions made by the intentional stance. However, it is not clear to what extent natural selection will tend to give rise to such organisms. For example, Stephen Stich (1990) has argued that natural selection will not necessarily favour true believers. Finding out the truth can be expensive, and under some circumstances natural selection may favour organisms which are satisfied with cheap approximation. The mouse which falsely concludes that the cat is present on the basis of scant evidence may have more reproductive success than the mouse which stubbornly refuses to form a judgment about the cat's whereabouts in the absence of incontrovertible evidence. The simple claim that natural selection favours agents which typically form true beliefs must be carefully qualified. Dennett (1981b) has, however, offered such qualifications, arguing that neither the theory of natural selection, nor intentional systems theory, naively predict that organisms will always and everywhere believe the truth. This is not the place, though, to further pursue these issues.

Notes

1. These two ways of understanding folk psychology (taken to be a theory) were originally distinguished in Stich and Ravenscroft (1994).
2. Pain is almost certainly *not* identical to c-fibre firing. This was, however, a common speculation at the time Place and others were writing.

3. Better: the person who *best* or *adequately* fits that description. If no one comes close to fitting the description, then "Aristotle" fails to refer.
4. For a very sophisticated discussion of these issues by someone sympathetic to the platitude approach to folk psychology, see Jackson (2000).
5. See for example Marr (1982) and Rock (1983) on vision; McCloskey (1983) and Hayes (1985), on our capacity to predict the movements of middle-sized objects.
6. For arguments in favour of the claim that grammar is largely innate, see Pinker (1994); for a highly sceptical discussion of the innateness claim, see Cowie (1999).
7. For an especially penetrating discussion of the evolution of folk psychology see Sterelny 2003, especially pt III.
8. The classic work in this area is Beck (1967).
9. See Elkin et al. (1989). Subsequent studies suggest that cognitive behavioural therapy is more effective than drug therapy at preventing the recurrence of depression. See Hollon et al. (1990).
10. For an extensive discussion of Churchland's eliminativist arguments see Horgan and Woodward (1995).

References

Armstrong, D. (1968) *A Materialist Theory of the Mind*, London: Routledge & Kegan Paul.

Baron-Cohen, S. (1995) *Mindblindness*, Cambridge, MA: MIT Press.

Baron-Cohen, S., Leslie, A., and Frith, U. (1985) "Does the Autistic Child Have a 'Theory of Mind'?" *Cognition* 21: 37–46.

Beck, A. (1967) *Depression*, New York: Hoeber.

Block, N. (1978) "Troubles with Functionalism," in W. Savage (ed.), *Perception and Cognition*, Minnesota Studies in Philosophy of Science, vol. 9, Minneapolis: University of Minnesota Press, pp. 261–325; repr. Block (1980).

—— (1980) *Readings in Philosophy of Psychology*, Cambridge, MA: Harvard University Press.

Braddon-Mitchell, D., and Jackson, F. (1996) *Philosophy of Mind and Cognition*, Oxford: Blackwell.

Carruthers, P. (1996) *Language, Thought and Consciousness*, Cambridge: Cambridge University Press.

Chomsky, N. (1959) Review of *Verbal Behavior*, by B. F. Skinner, *Language*, 35, 26–58; repr. Block (1980).

—— (1988) *Language and Problems of Knowledge*, Cambridge, MA: MIT Press.

Churchland, P. (1981) "Eliminative Materialism and the Propositional Attitudes," *Journal of Philosophy* 78: 67–90.

Cowie, F. (1999) *What's Within? Nativism Reconsidered*, Oxford: Oxford University Press.

Davidson, D. (1985) *Inquiries into Truth and Interpretation*, Oxford: Oxford University Press.

Dennett, D. (1971) "Intentional Systems," *Journal of Philosophy* 8: 87–106; repr. Dennett (1978a).

—— (1978a) *Brainstorms*, Montgomery: Bradford Books.

—— (1978b) "Beliefs about Beliefs," *Behavioral and Brain Sciences* 4: 568–70.

—— (1981a) "True Believers," in A. Heath (ed.), *Scientific Explanation*, Oxford: Oxford University Press; repr. Dennett (1987a): 13–37.

—— (1981b) "Making Sense of Ourselves," *Philosophical Topics* 12: 63–81.

—— (1983) "Intentional Systems in Cognitive Ethology," *Behavioral and Brain Sciences* 6: 343–90; repr. Dennett (1987a).

—— (1987a) *The Intentional Stance*, Cambridge, MA: MIT Press.

—— (1987b) "Real Patterns, Deeper Facts, and Empty Questions," in Dennett (1987a): 37–42.

Elkin, I., et al. (1989) "National Institute of Mental Health Treatment of Depression Collaborative Research Program: General Effectiveness of Treatments," *Archives of General Psychiatry* 46: 971–82.

Feigl, H. (1958) "The 'Mental' and the 'Physical'," in H. Feigl, M. Scriven, and G. Maxwell (eds) *Concepts, Theories and the Mind-Body Problem*, Minnesota Studies in Philosophy of Science, vol. 2, Minneapolis: University of Minnesota Press, pp. 370–497.

Fodor, J. (1983) *The Modularity of Mind*, Cambridge, MA: MIT Press.

—— (1985) "Fodor's Guide to Mental Representation," *Mind* 94: 76–100.

—— (1992) "A Child's Theory of the Mind," *Cognition* 44: 283–96.

Frith, C. (1992) *The Cognitive Neuropsychology of Schizophrenia*, Hove, NY: Erlbaum.

Goldman, A. (1989) "Interpretation Psychologized," *Mind and Language* 4: 161–85.

Gopnik, A., and Meltzoff, A. (1997) *Words, Thoughts and Theories*, Cambridge, MA: MIT Press.

Gordon, R. (1986) "Folk Psychology as Simulation," *Mind and Language* 1: 158–71.

Hayes, P. (1985) "The Second Naïve Physics Manifesto," in J. Hobbs and R. Moore (eds), *Formal Theories of the Commonsense World*, Norwood, NY: Ablex.

Hollon, S., de Rubeis, R., and Evans, M. (1990) "Combined Cognitive Therapy and Pharmacotherapy in the Treatment of Depression," in D. Manning and A. Francis (eds), *Combination Drug and Psychotherapy in Depression*, Washington, DC: American Psychiatric Press.

Horgan, T., and Woodward, J. (1985) "Folk Psychology Is Here to Stay," *Philosophical Review* 94: 197–226.

Jackson, F. (2000) *From Metaphysics to Ethics*, Oxford: Clarendon Press.

Knutson, B., Rick, S., Wimmer, G. E., Prelec, D., and Loewenstein, G. (2007) "Neural Predictors of Purchases," *Neuron* 53: 147–56.

Kripke, S. (1980) *Naming and Necessity*, Cambridge, MA: Harvard University Press.

Lewis, D. (1966) "An Argument for the Identity Theory," *Journal of Philosophy* 63: 17–25.

—— (1970) "How to Define Theoretical Terms," *Journal of Philosophy* 67: 427–46.

—— (1972) "Psychophysical and Theoretical Identification," *Australasian Journal of Philosophy* 50: 249–58; repr. Block (1980).

Marr, D. (1982) *Vision*, San Francisco: Freeman.

McCloskey, M. (1983) "Naïve Theories of Motion," in D. Gentner and A. Stevens (eds), *Mental Models*, Hillsdale, NJ: Erlbaum.

Pinker, S. (1994) *The Language Instinct*, New York: Morrow.

Place, U. (1956) "Is Consciousness a Brain Process?" *British Journal of Psychology* 47: 44–50.

Popper, K. (1968) *The Logic of Scientific Discovery*, London: Hutchinson.

Premack. D., and Woodruff, G. (1978) "Does the Chimpanzee Have a Theory of Mind?" *Behavioral and Brain Sciences* 4: 515–26.

Putnam, H. (1967) "Psychological Predicates," in W. Capitan and D. Merrill (eds), *Art, Mind, and Religion*, Pittsburgh: University of Pittsburgh Press, pp. 37–48; repr. Block (1980) as "The Nature of Mental States."

—— (1975) "The Meaning of 'Meaning'," in K. Gunderson (ed.), *Language, Mind, and Knowledge*, Minnesota Studies in Philosophy of Science, vol. 7. Minneapolis: University of Minnesota Press, pp. 131–93.

Quine, W. (1960) *Word and Object*, Cambridge, MA: MIT Press.

Ravenscroft, I. (1999) "Predictive Failure," *Philosophical Papers* 28: 143–68.

Rock, I. (1983) *The Logic of Perception*, Cambridge, MA: MIT Press.

Rumsey, J. (1985) "Conceptual Problem-Solving in Highly Verbal, Nonretarded Autistic Men," *Journal of Autism and Developmental Disorders* 15: 23–36.

Segal, G. (1996) "The Modularity of Theory of Mind," in P. Carruthers and P. Smith, *Theories of Theories of Mind*, Cambridge: Cambridge University Press, pp. 141–57.

Shoemaker, S. (1975) "Functionalism and Qualia," *Philosophical Studies* 27: 291–315; rev. repr. Block (1980).

Skinner, B. (1957) *Verbal Behavior*, New York: Appleton-Century-Crofts.

Smart, J. (1959) "Sensations and Brain Processes," *Philosophical Review* 68: 141–56.

Sterelny, K. (2003) *Thought in a Hostile World*, Malden, MA: Blackwell.

Stich, S. (1990) *The Fragmentation of Reason*, Cambridge, MA: MIT Press.

Stich, S., and Nichols, S. (1992) "Folk Psychology: Theory or Simulation?" *Mind and Language* 7: 35–71.

—— (2003) "Folk Psychology," in S. Stich and T. Warfield (eds), *The Blackwell Guide to the Philosophy of Mind*, Maldon, MA: Blackwell, pp. 235–55.

Stich, S., and Ravenscroft, I. (1994) "What *Is* Folk Psychology?" *Cognition* 50: 447–68; repr. S. Stich, *Deconstructing the Mind*, Oxford: Oxford University Press, 1996.

Wimmer, H., and Perner, J. (1983) "Belief about Belief: Representation and Constraining Function of Wrong Beliefs in Young Children's Understanding of Deception," *Cognition* 13: 103–28.

10
COMPUTATIONAL FUNCTIONALISM

Thomas W. Polger

Computational functionalism

To a first approximation, computational functionalism is the view that the mind is usefully thought of as a mechanical device, such as a computing machine. The core idea behind the mind-as-machine theory is that psychological entities should be understood in terms of what they do, rather than in terms of the stuff of which they are made. Thus computational functionalism departs from both traditional materialism and dualism, and exhibits some affinity with the behaviorist approach.

The core idea of computational functionalism has been developed in various ways so that functionalism now constitutes a whole family of theories. Functionalist theories vary along several dimensions, including (a) how broadly the theories apply; (b) how they unpack the notion of a computing device or machine; and (c) whether they take the mind-machine comparison literally or metaphorically. But functionalist theories also share some core commitments, and they are generally advanced on the basis of a few common arguments. In what follows we will explore these differences and similarities.

Before moving forward, two caveats are in order. First, computational functionalism should not be confused with other "functionalist" theories in psychology and philosophy of science. In particular, and despite some similarities, contemporary computational functionalism is distinct from the "Chicago" functionalism advocated by American pragmatist psychologists in the late nineteenth and early twentieth centuries.[1] Henceforth I will drop the qualification "computational" and speak generically of "functionalism," except where some confusion might arise from this terminological economy. Second, I cast my net widely when collecting together the family of functionalist theories. Some philosophers and psychologists reserve the term "functionalism" for only a subset of the variations to be discussed herein. For example, some philosophers take functionalism only to be a thesis about the narrow or internal relations among psychological states; on something like this basis, Fred Dretske (1995) denies that he is a functionalist. And Ned Block (1980) uses "Functionalism" (with a capital *F*) to refer to the particular version of the theory exemplified by the work of David Lewis (1966, 1972).[2] I trust that my less restricted use of the term will be vindicated if it allows us to systematize and explain a range of philosophical views. So let us now proceed to doing so.

Varieties of functionalism

Begin with Brentano's thesis, the idea that "intentionality is the mark of the mental." On the view associated with Brentano, to be a psychological (i.e., mental) entity is to be intentional, to have content. Take paradigmatic intentional states such as beliefs and desires. Plainly beliefs mediate our perceptions and actions differently than desires. My belief that it is a sunny day is usually caused by seeing or being told that the day is sunny but my desire that it be a sunny day is not caused in that way, for example. And beliefs mediate our perceptions and actions differently depending on their content. My beliefs about sunny days have different causes and effects than my beliefs about coffee. And my beliefs about sunny days are related to other beliefs — such as those about blue skies, about beaches, and so forth — which differ from those to which my beliefs about coffee are related.

Suppose that some physical state of a system mediates the perceptual inputs and behavioral outputs of the system in the ways that are characteristic of a belief, and that it is related to objects in the world and to other states of the system in the ways that are distinctive of a belief with a particular propositional content, say, that there is coffee in this mug. If so, then why should we not say that the physical state in question simply is the belief that there is coffee in this mug? If it looks like a duck and quacks like a duck, then it's a duck. So the platitude goes. The core functionalist idea is that a state that acts (all-things-considered) like a belief or a pain simply is a belief or a pain, respectively.

There are a number of attractive features of the functionalist view, not least of which is that it may seem like plain common sense. Second, functionalism makes the conditions for being or having a mental state quite independent of the material substance (or immaterial substance, for that matter) of which a system is composed. This seems to have the corollaries that there could be non-biological mental entities – naturally occurring aliens or artificially engineered robots – and that the study of psychology may proceed more or less independently of the study of the physical (or nonphysical) systems in which psychology is exhibited. Third, functionalism seems to bring the conditions for being a mental entity directly in line with ordinary and empirical criteria for determining what mental states a system has. Functionalists deny that anything could play the full role of a belief about coffee without thereby being such a belief. So functionalism provides a framework for psychological explanation, a methodological model for studying psychology, and a theoretically motivated response to skeptics about other minds.

All this is to say that, as illustrated above, functionalism promises to answer a bevy of philosophical questions about minds in one blow: We get a theory (or set of related theories) about (1) the *metaphysics* or ontology of mental states, (2) the *explanatory* and (3) the *theoretical* structures of psychological science, (4) the *intentionality* and (5) the *semantics* of mental states, and (6) the *methodology* for the study of psychology. As these different phenomena run the full range of those that have concerned philosophers of mind and psychology, functionalism promises to be a comprehensive theory.[3]

It is unclear whether any single theorist has ever endorsed the functionalist theory for all six of these phenomena. Determining the answer is troublesome because it is often difficult to discern when functionalism is put forth as a serious theory and when it is advanced as a metaphor or a convenient idealization. But each variety of functionalism can be found separately among contemporary theorists.

Metaphysical functionalism

Begin with functionalism as a metaphysical theory about the nature of psychological states or processes. The slogan "mental states are functional states" is often used to express the functionalist metaphysical thesis. Here the idea is that some states or properties are such that they are wholly constituted by their relations to one another and to certain inputs and outputs, and that mental states or properties are among these. For example, what makes something (a rock, say) into a doorstop is not its inner structure or essence (if any), but simply that it is suitable for playing the role of a doorstop – that it functions as a doorstop. Being a doorstop is wholly a matter of a thing's relations to certain other objects, especially floors and doors. Likewise, what makes something a calculator is that it functions as a calculator, regardless of the stuff of which it is made.

In the jargon of functionalism, doorstops and calculators are *realized* by various physical systems, but neither doorstops nor calculators are physical natural kinds. Their various potential realizers are a physically heterogeneous group, having in common only that they realize (equivalently: implement, function as, or play the role of) doorstops and calculators, respectively. The clearest examples of such "functional" kinds are artifacts. But a case can be made that biological kinds, such as hearts or eyes, are functional kinds in the same sense.

Metaphysical functionalism is the theory that the ontological nature of mental states is that they are realized by physical states of brains. Thus mental states are not identical to brain states, as the psychophysical identity theory holds; nor are mental states simply syndromes of behavior and behavioral dispositions, as some behaviorists held. Rather mental states are the functionally constituted internal states, e.g., brain states or machine states, whose symptoms are various bits of behavior and behavioral dispositions of their containing systems. Functional states are understood to be relational in nature. Being a mental state is thus like being on the left of something rather than like having a mass of five kilograms; it essentially involves a thing's relations to other things, not merely the properties of the thing in itself. The functionalist holds that a realizer of a psychological state must be a thing of some sort – for it must be able to enter into the correct functional relations – but it need not be a thing of any one particular sort. In this way, functionalism aims to plot a middle course between the "chauvinistic" excesses of the identity theory – which seems to imply that only things with brains relevantly like ours can have mental states – and the "liberal" excesses of behaviorism – which counts any apparently intelligent behavior as genuinely psychological regardless of how it is produced.[4]

Metaphysical functionalism does not merely claim that psychological states are like functional states or can be usefully thought of as such. Metaphysical functionalism takes the functionalist slogan that "mental states are functional states" to express a literal truth. Hilary Putnam, in his "The Nature of Mental States," is usually credited as the first functionalist, for advancing metaphysical functionalism as an empirical hypothesis (1975a [1967]).[5] Putnam characterized functional states in terms of probabilistic automata, a generalization of Alan Turing's finite state machines. He and others had for years thought of these computing devices as good models for human psychology. Indeed Turing himself had set forth a behavioral test for intelligence that he was sure such machines would be able to pass.[6] But it was Putnam who upgraded the idea from a metaphor or model and articulated it as an ontologically committed theory of the nature of mental states.

While the functionalist slogan that "mental states are functional states" can be used to express the thesis of metaphysical functionalism, it can also be used to express a variety of ontologically weaker claims. It is to these that we now turn.

Explanatory functionalism

Rather than taking the view that mental states are functional states to be an ontological thesis about the nature of psychological entities, one might take functionalism as an explanatory framework that allows us to remain neutral about the ontological status of psychological entities. This is one of the applications of explanatory functionalism.

I take it that explanatory functionalism is something like the view that a phenomenon *x* is best explained by reference to its function, or to the functioning of *x*'s constituents to enable its behavior. On this general formulation, every functionalist theory is a case of explanatory functionalism, where the variable *x* may be replaced by the ontology of mind, the intentionality of beliefs, and so on. Thus explanatory functionalism turns out to be the central kind from which all others can be formulated. There is something to this idea. But those who are realists about the phenomena in question – and functionalists have tended to be realists – will think that explanations of psychological ontology, intentional content, and so forth take the functional form precisely because those phenomena are essentially functional in themselves. So amenability to functional explanation does not constitute the truth of functionalisms, rather it is a sign of the common functional natures of their explananda.

For the purposes of the present taxonomy we are interested in a stronger form of explanatory functionalism, one that makes specific commitments about the explanatory structure of psychology. Classical behaviorism was the view that psychology is the science of behavior and psychological explanations should be stimulus-response explanations. Likewise, the explanatory versions of functionalism hold that psychological explanations should be functional explanations – explanations in terms of inputs, outputs, and relations among internal states. This means that one has not completed a psychological explanation merely by describing a lawful or lawlike regularity between inputs and outputs; in addition, psychological explanation requires a characterization of the mechanism that produces the outputs (and changes in other internal states) in response to the inputs. This kind of explanatory activity is what Robert Cummins (1975) calls "functional analysis" and Daniel Dennett (1981) calls "homuncular decomposition." A functional explanation succeeds in explaining how a system operates by showing how its component parts contribute to the operation (behavior) of the total system through their interactions with one another and with inputs and outputs. The best known account of functional explanation in psychology is due to David Marr, who describes how layers of functional explanation interact in a theory of human vision (1982).

The advantage of functional explanation is that it can proceed independently of most knowledge of the internal structure, if any, of the functional components. This independence is possible because the explanation appeals only to the relations of those components with one another and the inputs and outputs of the containing system. As a consequence, it is widely held, functional explanations capture regularities that are either invisible or practically intractable to explanations in terms of components' structures or substantial composition. To take a simple example, one can explain the operation of a vending machine by appeal to how the system responds to various inputs, e.g., coins, to produce certain outputs, e.g., bottles (e.g., Block 1980). The functional explanation will look very much like a program or decision procedure. And it depends only on the functional relations among the states of the machine and not on the particular physical processes in which the system is implemented. Explaining the vending behavior in terms of the laws of physics would be difficult or impossible, but it is an easy task for functional explanation (Dennett 1971; Putnam 1975b).

The net result is that functional explanations are often thought to be *autonomous* from the explanations of, say, physics. A functional explanation may be compatible with any of a variety of physical explanations of an explanandum, but its value does not await delivery of the physics explanation or depend on the explanatory terms or entities having any special relation to one another. The view that functional explanations are autonomous stands in contrast with classical reduction, according to which the "higher level" explanatory terms are required to be coextensive with those of the "lower level" explanation, so that the natural kinds of the higher level explanation are also natural kinds of the lower level explanation. Jerry Fodor (1974) and Philip Kitcher (1982) persuaded many philosophers that scientific and explanatory legitimacy does not require coextension of predicates. So if psychological explanations are functional explanations, that seems to show how they can eschew such constraints. Psychology, then, is vindicated as a science in its own right.

Theoretical functionalism

If psychological explanations are functional explanations, and if theories are sets of explanations, then there is a simple way in which psychological theory would turn out to be a functional theory: it would be constituted by functional explanations. This would be an interesting and important result. It is by no means obvious that actual scientific psychology is a functional theory of even this weak sort.

Yet there is a more demanding notion of functional theories that is widely applied in philosophy of psychology. This stronger idea of a functional theory begins with a psychological theory that is functional in the weak way, and then uses such a theory to define the theoretical terms of psychology (Lewis 1970, 1972). The resulting theory is a functional theory in that the theoretical terms of the science can be wholly defined by the role that they play in the total theory. Suppose, for example, that our psychological explanations include the following sorts of claims: For all creatures of kind *K*, when they are exposed to acute skin damage or . . ., etc., they experience pain, which causes them to form a belief that the stimulus is harmful and causes them to attempt to withdraw the affected area from the stimulus or remove the stimulus or . . ., etc. Of course there would be many such explanatory schemas or laws regarding pain, regarding memory, regarding belief, and so forth. The proposal of the theoretical functionalist is that we can conjoin the explanatory regularities of a completed psychology together and use them to define the meanings of its theoretical terms. So we can say the meaning of the term *pain* is "the state such that, for all creatures of kind *K*, when they are exposed to acute skin damage or . . ., etc., they experience pain, which causes them to form a belief that the stimulus is harmful and causes them to attempt to withdraw the affected area from the stimulus or remove the stimulus or . . ., etc."[7]

One might adopt theoretical functionalism but still hold that the functional theory does not explain the real natures of psychological states because it describes only their relational properties and none of their intrinsic properties. A substance dualist could think that theoretical functionalism is the right semantic account for the theoretical terms of psychology. But it will at least be tempting to hold that a term-defining functionalist theory implicitly says everything that there is to say about the entities to which the theoretical terms of psychology apply. After all, it will be a definitional or analytic truth that pain is the state such that, for all creatures of kind *K*, when they are exposed to acute skin damage or . . ., etc., they experience pain. And likewise that the pain causes creatures of kind *K* to form a belief that the stimulus is harmful and causes them to attempt to withdraw the affected area from the stimulus or remove the stimulus or . . ., etc. So while theoretical functionalism does not strictly entail metaphysical functionalism, it provides one natural route to the metaphysical view.

Intentional functionalism

Thus far I have focused on functionalism as an account of what it is to be a psychological state, and as an account of psychological explanation and the content and structure of psychological theories. But two important varieties of functionalism offer accounts of the contents of psychological states themselves. The first, which I call *intentional functionalism*, is the view that what makes some states into intentional states – states that have content, aboutness – is their functional role. I gave an example of this view earlier: One might think that beliefs have a distinctive role in modulating behavior, perhaps to be understood in terms of the characteristic ways that beliefs are caused by sensory stimulation and (when interacting with appropriate desires) result in characteristic actions. On this view, what makes some state an intentional state at all, and moreover the kind of intentional state that it is (a belief in the above example) is that it plays the belief-role: as Fodor explains the idea,

> to hold that to believe it's raining is to have a token of 'it's raining' play a certain functional role in the causation of your behavior and of your (other) mental states, said role eventually to be specified in the course of the detailed working out of empirical psychology . . ., etc., etc. This is, perhaps not much of story, but it's fashionable, I know of nothing better, and it does have the virtue of explaining why propositional attitudes are opaque.
>
> (Fodor 1978, in Block 1980: 53–4)

The difference, then, between distinct kinds of intentional states, e.g., beliefs and desires, will be a difference in their characteristic roles. Likewise, what distinguishes beliefs from non-intentional states that mediate stimuli and behaviors will be explained in terms of their distinctive role. States of the spinal nerves that mediate reflexive withdrawal from painful stimuli may be distinguished from beliefs by their functional role – for example, their general failure to interact with other beliefs and with desires, etc.

Of course, if one holds that what it is to be an intentional state is a matter of functional role and additionally holds Brentano's thesis that intentionality is the mark of the mental, then it follows that what it is to be a mental state is itself a matter of functional role. Thus intentional functionalism and Brentano's thesis entail metaphysical functionalism about psychological states.

Semantic functionalism

The second variety of functionalism about content is semantic functionalism. Semantic functionalism is the view that the particular content of a mental state is constituted by its functional role. I distinguish intentional functionalism from semantic functionalism. The first is a view about what makes some bits of the world into content bearing states at all, and of which kinds. The second is a view about what gives such intentional states their particular content. In the example I used earlier, semantic functionalism is illustrated by the idea that what makes my beliefs about sunny days distinct from my beliefs about coffee is that the different beliefs play different roles – one group typically mediates my interactions with weather, and the other with beverages.

It is attractive to think that the intentional and semantic questions can be answered at the same time, and even by the same relations: perhaps what makes something a belief about trees is that it plays the belief role relative to stimulation from and behavior toward trees, as well as relative to beliefs about leaves and bark and desires about shade and apples. And, indeed, some philosophers espouse both functionalism about intentionality and functionalism as a theory of psychosemantics, that is, of the semantic content of psychological states.

But it is also possible, and indeed common, to hold only one of the two functionalist theories. For example, one could have the idea that what gives a belief its specific content is the role that belief plays in a network of other mental states without paying any attention to the question of what makes something a belief in general. This would be an ordinary version of functional role semantics for mental states (cf. Van Gulick 1980). And, on the other hand, some prominent theorists who are functionalists about intentionality, e.g., William Lycan (1987) and Jerry Fodor (1986), reject functionalism and general accounts of psychosemantics. So whereas it is possible to hold both intentional and semantic functionalisms together, it is certainly not mandatory.[8]

Methodological functionalism

Like explanatory functionalism, methodological functionalism has generic and robust instances. Any method of studying a system by observing and characterizing its inputs and outputs will be functionalist in the generic sense. It is this generic usage that sometimes tempts philosophical supporters of functionalism to think it is ubiquitous and critics to think it is trivial. A method of psychological inquiry or analysis is robustly functional if it treats its objects as functional in one of the ways discussed above. Two such methods are common. The first is the method of functional analysis or decomposition, mentioned with respect to explanatory functionalism, in the subsection on explanatory functionalism, above. The second is the method of functionally defining theoretical terms, mentioned with respect to theoretical functionalism, in the subsection on theoretical functionalism, above.

Any activity that results in functional explanations is ipso facto a functionalist methodology in a way. This makes functionalist methods abundant. But this is also a very minimal claim. It amounts to little more than saying that functionalist methods are those that study how things function. Psychology is obviously functional in this sense – regardless of whether it is behaviorist, cognitive, or biological psychology we have in mind. But the claim is correspondingly weak and uninteresting. The more pressing questions concern whether psychology is functionalist in some more robust way. In particular, philosophers have been interested in whether psychology is metaphysically, intentionally, or semantically functionalist, and in whether the theoretical terms of psychology are susceptible to definition in the way hypothesized by theoretical functionalism.

But we must be cautious in evaluating the candidates. Take for example the methods of functional neuroimaging, including functional magnetic resonance imaging (fMRI). Such techniques have rightly received much attention of late. But is functional MRI a method that treats its object of study as essentially functional in nature? This is much less clear. Imaging studies try to give us a picture – literally and theoretically – of what is going on in subjects' brains when they perform various activities, e.g., remembering words, viewing visual stimuli, listening to auditory cues, etc. But none of this makes any assumption that the brain processes observed and the mental processes are essentially functional. While fMRI and similar techniques certainly study brains while they are functioning – in action, as it were – there is nothing intrinsic to the techniques or the resulting theories that requires a commitment to any distinctively functionalist thesis. Of course some theorists may propose functionalist hypotheses about neural and psychological functions, but that is another matter.

Functionalism, function, and realization

Thus far I have neglected two crucial questions about functionalism: What is a function? And what does it take to realize a function or play a functional role?

The most common notion of function employed in philosophy of mind is a causal notion of function. The function of a thing is characterized by its causes and effects, by what it does or is apt to do. It follows that to realize that sort of function or have that kind of functional role is to be a thing that has those characteristic causes and effects (e.g., Kim 1998; Shoemaker 2001, 2003; Melnyk 2003; Gillett 2002, 2003). My earlier examples of hearts and doorstops implicitly appealed to this idea: Hearts are things that pump blood; doorstops are things that hold open doors. I also employed this idea when I discussed the varieties of psychological function; for example I talked about beliefs mediating causal interactions with the world in characteristic ways, ways that differ from those in which desires mediate behavior.

But there are also other notions of function that have been employed in functionalist theories of psychology. Early proposals seem to have had in mind some kinds of abstract functional relations from mathematics, from semantics, or from information theory. If the salient functional relations are abstract like the relations among numbers, then realizing those in a physical system is usually held to be a matter of having physical states that are isomorphic to or map onto the abstract relations (Van Gulick 1988; Cummins 1989). And recently some philosophers have appealed to teleological and etiological notions of function drawn from evolutionary biology (Millikan 1984; Lycan 1987). According to these views, the function of a thing is (roughly speaking) the effect that its ancestors had for which they were naturally selected. For example, contrary to what was suggested earlier, it might be that being a heart requires neither actually pumping blood nor being apt to do so. Instead, being a heart requires being a thing of a kind that conferred an evolutionary benefit to its ancestral bearers because things of that kind in fact pumped blood in them. It follows that to realize this sort of function requires having a certain evolutionary history, rather than having some causal powers or standing in any mapping relation. One has to have had the right ancestors, and so forth.

There are no doubt other notions of function that could be explored, and hybrid variations as well (e.g., Lycan 1987; Dretske 1995). And there is no reason that any notion of function could not be tried in any variety of functionalism. Likewise there is no reason to suppose that functionalism is an all-or-nothing affair. One might be a functionalist about mental content but not about psychological ontology. One might apply the etiological account of function to psychosemantics and the causal account to one's psychological explanations.

As I've characterized functionalism, it may be formulated in terms of various kinds of functions, each of which carries its own conditions for realization. So realization is a matter of having a function of some sort (Polger 2004, 2007). But mine is not the only approach to understanding the realization relation; and its articulation is at least as controversial as that of functionalism (see, e.g., Poland 1994; Kim 1998, 2005; Wilson 2001; Shoemaker 2001, 2003; Gillett 2002, 2003; and Melnyk 2003).

Assessing the merits and demerits of all the varieties of functionalism is another matter; at present we are only concerned with identifying the variants. It seems obvious to me that an adequate account of functionalism ought to leave room for all of these variations, and that an adequate account of realization ought not to assume that only one kind of function can be realized. But I have already noted that my equanimity is controversial.

From metaphor to theory: arguments for functionalism

The slogan that psychological states are functional states is, on one reading, obvious. Psychological states are states that have functions in thinking. Psychological states are states that mediate between inputs and outputs of a system, and among other internal states of the system some of which may also be psychological states. This is just to say that psychological states do various things; but that observation is not very informative. It is certainly not a philosophical theory about psychology, psychological states, or their contents.

Even the somewhat more substantial thesis that psychological states are computational states leaves too many important details unspecified. It has been widely noted that on at least some conceptions of computation, every state of every object can be treated as a computational state (Putnam 1988; Searle 1990). Even if that conclusion does not follow from every account of computation, it at least shows that the computational functionalist owes us an explanation of his or her idea of computational states before we know what to make of the claim that psychological states are states of that sort.

But the deeper problem is that the mere claim that psychological states are functional states has a simple predicative use, saying of psychological states that they have a certain property, namely, a certain function. This account falls short of the claim that the property in question – being a functional state, as of a computing machine – is essential or even important to or explanatory of the state's being psychological, intentional, semantic, and so on.

A full blown functionalist theory goes beyond noticing certain commonalities between psychological states and functional states; it offers, as an explanation of those commonalities, the suggestion that mentality (or intentionality, or psychological explanation, etc.) is essentially functional in something like the ways discussed in the second section, on varieties of functionalism. There are many reasons for making the upgrade from the functional view of the mind as a metaphor to a fully formed functionalist theory of mind. I will focus on the three that have been most influential.

Probably the most well-known reason to adopt a functionalist theory is given by the *multiple realization* argument originated by Putnam (1975a [1967]). He argues that the best explanation for the prevalence of psychological states in nature given the heterogeneity of psychological systems is that mental states are internal states of creatures (contra behaviorism) but that they should be identified with functional states of whole organisms, rather than relatively local states of brains (contra the mind-brain type identity theory). This proposal accounts for the apparent fact that the same psychological state, e.g., pain, can be had by creatures that are quite different anatomically and neurologically, e.g., human beings, dogs, and octopi. That is, the fact that psychological states are realized by multiple physically diverse systems. Although the fact of multiple realization does not entail the truth of functionalism, it is highly suggestive. For it is widely thought that if the multiple realizability argument succeeds, then the identity theory is false. With the decline of behaviorism in psychology and philosophical psychology, the identity theory and functionalism are the main standing alternatives for a theory of the nature of metaphysics of psychological states and processes. So most philosophers regard Putnam's argument as more or less decisive against the type identity theory. In this context the multiple realizability argument can be treated as the most widely accepted argument for functionalism.

The second prominent argument in favor of functionalism in psychology is the autonomy argument articulated by Putnam (1975b) and Jerry Fodor (1974). According to Putnam and Fodor, the so-called special sciences (namely, the sciences other than physics and maybe chemistry) typically get their explanatory power by characterizing regularities with a kind of generality that abstracts away from the physical details of systems. Psychology is a paradigm special science in this sense. Take any example of folk psychological explanation in terms of belief and desire or of scientific psychological explanation in terms of information and representation. Belief, desire, information, and representation are all characterized in ways that do not even mention the physical properties of the systems that bear them.[9] (Because they are "topic neutral" the objects of these characterizations are also open to multiple realization, a connection not lost on Putnam and Fodor.) This seems to show that psychology should go about its business without much need to know about neurophysiology or whatever other "hardware" the psychological systems are implemented in. Psychology is thus vindicated as an autonomous and independent science.

But the autonomy of psychology is only one side of the coin. The other side is that since cognitive psychologists were already operating more or less independently of neuroscientists and because they were already inspired by computational models and metaphors, functionalism seems to provide the best description of the actual practices of psychologists. Work by Miller (1956), Chomsky (1965), and Shepard and Metzler (1971) were early influences; but the epitome of this apparent convergence is Marr's computational theory of vision (1982). The resemblance is clear enough in the cases of explanatory and methodological functionalism, and at least suggestive in the case of metaphysical functionalism. Thus the convergence of philosophical functionalism with the methods and practices of scientific psychology constitutes a third line of reasoning in support of the conclusion that functionalism is the correct philosophical theory of the mind. So to a philosopher of science it may seem obvious that both prescriptive and descriptive considerations support some form of functionalism about psychological states and psychological science.

Consciousness, causal power, and constraints: arguments against functionalism

Functionalism, however, is not without its critics. The best known family of objections center around the apparent failure of conscious experiences and sensations to yield to functional analysis or definition (e.g., Block 1978; Levine 1983). It seems as though two systems could be functionally identical (in whatever sense of function one chooses) and yet differ with respect to their states of consciousness. Most famously, we seem to be able to imagine creatures who are functionally indistinguishable from us but whose conscious states are inverted with respect to our own (e.g., Shoemaker 1982; Block 1990), or who lack consciousness altogether (Kirk 1974; Chalmers 1996; Polger 2000). If such scenarios can be sustained, then functionalism is not the correct theory of psychology in general, for there are at least some psychological differences – namely, differences in conscious experience – that are not accounted for by functional differences.

A second important class of objections to functionalism raises problems about the causal efficacy of functional states. The puzzle can be put intuitively using the example of the rock that realizes a doorstop. The rock is an object with a certain size, mass, and so forth. Presumably these physical qualities determine (or are determined by) the causal powers of the rock. Its having these powers is what makes it suitable to be a doorstop. But of course it has those powers whether or not it is playing the role of a doorstop; so the functional property of being a doorstop doesn't add any new causal powers to the rock. The functional property of being a doorstop seems to be epiphenomenal. We might try saying that the powers of the doorstop are simply the same as those of the rock; but then we would have two objects (a rock and a doorstop) with the same causal powers. So the powers of the thing qua doorstop are either none at all or else simply redundant of those of the rock.[10] Jaegwon Kim, in particular, has pressed this "causal exclusion" problem (1993, 1998, 2005).

Finally, recent critics of functionalism have focused directly on the alleged multiple realization of psychological states. If psychological states are multiply realized, then this is good news for functionalism. But if functionalists overestimate the degree of multiple realization, the theory will turn out to be overly liberal – assigning mental states to too many systems. For example, William Bechtel and Jennifer Mundale have argued that the practices of neuroscientists presuppose that psychological states are not multiply realized (1999), and Lawrence Shapiro has argued that the hypothesis that there are substantial physiological constraints on psychological states is biologically more probable given the evidence we have thus far (2000, 2004).[11]

So despite being the most widely held cluster of theories in philosophy of psychology, there are some serious challenges that the advocates of functionalism must face. This is hardly the curtain call for functionalism, however. After all, the competing theories all face hard questions as well. It should be no surprise that theories in psychology and philosophical psychology will not generally stand or fall based on philosophical arguments alone. Since functionalism is such a theory, we should expect that its evaluation will be a long-term and multidisciplinary project.

Functionalism, reduction, and the autonomy of psychology

Functionalism – as noted in the fourth section, "From metaphor to theory" – is widely thought to be the doctrine about psychological entities that is best able to vindicate psychology as the science of the mind. But this apparent consensus masks a deep divide over exactly how the result is achieved.

On one hand, some philosophers worry that the legitimacy of psychology requires bringing its entities and methods into the general framework of empirical sciences. In particular, they think that it needs to be shown that mental entities and processes are ultimately physical in nature, rather than being distinctively psychical and *sui generis*. For these philosophers, functionalism succeeds because it allows us to explain how physical states and processes can realize or implement psychological states and processes (Putnam 1975a [1967]; Kim 1998). Thus psychological states are in one way "nothing over and above" physical states, and psychological entities may be (in an important sense of the term) "reduced" to physical entities.

On the other hand, some philosophers worry that the legitimacy of psychology is threatened not only by the possibility that psychological states are essentially nonphysical, but also by the possibility – touted in the previous paragraph – that psychological states are nothing more than physical states. For they fear that if psychological states are "nothing over and above" physical states then one might do away with psychology altogether and simply go about the study of the physical realizers.[12] To these philosophers, the success of functionalism is that it shows how mental states can be in some sense physical states, namely, physically realized states, while also showing that they are not identical with and thus not "reducible" to merely physical states (e.g., Fodor [1974] and Kitcher [1982]). On this view, psychology is an independent and irreducible science, and the entities that it studies are ontologically real and explanatorily legitimate in their own right.

The lesson is that functionalism has an uneasy relationship with ontological and explanatory reductionism and the complementary autonomy or independence theses. The very consequences that some advocates tout are those that other advocates try to mitigate. While some theorists have questioned whether the connection between functionalism, reduction and autonomy runs as deep as the above sketches suppose (Richardson 1979; Polger 2004), there is no doubt that one of the main attractions of functionalism continues to be its promise to strike a balance between the reduction and autonomy of psychology.

Conclusion

I do not claim that my way of thinking about functionalism is the only one, but I've tried to provide one useful way of categorizing its varieties. Even more briefly, I've sketched a few of the most common lines of reasoning for and against functionalism. The sheer number of its varieties assures that there will be continued interest in the project of evaluating functionalism. I've also tried to point out some questions about functionalism that are yet to receive satisfactory answers. For example, recent attention to the central notions of realization and multiple realization show how much work remains to be done in even articulating a full theory, much less evaluating its application. And these issues appear to have consequences for metaphysics, explanation, and special sciences generally, not only psychology.

Notes

1. Space limitations prevent us from taking up herein the interesting question of the origins and history of functionalism. For some preliminary thoughts on the matter, see my 2004.
2. Lewis himself called this an "identity theory" early on (1966, 1972), and later asserted that it was a reductionist theory while deferring the question as to whether it is a functionalist theory (1994).
3. On the range of problems in philosophy of mind, see Paul Churchland (1988), from whom I adapt this list. The discussion in what follows relies heavily on the development of this taxonomy in chapter 3 of my 2004, where the characterization of each variety is developed more thoroughly.
4. The "liberal" versus "chauvinistic" distinction comes from Block (1978). Obviously the simplified representation of both identity theories and behaviorist theories is a caricature, but it is a useful one for seeing the general motivation behind functionalism.
5. There is an interesting question about whether various earlier philosophers – from Aristotle to Sellars – held a view that we would call functionalist. But Putnam appears to be the first to explicitly advocate the view, and he is the one who gave it its name and distinctive formulation in terms of computing machines.
6. Turing (1950) expected the machines to pass this test by the year 2000. To date, no machine has come close to satisfying the requirements of a generalized "Turing Test." Turing appears to have underestimated the technical challenges no less than the philosophical.
7. Some philosophers believe that every term that does not pick out a logical relation or a basic element of our ontology (the ontology of physics, if we are physicalists) must be defined in this way (Lewis 1994; Chalmers 1996; Jackson 1998).
8. Here I leave the functionalist theory of the semantics of words aside, but for the discussion of functional accounts of theoretical terms, above. But functionalism about linguistic meaning is clearly closely related to functionalism as a view of psychosemantics. Both the psychological and linguistic versions are influenced by Wittgenstein's doctrine of meaning as use (1953).
9. Not coincidentally, they all are characterized intentionally (see, e.g., Dennett 1971).
10. The problem only gets worse when we consider abstract or etiological notions of function, rather than the causal notion appealed to in this example.
11. For a general discussion of the state of play, see Polger (2000 [expanded in 2004]) and Bickle (2006).
12. And this fear is not mere paranoia, for the tactic has been endorsed by various philosophers (P. M. Churchland [1982], P. S. Churchland [1983], Bickle [1996, 1998]).

References

Bechtel, W., and Mundale, J. (1999) "Multiple Realizability Revisited: Linking Cognitive and Neural States," *Philosophy of Science* 66: 175–207.

Bickle, J. (1996) "New Wave Psychophysical Reductionism and the Methodological Caveats," *Philosophy and Phenomenological Research* 56, no. 1: 57–78.

—— (1998) *Psychoneural Reduction: The New Wave*, Cambridge, MA: MIT Press.

—— (2006) "Multiple Realizability," in Edward N. Zalta (ed.), *The Stanford Encyclopedia of Philosophy* (Fall 2006 edn); available: http://plato.stanford.edu/archives/fall2006/entries/multiple-realizability/

Block, N. (1978) "Troubles with Functionalism," in W. Savage (ed.), *Perception and Cognition*, Minnesota Studies in Philosophy of Science, vol. 9, Minneapolis: University of Minnesota Press, pp. 261–325; repr. Block (1980).

—— (ed.) (1980) *Readings in Philosophy of Psychology*, vol. 1, Cambridge, MA: Harvard University Press.

—— (1990) "Inverted Earth," in James Tomberlin (ed.), *Philosophical Perspectives*, vol. 4: *Action Theory and Philosophy of Mind*, Atascadero, CA: Ridgeview, pp. 53–79.

Chalmers, D. (1996) *The Conscious Mind: In Search of a Fundamental Theory*, New York: Oxford University Press.

Chomsky, N. (1965) *Aspects of the Theory of Syntax*, Cambridge, MA: MIT Press.

Churchland, P. M. (1982) "Is 'Thinker' a Natural Kind?" *Dialogue* 21, no. 2: 223–38.

—— (1988) *Matter and Consciousness*, rev. edn, Cambridge, MA: MIT Press.

Churchland, P. S. (1983) "Consciousness: The Transmutation of a Concept," *Pacific Philosophical Quarterly* 64: 80–93.

Cummins, R. (1975) "Functional Analysis," *Journal of Philosophy* 72, no. 20: 741–65.

—— (1989) *Meaning and Mental Representation*, Cambridge, MA: MIT Press.

Dennett, D. (1971) "Intentional Systems," *Journal of Philosophy* 68: 87–106.

—— (1981) *Brainstorms*, Cambridge, MA: Bradford Books-MIT Press.

Dretske, F. (1995) *Naturalizing the Mind*, Cambridge, MA: MIT Press.

Fodor, J. (1974) "Special Sciences, or the Disunity of Science as a Working Hypothesis," *Synthese* 28: 97–115.

—— (1986) "Banish DisContent," in J. Butterfield (ed.), *Language, Mind, and Logic*, New York: Cambridge University Press.

Gillett, C. (2002) "The Dimensions of Realization: A Critique of the Standard View," *Analysis* 64, no. 4: 316–23.

—— (2003) "The Metaphysics of Realization, Multiple Realizability, and the Special Sciences," *Journal of Philosophy* 100, no. 11: 591-603.

Guttenplan, S. (ed.) (1994) *A Companion to the Philosophy of Mind*, Oxford: Blackwell.

Jackson, F. (1998) *From Metaphysics to Ethics: A Defense of Conceptual Analysis*, Oxford: Oxford University Press.

Kim, J. (1993) *Supervenience and Mind*, New York: Cambridge University Press.

—— (1998) *Mind in a Physical World: An Essay on the Mind-Body Problem and Mental Causation*, Cambridge, MA: MIT Press.

—— (2005) *Physicalism, or Something near Enough*, Princeton, NJ: Princeton University Press.

Kirk, R. (1974) "Zombies v. Materialists," *Proceedings of the Aristotelian Society* 48: 135–52.

Kitcher, P. (1982) "1953 and All That: A Tale of Two Sciences," *Philosophical Review* 93: 335–73.

Levine, J. (1983) "Materialism and Qualia: The Explanatory Gap," *Pacific Philosophical Quarterly* 64: 354–61.

Lewis, D. (1966) "An Argument for the Identity Theory," *Journal of Philosophy* 63: 17–25.

—— (1970) "How to Define Theoretical Terms," *Journal of Philosophy* 68: 203–11; repr. Lewis (1983).

—— (1972) "Psychophysical and Theoretical Identifications," *Australasian Journal of Philosophy* 50: 249–58; repr. Lewis (1999).

—— (1983) *Philosophical Papers*, vol. 1, New York: Oxford University Press.

—— (1994) "Lewis, David: Reduction of Mind," in Guttenplan (1994): 412–21.

—— (1999) *Papers in Metaphysics and Epistemology*, New York: Cambridge University Press.

Lycan, W. (1987) *Consciousness*, Cambridge, MA: MIT Press.

Marcel, T., and Bisiach, E. (1988) *Consciousness in Contemporary Science*, New York: Oxford University Press.
Marr, D. (1982) *Vision: A Computational Investigation into the Human Representation and Processing of Visual Information*, San Francisco: W. H. Freeman.
Melnyk, A. (2003) *A Physicalist Manifesto: Thoroughly Modern Materialism*, Cambridge: Cambridge University Press.
Miller, G. (1956) "The Magical Number Seven, Plus or Minus Two: Some Limits on Our Capacity for Processing Information," *Psychological Review* 63: 81–97.
Millikan, R. (1984) *Language, Thought, and Other Biological Categories*, Cambridge, MA: MIT Press.
Poland, J. (1994) *Physicalism: The Philosophical Foundations*, New York: Oxford University Press.
Polger, T. (2000) "Zombies Explained," in D. Ross, A. Brook, and D. Thompson (eds) *Dennett's Philosophy: A Comprehensive Assessment*, Cambridge, MA: MIT Press.
—— (2004) *Natural Minds*, Cambridge, MA: MIT Press.
—— (2007) "Realization and the Metaphysics of Mind," *Australasian Journal of Philosophy*, vol. 85(2): 233–59.
Putnam, H. (1975a [1967]) "The Nature of Mental States," in *Mind, Language and Reality: Philosophical Papers*, vol. 2, New York: Cambridge University Press, pp. 429–40.
—— 1975b. "Philosophy and Our Mental Life," in *Mind, Language and Reality: Philosophical Papers*, vol. 2, New York: Cambridge University Press, pp. 291–303.
—— 1988. *Representation and Reality*, Cambridge, MA: MIT Press.
Richardson, R. (1979) "Functionalism and Reductionism," *Philosophy of Science* 46: 533–58.
Searle, J. (1990) "Is the Brain a Digital Computer?" *Proceedings and Addresses of the American Philosophical Association* 64: 21–37.
Shapiro, L. (2000) "Multiple Realizations," *Journal of Philosophy* 97: 635–54.
—— (2004) *The Mind Incarnate*, Cambridge, MA: MIT Press.
Shepard, R., and Metzler, J. (1971) "Mental Rotation of Three Dimensional Objects," *Science* 171, no. 972: 701-3.
Shoemaker, S. (1982) "The Inverted Spectrum," *Journal of Philosophy* 79, no. 7: 357–81.
—— (2001) "Realization and Mental Causation," in C. Gillett and B. Loewer (eds), *Physicalism and Its Discontents*, Cambridge: Cambridge University Press.
—— (2003) "Realization, Micro-Realization, and Coincidence," *Philosophy and Phenomenological Research* 67, no. 1: 1–23.
Turing, A. M. (1950) "Computing Machinery and Intelligence," *Mind*, 59: 433–60.
Van Gulick, R. (1980) "Functionalism, Information, and Content," *Nature and System* 2: 139–62.
—— (1988) "Consciousness, Intrinsic Intentionality, and Self-Understanding Machines," in Marcel and Bisiach (1988): 78–100.
Wilson, R. (2001) "Two Views of Realization," *Philosophical Studies* 104: 1–30.
Wittgenstein, L. (1953) *Philosophical Investigations*, trans. G. E. M. Anscombe, Oxford: Basil Blackwell.

Further reading

For further reading, see R. Cummins, *The Nature of Psychological Explanation* (Cambridge, MA: MIT Press, 1983); F. Jackson, "Epiphenomenal Qualia," *Philosophical Quarterly* 32, no. 127 (1982): 127–36; J. Kim, *Philosophy of Mind* (Boulder, CO: Westview, 1966); B. Loar, *Mind and Meaning* (New York: Cambridge University Press, 1981); H. Putnam, *Mind, Language and Reality: Philosophical Papers*, vol. 2 (New York: Cambridge University Press, 1975); G. Rey, *Contemporary Philosophy of Mind* (Boston: Blackwell, 1997); S. Shoemaker, "Some Varieties of Functionalism," *Philosophical Topics* 12, no. 1 (1981): 83–118; and R. Van Gulick, "Functionalism as a Theory of Mind," *Philosophy Research Archives* 1 (1983): 185–204.

11
THE INTERFACE BETWEEN PSYCHOLOGY AND NEUROSCIENCE

Valerie Gray Hardcastle

What is the relationship between psychology and neuroscience? Of course, some areas of psychological inquiry – leadership studies, for example – are quite removed from investigations into how the brain works. And some arenas in neuroscience – studies of thermoregulation, for example – have little connection with the human mind and its functions. But, there are subfields in both psychology and neuroscience that would appear to overlap exactly – studies of memory, imagery, emotion, perception, mental representation, to name a few. Interestingly enough, for much of their history, investigations into these matters proceed almost completely independently in psychology and neuroscience. We can point to the rise of the interdisciplinary field of cognitive science and the development of better brain imaging techniques as the two main reasons why psychologists and neuroscientists are now working much more closely with each other in trying to understand the human mind. Because psychology and neuroscience operated apart for so long, it should not be surprising that their theories do not always mesh neatly with one another to form one larger and more complete description of the mind or brain. Hence, the question: what is their connection to one another (and what should it be)?

As cognitive science appeared to be forming into a genuine discipline, philosophers typically answered that question in one of three ways. Neuroscience will either displace psychology entirely and psychology as we know it will disappear in favor of brain studies. This possibility is known as *eliminativism*. Or, neuroscientific and psychological theories will become more and more aligned with one another such that they merge into one thing. This possibility is a relative of eliminativism, but in this case, theories about psychological processes do not disappear, but instead, they are conjoined with neuroscientific theories. They "evolve toward a reductive consummation," as Patricia Churchland (1986: 374) describes it. Or, neuroscience and psychology will continue to operate largely independently of one another, with neuroscience merely describing how the brain implements well-defined psychological processes. This possibility is referred to as *psychological functionalism*.

I think it is safe to say that we now know that none of these possibilities are exactly correct and that the truth is much more complicated than any of them. But each of these possibilities contains some aspects that point to how psychology and neuroscience relate to one another today. My preferred way of talking about how psychology and neuroscience interact is in terms of *explanatory extension* (Hardcastle 1992), but there are many versions of this idea with different names. But before we can understand the complexities behind psychology and neuroscience's relationship, we need to understand what it means for one scientific theory to *reduce* another, for all these possibilities are really different answers to the question of whether psychology will be reduced by neuroscience.

Reduction in science

In 1961, Ernest Nagel formulated the notion of reduction that most philosophers rely on today. Nagel's idea is that if every name that one theory uses connects with another name in a different theory such that each object that the one theory names forms the same set of objects that the second theory names, then the more basic theory "reduces" the higher ordered theory. In our case, neuroscience would reduce psychology if all the things and processes that psychology picks out as important are the same things and processes that neuroscience identifies. Nagel said that if one theory reduces another, then we could create "bridge principles" between the two theories, laws that connect the things and processes in one theory with the things and processes in the other theory. And, once we have outlined all the bridge principles between the two theories, then there is nothing left over in either theory that remains unconnected. This means that, if we wanted to, we could logically derive the reduced theory from the bridge principles and the reducing theory.

In the 1960s and 1970s, philosophers argued that the point of reducing psychology to neuroscience is to explain psychological generalizations by showing that they are really the same generalizations of a more basic science, neuroscience. They presumed that by explicating the physical mechanisms underlying psychological events, they would thereby demonstrate that psychological generalizations are just special cases of neurological theories. It turns out that this version of reductionism is much too strong, however, for even cases of scientific reduction that everyone agrees has been successful cannot meet these conditions.

Consider electromagnetic theory reducing physical optics (for a more complete discussion, see Schaffner [1967]). We cannot, strictly speaking, deduce the laws of optics from Maxwell's equations once we specify the bridge principles for at least two reasons. First, Fresnel's laws of intensity ratios end up with an additional factor in them when derived from Maxwell's theory. In practice, this factor is negligible in most cases, but theoretically it is very important, for it tells us that the behavior of light in part depends upon the magnetic properties of the surrounding medium. Second, the perfectly legitimate concept of "black" in optics has no counterpart in electromagnetic theory, so it is impossible to formulate the nineteenth-century optical problem of calculating diffraction by a black screen in electromagnetism. Strict reduction fails here. At the same time, no one claims that this is not an example of some sort of reductionism or other.

The conclusion that some draw is that we can derive a theory closely resembling physical optics from Maxwell's theory, but not classically understood optics itself. That is, we have to "correct" the reduced theory to a new theory that is similar to the old one before we can derive it from the union of the reducing theory and the bridge principles. This new theory "corrects" the old one if the new one makes more accurate predictions than the old one.

The point to notice is that, even weakened, the notion of reduction still means that there is some lawlike correspondence between the entities of the reducing and the reduced theories, and that this correspondence helps explain why (some version of) the reduced theory is true. The reduction shows the corrected laws of optics to be special instances of the more general laws of electromagnetism and, in virtue of this demonstration, helps explain why Fresnel's laws of intensity ratios and Snell's laws of refraction give the results they do and why the problem of black screen diffraction is not a problem after all. So, if psychology is to reduce to neuroscience, then, for some version of most psychological names and processes, there must exist corresponding neuroscientific names and processes, and the generalizations that express this correspondence help explain why psychological generalizations are accurate.

However, this revised version of reductionism leaves many crucial questions unanswered, most obviously: How much may a new theory correct the old one before the new one stops being a version of the old one and becomes a different theory? This is the question behind eliminativism. If a new theory "corrects" an old one enough, then it is safe to say that we have simply eliminated the old theory in favor of the new one. If neuroscience eliminates psychology, then we will be choosing to use neuroscience's concepts instead of psychology's, for psychology's are simply too inaccurate to be correct.

On the other hand, if we continue to tweak psychological concepts so that we continue to create more and more bridge principles that connect psychology to neuroscience, then we are unifying the two theories as Churchland suggests we will. Psychology and neuroscience would simply meld into one another over time.

Elimination vs. unification

Eliminativists in psychology believe that our common-sense conception of mental events and processes, our "folk psychology," is false. In fact, it is so misguided that it will be replaced outright by a future neuroscience. Though most examples of folk psychology involve beliefs and desires, it actually contains an extensive collection of propositional attitudes in its explanatory toolkit: hopes, intentions, fears, imaginings, and so forth. As should be apparent, much of scientific psychology (and some of neuroscience) retains these explanatory tools as well. Proponents of eliminative materialism claim that they do so at their peril, for some future brain science will give the correct account of human behavior, and that future brain science will not rely on any of these things in its explanations.

Eliminativists hold that just as we now understand fire in terms of oxidation and not phlogiston and bizarre behavior in terms of mental illness and not demonic possession, so too someday will we understand the mind's interactions in terms of something else besides beliefs and desires. As previous scientists did with phlogiston and demons, current psychologists have done with the propositional attitudes: we did not carve Nature at her proverbial joints. And, just as phlogiston and demons were removed from our scientific vocabulary because they were radically false, so too shall the common-sense propositional attitudes be eliminated from explanations of behavior because they are completely wrong-headed.

To maintain this position, eliminativists must show two things. First, they have to show that folk psychology is indeed a failure as an explanatory theory. Second, they have to show that neuroscience might have something better to offer. Much has been written about the first point and I think it is safe to say that the jury is still out on how successful psychological theories actually are. Less has been said about point number two.

In fact, most of the arguments around what neuroscience can improve have focused on issues of representation (e.g., Churchland 1986; Jacobson 2003). Churchland, for example, argues that activity vectors comprise our brain's representations, and vector-to-vector transformations are the central kind of computation in the brain. This notion contrasts sharply with the assumptions of folk psychology: that our mind represents using propositions and thinks in virtue of logical or semantic computations over these propositions. The difference between the ideas of vector transformations and logical computations is as great as, if not greater than, that between the ideas of oxidation and phlogiston.

Of course, if the vectorial analysis of representation for the mind/brain is correct, then we will have to change our psychological concepts. Does it follow that psychology as we know it will be eliminated? It is possible that even if psychologists were grossly incorrect about how we represent the world to ourselves, there might be other parts of folk psychology that are right. Notions of reduction should allow for a range of possible connections between theories, ranging from relatively smooth through significantly revisionary to extremely radical (Hooker 1981; Savitt 1974). Might the reduction of folk psychology and a "vectorial" neurobiology occupy the middle ground between smooth and radical intertheoretic reductions and hence suggest more of a revisionary conclusion?

A revisionary connection would occur when bridge principles slowly relocate the posits of the reduced theory in the reducing theory. For example, our understanding of electromagnetic radiation gradually replaced our theory of light, our conception of light was dramatically transformed as we recognized ways in which are old conception was mistaken or incomplete. Nevertheless, at no point did we come to say that there is really no such thing as light. Rather, "light" became identified with a form of electromagnetic radiation. John Bickle (1998) argues that folk psychology appears to have gotten right the gross outlines of many of our cognitive states, especially those related to perception and behavior, among other things. He believes that, because of this, we will see significant conceptual change in our psychological concepts, but denies their total elimination. This slow change over time as psychology and neuroscience move closer and closer to one another is the option of reductive consummation.

Functionalism and multiple realizability

The third possibility for a proposed relationship between psychology and neuroscience is essentially peaceful coexistence. Neuroscience does not reduce psychology, nor does it eliminate it. Both psychology and neuroscience continue as separate fields, each working independently of the other. The clearest way to see why psychology and neuroscience might stay separate is via a discussion of functionalism and multiple realizability.

As discussed in "Computational Functionalism" (Polger, this volume), functionalists in psychology define mental states in terms of input to the system, the causal relationships that exist among the mental states, and the output those states generate. That is, my desire for ice cream shows itself by my ice-cream-getting behaviors. Others know that I have this desire by observing my behavior. A functionalist would claim that there really is nothing more to this desire than what it makes me do, think, and say.

Generally speaking, for functionalists, states that play the same (or similar enough) causal roles within or across systems are identical. Insofar as your ice-cream-gathering behaviors resemble mine, then we share the same desire for ice cream. Moreover, what is most important in functionally defined states is not the stuff out of which these systems are made – firing neurons and the like – but rather the internal relations among the states of those systems – what these states make the system do.

Arguments against reductionism and other sorts of lawlike connections between theories are very easy to generate if we adopt psychological functionalism. If we define mental states in terms of their causal relations, then we can generalize across mental states whose underlying physical descriptions might have nothing in common. You might have the same desire for ice cream, even though your brain might be configured very differently than mine. A number of different physical mechanisms might be the substrate for the same functionally defined interactions.

For real-life example, consider that both the owl and the cat have binocular vision. However, anatomically and evolutionarily distinct neural structures underlie the same ability in these two animals (Pettigrew and Konishi 1976). This tells us that we can have psychological descriptions of things that do not correspond to unique neurophysiological descriptions. That is, we would not be able to generate bridge principles from concepts in psychology to concepts in neuroscience. We would describe the neurophysiological underpinnings of owl stereopsis very differently than how we would describe it in cat vision. And this lack of correspondence prevents reduction between fields.

To push what functionalism entails even further, some argue that even if it were true that humans who have functionally identical mental states also have the same underlying neurological patterns, this would say nothing about the viability of reductionism. As Jerry Fodor points out, for functionalists, mental states are defined essentially in terms of their functional roles, so "*whether* the physical descriptions of the events subsumed by [psychological] generalizations have anything in common is, in an obvious sense, entirely irrelevant to the truth of the generalizations, or to their interestingness, or to their degree of confirmation, or, indeed, to any of their epistemologically important properties" (1983: 133). Functionalism inherently denies reduction between psychology and neuroscience in any important sense.

However, contrary to what the antireductionists often assume, there is no easy or obvious division of labor between psychology and neuroscience. A monolithic function/structure distinction, in which psychology investigates function and neuroscience worries only about underlying structure, simply does not exist. There are many points of investigation in neuroscience – membranes, cells, synapses, cell assemblies, circuits, networks, systems, and even behavior – and at each juncture, neuroscientists answer questions concerning capacity, the processing subserving the capacity, and the physical implementation of the processes.

In particular, we can find functional theories in lower level sciences. New levels of theory get inserted between those describing the structure of the lower level entities and those describing higher level functional entities, between the anatomy of individual neurons and the descriptors of cognitive psychology. Furthermore, there might be a common neurofunctional property for a given type of psychological object or event across a wide variety of distinct anatomical structures. In this way, reduction could be achieved despite vast multiple realizability at the neuronal level. The neurocomputational approaches discussed elsewhere in this book provide empirical examples for this suggestion.

Still, a relative function/structure distinction may be all the wedge antireductionists need to argue that explanations in psychology cannot reduce to explanations in neuroscience. If psychology sits at the top of this hierarchy of levels of investigation, then all of neuroscience may be structural relative to psychology's inquiries.

It is my contention that these antireductionist arguments rest on confusions about what reductionism really is, however. First, arguing from the idea that different psychical systems might underlie higher level objects or processes (an idea referred to in the philosophical literature as "multiple instantiability") to the impossibility of bridge principles depends upon a notion of reduction that even our best cases of reduction do not fulfill (Churchland 1987, 1986; Enc 1983; Richardson 1982). Quite often reduction is made specific to a domain, and domain-reduction is a normal part of science. Consider the classic example of the reduction of temperature to mean molecular kinetic energy. This reduction holds only for gases. Temperature in solids is something else, and temperature in plasma is something else again. "Piece-meal" reduction also seems intuitively correct. Suppose that scientists discovered that all psychological concepts could be mapped directly on to neuroscientific descriptions of human brains. Would we want to claim that a reduction had failed because there might be (or are) some creatures, like owls, that psychological principles would accurately describe, but for which we would have more than one neuroscientific description? I think not. It seems likely that we argue that human psychology maps directly to human neurology, that owl psychology maps on to owl neurology, and that we can point to several correlations between human and owl psychological feats.

Moreover, arguing from functional definitions to a denial of reduction misconstrues what reductionism is. Reducibility between scientific domains per se makes no claims about what either domain should do, e.g., that the reducing theory sets the definitional standards for the reduced domain. Rather, reduction merely sets out a relationship between the two domains (Richardson 1979). Just because electromagnetism reduces physical optics does not mean that optics as a field no longer exists, nor that how optics defines its terms is parasitic on electromagnetic theory. Similarly, if neuroscience ever reduces psychology, psychology could still functionally define its concepts. All that the reduction would add is a statement about the relationship between two sciences. Functionalism really cuts across the issue of reductionism.

Moreover, those who believe that multiple realizability is a reason that reduction will fail often rely on different amounts of "granularity" in picking out mental and neurobiological referents (Bechtel and Mundale 1999). Often philosophers of psychology are happy to analyze psychological states at a coarse-grained level, in which only the loosest input-output similarities across people are sufficient to call two mental states identical. We both have the same desire for ice cream, even though I buy a half-gallon of rocky road from my local grocery store and you purchase an ice cream cone from Ben and Jerry's™. We can claim that these two very different physical movements pick out the same desire only if we construe the movements very broadly and name both of them examples of ice-cream-gathering behavior. At the same time, these philosophers insist that brain states be individuated very finely, such that small differences across species, or even small differences within species, are enough to make the neural referents different.

But, as I am sure is no surprise, psychological explanations can use a finer grain, and neural explanations can use a coarser grain. A psychologist could say, for example, that my ice-cream-seeking behavior is more frantic today than it was yesterday (because my local grocery store was closed and I was unable to satiate my desire), noting that my own ice cream desire differs from day to day. A neuroscientist could say, for example, that behavioral planning activates prefrontal cortex, referring to a large set of neurons that can be identified across many species. It is unfair to require neuroscience only to use very fine grains, while permitting a very coarse grain for psychology. Once we align the grains across levels of analysis, it might be the case that reductive relations follow unproblematically.

But it gets more complicated than this. We know that neural systems differ significantly across species. But, as John Bickle (2003) points out, neuroscience does not stop at the systems level. As we move into the physiology of individual cells and then into the molecular biology of neurons, we find many identical structures and processes across species. Many of the molecular mechanisms behind neural transmission and plasticity are the same from invertebrates through mammals. Moreover, the principles of molecular evolution suggest that these commonalities should be rampant. Evolutionary changes to the amino-acid sequence of a given protein are much slower in functionally important domains than in functionally less important ones. And evolutionary changes in functionally constrained domains have almost inevitably been detrimental to the organism's survival and reproduction. These principles suggest that these molecules and their intracellular interactions should remain largely unchanged across existing biological species with a common ancestor. Obviously, psychological processes that influence behavior must fundamentally rely on the metabolic mechanisms in individual neurons, for that is just where the causal action is in the brain. But that is exactly the machinery that should be conserved across existing biological species. Bickle argues that as research into the molecular and cellular mechanisms underlying cognition proceeds, we should expect more examples of multi-species reductions of shared psychological processes.

Antireductionists believe that psychology is primary because psychology is more general, therefore, it explains more with its theories. Neuroscience, they believe, simply describes the neural underpinnings behind psychological generalizations. In this case, the best that can be said for the lower level theories is that their generalizations bring out more details. But, as Sober (1999) reminds us, science aims for both depth and breadth, so we cannot automatically conclude that one approach is superior to the other. Both reductionists and antireductionists often make the mistake of privileging one goal over the other.

Pragmatics in explanation

What seems to be behind the arguments from functionalism, however, is the idea that psychology cannot reduce to neuroscience because psychology and neuroscience worry about completely different types of questions. That is, even if bridge principles link psychology to neuroscience, neuroscience could not subsume explanation in psychology for pragmatic reasons (Fodor and Pylyshyn 1988; Pylyshyn 1980, 1984; Putnam 1983). Different levels of analysis in cognitive science attempt to answer fundamentally different sorts of why questions, each with its own contrast class and background context. Some questions revolve around the basic capacity of the system under investigation; other questions involve the processes subserving the capacities; and still others relate to the physical mechanisms that underlie the processes subserving the capacities (Marr 1982).

Suppose a pedestrian sees an automobile accident at a street corner. This pedestrian whips out her cell phone and pushes the button for nine and then for one. What will she do next? We can be fairly certain that she will push the button for one again. Why? We believe we know what she will do because of our background knowledge regarding cell phones, emergency calls, automobile accidents, and so forth. However, if we focus on the pedestrian's neurophysiology and resulting muscular contractions, we would not be able to draw this conclusion. That simply is the wrong level of investigation and analysis for our conclusion, for we have no good way to link neural sequences to larger social contexts (in today's neuroscience anyway). A neural explanation will miss everything that seems to be important in understanding this behavior.

This is an additional problem with the classic formulation of reduction – the notion of explanation it presupposes is much too weak. Explanations in science are more than just simple derivations from sets of theories and data. (One difficulty with this simple view of explanation is the problem of irrelevant factors [Salmon 1971]. For example, if we observe salt dissolving in water under a fluorescent light, we do not conclude that the fluorescent light caused the salt to dissolve, even though we could derive the fact that the salt would dissolve from the facts that salt was placed in water and it was placed under a fluorescent light. We would maintain that light is not a relevant factor in salt's dissolving. It turns out that we can derive explanations that appeal to all sorts of things that are actually irrelevant to the event; nonetheless, we know that explanations should pick out only the factors that are causally relevant in the event to be explained.)

There is no agreement about how to solve this and other problems in philosophical accounts of scientific explanation. There is however a rough consensus that we need a pragmatics of explanation (Hempel 1966; Kitcher 1988; Railton 1981; van Fraassen 1980), although whether pragmatics alone can solve the problem of irrelevant factors is doubtful (Kitcher and Salmon 1987). In any case, the following at least seems to be clear: Some explanations answer questions of the form "Why *F*?" that are short-hand for the question "Why *F* and not G, *H*, or *I*?" Investigators ask these elliptical questions against a background context of the relevant interested community. For example, a doctor might want to know why George died of a *heart attack* and not a *stroke*, while his wife wants to know why George *died* of a heart attack instead of *surviving* it. In each case, the interested parties could frame their question as, "Why did George die?," with the background context implicitly understood by their communities.

The essence of this conception of explanation is that explanations are three-way relations among theories, data, and context. Exactly how to specify the relations involved is beyond the scope of the chapter. All we need to know is that whether something is an explanation depends at least upon the speakers, the audience, and circumstances of the inquiry – explanations per se cannot be divorced from the particular community in which they arose.

Therefore, if neuroscience is going to reduce psychology, then there have to be neuroscientific equivalents to all relevant psychological statements. That is, if a scientific question is formulated and answered in psychological language, there have to be corresponding neurophysiological statements that express all the concepts involved, including those from the background context. To argue that psychology cannot be reduced by neuroscience, philosophers must show either that not all psychological names and predicates have neuroscientific equivalences or that, if there be such equivalences, then they cannot be used to reformulate psychological explanations. With these conceptual tools in hand, we turn once again to the question of whether psychology should reduce to neuroscience.

The difficulty, as I see it, is that linking terms in psychology to those in neuroscience would not thereby explain our psychological generalizations. For each functionally defined psychological term, there are two possible ways a bridge principle could link it to a neuroscientific one. Either there is some neurophysiological structure that is identical (or similar enough) across all instances of the psychological term, in which case neuroscience could define the psychological term as the structure itself; or there are no structural similarities, in which case the psychological term could be understood functionally in neuroscience, as discussed above.

Assume first that we get an easy link between a neurophysiological structure and a functionally-defined psychological term. Would this link now explain the psychological term? The answer has to be no. Why does the term refer as it does? Because this is a functional term, part of that answer depends upon how its referent is causally connected to other *psychologically defined* objects or processes. If we knew the structure underlying our cognitive terms down to the most minute detail, it still would not change our psychological explanation of some event, because knowing the structure would not change the relevance of the functional explanation to the query as determined by the background context of cognitive psychology. Outlining the structure would only bury the psychological explanation in a mass of irrelevant data. Why did I see the swinging knife as a threat? Knowing the neurophysiological structures that underlie my visual processing is not going to explain why I saw a threat. Knowing the social and cultural significance of a swinging knife, knowing how my beliefs about swinging knives are connected to my other beliefs, is.

Now let us suppose instead that we have functionally defined our psychological term in neuroscience by importing the necessary terms and predicates from psychology. Would the links between neuroscience and psychology now explain why I experience the swinging knife as I do? Again, the answer must be no. If the statements in neuroscience just are the statements in psychology, then the description of the experiential event must be the same in both fields. Furthermore, because the statements accepted by the two scientific communities concerning the psychological term are *ex hypothesis* the same, the background context for the term must also be the same. Hence, the explanation in neuroscience would be the same as well. The one-step derivation of the psychological from neuroscience would have nothing to add to the psychological explanation because the neuroscientific account would be exactly the same as the psychological.

We are seeing this situation all the time in neuroscience these days in brain imaging experiments. In many instances, cognitive neuroscience has simply imported psychological concepts wholesale into its conceptual framework. As a result, while an imaging study might tell us something about where in the brain a particular process is occurring, it does not say anything about the truth of the psychological claim purportedly under examination.

We have to conclude that traditional reductionistic approaches to understanding the relationship between psychology and neuroscience must fail. It is clear that the answer is more complicated than philosophers originally thought.

Explanatory extension

One type of solution to the failure of traditional reduction includes Schaffner's (1974) "inter-level" theories, which are theories that refer to entities on more than one level of abstraction or "aggregation" and which exhibit different organizing principles, and Mayr's (1982) "constitutive hierarchies," in which units at a lower level are combined into units at a higher level with different properties and functions. Both these ideas reflect Wimsatt's (1976) levels of organization and roughly parallel Bechtel's (1982,

1983) account of the relationship between psychology and neuroscience in which he argues that we should view ourselves as a single system composed of an assembly of processes. The composite processes can be decomposed into groups of different processes, each of which is specified differently. Psychological theories then would "describe the interactions of components whose operations are, in turn, studied by neuroscience" (Bechtel 1983: 325; see also Darden and Maull 1977; Maull 1977).

We find a different type of solution in Rosenberg's (1985) use of the relation of supervenience. However, this relation is agnostic about the different sorts of properties each level may have and so is a fairly minimalist account of the relationship among different domains of inquiry. A richer story, if possible, is preferable.

However, these suggestions gloss over the pragmatic aspects of explanation. Since what counts as an explanation depends upon the context of the scientific inquiry, we cannot simply assume that what one field examines could be related at all to the concerns of another discipline. On the contrary, our discussion suggests that at least aspects of neuroscience concern themselves with fundamentally different sorts of questions and answers than psychology.

We need a characterization that can remain faithful to the different sorts of why-questions, with the different sorts of explanations they entail, as well as to the many levels of investigation both within and across neuroscience and psychology. I offer the notion of explanatory extension as a good model for helping us to elucidate the relationship. Explanatory extension does not require that the fields involved share historical contexts or explanatory goals. Rather, explanatory extension rests on the idea that one field can "illuminate issues that were treated incompletely, if at all," in another (Kitcher 1984: 358).

Two ways in which an extending theory could illuminate an extended theory are by

(1) theoretically demonstrating the possibility of some antecedently problematic presupposition of the extended theory; or
(2) conceptually refining the extended theory by better specifying the objects that the concepts in the extended theory define, such that proponents of the extended theory change the ways in which the entities are specified by these concepts.

Let me give two examples of how explanatory extension works in psychology and neuroscience, both taken from studies in pain processing. The first example illustrates condition (1), that an extending theory theoretically demonstrates the possibility of some antecedently problematic presupposition of the extended theory. We can cash out an antecedently problematic presupposition as some statement that is implied by the accepted background of the extended theory and the theory itself, but for which there also exist reasonable counterarguments from other premises that the statement is false.

In 1911, Head and Holmes proposed that our pain processing system was really two systems masquerading as one. We have an "epicritic" system that processes information regarding intensity and precise location, and a "protopathic" system that delivers the actual pain sensations. To this day, pain specialists believe their proposal is largely correct. They typically divide our pain processing system into a "sensory-discriminative" subsystem that computes the location, intensity, duration, and nature (stabbing, burning, prickling) of stimuli, and an "affective-motivational" subsystem that supports the unpleasant part of painful sensations.

Various drugs, illnesses, and brain lesions make the separation between the two processing streams very clear. Opiates will block the affective-motivational system without blocking the sensory-discriminative system, such that patients on morphine, for example, will claim that they are in pain and can point to where the pain is, but will also claim that the pain does not bother them. Several autoimmune disorders, some dementias, and an occasional brain injury will apparently activate the affective-motivational system without activating (or will damp down) the sensory-discriminative systems, such that patients will claim to be in great pain yet be unable to identify where the pain is located or what it feels like exactly.

What is problematic in this story, however, is that, apart from systemic drugs, scientists and physicians have a very difficult time isolating one stream from the other, which makes treating patients with disembodied pain near impossible. In fact, it appears virtually impossible for anything less than a systemic interaction to knock out one system in favor of the other. If this is the case, then in what sense do we have two systems? But if we do not have two systems, then how can we explain the apparent separation we find between systems?

The hope was that imaging studies of live patients in neuroscience might shed some light on this dilemma. If we could see what brains look like when they are experiencing pain, then we would be able to see whether we have two separate processing streams. In this sense, brain images of pain processing could extend our psychological theories, for they would be able to demonstrate more-or-less definitively whether the antecedently problematic assumption of dual systems is true.

The first thing that becomes immediately clear when looking at imaging studies of pain is that it is a highly distributed process. The structures that are most consistently active during pain processing include the contralateral insula, anterior cingulate cortex, thalamus, premotor cortex, and the cerebellar vermis. This activation varies parametrically with perceived pain intensity (Apkarian 1995; Casey 1999; see also Downar et al. 2003). More specifically, we can see a central network for pain processing in imaging studies which runs from the thalamus to the primary and secondary sensory cortex, which probably code, among other things, sensory-discriminative information, and to the anterior cingulate cortex, which is tied to the sensation of unpleasantness and appears to integrate intensity information, affect, cognition, and response selection – our affective-motivational system, in other words (Buchel et al. 2002; Chen et al. 2002; Ringler et al. 2003; Schnitzler and Ploner 2000; see also Alkire et al. 2004). Then the information flows to prefrontal cortex (Treede et al. 1999). In short, we can find different areas in the brain that differentially process sensory-discriminative information and other areas that differentially process affective-motivational information.

However, in seeing the images of pain processing, we can also see pretty quickly that the original simple dichotomy into sensory-discriminative and affective-motivational processing streams is over simplified – our pain networks are in fact too interconnected to identify two or even three separate processing streams. Indeed, conservation of intensity information across multiple areas suggests that we have a genuine pain-processing network. This possibility would help explain why patients can still experience pain after multiple lesions in their alleged pain processing streams (Treede et al. 1999; Coghill, Talbot et al. 1994; Coghill, Sang et al. 1999). We literally cannot identify a discrete processing stream, for everything feeds into everything else. Hence, we cannot affect one "stream" over another, unless we somehow do it systemically. Imaging studies of pain processing have shown how we can seem to have two pain processing streams yet not be able to isolate one stream from the other. In virtue of doing this, neuroscientific studies of pain have extended our psychological explanations of pain perception and sensation.

In the second example, imaging studies of pain processing are conceptually refining our psychological theories of pain by better specifying what pain is, such that pain specialists change the ways in which they define pain itself. The 1986 International Association for the Study of Pain definition of pain as being "an unpleasant sensory and emotional experience associated with actual or potential tissue damage or described in terms of such damage ... Pain is always subjective ... Pain is always a psychological state" (IASP 1986: 216). This definition holds that we should identify pain by what people report and not by any physical condition they have. If someone claims to be in pain, then that person is in pain, regardless of how the pain sensors or the brain are activated.

In contrast, in 2004, the National Research Council of Canada, Institute for Biodiagnostics, indicated that its ultimate goal in supporting imaging studies of pain process "is to develop a clinical MR [magnetic resonance] tool that will allow a clinician to assess ... whether or not a patient is truly experiencing pain (either intermittent acute or chronic)" (NRC n.d.). In this new definition, pain has switched from being purely subjective to something purely physical. This agency is suggesting that we should now determine whether people are in pain by what is happening in their brains and not by what they claim they are experiencing.

This change in approach represents a complete transformation in how we are to think about pain, and is a change due largely to advances in imaging technology. We have gone from a purely mentalistic description of pain – pain is a sensation – to one that is purely physical: pain is brain activity. This change, obviously, should have enormous implications for how pain patients are evaluated and treated. I leave it for another day to discuss whether making pain into a brain response is a wise decision. The point is that brain studies of pain processing are changing how pain itself is defined. In virtue of this, it is extending our psychological understanding of pain. (Notice that what I have just outlined is not a reduction, however, for even though work in neuroscience might provide the referents for a term in psychology, it does not follow that the theory in psychology in which the term is embedded is now better explained or justified.)

It is possible that explanatory extension might be a bidirectional relationship in the mind and brain sciences. If true, this would go against the common wisdom that one or the other science must be primary. In the philosophical literature, we find several arguments to the effect that discovering what the processes are must come before discovering where they are (Hatfield 1988; Klein 1981; Pylyshyn 1980), but this was not the case in either example. Discovery of the location of the processes came simultaneously with a better understanding of the process itself. The mind and brain sciences may literally co-evolve after all, with each working to extend the other.

The real point behind this chapter is to suggest that we need to stop arguing over the possibility of reductionism in psychology. Something is undoubtedly right about both sides: there is unquestionably a close and interesting relationship among the mind and brain sciences, but that connection does not reflect explanatory dependence. Psychology and neuroscience do rely on one another for evidence for some problematic entities or processes as well as for additional and more detailed support for their already developed hypotheses; however, nothing seems to suggest that any of these areas should ultimately merge or that they will need to rely on another discipline's advances for fundamental support. Though they do share many important points of contact, psychology and neuroscience are separate and independent fields of inquiry – each has its own history, with its own set of important questions, research techniques, explanatory patterns, criteria for error analysis, and so on. How or whether one domain will ultimately reduce another is simply the wrong philosophical approach to take.

A model of explanatory extension more adequately expresses the historical independence of the fields, as well as the complex connections that have been forged among them. Although the extending theory may indeed alter how we understand the objects and processes posited by the extended theory, the change is neither significant enough to warrant replacing the extended theory outright, nor broad enough to count as a reducing correction. In the end, we are left with a fairly messy set of connections that can help to shape future questions and research projects but not force a fundamental change in identity. The examples I gave illustrate only a small range of possibilities of interaction for two rapidly growing domains of inquiry that may never be understood using simpler models of eliminativism, functionalism, or consummation.

References

Alkire, M. T., White, N. S., Hsieh, R., and Haier, R. J. (2004) "Dissociable Brain Activation Responses to 5-Hz Electrical Pain Stimulation: A High-Field Functional Magnetic Imaging Study," *Anesthesiology* 100: 939–46.

Apkarian, A.V. (1995) "Functional Imaging of Pain, New Insights Regarding the Role of the Cerebral Cortex in Human Pain Perception," *Seminars in the Neurosciences* 7: 279–93.

Bechtel, W. (1982) "Two Common Errors in Explaining Biological and Psychological Phenomena," *Philosophy of Science* 49: 549–74.

—— (1983) "A Bridge between Cognitive Science and Neuroscience: The Functional Architecture of Mind," *Philosophical Studies* 44: 319–30.

Bechtel, W., and Mundale, J. 1999. "Multiple Realizability Revisited: Linking Cognitive and Neural States," *Philosophy of Science* 66: 175–207.

Bickle, J. (1998) *Psychoneural Reduction: The New Wave*, Cambridge, MA: MIT Press.

—— (2003) *Philosophy and Neuroscience: A Ruthlessly Reductive Account*, Norwell, MA: Kluwer.

Buchel, C., Bornhovd, K, Quante, M., Glauche, V., Bromm, B., and Weller, C. (2002) "Dissociable Neural Responses Related to Pain Intensity, Stimulus Intensity, and Stimulus Awareness within the Anterior Cingulate Cortex: A Parametric Single-Trial Laser Functional Magnetic Resonance Imaging Study," *Journal of Neuroscience* 22: 970–6.

Casey, K.L. (1999) "Forebrain Mechanisms of Nociception and Pain: Analysis through Imagining," *Proceedings of the National Academy of Science, USA* 96: 7668–74.

Chen, J. I., Ha, B., Bushnell, M. C., Pike, B., and Duncan, G. H. (2002) "Differentiating Noxious- and Innocuous-Related Activation of Human Sensory Cortices Using Temporal Analysis of FMRI," *Journal of Neurophysiology* 88: 464–74.

Churchland, P.M. (1987) *Matter and Consciousness*, rev. edn, Cambridge, MA: MIT Press.

Churchland, P. S. (1986) *Neurophilosophy: Toward a Unified Science of the Mind/Brain*, Cambridge, MA: MIT Press.

Coghill, R. C., Talbot, J. D., Evans, A. C., Meyer, E., Gjedde, A., Bushnell, M. C., and Duncan, G. H. (1994) "Distributed Processing of Pain and Vibration by the Human Brain," *Journal of Neuroscience* 14: 4095–108.

Coghill, R. C., Sang, C. N., Maisog, J. M., and Iadarola, M. J. (1999) "Pain Intensity Processing within the Human Brain: A Bilateral, Distributed Mechanism," *Journal of Neurophysiology* 82: 1934–43.

Darden, L., and Maull, N. (1977) "Interfield Theories," *Philosophy of Science* 44: 43–64.

Downar, J., Mikulis, D. J., and Davis, D. K. (2003) "Neural Correlates of the Prolonged Salience of Painful Stimulation," *Neuroimage* 20: 1540–51.

Enc, B. (1983) "In Defense of the Identity Theory," *Journal of Philosophy* 80: 279–98.

Fodor, J. (1983) *Representations: Philosophical Essays on the Foundations of Cognitive Science*, Cambridge, MA: MIT Press.

Fodor, J., and Pylyshyn, Z. (1988) "Connectionism and Cognitive Architecture: A Critical Analysis," *Cognition* 28: 3–71.

Hardcastle, V. G. (1992) "Reduction, Explanatory Extension, and the Mind-Brain Sciences," *Philosophy of Science* 59: 408–28.

Hatfield, G. (1988) "Neuro-Philosophy Meets Psychology: Reduction, Autonomy, and Physiological Constraints," *Cognitive Neuropsychology* 5: 723–46.

Head, H., and Holmes, G. (1911) "Sensory Disturbances from Cerebral Lesions," *Brain* 34: 102–254.

Hempel, C. G. (1966) *Philosophy of Natural Science*, Englewood Cliffs, NJ: Prentice Hall.

Hooker, Clifford (1981) "Towards a General Theory of Reduction. III: Cross-Categorial Reductions," *Dialogue* 20: 496–529

IASP (International Association for the Study of Pain) Subcommittee on Classification (1986) "Pain Terms, a Current List with Definitions and Notes on Usage," *Pain* (suppl.) 3: 216–21.

Jacobson, A. J. (2003) "Mental Representations: What Philosophy Leaves Out and Neuroscience Puts In," *Philosophical Psychology* 16: 189–203.

Kemeny, J. G., and Oppenheim, P. (1967) "On Reduction," in B. Brody (ed.), *Readings in the Philosophy of Science*, Englewood Cliffs, NJ: Prentice Hall, pp. 307–18.

Kitcher, P. (1984) "1953 and All That: A Tale of Two Sciences," *Philosophical Review* 93: 335–73.

—— (1988) "Explanatory Unification and the Causal Structure of the World," in P. S. Kitcher and W. Salmon (eds) *Scientific Explanation*, Minnesota Studies in the Philosophy of Science, vol. 13, Minneapolis: University of Minnesota Press, pp. 410–505.

Kitcher, P. S., and Salmon, W. (1987) "Van Fraassen on Explanation," *Journal of Philosophy* 84: 315–30.

Klein, Peter (1981) *Certainty: A Refutation of Scepticism*, Minneapolis: University of Minnesota Press.

Marr, D. (1982) *Vision*, San Francisco: Freeman.

Maull, N. (1977) "Unifying Science without Reduction," *Studies in History and Philosophy of Science* 8: 143–71.

Mayr, E. (1982) *The Growth of Biological Thought*, Cambridge, MA: Harvard University Press.

Nagel, E. (1961) *The Structure of Science*, New York: Harcourt, Brace, & World.

NCR (National Research Council of Canada) (n.d.) NCR Institute for Biodiagnostics website; available: http://ibd.nrc-cnrc.gc.ca/main_e.html
Pettigrew, J. D., and Konishi, M. (1976) "Neurons Selective for Orientation and Binocular Disparity in the Visual World of the Barn Owl (*Tyto alba*)," *Science* 193: 675–8.
Putnam, H. (1983) "Reductionism and the Nature of Psychology," in J. Haugeland (ed.), *Mind Design: Philosophy, Psychology, Artificial Intelligence*, Cambridge, MA: MIT Press, pp. 205–19.
Pylyshyn, Z. (1980) "Computation and Cognition: Issues in the Foundation of Cognitive Science," *Behavioral and Brain Sciences* 3: 111–34.
—— (1984) *Computation and Cognition*, Cambridge, MA: MIT Press.
Railton, P. (1981) "Probability, Explanation, and Information," *Synthese* 48: 233–56.
Richardson, R. C. (1979) "Functionalism and Reductionism," *Philosophy of Science* 46: 533–58.
—— (1982) "How Not to Reduce a Functional Psychology," *Philosophy of Science* 49: 125–37.
Ringler, R., Greiner, M., Kohlloeffel, L., Handwerker, H. O., and Forster, C. (2003) "BOLD Effects in Different Areas of the Cerebral Cortex During Painful Mechanical Stimulation," *Pain* 105: 45–553.
Rosenberg, A. (1985) *The Structure of Biological Science*, New York: University of Cambridge Press.
Salmon, W. (1971) *Statistical Explanation and Statistical Relevance*, Pittsburgh: University of Pittsburgh Press.
Savitt, S. (1974) "Rorty's Disappearance Theory," *Philosophical Studies* 28: 433–6.
Schaffner, K. (1967) "Approaches to Reduction," *Philosophy of Science* 34: 137–47.
—— (1974) "Reduction in Biology," in R. S. Cohen, C. A. Hooker, A. C. Michalos, J. W. van Evra (eds), *PSA 1974: Proceedings of the 1974 Biennial Meeting of the Philosophy of Science Association*, Dordrecht; Boston: D. Reidel.
Schnitzler, A., and Ploner, M. (2000) "Neurophysiology and Functional Neuroanatomy of Pain Perception," *Journal of Clinical Neurophysiology* 17: 592–603.
Treede, R. D., and Kenshalo, D. R., Gracely, R. H., and Jones, A. K. (1999) "The Cortical Representation of Pain," *Pain* 79: 105–111.
van Fraassen, B. (1980) *The Scientific Image*, Oxford: Oxford University Press.
Wimsatt, W. C. (1976) "Reductionism, Levels of Organization, and the Mind-Body Problem," in G. Globus, G. Maxwell, and I. Savodnik (eds), *Consciousness and the Brain: A Scientific and Philosophical Inquiry*, New York: Plenum Press, 199–267.

12
CONNECTIONISM

Amanda J. C. Sharkey and Noel Sharkey

Connectionism has made an important contribution to the intriguing challenge of finding a physical basis for mind. To understand its contribution, we need to see it in the context of the surrounding views and knowledge at the time. Placing it in context inevitably leads to charting its rise in the mid-1980s, its period of ascendancy throughout the 1990s, and a plateau of interest in the 2000s. During its ascendancy, it was seen by many as providing a new paradigm for the study of mind. In what follows, we shall trace the beginnings, and strengths of connectionism before turning to a consideration of some of the issues and problems that began to beset it. As will become apparent, some characteristics of connectionism, such as its relatively abstract modelling of brain functions, can be seen as an advantage, or a limitation, depending on the current perspective of the scientific community. Finally, we shall seek to evaluate and assess its lasting contributions and present state.

Connectionism is based on both the alleged operation of the nervous system and on distributed computation. Neuron-like units are connected by means of weighted links, in a manner that resembles the synaptic connections between neurons in the brain. These weighted links capture the knowledge of the system; they may be arrived at either analytically or by "training" the system with repeated presentations of input-output training examples.

In the last two decades of the twentieth century, considerable effort was directed towards exploring the implications of the connectionist approach for our understanding and modelling of the mind. However, connectionism has a longer history, and its antecedents in fact predate classical artificial intelligence. As long ago as 1943, McCulloch and Pitts wrote a paper called "A Logical Calculus of the Ideas Immanent in Nervous Activity," in which they provided an influential computational analysis of what they believed to be a reasonable abstraction of brain-like systems. To make the step from the complexity of the brain to binary computation required them to make a number of simplifications.

The ground for McCulloch and Pitts was prepared by earlier work. Until a hundred and twenty years ago the scientific community still believed that the nervous system was a continuous network similar to the blood system through which electricity flowed. Then a most important discovery was made by the Spanish scientist Ramón y Cajal in the nineteenth century. He found that there were tiny gaps or synapses, approximately 0.00002 (1/50,000) millimetres across, in what had been considered to be a continuous neural tube. This discovery paved the way for the notion of separable neurons communicating with one another and quickly gave rise to the *doctrine of the neuron* (Waldeyer 1891). Cajal was also responsible for the suggestion that learning involved adjustments of the connections between neurons. And it was not long before William James (James 1961 [1892]), the great philosopher and psychologist, speculated about how and when neural learning might occur. His idea was that when two processes in the brain are active at the same time, they tend to make permanent connections (e.g. the *sight* of an object and the *sound* of its name). But this idea was not to go much further for over fifty years.

By ignoring the physical and chemical complexity of the nervous system, McCulloch and Pitts (1943) were able to build their abstract model neurons into networks capable of computing logical functions. In particular their paper showed how modifying weight coefficients and the thresholds in networks could result in different Boolean functions being computed. They proved this in an archaic proof to show that by gluing together simple functions such as AND, OR and NOT, all possible Boolean functions could be computed by their networks.

Although they did not take up James' challenging question of how and when synapses are modified by learning, McCulloch and Pitts' seminal work showed the possible utility of abstract computational analysis for the study of the mind/brain relation. They believed that they had cracked the problem of linking brain activity to George Boole's language of thought. This has not worked out as planned but nonetheless their paper remains a cornerstone of modern connectionist research and computer science.

Their first simplification arose from the observation that neural communication is thresholded. That is, the spike action potential is all or none; it is either active enough to fire fully or it does not fire at all (the amount of charge needed to fire a neuron is about 10 millivolts). Thus the neuron could be conceived of as a binary computing device, an idea said to have inspired von Neumann when designing the modern digital computer. The other important simplification was that the synapses had numerical weightings between the binary computing elements. Computation proceeded by summing the weighted inputs to an element and using the binary threshold as an output function (Figure 12.1).

Later in the same decade the Canadian psychologist Donald Hebb made James' learning proposal concrete. Although he cites neither James nor McCulloch and Pitts, Hebb (1949) took a step beyond them in attempting to causally relate memory and perception to the physical world. His idea was that the representations of objects may be considered to be states (or patterns) of neural activity in the brain. He proposed that, each time a neural pathway is used, there is a metabolic change in the synaptic connection between the neurons in the path that facilitates subsequent signal transmission. In this way the more often two neurons are used together, the stronger will be their strength of connection and the greater the likelihood of one activating the other. The synaptic connections come to *represent* the statistical correlates of experience. Thus in learning to recognise objects, groups of neurons are linked together to form

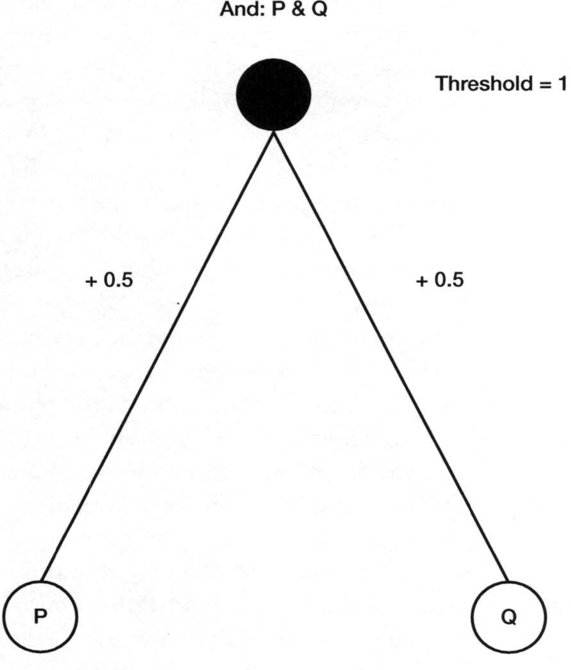

Figure 12.1 McCulloch and Pitts net for the Boolean function AND.

assemblies (the neurons in any assembly may come from many areas of the brain, e.g. visual and motor etc.).

This notion of modifiable synapses, or synaptic plasticity, and its role in learning and memory still persists today. Although to some in the neuroscience community Hebb's ideas are over simplistic, it has to be remembered that little was known about these issues in his day, and he did not have the technology to carry out the physiological experiments. Indeed, it was not until 1973 that Bliss and Lomo first reported, in detail, that, following brief pulses of stimulation, there is a sustained increase in the amplitude of electrically evoked responses in specific neural pathways. This is the now well known *long-term potentiation* phenomenon. Subsequent research has shown that one of a variety of synaptic types is indeed a Hebbian synapse (e.g. Kelso et al. 1986; Alkon 1987).

Taken together then, the approaches of Hebb and McCulloch-Pitts provided a new avenue to begin to study the physical basis of mind. On the one hand, the McCulloch-Pitts approach suggested a methodology for a computational analysis of the brain. On the other hand, Hebb's approach gave us an idea of how a device like the nervous system could learn the statistical correlates of the world needed to support perception

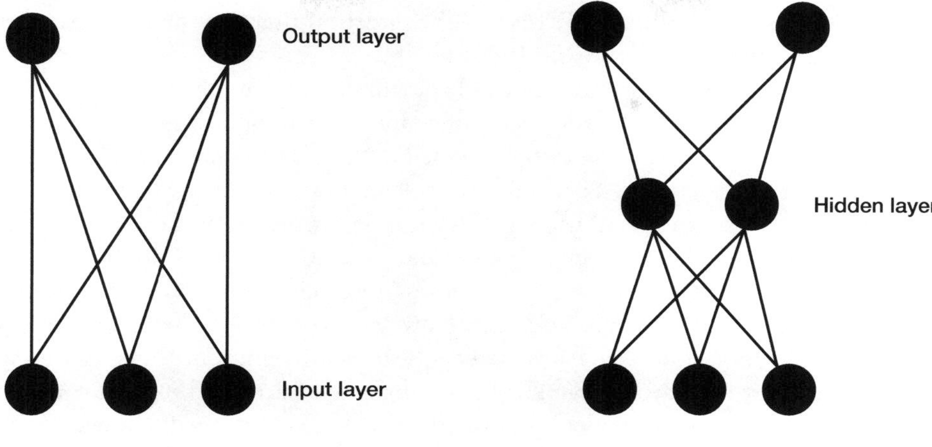

Figure 12.2 (a) Single-layer network; (b) two-layered network, with hidden units.

and memory. Here then is a history of ideas that arose from a slimmest of experimental evidence, and which has turned out to be correct in many ways or is at least consonant with current experimental work.

In fact, although work by McCulloch and Pitts, and by Hebb, cleared the ground for connectionism, its real heyday was to come later. Early enthusiasm for a neuron-based approach was fed by Rosenblatt's work on the perceptron; his development of the use of neurons for pattern recognition; and the publication of the perceptron convergence theorem (Rosenblatt 1962). The theorem demonstrated that if a set of weights existed that would produce the desired responses to a set of patterns, then a finite number of repetitions of his training procedure would find them. In other words, what Rosenblatt proved was that if a solution existed, his learning method would find it in a finite (although possibly large) number of steps.

However, research in the area received a severe setback following the publication of a book by Minsky and Papert (1969) that pointed out limitations on the kinds of problem that the perceptron could learn. In particular, they demonstrated that problems, such as the exclusive or (XOR), that were not linearly separable could not be solved with a perceptron. This did not invalidate the perceptron convergence theorem, since no solution existed for a single layer. The problem is that a perceptron has only one layer of weights and problems like XOR require a network with two-layers (see Figure 12.2 for an illustration of networks with and without hidden layers). At that time, there was no training procedure for networks with more than one layer.

Although some researchers were to persevere (e.g. Anderson 1972), mass interest in the field did not emerge until the latter half of the 1980s. In addition, there was a general tide of optimism about the possibilities offered by the symbol-processing approach for artificial intelligence. This was the direction that most researchers were moving in during the 1970s and early 1980s.

The re-emergence of connectionism can be attributed to a number of factors. One of these was the development of learning rules for training multilayer networks: in particular the backpropagation algorithm (Rumelhart, Hinton et al. 1986). This meant that the limitations identified by Minsky and Papert no longer applied: problems such as XOR could be learned. Another factor was a growing dissatisfaction with the classical symbolic approach to modelling mind and its relation to the brain. In between the first and second incarnation of connectionism, research in the symbolic paradigm of artificial intelligence had proceeded apace. However, even though theories of symbol manipulation could account for many aspects of human cognition, there was some concern about how such symbols might be developed or learnt and how they might be represented in the brain. Functionalism (Polger, this volume) was explicit in its insistence that details about how intelligence and reasoning were actually implemented were irrelevant. Concern about the manipulation of meaningless, ungrounded symbols is exemplified in Searle's Chinese-room thought experiment (1980). Connectionism, on the other hand, offered an approach that was based on learning, made little use of symbols, and was related to the way in which the brain worked.

Perhaps the biggest factor in the shift towards connectionism was the publication in 1986 of a two-volume edited work by Rumelhart and McClelland, on "parallel distributed processing" (PDP) (Rumelhart et al. 1986). The books contained a large number of connectionist models of different aspects of cognition that had been trained by exposure to samples of the required task. Although this work was indebted to earlier pioneering neural network research related to cognitive processing and memory (e.g. Anderson 1972), it was these two volumes that set the agenda for connectionist cognitive modellers and offered a methodology that became a standard. Following the publication of the PDP volumes, a legion of connectionist cognitive models were produced. The domains that were simulated included memory retrieval and category formation, and (in language) phoneme recognition, word recognition, speech perception, acquired dyslexia, language acquisition, and (in vision) edge detection, object and shape recognition.

Many of these models are based on supervised learning techniques. In the simplest case of supervised learning, a net consists of a set of input units, a layer of hidden units, and a set of output units, each layer being connected to the next via modifiable weights. This is a feed-forward net. When the net is trained on a set of input-output pairs, the weights are adjusted via a learning algorithm, e.g. backpropagation, until the required output is produced in response to each input in the training set. When tested on a set of previously unseen inputs, the net will, to a greater or lesser extent, display an ability to generalise. That is, to go beyond the data it was trained on, and to produce an appropriate response to some of the test inputs. The ability of the net to generalise depends on the similarity between the function extracted as a result of the original training, and the function that underlies the test set. Given a training set that is sufficiently representative of the required function, generalisation results are likely to be good. Where the inputs and outputs of such a net are given an interpretation relevant to the performance of a cognitive task, the net may be seen as a model of that task.

As well as their basic architecture and mode of operation, it is also possible to identify four typical features of connectionist models of cognition which, in combination, account for much of the popularity of the approach they exemplify: (i) they can be used both to model mental processes, and to simulate the actual behaviour involved; (ii) they can provide a "good fit" to the data from psychology experiments; (iii) the model, and its fit to the data, is achieved without explicit programming, or "handwiring"; and (iv) they often provide new accounts of the data.

The first two features, namely the way in which connectionist nets can both provide a model of a cognitive process and simulate a related task, and their ability to provide a good fit to the empirical data, can be seen as combining some of the characteristics of two earlier routes to modelling. One of these, taken by the cognitive psychology community, involved building models that could account for the results from psychology experiments with human subjects, but which did not incorporate simulations of experimental tasks. The second route, followed by the artificial intelligence community, was to build computer models that actually perform the task in ways that resemble human performance without regard to detailed psychological evidence. The connectionist approach, as described here, provides the benefits both of simulating the performance of human tasks, and at the same time, fitting the data from psychological investigations.

While it is possible to identify features of connectionist models that account for their popularity, stronger claims have been made about the suitability of connectionism for modelling the mind. Such claims are based in part on comparisons to the symbol-processing functional approach that preceded it. The stronger claims refer to the different form of computation that underlies connectionism.

For example, it has been claimed that connectionism offers a better account of learning and memory. Earlier approaches to network learning (e.g. Anderson 1983) tended to assume that the goal of learning is to formulate explicit rules that capture generalisations. By contrast, in a connectionist system, there is no central mechanism or place in which such rules could be formulated. A connectionist system is inherently decentralised. Memory and knowledge are captured in a distributed manner, in the form of the activations of units, or neurons, and the weighted links between such neurons. One advantageous consequence of this is that neural networks do not suffer from the brittleness that can afflict conventional rule-based artificial intelligence systems. They exhibit a robust flexibility in the face of noisy inputs or destruction of units. They show graceful degradation: a net's response to noisy input can be still appropriate, even if less accurate, where the response to noise or faults in classical computers can be catastrophic failure. Neural networks also provide a natural way of dealing with many conflicting constraints in parallel, in a way that is difficult for a rule-based system. And, it is argued, their performance here is closer to that of humans than conventional rule-based systems.

Connectionism provides an account of the way in which a rule can be inferred without the need for conscious inference, or externally imposed rules or heuristics.

Much of the excitement in the psychology community has been about the ability of neural nets to handle apparently rule-governed phenomena without any explicit rules: in particular, to account for the processing of regular and exceptional material. For example, learning to produce the appropriate past-tense form of verbs was always held as an example of a rule-governed phenomenon until McClelland et al.'s (1986) model showed that the behaviours could be trained in a model that did not contain any explicit rules. Here is an example of a connectionist approach resulting in a new model of existing data (see feature iv above), although it is now debated whether such networks still contain rules, albeit implemented in a different manner.

Questions have been raised about the extent to which connectionist nets provide a new account of learning, or merely implement a symbolic rule-based system. Different positions have been taken with respect to connectionism and symbol processing. "Eliminative connectionism" is a term coined by Pinker and Prince (1988) to describe the view that accounts of cognitive abilities such as rule-learning can be provided in a connectionist system that operates at the sub-symbolic level. "Implementational connectionism," by contrast, seeks to reconcile connectionism and symbol manipulation and to use connectionism to understand how symbol manipulation could be implemented in the brain. The burden of proof differs for these two approaches. As Marcus (1998) points out, an eliminative connectionist needs to show that a model is adequate, but also that it is not a covert implementation of a symbol manipulation model. An implementational connectionist, however, needs to show that the model is adequate, and that it serves as an implementation of a symbol-manipulating algorithm. The difficulty, as has been argued, is that some apparently eliminative connectionist models covertly implement symbol manipulation (Lachter and Bever 1988).

Apart from localist approaches in which each symbol is represented by a single network node, connectionist representations are distributed and non-symbolic. As such they are quite different from the symbolic representations employed in the classical approach. As the symbolists began to fight back in response to the growing enthusiasm for the connectionist paradigm, a detailed argument was made by Fodor and Pylyshyn (1988) to the effect that connectionism was incapable in principle of supporting higher mental processes, or that at the most it could only do so by implementing symbolic architectures. The question of whether or not connectionism is capable of supporting a cognitive architecture has mainly been addressed in the context of discussions about the novelty and value of connectionist representation. This question is considered below with particular reference to the concept of compositionality.

One of the seats of symbolic computing is in its ability to handle compositionality. Put briefly, compositionality is a reliable method for (a) producing an expression given its constituents; and (b) decomposing the expression back into those constituents. This is where the symbolic researchers launched their strongest attack on the connectionists. And this is also perhaps the area where the eliminative connectionists have been most successful in rebuffing the criticisms in demonstrating how their models differ from models employing standard symbol manipulation.

Proponents of the classical symbolic tradition have claimed that the distributed and non-symbolic representations developed through training neural nets are in principle incapable of supporting a cognitive architecture, because to account for the systematic nature of human thought, representations must be able to support structure-sensitive processes and this requires compositional representations. Their assumption was that there is only one kind of compositionality; namely the concatenative compositionality of symbolic strings. This permits structure sensitive operations because in their mode of combination the constituents of complex expressions are tokened whenever the complex expression is tokened. For example, to develop an expression from a sentence such as "John kissed Mary," arbitrary symbols representing the constituents JOHN, KISSED and MARY are combined in a contextually independent concatenation to produce the propositional representation KISS (JOHN, MARY). Whenever this latter complex expression is tokened, its constituents, KISS, MARY and JOHN, are also tokened. This makes the manipulation of the representations by a mechanism sensitive to the syntactic structure resulting from concatenative compositionality relatively easy.

Distributed representations, by contrast, do not exhibit this kind of compositionality. Instead, cognitive connectionists have identified an alternative form of compositionality, one that has been described as merely functional, non-concatenative compositionality (van Gelder 1990). Distributed representations combine tokens without those tokens appearing in the complex expression, since the tokens of the input constituents are destroyed in their combination. The point is that such representations can still be shown to be functionally compositional because there exist general and reliable procedures for combining constituents into complex expressions and for decomposing those expressions back into the constituents. It is possible, for example, to encode simple syntactic trees in terms of connectionist distributed representations, and to decode them back into the same syntactic trees (Pollack 1990). Thus the constituents of the tree have been combined into a form of representation that is non-concatenative, but which preserves the necessary information.

A considerable body of research has shown that distributed representations are not only compositional but can also enable systematic structure-sensitive operations. It started with Chalmers (1990), who demonstrated that it was possible to use connectionist nets to transform distributed representations for active sentences into distributed representations for passive sentences. Thus distributed representations allow at least a limited form of systematicity without emergence on to the symbol surface. Moreover, this is not just an example of "old wine in new bottles," i.e. a mere implementation. An interesting property of "uniquely connectionist representations" (Sharkey 1997) is that they are reusable, or portable for other tasks. This property is demonstrated by Chalmers' active-passive transformations. Similarly, Sharkey (1997) reported the development of a disembodied arm control system, in which the connectionist representations developed as a result of training a net to output transformationally invariant position classes were reused as input to a net trained to direct a mobile robotic arm to pick up objects.

There is then support for the claim that connectionist research is capable of supporting a different style of cognitive architecture from the symbolic approach that preceded it. Uniquely connectionist representations are capable of both compositionality and systematicity, and the representations are reusable for other tasks. And they accomplish these properties by very different means than those of Classical symbolic representations. It is arguments such as these, made by the more radical connectionists, which underlie claims that connectionism constituted a "paradigm shift" away from the symbol-processing account.

So far we have outlined a number of reasons for the enthusiastic adoption of the connectionist approach that took place from the late 1980s, and examined some of the debate about the extent to which connectionism could provide an adequate theory of cognition. By the turn of the millennium, this enthusiasm had largely evaporated. The fierce debates about the theoretical adequacy of connectionism seem to have subsided. Again, there are a number of reasons for this. One such reason is a growing dissatisfaction with the loose relationship between neuroscience, and neural nets. There has also been a gradual realisation of some of the limitations of neural nets, and recognition that there are aspects of cognition to which they do not easily provide a solution. In addition, the current zeitgeist places a much greater emphasis on the notion of "embodied cognition" and the role of the body and its interactions with the world, as well as the mind and the brain.

There has always been a clear difference between the use of brain-style computation and neuropsychological modelling. Connectionist models can be described as being "neurally inspired," but their relationship to neural processing is delicate and tenuous. In a model of cognitive processes, it is unlikely that the computation performed corresponds to what goes on at the neural level. Indeed, it has been suggested (Edelman 1987), that it may take units in the order of several thousand neurons to encode stimulus categories of significance to animals. Clearly, where the inputs to a net are things like noun phrases, or disease symptoms, or even the phonological representations of words, the inputs cannot be equated with neural inputs but must represent substantially pre-processed stimuli. In fact, there are few cases where actual facts about the nervous system are used to constrain the architecture and design of a model.

The relatively casual relationship between neural nets and what is known about the brain, can be viewed either as a strength, or as a weakness. In the heyday of connectionism it was surely seen as a strength. If one is concerned with cognition, rather than the details of neural processes, an appropriate research strategy is to use broader brush strokes; relying on computational abstractions. Indeed, it was probably the very paucity of "facts" about the nervous system that allowed Hebb, and McCulloch and Pitts to make what now seem to be the simplifying assumptions that enabled their abstract analyses. Their work, and connectionism in general, facilitated the uniting of cognition and brain theory. As Clark (1997) points out, connectionism saw the beginning of a shared vocabulary, and a movement towards understanding how a mind might emerge from a brain. Many neural net researchers ignore the details of the operation of real synapses in real brains and nervous systems, and the chemistry of neurotransmission. However, by examining what very simplified model neurons can compute, and the kinds of cognitive tasks they can simulate, answers to how a mind might emerge from a brain began to arise.

More recently, as knowledge about the workings of the brain has accumulated, and the surprise of being able to speak the same language as neuroscientists has dissipated, the differences between neural nets and the workings of the brain have become more apparent. Mainstream connectionists were not so interested in modelling the details of different types of neurons and synapses. And some, such as Hawkins (2004), have become impatient with the tendency of connectionists to concentrate on simple models with three layers of identical neurons and feed-forward connections, whilst ignoring the physical architecture of the brain and the way that inputs from the environment change over time, and making little use of feedback and prediction. There has similarly been concern about the lack of biological plausibility of the backpropagation algorithm commonly used to train neural nets. However, for many connectionists it is the representations that are developed as the result of training that are important, rather than the method used to arrive at them. In this way connectionism is more in line with associationism than neuroscience.

Another reason for the initial enthusiasm for neural nets was also that they seemed to provide a better account of the way that representations arise during natural learning rather than the explicit programming of rules common to the preceding symbolic approach. However, following the glory days of connectionism, there is a greater awareness of the way in which neural nets are indirectly programmed and of the idea that several aspects of the performance of a connectionist net are influenced by the researcher by means of extensional programming (A. Sharkey and N. Sharkey 2003). In particular, decisions are made about the selection and presentation of training data. Similarly, the architecture of the net is often decided upon by the researcher (although incremental constructive algorithms can automate the process). Some have argued for the greater biological plausibility of unsupervised, self-organising neural nets, but decisions still have to be made about a number of parameters, including the inputs to which they are exposed.

In addition to the preceding concerns, some of the limitations of connectionist nets have become more apparent. Backpropagation performs impressively when all of the training data are presented to the net on each training cycle. However, there are conditions in which "catastrophic interference" occurs. When neural net training is carried out sequentially, and a net is fully trained on one set of items, before being trained on a new set, results are not so impressive. The newly learned information often interferes with, and overwrites, previously learned information. For instance, McCloskey and Cohen (1989) used backpropagation to train a net on the arithmetic problem of + 1 addition (e.g. 1 + 1, 2 + 1, …, 9 + 1). They found that when they proceeded to train the same net to add 2 to a given number, it "forgot" how to add 1. Sequential training of this form results in catastrophic interference. Noel Sharkey and Amanda J. C. Sharkey (1995) demonstrated that it is possible to avoid the problem if the training set is sufficiently representative of the underlying function, or there are enough sequential training sets. In terms of this example, if the function to be learned is both + 1 and + 2, then training sets that incorporate enough examples of each could lead to the net learning to add either 1 or 2 to a given number. However, this is at the expense of being able to discriminate between those items that have been learned from those that have not.

In fact the McCloskey and Cohen example highlights another problem with neural nets. That is the ability to extrapolate beyond a given training set. Although humans can readily learn the idea of adding one to any given number, it is not so straightforward to train the net to extrapolate beyond the data on which it is trained. It has been argued (Marcus 1998) that this inability of neural nets trained using backpropagation to generalise beyond their training space provides a major limitation to the power of connectionist nets, an important one, since humans can readily generalise universal relationships to unfamiliar instances.

In many ways, the appeal of connectionism has weakened as the understanding of the strengths and limitations of neural nets has increased. Some of the attraction of the approach lay in its mystery. It is possible to identify three major new directions that have been taken in response to the demystification of connectionism. One is to see neural nets primarily as a statistical tool. Neural nets now form part of the arsenal of pattern recognition researchers who have little interest in their ability to provide a model of mind and cognition. Another response has been to pursue hybrid accounts, in which the strengths of connectionism are combined with higher level reasoning capabilities, making it possible to provide an account of most aspects of cognition. The third direction corresponds to a new emphasis on the role of the body of living creatures, and their interaction with the environment. The new fashion is for "embodied cognition."

Of the three directions identified above, it is the hybrid and embodied approaches that are most relevant to cognition. The hybrid approach recognises that there are strengths and weakness to both connectionist and symbolic approaches, and seeks to combine the best of both. The assumption is that there are some cognitive processes that are better captured by symbolic models, and some for which connectionist nets provide a better account. It has been suggested (Harnad 1990) that connectionism can provide a means of grounding the symbols in the world – distributed connectionist representations giving otherwise abstract symbols a meaningful grounding in the real world. Connectionism can provide an account of how the symbols were learned, and symbol processing systems can be used to reason with them. Hybrid models have been applied to a number of topics in cognitive science, including reasoning, skill learning, and natural language processing (Sun 2003).

The interest in embodied cognition, by contrast, reflects a new concern with the relationship between living organisms and their environment, and a view of the environment as "an active resource whose intrinsic dynamics can play important problem solving roles" (Clark 1997: 83). It represents another response to the dissatisfaction with traditional symbol processing and is generally accepted as being initiated by Rodney Brooks (1986, 1991) and a new emphasis on behaviour-based robots that are physically embodied and situated in the real world. Embodiment can be seen as providing a solution to the problems of symbol grounding: instead of the formal manipulation of abstract symbols, researchers subscribing to the embodied cognition approach are committed to the idea that any representations should be as action-centred and related to physical interactions between living organisms and the environment, as possible (see Aizawa and Adams, Schöner and Reimann, and Bickhard, each in this volume). Connectionism has paid little attention to the role of the body and its dynamic interaction with the environment.

Nonetheless, neural nets still seem to be surviving in the new paradigm of embodied cognition, since they can provide a useful means of capturing the relationships between inputs and outputs, or between sensorial inputs and motor outputs. Connectionist nets are often used by roboticists to form the basis of behavioural modules. They are not necessarily trained by means of learning algorithms such as backpropagation: instead their weights can be evolved using evolutionary algorithms, in response to measures of their effectiveness in the environment (see Nolfi and Floreano 2000). But their role here is much reduced, and bears only a small resemblance to the role they played whilst the connectionist approach was in ascendance.

In conclusion, we have charted the time course of connectionism over some sixty years and considered the contribution it has made to the study of mind. Clearly, connectionism constituted an influential step in the quest of understanding mind and cognition. Probably its main contribution results from the new view it offered of knowledge and learning, a view that took more account of their implementation in the brain and the way in which they might arise as the result of experience. Connectionism initiated a greater communication between disciplines associated with cognitive science, with the result that there is now a greater concern to take account of neuroscientific findings in models of cognition. As we have seen, the current position of neural nets is much reduced, and there is greater awareness of their strengths and limitations, but they possess a number of useful characteristics that have thus far ensured their survival.

References

Alkon, D. L. (1987) *Memory Traces in the Brain*, Cambridge University Press.

Anderson, J. A. (1972) "A Simple Neural Network Generating an Interactive Memory," *Mathematical Biosciences*, 8: 137–160.

—— (1983) *The Architecture of Cognition*, Cambridge, MA: MIT Press.

Bliss, T. V. P., and Lomo, T. (1973) "Long-Lasting Potentiation of Synaptic Transmission in the Dentate Area of the Anaethetised Rabbit Following Stimulation of the Perforant Path," *Journal of Physiology* 232: 331–56.

Brooks, R. A. (1986) "A Robust Layered Control System for a Mobile Robot," *IEEE Journal of Robotics and Automation*, RA-2, no. 1: 14–23.

—— (1991) "Intelligence without Reason," in Ray Myopoulos and John Reiter (ed.), *Proceedings of the 12th International Joint Conference on Artificial Intelligence, Sydney, Australia, August*, San Mateo, CA: Morgan Kaufmann, pp. 569–95.

Chalmers, D. J. (1990) "Syntactic Transformations on Distributed Representations," *Connection Science* 2, no. 1: 53–62.

Clark, A. (1997) *Being There: Putting Brain, Body and World Together Again*, Cambridge, MA: MIT Press-A Bradford Book.

Edelman, G. M. (1987) *Neural Darwinism*, New York: Basic Books.

Fodor, J. A., and Pylyshyn, Z. (1988) "Connectionism and Cognitive Architecture: A Critical Analysis," *Cognition* 28: 3–71.
Harnad, S. (1990) "The Symbol Grounding Problem," *Physica D* 42: 335–46.
Hawkins, J. (2004) *On Intelligence*, New York: Henry Holt & Company-An Owl Book.
Hebb, D. O. (1949) *The Organisation of Behavior*, New York: Wiley
James, W. (1961 [1892]) *Psychology: Briefer Course*, New York: Harper.
Kelso, S. R., Ganong, A. H., and Brown, T. H. (1986) "Hebbian Synapses in Hippocampus," *Proceedings of the National Academy of Science* 83: 5326–30.
Lachter, J., and Bever, T. G. (1988) "The Relation between Linguistic Structure and Associative Theories of Language Learning: A Constructive Critique of Some Connectionist Learning Models," *Cognition* 28: 195–247.
Marcus, G. F. (1998) "Rethinking Eliminative Connectionism," *Cognitive Psychology* 37: 243–82.
McClelland, J. L., Rumelhart, D. E., and PDP Research Group (1986) *Parallel Distributed Processing*, vol. 2: *Psychological and Biological Models*, Cambridge, MA: MIT Press.
McCloskey, M., and Cohen, N. J. (1989) "Catastrophic Interference in Connectionist Networks: The Sequential Learning Problem," *Psychology of Learning and Motivation* 24: 109–165.
McCulloch, W. S., and Pitts, W. H. (1943) "A Logical Calculus of Ideas Imminent in Nervous Activity," *Bulletin of Mathematical Biophysics* 5: 115–33.
Minsky, M., and Papert, S. (1969) *Perceptrons*, Cambridge, MA: MIT Press.
Nolfi, S., and Floreano, D. (2000) *Evolutionary Robotics: The Biology, Intelligence and Technology of Self-Organizing Machines*, Cambridge, MA: MIT Press-Bradford Books.
Pollack, J. B. (1990) "Recursive Distributed Representations," *Artificial Intelligence* 46: 77–105.
Pinker, S., and Prince, A. (1988) "On Language and Connectionism: Analysis of a Parallel Distributed Processing Model of Language Acquisition," in S. Pinker and J. Mehler (eds), *Connections and Symbols*, Cambridge, MA: Bradford-MIT Press, pp. 73–194.
Rosenblatt, Frank (1962) *Principles of Neurodynamics*, New York: Spartan.
Rumelhart, D. E., Hinton, G. E., and Williams, R. J. (1986) "Learning Internal Representations by Error Propagation," in D. E. Rumelhart and J. L. McClelland (eds) *Parallel Distributed Processing*, vol. 1, Cambridge, MA: MIT Press, pp. 318–62.
Searle, J. R. (1980) "Minds, Brains and Programs," *Behavioral and Brain Sciences* 3: 417–57.
Sharkey, A. J. C., and Sharkey, N. E. (2003) "Cognitive Modelling: Psychology and Connectionism," in M. A. Arbib (ed.), *The Handbook of Brain Theory and Neural Networks*, Cambridge, MA: MIT Press-A Bradford Book, pp. 219–22.
Sharkey, N. E. (1997) "Artificial Neural Networks for Coordination and Control: The Portability of Experiential Representations," *Robotics and Autonomous Systems* 22: 345–59.
Sharkey, N. E., and Sharkey, A. J. C. (1995) "An Analysis of Catastrophic Interference," *Connection Science* 7, nos. 3–4: 313–41.
Sun, R. (2003) "Hybrid Connectionist/Symbolic Systems," in M. A. Arbib (ed.), *The Handbook of Brain Theory and Neural Networks*, Cambridge, MA: MIT Press-A Bradford Book, pp. 543–6.
van Gelder, T. (1990) "Compositionality: A Connectionist Variation on a Classical Theme," *Cognitive Science* 14: 355–84.
Waldeyer, H. W. (1891) "Uber einige neuere Forschungen im Gebeite der Anotomie des Centrainervensystems," *Deutsche medizinische Wochenschrift* 17: 1352–6.

13
EMBODIED COGNITION AND THE EXTENDED MIND

Fred Adams and Ken Aizawa

The mind has an evolutionary history; it is an adaptation for coping with the environment. Perception and action are intimately related. Thinking is grounded in and inseparable from action. Mental representations do not play the role that traditional cognitive science has posited for them. The mind is shaped by, dependent upon, and bound up with the body and its environment. Each of these general ideas has made an appearance in the growing embodied cognition and extended mind (EC-EM) literature. Each of these components of this developing perspective is open-ended, subject to refinements or interpretations that make them more or less radical. They are also shaped, refined, and developed, in part, by the research interests of a diverse array of cognitive scientists from developmental psychologists to roboticists, philosophers, and vision scientists. Developmental psychologists within the EC-EM movement focus on the way in which infants mature and emphasize the role of action and perception in their development. Roboticists and vision scientists adopting the EC-EM perspective emphasize the role of the environment in guiding perception and action, minimizing the role of intensive centralized information processing. Philosophers have concerned themselves with arguments that attempt to undermine apparent cognitive differences between brain processes and processes that take place in the body and environment.

To sample and introduce some of the leading ideas of the EC-EM perspective, we will adopt an approach often taken by the proponents of the perspective, namely, we will contrast the EC-EM approach with the more mainstream cognitivist approach.[1] As we see it, the proponents of EC-EM have often sought to distance their new perspective from a more traditional cognitivist or "old-fashioned" artificial intelligence perspective according to which cognitive processes are processes operating on mental representations. At times, however, we think that these differences are overstated. For example, a cognitivist view of the mind is perfectly compatible with the idea that the mind has an evolutionary history and that it is an adaptation for coping with the organism's environment. Such an evolutionary cognitivist view is, in fact, developed at length by Steven Pinker.[2] One consequence of the attempt to distance the EC-EM approach from more mainstream ideas is that it exaggerates some differences. At times this threatens to create differences that do not really exist and, at others, to eclipse differences that do. What we propose to do in this chapter, after a brief introduction to cognitivism, is review and explain some of the leading ideas of the EC-EM approach, drawing attention to the diversity of ways in which these ideas might be developed further.

Cognitivism

Broadly construed, cognitivism is the view that cognitive processes consist of the manipulation of mental representations or symbols.[3] Among those interested in, and trying to develop, artificial intelligence, the cognitivist view is often associated with Alan Newell and Herbert Simon's "physical symbol system" hypothesis.[4] Among cognitive psychologists, cognitivism is perhaps closely associated with Noam Chomsky's theory of rules and representations.[5] Philosophers often attribute the view to Jerry Fodor or Zenon Pylyshyn, under the rubric of a computational theory of mind.[6] In these various guises, the common ground among cognitivists is that cognitive processes involve the manipulation of symbolic representations. Cognitivists differ among themselves in such matters as how symbolic representations get their meaning (how they are "semantically grounded"), what mental representations are to be found in cognitive economies, how symbolic representations are structured, and what kinds of manipulations are performed on these representations. We will comment on each of these points of difference.

One family of approaches to the genesis of meaning is the set of so-called "informational" approaches. These begin with the thought that a given brain state or action "X" might represent something X in virtue of some kind of causal coupling relation between "X" and X. Fred Dretske's (1988) theory of indicator functions and Jerry Fodor's (1990) theory of asymmetric causal dependencies are examples of this kind of approach. We can illustrate Dretske's theory as it might be applied to neuronal circuits. The firing of a particular neuron in Brodmann's area 17 (i.e., "X") might mean that there is an edge at roughly some particular orientation at roughly some particular place in the visual field (X) in virtue of the fact that this neuron fires when there is an edge of about that orientation at about that place in the visual field, and developmental processes in the brain have shaped the cell to have the function to indicate the presence of this kind of edge. Another kind of approach to the symbol grounding problem supposes that mental representations are like pictures, that neuronal states represent environmental states when the neuronal states mirror environmental states. We can illustrate Cummins' (1996) version of this picture theory with a neuronal circuit example. In this case, the idea is that the firing of a set of neurons in Brodmann's area 17 might represent a cube being in the environment if the pattern of firing in the set of neurons is isomorphic to the various edges of the cube and their relations. In other words, the firing neurons represents the cube, if there is a one-to-one and onto mapping between the firing neurons and the parts of the cube and between some feature of the neurons' firing and the corresponding relations among

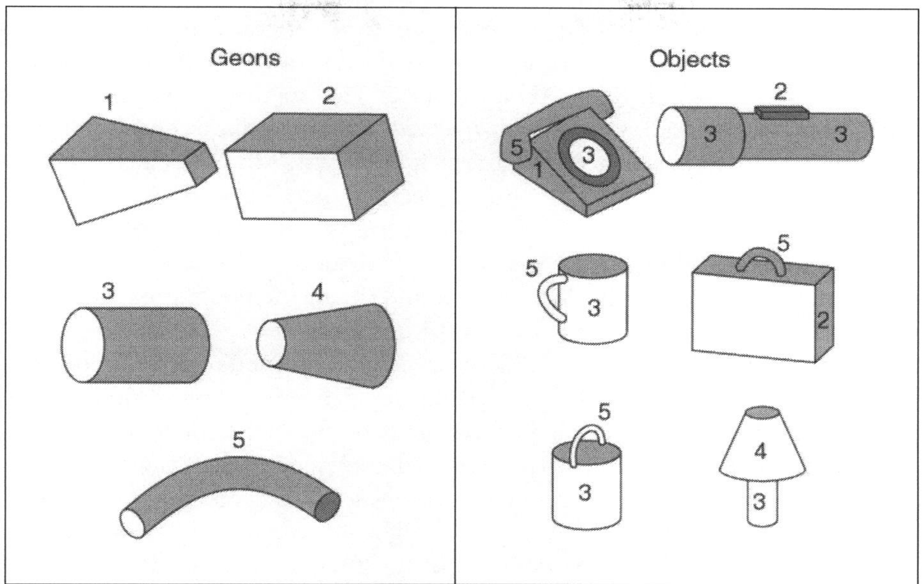

Figure 13.1 Geons and some constructions of geons (from Biedermann 1990).

parts of the cube.[7] Still other naturalized semantic theories begin with the idea that it is not relations between brain or neuronal state and the world that make a brain or neuronal state a representational state; it is relations among the brain/neuronal states that matter. A version of conceptual role semantics, such as that in Block (1986) and perhaps part of Newell and Simon's (1972) physical symbol system hypothesis, would exemplify this kind of approach. Applying these theories to brain circuits, one would maintain that it is relations among the firings of neurons that lead them to have their meanings.[8] Stich and Warfield (1994) contains an excellent collection of philosophy papers on the subject of the origins of mental representation.

Cognitivists can also differ among themselves about what is represented in this hypothetical system of mental representation; for example, they can differ over whether objects, Gibsonian affordances, or actions are represented.[9] As a more detailed illustration of one difference, we can note two theories of what is involved in object recognition. One theory, advanced by Irving Biedermann, hypothesizes that object recognition involves the assembly of a few, simple three-dimensional objects called geons (a contraction for **geo**metrical ico**ns**) (see Figure 13.1).[10] There are two important features of these atomic mental representations for object recognition. First, they can typically be discriminated from one another from almost any viewing angle. Second, they can be fairly readily discriminated even when partially occluded. Another theory, advanced by Bülthoff, Tarr, and their colleagues, however, postulates that object recognition involves matching a perspectival representation, or perspective-relative representation, to the object being viewed.[11] For most objects, these perspectival representations have a natural or canonical perspective. So, for example, the natural perspectival view of a car would be from the front, somewhat off to one side, and somewhat higher than the hood. This approach is meant to explain, among other things, findings in which it is easier to recognize a given object from some orientations than it is to recognize it from others. More familiar perspectives are supposed to facilitate recognition over less familiar perspectives (Palmer et al. 1981). Biedermann, on the one hand, and Tarr, Bülthoff et al., on the other, have in common a commitment to the existence of mental representations and operations on those representations. Where they differ is in the content of those mental representations.

One of the leading issues concerning the structure of mental representations begins with a concern about how one is to account for perception and mental imagery.[12] Think of a person looking at a warm sunny, sandy beach. Pre-theoretically, one might suppose that this person is having a perceptual experience and that this experience involves the formation of a mental picture in one's brain. Or, let this person *imagine* looking at a warm sunny beach. Again, one might suppose that this person is having an experience that includes the creation of an internal picture. Here the issue is not whether there are mental representations or what content they might have. It concerns the form or medium of the representations thought to underlie these experiences. Two kinds of hypotheses have been entertained here. One is that perception and imagination involve the creation of pictorial, or quasi-pictorial, analog mental representations, where the other involves sentential representations. The more theoretical or philosophical dimension of the debate concerns articulating the putative difference between these two forms of mental representations, while the more empirical dimension concerns what phenomena require an appeal to one format or the other. One of the phenomena most frequently cited in support of mental pictures is the following. Subjects are asked to memorize a map of an island with various landmarks on it. Subjects are asked to focus their attention on one of the landmarks, and then report when they "see" a second landmark. The central finding is that there is a linear relationship between the distance between the landmarks and the reaction times. This suggests to some that subjects possess a mental picture of the island which they scan across. Although psychological discussions of the existence of mental pictures date to at least the early part of the twentieth century, seminal experimental work by Kosslyn (1980, 1994) sparked renewed interest in the debate within the cognitivist tradition. Twenty years of vigorous debate and pronouncements to the contrary notwithstanding, the debate appears to be far from over.[13]

The issue of the format of mental representations is directly connected to the issue of the way in which cognitivists can think about the manipulation of mental representations. The most common cognitivist view of symbol manipulation is that it is carried out by some form of Turing-equivalent digital computation. Put very simply, cognitive processes are digital computations. It is quite common, for many purposes, to propose that cognitivism is defined by the hypothesis of digital computation. Such an approach is based on a circumscribed understanding of what is meant by "computation," i.e., that it means something like Turing-equivalent digital computation.

A broader understanding, however, would count analog computation as a type of computation. Thus, manipulation of analog images, such as images of islands, could count as a form of analog computation, hence those theories that postulate analog imagistic representations would count as *bona fide* cognitivist theories.

In the foregoing introductory comments on cognitivism, we have devoted more space to the topic of representation than to the topic of their manipulation. We have said more about representation than about rules.[14] This is because the topic of representation is so much more significant to our understanding of the multifarious relations between cognitivism, on the one hand, and the various components of the EC-EM perspective on the other.

Cognition and evolution

The mind has an evolutionary history; it is an adaptation for coping with the environment. As we said at the outset of the paper, this kind of claim is subject to multiple interpretations and there are various morals one might draw from it. Anderson (2005) claims that the embodied cognition approach foregrounds six ideas about cognition and evolution. To paraphrase, these ideas are that cognition has an evolutionary history, that cognition is an adaptation to specific environments in conjunction with specific organismal and environmental features, and that it builds on preexisting behaviors, instincts, needs, and purposes. Each of these claims, however, is perfectly consistent with a broadly construed cognitivist approach. Indeed, as we have noted, such claims are combined in detailed ways with cognitivism in Steven Pinker's book, *How the Mind Works*. This suggests that the combination of evolution and cognition is orthogonal to the issues separating the cognitivist and EC-EM approaches to mind.

The evolutionary history of cognition can, however, lead one to draw different conclusions. For example, one might conclude that the way to study cognition is to begin with the study of simpler minds, the minds of nonhuman animals.[15] Daniel Dennett (1978) proposed such a thing, and Dan Lloyd (1989) pursued it more extensively. It is also a theme in Rodney Brooks (1991a, b, 1997), works more closely allied with the EC-EM approach. Although a shift in methodological approach to the study of cognition, this idea need not constitute a break with cognitivism. Simpler minds might have fewer mental representations, mental representations with less structure, or simpler operations on those mental representations. Then again, a study of simpler minds could lead one to break ranks from cognitivism. It could lead one to a different research focus, a focus on adaptive behavior or behavior that enables an organism to cope with its environment. This can lead to a divergence in research interests between cognitivists and advocates of EC-EM – which is not necessarily the same as a theoretical difference – insofar as adaptive or coping behavior does not necessarily require intelligence or cognition. In other words, we should be prepared to find that the best way for an organism to adapt to its environment or cope with its environment is not to think.[16]

As a possible case in point, works by Brooks (1991a, b, 1997) are often cited as a source of inspiration or illustration of the embodied cognition approach. Consider

Brooks's interest in Creatures. He writes, "I wish to build completely autonomous mobile agents that co-exist in the world with humans, and are seen by those humans as intelligent beings in their own right. I will call such agents *Creatures*. This is my intellectual motivation. I have no particular interest in demonstrating how human beings work, although humans, like other animals, are interesting objects of study in this endeavor as they are successful autonomous agents" (Brooks 1991b: 86). By a "Creature" Brooks means the following:

- A Creature must cope appropriately and in a timely fashion with changes in its dynamic environment.
- A Creature should be robust with respect to its environment. Minor changes in the properties of the world should not lead to total collapse of the Creature's behavior; rather one should expect only a gradual change in capabilities of the Creature as the environment changes more and more.
- A Creature should be able to maintain multiple goals and, depending on the circumstances it finds itself in, change which particular goals it is actively pursuing; thus it can both adapt to surrounding and capitalize on fortuitous circumstances.
- A Creature should do *something* in the world; it should have some purpose in being (Brooks 1997: 402).

Brooks apparently expects that anything that meets these conditions will be a cognitive agent, that they will be "seen by those humans as intelligent beings in their own right." But, unless one takes care to interpret the conditions with this aim in mind, one should be prepared to discover that some organisms, such as plants or slime molds, that are normally construed as non-cognitive meet these conditions. Plants cope appropriately with their environments insofar as they can survive, reproduce, and even flourish. They often respond to their environments by sending out roots in appropriate directions and orienting their leaves and shoots toward the sun. Many can thrive in a wide range of climates or environments, at least as wide as some thinking animals. They can have multiple goals, if one counts producing leaves, roots, stems, taking in carbon dioxide, collecting water, and so forth. They also do something in the world and have some purpose in essentially the same sense in which cognitive animals do. What Brooks is proposing to study, while a legitimate enterprise in its own right, is evidently a departure from the subject of traditional artificial intelligence and cognitivism.

Notice that Brooks might simply insist that his conditions define or specify what he means by something's being intelligent/cognitive, so that he simply stipulates that plants and jellyfish are, in his sense, intelligent/cognitive. Perhaps the conditions on Creatures are supposed to provide an operational definition of intelligence/cognition. Even on this interpretation of what Brooks is up to there is an evident change in research. Where traditional cognitivism has supposed that plants are not organized in such a way as to have cognitive lives at all, Brooks does not share this presupposition. Thus, what Brooks proposes to study is apparently not what cognitivists propose to study. This is not to say that there is a conflict between cognitivism and EC-EM, only a parting of the ways.

Cognition and mental representations

In light of the prominent role of mental representations in the mainstream cognitivist view of cognition, it is not surprising that alternative theories of cognition or approaches to cognition will have something to say about mental representations. EC-EM, however, does not have a univocal position on the role of mental representations in the life of the mind. There are a number of different things that advocates of EC-EM mean when they claim that mental representations do not play the role that traditional cognitive science has posited for them.

At the more conservative end of the spectrum are theories that propose distinct contents and structures for mental representations. Lakoff and Johnson's (1999) theory of primary metaphor is a case in point. Lakoff and Johnson draw attention to what they believe are some underappreciated causal influences on cognition. They claim that the human mind is inherently embodied and that reason is shaped by the body. By this, they mean two principal things. In the first place, they mean *neural embodiment*. This is the claim that the structure of the neural networks making up the brain shapes the concepts and categories we use. As an example, they cite the fact that the human retina has about 100 million photoreceptors, but only about one million retinal ganglion cells leading out of the eye. This, they maintain, forces the nervous system to impose categories on the light information impinging on the retina. Further, what happens in the earliest stages of visual processing is characteristic of the brain as a whole. As another example of neural embodiment, they cite the role of our neural apparatus in the creation of color concepts. Without the particular combination of cones and other neural apparatus for processing electromagnetic radiation of specific frequencies, humans would not have color concepts or not the color concepts they do. In addition to neural embodiment, Lakoff and Johnson draw attention to *phenomenological embodiment*. This is the idea that the concepts we have are acquired and shaped through contingent features of our bodies. As an example of this, they cite the concepts of *front-of* and *back-of*. These are concepts we have and use as a result of the fact that our human bodies are asymmetrical, having a front and a back that mediate our interactions with the world. In our normal daily lives, we move in the direction our front faces and interact with others via our front side. We then project these concepts derived from our bodies on to other objects. Cars have a front in virtue of the direction they move. Televisions and stoves have a front because of the way in which one normally interacts with them. Following these principles, we can see that trees and rocks do not have fronts or backs. Shaun Gallagher (2005) presents another study of the ways in which cognitive processes (and conscious experience) are causally influenced by, or as he says shaped by, being embodied in the way they are. In Gallagher's account, the notions of *body image* and *body schema* are the principal theoretical posits. A *body image* consists of a set of perceptions, attitudes, and beliefs pertaining to one's own body. A *body schema* is a system of sensory motor capacities that function without perceptual monitoring or awareness.

Both Lakoff and Johnson (1999) and Gallagher (2005) offer new theories of the content of mental representations. They are theories of content that provide an articulation of the EC-EM idea that the mind is shaped by, dependent upon, and bound up with the body and its environment. These theories offer accounts of what the mind represents. Such theories, however, are perfectly consistent with the cognitivist view that cognitive processes are computational processes over mental representations. They count as distinct cognitivist theories of what the mind represents in just the way in which Biedermann's theory of geons and Tarr, Bülthoff et al.'s theory of perspectival representations constitute distinct cognitivist theories of what the mind represents.

Another EC-EM take on representations is to suppose that organisms need fewer of them than cognitivism has previously supposed. This theme plays out in various ways as well. Brooks's research again illustrates this theme. Although one might take the provocative title of Brooks's paper, "Intelligence without Representation," literally, what Brooks himself apparently means is that cognitive processing does not rely on representations as heavily or in the kinds of ways that cognitivism has traditionally presupposed.[17] Simple activities, such as navigating about some types of spaces, can be achieved without the construction of complex representations, or maps, of the environment. Navigation does not have to involve anything like a cycle of sensing the location of objects in the environment, constructing a map or model of the environment, then planning a route through the environment, then initiating the plan. Instead, navigation can be highly stimulus driven.

Two of Brooks's robots, Allen and Herbert, illustrate these ideas. Oversimplifying somewhat, Allen has a ring of twelve ultrasonic sonars that give it measures of distances to a dozen objects around it. Allen uses a "level-0" set of skills to compute the distances to objects around it, then moves in such a way as to avoid the objects. By using an additional "level-1" set of skills, Allen can pick random directions in which to move, then modify this choice of direction somewhat by gathering input from the level-0 apparatus that avoids collisions. By using a still further "level-2" set of skills, Allen can find distant walls and move down corridors without colliding with objects that might be in the way or that might move into it. Allen performs these tasks without creating an internal map of objects in its environment. Herbert, a successor to Allen, uses much the same reactive, stimulus driven approach in a more complex task. Herbert moves about the laboratory at MIT collecting soda cans. Herbert maintains no internal state for more than three seconds. Further, there is no communication between many of its distinct components. Herbert has, for example, several lower level modules that enable it to move about without running into objects. There are also several modules that guide the mechanical arm that actually grasps the soda cans. Yet, the movement modules and the grasping modules do not communicate with each other directly. The movement modules do not send a signal to the arm modules informing the arm that Herbert has arrived at a can. Instead, when Herbert's body is positioned appropriately by the stimulus driven moving modules, the grasping modules of the stimulus driven arm take over. When the arm detects a can, the arm in turn moves the hand into place. The arm does not signal to the hand that it has detected a can; rather, the hand simply closes when any object breaks a beam running between the fingers of the hand. The whole idea of the approach is to chain together environmentally reactive procedures in such a way as to have complex behaviors thereby emerge.

A modest construal of this behavior-based robotics is that it is an attempt to see what kinds of tasks might be accomplished without the more traditional approach of sensing, modeling, planning, and acting. As such, it can be seen as completely complementary to the traditional robotics approaches. Brooks, at least at times, seems to be satisfied with this kind of characterization. He sometimes describes it as modeling "insect-level intelligence." Perhaps insect-level intelligence is one thing and human intelligence quite another. Perhaps insect intelligence can be purely stimulus driven and lack complex mental representations, where human intelligence is not purely stimulus driven and does make use of complex mental representations. So conceived behavior-based robotics can exist happily alongside cognitivism. One might also maintain that many of the tasks humans perform in their normal daily routines are the product of environmentally cued responses of the sort found in Allen and Herbert. This, too, however, is consistent with cognitivism. Cognitivists might well concede that much of what humans do is thoughtless in the sense that it does not involve the kinds of information processing that cognitivists maintain constitute thought.

Then there are more radical conclusions one might draw from behavior-based robotics. One might propose that all of human behavior is entirely as reactive and stimulus driven as is Allen's method of moving around or Herbert's method of collecting soda cans. All of human behavior is produced without the mediation of complex mental representations in just the way that Allen's movement down a hallway or Herbert's soda can collecting is produced without the mediation of complex representations. One can, indeed, go farther and claim that cognition does not involve representations at all, complex or otherwise. Here there are two distinguishable ideas, that cognition is stimulus driven and that cognition does not involve complex representations, or even any representations at all. Each merits separate comment.

Clearly there are tasks that can be accomplished in the way suggested by the example of Herbert. But, there appear to be many other tasks that humans perform that cannot. If one proposes that behavior is purely stimulus driven, one needs some account of what is involved in the multifarious effects of what appear to be learning and memory. Surely no normal human being does anything like resetting its cognitive state every three seconds in the way Herbert does. Surely any moderately sophisticated conversation involves remembering information gathered outside the last three seconds. Surely reading with comprehension any moderately complicated paragraph in a book or newspaper article involves remembering what was read prior to the last three seconds. Surely humans going to the grocery without a shopping list remember more than Herbert does. Herbert need only wander about randomly waiting for the appropriate stimuli to guide it to soda cans and then guide it to their drop off point. No normal human going to the grocery wanders about until she finds the car keys, then wanders about the house until she finds the garage, then drives around randomly until finding a grocery, and so forth. Normal humans going to the grocery do seem to have short-term goals that are strung together to bring about complex, coordinated actions. To suppose that cognitive processing is mere stimulus driven processing is more apt to describe the sad condition of H.M., the subject of a bilateral hippocampectomy, who was largely unable to form long-term memories. H.M. had memories of numerous past events, but could form next to no new memories. So, for example, he could not recall from one day to the next the names of the members of the hospital staff who cared for him. He could not recall where the bathroom was or what he had eaten for lunch a half-hour after he had finished (Scoville and Milner 1957). How can EC-EM account for the apparent effects of learning and memory, without representations?

Beer (2003) apparently rejects the hypothesis that human behavior is entirely stimulus driven and proposes to explain the effects of learning and memory by appeal to nonrepresentational internal states. In other words, systems may take on different internal states as a function of experience and thereby modify their behavior as a result of experience, but we need not construe these different states as representational states. Beer backs up this proposal by appeal to the mathematical framework of dynamical systems theory, which allows one to have behaviors change in response to experience, without appeal to a change in representations. One might say that changes in the weights in a connectionist network, for example, are nonrepresentational changes of state that can enable a system to change its behavior as a result of experience.

Van Gelder (1995) supports much the same view and provides a simpler illustration of nonrepresentational processing than we find in Beer (2003). Van Gelder claims that there are two ways in which one might adjust a throttle valve from a steam engine to maintain a flywheel at constant speed. One is through one or another algorithm that measures the speed of the flywheel, compares that speed to a target speed, and then adjusts the throttle valve, if necessary. Another way is to link the flywheel to a vertical spindle. On this spindle, one can add rotating arms holding metal balls at their ends. The rotating mechanism of the arms can then be linked to the adjustable throttle. If the flywheel rotates too quickly, the centrifugal force on the rotating arms increases, extending the arms outward, thereby slowing the throttle. If the flywheel rotates too slowly, the centrifugal force on the rotating arms decreases, lowering the arms inward, thereby speeding up the throttle. In other words, one can attach a Watt governor to the engine. Van Gelder claims that the first method involves a computational method using representations, the kind of explanatory apparatus that a cognitivist might invoke to explain some human behavior, where the second is a non-computational method in a dynamical system that does not involve representations and that these are genuinely different methods.[18] The suggestion, then, is that if cognitive processing consists of changes in the state space of a dynamical system that does not use representations, then cognitive processing does not require representations.

Perhaps Beer and van Gelder are correct, that one can accomplish many tasks that are thought to be cognitive without appealing to representational states. Does this show that cognition does not involve representation? That is not so clear. Beer and van Gelder observe that there are two ways of completing or performing a task, such as regulating the flow of steam from a steam engine. Suppose this is so. Now compare the task of regulating the steam engine with a task such as obtaining food. One way to perform this task might be to deploy processing mechanisms of the sort proposed by cognitivists, namely, mechanisms for visual recognition, evaluating individual objects for edibility, planning a course through the environment, and so forth. But, another way to obtain food apparently involves no cognition at all. The Venus flytrap is not a cognitive agent, but it obtains food. This plant secretes a sweet mucus that attracts insects. When an insect appropriately triggers one of the hair structures in the trap, the trap snaps shut. The Venus flytrap can then proceed to digest the insect over the course of the next few days. Does the way that a Venus flytrap obtains food show that cognition does not require representation? No. A perfectly reasonable thing to say is that the task of obtaining food simply does not require cognition. The point, therefore, is that showing that some task is accomplished by some dynamical system that does not use representations does not show that cognition need not involve representations. Instead, it may show only that, prior expectations notwithstanding, the task does not need to be performed using cognitive processing at all, hence does not need to be performed using representations.

What Beer and van Gelder need is some theory of what a cognitive process is. What do they propose separates a cognitive process from a non-cognitive process? In virtue of what is it the case that an organism or machine, such as Allen or Herbert, is supposed to be cognizing? Cognitivists maintain that the use of representations is part of what sets cognitive processes apart from non-cognitive processes, but Beer and van Gelder have foresworn this theory. It does not suffice to say that cognitive processes are changes of state in some dynamical system. After all, even if one accepts this view, there presumably remains a need to discriminate between dynamical systems, such as coupled pendulums, that are non-cognitive from dynamical systems, such as human cognitive systems, that are cognitive. It might well be that in order to separate cognitive dynamical systems from non-cognitive dynamical systems, one has to say that the former involve representations. That, however, would undercut Beer and van Gelder's anti-representationalism. Nor will it do to say, as does van Gelder, that "the question here is not what makes something cognitive, but how cognitive agents *work*" (van Gelder 1998: 619). This only pushes the question of what processes are cognitive back on to the question of what a cognitive agent is. How can we determine how cognitive agents work, unless we have some sort of theory of what a cognitive agent is? The cognitivist answer is that, among other things, a cognitive agent uses representations. This, however, is precisely the answer that Beer and van Gelder reject.

Perception and action

As we saw in the last section, there is a strain of EC-EM thought that challenges the cognitivist view that a thinking robot would be one that senses, models, plans, and acts, by challenging the need for complex representations, or for any representations whatsoever.[19] Another EC-EM way of challenging this picture, however, is by challenging the apparently great separation between sensing and perceiving, on the one hand, and action, on the other. The EC-EM slogan here is that perception and action are intimately related. There are numerous very simple and thoroughly uncontroversial illustrations of ways in which actions generate important perceptual cues. In human audition, there are two primary cues for the localization of sounds, interaural time differences and interaural intensity differences. In humans, the ears are separated in space which will in many cases lead to differences in the times at which sound waves reach one ear versus the other and will lead to differences in the intensities of the sounds arriving at one ear versus the other. Sounds will arrive sooner and be more intense in the ear that is closer to the source of the sound. This gives humans important cues to the direction from which a sound is coming. These cues work well, except when the source of a sound falls near the plane of bilateral symmetry of the human head. When this happens, incoming sounds arrive at roughly the same time and with roughly the same intensity at both ears. In these cases, it is hard for people to localize the source of a sound. To address this problem, people often simply turn their heads. If the source of the sound is directly in front of or behind someone, this will enable localization. If, however, the sound is more or less directly above the person's head, the sound will still be difficult to localize. In olfaction, when smells are faint, humans, like other animals, will often sniff in an attempt to bring in more odorant. In vision, it is sometimes difficult to judge the distance of various objects in the visual field. Moving the head, however, induces motion parallax in which objects move differently relative to the fixation point. These motions provide depth cues that can be useful.

In the area of mobile robotics, or artificial intelligence, increased attention to the role of action in perception may well constitute a new approach to the design and construction of robots for interacting with the world.[20] Yet, it remains perfectly consistent with a cognitivist view insofar as the mechanisms of action and perception might still be held to be the manipulation of representations of objects, actions, their effects, etc. Within the field of sensation and perception, however, the foregoing kind of role of action in perception is relatively well studied. The various ways in which actions can be used to influence perception, or to collect additional perceptual cues, are familiar from textbooks on sensation and perception. In the study of vision, for example, Findlay and Gilchrist (2003), wish to draw attention to the role of eye movements in visual perception. Yet, it is clear as one works through the text and its many references that this approach draws heavily on an existing literature devoted to such things as the saccade and visual orienting. What we apparently have in this case is not so much a change in perspective or emphasis as a shift of attention. In Findlay and Gilchrist's "active vision," we are to pay greater attention to the role of eye motions in visual perception.

It is, however, possible to develop a more radical version of EC-EM that proposes an even tighter connection between action and perception. One might propose that the two are literally inseparable. It is not merely that there is a causal loop in which actions influence perceptions which in turn influence actions. Instead, actions might be said to be constitutive of perceptions. There is no perception without action. This is at the heart of Kevin O'Regan and Alva Noë's sensorimotor contingency theory of perception.[21] On this view, perception is the exercise of an individual's mastery of particular sensorimotor contingencies. Perceiving is acting, a kind of acting that involves the whole of the organism, an exercise of capacities of the entire agent. Different perceptual modalities, such as vision and touch, involve mastery of distinct sensorimotor contingencies. Vision involves mastery of the ways in which the motion of one's head and eyes will give rise to changes in the visual stimulus. Vision involves practical knowledge of such things as that turning one's head to the right will lead to a leftward motion of objects in the visual field, that the retinal projection of an object depends on its distance from the observer, that only the front face of an object is visible, and that the color and brightness of an object change in certain lawful ways as the object or the light source or the observer move around. Tactile perception by contrast does not depend on distance, it allows the whole of some objects to be embraced, and the feel of an object does not vary with illumination. The sensorimotor theory of perception suggests that cognition is embodied, not just in the brain, but in the whole of the organism, because it is the whole of the organism that is apparently needed to exercise the mastery of sensorimotor contingencies.

A fundamental problem for the sensorimotor theory, however, arises from observations of perception in spite of complete neuromuscular blockade.[22] There are any number of drugs, such as curare, that compete with acetyl choline for binding sites in the neuromuscular junction. If a subject is completely paralyzed by a sufficiently large dose of curare, then that subject cannot move a muscle. That subject cannot exercise mastery of most sensorimotor contingencies. Nevertheless, a subject's perceptual capacities are largely undisturbed. In one very clear study, Topulos et al. (1993) administered the muscle relaxer vecuronium to four subjects with tourniquets applied to one arm. The tourniquet prevented the vecuronium from reaching the neuromuscular junctions in the hand, hence allowed the subjects to continue to use their fingers to signal investigators. Subjects who were immobilized with vecuronium were capable of hearing and answering the investigators' questions, tasting a topical anesthetic, and feeling discomfort. As Topulos et al. report,

> Complete neuromuscular block caused no observable impairment of consciousness, sensation, memory, or the ability to think and make decisions. Objective evidence supported this assertion, as subjects responded promptly to questions. When the experimenter misunderstood their answers, subjects recognized this and made a correction. Subjects successfully used a questionnaire with many branching points to communicate their needs. Subjects also accurately recalled specific events that occurred in the room while they were paralyzed. This unimpaired mental function is consistent with the reports of previous investigators.
>
> (Topulos et al. 1993: 373)

So, the sensorimotor contingency theory of perception does represent a kind of break with traditional cognitivism in advancing a more intimate connection between perception and action than is standard. The problem with it, however, is that it founders on some rather simple and compelling experiments involving neuromuscular blockade.

Complementary processes in brain, body, and environment

Advocates of EC-EM often claim that cognition is shaped by, dependent upon, and bound up with the body and its environment. We have already seen one way of interpreting these claims in terms of the manner in which the content of one's concepts is derived in one way or another by reference to the body. Lakoff and Johnson (1999) and Gallagher (2005) each provide an example of this way of articulating these general claims. O'Regan and Noë's sensorimotor theory of perceptual experience provides another way of interpreting these claims. Yet another way of developing this general theme, however, is through what is sometimes described as the complementary relations between cognitive processes and environmental processes.[23]

The most familiar illustration of this kind of complementarity is found in the use of pencil and paper for the computation of large sums such as 736 + 877. The use of pencil and paper enables a normal human being to work around certain limitations on human cognitive processing, most particularly limits on short-term memory. Simply by writing the numbers down, one does not have to commit them to memory before starting to solve the problem. By writing "736" over "877" in the standard way, one can use relatively easy visual inspection to make sure that the numeral in the ones column in one expression is properly related to the numeral in the ones column in the other expression, that the numeral in the tens column in one expression is properly related to the numeral in the tens column in the other expression, and so forth. Again, this reduces the demands on short-term memory. In addition, as one proceeds in a step by step manner from the ones column to the tens column to the hundreds column, writing down each intermediate sum, one does not have to remember the results of past computations. This is yet another reduction in the demands on short-term memory.

Kirsh (1995) provides a classification of ways in which humans arrange objects and features of their environment in ways that help them compensate for the limitations of their relatively fixed cognitive resources. In Kirsh's scheme, we use the spatial arrangements of objects in order to regulate certain task choices, to simplify perception, and to simplify internal computation. By initially gathering all the ingredients one wants to put in a salad near the sink, one thereby simplifies subsequent task choices. This provides a visual cue concerning what items are to be used and what is to be done with them. Moving the washed items over to the knife and cutting board indicates what is to be done next. In stacking spare pieces of wood appropriately, a carpenter can facilitate the later choice of pieces for use in protecting the work piece when clamping and hammering. In working around a sink with a garbage disposal unit, it is often convenient to block the drain opening to prevent something from falling into the unit. This spares the user having to choose a safe place to put an object that might fall into the unit. These are cases in which the use of space facilitates certain task choices.

Spatial arrangements facilitate perception when like items are grouped together. Thus, when cooking, it is easier to distinguish the washed vegetables from the unwashed vegetables if they are kept in spatially separated clusters. When bagging groceries, the heavy items must go in the bottom of the bag, the intermediate items in the middle, and the light, fragile items on top. But, items do not reach the bagger prearranged for easy bagging. Not every item will immediately go into a bag, so the bagger must often sort the items by size and weight, prior to actually putting them in bags. It, therefore, makes sense to put the heavy items in one cluster, the medium sized items in another, and the light, fragile items in still another. This facilitates subsequent recognition of the weights of objects when they are finally to be bagged. The example of using pencil and paper to compute large sums illustrates this idea as well. By arranging the two numerals to be added one above another, rather than in a continuous line, it is easier to be sure to add ones to ones, tens to tens, etc. The long-range scanning that would be involved in the addition of the linearly arranged numerals is thereby avoided.

To illustrate how spatial arrangements simplify internal computation Kirsh refers to his work on playing the game Tetris. In this game, "tetrazoid" blocks of various shapes descend from the top of a computer screen and must be fitted into slots at the bottom of the screen. In order to assess the fit, experienced players do not imagine the blocks then mentally rotate them to check the fit. Instead, experienced players push a button on the game panel in order to rotate the block on the screen. Subjects, thus, spare themselves the effort of mentally rotating the objects by actually rotating the object on the screen. In another game context, playing Scrabble, subjects arrange the lettered tiles on their trays in an effort to cue possible uses of the tiles in words.

In describing his work, Kirsh generally offers a relatively conservative estimate of his research strategy. He takes it to be a shift in emphasis: "How we manage the space around us, then, is not an afterthought; it is an integral part of the way we think, plan, and behave, a central element in the way we shape the very world that constrains and guides our behavior" (Kirsh 1995: 31–2). Andy Clark (2002) and John Sutton (2010) adopt a potentially more radical interpretation of Kirsh's work. Cognitive processes do not occur only within the brain. They can also, under some circumstances, spread across physical and social environments. Both Clark and Sutton very deliberately rely upon the complementary relations between what goes on within the brain and what takes place in the environment in support of this view of the locus of mental processes.

What is potentially radical about Clark's and Sutton's proposal is not that cognitive processes *might* extend from the brain into the body and environment. This possibility stems from the cognitivist commitment to the idea that it is the functional organization of a process that determines whether or not that process is cognitive. That organization, whatever it may be, could, in principle, be realized in any number of material substrates. So, it could be realized only in the brain, or in combination with the brain and body, or in combination with the brain, body, and elements of the environment. What is radical in Clark and Chalmers's and Sutton's view, where it departs from cognitivist orthodoxy, is in the supposition that the complementary relations between brain processes and environmental processes are reason to think that the brain-body-environmental system would be cognitively equivalent to a cognitive process. The radical view maintains the whole assembly of complementary objects and processes constitutes a single thinking being, a single cognitive process. Although cognitivism allows for many sorts of things to realize a cognitive economy, mere complementarity with an environmental process does not enable a cognitive process to extend into the environment. While there is some value in noting the many types of complementary relationships between cognitive processes and environmental processes, it is a bold move to suppose that this gives us reason to suppose that cognitive processes extend from the brain into the body and environment.

To better appreciate the challenge to this radical EC-EM reasoning, consider other cases outside of cognitive science. A standard no. 2 pencil and a pencil sharpener work together to enable a person to write clearly. Writing wears down the point of the pencil, where the sharpener puts a finer point on it. Together the pencil and the sharpener enable a writer to write more and write more clearly and perhaps more attractively. Nevertheless, the pencil and sharpener remain distinct objects in which distinct processes take place. We do not suppose that writing takes place in, or with, both the pencil and the sharpener. In an air conditioner, the evaporator coil and the condenser serve complementary functions. In the evaporator coil a refrigerant evaporates causing a drop in temperature which cools the air. In the condenser, the refrigerant is pressurized which causes it to liquefy and heat up. These are complementary processes, each limited to a distinct portion of the air conditioner. We do not suppose that the cooling takes place in the whole of the system. In a vacuum cleaner, a fan generates a vacuum and a bag filters the air that passes through it. The appropriate arrangement of the vacuum generating device and the filtration device produces an object with capabilities not had by the individual parts. Nonetheless, suction generation takes place in one region of the vacuum cleaner; it does not pervade the whole of the device. All of which suggests that it is one thing to note the complementary relations between cognitive, bodily, and environmental processes, but quite another to suppose that, in virtue of these complementary relations, cognitive processes pervade brain, body, and environment.

The coupling between brain, body, and environmental processes

We have just seen that one way to interpret Kirsh's work is in terms of the complementary relations between brain, body, and environment. The interactions among brain, body, and environment open up possibilities that could not be realized by the brain acting in isolation. This is, however, still one more way to articulate the idea that the mind is shaped by, dependent upon, and bound up with the body and its environment. One can also think about Kirsh's work in terms of some sort of coupling between what takes place in the brain, the body, and the environment. Kirsh himself has this to say, "In many high speed interactions, the agent and environment can be so tightly coupled that it may be plausible to view the two as forming a single computational system. In that case, some elements of the computation are outside the agent, some are inside, and the computation itself consists in the dynamic interaction between the two" (Kirsh 1995: 63–4). This again invites the radical view according to which cognitive processes extend beyond the brain and span the brain, body, and environment.

Clark and Chalmers (1998), among others, pick up on the notion of coupling as one reason to think that cognitive processes are not to be found entirely within the head.[24] They claim that, "In these cases, the human organism is linked with an external entity in a two-way interaction, creating a *coupled system* that can be seen as a cognitive system in its own right. All the components in the system play an active causal role, and they jointly govern the behavior in the same sort of way that cognition usually does. If we remove the external component the system's behavioral competence will drop, just as it would drop if we removed part of its brain. Our thesis is that this sort of coupled process counts equally well as a cognitive process, whether or not it is wholly in the head" (Clark and Chalmers 1998: 8–9).[25] Here we have a familiar way of stating that cognitive processes extend into the body and environment.

This view is perhaps the boldest claim in the EC-EM literature, but it need not conflict with cognitivism. It could, in principle, be that processes that span the brain, body, and environment constitute a kind of computation on symbolic representations of just the sort found inside brains. In principle, a transcorporeal process could be cognitively equivalent to a cognitive process, hence be a cognitive process. Were there to be such an equivalence, we would have an instance of extended cognition.[26] Where Clark and Chalmers threaten to run afoul of cognitivism, however, is in thinking that creating a kind of coupling between a cognitive process and an environmental process is sufficient for bringing the environmental processes into a cognitive economy. Coupling relations appear to be insufficient to bring about a continuity of a process type. This is clear from some simple examples. Consider how Clark and Chalmers's reasoning might apply to a heating system. In these systems, a thermostat is linked with an external entity, the furnace, in a two-way interaction, creating a coupled system that constitutes the heating system. All the components in the system play an active causal role and they jointly govern the behavior. If we remove the furnace the system's behavioral competence will drop, just as it would drop if we removed part of the thermostat. Yet, contrary to what Clark and Chalmers would infer, the process of expansion of a bimetallic strip is limited to the thermostat and the process of generating heat by the combustion of a gas is limited to the furnace. As we noted above, in general, a coupling between two processes does not influence the typing of the process.[27]

Conclusion

The EC-EM approach to cognitive science is a work in progress, a work admitting of more conservative and more radical forms. Exactly what form the approach takes depends on how various slogans are developed in detail. Part of what makes the approach plausible is the ability to take on the milder versions of its slogans. The mind has an evolutionary history. Who but creationists deny this? Perception and action are intimately related. Of course, they can be integrated into a single cognitive economy. No one should doubt that. Mental representations do not play the role that traditional cognitive science has posited for them. There are many ways in which one can take exception to certain hypotheses concerning extant theories of mental representation. The mind is shaped by, dependent upon, and bound up with the body and its environment. Of course the mind causally interacts with the body and its environment. If the milder forms of these hypotheses make the EC-EM perspective seem plausible, it is the more radical forms that make it seem exciting. It is bracing to think that cognitive processes are to be found, not just in the brain, but in the body and environment as well. It is revolutionary to think that cognitive processes involve no representations at all. If the EC-EM approach is to stand as an alternative to cognitivism, however, it will need a way of articulating its slogans in ways that are both plausible and interesting.

Notes

1. For this mode of exposition of embodied cognition and extended mind, see, for example, Anderson (2003), Beer (1995), Brooks (1991a, b, 1997), Haugeland (1998), and Thelen (1995). For an exposition of cognitivism, see Garnham (this volume).
2. See, e.g., Pinker (1997).
3. For further exposition of cognitivism, see Garnham (this volume).
4. Newell and Simon (1972, 1976), Newell (1980, 1990).
5. See Chomsky (1980).
6. See Pylyshyn (1984) and Fodor (1987).
7. A one-to-one mapping between set A and set B is such that for each element of A, there is a distinct member of B. An onto mapping between set A and set B is such that for each member of B, there is a member of A mapped onto it.
8. There is a *prima facie* tension between the neuroscientific tendency to use single-cell-recording techniques to assign meaning to individual neurons on the basis of what environmental stimuli trigger them and the philosophical proposal that items in the mind get their semantic content in virtue of their interrelations.
9. Anderson and Perlis (2002) and Vera and Simon (1993), for example, review these options.
10. Biedermann (1987, 1990).
11. Blanz, V., Tarr, M. J., and Bülthoff, H. H. (1999), Bülthoff, H. H., Edelmann, S. Y., and Tarr, M. J. (1995), Tarr (1995).
12. Another issue concerns whether or not mental representations are compositional in the way that formulas in first-order logic are compositional, or whether they are in some sense "distributed" or "superposed." See, for example, Haugeland (1991) and van Gelder (1991).
13. See, for example, Kosslyn (1994), Kosslyn et al. (2003), Pylyshyn (2003a, b).
14. For still further discussion of representation, see Ryder, pts 1 and 2 (this volume).
15. Turing (1950) himself suggested studying and trying to implement a child's mind before trying to build an adult mind.
16. Chiel and Beer (1997), for example, focus on adaptive behavior, with ramifications much like those following from Brooks's work.
17. In truth, Brooks seems to us to take an equivocal attitude towards representations. On the one hand, he writes, "I must admit that the title is a little inflammatory – a careful reading shows that I mean intelligence without *conventional* representation, rather than without any representation at all" (Brooks 1999b: 79), and there are points in his text where this idea comes out clearly. There are, however, also points at which Brooks seems to want to claim that there are no representations at all: "we believe representations are not necessary and appear only in the eye or mind of the observer" (*ibid.*: 96).
18. Chemero (2000) challenges van Gelder's anti-representationalist interpretation of the Watt governor, where Glymour (n.d.) challenges van Gelder's anti-computationalist interpretation of the Watt governor. See also Bechtel (1998).

19. Within the EC-EM approach to vision, there is Ballard's (1991) proposal that, "[visual] behaviors may not require categorical representations of the 3-D world" (58). Churchland et al. (1994) also challenge what one might call "rich" representations of the environment. Noë (2004) argues that perception does not involve the formation of a mental image, photograph, or snapshot. Adopting these views is, of course, perfectly consistent with cognitivism. Merely challenging the need for complex representations of the environment in vision does not automatically put one beyond the pale of cognitivism. Pylyshyn (2003a, b), for example, provides an extended, cognitivist critique of the pictorial theory of vision. All of this can readily be construed as an in-house cognitivist debate over what representations are needed to explain vision, an in-house debate comparable to what is found in the imagery debate.
20. See Ballard (1991).
21. O'Regan and Noë (2001a, b) and Noë (2004).
22. For further discussion of this and other cases, see Adams and Aizawa (2008).
23. See Clark and Chalmers (1998).
24. The appeal to a coupling between environmental processes and brain processes is also at the heart of Haugeland's (1998) and van Gelder's (1995) version of the view that cognitive processes should be viewed as brain-body-world processes.
25. Not to oversimplify Clark and Chalmers's view, there are overtones of a commitment to the idea that the kinds of processing that take place in the environment are, in some sense, cognitively equivalent to the kind of processing that takes place within the brain.
26. For challenges to some putative examples of a cognitive equivalence between an internal cognitive process and the processes involving the use of a pencil and paper, see Adams and Aizawa (2001) and Rupert (2004).
27. For a much more extensive discussion of "coupling arguments" for extended cognition, see Adams and Aizawa (2001, 2008).

References

Adams, F., and Aizawa, K. (2001) "The Bounds of Cognition," *Philosophical Psychology* 14: 43–64.

—— (2008) *The Bounds of Cognition*, London: Blackwell.

Anderson, M. L. (2003) "Embodied Cognition: A Field Guide," *Artificial Intelligence* 149: 91–130.

—— (2005) "How to Study the Mind: An Introduction to Embodied Cognition," in F. Santoianni and C. Sabatano (eds), *Brain Development in Learning Environments: Embodied and Perceptual Advancements*, Newcastle upon Tyne: Cambridge Scholars Publishing, pp. 65–82.

Anderson, M. L., and Perlis, D. R. (2002) "Symbol Systems," in L. Nadel (ed.) *Encyclopedia of Cognitive Science*, New York: Nature Publishing Group, pp. 281–7.

Ballard, D. (1991) "Animate Vision," *Artificial Intelligence Journal* 48: 57–86.

Bechtel, W. (1998) "Representations and Cognitive Explanations: Assessing the Dynamicist's Challenge in Cognitive Science," *Cognitive Science* 22: 295–318.

Beer, R. D. (1995) "A Dynamical Systems Perspective on Agent-Environment Interaction," *Artificial Intelligence* 72: 173–215.

—— (2003) "The Dynamics of Active Categorical Perception in an Evolved Model Agent," *Adaptive Behavior* 11: 209–243.

Biedermann, I. (1987) "Recognition-by-Components: A Theory of Human Image Understanding," *Psychological Review* 94: 115–47.

—— (1990) "Higher-Level Vision," in D. N. Osherson, S. Kosslyn, and J. Hollerbach (eds), *An Invitation to Cognitive Science: Visual Cognition and Action*, Cambridge, MA: MIT Press, 41–72.

Blanz, V., Tarr, M. J., and Bülthoff, H. H. (1999) "What Object Attributes Determine Canonical Views?" *Perception* 28: 575–600.

Block, N. (1986) "Advertisement for a Semantics for Psychology," *Midwest Studies in Philosophy* 10: 615–78.

Brooks, R. (ed.) (1991a) "Intelligence without Reason," in Ray Myopoulos and John Reiter (ed.), *Proceedings of the 12th International Joint Conference on Artificial Intelligence, Sydney, Australia, August,*

San Mateo, CA: Morgan Kaufmann, pp. 569–95; repr. R. Brooks, ed., *Cambrian Intelligence: The Early History of the New AI*, Cambridge, MA: MIT Press, 1999, pp. 133–86.

—— (1991b) "Intelligence without Representation," *Artificial Intelligence Journal* 47: 139–60; repr. R. Brooks, ed., *Cambrian Intelligence: The Early History of the New AI*, Cambridge, MA: MIT Press, 1999, pp. 79–101.

—— (1997) "Intelligence without Representation," in J. Haugeland (ed.), *Mind Design II: Philosophy, Psychology, Artificial Intelligence*, rev. enlarged edn, Cambridge, MA: MIT Press, pp. 395–420.

Bülthoff, H. H., Edelmann, S. Y., and Tarr, M. J. (1995) "How Are Three Dimensional Objects Represented in the Brain?" *Cerebral Cortex* 5: 247–60.

Chemero, A. (2000) "Anti-representationalism and the Dynamical Stance," *Philosophy of Science* 67: 625–47.

Chiel, H. J., and Beer, R. D. (1997) "The Brain Has a Body: Adaptive Behavior Emerges from the Interactions of Nervous System, Body, and Environment," *Trends in Neuroscience* 20: 553–7.

Chomsky, N. (1980) *Rules and Representations*, New York: Columbia University Press.

Churchland, P. S., Ramachandran, V. S., and Sejnowski, T. J. (1994) "A Critique of Pure Vision," in C. Koch and J. S. Davis (eds), *Large-Scale Neuronal Theories of the Brain*, Cambridge, MA: MIT Press, pp. 23–60.

Clark, A. (2002) "Towards a Science of the Bio-Technological Mind," *International Journal of Cognition and Technology* 1: 21–33.

Clark, A., and Chalmers, D. (1998) "The Extended Mind," *Analysis* 58: 7–19.

Cummins, R. (1996) *Representations, Targets, and Attitudes*, Cambridge, MA: MIT Press.

Dennett, D. (1978) "Why Not the Whole Iguana?" (commentary on Pylyshyn), *Behavioral and Brain Sciences* 1: 103–4.

Dretske, F. (1988) *Explaining Behavior*, Cambridge, MA: MIT Press.

Findlay, J., and Gilchrist, I. (2003) *Active Vision: The Psychology of Looking and Seeing*, Oxford: Oxford University Press.

Fodor, J. (1987) *Psychosemantics: The Problem of Meaning in the Philosophy of Mind*, Cambridge, MA: MIT Press.

—— (1990). *A Theory of Content and Other Essays*, Cambridge, MA: MIT Press.

Gallagher, S. (2005) *How the Body Shapes the Mind*, Oxford: Oxford University Press.

Glymour, C. (n.d.) "Goethe to van Gelder: Comments on 'Dynamical Systems' Models of Cognition," PhilSciArchives; available: http://philsci-archive.pitt.edu/archive/00000139/ (accessed 20 December 2006).

Haugeland, J. (1991) "Representational Genera," in S. Stich, D. Rumelhart, and W. Ramsey (eds), *Philosophy and Connectionist Theory*, Hillsdale, NJ: Erlbaum, pp. 61–89.

—— (1998) "Mind Embodied and Embedded," in J. Haugeland (ed.), *Having Thought*, Cambridge, MA: Harvard University Press, pp. 207–37.

Kirsh, D. (1995) "The Intelligent Use of Space," *Artificial Intelligence* 73: 31–68.

Kosslyn, S. (1980) *Image and Mind*, Cambridge, MA: Harvard University Press.

—— (1994) *Image and Brain: The Resolution of the Imagery Debate*, Cambridge, MA: Harvard University Press.

Kosslyn, S., Ganis, G., and Thompson, W. L. (2003) "Mental Imagery: Against the Nihilistic Hypothesis," *Trends in Cognitive Sciences* 7: 109–11.

Lakoff, G., and Johnson, M. (1999) *Philosophy in the Flesh: The Embodied Mind and Its Challenge to Western Thought*, New York: Basic Books.

Lloyd, D. (1989) *Simple Minds*, Cambridge, MA: MIT Press.

Newell, A. (1980) "Physical Symbol Systems," *Cognitive Science* 4: 135–83.

—— (1990) *Unified Theories of Cognition*, Cambridge, MA: Harvard University Press.

Newell, A., and Simon, H. A. (1972) *Human Problem Solving*, Englewood Cliffs, NJ: Prentice-Hall.

—— (1976) "Computer Science as Empirical Inquiry: Symbols and Search," *Communications of the Association for Computing Machinery* 19: 113–26.

Noë, A. (2004) *Action in Perception*, Cambridge, MA: MIT Press.

O'Regan, J. K., and Noë, A. (2001a) "A Sensorimotor Account of Vision and Visual Consciousness," *Behavioral and Brain Sciences* 24: 939–1031.

—— (2001b) "What It Is Like to See: A Sensorimotor Theory of Perceptual Experience," *Synthese* 129: 79–103.
Palmer, S. E., Rosch, E., and Chase, P. (1981) "Canonical Perspective and the Perception of Objects," in J. Long and A. Baddeley (eds), *Attention and Performance*, vol. 9, Hillsdale, NJ: Erlbaum, pp. 135–51.
Pinker, S. (1997) *How the Mind Works*, New York: W. W. Norton & Sons.
Pylyshyn, Z. (1984) *Computation and Cognition: Toward a Foundation for Cognitive Science*, Cambridge, MA: MIT Press.
—— (2003a) "Return of the Mental Image: Are There Really Pictures in the Brain?" *Trends in Cognitive Sciences* 7: 113–18.
—— (2003b) "Explaining Mental Imagery: Now You See It, Now You Don't – Reply to Kosslyn et al.," *Trends in Cognitive Sciences* 7: 111–12.
Rupert, R. (2004) "Challenges to the Hypothesis of Extended Cognition," *Journal of Philosophy* 101: 389–428.
Scoville, W. B., and Milner, B. (1957) "Loss of Recent Memory after Bilateral Hippocampal Lesions," *Journal of Neurology, Neurosurgery, and Psychiatry* 20: 11–21.
Stich, S., and Warfield, T. (1994) *Mental Representation: A Reader*, Cambridge, MA: Blackwell.
Sutton, J. (2010) "Exograms and Interdisciplinarity: History, the Extended Mind, and the Civilizing Process," in R. Menary (ed.), *The Extended Mind*, Aldershot, UK: Ashgate.
Tarr, M. J. (1995) "Rotating Objects to Recognize Them: A Case Study in the Recognition of Three Dimensional Objects," *Psychonomic Bulletin and Review* 2: 55–82.
Thelen, E. (1995) "Time-Scale Dynamics and the Development of an Embodied Cognition," in R. Port and T. van Gelder (eds), *Mind as Motion: Explorations in the Dynamics of Cognition*, Cambridge, MA: MIT Press, pp. 69–100.
Topulos, G. P., Lansing, R. W., and Banzett, R. B. (1993) "The Experience of Complete Neuromuscular Blockade in Awake Humans," *Journal of Clinical Anesthesiology* 5: 369–74.
Turing, A. (1950) "Computing Machinery and Intelligence," *Mind* 59: 433–60.
van Gelder, T. (1991) "What Is the 'D' in 'PDP'? An Overview of the Concept of Distribution," in S. Stich, D. Rumelhart, and W. Ramsey (eds), *Philosophy and Connectionist Theory*, Hillsdale NJ: Erlbaum, pp. 33–59.
van Gelder, T. (1995) "What Might Cognition Be, If Not Computation?" *Journal of Philosophy* 91: 345–81.
—— (1998) "The Dynamical Hypothesis in Cognitive Science," *Behavioral and Brain Sciences* 21: 615–28.
Vera, A. H., and Simon, H. A. (1993) "Situated Action: A Symbolic Interpretation," *Cognitive Science* 17: 7–48.

14
CONCEPTUAL PROBLEMS IN STATISTICS, TESTING AND EXPERIMENTATION

David Danks and Frederick Eberhardt

Introduction

By virtue of the individuals and processes being studied, cognitive psychology is a methodologically challenging science. On the one hand, psychology aims to be a natural science, complete with testing of models by experimental evidence. On the other hand, the distinctive domain that psychology considers cannot be studied with many standard experimental techniques. This chapter explores some of the methodological and statistical challenges confronting present-day psychology, with a principal focus on problems that are particular to psychology, as opposed to the general problems of experimental design, confirmation, inference, and so on that confront essentially all sciences. We focus on problems for which no full and complete solution is known. Where appropriate, we have indicated various possibilities or proposals, but many of these challenges remain open questions for the practice of psychology.

There is one important body of difficulties that we will not explore in detail: namely, the relative inaccessibility of the target phenomena of psychology. Psychological objects such as beliefs and desires are not directly accessible to experimenters, either for manipulation or measurement. We cannot directly intervene on psychological states; at most, we can provide stimuli designed to induce a particular mental state, though those interventions are rarely as precise as desired (Campbell 2007). We thus confront a host of methodological concerns (e.g., Do our manipulations affect their target, but not other causally relevant variables?) and conceptual concerns (e.g., Are mental states causal variables at all? Does multiple realizability (if correct) preclude the very possibility of unambiguous interventions?). The lack of direct accessibility also presents a measurement challenge: we cannot directly observe mental states, but rather must measure various proxies, typically readily observable behavior. We note this measurement difficulty not as any sort of call for behaviorism; inference about unobserved entities is difficult, but certainly not impossible. Rather, our inability to directly observe mental states places an additional methodological burden on the psychologist: she must ensure that proxy measurements are suitably correlated with the mental states that she is trying to investigate. As a practical example, one should be skeptical when interpreting data obtained from surveys, as they are typically only (very) noisy proxies for the relevant underlying mental states. Furthermore, the measurement and manipulation challenges interact: if we could directly measure mental states, then our inability to directly manipulate them would pose less of a problem; if we could directly manipulate mental states, then we could use those manipulations to help directly measure them.

These two challenges are significant but have also been the target of many different philosophical debates (e.g., about the nature of mental causation). In contrast, we focus on conceptual and methodological challenges that are more specific to the practice of contemporary psychology, and that have either not received as much attention or continue to be the subject of methodological debate. In particular, our discussion will center on issues raised by the significant variability found in psychological data, the challenges presented by unconscious cognition, and important methodological issues in experiment design and analysis.

Variability in psychological data

One of the most noticeable features of psychological data – particularly to newcomers to the field – is the combination of large variability in the data and (relatively) small sample sizes. In general, we have neither sufficiently clean data to make precise predictions nor sufficient sample sizes to overcome data noise from many different sources. As a result, we must accept the fact that theoretically distinguishable theories will sometimes not be distinguishable, given the data at hand, and may not be distinguishable given *any* plausible future data. For example, exemplar- and prototype-based theories of categorization make differing predictions for certain experimental designs, but experiments using those designs do not discriminate between the theories. Superior performance by one or the other model type is almost certainly due to superior fitting of noise in people's response mechanisms, rather than underlying features of their categorization mechanisms (Minda and Smith 2001; Nosofsky and Zaki 2002; Olsson et al. 2004). Of course, all sciences face the noise vs. sample size tradeoff in one form or another; psychology is not special in this regard, though the problem is more extreme here. Psychology also has distinctive *reasons* for the variability. In general, we can think about this variability as arising from three distinct sources: (1) participant interest; (2) individual differences; and possibly (3) stochastic mechanisms. In this section, we examine conceptual issues that arise from each of these sources of variability, as well as their interaction.

A persistent (though rarely discussed) challenge of psychological experimentation is the obvious fact that the data points come from intentional agents with their own desires, beliefs, etc. In particular, there is a general, unstated recognition that some subset of the experimental participants will either (i) fail to understand the experiment instructions or (ii) not be sufficiently motivated to actually follow the instructions. This problem is arguably exacerbated by the common failure to check whether an experiment provides an appropriate incentive structure to elicit a participant's "best" behavior, as well as the widespread use of undergraduate students as experimental participants. The prototypical "problem participant" here is one who answers "No" or "0" for every question in an effort to leave as quickly as possible. A more difficult case is a participant in an experiment on arithmetic ability who aims to finish quickly by providing approximately correct answers, such as "101 × 59 = 5900." These responses do not accurately measure the participant's ability, and so should presumably be excluded from our analyses and theorizing. But what distinguishes this individual from the participant who simply is not very good at arithmetic?

Various experimental techniques can mitigate this problem, but it is rarely possible to eliminate it completely for interesting experiments. Instead, we need a method for classifying some participants as "unresponsive" or "failing to follow instructions." Such a method will necessarily depend on a normative model of how people *ought* to behave in this experimental setting (e.g., that no one should ever say "101 × 59 = 0"). The problem is that normative models of higher level cognition should be sensitive to the particular limits and constraints of our cognitive system, at least if one believes that normative models should not require behavior that is in principle unattainable (i.e., if one thinks that "ought implies can"). We thus face a potential conceptual circle: namely, our normative models of human cognition should be sensitive to descriptive capacities, but to develop models of descriptive capacities, we use the same normative models to interpret and identify relevant experimental data (see also Harré 1996).[1] Other sciences typically avoid this circle by finding an independent ground for the normative model in its more general applicability (e.g., using Newtonian mechanics to predict the specific behavior of a pendulum); it is not clear that normative models in psychology have the necessary independent grounding, or that there exist framework theories with the appropriate generality.

This circularity need not be a vicious one. There are at least two alternatives, though neither has been carefully explored. First, one could provide a bootstrap account in which descriptive accounts of cognitive phenomena at a "lower" level (e.g., short-term memory) are used to justify normative theories of "higher" phenomena (e.g., causal learning), which are then used to inform the development of descriptive theories at that same higher level. This approach requires an independently justified "ground level" theory (e.g., a descriptive account of working memory based on neuroscientific data), as well as evidence that the bootstrapping could actually work in practice. A second response to the circularity would aim for equilibrium between the various theories: the data deemed "acceptable" by the normative model N at one level would support a descriptive model D at the same level whose constraints are consistent with N. An equilibrium-based account would then need to establish a connection between this type of equilibrium and the truth about cognitive mechanisms, and it is not obvious that any such connection must hold. In practice, psychology almost certainly involves a mix of responses to the general conceptual circle. Regardless of approach, though, we need a more rigorous understanding of the relationship between normative and descriptive theories of cognition (see also Colyvan, 2008).

Even if we solve this general problem of "outlier" detection, the other sources of variability complicate discovery and inference from psychological data. Most of cognitive psychology is individualistic in target: it aims to develop models of cognitive functioning in particular individuals, for purposes of prediction, explanation, and understanding. At the same time, the significant variability of even "clean" data naturally leads to the use of population-level statistics (e.g., mean rating) for testing experiments. Since data about the whole group of participants are more robust against some of the problems of (random) noise, psychologists frequently use such data to make inferences about features of the cognitive mechanisms in a particular individual. There are, however, serious challenges in making inferences from features of the population to features of the individual. For example, some population-level statistics provably do not match the individual-level statistics, even if every individual in the population is identical (Chu et al. 2003; Danks and Glymour 2001).

Theories are also frequently tested by checking model fit, but the best-fitting model for populations need not be the same as the best-fitting model for individuals, either in theory (Brown and Heathcote 2003; Myung et al. 2000) or in practice. For example, participants in many categorization experiments learn novel categories, provide ratings (e.g., the likelihood of some new object being an *A*), and then those mean ratings are compared with the predictions of various theories. One of the most commonly used category structures is the so-called 5/4 structure (Medin and Schaffer 1978), and exemplar-based theories provide the best model fit for the mean ratings of most experiments with this structure. In contrast, Minda and Smith (2002) argue that prototype-based models provide a better fit for each *individual* (though see Zaki et al. 2003). Thus, the best-fitting categorization model for the population might not be the best model for each of the individuals.

Moreover, simple uses of population-level statistics to make inferences about individuals require an assumption of population uniformity, and there are numerous cautionary tales of empirical failures of this assumption. As just one example, in a standard type of causal learning experiment, participants observe a sequence of cases and then provide judgments about the causal strength of one factor to bring about another. The psychologist is principally interested in the way judgments vary as a function of the statistics of the sequence, and so the standard data analysis is to compare the mean ratings of causal efficacy against various theories. However, multiple studies provide evidence that participants are actually using a range of strategies (Anderson and Sheu 1995; Buehner et al. 2003; Lober and Shanks 2000), and so mean ratings are not necessarily informative about features of the individual learners. And the method of analysis matters for the conclusion: a single-group reanalysis of data from Buehner and Cheng (1997) supported Bayesian causal support (Griffiths and Tenenbaum 2005), while a two-group reanalysis supported a mixture of causal power and conditional ΔP (Buehner et al. 2003).

The standard response to all of these worries is to pursue so-called individual differences research. There are two distinct types of individual differences research: one in which all individuals are assumed to have the same algorithm, but different parameter values; and a second in which individuals are allowed to have different underlying algorithms. Research in the first vein has a long history in psychometrics (including seminal work such as Spearman 1904) and assumes that differential performance arises because people differ in some underlying attribute that plays an important role in cognitive function. The approach is analogous to understanding differential performance as arising from the same program running on two computers that have hardware differences (e.g., processor speed). This line of research has typically focused on "important" individual-specific parameters, such as working memory capacity, processing speed, or general intelligence, as well as their interaction (e.g., Ackerman 1988; Barrett et al. 2004; Just and Carpenter 1992; Schunn et al. 2001; Sternberg 1977; Taatgen 2002). The standard experimental design for this type of research is to provide people with a battery of psychometric tests to estimate the relevant global parameter(s), and then to correlate those estimates with performance on a subsequent, more complicated task. Since this research assumes that people all use fundamentally the same algorithm or underlying cognitive mechanism, performance differences must be due to differences in the global parameter(s).

In contrast, the second type of individual differences research allows for the possibility that people use completely different algorithms to solve problems. There is a significant body of research in a wide range of domains and for many different populations showing that people use a variety of strategies (e.g., Chi et al. 1981; Ericsson and Charness 1994; Payne et al. 1993; Siegler 1996; Stanovich 1999). This type of individual differences research uses an individual's behavior pattern to determine which strategy she is most likely using and, if relevant, the parameters for that algorithm (e.g., Lee 2006; Schunn and Reder 1998). Continuing the analogy with computers, this type of analysis models differential performance as resulting from the same computer (or same hardware) running different programs that achieve similar goals (e.g., MATLAB vs. Excel).

Regardless of focus, individual difference analyses must provide a model for each individual participant. Given the relative noisiness of psychological data, one typically must collect many more data points for an individual differences analysis than for a more traditional population-level analysis. Moreover, modeling each individual separately can make it difficult to balance both goodness of fit and generalizability for the model, as it becomes even more difficult to know which variations are due to noise, and which reflect actual features of the underlying cognitive mechanisms (Pitt et al. 2002). Thus, a promising line of recent research assumes that there is some small number of distinct groups, where every individual within a group has the same algorithm and parameters. Since groups have multiple members, one gains the benefits of multiple measurements to offset noise; at the same time, one is not locked into the assumption that every individual is identical. The tricky part is, of course, determining the appropriate number of groups, as well as which participant belongs to which group. There are a number of sophisticated statistical techniques that have recently been proposed, including Dirichlet process models (Navarro et al. 2006), a hierarchical Bayesian framework (Rouder et al. 2003), or maximum likelihood partition generation (Lee and Webb 2005). At their core, they are all structurally similar, finding (i) the number of groups; (ii) allocation of individuals to groups; and (iii) characteristics of each group that maximizes the likelihood of observing data such as these. As such, they are typically quite computationally complex but have the potential to establish a middle ground between population-level and individual differences analyses.

Finally, the possibility of stochastic cognitive mechanisms raises important questions about what types of predictions we ought to expect from psychological models. Deterministic psychological models are straightforward to confirm, at least from a theoretical point of view. Since precise predictions are made for each individual and each situation, we can generate the proper predictions (perhaps with noise) and check whether the observed data match those predictions (up to noise). In contrast, models that posit stochastic cognitive mechanisms cannot be confirmed in the same manner, since there is no determinate prediction for each situation. As just one example of many, the category learning model RULEX (Nosofsky and Palmeri 1998; Nosofsky et al. 1994) includes stochastic choice points during learning. If the same individual saw the exact same sequence of data on two separate occasions, she would not necessarily learn the same category, and so RULEX predicts only a distribution of learned categories for any individual. Thus, one is almost forced to confirm the RULEX model – or any other model that posits inherently stochastic elements – by comparing a predicted distribution of responses against the population as a whole, particularly since one can only provide an experimental participant with the same sequence multiple times by changing experimental features that might be relevant to their learning (e.g., cover story). Of course, the difficulty of confirmation will depend on the precise nature of the stochastic elements. Individual difference analyses are (almost) ruled out from the start, and even group-level analyses are more difficult.

The possibility of stochastic cognitive mechanisms raises one final issue: namely, the fact that we rarely are able to test psychological theories in isolation. The worry is not a general, Quine-Duhem one about the testability of theories, but rather that almost any theory of learning or reasoning must be supplemented by a choice or response theory in order to make predictions about observable behavior. Consider a standard categorization problem in which a psychological model might predict that $P(\text{Object } X \text{ is in Category } A) = 0.75$ and $P(\text{Object } X \text{ is in Category } B) = 0.25$, but where the experimental participant must make a forced-choice of X as definitely an A or a B. The categorization theory alone does not make any particular prediction about the participant's response; rather, one must also state how the participant's beliefs are converted into a response. The standard choice model (assumed without discussion in many cases) is probability matching: the probability of any response is equal to the probability of that possibility. In the example above, probability matching predicts $P(\text{Respond “A”}) = 0.75$ and $P(\text{Respond “B”}) = 0.25$. When the assumption of probability matching has actually been tested, however, it has not fared well, at least in the domain of categorization (Ashby and Gott 1988; Nosofsky and Zaki 2002; Wills et al. 2000). More generally, stochastic mechanisms mean that one must test multiple models simultaneously.

Implicit vs. explicit mental states

Although no mental states are directly observable by psychologists, we nonetheless think that we can frequently obtain close-to-direct measurements of them. In particular, many experiments in cognitive psychology assume that verbal reports (e.g., ratings on a seven-point Likert scale, descriptions of current beliefs, etc.) give more-or-less direct access to the relevant mental states. The discussion in the previous section implicitly made precisely this type of assumption. At the same time, clearly not all mental states can be reported in this manner. Some behavior is generated by unconscious cognitive mechanisms about which we cannot give verbal reports. These unconscious processes can be quite simple and mundane; we are not referring here to the elements of, say, Freudian psychology. For example, one early experiment on so-called implicit learning (Reber 1967) asked participants to learn letter sequences based on an unknown-to-the-participant artificial grammar. Participants were subsequently able to distinguish letter sequences satisfying the artificial grammar with better-than-chance accuracy, even though they were completely unable to articulate the method by which they performed the classification. The general tactic of finding significant differences in behavior without any corresponding reports of awareness has led to an astonishingly large body of research on unconscious processing, including implicit learning (Goschke [1997] and Shanks [2005] provide reviews), implicit memory (Schacter [1987] and Schacter et al. [1993] provide reviews), and other types of implicit cognition (e.g., Dienes and Perner 1999; Fazio and Olson 2003; Underwood 1996).

Implicit cognition is variously understood roughly as cognition that either has no accompanying awareness, or is not affected by lack of awareness. The central methodological challenge is thus to use either reliable measures or careful experimental design to determine whether some cognition occurs with absolutely no awareness. While careful experimental design is important, it seems highly unlikely that any experimental design can *guarantee* that participants will have no awareness of the relevant information. With regards to the first possibility, an open research question is precisely whether various subjective and objective measures are reliable indicators of *actual* lack of awareness (e.g., Dienes et al. 1995; Dienes and Scott 2005; Tunney and Shanks 2003). Not surprisingly, many subjective measures, such as introspective reports or the ability to explain one's own behavior, are not reliable measures of level of awareness (Shanks 2005). In contrast, objective measures of the implicitness of some cognition aim for a behavioral measure of lack of awareness (e.g., inability to use some information for a basic forced-choice task), but where the information affects their behavior in more subtle ways. Perhaps the best-known example of such an effect is the "mere exposure effect" (Kunst-Wilson and Zajonc 1980; Mandler et al. 1987). In the classic version of this experiment, participants were briefly shown various geometric figures, and then later shown each figure with a novel geometric figure and asked to choose which figure they recognized, and which they liked more. Participants performed at chance in terms of recognizing which figure of the pair had previously occurred but were significantly more likely to "like" the previously observed figure. Such effects have been shown to last for as long as 17 years (Mitchell 2006). The standard interpretation is that participants have no explicit memory of seeing the figure, but do have some type of implicit memory of the previous exposure, which then influences their "liking." Alternative explanations for these findings (e.g., Whittlesea and Price 2001) do not posit lack of awareness, though, and so the possibility of objective measures remains an open question.

More generally, the possibility of implicit cognition raises serious methodological concerns about the common psychological practice of using verbal reports as a major source of experimental data. If significant elements of our cognition occur without any corresponding awareness, then the assumption that verbal reports provide reliable measurements of underlying mental states might be less justified than is typically thought. Similar concerns are raised by experiments demonstrating a range of metacognitive failures, including evidence that people often act for reasons of which they are unaware (Kruger and Dunning 1999; Nisbett and Ross 1991). One response to these concerns has been a shift towards experiments that are grounded in behavioral measures, rather than verbal ones. This move is not without cost, however, as it creates a pressure to interpret our theories in a purely instrumentalist manner: the focus on behavioral measures and relative distrust of verbal reports makes it more difficult to interpret the functional forms of our theories in a realist manner. If we only trust measurements of behavior, then why think that our theories capture anything other than the perception-behavior functions? Of course, this pressure does not move us entirely to behaviorism, but it does force a greater degree of explicitness about exactly which parts of our theories are supposed to correspond to actual cognitive functions.

Designing experiments that work

Despite the wide variety of experimental designs in psychological research, there are important, general issues about the design of controlled experiments, particularly in light of data variability and the need to (sometimes) make inferences from population-level phenomena to individual features. Suppose we want to investigate the effect of a particular treatment (e.g., the use of graphical representations) on some cognitive outcome (e.g., learning argument structure). A standard experimental approach is a between-group design with (at least) two conditions: one, the treatment, in which participants are given graphical representations; and another, the control, in which they are not. Participants are randomized to one of the conditions and the effect size is calculated from differences in some comprehension task. The randomization aims to assign participants to the treatment or control group independently of any feature of the individual or the experimental setup. If successful, randomization ensures that any other feature that might obscure the effect of the treatment on the outcome will be equally prevalent in both the treatment and control condition, and so their effects will be balanced across the two conditions. Any observed difference between the treatment and control conditions can then be attributed to the treatment itself. (There are other advantages of randomization, such as for blinding the study, but we leave those aside here.)

This procedure is a completely standard experimental design found in many sciences. But due to the particular nature of psychological research, care needs to be taken about the inferences it supports. In particular, inferences from the experiment depend on how the effect is measured. If the effect is measured as a difference in mean between the control and the treatment condition, then the inference it supports is about a population-level phenomenon: the average effect of the treatment. No inference to any individual is necessarily licensed, since a positive difference in means can arise even if the majority of participants in the treatment group experienced a negative effect (compared with control), as long as that was outweighed by a strong positive effect of a minority. Various techniques, such as checking for extreme outliers and satisfaction of distributional assumptions of statistical tests, can help support inferences to the individual, but there is no completely satisfactory basis for inference from population-level findings to an individual. Further, even if the effect is positive for every individual in the treatment group, any inferences depend on the assumption that both the treatment and control group are representative of the wider population and – except for the treatment – of each other. This assumption will plausibly be true for large enough samples, but if the sample size is small (as it often is in psychology), we have no such assurances. It is unlikely, but not impossible, that 10 consecutive fair coin flips all come up heads. Similarly, it is unlikely but possible that randomization results in an assignment of treatment that is correlated with some causally relevant variable. Thus, even if we randomize, we still run the risk in small samples of not being able to identify the treatment's effects, and so we must be cautious about the correct causal assignment of the effect we observe. The possibility of spurious correlations despite randomization is not peculiar to psychology, but is exacerbated by the relatively small sample sizes.

Similarly, there are many possible explanations of a finding of no difference between the treatment and control conditions: there might not be any treatment effect, as the experimental outcome suggests, or there may be a mixture of populations in the treatment group, some for whom the treatment had a negative effect and others for which it was positive. Randomization does not help in this latter case, since if these subpopulations are suitably balanced in the general participant population, then randomization would also lead to balance across experimental conditions. In this case, the conclusion that there is no overall *average* effect is actually correct, but the inference to any particular individual might be quite incorrect. In addition, we might find no effect if the influence of the treatment is very weak relative to the noise (from any source) in the data. Randomization of treatment does not reduce outcome variance since (put intuitively) the randomization ensures only that both the treatment and the control condition contain a "good mix" of different participants, and not necessarily a mix with low variance in performance.

In these cases, we might use an experimental design referred to as "matching" that goes back to the philosophers Mill (1950) and Bacon (1854). The basic idea is to find two individuals that are identical on all relevant measures, but where we can observe or impose a difference in the cause variable of interest. Since the two individuals are otherwise the same, we can properly attribute any outcome differences to the treatment. More concretely, given pairs of individuals that resemble each other with respect to all variables we deem relevant, one of each pair (determined randomly) is assigned to the treatment group and the other to the control. The comparison in the outcome measurement is then performed between the matched individuals. If a significant difference is found for each pair of matched individuals (or a large proportion of them), then we have good evidence that there is an effect of the treatment on the outcome. The great advantage to this method is that the relevant variable – namely, the performance *difference* within a pair – will typically have much smaller variance, and so we will be able to identify much smaller treatment effects.

Matching provides excellent control of the noise in the data, but there are problems for both the validity of the causal inference and inferences about the effect of treatment for an individual. The validity of the causal inference hinges on whether or not we are able to match participants properly, and whether we have matched them on all the relevant variables. If we fail to match individuals on a causally relevant variable, then we cannot attribute all effects to the treatment. Therefore, matching only works if we are in the rare situation of knowing all of the causally relevant variables for E, except for some uncertainty about whether the treatment is relevant for E. And even if the matching is perfect, differences between individuals can lead to differences in outcome performance.

In practice, we can never match perfectly, and so can never completely exclude all explanations other than "treatment causes effect" using the small sample sizes of standard psychology experiments. One might turn instead to a within-participant experimental design in which each participant is placed in every experimental condition. The match is plausibly perfect, since the same individual is compared in different conditions. Moreover, we have a large sample size because each participant can be "reused," and we can make claims about the treatment effect on each individual. However, the application of multiple treatments is not always possible, either for practical reasons, or because exposure to one condition changes behavior in another.

The interactions in experimental design are subtle. For noise reduction, one wants homogeneous, carefully selected participants; for causal inference from treatment to outcome, one wants a large sample with a proper randomized treatment assignment. For inference to the individual from population-level data, large sample tests require uniformity assumptions; for tests on the individual, we need to know the other active causal effects. There is no perfect experimental design, but only a set of tradeoffs involving sample size, effect size, sample noise, and prior knowledge.

Data analysis and null hypothesis testing

Even for "perfect" data, statistical analysis faces its own problems. Often, though not always, statistical tests are used to investigate whether there is a difference in the value of a particular parameter between the treatment and control group. Results are reported and deemed publishable if a certain statistical significance (generally $p < 0.05$) is achieved. There has been a long, ongoing debate in the psychology literature on the value of null hypothesis significance tests (NHSTs) as measures of successful or relevant research (Gigerenzer 1993; Harlow et al. 1997; Huberty and Pike 1999; Kline 2004; Krantz 1999; Oakes 1986). The core issues arise as early as Berkson (1938) and were known to psychologists in the 1960s (Rozeboom 1960). A ban on the use of NHSTs in psychology was discussed in the 1990s (Harlow et al. 1997; Harris 1997; McLean and Kaufman 1998), and the debate about alternatives to using NHSTs continues today (Harlow et al. 1997; Kline 2004; Thompson 1999; and many others).

In an NHST, one tests a null hypothesis, H_0, of the baseline value of a particular parameter in the control population against an alternative hypothesis, H_1. H_1 can either be nonspecific (H_1 = not-H_0) or specific (H_1 = parameter γ has value q). Informally, NHSTs are performed at a particular significance level α that specifies the so-called rejection region of the parameter space: if the estimate of the parameter of interest falls within this region, then H_0 is rejected as a correct description of how the data were generated. The rejection region corresponds to data deemed so surprising in light of H_0 that they are taken as sufficient to reject H_0 as true. An NHST is typically reported by a *p*-value that indicates how small the significance level α could have been such that the observed data would still have led to a rejection of H_0; that is, the *p*-value is a measure of just how surprising the data would be if H_0 were true. The standard threshold of $p < 0.05$ is arbitrary; there is no fundamental justification for that standard. In particular, there is no reason to think that nature's effects are all at least so strong that they can be discriminated by a test with significance level of 0.05. Moreover, with sufficient sample size, all effects become significant because the slightest approximation errors of the model become detectable.

The debate about NHSTs in psychology has mainly been concerned with the danger of misinterpretation of the results of such a statistical test. There are many other, more technical issues relating to hypothesis testing, but we will not touch on them here (though see Cox 1958; DeGroot 1973). At least four systematic misunderstandings of aspects of NHSTs have featured prominently in the debate in psychology:

1 The *p*-value is taken as the probability that H_0 is true.
2 Rejection of H_0 is taken as confirmation of H_1.
3 $(1 - p)$ is taken as the probability that rejection of H_0 will be replicated.
4 Failure to reject H_0 repeatedly is interpreted as failure to replicate an earlier study.

We will briefly cover each of these errors. First, the *p*-value is technically the smallest α value such that the observed data would result in rejection of H_0. That is, a small *p*-value indicates that the data are very unlikely given H_0: $P(D \mid H_0)$ is almost zero. But that does not imply that H_0 is very unlikely given the data, since that conclusion requires that $P(H_0 \mid D)$ be almost zero. In general, $P(H_0 \mid D) = P(D \mid H_0) \times P(H_0) / P(D)$, and so the *p*-value, $P(D \mid H_0)$, is only informative about the probability of the hypothesis given the data, $P(H_0 \mid D)$, when we also know (at least) something about the prior probability of the hypothesis, $P(H_0)$.

The second misconception is that rejection of H_0 is tantamount to confirmation of H_1. This fallacy arises from thinking about rejection of H_0 in an NHST in the context of an over-simplified logical argument: H_0 or H_1; not H_0; therefore H_1. This argument is valid, but sound only if two conditions are met. First, H_0 and H_1 must exhaust the hypothesis space, which will happen only when H_1 = not-H_0. In general there might be infinitely many other alternative hypotheses that might be true or equally confirmed. For example, if H_0 = "*T* and *E* are uncorrelated," then rejection of H_0 only confirms "*T* and *E* are correlated," not any hypothesis about the specific degree of correlation. In this sense, NHSTs typically provide little positive information. Second, we must be able to test the theories in isolation from other commitments (Duhem 1954), but essentially all NHSTs require auxiliary assumptions about the distribution of the data. Consequently, if our test assumptions (e.g., unimodality) are faulty, then we might reject H_0, even though H_0 is correct.

The third and fourth misinterpretations focus on the replication of experimental results. The quantity $(1 - p)$ does not provide any probability for replicating the observed results, largely because *p*-values depend on both the data and H_0. Suppose H_0 is actually true, but statistical variation led to an unrepresentative data sample from H_0, which resulted in a small *p*-value. The probability of replication in this case is quite small, since an extremely unlikely event occurred, even though $(1 - p)$ is quite large. Alternatively, if H_1 is true, then a replication probability should give the likelihood of H_1 generating such a sample again. Such a probability should not depend on H_0, but the *p*-value does depend on H_0. More generally, it is not entirely clear what is meant by replication. Surely, an exact replication of the parameter estimate (or even worse, the data) cannot be a requirement. Rather, the probability of replication should be something akin to an estimate of the likelihood of repeated rejection of H_0 or H_1, but $(1 - p)$ is not a measure of this. Moreover, *contra* misconception 4, there are many reasons why one experiment could result in data that reject H_0, while a second experiment leads to data that fail to reject H_0. For example, failure to reject might be due to a sample (in either experiment) that happens to be improbable if H_0 is true. More importantly, if the alternative hypotheses (H_1) differ in the two experiments or if distributional features change, then the rejection region will change and consequently even the exact same data can lead to rejection in one experiment and failure of rejection in another.

These are all issues of misinterpretation and so suggest a sociological solution: simply help psychologists (as a community) have a more thorough understanding of statistical theory. However, the main issue emerging from the debate is that NHSTs do not really give the psychologist the information that she wants. In particular, psychologists are presumably most interested in the questions, "How likely is a particular hypothesis given the data?" and "How likely is replication of the results of a particular experiment?" In fact, neither question is directly addressed by a hypothesis test as described. In more recent years, the debate on NHSTs has turned to providing suggestions of methods that do answer these questions (Harlow et al. 1997; Kline 2004; and references therein). The emphasis has been on moving away from a single, numeric representation of the experimental effect and towards the use of a variety of different tools for evaluation. One suggestion has been to compute confidence intervals, which represent the set of unrejected null hypotheses and so indicate the entire space of values consistent with the data at a given significance level. However, with regard to rejection or failure of rejection, confidence intervals provide no more information than is already represented by the *p*-value, since the *p*-value corresponds to the largest confidence interval that does not include the original null hypothesis. Furthermore, confidence intervals also run the risk of serious misinterpretation: they do not provide a $1 - \alpha$ probability assurance that the true value of the parameter lies within the confidence interval, but rather only assurance that the confidence interval covers the true parameter $1 - \alpha$ percent of the time (Belia et al. 2005).

The other major response to these concerns about NHSTs has been a move towards Bayesian methods (Harlow et al. 1997; Kline 2004; and references therein). Bayesian methods allow an explicit calculation of the probability of the hypothesis given the data, $P(\mathrm{H} \mid \mathrm{D})$, and Bayesian confidence sets provide intervals which do represent the probability of the true parameter being contained within their boundaries. However, there are different concerns about using Bayesian methods. Bayesian methods require a prior probability for each hypothesis, i.e. for each hypothesis under consideration one has to specify *a priori* how likely it is. Two senses can be given to such a "prior": it can either be a representation of a researcher's subjective degree of belief in each hypothesis, or it could be some kind of objective measure of the hypothesis's likelihood. In the former case, it has been argued that we should not introduce a subjective component to the science. In the latter case, it remains unclear how such objective priors can be obtained. In addition, there is some concern that these methods are much more difficult to implement, although this is becoming less of a problem.

A more general lesson from the NHST debate is that experimental results should be subject to more careful data analysis and reported more precisely, ultimately with the goal of making the claims based on experimental research more testable and/or more highly corroborated. We can clarify our results by the use of explicit models that capture the relations between multiple variables (such as structural equation models), the use of tests of model fit, and the estimation of effect sizes. Model fitting has the advantage that the aim is not to reject H_0, but rather to fit the model it represents as well as possible. This avoids the misinterpretation problems that can arise from a focus on rejection. Estimation of effect sizes provides a quantitative estimation of the difference between treatment and control conditions that can be further tested. Alternatively, various measures for corroboration of a hypothesis and measures of model fit have been suggested (McDonald 1997), but there are currently no explicit accounts of corroboration that ensure that a highly corroborated theory is in some sense approximately true. Lastly, most scientists would agree that a result is a significant finding if it can be replicated. Consequently, rather than emphasizing the significance found in one experiment, more emphasis should be placed on the meta-analysis of several or repeated experiments. There is a vast literature on meta-analytic techniques (Kline 2004: Ch. 8, and references therein), although no particular theoretical account of replicability has found broad acceptance or usage (see Killeen 2005 and accompanying discussions).

Conclusion

Most of the discussions and debates in the philosophy of psychology focus on high-level conceptual challenges, such as the nature of mental properties, the possibility of mental causation, and so forth. Our aim in this chapter has been to show that the more mundane, everyday aspects of the practice of psychology – experimental design, model development, statistical analysis, and so on – also provide a rich ground of conceptual and methodological challenges. The large variability of psychological data, the possibility of implicit cognitive mechanisms and individual differences, difficulty of experimental design and control, and the widespread use (and misuse) of null hypothesis statistical testing all stand to benefit from serious philosophical investigation. Almost certainly, there are no perfect solutions for any of these problems, only better and worse alternatives. But much work is needed to determine which responses are appropriate for which situations, and to find novel methods for handling these challenges.

Notes

1. Note that this problem is distinct from various debates in psychology about which normative model is appropriate for a particular experimental design (e.g., predicate logic vs. Bayesian hypothesis confirmation in the Wason selection task).

References

Ackerman, P. L. (1988) "Determinants of Individual Differences during Skill Acquisition: Cognitive Abilities and Information Processing," *Journal of Experimental Psychology* (General) 117: 288–318.

Anderson, J. R., and Sheu, C.-F. (1995) "Causal Inferences as Perceptual Judgments," *Memory and Cognition* 23: 510–24.

Ashby, F. G., and Gott, R. E. (1988) "Decision Rules in the Perception and Categorization of Multidimensional Stimuli," *Journal of Experimental Psychology: Learning, Memory, and Cognition* 14: 33–53.

Bacon, F. (1854) *Novum organum*, Philadelphia: Parry & MacMillan.

Barrett, L. F., Tugade, M. M., and Engle, R. W. (2004) "Individual Differences in Working Memory Capacity and Dual-Process Theories of The Mind," *Psychological Bulletin* 130: 553–73.

Belia, S., Fidler, F., Williams, J., and Cumming, G. (2005) "Researchers Misunderstand Confidence Intervals and Standard Error Bars," *Psychological Methods* 10: 389–96.

Berkson, J. (1938) "Some Difficulties of Interpretation Encountered in the Application of the Chi-Square Test," *Journal of the American Statistical Association* 33: 526–42.

Brown, S., and Heathcote, A. (2003) "Bias in Exponential and Power Function Fits Due to Noise: Comment on Myung, Kim, and Pitt," *Memory and Cognition* 31: 656–61.

Buehner, M. J., and Cheng, P. W. (1997) "Causal Induction: The Power PC Theory versus the Rescorla-Wagner Model," in M. G. Shafto and P. Langley (eds), *Proceedings of the 19th Annual Conference of the Cognitive Science Society*, Mahwah, NJ: LEA Publishers, pp. 55–60.

Buehner, M. J., Cheng, P. W., and Clifford, D. (2003) "From Covariation to Causation: A Test of the Assumption of Causal Power," *Journal of Experimental Psychology: Learning, Memory, and Cognition* 29: 1119–40.

Campbell, J. (2007) "An Interventionist Approach to Causation in Psychology," in A. Gopnik and L. E. Schulz (eds), *Causal Learning: Psychology, Philosophy, and Computation*, Oxford: Oxford University Press, pp. 58–66.

Chi, M. T. H., Feltovich, P. J., and Glaser, R. (1981) "Categorization and Representation of Physics Problems by Experts and Novices," *Cognitive Science* 5: 121–52.
Chu, T., Glymour, C., Scheines, R., and Spirtes, P. (2003) "A Statistical Problem for Inference to Regulatory Structure from Associations of Gene Expression Measurement with Microarrays," *Bioinformatics* 19: 1147–52.
Colyvan, M. (2008) "Naturalising Normativity," in D. Braddon-Mitchell and R. Nola (eds), *Conceptual Analysis and Philosophical Naturalism*, Cambridge, MA: MIT Press.
Cox, D. R. (1958) "Some Problems Connected with Statistical Inference," *Annals of Mathematical Statistics* 29: 357–72.
Danks, D., and Glymour, C. (2001) "Linearity Properties of Bayes Nets with Binary Variables," in J. Breese and D. Koller (eds), *Uncertainty in Artificial Intelligence: Proceedings of the 17th Conference*, San Francisco: Morgan Kaufmann, pp. 98–104.
DeGroot, M. H. (1973) "Doing What Comes Naturally: Interpreting a Tail Area as a Posterior Probability or as a Likelihood," *Journal of the American Statistical Association* 68: 966–9.
Dienes, Z., Altmann, G. T. M., Kwan, L., and Goode, A. (1995) "Unconscious Knowledge of Artificial Grammars Is Applied Strategically," *Journal of Experimental Psychology: Learning, Memory, and Cognition* 21: 1322–38.
Dienes, Z., and Perner, J. (1999) "A Theory of Implicit and Explicit Knowledge," *Behavioral and Brain Sciences* 22: 735–55.
Dienes, Z., and Scott, R. (2005) "Measuring Unconscious Knowledge: Distinguishing Structural Knowledge and Judgment Knowledge," *Psychological Research* 69: 338–51.
Duhem, P. (1954) *La théorie physique: son objet, sa structure*, trans. P. P. Wiener, Princeton, NJ: Princeton University Press.
Ericsson, K. A., and Charness, N. (1994) "Expert Performance: Its Structure and Acquisition," *American Psychologist* 49: 725–47.
Fazio, R. H., and Olson, M. A. (2003) "Implicit Measures in Social Cognition Research: Their Meaning and Use," *Annual Review of Psychology* 54: 297–327.
Gigerenzer, G. (1993) "The Superego, the Ego and the Id in Statistical Reasoning," in G. Keren and C. Lewis (eds), *A Handbook for Data Analysis in the Behavioral Sciences*, Methodological Issues, vol. 1, Hillsdale, NJ: Erlbaum, pp. 311–39.
Goschke, T. (1997) "Implicit Learning and Unconscious Knowledge: Mental Representation, Computational Mechanisms, and Brain Structures," in K. Lamberts and D. R. Shanks (eds), *Knowledge, Concepts, and Categories*, Hove, UK: Psychology Press, pp. 247–333.
Griffiths, T. L., and Tenenbaum, J. B. (2005) "Structure and Strength in Causal Induction," *Cognitive Psychology* 51: 334–84.
Harlow, L. L., Muliak, S. A., and Steiger, J. H. (ed.) (1997) *What If There Were No Significance Tests?* Mahwah, NJ: Erlbaum.
Harré, R. (1996) "AI Rules: Okay?" *Journal of Experimental and Theoretical Artificial Intelligence* 8: 109–20.
Harris, R. J. (1997) "Ban the Significance Test?" *Psychological Science* 8: 1–20.
Huberty, C. J., and Pike, C. J. (1999) "On Some History Regarding Statistical Testing," in B. Thompson (ed.), *Advances in Social Science Methodology*, vol. 5, Stamford, CT: JAI Press, pp. 1–22.
Just, M. A., and Carpenter, P. A. (1992) "A Capacity Theory of Comprehension: Individual Differences in Working Memory," *Psychological Review* 99: 122–49.
Killeen, P. R. (2005) "An Alternative to Null-Hypothesis Significance Tests," *Psychological Science* 16: 345–53.
Kline, R. B. (2004) *Beyond Significance Testing*, Washington, DC: American Psychological Association.
Krantz, D. H. (1999) "The Null Hypothesis Testing Controversy in Psychology," *Journal of the American Statistical Association* 94: 1372–81.
Kruger, J., and Dunning, D. (1999) "Unskilled and Unaware of It: How Difficulties in Recognizing One's Own Incompetence Lead to Inflated Self-Assessments," *Journal of Personality and Social Psychology* 77: 1121–34.
Kunst-Wilson, W. R., and Zajonc, R. B. (1980) "Affective Discrimination of Stimuli That Cannot Be Recognized," *Science* 207: 557–8.

Lee, M. D. (2006) "A Hierarchical Bayesian Model of Human Decision-Making on an Optimal Stopping Problem," *Cognitive Science* 30: 1–26.

Lee, M. D., and Webb, M. R. (2005) "Modeling Individual Differences in Cognition," *Psychonomic Bulletin and Review* 12: 605–21.

Lober, K., and Shanks, D. R. (2000) "Is Causal Induction Based on Causal Power? Critique of Cheng (1997)," *Psychological Review* 107: 195–212.

Mandler, G., Nakamura, Y., and van Zandt, B. J. (1987) "Nonspecific Effects of Exposure on Stimuli That Cannot Be Recognized," *Journal of Experimental Psychology: Learning, Memory, and Cognition* 13: 646–8.

McDonald, R. P. (1997) "Goodness of Approximation in the Linear Model" in L. L. Harlow, S. A. Muliak, and J. H. Steiger (eds), *What If There Were No Significance Tests?* Mahwah, NJ: Erlbaum, pp. 199–219.

McLean, J., and Kaufman, A. S. (eds) (1998) *Statistical Significance Testing*; special issue of *Research in the Schools* 5, no. 2.

Medin, D. L., and Schaffer, M. M. (1978) "Context Theory of Classification Learning," *Psychological Review* 85: 207–38.

Mill, J. S. (1950) *Philosophy of Scientific Method*, New York: Hafner.

Minda, J. P., and Smith, J. D. (2001) "Prototypes in Category Learning: The Effects of Category Size, Category Structure, and Stimulus Complexity," *Journal of Experimental Psychology: Learning, Memory, and Cognition* 27: 775–99.

Minda, J. P., and Smith, J. D. (2002) "Comparing Prototype-Based and Exemplar-Based Accounts of Category Learning and Attentional Allocation," *Journal of Experimental Psychology: Learning, Memory, and Cognition* 28: 275–92.

Mitchell, D. B. (2006) "Nonconscious Priming After 17 Years: Invulnerable Implicit Memory? *Psychological Science* 17: 925–9.

Myung, I. J., Kim, C., and Pitt, M. A. (2000) "Toward an Explanation of the Power-Law Artifact: Insights from Response Surface Analysis," *Memory and Cognition* 28: 832–40.

Navarro, D. J., Griffiths, T. L., Steyvers, M., and Lee, M. D. (2006) "Modeling Individual Differences Using Dirichlet Processes," *Journal of Mathematical Psychology* 50: 101–22.

Nisbett, R. E., and Ross, L. (1991) *The Person and the Situation: Perspectives of Social Psychology*, New York: McGraw-Hill.

Nosofsky, R. M., and Palmeri, T. J. (1998) "A Rule-Plus-Exception Model for Classifying Objects in Continuous-Dimension Spaces," *Psychonomic Bulletin and Review* 5: 345–69.

Nosofsky, R. M., Palmeri, T. J., and McKinley, S. C. (1994) "Rule-Plus-Exception Model of Classification Learning," *Psychological Review* 101: 53–79.

Nosofsky, R. M., and Zaki, S. R. (2002) "Exemplar and Prototype Models Revisited: Response Strategies, Selective Attention, and Stimulus Generalization," *Journal of Experimental Psychology: Learning, Memory, and Cognition* 28: 924–40.

Oakes, M. W. (1986) *Statistical Inference: A Commentary for the Social and Behavioral Sciences*, New York: Wiley.

Olsson, H., Wennerholm, P., and Lyxzèn, U. (2004) "Exemplars, Prototypes, and the Flexibility of Classification Models," *Journal of Experimental Psychology: Learning, Memory, and Cognition* 30: 936–41.

Payne, J. W., Bettman, J. R., and Johnson, E. J. (1993) *The Adaptive Decision Maker*, Cambridge: Cambridge University Press.

Pitt, M. A., Myung, I. J., and Zhang, S. (2002) "Toward a Method of Selecting among Computational Models of Cognition," *Psychological Review* 109: 472–91.

Reber, A. S. (1967) "Implicit Learning of Artificial Grammars," *Journal of Verbal Learning and Verbal Behavior* 6: 855–63.

Rouder, J. N., Sun, D., Speckman, P. L., Lu, J., and Zhou, D. (2003) "A Hierarchical Bayesian Statistical Framework for Response Time Distributions," *Psychometrika* 68: 589–606.

Rozeboom, W. W. (1960) "The Fallacy of the Null Hypothesis Significance Test," *Psychological Bulletin* 57: 416–28.

Schacter, D. L. (1987) "Implicit Memory: History and Current Status," *Journal of Experimental Psychology: Learning, Memory, and Cognition* 13: 501–18.

Schacter, D. L., Chiu, C.-Y. P., and Ochsner, K. N. (1993) "Implicit Memory: A Selective Review," *Annual Review of Neuroscience* 16: 159–82.

Schunn, C. D., Lovett, M. C., and Reder, L. M. (2001) "Awareness and Working Memory in Strategy Adaptivity," *Memory and Cognition* 29: 254–66.

Schunn, C. D., and Reder, L. M. (1998) "Strategy Adaptivity and Individual Differences," in D. L. Medin (ed.), *The Psychology of Learning and Motivation*, vol. 38, New York: Academic Press, pp. 115–54.

Shanks, D. R. (2005) "Implicit Learning," in K. Lamberts and R. L. Goldstone (eds), *Handbook of Cognition*, London: Sage, pp. 202–20.

Siegler, R. S. (1996) *Emerging Minds: The Process of Change in Children's Thinking*, New York: Oxford University Press.

Spearman, C. (1904) "The Proof and Measurement of Association between Two Things," *American Journal of Psychology* 15: 72–101.

Stanovich, K. E. (1999) *Who Is Rational? Studies of Individual Differences in Reasoning*, Mahwah, NJ: Erlbaum.

Sternberg, R. J. (1977) *Intelligence, Information Processing, and Analogical Reasoning*, Hillsdale, NJ: Erlbaum.

Taatgen, N. A. (2002) "A Model of Individual Differences in Skill Acquisition in the Kanfer-Ackerman Air Traffic Control Task," *Cognitive Systems Research* 3: 103–12.

Thompson, B. (1999) "If Statistical Significance Tests Are Broken/Misused, What Practices Should Supplement or Replace Them?" *Theory and Psychology* 9: 165–81.

Tunney, R. J., and Shanks, D. R. (2003) "Subjective Measures of Awareness and Implicit Cognition," *Memory and Cognition* 31: 1060–71.

Underwood, G. (1996) *Implicit Cognition*, New York: Oxford University Press.

Whittlesea, B. W. A., and Price, J. R. (2001) "Implicit/Explicit Memory versus Analytic/Nonanalytic Processing: Rethinking the Mere Exposure Effect," *Memory and Cognition* 29: 234–46.

Wills, A. J., Reimers, S., Stewart, N., Suret, M., and McLaren, I. P. L. (2000) "Tests of the Ratio Rule in Categorization," *Quarterly Journal of Experimental Psychology* 53A: 983–1011.

Zaki, S. R., Nosofsky, R. M., Stanton, R. D., and Cohen, A. L. (2003) "Prototype and Exemplar Accounts of Category Learning and Attentional Allocation: A Reassessment," *Journal of Experimental Psychology: Learning, Memory, and Cognition* 29: 1160–73.

Part III

Cognition and representation

15
PROBLEMS OF REPRESENTATION I: NATURE AND ROLE

Dan Ryder

Introduction

There are some exceptions, which we shall see below, but virtually all theories in psychology and cognitive science make use of the notion of *representation*. Arguably, folk psychology also traffics in representations, or is at least strongly suggestive of their existence. There are many different types of things discussed in the psychological and philosophical literature that are candidates for representation-hood. First, there are the propositional attitudes – beliefs, judgments, desires, hopes etc. (see Chapters 9 and 17 of this volume). If the propositional attitudes are representations, they are person-level representations – the judgment that the sun is bright pertains to *John*, not a sub-personal part of John. By contrast, the representations of edges in V_1 of the cerebral cortex that neuroscientists talk about and David Marr's symbolic representations of "zero-crossings" in early vision (Marr 1982) are at the "sub-personal" level – they apply to parts or states of a person (e.g. neural parts or computational states of the visual system). Another important distinction is often made among perceptual, cognitive, and action-oriented representations (e.g. motor commands). Another contrast lies between "stored representations" (e.g. memories) and "active representations" (e.g. a current perceptual state). Related to this is the distinction between "dispositional representations" and "occurrent representations." Beliefs that are not currently being entertained are dispositional, e.g. your belief that the United States is in North America – no doubt you had this belief two minutes ago, but you were not consciously accessing it until you read this sentence. Occurrent representations, by contrast, are active, conscious thoughts or perceptions. Which leads us to another important distinction: between conscious and non-conscious mental representations, once a bizarre-sounding distinction that has become familiar since Freud (see Chapter 4 of this volume).

I mention these distinctions at the outset to give you some idea of the range of phenomena we will be considering, and to set the stage for our central "problem of representation": what is a mental representation, exactly, and how do we go about deciding whether there are any? We know there are public representations of various kinds: words, maps, and pictures, among others. Are there any representations that are properly thought of as *psychological*?

Minimally, a representation is something that possesses *semantic* properties: a truth value, a satisfaction value (i.e. satisfied or not), truth conditions, satisfaction conditions, reference, or content. So here is one way we might proceed, which we can call "the simple strategy": first, figure out what endows something with semantic properties, and then see if any of the objects that have semantic properties are mental or psychological. The simple strategy might ultimately work, but there are at least two *prima facie* problems with it. First, there is substantial disagreement over what endows an object with semantic properties, and even whether such properties are scientifically accessible at all. Debates about whether thermostats or dogs harbour real representations are often just disputes about whether these things possess states with semantic properties. (The subject of what, if any, natural properties ground semantic properties is the topic of the next chapter.) The second problem with the simple strategy is that there is a danger of talking past one another: not everyone accepts that if something has semantic properties, it must be a species of representation. Many notions of representation require something more. Let us now look at the various notions of representation in common use.

Notions of representation

The degree-of-structure axis

The minimalist or purely semantic notion

The most general notion has already been given: the purely semantic notion, i.e. if it has semantic properties, then it is a representation. On this notion, if folk psychological ascriptions of belief, desire, perception, and intention are true, and such states have semantic properties (which is uncontroversial), then there exist mental representations. Suppose John judges that the sun is bright. On the purely semantic notion, that judgement of John's is a mental representation. Indeed, on the purely semantic notion, mental representation is implied by any true application of a predicate that is both psychological and semantic.

On this minimalist notion, only a radical eliminativist would deny that there are mental representations. It is not clear that there are any such radical eliminativists. The Churchlands are well-known as eliminativists, but they accept that there are mental representations, denying only the existence of the mental representations countenanced by folk psychology (P. S. Churchland 1986; P. M. Churchland 1989). Both Quine (at least in some moods – see his 1960) and Stich (in his 1983) deny semantic properties any scientific credentials. However, Quine is neutral between an eliminativist and a reductionist line, arguing that there is no clear distinction between the two; in more recent work, Stich has made a similar response (Stich 2001). Even in his (1983), Stich seems to accept the existence of mental representations, though maintaining that for scientific purposes they must be individuated syntactically. Why these syntactically individuated types should count as representations is less clear – so the early Stich may come as close as anyone has to denying the existence of mental representations on the purely semantic notion of representation. That said, he acknowledges that, although content-bearing states may play no role in a correct psychological theory, room could be made for them in common-sense, just as there is room in common sense for tables and chairs, although no scientific theory adverts to them.

A purely instrumentalist view, according to which contentful attributions in psychology (whether folk or scientific) are merely a useful fiction, also does not have any clear advocates. Some take Dennett to flirt with such a view (Baker 1995), but in recent times, Dennett has tried to make clear that his "intentional stance" theory does not question the truth of contentful mental state ascriptions (Dennett 1991), which would make him a mental representationalist on the minimalist purely semantic notion.

The thin notion

Let us move now to a somewhat more stringent notion of representation, one that includes fewer theorists under the mental representationalist umbrella. On the purely semantic notion, mental representation requires only the true application of predicates that were both psychological and semantic. On a less minimalist but still rather thin notion of representation, application of a predicate that is both psychological and semantic must be made true by an identifiable state or object harboured by the agent possessing the representation. On this "thin" (as opposed to minimalist, purely semantic) notion, if the fact that John judges that the sun is bright is made true by an identifiable, repeatable neurological state of John, for instance, this neurological state would count as a representation.[1]

The thin notion of representation is strong enough to push some versions of behaviourism out of the representationalist realm (see Chapter 6 of this volume). A Ryleian behaviourist, for example, maintains that mental state attributions are true in virtue of the obtaining of certain counterfactuals concerning behaviour. There need be no identifiable state of the agent that makes them true. So the Ryleian behaviourist denies that beliefs and desires, for instance, need be representations or composed of representations.

Dennett's theory of propositional attitudes also falls on the non-representationalist side of the divide as determined by the thin notion. (It is less clear that the sub-personal-level "representations" Dennett talks about are not representations on the thin notion – see Millikan [2000] and Dennett's response, contained there.) According to Dennett (1987b), semantic, psychological predicates are applied from the "intentional stance," which may legitimately be adopted towards any object whose behaviour is best predicted by assuming that it is trying to get what it wants, in light of what it believes. Such a stance is legitimately adopted when it offers advantages in terms of predictive power over two alternative stances, namely the physical stance and the design stance. (Predictive power is a function of both accuracy and simplicity.)

The physical stance predicts by appeal to physical properties and laws; the design stance predicts by assuming intelligent design for a purpose. For instance, consider a simple thermostat based upon a bimetallic strip. Its behaviour may be predicted from the physical stance by appeal to laws concerning the expansion of different metals as well as electric circuits. Its behaviour may also be predicted from the design stance, by assuming that it is designed to keep the temperature at its set point. Its behaviour may further be predicted from the intentional stance, by assuming that it *wants* to keep the temperature at its set point. If it believes that the temperature is higher than its set point, it engages its cooling system because it believes that will bring the temperature back to its set point. In this case, there may be some advantage in predictive power by adopting the design stance over the physical stance: less input information is needed to make the prediction (one doesn't need to know the composition of the lead wires, for instance) and the inferences involved are simpler. However, nothing is gained by adopting the intentional stance rather than the design stance. Neither is the predictive process any simpler, nor is it any more accurate.

Things are otherwise, though, when a dog owner pronounces "Walkies!" within earshot of her Labrador retriever. Adopting the intentional stance allows us to predict that the dog will become excited and perhaps go to fetch a leash. Predicting this behaviour accurately from the physical stance or design stance would require vastly more input information, about the internal structure or design of the dog, and its relation to its environment. (For instance, a separate calculation would have to be made in order to predict that the dog would proceed *around* the table rather than crashing into it, or one would have to know the design details of its navigational mechanisms.) This is a clear case, then, in which the intentional stance may legitimately be adopted.

On Dennett's view, what makes the adoption of the intentional stance legitimate, and therefore what makes the application of semantic, psychological predicates true, are the patterns of behaviour that an object (whether thermostat, dog, or person) exhibits (Dennett 1991). In particular, these patterns must be characterizable in semantic, rational terms. However, as for Ryle (Dennett's intellectual father), there need be no identifiable internal state that is causally responsible for the emergence of this pattern. In principle, every time its owner utters "Walkies!," it could be a *different* condition of the dog that leads to its excited retrieval of its leash, and this would not impugn the attribution of a belief to the dog that it is about to go for a walk, nor its having retrieved the leash for this reason. Thus satisfying Dennett's conditions for legitimate use of the intentional stance is not sufficient for an agent to harbour mental representations, on the thin notion.

There are other theoretical positions that the thin notion deems non-representational. Some dynamical systems theories of cognition claim that there is such a large degree of interdependence among parts of the system, that nothing less than the whole system may be identified as the possessor of semantic properties. On this view, there is no individuable internal state or process than can be separated out from the rest of the system and identified as serving the representational role in question. Any such candidate state or process is causally coupled with so many other states or processes in the system that it would be arbitrary to assign *it* the representational role rather than some other part (Thelen and Smith 1994; Kelso 1995; van Gelder 1995, possibly Brooks, 1991). To the extent that these dynamicists are anti-representational, they are so based on the thin notion of representation. There is a problem in evaluating such a claim, however, since dynamicists frequently model a system only using abstract systems of mathematical equations, while eschewing any discussion of mechanism (Abrahamsen and Bechtel 2006). Despite their claims to the contrary, it seems reasonable to expect a complete explanation to include details of how these equations are realized in a physical system, and once those details become available it may prove possible to identify physical entities that play representational roles. Dynamicists counter that such representations are explanatorily otiose, and so there is no reason to admit them into a scientific theory of the mind.

This dispute highlights an important division in the sorts of reasons that have been advanced for believing in mental representations. On the one side, there are *explanatory* reasons: do mental representations earn their keep as explanatory postulates? Are they necessary parts of a complete science of the mind (see Stich 1983)? On the other side, there are *ontological* reasons: whatever their explanatory import, given a certain notion of mental representation, are there any such things? It could be, for instance, that the anti-representationalist dynamicists are right about the explanatory question, but the representationalists are right about the ontological question. That said, the two types of reasons are not entirely insulated from one another: one of the best reasons for believing in the existence of something is if it makes a causal contribution to the system of which it is a part. Indeed, on some views, for a property to exist it *must* be causally relevant to something (Alexander's dictum; see Kim 1998). Depending upon how closely causal contributions map on to explanatory contributions, this could tie the two sorts of reasons for believing in representations very closely indeed. Further, often the only reason we have for believing in something is that it is a theoretical postulate (and thus an explanatorily relevant component) of a well-confirmed scientific theory. If one does not take introspective evidence very seriously, this could also unify the explanatory and ontological reasons for believing in mental representation. These issues take us into the vast literature on mental causation and psychological explanation (see Chapter 8 of this volume), which we will only touch upon here. They also take us deep into fundamental areas of philosophy of science, epistemology, and metaphysics, where we shall tread hardly at all.

Continuing with the thin notion of representation, the claim that nothing less than the whole system may be identified as the possessor of semantic properties comes not only from some dynamicists, but also from a very different quarter. The thin notion of representation also classifies as anti-representationalists those Wittgensteinians who maintain that it is a mistake to speak of semantic properties pertaining to subpersonal states (e.g. Bennett and Hacker 2003). They maintain that "believes that ..." and other semantic psychological predicates apply only to whole persons, and never to parts or aspects of persons, defending this position on ordinary language grounds. Thus they would deny that there could be any such internal state of John which is his judgement, and more generally that there could be internal representations. (Perhaps their arguments allow that there could be identifiable *person*-level states of John – e.g. beliefs – that were representations, though it is hard to see how that story would go.) This literature has not had much of an impact on psychology and cognitive science, due to scepticism concerning the intuitions revealed through the analysis of ordinary language. Cognitive scientists and naturalistically inclined philosophers doubt that these intuitions have an evidential weight that could challenge any reasonably supported scientific theory. Wittgensteinians retort that since the scientists use ordinary language, their "theories" are literally nonsense, leading to a standoff.

Some cognitive scientists working in the tradition of *embodied cognition* deny that there are mental representations, on the basis of the thin notion, because they deny that there are any identifiable *internal* representations. The brain, body, and environment are so closely coupled that it would be arbitrary to assign semantic properties only to some restricted internal component (this is partly what Rodney Brooks [1991] has in mind; see also Varela et al. [1991]). Such a view is often closely allied with the dynamicist view summarized above. Alternatively, such theorists sometimes insist that there are indeed mental representations, but that they incorporate portions of the environment. (See Chapter 13 of this volume for further details.) This division in embodiment theorists may coincide with their views on whether the individuation strictures of the thin notion can be satisfied by relevant brain-body-environment entities.

Another sort of theory that the thin notion puts into the non-representationalist camp is a social context theory. On this view, what makes the application of a semantic psychological predicate correct is that the agent to whom the predicate is applied is a member of a certain community, subject to certain rules. Usually the community in question is a *linguistic* community. Since being a member of a certain linguistic community and being thereby subject to certain rules is not a matter of harbouring any particular kinds of internal states (even internal states characterized by relations to the environment), a social context theory does not entail that believers harbour representations, on the thin notion. The theory advocated by Robert Brandom (1994) is a good example.

The notion of representation in the representational theory of mind

We now proceed to a yet thicker notion of representation, which characterizes the representational theory of mind proper (RTM) (Fodor 1975; Sterelny 1990). John is not only capable of judging or believing that the sun is bright, he is also capable of hoping that the sun is bright, wanting the sun to be bright, pretending that the sun is bright, fearing that the sun is bright, etc. These mental states differ, but not in their contents. Following Russell (1918), we can say that John can take the "attitudes" of belief, hope, desire, pretence, fear, etc., toward the proposition that *P*. This possibility for mix-and-match of contents with attitudes seems to apply to any proposition *P* that John can entertain. This would be (best?) explained if there existed, in our minds, a representation which meant that-*P*, such that this representation could somehow be "attached" to the different attitudes (or put, as it were, into the "belief-box," or the "desire box," etc.; Schiffer 1981). If John's mind contained a single representation that the sun is bright[2] ready for melding with different attitudes at different times, we would *expect* John to be capable of hoping or wanting the sun to be bright if he is capable of judging that the sun is bright. By contrast, this mix-and-match would be utterly surprising if John's attitudes had no such representational part or aspect in common. It would be surprising for the same reason that it would be surprising if Billy could produce, on demand from his box, any of the Mr Potato Head combinations, but it turned out that inside the box was not a potato with interchangeable parts, but rather thousands of complete figurines.

The RTM notion of representation, then, is of an identifiable internal state with semantic properties (as on the thin notion), with the additional requirement that this state can mix-and-match with the attitudes. An example of a theory that is non-representational on the RTM notion is a traditional functionalist theory of the attitudes, which treats them as states that may be compositionally unrelated. On David Lewis's theory, for example, the belief that it is raining is characterized *holus-bolus* as the type of physical state that enters into certain causal tendencies with other mental states (e.g. the belief that there is an umbrella in the corner, and a desire to avoid getting wet) as well as perceptual inputs and behaviour (e.g. seeing and getting the umbrella). While the *hope* that it is raining may be characterized by its causal relations with some of the same items as the *belief* that it is raining, by contrast with RTM there is no assumption that the two attitudes literally share a part or aspect corresponding to the representation "that it is raining."

Syntactic structure

To generate an even more restrictive notion of representation, the Mr Potato Head argument may be applied for one more iteration, producing the view that true representations must possess *syntactic structure*. (Sometimes the term "representational theory of mind" is reserved for a theory that takes mental states to exhibit this level of structure, but usually it is meant more broadly, as above.) Just as the observation that John has the capacity to believe that it is raining as well as the capacity to hope that it is raining (etc.) may lead one to postulate the existence of a separable representation "that it is raining," the observation that John may think "the rain is wet," "the rain is cold," "the snow is wet," and "the snow is cold" (etc.) may lead one to postulate the existence of separable representations of rain, snow, wetness, and coldness. These separable representations, on the syntactic structure view, may be structured to produce more complex representations that express complete thoughts – just as words in a language may be structured to produce sentences. The meanings of the complex structure are a function of the meanings of the parts and the syntactic rules for putting the parts together. Such structure is the leading feature of the "language of thought" theory of mental states, found in Sellars (e.g. his 1969) and fully developed by Fodor (1975) (also see Chapter 17 of this volume). (We should also acknowledge that a system of representation that shares features with representational formats that are non-linguistic [e.g. pictures or models] may also exhibit syntactic structure in this minimal sense.) Some authors reserve the term "representation" for psychological states that exhibit some such structure, e.g. Millikan (1984) (though in more recent work she uses the term more liberally).

Related problems: explicit vs. implicit representation

We have now surveyed one axis on which one might draw a line between the representational and the non-representational. Let us call this axis the "degree-of-structure" axis. It goes from zero structure (the minimalist, purely semantic notion of representation) to a high degree of structure (syntactic structure). One of the many "problems of representation" takes place in the degree-of-structure arena. To what extent are our mental representations (if any) structured? The question may be asked of all the various types of candidate mental representations mentioned initially: personal-level representations and sub-personal-level representations; perceptual, cognitive, and action-oriented representations; stored, active, dispositional, and occurrent representations; and finally, conscious and non-conscious representations. Obviously, different answers may be given for the different types. There is a vast amount of literature on such topics; for illustrative purposes, we shall consider one representative issue.

Sometimes a distinction is drawn between a system representing something *explicitly* vs. representing it *implicitly* or *tacitly*. One of the distinctions these terms are used to mark may be drawn on the degree-of-structure axis. (The terms are also used to mark a somewhat related distinction, between a set of representations and the logical consequences of those representations.) As he often does, Dennett gives a nice illustrative case (Dennett 1978; see also Fodor 1985). You might play chess against a computer many times, and come to be familiar with its strategies. You might say, for instance, that it thinks it should get its queen out early. The computer's program involves a complex evaluation of possible moves; after considering its consequences, each move is given a numerical value, and the move with the highest value is chosen. As it happens, the programmer did not include a line in the program that assigns a higher value to a move that tends to bring the queen out early. Bringing the queen out early is never used as a factor in evaluating moves. However, it turns out that given other lines of the program, the tendency to bring its queen out early emerges naturally; this is indeed an accurate way of summarizing one aspect of the computer's behaviour. But (so the story goes) the computer does not explicitly represent "It is good to bring your queen out early." Only lines in the program (or data structures in memory) are explicitly represented; the computer only implicitly represents that it should get its queen out early.

There are a number of places one might draw this version of the implicit/explicit distinction on our degree-of-structure axis, but it should be clear that this is an appropriate axis on which to draw it. A line in a computer program will have syntactic structure, but the complex state underlying the computer's tendency to bring its queen out early will not. (Perhaps it is representational only on the minimal notion, or only on the thin notion.) A similar sort of distinction could apply to a system that represents in a non-linguistic manner. A model of the solar system (an "orrery") might represent explicitly that Mercury is in such-and-such a position in its orbit, but only represent implicitly the relative speeds of Mercury and Venus. Its representation that Mercury moves more quickly than Venus is a consequence of the dispositional setup of its gears; there is no discrete structure that varies with the relative speeds of the various planets.

The issue with respect to mental representation is whether different types of mental representations are explicit or implicit. (Of course, if one draws the representational–non-representational line at a different position on the degree-of-structure axis, the issue could become one between representing and not representing.) Is a subconscious Freudian desire to kill your father explicit or implicit? Are the rules hypothesized to explain how the visual system arrives at an interpretation of the incoming light explicit or implicit? And even: is your belief that your name is such-and-such explicit or implicit? In a later paper (Dennett 1987a), Dennett remarks that the dispositions built into the hardware of a common calculator ought to be thought of as representing the truths of arithmetic only implicitly (though he uses the term "tacitly"), and connectionists have sometimes claimed that all representation in connectionist systems is merely implicit. Both of these claims ought to be evaluated empirically by examining the degree of structure that is present in these systems.[3] Similarly for our psychological systems.

The degree-of-systematicity axis: from detectors to speakers

Let us now return to our central issue of what counts as a mental representation. The degree-of-structure axis is only one of many. We shall now briefly examine several other such axes upon which one might draw a line between the representational and the non-representational.

Related to the degree-of-structure axis is the degree-of-systematicity axis. On all views of representation, it seems, in order to represent something, a system must be capable of representing other things as well, in ways that are systematically related to one another. The minimal degree of systematicity required has been described by Ruth Millikan (1984). This minimal degree is such that some possible variation in the representation maps on to some possible variation in the represented. This applies to even the simplest representers, for instance a metal detector. The metal detector beeps when it is brought near metal; on some views this means that it represents the presence or absence of metal here now. The beeping varies in the following ways: presence/absence, time, and place. These variations map on to the presence/absence of metal, the time, and the location.[4] Thus on this very weak account of systematicity, even simple detectors have it. One can imagine even (semantically) simpler detectors that are insensitive to place – they detect the presence of something anywhere in the universe. Perhaps it is even conceptually possible (though surely physically impossible) to have a sort of detector that detects the presence of something anywhere at anytime – e.g. something that detects whether the element with atomic number 369 has existed or will ever exist. Still, such a detector would exhibit a minimal sort of systematicity – it is capable of representing *either* the presence or absence of the element with atomic number 369. Any token representation in such a detector is a member of a (very small) system of possible representations.

Systematic relations are a common requirement for something to count as a mental representation (see e.g. Clark 1997: Ch. 8; Haugeland, 1991). The degree-of-systematicity axis starts with very simple detectors, extends to systems of such detectors, and further runs to complex models with many interrelations (think of a model of terrestrial weather). At the extreme end, we have *extreme representational holism*, which requires the presence of a vast system of representations possessing sophisticated inferential relations, on the order of the sort of system of belief possessed by a normal adult human (see e.g. Davidson 1973).[5] According to the representational holist, you cannot judge that the sun is bright unless you are capable of judging a host of other things, for example that the sun is circular, and therefore that something circular is bright; that the sun is brighter than a match; that the sun is called "the sun," and therefore that something called "the sun" is bright; etc. According to Davidson, there are no *particular* judgements one must be capable of making if one is to judge that the sun is bright, but one must be capable of making a large number of related judgements and acting on them (including expressing them linguistically). Only a holistic representational system like this is capable of being *interpreted* by an observer, and there is no representation without the possibility of interpretation. (You will note the similarity between Davidson's view and Dennett's. One difference is that Dennett does not make such an holistic systematicity criterial of representation, although one might suspect that the advantages of the intentional stance apply exactly to a complex system like this.)

Similarity and iconic representations

Another dimension that is sometimes taken as criterial of representation is *similarity to what is represented*. In medieval philosophy (particularly in Aquinas, following translations of Avicenna and ultimately derived from Aristotle), the term "representation" in psychology is restricted to mental images, which were thought to resemble their objects (Lagerlund 2004). When Aquinas discusses concepts, he calls them *verba* or mental words, and never refers to them with the term "representation." In the modern sense of representation under discussion here, this difference is typically thought to mark a distinction between *types* of representations, rather than between representation and non-representation. That said, some philosophers require that representations resemble what they represent, where the resemblance is usually *relational* resemblance, or isomorphism/homomorphism (Millikan 1984; Gallistel 1990; Swoyer 1991; Cummins 1996).

The debate over whether there are any mental representations that resemble what they represent ("iconic representations") has been a long and heated one. To understand this debate, it is essential to distinguish between a representational *vehicle* and that vehicle's content. A representational vehicle is a (physical) object or event, like a slab of marble, a written word, or a neural firing pattern. (These can be tokens or types.) If that object or event is a representational vehicle, it will also have a meaning or content. The debate under consideration is about representational vehicles, not their contents. A bust of Julius Caesar is an iconic representation if the shaped slab of marble that constitutes it resembles (or is supposed to resemble) Julius Caesar as he was when he was alive. By contrast, the name "Julius Caesar" exhibits no such resemblance, nor is it supposed to – it exhibits an arbitrary structure *vis-à-vis* its object, and is "symbolic" rather than iconic.

A naïve argument in favour of the existence of iconic representations is an introspective one: when one introspects one's mental images, one can see that they resemble their objects. My image of my mother looks just like my mother, one might say. However, while introspection may be a reliable way of registering the *contents* of representations, it is at least highly doubtful that it also registers the intrinsic properties of those representations' vehicles (e.g. the intrinsic properties of neural states). So this introspective argument is little evidence that the representational *vehicles* of mental imagery are iconic. More theoretical arguments are needed, such as those based on the Shepard and Metzler rotation experiments (Shepard and Metzler 1971). In these experiments, subjects were given two pictures of three-dimensional objects that might or might not be rotations of each other, and they had to judge whether they were or not. Shepard and Metzler found that the length of time it took to make the judgement was predicted by a model under which there was a transformation of the representational vehicle corresponding to a rotation of one of the objects to look for a "match." The further the rotation, the longer the judgement took. This suggests that the underlying vehicle is iconic. This sort of argument has also been defended by Stephen Kosslyn (1994), who, in addition, cites brain imaging evidence (i.e. looking at the actual vehicles). The iconic view is opposed most prominently by Zenon Pylyshyn (see e.g. his 2003 and 1999).

Use: causal role and function

We now turn to a series of distinctions related to how an internal state is *used* in the psychological economy. It is quite plausible that, for instance, representation-hood cannot be determined on the basis of degree of structure or degree of similarity alone. For example, a building-hating but sky-loving city dweller might trim his hedge to block out, very precisely, the downtown skyline, and his hedge would then resemble the downtown buildings. But it is far from obvious that the hedge thereby represents the downtown buildings. If, however, someone were to make *use* of the similarity to choose their afternoon destination (the tallest skyscraper), then the representational status of the hedge becomes more plausible. It is not a map of the downtown skyline unless it is *used* as such. Similarly, the map-like organization of a bunch of neurons in somatosensory cortex does not necessarily represent the relative positions of the limbs unless that mapping can be *used* by higher areas, so that it has functional import (see also Chapter 23 of this volume).

There are two main ways of understanding use naturalistically, as causal role or as normative or teleological functional role (corresponding to two broad types of functionalism – see Chapter 10 of this volume). For a representation to occupy a particular type of (pure) *causal role* is for it to be located in a particular pattern of causes and effects (which might extend many causal steps upstream and/or downstream). (Usually the requirement will be for the representation to be *disposed* to enter into a particular causal pattern, rather than for it actually to be occupying it right now.) Typically a *teleological* functional role is also a causal role, but it is one that the representation is *supposed* to enter into; that is its job or function. In artificial systems, that job is usually assigned by a designer. In natural systems (e.g. human cognitive systems), that job is alleged to be assigned by evolution and/or learning (see the next chapter for details). Any of the bases for dividing representations from non-representations that are related to use might be given a pure causal or, alternatively, a teleological reading.

Representation hungriness

We can use a nice term from Andy Clark (1997) to name our first use-based axis often suggested to mark the representational/non-representational divide: the degree of "representation hungriness" of the task for which a putative representation is deployed. Following Haugeland (1991), Clark suggests that one type of representation-hungry problem arises when a system "must coordinate its behaviors with environmental features that are not always reliably present to the system" (1997: 167). Some examples would be having the capacity to plan a route ahead of time, or to recall my distant lair, or to imagine what would happen if I tipped this rock off the cliff on to Wily Coyote. This idea of representation is strongly connected to the notion of a representation as a stand-in for an absent feature or state of affairs. The intuition here is that in the absence of what a representation is about, there is a need for some sort of internal "stand-in" to have a psychological effect. My distant lair cannot *directly* affect my thinking or behaviour if it is not present to me, so if my lair appears to affect my thinking or behaviour it must do so via some intermediary. (A real example from the psychological literature: C. R. Gallistel [1990] argues that ants have a representation of their location with respect to their lair, since, in a featureless desert, they can walk the correct distance in a straight line no matter what their previous path was.) By contrast, when a flower adjusts its position to keep constantly facing the sun, no "stand-in" is needed. The sun can directly cause the change in the sunflower's position.

The other type of representation-hungry problem, according to Clark, "involves selective sensitivity to states of affairs whose physical manifestations are complex and unruly" (1997: 167). If someone has the capacity to respond to or reason about events that are characterized by moral turpitude, for instance, it is reasonable to expect their cognitive system to be set up in such a way that "all the various superficially different inputs are first assimilated to a common inner state or process such that further processing (reasoning) can be defined over the inner correlate." Events that are extremely dissimilar physically may all be perceived by a cognitive system as infected by moral turpitude. Treating them the same in this way would seem to require an internal stand-in for moral turpitude. By the same token, two very similar events, physically speaking, might *fail* to share the characteristic of moral turpitude (if one act is committed by a large but young child, for instance). This time the system must be able to treat very similar perceptual encodings as calling for entirely different responses, and again, an internal state seems necessary "to guide behavior despite the effective unfriendliness of the ambient environmental signal" (168).[6]

Clark does not exactly present it this way, but involvement in representation-hungry problems is sometimes taken to be criterial of genuine representation. Following Gibson (1979), ecological psychologists deny that there are internal representations mediating many psychological processes, precisely because they maintain there are few if any representation-hungry problems (and so no need for an internal "stand-in").[7] They claim that there is always some invariant feature of the environment that is available to be perceived and to drive behaviour directly, as long as the system is sensitive to that feature. If this seems implausible, consider that some of the features that can be directly perceived, according to ecological psychologists, are certain dispositional or relational features called "affordances" – so that I can directly perceive that the rock on the cliff "affords" the squishing of Wily Coyote. To take a simpler example, consider when I look at some steps, and judge whether they are climbable (in the normal way) or not. It turns out that there is information directly available to me (step frequency, riser height, stair diagonal, leg length, strength and flexibility, and body weight) that fully specifies whether those steps are climbable for me (Konczak et al. 1992; Warren 1984). I need not *imagine* myself climbing the stairs to discover this (thus making use of an internal stand-in); I can simply register the combination of specifying information. (Hubert Dreyfus [2002] seems to have something similar in mind when he critiques representationalism, and it is also part of what Rodney Brooks [1991] contends.)

So judging climbability turns out *not* to be a representation-hungry problem, in Clark's sense, at least not for the reason of an *absent* (as opposed to unruly) environmental signal.[8] Whether more complicated cases, like the Wily Coyote case, or spatial navigation, will also turn out not to be representation-hungry is something that the ecological psychologists have yet to demonstrate to sceptical mainstream cognitive scientists. And since ecological psychologists in general eschew talk of mechanisms, they have not provided much reason to doubt that internal stand-ins are sometimes necessary in order to deal with an *unruly* environmental signal, Clark's second type of representation-hungry problem.

Other suggested typifying roles

What exactly *is* the typifying causal role or teleological function of representation? As we have just seen, disagreements may arise as to an item's representational status based on a fundamental disagreement about what sort of functional role makes a representation a representation.[9] The ecological psychologists seem to assume that representation occurs only when the cognitive system is not driven by some ambient signal in the environment, whereas mainstream cognitive scientists allow that representation may occur when the system responds to an environmental signal that is present but unruly. A number of other typifying functional roles of representation have been implied or suggested in the literature.

One obvious one is storage in memory. Information about the environment is collected, but not lost – it is kept for later use. This is one major role often envisioned for representation, and it is clearly linked to Clark's first representation-hungry problem (sensitivity to absent stimuli). Another major role commonly envisioned for representation is information processing – once stored, the information may be manipulated in combination with other pieces of information to generate new representations. A third major role is in problem solving, especially problem solving that involves hypothetical reasoning (e.g. the Tower of Hanoi problem). For example, Soar is a cognitive architecture from artificial intelligence that is primarily designed for problem-solving, and its leading characteristic is the manipulation of representations to explore (in "working memory") the various options in a "problem space," eventually settling on a procedure that will accomplish the task it has been set (Rosenbloom et al. 1992). (This is another instance of introducing representations to address Clark's first representation-hungry problem.) However, sometimes much simpler functional roles are taken to be criterial of representation. In the neuroscientific literature, the term "representation" is often used just in case there is a neural "detector" of some type of environmental stimulus, which need not be particularly unruly. (For instance, ganglion cells in the retina are sometime said to "represent" the impingement of multiple photons in a single location.) Usually it is also (implicitly) required that the signal thus generated can be used in further processing, though not necessarily computational processing in any robust sense.

In the psychological literature, representations (especially concepts) are often assumed to have the role of "classifiers," with the role of assimilating a number of (possibly unruly) environmental signals. These classifiers then may play a number of other roles, including, for example: (1) Economy of storage: Rather than remembering each experience individually, a cognitive system may remember features as pertaining to a small number of situation types (thus "dogs are furry" rather than "Rover is furry, Spot is furry, Snoopy is furry…"). (2) Economy of interface: This proposed function is closely related to the handling of "unruly" environmental signals, as above. Perceptual inputs need to be organized to facilitate action, and this can require the involvement of simplifying intermediaries. The sort of reasoning implemented by a classical "symbol manipulation" cognitive architecture (see Chapter 7 of this volume) can be seen as this kind of action-facilitating interface. (3) Communication: One of the actions facilitated by representations understood as classifiers is communication. Language is a small bandwidth system, so the economy introduced via classification also helps enable communication. (4) Identification of kinds and induction: If the features unified by a single representation are features of a real kind (e.g. dogs rather than the arbitrary class of red balloons, cups, and asparagus), the representation will be useful for inductive inference (if one dog is furry and brown, it is more likely that another dog is furry and brown; whereas the pointiness and greenness of asparagus does not make it more likely that a red balloon will be green and pointy). It will also be useful for organizing action, since items that share fundamental similarities are more likely to be appropriately subjected to similar actions.

Combination approaches

As one might expect, researchers often make use of multiple criteria simultaneously in wielding the term "representation." This is particularly true in the scientific literature, and often the criteria being used are merely implicit. Gallistel and Gibbon (2001) provide a nice exception, which I will present as an example of the combination approach. In arguing for their view that classical (Pavlovian) conditioning is a representational process, they contrast a computational/representational process with a process of simple association. They rely on a multi-pronged account of what makes something a representation. First, it must have a semantic content, or as they put it, it must "encode information about objectively specifiable properties of the conditioning experience." If classical conditioning were implemented by an associative process, there would be no representational separation of the variables that can affect the strengthening and weakening of the association between the conditioned and unconditioned stimuli (in Pavlov's famous experiments, CS = bell, US = food). There are many such variables, including (for example) the length of time between trials, the length of time between reinforcements, the number of reinforcements, and the delay in reinforcement. Because all of these variables would be confounded together in one association (a process of strengthening or weakening a connection), Gallistel and Gibbon maintain there is no determinate semantic content (about time, or number of trials, etc.) that could be attached to that associative process, or aspects of it. Since it would not have a determinate semantics, then, such a process could not be representational. They go on to argue that the experimental results suggest that what is going on is not in fact associative, but rather involves real representational separation. In particular, conditioning is insensitive to the time scale of the various intervals in the experimental protocol. As long as the ratios between the length of time between reinforcements, reinforcement delay, etc., are kept constant, the same effects on reinforcement strength are observed. The best explanation for this, they argue, is that the system keeps *separate* track of the various time intervals involved. This separation allows for determinate semantics and thus genuine representation.

The second part of their combination requirement for representation is a functional one: storage in memory. This is so that the third part may be satisfied: subsequent manipulation to generate new representations ("information processing"). In their representational account of conditioning, the various time intervals involved are "recorded in memory for later use in the computation of the decision variables on which conditioned responding is based." By contrast, "the associative bond does not participate in information processing (computational) operations. Associations, unlike symbols, are not added, subtracted, multiplied, and divided in order to generate new associations."

So here we have a nice example of the combination approach. It is also a nice example of when explanatory value grounds the postulation of representations. In Gallistel and Gibbon's model of conditioning, the question they try to answer is this: how does the animal manage to display time-scale invariance in its learning? They argue that it requires (1) variable separation; (2) variable storage; and (3) variable manipulation – and it is those related explanatory needs that lead them to postulate the existence of representations in the conditioning process (given their criteria for representation-hood). By contrast, if an associative model were explanatorily sufficient, no representations would need to be postulated.

Conclusion: other problems of representation

This review has been organized around the central strategy of figuring out what makes something count as a representation, and from there deciding what things count as *mental* representations. We have seen a wide variety of proposed criteria for representationhood, including degree of structure, degree of systematicity, similarity/isomorphism, representation hungriness, playing a role in detection, in storage, in information processing, in problem solving, or in classification. Many debates about the nature and role of various kinds of mental representations can be illuminated by paying careful attention to the participants' assumptions about what makes something a representation. We saw a few examples, but we have neglected many others. Fortunately most of these are treated elsewhere in this volume.

For example, there is controversy over the extent to which the outside world is in some sense a part of mental representation. Some advocates of embodied cognition claim that the outside world is literally a part of our mental representations (see Chapter 13 of this volume), and content externalists argue that a representation's content – and therefore the representation's identity – depends on things external to the mind (see the next chapter). There have also been and continue to be extensive debates about the format and nature of the various types of mental representations: are they classical, connectionist, or dynamical (Chapters 7, 12, and 28)? Are they digital or analog (Chapter 13)? Is there a language of thought, and is that language *sui generis* or is it a public language (Chapter 17)? If there are mental modules, do these modules share a *lingua franca*, or each "speak" a different language (Chapter 18)? Are there stored mental "rules" that dictate psychological processing (Chapter 12)? Are there both conceptual and non-conceptual representations (Gunther 2003)? Are there non-representational mental states, e.g. are sensory states non-representational (Chapters 29 and 35)? Are all mental representations consciously accessible (Chapter 31)? Are there innate mental representations (Chapter 19)? All of these other problems, though, will require an answer to the central question of what counts as a mental representation.

Notes

1. This requirement is imposed by, among others, John Haugeland (1991) and Andy Clark (1997).
2. Or alternatively, if something that could produce invariant that-the-sun-is-bright representations on demand.
3. It is precisely the lack of structure in connectionist systems that forms the basis for Fodor and Pylyshyn's famous attack on them – see Sharkey and Sharkey (this volume).
4. Millikan calls this corresponding variation an "isomorphism," though it should be understood that the isomorphism is not between a set of currently active representations and a set of circumstances in the world; rather it is an isomorphism between a set of possible currently active representations (beeps at different times and places) and a set of possible circumstances – the isomorphism could be called a "modal isomorphism." This contrasts with a picture, or more generally an "iconic" representation, in which the structure of a single representation maps on to the structure of some bit of the environment. This sort of isomorphism shall be considered below.
5. Although they often go hand-in-hand, representational holism, according to which representational status depends on holistic systematic relations, should be distinguished from content holism, according

to which a representation's content depends upon these relations. One could be a representational holist, and still accept Fodor and Lepore's (1992) central argument against *content* holism, to the effect that content holism is incompatible with a compositional syntactic structure.

6. As Clark notes, the classical computational model of vision has developed the view that even ordinary cases of perception, like perceiving distance, in fact involve dealing with similarly unfriendly environmental signals, thus their invocation of a multitude of internal representations.
7. Sometimes ecological psychologists talk as though representation hungriness is *criterial* for genuine representation, but other times they seem to take it as merely *evidence* for it, i.e. an internal "stand-in."
8. Gibson also makes the point that the registration of an environmental signal takes time – if that time can be indefinitely long, we may even obviate the need for memory, if memory is to be understood as the storage of representations. Instead, we may think of the cognitive system as registering the presence of information in the environment over the course of seconds, hours, days, or even years.
9. I'll now use this term, "functional role," generically to include both causal role and teleological role readings.

Reference

Abrahamsen, A., and Bechtel, W. (2006) "Phenomena and Mechanisms: Putting the Symbolic, Connectionist, and Dynamical Systems Debate in Broader Perspective," in Stainton, R. J. (ed.), *Contemporary Debates in Cognitive Science*, Oxford: Blackwell, pp. 159–86.

Baker, L. R. (1995) *Explaining Attitudes: A Practical Approach to the Mind*, Cambridge: Cambridge University Press.

Bennett, M. R., and Hacker, P. M. S. (2003) *Philosophical Foundations of Neuroscience*, Malden, MA: Blackwell.

Brandom, R. (1994) *Making It Explicit*, Cambridge, MA: Harvard University Press.

Brooks, R. (1991) "Intelligence without Representation," *Artificial Intelligence* 47: 139–59.

Churchland, P. M. (1989) *A Neurocomputational Perspective: The Nature of Mind and the Structure of Science*, Cambridge, MA: MIT Press.

Churchland, P. S. (1986) *Neurophilosophy: Toward a Unified Science of the Mind-Brain*, Cambridge, MA: MIT Press.

Clark, A. (1997) *Being There*, Cambridge, MA: MIT Press.

Cummins, R. (1996) *Representations, Targets, and Attitudes*, Cambridge, MA: MIT Press.

Davidson, D. (1973) "Radical Interpretation," *Dialectica* 27: 314–28.

Dennett, D. (1978) "A Cure for the Common Code," in *Brainstorms*, Cambridge, MA: MIT Press, pp. 90–108.

—— (1987a) "Styles of Mental Representation," in *The Intentional Stance*, Cambridge, MA: MIT Press, pp. 213–25.

—— (1991) "Real Patterns," *Journal of Philosophy* 88, no. 1: 27–51.

—— (1987b) *The Intentional Stance*, Cambridge, MA: MIT Press.

Dreyfus, H. (2002) "Intelligence without Representation," *Phenomenology and the Cognitive Sciences* 1, no. 4: 367–83.

Fodor, J. A. (1985) "Fodor's Guide to Mental Representation: The Intelligent Auntie's Vade-Mecum," *Mind* 94: 55–97.

—— (1975) *The Language of Thought*, New York: Thomas Y. Crowell & Co.

Fodor, J., and Lepore, E. (1992) *Holism: A Shopper's Guide*, Oxford: Blackwell.

Gallistel, C. R. (1990) *The Organization of Learning*, Cambridge, MA: MIT Press.

Gallistel, C. R., and Gibbon, J. (2001) "Computational vs. Associative Models of Simple Conditioning," *Current Directions in Psychological Science* 10: 146–50.

Gibson, J. J. (1979) *The Ecological Approach to Visual Perception*, Boston: Houghton-Mifflin.

Gunther, Y. H. (ed.) (2003) *Essays on Nonconceptual Content*, Cambridge, MA: MIT Press.

Haugeland, J. (1991) "Representational Genera," in W. Ramsey, S. Stich, and D. E. Rumelhart (eds), *Philosophy and Connectionist Theory*, Hillsdale, NJ: Erlbaum, pp. 61–89.

Kelso, J. A. S. (1995) *Dynamic Patterns: The Self-Organization of Brain and Behavior*, Cambridge, MA: MIT Press.
Kim, J. (1998) *Mind in a Physical World*, Cambridge, MA: MIT Press.
Konczak, J., Meeuwsen, H. J., and Cress, M. E. (1992) "Changing Affordances in Stair Climbing: The Perception of Maximum Climbability in Young and Older Adults," *Journal of Experimental Psychology: Human Perception and Performance* 18, no. 3: 691–97.
Kosslyn, S. M. (1994) *Image and Brain*, Cambridge, MA: MIT Press.
Lagerlund, H. (2004) "Mental Representation in Medieval Philosophy"; available: http://plato.stanford.edu/archives/sum2004/entries/representation-medieval/
Marr, D. (1982) *Vision: A Computational Investigation into the Human Representation and Processing of Visual Information*, San Francisco: W. H. Freeman.
Millikan, R. (1984) *Language, Thought, and Other Biological Categories*, Cambridge, MA: MIT Press.
—— (2000) "Reading Mother Nature's Mind," in D. Ross, A. Brook, and D. Thompson (eds), *Dennett's Philosophy: A Comprehensive Assessment*, Cambridge, Mass.: MIT Press, pp. 55–76.
Pylyshyn, Z. W. (2003) "Return of the Mental Image: Are There Really Pictures in the Brain?" *Trends in Cognitive Sciences* 7(3): 113–18.
—— (1999) "Is Vision Continuous with Cognition? The Case for Cognitive Impenetrability of Visual Perception," *Behavioral and Brain Sciences* 22, no. 3: 341–423.
Quine, W. V. O. (1960) *Word and Object*, Cambridge, MA: MIT Press.
Rosenbloom, P. S., Laird, J. E., and Newell, A. (1992) *The Soar Papers: Research on Integrated Intelligence*, Cambridge, MA: MIT Press.
Russell, B. (1918) "The Philosophy of Logical Atomism," *Monist* 28: 495–527.
Schiffer, S. (1981) "Truth and the Theory of Content," in H. Parret and J. Bouveresse (eds), *Meaning and Understanding*, New York: De Gruyter, pp. 204–22.
Sellars, W. (1969) "Language as Thought and as Communication," *Philosophy and Phenomenological Research* 29: 506–27.
Shepard, R. N., and Metzler, J. (1971) "Mental Rotation of Three-Dimensional Objects," *Science* 171: 701–3.
Sterelny, K. (1990) *The Representational Theory of Mind*, Oxford: Blackwell.
Stich, S. P. (1983) *From Folk Psychology to Cognitive Science*, Cambridge, MA: MIT Press.
—— (2001) *Deconstructing the Mind*, New York: Oxford University Press.
Swoyer, C. (1991) "Structural Representation and Surrogative Reasoning," *Synthese* 87: 449–508.
Thelen, E., and Smith, L. B. (1994) *A Dynamic Systems Approach to the Development of Cognition and Action*, Cambridge, MA: MIT Press.
van Gelder, T. (1995) "What Might Cognition Be, If Not Computation?" *Journal of Philosophy* 91: 345–81.
Varela, F., Thompson, E., and Rosch, E. (1991) *The Embodied Mind: Cognitive Science and Human Experience*, Cambridge, MA: MIT Press.
Warren, W. H. (1984) "Perceiving Affordances: Visual Guidance of Stair Climbing," *Journal of Experimental Psychology: Human Perception and Performance* 10: 683–703.

16
PROBLEMS OF REPRESENTATION II: NATURALIZING CONTENT

Dan Ryder

Introduction

The project

John is currently thinking that the sun is bright. Consider his occurrent belief or judgement that the sun is bright. Its content is that *the sun is bright*. This is a *truth-evaluable content* (which shall be our main concern) because it is capable of being true or false.[1] In virtue of what natural, scientifically accessible facts does John's judgement have this content? To give the correct answer to that question, and to explain *why* John's judgement and other contentful mental states have the contents they do in virtue of such facts, would be to naturalize mental content.

A related project is to specify, in a naturalistically acceptable manner, exactly what contents *are*. Truth-evaluable contents are typically identified with abstract objects called "propositions," e.g. the proposition that *the sun is bright*. According to one standard story, this proposition is constituted by further abstract objects called "concepts": a concept that denotes the sun and a concept that denotes brightness. These concepts are "combined" to form the proposition that *the sun is bright*. This proposition is the content of John's belief, of John's hope when he hopes that the sun is bright, of the sentence "The sun is bright," of the sentence, "Le soleil est brillant," and possibly one of the contents of John's perception that the sun is bright, or of a painting that depicts the sun's brightness.[2] This illustrates the primary theoretical role of propositions (and concepts). Saying of various mental states and/or representations that they express a particular proposition P is to pick out a very important feature that they have in common. But what exactly is this feature? What are propositions and concepts, naturalistically speaking? Having raised this important issue, I will now push it into the background, and focus on the question of how mental states can have contents, rather than on what contents are, metaphysically speaking. (That said, the most thoroughly naturalistic theories of content will include an account of propositions and concepts – compare the thoroughly naturalistic Millikan [1984], for instance, with McGinn [1989].)

Whatever the ultimate nature of contents, the standard view among naturalists is that content is at least *partly* constituted by truth conditions (following e.g. Davidson [1967] and Lewis [1970] on the constitution of linguistic meaning). This review, then, will focus on naturalistic accounts of how mental states' truth conditions are determined. That said, "content" is clearly a philosophical term of art, so there is a large degree of flexibility as to what aspects of a mental state count as its content, and therefore what a theory of content ought to explain. For example, is it possible for me, you, a blind person, a robot, a chimpanzee, and a dog to share the belief "that the stop sign is red," concerning a particular stop sign? Clearly, there are differences among the mental states that might be candidates for being such a belief, but it is not immediately obvious which of those differences, if any, are differences in *content*.

It seems that contents pertain both to certain mental states (like John's judgement) and to representations (like a sentence).[3] It would simplify matters a lot if contentful mental states turned out to be representations also. This is a plausible hypothesis (see Chapters 7, 10, 17, and 23 of this volume), and almost universally adopted by naturalistic theories of content. On this hypothesis, the content of a particular propositional attitude is inherited from the content of the truth-evaluable mental representation that features in it. What we are in search of, then, is a naturalistic theory of content (including, at least, truth conditions) for these mental representations, or in Fodor's (1987) terms, a "psychosemantic theory," analogous to a semantic theory for a language. Soon we will embark on a survey of such theories, but first, a couple of relatively uncontroversial attributive (ATT) desiderata.

The attributive desiderata

On one view, we begin philosophical study with an a priori grasp of our subject matter; in this case, mental content. Our task is then to elucidate exactly what it is that we have in mind by coming up with a list of *a priori* accessible necessary and sufficient conditions for something to, say, have a particular mental content. But the naturalistic philosopher need not accept this *modus operandi* in order to come up with a list of conditions that a theory of content ought to meet (if it is possible to meet them jointly). We have no *a priori* accessible definition of water, but we would be rightly suspicious of a theory that claimed none of the things we thought were water were actually water. Absent a convincing explanation for our massive error, we would rightly accuse such a theory of changing the subject. A theory of content that said we were massively mistaken about some central aspects of ordinary content attributions should receive the same treatment. This gives rise to two relatively uncontroversial desiderata for a psychosemantic theory:

ATT_{Self} – A theory of mental content ought not have the consequence that we are usually radically mistaken about the contents of our own mental states.

ATT_{Others} – A theory of mental content ought not have the consequence that we are usually radically mistaken about the contents of the mental states of others.

Any theory of content can rescue itself by rejecting the two ATT desiderata, including the theory that the content of all our mental states is *that Bozo is a clown*, or the radical eliminativist option that none of our mental states have content. Absent a convincing explanation for our radical error, any theory of content that fails to satisfy one or both of the ATT desiderata should stand accused of either being false or changing the subject. As it turns out, all extant theories have been so accused based on strong reasons. Psychosemantics isn't easy.

Informational theories

Information

At least at first glance, perceptual systems resemble measuring devices or indicators. An alcohol thermometer is a very simple measuring device, but there are of course measuring devices of much greater complexity. A gel electrophoresis unit, for instance, can measure the relative charges and sizes of DNA molecules in a sample, and a cell phone can measure the level of the local cell's carrier signal ("signal strength," typically shown on the phone's LCD display). It is natural to suppose that perceptual systems – and perhaps even the mechanisms that give rise to judgements and beliefs – are best thought of as highly sophisticated measuring devices. For instance, perhaps the auditory system measures (among other things) the loudness, pitch, and timbre of emitted sounds, while the visual system measures (among other things) the spatial location and extent of objects in the observer's view.

Measurement yields *information* (in a sense to be explained below), and information can be further *processed*. For instance, visual information about the spatial layout and auditory information about timbre could be combined to yield information about the identity of the musical instrument in front of one: a tuba. In a way, the identification of the tuba may be thought of as just another form of measurement, with graduations (regions in multivariate spaces) marked "tuba," "trumpet," "violin" etc., just as the thermometer's tube is marked "5°," "10°," and "15°." Or perhaps the identification of a tuba may be thought of as a light flashing on a "tuba indicator," preceded by a lot of complicated measurement and information processing, like an airport security door beeps to indicate metal. Concepts could then be thought of as banks of indicators preceded by specialized information processing. (Henceforth nothing important will hang on whether I talk about indication or measurement.)

No doubt you are inclined to say that the thermometer doesn't represent anything, only the person *reading* the thermometer does. Perhaps; but the thermometer can be read only because the state of its alcohol column is so intimately related to the temperature, i.e. to the content of the representation in question. This intimate relationship between an indicator's state and its content is suggestive. The hope of the information-based theorist is that this intimate relation, assuming it can be characterized naturalistically, may ultimately serve as a reductive base for content generally – including the content of your belief when you read the thermometer.

The naturalistic relation available is that of *carrying information about* or *carrying information that*. This relation has been elucidated in many different ways. (Related views date back at least to Reichenbach and possibly to Locke and even Ockham, but modern versions are due to Stampe [1977], Dretske [1981, 1986, 1988], Barwise and Perry [1983], Fodor [1987, 1990], Stalnaker [1984], Matthen [1988], Jacob [1997], and Neander [1995]). It is beyond the scope of the present chapter to examine these in detail, but the general idea can be conveyed quite easily. It is best expressed as a relation between facts or states of affairs: for instance, the fact that the thermometer's alcohol column is 3.5 centimetres carries the information that the ambient temperature is 10° Celsius (C). (Note that the formulation in terms of that-clauses makes information *truth evaluable*.) More generally, the fact that *r* is G carries the information that *s* is *F* if and only if the fact that *r* is G *guarantees* or *makes probable* the fact that *s* is *F*. If you *knew* that the thermometer's height was 3.5 centimetres, you would be in a position to know or predict with reasonable confidence that the ambient temperature is 10°C because there exists a certain dependence between those two facts. As it is often put, *r*'s being G "indicates," or "is a sign of," *s*'s being *F*.

As Paul Grice noted in 1957, there is a sense of "means" that is correctly applied to this sort of "natural sign." When we say that "smoke means fire," we are using the term in this sense. However, there are a number of reasons why the contents of our mental representations cannot just be what they mean as natural signs, at least if we are to take the ATT desiderata seriously.

Violating the ATT desiderata: let me count the ways

The specificity problem

First, suppose a thermometer's alcohol column currently carries the information that the ambient temperature is 10°C. Then it *also* carries the information that the ambient temperature is between 5 and 15°C, since the former entails the latter. Or suppose a flashing indicator carries the information that a tuba is present; it will also carry the information that a brass instrument is present. Similarly, if I perceive a tuba as such, my perception will also carry the information that a brass instrument is present. Yet I need not recognize that a brass instrument is present; I may not even know what a brass instrument is. This "specificity problem" (or "qua problem" – Devitt [1981]) will obviously be quite general; if a signal carries some piece of information, it will usually carry many pieces of more general information. In such a case, the informational content of my perception does not match what I shall call its "intuitive content," i.e. the content that one would normally apply to it introspectively, or attribute to someone else in the same perceptual state. This mismatch violates the ATT desiderata.[4]

Disjunction problems

How strong a guarantee must *r*'s being G provide of its representational content, i.e. of *s*'s being *F*? On Dretske's formulation, the conditional probability of *s*'s being *F*, given that *r* is G, must be equal to 1: in this case, call *s*'s being *F* part of the "strict informational content" of *r*'s being G. Then for the thermometer's alcohol column to carry the strict information that the ambient temperature is 10°C, the column's being at that height must *absolutely guarantee* that the temperature is 10°C. Which it doesn't: if the glass has a small hole in it, some of the alcohol will leak out as it moves, and the column's height will be at that level even if the temperature is 12°C. So it seems that the column's being at that height *doesn't* carry the (strict) information that the temperature is 10°C. Rather it carries the strict information that either there is no hole in the glass and the temperature is 10°C, or there is a hole of size *x* in the glass and the temperature is 10.5°C, or there is a hole of size *y* in the glass and the temperature is 11°C, etc. This strict informational content is a long disjunction (*very* long, considering there are many other things that might interfere with the column's height other than a hole in the glass).

Identifying our mental states' representational content with their strict informational content is not an attractive option. There are even more ways that our perceptual systems can go wrong than the thermometer can, and it would be a significant breach of the ATT desiderata to admit that our conscious visual states have massively disjunctive content, with part of that content being that our retina is not currently being interfered with (by analogy with a hole in the thermometer) and that we are not dreaming. This is an example of a "disjunction problem."

The most famous disjunction problem is the problem of misrepresentation, where some of the states of affairs included in the long disjunction of strict informational content are misrepresentations – and so should not be included – according to the intuitive content of that representation. For example, the holed thermometer intuitively misrepresents the temperature, and (to use a famous example of Fodor's) a perceptual representation that a horse is present intuitively misrepresents things when it is caused by a cow on a dark night. These misrepresented states of affairs will be included in strict informational content, however, with the ATT-violating consequence that misrepresentation is impossible.

Any type of state of affairs that is disposed to cause the tokening of a representation will be found among the disjuncts of that representation's strict informational content. Some of those states of affairs will intuitively be cases of misrepresentation. Others do not fit that description very well, e.g. when bone thoughts are disposed to cause dog thoughts (so one strict informational disjunct for dog thoughts will be that there is a bone thought present). So the disjunction problem is broader than just the problem of misrepresentation (Fodor 1990).

The distality problem

A related problem faced by information-based theories is the "chain problem" or "distality problem" or "transitivity problem" (Jacob 1997: Ch. 2; Prinz 2002: 120–21, 2002). Consider a gas gauge: it measures and represents the level of gasoline in a car's tank. However, the level of gas in the tank is not the only state of affairs type included among the strict informational disjuncts of a state of the gas gauge: also included are other states in the causal chain leading to the response of the gauge, for example the amount of electrical current in its lead wire. (These other states of affairs are not *alternative* causes for the representation; they will all be present simultaneously with its intuitive content – so Jacob [1997] calls this a "conjunction problem," as opposed to a disjunction problem.) The analogues in the mental case are the various proximal stimuli responsible for a perceptual judgement, e.g. the state of the intervening light or sound waves, the state of the sensory receptors, etc. So this is yet another way in which strict informational content includes states of affairs that are not part of the intuitive content of measuring instruments, indicators, or mental states.

Proposed fixes for ATT violations

One legitimate way to get from the thermometer's strict informational content to its intuitive representational content would be *via* the *user's* intentional states. We, as the thermometer's user or interpreter, read the thermometer as saying the temperature is 10°C, thus our own mental representations reduce the disjunction. However, an infinite regress threatens if we apply the same move to our perceptual states and other mental representations; it seems that *some* representations must not depend on use or interpretation in order to have content. These representations have *original* rather than *derived* intentionality (Searle 1983). (The interpretivist [e.g. Dennett, see below] may be seen as rejecting that apparent implication.) There have been a number of proposals for how an informational psychosemantics could "get the contents right."

Nomic dependence

The theoretical tweak normally introduced to deal with the specificity problem appeals to nomic dependence. Fodor, for instance, requires that the tokening of a representation be nomically dependent on its content, e.g. the instrument's property of being a tuba (Fodor 1990: 102). This means the representation is insensitive to French horns and trombones, but is tokened in the presence (but not the absence) of a tuba. It exhibits a causal or nomic dependence on tubas, not brass instruments. Dretske (1981: Ch. 7) achieves much the same result by constraining the content of a mental representation to being among the most *specific* information it carries, which happens also to be the information to which it is causally sensitive (180).[5]

Fodor makes use of the nomic dependency condition in response to the distality problem as well (Fodor 1990: 108–10). In general, there is no particular pattern of sensory receptor activations necessary for identifying an object. For belief-level representations, in fact, almost *any* pattern of receptor activations at all can cause a "there is a tuba" representation, since having the thought "There is a tuba" can be highly theory mediated. To borrow his figure of speech, all one would need is a ripple in tuba-infested waters – or, for that matter, a report that there's a tuba in any language whatsoever (even an alien one), as long as one understands it. This means that the disjunction of receptor activations that can cause "there is a tuba" representations is open-ended. Fodor reasonably asserts that open-ended disjunctions cannot participate in laws, so the open-ended disjunction of receptor activations fails the nomic dependency requirement and is not a legitimate content. Tubas (the distal item), by contrast, are. Of course, this response could only work for belief-level (i.e. theory-mediated) representation, it does not work for hardwired, modular perceptual representation. (But that is perhaps a bullet one could bite – perhaps perceptual representations really *do* mean the disjunction of receptor activations.)

"Lax" information

In order to (partially) avoid the disjunction problems, many informational psychosemanticists reject Dretske's (claimed) exclusive reliance on strict information (Jacob 1997; Fodor 1998; Usher 2001; Prinz 2002). On the "lax information" view, representation does not require that *r*'s being G *guarantee* *s*'s being *F*. For instance, one might say that the height of the alcohol column in the thermometer represents that single state of affairs type with which it exhibits the highest correlation, or the one that is most probable given that height. (See e.g. Usher [2001]. Usually, however, the exact nature of this relaxation from a probability of one is not fully explained.) If it is not very probable that there is a hole in the thermometer, then the disjunct "there is a hole of size *x* in the glass and the temperature is 10.5°C" will not be included in the representation's content.

A major problem for this kind of move is in identifying what counts as "the" state of affairs type with which the representation is most highly correlated. Think of the set of all states of affairs that are nomically/causally related to "there is a tuba," and which exhibit some correlation with that representation: tuba sideways at distance d_1 in bright light, tuba vertical at distance d_2 in dim light, French horn at d_3 in dim light next to a piccolo ... an extremely large set. Isolating "the" state of affairs type that is the representation's content involves picking out just the right subset of this large set, and in a non-question-begging manner. This is a tall order. Those states of affairs that exhibit the highest correlation will include optimal epistemic conditions (e.g. "there's a tuba in close range in good light"), but these conditions are not part of the intuitive content ("the problem of ideal epistemic conditions"). As we move to lower correlations, we include more states of affairs that are misrepresentations (some of which may be highly probable, e.g. if a small person holds a euphonium). On top of all this, the probability of a judgement being true *depends on what is being measured or judged.* (Compare judging temperature with judging anger.) Therefore it is impossible to define content-determining levels of correlation piecemeal, representation by representation, without cheating and taking a peek at each representation's content in advance – a circularity that violates the naturalism constraint. (See also Godfrey-Smith [1989].)

Channel conditions/optimal conditions

Dretske's early response (1981) to disjunction problems was to maintain informational strictness but to make the information carried relative to certain *channel conditions*, for instance the channel condition that the thermometer's glass tube be intact. The channel conditions for the perceptual judgement "There is a tuba" to carry information about the presence of a tuba would perhaps include good light, the subject being awake and attentive, the absence of trick mirrors, the absence of pesky neurophysiologists injecting neurotransmitters into one's retina, etc. Different channel conditions would of course determine different representational contents for the indicator; the trick is to find some non-question-begging way of assigning the channel conditions that make "There is a tuba" carry non-disjunctive information about the presence of tubas, and thus match intuitive content.[6] This presents a challenge because, as for the probability of a representation being true, the relevant channel conditions seem to depend on the content of the representation: recognizing tubas may require good light, but recognizing stars requires the opposite. (The problem is only exacerbated when we consider theory-mediated judgements – see McLaughlin [1987].) It seems we need to know the content of a representation in order to know which channel conditions to specify, but this violates the naturalism constraint.[7]

Incipient causes

Dretske (1981) pursues the "incipient-cause" strategy in order to try to isolate the intuitive content from informational content, and solve the problem of misrepresentation; a more recent proponent of this strategy is Prinz (2002) (from whom I take the term).[8] On this view, the content of a mental representation is limited to the thing or kind of thing that caused (or, on Dretske's view, *could* have caused) the representation to be acquired. For example, although the strict informational content of a judgement might be disjunctive between "there is a Monarch butterfly" and "there is a Viceroy butterfly," if the concept figuring in the judgement was acquired through exposure to Monarchs (and not Viceroys), this rules out the Viceroy disjunct (at least on Prinz's view, if not Dretske's). While this move can help with the problem of misrepresentation (since it is plausible that misrepresented items rarely play a role in representation acquisition), it cannot rule out items that normally do play a role in acquisition: for instance proximal stimuli (the distality problem) and epistemic conditions like "in good light" (the problem of ideal epistemic conditions). (Prinz handles the distality problem by appeal to nomic dependence, but it seems he still faces the problem of ideal epistemic conditions.)

One final point: the incipient-cause approach promises to handle the tricky matter of reference to individuals, something we have not yet considered. Two individuals can be exact duplicates, yet it is possible to have a concept that is determinately about a particular individual rather than any of its duplicates (parents will be familiar with a child who wants *that very toy that was lost*, not another one exactly the same). It seems, however, that informational and nomic relations are ill-suited for distinguishing between duplicates. Supplementing the informational theory with an historical factor like incipient causation might be a sensible way to link a representation to an individual.

Asymmetric dependence

Fodor's attempts to wrestle with the disjunction problems centre on his asymmetric dependence approach (original version in Fodor [1987]; later version in Fodor [1990: Ch. 4]). Fodor focuses on the sub-propositional components of truth-evaluable representations (e.g. concepts). According to the asymmetric dependence theory, the content-determining informational relation between a representation and its object is fundamental, in the sense that any other causal or nomic relations between the representation and the world depend on the fundamental nomic relation, but not the other way around (thus the dependence is asymmetric).

This approach can be made intuitive in the case of perceptual error, for example when a carrot looks misleadingly like a pencil. Since "pencil"s (the mental representations that denote pencils) can be caused either by pencils or by carrots, there must be laws connecting "pencil"s to both pencils and carrots. There's some pencil → "pencil" law that obtains because of the way pencils look, and there's also a carrot → "pencil" law that obtains because of the way carrots sometimes look – they sometimes look like pencils. That carrots can sometimes cause "pencil"s depends on some shared appearance that carrots and pencils have. Thus the carrot → "pencil" law rides piggyback on the pencil → "pencil" law, via a shared appearance. If there were no pencil → "pencil" law there would not be the carrot → "pencil" law. So the existence of the carrot → "pencil" law depends on the existence of a pencil → "pencil" law. However, the reverse does not hold. There could perfectly well be a pencil → "pencil" law even if, for instance, carrots and pencils did not share an appearance, so carrots did not cause "pencil"s. So although the carrot → "pencil" law depends on the pencil → "pencil" law, the pencil → "pencil" law does not depend upon the carrot → "pencil" law. That is, dispositions to commit perceptual errors are dependent upon dispositions to correctly apply a representation, but not the other way around. If you extend this to epistemic routes that go beyond shared appearances (e.g. theory-mediated routes), then you get Fodor's theory.

Fodor's theory spawned a small industry producing counterexamples to it (Adams 2000; Mendola 2003). Whether any of these counterexamples succeed is a controversial matter, and beyond the scope of this chapter. But one concessive response that Fodor makes should be mentioned: he points out that his theory presents merely *sufficient* conditions for content, not *necessary* ones. So if a blow-to-the-head → "pencil" law applies to someone (why not?), and this law does not depend on the pencil → "pencil" law, violating asymmetric dependence, Fodor can just say "That's just not a case to which my theory applies – I didn't say it applied to *all* representations." This reduces the interest of the theory significantly, perhaps even rendering it vacuous (if, for example, all of our representations can be caused in non-standard ways, like blows to the head, or specifically designed electromagnetic apparatus – Adams [2000]). See also Mendola (2003) for a general critique of all asymmetric dependence approaches.

Basic representations plus composition

It might be thought that there are some basic, perceptual representations (e.g. colours, tastes, sounds) that fit informational semantics rather well, i.e. they are less susceptible to problems of misrepresentation, distality, etc. Perhaps the informational psychosemantic story applies only to these primitives, and other mental representations are simply constructed out of these basic ones; in this way, the various violations of ATT might be avoided (Dretske 1986; Sterelny 1990). This compositional strategy is also the preferred response to an as-yet-unmentioned difficulty for informational theories, the problem of empty representations, like the empty concept of unicorns. It is unclear how information can be carried about the nonexistent, but if these concepts can be decomposed into more basic ones that are susceptible to an informational treatment (e.g. of horses and horns), there's no problem (Dretske 1981).

To succeed with this compositional project, we would need plausible analyses of complex concepts, and given the poor track record of conceptual analysis (Fodor 1998), this appears unlikely. Consider also the evidence that we need not know the individuating conditions for kinds or individuals (including mythical or fictional kinds and individuals) in order successfully to refer to them (Kripke 1972; Putnam 1975; Burge 1979; Millikan 1984). This suggests that conceptual analysis cannot individuate such concepts, perhaps explaining its poor track record. Overall, the compositional strategy does not seem very promising. The right balance of a range of primitive contents and a plausible individuating analysis of complex concepts would have to be found, and we are certainly nowhere near that.

Informational teleosemantics

One possible panacea for all of these problems is teleology. Returning to the thermometer, we could say the teleological function or job of the thermometer is to make the height of its mercury column co-vary with temperature such that the mercury column's being at "12" is *supposed* to carry the information that the temperature is 12°C. While its informational content is disjunctive, its semantic content is just the disjunct singled out by the teleology. If the thermometer has a leak, it is failing to do what it is supposed to do, and therefore misrepresenting. Also, the mercury column is not representing any proximal cause of its height (e.g. the pressure and volume of the glass tube), because that is not what it is supposed to carry information about. This teleological version of "informational thermosemantics" seems to match intuitive content quite easily – thus the pursuit of a plausible teleological version of informational *psychosemantics*. The most familiar version of such a psychosemantics comes from Dretske's more recent work (1986, 1988, 1995; see also Neander 1995; Jacob 1997; Shea 2007).

The most difficult task is to justify the teleology. In the case of the thermometer, it is the designer's and/or user's intentions that endow it with its function, but the psychosemanticist must look elewhere, usually to some selective process, like evolution by natural selection or some variety of trial-and-error learning.[9] A human designer might select a variety of materials in a particular arrangement to pump water out of a cistern – so that the artefact produced has the function of pumping water, and not of making thumping noises (although it does both). Similarly, Darwinian evolution selects a variety of materials in a particular arrangement in order to pump blood through the body – so that the heart has the function of pumping blood, and not of making thumping noises, although it does both (Wright 1973; Millikan 1984). In both cases, the object (pump or heart) is there *because* it does the thing that is its function (pumping). In both cases, there are limitations on what materials are available, and what arrangements are possible. In both cases, there are random elements involved: what ideas the designer happens across (discarding most of them), and what mutations occur. The contention is that the analogy is close enough to justify applying teleological terminology in the biological world quite generally, even if it rests most naturally upon artefacts (Millikan [1984]; for refined analyses, see Neander [1991], Allen et al. [1998]; for discussion, see Ariew et al. [2002]).

Assuming we are willing to accept natural teleology, how do we get natural *informational* teleology? We need an indicator to be naturally selected for indicating its intuitive content, just as a gas gauge is selected (by a car's designer) for indicating the level of gas in the tank (Dretske 1988). The gas gauge represents the level of gas in the tank (and not the current in its lead wire, or the incline of the slope the car is on) because that is what it is supposed to indicate, that's its job or function. For mental representations that are a product of development (as opposed to learning), the relevant selection may be accomplished by evolution (Dretske 1995). "Hardwired" visual circuits for detecting edges might be an example. A mutation results in a particular type of visual neuron being sensitive to edges in a single animal. This results in improved vision in that animal, which navigates its environment very successfully and consequently leaves many offspring, more than its average competitor. These offspring also compete well, and the presence of the modified gene gradually predominates in the population. So that neuron type is there (in the population) because it carries information about edges; that is its function. If one of these neurons responds instead to a bright flash, it is falsely representing the presence of an edge – this counts as an error because the neuron is not doing what it is supposed to do. *That* detection disposition of the neuron type did not confer any advantage on its host organisms, and so was not causally responsible for the spread of that neuron type through the population.

That is the informational teleosemantic story for innate indicators, indicators that are products of development. Learned representations may be accommodated in one of two ways: either (1) analogously to innate representations, but where the selective process is trial-and-error learning (Dretske 1988; Papineau 1987); or (2) by attributing to the learning mechanism an evolutionarily derived generic function of creating mechanisms with more specific indicator functions (i.e. an informational version of Millikan 1984 – it should be emphasized that Millikan's theory is *not* informational).[10]

Objections to teleosemantics

There are many objections that have been raised against teleosemantic accounts of content generally, and some against informational teleosemantic accounts. However, the two principle problems are Swampman and the disjunction/distality problems.

Swampman is a molecular duplicate of (usually) Davidson, who arises by a massively improbable chance in the Florida Everglades, after a lightning strike perhaps.[11] Since Swampman lacks any evolutionary or learning history, none of his "mental representations" have any content, on the standard teleosemantic views. Yet he behaves exactly like Davidson, successfully navigating his environment and (apparently, at least) engaging in philosophical conversation. Ignorant of his past, we would unhesitatingly attribute mental states to Swampman, so the example is meant to show that teleosemantics violates the $\text{ATT}_{\text{Others}}$ desideratum (albeit for a rather unusual "other").

Swampman is a problem for teleosemantics only if teleology depends upon *historical* facts, e.g. evolutionary or learning facts. Therefore some teleosemanticists have responded to the Swampman objection by attempting to formulate a non-historical teleology, usually dependent upon cybernetic ideas of feedback and homeostasis (see Chapter 21 of this volume; Schroeder 2004a, b). Another response is a thorough-going externalism (like Millikan's, for instance). It is relatively uncontroversial that Swampman lacks a concept of Davidson's mother, since he has never had any causal contact with her. If it could be made intuitive that prior causal contact (or other relation) is necessary for *any* concept (Burge 1979; Millikan 2000; Ryder 2004), then it should be intuitive that Swampman's concepts don't refer and so his mental states lack truth-conditional content (though they could have *narrow* content – see below). In addition, Millikan (1996), and Papineau (1993: 93) insist that their teleological theory (among others) is a "real-nature" theory, rather like the chemical theory that water is H_2O. While it might seem to us that water could be composed in some other way – it is imaginable to us – it is not really possible. Similarly, while a content-possessing Swampman is imaginable, he is not really possible. (See Braddon-Mitchell and Jackson [1997], Papineau [2001], and Jackson [2006] for further discussion.)

Note that the teleosemanticist can agree with her opponent that Swampman has *conscious* states, at least phenomenally conscious states (see Chapter 29 of this volume), as long as those are not essentially intentional. (So this move is not available to Dretske, for instance; see his 1995.) Perhaps that is enough shared mentality to account for the problematic intuition that Swampman is mentally like us. Nevertheless, the Swampman issue remains a contentious one – it is probably the most common reason for rejecting a teleological approach to content.

The second main problem for teleosemantics is that it isn't clear that it can fully overcome the disjunction and distality problems. Fodor (1990: Ch. 4) is particularly hostile to teleosemantic theories for this reason. Much of the discussion has focused on the case of the frog's "fly detector." The detection of flies, nutritious blobs, small dark moving spots, or a disjunction of receptor activations could all be implicated in the selectional explanation for why frogs have such detectors, so it seems that a teleosemantic theory cannot decide among those content assignments. The nomic dependency condition may help a little here, since the frog's representation arguably exhibits a nomic dependence on small dark moving dots, but not on nutritious blobs. However, proximal stimuli exhibit both the requisite nomic dependence (albeit a disjunctive one) and selectional relevance, so the distality problem appears to be particularly problematic for informational teleosemantics (Neander 2004; see also Godfrey-Smith 1994). Millikan claims a teleosemantic solution is available only if we abandon the informational approach (see below).

The grain problem

In this, the final section on informational semantics, I turn to a rather different problem. It will take us in new directions entirely, towards a variety of psychosemantics that is not information based: conceptual or causal role psychosemantics.

Frege noted how fine grained the contents of linguistic utterances and propositional attitudes are, in that it is possible to believe that *P* and disbelieve that *Q* even though *P* and *Q* are equivalent in one of multiple ways: extensional, nomological, or logical. The nomic-dependence condition allows informational semantics to distinguish judgements that are extensionally equivalent. For example, creatures with hearts and creatures with kidneys might *actually* cause all the same representations to be tokened, but nomicity requires that they exhibit the same *counterfactual* tendencies as well, which they do not. However, for equivalence stronger than extensional, information-based theories run into trouble. Consider the following pairs of predicates: "is an electron" and "has charge *e*"; "is fool's gold" and "is iron pyrite"; "is equilateral" and "is equiangular"; and the following pairs of concepts: "the morning star" and "the evening star," "Clark Kent" and "Superman," and "silicone" and "polysiloxane." None of these can be distinguished counterfactually.

One possible response is to say that these representations are not really distinct, at least not in terms of their contents (roughly equivalent to the modern "Russellian" position in philosophy of language [Richard 1983; Salmon 1986; Soames 1989; Braun 2000]). (In a few cases they may be distinguished syntactically: this is particularly plausible for the "is an electron"–"has charge *e*" pair.) The usual response, though, is to maintain that the distinct representations that are strongly equivalent play different causal roles in the cognitive economy (e.g. Prinz 2002; Neander 2004). (This corresponds roughly to the Fregean position in philosophy of language [Church 1951; Evans 1982; Peacocke 1992], where the causal roles are to be identified with Fregean senses.) Although the concepts linked to the words "silicone" and "polysiloxane" denote the same thing, they might be differentiated by their internal cognitive roles.

Controversially, informational content and cognitive role are sometimes divided into explanations of two kinds of content, external or *broad content* and internal or *narrow content*. Broad content is linked to the phenomena of reference, truth, and (more generally) satisfaction conditions, while narrow content is linked to the phenomenon of cognitive significance (e.g. the different cognitive significance of "morning star" and "evening star," despite common reference). Narrow content, by definition, supervenes upon the intrinsic state of the representing mind, while broad content does not so supervene. On hybrid informational-cognitive role theories, narrow content is only related to truth (and satisfaction) by attaching to representations that also have broad contents *via* external informational relations (Field 1977; Loar 1982). Because of its distant relation to truth conditions, and (on the standard view) the intimate link between truth conditions and content, it is questionable whether narrow content deserves the name of "content" on such "hybrid" or "two factor" theories. (Recall, however, that "content" is a philosophical term of art.) By contrast, there are theories on which internal cognitive role is supposed to be much more directly related to truth conditions – we now turn to those.

Conceptual role semantics

Naturalistic versions of conceptual role semantics (CRS) descend directly from functionalism in philosophy of mind (Chapter 10 of this volume) and "use" theories of meaning in philosophy of language (Wittgenstein 1953; Sellars 1963). Use theories of meaning say that the linguistic meaning of an expression is determined by its use or role in a language (in inference and other aspects of the "language game"). Functionalism says that the identity of a mental state is determined by its causal role in the perceptual, cognitive, and behavioural system. Since the content of a mental state is essential to its identity, and since linguistic meaning and mental content share deep analogies (e.g. similar belief contents and linguistic meanings are typically expressed using the same "that" clauses), the two theories naturally come together to say: mental content is determined by causal role (especially inferential role) in the perceptual, cognitive, and behavioural system.

For example, take the thought "it is raining." The CRS theory will characterize the content of this thought (at least in part) by the inferences that it is disposed to participate in (either as premise or conclusion). For instance, if one has the thought "it is raining," perhaps one is disposed to infer the thought "there are clouds outside." This thought will also have its own content-characterizing inferences, to other thoughts which will, in turn, have their own content-characterizing inferences, etc. Depending on the type of theory, any of these inferential-cum-causal patterns might be relevant to the content of the thought "it is raining." Again depending on the type of theory, causal relations to items in the external environment may also be relevant.

There are several ways to divide CRS theorists. First, there are those who accept the representational theory of mind (RTM), and those who do not (Armstrong 1973; Lewis 1994; see previous chapter). Naturalists have generally found the arguments in favour of RTM persuasive, so most naturalistic CRS advocates apply the theory to mental representations; however, most of the discussion below will apply to similar non-RTM theories as well. Another division is into the teleological and non-teleological camps, a distinction we shall consider later when looking at objections to CRS. Finally, there are different ways of characterizing the content-determining causal roles, in terms of their density and whether they extend beyond the mind into the environment.

Characterizing causal roles

Short vs. long armed

CRS theorists divide on whether content-determining causal roles extend into the environment. A long-armed theory (externalist, e.g. Harman 1982, 1987) allows external objects to enter into the functionalist analysis, while a short-armed theory (internalist, e.g. internalist computational functionalism [see Ch. 10 of this volume]) analyses contents only in terms of perceptual states, motor commands, and the complex systemic causation that occurs in between.

On a short-armed theory, causal roles are initially characterized as relations among mental states characterized by their contents ("it is raining" is disposed to cause "it is cloudy," etc.). These contents are then abstracted away and one is left with particular causal patterns. These content-characterizing causal patterns are entirely abstract, or purely relational (*a*, *b*, and *c* jointly cause *d*; *d* and *e* jointly cause *f*, etc.). Such a theory is particularly vulnerable to complaints of being too liberal – perhaps the molecules in my wall exhibit the relevant causal pattern, or a set of water pipes could be set up to exhibit the pattern, but these things do not represent that it is raining (or so goes the intuition; see Searle 1980, 1992). A possible response is to require that the variables denote *representations*, with some stringent additional requirements for what counts as a representation (e.g. that they enter into *computations* [Chapter 10 of this volume]; see the previous chapter for some approaches).

While CRS is designed neatly to solve the grain problem, a short-armed theory runs into trouble with the flipside: twin cases. Kripke (1972) (on individuals) and Putnam (1975) (on kinds) persuaded most philosophers of mind (and language) that at least some mental contents are determined, in part, by conditions external to the mind. Oscar, who lives on Earth (where the rivers, lakes, and oceans are filled with H_2O) is a functional duplicate of twin Oscar, who lives on twin Earth (where the rivers, lakes, and oceans are filled with XYZ). Yet (Putnam persuades most of us) Oscar's water-role thoughts are of H_2O, while twin Oscar's water-role thoughts are of XYZ. A short-armed CRS, being an internalist theory, does not appear to have the resources to account for this difference in content.

A long-armed theory is somewhat resistant to the charge of liberalism and twin-case worries. The charge of liberalism is not as problematic because the causal pattern characterizing a particular content is less abstract. Included in it are causal links to types of items in the environment, which need not be abstracted away (Cummins 1989: 122). Furthermore, as long as those causal links to external items are not construed purely dispositionally (e.g. a disposition to respond perceptually to clear, potable liquids), a long-armed theory may not be vulnerable to the twin problem either. The causal role of Oscar's thoughts may link him only to H_2O, while the causal role of twin Oscar's thoughts may link him only to XYZ (Block 1998).

Causal role density

There are several choices as to what sorts of causal relations to include in the content-determining causal patterns. One possibility is to include, as content-determining, *all* the causal relations that a token contentful mental state enters into. This is not very plausible – a mental state token's disposition to reflect light is clearly not relevant to its content. How to narrow down the relevant dispositions, though?

One very restrictive possibility is to include only relations that are definitional, so that the representation "*x* is a bachelor" is characterized by the disposition to infer, and be inferred by, "*x* is an unmarried adult male person." On a naturalistic theory, these contents would then be abstracted away, leaving a causal pattern. There are three serious problems with this idea. First, after decades of effort in the twentieth century alone, very few concepts seem to be definable (Fodor 1998). Some of the few exceptions include logical concepts, for which a CRS theory is particularly plausible.[12] The second major problem with the definitional route is that the possibility of isolating definitional relations depends upon there being a determinate difference between claims that are analytic, and those that are synthetic (Fodor and Lepore 1991) – and it is far from clear that the analytic-synthetic distinction can be maintained in the face of the objections raised by Quine (1953, 1976). Third, the meagre causal roles that are supposed to be content determining are highly vulnerable to the charge of excessive liberalism. This problem will also apply to possible alternative "sparse-role" versions of CRS, for example a naturalized version of Peacocke's theory, where the content-determining roles are only those that are "primitively compelling."

Perhaps a better option is to be less restrictive about what causal relations are content-determining. Armchair philosophy might be given the task of elucidating all manner of conceptual relations and platitudes that individuate contents (a tall order!) (Lewis 1994; Jackson 1998), and these conceptual roles could then be naturalized by mapping them on to causal ones. Alternatively, it could be left to psychology to determine what causal roles characterize states with particular contents. These roles may have a probabilistic structure, as in prototype theory, for instance (Rosch 1978). On prototype theory, no particular perceptual or other sort of representation, or set of such representations, need be necessary and sufficient to make a thinker token a mental state with a particular content. Rather, such an inference will occur only with a certain probability. Alternatively, the causal roles may be characterized somewhat as one characterizes the role of a concept in a scientific theory (Gopnik and Meltzoff 1997), with a many-layered and revisable inferential structure.

CRS theories and truth conditions

One fundamental problem for naturalistic CRS theorists is in relating causal roles to truth conditions. Prima facie, a psychosemantic theory ought to make plain the general principles by which internal, physical states are mapped on to truth conditions. This mapping is made relatively transparent by informational theories. On a CRS theory, by contrast, the mapping is difficult to make explicit. On a short-armed theory, there are no content-determining relations to external items that could be used to identify truth conditions, and on long-armed theories, there are *too many* such (potentially) content-determining relations – as Fodor observed (see the section, above, "Disjunction problems"), a contentful mental state can be tokened in response to multifarious external conditions.

One strategy is to make use of informational relations as determinative of truth conditions, producing the hybrid theory mentioned at the end of the section, "The grain problem," above. This theory will inherit most of the virtues and problems that come with informational theories, and will not be further discussed here. Another strategy is to take the mass of related inferences to be similar or *isomorphic* to related states of affairs in the environment. This isomorphism-based strategy will be considered below. The third strategy, which comes in two forms, is to reject the demand for a general naturalistic formula or "recipe" for determining truth conditions. That is the strategy we shall examine first.

"No-recipe" CRS theories

The most radical rejection of the demand for a general formula for determining truth conditions is *deflationism* (e.g. Field 1994; Horwich 1998). The CRS deflationist denies that "the problem of content" relates to any genuine mind-world connection that needs explaining. The deflationist accepts the standard schemata,

> "*P*" is true if and only if *P*
>
> If *b* exists then "*b*" refers to *b* and nothing else; if *b* doesn't exist then "*b*" doesn't refer to anything

and claims that that is all there is to say about truth and reference (whether for language or for mental representations). Meaning and content are determined by use, and there is no need for a theory of content to provide a substantive account of how truth conditions are determined. The debate between deflationists and "inflationists" (primarily in the arena of language) is voluminous and complex, defying any quick summary here (see Blackburn and Simmons [1999] and Lynch [2001] for discussion). If deflationism works, however, it would in one fell swoop remove all the difficulties we have seen in matching intuitive content. The major cost is that our success in dealing with the environment could not be explained by our mental states "corresponding to the facts" in any robust sense (e.g. carrying information about or being isomorphic to the facts).

The second version of the "no recipe" strategy effectively takes the relation between a causal role and a truth condition to be real, but primitive and unexplained. Certain causal roles or patterns determine certain truth-conditional contents, and that is all there is to say. However, this sort of primitivist theory is severely hampered in trying to characterize content-determining causal roles. A recipe for determining truth conditions would provide a test for whether one has got the right causal role for a particular content or set of contents. If it is the right causal role, it must determine the right (i.e. intuitive) truth conditions. This introduces a welcome constraint. Without such a recipe, one has only raw intuition to go by in figuring out what aspects of a mental representation's causal role are content-determining. Given the clash of intuitions one finds in the literature, one's hopes should not be high that philosophers of mind will ever settle on a particular "no-recipe" CRS theory. That, by itself, is reason to hope for a truth-condition determining recipe. Luckily, there is a very ancient one available for the CRS theorist to make use of: *resemblance*.

Relational resemblance as a recipe for determining truth conditions

While first-order resemblance between mental states (e.g. brain states) and represented states of affairs is clearly a non-starter, the *relational* resemblance that fits with a CRS theory is much more plausibly a content-determining one. On this view, the complex, internal web of causal roles resembles (is isomorphic or homomorphic to) the complex structure of that which is represented. That which is represented could be the causal or regularity structure of the environment (Cummins 1989; McGinn 1989; P. S. Churchland 2002; Ryder 2004), or (less naturalistically) computational functions or entailment structures among propositions (Cummins 1989; McGinn 1989). The key point is that CRS, on this version, turns out to be a species of "structural representation," where a pattern of relations among a group of representations mirrors a pattern of relations in what is represented (Swoyer 1991).

A nice example is a solar system model, or orrery. The gears in the orrery ensure that the pattern of regularities in the motions of the model planets mirrors the motions of the real planets. As Swoyer points out, this allows for the process of "surrogative reasoning": if you don't know the position of Venus in two months, but you do know where the Earth will be, simply rotate the Earth into that position and read off the future position of Venus. Similarly, if the pattern of inferences we make about the world mirrors real regularities in the world, we can understand how we are able to make predictions (this is the key insight of the internal-model theory of thinking [Craik 1943]).

If the relational resemblance is meant to serve as a recipe for determining referential content and truth conditions, however, it runs into serious trouble. The problem is that relational resemblance (whether isomorphism or homomorphism) is too cheap. Given a set of representations exhibiting a number of causal relations, this structure will be mirrored by an indefinitely large number of environmental (or propositional entailment) structures. Thus the relational resemblance strategy faces a serious problem of indeterminacy. Some other element would need to be added – perhaps causal, informational, or teleological. Thus, for example, McGinn (1989) and Ryder (2004) propose teleological isomorphism theories, and must contend with the standard problems for teleosemantics (especially Swampman and indeterminacy).

Further problems with CRS

Holism

Perhaps the central problems for non-definitional versions of CRS that appeal to fairly dense causal roles are those that arise as a result of their *content holism* (to be contrasted with the *representational holism* described in the previous chapter). With the rich conceptual cum causal relations that are content-determining on such theories, each mental representation gets constitutively linked to many others, which are linked to many others, and pretty soon the content of a single mental state gets determined by the entire web of conceptual relations. Since no two actual thinkers believe all the same things, the theory dictates that no two thinkers have *any* beliefs in common. This clearly violates ATT_{Others}; we regularly say that two people believe the same thing.

CRS theorists typically respond that our attributive practice requires only *similarity* of content (e.g. P. M. Churchland 1996). For practical purposes, we need not pay attention to the small differences in belief contents when attributing the judgement "the puppy is black" to two people, only one of whom also believes that dog hair is made of protein and that Jung was a charlatan. The conceptual and/or causal webs of these two people are similar enough to justify treating them as the same, for ordinary psychological explanation and other purposes. The problem, then, is to define a measure of similarity, and then to determine how similar is "similar enough." Critics, most notably Fodor, deny this can be done. Part of the problem is that complex relational structures are extremely difficult to compare objectively, especially if they differ in a large number of respects (e.g. number of nodes as well as pattern of connectivity). And webs that *do* differ in a large number of respects nevertheless seem to be able to support the same mental contents: both you and Helen Keller can believe that the sun is shining, for instance. This debate is unresolved, with CRS advocates turning to the details of neural network theory for help (P. M. Churchland 1998; Goldstone and Rogosky 2002), and critics responding that this doesn't change a thing (Fodor and Lepore 1999).

Compositionality

Fodor and Lepore have pressed another issue faced by non-definitional CRS, which is compositionality. We are able to think an indefinite variety of thoughts that are systematically related by their contents; the most obvious explanation for this capacity is that our thoughts have components (e.g. concepts), and the propositional contents of our thoughts are a function of the sub-propositional contents of those components (see the section "Syntactic structure," in the previous chapter, and Chapter 17 of this volume). The problem for non-definitional versions of CRS is that conceptual roles do not seem to compose in the right way – for example, the conceptual role of a complex concept need not be a function of the conceptual roles of its component, simpler concepts. One of Fodor's favourite examples is the complex "pet fish." Take, for example, an aspect of conceptual role focused on by prototype theorists: typicality judgements. The typical pet is a cat or dog, and the typical fish is a trout or salmon. But the typical pet fish is not the average between cat/dog and trout/salmon; rather it is a goldfish or guppy. More generally, it is hard to see how the non-definitional conceptual role of "pet fish" could be *any* function of the conceptual roles of "pet" and "fish" – it is certainly not a simple additive function. Perhaps some more complex function could be determined (see Prinz [2002] for an attempt), but the holistic nature of the content-determining roles makes it a difficult task. It is fair to say that the compositionality problem is an unresolved issue, with CRS (at least the "no-recipe" sort) on the defensive. (The relational resemblance strategy might provide a solution, since truth conditional/referential content *is* compositional.)

Normativity

CRS also runs into an analogue of one of the principal problems that plagues informational semantics, namely the problem of misrepresentation, or more generally the problem of error. It rears its ugly head in even broader form: people make inferential errors not only when the conclusion involves *applying* some representation to an item or state of affairs (giving rise to the classic problem of misrepresentation), but when making other sorts of inferences as well (e.g. inferences in practical reasoning). A naturalistic version of CRS needs to make sense of these inferences as being erroneous, and as Kripke has famously argued (Kripke 1982), it is far from obvious how this is to be done with only causal notions at one's disposal. Kripke asks, what distinguishes between two people who are both disposed to infer "5" from "57 + 65," one of whom does so incorrectly (meaning by "+" the plus function), the other correctly (since she means something else by "+," call it "quus"). What aspect of their functional profile could distinguish them? Perhaps the "plusser" is disposed to correct himself, but that seriously risks begging the question – why suppose that this is disposition to "correct" as opposed to, say, second-guess incorrectly?

This is the classic problem of the normativity of content, a challenge for any naturalistic psychosemantics. Similar responses are available to the CRS theorist as to the informational theorist, accompanied by much the same problems (see the sections, "Proposed fixes for ATT violations," and "Informational teleosemantics," above). Appeal may be made to "ideal conditions" (in an individual or population) of some sort, though it is unclear how this is to be done in a non-question-begging manner. Alternatively, the correct inference could be determined in some way by its incipient cause, although isolating "the" incipient cause would be difficult. (Explanations for our acquisition of inferential habits are typically rather complex, not a matter of simple conditioning.) Perhaps the incorrect inferences are asymmetrically dependent on the correct ones (Mendola 2003). Finally, one might introduce naturalistic teleology (also further dulling the charge of liberalism) (Sober 1985), and face Swampman and disjunction/distality problems.[13]

Success psychosemantics

Mental representation is involved in perception, inference, and action. We have seen psychosemantic theories founded upon the first two (informational and conceptual role theories); what about the last one? We now turn to this action-oriented strategy, which I call, following Peter Godfrey-Smith (1994), "success (psycho)semantics."

Papineau and success as desire satisfaction

The pragmatist view is that beliefs are true when they are *successful* in some sense. Given a naturalistic definition of success, we can get a psychosemantics out of the pragmatist view of truth. One plausible account of success is desire satisfaction; but desires are intentional mental states themselves, and so must have their contents accounted for in turn. David Papineau (1987, 1993) turns to teleology to solve this problem. He claims that a desire's satisfaction condition is the effect it is selected (by evolution or learning) to produce. So, for example, the desire for food was designed (presumably by natural selection) to produce the effect of the animal ingesting food. The function of the desire is to bring about that state of affairs, which is also the desire's satisfaction condition.

Of course, desires can only bring about their satisfaction conditions with the cooperation of beliefs (following a standard belief-desire explanation for action). Beliefs, then, also must have a general function of bringing about desires' satisfaction conditions – the satisfaction conditions of the desires with which they are cooperating. Each belief does this in its own particular way: it has the function of causing actions that will satisfy desires *if a particular condition* obtains. This condition is that belief's truth condition.

When Papineau says that beliefs will lead to desire satisfaction if their truth conditions obtain, he means something quite strong: that desire satisfaction is *guaranteed* if the belief is true. (So a belief's truth condition is "that condition which guarantees that actions generated by that belief will fulfil its biological purpose of satisfying desires" [1993: 80].) This might seem obviously false: if I believe that the sun is 93 million miles away (true), but I also believe that I can jump that far, a desire to jump to the sun will fail to be satisfied (in magnificent fashion!) by my ensuing action. His response to this problem is to go holistic (1993: 72–3): a belief is guaranteed to satisfy desires if it is true *and* if the other beliefs it is acting in concert with are also true. This approach makes the truth conditions of whole sets of potentially related beliefs interdependent, to be determined simultaneously. This helps with the counterexample above, where I have a false belief that I can jump 93 million miles high. But it seems that there are other cases where the fix will fail. Perhaps all my beliefs are true of the situation I'm involved in, but some outside circumstance conspires to interfere with satisfaction of my desires, e.g. a meteorite knocks my ice cream to the ground. The truth of my operative beliefs has failed to guarantee satisfaction of my desires, unless we maintain, implausibly, that I had a belief operating to the effect that no meteorite would knock my ice cream to the ground. (Perhaps I had a belief to the effect that nothing would interfere with the satisfaction of my desire to eat ice cream – but this threatens to trivialize the identification of a belief's truth condition. For instance, we could say that my belief that I can jump 93 million miles high is true, except for the interference of my weakness.)

Millikan and representation consumers

Ruth Millikan (Millikan 1984, 1989, 2004) offers a version of success semantics that forges a weaker link with success than the pragmatists or Papineau. Hers is probably the most ambitious theory in our survey, attempting, as it does, to account for the contents of representations in simple animals all the way to high-level cognitive contents, and linguistic meaning as well. Unlike Papineau, she does not define success in terms of desire satisfaction. Rather, she divides a system up into representation *producers* and representation *consumers*. The notions of "producer" and "consumer" are very broad: they include two honeybees communicating via a dance, a speaker and a listener, two parts of a cognitive system, or a cognitive system and its attached motor system. (We will be focusing on psychosemantic cases like the latter two, of course.) For Millikan, success is defined in terms of the proper performance of the representation consumer's function(s).

For instance, if the representation consumer is the motor system, and one of its functions is to bring food to the mouth, success may be defined as actually performing that function. She also does not require that a representation's truth condition *guarantee* proper performance of the consumer's function. It just needs to be an "historically Normal condition" for the performance of the consumer's function. This means that it forms part of an explanation for how it was that the consumer managed to perform its function in the past, which performance explains why this producer-consumer pairing was selected. For example, the function of eating was accomplished in the past by the belief that I'm holding an ice cream being compresent with the condition of my actually holding an ice cream, and this accomplishment selectionally explains why my belief and the motor system have the interaction that they do. If Papineau were to adapt his account to be similar to Millikan's in this respect, he would say, not that a belief's truth condition guarantees satisfaction of desires (which causes trouble), but that a belief's truth condition is an essential part of an explanation for why that belief was selected for desire satisfaction.

Millikan complicates things further. On Papineau's model, beliefs have the function of aiding in desire satisfaction, and they do so by covarying with a particular state of affairs type. On Millikan's model, representation producers have the function of aiding in consumer function satisfaction, and they do so by producing representations that *map* on to world affairs according to a particular *rule*. The representations that are produced are articulated or complex (see previous chapter, the section, "The degree-of-systematicity axis: from detectors to speakers"), such that aspects of the representation that may vary can be mapped on to ways in which the world can vary. For example, activity in visual areas of the cerebral cortex may vary in intensity and location, where those aspects of the representation map on to variations in contrast and location of discontinuities (lines) in the environment. So it is not compresence with a truth condition that selectionally explains the satisfaction of consumer function, but mapping according to a particular rule. This allows for novel representations, that never before occurred in history, e.g. a novel combination of a line in a particular location at a particular contrast.

Selected mapping rules, according to Millikan, may be extremely broad and general. For instance, her theory can apply to a general-purpose learning system, such as that presented in Ryder (2004). On that theory, the cerebral cortex was selected for structuring itself isomorphically with particular regularities (of a certain type) upon encountering them in the environment, just as a camera's film was selected for structuring itself isomorphically with reflected light patterns that enter the camera's lens. Just as a camera's film can represent many different patterns of light, so the cerebral cortex can represent many regularities (and the items that participate in them).

While Papineau's link between representation and success seems too strong to yield correct truth conditions, it may be that Millikan's is too weak. Pietroski (1992) has objected that her theory violates the ATT desiderata because the selected mapping rule may identify contents that, intuitively, a creature is incapable of conceiving. In his example, the simple kimus evolve a producer-consumer mechanism that causes them to pursue red light, allowing them to avoid their predators (the snorfs) at sunrise and sunset. Intuitively, the kimus know nothing of snorfs (they wouldn't even recognize one), they are just following red light. But the mapping rule that applies to their representations maps on to the presence/absence of snorfs, so their representations (according to Millikan's theory) are about the presence/absence of snorfs. Millikan accepts this consequence with equanimity (Millikan 2000); others claim that the problem does not infect complex belief-desire psychologies (Rountree 1997).

Problems for consumer semantics

Both Papineau's and Millikan's theories are subject to the standard worries about teleosemantics, namely Swampman and disjunction/distality. I commented earlier (the section, "Objections to teleosemantics") on their responses to the Swampman problem. Millikan believes that her particular focus on consumer functions solves the disjunction and distality problems. Turning to the fly/frog example, it must be a Normal condition for the representation consumers to perform their function that the frog's active detector map on to the presence-of-a-fly-now, while the silent detector map on to the absence-of-a-fly-now. However it is not clear how this is supposed to resolve the disjunction (or specificity) problem, for it seems that the fly-now mapping and the nutritious-blob-now mapping are equally good candidates for being Normal conditions for the representation consumer (the frog's motor and digestive system?) performing its function. This is because the representation consumer's function is equally indeterminate – is it supposed to ingest and digest flies, or is it supposed to ingest and digest nutritious blobs? As Fodor puts it, "Millikan's strategy is to solve the disjunction problem for the signals by describing the 'consumers' of the signals in intentional terms (in terms of what they 'care about') and then to beg the disjunction problem for the consumers" (Fodor 1991). Papineau concedes that indeterminacy attends to simple systems like the frog, but believes there is no such indeterminacy in the case of complex belief-desire systems like ours, because of the specificity of desire functions (1998, 2003). However, it isn't clear that he solves the disjunction problem either, because he doesn't consider the possibility of a desire's content being a disjunction of all the various means historically used to satisfy it, rather than the desire's intuitive end.

Further issues

A set of problems that tend to cause trouble for *any* naturalistic psychosemantics is accounting for seemingly abstract concepts, like numbers, causation, logical concepts, democracy, etc. These things are either very difficult to fit into the causal order (e.g. numbers), or, in one case (causation), they *constitute* the causal order. Either way, it is far from obvious how they could participate in informational relations, be selectionally relevant, or participate in long-armed causal roles. It is only slightly more promising to suppose that they could be isomorphic to mental representations, or somehow contribute to success. Here, we hearken back to age-old disputes between rationalism and empiricism, with most naturalized psychosemantics tending towards the empiricist camp. In general, psychosemanticists have focused on solving the "easy problems" of representing everyday physical states of affairs, saving these more difficult cases for later. For some sample attempts, however, see Millikan (1984) and Prinz (2002).

Some philosophers maintain that there is a necessary connection between intentionality and consciousness (Searle 1983). If this is true, and it turns out that consciousness cannot be naturalized, then the prospects of naturalizing representational content would be dim indeed. However, the arguments for this necessary connection are based upon intuitions that naturalists have not found compelling.

This chapter has been organized around the ATT desiderata, but there are other important desiderata for a theory of content. Some we have come across along the way, e.g. that there be a general formula for determining a representation's truth (or satisfaction) conditions, and that content be shareable. However, there is one important desideratum that has not made an explicit appearance, although it is related to the ATT desiderata:

> A theory of content ought to cohere with our everyday content-dependent explanations of behaviour.

We explain behaviour by appeal to what people think, believe, and want, not by what is actually the case extra-mentally. For example, we might explain Fred's behaviour in opening the fridge by saying "he wanted a beer, and he thought there was a beer in the fridge." Actual beer in the fridge need not figure in this explanation at all; rather it is the content of Fred's belief that figures in it. After all, there need not have been any beer in the fridge, perhaps Fred was mistaken. This is why our explanations of behaviour are typically "content-involving" (and why the problem of misrepresentation is so crucial – misrepresentations play an essential role in the explanation of behaviour). It seems that a theory of content which made this sort of explanation unfathomable could not be about our target phenomenon: the content of the propositional attitudes and other truth-evaluable mental states. The problem is made particularly pressing in view of the fact that it is unclear how broad, truth conditional content – which involves states of affairs external to the mind – can causally explain what a mind does (Braun 1991; Yablo 1997).

Almost all of the theories we have examined or mentioned have something to say about how they can accommodate the explanation of behaviour (Fodor 1987; Dretske 1988; Cummins 1989; Block 1990; Millikan 1993). There are also serious problems that attend to the proposed solutions (Stich 1983; Godfrey-Smith 1994; Melnyk 1996). Clearly this issue will be of fundamental importance in evaluating the various psychosemantic proposals, but unfortunately it would require its own chapter for a proper treatment (see Heil and Mele [1993] for a good introduction).

Finally, I should explain why I have not examined interpretivism (e.g. Dennett's "intentional stance" theory; see the section in the previous chapter, "The thin notion"): it is because such theories are not reductive. For the interpretivist, "all there is to really and truly believing that *P* (for any proposition *P*) is being an intentional system for which *P* occurs as a belief in the best (most predictive) interpretation" (Dennett 1987: 29). As Dretske (1986) and Byrne (1998) point out, interpretations involve beliefs with various contents, so there is no analysis here of belief content in terms of something *else*. That said, such theories are quite friendly to naturalism since they maintain a strong supervenience of mental representational content upon the physical, plus they clearly have no problem meeting the ATT desiderata. Thus interpretivism might be an attractive backup option if no reductive account can be made to work. However, I hope the reader has not concluded from this review that it is time to give up on the reductive project.

Notes

1. I shall paper over the distinction between conceptual and non-conceptual truth-evaluable content because it has not played a prominent role in debates about naturalizing content. For a nice discussion of the distinction, see Heck (2007).
2. The latter two are often taken to be non-conceptual, so not involving concepts (see note 1).
3. It is controversial to what extent sensations and emotions, for example, are contentful mental states. Some maintain that the sensation of pain, for instance, represents that there is damage to tissue in a certain location, and so that it is contentful (Tye 1995), while most deny that pain represents anything.
4. The specificity problem is what makes "the causal theory of reference" a nonstarter for our purposes. This "theory," whose recent history traces back to the work of Kripke (Kripke 1972), is really just a programmatic suggestion and does not provide reference-determining conditions (see Devitt 1981; Kim 1977).
5. In Dretske's terminology, this is the information it carries "digitally."
6. Some identify representational content with the information a representation carries "under ideal epistemic circumstances" (or "fidelity conditions" [Stampe 1977] or "relevant normal conditions" [Stalnaker 1984]). This is essentially the same strategy, and suffers from the same problem.
7. See Dretske (1981) and Jacob (1997) for attempts to specify the channel conditions as those which lack relevant alternative possibilities, i.e. whose reliability is such that the *fact* that they are reliable isn't news to the receiver of the information.
8. Fodor suggested something similar in his 1990 book, but later repudiated the idea.
9. For the rest of this section, "function" will mean "teleological function" unless specified otherwise.

10. On Dretske's view, the indicator is selected to cause some movement, via operant conditioning. This is, in effect, a selectional explanation for its presence in the cognitive system, since Dretske agrees with Ramsey (Ramsey 1931) that it isn't a belief unless it "steers."
11. The original idea is due to Boorse (in the form of "swamprabbits") (1976) and made famous by Davidson in his 1987.
12. See Peacocke (1992) for a detailed account, though he stops short of making the move to naturalistic causal roles. Even Fodor takes CRS to be the correct theory for logical concepts (Fodor 1994: Ch. 3).
13. Another source of teleology besides the biological and the cybernetic should be mentioned in this connection: linguistic norms. On Sellars' account (1963), norms have their primary place in a public language using community, and the norms that apply to mental representations are derived from the public ones. See Gillett (1997) for an attempt to naturalize this sort of strategy.

References

Adams, F. (2000) "Asymmetrical Dependence"; available: http://host.uniroma3.it/progetti/kant/field/asd.htm

Allen, C., Bekoff, M., and Lauder, G. (eds) (1998) *Nature's Purposes: Analyses of Function and Design in Biology*, Cambridge, MA: MIT Press.

Ariew, A., Cummins, R., and Perlman, M. (eds) (2002) *Functions: New Essays in the Philosophy of Psychology and Biology*, Oxford: Oxford University Press.

Armstrong, D. M. (1973) *Belief, Truth and Knowledge*, Cambridge: Cambridge University Press.

Barwise, J., and Perry, J. (1983) *Situations and Attitudes*, Cambridge, MA: MIT Press.

Blackburn, S., and Simmons, K. (eds) (1999) *Truth*, Oxford: Oxford University Press.

Block, N. (1990) "Can the Mind Change the World?" in G. Boolos (ed.), *Meaning and Method: Essays in Honor of Hilary Putnam*, Cambridge: Cambridge University Press, pp. 137–70.

—— (1998) "Conceptual Role Semantics," in E. Craig (ed.), *The Routledge Encyclopedia of Philosophy*, London: Routledge; available: http://www.rep.routledge.com/article/W037 (accessed September 14, 2007).

Boorse, C. (1976) "Wright on Functions," *Philosophical Review* 85: 70–86.

Braddon-Mitchell, D., and Jackson, F. (1997) "The Teleological Theory of Content," *Australasian Journal of Philosophy* 75: 474–89.

Braun, D. (1991) "Content, Causation, and Cognitive Science," *Australasian Journal of Philosophy* 69: 375–89.

—— (2000) "Russellianism and Psychological Generalizations," *Nous* 34: 203–36.

Burge, T. (1979) "Individualism and the Mental," *Midwest Studies in Philosophy* 4: 73–122.

Byrne, A. (1998) "Interpretivism," *European Review of Philosophy* 3: 199–223.

Church, A. (1951) "A Formulation of the Logic of Sense and Denotation," in P. Henle, M. Kallen, and S. K. Langer (eds), *Structure, Method, and Meaning: Essays in Honor of Henry M. Scheffer*, New York: Liberal Arts Press, pp. 3–24.

Churchland, P. M. (1996) "Fodor and Lepore: State-Space Semantics and Meaning Holism," in R. McCauley (ed.), *The Churchlands and their Critics*, Cambridge, MA: Blackwell pp. 272–7.

—— (1998) "Conceptual Similarity and Sensory/Neural Diversity: The Fodor/Lepore Challenge Answered," *Journal of Philosophy* 95: 5–32.

Churchland, P. S. (2002) *Brain-Wise: Studies in Neurophilosophy*, Cambridge, MA: MIT Press.

Craik, K. J. (1943) *The Nature of Explanation*, Cambridge: Cambridge University Press.

Cummins, R. (1989) *Meaning and Mental Representation*, Cambridge, MA: MIT Press.

Davidson, D. (1967) "Truth and Meaning," *Synthese* 17: 304–23.

—— (1987) "Knowing One's Own Mind," *Proceedings and Addresses of the APA* 60: 441–58.

Dennett, D. C. (1987) *The Intentional Stance*, Cambridge, MA: MIT Press.

Devitt, M. (1981) *Designation*, New York: Columbia University Press.

Dretske, F. (1981) *Knowledge and the Flow of Information*, Stanford: Center for the Study of Language and Information Publications.

—— (1986) "Misrepresentation," in R. J. Bogdan (ed.), *Belief: Form, Content and Function*, Oxford: Oxford University Press, pp. 17–36.
—— (1988) *Explaining Behavior*, Cambridge, MA: MIT Press.
—— (1995) *Naturalizing the Mind*, Cambridge, MA: MIT Press.
Evans, G. (1982) *The Varieties of Reference*, Oxford: Oxford University Press.
Field, H. (1977) "Logic, Meaning and Conceptual Role," *Journal of Philosophy* 69: 379–408.
—— (1994) "Deflationist Views of Meaning and Content," *Mind* 103: 249–85.
Fodor, J. (1987) *Psychosemantics*, Cambridge, MA: MIT Press.
—— (1990) *A Theory of Content and Other Essays*, Cambridge, MA: MIT Press.
—— (1991) "Reply to Millikan," in B. Loewer and G. Rey (eds), *Meaning in Mind: Fodor and his Critics*, Oxford: Blackwell, pp. 293–6.
—— (1994) *The Elm and the Expert*, Cambridge, MA: MIT Press.
—— (1998) *Concepts: Where Cognitive Science Went Wrong*, Oxford: Oxford University Press.
Fodor, J. A., and Lepore, E. (1991) "Why Meaning Probably Isn't Conceptual Role," *Mind and Language* 6, no. 4: 329–43.
—— (1999) "All at Sea in Semantic Space: Paul Churchland on Meaning Similarity," *Journal of Philosophy* 96: 381–403.
Gillett, G. (1997) "Husserl, Wittgenstein and the Snark: Intentionality and Social Naturalism," *Philosophy and Phenomenological Research* 57, no. 2: 331–49.
Godfrey-Smith, P. (1989) "Misinformation," *Canadian Journal of Philosophy* 19, no. 4; 535–50.
—— (1994) "A Continuum of Semantic Optimism," in S. Stich and T. Warfield (eds), *Mental Representation*, Oxford: Blackwell, pp. 259–77.
Goldstone, R. L., and Rogosky, B. J. (2002) "Using Relations within Conceptual Systems to Translate across Conceptual Systems," *Cognition* 84: 295–320.
Gopnik, A., and Meltzoff, A. (1997) *Words, Thoughts, and Theories*, Cambridge, MA: MIT Press.
Grice, P. (1957) "Meaning," *Philosophical Review* 66: 377–88.
Harman, G. (1982) "Conceptual Role Semantics," *Notre Dame Journal of Formal Logic* 23: 242–56.
—— (1987) "(Nonsolipsistic) Conceptual Role Semantics," in E. Lepore (ed.), *Semantics of Natural Language*, New York: Academic Press, pp. 55–81.
Heck, R. (2007) "Are There Different Kinds of Content?" in J. Cohen and B. McLaughlin (eds), *Contemporary Debates in Philosophy of Mind*, Oxford: Blackwell, 117–38.
Heil, J., and Mele, A. (eds) (1993) *Mental Causation*. Oxford: Oxford University Press.
Horwich, P. (1998) *Meaning*, Oxford: Clarendon Press.
Jackson, F. (1998) *From Metaphysics to Ethics: A Defense of Conceptual Analysis*, Oxford: Oxford University Press.
—— (2006) "The Epistemological Objection to Opaque Teleological Theories of Content," in G. Macdonald and D. Papineau (eds), *Teleosemantics*, Oxford: Oxford University Press, pp. 85–99.
Jacob, P. (1997) *What Minds Can Do*, Cambridge: Cambridge University Press.
Kim, J. (1977) "Perception and Reference without Causality," *Journal of Philosophy* 74: 606–20.
Kripke, S. (1972) *Naming and Necessity*, London: Blackwell.
—— (1982) *Wittgenstein on Rules and Private Language*, Cambridge, MA: Harvard University Press.
Lewis, D. (1970) "General Semantics," *Synthese* 22: 18–67.
—— (1994) "Reduction of Mind," in S. Guttenplan (ed.), *A Companion to the Philosophy of Mind*, Oxford: Blackwell, pp. 412–31.
Loar, B. (1982) "Conceptual Role and Truth-Conditions," *Notre Dame Journal of Formal Logic* 23, no. 3: 272–83.
Lynch, M. (ed.) (2001) *The Nature of Truth*, Cambridge, MA: MIT Press.
Matthen, M. (1988) "Biological Functions and Perceptual Content," *Journal of Philosophy* 85: 5–27.
McGinn, C. (1989) *Mental Content*, Oxford: Blackwell.
McLaughlin, B. (1987) "What Is Wrong with Correlational Psychosemantics," *Synthese* 70: 271–86.
Melnyk, A. (1996) "The Prospects for Dretske's Account of the Explanatory Role of Belief," *Mind and Language* 11, no. 2: 203–15.
Mendola, J. (2003) "A Dilemma for Asymmetric Dependence," *Nous* 37: 232–57.
Millikan, R. (1984) *Language, Thought, and Other Biological Categories*, Cambridge, MA: MIT Press.

—— (1989) "Biosemantics," *Journal of Philosophy* 86, no. 6: 281–97.
—— (1993) "Explanation in Biopsychology," in J. Heil and A. Mele (eds), *Mental Causation*, Oxford: Oxford University Press, pp. 211–32.
—— (1996) "On Swampkinds," *Mind and Language* 11, no. 1: 103–17.
—— (2000) *On Clear and Confused Ideas*, Cambridge: Cambridge University Press.
—— (2004) *Varieties of Meaning: The 2002 Jean Nicod Lectures*, Cambridge, MA: MIT Press.
Neander, K. (1991) "Functions as Selected Effects," *Philosophy of Science* 58: 168–84.
—— (1995) "Malfunctioning and Misrepresenting," *Philosophical Studies*, 79, 109–41.
—— (2004) "Teleological Theories of Mental Content"; available: http://plato.stanford.edu/archives/sum2004/entries/content–teleological/ (accessed summer 2004)
Papineau, D. (1987) *Reality and Representation*, Oxford: Blackwell.
—— (1993) *Philosophical Naturalism*, Oxford: Blackwell.
—— (1998) "Teleosemantics and Indeterminacy," *Australasian Journal of Philosophy* 76, no. 1: 1–14.
—— (2001) "The Status of Teleosemantics, or How to Stop Worrying about Swampman," *Australasian Journal of Philosophy* 79, no. 2: 279–89.
—— (2003) "Is Representation Rife?" *Ratio* 16, no. 2: 107–23.
Peacocke, C. (1992) *A Study of Concepts*, Cambridge, MA: MIT Press.
Pietroski, P. (1992) "Intentionality and Teleological Error," *Pacific Philosophical Quarterly* 73: 267–82.
Prinz, J. (2002) *Furnishing the Mind: Concepts and Their Perceptual Basis*, Cambridge, MA: MIT Press.
Putnam, H. (1975) "The Meaning of 'Meaning'," in K. Gunderson (ed.), *Language, Mind and Knowledge*, Minneapolis: University of Minnesota Press, 131–93.
Quine, W. V. O. (1953) "Two Dogmas of Empiricism," in *From a Logical Point of View*, Cambridge, MA: Harvard University Press, pp. 20–46.
—— (1976) "Carnap and Logical Truth," in *The Ways of Paradox and Other Essays*, Cambridge, Mass.: Harvard University Press, 107–32.
Ramsey, F. P. (1931) *The Foundations of Mathematics and Other Logical Essays*, London: Routledge & Kegan Paul.
Richard, M. (1983) "Direct Reference and Ascriptions of Belief," *Journal of Philosophical Logic* 12: 425–52.
Rosch, E. (1978) "Principles of Categorization" in E. Rosch and B. Lloyd (eds), *Cognition and Categorization*, Hillsdale, NJ: Erlbaum, pp. 27–48.
Rountree, J. (1997) "The Plausibility of Teleological Content Ascriptions: A Reply to Pietroski," *Pacific Philosophical Quarterly* 78, no. 4: 404–20.
Ryder, D. (2004) "SINBAD Neurosemantics: A Theory of Mental Representation," *Mind and Language* 19, no. 2: 211–40.
Salmon, N. (1986) *Frege's Puzzle*, Cambridge, MA: MIT Press.
Schroeder, T. (2004a) "Functions from Regulation," *The Monist*, 87, 115–35.
—— (2004b) "New Norms for Teleosemantics," in H. Clapin, P. Staines, and P. Slezak (eds), *Representation in Mind: New Approaches to Mental Representation*, Amsterdam: Elsevier, pp. 91–106.
Searle, J. (1980) "Minds, Brains, and Programs," *Behavioral and Brain Sciences* 3: 417–24.
—— (1983) *Intentionality: an Essay in the Philosophy of Mind*, Cambridge: Cambridge University Press.
—— (1992) *The Rediscovery of the Mind*, Cambridge, MA: MIT Press.
Sellars, W. (1963) *Science, Perception and Reality*, London: Routledge & Kegan Paul.
Shea, N. (2007) "Consumers Need Information: Supplementing Teleosemantics with an Input Condition," *Philosophy and Phenomenological Research* 75, no. 2: 404–35.
Soames, S. (1989) "Direct Reference, Propositional Attitudes and Semantic Content," *Philosophical Topics*, 15, 44–87.
Sober, E. (1985) "Panglossian Functionalism and the Philosophy of Mind," *Synthese* 64, no. 2: 165–93.
Stalnaker, R. (1984) *Inquiry*, Cambridge, MA: MIT Press.
Stampe, D. (1977) "Toward a Causal Theory of Linguistic Representation," in P. French, T. Uehling, and H. Wettstein (eds), *Contemporary Perspectives in the Philosophy of Language*, Midwest Studies in Philosophy, vol. 2, Morris, MN: University of Minnesota, pp. 42–63.
Sterelny, K. (1990) *The Representational Theory of Mind*, Oxford: Blackwell.
Stich, S. P. (1983) *From Folk Psychology to Cognitive Science*, Cambridge, MA: MIT Press.

Swoyer, C. (1991) "Structural Representation and Surrogative Reasoning," *Synthese* 87: 449–508.
Tye, M. (1995) *Ten Problems of Consciousness: A Representational Theory of the Phenomenal Mind*, Cambridge, MA: MIT Press.
Usher, M. (2001) "A Statistical Referential Theory of Content: Using Information Theory to Account for Misrepresentation," *Mind and Language* 16, no. 3: 311–34.
Wittgenstein, L. (1953) *Philosophical Investigations*, Oxford: Blackwell.
Wright, L. (1973) "Functions," *Philosophical Review*, 82: 139–68.
Yablo, S. (1997) "Wide Causation," *Philosophical Perspectives* 11: 251–81.

17

THE LANGUAGE OF THOUGHT

Susan Schneider

According to the language-of-thought (or LOT) hypothesis, conceptual thinking occurs in an internal language-like representational medium. However, this internal language is not equivalent to one's spoken language(s). Instead, LOT is supposed to be the format in which the mind represents concepts, rather than merely the natural-language words for the concepts themselves. The LOT hypothesis holds that the mind has numerous internal "words" (called "symbols") which combine into mental sentences according to the grammatical principles of the language. Conceptual thinking has a computational nature: thinking is the processing of these strings of mental symbols according to algorithms. The LOT program and the connectionist program are often viewed as competing theories of the format, or representational medium, of thought (see Sharkey and Sharkey, this volume; and Ryder, this volume).

Why believe in LOT? As we shall see, many of the most well received motivations arise from the following crucial and pervasive feature of conceptual thought: thought is essentially combinatorial. Consider the thoughts *the cappuccino in Florence is better than in New Brunswick* and *Surprisingly, Bush thought about Einstein*. You have probably not had any of these thoughts before, but you were able to understand these sentences. The key is that the thoughts are built out of familiar constituents, and combined according to rules. It is the *combinatorial* nature of thought that allows us to understand/produce these sentences on the basis of our antecedent knowledge of the grammar and atomic constituents (e.g., *Einstein*, *Italy*). Clearly, explaining the combinatorial nature of thought should be a central goal of any theory of the cognitive mind. For, as Gary Marcus puts it, "what is the mind such that it can entertain an infinity of thoughts?" (Marcus 2001: 1). LOT purports to be the only explanation for this important feature of thought.

In this overview of the LOT program, I shall begin by laying out its three central claims, as well as stressing the key philosophical issues which the LOT project is supposed to inform. I then discuss the main motivations for believing that there is a LOT. Finally, I close by exploring some "skeletons" in the LOT closet: relatively ignored issues that the success of LOT depends upon.

What is LOT?

The idea that there is a LOT was developed by Jerry Fodor, who defended this hypothesis in an influential book, *The Language of Thought* (1975). As Fodor has emphasized, the LOT hypothesis was inspired by the ideas of Alan Turing, who defined computation in terms of the formal manipulation of uninterpreted symbols according to algorithms (Turing 1950; Fodor 1994). In his "Computing Machinery and Intelligence," Turing had introduced the idea that symbol-processing devices can think, a view which many in cognitive science are sympathetic to, yet which has also been the focus of great controversy (e.g., Searle 1980; Dreyfus 1992). The symbol-processing view of cognition was very much in the air during the time in which the LOT hypothesis was developed. Around the same time that *The Language of Thought* came out, Allen Newell and Herbert Simon suggested that psychological states could be understood in terms of an internal architecture that was like a digital computer (Newell and Simon 1972). Human psychological processes were said to consist of a system of discrete inner states (symbols) which are manipulated by a central processing unit (or CPU). Sensory states served as inputs to the system, providing the "data" for processing according to the rules, and motor operations served as outputs. This view, called "classicism," was the paradigm in the fields of artificial intelligence, computer science, and information-processing psychology until the 1980s, when the competing connectionist view also gained support. LOT, as a species of classicism, grew out of this general trend in information-processing psychology to see the mind as a symbol-processing device.

Now let us turn to a more detailed discussion of the LOT hypothesis. In essence, the LOT position consists in the following claims:

> 1. Cognitive processes consist in causal sequences of tokenings of internal representations in the brain.

This claim has enormous significance, for it provides at least a first approximation of an answer to the age old question, "how can rational thought ultimately be grounded in the brain?" At first pass, rational thought is a matter of the causal sequencing of tokens (i.e., patterns of matter and energy) of representations which are ultimately realized in the brain. Rational thought is thereby describable as a physical process, and further, as we shall see below, both a computational and semantic process as well.

In addition,

> 2. These internal representations have a combinatorial syntax and semantics, and further, the symbol manipulations preserve the semantic properties of the thoughts (Fodor 1975; Fodor and Pylyshyn 1988).

This claim has three components:

> 2a. Combinatorial syntax.

As noted, complex representations in LOT (e.g., #take the cat outside#) are built out of atomic symbols (e.g., #cat#, #outside#), together with the grammar of the LOT.

2b. Combinatorial semantics.

The meaning or content of a sentence in the LOT is a function of the meanings of the atomic symbols, together with their grammar.

2c. Thinking, as a species of symbol manipulation, preserves the semantic properties of the thoughts involved (Fodor 1975; Fodor and Pylyshyn 1988).

To better grasp (2c), consider the mental processing of an instance of *modus ponens*. The internal processing is purely syntactic; nonetheless, it respects semantic constraints. Given true premises, the application of the rule will result in further truths. The rules are *truth preserving*. John Haugeland employs the following motto to capture this phenomenon:

> Formalist motto – "If you take care of the syntax of a representational system, the semantics will take care of itself" (Haugeland 1989: 106).

And lastly,

3. Mental operations on internal representations are causally sensitive to the syntactic structure of the symbol (Fodor and Pylyshyn 1988).

Computational operations operate upon any symbol/symbol string satisfying a certain structural description, transforming it into another symbol/symbol string that satisfies another structural description. For example, consider an operation in which the system recognizes any operation of the form "(*P*&*Q*)" and transforms it into a symbol of the form "(*P*)." Further, the underlying physical structures on to which the symbol structures are mapped are the very properties that cause the system to behave in the way it does (Fodor and Pylyshyn 1988: 99). (It turns out that this feature of classical systems – that the constituents of mental representations are causally efficacious in computations – plays a significant role in the LOT-connectionism debate. For in contrast to symbolic systems, connectionist systems do not operate on mental representations in a manner that is sensitive to their form (for discussion see Fodor and Pylyshyn 1988; Macdonald 1995: Ch. 1; Marcus 2001: Ch. 4; Smolensky 1988, 1995).

(1)–(3) combine in a rather elegant way. For they generate a view which is closely related to the LOT hypothesis, called "the computational theory of mind" (or put simply, CTM). CTM holds the following:

> CTM – Thinking is a computational process involving the manipulation of semantically interpretable strings of symbols which are processed according to algorithms (Newell and Simon 1972; Fodor 1994; Pinker 1999; Rey 1997).

Stephen Pinker captures the gist of the manner in which (1)–(3) give rise to CTM:

> arrangements of matter . . . have both representational and causal properties, that is . . . [they] simultaneously carry information about something and take part in a chain of physical events. Those events make up a computation, because the machinery was crafted so that if the interpretation of the symbols that trigger the machine is a true statement, then the interpretation of the symbols created by the machine is also a true statement. The Computational Theory of Mind is the hypothesis that intelligence is computation in this sense.
> (Pinker 1999: 76)

This statement aptly connects the CTM hypothesis to the aforementioned age old question, "How can rational thought be grounded in the brain?" We've already noted that on the present view, rational thought is a matter of the causal sequencing of symbol tokens which are ultimately realized in the brain (thesis [1]). To this we add: these symbols, which are ultimately just patterns of matter and energy, have both representational (thesis [2b]) and causal properties (thesis [3]). Further, the semantics mirrors the syntax (thesis [2c]). This leaves us with the following picture of the nature of rational thought: thinking is a process of symbol manipulation in which the symbols have an appropriate syntax and semantics (roughly, natural interpretations in which the symbols systematically map to states in the world).

This account of the nature of rational thought has been summoned to solve an important puzzle about intentional phenomena. By "intentional phenomena" what is meant is a thought's "aboutness" or "directedness," that it represents the world as being a certain way. It has long been suspected that thought is somehow categorically distinct from the physical world, being outside the realm that science investigates. For how is it that a thought (e.g., the belief that the cat is outside, the desire to eat pizza), which, as we now know, arises from states of the brain, can be about, or directed at, something in the world? The LOT-CTM framework has been summoned to answer to this question. In essence, the proponent of LOT approaches this question in a "naturalistic" way, trying to ground intentionality in the world which science investigates. Now, we've already noted that symbols have a computational nature. As such, they are clearly part of the domain that science investigates. But the proponent of LOT has a naturalistic story about the aboutness, or intentionality, of symbols as well. Symbols refer to, or pick out, entities in the world, in virtue of their standing in a certain causal or nomic relationship that exists between the symbols and property tokens/individuals in the world. Simply put, the symbols are "locked on to" properties or individuals of a certain sort in virtue of standing in a certain nomic or causal relationship specified by a theory of meaning or mental content (for further discussion see Ryder, this volume). So the intentionality of a thought, e.g., *the espresso is strong*, is a matter of a causal, and ultimately physical, relationship between symbolic computational states and entities in the world (e.g., espresso).

This, then, is the gist of the LOT picture. At least at first blush, the LOT project seems to be a coherent naturalistic picture of the way the cognitive mind might be.

But, importantly, is it true? That is, is the cognitive mind really a symbol-manipulating device? Let us turn to the major reasons that one might have for suspecting that it is.

The key arguments for LOT

The most important rationale for LOT derives from the following observation: any empirically adequate cognitive theory must hold that cognitive operations are sensitive to the constituent structure of complex sentence-like representations (Fodor 1975; Fodor and Pylyshyn 1988). This observation has been regarded as being strong evidence for a LOT architecture. To develop this matter in more detail, there are the following closely related features of cognition that seem to require that any theory of cognition appeal to structure-sensitive representations: productivity, systematicity, and inferential coherence.

The productivity of thought

Consider the sentence, "The nearest star to Alpha Centauri is dying." As noted earlier, despite the fact that you've never heard a novel thought before, you are capable of understanding it. Thought is productive: in principle, you can entertain and produce an infinite number of distinct representations. How can you do this? Our brains have a limited storage capacity, so it cannot be that we possess a mental phrase book in which the meaning of each sentence is encoded. Instead, there must be a system with a combinatorial syntax. This allows for the construction of potentially infinitely many thoughts given a finite stock of primitive expressions (Fodor 1975: 31; Fodor and Pylyshyn 1988: 116; Fodor 1985, 1987).

The systematicity of thought

A representational system is systematic when the ability of the system to entertain/ produce certain representations is intrinsically related to the ability to entertain/ produce other representations (Fodor and Pylyshyn 1988). Conceptual thought seems to be systematic; e.g., one doesn't find normal adult speakers who understand, "Mary loves John" without also being able to produce/understand "John loves Mary." How can this fact be explained? Intuitively, "Mary loves John" is systematically related to "John loves Mary" because they have a common constituent structure. Once one knows how to generate a particular sentence out of primitive expressions, one can also generate many others that have the same primitives (Fodor 1987; Fodor and Pylyshyn 1988; Fodor and McLaughlin 1990).

Inferential coherence

As Fodor and Pylyshyn have observed, we do not encounter normal human minds which are always prepared to infer from *P&Q&R* to *P* but not infer from *P&Q* to

P (1995: 129). Thought is inferentially coherent: given that a system can draw a particular inference that is an instance of a certain logical rule, the system can draw any inferences that are instances of the rule. And again, this has to be due to the fact that mental operations on representations are sensitive to their form (Fodor and Pylyshyn 1988).

In sum, these three features of thought all seem to arise from the fact that mental representations have constituent structure. As noted, they have been regarded as providing significant motivation for LOT. It is currently a source of great controversy whether connectionist systems can explain these important features of thought (see, e.g., Calvo and Colunga 2003; Fodor and Pylyshyn 1988; Fodor and McLaughlin 1990; Elman 1998; van Gelder 1990; Marcus 2001; Smolensky 1988, 1995). Connectionist models are networks of simple parallel computing elements, with each element carrying a numerical activation value which the network computes given the values of neighboring elements, or units, in the network, employing a formula (see infra, Sharkey and Sharkey, this volume). In very broad strokes, critics claim that a holistic pattern of activation doesn't seem to have the needed internal structure to account for these features of thought. Critics have argued that, at best, connectionist systems would provide models of how symbol structures are implemented in the brain, and would not really represent genuine alternatives to the LOT picture (Fodor and Pylyshyn 1988). There is currently a lively debate between this "implementationalist" position and radical connectionism, a position which rejects the view that connectionism, at best, merely implements LOT, advancing connectionism as a genuine alternative to the LOT hypothesis.

In addition to arguments for LOT based on the combinatorial structure of thought, the following two arguments are well-known arguments as well.

Fodor advances the first argument as the central argument of his 1975 book. The rough argument is as follows: (P_1) The only plausible psychological models of decision making, concept learning and perception all treat mental processes as computational. (P_2) Computation presupposes a medium of computation – a representational system in which computations are carried out. (P_3) Remotely plausible theories are better than nothing. (C) Therefore, we must take seriously the view that the mind has a LOT (Fodor 1975: 27). Much of Fodor's defense of the argument is devoted to exploring the basic form of information-processing models of learning, decision-making, and perception (Fodor 1975).

It is important to bear in mind that the argument, which dates back to 1975, preceded the rise in popularity of connectionism. LOT is no longer "the only game in town" (as Fodor used to boast) (Fodor 1975). While the view that contemporary cognitive science is computational is still very well received, nowadays, a computationalist need not be a classicist; she can be a connectionist instead. These issues are subtle: As mentioned, "implementational connectionists" actually believe in LOT, holding that connectionist networks merely implement LOT. It is likely that they would agree with something like the above argument. Radical connectionists, by contrast, would likely object that the conclusion does not follow from the premises;

(P_1) and (P_2) are compatible with connectionism as well. Whether the connectionist response is effective depends upon nuances of the LOT-connectionism debate which we cannot delve into here (for a helpful introduction to these issues see Macdonald and Macdonald [1995]). Suffice it to say that the proponent of LOT, armed with arguments along the lines of (1)–(3), would likely charge that any connectionist model of psychological phenomena that purports to be a genuine alternative to (rather than mere implementation of) LOT will not satisfy the demands of these arguments.

A second challenge to this argument was raised, ironically, by Fodor himself, who, after publishing *The Language of Thought*, has expressed doubts about the plausibility of computational explanation of decision-making, and conceptual thought more generally, and has offered arguments which can be viewed as an attack on P_1 (Fodor 2000). This important issue will be discussed below.

Finally, a fifth argument for LOT is Fodor's well-known argument for nativism (Fodor 1975, 1981). Because Fodor's (1975) emphasized this argument, and because Fodor himself has been associated with extreme concept nativism, extreme concept nativism has become unduly wedded to the LOT program. Indeed, many assume that if there's a LOT, then vocabulary items in the LOT must be innate. But notice that nativism is not entailed by theses (1)–(3); nor is it invoked in any of the aforementioned motivations for LOT.

In very broad strokes, Fodor's nativist argument for LOT is along the following lines. Since concept learning is a form of hypothesis formation and confirmation, it requires a system of mental representations in which the formation and confirmation of hypotheses is to be carried out. But then one must already possess the concepts in one's LOT in which the hypotheses are couched. So we must already have the innate symbolic resources to express the concepts being learned (Fodor 1975: 79–97, 1981).

The above argument, as it stands, is open to the possibility that many lexical concepts are constructed from more basic, unstructured, concepts. These lexical concepts can be learned concepts because they have internal structure, being assembled from more basic, innate concepts. These lexical concepts are thus not innate. So, strictly speaking, the above argument does not entail the extreme concept nativism associated with Fodor's project. However, Fodor famously rejects the view that lexical concepts are structured, arguing in his (1981) that lexical concepts do not have internal structure, as the leading theories of conceptual structure are highly problematic. If Fodor is correct, we are left with a huge stock of lexical primitives (Fodor 1981). And, according to Fodor, primitive concepts are innate. If this is correct, then the above rough argument presents a case for radical concept nativism.

Critics and proponents of LOT uniformly reject radical concept nativism (including Fodor himself in his [1998]). After all, it is hard to see how concepts that our evolutionary ancestors had no need for, such as [carburetor] and [photon], could be innate. Of course, proponents of LOT generally believe that LOT will turn out to have some empirically motivated nativist commitments invoking both certain innate modules and primitive symbols. However, it is important that LOT be able to accommodate any well-grounded empirically based view of the nature of concepts that cognitive science develops, even one in which few or no concepts are innate. Nonetheless,

Fodor's argument and concerns about conceptual structure are intriguing, for they raise some very important questions: What is wrong with the argument? Can primitive (unstructured) concepts be learned? Are many lexical concepts structured?

While I've stressed that LOT shouldn't require the truth of radical concept nativism, it should be mentioned that there is a nativist commitment that seems reasonable to wed to the LOT program. LOT can be regarded as an innate cognitive capacity, because, according to the proponent of LOT, any sophisticated language-like computational system requires an internal language that has primitive vocabulary items obeying rules enabling the language to be systematic, productive, and compositional. But this sort of nativism is distinguishable from concept nativism; for this innate capacity can exist, while the stock of symbols in each person's inner vocabulary may differ. In such a scenario, we each have a cognitive system which satisfies (1)–(3), but some, or even all, of the primitive vocabulary items differ.

Some important qualifications

Needless to say, with such a bold view of the nature of thought, numerous qualifications are in order. First caveat: I have thus far said nothing about the nature of consciousness. Even philosophers who are sympathetic to computational accounts of the mind suspect that computational theories may fall short as explanations of the essential nature of consciousness (Block 1991; Chalmers 1995). LOT does not aspire to be a theory of consciousness or to answer the hard problem of consciousness; instead, it is a theory of the nature of language-like mental processing that underlies higher cognitive function, and more specifically it is designed to account for the aforementioned combinatorial features of thought, issues which are, of course, important in their own right.

Indeed, it is important to bear in mind that the scope of the LOT hypothesis is itself a matter of significant controversy. LOT is not primarily concerned with the nature of mental phenomena such as perceptual pattern recognition, mental imagery, sensation, visual imagination, dreaming, hallucination, and so on. While a LOT theorist may hold views that explain such phenomena by something similar to LOT, it is likely that even if LOT is correct, it does not apply to all the above domains. Indeed, it may turn out that certain connectionist models better explain some of these phenomena (e.g., pattern recognition) while the symbol-processing view offers a superior account of cognition. Such a "hybrid" view is sympathetic to a connectionist picture of sensory processes, while claiming that when it comes to explaining conceptual thought, the symbol-processing account is required (Wermter and Sun 2000). Fodor himself rejects hybrid models, suggesting instead that modular input systems have their own LOT (1983); they do not have a full-blown LOT, but for Fodor, it is a matter of degree.

Second qualification: although the LOT hypothesis holds that the mind is computational, this view should not be conflated with the view that the mind is like a commercially available computer, having a CPU in which nearly every operation is executed. Although symbolicists in the 1970s and '80s seem to have construed classicism in this way, this view is outdated. As Stephen Pinker notes, LOT is implausible when it is aligned with the view that the mind has a CPU in which every operation is executed in a serial fashion (Pinker 2005). Although introspectively our thoughts seem to be sequential, introspection only reveals a portion of the workings of the mind; it is uncontroversial that the brain has multiple non-conscious processes that operate in a massively parallel manner. Classicism and LOT merely require the weaker view that the brain has a "central system." On Fodor's view, the central system is a non-modular subsystem in the brain in which information from the various sense modalities is integrated, deliberation occurs, and behavior is planned (Fodor 1983). Crucially, a central system need not be a CPU; for it is not the case that every operation needs to be executed by a central system, as it does with a CPU. Instead, the central system may only be involved in higher cognitive tasks, e.g., planning, deliberation, categorization, not in mental operations that do not involve consciousness or reasoning.

Indeed, it is well worth getting clear on the nature of the central systems. For, as we shall see below, when we consider some issues requiring further development by the proponent of LOT, *inter alia*, the proponent of LOT seems to owe us a positive account of the nature of the central systems. Let us now turn to these outstanding issues.

Looking ahead: issues in need of future development

Back in 1975 Fodor has noted that characterizing the LOT, "is a good part of what a theory of mind needs to do" (Fodor 1975: 33). Unfortunately, even today, certain key features of the LOT program remain unexplained. Herein, I shall consider two important problems that threaten the success of the LOT program. The first issue concerns the notion of a symbol in LOT. While the notion of a symbol is clearly key to the LOT program, unfortunately, the program lacks a well-conceived notion of the symbolic mental states that are supposed to be the very basis of cognition. Second, as noted, Fodor himself has expressed doubts about the plausibility of computational explanation. More specifically, he suspects that the central systems will defy computational explanation and has offered two arguments in support of this pessimistic view (Fodor 2000). It is rather important whether these two arguments are correct; if Fodor is correct, then we should surely reject the LOT hypothesis. For, as noted, the central system is supposed to be the system in which deliberation and planning occur. So it is reasonable to regard it as the primary domain which LOT characterizes. But LOT is obviously a computational theory, so how can it correctly characterize the central systems if they are not, in fact, computational to begin with? Further, if LOT fails to characterize the central systems, it is difficult to see why we should even believe that it applies to the modules.

Symbols

Let us first consider where LOT stands concerning the nature of mental symbols. To provide a theory of the nature of symbols, one needs to locate features of symbols according to which the symbols should be taxonomized, or classified. For instance, should two symbol tokens be regarded as being of the same type when they have the same semantic content? Or perhaps, instead, symbols should be type-individuated by computational properties, such as computational roles? If so, what properties or roles? For the proponent of LOT the stakes are high: without a plausible theory of primitive symbols, there cannot be a complete understanding of what the LOT hypothesis is supposed to be. After all, without a theory of symbol natures, it remains unclear how patterns of neural activity could be, at some higher level of abstraction, accurately described as being symbol manipulations. For what is it that is being manipulated? Further, without an adequate theory of symbol natures, related philosophical projects that draw from the LOT approach are undermined. First, the aforementioned attempt to naturalize intentionality will be weakened, for such accounts will lack an account of the nature of the internal mental states that are appealed to as the computational basis of intentionality. For according to the proponent of LOT, these mental states are the symbols themselves. Second, as noted, those who are interested in LOT frequently say that meaning is determined by some sort of external relation between symbols and properties or individuals in the world. Unfortunately, since symbols are the internal mental states, or "vehicles" that the meanings lock on to, such theories of mental content will be radically incomplete.

Existing theories of the nature of symbols include individuation by (externalist) semantic content and individuation by the role that the symbol plays in the computational system, where the notion of "computational role" is fleshed out in various ways. Concerning semantic proposals, it has been objected that a semantic manner of typing LOT expressions ruins the prospects for naturalism (Pessin 1995). For the externalist hopes to naturalize intentionality by taking the intentionality of thought to be a matter of a symbol bearing some sort of external relationship (e.g., historical, informational) to a property or thing in the world. But if the intentionality of thought is supposed to reduce to a physical relation between the symbol and the world, the symbol itself cannot be typed semantically. For this is an intentional phenomenon, and in this case, the intentionality of thought couldn't reduce to the physical (Pessin 1995).

Computational-role proposals also seem to be problematic. The "computational role" of a symbol is the role that the symbol plays in computation. As mentioned, there are different ways that computational role can be construed. Proposals can be distinguished by whether they consider all, or merely some, elements of a given symbol's role as being built into the nature of a symbol. A "molecularist" claims that in defining the nature of a symbol, only a certain privileged few computational relations are required for a given symbol to be of a certain type. To consider a tinker toy example, a molecularist view could hold that to have a token of the symbol, [cat], the system in question must have thoughts such as [furry] and [feline], but the system need not have others, e.g., [likes cat treats], [black cats are timid]. The advantage of molecularism is that because only some elements of a symbol's computational role constitute the symbol's nature, many individuals will have common symbols, so groups of individuals can figure in psychological explanations in virtue of the symbols they have. For there will be equivalence classes of systems which, when tokening a given symbol and in common conditions, will behave in similar ways.

Although this would surely be a virtue of the molecularist theory, many would say that molecularism faces insurmountable obstacles. For consider the related molecularist theories of narrow content. In the context of debates over the nature of mental content, molecularist views attempted to identify certain conceptual or inferential roles as being constitutive of narrow content. Such views were criticized because, according to the critics, there is no principled way to distinguish those elements of conceptual or inferential role that are meaning constitutive from those which are not (Fodor and LePore 1992; Segal 1999; Prinz 2002). Unfortunately, similar issues seem to emerge for molecularism about symbol types, although the issues do not concern meaning; instead, the issue concerns whether there can be a select few symbol-constitutive computational relations (Aydede 2000; Schneider n.d.). A natural reaction is to embrace the view that all of the computational relations individuate the symbol. But if a symbolic state is individuated by all the computational relations it participates in, a natural concern is that symbolic states will not be shared from person to person (Aydede 2000; Prinz 2002; Schneider n.d.).

In sum, the nature of symbols is very much an open question.

The computational nature of the central systems

A second major challenge to the LOT approach stems, ironically, from Fodor's aforementioned view that the cognitive mind is likely to *not* be computational. His first argument involves what he calls "global properties," features that a sentence in the LOT have which depend on how the sentence interacts with a larger plan (i.e., set of LOT sentences), rather than merely depending upon the nature of the LOT sentence itself. For example, the addition of a new LOT sentence to an existing plan can complicate (or alternately, simplify) a plan. Since the added simplicity/complexity varies according to the context, that is, according to the nature of the plan the new sentence is added to, simplicity/complexity seems to be a global property of the mental sentence (Fodor 2000). Global properties, according to Fodor, give rise to the following problem for CTM:

> The thought that there will be no wind tomorrow significantly complicates your arrangements if you had intended to sail to Chicago, but not if your plan was to fly, drive or walk there. But, of course, the syntax of the mental representation that expresses the thought #no wind tomorrow# is the same whichever plan you add it to. The long and short is: the complexity of a thought is not intrinsic; it depends on the context. But the syntax of a representation is one of its essential properties and so doesn't change when the representation is transported from one context to another. So how could the simplicity of a thought supervene on its syntax? As please recall, CTM requires it to do.
>
> (2000: 26)

In a bit more detail, Fodor's argument is the following: cognition is sensitive to global properties. But CTM holds that cognition, being computational, is only sensitive to the "syntax" of mental representations. That is to say that cognition is sensitive to the type identity of the primitive symbols, the way the symbols are strung together into well-formed sentences, and the algorithms that the brain computes. And these "syntactic" properties are *context insensitive* properties of a mental representation. That is, what a mental representation's syntactic properties are does not depend on what the other mental representations in a plan are: it depends only on the type identity of the LOT sentence. But whether a given mental representation has the global properties that it has will typically depend upon the *context* of the other representations in a plan (that is, it depends upon the nature of the other LOT sentences in the relevant group, as in Fodor's example involving it being windy). So it seems that cognition then cannot be wholly explained in terms of computations defined over syntactic properties (Fodor 2000; Ludwig and Schneider 2008; Schneider 2007).

The second problem concerns what has been called, "The Relevance Problem." According to Fodor, this is the problem of whether and how humans determine what is relevant in a computational manner. Fodor suspects that if one wanted to get a machine to determine what is relevant, the machine would need to walk through virtually every item in its database, to see whether a given item is relevant or not. This is a huge computational task, and it could not be accomplished quickly enough for a system to act in real time. However, humans make quick decisions about relevance all the time. Hence, it looks like human domain general thought (i.e., the processing of the central systems) is not computational (Fodor 2000).

Elsewhere, Kirk Ludwig and I have argued that the problem that Fodor believes global properties pose for CTM is a non-problem (Ludwig and Schneider 2008; Schneider 2007). And concerning the relevance problem, elsewhere I've argued that while the relevance problem is a serious research issue, it does not justify the overly pessimistic view that cognitive science, and CTM in particular, will likely fail to explain cognition (Schneider 2007). Although we do not have time to consider all of these issues, I will quickly raise one problem with each of Fodor's two concerns. Both problems rely on a common example. Before entertaining this example, let us try to answer an important question: suppose that both problems can exist in the context of uncontroversially computational processes. What would this fact show? The following answer seems plausible: It would mean that the presence of a globality or relevance problem does *not* entail that the system in question is non-computational.

Now, bearing this in mind, notice that each of Fodor's arguments maintains that, as a result of the given problem, the central systems are non-computational. However, I shall now proceed to show that both problems exist in uncontroversially computational systems. We are now ready to consider our example. Consider a chess-playing program. Suppose that a human opponent makes the first move of the game, moving a certain pawn one square forward. Now, the program needs to decide, given the information of what the previous move was, which future move to execute. Even in an uncontroversially computational system like this one, we can quickly see that Fodor's globality problem emerges. Let us suppose that there are two game strategies/plans in the program's database and the program needs to select one plan, given information about what the first move is. Let one plan involve taking the bishop out early in the game, while the other plan involves taking the rook out early in the game (where "early" means, say, within four turns). Now, it is important to notice that the impact that the addition of the information about what the opponent's first move was on the simplicity of each of the two plans does not supervene on the type identity of the string of symbols that encodes the information about the opponent's first move. Instead, the impact of the addition of the string of symbols on the simplicity of each plan depends on the way that the string interacts with the other sentences in the plan. Thus (our new globality argument continues), the processing of the chess program is not syntactic, and thus, not computational. Hence, it appears that a globality problem emerges in the context of highly domain-specific computing (Schneider 2007).

Using this same simple example, we can also quickly see that a relevance problem emerges. Notice that skillful chess playing involves being able to select a move based on the projected outcome of the move as far into the future of the game as possible. So chess programmers deal with a massive combinatorial explosion all the time, and in order to quickly determine the best move, clever heuristics must be employed. This is precisely the issue of locating algorithms that best allow for the quick selection of a future move from the greatest possible projection of potential future configurations of the board (Marsland and Schaeffer 1990). And this is just the relevance problem as it has been articulated by Fodor and other philosophers (Schneider 2007). The upshot: both problems emerge at the level of relatively simple, modular, and uncontroversially computational processes. But if both problems can occur in the context of uncontroversially computational processes, the presence of a globality or relevance problem does not entail the conclusion that the relevant system is non-computational. And this is the conclusion that was needed to undermine the possibility that the central systems are computational.

Perhaps Fodor could say that the relevance problem, as it presents itself to the central systems, is somehow different. And moreover, it is different in a way that suggests that relevance determination in the central systems is non-computational. An obvious point of difference is that unlike modular processing, central processing is supposed to be domain general. However, this point of difference doesn't seem to warrant the extreme view that the processes in question would be non-computational. For one thing, there are already programs that carry out domain-general searches over immense databases. For consider your own routine Google searches. In about 200 milliseconds you can receive an answer to a search query involving two apparently unrelated words that involved searching a database of over a billion Web pages (Schneider 2007). Second, Fodor's relevance problem concerned how the brain could sift through massive amounts of data given the constraints of real time, and domain generality entails nothing about the size of a database that a relevance search draws from. A database that records the mass of every mass-bearing particle in the universe would be topic specific, yet still be of a much greater size than a human's memory (Schneider 2007).

Now, in contrast to the globality problem, which I suspect is merely a non-problem (Ludwig and Schneider 2008), the relevance program does present a challenge to programmers. The challenge for programmers is to find judicious algorithms which maximize the amount of information subject to the constraints of real time. However, if my above argument concerning relevance is correct, it is implausible to claim that a relevance problem entails that the system in question is non-computational. Yet it is natural to ask whether there are better ways of formulating the problem that relevance presents for CTM. Elsewhere, I discuss and rule out different formulations (Schneider 2007). But for now, let me suggest that a very different way to proceed with respect to the relevance problem is to assume that the presence of a human relevance problem is not terribly different from relevance problems existing for other *computational* systems. But, in the human case, the "solution" is a matter of empirical investigation of the underlying brain mechanisms involving human searches. This alternative approach assumes that evolution has provided *Homo sapiens* with algorithms that enable quick determination of what is relevant, and further, it is the job of cognitive science to discover the algorithms. On this view, Fodor's injunction that research in cognitive science rest at the modules must be resisted (Fodor 2000; Schneider 2007). Proponents of LOT should instead seek to provide detail concerning the nature of the central systems, in order to understand the nature of symbolic processing, including, especially, what the algorithms are that symbolic systems compute. An additional bonus of this more optimistic approach is that locating a computational account of the central systems could help solve the problem of symbol individuation, for once algorithms that the central systems compute are well understood, it is possible that they can be summoned to individuate symbols by their computational roles in the central systems.

Conclusion

Well, where does all this leave us? I still have not answered the question I posed earlier, "Is LOT true?" But doing so would be premature: for cognitive science is now only in its infancy. As cognitive science develops, we will learn more and more about the various representational formats in the brain, sharpening our sense of whether LOT is a realistic theory and how the different representational formats of the brain interrelate. And, in the course of our investigations, it is likely that new and intriguing issues will come to the fore. In addition, we've canvassed a number of existing controversies still awaiting resolution. *Inter alia*, we've noted that many individuals are drawn to the symbol-processing program because it provides insight into the mind's combinatorial nature. But, as discussed, LOT is no longer the "only game in town," and it still remains to be seen whether connectionist models will be capable of explaining the combinatorial nature of cognition in a way that supports a genuine alternative to LOT. We've also discussed two other pressing issues which currently require resolution: first, the LOT/symbol-processing view requires a plausible account of the nature of symbols; and second, as discussed, there are the well-known worries about the limits of computational explanation of the cognitive mind which were posed by Fodor himself.

It is also worth mentioning that our discussion of presently known issues requiring more development is not intended to be exhaustive. Also of key import, for instance, are issues involving the modularity of mind and the nature of mental content (these issues are canvassed in the present volume, Chapters 17 and 18). For instance, any proponent of LOT would be interested in Peter Carruthers' recent book on modularity, which has recently developed the LOT approach within a modularist view of the central systems (Carruthers 2006). And intriguingly, Jesse Prinz has recently challenged the very idea that the mind is modular (Prinz 2006). And, as mentioned, the proponent of LOT will need a plausible theory of mental content in order to provide a complete account of the nature of intentionality. Yet the debate over mental content rages on. In sum, thirty years after the publication of Fodor's seminal book, *The Language of Thought*, there are still many areas to investigate. So in lieu of a firm answer to our question, we can at least acknowledge the following: the LOT program, while no longer the only game in town, is an important and intriguing proposal concerning the nature of conceptual thought.

Acknowledgements

Thanks very much to Mark Bickhard, Paco Calvo and John Symons for helpful comments and suggestions on an earlier draft of this essay.

References

Aydede, Murat (2000) "On the Type/Token Relation of Mental Representations," *Facta Philosophica* 7 (March): 23–49.

Block, Ned (1991) "Troubles with Functionalism," in David M. Rosenthal (ed.), *The Nature of Mind*, Oxford: Oxford University Press, chapter 23, pp. 211–28.

Calvo, Paco, and Colunga, Eliana (2003) "The Statistical Brain: Reply to Marcus' *The Algebraic Mind*," *Proceedings of the American Twenty-Fifth Annual Conference of the Cognitive Science Society*, London: Routledge, pp. 210–15.

Carruthers, Peter (2006) *The Architecture of the Mind*, Oxford: Oxford University Press.

Chalmers, David (1995) "Facing Up to the Hard Problem of Consciousness," *Journal of Consciousness Studies* 2, no. 3: 200–19.

Dreyfus, Hubert (1992) *What Computers Can't Do: A Critique of Artificial Reason*, New York: Harper.

Elman, Jeffrey (1998) "Generalization, Simple Recurrent Networks, and the Emergence of Structure," in M. A. Gernsbacher and S. Derry (eds), *Proceedings of the 20th Annual Conference of the Cognitive Science Society*, Mahwah, NJ: Erlbaum.

Fodor, Jerry A. (1981) "The Present Status of the Innateness Controversy," in J. A. Fodor (ed.), *Representations: Philosophical Essays on the Foundations of Cognitive Science*, Brighton, UK: Harvester Press, pp. 257–316.

—— (1983) *The Modularity of Mind*, Cambridge, MA: MIT Press.

—— (1985) "Fodor's Guide to Mental Representation: The Intelligent Auntie's Vade-Mecum," *Mind* 94: 76–100; also in J.A. Fodor (1990).

—— (1987) *Psychosemantics: The Problem of Meaning in the Philosophy of Mind*, Cambridge, MA: MIT Press.

—— (1990) *A Theory of Content and Other Essays*, Cambridge, MA: MIT Press.

—— (1994) *The Elm and the Expert*, Cambridge, MA: MIT Press.

—— (1998) *Concepts: Where Cognitive Science Went Wrong*, Oxford: Oxford University Press.

—— (2000) *The Mind Doesn't Work That Way*, Cambridge, MA: MIT Press.

Fodor, Jerry A., and LePore, E. (1992) *Holism: A Shopper's Guide*, Oxford: Blackwell Publishing.

Fodor, Jerry A., and McLaughlin, B. (1990) "Connectionism and the Problem of Systematicity: Why Smolensky's Solution Doesn't Work," *Cognition* 35: 183–204.

Fodor, Jerry A., and Pylyshyn, Zenon W. (1988) "Connectionism and Cognitive Architecture: A Critical Analysis," in S. Pinker and J. Mehler (eds), *Connections and Symbols* (*Cognition* special issue), Cambridge, MA: MIT Press; also in Macdonald and Macdonald (1995).

Haugeland, J. (1989) *Artificial Intelligence: The Very Idea*, Boston: MIT Press.

Ludwig, Kirk, and Schneider, Susan (2008) "Fodor's Challenge to the Classical Computational Theory of Mind," *Mind and Language*, 23: 123–43.

Macdonald, Cynthia, and Macdonald, Graham (1995) *Connectionism: Debates on Psychological Explanation*, vol. 2, Oxford, Basil Blackwell.

Marcus, Gary (2001) *The Algebraic Mind*, Boston, MIT Press.

Marsland, T. Anthony, and Schaeffer, Jonathan (ed.) (1990) *Computers, Chess, and Cognition*, New York: Springer-Verlag.

Newell, Allen (1980) "Physical Symbol Systems," *Cognitive Science* 4: 135–83.

Newell, A., and Simon, H. A. (1972) *Human Problem Solving*, Englewood Cliffs, NJ: Prentice-Hall.

Pessin, A. (1995) "Mentalese Syntax: Between a Rock and Two Hard Places," *Philosophical Studies* 78: 33–53.

Pinker, S. (1999) *How the Mind Works*, New York: W. W. Norton.

—— (2005) "So How *Does* the Mind Work?" (Review and reply to Jerry Fodor [2000]), *Mind and Language* 20: 1–24.

Prinz, J. (2002) *Furnishing the Mind: Concepts and Their Perceptual Basis*, Cambridge, MA: MIT Press.

—— 2006. "Is the Mind Really Modular?" In Bob Stainton (ed.), *Contemporary Debates in Cognitive Science*, New York: Blackwell.

Pylyshyn, Z. (1986) *Computation and Cognition*, London: MIT Press.

Rey, Georges (1997) *Contemporary Philosophy of Mind*, New York: Blackwell.

Schneider, S. (2005) "Direct Reference, Psychological Explanation, and Frege Cases," *Mind and Language* 20, no. 4: 423–47.

—— (2007) "Yes, It Does: A Diatribe on Jerry Fodor's *The Mind Doesn't Work That Way*," *Psyche* 13, no. 1: 1–15.

—— (n.d.) "The Nature of Primitive Symbols in the Language of Thought: A Theory," unpublished manuscript.

Searle, John R. (1980) "Minds, Brains, and Programs," *Behavioral and Brain Sciences* 3, no. 3: 417–24.

Segal, Gabriel (1999) *A Slim Book on Narrow Content*, Cambridge, MA: MIT Press.

Smolensky, Paul (1988) "On the Proper Treatment of Connectionism," *Behavioral and Brain Sciences*, 11: 1–23.

—— (1995) "Reply: Constituent Structure and Explanation in an Integrated Connectionist/Symbolic Cognitive Architecture," In Macdonald and Macdonald (1995).

Turing, A. M. (1950) "Computing Machinery and Intelligence," *Mind* 59: 433–60.

van Gelder, Tim (1990) "Why Distributed Representation Is Inherently Non-Symbolic," in G. Dorffner (ed.), *Konnektionismus in Artificial Intelligence und Kognitionsforschung*, Berlin: Springer-Verlag, pp. 58–66.

Wermter, Stephan, and Sun, Ron (2000) "An Overview of Hybrid Neural Systems," in Stephan Wermter and Ron Sun (eds), *Hybrid Neural Systems*, Heidelberg: Springer, pp. 1–13.

18
MODULARITY

Verena Gottschling

The modularity of the human mind is a hotly debated issue in philosophy of psychology and cognitive science. It's a debate about the cognitive architecture of the mind. Recently, it was argued that the mind is not structured the way it's assumed to be in (classical) cognitive science, but rather consists of several modules. This is often called the massive modularity hypothesis (MMH) and referred to as the modern modularity debate. MMH is a specific claim about the functional decomposition of the human mind: the idea that the human mind is a massive modular, instead of a general-purpose, device. It contains a huge number of modules, which interact and together give us an explanation not only of peripheral cognition, but also of central cognitive capacities. The account is often colorfully labeled as "the Swiss Army knife account" – instead of one general-purpose device the human mind contains a large number of tools, which are designed to be useful for very specific tasks – like screw-drivers, knives, and rasps. The modules at issue are thereby not simply small groups of neurons, but rather complex processing structures; we find them not only at very low levels of analysis, but also at higher levels of processing and complexity. For example, modular systems are claimed to deal with cheater detection, language, mindreading, or finding a mate. Thus, the hypothesis of massive modularity contains three elements: plurality of the modular components, their compositionality, and their centrality in explanations of higher cognitive capacities (see Samuels 2006). In other words, there are many such modules, together explaining cognition, and especially higher order cognitive capacities, and they are not limited to lower levels of analysis.

The spectrum of modularist positions

The literature contains a whole spectrum of modularist positions. At one extreme we find the claim that the mind contains no modules at all (Prinz 2006; Woodward and Cowie 2004). It is argued not only that the arguments for the existence of modules are flawed but also that there cannot exist any modules. Another view, proposed by Fodor (1983, 2000), argues for minimal modularity, called *peripheral-systems modularity*. This view refers to the traditional debate many philosophers associate with modularity. This view holds that there are modules, but they are limited to input and output systems for cognition. Such modular systems include the sensory systems like audition, vision, face recognition, and also various motor-control systems. According to this view, the mind's central processes are "informationally unencapsulated," meaning that they can in principle draw on information from almost any source (see the frame problem, Fodor 1983, 2000). Thus, *central* cognition, the area for belief/desire psychology, concept deployment, inferences and decision-making, is *non*-modular.

At the other extreme we find the hypothesis of *massive modularity*. This hypothesis is the focus of the contemporary debate and is often proposed and defended by evolutionary psychologists (for example Tooby and Cosmides 1992; Pinker 1997; Sperber 1996, 2002, 2005). According to this view, the mind consists *entirely*, or at least *almost entirely*, of modular systems. The processes that generate beliefs, desires and decisions, are all (or almost all) modular in nature. On this view, the traditional Cognitive Science assumption of general learning mechanisms is false. There exists probably no such thing as "general learning."

In between these more radical views there are a variety of positions, which posit peripheral input and output modules as well as *some central* or *conceptual modules*. Nonetheless, what these views share is the claim that the mind contains both modular and non-modular systems or processes. Depending on which systems and processes are assumed to be modular or non-modular, these views can differ substantially (Carey 1985; Carey and Spelke 1994; Carruthers 1998; Cosmides and Tooby 2001; Hauser and Carey 1998; Spelke 1994). Recently, Carruthers introduced the term "moderate modularity" for these views. This is a bit confusing, since the peripheral view is also labeled as moderate modularity in the literature.

What is a module?

The classical characterization of modules goes back to Fodor (1983). Fodor introduced the term by using several criteria: information encapsulation, missing access from other processes, mandatoriness, fast output, "shallow" output, characteristic breakdown, neural localization, domain specificity, and innateness. Modules are assumed to be domain-specific processing systems which are innately specified. They also have their own transducers on the input side, and they deliver a "shallow" (roughly a non-conceptual) output. Also, the subject cannot voluntarily influence whether the modules work or not. Relatedly, the information processes in modules are isolated from the rest of cognition (encapsulated), and inaccessible to the rest of cognition. Further, once triggered, the operations of a module cannot be influenced: modules are assumed to be mandatory in their operation. Modules are also assumed to be swift in their processing, which together with mandatoriness and encapsulation, goes well with evolutionary explanations, because acting fast, and not losing time with unnecessary mental processes, can increase the chances for survival in several situations (see Fodor 1983). Moreover, modules are assumed to be associated with particular neural structures. Together with the criterion of encapsulation, this implies a further characteristic: modules are liable to characteristic patterns of breakdown. But not only the breakdown of modules is characteristic; their development is as well. In modules we find a sequence of growth that is both paced and distinctively arranged.

Besides this classical understanding, there is an intuitive understanding of modules as dissociable components that is based on the everyday meaning of "module." Consider the classical example, a tape deck. It is a dissociable component of a hi-fi system with its own specific function. It also can be damaged without affecting the whole hi-fi system. The intuitive interpretation predicts that if the human mind contains several modules people can have one module damaged while much of the remainder of cognition is still intact. In artificial intelligence (AI) and/or engineering, this understanding of software modules as function blocks is also common. Every block that is a dissociable functional component or a specific function qualifies as a "module."

It is important to be aware that neither the Fodorian way nor the intuitive or AI way is how modules are characterized in the recent debate. According to the intuitive interpretation, almost every dissociable element in cognition with its own function qualifies as a module. This notion is clearly too broad. Every system that is the result of a functional decomposition would qualify as a module. Since it is uncontroversial in cognitive science that we need to break up complex systems like the mind *somehow* into subsystems, nobody would oppose this view. As a result, massive modularity would not be an interesting claim about cognitive architecture anymore.

The initial Fodorean characterization, however, was designed to apply to input and output systems; in other words, at best it turns out to be suitable for peripheral modules. Since the recent debate is mainly one about whether central cognition is modular (and if it is, in which sense), the recent debate uses a more restricted set of characteristics or understands the characteristics less strictly. For example, advocates of central modularity (like Carruthers, Carston, Pinker, Sperber, any many others) can no longer believe that central modules are completely isolated from the rest of cognition. Modules in central cognition must be both capable of taking conceptual inputs (capable of operating upon beliefs and desires for example), and able to generate conceptual outputs (like beliefs or desires). So, not all modules always deliver shallow outputs. But it can still be maintained that central modules are encapsulated to a certain degree, largely inaccessible to the remainder of cognition. Perhaps they are even largely unalterable by other cognitive processes. And it can still be held that modules are innately channeled and that they are processing systems which follow distinctive patterns of growth in development. It can also still be assumed that modules operate based on their own distinctive processing algorithms, and that modules are fast and mandatory as well as liable to specific patterns of breakdown. To summarize, in the recent debate about MMH, modules are either characterized by a bundle of characteristics, while domain specificity, innateness and encapsulation play an important role; or domain specificity is seen as a necessary condition for something to be a module. Which other elements in the Fodorean bundle are involved in central modularity is controversial. It is also disputed whether some elements should be excluded from the list or understood in a broader way. For example, there is hot debate about whether central cognitive modules have only their own proprietary transducers, and their own exclusive information processes or not. But even if one focuses on the three main characteristics and leaves additional criteria aside, one runs into problems, for all three criteria are used in ambiguous ways as well. Thus the unclear term "module" is going to be explained by using terms that don't range behind "module" in their ambiguity.

Innateness

Let us begin with innateness. One of the central ideas behind modularity is that modules are innate. But it is unclear what "innateness" means and what it means to claim that modules are innate. It has even been argued that innateness is a confused concept that confounds, under one term, several meanings and that therefore we should in general avoid talking about innateness (see Griffiths 1997: 104). Griffiths claims that being innate can refer to at least four independent properties:

1 The trait is found in an individual because of their ancestry rather than the current environment.
2 The trait's growth or development does not depend on the environment.
3 The trait is present at birth or at least very early in development.
4 The trait is part of the nature of the species.

Whether the situation is that desperate is not clear either. Griffiths is right that different readings of innateness are to be found and not distinguished accordingly. But that does not necessarily imply that it is impossible to clarify what we mean in using the term, at least in the context of modularity. The core idea is that in the case of innate capacities, we are biologically prepared to develop these abilities. In the literature, there are two promising accounts which specify this core idea. First, according to the primitiveness account (Samuels 2002; Cowie 1998), innate knowledge is psychologically *primitive*, i.e. it is not acquired by any psychological process, by any process of perception or inference. Rather, it has to be considered primitive from the psychological point of view – something that we assume that the learner is equipped with before the process of learning starts. Clearly, the burden of this account is carried by the "not." We are confronted with the problem of specifying what exactly is there before the process of learning starts.[1] The second is the canalization account introduced by Andre Ariew (1996, 1999). A trait is assumed to be canalized to the extent that its development is causally insensitive to environmental and genetic variation. For example, the development of toes or wings is highly canalized, since it is relatively insensitive to the relevant influences. Development of human hair color is less so, since it is causally affected by exposure to sunlight. We can think of a trait as innate to the extent that it is developmentally canalized.

Innateness is also the element in the Fodorean bundle that related the MMH debate to the nativism/empiricism debate. The traditional disagreement between nativists and empiricists regards the existence, richness and complexity of the pre-specified contents, structures and processes of the mind. Their disagreement is not about the question whether the human mind or even some capacity itself is innate or not. Rather, it's a debate about different kinds of learning methods, different ways of acquiring a capacity. Empiricists commit themselves to the idea of "general-purpose learning methods" we use to acquire a capacity. These empiricist "learning methods" include acquisition by induction, abduction, deduction, perception, statistical inference, conditioning, etc. Empiricists tend to favor faculties or principles of inference not specifically designed for the acquisition and performance of *one* particular task but for a whole bundle of tasks, i.e. they favor a different architecture, one that is both less detailed and less task specific.

Nativists, in contrast, assume that the capacity in question was acquired differently and tend to reject pure general-purpose learning methods: what is necessary for learning is the aid of an innate, domain-specific cognitive endowment. Again, two issues play a role: being innate and being domain specific. Both characteristics are familiar from the modularity debate.

Thus the empiricism/nativism debate is clearly related to the modern debate about massive modularity. But nativism comes in various versions. One can be a nativist regarding one capacity but not regarding another, and what is contained in the proposed innate endowment – knowledge, concepts, mechanisms – might vary as well. Thus massive modularity is nativism of a special flavor.

So acquisition and innateness are not really opposed. Even some modularists argue that learning and innateness are not really opposed. Carruthers (2004) claims that it is not the learning methods themselves that are innate, but only that the postulated modular systems are systems *of* learning. The language system is modular, because it is "designed *for* learning the syntax and vocabulary of the surrounding environment" (Carruthers 2004: 297), and because these learning algorithms are assumed to be unique to this system. But they would even be modular if it turns out that the same algorithms are used in other modules. According to this view, the innate endowment seems to be restricted to the *underlying design plan* of the cognitive systems that interact to *produce the disposition to learn* language. An innate module for language does *not* mean (i) language is there from the beginning, nor (ii) its development is independent from the environment. It also does *not* mean that (iii) the disposition to learn language is innate. The claim is less strong, that language is innate only means that the design plan to develop a system that produces this disposition to learn a language is innate. Thus, it is not the learning method that is innate, but the underlying structure (the design plan) to develop a learning method designated to language.[2] But this learning method might be used in the development of different capacities; it might not be exclusively a language learning method.

Domain specificity

Domain specificity is either an important feature in a bundle of characteristics, or domain specificity is seen as a necessary condition for something to be a module. Further, domain specificity is often regarded as the essence of modularity. Thus, obviously, it deserves careful consideration. But on a closer look, it turns out to be hard to characterize this feature in more detail and specify its underlying intuitive understanding.

Obviously, domain specificity and innateness are related: To say that a capacity is innate entails that it is domain specific in one reading. We have seen that innate capacities are capacities we are prepared for biologically, capacities that are relatively independent of environmental change. But it does not work the other way around: domain specificity does not entail innateness.

Unfortunately, the agreement ends there. It is controversial how large domains are and what constitutes a domain. And it is controversial as well about what being specific entails.

One problem is the ambiguity of "domain." In psychology, a domain is often simply a domain of facts of a certain kind, or a certain class of contents. And modularists believe, indeed, that each of these early emerging competencies is underpinned by a distinct cognitive module. Thus, according to some views, mindreading, for example, qualifies as domain specific just because it deals with a class of contents, for example the mental states of conspecifics (Carruthers 2004: 260). On this reading, if a cognitive subsystem concerns a domain, this means that it deals with a class of certain contents, or has a subject matter. Unfortunately, on this broadest reading, just about anything qualifies as a domain because a subject matter might be anything. The subject matter might be a class of related behaviors, a skill, or a class of some objects in the world. In fact, it can be any coherent category.

In contrast, others define domain specificity in evolutionary terms; a domain is an adaptation to a specific environmental problem, a capacity, which has been selected in evolution to fulfill a specific function, to solve a specific evolutionary problem. But it is also a capacity that deals with a specific restricted set of inputs, hints from behavior, facial expressions, character traits.

"Specific" also has different readings. First, "specificity" has a broad reading: it could mean no more than that we talk about the resources underlying our ability, i.e. the resources used to process the relevant information. In other words, every mental resource underlying that ability would qualify, and domain specificity would not require exclusivity. Presumably, the mental resources underlying one ability will overlap with resources used in others. The problem is that the broad reading does not give us an interesting claim about modularity anymore – almost everything would qualify as domain specific.

One central question here is whether "specific" has to be interpreted as implying exclusiveness. If exclusiveness is required (see Prinz 2006; Gottschling, in prep.), the claim of massive modularity is stronger. But at the same time, it is less plausible because the empirical evidence for these kinds of modules seems limited to relatively low-level modules. Higher level capacities would not be modular anymore, because they mostly – though not exclusively – process information dedicated to their domains. Vision, taken as a coherent whole, would not be domain specific in the strong sense. Some subsystems in vision, like edge detectors, may be domain specific, but other resources used for processing visual information seem to be more general. For example, the visual system can be recruited in problem solving, as when one uses mental visual imagery. The activity in cells can be bimodal. Even low-level vision would not be domain specific in this strong sense, because visual subsystems are also used in mental visual imagery. How we decide this issue has important consequences: if the combination of non-overlapping modules for central cognitive capacities must be an indispensable part of MMH to be an interesting and new hypothesis about cognitive architecture, MMH seems a very strong, but implausible claim. However, if exclusiveness is not required, modules can overlap or share both processes and brain areas with other modules (see Carruthers 2004: 296). But then, one of the central constraints for modularity turns out to be banal. Thus, if this is the criterion to distinguish modules from non-modules, lots of structures end up as modular. In other words, on some interpretations, both "domain" and "specificity" turn out as trivial properties. As a result, the claim that the mind is massively modular is not a very strong one. On other interpretations, domain specificity requires more. But if we think about large-scale domains – paradigm cases of what is treated as a module – such as language, vision or folk psychology, we run into a problem. The problem arises because the modularity debate is a debate about complex processing structures we find at higher levels of analysis (not just small groups of neurons). Thus we need to include large-scale domains. If we use domain specificity in a stronger reading, we are looking for systems that are exclusively dedicated to broad domains. But there is little evidence for such large-scale modules. In fact, the larger the domain, the harder it seems to find exclusive processing. Still, large-scale domains are essential for MMH, we need large-scale modules to play an essential role in the performance of central cognitive tasks. However, for large-scale domains, exclusiveness is not fulfilled.

As a result, MMH is an interesting but less convincing claim. It should not surprise that most opponents to massive modularity use the stricter interpretations, whereas many proponents of the view have a broader understanding in mind.

A promising move could be to define domains in terms of adaptive problems, thereby including evolutionary considerations.[3] Adaptive problems are the phenomena in respect to which modules are domain specific. In the literature, these are often described as the problems humans were confronted with during the Pleistocene epoch (between two million and ten thousand years ago). These include finding a mate, communication via language, social exchange, and prediction and explanation of the behavior of others. So we talk in fact about very large-scale domains. Unfortunately, this raises another problem. A definition in terms of evolutionary challenges faces a related problem called the grain problem (Sterelny and Griffiths 1999). Attempts to identify a module would require a fixed level of description at which the selection pressures in play are specified. But the process of fixing that level is in principle arbitrary in evolutionary descriptions. Why shouldn't we describe the evolutionary challenge as visually perceiving depth or discriminating between low and high contrast in the visual field? If the level of description that fixes the decision of whether an architectural feature is domain general or domain specific is arbitrary, there might be no robust distinction between domain generality and domain specificity. As a result, the debate of domain-general versus domain-specific cognition is in danger of being vacuous. As Atkinson and Wheeler pointed out, the full grain problem is even more severe and has two dimensions: the first is the difficulty of matching psychological capacities to adaptive problems or selection pressures, because the latter are hierarchical and nested. The second is the difficulty of matching adaptive problem and selection pressures with psychological capacities, because these capacities are hierarchical and nested as well (Atkinson and Wheeler 2003: 69f., 2004: 162).

If domain is characterized in terms of evolutionary challenges, the connection between innateness and domain specificity turns out to be more complex as well. Suppose that we accept the evolutionary strategy and assume, in consonance with a very broad MMH approach, that only the resources to develop systems, which solve these challenges, are innate. Thus the domains are seen as the large-scale domains described above. What reasons do we have to assume that these resources are specific to these domains? Again, if specificity entails no shared recourses, the claim is clearly in need of additional arguments. However, if specificity is only understood as referring to the underlying structures, the claim is trivial again.

It has been argued that there are ways to define domains in terms of sets of adaptive problems by using a multilevel approach – as long as large-scale domains are included. Thus, we postulate domains at many levels, small-scale modules as well as large-scale modules. The core idea is to combine two aspects. First, it can be shown that at different levels of description we can develop component theories. At each of these levels, we find modular components. Second, the modular components in these theories can be shown to be consistent, and the components at the different levels stand in the right relation to components at other (higher or lower) levels of description (see Atkinson and Wheeler [2003, 2004] for a more detailed discussion). An obvious danger that needs to be avoided is the danger of treating large-scale domains differently than small-scale domains. If there are different criteria for modularity at different levels of description, we would introduce different meanings of "module." But even if this can be avoided, such an account would link MMH to evolutionary psychology, a concession not everybody would be willing to make.

There is another ambiguity. Within the modularity debate, it is not always clear whether we are talking about the underlying mechanisms as domain specific, or the information which is relevant to the task in question. In principle, we have four systematical options:

Mechanisms/ Information	**Domain general**	**Domain specific**
Domain general	Classical cognitive science: domain-general mechanisms and domain-general information	Domain-general mechanisms and domain-specific information
Domain specific	Domain-specific mechanisms and domain-general information (computational modules)	Domain-specific mechanisms and domain-specific information (representational computational modules)

The classical approach in cognitive science (CCS) has been seen as a combination of general-purpose or domain-specific mechanisms and domain-general information. Evolutionary psychologists and modularists often discuss domain generality and domain specificity in general and do not distinguish whether they are talking about domain-specific mechanisms or information. Moreover, they sometimes seem to assume that both go hand in hand. But in fact they don't necessarily. Moreover, if they are not kept apart accordingly, this often results in an entangling of different arguments and issues. Samuels (1998, 2000) pointed out this important difference. Regarding innate domain-specific aspects, he distinguishes a pure innate database (Chomskian or representational modules) from pure innate mechanisms (Darwinian or computational modules, CM), and combinations of both, i.e. a domain specific database plus mechanisms (called computational representational modules, CRM). Because MMH is a claim about cognitive architecture, it *could* in principle be developed to be a claim about either pure mechanisms or about computational representational modules. What is excluded is to interpret it as a claim about representational modules (Samuels 2000, see also Atkinson and Wheeler 2004: 152). Traditionally, MMH was interpreted as a CRM claim. But since there are other ways to make sense of the claim, one can find renewed interest in CMs in recent publications.

Encapsulatedness

The third feature of modularity is its being encapsulated. Essential properties of modules seem to be that they do not let much information in (encapsulation in a stricter reading) and they do not let much information out (inaccessibility). Several authors regard encapsulation as the very core of any useful notion of modularity (Carruthers 2003; Currie and Sterelny 2000; Fodor 2000). For example, for Scholl and Leslie (1999) encapsulation is the essence of modularity:

> The essence of architectural modularity is a set of restrictions on information flow. The boundaries of modules in this sense are [...] informational filters: Either some of the information inside the module is not accessible outside the module, or some of the information outside the module is not accessible inside the module.
>
> (Scholl and Leslie 1999: 133)

More precisely, inaccessibility means that systems outside a module have no access to the internal operations and data within that module. Pure encapsulation works in the other direction, but also with the isolation of modules: modules have no access to the internal operations and data within other informational systems.[4] Encapsulation requires that operations within the module can't be affected by the information held elsewhere in the mind. As a result, if a system's internal operations can't be affected by *any of* the information held elsewhere in the mind, we have a completely encapsulated system. Another reading would be that in an encapsulated system the internal operations of the system can't be affected by *most* of the information held elsewhere in the mind.

Further, a module has its own limited database that gets consulted *only* by the computational processes within the encapsulated system. In contrast, inaccessibility works in the other direction; the operations elsewhere in the mind can't be affected by the information held within a modular system. So encapsulation and inaccessibility are actually linked to the debate of domain-specific information.

If we consider modules in central cognition, the question arises immediately, whether anything can remain of the isolation of modules. Obviously, encapsulation cannot mean full encapsulation with regard to central cognitive capacities. But, as we have seen, encapsulation might come in degrees. The extreme interpretation turns out to be implausible with regard to central cognitive capacities and massive modularity.

One might understand encapsulation in the broad sense as information processing whose internal operations can't be affected by *everything* outside the modular system. But this criterion would obviously be inadequate and too weak. All information processing in the brain turns out to be encapsulated in this sense for it can't use *all* the information to be found in the mind – at least not at the same time. There is a danger of triviality in this reading.

At the other end of the spectrum, one might interpret encapsulation as requiring that modular information processing systems in the brain can't in principle use *any* of the information to be found elsewhere in the mind. Encapsulation in this sense would be information processing whose internal operations can't be affected by *anything* outside the modular system. This is obviously too strong. Only very low-level systems at the periphery of cognition would qualify, for example edge detection in low-level vision (and perhaps not even these). And as we have seen, a sufficient degree of complexity is necessary for something to count as modular in an interesting sense.

The only remaining option here is to postulate that in central modules we find partial encapsulation. It's tempting to specify it as having access only to those beliefs and other informational states that involve their own proprietary concepts. But this turns out to be insufficient. These beliefs themselves would not be encapsulated and there might not be restriction to their connections. Thus it is not clear whether such a move simply shifts the problem.

Something similar holds for inaccessibility. To get a more precise criterion that is compatible with the intuitive understanding of modularity, we might require the following: There is no conscious access possible to the internal processing of modules.

Introspectively, this criterion seems convincing. We cannot consciously access low-level information processes in the visual system (edge detection), for example. Unfortunately, "no conscious access" is not identical with "no access." Inaccessibility cannot simply mean no conscious accessibility. After all, several processes are not consciously accessible, but are highly connected with other processes. Consider visual mental imagery, for example. An interpretation of inaccessibility in terms of conscious inaccessibility seems to dismiss the main underlying intuitive idea of the isolation of modules, even if understood as partial isolation.

In other words, both encapsulation and inaccessibility come in degrees. Both elements of the isolation of modules do not give us sharp criteria for distinguishing modules from other processing systems. However, limited accessibility and encapsulation are artificial terms that need to be characterized more precisely. But at present, such a characterization is missing.[5]

Modularity: arguments in favor, objections, and problems

The arguments in favor of MMH can be understood as belonging to two groups. First, some arguments are presented for massive modularity. Second, proponents of modularity argue that one specific capacity is modular and that this capacity is clearly a part of central cognition. In these arguments, an existence claim is made. This then points to moderate modularity. If this could be shown for several central cognitive capacities, the case for massive modularity is strengthened.

Arguments for massive modularity

Evolutionary biology arguments

Evolutionary arguments are frequently presented in the modularity debate. The general idea is that we should expect systems to be hierarchically constructed. They contain dissociable elements. And this hierarchical construction is done in such a way that the functionality of the whole system is buffered, to some extent at least, from damage to some of its parts. Further, it is argued that under specific evolutionary pressure it is adaptively useful for a system to be able to find a quick and reliable solution to deal with the problem. This will confer a fitness advantage on those systems which possess the ability to solve this specific problem. The solution to the problem is therefore most likely a domain-specific system in the organism, designed to solve the evolutionary problem. In other words, distinct functions predict distinct mechanisms that fulfill these functions. Tooby and Cosmides (1992: 104) present an example of this style of reasoning in terms of domain-general information: The more general the information available for a subject, the less useful this information will be for solving a specific problem. Therefore, genuinely domain-general information is adaptively worthless. One problem with this argument is simply that it presupposes that domain-general versus domain-specific information is either given or not. But in fact, domain specificity comes in degrees.[6] Another problem is that in its presented form, the argument deals with *information*. We need to transfer it to domain-specific *processes*. But then, the same problem arises.

Another but related line of evolutionary arguments concerns the learning mechanisms used for different tasks. These arguments are also called optimality arguments. Many problems with which systems are confronted pose serious computational challenges. These challenges differ from case to case. For this reason, it is argued, we should assume the existence of a distinct learning mechanism for each of these distinct problems. The reason is that distinct problems require different optimal solutions and, thus, different learning mechanisms. According to this picture the mind contains a whole host of specialized learning systems. Note that this does not commit us to the claim that the mind is composed exclusively of such distinct modular systems. This also does not imply that each of these processing systems employs a unique processing algorithm. Massive modularists can be open to the possibility that the same or similar algorithms (different tokens) may be optimal solutions for different given problems. Therefore, they might be replicated many times over in the human mind/brain.

There are several problems with this argument. One problem is that one might question the underlying principle that evolution does necessarily come up with optimal solutions (Stich 1990; Sober 1993; Kitcher 1985; regarding psychological traits, Fodor 1996). What we find might rather be suboptimal solutions, which nonetheless solve the problem in a sufficiently efficient way. Without this presupposition, the conclusion that we can expect specialized learning systems does not follow. If the solutions for different problems are not necessarily optimal, they are not necessarily different.

Another problem with this view is obviously that modularists are committed to modular mechanisms. But the arguments presented seem to give only reasons for an innate, domain-specific endowment of some kind. We might accept that different tasks require different systems. But the second step from different systems to different mechanisms is much more problematic. Even if we accept the first step, it seems a genuine possibility that it is not the mechanisms, but rather the information, that is domain specific. So far, the innate cognitive endowment as a whole might be a mixture of domain-specific and domain-general recourses. And the domain-specific recourses would be restricted to information instead of mechanisms. As Samuels (1998) put it, instead of a large number of specialized learning systems, there might be just *one* single general-learning/general-inference mechanism, which operates on several distinct bodies of innate information. In other words, the argument does not rule out the option that we might deal with pure representational modules. Samuels called this "informational modularity," and contrasted it with computational modularity. In other words, he raises the possibility of postulating subsystems, denies any modular processing, and assumes parallel processing. These arguments do not clearly indicate massive modularity.

A solution for the frame problem

Related to evolutionary arguments, i.e. arguments that domain-specific recourses are better suited to deal with evolutionary challenges, is an argument often mentioned, called the "solvability argument." It is claimed that domain-general strategies alone *must* fail. Thus, a genuine general-purpose problem solver without the assistance of domain-specific mechanisms is improbable and cannot evolve. The reason is not only that a suite of special-purpose modules would always be more effective than a general-purpose problem-solving system. Rather, a general-purpose problem solver would even be inefficient; it has, by definition, access to all kinds of information within the system. This results in the well-known frame-problem. As Fodor put it in his classical formulation (Fodor 1983: 112ff.), the frame problem is "the problem of putting a 'frame' around the set of beliefs that may need to be revised in the light of specified newly available information." Domain-specific encapsulated modules seem to solve the frame-problem. There is no need to decide which mental states play a role in a given situation and revise just these states, simply because domain-specific mechanisms are restricted in their domains and encapsulated anyway. Therefore, an optimally designed set of domain-specific mechanisms processes information faster and more reliably. In contrast, a pure domain-general problem solving system runs into the frame problem. Moreover, a general-purpose problem solver can only solve one problem at a time. It cannot solve several problems in parallel, which is an additional evolutionary disadvantage. As Tooby and Cosmides (1994: 90) put it, "It is in principle impossible for a human psychology to contain nothing but domain-general mechanisms to have evolved, because such a system cannot consistently behave adaptively."

This argument is confronted with a similar problem to the former ones. Domain specificity and encapsulation come in degrees. Even if the argument were successful, it would only show that a *pure* general-purpose problem solving system with access to *all* information fails. In other words, this seems to attack a straw man. It is relatively uncontroversial that there is some specialization, and some splitting up of subsystems within the mind and brain. But to establish massive modularity, modularists have to show more than that. If massive modularity is a new view about cognitive architecture that differs from the traditional cognitive science view, modularists need to show that *only* modular systems can solve some challenges. Moreover, "modular" needs to mean more than simply "not purely domain general." In contrast, moderate modularists only need to establish a more moderate claim. Moderate modularists need to show which modules are necessary for which central cognitive tasks.

Samuels (2000) points out that the argument runs into another problem, even if we understand the argument as one about mechanisms. Domain specificity can be stated in terms of information as well as in terms of mechanisms. Samuels (1998, 2000) argues that Cosmides and Tooby conflate two different notions of "domain-general computational mechanism." They don't differentiate between domain specificity regarding problem solving in general and domain-specific knowledge versus mechanisms. Again we are confronted with an overlooked possibility that we mentioned earlier. If we assume innate domain-specific information, but domain-general processes, we can resist the conclusion of the argument.

The tractability argument

Another related and well-known argument for massive modularity is the argument from computational tractability (Fodor 1983, 2000).[7] This argument, if successful, aims to show that the mind is (at least mainly) composed of encapsulated processing systems. Therefore, it would support the stronger forms of massive modularity. The argument starts with the relatively uncontroversial claim in cognitive science that the mind is computational in character. So, cognitive processes must be realized computationally. But if that is given, they can be carried out within finite time (at least in principle). In other words, these computations must be tractable in every implementation. This tractability requires that the processes will have to be "frugal" in two respects: (i) the algorithms used in these computations are suitable regarding their complexity; and (ii) the computations use in their normal operations only a limited amount of information. But if these processes are tractable, it seems the computations can only consult a limited amount of information relevant for the computations, and must ignore all other information held in the system. Otherwise, we cannot guarantee that they can be carried out within a finite amount of time. As Carruthers puts it: to be tractable, "computations need to be encapsulated; for only encapsulated processes can be appropriately frugal in the informational and computational resources that they require" (Carruthers 2006: 18). In Fodor's (2000) terms, computationally tractable processes only use a limited amount of information, information that is relevant in a given situation; they are, in a sense at least, local processes. So this constraint can be formulated in terms of locality. Obviously, if these processes would consult all (or even a significant amount) of the total information available, this would result in a combinatorial explosion. Thus tractability requires encapsulated computational processes. Since it holds for all these computations that they must be tractable in every implementation, the mind itself must be realized in a large set of many modules, encapsulated computational processes.

The tractability argument differs from the argument mentioned before. It neither claims that the degree in which the processes are frugal is an optimal solution, nor assumes that access to information held elsewhere in the system is all-or-nothing.

There are difficulties with the tractability argument. Samuels (2005) discusses it in detail. He argues that tractability does not require encapsulation in any sense. Rather, what it requires is frugality. We need a way to restrict the information used to restrict our search. But encapsulation is only one way to achieve this goal. Heuristics are another option, one that is familiar from computer science and AI.

In discussing this response, Carruthers (2006) introduced another way of specifying the sense in which sense modules are encapsulated. He distinguished "narrow-scope encapsulation" and "wide-scope encapsulation." Narrow-scope encapsulation is the traditional notion of encapsulation: it requires only that *most* of the information held in the mind can't affect the processes in the modular system. In contrast, wide scope encapsulation of a system means that the system "*can't* be affected by *most* of the information held in the mind in the course of its processing" (Carruthers 2006: 16). According to Carruthers, this is the way in which modular systems are encapsulated.

What he has in mind is the requirement that the system's algorithms are set up in a way such that *during the task* in question only a limited amount of information is consulted. Samuels is right, Carruthers argues: encapsulation understood in the traditional way is only one way to achieve frugality. According to Carruthers, frugal search heuristics combined with stopping rules, like the ones some evolutionary psychologists assume, is another way. In effect, Carruthers tries to incorporate heuristics as another form of encapsulation, which he calls wide-scope encapsulation.

The usefulness of this distinction has been questioned. Samuels (2006) argues that wide scope encapsulation gives us no interesting notion of encapsulation. He complains that this notion simply denies exhaustive search (Samuels 2006: 45). Similarly, Prinz concedes that wide-scope encapsulation is plausible, but complains that it doesn't give us a useful notion for explaining in which sense systems are encapsulated; it allows that encapsulated systems are accessible – they just aren't accessed all at once (Prinz 2006: 33). Again, we fail to find a characterization of encapsulation that might be relevant for modules. Moreover, the conclusion drawn in the argument seems too hasty.

Arguments for modular capacities

There is a second class of arguments for modularity. Arguments in this class are mostly empirical in character. The idea behind them is to give evidence that a capacity, which clearly belongs to the cognitive capacities, is modular in structure. The moderate cognitive modularist is only committed to showing that some important capacities are modular to establish that the mind is modular (see above). The capacities mentioned frequently are language, mindreading, reasoning, and moral judgments. The arguments to be found differ in strength. Moreover, they often only argue for one feature in the modularity characteristics bundle. Obviously, the idea is that they together support that the whole capacity in question is modular.

Universality arguments

The innateness claim entails that some mechanisms which acquire a specific capacity and/or some concepts involved are innate and thus universal in the sense of being pan-cultural. If we put it in evolutionary terms, we could say that evolution has predisposed everyone to come up with the same capacity; hence, we will find this capacity in all cultures and times, and all normally functioning people have this module. This argument is also an argument for modular capacities, not for massive modularity as such.

If we actually find universality, this hints at innate endowment. But universality is only evidence (not proof) for innate endowment. Universality of the phenomenon in question could also be the result of constant conditions in the environment. There is a second problem. Universality of the phenomenon does not allow us to infer a special kind of innate endowment, innate mechanisms. Therefore, even if universality could be taken to argue for innate endowment, universality alone is insufficient evidence in favor of modularity of a specific capacity.

One might expect that the argument works in the other direction as an argument against modularity: if we find no universality, the chances for modularity of the relevant elements might be minimized. But on a closer look, modularists are not committed to universality of the phenomenon in question. Some moderate modularity views allow for differences among adults. Gopnik (1996) introduced the analogy of Neurath's boat to describe a version of "theory-theory" accounts of mentalizing, for which these kinds of differences do not present any difficulties. According to Gopnik, we can understand the theory of mind module as a general frame we start with, but during the journey (the course of development) the ship is rebuilt continually. As a result, the adult may end up with a completely different theory of mind than the one the child had. Nonetheless, according to this view, it is legitimate to dub this capacity modular, because at any point of the development there is only a limited set of possible alternatives. Thus, cultural diversity in adults is compatible with a modular view regarding learning mechanisms. It is also compatible with Carruthers' moderate modularity, the idea that only the underlying structure, the design plan, to develop a learning method designated to this capacity, is innate.

But other – stronger – interpretations of modularity refer to the fully developed capacity in question. For these readings, we seem to run into an explanatory problem. Sometimes modularity of a capacity is meant to mean that a system contains exclusively modular subcomponents, which are linked in a specific way. To say that the capacity in question is modular means not that it is itself modular, or that the learning mechanisms which determine its development are modular. Rather, it means that only modules are contained in it. We do not know much about the "links" between these modules, other than that they allow flexibility to some degree. If we don't find universality of the capacity, this would show that there is a lot of flexibility in the way the relevant capacity might develop. Again, this is no conclusive argument against this reading of modularity of the capacity in question, for the very point of massive modularity is that even very flexible capacities can be explained by using many interacting modules. Some or all elements that the capacity contains might be modular. But it shows something else. Advocates of this view need to explain these "links," the interface between the modules they postulate. They need to specify the exact interface between all the components they posit, otherwise the explanatory value of such an account would turn out to be empty. If we have empirical evidence for flexibility of one kind in a particular capacity, we need to understand exactly *how* the combination of *these* involved modules, linked in *this specific way*, allow for the flexibility we find.

Developmental arguments: poverty arguments, fixed-schedule arguments

Poverty (POV) arguments are a class of arguments that can be used to argue for the modularity of a specific capacity or property. The general consideration of this class of arguments is that a significant group of subjects have a specific psychological property and this property is to be found within a specific time window. There are two possibilities how this property might be acquired: either (1) via general-purpose learning mechanisms; or (2) with the aid of an innate domain-specific cognitive endowment. If it can be shown that the stimuli are too poor for the subjects to acquire this property (only) by general-purpose learning methods – thus by using the classical empiricists kit bag (induction, abduction, deduction, perception, statistical inference, conditioning etc.) – it follows that the subjects do not acquire this property (only) by using the empiricists kit bag but acquire it with the aid of some domain-specific cognitive endowment.[8]

POV arguments were introduced by Chomsky with regard to language acquisition: the classical evidence for innate language modules and POV arguments consists of errors, alternative rule-sets, theory complexity, and empirical evidence for fixed schedule. Language acquisition works on different levels; finding word boundaries differs from universal grammar, and even different semantic/pragmatic inferences differ. So what we find is in fact POV arguments for these aspects of language, not for language as such. In the meantime, language and universal grammar are not assumed to be innate rule systems but only certain parameters or biases that govern the acquisition. Transferred to other properties or capacities, the general idea would be that there are some parameters that govern the development of the capacity in question. But what these parameters are might differ in different capacities. In other words, the acquisition of the capacity in question is somehow innately channeled.

The problem with POV arguments is an already familiar one. POV arguments concern the extent of an *innate domain-specific* cognitive endowment that is necessary for learning. But the MMH is not only about innateness, but more specifically about domain specificity and encapsulation *of mechanisms*. Therefore, POV arguments do not support the modularity of mindreading, or the three-component MMH, but support nativism in general, for MMH proponents are committed to computational modules or representational computational modules. As an argument for modularity POV arguments alone do not suffice. The situation is even worse. Even if we assume that POV arguments could give us evidence for innate mechanisms, they don't give us reasons to assume that these mechanisms are not limited to very low-level mechanisms. But innate low-level mechanisms are not sufficient support for MMH.

Other classes of arguments are also special cases of developmental arguments. Fixed-schedule arguments do not deal with the impoverished information in the environment, but argue that the schedule of the development is fixed. Sub-capacities develop in a fixed hierarchical order. Therefore, this hierarchy of sub-capacities must be innately channeled. Consider language acquisition. Children normally master skills like language acquisition or mindreading within a certain developmental time frame. Moreover, these abilities develop in different steps. Language acquisition is mastered at different ages in different cultures and there are also huge individual differences to be found. Nonetheless the pattern itself remains remarkably constant. All that must be shown for the fixed-schedule argument to work is that there be fixed patterns in the development of this ability. This is certainly the case in language acquisition and mindreading. Both are rather complex abilities that involve hierarchical structured components. For example, shared attention is an important element or precondition in mindreading. To share attention, I have to be able to attend to faces. In language acquisition, children need to be able to master one-word-sentences before they are able to master more complex sentences. The argument though states that the ability in question develops in specific hierarchical steps and on a fixed schedule. It starts with lower level abilities in infants and ends with a full-blown ability. Thus, the development of this ability is highly canalized, and therefore innate. Moreover, it is domain specific. And the domain in question is a large-scale domain. Thus, it is modular or at least composed of modular components.

The fixed-schedule argument differs from the universality argument. Universality deals with the full-blown capacity whereas fixed-schedule arguments deal with the individual development of the capacity. Therefore, fixed schedule would give an explanation for universality. But the fixed-schedule argument is independent of the universality argument. Even if we find cultural differences, the capacity might develop on a fixed schedule. And modularity of the capacity would give us an explanation for this fixed schedule.

Nonetheless, there are problems looming. Abilities like mindreading or language are acquired in childhood, and of course cultural influences, social experience and language training play an important role. It is tempting to assume most complex skills are acquired through social experience and language training. For example, individual differences in belief attribution are highly correlated with language skills and exposure to social interaction (Garfield et al. 2001). It is highly controversial whether mindreading guides language or the reverse. But for our purposes here it is enough to see that the *separation* of both for empirical research turns out to be very difficult. Mindreading exploits a number of structures that are also used for other capacities. This seems enough to cast doubt on the modularity and encapsulation of these capacities.

It is also clear that fixed schedule alone does not establish modularity, for it does not show that these substructures depend on domain-specific, innate and encapsulated mechanisms. All it shows is a hierarchy in the involved sub-capacities. Thus, the problems are similar to those POV arguments face. An innate endowment of some kind is not sufficient for modular mechanisms. And a hierarchical organization into dissociable components is compatible with all kinds of accounts, modular as well as non-modular accounts.

Modularists may allow for cultural influences and individual differences in the development of abilities. As we have seen, cultural influences, to which one is exposed from birth, are not, in principle, a problem for the modularity of mindreading or language acquisition. If only the development of learning mechanisms is claimed to be modular, cultural influences and individual differences propose no problem for modularists. What seems more problematic for modularists is that candidates for modular capacities (language and mindreading, for example) might develop in relation to each other and depend on each other in their development as well as in their processing. If this turns out to be true, encapsulation and inaccessibility might not be maintained to an interesting degree. This would probably be a serious concession for modularists to make. Further, if modularity requires domain specific non-overlapping modules and exclusiveness of the relevant processes, both are obviously problematic if we find a strong relation between the full-blown capacities. Maybe the hierarchically lower components in developments are rather precursor abilities which play a role as preconditions for the ability to develop, but are not actually components of this capacity. Consider mindreading again. Maybe imitation, joint attention, and social referencing are not components of theory of mind but rather precursors to theory of mind. Modularists must exclude such an alternative interpretation in order for the fixed-schedule argument to work, for if it is sufficient for modularity that the capacity has only modular precursors, modularity of capacities would be a trivial claim.

Arguments from double dissociation

Another class of arguments is arguments from double dissociation. For example, García (2007) recently argues that most connotations and features discussed regarding modularity turn out to be irrelevant, and that only cognitive dissociations can be considered as strong indicators of modular structures. If we find conclusive evidence that the capacity in question can be delayed or impaired without any other capacity being impaired this would show domain specificity and encapsulation of the capacity, and thus would be good evidence for its modular structure. If we can also find cases where all the other capacities are impaired and only the capacity in question is intact, this is further evidence for its domain specificity and encapsulation. Double dissociation, further, would give evidence for the stronger modular readings, because shared processes and overlapping modules are avoided.

Let us consider mindreading again. Autism is a disorder that is diagnosed basically with behavioral criteria and associated with lack of pretend play, language delay, and stereotyping. Approximately 75 percent of autistic children are also mentally retarded. Often, a triad of impairments is mentioned (Leslie 2000), which includes social incompetence, poor communicative skills (both verbal and nonverbal), as well as a lack of pretend play. The remaining 25 percent of autistic children are not mentally retarded. But, compared with other children, these children still show the mentioned triad of impairments. Therefore, it has been argued, the triad cannot be the result of general mental retardation, although it is central to the syndrome of autism. Rather, it is assumed that the triad reflects a more specific impairment, an impairment of the theory of mind mechanism (Leslie 1991; Leslie and Roth 1993; Leslie 1987). There is also very good evidence that autism is a biological disorder; it is generally seen as genetic in origin (Gillberg and Coleman 1992). After all, "theory of mind" abilities underlie the mentioned triad of social incompetence, poor communicative skills, and the lack of pretending, thus this triad might be the result of an impaired mindreading mechanism (Leslie 2000) while the remainder of cognition is intact. In addition, autistic children fail the false-belief task. Success at this task is often seen as the criterion establishing mindreading. This seems further evidence for an impaired mindreading module.

I think the last conclusion is too hasty. First, whereas success at the false-belief task clearly demonstrates mindreading abilities, failure in the task is no evidence of a total lack of mindreading abilities. For mindreading is a complex ability. It develops in stages from infancy; it is not an all-or-nothing affair. People with autism lack the ability to a greater or lesser degree and for different reasons (Frith 1989; Happé 1994). If mindreading is a complex and hierarchically structured ability, different sorts of damage might result in impairment to different aspects of mindreading. And that we find *some* behavioral impairment is not surprising, given that autism is attributed on behavioral grounds, including the mentioned triad. But in some cases of autism, there is evidence that higher level mindreading is selectively impaired independently of other practical reasoning and problem solving functions. Contrariwise, mindreading can be selectively spared despite significant degradation of other higher order cognitive functions involved in practical reasoning and problem solving (as evidenced perhaps in Williams Syndrome). This double dissociation is a good hint for encapsulation and domain specificity of the large-scale domain. But again, we find a strong connection to language. Moreover, how one explains our ability to mindread turns out to be important. Some authors link mindreading to imagination (Goldman 1989, 2006; Gordon 1986), and thus see it as part of our general executive working memory capacity. We have the ability to imagine situations which do not actually occur. These mindreading accounts would also predict that mindreading would be impaired in cases of autism, but general problem-solving and practical reasoning would not necessarily be affected too. In other words, findings like these are open to multiple interpretations, and it turns out to be hard to specify conditions under which only one interpretation is possible. Moreover, we run into the same problems developmental arguments face. These remarks are not intended to count against the possibility of a mindreading module. They merely demonstrate that how convincing the evidence appears is crucially dependent on (i) the explanatory theory of the capacity in question being taken for granted; (ii) what we require a nativist of some sort to show (whether she needs to rule out all other options); and (iii) the interpretation of the modularist position we focus on. Again, stronger modularist interpretations are less plausible than the weaker ones, since they require encapsulation and exclusive processing.

Objections to MMH

MMH has been criticized vehemently by those who are skeptical of evolutionary accounts. But it also receives a lot of critical fire from authors who are broadly sympathetic to evolutionary psychology projects. An important problem pointed out frequently is the imprecise and undifferentiated use of many central terms including "domain," "evolutionary problem," "innateness," and "module." We have already seen some of these problems. Another important problem is that the arguments in favor of modularity often argue only for modularity according to one understanding. Evidence for modularity in one sense is then used as evidence for modularity in other, typically stronger, senses. Researchers also switch between notions of modules frequently, and then use "module" in a sense that is not supported by the argument presented. Therefore, MMH is hard to assess.

Another frequently mentioned problem is the flexibility problem. It can be summarized as follows. Human behavior is highly flexible in most cases, especially when it comes to central cognitive capacities. I can think about almost anything and include in my thinking all kinds of information and concepts. For example, while I am considering arguments against modularity, I include thoughts about the film I am going to see tonight. Per definition, modular information processing is not flexible. Therefore, human flexible capacities cannot be realized by modules. Moreover, we find correlations between different tasks; our performance in one central cognitive task gives us a reliable basis for predictions about performance in a wide range of other cognitive tasks. For example, spatial reasoning, mental visual imagery, and perception performance co-vary. This seems incompatible with the existence of different modules. Moreover, there are cases where we find deficits in the performance of these highly correlated tasks and where there is good evidence for something like general mental retardation. How is that possible, if the mind consists (at least mostly) of innate, domain-specific encapsulated systems?

The classical answer from MMH proponents is that the flexibility is the result of the combination of different modules. The interplay between these modules allows for flexibility. It also explains the co-variation and general mental retardation, because being modular comes in degrees. If exclusiveness is not required, this proposes no problem. But is this really a convincing answer? How exactly does this work? First, if the capacity itself only has to contain modules to be called modular, the central terms are used with a different meaning and we no longer have an interesting claim about cognitive architecture any more. Second, if overlapping modules and a lot of cross-talk between systems is allowed, the question arises how much is left of the initial new idea about cognitive architecture.

Massive modularity and evolutionary psychology

Evolutionary psychology is a new field in philosophy of mind. Like its predecessor, sociobiology, evolutionary psychology is the application of evolutionary theory to social behavior and mental capacities. In other words, evolution encompasses not just genes and bodies, but also psychological, social, and (in some versions) cultural features. The human mind and brain are understood as shaped by natural selection. The mind consists of many distinctive components – modules – which developed as solutions to specific adaptive problems. Therefore, MMH is often seen as the central claim of evolutionary psychology. In other descriptions, MMH is at least a claim evolutionary psychology seems to be committed to. As a result, it is a common strategy to attack MMH to show that there are serious problems with evolutionary psychology in general. It also works the other way around: by objecting to the methodology of evolutionary psychology, authors present objections against the evolutionary arguments in favor of MMH.

But on a closer look, the relationship between both is not as clear as it seems at first glance. Certainly both views are on good terms. They might even supplement each other. But they do not conceptually depend on each other.

On the one hand, one can certainly posit the existence of many functional modular units, without being an advocate of an evolutionary explanation of this fact. It might just be a coincidence, or there may be other reasons for it. A claim about cognitive architecture does not commit one to an evolutionary explanation of this fact. Moreover, the plausibility of MMH obviously depends on what you mean by massive modularity. If it is simply the view that – at some level of analysis – the mind and brain contain components that have different functions, i.e. they operate according to distinct principles, the view is very convincing. In fact, this is uncontroversial. But this is not a new view about cognitive architecture. But if massive modularity as a new hypothesis about cognitive architecture means more than this, and we want to require additional properties to be fulfilled, MMH is a more interesting but at the same time a more controversial claim.

On the other hand, one can believe that the human mind and brain are shaped by natural selection (like other organs), without believing that the result is the cognitive architecture MMH advocates posit. Most critics of evolutionary psychology accept that the brain and the mind are shaped by natural selection. But they object to the conclusion that this commits us to a specific view about the relationship between evolution and the structure of the mind and brain. The problem is the methodology of "reverse engineering" used by evolutionary psychologists. In philosophy of biology, there is a hot debate about the legitimacy of this methodology.[9] We have discussed some of these evolutionary arguments for establishing MMH earlier. Evolutionary psychologists assume that a behavior, a capacity or a competence we find today is a solution for an adaptive problem our ancestors were confronted with in the Pleistocene Epoch. Further, they presuppose that natural selection therefore engineered a module, a specialized psychological mechanism, to solve this specific adaptive problem. Both steps in this argument are disputed. First, such an explanation neglects other factors that might have shaped our capacities. Psychological traits depend on other factors than just adaptive problems; developmental and physiochemical factors, to mention just two, play a role as well. Second, it is not clear that only specialized psychological mechanisms are solutions for these adaptive problems. It is presupposed that one module performs only one function. As we have seen, this assumption might turn out to be a dispensable part of evolutionary psychologists' methodology, given that a convincing hierarchical account could be developed. But at present it is a serious worry. There are other problems looming. These include the problem of specifying the adaptive problems of an organism independent of its cognitive capacities (Stotz and Griffiths 2002), to ensure that some trait is an adaptation and not just a second order adaptation, and many others. So there are good reasons to treat many evolutionary arguments very carefully. But it would be hasty to conclude that MMH cannot be defended at all. For both views are conceptually independent.

Yet, both views seem to complement each other. MMH seems to depend to a certain degree on evolutionary accounts. Several of the arguments in favor of modularity (see above) start from an evolutionary perspective. A promising solution for the pressing problem of specifying the core characteristics of modular systems seems to define it in evolutionary hierarchical terms. If such an account could be presented, we would end up with a more intimate relationship between the two views. At present, the jury is still out on the relationship between modularity and evolutionary psychology.

Where does the debate stand?

The intention of this article was not – and cannot be – to give a final answer to the question of whether the mind is modular. The reason is that the key concepts and arguments have to be refined before such a project can even be addressed properly. The most pressing problem in the debate is that the notion of a module is unclear and that proponents do not use the same characterization of "module." In other words, the central term in the debate is used both vaguely and ambiguously. In fact, different authors explicitly use different characterizations. Moreover, as I have shown, these characterizations are probably incompatible. The situation seems even more unfortunate. Indeed, some consistent characterizations have been proposed, but they either don't seem to be supported by the arguments presented, or they are relatively trivial claims with respect to cognitive architecture. A second urgent problem that needs to be addressed is that of providing a more detailed clarification of the relation between the arguments presented and the view defended. A third one is the clarification of the relationship between evolutionary psychology and massive modularity.

As a result, the debate is confusing and it is hard to find out whether it is actually about one particular question. Even if it were about a particular question, to judge the situation we need to consider the arguments. But how these arguments relate to the characteristics and different views of modularity is unclear as well. Hence, the modularity debate is still in its early stages at best. There is a lot of work to do. But this is not a decisive argument against modularity, for this does not imply that there is no possible understanding of "module" that is on the one hand an interesting claim about cognitive architecture, and which, on the other hand, uses a non-trivial characterization of "module." After all, "module" is an artificial term borrowed and developed from the everyday meaning of the term.

Some participants in the recent debate (Woodward and Cowie 2004; Prinz 2006) make the stronger claim that there is no unambiguous sense of module possible that would be faithful and useful for MMH advocates. Even given the recent confusing debate, this claim seems too strong. Sure enough, at present, the stance of MMH is far from being convincing. The view was introduced to establish a new position regarding cognitive architecture, a view that radically differs from the standard cognitive science view. To live up to the expectations such a full-bodied pronouncement generates, advocates of MMH need first to develop a clear understanding of the newly postulated entity, "module." Second, they have to make sure that the new view differs in important aspects from the standard view. Third, they have to develop convincing arguments in favor of their view, or against the traditional view respectively. None of these three aims have been achieved yet. But that does not imply that it is impossible to develop such a view or that there are not the slightest prospects of developing one. Nonetheless, at present, the ambitious claims of MMH seem unwarranted. There is a long way to go for MMH advocates.

In my view, necessary conditions for more fruitful lines of investigation include several important issues: First, a more comprehensive understanding of the core characteristics of the modules and their relation to each other is the most urgent demand in the MMH debate. Second, the relation between the arguments for and against modularity needs to be related to these characteristics in question, instead of being arguments for or against modularity as such. Third, the relation between evolutionary psychology and MMH needs to be analyzed in more detail.

It seems to me that we can rule out some radical readings of MMH. Complete massive modularity, combined with a strong interpretation of the strong characteristics of modules, is unpersuasive. When it comes to central cognitive capacities, complete encapsulation for example, is not an option. Moreover, an absolute denial of modularity independent of the characterization is not convincing either. That a view is seriously underdeveloped does not imply that it cannot be developed in detail, at least not in the absence of serious conceptual inconsistencies within it. In my view, these conceptual inconsistencies concern mainly the methodology of evolutionary psychology. But if MMH could be developed in a way that is conceptually independent of evolutionary psychology, it might not present a serious problem. Therefore, the remaining interesting question is, are there any intermediate non-trivial understandings of modularity, for which there is both conceptual and empirical evidence? At present, this seems an open question.

Notes

1. See the entry on innateness (Samuels, this volume).
2. Note that there is no tension in primitiveness accounts of innateness here. The knowledge and the capacity could still be acquired by psychological processes – thus learned. Only the design plan for the learning methods is claimed to be innate.
3. But this involves concessions on the role evolutionary explanations play for a central term in MMH, and not all proponents of MMH would approve of this strategy, for it closely links MMH to evolutionary psychology.
4. Often, both directions are run together and the label "encapsulation" is used as well (see Scholl and Leslie 1999); the internal operations of a module may be both encapsulated from the remainder of cognition and inaccessible to it. I use the term in the stricter sense.
5. But see the discussion of the tractability argument for another account specifying encapsulation.
6. For a more detailed discussion see Atkinson and Wheeler (2004: 154f.).
7. For a more detailed systematic overview, see Carruthers (2006).
8. For an overview from different perspectives, see Pinker (1994), Cowie (1999), and Segal (2007).
9. Unfortunately, a general discussion of these issues is far beyond the possibilities of this entry.

References

Ariew, A. (1996) "Innateness and Canalization," *Philosophy of Science* 63, no. 3 (suppl.): S19–S27.

—— (1999) "Innateness Is Canalization: In Defense of a Developmental Account of Innateness," in V. Hartcastle (ed.), *Biology Meets Psychology: Conjectures, Connections, Constraints*, Cambridge, MA: MIT Press, pp. 117–38.

Atkinson, A. P., and Wheeler, M. (2003) "Evolutionary Psychology's Grain Problem and the Cognitive Neuroscience of Reasoning," in D. Over (ed.) *Evolution and the Psychology of Thinking: The Debate*, Current Issues in Thinking and Reasoning, Hove: Psychology Press, pp. 61–100.

—— (2004) "The Grain of Domains: The Evolutionary-Psychological Case against Domain-General Cognition," *Mind and Language*, 19, no. 2: 147–76.

Baron-Cohen, S., Tager-Flusberg, H., and Cohen, D. J. (ed.) (1996) *Understanding Other Minds: Perspectives from Autism*, Oxford: Oxford University Press.

Carey, S. (1985) *Conceptual Change in Childhood*, Cambridge, MA: MIT Press.

Carey, S., and Spelke, E. (1994) "Domain-Specific Knowledge and Conceptual Change," in L. Hirschfeld and S. Gelman (eds), *Mapping the Mind: Domain Specificity in Cognition and Culture*, Cambridge: Cambridge University Press, pp. 169–200.

Carruthers, P. (1998) "Thinking in Language? Evolution and a Modularist Possibility," in P. Carruthers and J. Boucher (eds), *Language and Thought*, Cambridge: Cambridge University Press, pp. 94–120.

—— (2003) "Moderate Massive Modularity," in A. O'Hear (ed.) *Mind and Persons*, Cambridge: Cambridge University Press, pp. 67–90.

—— (2004) "The Mind Is a System of Modules Shaped by Natural Selection," in C. Hitchcock (ed.), *Contemporary Debates in Philosophy of Science*, Oxford: Blackwell, pp. 293–311.

—— (2006) "The Case for Massively Modular Models of Mind," R. Stainton (ed.), *Contemporary Debates in Cognitive Science*, Oxford: Blackwell, pp. 3–21.

Carston, R. (1996) "The Architecture of the Mind: Modularity and Modularization," in D. Green (ed.), *Cognitive Science*, Oxford: Blackwell, pp. 53–83.

Cosmides, L., and Tooby, J. (2001) "Unraveling the Enigma of Human Intelligence," in R. Sternberg and J. Kaufman (eds) *The Evolution of Intelligence*, Mahwah, NJ: Erlbaum, pp. 145–98.

Cowie, F. (1998) *What's Within? Nativism Reconsidered*, Oxford: Oxford University Press.

Currie, G., and Sterelny, K. (2000) "How to Think about the Modularity of Mind-Reading," *Philosophical Quarterly* 50, no. 199: 145–60.
Fodor, J. A. (1983) *The Modularity of Mind*, Cambridge, MA: MIT Press.
—— (1996) "Deconstructing Dennett's Darwin," *Mind and Language* 11: 246–62.
—— (2000) *The Mind Doesn't Work That Way*, Cambridge, MA: MIT Press.
Frith, U. (1989) *Autism: Explaining the Enigma*, Oxford: Blackwell.
García, C. L. (2007) "Cognitive Modularity, Biological Modularity, and Evolvability," *Biological Theory, Development, Evolution, and Cognition* 2, no. 1: 62–73.
Garfield, J. L., Peterson, C., and Perry, T. (2001) "Social Cognition, Language Acquisition and the Development of the Theory of Mind," *Mind and Language*, 161, no. 5: 494–541.
Gillberg, C., and Coleman, M. (1992) *The Biology of the Autistic Syndromes*, 2nd edn, London: MacKeith Press.
Goldman, A. (1989) "Interpretation Psychologized," *Mind and Language* 4: 161–85; repr. M. Davies and T. Stone (eds), *Folk Psychology: The Theory of Mind Debate*, Oxford: Blackwell, 1995.
—— (2006) *Simulating Minds: The Philosophy, Psychology, and Neuroscience of Mindreading*, New York: Oxford University Press.
Gopnik, A. (1996) "Theories and Modules: Creation Myths, Developmental Realities and Neurath's Boat," in P. Carruthers and P. Smith (eds), *Theories of Theories of Mind*, Cambridge: Cambridge University Press.
Gordon, R. (1986) "Folk Psychology as Simulation," *Mind and Language* 1: 158–171; repr. M. Davies and T. Stone (eds), *Folk Psychology: The Theory of Mind Debate*, Oxford: Blackwell, 1995.
Gottschling, V. (in prep.) "Massive Modularity, Nativism and Mindreading."
Griffiths, P. E. (1997) *What Emotions Really Are*, Chicago: Chicago University Press.
Happé, F. (1994) *Autism: An Introduction to Psychological Theory*, London: UCL Press.
Hauser, M., and Carey, S. (1998) "Building a Cognitive Creature from a Set of Primitives," in D. Cummins and C. Allen (eds), *The Evolution of Mind*, Oxford: Oxford University Press.
Kitcher, P. (1985) *Valuing Ambition*, Cambridge, MA: MIT Press.
Leslie, A. M. (1987) "Pretence and Representation: The Origins of 'Theory of Mind'," *Psychological Review* 94: 412–26.
—— (1991) "The Theory of Mind Impairment in Autism: Evidence for a Modular Mechanism of Development?" in A. Whiten (ed.), *Natural Theories of Mind*, Oxford: Basil Blackwell, pp. 63–78.
—— (2000) "'Theory of Mind' as a Mechanism of Selective Attention," in M. S. Gazzaniga (ed.), *The New Cognitive Neurosciences*, 2nd edn, Cambridge, MA: MIT Press, pp. 1235–47.
Leslie, A. M., and Roth, D. (1993) *What Can Autism Teach Us about Metarepresentation?* Oxford: Oxford Medical.
Pinker, S. (1997) *How the Mind Works*, London: Penguin.
Prinz, J. J. (2006) "Is the Mind Really Modular?" in R. Stainton (ed.), *Contemporary Debates in Cognitive Science*, Oxford: Blackwell, pp. 22–36.
Samuels, R. (1998) "Evolutionary Psychology and the Massive Modularity Hypothesis," *British Journal for the Philosophy of Science* 49: 575–602.
—— (2000) "Massively Modular Minds: Evolutionary Psychology and Cognitive Architecture," in P. Carruthers and A. Chamberlain (ed.), *Evolution and the Human Mind*, Cambridge: Cambridge University Press, pp. 13–46.
—— (2002) "Nativism in Cognitive Science," *Mind and Language* 17, no. 3: 233–65.
—— (2005) "The Complexity of Cognition: Tractability Arguments for Massive Modularity," in P. Carruthers, S. Laurence, and S. Stich (eds), *The Innate Mind: Structure and Contents*, Oxford: Oxford University Press, pp. 107–21.
—— (2006) "Is the Mind Massively Modular?" in R. Stainton (ed.), *Contemporary Debates in Cognitive Science*, Oxford: Blackwell, pp. 37–56.
Scholl, B. J., and Leslie, A. M. (1999) "Modularity, Development, and 'Theory of Mind'," *Mind and Language* 14, no. 1: 131–53.
Segal, G. (1995) "The Modularity of Theory of Mind," in P. Carruthers and P. Smith (eds), *Theories of Theories of Mind*, Cambridge: Cambridge University Press, pp. 141–8.
—— (2007) "Poverty of Stimulus Arguments Concerning Language and Folk Psychology," in P.

Carruthers, S. Laurence, and S. Stich (eds), *The Innate Mind: Foundations and Future*, Oxford: Oxford University Press, 90–107.

Sober, E. (1993) *Philosophy of Biology*, Oxford: Oxford University Press.

Spelke, E. (1994) "Initial Knowledge: Six Suggestions," *Cognition* 50: 431–45.

Sperber, D. (1996) *Explaining Culture: A Naturalistic Approach*, Oxford: Blackwell.

—— (2002) "In Defense of Massive Modularity," in I. Dupoux (ed.), *Language, Brain and Cognitive Development*, Cambridge, MA: MIT Press, pp. 47–57.

—— (2005) "Massive Modularity and the First Principle of Relevance," in P. Carruthers, S. Laurence, and S. Stich (eds), *The Innate Mind: Structure and Contents*, Oxford: Oxford University Press, pp. 53–68.

Sterelny, K., and Griffiths, P. E. (1999) *Sex and Death: An Introduction to the Philosophy of Biology*, Chicago: University of Chicago Press.

Stich, S. (1990) *The Fragmentation of Reason*, Cambridge, MA: MIT Press.

Stotz, K., and Griffiths, P. E. (2002) "Dancing in the Dark: Evolutionary Psychology and the Problem of Design," *Evolutionary Psychology: Alternative Approaches*, S. Scher and M. Rauscher (eds), Dordrecht: Kluwer, pp. 135–60.

Tooby, J., and Cosmides, L. (1992) "The Psychological Foundations of Culture," in J. Barkow, L. Cosmides, and J. Tooby (eds) *The Adapted Mind*, Oxford: Oxford University Press, pp. 19–136.

—— (1994) "Origins of Domain Specificity: The Evolution of Functional Organization," in L. Hirschfeld and S. Gelman (eds) *Mapping the Mind: Domain Specificity in Cognition and Culture*, Cambridge: Cambridge University Press, pp. 85–116.

Woodward, J., and Cowie, F. (2004) "The Mind Is Not (Just) a System of Modules Shaped (Just) by Natural Selection," in C. Hitchcock (ed.), *Contemporary Debates in Philosophy of Science*, Oxford: Blackwell, pp. 312–34.

19
NATIVISM

Richard Samuels

Introduction

Nativism has a long intellectual heritage going back at least as far as Plato and the claim that we possess innate knowledge. More recently, it has played a pivotal role in the development of cognitive science, where largely under Chomky's influence, innateness hypotheses have been invoked to explain a broad array of psychological phenomena, including concept acquisition, theory of mind, arithmetic and language. Though there are many interesting issues about the history of nativist thought and its connections to more recent concerns (Scott 1995; Stich 1975; Cowie 1999), in what follows I focus primarily on recent incarnations of nativism and the debates in which they figure.

What is nativism?

Though one could be a nativist about many things, contemporary debates are primarily concerned with a range of issues about the nature and extent of our innate psychological endowment: roughly put, with those mental traits that are acquired in the normal course of development, though not as a result of any kind of learning process. By addressing such issues in sufficient detail, researchers seek to illuminate the nature of our psychological capacities – for language, perception, reasoning, and the like – and to help explain how we come to possess such capacities.

To a first approximation, those positions labeled "nativist" maintain that our innate psychological endowment is relatively rich, whilst those labeled "empiricist" – though "non-nativist" would perhaps be more accurate – advocate a relatively austere conception of our innate endowment. But "nativism" – and "empiricism" for that matter – is not a label for some single well-defined position, but instead characterizes a broad array of claims. Most obviously, some of these claims are quite *local* in the sense that they concern relatively specific psychological traits, whilst others are *global* in the sense that they are very general claims about the overall composition of the mind.

When used to express a local hypothesis, the term "nativism" is typically used in an explicitly relational fashion: one endorses nativism *about* some trait or class of psychological traits. Typically, what this amounts to is the claim that the trait in question is largely or perhaps entirely innately specified. In contrast, those who advocate empiricism (or non-nativism) about a given trait, claim that it is not innately specified. Clearly, there are many possible nativisms of this local variety. But what is most commonly at issue is the innateness of *concepts* (ONE, OBJECT, IDENTICAL, etc.), *mentally represented bodies of information* (e.g. about physical objects, number and biological kinds), and *psychological mechanisms* (e.g. for language acquisition, reasoning and perception). Some local innateness hypotheses are concerned exclusively with one of the above sorts of structure. But it is equally common for hypotheses to incorporate claims about some combination of psychological structures.

In contrast to local forms of nativism, global nativism involves a claim about the overall nature and extent of our innate psychological endowment. Precisely how such a view should be formulated remains a point of some dispute (Cowie 1999). Some have even suggested that no such view has ever been coherently formulated, let alone defended (Chomsky 2003). But within cognitive science there currently appears to be a widely endorsed – though to be sure, vague and underspecified – general nativist perspective that subsumes a confederation of more specific proposals (Simpson et al. 2005). What such proposals share is a relatively *rich* conception of our innate psychological endowment, where this characteristically involves the following pair of commitments:

- Our minds contain *lots* of innate psychological structure – concepts, bodies of information, psychological mechanisms, biases, and so on.
- Much of this innate structure is *domain specific* – as opposed to domain general – in roughly the sense that it is dedicated to addressing problems with quite specific subject matters – e.g. arithmetic, folk biology, naïve physics, language, and so on.

The two commitments are connected. In particular, contemporary nativists posit lots of innate structure in large measure because they are pessimistic about the prospects for explaining our psychological development in terms of domain-general structures and processes. As a consequence, advocates of global nativism contend that a satisfactory account of the human mind is likely to require a large inventory of innate, domain-specific structures.

In contrast to nativism of this global variety, global empiricism advocates a far more austere conception of our innate psychological endowment. Though empiricists seldom reject all innate mental structure – among other things, it is hard to see how learning could occur at all without at least some innate learning mechanisms – they do insist that our minds contain relatively little innate structure (Block 1981). Moreover, they do so in large measure because they think that the acquisition of our mature psychological capacities – for language, reasoning, face recognition, and so on – can be explained without positing much in the way of innate, domain-specific structure. On this view, then, most specialized mental structure is acquired in the course of development, typically by general-purpose or domain-general learning processes. For example, according to one rather extreme version of empiricism, our minds come equipped with little more than a set of innate perceptual systems and a few domain-general learning mechanisms, such as those for induction and associative learning. As a consequence, global empiricists posit far less innate domain-specific structure than their nativist counterparts.

Some arguments for global nativism

Why be a global nativist? Though the case typically rests on the accumulation of evidence for more local innateness hypotheses – some of which we will consider in the third section ("Local nativism: two examples") – there are also various general arguments that have been influential in motivating nativism about psychological structure. Here are two examples.

Methodological continuity with other sciences

Empiricists suppose that our minds contain relatively little innate structure; and that what specialized structure they have is largely a product of general learning processes. Though deeply entrenched in many regions of social science, nativists often maintain that this assumption is highly implausible. One reason is that research in many adjacent fields of enquiry – e.g. anatomy, physiology, and comparative psychology – would appear to suggest that an organism's capacities very often depend on innate, specialized systems and structures. Hearts and kidneys, for example, though influenced by environmental factors, are not acquired by some kind of general-purpose learning process but instead result from biological processes of growth. According to Chomsky and others, parity of reason should lead us to the default assumption that mental capacities are similarly dependent on specialized, unlearned systems or "organs" (Chomsky 1980). To assume otherwise, they maintain, is to adopt a view that treats minds as somehow separate from the rest of the biological world.

The above argument, though suggestive, is inconclusive. Empiricists need not reject the demand for mental specialization. Rather, their disagreement with nativists concerns the *extent* of this specialization. For example, they typically acknowledge the need for innate perceptual mechanisms and for systems specialized for learning. What they deny is the need for lots of innate, domain-specific structure. The present objection would thus seem to involve an uncharitable construal of the empiricist position. To put the point bluntly, the present objection is akin to complaining that physiologists of the circulatory system reject innate specialization because they fail to posit *multiple* hearts – say, one for pumping red blood cells and another for pumping white cells. Such a complaint would clearly be misplaced. Likewise, the empiricist will object that the analogous criticism is similarly misplaced. It is not that they reject the existence of mental specialization. It is merely that they deny that it is as extensive as nativists would have us believe.

General computational considerations

Contemporary nativists tend to think of cognitive tasks in general and learning tasks in particular as *computational* problems. But from a computational viewpoint, so the argument continues, cognitive tasks require computational processes that are tailored both to the inputs they receive and the function they are supposed to compute. From this vantage, then, the idea of general-purpose cognitive processes – e.g. for learning – "makes no more sense than the notion of a general-purpose sensing organ" (Gallistel 2007). Compare: There is no such thing as a general-purpose sense organ because picking up information from different stimuli – light, sound, chemical etc. – requires organs with structures shaped by the specific properties of the input that they process. According to the present argument, the same is true of learning and cognition.

Again, the argument is inconclusive. For one thing, many empiricists are not computationalists in the relevant sense, but instead endorse some form of associationism about learning and cognition (Gallistel 2007). As a consequence, the relevance of computational considerations is less clear; and debates over the existence of innate structure frequently devolve into disputes over whether or not to be a computationalist about cognition (Samuels 2002). But even if one accepts computationalism, the general argument is hard to sustain without a plethora of specific cases in which learning and cognition plausibly require innate, specialized structure. To assess the case for global nativism, then, we need to turn from theoretical arguments concerned with cognition in general to more specific hypotheses about the existence of innate, domain-specific mental structure.

Local nativism: two examples

Disputes over innateness have emerged in connection with a broad array of psychological phenomena, including our intuitive understanding of the physical world, arithmetic and theory of mind. But it is in relation to language that the issues have been most extensively explored.

Linguistic nativism

To appreciate the character of the debate over linguistic nativism, it is worth first noting some widely shared assumptions about the acquisition of language. Researchers working on language tend to suppose that when acquiring a language one comes to possess an internal grammar – or an internal representation of a grammar – for that language. (Amongst other things, this helps explain the systematicity and productivity of language.) Clearly, it is implausible that the grammar possessed by a competent speaker – e.g. a grammar for English as opposed to French or Hindi – is innately specified, since what grammar one acquires depends on which linguistic environment one inhabits. Nonetheless, in contrast to other organisms, all humans everywhere – save those suffering extreme pathology or environmental deprivation – reliably acquire competence in some natural language within the first few years of life. This suggests, with only a hint of idealization, that humans share some set of innate resources – some *initial state* – that permits the acquisition of a grammar for the language they speak. A central problem for any account of language acquisition is thus to characterize the initial state: those innate resources that reliably enable a grammar to be acquired on the basis of the available environmental information.

What are the options? One broad distinction is between linguistic empiricism, on the one hand, and linguistic nativism, on the other. To a first approximation, linguistic empiricists claim that language acquisition depends on the same innate, mechanisms that are responsible for cognitive development in other domains. In contrast, linguistic nativists claim that at least some of the innate resources on which language acquisition depends are specific to the domain of language. Within these broad categories, however, there are many more finely articulated positions that one might occupy. For instance, even if one endorses some version of linguistic nativism, there is still plenty of room for disagreement over the precise nature and extent of our innate language-specific resources. For instance, one claim widely associated with the work of Chomsky and his followers is that humans possess an innate, domain-specific *language faculty* which incorporates a universal grammar: a rich body of innate knowledge that specifies the properties shared by all natural languages (Chomsky 1980). But one might be a linguistic nativist without endorsing the existence of universal grammar. For example, one might think there is an innate, language-specific learning mechanism or module, whilst also denying that we possess an informationally rich body of innate, language-specific knowledge of the sort associated with universal grammar. Indeed, there are various strands in Chomsky's more recent work – within the so-called "minimalist program" – that would suggest just such a rejection of rich innate knowledge of language (see, for example, Fitch et al. 2005).

Poverty-of-the-stimulus arguments

The debate over linguistic nativism is a largely empirical one; and like other empirical debates, different proposals are assessed in terms of their overall ability to accommodate evidence in a simple, powerful and conservative manner. Here, there are many sorts of evidence that are relevant (Pinker 1994; Cowie 2008). But perhaps the most influential argument for linguistic nativism – and the one that has received most attention from philosophers – is what has come to be known as the *poverty-of-the-stimulus argument* (PoSA).

The PoSA has been formulated in a number of different ways. But the rough idea is that some version of linguistic nativism must be right because the information that children receive from the environment is too impoverished to permit an *empiricist learner* – one lacking any innate, language-specific knowledge, mechanisms or biases – to reliably acquire the grammar for their language (for further details see Cowie [1999, 2008] and Laurence and Margolis [2001]).

Though the PoSA is widely accepted by linguists, it has also been subjected to sustained criticism. One major challenge concerns the issue of what environmentally derived information is available in the course of language acquisition. For example, nativists have tended to suppose that children are seldom provided with negative data – roughly, information about when an utterance is *not* grammatical. But recently this assumption has come under scrutiny; and researchers have argued that such data is both available to and used by children in the course of language development (Chouinard and Clark 2003).

Another major challenge concerns the nature of empiricist learners. Almost everyone agrees that traditional empiricist accounts of language learning, such as those that have emerged from the behaviorist tradition, are inadequate. But in recent years there has been an explosion of research on statistical learning (Pereira 2000); and some have suggested that this research may form the basis for a satisfactory non-nativist account of language acquisition (Scholz and Pullum 2005).

Though a systematic assessment of these methods is beyond the scope of the present chapter, it's far from clear they undermine the PoSA for linguistic nativism. Recall: What the PoSA purports to show is merely that language acquisition requires some set of innate, language-specific structures or biases. But the current state of research on statistical learning seems wholly compatible with this claim. Specifically, our most successful computational models of language learning invariably assume language-specific constraints. For example, they assume some model (or representational scheme) relevant to the domain of language; and they presuppose constraints on the inputs that the learning system receives (e.g. sentences in the target language as opposed to the myriad other kinds of inputs that a learning device might receive). Though there is much more to say on the matter, it is far from clear that without an account of how such constraints are acquired by empiricist learning these models vindicate empiricism as opposed to suggesting a variant on linguistic nativism: one which posits an innate, language-specific statistical learning mechanism or module.

Other arguments

Whether or not PoSAs succeed in establishing linguistic nativism, it is important to stress that such arguments are located within a rich network of other considerations intended to support a nativist view of language. The general idea is that nativist views do better at accommodating this range of data, and for this reason are to be preferred to alternative accounts. Here are few examples of such phenomena.

Linguistic universals

According to many linguists, the existence of linguistic universals – roughly, properties possessed by all possible natural languages – militates in favor of linguistic nativism, since the existence of such universals is readily explained on the assumption that we possess an innate language faculty or universal grammar (Crain et al. 2005). In response, some non-nativists have questioned the assumption that there are any substantive linguistic universals, noting both that there is considerable variation in what different nativists take the universals to be and, moreover, that many proposed universals turn out on further scrutiny not to be possessed by all natural languages (Tomasello 2004; Newmeyer 2005). Others argue that even if there are universal features of language, it does not follow that such features are innate and specific to language. So, for example, it may be that they reflect facts about the historical development of natural languages – for example, that current world languages share certain features because they evolved from a common ancestral language (Putnam 1971). Alternatively, it may be that linguistic universals do not reflect language-specific features of our minds but instead result from constraints imposed by general facts about cognition. So, for example, it has been variously suggested that they reflect facts about the structure of thought, the character of human memory, or our possession of some general capacity for symbolic communication (Tomasello 2003).

Sensitive periods

Another familiar kind of argument for linguistic nativism turns on the existence of sensitive/critical periods. In brief, though we are capable of learning many things throughout the entire course of our lives, our facility for language acquisition appears to diminish dramatically after the age of about twelve; and in those unfortunate cases where a child is denied any significant access to normal linguistic inputs prior to puberty – as in the case of so-called "wild children" – they appear never to attain a mastery of natural language (Skuse 1993). Nativists maintain that this kind of phenomenon is readily explained on the assumption that we have an innate language faculty with its own specific developmental timetable. Non-nativists have responded in a variety of ways. So, for example, it has been argued that there are methodological problems with the evidence for sensitive periods. Among other things, the case rests largely on evidence from the study of wild children. But according to critics, such evidence is problematic both because there are relatively few well-studied instances of such children, and because in those cases that have been studied, the absence of normal linguistic input is confounded with many other, often more egregious, forms of deprivation.

Developmental disorders

A final consideration in support of linguistic nativism that I consider here concerns the putative existence of various heritable, developmental disorders involving either the selective impairment or sparing of linguistic abilities. For example, it has been claimed that the linguistic abilities of children with Williams syndrome are relatively spared, despite profound deficits in general cognitive capacity (IQ < 60) (Pinker 1994, 1999). Conversely, it has been argued that people with a syndrome known as Specific Language Impairment (SLI) exhibit selectively impaired linguistic abilities, despite otherwise normal cognitive capacities (van der Lely, 2005). Nativists argue that the existence of such disorders suggests that some version of linguistic nativism is correct. Specifically, it is argued that the (putative) fact that these genetic disorders involve the selective sparing or impairment of linguistic abilities is most readily explained on the assumption that language depends on innate, domain-specific cognitive structures.

Once more, non-nativists have challenged this line of argument in a variety of ways. Most importantly, it is has been argued that, contrary to what some nativists maintain, Williams syndrome, specific language impairment (SLI), and other developmental disorders, do not clearly involve the selective sparing or impairment of linguistic abilities. For example, opponents of the argument maintain that subjects with Williams syndrome not only exhibit a range of syntactic and morphological deficits but also have islands of relatively spared nonlinguistic abilities as well (Karmiloff-Smith, Brown et al. 2003). Similarly, it has been argued that people with SLI not only exhibit language-specific impairments, but also a range of nonlinguistic deficits (Karmiloff-Smith, Scerif et al. 2003).

Nativism about folk psychology

In addition to the case of language, debates over innateness have arisen in connection with a broad array of other cognitive capacities. One that has been of considerable interest to philosophers is our capacity for "mindreading" or folk psychology – i.e. the capacity to attribute beliefs, desires and other mental states to agents (Nichols and Stich 2003). Nativists about mindreading are all committed to the thesis that we possess innate domain-specific psychological structures for folk psychology. But as with linguistic nativism, nativism about folk psychology can take a variety of forms (Segal 2007). According to some views, for example, we possess both innate domain-specific mechanisms dedicated to folk psychological inference and various explicit representations expressing core folk psychological concepts, such as BELIEF, PRETENCE and DESIRE (Leslie 1994; Scholl and Leslie 1999). Other views assume merely that we possess some limited set of innate, domain-specific conceptual resources for folk psychology that are deployed by domain-general systems for learning and reasoning (Wellman 1990). Finally, some views are largely empiricist in character and posit no innate cognitive structures that are specialized for folk psychology as such. Instead they maintain that the acquisition of our mature mindreading capacities depends largely on general-purpose learning systems, perhaps aided by various low-level perceptual and action-guiding mechanisms – such as devices for detecting eye-direction and for engaging in imitation (Karmiloff-Smith, 1997; Sterelny 2003).

Arguments

As with the case of language, there are many considerations that have been invoked in support of nativism about folk psychology. First, nativists about folk psychology have attempted to provide PoSAs in support of their views (see Segal [2007] for an excellent discussion of such arguments). Second, it has been argued that evidence from autism supports nativism about folk psychology, since the disorder is a genetic one in which even high functioning subjects have a significantly impaired ability to attribute beliefs and other mental states. Third, though the details of folk psychology vary from culture to culture, the "core" capacity to attribute beliefs and desires appears to be a universal human trait (Scholl and Leslie 1999). Finally, recent evidence would appear to suggest that the capacity for mental state attribution emerges very early in development (Onishi and Baillargeon 2005; Surian et al. 2007). Nativists claim that such facts are best explained on the assumption that we possess innate resources specialized for folk psychology.

Unsurprisingly, the above kinds of considerations remain a subject of heated debate. For example, in response to PoSAs, some non-nativists about folk psychology maintain that we are embedded in environments that provide a rich source of data concerning the nature of mental states (Sterelny 2003). Similarly, in response to the data concerning autism and universality, non-nativists maintain that alternative hypotheses better explain the data (Prinz 2005). The extent to which our folk psychological capacities depend on innate domain-specific structure thus remains a topic of active and ongoing debate.

Some arguments for global empiricism

As we have already seen, most contemporary research into our innate psychological endowment is concerned with quite specific empirical hypotheses. Even so, just as nativists have sought to make their views plausible on the basis of quite general considerations, empiricists have developed similarly general arguments against nativism.

Perhaps the most well known of these argument is the *argument from cultural variability*. This argument was commonplace in the work of mid-twentieth-century anthropologists, such as Margaret Mead and Franz Boas; and it continues to command widespread acceptance in many areas of the social sciences. According to the argument, when we survey the anthropological record, we see enormous variation in human psychology and behavior: in technology, languages, social conventions, emotional responses, gender relations, religious practices, and so on. But this kind of malleability would not occur, it is claimed, if our minds possessed a rich innate structure. Instead, we should expect substantial uniformity across cultures. Thus advocates of the argument conclude that biology imposes few constraints on our mental development and that our minds are (almost) entirely the products of our environments. As Mead famously claimed, "we are forced to conclude that human nature is almost unbelievably malleable, responding accurately and consistently to contrasting cultural conditions" (Mead 1935: 280).

Nativists have responded to the argument from cultural variability in a number of ways. One common response is that the argument overstates the extent of cultural differences. Though there is, of course, considerable cross-cultural variation, there are also literally hundreds of pan-cultural "human universals" – characteristics of behavior and cognition that appear stable across all cultures (Brown 1991, 2000). So far as we know, for example, all cultures communicate in a natural language, engage in religious/spiritual practices, categorize flora and fauna, have beliefs about the minds of others, and so on. Second, nativists argue that the observed cultural variability is wholly compatible with the existence of a rich innate psychology. What the anthropological record suggests is that there is considerable variability in *overt* responses. But for all the argument shows, these different outputs could be produced by richly structured innate mechanisms that produce different responses under different environmental circumstances (Tooby and Cosmides 1992). Indeed, it is widely assumed by nativists that many innate structures – those for vision and language, for example – exhibit precisely this sort of sensitivity to environmental inputs.

Another, though rather different, objection to nativism is sometimes called the *"gene shortage" argument* (Marcus 2004). According to this argument, the human genome is too small to allow for much innate psychological structure (Bates et al. 1998; Ehrlich and Feldman 2003). For while we have only about 30,000 genes, our brains contain literally billions of neurons. In which case, it is unlikely that the fine-grained structure of the brain is strongly influenced by genetic factors; and since cognition depends on this fine-grained organization, it is thereby unlikely that it is under genetic control. In which case, though genes may be responsible for the general morphology of the human brain, it is very unlikely that much cognitive structure is innately specified.

What are we to make of this argument? One initial observation is that the argument clearly shows too much. For if it were sound, then exactly analogous considerations would also show that kidneys, lungs, legs and the like are not innate. Such physiological structures also contain many more cells than there are human genes. But this alone surely doesn't show that such structures are not innate. On the contrary, they are prototypical examples of what nativists have in mind when speaking of innate structures. Now what the argument may well show is that brains are not solely a product of genetic factors and that the structure/function of each neuron is not coded in the genome. But this should be no cause of concern for nativism, since no (sane) nativist would endorse such a view. On the contrary, nativists routinely accept the banal interactionist thesis that cognitive development – as with every other aspect of human development – depends on both innate and environmental factors. In short: the present argument only succeeds in refuting a view that no one actually endorses.

What is Innateness?

Most debates over nativism in psychology and cognitive science proceed under the assumption that the notion of innateness is clear enough to permit the framing of substantive empirical issues. But there are, in fact, considerable difficulties with trying to understand what innateness is; and some prominent theorists have suggested that the very concept is "fundamentally confused" (Bateson 2000; Griffiths 2002). If such a claim could be sustained, it would appear to have important implications for psychological research. For not only would it undermine nativism in its various forms, it would also threaten the main empiricist alternatives, since they too presuppose the coherence of the innateness concept (Samuels 2007).

One standard reason for claiming that innateness is a confused concept is that it is said to confound several properties under a single term: properties that are neither co-extensive nor, by themselves, adequate to characterize what we mean by "innate." So, for instance, it is sometimes claimed that innate traits are ones that are *present at birth*, even though presence at birth is neither necessary nor sufficient for innateness. It is not sufficient because prenatal learning is possible (Gottlieb 1997); and it is not necessary because, as Descartes observed long ago, innate characteristics can be acquired quite late in development. (Illustration: Secondary sexual characteristics are plausibly innate but clearly not present at birth.) Similarly, it is sometimes said that innate traits are solely the products of internal (including genetic) causes, even though this is clearly not necessary for innateness, since, like all contemporary theorists, nativists wholeheartedly accept the banal thesis that cognitive traits are caused jointly by internal *and* environmental factors.

In view of the problems with standard claims about innateness, theorists have responded in a variety of ways. One response is to conclude that innateness is a confused concept, and map out the implications of this for future psychological research (Mameli and Bateson 2006). Another response is to try and make systematic sense of the notion of innateness that figures in psychology and allied sciences. Though there is not the space here to discuss the issue at great length, a number of proposals seem worthy of further consideration.

Innateness as canalization

One such view invokes the notion of environmental *canalization* (Waddington 1940). According to this proposal, a trait of an organism (with a given genotype G) is innate to the extent that it is environmentally canalized in organisms with G; and the trait is highly canalized to the extent that its development is insensitive to the range of environmental conditions under which it emerges (Ariew 1999). So, for example, my possession of legs is (highly) innate on this view because, for organisms with the same genotype as me, the development of legs is highly insensitive to variation in environmental conditions.

The canalization account of innateness has been criticized on several grounds. One standard concern, for example, is that it threatens to trivialize debate over innateness (Cowie 1999). The worry is, in brief, that assessments of canalization depend on what sorts of environmental variability one takes to be relevant to the process at hand; and this, in turn, appears to depend on the explanatory interests of those who use the concept of canalization in the first place. (Example: The development of normal facial features is likely to seem more highly canalized where we are interested only in those environments capable of sustaining human life than it will to, say, an obstetrician interested in a wide range of *in utero* environments, many of which may interfere with normal facial development.) The concern is thus that disputes over innateness end up merely reflecting differences of explanatory emphasis.

For the present objection to pose a genuine obstacle to understanding nativist/empiricist debates in terms of canalization, however, it would need to be the case that these debates do, in fact, turn on such differences in explanatory emphasis (Segal 2007). Fortunately for the canalization account, it is unclear that this is so. On the contrary, it would seem that whilst nativists and empiricists disagree about the processes responsible for psychological development, they nevertheless share much the same assumptions about which range of environments is relevant to understanding such processes (Segal 2007). Thus it is far from clear that the canalization account does trivialize the debate between nativists and empiricists.

Innateness as psychological primitiveness

A second approach to understanding the notion of innateness as it figures in contemporary nativist/empiricist debates is one that invokes the notion of *psychological primitiveness* (Cowie 1999; Samuels 2002). According to this view, innate psychological traits are primitive in roughly the sense that they are (a) acquired in the normal course of development, whilst (b) not being acquired by any kind of psychological process, such as perception or inference. Or to put the point slightly differently, according to the present view, the innate mind consists of those reliably developing psychological traits whose acquisition psychology cannot explain.

One virtue of the psychological primitiveness account is that it explains the peculiar significance of innateness hypotheses to psychology and cognitive science. Though many areas of biology have dispensed with the notion of innateness altogether – in large measure because it plays no useful theoretical role – it continues to have widespread application in psychology and cognitive science (Johnson 1997). Why is this? One possibility is that it results from an unfortunate oversight that should be remedied immediately (Griffiths 2002). But if the present proposal is correct, then the notion of innateness in fact functions to frame two issues of genuine importance to psychology and cognitive science. First, it delimits the scope of psychological explanation: once we know that a given structure is innate, we also know that our scientific psychology should not – indeed cannot – explain how it was acquired, and that we must instead look to biology or some other science for an explanation. Second, discovering which structures are innate also furnishes us with the resources – the "building blocks" – from which to construct developmental psychological theories. Such theories must – on pain of regress – presuppose the existence of structures whose acquisition is not explained by psychology. So, if we know that a given structure is innate, then it can be invoked by psychological theories to explain the development of other psychological traits.

As with the canalization view of innateness, the primitiveness account has also been subject to a variety of criticisms. One common complaint, for example, is that it invokes an unduly vague notion of normal development (Mameli and Bateson 2006). There is something to this. Clearly, there are many possible notions of normalcy that might be invoked here. But one should be careful not to overplay the point. Though it would no doubt be desirable to provide a more precise account of normalcy, it is unclear that the task is any more pressing here than it is in understanding the claims made in many other areas of science. All sciences – with the possible exception of physics – typically assume some largely unarticulated set of normal conditions in formulating their laws and generalizations. In the jargon of philosophy, they are *ceteris paribus* generalizations that apply only when all else is equal (Carroll 2003). According to the present view, much the same is true of innateness hypotheses in developmental psychology and other areas of cognitive science. In effect, they are generalizations that, like virtually all other scientific generalizations, tacitly assume some set of background normal conditions. So, for example, the claim that humans possess an innate object concept is tantamount to the claim that, *ceteris paribus* –

i.e. given standard background conditions – humans acquire the object concept via some non-psychological process. On this view, then, notions of normalcy are no more important to understanding innateness hypotheses in cognitive science than they are to understanding hypotheses in geology, economics, or, for that matter, aerodynamics.

References

Ariew A. (1999) "Innateness Is Canalization: A Defense of a Developmental Account of Innateness," in V. Hardcastle (ed.), *When Biology Meets Psychology*, MIT Press, Cambridge, pp. S19–S27.

Bates, E., Elman, J., Johnson, M., Karmillof-Smith, A., Parisi, D., and Plunkett, K. (1998) "Innateness and Emergentism," in W. Bechtel and G. Graham (eds), *A Companion to Cognitive Science*, Oxford: Blackwell, pp. 590–601.

Bateson, P. (2000) "Taking the Stink Out of Instinct," in H. Rose and S. Rose (eds), *Alas, Poor Darwin*, London: Cape, pp. 157–73.

Block, N. (1981) "Introduction: What Is Innateness?" in N. Block (ed.), *Readings in the Philosophy of Psychology*, vol. 2, London: Methuen, pp. 279–81.

Brown, D. E. (1991) *Human Universals*, New York: McGraw-Hill.

—— (2000) "Human Universals and Their Implications," in N. Roughley (ed.), *Being Humans: Anthropological Universality and Particularity in Transdisciplinary Perspectives*, New York: Walter de Gruyter.

Carroll, J. (2003) "Laws of Nature," in Edward N. Zalta (ed.), *The Stanford Encyclopedia of Philosophy*; available: http://plato.stanford.edu/entries/laws-of-nature

Chomsky, N. (1980) *Rules and Representations*, New York: Columbia University Press.

—— (2003) "Replies," in L. Antony and N. Hornstein (eds), *Chomsky and His Critics*, Oxford: Blackwell.

Chouinard, M. M., and Clark, E. V. (2003) "Adult Reformulations of Child Errors as Negative Evidence," *Journal of Child Language* 30: 637–69

Cowie, F. (1999) *What's Within? Nativism Reconsidered*, Oxford: Oxford University Press.

—— (2008) "Innateness and Language," in Eward N. Zalta (ed.), *The Stanford Encyclopedia of Philosophy* (Winter 2008 edn); available: http://plato.stanford.edu/entries/innateness-language/

Ehrlich, P., and Feldman, M. (2003) "Genes and Cultures: What Creates Our Behavioral Phenome," *Current Anthropology* 44: 87–107.

Fitch, W., Hauser, M., and Chomsky, N. (2005) "The Evolution of the Language Faculty," *Cognition* 97: 179–210.

Gallistel, C. R. (2007) "Learning Organs," in J. Bricmont and J. Franck (eds), *Cahier 88: Noam Chomsky*, Paris: L'Herne, pp. 181–7.

Gottlieb, G. (1997) *Synthesizing Nature-Nurture: Prenatal Roots of Instinctive Behavior*, Hillsdale, NJ: Erlbaum.

Griffiths, P. (2002) "What Is Innateness?" *Monist* 85, no. 1: 70–85.

Johnson, M. (1997) *Developmental Cognitive Neuroscience*, Oxford: Blackwell.

Karmiloff-Smith, A., Brown, J. H., Grice, S., and Paterson, S. (2003) "Dethroning the Myth: Cognitive Dissociations and Innate Modularity in Williams Syndrome," *Developmental Neuropsychology* 23: 229–44.

Karmiloff-Smith, A., Scerif, G., and Ansari, D. (2003) "Double Dissociations in Developmental Disorders? Theoretically Misconceived, Empirically Dubious," *Cortex* 39: 161–3.

Laurence, S., and Margolis, E. (2001) "The Poverty of the Stimulus Argument," *British Journal for the Philosophy of Science* 52: 217–76.

Leslie, A. (1994) "ToMM, ToBY, and Agency: Core Architecture and Domain Specificity," in L. Hirschfeld and S. Gelman (eds), *Mapping the Mind*, Cambridge: Cambridge University Press, pp. 119–48.

Mameli, M., and Bateson, P. (2006) "Innateness and the Sciences," *Biology and Philosophy* 21, no. 2: 155–88.

Marcus, G. (2004) *The Birth of the Mind*, New York: Basic Books.
Mead, M. (1935) *Sex and Temperament in Three Primitive Societies*, New York: Morrow.
Newmeyer, F. (2005) *Possible and Probable Languages*, Oxford: Oxford University Press.
Onishi, K. H., and Baillargeon, R. (2005) "Do 15-Month-Old Infants Understand False Beliefs?" *Science* 308, no. 5719: 255–8.
Pereira, F. (2000) "Formal Grammar and Information Theory: Together Again?" *Philosophical Transactions of the Royal Society* A358: 1239–53.
Pinker, S. (1994) *The Language Instinct*, New York: William Morrow & Co.
—— (1999) *Words and Rules*, London: Weidenfeld & Nicolson.
Putnam, H. (1971) "The 'Innateness Hypothesis' and Explanatory Models in Linguistics," in J. Searle (ed.) *The Philosophy of Language*, London: Oxford University Press, pp. 130–9.
Samuels, R. (2002) "Nativism in Cognitive Science," *Mind and Language* 17, no. 3: 233–65.
—— (2007) "Is Innateness a Confused Concept?" in P. Carruthers, S. Laurence, and S. Stich (eds), *The Innate Mind: Foundations and the Future*, Oxford: Oxford University Press.
Scholl, B. J., and Leslie, A. M. (1999) "Modularity, Development and 'Theory of Mind,'" *Mind and Language* 14: 131–53.
Scott, D. (1995) *Recollection and Experience*, Cambridge: Cambridge University Press.
Segal, G. (2007) "Poverty of the Stimulus Arguments Concerning Language and Folk Psychology," in P. Carruthers, S. Laurence, and S. Stich (eds), *The Innate Mind: Foundations and the Future*, Oxford: Oxford University Press.
Simpson, T., Carruthers, P., Laurence, S., and Stich, S. (2005) "Introduction: Nativism Past and Present," in P. Carruthers, S. Laurence, and S. Stich (eds) *The Innate Mind: Structure and Contents*, Oxford: Oxford University Press.
Sterelny, K. (2003) *Thought in a Hostile World: The Evolution of Human Cognition*, Oxford: Blackwell.
Stich, S. (ed.) (1975) *Innate Ideas*, Berkeley: University of California Press.
Surian, L., Caldi, S., and Sperber, D. (2007) "Attribution of Beliefs by 13-Month-Old Infants," *Psychological Science* 18, no. 7: 580–6.
Tomasello, M. (2003) *Constructing a Language: A Usage-Based Theory of Language Acquisition*, Cambridge, MA: Harvard University Press.
—— (2004) "What Kind of Evidence Could Refute the UG Hypothesis?: Commentary on Wunderlich," *Studies in Language* 28, no. 3: 642–4.
Tooby, J., and Cosmides, L. (1992) "The Psychological Foundations of Culture," in J. Barkow, L. Cosmides, and J. Tooby (eds), *The Adapted Mind*, Oxford: Oxford University Press, 19–136.
van der Lely, H. K. J. (2005) "Domain-Specific Cognitive Systems: Insight From Grammatical Specific Language Impairment," *Trends in Cognitive Sciences* 9, no. 2, 53–9.
Waddington, C. H. (1940) *Organizers and Genes*, Cambridge: Cambridge University Press.

Further reading

For further reading, see J. Elman, E. Bates, M. Johnson, A. Karmillof-Smith, D. Parisi, and K. Plunkett, *Rethinking Innateness: A Connectionist Perspective on Development* (Cambridge, MA: MIT Press, 1996); S. Oyama, *The Ontogeny of Information* (Cambridge: Cambridge University Press, 1985); and R. Samuels, "Innateness and Cognitive Science," *Trends in Cognitive Sciences* 8, no. 3 (2004): 136–41.

20
MEMORY

Mark Rowlands

The concepts of memory

Wittgenstein once wrote, "If I say rightly, 'I remember it', the most different things can happen, and even merely this: that I say it" (1974: §131). Wittgenstein is drawing our attention to the heterogeneity of the category of memory, and the corresponding unlikelihood that the variegated phenomena we refer to with the term "memory" will be amenable to any unified explanatory model. Recent cognitive science acknowledges, indeed reinforces, this heterogeneity with the common tripartite distinction between *procedural*, *semantic*, and *episodic* memory.

Procedural memory is the mnemonic component of learned – as opposed to fixed – actions patterns: to have procedural memory is to remember *how* to do something that one has previously learned. For this reason, it is sometimes referred to as *knowing how* (Ryle 1949) or *habit memory* (Bergson 1908; Russell 1921). The most obvious examples of procedural memory are embodied skills such as riding a bicycle, playing the piano, or skiing. Procedural memory has nothing essentially to do with conscious recall of prior events: one can, in principle, know how to do something while having completely forgotten learning to do it.

Semantic memory is memory of facts (Tulving 1983). It is not immediately clear that this category is genuinely distinguishable from the category of *belief*. What is the difference between, for example, believing that Ouagadougou is the capital of Burkina Faso and remembering this fact? Beliefs are dispositional, rather than occurrent, items (Wittgenstein 1953: 59). Neither beliefs nor memories need be consciously recalled or apprehended by a subject in order to be possessed by that subject. Therefore it is difficult to avoid the conclusion that semantic memories are simply a subset of beliefs. Not all beliefs qualify as semantic memories. If I perceive that the cat is on the mat, and form the belief that the cat is on the mat on this basis, it would be very odd to claim that I remember that the cat is on the mat. However, all semantic memories do seem to be beliefs: the claim that I remember that *P* without believing that *P* seems to be contradictory. And the most obvious explanation of this is simply that to remember that *P* is the same thing as to believe that *P*.

Episodic memory, sometimes called "recollective memory" (Russell 1921), is a systematically ambiguous expression. Often it is used to denote memory of prior *episodes* in a subject's life (Tulving 1983, 1993, 1999; Campbell 1994, 1997). However, it is also sometimes taken to denote memory of prior *experiences* possessed by that subject. For example, Locke understood (episodic) memory as a power of the mind "to revive perceptions which it has once had, with this additional perception annexed to them, that it has had them before" (1975 [1690]: 150). In a similar vein, Brewer defines episodic memory as a reliving of one's phenomenal experience from a specific moment in their past, accompanied by a belief that the remembered episode was personally experienced by the individual in their past (1996: 60). The ambiguity embodied in the concept of episodic memory, then, is that between the episode experienced and the experience of the episode. This ambiguity is significant but can be accommodated in a sufficiently sophisticated account of episodic memory.

Suppose you fell out of a tree when you were eight years old. It is, let us suppose, a fact that you did so. However, when you recall this episode, it is not in the manner typical of recalling a fact – in the same way that you might recall that Ouagadougou is the capital of Burkina Faso. You do not recall it even in the manner you might recall personal facts about yourself – such as the fact that you were born on a certain date. You recall this episode in a certain distinctive manner. That is, you recall this past episode by way of certain experiences you had, or purport to have had, when the episode took place. You recall the episode of falling from the tree through, or by way of, the feelings of vertiginous terror you experienced, or take yourself to have experienced, during that episode. In particular, you experience the episode as something that happened to you, or as an event otherwise presented to you in some specific experiential way (for example, you can remember the episode of someone else falling out of a tree).

In short, that episodic memory involves recall of past episodes is not, by itself, sufficient to distinguish it from semantic memory – for these episodes can also be understood as a species of fact. What is distinctive of episodic memory is the way in which facts are presented: they are presented by way of experiences. And these experiences, in turn, are presented as ones that the subject had at the time of the episode. It is this sort of *structured double* mode of presentation that seems to essentially characterize episodic remembering. In such remembering, episodes are presented via experiences, and these experiences are presented – rightly or wrongly – as ones that occurred at the time of the episode. The defining characteristic of episodic memory, therefore, is its *mode of presentation* of facts. In veridical episodic memory, we remember both the episode and the experience. What is crucial is that we remember the episode via the experience: by the way the experience presents the episode and the way the experience that presents the episode is in turn presented.

This has one clear and important entailment: the distinction between episodic and semantic memory is one of degree not kind. What would the memory of your falling out of the tree amount to if it were not presented by way of experiences that are themselves presented as occurring at the time of the episode? It would, it seems, amount to little more than the apprehension of the fact that you fell out of tree at some point in the past – akin to remembering that you were born on a certain date. Generally, episodic memory would be gradually transformed into semantic memory if its specific and concrete experiential content becomes sufficiently abstract and attenuated that its situational specificity is lost (Rowlands 1999: 126). If this is correct, then the common claim that semantic memory is found only in humans (Donald 1991: 152) might be difficult to sustain.

Procedural memory is a sub-species of knowledge. Semantic memory is a sub-species of belief. To the extent that memory engenders a specific and distinctive set of philosophical and scientific issues, these turn on the core concept of episodic memory – even though this is a *range* rather than *rigid* concept. Accordingly, this paper will focus primarily on this latter form of memory.

Normativity and representation

In its everyday deployment, "memory" is not always used as a success term. We might speak of someone "remembering" being abused by their father, even though we know these "memories" are, in fact, false ones. However, in both philosophical and scientific contexts, it is more usual to find the term "memory" employed in a success-dependent manner: false memories are not, in fact memories at all. When it is used in this way, the expression "episodic memory" denotes a clearly *normative* concept. A claim of episodic memory makes a normative claim about the way the world once was. If I remember falling out of a tree when I was eight years old, then the world *should*, tenselessly, be such that it contains an episode of me falling out of the tree when I was eight. If it does not, then something has gone wrong, and my memory is not a real memory at all. In this, episodic memory is similar to belief in one way and dissimilar in another. Beliefs also make normative claims: claims about the way the world should be. However, failure of the world to be this way is not, in general, regarded as sufficient to disqualify the belief as a belief.

There is a familiar explanatory apparatus that is used to account for the normativity of states such as this, the apparatus of *mental representations*. The core idea of mental representation is of a state, *R*, that *stands in* or *goes proxy* for another distinct state or circumstance, and that can, in virtue of this, be used to guide a subject in the absence of that state or circumstance (Haugeland 1991). Crucial to understanding the idea of representation is understanding the relation between *R* and the state for which it goes proxy in virtue of which *R* can be *about* that state or have that state as its *content*.

The idea of an episodic memory as a *trace* of the episode of which it is a memory conforms to this general schema quite closely. The key to understanding the putative role of representation in memory is, therefore, to understand the relation between the memory trace and what it represents in virtue of which it represents it. Sometimes, the connection is understood in *causal* terms: an episodic memory trace is a memory of an episode in virtue of its being caused, in an appropriate way, by that episode. However, while causal relations are *arguably* necessary for representation, they are notoriously insufficient.

Teleological approaches to representation are designed, in part, with the failure of causal approaches in mind. On a teleological approach, the idea would be that the memory trace has the *proper function* of tracking the episode that produced it, and it is in virtue of this function that it is about that episode or takes that episode as its content (Millikan 1984, 1993; Dretske 1986). There are, however, unresolved problems with this approach. Nevertheless, the attractions of the appeal to memory traces as representational items are obvious ones: they locate the problem of accounting for the normativity of memory in terms of a framework – a familiar and reasonably well-understood framework – that seeks to account for the normativity, and other characteristic features of representation more generally.

The representational account of memory has met with vociferous dissent on several fronts. Some of this dissent is clearly based on a misunderstanding of what the representational model does and does not entail. One popular objection to the representational account is based on the mistaken assumption that the account is committed to the claim that, in episodically remembering an experience, we are directly aware only of the memory trace – the representation of the experience – and only indirectly aware of the experience itself. That is, according to this objection, the representational account is committed to the claim that our awareness of our past experiences is always mediated by way of our awareness of a representation of those experiences. Thus, Reid objects to the memory trace model on the grounds that (episodic) memory is "an immediate awareness of something past" (1849 [1785]: 357). This sort of objection was also advanced by Gibson (1979: 223).

However, the representational model is not committed to this idea: it can accept that our awareness of past experiential episodes is direct and unmediated by way of our awareness of a representation. There are two quite different ways of thinking about a representation. One is to think of it as an item *of* which we are aware in the having of an experience. Someone who thinks of representations as akin to consciously entertained mental images, for example, is going to think of mental representations in this way. Thus, on a mediational account of perception, in having a visual experience of a dog, I am directly aware of a mental image and indirectly aware – via, say, a process of inference – of the dog itself. The corresponding account of memory would claim that in episodically remembering an experienced episode, I am aware of my representation of the episode, and from this I infer the presence of the original episode.

However, this is not the only way of thinking about representations. It is also possible to regard them not as items *of* which we are aware, but as items *in virtue of* which we are aware. Thus, in having a visual experience of a dog, I am aware of the dog, and I am aware of the dog in virtue of having a representation of it. Similarly, it is possible to hold that the memory trace is that in virtue of which I can become aware of my past experiences, and is so without my being aware of the trace itself. This way of thinking about representations lends itself far more naturally to the idea that representations are brain states rather than conscious items – since it is implausible to suppose that we are aware of such states in the process of remembering. However, it is also possible to think of representations as mental items – indeed, conscious mental items – that make us aware of things outside them without supposing that we are aware of the representations themselves (Rowlands 2001).

However, while some objections to the representational account are clearly misguided, some are altogether more serious.

Realism and constructivism

The representational account of episodic memory is a *realist* account in two senses. First, it is realist about the past: it assumed that at some point in the past, episodes of certain sorts occurred. This is a necessary feature of the representational account. Its goal is to explain memory in terms of the representation of the past. It cannot, therefore, attempt to explain the past in terms of our representations of it. Second, it is realist about the possibility of representation of the past. This is not to claim, of course, that episodic memory is infallible. But it is to claim that it is *possible*. If our memories are functioning correctly, and the environmental circumstances are appropriately benign, then it is, in principle, possible to accurately remember past experiential episodes.

One can be a *constructivist* about memory in two corresponding ways. On the one hand, one might be an antirealist about the past in general – seeing it as, in one way or another, a construction of human retrospective states. On the other hand, one might be a sceptic not about the past but about the possibility of accurate recall of past experiential episodes. If such recall is not, in general possible, then there is little point inventing an apparatus of representations whose function is to underwrite this recall. Therefore, the starting point for this second, and more interesting, form of constructivism lies in the transience and unreliability of episodic memory.

Schachter claims that, "a variety of conditions exist in which subjectively compelling memories are grossly inaccurate" (1995: 22). More generally, cognitive and developmental psychologists have now reached a broad, but significant, consensus that episodic remembering is to a considerable extent a constructive process (Sutton 2003: 9). This claim, however, suffers from the systematic ambiguity we have already identified in the concept of episodic memory. Inaccuracy in episodic memory might pertain to the experience of remembered episodes, or it might pertain to the episodes themselves.

With regard to the latter possibility, there is little reason for supposing that episodic memories are *systematically* false, inaccurate, or otherwise misleading – although, obviously, they may be so in particular cases. In general, episodic memory should not be understood as a reporting of episodes that never took place. Rather, on its most sensible interpretation, the expression "constructive remembering" designates the way in which memories can re-organize, embellish, and transform the original experienced episodes. Here, we should bear in mind the distinction we introduced earlier between the *episode* experienced and the *mode of presentation* of that episode. The constructivist account of remembering applies most naturally, and plausibly, to the experiences that provide the mode of presentation of the remembered episode.

For example, in fairly quotidian forms of episodic remembering, most people can *switch perspectives* (Sutton 2003: 9). You can remember yourself falling from the tree when you were eight years old. But you can also alter your perspective, and apparently remember yourself as you must have looked to others during your fall. In this sort of case, you may well be accurately remembering the episode itself – you did indeed fall from the tree, and in the manner at least roughly specified in the experiences.

However, you do not accurately remember the experiences that presented the episode in its occurrence. You seem to be remembering visual experiences that you could not have had – assuming it was indeed you who fell from the tree. Therefore it could be argued, the principal evidence for the constructive character of remembering pertains largely, perhaps exclusively, to the experiences that provide the modes of presentation for the factual episodes remembered in cases of episodic memory.

Then, the obvious question is this: what are the mechanisms that allow the same remembered episodes to be designated, or picked out, by different, and perhaps wildly divergent, modes of experiential presentation? One plausible account is provided by *connectionist* or *neural network* models of memory.

Distributed memory

The idea that episodic remembering is, at least in part, a constructive process, sits uncomfortably with a certain conception of the memory trace. The conception in question is that of the trace as a stable, static structure, causally produced by the original experiences, and stored in the brain in a manner that is fixed and independent of current environmental circumstances that might occasion its activation. However, commitment to memory traces itself does not commit one to this conception of their nature. Connectionist, or neural network, models of memory seem to capture the more flexible and dynamic understanding of memory traces required to accommodate constructivist pressure.

Neural network approaches to modelling episodic remembering understand this process as the temporary reactivation of a particular pattern or vector of activity across the nodes of a neural network. This reactivation is a function of the interaction between current input to the network, and certain dispositions to propagate patterns of activation laid down in the network's history – these dispositions being realized in the patterns of connectivity and connection weights obtaining between individual nodes. According to such models, memory traces of prior experiences are not stored statically, but are *superposed* in the relevant set of weights. Thus, in a classic statement of the position, Rumelhard et al. (1986: 193) write,

> We see the traces laid down by the processing of each input as contributing to the composite, superimposed memory representation. Each time a stimulus is processed, it gives rise to a slightly different memory trace – either because the item itself is different or because it occurs in a different context that conditions its representation – the traces are not kept separate. Each trace contributes to the composite, but the characteristics of particular experiences tend nevertheless to be preserved, at least until they are overridden by cancelling characteristics of other traces.

On this kind of model, remembering does not consist in the retrieval of a discrete and fixed stored symbol. Rather, it consists in the completion, or filling in, of a pattern of activation, where this process occurs on the basis of a particular input. Crucially, this input can be incomplete, can vary over time, and can even be severely distorted. This allows us to understand the mechanism that allows the same experienced episode to be picked out by significantly divergent experiential modes of presentation. However, this superposition model of memory does engender problems of its own. Most notably, the model has a clear and important entailment. In this model, data that has been previously processed persist not as stored symbols, but only implicitly, as connection weights and resulting dispositions. Thus, within the network itself, there is no *essential* difference between *reconstructing* a previous state and *constructing* a new one (Bechtel and Abrahamsen 1991: 64; McClelland 1995: 69–70). Thus, when the superposition model is applied to remembering, it seems to entail there is no essential difference between memory and fantasy.

The problem is not simply one of accounting for *truth* in memory – it goes deeper than that. The problem is one of accounting for the *normativity* of memory – for the *possibility* both of its truth and falsity. Thus, one can agree with Sutton (2003: 11), that "experienced sedimentations of memory in the body, and of emotion in memories, make it blindly obvious that the real past, for all its occasional obscurity and its opacity to conscious or complete capture, does affect the present." However, the issue is not simply whether the real past does affect the present, but whether it affects it in the *right* way, that is, in such a way that respects the normative claims memory makes on the world. The root of the problem, once again, is the gap between causation and normativity.

Connectionist models have a simple way of getting around this problem: they employ what are known as *supervised learning rules*. These rules function by giving the network explicit feedback in response to its output as its weights are adjusted. However, while supervised learning obviously plays an important role in human cognitive development, we cannot, of course, rely on it to supply a general solution to the problem of accounting for truth in memory. This is because we cannot, in general, compare our current memories with some independent version of the past.

Embedded and extended memory

This problem is, in fact, an instance of a more general problem for neural network models of cognition. Neural networks are very good at modelling some types of cognitive process – essentially, processes (for example, facial recognition) that reduce quickly and easily to some form of pattern-mapping operation. However, they are far less successful at modelling other types of cognitive process, including formal and informal reasoning, and the processes involved in speaking and understanding language. The root of the problem in these cases seems to be that the processes must adhere to a certain kind of *structure*, and so possess a certain kind of *stability*, that the dynamic and transient patterns of activity embodied in a neural net seem ill-equipped to accommodate.

One type of response to this problem is particularly pertinent to the case of memory. Instead of attempting to get the neural network to model the relevant kind of structure and so reproduce the relevant sort of stability, we instead try to give it the means for *utilizing* stable, structured items in the world around it. That is, in these sorts of problematic cases, the goal is to *embed* neural networks in a wider environment that contains the sorts of stable and structured items that the network was initially being required to model. The goal of the network is, then, not to model these structures directly, but to learn how to use these structures to facilitate achievement of its tasks.

Thus, at least some of the problems endemic to neural networks might, it is argued, be overcome by suitably embedding them in wider, structured environments. In the case of human memory, by far the most important external structure would be *language*. This general theme has been developed, in slightly different ways, by Luria and Vygotsky (1992), Donald (1991), and Rowlands (1999). The core idea is that language – most obviously, but not exclusively, in its written forms – is an external information-bearing structure to which a subject can "plug in." In a classic development of the position, Luria and Vygotsky point to the differences in the information-processing tasks facing, on the one hand, an African envoy who has to remember word-for-word the message of his tribal chief and, on the other, the Peruvian *kvinu* officer, who can tap into a potentially unlimited supply of information by learning the code or language of *kvinus* – conventional knots used to represent important information of state (taxes, the state of the army, etc.). The *kvinu* officer simply needs to learn the code, and this can allow him to use and interpret an unlimited number of messages. The envoy, on the other hand, must redeploy his memory resources each time a new message is given to him. In this way, embedding in an appropriate environment can be used to reduce the internal information-processing task facing the subject.

The idea is that external information-bearing structures – of which human language is perhaps the best and most sophisticated example – might play a role in memory processing akin to that played by supervised learning rules in neural networks. That is, language can be used to provide a version of the past that is sufficiently objective and independent of present episodic recall to mitigate the transformative impact of that recall. By plugging into the language that exists in its environment, a subject can tap into a store of facts that are subject to standards of conventional acceptance or rejection. Their content is, to this extent, less dependent on the vicissitudes of individual episodic recall.

Three further points are worth noting. First, the role of environmental embedding is not, necessarily, restricted to semantic memory. Language is, of course, a repository of (statements of) facts (among many other things). And our ability to access these facts at will – once we have learned the "code" that allows us to do so – can therefore enhance our semantic memory capacities. But the implications of this for episodic memory are unclear. Luria and Vygotsky (1992) claim to have traced a gradual withering away, or vestigialization, of episodic memory, as the members of modern literate cultures come to rely more and more in their memory tasks on external storage of facts (see Rowlands 2003: 134). However, if the difference between semantic and episodic memory is best thought of as one of degree, not kind, then this general picture of the inverse effect of environmental embedding on semantic and episodic memory may be too simplistic.

Second, the most obvious way in which language can be an external information store is when it is written down. However, in this respect at least, the difference between written and spoken language is one of degree, not kind. Spoken linguistic forms, no less than written ones, are external to subjects, and carry information. Moreover, they can be employed by subjects to reduce the amount of internal information processing required in the performance of a memory task (Rubin 1995; Rowlands 1999). The difference between written and spoken linguistic forms is one of relative permanence. While this is important, it does not point to any difference of *kind* between the role played by written and spoken language in the facilitation of memory tasks – particularly when token utterances can be reiterated an indefinite number of times. This underlines the importance of the role played by *narrative rehearsal* and *revisiting* – both verbal *and* mental – in the constitution of memory.

Finally, studying the way in which cognitive processes can be *embedded* in appropriately structured environments constitutes one of the most interesting areas of current research in cognitive science. Some have gone further, and argued that cognitive processes are literally *constituted*, in part, by processes of deploying, manipulating, and exploiting relevant structures in the *world* (Clark 1997; Clark and Chalmers 1998; Hurley 1998; Rowlands 1999, 2003; Wilson 2004). If this thesis of the *extended mind* or *vehicle externalism* is true, then remembering is not just a process that a subject achieves in his or her head. Equally fundamentally, it is a process that a subject achieves in his or her world.

References

Bechtel, W., and Abrahamsen, A. (1991) *Connectionism and the Mind*, Oxford: Blackwell.

Bergson, H. (1908) *Matter and Memory*, trans. N. M. Paul and W. S. Palmer, New York: Zone Books.

Brewer, W. (1996) "What Is Recollective Memory?" in D. C. Rubin (ed.), *Remembering Our Past*, Cambridge: Cambridge University Press, 19–66.

Campbell, J. (1994) *Past, Space, and Self*, Cambridge, MA: MIT Press.

—— (1997) "The Structure of Time in Autobiographical Memory," *European Journal of Philosophy* 5: 105–18.

Clark, A. (1997) *Being-There: Putting Brain Body and World Back Together Again*, Cambridge, MA: MIT Press.

Clark, A., and Chalmers, D. (1998) "The Extended Mind," *Analysis* 58: 7–19.

Donald, M. (1991) *Origins of the Modern Mind*, Cambridge, MA: Harvard University Press.

Dretske, F. (1986) "Misrepresentation," in R. J. Bogdan (ed.), *Belief*, Oxford: Oxford University Press, pp. 17–36.

Gibson, J. (1979) *The Ecological Approach to Visual Perception*, Boston: Houghton-Mifflin.

Haugeland, J. (1991) "Representational Genera," in S. Stich, D. Rumelhart, and W. Ramsey (eds) *Philosophy and Connectionist Theory*, Hillsdale, NJ: Erlbaum, pp. 61–89.

Hurley, S. (1998) *Consciousness in Action*, Cambridge, MA: Harvard University Press.

Locke, J. (1975 [1690]) *An Essay Concerning Human Understanding*, ed. P. H. Nidditch, Oxford: Oxford University Press.

Luria, A., and Vygotsky, L. (1992) *Ape, Primitive Man, and Child*, Cambridge, MA: MIT Press.

McClelland, J. (1995) "Constructive Memory and Memory Distortions: A Parallel Distributed Processing Account," in D. L. Schachter (ed.), *Memory Distortion: How Minds, Brains and Societies Reconstruct the Past*, Cambridge, MA: Harvard University Press, pp. 69–90.

Millikan, R. (1984) *Language, Thought and other Biological Categories*, Cambridge, MA: MIT Press.

—— (1993) *White Queen Psychology, and Other Essays for Alice*, Cambridge, MA: MIT Press.

Reid, T. (1849 [1785]) *Essays on the Intellectual Powers of Man* in *The Works of Thomas Reid*, ed. W. Hamilton, Edinburgh: McLachlan, Stewart and Co.

Rowlands, M. (1999) *The Body in Mind: Understanding Cognitive Processes*, Cambridge: Cambridge University Press.

—— (2001) *The Nature of Consciousness*, Cambridge, MA: Cambridge University Press.

—— (2003) *Externalism*, Chesham, UK: Acumen.

Rubin, D. (1995) *Remembering in Oral Traditions*, Oxford: Oxford University Press.

Rumelhart, D., McClelland, J., and PDP Research Group (1985) *Parallel Distributed Processing: Explorations in the Microstructure of Cognition*, vol. 1: *Foundations*, Cambridge, MA: MIT Press.

Russell, B. (1921) *The Analysis of Mind*, London: Allen & Unwin.

Ryle, G. (1949) *The Concept of Mind*, London: Penguin.

Schachter, D. L. (1995) "Memory Distortion: History and Current Status," in D. L. Schachter (ed.), *Memory Distortion: How Minds, Brains and Societies Reconstruct the Past*, Cambridge, MA; Harvard University Press, pp. 1–43.

Sutton, J. (2003) "Memory," in Edward N. Zalta (ed.), *The Stanford Encyclopedia of Philosophy*; available: http://plato.stanford.edu

Tulving, E. (1983) *Elements of Episodic Memory*, Oxford: Oxford University Press.

—— (1993) "What Is Episodic Memory?" *Current Directions in Psychological Science* 2: 67–70.

—— (1999) "Episodic versus Semantic Memory," in R. A. Wilson and F. C. Keil (eds), *The MIT Encyclopaedia of the Cognitive Sciences*, Cambridge, MA: MIT Press.

Wilson, R. (2004) *Boundaries of the Mind: The Individual in the Fragile Sciences*, Cambridge: Cambridge University Press.

Wittgenstein, L. (1953) *Philosophical Investigations*, Oxford: Blackwell.

—— (1974) *Remarks on the Philosophy of Psychology*, vol. 1, ed. G. E. M. Anscombe and G. H. von Wright; trans. C. G. Luckhardt and M. A. E. Aue, Oxford: Blackwell.

21
INTERACTIVISM

Mark H. Bickhard

The historical core of interactivism is a model of the nature of representing and representation. This model differs from alternatives in at least two interrelated ways: (1) it offers a dynamic, pragmatic, future-oriented, model of representation, in contrast to most alternatives, with far-ranging consequences for phenomena that involve representation, such as perception, language, rationality, learning, memory, motivation, emotions, consciousness, and sociality; and (2) it involves assumptions and positions regarding underlying metaphysical issues, such as normativity, emergence, process metaphysics, and naturalism, that also have ramified consequences and deep historical roots. I will focus, in this chapter, primarily on the model of representation.

Primitive representation

The evolution of complex animals required solving a general problem for agents: agents interact with their worlds, and agents must therefore select which interactions to engage in. I argue that representing, and later representations, emerged in the solutions to this problem. In simple animals (inter)action selection could be itself relatively simple, such as a triggering of action upon detection of sufficient triggering conditions. A bacterium that finds itself swimming down a sugar gradient, for example, will trigger tumbling for a moment in place of swimming; if it is swimming up a sugar gradient, it will tend to keep swimming. In more complex agents, however, the task of interaction selection begins to split into two related parts: (1) indications of what interactions are currently possible; and (2) selection among those possible of the "best" interaction relative to current goals and other internal states. A frog, for example, might have two flies that it could flick its tongue at in an attempt to eat, also a worm, and still further the shadow of a hawk flying overhead that invites jumping into the water. The frog must select among multiple possibilities, and it must keep some ongoing functional account of what those possibilities are. According to the interactivist model, representation originates in such indications of interaction possibilities, and the shift from triggering to selection among possibilities begins the evolution toward more complex (and more familiar) kinds of representation.[1]

Intentionality

Even in these simple versions, however, we have the emergence of a primitive intentionality: truth value and aboutness. Indications that some (type of) interaction is possible in the current situation might be true or might be false. Such an indication is a kind of dynamic predication concerning the current situation: this is one of those situations in which this (type of) interaction is possible. That dynamic predication can be true of the current situation or it can be false: this is one aspect of the emergence of truth value. Furthermore, if an indicated interaction is engaged and fails to proceed as indicated, it is not only false, it is falsified for the organism itself. Such system- (organism-) detectable error is of central importance, and will be addressed again later.

Some situations will realize conditions sufficient for an interaction type to proceed as "anticipated," and some will not. Some sufficient set of such interaction-supporting conditions is presupposed about the current situation in any indication that the interaction type is possible in that situation. The predication that an interaction type is possible in a situation constitutes a predication that some set of sufficient conditions hold in that situation. These sufficient conditions are presupposed. They are implicit, not explicit. They are the *content* that is presupposed *about* the situation, about the current environment.[2] They constitute what is true about the environment if the interaction-indication is correct.[3]

More complex representation

Resources

Functional indications of interaction potentialities possess two crucial characteristics of intentionality, but they don't look much like familiar representations. Nevertheless, we already have the beginnings of the resources that account for more complex representation and for the evolution of such more complex representation. The first part of these resources is the split already mentioned between indications of interaction potentialities and selections between such potentialities. In particular, the frog example is, among other things, an example of the sense in which interactive potentialities can branch into multiple possibilities.

The next resource arises from the point that the setting up of such indications requires that the organism have appropriate sensitivities to the environment, that the organism be able to differentiate environments in which it is appropriate to set up various interaction potentiality indications from environments in which it is not appropriate. That is, setting up interaction indications must be conditional.

Differentiation

Such conditions most generally arise in interactive differentiations: an interaction with the environment will proceed in part in accordance with the functional organization of the system engaging in the interaction, and in part in accordance with the environment being interacted with. Internal flows of such interaction, therefore, including culminating internal states of such interactions, can serve to differentiate types of environments from each other. If the interaction yields internal outcome A, say, rather than B, then the organism is in an A-type environment. Note that there is nothing in such an interaction to represent what constitutes an A-type environment: it is simply differentiated from B-types (and perhaps other possibilities). But the organism may learn, or have already innate, that A-type environments are a kind of environment in which it is possible to flick one's tongue a certain way and eat, while B-type environments permit, perhaps, a different sort of tongue flicking and eating. The outcomes of past interactions, then, serve the differentiating function that is necessary to successfully set up further indications of interactive potentiality. Whatever kinds of environments that happen to yield internal outcomes of A will, in this scenario, evoke indications of particular sorts of tongue flicking, and eating. For the frog, those kinds of environments will, hopefully, mostly be those that contain a fly with a certain position and direction. Note, however, that this requirement that A-type environments be fly-in-certain-circumstances environments is *factual* requirement on the frog's success. It is not something that the frog needs to able to represent for itself. So long as the conditions for setting up tongue flicking indications are *factually* appropriately sensitive to actual environments, the frog can survive. More will be said about such differentiations later; for now, what is crucial is the recognition that interaction indications are *conditional*.

Furthermore, those conditionalities are present even if the conditions per se are not satisfied. It is a property of the way in which the frog functions that, if a differentiation *were* to yield an A internal outcome, then an indication of the potentiality of tongue flicking and eating *would* be set up. And this conditionality is a fact about the functional organization of the frog, even when there is no support for an A-type differentiation present.

Indications of interaction potentialities, then, can branch and they are conditional. Their conditionality yields the possibility, if the organism is sufficiently complex in the right kinds of ways, that interaction indications can iterate. They can iterate in the sense that one interaction may yield the conditions under which another potentiality becomes indicated. Interaction X may yield the possibility for interaction Y, which, in turn, may yield the possibility of interaction Z.

Situation knowledge and apperception

In more complex organisms, such indications may branch and iterate into vast webs of organizations of conditional indications of interactive potentiality. This web is the basic resource for complex representation. Such a web constitutes the organism's *situation knowledge*: knowledge of the potentialities constituting the current situation. A web of any complexity will of necessity be ongoingly changing, due to processes in the environment, new interactions and differentiations, and just from the passage of time: the environment is not, in general, static. The processes of creating, maintaining, and updating situation knowledge are those of *apperception*.

Objects

As an example of how a situation knowledge web can account for more familiar forms of representation, consider a child's toy block. The block offers many interactive potentialities, of visual scans, manipulations, dropping, and so on, that can form a sub-web within the overall situation knowledge. These potentialities, furthermore, are all reachable from each other: e.g., any visual scan is reachable from any other via, perhaps, one or more intermediate manipulations of the block to bring the side into view. Still further, this sub-web of internally mutually reachable interactive potentialities is invariant under a large class of other interactions and changes that can take place. If the child leaves the room, or puts the block in the toy box, the sub-web is still reachable via the requisite intermediaries of going back into the room or opening the toy box. It is not invariant under all possible changes, however: crushing or burning the block destroys the interactive possibilities. In this general manner, the situation knowledge web can account for representations of manipulable objects.[4] Other complex representations, such as concepts, particulars, ideals, and so on, can similarly be modeled within situation knowledge.[5]

Some properties of representation

The interactivist model of representation can account for the emergence of truth value, content, and complex representations, such as of objects. There are a number of additional properties that follow from the interactivist account, some familiar, but some less familiar.

Embodiment

Recent discussions have emphasized several properties that follow directly from the interactivist model. Representation, on this account, is inherently embodied: only an embodied agent can interact with its environment. It is naturally situated in that environment, and its orientations to the environment are inherently indexical and deictic, with reference to the agent's possible actions and orientations.

Implicitness and modality

The implicitness of content has already been mentioned. This is in strong contrast to most models, for which content must be explicit if the representation is to exist at all. Another related property is that interactive content is inherently modal: it is of interaction *potentialities*. This is in contrast to focusing on representations of past or present actualities, with modality, if addressed at all, being added on with ad-hoc supplement.

Evolutionary epistemology

An action or interaction-based model forces a constructivism. It may be tempting to consider that representations are impressed into a passive mind like a signet ring into wax, or light transduced into unconscious propositions, or longer term inductive scratchings into the wax of the mind. But, if representation is in fact emergent in *interaction* systems, there is no temptation to assume that the environment can impress a competent interactive organization into a passive mind. Representation must be constructed.

Furthermore, if such constructions are not prescient, then they must be tried out, and selected out if they fail. There must be a variation and selection process: the interactive model forces an *evolutionary epistemology*.

In more complex organisms, this constructivism will be recursive in the sense that future constructions can make use of past constructions as units or foci of variation. In humans, at least, the processes of construction, not just what is constructed – learning and development – are themselves (recursively) constructed. Learning is the constructive process *per se*, while, for any recursive constructivism, the resources of past constructions introduce a historicity (and hysteresis) into possible trajectories of further construction that constitutes developmental constraints and enablings.

Emergent

Still further, representation is *emergent* in the constructions of interactive organization. Interactive organization that involves anticipations of what is or would be possible under indicated differentiation conditions constitutes representation, but it is constructed out of functional, control system organization that is not itself representational. Representation is emergent out of nonrepresentational phenomena.

Recognizing the possibility of emergent representation eliminates arguments for the *necessity* of innateness (such arguments fail anyway in that, if evolution can create representation, there is no argument offered why learning and development could not similarly create emergent representation). Further, if representation is emergent, the possibility is opened of ongoing nonrepresentational mental dynamics out of which representations emerge as a kind of generative foam, perhaps most of which fade out of existence, but some of which – those that are supported by or satisfy other considerations, perhaps – are stabilized sufficiently to participate in and influence further processes of thought. Such a dynamic of representationally emergent constraint satisfaction is utterly contrary to anything in the current literature, and yet fits the phenomenology of thought much better than alternatives.[6]

What about input processing?

The interactive, future-oriented modal character of representation, according to the interactive model, is diametrically opposite to standard models, which construe, for example, perception as beginning with the encoding of sensory inputs. Indeed, every introductory text in physiological psychology contains multiple chapters on "sensory encoding." It would seem to be the case, then, that at least some basic representation is not of the interactive kind. If that is *not* so – if all representation *is* interactive in nature – then the question arises of how the phenomena of, for example, frequency and line encoding discussed in such texts can be accounted for within the interactive framework?

The basis for the answer to this question has already been introduced. All agents must have differentiating contact with their environments in order to be able to appropriately set up indications of further interaction potentialities. Such differentiations are, in their most general form, full interactions in which the internal flow of the interactions and the internal outcomes of the interactions serve to differentiate types of environments encountered in those interactions. In general, *any* interaction that has concluded – that has already happened – can serve as the basis for such differentiation and, therefore, for apperception regarding situation knowledge. A limit case of such differentiating interaction, however, is that with null outputs: pure passive input processing. An input processing "interaction" can serve to differentiate in virtue of its internal outcome just as well as a full interaction. And it is such passive input processing differentiations that are called sensory encoding when they take place in physiologically specialized neural subsystems.

Sensory "encoding," then, is the input aspect of interactions that differentiate environments: frequency and line differences are differentiators. They constitute the necessary *contact* with the environment for appropriate orientation to the future. They do not, however – contrary to standard interpretation and to the standard meaning of "encoding" – constitute representations of what they differentiate. They do not constitute *content*.[7]

Contact and content

This distinction between contact and content is not familiar. It is not familiar because most models, especially information semantics and related approaches, equate the two. Whatever the differentiating contact is in fact with in the environment is taken to be what is represented by the differentiating internal states and processes. The (factual) *contact* is taken to be the (normative) *content* of the differentiating internal phenomena: the differentiation is taken to be a representation. This is one of the powerful sources, especially regarding perception, for the intuitions underlying standard models of representation. The assumption is made that a differentiating contact *encodes* what the contact is with.

Troubles with encodingism

Versions of this assumption are so common that I have come to call the assumption that all representation is encoding *encodingism*. The point is not that encodings do not exist, but that, when examined carefully, encodings are always and necessarily derivative representations – they are always stand-ins for already available representations.

Encodings, therefore, cannot serve any primary epistemic functions: they cannot be the ground of, for example, perception.

Consider "..." encoding *s* in Morse code. That encoding relationship certainly exists, and it is quite useful in that, e.g., "..." can be sent over telegraph wires while *s* cannot. But the encoding relation only exists for those who already represent the dot patterns, the characters, and the relationships among them. All relevant representations must already exist and be available in order for the encoding relation to exist. The encoding changes the form of representation by standing-in for some other representation, and such changes in form and other forms of stand-in can be useful, but encodings do not provide new representation.

If the conventionality of this example is troubling, consider the sense in which the neutrino count in some mine encodes properties of fusion processes in the sun. Here the encoding relationship is based on strictly natural phenomena and relations among them, but it is still the case that such encoding relationship itself exists only for those who already represent the neutrino-count process, the fusion process, and the relationships between them. Again, a natural information-based encoding relationship can enable our coming to know more about fusion in the sun without having to directly access that fusion, but it can do so only for those who already have all of the relevant representations.

In general, representation is held to be constituted by some favored special kind of relationship between the representation and that which it represents. This might be an informational relationship (in the strictly factual sense of co-variation, for example), or a causal relationship, or a nomological relationship, or a structural relationship. The favored kind of relationship is taken to constitute an encoding representational relationship. There is a large family of problems with any such approach – I will outline a few of them, but focus on one in particular.

Unbounded correspondences

For any particular instance of any one of these kinds of relationships, there are an unbounded number of additional instances, and it is not clear which one is to be taken as the "representational" instance. A causal relationship between activities in the retina and a table, for example, is accompanied by causal relationships with the light, with the quantum activities in the surface of the table, with the table a minute ago, with the trees out of which the table was constructed, with the fusion processes in the sun that fueled those trees, and so on, extending back several billion years. Which one is representational? And how does the organism determine which one is representational? And, however, it might be determined, how does the organism represent the favored one – clearly the relational instance per se cannot suffice, because it is at minimum ambiguous within an unbounded set. As before, the organism has to already have the crucial representation(s) in order for any kind of encoding to exist for that organism.

The copy argument

Piaget has an argument against any copy model of representation that provides a different aspect of these circularities: if our representations of the world are copies of the world, we would have to already know how the world is in order to construct our copies of it. Similarly, if we have an internal state or process that is in an informational relationship with something in the world, how does the organism determine that this state or process is in *any* informational relationship, and how does the organism determine what those informational relationships are with (there will be an unbounded number of them), how does the organism determine which of those is the "representational" instance, and how does the organism determine what that particular informational relationship is with? The same circularity as before.

Stand-ins

Because encodings are stand-ins, they cannot generate emergent representation – they must borrow their representational content. So, if *all* representations were encodings, then there would be nothing to borrow content from, so no representations could exist at all. Representation did not exist a dozen or more billions year ago, and it does now, so representation has to have emerged. Any model that renders such emergence impossible is thereby refuted. So, if arguments for innatism, for example, on the basis that it is not possible for learning or development to generate emergent new representations were *a priori* sound, then representation would simply be impossible.

Representational error

A crucial problem that highlights the confounding of representational models by normative considerations is that of accounting for the possibility of representational error. If the favored representation-constituting relationship exists, then the representation exists, and it is correct. But if the favored representation-constituting relationship does not exist, then the representation does not exist. Unfortunately, there is a third possibility that must be accounted for, but there are no remaining resources to deploy in any such account: the possibility is that of the representation existing but being false. There has been a minor industry in the literature for a couple of decades attempting to address this problem, but without success. At best, they can account for some external observer of the organism and its environment, who somehow knows what the organism's internal states are supposed to represent (knows their content), and can compare that with the "real" world to determine if the content fits the actual represented. In general, they don't accomplish even this much, but, even if they did, this account would leave the representations of the external observer unaccounted for – the external observer's representations have to be capable of truth and falsity too.

System-detectable representational error

There is an even stronger version of the error problem that is simply not addressed at all in the literature: the possibility of system-, or organism-, detectable error – that is, not just error in some God's eye view, but error that can be detected by the organism itself. This may at first seem to be not directly relevant – perhaps too strong a criterion that should be postponed 'till further progress has been made. But, if organism-detectable error is not possible, then error-guided behavior and learning are not possible. We know that error-guided behavior and learning occur, so any model that cannot account for system-detectable error is thereby refuted.

Furthermore, the problem of system-detectable error is the core of the radical skeptical argument: you cannot determine the correctness or incorrectness of your own representations, so the argument goes, because you would have to step outside of yourself (become your own external observer) to compare your representations with the actual world, and you cannot do that. This argument has been around for a very long time and has remained unrefuted to the point that it is most often ignored as unsolvable, so why bother. But, again, there has to be something wrong with the argument, because, if its conclusion were correct, error-guided behavior and learning would not be possible.

The interactive model of representation accounts for both the possibility of error and the possibility of system-detectable error in fairly simple ways: the functional anticipations or indications that constitute representation can easily exist but nevertheless be in error, and furthermore if an indicated interaction is engaged and it fails to proceed as indicated, then it is false and it is falsified in a manner functionally accessible by and for the organism itself. The key difference is that (interactive) representation is future oriented and can be false about the future and be discovered to be false about that future. I will use this criterion of system-detectable error as a universal perspective within which to show that the major alternative approaches to representation in the literature cannot possibly be correct.

Representation still resists naturalism

Millikan

According to the interactivist model, normativity emerges most primitively in biological function, and representation emerges in the serving of particular functions. In this macro-architecture, the interactivist model is similar to Millikan's etiological model (1984, 1993, 2004, 2005), but there are wide divergences at more detailed levels. I will outline a few of them.

Having a biological function, according to Millikan's model, is constituted in having the right kind of evolutionary history of selections. Kidneys have the function of filtering blood because that's what ancestral kidneys were selected for doing. This is a powerful model with strong appeal, though it does have some counterintuitive consequences. Consider, for example, the thought experiment of Millikan's lion that pops into existence in the corner via a coalescence of molecules, and that is, by assumption, molecule-by-molecule identical to a lion in the zoo. Or, for a less science-fictional example, consider the first time that something emerges in evolution that is useful to the organism that it is a part of.

The zoo lion has organs that have the right evolutionary history and, therefore, have functions; the lion in the corner, even though identical in its current state, has organs with *no* evolutionary history and, therefore, no function. Similarly, the brand new evolutionary emergent has no evolutionary history and, therefore, no function, while a sufficiently generationally removed descendent, even if identical in other respects, will (or may) have the right evolutionary history and, therefore, will have a function. These kinds of examples are acknowledged as counterintuitive but are considered to be quite acceptable, given the overall power of the model.

But what is not often remarked is that the lion in the corner is identical in state to the lion in the zoo, therefore the two lions are dynamically, causally, identical, yet one has functions while the other does not. Similarly, the fresh evolutionary emergent might be identical in causal dynamics to its descendent, yet one has functions while the other does not. In such cases we see that having or not having etiological function has no consequence for causality: etiological function is, causally, epiphenomenal.

Consequently, representation based on etiological function is causally epiphenomenal. Etiological history may explain etiology, but it is otherwise irrelevant to causality. This constitutes a failure of naturalism.[8]

Even if we overlook this problem, however, the etiological model faces, among other things, the system-detectable error problem. Representation is constituted as a kind of function, and function is constituted in having the right kind of evolutionary history. But no organism has access to its relevant evolutionary history, therefore no organism has access to the contents of its own representations.

And even if it did, system-detectable error would require that the organism compare that content with what was currently being represented, and that poses the representational problem all over again: circularity. The radical skeptical argument applies in full force: system-detectable error is not possible on this account, therefore error-guided behavior and learning are not possible.

Dretske

Dretske's model (1988) is also an etiological model, though the relevant etiology is a learning history, not an evolutionary history. Nevertheless, the same point about causal epiphenomenality applies: something *constituted* in the past history (not just explained by that past history) cannot have causal consequences for the present – only current state is causally efficacious.

Also similarly, organisms do not in general have access to their own learning history (certainly not simpler organisms nor infants, for example), and therefore do not have access to their own representational contents. And, as before, even if they did, system-detectable error would require that they compare those contents with what is currently being represented and we yet again encounter the basic circularity of correspondence models of representation.

Fodor

Fodor's model of representation (1987, 1990a, b, 1998, 2003) is an explicitly informational semantics model: representation is constituted in having the right kind of informational relationship with what is being represented. For Fodor, this right kind of relationship is a nomological relationship, with a few additional criteria.

Of particular importance for current purposes is Fodor's attempt to address the problem of representational error. He points out that cases of incorrect representation are derivative from cases of correct representation in an asymmetric manner. A representation of a cow, for example, that is *incorrectly* applied to what is in fact a horse (perhaps on a dark night), is dependent on the possibility of the cow representation being *correctly* applied to cows, but the reverse dependency does not hold: The cow representation could apply to cows perfectly well even if it were never incorrectly applied to horses.

This asymmetric dependency criterion has counterexamples, even as a criterion for representational error *per se*. A poison molecule, for example, that mimics a neurotransmitter and docks on the same receptor molecule as the neurotransmitter molecule manifests the same asymmetric dependencies as the "cow" and "horse" example, but there is no representation at all. At best, the asymmetric dependency criterion captures a property of functional error, not representation.

Even if it did capture representational error, however, it still does not even address system-detectable representational error. As before, no organism has access to its relevant asymmetric dependencies among classes of counterfactual possibilities of correct and incorrect applications, therefore, no organism has access to its own contents. And, also as before, even if it did, system-detectable error would require that such contents be compared with what is being currently represented, and that poses the representation problem yet again: circularity yet again.

The symbol system hypothesis

Cognitive science was long dominated by the symbol system hypothesis. This hypothesis held that symbols represented via some kind of "designation" relationship, usually relatively unspecified. Whatever the special favored relationship – pointer, transduction, structural isomorphism, etc. – this framework does not have any response to the problem of representational error, and certainly none to the problem of system-detectable representational error.

Connectionism

Connectionism holds that representation is constituted in vectors of activations of nodes, usually in connectionist nets that have been trained to be evoked in response to favored classes of input patterns. There is certainly important power available in the properties of distributedness and trainability in these models, but, with regard to representation per se, a connectionist activation vector "representation" is "just" a trained transduction, and provides no new resources for addressing genuine representational issues.

Dynamics

Connectionism was overtaken as the frontier of cognitive science in the 1990s by various dynamic and agentive approaches. These were advances in multiple ways, but the debates concerning representation generally fell into either a pro- or an anti-representationalist camp, but with the notions of representation at issue being the same familiar correspondence-encoding models as before. There was no progress regarding such issues as error or system-detectable error – with respect to normativity.

Convergences

The interactivist model is clearly a kind of dynamic model. In fact, it is rooted in a process metaphysics at the most fundamental level. But the interactivist model introduces notions of normativity, agency, and an agent-interaction-based model of representation, among others – issues that are not generally addressed within dynamic approaches.[9] Issues of error-guided behavior and learning, among others, require addressing such phenomena of normative intentionality.

In its interaction framework, the interactivist model makes strong connections with Piaget and Gibson as well as the pragmatist philosophers – especially Peirce and Dewey – and the pragmatically oriented existentialists, such as (early) Heidegger and Merleau-Ponty. These movements away from the substance-and-particle frameworks of antiquity are still historically very recent, and the relevant conceptual and theoretical spaces still only sparsely explored. The interactivist model has developed within this overall framework, thus the convergences and borrowings. The interactivist model of interactive *representation*, with truth value and aboutness (intentionality), is among its *unique* developments within that framework.

Conclusion

Representation emerges as part of the solution to the problem of interaction guidance and selection. It is a necessary aspect of the dynamics of agents. Unlike standard past-oriented correspondence-encoding models, it is future-oriented, action-based, modal, and explains the possibilities of representational error and system-detectable representational error in simple and natural ways. It grounds more complex forms of representation and cognition with resources that emerge naturally as primitive representation evolves.

Notes

1. This evolution of representation is a natural progression in the evolution of agents, *including the evolution of artificial agents*: robots.

2. In being presupposed and implicit, such content is unbounded: there is no explicit bound on what such conditions might be. Any attempt to render such unbounded ranges explicitly, therefore, will encounter the inherent problem that there is no bound on what or how many explicit renderings are required to exhaust the implicit content. Elsewhere I argue that this is the source of the frame problems.
3. It should be noted that this model of truth value and content depends on the normative notion of "indication" or "anticipation." Such normativity must itself be accounted for. The interactivist model shows that such normative properties can be emergent as particular kinds of normative function (function in the service of interaction selection). Normative function, in turn, is emergent in particular kinds of far-from-thermodynamic-equilibrium processes. Such emergence must be a genuine metaphysical emergence, and, the argument continues, metaphysical emergence requires abandoning the substance and particle metaphysics that have descended from Parmenides and his successors in favor of a process metaphysics. These issues are addressed elsewhere.
4. This is basically Piaget's model of the representation of manipulable objects stated in interactivist terms. It is possible to borrow such models from Piaget because both approaches are action-based, pragmatic approaches. Piaget's model and interactivism, however, diverge in important respects.
5. Some representational phenomena require reflection, which, in turn, requires significant additional architecture.
6. Note that the foam of emergents would constitute a source of variable candidates, while the constraints would constitute selection criteria for those candidates: the overall dynamic would constitute an internal evolutionary epistemology.
7. Perception, in the interactive model, is constituted by interactions that are undertaken primarily for the sake of their apperceptive consequences rather than for the changes they might induce in the environment. This is especially the case for apperceptively oriented interactions involving physiologically specialized subsystems for such interactions: the classical sensory modalities. Perception in this sense can also accommodate non-specialized processes, such as reading X-rays or sonar. Perception involves passive input processing, but cannot be fully captured by passive models: perceiving is itself an active, ongoing interactive process and is much more akin to Gibson's model than to standard passive encoding models.
8. Note that if the etiological model of function were correct, it would violate Hume's argument that norms cannot be derived from facts – the argument that Kant, Hegel and the idealists, the logical positivists, and the Quinean "sciencists" alike have all accepted and based their work on. The interactive model of function faces the same apparent barrier: Hume's argument precludes the possibility of a naturalistic model of any kind of normativity. Hume's argument, however, is unsound. This point is developed elsewhere.
9. Note that any dynamic model of interactive agents will of necessity include a model of interaction guidance and selection and, therefore, of at least the primitive versions of interactive representation. This holds even if, as has been typical, there are explicit arguments *against* the inclusion or relevance of representation in the model in any of the classical correspondence encoding senses. That is, modeling agents requires modeling representation in the sense of phenomena with truth value and aboutness, whether or not any such vocabulary is used.

References

Dretske, F. I. (1988) *Explaining Behavior*, Cambridge, MA: MIT Press.
Fodor, J. A. (1987) *Psychosemantics*, Cambridge, MA: MIT Press.
—— (1990a) *A Theory of Content*, Cambridge, MA: MIT Press.
—— (1990b) "Information and Representation," in P. P. Hanson (ed.), *Information, Language, and Cognition*, Vancouver, Canada: University of British Columbia Press, pp. 175–90.
—— (1998) *Concepts: Where Cognitive Science Went Wrong*, Oxford: Oxford University Press.
—— (2003) *Hume Variations*, Oxford: Oxford University Press.
Millikan, R. G. (1984) *Language, Thought, and Other Biological Categories*, Cambridge, MA: MIT Press.
—— (1993) *White Queen Psychology and Other Essays for Alice*, Cambridge, MA: MIT Press.

—— (2004) *Varieties of Meaning*, Cambridge, MA: MIT Press.
—— (2005) *Language: A Biological Model*, Oxford: Oxford University Press.

Further reading

An interesting exchange between some commentators and critics, with Fodor's replies, can be found in B. Loewer and G. Rey, *Meaning in Mind: Fodor and His Critics* (Oxford: Blackwell, 1991). A good overview of Fodor's philosophy is M. J. Cain, *Fodor* (Oxford: Blackwell, 2002). The seminal work on evolutionary epistemology (though the idea is some years older) is D. T. Campbell, "Evolutionary Epistemology," in P. A. Schilpp (ed.), *The Philosophy of Karl Popper* (LaSalle, IL: Open Court, 1974), pp. 413–63. One (of many) of Piaget's classics, this one focuses the child's construction of reality, including that of objects: J. Piaget, *The Construction of Reality in the Child* (New York: Basic Books, 1954).

The following are suggestions for pursuing some of the connections between the interactivist model and various issues and domains in the broader literature. A detailed presentation of the early model of language and cognition is M. H. Bickhard, *Cognition, Convention, and Communication* (New York: Praeger, 1980). For the basic model of representation, including normative issues, and an extended critique of Fodor, see M. H. Bickhard, "Representational Content in Humans and Machines," *Journal of Experimental and Theoretical Artificial Intelligence* 5 (1993): 285–333. A brief introduction to the interactivist model of motivation and emotion is M. H. Bickhard, "Motivation and Emotion: An Interactive Process Model," in R. D. Ellis and N. Newton (eds), *The Caldron of Consciousness* (Amsterdam: J. Benjamins 2000), pp. 161–78. In this model, motivation and cognition are differing aspects of the same underlying system organization, as discussed in M. H. Bickhard, "An Integration of Motivation and Cognition," in L. Smith, C. Rogers, and P. Tomlinson (eds), *Development and Motivation: Joint Perspectives*, Monograph Series II (Leicester, UK: British Psychological Society, 2003) pp. 41–56. A model of metaphysical emergence based on process metaphysics, with applications to function and representation, is M. H. Bickhard, "Process and Emergence: Normative Function and Representation," *Axiomathes – An International Journal in Ontology and Cognitive Systems* 14 (2004): 135–69; originally published in J. Seibt (ed.), *Process Theories: Crossdisciplinary Studies in Dynamic Categories* (Dordrecht: Kluwer, 2003), pp. 121–55. On how the interactivist framework yields a model of emergent social ontology, and of persons as social-level emergents, see M. H. Bickhard, "The Social Ontology of Persons," in J. I. M. Carpendale and U. Muller (eds), *Social Interaction and the Development of Knowledge* (Mahwah, NJ: Erlbaum, 2004), pp. 111–32; "Are You Social? The Ontological and Developmental Emergence of the Person," in U. Müller, J. I. M. Carpendale, N. Budwig, and B. Sokol (eds), *Social Life and Social Knowledge* (New York: Taylor & Francis, 2008), pp. 17–42; and "Social Ontology as Convention," *Topoi* 27, no. 1–2 (2008): 139–49.

The model accounts for multiple phenomena of consciousness in M. H. Bickhard, "Consciousness and Reflective Consciousness," *Philosophical Psychology* 18, no. 2 (2005): 205–18. A basic outline of the developmental aspects of the interactivist model is found in R. L. Campbell and M. H. Bickhard, *Knowing Levels and Developmental Stages*, Contributions to Human Development (Basel, Switzerland: Karger, 1986). Issues of normativity are central to the development of children in M. H. Bickhard, "Developmental Normativity and Normative Development," in L. Smith and J. Voneche (eds), *Norms in Human Development* (Cambridge: Cambridge University Press, 2006), pp. 57–76. Later discussions of language and its properties are covered in M. H. Bickhard and R. L. Campbell, "Some Foundational Questions Concerning Language Studies: With a Focus on Categorial Grammars and Model Theoretic Possible Worlds Semantics," *Journal of Pragmatics* 17, no. 5–6 (1992): 401–33; and "Intrinsic Constraints on Language: Grammar and Hermeneutics," *Journal of Pragmatics* 23 (1995): 541–54. The model has fundamental convergences with James Gibson's model of perception, as well as some important divergences, as shown in H. M. Bickhard and D. M. Richie, *On the Nature of Representation: A Case Study of James Gibson's Theory of Perception* (New York: Praeger, 1983). The model has critical relevance to multiple positions, frameworks, and assumptions in the fields of artificial intelligence and cognitive science, as shown in M. H. Bickhard and L. Terveen, *Foundational Issues in Artificial Intelligence and Cognitive Science: Impasse and Solution* (Amsterdam: Elsevier, 1995). For a presentation of the central model of normative function, see W. D. Christensen and M. H. Bickhard, "The Process Dynamics of Normative Function," *Monist* 85, no. 1 (2002): 3–28.

22
THE PROPOSITIONAL IMAGINATION

Shaun Nichols

Propositional imagination is the capacity we exploit when we imagine that there is an evil demon or that Iago deceived Othello. This capacity is centrally implicated in thought experiments, modal judgment, and counterfactual reasoning. As a result, the capacity plays a central role in philosophical inquiry. The propositional imagination also figures greatly in everyday life. We use it to understand others, to develop plans for action, and for hypothetical reasoning more broadly. Indeed, the propositional imagination is implicated in such a vast and fundamental set of practical and philosophical endeavors that it's a wonder that the topic received little systematic attention for the bulk of the twentieth century. Fortunately, over the last two decades, there has finally been a concerted research effort to develop a cognitive account of the propositional imagination.

Motivation

Perhaps the most obvious reason for studying the propositional imagination is that it plays such a fundamental part in our lives. Insofar as we want to understand the human mind, we had better understand our capacity for imagination. In addition, the propositional imagination is of special interest to philosophers for several reasons.

Thought experiments

Thought experiments have played a central role in philosophy at least as far back as Plato. Imagine that you had the Ring of Gyges and could turn yourself invisible – would you still refrain from stealing and killing? Obviously we can't begin to entertain such thought experiments without the propositional imagination. The use of thought experiments is hardly restricted to antiquity. It is central to philosophical inquiries as diverse as reference and politics.

Since these philosophical pursuits directly involve the propositional imagination, it can be important to know how the propositional imagination works. For we might discover that the propositional imagination is a reliable mechanism for certain kinds of thought experiments but not others. That is, some thought experiments might turn out to be systematically misleading because of quirks in the cognitive structure of the propositional imagination. But we would be unable to determine this until we had a good psychological characterization of the propositional imagination.

Imagination and modality

Propositional imagination is especially central to the philosophy of modality. It's an old idea in philosophy that the imagination reveals possibilities. In his 1739 *Treatise*, David Hume maintained that it was an "establish'd maxim" that "*whatever the mind clearly conceives, includes the idea of possible existence*, or in other words, *nothing we imagine is absolutely impossible*" (1964 [1739]: Bk 1, pt 2, sec. 2, para. 8). The idea is old, but it continues to exercise a powerful hold in philosophy. In his recent discussion of this maxim, Stephen Yablo maintains that philosophers have not discovered any "seriously alternative basis for possibility theses" (1993: 2). If the imagination doesn't tell us what things are possible, then it's not clear what does.

As an empiricist, Hume holds that all ideas are copies from sensory impressions. As a result, it's natural to interpret Hume's notion of "imagination" as *imagistic*, i.e., as requiring sensory-like images. Some philosophers might thus maintain that since imagining is imagistic, it is an entirely distinct faculty of *conceiving* that informs us about possibility. However from the perspective of recent discussions of propositional imagination, this is largely a terminological dispute. As we'll see below, contemporary cognitive accounts of the imagination tend *not* to treat the imagination as imagistic. Similarly in the philosophical literature, the faculty of conceiving tends to be characterized in terms of a faculty of propositional imagination for which sensory-like images are not required.

Philosophers have, of course, challenged the use of the imagination to establish modal theses. But these issues about the relation between imagination and modality continue to occupy a central place in philosophical debates.

Imaginative resistance

The next topic also traces a history to Hume. Hume concludes "On the Standard of Taste" by raising puzzles that are now known under the label "imaginative resistance." In a key passage, Hume writes, "where vicious manners are described, without being marked with the proper characters of blame and disapprobation; this must be allowed to disfigure the poem, and to be a real deformity. I cannot, nor is it proper I should, enter into such sentiments" (Hume (1985 [1757]: Para. 32). Part of the idea here is that when I read a poem that makes pronouncements that run deeply against my own moral values, I can't bring myself to share the reactions.

Richard Moran (1994), Kendall Walton (1990, 1994, 2006), and Tamar Gendler (2000, 2006) resurrected Hume's issues in the context of the aesthetics of fiction. In his illuminating discussion of the issue, Moran sets the problem as follows:

> If the story tells us that Duncan was *not* in fact murdered on Macbeth's orders, then *that* is what we accept and imagine as fictionally true ... However, suppose the facts of the murder remain as they are in fact presented in the play, but it is prescribed in this alternate fiction that this was unfortunate only for having interfered with Macbeth's sleep that night.
>
> (Moran 1994: 95)

In the former case, in which the story says that Duncan wasn't murdered, we happily go along; but in the latter case, Moran suggests, we would not accept it as true in the fictional world that murdering one's guest is morally okay. In most cases, it seems, we imagine whatever the fiction directs us to imagine, and we also accept it as fictionally true. But in cases of moral depravity, we often refuse to let our imaginations and judgments of fictional truth follow. Thus, the problem of imaginative resistance.

Fictional truths, according to Walton's prominent account, are defined by prescriptions to imagine (Walton 1990). So, it is fictionally true that Desdemona is innocent just because the play prescribes that we imagine this. If we adopt this view of fiction, it's clear that there are importantly different issues implicated in the discussion of imaginative resistance. One question concerns why we refuse to accept some things as fictionally true. That is, we seem to reject the idea that we *ought* to imagine that murdering Duncan was okay (even if the play said so). A different question concerns why we in fact seem to find ourselves unable to imagine that Duncan's murder was okay. The first puzzle, about the fiction, and the second puzzle, about the psychology, are at least partly independent. But both involve considerations about the propositional imagination.

Although the issue of imaginative resistance was initially raised in the context of the aesthetics of fiction, once the puzzles about fiction and psychology are distinguished, it becomes clear that the psychological puzzle exceeds the boundaries of fiction. The fact that we seem to resist imagining certain contents applies even when we aren't consuming fiction. It is a more general, striking, fact about our minds that the imagination rebels against certain contents.

Imagination and emotion

The final topic to be considered – emotions and the propositional imagination – also emerged in the context of the aesthetics of fiction (Radford 1975; Walton 1990). The philosophical literature here has largely been driven by the "paradox of fiction," which is generated by a triad of claims, each of which seems plausible:

(a) We often feel emotions for fictional characters (e.g. I pity King Lear).
(b) To feel emotions for something, you have to believe it exists.
(c) We don't believe in the existence of characters that we know are fictional (e.g., I don't believe King Lear exists).

While some treatments of the paradox do not invoke considerations about the imagination, the literature on the paradox has raised several interesting questions about emotions and the imagination. The central questions are the following: (i) Are the affective responses to fiction caused by imaginative activities, and if so, how does the imagination generate these effects? (ii) Under what conditions (if any) is it rational to have affective responses to imaginative activities concerning fictions? And (iii) Do the affective responses to fiction count as instances of genuine emotions like pity and indignation, or are we imagining that we have those emotions, as part of a broader game of make-believe? For example, do we literally feel pity when seeing *King Lear* or do we imagine, as part of a broader game of make-believe, that we feel pity?

Although the philosophical concerns about imagination and emotion have primarily been discussed in the aesthetics of fiction, the psychological phenomena again exceed the boundaries of aesthetics. For the imagination apparently drives affective responses, even when there is no associated fiction. Many of the same questions arise when we detach from fiction: How does the imagination cause affective responses in everyday life? Under what conditions is it rational to have those affective responses from the imagination? And are the affective responses we have to imagination instances of genuine emotions?

Towards a cognitive account of the propositional imagination

To address the philosophical questions reviewed above, it would obviously be beneficial to draw on cognitive characterizations of the capacity for propositional imagination. But until recently, there was little to draw from. Fortunately, philosophers and psychologists finally applied themselves to the task beginning in the 1980s.

One of the key developments that led to cognitive theorizing about the imagination was the reemergence of the representational theory of mind. According to the representational theory of mind, beliefs (among other mental states) are internal representations. To believe that *P* is to have a representation token with the content *P* stored in some functionally appropriate way in the mind. This broad view of cognition was one central assumption that underpinned the early cognitivist accounts of the imagination.

A second key background assumption for the cognitive accounts is the view that some different kinds of psychological states are distinguished by their *functional role*. To take one familiar example, many philosophers maintain that beliefs and desires are distinct kinds of mental states, but what distinguishes them is not the *content* of the mental state, but rather the *functional role* the two states play. That is, beliefs and desires have different causal interactions with stimuli, behavior and other mental states. So, if we allow that the desire that *P* is a representation stored in the mind, this representation exhibits a significantly different functional profile from the belief that *P*, despite the fact that they both represent the same content. These differences in functional role are what make *belief* and *desire* different kinds of mental state.

These background assumptions about representations and functional roles set the stage for the development of cognitive accounts of the imagination. In addition to these high-level theoretical assumptions, there are several central facts about the propositional imagination that have shaped nearly all of the theorizing in the recent literature. Here is a brief overview.

(i) Early emergence of the imagination.

Most children engage in pretend play before their second birthday. Their pretend play actually is really rather remarkable. Consider, for instance, the common childhood activity of pretending to talk on a phone using a banana as a prop. In these instances, even very young children don't confuse their pretense with reality; even when they are pretending that the banana is a telephone, they don't seem to think that the banana really *is* a telephone. Two-year-old children certainly don't seem to confuse bananas with telephones, and a bit later, when it's easier to test them, it becomes quite clear that children do indeed distinguish what is imagined from what is real. For instance, in one experiment, children were told about two individuals, one of whom has a cookie and one of whom pretends to have a cookie. Even three-year-olds were more likely to say that the person who was merely pretending to have a cookie couldn't see it or touch it (Wellman and Estes 1986). In a different paradigm, researchers found that children distinguished between what the experimenter was pretending an object to be (e.g., a telephone) and what it really was (a pen) (Flavell et al. 1987; see also Harris et al. 1994). More recently, developmental psychologists have shown that young children even distinguish between different fictional worlds, like the world of SpongeBob vs. that of Batman (Skolnick and Bloom 2006).

(ii) It's possible to imagine that P and believe that P simultaneously.

Typically when we engage in the propositional imagination, we imagine things that we don't believe. One might thus be tempted to assume that it's impossible for a person to imagine and believe the same thing at the same time. In contemporary work on the imagination, this assumption is widely rejected, both by the philosophers and the psychologists. For instance, Walton writes, "imagining something is entirely compatible with knowing it to be true" (Walton 1990: 13). In psychology, an experiment from Alan Leslie (1994) provides a particularly nice illustration. An experimenter plays a tea party game with young children. The experimenter pretends to fill a cup with tea, then proceeds deliberately to overturn the cup. The children now imagine that the cup is empty, and they also, of course, believe that the cup is empty.

(iii) Imagination and belief generate different action tendencies.

When children engage in pretend play, they carry out behavioral sequences that conform in important ways to the actions they would perform if they really had the beliefs. For example, if a child believes that Grandma is on the telephone, he would really talk to her; and when the child pretends that the banana is a telephone with Grandma on the line, he talks into the banana. Nonetheless, there are important behavioral discontinuities. When pretending that mud globs are delicious pies, even hungry children don't consume the "pies." Moreover, as adults, when we consume fiction, daydream, or fantasize, we don't typically produce actions that would be produced if we really believed what we are imagining.

(vi) Intentions direct the imagination.
The previous point was that imagination and belief produce different outputs; imagining and believing are also distinguished by how they are generated. Belief is not at the whim of our intentions, but imagination is. While some philosophers maintain that we can to some extent shape our beliefs by our intentions, presumably we can't believe that the moon is made of cheese by dint of a simple intention to believe that. By contrast, the imagination is much more amenable. We typically decide when to engage in an imaginative episode, and in many ways we can also control the particular contents that we imagine. As a result, we can fill out an imaginative episode in all kinds of surprising ways.

(v) Imagination exhibits inferential orderliness.
Although the imagination is flexible in some ways, it's fairly rigid and predictable in other ways. In particular, when people engage in imaginative activities, they often follow orderly inference chains. When I read that Charlotte is a spider, I infer (in imagination) that Charlotte has eight legs. When I hear that Lear is a king, I infer (in imagination) that he is not a peasant. These inferences track the kinds of inferences that I would have if I really believed that Charlotte was a spider and Lear was a king.[1] Such orderly inferences emerge on the scene very early in childhood. In one study, the experimenter introduces two-year-old children to several toy animals, including "Larry Lamb," and tells them that the animals are going outside to play. The experimenter designates part of the table top as "outside," points to a smaller part of this area, and says "Look, there's a muddy puddle here." Then the experimenter takes Larry Lamb and makes him roll over and over in this area. The children are asked, "What has happened? What has happened to Larry?" Nearly all of the children indicated that Larry got muddy. Here then, they are apparently drawing inferences over the contents of what they are pretending, and the inferences parallel the inferences that the children would draw if they had the corresponding beliefs (Leslie 1994).

(vi) The imagination activates affective systems.
It is common wisdom in psychology that imagining scenarios can have significant affective consequences. Indeed, one traditional experimental technique for inducing affect is precisely to have subjects imagine scenarios that are expected to produce particular kinds of affective responses. Furthermore, the research suggests that the affective response to imagining a scenario closely tracks the affective response that would occur if the subject came to believe that the scenario was real (for reviews see, e.g., Lang 1984; Harris 2000).

Convergences

In light of the background assumptions about representational theory of mind, as well as the central facts listed above, cognitive scientists and philosophers of psychology have largely arrived at a consensus for a basic cognitive account of the imagination. There are, of course, important disagreements (see below) but most people working in this area agree on several substantive claims about the nature of the imagination.

The first point of convergence is that recent theorists adopt a representationalist approach to the propositional imagination. To believe that *P* is to have a "belief" representation with the content *P*. Analogously, to imagine that Iago is wicked is to have an "imaginational" representation with the content *Iago is wicked*.

The second point of agreement is that imaginational representations are distinguished from belief representations by their *functional roles*, not by their *contents*. Just as desires are distinguished from beliefs by their pattern of causal interaction, so too are imaginings distinguished from beliefs by their pattern of causal interaction. The appeal to a distinction at the level of function rather than content can accommodate the fact that it's possible to believe and imagine the same thing (as noted in point [ii], above). Further, the central facts reviewed above provide us with some of the critical functional differences between believing and imagining. The inputs to the imagination are at the whim of intention, but this is not the case for belief, and the imagination and belief make different causal contributions to action tendencies (points [iii] and [iv]). These are major differences in the causal roles of imaginational representations and belief representations. In addition, though this is somewhat less explicit, most theorists assume that the capacity for propositional imagination is a basic part of human psychology. This makes sense of the early emergence of pretend play and the early ability to distinguish fantasy and reality (point [i]). It also accommodates the widespread presumption that imagining cannot be reduced to other mental states like believing or desiring.

The third important point of agreement is that imaginational representations interact with some of the same mental mechanisms that belief representations interact with, and these shared mechanisms treat imaginational representations and belief representations in much the same ways. That is, imagining and believing have shared pathways in the mind, and those pathways process imaginational input and belief input in similar ways. For instance, most theorists maintain that our inferential mechanisms process input from both beliefs and from the imagination. Further, most theorists maintain that some affective systems can be activated by both beliefs and by imaginational representations. The consensus view holds that the shared mechanisms will treat the imaginational representation *P* and the belief representation *P* in much the same way. This then makes sense of the fact that we see inferential orderliness in imagination (point [v]) and that we see similar affective responses to believing that *p* and imagining that *P* (point [vi]).

Divergences

While we have seen an impressive degree of convergence in theorizing about the imagination, there are also important areas of disagreement. Perhaps the most important fault line is the dispute over the existence of "pretend desires."

For those familiar with the debates over "simulation theory" (e.g., Davies and Stone 1995a, b), it will be evident that the foregoing celebration of convergence tells no more than half of the story. According to one influential version of simulation theory (Gordon 1986; Goldman 1989), when I predict another's behavior, I don't exploit a specialized body of knowledge about psychology; rather, I insert "pretend" versions of the target's beliefs and desires into my practical-reasoning mechanism, which then generates a "pretend" decision which I use to predict the decision of the target. Thus, for this version of simulation theory, one important notion is "pretend belief," and something like the notion of "pretend belief" might be identified with the kind of propositional imagination that we've been considering. However, many simulation theorists also defend the existence of pretend *desires* – imaginational states that are related to real desires in much the way that pretend beliefs are related to real beliefs. On that topic, there is serious disagreement.

If there are pretend desires, this counts as a profound addition to the architecture of the imagination. It also greatly expands the available resources for explaining the phenomena surrounding the imagination. So the stakes in this debate are high. Advocates of pretend desires invoke them to explain pretend play behavior, emotional responses to fiction, and imaginative resistance. Most centrally, however, advocates of pretend desires maintain that such states play a crucial role in the prediction and explanation of others' behavior. When we try to predict or explain the behavior of a target, we must accommodate her differing mental states in some way. Our predictions will often go wrong if we are insensitive to the different beliefs and desires of the target. It is widely agreed that one often accommodates the target's discrepant belief that *P* by imagining that *P*. However, how do we accommodate the target's discrepant desire that *Q*? According to many simulation theorists, we do this by taking on the pretend desire that *Q*. In parallel with the case of pretend belief, the pretend desires get processed much like real desires. This explains how we succeed at predicting and explaining the behavior of those with discrepant desires.

On the other side of the theoretical divide, skeptics about pretend desires maintain that pretend desires play no role in predicting behavior (or anything else) (e.g., Carruthers 2003; Nichols 2004b; Nichols and Stich 2003; Weinberg and Meskin 2005). These theorists maintain that there are several ways in which a predictor can accommodate another's discrepant desire. For instance, I can believe that the person has a certain desire; I can imagine that the person has the desire; I can imagine that *I* have the desire. But none of this requires having pretend desires.

Each side in this debate holds a well entrenched position, and the issue continues to be an important rift among prevailing theories of the propositional imagination. Nonetheless, it shouldn't obscure the widespread agreement that has been reached about the architecture of the imagination.

Given the recency of these new accounts of the imagination, the philosophical implications are only beginning to be explored. To return to the philosophical matters, there has been some work applying the new accounts of the imagination to fiction and the emotions (Currie 1997; Currie and Ravenscroft 2002; Meskin and Weinberg 2003). There has also been a bit of work applying these accounts to the problem of imaginative resistance (Nichols 2004a; Weinberg and Meskin 2006). And there is a modicum of work on modal judgment and the propositional imagination (Nichols 2006). But clearly there remains much to do in exploring the philosophical lessons that flow from the cognitive accounts of the imagination.

Notes

1. Of course, there are many exceptions to this, some of which are to be explained by the fact (noted in point [iv], above) that intentions can direct (and redirect) the contents of our imaginings.

References

Carruthers, P. (2003) Review of *Recreative Minds*, by G. Currie and I. Ravenscroft, *Notre Dame Philosophical Reviews* 11(12); available: http://ndpr.icaap.org/content/archives/2003/11/carruthers-currie.html

Currie, G. (1997) "The Paradox of Caring," in M. Hjort and S. Laver (eds), *Emotion and the Arts*, Oxford: Oxford University Press.

Currie, G., and Ravenscroft, I. (2002) *Recreative Imagination*, Oxford: Oxford University Press.

Davies, M., and Stone, T. (eds) (1995a) *Folk Psychology: The Theory of Mind Debate*, Oxford: Blackwell.

—— (eds) (1995b) *Mental Simulation: Evaluations and Applications*, Oxford: Blackwell.

Flavell, J. H., Flavell, E. R., and Green, F. L. (1987) "Young Children's Knowledge about the Apparent-Real and Pretend-Real Distinctions," *Developmental Psychology* 23: 816–22.

Gendler, T. (2000) "The Puzzle of Imaginative Resistance," *Journal of Philosophy* 97: 55–81.

—— (2006) "Imaginative Resistance Revisited," in S. Nichols (ed.), *The Architecture of the Imagination*, Oxford: Oxford University Press, pp. 135–37.

Goldman, A. (1989) "Interpretation Psychologized," *Mind and Language* 4: 161–85.

Gordon, R. (1986) "Folk Psychology as Simulation," *Mind and Language* 1: 158–70.

Harris, P. (2000) *The Work of the Imagination*, Oxford: Blackwell.

Harris, P. L., Kavanaugh, R. D., and Meredith, M. C. (1994) "Young Children's Comprehension of Pretend Episodes: The Integration of Successive Actions," *Child Development* 65: 16–30.

Hume, D. (1964 [1739]) *A Treatise of Human Nature*, Oxford: Clarendon Press.

—— (1985 [1757]) "Of the Standard of Taste," in *Essays: Moral, Political and Literary*, ed. Eugene Miller, Indianapolis: Liberty.

Lang, P. (1984) "Cognition and Emotion: Concept and Action," in C. Izard, J. Kagan, and R. Zajoncs (eds), *Emotions, Cognition and Behavior*, Cambridge: Cambridge University Press.

Leslie, A. (1994) "Pretending and Believing: Issues in the Theory of ToMM," *Cognition* 50: 211–38.

Meskin, A., and Weinberg, J. (2003) "Emotions, Fiction, and Cognitive Architecture," *British Journal of Aesthetics* 43: 18–34.

Moran, R. (1994) "The Expression of Feeling in the Imagination," *Philosophical Review* 103: 75–106.

Nichols, S. (2004a) "Imagining and Believing: The Promise of a Single Code," *Journal of Aesthetics and Art Criticism* 62: 129–39.

—— (2004b) Review of *Recreative Minds*, by G. Currie and I. Ravenscroft, *Mind*, 113: 329–34.

—— (2006) "Imaginative Blocks and Impossibility: An Essay in Modal Psychology," in S. Nichols (ed.), *The Architecture of the Imagination*, Oxford: Oxford University Press, pp. 237–57.

Nichols, S., and Stich, S. (2003) *Mindreading*, Oxford: Oxford University Press.

Radford, C. (1975) "How Can We Be Moved by the Fate of Anna Karenina?" *Proceedings of the Aristotelian Society* 49 (suppl.): 67–80.

Skolnick, D., and Bloom, P. (2006) "The Intuitive Cosmology of Fictional Worlds," in S. Nichols (ed.), *The Architecture of the Imagination*, Oxford: Oxford University Press, pp. 73–87.

Walton, K. L. (1990) *Mimesis as Make-Believe: On the Foundations of the Representational Arts*, Cambridge, MA: Harvard University Press.

—— (1994) "Morals in Fiction and Fictional Morality," *Proceedings of the Aristotelian Society* 68 (suppl.): 27–50.

—— (2006) "On the (So-called) Puzzle of Imaginative Resistance," in S. Nichols (ed.), *The Architecture of the Imagination*, Oxford: Oxford University Press, 137–49.

Weinberg, J., and Meskin, A. (2005) "Imagine That!" in M. Kieran (ed.), *Contemporary Debates in Aesthetics and the Philosophy of Art*, Oxford: Blackwell, pp. 222–35.

—— (2006) "Puzzling over the Imagination: Philosophical Problems, Architectural Solutions," in S. Nichols (ed.), *The Architecture of the Imagination*, Oxford: Oxford University Press, pp. 175–203.

Wellman, H. M., and Estes, D. (1986) "Early Understanding of Mental Entities: A Reexamination of Childhood Realism," *Child Development* 57: 910–23.

Yablo, S. (1993) "Is Conceivability a Guide to Possibility?" *Philosophy and Phenomenological Research* 53: 1–42.

23

BELIEF AND REPRESENTATION IN NONHUMAN ANIMALS

Sarah Beth Lesson, Brandon Tinklenberg, and Kristin Andrews

1 Introduction – the value and challenges associated with animal belief

It's common to think that animals think. The cat thinks it is time to be fed; the monkey thinks the dominant is a threat. In order to make sense of what the other animals around us do, we ascribe mental states to them. The cat meows at the door because she wants to be let in. The monkey fails the test because he doesn't remember the answer.

We explain animal actions in terms of their mental states, just as we do with humans. One of us has argued that our science of animal minds requires that animal behavior be explained in such terms and that doing so doesn't lead to anthropomorphism or a problematic use of folk psychology (Andrews, 2016, forthcoming). By "anthropomorphism" we mean the attribution of human psychological, social, or normative properties to nonhuman animals "usually with the implication it is done without sound justification" (Shettleworth, 2010a, p. 477). And by "folk psychology" we mean the commonsense practice of seeing action as caused or accompanied by mental states like belief and desire, emotions, and seeing others in terms of their moods or personality traits, as well as categorizing complex behaviors as examples of grieving, communicating, or teaching (Andrews, 2012, 2017a). Psychologists routinely describe human behaviors in folk psychological terms, so it's not that the categories are unscientific. The issue with using folk psychology to describe animal behavior is whether observable similarities between human and nonhuman behavior warrants the claim that the behaviors involve the same psychological kinds. Applying folk psychology to animals need not be problematically anthropomorphic so long as we have an evidentiary basis for filing animal behavior under folk psychological categories.

Although it is commonplace for humans to attribute thoughts to animals, and despite there being arguments in favor of doing so in science, the nature of the mental states we attribute to animals remains unclear. To make this issue more exact, we will examine the attitude of belief. In this chapter we will examine the various possible views on animal beliefs and their implications for our folk practice as well as our scientific investigations.

2 Representational belief

Use of the term "belief" pervades our everyday discourse. We sometimes use talk of belief to express trust (I believe in her) or as a testament of faith (I believe in God) or to indicate uncertainty (I believe the subway is two blocks north). The philosophical and scientific sense of belief is rather different. Most generally, a belief is an attitude toward a proposition whereby the proposition is taken to be true. There are some features of belief that all theories aim to capture:

- **Direction of fit**: Beliefs are thought to have a "mind-to-world" direction of fit, meaning that the accuracy of beliefs depends on them depicting the world in the right way. Beliefs are thus contrasted with desires, which have a "world-to-mind" direction of fit: Desires are satisfied whenever the world changes to accord with my mental states. (Anscombe, 1957)
- **Epistemic endorsement**: Beliefs often express some internal commitment to their accuracy. What you "believe" is thus often what you "think" is right. Recent research finds that the folk use of the term "think" comes in at least two varieties – a thin belief "involves representing and storing P as information" and a thick belief that adds an attitude to the representation of P; one might "like it that P is true, emotionally endorse the truth of P, explicitly avow or assent to the truth of P, or actively promote an agenda that makes sense given P" (Buckwalter, Rose and Turri, 2015, p. 2).
- **Aspectuality/opacity**: Beliefs are a species of propositional attitudes, or, mental attitudes we can take toward propositions or statements, and propositional attitudes have the property of referential opacity. This means that even if "Superman" and "Clark Kent" refer to the same person, but Alice doesn't know this to be so, we would be in error if we attributed to her a belief that Superman has some typical Clark Kent property. We can't correctly say that Alice believes that Superman is a reporter. Beliefs respect the fact that we encounter the world from different perspectives.
- **Conscious availability/verbal report**: Whenever we talk about what we think, it's intuitive to think that we're expressing our beliefs. Since we are conscious when we speak, we are thus aware of what we believe. That said, not all my beliefs are immediately available to conscious awareness (Thompson, 2016).
- **Inferential integration**: Beliefs are thought to be related by patterns of reasoning. If I believe humans are mortal, and I also believe Cher is a human, then most would posit that I believe Cher is mortal. This doesn't mean that all my beliefs are the result of sound reasoning, but they should relate to the way I make inferences in some fashion.

(Stich, 1978)

The typical way theorists try to capture these features is by thinking of beliefs as mental representations. Representationalists all hold that beliefs are internal mental states that carry content. There is a healthy variety of representationalist views. Theories differ in two main ways: they differ on how the content or meaning of beliefs are fixed and on what representational vehicles (or what medium) beliefs use. Here we will focus on how representationalists differ with regards to representational vehicles.

2.1 A classic worry about representational belief in animals

Taking belief to be an attitude toward a proposition raises an immediate question for animal belief – how can we correctly attribute a proposition to an individual who does not use language? Can we translate animal concepts into human concepts? If we cannot attribute content to animals' beliefs, should we conclude that animals don't have beliefs?

A number of philosophers have raised these sorts of questions (e.g. Beck, 2013; Stich, 1979; Dummett, 2010). For example, Michael Dummett raises this worry in his discussion of a dog who is routinely attacked by other dogs when traveling a particular path (Dummett, 2010). As the dog walks the path, sometimes he is attacked by one dog, sometimes by a pack, and the victim learns to use different techniques in these different situations; he stands his ground when there is only one aggressor and turns and runs when there are more. We might want to explain the standing-his-ground behavior by saying he thinks there is only one dog on the path. But to make that attribution, the dog would need all the concepts that we attribute to him, including the concept "one," which requires corresponding numerical concepts that we might never have had reason to attribute to a dog. This is because linguistic phenomena are thought to be compositional: complex linguistic elements like sentences are constructed out of strings of words that obey grammatical rules. Similarly, if beliefs are language-like, they must be constructed out of concepts in a way that respects the linguistic structure of thought. This requires competence with all the concepts that constitute a belief. If we think that Dummett's dog has the concept "one," then he should be able to generalize to other numbers, to single objects in other contexts, etc., but such generalizations would lead to false predictions. Furthermore, there is no substitute concept we can attribute to the dog. As Dummett puts it, "So the dog does *not* have the very thought by which we express the feature of the situation he has recognized. Conversely, we have no linguistic means of expressing just what it is he recognizes. Animals without language cannot have the very same thoughts we express in language" (Dummett, 2010, p. 118).

If we cannot articulate the content of an animal's belief, but we still think an animal has a belief, we demonstrate a misunderstanding of the nature of belief, or so goes this worry. A belief attribution that doesn't capture the aspectual character of the mental state fails to be a belief.

2.2 Responses to the worry

There are a number of ways to respond to the classic worry – both empirical and philosophical. First, similar worries arise when attributing content to other humans – children who do not yet have the adult concept, other cultural groups who use unfamiliar concepts, and even adults of our own culture who disagree about the nature of the concept, such as "life" or "murder" (Dworkin, 1986; Plunkett and Sundell, 2013). But this fact doesn't raise serious problems for attributing beliefs to humans.

Some philosophers argue that we can preserve the aspectuality of attributions to animals without assuming animals can use the same concepts we use when we state the content of their beliefs. It might be that animals don't need to understand the contents of their beliefs. Or it might be that the relevant similarities in how animals and humans conceive of the world justifies belief attribution.

For instance, Mark Rowlands (2012) thinks we can attribute beliefs to animals without using concepts that the animals themselves use or understand via a specific kind of de dicto content he calls tracking:

> (*Tracking*): Proposition *p* tracks proposition *p** if the truth of *p* guarantees the truth of *p** in virtue of the fact that there is a reliable asymmetric connection between the concepts expressed by the term occupying the subject position in *p* and the concept expressed by the term occupying the subject position in *p**.
> (Rowlands, 2012, p. 58)

Tracking allows us to attribute beliefs to animals without assuming they have any understanding of the concepts involved.

José Bermúdez (2003) relies on a similar insight about the relationship between beliefs and patterns of behavior in his development of a success semantics, in which the content of a belief is that which would satisfy the animal's desire by causing the appropriate action. Bermúdez thinks that that we have already learned a lot about the content of animal beliefs via research in cognitive science. Since "nonlinguistic creatures are perfectly capable of perceiving a structured world" (p. 81), Bermúdez thinks we can attribute belief to them in this way. However, there remains an open question as to whether animals understand any of the structure that they're receptive to.

The second approach is to say that animals do have belief states that resemble the content that we attribute. The clearest example of this approach is seen in Jerry Fodor's suggestion that animals, while lacking an external language, think in a language of thought (Fodor, 1975). If the structure of their concepts roughly matches our own, our attributions of content can be as correct as any translation from one human language to another.

Other philosophers don't adopt a language of thought perspective but still conclude that animals can think in ways comprehensible to humans. In defense of the idea that animals have beliefs that we can explicate in human concepts, Colin Allen argues that we shouldn't worry about capturing the exact content of a thought in our belief attributions to humans or other animals. After all, language only approximates our cognitive states, which are fluid and come in more shades and degrees than our language can accommodate (Allen, 2013). What I mean when I say, "I like to swim," may differ depending on the context; for example, sometimes I'm expressing a thin belief that isn't associated with any affect and other times a thick belief with some commitments and motivations associated with it. Even if we kept contexts fixed my assertion still underdetermines what follows in terms of actual commitments and motivations I might have.

Allen (2013, 2014) suggests we should abstract away from the details of our representations and treat them as multidimensional objects. He proposes that we use a transformational rule to show that two cognitive systems are thinking the same thing. This method suggests that for adults, children, and animals, at least some beliefs utilize nonlinguistic representational vehicles. To see this idea at work, let's return to Dummett's dog. While the first pass attempt to ascribe content to the dog referred to the number concept "one," it may be that the dog represents quantities without understanding the nature of integers. As with humans, many species can discriminate between arrays of objects, which is evidence of numerosity without language. Pigeons (Rilling and McDiarmid, 1965), rats (Mechner, 1958), monkeys (Hauser et al., 2003), chimpanzees (Biro and Matsuzawa, 2001), orangutans (Shumaker et al., 2001), and dolphins (Kilian et al., 2003) are among the species that have demonstrated some understanding of number. The cognitive systems responsible for these behaviors all involve nonlinguistic representations of numerosity.

Other representationalists who think that animals have beliefs that do not take a linguistic representational vehicle include Elisabeth Camp (2009) and Michael Rescorla (2009). For example, Camp argues that beliefs can be represented as images such as diagrams or maps. In response to primatologists Dorothy Cheney and Robert Seyfarth (2007), Camp claims that we can understand the baboon's features of thought not as a language-like understanding but rather as a nonsentential representation with a tree-like structure. The view that animals can have perceptual beliefs that ought not be understood in terms of propositional attitudes has also been defended by Glock (2000, 2010).

Finally, one might argue that animals are capable of representing their world, but they do so without beliefs. Maybe animal thinking involves nonconceptual, representational states that are similar but not identical to beliefs. But then the onus is on the representationalist to explain what lies within and outside the scope of belief: which subset of the features listed at the beginning of this section is necessary for belief attribution? Such questions may lead us to expand our cognitive ontology so as to include mental states like "interpretation" and "anticipation," "monitoring" and "registering," etc. (Butterfill and Apperly, 2013; Westra and Carruthers, 2017; De Bruin and Newen, 2014).

2.3 Conclusions about animal representational belief

The worries about ascribing belief to nonlinguistic animals are based largely on the intuition that beliefs expressed in language are stereotypical of all forms of belief. Treating beliefs as nonlinguistic representations helps avoid the worry about language but doesn't explain our practice of ascribing beliefs to animals linguistically and can't immediately vindicate our inclusion of nonlinguistic creatures in the set of folk psychological objects. Of the views presented earlier, Allen's best accommodates our typical practice of ascribing beliefs to animals, babies, people with cognitive disorder, and people across cultures who might lack our battery of concepts.

One may adopt Allen's comparative methodology but still deny that beliefs are representational. Treating beliefs as representations neatly accommodates some but not all of the features associated with our ordinary belief attributions listed earlier. As with beliefs that are partially inferentially integrated or not immediately consciously available, there are many cases of legitimate belief attribution that do not entail an agent that has all the features of belief.

3 Non-representational accounts of belief

While representationalism remains the most widely accepted view about the nature of belief, there are a number of nonrepresentational accounts that have recently gained popularity. In this section we discuss some of the main nonrepresentational accounts of belief and how they might help us study animal minds. In particular, we will look at dispositionalist and interpretationist views of belief and what these theories can say about the question of animal minds.

3.1 Behaviorism and dispositionalism

Understood broadly, analytic behaviorism claims that beliefs can best be understood in terms of observable behavior and dispositions to behave – patterns of behavior that can reliably be correlated with specific beliefs. Gilbert Ryle, viewed by many as the main proponent of behaviorism (although some have argued this label is ill fitting, see Tanney, 2012), argued that it is a category mistake to take the referents of terms like "belief," "thinking," and "imagine" to be privately accessible, internal states of a subject. Ryle argued that the meaning of any mental predicate is some behavioral disposition or loosely connected collection of behavioral tendencies in a given situation. As Ryle (1949) says,

> Dispositional words like "know," "believe," "aspire," "clever," and "humorous" are determinable dispositional words. They signify abilities, tendencies or pronenesses to do, not things of one unique kind, but things of lots of different kinds. Theorists . . . are apt to notice this point, but to assume that there must be corresponding acts of knowing or apprehending and states of believing; and the fact that one person can never find another person executing such wrongly postulated acts, or being in such states is apt to be accounted for by locating these acts and states inside the agent's secret grotto.
>
> (Ryle, 1949, pp. 118–19)

Behaviorism suggests that we can take the same approach to explaining the mental states of both humans and animals. However, two early advocates of behaviorist-friendly views, Wittgenstein (1953) and Sellars (1963), put a lot of emphasis on the role language plays in creating mental states, challenging our ability to say *what* animals think even if we want to accept *that* they think. For example, Wittgenstein famously wrote in *Philosophical Investigations* that "if a lion could talk, we could not understand him" (Wittgenstein, 1953, p. 223). The received interpretation of this aphorism is that even if a lion were able to speak human language, the lack of shared practices, experiences, and living conditions between us and the lion would make the lion's utterances untranslatable. If we extrapolate that in order for creatures to understand one another, their verbal and nonverbal behaviors must be embedded in shared ways of life, the idea that we could ever say much about the minds of nonhuman animals is hopeless.

Sellars's skepticism about our ability to know animal minds comes from his inferentialist semantics, which places the source of meaning in publicly accessible, intersubjective, linguistic practice. On this view, the meaning of any given word/phrase can only be parsed by tracing out its inferential relations to other words/phrases in the language. States of belief and knowledge are individuated by the same sort of inferential relations – to believe a tie is green is, among other things, to believe that it is colored and that it is not red or blue. Sellars says,

> The essential point is that in characterizing an episode or a state as that of *knowing*, we are not giving an empirical description of that episode or state; we are placing it in the logical space of reasons, of justifying and being able to justify what one says.
>
> (Sellars, 1963, p. 169)

Since nonhuman animals will presumably not have mastered such rich inferential relations, they might be said to have brute sensory concepts but not beliefs in the robust way humans do. The same will be true of human infants.

While most researchers in the field have rejected behaviorism as an overarching theory of mind, elements of the view have been preserved in some contemporary accounts of belief and recent approaches are more optimistic about attributing content to animal belief.

Dispositionalism is the view that belief attributions refer to the likelihood that the target will act in certain ways. How do we know if Tamara believes that her cat got out of the house? If she runs out the front door calling the kitty's name, scanning the street and the nearby yards with her eyes, and says that she's lost her cat, we can conclude that she believes the cat got out. Dispositionalism differs from classic behaviorism in that it purports only to be an analysis of belief (and sometimes other propositional attitudes), making no claims about the nature of other mental states, such as emotion, sensation, imagination, or memory.

Dispositionalism takes both a conservative and liberal form. A conservative dispositionalist, like Braithwaite (1933), typically has physicalist motivations, seeking to get a full reduction of mentalistic concepts into behaviors, along the lines of analytic behaviorism. On the other hand, a liberal dispositionalist does not seek any clean reduction and allows appeals to other mental states in analyses of belief. The goal of liberal dispositionalism is to rightly characterize the logic of belief attributions. Some notable liberal dispositionalists include Marcus (1990, 1995) and Schwitzgebel (2002, 2015). On Marcus's account, the state of believing is necessarily action guiding, since to believe something is simply to behave in a way that is consistent with obtaining that thing. Since believing is a nonlinguistic relation between a subject and a way the world can be, beliefs can be properly attributed to animals and young children alike. Eric Schwitzgebel develops and defends a neo-Rylean view called *phenomenal dispositionalism* (2002). Phenomenal dispositionalism breaks with classic behaviorism by allowing not only observable behaviors but also cognitive and phenomenal processes in its analysis of belief. Illustrating his notion of disposition, Schwitzgebel says,

> Consider a favorite belief of philosophers: the belief that there is beer in the fridge. Some of the dispositions associated with this belief include: the disposition to say, in appropriate circumstances, sentences like 'There's beer in my fridge'; the disposition to look in the fridge if one wants a beer; a readiness to offer beer to a thirsty guest; the disposition to utter silently to oneself, in appropriate contexts, "There's beer in my fridge'; an aptness to feel surprise should one go to the fridge and find no beer; the disposition to draw conclusions entailed by propositions that there is beer in the fridge (e.g. that there is something in the fridge, that there is beer in the house); and so forth.
>
> (2002, p. 251)

For Schwitzgebel, the possession of a belief is not all or nothing. Instead, depending on how many of the stereotypical behaviors associated with the given belief someone exhibits, we are able to say that she *really* believes that p, doesn't believe that p at all, or perhaps only half-heartedly or semi-believes that p. Phenomenal dispositionalism seems well equipped to be extended to other animals. While verbalization is *one* type of behavior, it's not necessary or exhaustive of a belief state. This view renders a common-sense result – that animals have beliefs in many of the same ways humans do but simply lack one of the stereotypical behaviors humans often engage in, namely sophisticated verbal behavior. On this view, an animal possesses certain beliefs to certain degrees.

3.1 Interpretationism

Another brand of nonrepresentationalism about belief is interpretationism. Interpretationism captures dispositionalism's focus on patterns of behavior but emphasizes the pragmatic and practical elements of belief attribution, not just those related to predicting behavior. For the interpretationist, believing is a matter of being able to locate behavior (whether it's your own, a neighbor's, or a llama's) within a "web of reason," i.e. a holistic picture of what an agent is doing and why. Dennett (1978a, 1991) and Davidson (1975, 1982) are the most prominent proponents of this strategy, though they disagree about the question of animal beliefs.

For Davidson, linguistic activity is necessary for interpreting an agent as a believer (1982). Propositional attitudes like belief, desire, and intention depend on similar states, and without the presence of a complex pattern of behavior realized in language, genuine thought is impossible. Davidson writes,

> My thesis is not . . . that each thought depends for its existence on the existence of a sentence that expresses that thought. My thesis is rather that a

> creature cannot have a thought unless it has language. In order to be a thinking, rational creature, the creature must be able to express many thoughts, and above all, be able to interpret the speech and thoughts of others.
>
> (1982, p. 100)

While the linguistic constraint present in Davidson's interpretationism may not be essential in order to understand others as mental creatures (Bar-On and Priselac, 2011), Davidson stresses that attributing beliefs implies they are governed by rationality in some sense.

Dennett's intentional systems theory offers a form of interpretationism more congenial to nonhuman animals (2009). According to this account, being able to interpret others and ourselves as minded beings has evolutionary value, because adopting an "intentional stance" toward another creature affords unique predictive and explanatory powers. We are more likely to understand a "rational" creature's actions and predict what it will do next if we attribute certain beliefs (and other mental states). And when it comes to both other people and nonhuman animals, couching behavior in terms of mental states *does* seem to help us predict and explain. When my cat scratches at the cabinet door, it's not random, senseless behavior. There are treats in the cabinet, and saying Meursault *believes* the treats are in the cabinet and *wants* to have some is a helpful interpretation of her observable behavior. Dennett calls this strategy of attributing beliefs and desires "taking the intentional stance" (1989). While there is some criticism of the view that belief attribution is necessary for predicting and explaining (Andrews, 2012), there's something novel and potentially promising in the interpretationist's insistence that believing is more a matter of how we *treat* certain beings and less a matter of their *possessing* the right kind of states or physical structure.

Interpretationists, like representationalists, disagree about whether legitimate belief attribution depends on believers' capability of understanding the contents of their beliefs. In his recent work, Dennett (2017) claims that while taking an intentional stance on animal behavior is sufficient to generate predictions, if we are actually interested in what explains behavior we should look elsewhere. Just as we can interpret a calculator as competent at computing complex arithmetic formulas without assuming it understands arithmetic, we can interpret animals as strategically responding to the world, regardless of whether they "comprehend" how and why they are acting. This is because animals can have a truncated form of behavioral comprehension without any of the reflective capacities we ordinarily associate with thought:

> In animals with more complex behaviors, the degree of versatility and variability exhibited can justify attributing a sort of behavioral comprehension to them so long as we don't make the mistake of thinking of comprehension as some sort of stand-alone talent, a source of competence rather than a manifestation of competence.
>
> (Dennett, 2017, p. 101)

The difference between behavioral competence and behavioral comprehension is underspecified. Nonetheless, it appears that Dennett now thinks that reflective access to one's beliefs – that is, the ability to take the intentional stance toward oneself – is needed for an individual to count as a believer in an interpretationist framework. Dennett thinks that this reflective capacity admits of degrees, and humans have it in spades. This is because Dennett assigns an important role for language in the development of reflection and comprehension – language is a cognitive tool that not only structures the thoughts we might have but also allows us to represent our thoughts to ourselves in order to explore and sculpt our own interpretations of events. While Dennett is open to the idea that nonhuman animals might engage in some form of evidence-monitoring, it's unclear exactly what that would mean for his overall picture of cognitive evolution, since it's our unique ability to reflect on our own thoughts that allows us to purposefully exploit our own patterns of thinking.

3.2 *Conclusions about nonrepresentational beliefs*

While few scholars accept behaviorism as an overarching theory of the mind, contemporary offshoots of that view, such as dispositionalism or interpretationism, may offer a plausible and promising account of a subset of mental states – propositional attitudes in general and belief in particular. These nonrepresentationalist views claim to have the benefit of avoiding some of the more serious metaphysical problems that representational views face, such as the mental causation problem and the challenge of naturalizing the mind. Perhaps most attractively, nonrepresentational theories tout the intuitive idea that observable behavior is intimately involved in what it means to believe, not in a merely contingent way but rather in some essential sense. Further, by viewing verbal behavior as *just one* of the many types of actions and cues we assess when deciding what someone believes, nonrepresentationalist views offer perhaps the most promising path forward in understanding the nature of animal thought as different only in degree, not in kind, from human thought.

4 Animal belief in comparative psychology

Despite the plausibility of nonrepresentational views of belief, representationalism is the default assumption in the empirical sciences. This is likely due to the fact that the cognitive revolution was late in coming to the study of animal behavior, as well as the acceptance of what psychological behaviorists such as B. F. Skinner denied, namely the importance of intervening variables with causal power. Cognitive psychologists such as Charles Gallistel (1993) urge us to understand animal minds in terms of computational representations rather than associative learning. Even some psychologists who think associative learning can go a long way in understanding animal minds still point to an essential role for internal representations (Shettleworth, 2010b).

While it is largely assumed that animals have representational mental states, such as beliefs, a question of much interest has been whether other animals have beliefs about others' beliefs. This ability is called "mindreading" or "theory of mind." In 1978 the psychologists David Premack and Guy Woodruff asked whether chimpanzees do what Premack and Woodruff presumed humans do – namely attribute mental state in order to predict and explain others' behavior. The question stems from the assumption that in order to predict and explain behavior, we have to determine the beliefs and desires that cause action.

Following a suggestion stemming from commentaries on Premack and Woodruff's original paper, Daniel Dennett (1978b), Jonathan Bennett (1978), and Gilbert Harman (1978) suggested that the real way to find out if chimpanzees can think about others' beliefs is to determine whether chimpanzees can think that others have *false* beliefs. This suggestion led to the false belief task, which was designed to examine when children start developing the concept of belief. As developed by psychologists Hans Wimmer and Josef Perner (1983), the classic test involves presenting children with a puppet show that goes like this: Maxi hides a piece of chocolate and leaves the room. While Maxi is out, his mother finds the chocolate and moves it to another location. When Maxi comes back in the room to get his chocolate, the child is asked where Maxi will go to look for his chocolate. If children predict that Maxi will look for the chocolate where he left it, they then pass the test. But the child who predicts that Maxi will look for the chocolate where it really is fails. Passing the test is interpreted as evidence of being able to reason about beliefs. Children pass the test around 4 to 5 years of age (Wellman, Cross, & Watson, 2001).

Though chimpanzees failed at versions of this task for many years (Call and Tomasello, 1999; Krachun et al., 2009; Kaminski, Call, and Tomasello, 2008), a recent pair of studies found evidence that chimpanzees can get the right answer on a chimp version of the task (Krupenye et al., 2016; Buttlemann et al., 2017). While these studies show that apes can anticipate people's actions when they have a false belief, we don't know how the apes make these predictions.

Figure 23.1 False belief 2 condition from Krupeyne's *et al.* experiment 1. The chimpanzee subject watches as the human sees King Kong hide in the right haystack and then goes inside to get the stick, closing the door behind him. While the human isn't watching, King Kong moves from the right haystack to the left and then leaves the scene. Then the door opens, and the human comes out with the stick. Subjects tend to look toward the rightmost haystack, where the human last saw King Kong.

While chimpanzees pass the task, we may still wonder whether they have belief with the features listed in section 1. We may ask whether chimpanzees demonstrate the ability to formulate and ascribe propositional attitudes that can be true or false, we can ask whether they demonstrate aspectuality in their attributions of beliefs, and we can ask whether they show evidence of inferential integration (Andrews, 2017b, 2018).

Furthermore, we might challenge the view that belief attribution has the kind of direction-of-fit relationship that it is usually taken to have. For example, humans attribute beliefs in ways that do not explicitly aim at accuracy, much less in ways that neatly conform with norms of practical reasoning (Spaulding, 2016). An interpretationist or dispositionalist might also conclude that these studies must be complemented by different types of tests that seek to find robust patterns of behavior that are "usefully and voluminously" (Dennett, 2009) predicted and explained through the attribution of a mindreading capacity.

Instead of focusing on false belief tasks involving moved objects, researchers can examine those situations that might naturally elicit belief reasoning in chimpanzees. We can look at chimpanzees' natural life to examine whether there are specific conditions in which they would benefit from thinking about others' beliefs. Chimpanzees have a fission-fusion social structure, which means they often spend time away from one another. During that time chimpanzees might learn something that another doesn't know. It might be useful to share new information in such a context, or it might be useful to hide it. Chimpanzees who hunt in groups might need to share information in order to better coordinate behavior. Chimpanzees might act oddly, and others may want to explain their odd behavior. Odd behavior may be beneficial to the group, as it might be a cultural innovation that is worth understanding (Andrews, 2012).

5 Conclusion

In this chapter we've outlined some of the central ways theorists approach the study of animal minds, trying to make sense of the seemingly uncontroversial claim that animals think. There is evidence in support of the idea that when we attribute beliefs to our fuzzy, feathered, and finned friends, we're not merely anthropomorphizing but describing a basic fact. Despite the common practice of attributing thought to animals and the scientific evidence in favor of doing so, the exact nature of the mental states we observe in other animals remains unclear. To be fair, there is still a lot of contentious debate about the nature of *human* belief, so we shouldn't be too discouraged by the lack of consensus on animal minds. We can note that the past century has seen revolutionary progress in the way we approach the study of animal minds and that there are now a number of promising theoretical paths to take toward a more comprehensive understanding of the topic.

Bibliography

Allen, C. (2014) "Models, Mechanisms, and Animal Minds." *The Southern Journal of Philosophy* 52: 75–97.

Allen, C. (2013) "The Geometry of Partial Understanding." *American Philosophical Quarterly* 3(50): 249–62.

Andrews, K. (forthcoming) *How to Study Animal Minds*. Cambridge: Cambridge University Press.
Andrews, K. (2018) "Apes Track False Beliefs But Might Not Understand Them." *Learning and Behavior* 46(1): 3–4.
Andrews, K. (2017a) "Pluralistic Folk Psychology in Humans and Other Animals." In J. Kiverstein, ed., *The Routledge Handbook of the Social Mind*. New York: Routledge.
Andrews, K. (2017b) "Do Chimpanzees Reason about Belief?" In K. Andrews & J. Beck, eds., *The Routledge Handbook of the Philosophy of Animal Minds*. New York: Routledge.
Andrews, K. (2016) "A Role for Folk Psychology in Animal Cognition Research." In A. Blank, ed., *Animals: Basic Philosophical Concepts*. Philosophia: Munich.
Andrews, K. (2012) *Do Apes Read Minds? Toward a New Folk Psychology*. Cambridge, MA: MIT Press.
Anscombe, G.E.M. (1957) *Intention*. Oxford: Oxford University Press.
Bar-On, D. & Priselac, M. (2011) "Triangulation and the Beasts." In C. Amoretti & G. Preyer, eds., *Triangulation: From an Epistemological Point of View*. Frankfurt: Ontos Verlag.
Beck, J. (2013) "Why We Can't Say What Animals Think." *Philosophical Psychology* 26(4): 520–46.
Bennett, J. (1978) "Commentary on Three Papers about Animal Cognition." *The Behavioral and Brain Sciences* 1: 556–60.
Bermúdez, J. L. (2003) *Thinking without Words*. Oxford: Oxford University Press.
Biro, D. & Matsuzawa, T. (2001) "Use of Numerical Symbols by the Chimpanzee (Pan Troglodytes): Cardinals, Ordinals, and the Introduction of Zero." *Animal Cognition* 3(4): 193–99.
Braithwaite, R. B. (1933) "VI: The Nature of Believing." *Proceedings of the Aristotelian Society* 33(1): 129–46.
Buckwalter, W., Rose, D., & Turri, J. (2015) "Belief through Thick and Thin." *Noûs* 49(4): 748–75.
Butterfill, S. & Apperly, I. (2013) "How to Construct a Minimal Theory of Mind." *Mind and Language* 28(5): 606–37.
Buttlemann, D., Buttlemann, F., Carpenter, M., Call, J., & Tomasello, M. (2017) "Great Apes Distinguish True from False Beliefs in an Interactive Helping Task." *Plos One* 12(4).
Call, J. & Tomasello, M. (1999) "A Nonverbal False Belief Task: The Performance of Children and Great Apes." *Child Development* 70: 381–95.
Camp, E. (2009) "A Language of Baboon Thought?" In R. Lurz, ed., *Philosophy of Animal Minds*. New York: Cambridge University Press.
Cheney, D. L. & Seyfarth, R. M. (2007) *Baboon Metaphysics: The Evolution of a Social Mind*. Chicago: University of Chicago Press.
Davidson, D. (1982) "Rational Animals." *Dialectica* 36(4): 317–27.
Davidson, D. (1975) "Thought and Talk." In S. Guttenplan, ed., *Mind and Language*, 7–24. Oxford: Oxford University Press.
De Bruin, L. C. & Newen, A. (2014) "The Developmental Paradox of False Belief Understanding: A Dual-System Solution." *Synthese* 191(3).
Dennett, D. C. (2017) *From Bacteria to Bach and Back: The Evolution of Minds*. New York: W. W. Norton & Co. Press.
Dennett, D. C. (2009) "Intentional Systems Theory." In B. McLaughlin, A. Beckermann, & S. Walter, eds., *The Oxford Handbook of Philosophy of Mind*. Oxford: Oxford University Press.
Dennett, D. C. (1991) "Real Patterns." *Journal of Philosophy* 87: 27–51.
Dennett, D. C. (1989) *The Intentional Stance*. Cambridge, MA: MIT Press.
Dennett, D. C. (1978a) *Brainstorms*. Cambridge, MA: MIT Press.
Dennett, D. C. (1978b) "Beliefs about Beliefs." *Behavioral and Brain Sciences* 4: 568–70.
Dummett, M. (2010) *The Nature and Future of Philosophy*. New York: Columbia University Press.
Dworkin, R. (1986) *Law's Empire*. Cambridge, MA: Belknap Press.
Fodor, J. A. (1975) *The Language of Thought*. New York: Crowell.
Gallistel, C. (1993) *The Organization of Learning*. Cambridge, MA: A Bradford Book.
Glock, H. (2010) "Can Animals Judge?" *Dialectica* 64: 11–33.
Glock, H. (2000) "Animals, Thoughts and Concepts." *Synthese* 123: 35–64.
Harman, G. (1978) "Studying the Chimpanzees' Theory of Mind." *Behavioral and Brain Sciences* 1: 576–77.
Hauser, M. D., Tsao, F., Garcia, P., & Spelke, E. (2003) "Evolutionary Foundations of Number: Spontaneous Representation of Numerical Magnitudes by Cotton-Top Tamarins." *Proceedings of the Royal Society of London. Series B: Biological Sciences* 270(1523): 1441–46.

Kaminski, J., Call, J., & Tomasello, M. (2008) "Chimpanzees Know What Others Know, But Not What They Believe." *Cognition* 109: 224–34.

Kilian, A., Yaman, S., von Fersen, L. & Güntürkün, O. (2003) "A Bottlenose Dolphin Discriminates Visual Stimuli Differing in Numerosity." *Animal Learning & Behavior* 31(2): 133–42.

Krachun, C., Carpenter, M., Call, J., & Tomasello, M. (2009) "A Competitive Nonverbal False Belief Task for Children and Apes." *Developmental Science* 12(4): 521–35.

Krupenye, C., Kano, F., Hirata, S., Call, J., & Tomasello, M. (2016) "Great Apes Anticipate That Other Individuals Will Act According to False Beliefs." *Science* 354: 110–14.

Marcus, R. B. (1995) "The Anti-Naturalism of Some Language Centered Accounts of Belief." *Dialectica* 49: 113–29.

Marcus, R. B. (1990) "Some Revisionary Proposals about Belief and Believing." *Philosophy and Phenomenological Research* 50: 132–53.

Mechner, F. (1958) "Probability Relations within Response Sequences under Ratio Reinforcement." *Journal of the Experimental Analysis of Behavior* 1(2): 109–21.

Plunkett, D. & Sundell, T. (2013) "Dworkin's Interpretivism and the Pragmatics of Legal Disputes." *Legal Theory* 242(19).

Premack, D. & Woodruff, G. (1978) "Does the Chimpanzee Have a Theory of Mind?" *Behavioral and Brain Sciences* 1: 515–26.

Rescorla, M. (2009) "Chrysippus' Dog as a Case Study in Non-Linguistic Cognition." In R. W. Lurz, ed., *The Philosophy of Animal Minds*, 52–71. Cambridge: Cambridge University Press.

Rilling, M. & McDiarmid, C. (1965) "Signal Detection in Fixed-Ratio Schedules." *Science* 148(3669): 526–27.

Rowlands, M. (2012) *Can Animals Be Moral?* Oxford: Oxford University Press.

Ryle, G. (1949) *The Concept of Mind*. London: Hutchinson & Co. Press.

Schwitzgebel, E. (2015) "Belief." In E. N. Zalta, ed., *The Stanford Encyclopedia of Philosophy*. Accessed at https://plato.stanford.edu/entries/belief/.

Schwitzgebel, E. (2002) "A Phenomenal, Dispositional Account of Belief." *Nous* 36: 249–75.

Sellars, W. (1963) *Sense, Perception, and Reality*. New York: Humanities Press.

Shettleworth, S. J. (2010a) "Clever Animals and Killjoy Explanations in Comparative Psychology." *Trends in Cognitive Sciences* 14(11): 477–81.

Shettleworth, S. J. (2010b) *Cognition, Evolution, and Behavior* (2nd ed.). New York: Oxford University Press.

Shumaker, R. W., Palkovich, A. M., Beck, B. B., Guagnano, G. A., & Morowitz, H. (2001) "Spontaneous Use of Magnitude Discrimination and Ordination by the Orangutan (Pongo Pygmaeus)." *Journal of Comparative Psychology* 115(4): 385–91.

Spaulding, S. (2016) "Mind Misreading." *Philosophical Issues* 26(1).

Stich, S. (1979) "Do Animals Have Beliefs?" *Australasian Journal of Philosophy* 57: 15–28.

Stich, S. (1978) "Beliefs and Subdoxastic States." *Philosophy of Science* 4(45): 499–518.

Tanney, J. (2012) *Rules, Reason, and Self-Knowledge*. Cambridge, MA: Harvard University Press.

Thompson, J. R. (2016) "Believe It or Not: On Multiplying Classes of Belief-Like States." *Studia Philosophica Estonica* 9(1): 79–110.

Wellman, H. M., Cross, D., & Watson, D. (2001) "Meta-Analysis of Theory-of-Mind Development: The Truth about False Belief." *Child Development* 72: 655–84.

Westra, E. & Carruthers, P. (2017) "Pragmatic Development Explains the Theory of Mind Scale." *Cognition* 158: 165–76.

Wimmer, H. J. & Perner, J. (1983) "Beliefs about Beliefs: Representation and Constraining Function of Wrong Beliefs in Young Children's Understanding of Deception." *Cognition* 13: 103–28.

Wittgenstein, L. (1953) *Philosophical Investigations*. G.E.M. Anscombe & R. Rhees, eds., G.E.M. Anscombe, trans. Oxford: Blackwell Publishing.

24
REPRESENTATION IN THE PREDICTION ERROR MINIMIZATION FRAMEWORK

Alex Kiefer and Jakob Hohwy

Introduction

The prediction error minimization (PEM) framework in cognitive science is an approach to cognition and perception centered on a simple idea: organisms represent the world by constantly predicting their own internal states. Predictions consist of efferent signals traveling via "top-down" synaptic connections from higher (e.g. frontal and temporal) cortical regions to lower-level sensory and motor cortices. Cascades of predictions are matched against incoming sensory signals, which act as negative feedback to correct a generative model encoded in the top-down and lateral connections. Comparisons between predictions and bottom-up signals occur at each stage of hierarchical cortical processing, and only the "error signal," the unpredicted portion of the bottom-up input, feeds forward to the next stage (as a process theory, this hypothesized mechanism is known as "predictive coding" – see e.g. Rao and Sejnowski 2002; Friston 2005; Clark 2013; Hohwy 2013; Clark 2016b for details and discussion).

In this chapter, we focus on what's novel in the perspective that the PEM framework affords on the cognitive-scientific project of explaining intelligence by appeal to internal representations.[1] The core representational structure posited by such theories is the hierarchical generative model. Generative models have long been informally hypothesized to play a role in perception (Helmholtz 1860) and have been proposed as a unifying framework for understanding unsupervised learning within neural networks (Hinton and Sejnowski 1999). More recently, the PEM framework and predictive coding theories have drawn long-deserved attention within wider cognitive-scientific circles to generative statistical modeling as a powerful overarching theoretical approach to mental and neural representation.

Generative models are a philosophically interesting class of representations in part because they can be understood both in terms of Bayesian updating of subjective probabilities in light of evidence, and thus as part of a hypothesis-testing model of cognition (Fodor 1975), and in terms of simulation or (exploitable) structural resemblance to modeled sets of causes (Cummins 1994; Gładziejewski 2016; Gładziejewski and Miłkowski 2017). By the close of the chapter we aim to have shown how truth-conditional and resemblance-based approaches to representation in generative models may be integrated.

Generative models are also appealing for cognitive science because their (typically hierarchical) structures can be mapped relatively easily onto the physical structures of neural vehicles. While the empirical jury is still out with respect to some of the finer details of PEM models (such as Friston's hypothesis that distinct neuronal populations encode predictions and errors respectively – see (Friston 2005)), the way in which such models could in principle be neurally implemented is well understood. A consistent theme in cognitive theories that appeal to generative models is the possibility of implementing them using only biologically plausible local synaptic (e.g. Hebbian and anti-Hebbian) update rules (Hinton and Sejnowski 1983; Hinton et al. 1995; Friston 2005; Bogacz 2017).

It understates the case for such theories, however, to point out merely that it is easy to implement generative models in brain structures. It is more accurate to say that it would be difficult *not* to implement a statistical model, given basic properties of neural computation and learning and exposure of the network to signals from external information sources. Such matters of implementation will be kept constantly in view in the ensuing discussion. Relatedly, there is a surprisingly short route from potential energy minimization in self-sustaining systems to learning and inference in generative models (Hinton and Zemel 1994, Neal and Hinton 1998, Friston 2009, also discussed below).

We begin in section 1 with a discussion of generative models in some depth, starting with conceptual foundations and outlining the essential role that generative models (and their inverses, recognition models) are hypothesized to play in explanations of psychological phenomena. We illustrate the interplay between generative and recognition models by appeal to a pioneering computational model of perceptual inference proposed by Hinton and colleagues (1995). In section 2, we discuss what predictive coding models such as Friston's (2005) add to this picture, and then sketch one route via which the connection between Bayesian inference and energy minimization can be understood, again by appeal to an early proposal in machine learning (Hinton and Sejnowski 1983). In section 3, we build on recent work on the theory of structural representation (Gładziejewski 2016; Gładziejewski and Miłkowski 2017) to develop an account of representation within generative models that is responsive to traditional philosophical concerns about mental representation.

1 Generative models

Despite its importance in contemporary cognitive science, the notion of a generative model has seldom received extensive philosophical treatment in its own right. In this section we first provide an intuitive conceptual overview of generative models and then consider how they are distinguished from discriminative models, on the one hand, and from recognition models, on the other, in theoretical contexts. Both dimensions of comparison play important roles in understanding representation and learning within the PEM framework. We then discuss the Helmholtz machine (Hinton et al. 1995), a particular model of perceptual inference that implements generative and discriminative models.

1.1 (Hierarchical) generative models

The term "generative model" is used in a variety of related ways in machine learning, statistics, and related disciplines. A paradigmatic concrete example is a program that generates realistic 2D images of human faces, based on a handful of input variables representing relevant parameters, e.g. the positions of facial muscles, skin texture, pose, and lighting or more generally, any 3D graphics engine. Such a program (a) implements a generative *process* capable of producing a range of phenomena (images of human faces, (b) in a way that *models*, i.e. represents or stands in in some relevant way for, a distinct generative process (e.g. the process by which the underlying variables in the real world contribute to the appearance of actual human faces).

The degree to which one generative process is capable of modeling another depends on the similarity between the two. Similarity was built into the description of the toy example just considered, in the claim that the model contains representations of relevant environmental variables underlying facial appearances. But generative models are best understood as representing what they do in virtue of purely structural similarities. It could not sensibly be stipulated that some state within the model represented the position of a certain facial muscle unless that state contributed – along with other variables in the model – to the resulting image in an analogous way to that in which the position of the relevant muscle contributes to the appearance of a real face in the context of other relevant factors. Consistent with this, Gładziejewski (2016) argues, following Hohwy (2013) and others, that the generative models posited by PEM-style theories are "structural representations": representations in which "the representation itself and what is represented are related in terms of structural similarity" (this idea is critically discussed in Part 3).

A generative model is also often described, in similar contexts, as a model that *explains* some phenomenon by *specifying* a set of causes that could have produced the phenomenon (see e.g. Nair et al. 2008).[2] These two notions of generative model – as (1) a *causally efficacious* compact structure that produces a range of phenomena and (2) as a model that *causally explains* the same phenomena – are of course intimately related. The idea is that a structure of causes capable of producing X (assuming it is independently plausible) can be appealed to in an abductive explanation of X.

PEM theories often stress the hierarchical structure of the generative models they posit. Hierarchical representations have long been supposed to underlie cognitive and perceptual capacities of all sorts for diverse reasons, and there is ample theoretical and experimental evidence for them (see e.g. Chomsky 1957; Marr 1982). That aside, it is clear *a priori* that good hierarchical generative models should be capable of producing better "synthetic data" than shallower models for domains of any complexity. A hierarchical version of the face-image generator discussed earlier, for example, may include (a) a generative model of facial appearance based on muscular positions and other variables and (b) a generative model of facial muscle positions based on affective state. The resulting two-level model is more likely to produce realistic face images than a single-level model in which the allowed combinations of muscle positions are unconstrained.

This example makes explicit a key feature of hierarchical generative models that partially explains their representational capacity: a hierarchical generative model is, essentially, a hierarchy *of* generative models of interrelated phenomena. Hierarchy (and model complexity more generally) are also important for constraining the contents of generative models. As the complexity of the causal process being modeled (and of a corresponding adequate model) increases, the chances of being able to generate the relevant phenomenon using highly structurally dissimilar sets of causes decreases.

1.2 Generative and discriminative models

In the previous section we discussed generative models from a broad, conceptual point of view. In a narrower sense, a generative model is a species of statistical model. Statistical models, for present purposes, can be defined as mathematical models that capture the dependencies that obtain among the values of a set of random variables. The dependencies are represented by the parameters of the model, and variables may be observed (i.e. have some of their values supplied directly by data) or hidden (latent).

A simple linear regression model, for example, might be defined by an equation such as $y = P_1x_1 + P_2x_2 + P_3x_3 + P_4x_4$, where y is a variable whose value we are interested in predicting, $P_1 \ldots P_4$ are the parameters of the model, and $x_1 \ldots x_4$ are observed variables on which the prediction is based. The parameters determine how each variable influences the final prediction. Logistic regression is a slightly more complex case in which the observed variables are mapped to a real value between 0 and 1, using a nonlinear function[3] g of the linear combination of x's weighted by P's: $y = g(P_1x_1 + P_2x_2 + P_3x_3 + P_4x_4)$. Here, y can be interpreted as the expected probability of some state of affairs obtaining, given values of x.

Statistical models in general exhibit many of the features of generative models that are appealed to in PEM accounts of representation and learning. With respect to representation, statistical models may be thought of as (often extremely low-fidelity or idealized) simulations (Cummins 1994). For each relevant aspect of the modeled situation, there is a representation in the model whose relations to other representations mirrors the relations that obtain between that represented aspect of the situation and the other represented aspects. Representation in statistical models can thus be understood in terms of structural similarity. To make the structure of statistical models explicit, it is useful to depict them as graphical models, as in Figure 24.1.

Statistical models are only as good as their predictions, which in turn are only as good as the model parameters, which can be learned from data. In the regression models discussed previously, optimal parameters can be discovered by supplying values

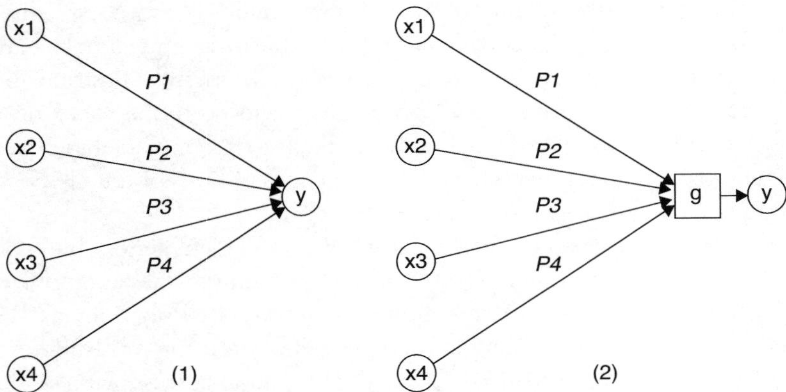

Figure 24.1 (1) Linear regression and (2) logistic regression, depicted graphically. The values of the parameters P determine the influence of the corresponding x values on the overall prediction for y. In (1), y is the sum of the input multiplied by the parameters. In (2), the function g converts the summed, weighted input into a real value between 0 and 1

of the observed variables x from data, deriving predictions $F(x)$ for y, comparing the predictions to known values of y given the same values of x in the dataset to obtain a measure of error, and adjusting the parameters so as to minimize the error across examples (captured in a "cost function" that defines a mapping from model parameters to average error).

A conceptually simple and widely used method for doing this is stochastic gradient descent: given a data point x, derive a prediction for y, adjust each parameter in proportion to its contribution to the cost for that example, and repeat.[4] This gradient descent learning is Bayesian in a broad sense: predictions based on prior knowledge, encoded in the parameters, are compared against incoming evidence and used to update the parameters, determining a new posterior distribution over (or estimate of, depending on the type of model) the values of the variables at each step. In later sections, we consider models that employ Bayesian reasoning more explicitly.

The discussion thus far shows that two core principles of the PEM framework, structural representation and Bayesian learning by prediction error minimization, are already operative in the simplest statistical models. It remains to be seen what distinguishes generative statistical models from other sorts. Informally, there is a sense in which any statistical model is a generative model: given values of some of the variables in the model, predicted "synthetic" values of other variables can be derived based on the parameters. David Danks makes a similar point regarding graphical models: "Essentially all graphical models make predictions about how the world should be. That is, they are almost all generative models: representations that can be used to generate 'typical' data (according to the model)" (Danks 2014: 44).

In a technical sense commonly employed in statistics and machine learning, however, a generative model is one that determines a joint probability distribution[5] over a set of variables, in contrast to a *discriminative* model, which determines a distribution over a target variable (often representing a class label) conditioned on the value(s) of observed variable(s) (Jebara 2002; Bishop and Lasserre 2007). Discriminative models are so called because they are typically (and naturally) used for discrimination and classification. Neural networks used in computer vision, for example, determine $p(Y \mid X)$, where Y is an image label and X is a matrix of pixel intensities for the image. Generative models are so called because they can be used to generate data similar to a set of observed values, as previously discussed. A generative image model, for example, may determine a distribution over pixel intensities $p(X)$, or perhaps $p(X, Y)$, where Y is a label, if it is a joint model of both images and their labels (for an example of the latter, see (Hinton 2007)). Generative models of any interest typically include latent variables.

Since relevant marginal and conditional probabilities can always be computed from a joint distribution (Jebara 2002: 27), generative models are in a sense more powerful than discriminative models, and each multivariate generative model may be thought of as containing implicit discriminative models of its variables. However, in practice, given constraints due to limited data and the difficulty of learning arbitrary full generative models, it is often more efficient and effective to train a discriminative model directly if one's goal is classification or discrimination. Clearly, cognitive agents learn the functional equivalents of good discriminative models based on sensory data. They are hypothesized to do so within the PEM framework by inverting a generative model, as discussed in the next section.

1.3 Generative and recognition models in the Helmholtz machine

In order to understand how relevant hypotheses can be selected conditional on sensory input, we need not only the generative model (i.e. a mapping from underlying causes to the sensory input) but a recognition model (i.e. the inverse mapping from sensory input to causes) (Dayan et al. 1995: 889; Nair et al. 2008: 1). A recognition model in this sense is of course the essential component of any perceptual system. The novel explanatory power of the PEM account (and of theories of perception based on generative models more generally) derives largely from the way in which pairs of generative and recognition models interact.

This interaction is illustrated particularly clearly in an artificial neural network model called the "Helmholtz machine" (Dayan et al. 1995; Hinton et al. 1995; Frey et al. 1997) (Figure 24.2), a model of perceptual inference and learning that incorporates many of the core features of PEM models and in large part inspired them. The Helmholtz machine consists of layers of binary stochastic processing units ("neurons") – that is, units that may be in one of two states, 0 and 1, and whose states at any moment are determined probabilistically using an activation function that computes the probability of a neuron being in the "1" state as a function of its weighted, summed input (plus a bias term) and then sets the state to "1" with that probability.[6] The "bottom" layer is an input layer L whose units may have their activities fixed directly by an external input source, and subsequent layers are fully connected to the layers above and below.

Elsewhere, Hinton and Sejnowski (1983) propose a simple interpretation of a binary stochastic network (discussed in section 2.2 below) as a representation of the source of its external input signals: the state of each unit is interpreted as the truth-value assigned to a proposition, and the probability of a unit's being in the "True" (or "1") state at a given moment corresponds to the probability the system assigns to the corresponding proposition at that moment ("probabilities are represented by probabilities" (Hinton and Sejnowski 1983: 448)). Under this interpretation, the "input" nodes correspond to pieces of sensory evidence, and the rest correspond to hypotheses invoked to explain the evidence. Except for the input units, the probability of each unit (and thus each hypothesis) depends only on the states of the other units (hypotheses) plus the strength and sign of the connections between them. Such a network can thus represent complex probabilistic dependencies among hypotheses.[7]

A trained Helmholtz machine encodes a hierarchical generative model of the source of the input to L in its top-down connections and a recognition model in its bottom-up connections.[8] To "infer" a set of hypotheses on the basis of input supplied at L, one simply activates the units in $L + 1$ using the bottom-up weights and then uses those activities to calculate activities for units in $L + 2$ and so on to the top layer of the model. Thus, "perceptual inference" in this model is purely feed-forward. The generative model can be run by choosing a top-level state using the biases or beginning with the top-level state induced by a previous bottom-up pass and then using the same activation function to choose states for successively lower layers, down to L.

Fitting the model to data piggybacks on the processes of perceptual inference from data and generation of "fantasies" using the top-down connections. An effective learning algorithm (the "wake-sleep" algorithm) alternately (a) uses data supplied at the input layer and the current recognition model to cause a series of hidden-layer activities and then adjusts the generative model's connections so that it will be more likely to produce those same activities; then, (b) generates states of the entire model top-down using the current generative model and adjusts the bottom-up connections so that they're more likely to produce those states next time perceptual inference is performed from data (Hinton et al. 1995).

In this way, "bottom-up and top-down models can train each other" – "given a *poor* graphics network, we use the images it generates to train a vision network. When this vision network is then applied to *real images* we can use it to improve the graphics network" (Frey et al. 1997: 3–5). From a statistical perspective, the generative model at any stage of learning determines a prior distribution P over both "hidden causes" of sensory input represented by hidden-layer states and, via those, over states of the input layer, and we would like to update this distribution after receiving input to yield a posterior generative distribution. The recognition model determines a distinct distribution Q over causes given data. P and Q converge over the course of learning so that the probability of alternative configurations of the network under the recognition model comes to approximate the posterior distribution under the generative model.[9]

Since the hidden-layer states induced by the recognition model are systematically related to (i.e. carry information about) the input and the generative model is trained on the recognition model, we may expect this process to work for essentially the same (broadly Bayesian) reason that simple regression models work. In effect, the parameters come to store compressed information about the average relationships among variables observed in the data. In this case, however, rather than learning a mapping from input variable X to distinct output variable Y, the model is learning a mapping from X, through a latent "neural code" H (the set of hypotheses) and back down to X – i.e. a generative model of X.

We hope that the foregoing gives some indication of the explanatory power of a theory of mental (in particular, perceptual) representation based on pairs of generative and recognition models. Arguably, the key breakthrough is in the explanation of how a recognition model could be learned in an unsupervised way, i.e. without explicit feedback about the real causes of the sensory input. This explanation depends essentially on generative models and the bootstrapping process that improves generative and recognition models simultaneously. But generative models afford theoretical benefits independently of this: they offer an account of endogenously generated psychological phenomena such as dreaming and mental imagery, and they are well suited to play the essential role in the explanation of action, analogous to the essential role played by recognition models in the explanation of perception.[10]

We concluded this first part of the paper with a discussion of the Helmholtz machine because of the transparency with which it implements core concepts relevant to the PEM framework, and because of its historical importance. But the Helmholtz machine has important limitations. For one thing, as its creators acknowledge (Frey et al. 1997: 21), it lacks a role for top-down signals during online perceptual processing. It thus does not implement the idea, surely one of the more well-known features of Friston's model (Friston 2005), that certain hypotheses may be contextually favored over others by having their prior probabilities dynamically raised over short timescales by various sorts of priming and collateral information, including preceding sensory input. It also therefore lacks the efficiency of an online "prediction-subtraction" mechanism, whereby *only* the unpredicted, un-"cancelled" portion of the sensory signal is passed up the hierarchy (as discussed in the next section).

It is also limited in its modeling power, since it can learn only factorial distributions (Hinton et al. 1995: 4). That said, though the Helmholtz machine architecture employed in combination with the wake-sleep algorithm is far from the best-performing approach to unsupervised learning at present, it is able to learn to recapitulate the structure of the generative process that produces its inputs in simple toy problems (Hinton et al. 1995: 5; Frey et al. 1997), and it learns useful compressed representations on real datasets by minimizing the Shannon description length of the neural codes inferred from input, which is equivalent to minimizing the Helmholtz free energy associated with alternative codes (Hinton et al. 1995). It thus constitutes a powerful proof-of-concept for the generative models approach to perception and learning as well as the narrower idea that Bayesian inference can be accomplished via the minimization of free energy (Hinton and Zemel 1994; Friston 2009).

2 Predictive coding, Bayesian inference, and energy minimization

More remains to be said about how precisely representation and hypothesis-testing get off the ground on the picture previously sketched and about the notion of representation involved. The latter will be discussed in Part 3. In this section, we discuss hierarchical models that incorporate the mechanism of predictive coding (Rao and Ballard 1999; Rao and Sejnowski 2002; Friston 2005; Huang and Rao 2011), focusing on the respects in which they differ from the Helmholtz machine. We then attempt to elucidate the conceptual link between Bayesian inference and energy minimization exploited by such models, appealing to an early proposal by Hinton and Sejnowski (1983).

2.1 Prediction error minimization versus predictive coding

"Predictive coding" (PC) refers to an encoding strategy in which predicted portions of an input signal are subtracted from the actual signal received, so that only the difference between the two is passed as output to the next stage of information processing. Early proposals such as that in Srinivasan et al. (1982) suggest that the center-surround antagonism characteristic of the receptive fields of some neurons in visual cortex implement predictive coding: "The antagonistic surround takes a weighted mean of the signals in the neighboring receptors to generate a statistical prediction of the signal at the centre. The predicted value is subtracted from the actual centre signal" (p. 427). In this case, part of the signal from a given neural population is used to predict other parts of the same signal, all via feed-forward connections. In what follows, we will focus on PC theories that implement a similar mechanism within hierarchical cortical structures, where neural populations higher in the hierarchy predict the activities of those at lower levels via top-down connections.

Both the Helmholtz machine discussed in section 1.3 and the hierarchical PC models in question implement generative models that provide top-down explanations of sensory input, as well as recognition models, which are used for approximate perceptual inference. Learning in both models proceeds via prediction error minimization. Although prediction error is nowhere explicitly represented in the Helmholtz machine, we can regard the difference between states produced bottom-up and states likely to be produced top-down as an error term – this term is used to optimize the top-down generative weights during training. As already sketched, a mirror-image process is used during the "sleep" phase of the wake-sleep algorithm to update the parameters of the recognition model using "fantasized" data produced by the generative model as a target.

One of the main differences between PC models and the Helmholtz machine is that in the former, prediction errors are represented explicitly. In Friston's predictive coding model (see (Bogacz 2017) for an accessible exposition), there are two distinct types of explicit representations encoded in neural activities: expectations about properties in the environment ("representation units") and prediction errors encoded in "error units." Top-down connections run from the representation units at level L_{i+1} in the hierarchy to the error units at L_i and bottom-up connections run from the error units at L_i to the representation units at L_{i+1} (thus, only the error signal is passed up the hierarchy). The same connectivity exists at each L_i (so, for example, representation units at L_i feed predictions down to error units at L_{i-1}, and error units at L_{i+1} pass prediction errors up to representation units in L_{i+2}).

Another important difference is that Friston's model includes lateral connections, between the error and representation units at a given level. The Helmholtz machine, and related neural network models, such as Restricted Boltzmann Machines (RBMs) (Hinton 2012), eliminate within-layer connections, increasing tractability but sacrificing biological plausibility as well as representational power. In Friston's model, lateral connections among error units are used to de-correlate competing causal explanations (Friston 2005: 823) and those between error and representation units at a given level mediate comparisons of approximate bottom-up inferences with top-down predictions.

There is also an important difference in the way probability distributions are represented in Friston's model: namely in terms of their sufficient statistics (for Gaussian distributions, mean and variance). The state of each representation unit represents the mean of the approximate recognition distribution over the represented property, and the top-down influence on each error unit represents the predicted mean. In addition to its other connections, each error unit contains an inhibitory self-connection whose weight is proportional to the variance of the unit. In the Helmholtz machine, by contrast, the probability that the network assigns to a hypothesis under the generative and recognition distributions is determined directly by the probability of the corresponding code's being produced either top-down or bottom-up, respectively, by the stochastic activation function.

In summary, the state of each representation unit at a given level of the predictive coding model is determined by its bottom-up input minus weighted input from the error units at that level, and the state of each error unit is given by its lateral input from representation units at that level minus both top-down input and self-inhibition in proportion to the unit's variance. Unlike in the Helmholtz machine, top-down and bottom-up influences in the predictive coding model are computed simultaneously and used to update both the generative and recognition models as sensory data comes in.

We mentioned earlier the Helmholtz machine's limitation to factorial distributions (which arises from its lack of lateral connections). The model considered here, too, is limited in that the distributions are assumed to be Gaussian. But this limitation does not matter much in practice, since multiple layers of predictions, each individually subject to this constraint, can give rise to more complicated distributions over representations at lower levels of the model.

Friston's model is notable both for its incorporation of lateral connections and for the role it gives top-down connections in online perceptual processing. The latter feature allows predictive coding accounts to take on board not only the biological plausibility of unsupervised learning schemes but also the idea that epistemic context can affect perceptual information processing and content, an idea that seems to enjoy broad empirical support (see e.g. (Harrison et al. 2007; Newen et al. 2017)).

2.2 Bayesian inference and energy minimization

Hinton and Sejnowski (1983) pioneered a model of "optimal perceptual inference" inspired in part on earlier work by J. J. Hopfield (1982).[11] Though different from the models discussed so far in important ways, it implements the idea that Bayesian inference can be accomplished via the minimization of potential energy within a generative model in a particularly transparent way. We first briefly describe the dynamics of the network, treating it simply as a physical model of the brain, and then discuss the interpretation of the model as performing statistical inference.

Like the Helmholtz machine, the model consists of a large collection of binary stochastic processing units. Each pair of units is reciprocally connected via symmetric synaptic weights (that is, for all units *i* and *j*, the weight from *i* to *j*, w_{ij}, = the weight from *j* to *i*, w_{ji}). A subset of the units (the "input nodes") can receive additional input directly from an external information source. The network is otherwise unstructured. Its state at any given moment is determined by the connections between the units, together with external input. Hinton & Sejnowski define an "energy function" that assigns a scalar value, the "energy," to each state of the network, based on the states of each unit and the strength and sign on the connections between them (as well as external input).

One way to see why energy functions make sense in this context begins by considering simple properties of biological brains. Action potentials in a biological neuron are likely to occur in proportion to the voltage difference that has built up across its cell membrane (the "membrane potential," which is a type of potential energy). This suggests that, as Hopfield (1982: 2555) puts it, "The mean rate at which action potentials are generated is a smooth function of the mean membrane potential." This function turns out to be nonlinear and, in particular, sigmoidal in shape. The logistic activation function (discussed in section 1.3 above) is employed in Hinton & Sejnowski's network (Figure 24.2) to model such a function from membrane potential to firing rate stochastically.

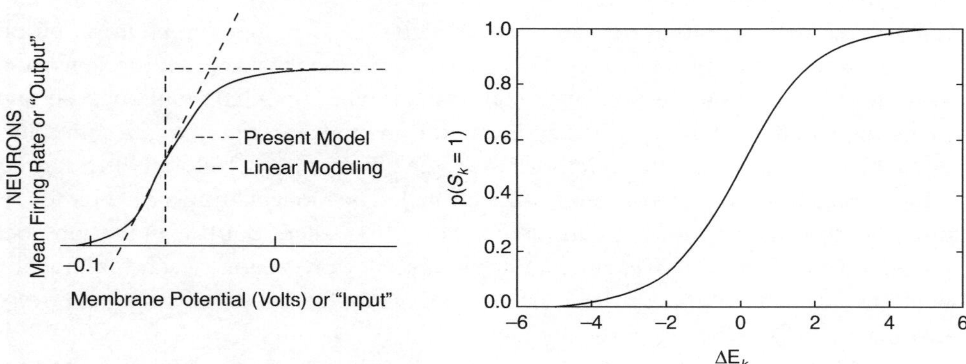

Figure 24.2 (a) The relationship between firing rates and membrane potential (Hopfield 1982, Fig.1, reprinted with permission of the author). (b) (after Hinton and Sejnowski 1983, Fig. 1) The logistic activation function maps an artificial neuron's contribution to potential energy to its stochastic state. ΔE_k = the network's global energy with $s_k = 0$ – the global energy with $s_k = 1$, where s_k is the binary state of unit *k*.

The global energy of a configuration (assignment of "1" and "0" states) of the units then depends linearly on the energy contributed by each pair of neurons, which can be determined locally for each given the current synaptic weights. In the model, each neuron's contribution to the total potential energy of the network is a function of (a) its weighted, summed input from its neighbors and (b) its current state. This make sense, since in real brains, these together determine the difference in voltage across the cell membrane and thus the membrane potential.

Starting from an arbitrary initial configuration (choice of "0" or "1" states for all neurons) and assuming a fixed set of weights, the network can be run so as to minimize its potential energy by choosing states for each unit based on the sigmoid activation function described above. Choosing states for the units in this way updates the states of the units so that they take the states of their neighbors into account, thus lowering the potential energy relative to the starting-point. Neurons receiving large negative (inhibitory) input minimize the potential energy when turned "off", and those receiving large positive input minimize it when firing, as is reflected in the energy equation for the network (Hinton and Sejnowski 1983, Eq.1).

Repeating this process simulates (in a very coarse-grained way) the brain's settling into thermodynamic equilibrium. To see this, consider that since potential energy is generated when a system is forced out of equilibrium, significant membrane potentials are local nonequilibrium states. Running the network so as to discharge these potentials then brings it closer to (internal) equilibrium. If external input is added, the network can simulate the brain's settling back into an equilibrium state after the absorption of sensory signals.

Thus far, our description of this network has been motivated purely by its intrinsic physical properties. Given a propositional interpretation of the nodes as discussed in section 1.3, the process of updating each node's state is equivalent to Bayesian inference. For hypothesis H and evidence E, Bayes's theorem can be written in terms of the natural logarithms of the prior and likelihood ratios by expanding p(E) into the terms used to calculate it, simplifying, and using the reciprocal properties of exponentiation and the natural logarithmic function (see Figure 24.3). Once Bayes's theorem is rewritten in this way, it is identical in form to the sigmoid activation function.[12]

To consider a simple example: suppose we have sensory evidence E (an array of inputs to the "input nodes" that determines states of the nodes, e_1, e_2, . . . e_n) and two alternative configurations of the network, H and H', consisting of two different assignments of activities to the remainder of the nodes, h_1, . . . h_n. According to Bayes's theorem, the posterior probability of H given E should increase relative to the prior probability of H when the likelihood p($E \mid H$) is greater than chance, and it should decrease otherwise. This is captured in the dynamics of the neural network. Unit h is more likely to be turned on after E is observed (that is, after e_1, . . . e_n take on the states determined by E) than it was prior to observing E only if the summed weighted input from e_1, . . . e_n to h is positive, which in turn guarantees that the likelihood is greater than 0.5, as inspection of the logistic function shows.

$$\text{(a) } p(H|E) = \frac{1}{1 + e^{-(\ln \frac{p(H)}{p(\neg H)} + \ln \frac{p(E|H)}{p(E|\neg H)})}} \qquad \text{(b) } p_h = \frac{1}{1+e^{-\Delta E_h}}$$

$$\text{(c) } \Delta E_h = \textstyle\sum_e w_{he} s_e - \theta_h$$

$$\text{(d) } -\theta_h = \ln \frac{p(H)}{p(\neg H)}, \quad w_{he} = \ln \frac{p(E|H)}{p(E|\neg H)}, \quad p_h = p(H|E)$$

Figure 24.3 Equations adapted from (Hinton and Sejnowski 1983). (a) Bayes's rule, expressed in terms of the natural exponential function. (b) The sigmoid activation function used in Hinton & Sejnowski's network (with temperature parameter T omitted), where p_h is the probability of unit h firing, i.e. being in the "True" state and ΔE_h is the difference between the energy of the network with unit h in the "False" state and the energy with h in the "True" state. (c) ΔE_h is determined locally for each unit by its weighted, summed input minus its threshold term, where w_{he} is the symmetrical weight between unit h and unit e, s_e is the binary state of unit e, and θ_h is the threshold for unit h (the term for direct external input is omitted here for simplicity). (d) Interpreting variables in the model as representing the probabilities of relevant pieces of evidence yields a formal equivalence between energy minimization in the network and statistical inference using Bayes's rule. The weights and biases of the network are interpreted as log probability ratios, while the probability of unit h being "on" is interpreted as the probability assigned to hypothesis H.

Since the network's settling into equilibrium can thus be interpreted as massively parallel Bayesian inference, the potential energy of a global state is a measure of the incoherence of the corresponding collection of hypotheses. As Hinton & Sejnowski put it,

> The energy of a state can . . . be interpreted as the extent to which a combination of hypotheses fails to fit the input data and violates the constraints between hypotheses, so in minimizing energy the system is maximizing the extent to which a perceptual interpretation fits the data and satisfies the constraints.
>
> (p. 449)

Obviously, there is no reason to suppose that an arbitrary collection of weights will result in a very coherent set of hypotheses. Learning can be accomplished in the network by adjusting the weights so as to minimize the difference between the network's equilibrium (high-probability, low-energy) states when running independently of external input and its equilibrium states given fixed external input (p. 452). Adjusting the weights in this way amounts to fitting a generative model to the data supplied at the input nodes.

To expand on this point: the prior probability of a set of hypotheses under the generative model is given by the probability of the corresponding configuration of nodes occurring at thermal equilibrium, when the network is running free of external input (Hinton and Sejnowski 1983; Hinton et al. 1995). The equilibrium distribution with external input held fixed corresponds to the posterior under the generative model (since it favors states that are low in energy given the states of the input units). The learning scheme thus ensures that the prior distribution becomes more similar to the posterior distribution after each input (a form of stochastic gradient descent, discussed in section 1.2 above).

Although this network contains no explicit, distinct generative and recognition models, by supplying sustained input and letting the network settle into equilibrium, one implicitly inverts the generative model. Inversion of a generative model is simply any process that, given a generative mapping from causes to effects, finds the inverse mapping from effects back to causes. In the context of perception, a generative model would produce predictions for peripheral sensory states from internal causes (each of which represents a corresponding external cause). Its inversion selects (representations of) causes on the basis of peripheral states (i.e. sensory inputs). This is just what energy minimization given fixed external input accomplishes in Hinton and Sejnowski's model.

2.3 Generalizing the link between energy and inference

The model just discussed provides a particularly perspicuous, but highly idealized and abstract, account of the way in which Bayesian inference may be implemented neurally. It also affords a clear view of the link between statistical inference and energy minimization. Here, we briefly review that link, and then consider how a similar story can be told for the other models considered in previous sections.

In brief, we've seen that if (1) alternative physical configurations of a cognitive system are neural representations, (2) the probability of a given representation occurring represents the subjective probability that the system assigns to the associated hypothesis, and (3) low-energy states are more probable than high-energy states (as is guaranteed by thermodynamics), then some hypotheses will be assigned higher prior probability than others. If this prior distribution is shaped during learning so that it is close to the posterior given sensory input, then the impact of such input will tend to be minimized and will not push the system far out of equilibrium, so the energy will remain low, which ensures that the system must have learned a decent generative model of its environment.

This story clearly applies even to "broadly Bayesian" systems that can be understood as integrating prior and incoming information but in which Bayes's theorem is not explicitly implemented. We saw earlier that the Helmholtz machine is able to improve a generative model by leveraging an initially poor system for approximate inference. Learning in the Helmholtz machine via the "wake-sleep" algorithm, as described in section 1.3, minimizes a measurement from statistical physics of the potential energy available for work in a system, called the Helmholtz free energy. This energy is minimized at thermal equilibrium and is defined in terms of the probabilities of alternative configurations of the system and the entropy of the distribution over configurations (Hinton et al. 1995; Frey et al. 1997).

As Hinton and Zemel put it in discussing nonlinear generative models generally,

> Given an input vector, each possible code [i.e. latent neural representation] acts like an alternative configuration of a physical system . . . the Helmholtz

> free energy . . . is minimized by the thermal equilibrium or Boltzmann distribution. The probability assigned to each code at this minimum is exactly its posterior probability given the parameters of the generative model.
>
> (Hinton and Zemel 1994: 8)

The two distinct sets of "synaptic" weights in the Helmholtz machine make different contributions to the free energy. Specifically, the generative weights define the probability of generating input vectors (or, equivalently, the cost in bits of representing them) using alternative states of the generative model, and the recognition weights define the probability of those states of the model being selected given the input vectors. Learning improves both sets of weights so that (a) the recognition distribution over internal states approaches the generative model's equilibrium distribution and (b) the log probability of the data under the generative distribution is improved.[13]

As discussed in section 2.1, Friston's predictive coding model (Friston 2005) represents probability distributions in a very different way from these stochastic models (in terms of explicitly encoded Gaussian sufficient statistics) so that assumption (2) discussed previously does not hold. But learning and inference can still be understood in terms of energy minimization. In Friston's model, the energy is minimized when the means of the top-down predictions and bottom-up approximations coincide, i.e. when the explicitly represented prediction errors are minimized. Energy is increased whenever one representation needs to be revised in light of others, so a state of the model in which the priors generate accurate predictions (both for sensory input and for representations at intermediate levels) will be comparatively low in energy.

Thus, the same basic reasoning that applies in the case of Hinton and Sejnowski's model applies also to predictive coding models: the better the generative model, the more a state that the network will be in subsequent to sensory input, *S*', resembles a state *S* that it would likely have been in anyway, if left to its own devices (i.e. *S*', like *S*, is relatively low in potential energy). Similar arguments can be made in the case of any generative model that is learned online from data, including a wide range of models implemented in unsupervised learning schemes in machine learning (see e.g. (Neal and Hinton 1998; Carreira-Perpiñán and Hinton 2005; Bengio 2009)).

We should note that the connection between statistical mechanics and optimization problems was historically taken to be one of analogy: it was discovered that techniques for analyzing physical systems composed of large numbers of interacting parts can fruitfully be applied to the analysis of functions of large numbers of interacting variables (Kirkpatrick et al. 1983). In the foregoing we take an approach that is (so far as we know) somewhat novel, motivating the free energy formulation of Bayesian inference more directly by appeal to the idea that a system's internal representations supervene on its physical states so that there may exist a tight relationship between the physical and the epistemic interpretations of the energy in neurally implemented generative models.

However, energy minimization is well motivated as an optimization strategy independently of this argument. The approach taken here complements existing approaches in the literature, which focus on the framework of variational Bayesian inference (Neal and Hinton 1998; Bishop 2007). Formally, the free energy provides a lower bound on the log probability of the evidence under a model, and minimizing the energy is equivalent to minimizing the KL divergence between generative and recognition distributions, as mentioned previously (see also (Bogacz 2017)).[14]

3 Representation

It was assumed in our exposition thus far that the states of a generative model are representations of the environmental causes of perceptual inputs, but little has been said so far to justify this assumption beyond a nod to the notion of representation via structural resemblance. In the following sections we unpack the notion of structural representation as it is hypothesized to occur in generative models, and attempt to situate this proposal with respect to more mainstream accounts of mental representation. We consider how the contents of individual representations within generative models are determined, and argue that structural representation and functional role approaches to content (as against causal and teleological approaches) have much in common. We then discuss measures of structural similarity, and a measure of misrepresentation in hierarchical generative models consistent with these ideas.

3.1 Structural representation

As previously mentioned, a core assumption within the PEM framework is that, as Gładziejewski (2016) puts it, following Hohwy (2013) and others,

> The generative model "recapitulates" the causal – probabilistic structure of the external environment that impinges on the organism's sensory apparatus. It constantly generates, in a top – down manner, a flow of virtual or mock sensory signals that predicts the unfolding of sensory signals generated by external causes.

This recapitulation of causal structure can be considered the basis of a form of representation by "simulation" as it occurs broadly in statistical models (see Section 1.3). Recently, the theory that mental representation consists fundamentally in structural similarity between the representation and what is represented has been elaborated considerably, most notably in (Gładziejewski 2016; Gładziejewski and Miłkowski 2017). As applied to the PEM framework, this approach suggests that not only do generative models mimic the causal structure of the world, but it is in virtue of doing so that they represent it.

As is often emphasized in discussions of the structural resemblance theory, however, resemblance is not sufficient for representation in any intuitive or theoretically useful sense. Any two items resemble one another in some respect, so an account of representation based on similarity alone would be trivial. It also seems clear that representation is an asymmetric relation, while resemblance is not. Both of these problems can be solved by requiring that the structural resemblance be *used* or exploited by a cognitive system in order to make cognitive functioning effective (see e.g. (Godfrey-Smith 1996; Shea 2014; Gładziejewski and Miłkowski 2017)). This captures the intuitive idea that a representation (mental or otherwise) serves as a proxy or stand-in for what is represented.

Following Gładziejewski and Miłkowski, we may spell out this "proxy" condition at least in part by requiring that the similarity between a structural representation and a represented system be causally responsible for the successful operation of cognitive capacities directed at the latter. This of course presupposes some notion of success, which may vary depending on the capacity in question. A compelling example is the ability of rats to navigate mazes using hippocampal "place cells," which form a map of the environment whose utility depends not just on intrinsic features of the map or of the environment alone, but on the similarity between the two (Gładziejewski and Miłkowski 2017).

In addition to playing basic action-guiding roles, paradigmatic structural representations such as maps have additional features that we may want to require of structural representations generally, as Gładziejewski (2016) notes. For one, they can be recruited for "offline" use when a represented system is not immediately present, for example when a map is used to plan a future route through a city. They also afford the possibility of detecting representational errors. Importantly, both of these features depend on structural resemblance.[15]

The notion of structural representation is of course only as clear as the relevant notion of structural similarity. Gładziejewski and Miłkowski adopt the definition offered by O'Brien and Opie (2004: 11), which may be paraphrased as follows: suppose that a system S consists of a set of elements E and a set of relations R defined on those elements. We may say system S_1 is structurally similar to S_2 just in case there is a mapping from members of E_1 to those of E_2 and a mapping from R_1 to R_2 that together preserve the relational structure among the elements of S_1 for "at least some" elements and relations in E_1 and R_1.

This definition is vague thanks to the quantifier "at least some." Plausibly, structural similarity is a graded notion that scales with amount of relational structure preserved, but there are special cases of "exact" matching that may be of interest: *homomorphisms* may be defined as mappings that preserve *all* relevant relational structure among the elements, while *isomorphisms* are homomorphisms that are bijective and therefore involve perfect structural correspondence (i.e. each member of E_1 is mapped to a unique member of E_2, and at least one member of E_1 maps to every member of E_2).

Statistical models can be perspicuously represented as graphical models, as can many other structures, including the causal structure of an environment (at least in principle). Graph comparisons may thus be useful in assessing structural similarity in the present context (the definitions of homomorphism and isomorphism previously given yield the relevant definitions for graphs as special cases, where the elements are vertices and the relations are captured by edges or arcs). However, to adequately represent a statistical model, one needs to keep track not just of the existence or nonexistence of dependencies between variables (which are captured in the topology of the graph) but of the possible values of each variable and the type and degree of value-dependent influence (in this case, conditional probability) between them. This complicates things relative to the definition previously given because similarity between two such graphical models depends on the dependency structures captured by each model, not just the topology, so that there is in general no simple, exact mapping from R_1 to R_2.

Fortunately, methods for the kind of "inexact" graph matching needed here (and needed in any case to define a notion of similarity weaker than homomorphism) are an active area of research, and those interested in developing more exact general definitions of similarity have many options to choose from (see (Gallagher 2006; Gao et al. 2010) for recent surveys). We need not commit to any particular precisification of the general definition of structural similarity for structural representations considered here, but will consider a more precise proposal for evaluating the representational accuracy of generative models in section 3.3.

3.2 *Content in structural representations*

One fundamental question about mental representations concerns how precisely they get their contents – that is, in virtue of what they represent what they do or are about what they are about. Here, we consider in more depth how this question may be answered within the structural representation paradigm, and compare what we take to be the most promising answer with the answers given by more historically mainstream accounts of representation. We begin with a very brief discussion of the latter.

One widely discussed theory of content, advocated in various ways by (Field 1977; Block 1994; Brandom 1994; Harman 1999; Sellars 2007) and many others, proposes that the contents of mental representations depend in some way on their overall functional (inferential, causal, conceptual, or evidential) roles within a cognitive system. Another, advocated by (Dretske 1981; Millikan 1984; Papineau 1984; Millikan 1989; Fodor 1990) and, again, many others, identifies the contents of a representation, at least in the basic case, with (some subset of) its regular causes or what amounts to the same thing, with (some subset of) the causes about which the representation carries information (Millikan 1984; Papineau 1984). Under this second umbrella we wish to include teleological theories, which, because of well-known theoretical problems for the pure causal/informational theory, such as the "disjunction problem" (Fodor 1990), appeal to facts about the etiology of representations – in particular, the learning histories that gave rise to them (Dretske 1981) or the evolutionary history in virtue of which the capacity to carry information about certain things was favored by selection pressures (Millikan 1984; Papineau 1984) – to fix their contents.[16]

The structural representation theory seems to give a clear and distinct third answer to the content-determination question: representations get their content via structural resemblance to what they represent. There are two reasons to qualify this answer, however. First, while the structural representation as a whole gets its content via resemblance, the same need not be true of its parts (for example parameters of a generative model). These get their content via the overall structural resemblance, as discussed in section 1.1, but the part-part relations themselves are not resemblance relations.[17] This shows that a form of *content holism* is entailed by the structural representation proposal: the content of one part of the overall representation depends on the structure of the whole and thus cannot be determined without simultaneously fixing the contents of the other parts.

Second, if cases like maze navigation in rats are taken as a general model for structural representation, the exploitability or "proxy" constraint previously considered may be read as restricting the possible contents of any structural representation to things in the environment with which its owner causally interacts. However, our cognitive capacities can plausibly be directed at merely imaginary or hypothetical environments, as happens normally in cases of imagination and daydreaming and perhaps during radical cases of perceptual misrepresentation (cases of misrepresentation may be distinguished from nonrepresentational failures precisely in that, in a sense, *the wrong thing* is represented).

Moreover, we can engage with merely imagined environments cognitively, for example by reasoning about them or finding routes through them. Of course, genuine representation arguably requires the possibility of error, but error need not in every case be assessed against one's immediate environment. The standard for error may be goal- or capacity-dependent. Therefore, if structural representations underlie mental representation generally (including cases of imagination and the like), they must first and foremost be proxies for (i.e. have as contents) hypothetical worlds or states of affairs (picked out in terms of their relevant structures), encompassing representation of the actual environment as a special case.[18] This suggests a surprisingly "internalist" reading of the structural representation proposal.

The considerations thus far suggest similarities (holism and, at least arguably, internalism) between structural representational and functional role approaches to content.[19] As O'Brien and Opie (2004) note, the way in which content is determined in functional role theories is also sometimes cast as relying on structural resemblance (e.g. between a system of causally related vehicles and a system of inferentially related propositions – see (Fodor 1990), chapter 1). It is thus tempting to assimilate structural representation (as conceived of here) to the paradigm of functional role semantics.

Although functional role approaches do not in themselves entail structural similarity between representation and environment, the latter may be conceived of as mediated by inferential roles when it does occur. In particular, the inferential relations in terms of which contents are implicitly defined may encompass *inductive* inferential transitions – what Sellars (Sellars 1953) called "material inferences," such as that from "it's raining" to "the street is wet." Such inductive inferences keep track, in effect, of causal regularities. Thus, the relevant inferential structure will be similar to the structure of the environment insofar as the latter is captured by the representation. Crucially, this view is consistent with the requirement that the resemblance between vehicle and environment causally explains the success of behavior based on the representation (Gładziejewski and Miłkowski 2017), while allowing that in some cases merely possible environments are represented.

Even if one resists treating structural representation as a species of functional role semantics,[20] the preceding considerations seem to show that such representations cannot be assimilated to representations understood on the model of causal or teleological theories.[21] It should be noted that one may reject the latter without supposing, implausibly, that the information that representations carry about environmental conditions is irrelevant to their content. A generative statistical model guided by the online minimization of prediction error, for example, is bound to carry information about the phenomena it models in its learned parameters (and latent variables) (Hohwy 2013). This ensures that the parameters will tend to covary with individual causes and such covariation may be heuristically useful in identifying the contents of a representation without such covariation being constitutive of representation.[22]

3.3 *Misrepresentation in generative models*

As discussed earlier, generative and recognition models can be understood as probabilistic statistical models, which can, like the structure of the environment, be represented as graphical models. We can then, in principle, determine the similarity between a generative model and the environment by comparing two graphical models. This comparison should capture similarities between priors and likelihoods encoded in the model and those in the environment, on which Gładziejewski's discussion of structural similarity in generative models focuses (Gładziejewski 2016).[23]

One appealing way of defining representational content in terms of structural similarity is to combine a binary, all-or-nothing representation-relation determined by the "proxy" condition with (dis)similarity to yield a graded overall notion of (mis) representation. Note, however, that there seem to be at least two different ways in which misrepresentation may occur in a structural representation: the structures may fail to match, or the model may fail to be registered properly with the represented system even if it is structurally similar, as plausibly happens when one locates oneself incorrectly on a map or infers an incorrect explanation within a generative model (Gładziejewski 2016). We may add that in a generative model, an incorrect hypothesis may sometimes be selected to explain the sensory input even when there is no flaw in either the model or its application: a good statistical model will usually select the most likely cause, but sometimes the unexpected occurs.

Fortunately, at least in the case of statistical models, there is a fairly simple relationship between the two types of misrepresentation. Registering the model with respect to the represented system involves supplying values of the observed variables from real data (in the case under consideration, receiving sensory input), from which statistical inference proceeds. Assuming that the model is correctly registered, such inferences will tend to yield accurate results in proportion to the extent to which the model captures the structure of the target domain. So, degree of structural representation also measures the *average* amount of misrepresentation in this second sense. Importantly, the latter kind of misrepresentation is of the familiar truth-conditional sort: given an overall structural similarity sufficient to ground content, individual representations in the model are veridical just in case the modeled causal structure is present in the actual environment that caused the sensory input.

As discussed earlier, it is not simple to compare the structure of two statistical models, since such structure may vary along many dimensions. Even without directly comparing such structures, however, there is a heuristic of sorts that can be derived from the paradigm of variational Bayesian inference (previously mentioned in connection with energy minimization) to provide a philosophically satisfying perspective on representation and misrepresentation and their connections to learning within the PEM framework. Namely, we suggest taking the KL divergence (defined earlier in section 1.3) between the generative model's posterior distribution, $p(h \mid e)$, and the causal structure in the world, in principle captured in a joint distribution over causes, $c(h)$, as a measure of *misrepresentation* of the environment.

Finally, recall that learning occurs in the model by reducing the KL divergence between the posterior generative and approximate recognition distributions, $p(h \mid e)$ and $q(h)$. Thus, the better the model of the environment, the lower this KL divergence should be. We should thus expect it to track structural similarity as well. We can use the "internal" KL divergence, $KL(p(h \mid e) \,||\, q(h))$, as an internally accessible measure of misrepresentation that can be leveraged for learning and acts as a proxy for the objective misrepresentation just defined. We learn $p(h \mid e)$ by "bootstrapping" grounded in the sensory data – i.e. by simultaneously refining generative and discriminative models – as mentioned in section 1.3, i.e. reducing $KL(p(h \mid e) \,||\, q(h))$, so by doing this we will also reduce $KL(p(h \mid e) \,||\, c(h))$.

To supplement this argument, there is a more intuitive way of thinking about how the "internal" and "external" measures of misrepresentation are related. The generative and recognition models each define a joint distribution over the same hypothesis space, though they factor this joint distribution differently.[24] Conceptually, then, the internal measure amounts to comparing one representation of the world to another (presumed at least provisionally to be accurate) to assess accuracy. When the KL divergence is above zero, there is some degree of "misrepresentation" in the sense that the recognized causes are not the causes for which there is the best (in Bayesian terms) evidence. The "bootstrapping" process by which the two representations are used to improve each other is then analogous to that via which theories in science are refined not just by confrontation with observation but by comparison with other well-evidenced theories.

Conclusion

This chapter has introduced the essentials of the prediction error minimization framework, with an emphasis on the notion of mental representation as statistical modeling. The approach to representation we propose is quite general, as it is based on any system relying on generative models in the ways previously described. We have shown in some detail how the computational tools used in research on generative models can be used to address philosophical issues about content and representation. The proposal is that this overall computational approach to perception and representation is a natural fit with a functional role semantics, but with room for causal and informational relations to the external world to play roles in the explanations of particular representation-based cognitive and perceptual capacities.

Importantly, we take this perspective to cover perceptual representational content as well as paradigmatically conceptual representation. As we have seen, perceptual inference under predictive coding schemes can be updated online, that is, as sensory input is received by the system, and so employs priors in the same way that ordinary Bayesian reasoning does. There may yet be important differences between conceptual and perceptual representation, and the overall theoretical perspective defended here allows for much more complexity to be added to the structure of relevant models. We hope to have shown, however, that a unified representationalist approach to perception and cognition as a matter of prediction error minimization within generative models is not only intelligible but also appealing for many reasons.

This chapter has necessarily excluded many topics worthy of philosophical consideration, all of which relate to the ideas we have presented here. The PEM framework arguably challenges many of the obvious ways in which perception can be distinguished from cognition, and the view that perception delivers unbiased information to the rest of the cognitive system (Jenkin and Siegel 2015; Lupyan 2015; Newen et al. 2017). Relatedly, there is discussion about whether and how the view that the mind is "modular" (Fodor 1983) can be retained in light of such theories (Hohwy 2013, Ch 7; Drayson 2017). PEM also engages general, theoretical debates about how traditional approaches to representation contrast to the family of embodied, extended, and enactive approaches to cognition (for discussion, see (Bruineberg 2016; Clark 2016a; Hohwy 2016; Orlandi 2016; Clark 2017; Hohwy 2017)).

Our treatment is in need of development in its own right, along several dimensions. As this happens, it should be possible to address in more detail these wider philosophical debates. We hope this chapter has suggested lines of future research for philosophers and cognitive scientists interested in the PEM framework and the statistical modeling approach to mental representation more generally.

Notes

1. Here, we *assume* representationalism as a background approach to cognitive science and do not explicitly address anti-representationalist arguments. That said, the somewhat novel way in which representations are treated within the PEM framework, outlined here, may provide a basis for responding to such arguments, which are often based on certain philosophical assumptions about representation (see Gładziejewski and Miłkowski 2017).
2. There may be generative processes that are not causal, i.e. that rely on purely abstract mathematical relations, but for the purposes of theories of cognition and perception the causal case is clearly the most salient one. As such we use the terms "generative model" and "causal generative model" interchangeably.
3. A version of the logistic function is commonly used for this purpose: $g = \frac{1}{1+e^{-z}}$, where z is the sum of the x values weighted by parameters P.
4. The contribution of each parameter to the prediction error is given by its partial derivative with respect to the cost function. The sign of the derivative determines whether the current value of the parameter lies uphill (+) or downhill (−) on the error surface defined by the cost function (along the dimension corresponding to that parameter), and its magnitude determines the steepness of the slope. So the cost function can be minimized by subtracting the partial derivative (usually scaled by a learning rate term) from the current value of the parameter.
5. For ease of exposition we use "distribution" in a way intended to cover both continuous and discrete distributions since the difference is unimportant at this level of abstraction.

6. The stochastic activation function used in the Helmholtz machine and many other stochastic networks employs the logistic function discussed in connection with logistic regression (Section 1.2) to determine the relevant probabilities.
7. The claim that these are really *representations* may be philosophically contentious and will be substantiated in Part 3.
8. The generative model also includes the generative bias for each unit, and the recognition model includes a distinct set of recognition biases.
9. The Kullback-Leibler (KL) divergence or relative entropy between Q and P, $D_{KL}(Q||P) = \sum_i Q(i)\log\left(\frac{Q(i)}{P(i)}\right)$, allows for precise quantification of the difference between the distributions.
10. Action is not a focus of the present paper, but in brief, it has long been supposed that motor control systems test generative models that predict sensory input consequent to action against actual input (Aggelopoulos 2015). Moreover, we may suppose that our generative models include mappings between states of the world and proprioceptive states, learned in the same way as in the case of vision. We can then exploit high-level representations of worldly states to execute actions by holding them fixed until the rest of the model (including the peripheral motor system and the perceptual systems) falls into line, at which point the "fantasized" state of the world will have become reality. This is the essence of "active inference" (Friston 2011; Hohwy 2013, Ch 4).
11. Much of the material in this section is presented in slightly modified form in (Kiefer 2017).
12. See (Hinton and Sejnowski 1983), equation 5, for the full derivation. For simplicity, we ignore the term for external input and the "temperature" parameter in the sigmoid function, which is assumed to be set to 1. The authors point out two important issues with this simple model: (a) symmetrical weights are required if each unit is to implement inference using only local information, but the relation between evidence and hypothesis described by Bayes's theorem is not symmetrical; and (b) the weights and thresholds must be so designed as to capture the effect of the negation of the evidence on a hypothesis. These issues are surmountable, but we omit the details here (see pp. 450–451 & 453 of the paper).
13. This is reflected in equations (3) and (5) in (Hinton et al. 1995), which define the cost functions for learning.
14. $D_{KL}(Q(h)||P(h|e)) + \sum_h Q(h)\log\left(\frac{P(e,h)}{Q(h)}\right) = \log P(e)$, where the first term on the left is the KL divergence between the recognition and posterior generative distributions over hypotheses, and the second term is the negative free energy (see Bogacz [in press], equation 32). Since KL divergences are always positive, the log probability of the evidence is equal to or greater than the negative free energy, i.e. by minimizing the free energy one maximizes a lower bound on the log probability of the evidence under the model. Further, given a fixed $P(e)$, minimizing the energy entails minimizing the KL divergence term.
15. The possibility of detecting mismatches between map and terrain of course depends essentially on the map's being a largely accurate guide to the terrain in the first place.
16. Also included under this umbrella is Fodor's (1990) solution to the disjunction problem, based on asymmetries among nomic relations.
17. Of course, we do not mean to rule out that parts may also be structured and function themselves as structural representations. Indeed, this is likely the case in hierarchically organized systems like those considered in this chapter, but we lack space to consider this issue here.
18. This way of putting things may go to the heart of some of the more radical claims about how the generative models paradigm informs the nature of the mind-world relation – for example, claims that perception is "controlled hallucination" (Grush 2004). Similarly, Geoff Hinton (one of the originators of contemporary models of perceptual inference involving generative models) claims in essence that the contents of mental states are hypothetical worlds (Hinton 2005), suggesting a possible link to more traditional "possible-worlds" approaches to content (see e.g. (Lewis 1986)).
19. It should be noted that there are "wide" versions of functional role semantics as well (see e.g. (Harman 1973)), though the paradigm is often associated with "narrow" content (see (Block 1994) for more on this distinction).
20. O'Brien and Opie (2004) distinguish strictly between functional role semantics and their preferred version of structural representation theory on the grounds that the former appeals to causal relations

among vehicles while the latter appeals to physical relations. It is not obvious, however, why the latter category should preclude the former.

21. Gładziejewski and Miłkowski (2017) draw a similar conclusion for different reasons.
22. This accommodates the fact that neuroscientists often take neural activities to represent whatever they carry information about – see e.g. (deCharms and Zador 2000).
23. To capture diachronic causal relations, the graph would have to include relations between sets of causes at one moment and sets of causes at the next, as well as synchronic relations among causal regularities at different temporal scales, all of which conspire to produce sensory input at any given moment. This presents no problem in principle since Bayesian networks may be used to capture such temporal dependencies as well. Some of the models we have discussed do not take statistical dependencies across time into account, but they can easily be generalized to do so (see for example (Hinton et al. 1995)).
24. This of course *assumes* sufficient structural similarity to assign the same contents to the nodes for both models and thus will only work for idealized cases. A full account of (mis)representation would in any case need to account for less-than-perfect topological similarity between the relevant networks – particularly in light of Gładziejewski and Miłkowski's (2017) point that useful models *must* be less than fully detailed ones with respect to the environment in order to avoid overfitting and allow for generalization.

Bibliography

Aggelopoulos, N. C. (2015). "Perceptual inference." *Neuroscience & Biobehavioral Reviews* **55**: 375–392.

Bengio, Y. (2009). "Learning deep architectures for AI." *Foundations and Trends in Machine Learning* **1**(2): 1–127.

Bishop, C. M. (2007). *Pattern Recognition and Machine Learning*. Cordrecht, Springer.

Bishop, C. M. and J. Lasserre (2007). "Generative or discriminative? Getting the best of both worlds." *Bayesian Statistics* 8. J. M. Bernardo, M. J. Bayarri, J. O. Berger, A. P. David, D. Heckerman, A. F. M. Smith, and M. West, eds., Oxford: Oxford University Press, pp. 3–24.

Block, N. (1994). "Advertisement for a semantics for psychology." *Mental Representation: A Reader*. S. P. Stich and T. Warfield, eds. Oxford, Blackwell.

Bogacz, R. (2017). "A tutorial on the free-energy framework for modelling perception and learning." *Journal of Mathematical Psychology* **76, Part B**: 198–211.

Brandom, R. (1994). *Making It Explicit*. Cambridge, Harvard University Press.

Bruineberg, J. (2016). "The anticipating brain is not a scientist: The free-energy principle from an ecological-enactive perspective." *Synthese* **195**(6): 2417–2444.

Carreira-Perpiñán, M. A. and G. E. Hinton (2005). *On Contrastive Divergence Learning*. Proceedings of the Tenth International Workshop on Artificial Intelligence and Statistics, Bridgetown, Barbados.

Chomsky, N. (1957). *Syntactic Structures*. The Hague: Mouton Publishers.

Clark, A. (2013). "Whatever next? Predictive brains, situated agents, and the future of cognitive science." *Behavioral & Brain Sciences* **36**(3): 181–204.

Clark, A. (2016a). "Busting out: Predictive brains, embodied minds, and the puzzle of the evidentiary veil." *Noûs*: n/a–n/a.

Clark, A. (2016b). *Surfing Uncertainty*. New York, Oxford University Press.

Clark, A. (2017). "How to knit your own Markov blanket." *Philosophy and Predictive Processing*. T. K. Metzinger and W. Wiese, eds. Frankfurt am Main, MIND Group.

Cummins, R. (1994). "Interpretational semantics." *Mental Representation: A Reader*. S. Stich and T. Warfield, eds. Oxford, Blackwell.

Danks, D. (2014). *Unifying the Mind: Cognitive Representations as Graphical Models*. Cambridge, MA, MIT Press.

Dayan, P., G. E. Hinton, R. M. Neal and R. S. Zemel (1995). "The Helmholtz machine." *Neural Comput* **7**(5): 889–904.

deCharms, R. C. and A. Zador (2000). "Neural representation and the cortical code." *Annual Review of Neuroscience* **23**: 613–47.

Drayson, Z. (2017). "Modularity and the predictive mind." *Philosophy and Predictive Processing*. T. K. Metzinger and W. Wiese, eds. Frankfurt am Main: MIND Group.
Dretske, F. (1981). *Knowledge and the Flow of Information*. Camebridge, MA, MIT Press.
Field, H. (1977). "Logic, meaning and conceptual role." *Journal of Philosophy* (69): 379–409.
Fodor, J. A. (1975). *The language of thought*. Cambridge: Harvard University Press.
Fodor, J. A. (1983). *The Modularity of Mind*. Cambridge, MA, MIT Press.
Fodor, J. A. (1990). *A Theory of Content and Other Essays*. Cambridge, MA, MIT Press.
Frey, B. J., P. Dayan and G. E. Hinton (1997). "A simple algorithm that discovers efficient perceptual codes." *Computational and Biological Mechanisms of Visual Coding*. M. Jenkin and L. R. Harris, eds. New York: Cambridge University Press.
Friston, K. (2009). "The free-energy principle: A rough guide to the brain?" *Trends in Cognitive Sciences* **13**(7): 293–301.
Friston, K. (2011). "What is optimal about motor control?" *Neuron* **72**(3): 488–98.
Friston, K. J. (2005). "A theory of cortical responses." *Philosophical Transactions: Biological Sciences* **369**(1456): 815–36.
Gallagher, B. (2006). *Matching Structure and Semantics: A Survey on Graph-Based Pattern Matching*. AAAI Fall Symposium on Capturing and Using Patterns for Evidence Detection, American Association for Artificial Intelligence, Arlington, VA.
Gao, X., B. Xiao, D. Tao and X. Li (2010). "A survey of graph edit distance." *Pattern Analysis and Applications* **13**: 113–29.
Gładziejewski, P. (2016). "Predictive coding and representationalism." *Synthese* **193**(2): 559–82.
Gładziejewski, P. and M. Miłkowski (2017). "Structural representations: Causally relevant and different from detectors." *Biology and Philosophy* **32**(3): 337–55.
Godfrey-Smith, P. (1996). *Complexity and the function of mind in nature*. Cambridge, Cambridge University Press.
Grush, R. (2004). "The emulation theory of representation: Motor control, imagery, and perception." *Behavioral and Brain Sciences* **27**: 377–442.
Harman, G. (1973). *Thought*. Princeton, Princeton University Press.
Harman, G. (1999). *Reasoning, Meaning and Mind*. Oxford, Oxford University Press.
Harrison, L. M., K. E. Stephan, G. Rees and K. J. Friston (2007). "Extra-classical receptive field effects measured in striate cortex with fMRI." *NeuroImage* **34**(3): 1199–208.
Helmholtz, H. V. (1860). *Treatise on Physiological Optics*. New York, Dover.
Hinton, G. E. (2005). *What kind of graphical model is the brain?* International Joint Conference on Artificial Intelligence, Edinburgh.
Hinton, G. E. (2007). "Learning multiple layers of representation." *Trends in Cognitive Sciences* **11**(10): 428–34.
Hinton, G. E. (2012). "A practical guide to training restricted Boltzmann machines." *Neural Networks: Tricks of the Trade. Lecture Notes in Computer Science*, vol 7700. G. Montavon, G. B. Orr, & K. R. Müller, eds. Berlin, Heidelberg: Springer.
Hinton, G. E., P. Dayan, B. J. Frey and R. Neal (1995). "The wake-sleep algorithm for unsupervised neural networks." *Science* **268**(5214): 1158–61.
Hinton, G. E., P. Dayan, A. To and R. M. Neal (1995). "The Helmholtz machine through time." *International Conference on Artificial Neural Networks*. F. Fogelman-Soulie and R. Gallinari, eds., pp. 483–90.
Hinton, G. E. and T. J. Sejnowski (1983). *Optimal Perceptual Inference*. Proceedings of the IEEE Conference on Computer Vision and Pattern Recognition, Washington, D.C.
Hinton, G. E. and T. J. Sejnowski (1999). "Unsupervised learning: Foundations of neural computation." *Unsupervised Learning: Foundations of Neural Computation*. G. E. Hinton and T. J. Sejnowski, eds. Cambridge, MA, MIT Press.
Hinton, G. E. and R. Zemel (1994). "Autoencoders, minimum description length and Helmholtz free energy." *Advances in Neural Information Processing Systems* **6**: 3–10.
Hohwy, J. (2013). *The Predictive Mind*. Oxford, Oxford University Press.
Hohwy, J. (2016). "The self-evidencing brain." *Noûs* **50**(2): 259–85.
Hohwy, J. (2017). "How to entrain your Evil Demon." *Philosophy and Predictive Processing*. T. K. Metzinger and W. Wiese, eds. Frankfurt am Main, MIND Group.

Hopfield, J. J. (1982). "Neural networks and physical systems with emergent collective computational abilities." *Proceedings of the National Academy of Sciences USA* **79**: 2554–58.

Huang, Y. and R. P. N. Rao (2011). "Predictive coding." *Wiley Interdisciplinary Reviews: Cognitive Science*: n/a–n/a.

Jebara, T. (2002). *Discriminative, generative, and imitative learning*. Ph.D. thesis, Massachusetts Institute of Technology, Cambridge, MA.

Jenkin, Z. and S. Siegel (2015). "Cognitive penetrability: Modularity, epistemology, and ethics." *Review of Philosophy and Psychology* **6**(4): 531–45.

Kiefer, A. (2017). *Literal Perceptual Inference. Philosophy and Predictive Processing*. T. K. Metzinger and W. Wiese. Frankfurt am Main: MIND Group.

Kirkpatrick, S., C. D. Gelatt and M. P. Vecchi (1983). "Optimization by simulated annealing." *Science, New Series* **220**(4598): 671–80.

Lewis, D. (1986). *On the Plurality of Worlds*. Oxford: Basil Blackwell.

Lupyan, G. (2015). "Cognitive penetrability of perception in the age of prediction: Predictive systems are penetrable systems." *Review of Philosophy and Psychology* **6**(4): 547–69.

Marr, D. (1982). *Vision: A Computational Investigation into the Human Representation and Processing of Visual Information*. San Francisco, CA: W. H. Freeman.

Millikan, R. (1984). *Language, Thought, and Other Biological Categories*. Cambridge, MA, MIT Press.

Millikan, R. (1989). "Biosemantics." *The Journal of Philosophy* **86**(6): 281–91.

Nair, V., K. Susskind and G. E. Hinton (2008). "Analysis-by-synthesis by learning to invert generative black boxes." *ICANN '08 proceedings of the 18th international conference on Artificial Neural Networks, Part I*. V. Kurkov, R. Neruda, and J. Koutn, eds., pp. 971–81. Berlin, Heidelberg: Springer.

Neal, R. M. and G. E. Hinton (1998). "A view of the EM algorithm that justifies incremental, sparse, and other variants." *Nato Asi Series D Behavioural and Social Sciences* **89**: 355–70.

Newen, A., F. Marchi and P. Brössel (2017). "Consciousness and cognition: Cognitive penetration and predictive coding." *Consciousness and Cognition* **47**: 1–112.

O'Brien, G. and J. Opie (2004). "Notes toward a structuralist theory of mental representation." *Represenation in Mind: New Approaches to Mental Representation*. H. Clapin, P. Staines and P. Slezak, eds. Oxford, Clarendon Press.

Orlandi, N. (2016). "Bayesian perception as ecological perception." *Philosophical Topics* **44**(2): 327–51.

Papineau, D. (1984). "Representation and explanation." *Philosophy of Science* **51**(4): 550–572.

Rao, R. P. N. and D. H. Ballard (1999). "Predictive coding in the visual cortex: A functional interpretation of some extra-classical receptive field effects." *Nature Neuroscience* **2**(1): 79–87.

Rao, R. P. N. and T. J. Sejnowski (2002). "Predictive coding, cortical feedback, and spike-timing-dependent plasticity." *Probabilistic Models of the Brain: Perception and Neural Function*, R. P. N. Rao, B. A. Olshausen and M. S. Lewicki, eds. Cambridge, MA, MIT Press.

Sellars, W. (1953). "Inference and meaning." *Mind* **62**(247): 313–38.

Sellars, W. (2007). *In the Space of Reasons*. Cambridge, Harvard University Press.

Shea, N. (2014). "Exploitable isomorphism and structural representation." *Proceedings of the Aristotelian Society Supplementary Volume* **114**(2): 123–44.

Srinivasan, M. V., S. B. Laughlin and A. Dubs (1982). "Predictive coding: A fresh view of inhibition in the retina." *Proceedings of the Royal Society of London B: Biological Sciences* **216**: 427.

Part IV

The biological basis of psychology

25
REPRESENTATION AND THE BRAIN

Arthur B. Markman

Representation and the brain

The fundamental premise on which the information-processing revolution in psychology was built is that the mind/brain can be profitably understood as a computational device. Central to this notion of computation is that there are data structures in the mind that format the information used in psychological processing, and that these data structures are processed by procedures that make use of this information (Markman 1999; Palmer 1978). Many theories in psychology focus on representation in a functional sense (see the chapter in this volume by Polger). That is, they talk about the ways that people represent and process information independently of the physical implementation of those representations and processes within the brain. In contrast, this chapter is explicitly concerned with issues relevant to thinking about representation and the brain.

To accomplish this goal, the chapter begins with a brief discussion of the concept of representation (see also the chapters in this volume by Ryder, and Adams and Aizawa). Then, we examine two ways of thinking about representational issues in the brain. The first examines representation at the level of individual neurons and groups of neurons. The second focuses on broad implications of the regions of the brain that are active during cognitive processing for the content of mental representations. In both of these sections we focus primarily on philosophical issues that affect our ability to make claims about mental representation rather than on current beliefs about the way the brain is representing particular kinds of information. The reason for this focus is that neuroscience is a rapidly developing field. Specific claims about the functionality of particular brain regions will undoubtedly become outdated quickly, but the philosophical issues underlying our understanding of representation in the brain remain more constant.

Representation and explanation

Computational systems represent and process information. Markman (1999) gives an extensive definition of the concept of psychological representation (see also Palmer 1978). For the purpose of the present discussion, a representation is some aspect of a computational or neural system that stands for some aspect external to the system or to another element within the system. The information in these representations must be used by some process to carry out a task.

As an example, Tversky's (1977) contrast model is a classic theory of psychological similarity. On this model, concepts are represented by features that describe the concept. So, this model would suggest that a bird is represented by internal symbols like *has feathers* or *flies* that are assumed to stand in a lawful relation to the properties in the world that birds have feathers and that birds fly, respectively. These features are processed by comparing the feature lists for two different concepts. Matching features are commonalities of a pair, and mismatching features are differences. Perceived similarity increases with the number of matching features and decreases with the number of mismatching features. Of importance, any theory of representation must be concerned both with the representations themselves and with the processes that operate on them.

As this example makes clear, theories in psychology can make claims about representations without making reference to the brain. This issue is made explicit in discussions of levels of explanation within cognitive science. Marr (1982) pointed out that psychological systems can be described at a variety of levels (see also Pylyshyn 1980). Scientists can explain psychological processes in terms of representations and processes that do not connect directly to claims about the way those representations and processes are implemented in the brain. These explanations are called *computational level* explanations when they describe the functional relationships between inputs and outputs of the processes and *algorithmic level* explanations when they focus on representations and specific procedures for processing those representations. The contrast model just described falls somewhere between a computational and algorithmic level theory. It does make a proposal for the nature of mental representation, though it does not make specific claims about the process that matches up the features from the representations of different concepts. A firm distinction between the computational and algorithmic levels of explanation is not crucial for the issues discussed here.

More central is that, on Marr's view of explanation, there are also explanations that are explicitly concerned with the way that a particular process is implemented. Proposals of this type fall at what he called the *implementational level* of explanation. Discussions of neural mechanisms involved in particular psychological processes are one possible implementational-level explanation, though across cognitive science one might also posit other implementations like robots. Proposals for neural mechanisms are important, of course, because they help to illuminate the way the brain works. In addition, our growing understanding of the brain may place constraints on explanations of cognition at other levels of abstraction. That is, an implementational level explanation may suggest ways to refine a computational or algorithmic level explanation of the same process.

To summarize, then, proposals about mental representations assume that the mind represents information in some format, and that mental processes make use of this information. Most proposals about the nature of mental representation are made without regard to the way the brain might handle these processes. There is work on neural bases of behavior, however, and these proposals may make claims about the way that information is represented and processed by the brain.

Representation and processing in the brain

Advances across the sciences have sped progress in neuroscience. Research in genetics has paved the way for a more detailed understanding of the growth of neurons and the expression of receptors for neurotransmitters. Advances in microscopy have opened up new ways to image individual neurons in fine detail. New techniques for recording from many different neurons simultaneously have created ways to correlate signals from many different brain cells and brain regions in awake-behaving animals. Finally, methods for noninvasive brain imaging have supported views of brain activity in humans.

These advances have provided windows into the nature of representation in the brain both at the level of populations of neurons and at the level of brain systems. Interestingly, this work tends to appear in different scientific literatures. Research at the level of the individual neuron or small populations of neurons tends to be done in animals where invasive techniques can be performed. Research on brain systems is done with both humans and other animals. In contrast, work on brain systems, and the functionality of particular brain regions, has historically involved studies of the effect of brain lesions on behavior. In humans, these lesions are the result of brain damage arising from accident or stroke, while animal research looks at lesions that are created experimentally. The research with humans often appears in clinical and medical journals, because it describes results taken from observations of patients. More recently, research on brain systems and the functionality of regions has been spurred by the development of noninvasive techniques of brain imaging. These techniques support measurements of brain activity in humans. Making representational claims on the basis of research on neurons and on brain systems involves quite different philosophical issues, and so we treat these aspects of research in different sections. We begin with a discussion of representation and neurons.

Some basic facts about neurons

In order to discuss representation and the brain, it is important to consider some basic facts about the brain that are relevant to our discussion. Figure 25.1a shows a diagram of a whole brain. The brain itself looks like a pair of boxing gloves set side-by-side with the thumbs pointing outward. Because the two sides of the brain look similar, we

(a)

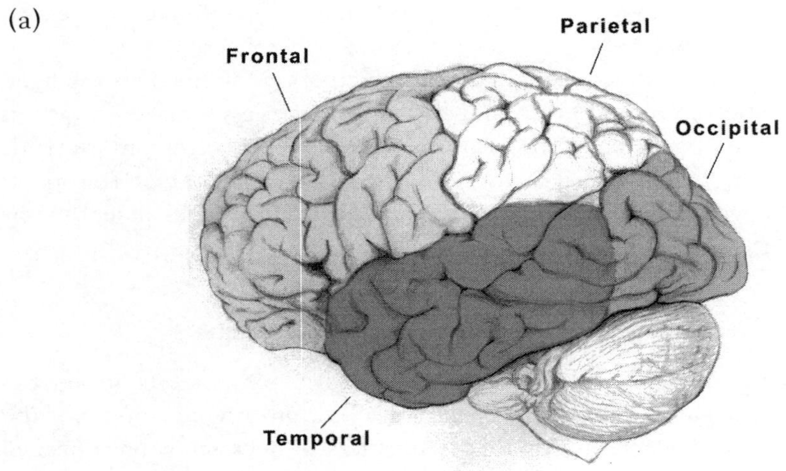

(b)

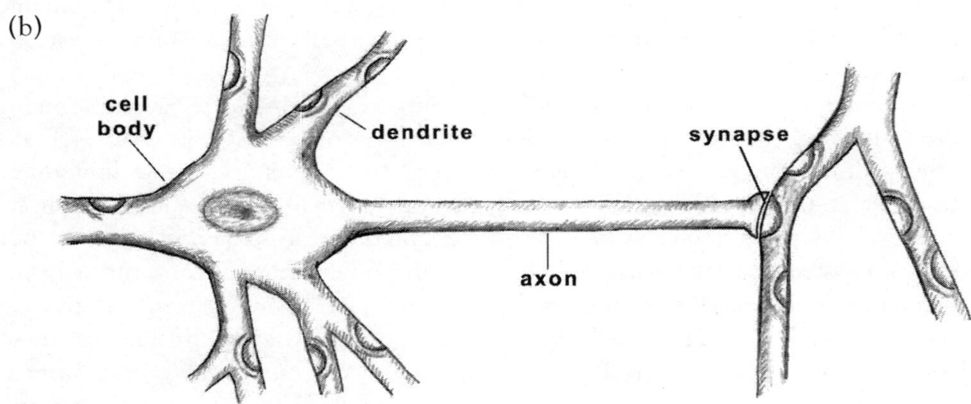

Figure 25.1 (a) Diagram depicting a brain with the four lobes labeled; (b) Schematic neuron showing the major components of the neuron.

say that the brain has two *hemispheres*, each of which is anatomically similar. Based on studies of physiology, the brain is divided into four regions or lobes, which are labeled on Figure 25.1a.

The brain is made up of many different kinds of cells. Of primary importance from a processing standpoint are *neurons*. These basic cells are the carriers of information signals in the brain. A schematic picture of a neuron is shown in Figure 25.1b. In particular, the body of the nerve cell (where the nucleus is found) has small projections called *dendrites*. These dendrites are the home of *receptors* that serve as gates between the inside and the outside of a cell. When particular chemicals called *neurotransmitters* attach themselves to the receptors, the gates allow positively or negatively charged ions to pass across the membrane that separates the inside from the outside of the cell. This flow of charged particles changes the relative electrical charge between the inside and the outside of the cell.

When the electrical charge of the neuron reaches a particular level, an electrical signal is sent from the cell body down the length of the long projection of the neuron (called the *axon*). This signal is called an action potential. When an action potential is sent down an axon, the neuron is said to *fire*. When the action potential reaches the end of the axon, it causes the release of neurotransmitters stored inside the cell. These neurotransmitters then affect the receptors of neighboring neurons, making them either more or less likely to fire. This active space between cells where neurotransmitters are released is called the *synapse*. Once a given neuron fires, there is often some period of time after that in which the neuron must "reset" itself before it can fire again. Thus, there is a maximum firing rate for any given neuron.

In humans, most behaviors are not driven by the individual firing of single neurons. It would be dangerous for any individual neuron to play too strong a role in controlling behavior, because the death of that neuron would be catastrophic for the individual. Furthermore, each individual neuron fires at best 100 times per second, and so it is not capable of carrying too much information on its own. Instead, there are a few key aspects of neural organization that are relevant. First, the cell bodies of neurons (and consequently the synapses) are concentrated primarily in the gray-matter areas of the brain. The white-matter areas of the brain generally contain insulated axons that travel longer distances between brain areas. Because the cell bodies are located in particular regions, it is the coordinated firing of neurons in a region that seems to carry information.

Second, many brain areas have been identified that have primary responsibility for particular aspects of psychological functioning. For example, the eyes project signals through the thalamus (which serves as a kind of relay station for sensory signals) to the rear portion of the brain (the occipital lobe). Many areas of the occipital lobe are assumed to be involved primarily in visual processing. This conclusion is based on many strands of data. For example, if electrodes are placed in areas of the occipital lobe of the brains of cats, neurons can be identified that fire most strongly in response to particular visual stimuli, such as lines of particular orientations or fields of dots moving in particular directions (e.g., Hubel and Wiesel 1965). This selective firing of neurons in response to particular stimuli is used to draw conclusions about the function of the brain area.

Representation and neurons

There are two core difficulties with trying to identify what it is that particular neurons in the brain are representing. The first is that our interpretation of the firing of neurons is based on our prior expectations about how the brain operates. That is, our interpretations of the data we collect on the firing of neurons are just as theory laden as our interpretation of any other data about the mind. Just because we have collected data from the brain itself does not mean that interpretation of that information is more straightforward than if we observed some aspect of behavior.

For example, we just mentioned that there are neurons that fire when a line of a particular orientation appears in a particular region of a cat's visual field. We are able to identify these neurons because we believe that orientation is a salient aspect of a line, and so we can easily notice the correlation between the firing of a particular neuron and the orientation of the line. It is quite possible, however, that some neurons are responding to stimuli in the environment but are coding information about more complex properties that we (as researchers) do not notice explicitly or do not believe are relevant to visual processing. If so, then we are much less likely to find the relationship between the firing of these neurons and the stimuli in the environment.

Even when we do successfully identify a correlation between the firing of a neuron and an aspect of an animal's environment, it is still difficult to interpret what that firing means because the brain does not make a clean separation between representation and process. This separation is obvious in most computer languages that have data structures and then procedures that operate on those data structures. In contrast, the firing of neurons in the brain both transforms the information that is available and also makes use of that information. This aspect of brains makes it difficult to make a purely representational interpretation of the firing of neurons. This issue can be illustrated with an example.

Much research in neuroscience has focused on the functioning of a brain structure called the *hippocampus* (see, e.g., Cohen and Eichenbaum 1993). Figure 25.2 shows the location of the hippocampus in the brain of a rat. As this figure shows, the hippocampus is a gray-matter area that is below the surface of the brain, and so it is called a *subcortical* structure. The hippocampus is an area of interest, in part because of a classic case study of the human patient H.M. H.M. was a teenager who had epileptic seizures that could not be controlled. To try to prevent those seizures from occurring, surgeons removed H.M.'s hippocampus from both sides of his brain. As soon as it was removed,

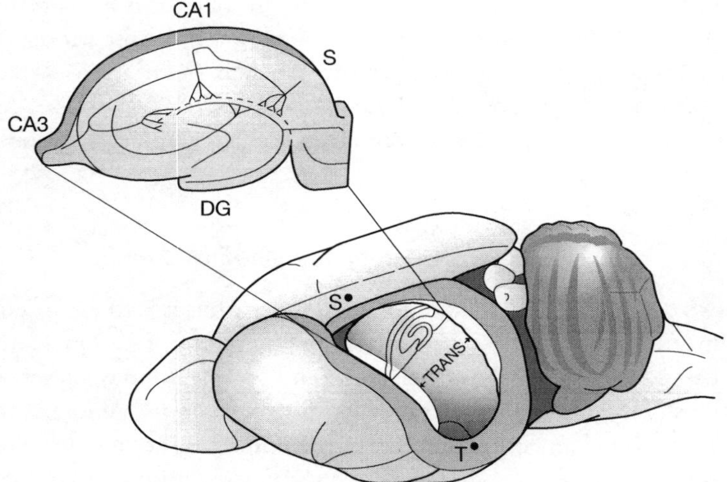

Figure 25.2 Location of the hippocampus in the brain of a rat (Fuster 1995).

H.M. was no longer able to remember new facts. For example, he was unable to learn the names of new doctors or to learn about current events. We say that H.M. had severe *anterograde* amnesia, which just means that he could not learn new information. On the basis of observations like this, psychologists concluded that the hippocampus plays a crucial role in the storage of new memories.

This interest in the hippocampus naturally led to single-cell recording studies with rats (see Redish [1999] for a review). A striking finding in these studies is that neurons in the hippocampus fire selectively when a rat is walking in a particular location in a familiar environment. Because of the correlation between the firing of these neurons and the rat's location, initially these cells were called *place cells* (O'Keefe and Nadel 1978). On the basis of these findings, it was hypothesized that the hippocampus in rats creates a spatial representation of the surrounding environment. Of importance for us, though, this interpretation is based on the correlation between the firing of these neurons and the location of the rat at the time the measurement was taken.[1]

However, in order to make a representational interpretation of the firing of these neurons, it is crucial to know both what factors of the rat's external (and internal) environment are correlated with the firing of these cells and the function of the activity of these neurons in the brain of the rat. For example, it may be that rats have to learn to associate particular regions of space with danger or reward. If so, and if the hippocampus is playing a role in creating memories, then perhaps researchers were observing cells that fired selectively to particular locations, because those locations were important for what the rat had to learn. As this example demonstrates, it can be difficult to tease apart the representational and functional roles of the firing of individual neurons.

Making claims about the representational status of the firing of neurons has been easier for neural systems that are closer to the input and output ends of processing. For example, much work has been done on the firing of cells in the occipital lobe (see Figure 25.1a) where activity from retinal cells is sent first. Classic work by Hubel and Wiesel (1965) demonstrated that particular cells in the cortex of visual areas of the occipital lobe of cats fire to lines of particular orientations presented to the cat's visual field. Interestingly, the visual cortex is organized in a way where neighboring cells seem to be sensitive to properties that are similar to each other. For example, Hubel and Wiesel demonstrated that the primary visual cortex has columns of cells that fire to lines oriented in a particular direction. Cells in neighboring columns fire most strongly to lines that differ slightly in orientation. On the basis of these data, vision researchers have concluded that the visual system is extracting orientation information from edges in the visual environment.

This notion of a topographical organization of the brain where neighboring regions encode similar information is also found in motor cortex. Classic work on this topic was done by Penfield and colleagues (Penfield and Boldrey 1938). During brain surgery, Penfield stimulated areas of the frontal lobe and found that this stimulation caused movements in areas of the body. Similar to the finding for visual cortex, neighboring regions of this area (now called *motor cortex* to highlight its role in causing body movements) caused nearby parts of the body to move. Furthermore, the size of the brain area required to control movements of an area was proportional to the complexity of the movements required by that body part. So, the motor areas associated with the hands and fingers are substantially larger than the areas associated with movements of the feet and toes.

It is important to remember that in early visual cortex and primary motor cortex, there is still a functional component to the firing of neurons. For example, rapid firing of cells in motor cortex is an important part of the causal chain that leads to body movements in the associated regions. The firing of neurons in early visual cortex integrates information from the retina and passes that information to other regions that provide further processing.

That said, brain regions close to the input and output ends of the information flow are relatively insulated from activity in other areas. Thus, there is a more direct correlation between observable events in the environment and neural firing. For many other areas of cortex, the firing of neurons reflects the integration of neural inputs from a variety of regions. Consequently, the representations in these areas correlate less with externally observable events than with other events internal to the brain.

This ease of identifying sources of neural activity in early visual and late motor areas relative to more central areas is reminiscent of an argument made by Fodor (1983) in his work on modularity. He argued that relatively peripheral systems are more likely to be informationally encapsulated than are central systems. That is, these peripheral systems will take information from a limited number of areas, and processing within these systems will not be affected by processing in other areas. He argued that modular systems were the only ones that cognitive science could hope to understand, because the dynamics of central systems would make them difficult to comprehend. Translating this view to the brain, we would expect it to be easier to identify the representations used by peripheral systems (like early visual and late motor cortex) than by central systems (like the hippocampus).

There are two caveats to make to this generalization. First, no area of the brain is truly insulated from the influence of other areas. Even the earliest areas of visual processing in the occipital lobe, for example, have connections that feed back to it from areas that process more complex visual information. Thus, while it is easier to interpret aspects of neural representation in early visual areas, there is much complexity that has yet to be understood.

Second, the difficulty of interpreting activity in central brain areas is not a cause for despair. There are a number of important advances being made in neural representation as a result of new techniques for measuring brain activity. Early studies of neural firing measured from a single electrode, and thus the data evaluation was limited to correlations between the firing of particular neurons and observable aspects of an animal's environment. More recently, techniques have been developed to record from many neurons at once, and from neurons in different brain areas. Thus, it is now possible to look at relationships in neural firing both within and across brain areas. These techniques hold great promise for helping us to better understand how information is represented and processed in the brain.

Representation and brain systems

In the background of our discussion so far is that different areas of the brain are typically involved in different functions. This distribution of labor arises because of the way that neurons are interconnected in the brain. Neurons in the brain are not randomly interconnected. Instead, there are distinct neural pathways throughout the brain that provide initial developmental constraints on information processing in the brain. Furthermore, studies of the results of brain lesions in humans and animals make clear that brain damage in different areas results in distinct deficits. We already saw, for example, that H.M. was impaired in a specific way when the hippocampus was removed from each hemisphere of his brain. In addition, there are enough similarities in the effects of lesions in certain areas across individuals to believe that there is at least some similarity in the way different people's brains process some kinds of information.

Interpreting data from brain-lesion studies is complicated by a number of factors. When an ability or behavior is disrupted as a result of a brain lesion, researchers are tempted to conclude that this brain region is responsible for the process that has been affected. This conclusion is strengthened if other lesions do not produce the same problems. Logically speaking, however, there are a number of reasons why a particular lesion might affect behavior. Obviously, it is possible that a lesion has destroyed the area responsible for carrying out a specific function. However, there are also regions of the brain that inhibit activity in other areas. Thus, it is possible that a lesion of one brain region caused a disinhibition of another area, which in turn caused a disruption of behavior. A third possibility is that information that is crucial for the desired behavior passes through the affected brain region on its way to another area in which the crucial processing is done. A fourth problem is that the brain is designed for learning. As soon as someone recovers from a brain lesion, the remaining brain areas will attempt to function as well as possible, and so observing a damaged brain in operation is not the same as observing an intact brain. For all of these reasons, it is important to treat lesion data with some caution, and to seek converging evidence for conclusions drawn from such studies.

One source of converging evidence about the function of brain regions comes from advances in noninvasive techniques for imaging the human brain that have supported additional theories of the functions of particular brain regions. The most common technique currently in use is functional magnetic resonance imaging (fMRI). This technique exploits changes in the magnetic properties of hemoglobin, depending on whether it is carrying oxygen. Tracking these magnetic properties identifies the volume of blood flowing to different regions of the brain. This technique assumes that neurons require substantial energy to fire, and so areas of the brain that are highly active at any given moment will require lots of blood flow. Interpretation of these data typically assumes a particular brain region will draw more blood when the neurons in that region are active than when they are inactive.

Imaging data have a very different character than data on neural firing discussed in the previous section. Blood flow in the brain changes fairly slowly (on the order of a few seconds). Thus, it is possible to identify where in the brain there have been changes in activity, but not precisely when activity changed with respect to changes in activity in other brain areas or with respect to changes in the environment. That is, fMRI is said to have excellent *spatial resolution* (where there is activity), but poor *temporal resolution* (when the activity occurred).

With all of these caveats in place, I discuss two interesting aspects of representation in different brain systems. These cases illustrate both the power of considering representational hypotheses about the brain, and also the limitations in our ability to interpret the representations involved in different brain regions.

The first case involves hemispheric differences in processing. As shown in Figure 25.1, the whole brain consists of two hemispheres that, to the naked eye, look virtually identical. On the basis of a variety of studies, however, it has become clear that these hemispheres do not function identically in most people.

The most obvious difference between hemispheres is that the left hemisphere is crucial for human language abilities (in right-handed people and many left-handed people). This observation is based on a number of sources. First, starting in the nineteenth century, neurologists correlated areas of brain damage with patterns of language deficiencies that occur after a stroke damages the brain (Benson and Ardila 1996; Benton 1981). These studies revealed that language difficulties were typically caused by damage to the left hemisphere of the brain. Lesions to different regions of the left hemisphere cause different kinds of language deficits, though a catalog of these deficits goes beyond the scope of this chapter.

Converging evidence for this conclusion came following another type of surgical procedure used to control epilepsy in which a band of fibers that connects the two hemispheres (called the *corpus callosum*) was severed (Gazzaniga 2005). Cutting the corpus callosum did effectively stop the seizures, but it also left the hemispheres of patients' brains unable to communicate. Patients who have had this surgery are typically called *split-brain* patients to emphasize that the hemispheres of their brains are acting independently.

An interesting aspect of the connectivity of the brain allowed these patients to be studied experimentally. The brain is wired so that visual information presented to a person's left side is sent first to the right hemisphere of the brain, and information presented to a person's right is first sent to left hemisphere.[2] Likewise, motor cortex on the right side of the brain controls the left arm and leg, while motor cortex on the left side of the brain controls the right arm and leg.

One of the most striking observations from split-brain patients is that they are able to name objects presented to their right visual field but not objects presented to their left visual field. The visual information from the right visual field goes to the left hemisphere, which appears to do most of the language processing. Split-brain patients are able to identify objects presented to the left visual field, because they are able to demonstrate (with their left hands) how the objects would be used. They are just not able to say the name of the object, because the information from the right hemisphere cannot cross over to the left hemisphere.

This observation has naturally led to much research about ways that the left and right hemispheres differ in their representational capacities. Many of these proposals focus on aspects of representation that might differentiate linguistic from nonlinguistic representational abilities. For example, Marsolek (1999) argues that the left hemisphere is biased toward abstract representations, and the right hemisphere is biased toward representations of specific items.

Related to this approach is the suggestion that the left hemisphere creates categorical representations of space that preserve relationships among elements in visual scenes (e.g., left-of or right-of). In contrast, the right hemisphere creates representations of space that preserve the distance and orientation between elements (Kosslyn et al. 1989). Taken together, these two proposals suggest that language is processed in the left hemisphere because it requires abstracting across many different presentations of sentences to form a grammar, and across many different specific exemplars to form categories that can be labeled by words.

However, the interpretation of hemispheric differences may not be so simple. Ivry and Robertson (1998) provide a very different interpretation of hemispheric differences in processing. They posit that the hemispheres differ primarily in the relative *spatial frequencies* to which they attend. In a visual image, the spatial frequency is the width of a line that can be detected or discriminated. Low spatial frequencies are thick lines, while high spatial frequencies are thin lines. So, the fine detail in an image is contained in the high-spatial-frequency information, while the broad outlines are contained in the low-spatial-frequency information. Ivry and Robertson argue that the left hemisphere focuses on relatively lower spatial frequencies than does the right hemisphere. For this reason, it appears that the left hemisphere is forming more abstract visual categories, because only the broad outlines of visual images are available to it relative to the information available to the right hemisphere.

The point of this discussion is not to evaluate these two possible claims for the nature of hemispheric differences in representation. The main idea is that there is a tendency to create proposals about mental representation that fit in obvious ways with what we know about behavior. For example, we know that language behavior requires using some symbols (such as words). Thus, we posit that the left hemisphere must be more likely than the right hemisphere to represent things symbolically. However, there are many potential ways that a particular behavior might be carried out, and there is a potential danger in imposing our current theoretical beliefs about algorithmic-level explanations for a cognitive process on the interpretation of data about neural processes.

Conflating processes and tasks

The influence of our theoretical beliefs on our interpretation of the activation of brain systems deserves more discussion. Uttal (2001) refers back to the phrenologists of the nineteenth century. It is easy to laugh at the pictures of heads with the brain divided up into squares labeled with personality traits like "gratitude" and "generosity." What seems quaint about these pictures, however, is not the basic premise that the brain is divided into regions of specialization. Instead, it is the labels on the boxes that do not mesh with current theories about cognitive processes. Uttal warns, however, that there is a tendency to identify cognitive processes with the tasks that psychologists use to study them. Thus, we have theories of categorization, decision-making, problem-solving, attention, and implicit memory, because psychologists give research participants categorization, decision-making, problem-solving, attention, and implicit-memory tasks. While we may think of some of these complex cognitive tasks as constructed from simpler ones (e.g., categorization may involve perceptual and memory processes), others seem to be more basic processes (e.g., attention).

Our ability to identify the functions of brain regions is only as good as the taxonomy of cognitive processes that we have. If we are unsure of the component processes of a particular cognitive task, then this uncertainty will carry over to our interpretation of fMRI data. We must, therefore, be careful in evaluating claims about the function of particular brain regions to ensure that the cognitive analysis on which it is based is acceptable. Thus, while brain-imaging techniques hold great promise for the development of cognitive neuroscience, these measures are but one of many methods for collecting psychological data.

Conclusions

It is clearly impossible to summarize all of what we know about representation and the brain in a single chapter. Indeed, whole books have been written on the topic of representation generally (e.g., Gärdenfors 2000; Markman 1999; Sowa 1984). Furthermore, the field of neuroscience is in a period of tremendous growth. Thus, current beliefs about the way information is represented in the brain will change rapidly. For this reason, I focused on issues that make it difficult to identify the bases of neural representation. These issues are ones that must be considered when evaluating any proposal about representation and brain. I summarize the main issues here.

First, neurons integrate inputs from a variety of sources and then convey the results of that integration to other neurons through a process of neural firing. Each neuron is both processing (i.e., integrating) information and also passing along information that will be integrated elsewhere. Thus, unlike computer programs, which often treat data structures and procedures separately, the brain makes no clear distinction between representation and process. This confounding of representation and process complicates the task of identifying the way the brain is representing information. We must strive to understand the role each brain region plays within a system to be confident in claims about neural representation.

Second, it is clear that there is a complex division of labor in the brain. Different brain regions are responsible for processing different aspects of information. However, there is no guarantee that this brain organization is broken down along the same lines as our descriptive theories of cognitive processing. Thus, there is a danger that if we identify particular brain regions with processes derived from our current taxonomy of cognitive processing, that we may misidentify the functions of these brain areas.

Third, there is a tendency to assume that the representations developed by the brain match our intuitions about the cognitive processes in which those brain regions are involved. For example, we may seek neurons whose firing correlates with the presence of particular visual features in the environment, because we believe that those features are likely to be identified by the visual system. We may assume that areas of the brain associated with language are more likely to develop symbolic representations than are areas of the brain that are not associated with language. However, there are many ways that a given process might be implemented, and there is no reason to believe that the brain has done so in an intuitively obvious way. For example, the concept of spatial frequency analysis described above is deeply counterintuitive, and yet there is significant evidence that visual representations are strongly influenced by the analysis of spatial frequencies (Graham 1989; Oliva and Schyns 1997). Thus, great care must be exercised in labeling the representations we assume that the brain is using.

While much of this chapter advises caution, this must be taken in the context of this period of growth in neuroscience. We have learned much about the way the brain operates from the fine details of the relationship between genes and the development of receptors for neurotransmitters all the way to the patterns of coordinated activity across brain regions. The data being collected across the areas of neuroscience will fundamentally change the way we think about brain and behavior. In this spirit, it is important to be aware of the logical pitfalls into which one can fall while interpreting what the brain is doing.

Notes

1. It is important to point out that this discussion looks at the likelihood that a particular pattern of firing would occur given a particular stimulus in the environment. An alternative way of looking at the interpretation of neural representations has been to assume that the brain only has access to the existing pattern of firing. Thus, it may be more appropriate to focus on decoding the likelihood that a given stimulus appeared in the environment given the observed pattern of neural firing (Rieke et al. 1997).
2. Both eyes take in information about the right and left sides of space, but the activity of the retina corresponding to regions in the left side of space from both eyes goes to the right hemisphere and that from the right side of space goes to the left hemisphere.

Acknowledgements

The author thanks Jeff Laux, Lisa Narvaez, and Jon Rein for helpful comments on previous drafts of the manuscript. Special thanks to Susanna Douglas, who prepared Figure 25.1. Preparation of this chapter was supported by National Science Foundation grant DMI–05–55851, Air Force Office of Scientific Research grant FA9550–06–1–0204, and a fellowship to the IC2 Institute at the University of Texas.

References

Benson, D. F., and Ardila, A. (1996) *Aphasia: A clinical perspective*, New York: Oxford University Press.

Benton, A. (1981) "Aphasia: Historical Perspectives," in M. T. Sarno (ed.), *Acquired Aphasia*, New York: Academic Press, pp. 1–25.

Cohen, N. J., and Eichenbaum, H. (1993) *Memory, Amnesia, and the Hippocampal System*, Cambridge, MA: MIT Press.

Fodor, J. A. (1983) *The Modularity of Mind*, Cambridge, MA: MIT Press.

Fuster, J. M. (1995) *Memory in the Cerebral Cortex: An Empirical Approach to Neural Networks in the Human and Nonhuman Primate*, Cambridge, MA: MIT Press.

Gärdenfors, P. (2000) *Conceptual Spaces: The Geometry of Thought*, Cambridge, MA: MIT Press.

Gazzaniga, M. S. (2005) "Forty-five Years of Split-Brain Research and Still Going Strong," *Nature Reviews Neuroscience* 6, no. 8: 653–59.

Graham, N. V. (1989) *Visual Pattern Analyzers*, New York: Oxford University Press.

Hubel, D. H., and Wiesel, T. N. (1965) "Receptive Fields and Functional Architecture in Two Nonstriate Visual Areas (18 and 19) of the Cat," *Journal of Neurophysiology* 28: 229–89.

Ivry, R. B., and Robertson, L. C. (1998) *The Two Sides of Perception*, Cambridge, MA: MIT Press.

Kosslyn, S. M., Koenig, O., Barrett, A., Cave, C. B., Tang, J., and Gabrieli, J. D. E. (1989) "Evidence for Two Types of Spatial Representations: Hemispheric Specialization for Categorical and Coordinate Relations," *Journal of Experimental Psychology: Human Perception and Performance* 15, no. 4: 723–35.

Markman, A. B. (1999) *Knowledge Representation*, Mahwah, NJ: Erlbaum.

Marr, D. (1982) *Vision*, New York: W. H. Freeman & Co.

Marsolek, C. J. (1999) "Dissociable Neural Subsystems Underlie Abstract and Specific Object Recognition," *Psychological Science* 10, no. 2: 111–18.

O'Keefe, J., and Nadel, L. (1978) *The Hippocampus as a Cognitive Map*, London: Clarendon Press.

Oliva, A., and Schyns, P. G. (1997) "Coarse Blobs or Fine Edges? Evidence that Information Diagnosticity Changes the Perception of Complex Visual Stimuli," *Cognitive Psychology* 34: 72–107.

Palmer, S. E. (1978) "Fundamental Aspects of Cognitive Representation," in E. Rosch and B. B. Lloyd (eds), *Cognition and Categorization*, Hillsdale, NJ: Erlbaum, pp. 259–302.

Penfield, W., and Boldrey, E. (1938) "Somatic Motor and Sensory Representation in the Cerebral Cortex of Man as Studied by Electrical Stimulation," *Brain* 15: 389–443.

Pylyshyn, Z. W. (1980) "Computation and Cognition: Issues in the Foundations of Cognitive Science," *Behavioral and Brain Sciences* 3, no 1: 111–69.

Redish, A. D. (1999) *Beyond the Cognitive Map: From Place Cells to Episodic Memory*, Cambridge, MA: MIT Press.

Rieke, F., Warland, D., de Ruyter van Steveninck, R., and Bialek, W. (1997) *Spikes: Exploring the Neural Code*, Cambridge, MA: MIT Press.

Sowa, J. F. (1984) *Conceptual Structures: Information Processing in Mind and Machine*, Reading, MA: Addison-Wesley.

Tversky, A. (1977) "Features of Similarity," *Psychological Review* 84, no. 4: 327–52.

Uttal, W. R. (2001) *The New Phrenology*, Cambridge, MA: MIT Press.

26

LEVELS OF MECHANISMS: A FIELD GUIDE TO THE HIERARCHICAL STRUCTURE OF THE WORLD

Carl F. Craver

Introduction

The intuition that the world can be ordered into a hierarchy of levels is nearly ubiquitous in cognitive neuroscience and the special sciences generally. However, scientists and philosophers use the term "level" to describe a wide variety of relations, and considerable confusion arises from a failure to keep them distinct. For this reason, it is best not to speak of "levels" *simpliciter*, but rather to speak of "levels of *R*," where *R* is some explicit specification of a relation between levels or of the *relata* at different levels.

Here I develop a field guide to different senses of level in the special sciences. My ultimate goal is to focus on levels of mechanisms, which play a central explanatory role in sciences such as experimental biology and neuroscience. I extract some features of this variety of levels by looking at a well-understood exemplar, which I call the levels of learning and memory. These levels (sketched in the third section) are described as aspects of one of the most successful, if controversial, explanations in contemporary cognitive neuroscience. I develop a taxonomy of different senses of level, and I show that each is either inappropriate or incomplete as a description of the levels of learning and memory. I then argue that levels of mechanisms capture most clearly the explanatory sense of levels ubiquitous in contemporary cognitive neuroscience. I close by contrasting levels of mechanisms with levels of realization, the target of much recent debate in the metaphysics of mind.

The levels metaphor: three questions

The levels metaphor is spatial. Application of the metaphor requires only a set of items and a procedure for ranking them as higher or lower than one another. Consequently, the levels metaphor is used in different domains to relate different items by different relations. One can keep these different uses of the metaphor distinct by answering three questions. The first is the *relata question*: What items are sorted into levels? Different construals of the levels relationship relate different things, e.g., scientific fields, functions, entities, events, sciences, and theories. It is not at all obvious, and certainly should not be assumed from the start, that the levels used to sort these different relata will bear any similarity to one another. The second question is the *relations question*: By virtue of what are any two items at different levels? Different relations are often postulated in different accounts of levels: relations of complexity, control, dominance, explanation, and size are examples. The third question is the *identification question*: By virtue of what are any two items at the same level? Not every account of levels can answer all of these questions. (My own view, for example, provides no unique answer to the identification question.) Still, to answer these questions is to add content to the levels metaphors used in different contexts.

Levels in the neuroscience of memory

Gordon Shepherd opens his classic neurobiology textbook with a call for multilevel research in the neurosciences:

> From these considerations we can deduce a basic premise, that an understanding of nervous function requires identifying the elementary units at different levels of organization and understanding the relations between different levels. We can summarize this view with a more precise definition of the subject matter of modern neurobiology and of this book: Neurobiology is the study of nerve cells and associated cells and the ways that they are organized into functional circuits that process information and mediate behavior.
>
> (1994: 4–5)

Shepherd's perceptive characterization of levels is the intended target for my positive analysis. Recent work on the neuroscience of spatial memory exemplifies the multilevel structure that Shepherd emphasizes (for reviews see Squire and Kandel 2001; Lynch 2004; for philosophical discussion, see Craver 2003; Bickle 1998, 2003; Churchland and Sejnowski 1992; Schaffner 1993). This work serves as a brief and familiar example of one notion of "level" that recurs across the cognitive neurosciences and the special sciences generally.

The theories of learning and memory in contemporary neuroscience bridge roughly five levels (henceforth LM levels). Behaviors (1) are explained in terms of neural computations (2), which are explained in terms of synaptic changes and activity levels (3), which are explained in terms of intracellular molecular mechanisms (4), which are explained in terms of linear sequences of amino acids and base pairs (5).

At the highest level is the behavioral or cognitive phenomenon of spatial memory, studied as the capacity of animals to solve different types of maze (e.g., the Morris water maze). At this level, an organism is described as, for example, engaged in dead reckoning or in the recognition of cues. The next level down is the level of computation in the hippocampus, one among many neural structures involved in spatial memory. The hippocampus is thought to be special because it houses a "spatial map." Individual cells in the hippocampus (and the entorhinal cortex) fire preferentially when the animal enters a specific region of space in a specific orientation. Computational models of the formation of the spatial map have now been shown to accurately describe certain crucial aspects of the organization of the functional architecture of the hippocampus (Samsonovich and McNaughton 1997; Hafting et al. 2005). At this level, maps are created, encoded, stored, updated, and replaced. Next down is the level of the synapse. Neuroscientists think of spatial maps as created, encoded, stored, updated, and replaced through the behavior of organized collections of individual cells coupled by plastic synapses. Synaptic adjustments, in the form of long-term potentiation (LTP) and long-term depression (LTD) (or, more properly, in the form of physiological adjustments analogous to these laboratory phenomena), are thought to change the organization of this network. The map is stored in patterns of connection strengths across the entire population. Finally, at the molecular level are the diverse activities of ion channels and intracellular signal cascades that explain these synaptic phenomena.

These are, roughly, the levels of learning and memory. One might posit levels between them, such as a level for molecular cascades or neuronal micronetworks. One might also extend the hierarchy to include the role of social networks and culture in memory at one end and the details of protein folding at the other. What matters is not how many levels there are but the principle by which the levels are individuated and distinguished. What sense can we make of the claim that these different components of the spatial memory mechanism are at different levels?

A field guide to levels

Below are eight different senses of "level":

1 Levels of control
2 Levels of processing
3 Levels of sciences
4 Levels of theories
5 Levels of regularity and predictability
6 Levels of mereology
7 Levels of mere aggregates
8 Levels of mechanisms.

I believe that LM levels are most perspicuously described as levels of mechanisms. I explain why by working through this list from beginning to end, pausing at each step to reflect on the match and mismatch with LM levels.

Levels of control and levels of processing are species of causal levels, which are defined by a particular asymmetrical causal relation among the hierarchically ordered items.[1] In *levels of control*, the relata are agencies and the relation is some sort of dominance or subordination. Higher levels of control, direct, or regulate the goings-on at lower levels. Bosses and employees, sheriffs and deputies, and queen bees and drones are at different levels of control. Analogous relations are sometimes found among physiological systems as well. When one speaks of "executive function" in cognition, one is describing levels of control. I suspect that not even the most ardent antireductionist will champion the idea that the mouse is in any sense controlling the magnesium ion. The reason to be reluctant about this idea is that the mouse and the magnesium ion are related as whole to part whereas levels of control relate wholly distinct items. In LM levels, the relata are logically dependent in the sense that one item is part of the other. They also overlap in space and time. These disanalogies help to underscore some of the reasons that talk of interlevel causation seems to many of us to be deeply confused. In levels of control, by contrast, the relata are logically independent and spatiotemporally distinct interactors.[2] It is not implausible for one to control the other causally (more on this below; see Craver and Bechtel 2007).

Levels of processing and LM levels are disanalogous in exactly the same way. In *levels of processing*, the relata are processing units of some sort (such as brain regions or computational modules), and they are related as "upstream" or "downstream" in the "flow of information," or in the order of production. If one idealizes feedback connections out of the early visual system ("early" and "late" also denoting order of processing), one can describe visual information as passing from lowest-level processing in the retina to higher-level processing in the lateral geniculate nucleus (LGN) and, still higher, in the primary visual cortex. This sort of relation does not hold in LM levels. The mouse is not in any sense downstream in the flow of information from the NMDA (N-methyl-D-aspartic acid) receptor. Again, this is because the mouse and the NMDA receptor are, whereas the retina and the LGN are not, related as part to whole.

Many common assumptions about the nature of causation preclude the possibility of causal relations between parts and wholes. Consider, for example, the view that all causation involves transmitting something such as a mark (Salmon 1984) or a conserved quantity (Dowe 2000) from one event, object, or process to one another. This is a minority view to be sure, but it represents a core idea about causation that is implicit in many of the metaphors used to describe causal connections. Causation is frequently described as a kind of cement, glue, spring, string, or some other physical transmission or exchange from one object, process, or event to another through contact action or through a propagated signal (see Hitchcock 2003). Such a conception of causation as a physical connection between two things does not accommodate interlevel causes between mechanisms and their components (for one account of mechanisms, see Craver 2007; 2007). Mechanisms and their components are not distinct events, objects, or processes. Given the compositional relations between mechanisms and their components, the space-time path of the mechanism includes the space-time path of its components. They coexist with one another, and so there is no possibility of their *coming to* spatiotemporally intersect with one another. If a conserved quantity is possessed by one of the components (say, a certain mass or a charge), that component conserved quantity is also possessed by the whole (if only by virtue of being possessed by the part).

The componency (or constitutive; Salmon 1984) relation between mechanisms and their components conflicts with many other common assumptions about causation. Most theories of causation, at least since Hume, have assumed that causes and effects must be wholly distinct. Lewis is explicit:

> C and E must be distinct events – and distinct not only in the sense of nonidentity but also in the sense of nonoverlap and non-implication. It won't do to say that my speaking this sentence causes my speaking this sentence causes my speaking this sentence; or that my speaking the whole of it causes my speaking the first half of it; or that my speaking causes my speaking it loudly, or vice versa.
>
> (2000: 78)

Strictly speaking, the opening of the NMDA channel is not a cause of the induction of LTP. Rather, it is part of its induction. LTP is induced through the opening of NMDA receptors, not as a consequence of their opening. Of course, there is no stopping someone who wants to use the word "cause" in this way, but to use "cause" so loosely is to expand its extension to cover relationships that are already characterized without remainder by the word, "component."

As Kim (2000) argues, the possibility of bottom-up and top-down influence "propagated" simultaneously across levels results in problematic causal circles. For example, one might believe that if an object, X, has its causal powers in virtue of possessing a property, P, then if X is to exercise its powers at time t, X must possess P at t. And one might believe further that if something causes X to acquire P at t, then X does not already possess P at t until that something has acted. If X's acquiring P at t is a cause of S's having ψ (pronounced "sigh") at t, and S's having ψ at t is a cause of X's having P at t, then it appears that X's acquiring P at t cannot cause S to have ψ until S's having ψ causes X to acquire P. In that case, it is little wonder that talk of interlevel causation strikes many of us as mysterious.

To avoid this problem, one might assume that causal transactions across levels take time: the effects of changes to a component alter the behavior of the mechanism as a whole at some later time, and vice versa. This would ameliorate some of the worry about the temporal order of causation, but it raises a related worry about the asymmetry of causation.[3] It is a widely accepted condition on accounts of causation that they account for the asymmetry of causal dependency. The sun's elevation causes the length of the shadow, but the length of the shadow does not determine the elevation of the sun. Causes produce their effects, and (at least in many cases) *not* vice versa. While at least some cases of intralevel causation are asymmetrical, all of the interlevel relations are symmetrical: components act as they do because of factors acting on mechanisms, and mechanisms act as they do because of the activities of their lower level components. For these reasons, one should not confuse a *causal* way of thinking about levels with a constitutive, or componential, way of thinking about levels. Levels of control and processing are causal levels. LM levels are componential levels. (For a similar but fuller discussion of interlevel causation, see Craver and Bechtel [2007].)

Returning to the above list, philosophers sometimes describe levels in terms of units of science or products of science associated with each level. In levels of units of science (*levels of science*), the levels are fields or sciences. One is implicitly speaking of levels of science when one says that, for example, physics is at a lower level than chemistry, or that psychology is at a lower level than economics. *Levels of theories* (description, explanation, or vocabulary) are levels of scientific products. Precisely how the ranking within a hierarchy of sciences or theories is to be defined (systematicity or unification, perhaps) can be left ambiguous for now. My point about levels of theories does not depend on settling the matter.

Oppenheim and Putnam's (1958) influential view of the unity of science presumes a tidy correspondence between levels of nature (levels in the ontological structure of the world), levels of theory (levels among descriptions or models of the world), and levels of science (levels among fields of scientific investigation). They divide the world into six ontological strata (societies, organisms, cells, molecules, atoms, and elementary particles), with distinct sciences and complete theories for each. The unity of science, on their view, is to be achieved by the explanation of the items in the domain of one science in terms of the items in the domain of a more fundamental science.

LM levels do not conform to this tidy image of science. Most special sciences are composed of a reticulate network of interfield connections and interfield theories. LM levels are but one example of how researchers in a single field can integrate phenomena at multiple ontological levels by linking them within a single explanation. Levels of theory (and description, and explanation) break down in interfield climates such as the cognitive neurosciences and other special sciences. The fields of contemporary cognitive neuroscience (and the other special sciences) are structured in large part to form interlevel bridges and connections. Levels of science and levels of theory are too much in flux and too much under the influence of sociological factors (such as who travels and publishes with whom) to serve any precise ontological purpose. If one intends the metaphor of levels to describe structures in the world, levels of theories and levels of sciences are constructs derivative from, if they reflect at all, the ontological levels that they are designed to describe and explore. LM levels are more like Wimsatt's "biopsychological thicket" (1976), with reticulate connections among items at different levels and explanatory relationships moving up and down as the narrative of the mechanism unfolds. Activities in the special sciences span phenomena at different levels (as, for example, one intervenes to delete a component at one level and measures the consequences at another) and there is nothing like a complete theory (or the prospects for such) to be found at any of the LM levels (Figure 26.1).

Wimsatt's (1976) discussion of levels is an underappreciated classic in the philosophy of science. Wimsatt understands levels as features of the natural world. They are local maxima of *regularity and predictability* in the phase space of possible organizations of matter. These levels appear as peaks of regularity and predictability

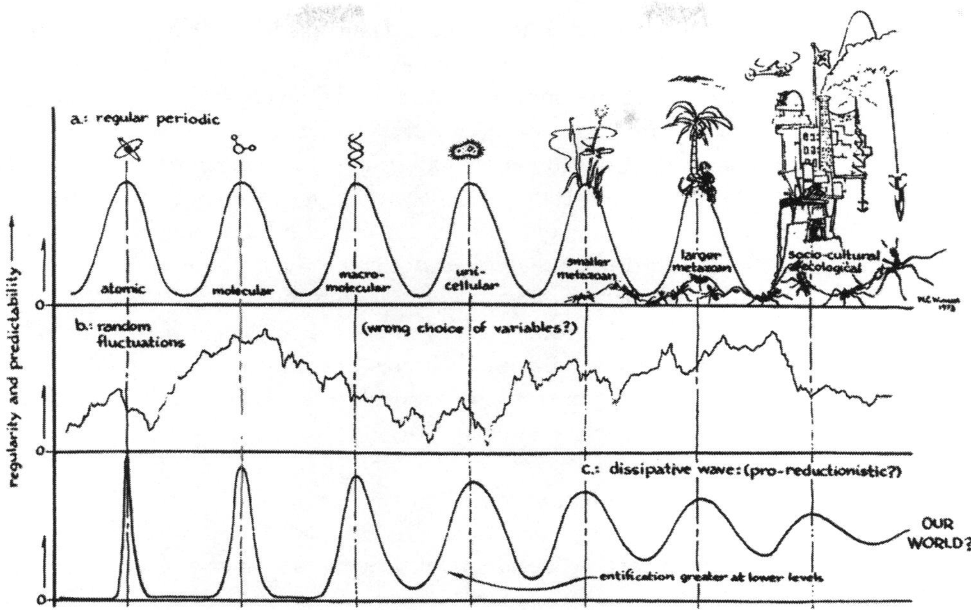

Figure 26.1 Wimsatt's representation of levels as peaks of regularity and predictability. At the top (a) is a world with well-defined peaks at some size scales. In the middle (b) is a world without levels. At the bottom ("Our World?") is a world characterized by a dissipating wave, with well-defined peaks that get shorter and less well-defined as size increases.

when graphed against size. See Figure 26.1. The relata in Wimsatt's picture are entities, and they are related as smaller or larger. Wimsatt points out in addition that items at the same level tend to act and interact with one another in regular ways, that forces of different strengths act at different levels, and that phenomena at different levels operate at different time scales (consider the difference in temporal scale among subatomic, biochemical, and behavioral phenomena). Size differences explain or at least are correlated with differences in laws and regularities, forces, and strength or frequency of interaction. This is why, on Wimsatt's view, there tend to be peaks of regularity and predictability at different size scales. Wimsatt thus develops a prototype view of levels structured around levels of regularity and predictability at different size scales.

Note that the levels in Figure 26.1 are not related as parts to wholes. Some of these levels stand in part-whole (or compositional) relationships of some sort. Molecules are composed of atoms, and atoms are composed of elementary particles, but larger metazoan animals are not composed of smaller metazoan animals. LM levels are of the first, not the second, sort. They are mereological. The NMDA receptor is part of the synapse, which is part of the hippocampus, which is part of the mouse. If "part of" is understood in spatial terms, then levels so defined will automatically be ranked according to size; no part can be larger than the whole. However, the size relation among the relata in the levels of contemporary neuroscience will then be seen as derivative from the part-whole relationships among items at different levels.

For reasons discussed above in connection with causal levels, it is crucial that one distinguish compositional from non-compositional varieties of levels. There is no difficulty imagining small things (even very small things) interacting with large things (even very large things). Planets attract molecules into atmospheres; elephants squash fleas. But there is considerable difficulty conceiving causal interactions between parts and wholes. The mouse's learning a maze does not cause the synapses to induce LTP. The induction of LTP is part (in some sense) of that learning.

In saying that LM levels are mereological, however, one must specify the intended sense of mereology. For example, certain theorems of classical mereology have no application to, or are misleading in thinking about, LM levels and similar multilevel explanations. Consider three such theorems:

1 *Reflexivity* – Every object is a part of itself.
2 *Extensionality of the part relation* – An "object" is completely determined by the set of its parts; i.e., for "objects" to be identical, it suffices that they have the same parts.
3 *Summation* – Any pair of objects (x, y) is itself an object z, which is their sum.

These theorems, found in many formal systems of mereology, are inappropriate for describing LM levels. First, LM levels are space, structure, and time involving in ways that most classical mereology is not intended to be. The set of integers is part of the set of real numbers, and *Fresh Fruit for Rotting Vegetables* is part of the Dead Kennedys corpus, but not in the same way that the NMDA receptor is part of the synapse. The NMDA receptor takes up part of the space occupied by the synapse as a whole. Its opening is part of the extended process that is the induction of LTP.

Though reflexivity is involved in certain theoretical applications of mereology, it confuses unnecessarily the concept of levels in examples from the sciences. If levels are related as a part to whole and everything is a part of itself, then everything is at both higher and lower levels than itself. LM levels are proper parts, not parts in the more inclusive sense described in many mereological systems.

The extensionality and the summation theorems call attention to a different disanalogy between some systems of formal mereology and the part-whole relation in LM levels. The extensionality theorem allows one to treat as the same object both a hippocampus and a bust of Chairman Mao formed by rearranging the cells of the hippocampus just so. The cells are at a lower level than anything that might be formed by aggregating the cells. In contrast, the precise organization of the parts within the whole is crucial to the explanatory force of LM levels, and so to the very structure of LM levels. The cells of the hippocampus differently arranged would not be components of, and so would not be at a lower level than, a working hippocampus. Any aggregation of cells in the form of the Chairman would represent him equally well.

The summation theorem is likewise too permissive for the purposes of characterizing LM levels. Together, the summation and the extensionality theorems allow for arbitrarily many gerrymandered wholes, wholes collected out of disparate and unconnected parts that have no functional role within the mechanism (in the sense of Craver [2001]). Lewis (1991) calls this "unrestricted composition": Whenever there are some things, then there exists a fusion of those things. But although the NMDA receptor, CREB, and glutamate are all parts of the LTP mechanism, it is not clear that the set composed of these is itself a component of the mechanism; these parts do not work together in any interesting sense; they can be merely gerrymandered into a whole. A similar issue arises for any mere fraction of a whole, such as the first third of my dog, Spike. Such haphazard parts are not parts in the same sense that the NMDA receptor is part of the LTP mechanism. The parts in LM levels are not just proper parts; they are working parts. I do not intend to claim that no formal mereology can represent adequately the crucial feature of LM levels; perhaps such a formal system exists. Rather, I claim that any adequate formal system will have to satisfy these descriptive restrictions on the special kind of part-whole relation involved in LM levels.

One way to bring this out is to compare LM levels with *levels of mere aggregates* (see Wimsatt 1997; Craver 2001). Aggregative properties are simple sums of the properties of their parts (such as the mass of a pile of sand and the masses of the individual grains). Aggregative properties do not change with the addition, removal, or intersubstitution of parts, and the parts have no significant interactions among them (Wimsatt 1997). LM levels, in contrast, depend precisely upon the organization of the components. In this sense, and this sense alone, mechanisms are greater than the sums of their parts: they have features and engage in activities that their parts alone cannot have and cannot engage in. The lower-level parts in LM levels are not summed into mere aggregates; they are organized into mechanisms. (This is why Kim's well-rehearsed overdetermination/exclusion arguments against higher-level causation do not apply to levels of mechanisms. Parts organized often work in ways that parts alone cannot and so, as Kim notes, have causal properties that the parts alone do not.)

Of course, there is something right about the idea that LM levels are mereological levels of some sort. NMDA receptors are spatial parts of hippocampal synapses, which are within the hippocampus, which is within the spatial memory system. The activities of these entities are also related as temporal part to whole: the binding of glutamate is a temporal component in the activity of the NMDA receptor. Spatially, the objects at lower levels are smaller than (or at least no larger than) the whole, giving the hierarchy a derivative size-ordering. Temporally, the lower level activities have shorter (or at least not longer) duration than the higher-level activities, giving the levels a derivative temporal ordering. But the important point is that relations of size and temporal inclusion, rather than defining what it is for an item to be at a level (the identification question), are derivative from the more fundamental relationship between levels (the relations question): namely, their relationship as mechanism to component.

Levels of mechanisms

Informally, the notion of level appropriate to the LM case is "levels of mechanisms," levels that are related as parts to wholes with the additional restriction that the parts are components. The relata are mechanisms and components, and the relationship is organization: lower level components are organized to make up a higher-level mechanism. By organization, I mean that the parts have spatial (e.g., location, size, shape, motion), temporal (e.g., order, rate, duration) and causal relations (e.g., feedback) with one another such that they work together to do something. Three levels of mechanisms are represented in Figure 26.2. At the top is a mechanism *S* engaged in behavior ψ. Below it is the ϕ-ing (pronounced phi-ing) of *X*s organized in *S*'s ψ-ing. Below that is the ρ-ing (pronounced rho-ing) of *P*s organized in one of the *X*'s ϕ-ing.

To say that *S* and ψ are at a higher-level than the *X*s and ϕs, is to say something of only local significance. Mechanistic levels are defined in part by a topping-off point, that property or activity to which all lower level components are constitutively relevant. Figure 26.2 depicts a three-leveled mechanism that, like the hierarchy of LM levels, traces only a single (local) strand: from the mechanism as a whole, to one

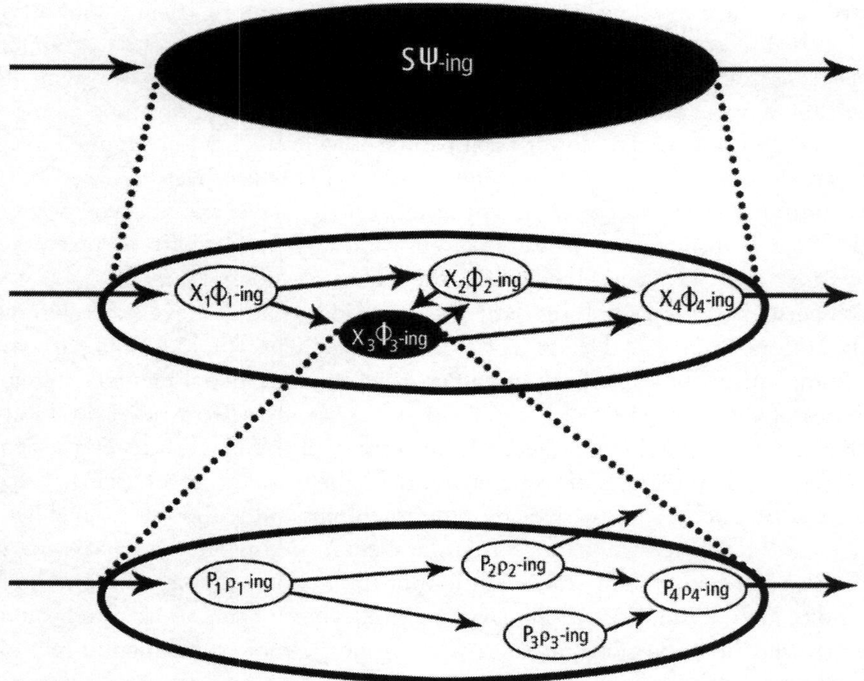

Figure 26.2 Three levels of mechanisms. At the top is the phenomenon. One level down (–1) is an organized set of entities and activities for that phenomenon. One level below that (–2) is the mechanism for one of the (–1)-level activities. Levels thus described are local, defined only within a mechanism.

of its components, on to one of *its* components, and so on. Levels as such are defined within mechanisms and not across mechanisms. They are not single strata across all of nature; they are local component/subcomponent relations.

Three immediate consequences follow from placing levels of mechanisms centrally in thinking about the causal structure of the world.

First, to think of levels in this way weakens one's inclination to think of levels as monolithic divides in the furniture of the world. This temptation is explicit in Oppenheim and Putnam's vision of the unity of science, and it is also retained as a vestige in Wimsatt's vision of levels, according to which causes, forces, and laws cluster at size levels. Mechanistic levels are defined within a system or subsystem, and there is no basis for comparing levels between systems. The question of whether molecules and cells are "at different mechanistic levels" can be asked only in the context of a given mechanism and a given decomposition of that mechanism. Is my heart at a different level than my car's engine? I do not know what such a question asks, and I do not know precisely because the heart and the engine are in different systems. It is not "molecules" in general that are at a lower level than "cells" in general, but the molecules composing systems of a type and the cells composing systems of a type.

Second, higher levels of mechanisms are, by definition, mechanistically explicable. This notion of levels thereby excludes spooky emergence by fiat. A defining mark of spooky emergence is that *spooky emergent properties and activities have no mechanistic explanation*.[4] The organization of components in a mechanism might in some sense allow the novel property to "emerge," but the property, it is said, has no explanation in terms of the operation of that mechanism. There can be no levels of mechanisms when decomposition is impossible in principle. This has two implications. First, the notion of "level" involved in discussions of emergence is not the same as the notion of level that is so ubiquitous in biology. Levels of mechanisms are componential levels; levels of spooky emergence are not. For this reason, the notion of strong emergence can borrow no legitimacy from its loose association with the levels of mechanisms so ubiquitous in biology and elsewhere. Second, the defender of strongly emergent properties must explain why top-down causation from emergent to non-emergent properties is different from mundane causation between two distinct properties. It is best to separate the question of whether strongly emergent properties are possible (in some sense of the word possible) from the question of whether interlevel causation is possible. The problem of interlevel causation can arise without strong emergence, and the possibility of strongly emergent properties does nothing to make that problem more difficult to solve. Indeed, if the second conclusion above is correct, the problem of interlevel causation is considerably easier to solve for emergent properties.

Finally, levels of mechanisms should also be distinguished from levels of realization. Much debate in contemporary philosophy of mind has centered on the question of whether higher-"level" items (usually properties or events) can have causal powers over and above those of lower-"level" items. This argument applies to levels of (or orders of) realization, not levels of mechanisms (see Craver 2007). In levels of realization, the relata are two properties, ψ and $\phi\#$ (pronounced phi-pound), both ψ and $\phi\#$ are properties of one and the same thing (S), and S has ψ in virtue of having $\phi\#$.

This is the way that Kim (1998) thinks of realization. For example, the hippocampus is a spatial map (ψ) in virtue of the precise spatial, temporal, and active organization of its component cells ($\phi\#$). It is easy to see how ψ and $\phi\#$ might compete as causes. ψ is the behavior of a mechanism as a whole, and $\phi\#$ is the organization and behavior of all of its components. Any causal power of ψ must, says Kim, be inherited from the causal powers of $\phi\#$, and it is therefore difficult to see what ψ could add to the causal structure of the world over and above what $\phi\#$ already contributes. ψ appears to be epiphenomenal. Whatever the merits of this argument (see Craver 2007: Ch. 6), it does not apply to levels that are related as part to whole. This is for the simple reason that parts do not compete with wholes as sufficient causes. It is uncontroversial and obvious, Kim notes, that wholes can do things that their parts cannot. Lawnmowers mow lawns; spark plugs do not. Hippocampi form spatial maps; individual cells do not. Kim's argument is not threatening to higher levels of mechanisms. At best, his argument threatens levels of realization. Thus the causal exclusion arguments widely discussed concerning the metaphysics of mind have no bearing upon the levels that are so important to the explanatory structure of contemporary neuroscience and other special sciences.[5]

Conclusion

Despite the ubiquity of levels talk in contemporary science and philosophy, very little has been done to clarify the notion. Here I develop a taxonomy of different senses of level, and I focus on one sense – levels of mechanisms – that seems especially relevant to the explanations in contemporary cognitive neuroscience and other special sciences. If one thinks of levels in this way, one can easily see why interlevel causation should seem so problematic (indeed, it is problematic), one is free to jettison Oppenheim and Putnam's idea of monolithic levels of nature, and one can see room in the causal structure of the world for the existence and legitimacy of higher-level causes and explanations.

Notes

1. Churchland and Sejnowski mention levels of control and distinguish them from levels of description (Marr's levels) and levels of organization (in my schema, these are described as size levels but should be interpreted as levels of mechanisms).
2. Bosses and employees are, in a sense, functionally defined in terms of one another and are, in this sense, logically dependent upon one another. However, the occupiers of those roles are logically independent.
3. This principle has been questioned. See Price (1996) for a lengthy review. I am merely noting that many causal intuitions conflict with interlevel causes. I cannot demonstrate that they are metaphysically impossible on all notions of causation.
4. Others use "emergence" to describe properties of complex wholes that cannot be predicted from knowledge of the parts. Such epistemically emergent properties might be mechanistically explained even if they are unpredictable.
5. I believe that one can make the case for causal relevance of higher levels of realization, but I do not discuss that here. See Craver (2007).

Acknowledgements

Thanks to Phillip Robbins, Anthony Dardis, Donald Goodman, and Eric Marcus for comments on earlier drafts.

References

Bickle, J. (1998) *Psychoneural Reduction: The New Wave*, Cambridge, MA: MIT Press.

—— (2003) *Philosophy of Neuroscience: A Ruthlessly Reductive Approach*, Dordrecht: Kluwer.

Churchland, P. S., and Sejnowski, T. J. (1992) *The Computational Brain*, Cambridge, MA: MIT Press.

Craver, C. F. (2001) "Role Functions, Mechanisms and Hierarchy," *Philosophy of Science* 68: 31–55.

—— (2003a) *Explaining the Brain: Mechanisms and the Mosaic Unity of Neuroscience*, London: Oxford University Press.

—— (2003) "The Making of a Memory Mechanism," *Journal of the History of Biology*, 36: 153–95.

—— (2007) *Explaining the Brain: Mechanisms and the Mosaic Unity of Neuroscience*, Clarendon Press: Oxford, UK.

Craver, C. F., and Bechtel, W. (2007) "Top-Down Causation without Top-Down Causes," *Biology and Philosophy* 22: 547–63.

Dowe, P. (2000) *Physical Causation*, New York: Cambridge University Press.

Hafting, T., Fyhn, M., Molden, S., Moser, M., and Moser, E. I. (2005) "Microstructure of a Spatial Map in the Entorhinal Cortex," *Nature* 436: 801–6.

Hitchcock, C. (2003) "Of Humean Bondage," *The British Journal for the Philosophy of Science* 54: 1–25.

Kim, J. (1998) *Mind in a Physical World*, Cambridge, MA: MIT Press.

—— (2000) "Making Sense of Downward Causation," in Peter Bogh Andersen, et al. (eds), *Downward Causation*, Aarhus, Denmark: Aarhus University Press, pp. 305–21.

Lewis, D. (1991) *Parts of Classes*, Oxford: Blackwell.

—— (2000) "Causation as Influence," *Journal of Philosophy* 97: 182–98; repr. J.Collins, N. Hall, and L. Paul (eds), *Causation and Counterfactuals*, Cambridge, MA: Bradford-MIT Press.

Lynch, M. A. (2004) "Long-Term Potentiation and Memory," *Physiological Review* 84: 87–136.

Oppenheim, P., and Putnam, H. (1958) "Unity of Science as a Working Hypothesis," in H. Feigl, M. Scriven, and G. Maxwell (eds) *Concepts, Theories, and the Mind-Body Problem*, Minnesota Studies in the Philosophy of Science, vol. 2. Minneapolis: University of Minnesota Press, pp. 3–36.

Price, Huw (1996) *Time's Arrow and Archimedes' Point*, Oxford: Oxford University Press.

Salmon, W. (1994) "Causality without Counterfactuals," *Philosophy of Science* 61: 297–312.

Samsonovich, A., and McNaughton, B. (1997) "Path Integration and Cognitive Mapping in a Continuous Attractor Neural Network Model," *Journal of Neuroscience* 17: 5900–20.

Schaffner, K. F. (1993) *Discovery and Explanation in Biology and Medicine*, Chicago: University of Chicago Press.

Shepherd, G. (1994) *Neurobiology*, 3rd edn, London: Oxford University Press.

Squire, L. R., and Kandel, E. R. (2000) *Memory: From Mind to Molecules*, New York: Scientific American Library.

Wimsatt, W. (1976) "Reductionism, Levels of Organization, and the Mind Body Problem," in G. Globus, I. Savodnik, and G. Maxwell (eds) *Consciousness and the Brain*, New York: Plenum Press, pp. 199–267.

—— (1997) "Aggregativity: Reductive Heuristics for Finding Emergence," in L. Darden (ed.), *PSA-1996*, vol. 2, *Philosophy of Science* (proc.), S372–84.

27 CELLULAR AND SUBCELLULAR NEUROSCIENCE

John Bickle

Cellular and subcellular neuroscience

Cellular and subcellular neuroscience is the realm of action potentials, selectively permeable membranes, enzymes, voltage-gated ion channels, intra-neuronal molecular signaling, second messengers, configured proteins, and the like. So why include an entry on this topic in a *Companion* volume to the philosophy of psychology? An initial reason stems from recent trends in neuroscience itself. Over the past fifteen years neuroscience has been washed by a "molecular wave" that has now even reached the discipline's principal textbooks. A half decade ago, in the introduction to the fourth edition of their monumental *Principles of Neural Science*, Eric Kandel, James Schwartz, and Thomas Jessell announced accomplished "mind-to-molecules linkages":

> This book . . . describes how neural science is attempting to link molecules to mind – how proteins responsible for the activities of individual nerve cells are related to the complexity of neural processes. Today it is possible to link the molecular dynamics of individual nerve cells to representations of perceptual and motor acts in the brain and to relate these internal mechanisms to observable behavior.
>
> (2001: 3–4)

This emphasis on molecular mechanisms is not limited to "basic" research into neuronal activities. It has already entered into the search for mechanisms of cognition. There now exists a professional society, the Molecular and Cellular Cognition Society, with over 800 members worldwide from more than 100 laboratories conducting research on the molecular and cellular basis of cognitive function. Learning and memory research has been this young field's most productive area to date, but work is underway on awareness, attention, anxiety, sensation, and motor control – phenomena that collectively define the research agenda of cognitive science.

Most philosophers of psychology recognize that they have a professional interest in keeping their work "scientifically realistic." In the first decade of the twenty-first century, doing so requires recognizing the impact that molecular biology has had on neuroscience. So to start this chapter, I will describe two paradigmatic examples of experimental work from molecular and cellular cognition. These two are selected out of at least one hundred examples, published over the past fifteen years, which would equally serve my expository purposes. They will give readers a sense of some of the hottest experimental work now underway in this field. I'll then present a new account of scientific reductionism derived from a metascientific analysis of the practices of molecular and cellular cognition, and contrast this novel account with the two accounts that have dominated recent philosophical discussions of reduction: inter-theoretic reduction and functional reduction.

Cortical microstimulation

We begin with experimental interventions directly into cellular activity – namely, into action-potential frequency in tiny clusters (250–500 microns) of neurons responsive to similar sensory stimuli or motor outputs. In 1963 neurosurgeons Wilder Penfield and Phanor Perot published case histories of forty patients (out of over 1,100 during twenty-five years of surgeries at the Montreal Neurological Institute) who reported "experiential responses" to mild cortical stimulation while undergoing neurosurgery while awake. Penfield and Perot noted the similarities of these electrically induced experiences with the experiential hallucinations that sometimes accompanied epileptic patients' spontaneous seizures. These induced experiences ranged from fragmentary to extensive and often included sights, sounds, and accompanying emotions. They were often recognized by the patient as a past instance of his or her personal history. For example, one case (Case 5, D.F.) involved a woman experiencing a tune from her childhood played on a piano; another involved a man (Case 14, R.R.) experiencing parts of a conversation that took place earlier in his life when he resided in South Africa.

That such complex, multi-modal, episodic memories can be induced at all by mild cortical stimulation to selective locations is remarkable, especially given Penfield's crude techniques (surface cortical stimulation using monopolar silver ball electrodes, contact area of roughly 1.5 mm^2, yielding a current ranging from 50–500 milliamperes). But there are reasons for being philosophically cautious in interpreting these results. Full-blown experiential responses (as compared with simple sensory experiences and motor twitches) were only evoked via temporal lobe stimulation, and in only a small minority of temporal-lobe cases (7.7 percent of the 520 temporal-lobe cases; Penfield and Perot 1963: Table 3). Experiential responses were typically evoked near epileptic seizure origin sites, where neural activity was facilitated by tissue damage. Only a small number of types of memory content were evoked, mostly having to do with conversations, music, and audiovisual scenes. Penfield and Perot (1963) even catalogued a large variety of types of memory experiences that were, surprisingly, never evoked by temporal lobe stimulation. Finally, these results don't even provide evidence for the cortical localization of the limited types of memory contents evoked. This was displayed by follow-up interviews after surgical recovery. Patients often reported memories of the experiences evoked by cortical microstimulation during the surgery – even when the site of stimulation where the memory was evoked was ablated later during the surgical procedure.

These cautions might deflate all philosophical interest in cortical microstimulation. But its impact is more substantial when we fast-forward a quarter century to its experimental use on non-human primates. Breakthroughs in microelectrode technology were crucial. Contrasted to the physical dimensions of Penfield's stimulating electrodes (mentioned above), William Newsome began using tungsten tipped electrodes, with an exposed tip length of 20–30 microns, capable of being embedded into cortical layers. These electrodes' physical dimensions yielded a stimulating current of approximately 10 microamperes, more than three orders of magnitude less than Penfield's. Current mathematical estimates suggest that only neurons within 85–100 microns of the electrode tip are stimulated directly by the electrical stimulus (typically less than 100 neurons). These dimensions permit investigators to embed a stimulating electrode into 250–500 micron clusters of neurons with similar response properties. Such clustering of similarly "tuned" neurons (into cortical microcolumns) is a common microarchitectural feature across mammalian cortex.

A paradigmatic recent example of cortical microstimulation research is work by Ranolfo Romo and colleagues. They embedded stimulating microelectrodes into clusters of neurons in the primary somatosensory cortex (S_1), whose receptive fields cover small patches of skin on fingertip surfaces on the contralateral hand (the hand on the opposite side of the body). These neurons respond to pressure changes on the skin induced by vibratory stimuli. (More technically, they microstimulated quickly adapting [QA] neurons in area 3b of S_1.) Conveniently, higher action-potential frequencies in these neurons code for higher vibratory stimulus frequencies. Rhesus monkeys outfitted for cortical microstimulation at right-hemisphere S_1 sites were first trained on a stimulus comparison task. A vibratory "base" mechanical stimulus at a particular frequency (measured in cycles per second, or hertz [Hz]) was applied to a left-hand fingertip site for 500 milliseconds (ms). A delay period of a few seconds began as soon as the base stimulus ended. Then a "comparison" mechanical stimulus at a different frequency was applied to the fingertip site for 500 ms. Within 600 ms of the end of the comparison stimulus, the monkey had to press one of two buttons with his right hand to indicate which stimulus, base or comparison, was of the higher frequency. (The monkey received a drop of fruit juice reward only for correct judgments.) Trained monkeys can reliably discriminate base and comparison frequencies that differ by as little as 4 Hz, with roughly 75-percent accuracy. With differences of 8 Hz or more, their accuracy typically exceeds 90 percent (Romo, Hernández, Zainos, and Salinas 1998).

Once trained, monkeys are ready for the first experimental manipulation. On all trials, the base stimulus remained mechanical vibration at some frequency to a fingertip site. On half of the trials, the comparison stimulus was also mechanical vibration at a different frequency. But on the other half, the mechanical comparison frequency was replaced by direct cortical microstimulation to produce action-potential frequencies correlated with particular mechanical vibratory stimuli in the appropriate neurons. Based on their performance on the sensory stimulation-working memory-comparative judgment task, could monkeys tell the difference between mechanical comparative stimuli and cortical microstimulation? Would cortical microstimulation comparison stimuli affect their performance on the comparative judgment task?

Apparently not. There were no statistical differences in the monkeys' performances on mechanical and cortical microstimulation comparison trials to each of 10 different base-comparison stimulus pairs (10 trials per pair) where base and comparison stimuli differed by 8 Hz. There were no differences in their performances on mechanical and cortical microstimulation comparison trials to each of 10 different base-comparison stimulus pairs in which the base frequency was held constant at 20 Hz and the comparison frequency (half-mechanical fingertip stimulation, half-cortical microstimulation) varied from 8 to 32 Hz. Finally, there were no differences on mechanical and cortical microstimulation comparison trials on 10 other pairs mixed randomly among the pairs, where the base frequency was held constant at 20 Hz. (For these data, see Romo, Hernández, Zainos, and Salinas [1998: Figure 2].) In their discussion section, Romo and colleagues draw an explicit connection with subjective conscious sensation:

> Such high accuracy, based on the interaction between natural and artificially evoked activity, is consistent with the induction of a sensory percept . . . Here the evoked discharges from S_1 provided the substrate for higher-order processes leading to frequency discrimination in those cortical areas that are anatomically linked to S_1. Thus, the microstimulation patterns used may elicit flutter sensations referred to the fingertips that are not unlike those felt with mechanical vibrations.
>
> (1998: 389–90)

These results suggested numerous follow-up experiments. What if the base stimuli are varied between mechanical fingertip vibratory stimuli and cortical microstimulation (while comparison stimuli remain mechanical fingertip vibrations on every trial)? Again, this had no statistical effect on trained monkeys' performances on the stimulus comparison task, either with frequency pairs that differed by 8 Hz or with pairs in which the mechanical comparison stimuli were held constant at 20 Hz and base stimuli (half-mechanical fingertip vibrations, half-cortical microstimulation) varied between 8 and 32 Hz (Romo, Hernández, Zainos, Brody et al. 2000). This result is important because it shows that cortical microstimulation can drive all aspects of the task, including working memory for the base stimulus during the delay period and its role in comparative judgment and decision-making. What if monkeys' performances are compared on trials in which both base and comparison stimuli are mechanical fingertip vibrations with trials where the analogues of those same base and comparative frequencies are both cortical microstimulation? Except on trials where base and comparison frequencies differed by less than 4 Hz, the monkeys again showed no statistical differences in their performance on the task (Romo, Hernández, Zainos, Brody et al. 2000). Romo and his colleagues conclude,

> Correct behavioral performance after replacement of both base and comparison stimuli by cortical microstimulation demonstrates that activation of the QA circuit of S_1 is, by itself, sufficient to initiate all neural processes that underlie this cognitive task . . . This study, therefore, has directly established a strong link between neural activity and perception.
>
> (2000: 276)

At the time of this writing, cortical microstimulation is being used in numerous labs to explore the cellular basis of cognitive phenomena ranging from visual motion detection and depth judgments to heading direction through space, multiple-joint limb movements and motor plans, working memory, and neuroeconomic decision-making. (In Bickle [2003: Ch. 4], I survey results through the early 2000s and stress their importance for the search for cellular physiological mechanisms of consciousness, describing and citing numerous articles from the primary experimental literature.) One elegant feature of these experiments is that the behaviors used as measures of perceptual content are induced to occur – by the direct electrical stimulation of probably less than 100 neurons!

Molecular genetic manipulations in mammals

Learning and memory have been targets of neuroscientific research for decades. This includes the search for molecular mechanisms. Beginning in the late 1960s Seymour Benzer and his collaborators began using genetic manipulation techniques from molecular biology to create fruit fly mutants with specific learning and memory deficits. (For some details with numerous references to the primary scientific literatures, see Bickle [2003: Ch. 3].) But it wasn't until the early 1990s that these intervention techniques were applied to mammalian nervous tissue. Working in nobel laureate Susumu Tonegawa's lab, Alcino Silva and collaborators (Silva, Paylor et al. 1992) "knocked out" in mice-embryonic stem cells the gene expressing α-calcium-calmodulin-dependent kinase II (αCaMKII). This protein was known to occur in high concentrations in post-synaptic densities and had been implicated in the molecular mechanisms of long-term potentiation (LTP, a well-studied form of activity-dependent synaptic plasticity that had been correlated with learning and memory for more than two decades by that time). The mutants were viable, phenotypically (including behaviorally) normal and survived for durations that matched their "wild-type" littermate controls (whose αCaMKII gene was not disrupted). Yet hippocampal slices from the mutants showed deficient LTP, and intact mutants showed impaired spatial learning (compared with wild-type littermate controls) on a variety of Morris water maze and plus (+) maze tasks (Silva, Paylor et al. 1992). The paper just cited is now widely recognized as having launched "molecular and cellular cognition" and has been cited more than 1,300 times.

The use of living, behaving genetically altered mice to study the molecular mechanisms of cognitive function has blossomed over the past fifteen years. To provide some sense of the experimental strategies now standard in this field, I will describe in detail one early study. This study induced an especially elegant genetic mutation, employed important controls to isolate the cognitive deficit to memory consolidation, and generated very significant results; but in terms of overall methodology it is similar to probably any one of a hundred other studies I could describe to illustrate this work.

In the mid-1990s Ted Abel, working in Eric Kandel's lab, developed a transgenic mouse that over-expressed a regulatory subunit (R) of protein kinase A (PKA). Since the transgene was inserted into embryonic stem cells, it was present in all cells of the mutants' bodies. But it was linked to a promoter region selective for αCaMKII, so the PKA R transgene was highly expressed only in neurons in forebrain regions, including hippocampus. Specifically, its expression was much lower in amygdala (Abel et al. 1997). In simpler terms, this specific subunit of the PKA protein was present in highest amounts only in forebrain neurons. *In vitro* studies had already suggested that PKA was important in the induction of late (L-) LTP, a gene expression and protein synthesis-dependent form of synaptic plasticity lasting many hours, up to weeks, in living animals. Concentrations of cyclic adenosine monophosphate (cAMP), the classic second messenger of molecular biology, rise in the active post-synaptic neuron following multiple, properly timed stimulus pulses in pre-synaptic axon fibers. This rise is due (in mammals) to dopaminergic interneurons also activated by the pre-synaptic stimulus trains. Released dopamine binds to post-synaptic receptors that activate an intracellular G-protein complex, priming adenylyl and adenylate cyclase molecules to convert adenosine triphosphate into cellular energy and cAMP. The cAMP molecules bind to PKA R subunits, freeing catalytic PKA subunits. When a high enough concentration of cAMP molecules becomes available, freed catalytic PKA subunits translocate to the post-synaptic neuron's nucleus. There they phosphorylate cAMP-response element-binding protein (CREB) molecules. Phosphorylated CREB, particularly the α and δ isoforms, serve as gene transcription enhancers, turning on new gene expression and synthesis of both regulatory and effector proteins. The end results are proteins that restructure the cytoskeleton of active post-synaptic synapse sites, keeping the activated synapses potentiated for hours to days. However, PKA appears to play no role in early (E-) LTP, a short-term (1- to 3-hour) form of synaptic enhancement, whose molecular mechanisms are contained entirely within the dendritic spines associated with active synapses. Cellular physiology comparing activity in slices of hippocampus tissue from the PKA R transgenic mice with that in slices from wild-type littermate controls revealed that L-LTP was attenuated, while E-LTP was intact, in the mutants (Abel et al. 1997). (See Bickle [2003: Ch 2], for a non-technical explanation of some details of these molecular cascades and the transgenic bioengineering procedures used to generate the transgenic mutants.)

Abel and Kandel's PKA R transgenic mice thus offered a unique experimental model for testing whether the molecular mechanisms of LTP directly affected hippocampus-dependent ("explicit," "declarative") memory. If E-LTP is a mechanism for certain forms of short-term memory, then PKA R transgenics should be intact in both hippocampus- and non-hippocampus- (e.g., amygdala-)-dependent short-term memory tasks. And if L-LTP is a mechanism for the consolidation of short-term memories into long-term form, then the PKA R transgenics should be impaired on long-term versions of hippocampus-dependent tasks but intact on amygdala-dependent tasks (where the

PKA R transgene was expressed in lesser amounts due to the specific promoter region [αCaMKII] attached to it).

These were exactly the experimental results that Abel et al. (1997) obtained. Mice were placed in a novel environment and permitted to explore it for 2 minutes. Next a tone was played for 30 seconds. Mice then received a foot shock from a floor grid. Two minutes after the shock, mice were returned to their home cages. The context-shock conditioning is the hippocampus-dependent component. Rodents whose hippocampuses have been ablated bilaterally cannot acquire the context-shock association. The tone-shock conditioning is the amygdala-dependent component. (Rodents with bilateral hippocampus ablations can acquire and retain the tone-shock association.) Mice from both groups were then either placed back into the training environment 1 hour later (to test for short-term hippocampus-dependent memory) or 24 hours later (to test for the consolidation to long-term hippocampus-dependent memory). Or they were played the conditioning tone in their home cages, either 1 hour later (to test for short-term amygdala-dependent memory) or 24 hours later (to test for the consolidation to long-term amygdala-dependent memory). The behavioral measure used to indicate strength of memory association was the amount of time animals spent freezing during the first 2 minutes after the stimulus (novel environment, conditioned tone) was repeated. Freezing is a stereotypic rodent fear response where the animal crouches, tucks its front paws underneath its chest, and remains immobile except for breathing.

As predicted, both generations of PKA R transgenic mice that were tested were intact in their fear response to the training shock itself. There were no statistical differences in the average amount of time they spent freezing during the 2 minutes after the training shock, compared with wild-type littermate controls. They were also fully intact on both short-term and long-term versions of the amygdala-dependent classical fear conditioning task. That is, they spent just as much time freezing as did controls when the conditioned tone was repeated after 1 hour and after 24 hour delays. And they were intact on the short-term version of the hippocampus-dependent task. But they were significantly impaired on the long-term version of the hippocampus-dependent task, spending only about half as much time freezing as controls when put back into the novel environment 24 hours later. The intact long-term amygdala-dependent results are important because they control for motivational or motor effects of transgene expression. (Transgene expression did not simply inhibit the mutants' long-term motivation or capacity to freeze.) The intact immediate responses following training shocks are important because they control for sensory and attentional effects of transgene expression. Abel et al. (1997) also report similar intact short-term and deficient long-term effects by the PKA R mutants on another hippocampus-dependent memory task, the Morris water maze. In light of these results, Abel and his collaborators boldly conclude:

> Our experiments define a role for PKA in L-LTP and long-term memory, and they provide a framework for a molecular understanding of the consolidation of long-term explicit memory in mice … The consolidation period is a

> critical period during which genes are induced that encode proteins essential for stable long-term memory. The long-term memory deficits in R(A,B) transgenic mice demonstrate that PKA plays a role in the hippocampus in initiating the molecular events leading to the consolidation of short-term changes in neuronal activity into long-term memory.
>
> (1997: 623–4)

Readers should note that this paper was published in *Cell*, one of molecular biology's highest impact-factor journals and certainly not one given to rhetorical flourishes. "Mind-to-molecular-pathways" reductionism is now well underway in mainstream neuroscience, despite the nearly complete ignorance of it by philosophers and cognitive scientists.

Molecular mechanisms of consciousness?

Are features of phenomenal consciousness addressable by the experimental and interventionist techniques of cellular and molecular neuroscience? Few in consciousness studies have suggested that such investigations will bear much fruit; this includes physicalists about consciousness, who tend to bank on higher level neuroscientific investigations into more global brain processing in their search for "neural correlates of consciousness." However, cellular and molecular neuroscience has already uncovered mechanisms of working memory, selective visual attention, and even phenomenally rich features like awareness, arousal state, and anxiety level. Of real interest are some recent results using bioengineered mice. Single amino acid replacements in specific subunits of "fast" γ-aminobutyric acid type A ($GABA_A$) receptor proteins (components of the most prominent inhibitory neurotransmitter system in mammalian brains) have yielded mutant mice with specific changes in behavioral measures of loss of awareness or recovery of normal arousal state after selective anesthetic drug dosages, and in behavioral measures of anxiety reduction and sedation after anxiolytic drug dosages. Space limitations in this chapter prohibit a detailed discussion, though I will say a bit more about philosophical debates about qualia when I discuss functional reduction later in this chapter. I refer the interested reader to my 2007 paper for details of these experiments and results, and arguments for their philosophical relevance.

Reductionism reconceived: the case for pursuing metascience

Beyond educating philosophers and cognitive scientists about the kinds of investigations that are already underway and yielding fruit in cellular and molecular neuroscience, what philosophical lessons does this research offer? In the remainder of this chapter I'll elaborate on one consequence: a novel account of the nature and scope of psychoneural reduction(ism). Two models of reduction have figured prominently in philosophy of mind and psychology over the past four decades. The first is *intertheoretic* reduction, especially in the form first articulated by Ernest Nagel (1961) and refined in various ways by other philosophers of science (including me, in my 1998 book). This picture characterizes the key components of science as *theories* – sets of laws or explanatory generalizations. With regard to psychoneural intertheoretic reductions, such theories pertain to different "levels" of psychological and biological organization – to behavior, information processing, neural regions, neural circuits, on down to neurons and their components. Like the levels of biological organization they address, theories are also arranged into a hierarchy. On Nagel's original account, reduction is the relationship of deduction or derivability of a higher level theory (e.g., a theory from psychology) with a lower level theory serving as a key premise (e.g., a theory from cognitive neuroscience); soon after Nagel's original account was published, numerous philosophers of science proposed relations that were weaker than derivability in order to account for some recalcitrant cases from the history of science. These cases were widely acknowledged to be accomplished reductions, and yet they implied nontrivial correction to the reduced theory by way of the reducing theory. Obviously, a false conclusion (reduced theory) cannot be derived validly from a presumably true premise (reducing theory). Interestingly, a nontrivial amount of correction was even present in the scientific example Nagel himself used to illustrate his "reduction as deduction" account: the reduction of the ideal gas laws to statistical mechanics and the kinetic model of gases.

Further investigations by historically oriented philosophers of science led to further refinements of Nagel's basic account. In many examples of "textbook" scientific theory reductions, additional premises (besides the reducing theory) would be necessary to achieve a derivation of the reduced theory (or even an approximation of a derivation). These include assumptions or conditions limiting the scope or boundaries of the reducing theory's application, and "bridge principles" linking components of the reduced theory's theoretical vocabulary that do not occur within the reducing theory's vocabulary to components that do occur. Nagel's original account acknowledged the existence of both of these additional premises, but their status and complications became more pronounced as historians and philosophers of science examined historical intertheoretic reductions more closely. Nevertheless, Nagel's principal motivation held sway among many reductionists, especially those looking to apply work on intertheoretic reduction in science generally to emerging psychology-to-neuroscience cases. By focusing first on the intertheoretic reduction obtaining or developing in these cases, we can learn about the ontological status of the purported referents of psychology's or cognitive science's vocabulary (autonomy, identity, revision, or elimination) in the same way we learned about the ontological status of other potentially reduced theories' posits throughout the history of science. Namely, by the relative "smoothness" or "bumpiness" of the emerging intertheoretic reduction: the extent of the corrections implied to the reduced theory, the number and counterfactual nature of the required limiting assumptions and boundary conditions, the extent to which the relationship between reducing and reduced theory approximates deductive validity, the strength of the analogy between the reduced theory itself and the structure that could actually be deduced validly from the reducing theory, and so on. (See Bickle [1998: Chs 1 and 2], for a detailed overview of this episode in late-twentieth-century philosophy of science and its application to reductionism in the philosophy of mind.)

The second popular philosophical model of scientific reductionism, functional reduction, is of more recent vintage. It has emerged as the accepted account of reduction within consciousness studies – even though it was introduced, ironically, by *anti*-reductionists about features of qualitative consciousness. The principal idea is that reduction is a two-stage process. The first stage involves working the concept to be reduced "into shape" by characterizing it exhaustively in terms of its causes and effects ("functionalizing" it). The second stage is the purely empirical, scientific search for the mechanisms in this world that actually perform (or at least approximate) that set of causes and effects. (Levine [1993] contains an especially clear and straightforward account of this model, but it has also been offered as the correct general account of reduction by as prominent a reductionist as Jaegwon Kim [2005].)

Both of these popular accounts face serious shortcomings as models of actual reductionism in scientific practice. Most emerging reductions in science, especially in psychology and neuroscience, aren't affiliated with anything matching the grandiose structure of "theories" that are parts of the historical reductions that serve as the basis of the analysis by accounts of intertheoretic reduction. This holds even for the lower level, reducing sciences. Recalling the two neuroscientific examples discussed earlier in this chapter, neither cellular neurophysiology nor molecular genetics provides a set of "lawlike" generalizations that explain the behavior of neurons or intra-neuronal molecular components in all circumstances (not even in all biologically realistic circumstances). As is well known, biochemistry does not yet provide a comprehensive account about how a protein's tertiary structure emerges from the sequence and interactions of its amino acid constituents. Even if we understand theories of intertheoretic reduction to be accounts of *accomplished* scientific reductions, rather than accounts of how a reduction develops, existing accounts still assume tacitly, not only that reduction is similar across sciences, but also that the relationship hasn't changed over time. This tacit assumption is illustrated by the historical cases from which accounts of the intertheoretic reduction relation were culled. The reduction of the ideal gas laws of classical equilibrium thermodynamics to principles of statistical mechanics and the corpuscular-kinetic theory of gases, certainly the most influential case in the literature, was a reduction *from nineteenth-century physics*. No proponent of intertheoretic reduction has defended the assumption that the results that counted for an accomplished scientific reduction in nineteenth-century physics ought still to be expected in cognitive science today. Even the second favorite historical example of accomplished intertheoretic reduction, that of Mendelian principles of inheritance to the molecular mechanisms of gene expression and protein synthesis, is drawn from the history of biology *from one-half century ago*. It is clear that biology itself changed during this period. Why think that the sense of reduction within it stayed constant?

With regard to functional reduction, a focus on the scientific case studies appealed to by proponents is even more revealing. For the scientific examples offered are not even drawn from any science's genuine history. Instead they are drawn from *elementary-school* science education. A favorite example is the explanation of thermal properties of water via the dynamics of H_2O molecules – literally told with the limited detail we use to instruct children about science. One can be excused for thinking that reductive practices in actual present science, and even recently accomplished reductions, might differ considerably from the relationship exhibited in the examples we use to inculcate children into our scientific worldview!

What if, in an attempt to articulate an accurate account of reductionism in actual scientific practice, we instead turned to examples of actual ongoing investigations (in all their details and nuances) from a branch of science characterized as "reductionistic" by both its practitioners and other scientists working on similar phenomena in less reductionistic branches? And what if we focused our analysis on recent experimental results deemed paradigmatically successful by that field's proponents? And what if we conducted our analysis by simply looking for common experimental practices and theoretical interpretations of results across these cases, as unencumbered as we can render ourselves by philosophical assumptions about "what reduction has to be," or even about what it has seemed to be in a few accomplished historical examples? We'd then be doing *metascience* and presumably would be giving ourselves the best opportunity to discover what real reductionism is in actual scientific practice. Armed with such an account, we could then turn to questions about whether it delivers the goods that philosophers have expected from a psychoneural "reductionism."

A first metascientific hypothesis: real reductionism in genuinely reductionistic neuroscience

Based on a number of scientific cases like the ones described earlier in this chapter, neurobiologist Alcino Silva was first to sketch four principles (mostly in unpublished writings, although see Silva, Elgersma, and Costa [2000] for a kernel of each) that together comprise sufficient experimental evidence for establishing a cellular or molecular mechanism for a cognitive phenomenon – at least within the accepted practices of clearly reductionistic molecular and cellular cognition. Our recent collaborations have produced more detailed accounts of these convergent four (Silva and Bickle, forthcoming). The novel account of reductionism I began developing in my 2003 book and have elaborated on in publications since then (especially Bickle 2006a, b) serendipitously emerged as a metascientific consequence of two of these principles.

Principle 1: Observation

Occurrences of the hypothesized mechanism are strongly correlated with occurrences of the behaviors used as experimental measures of the cognitive phenomenon. The scientific examples described above demonstrate numerous results that illustrate this principle. Before Romo and collaborators' cortical-microstimulation experiments, researchers had *observed* that vibratory stimuli to fingertip sites were followed by increased action-potential frequencies in specific neurons in S_1 (the very neurons that Romo and collaborators microstimulated), and that specific action-potential frequencies in these neurons correlated strongly with the frequency of the vibratory stimuli applied. Before Abel and Kandel's experiments with PKA R transgenic mice, researchers had *observed* cAMP-PKA interactions and increased levels of PKA catalytic subunits freed from regulatory R subunits and translocated to the neuron nucleus following increased activity in pre-synaptic fibers that induced L-LTP in active synapses, and that learning was accompanied by long-lasting changes in synaptic plasticity in the very brain regions known to be crucial for the type of learning and memory involved (e.g., hippocampus for contextual memory, amygdala for tone-fear conditioning).

Principle 2: negative alteration

Intervening directly to decrease activity of the hypothesized mechanisms must reliably decrease the behaviors used as experimental measures of the cognitive phenomenon. Experiments that establish negative alteration are currently the centerpieces of molecular and cellular cognition investigations. Results with Abel and Kandel's PKA R subunit transgenic mice are clear instances. By intervening to block the translocation of freed catalytic PKA subunits to the nuclei of forebrain neurons, they intervened to block a key step in the gene expression and protein synthesis that produces L-LTP. The increased number of PKA R subunits available in the cytoplasms of these neurons enabled these regulatory units to quickly rebind catalytic PKA subunits freed by the upsurge in cAMP. Experimenters then tracked the negative behavioral effects of this intervention on standard tests of hippocampus-dependent long-term memory consolidation.

Principle 3: positive alteration

Intervening directly to increase activity of the hypothesized mechanisms must reliably increase the behaviors used as experimental measures of the cognitive phenomenon. Although positive alterations of learning and memory have been carried out successfully in insect studies for decades, successful cases in mammals are still few and far between. Romo's microstimulation work discussed above is a kind of positive alteration (at the cell-physiological level). By directly intervening into similarly-tuned cortical neurons to mimic action-potential frequencies typically generated by a specific kind of sensory stimulus, the experimenters were able to measure behavior (in the base-comparison stimuli judgment task) statistically identical to that generated by actual mechanical fingertip stimuli, in its complete absence. And although the Abel and Kandel study did not attempt to establish positive alteration, more recent work by Alcino Silva, Sheena Josselyn, and their collaborators (Han et al. 2007) have used viral vector gene targeting techniques to increase CREB functioning in lateral amygdala neurons to both rescue long-term fear conditioning in CREB knock-out mice and generate increased freezing in wild-type mice to conditioned tones paired with shocks that produce less than maximal conditioned responses.

Principle 4: integration

The hypothesis that the proposed mechanisms are key components of the causal nexus that produces the behaviors used as experimental measures of the cognitive phenomenon must be connected up with as much experimental data as is available about both the hypothesized mechanism and the cognitive phenomenon. Principle 4 is the most abstract of these jointly sufficient conditions on experimental evidence, and certainly the one requiring the most extensive explication. (See Silva and Bickle [2009] for a start.) Experimental results that meet it typically provide the empirical justifications for the specific negative and positive alteration experiments that investigators attempt, down to the particular gene expression and protein synthesis manipulated (including the particular molecular-biological techniques employed) and the behavioral measures used to track the effects of their manipulations. A lot of information is usually known about the cellular physiology or molecular biology and the behavioral measures that molecular and cellular cognitivists combine in their negative and positive alteration studies. This information goes far beyond the observational correlations that fall under principle 1. In the Romo study discussed above, for example, this integrative background included (but was not limited to) the microarchitectural details of the distribution of QA neurons in S_1, the effects of cortical microstimulation on neuronal action-potential frequencies, the capacities of rhesus monkeys to perform the stimuli comparison judgment task, and the use of that task as an effective measure of perceptual content. In the Abel and Kandel study, this integrative background included the role of PKA subunits in the mechanisms of L-LTP, the use of an αCaMKII promoter to limit expression of the transgene to forebrain regions, and the use of the different memory tasks as effective behavioral measures of hippocampus- and non-hippocampus-dependent memory consolidation. Components of a study's integrative background often come from prior experimental work; through this principle that work gets incorporated seamlessly into ongoing research. This incorporation is what philosophers and cognitive scientists typically refer to as "relating different levels of theory and explanation." Principle 4 thus reflects the way that new experiments often build on prior results – where the prior results themselves often meet at least some of the convergent four principles on their own.

Notice that meeting principles 1 and 4 requires "higher level" investigations. To establish the required observational correlations between hypothesized mechanisms and behaviors, and to integrate knowledge of molecules and behavior to establish the theoretical plausibility of the proposed mechanisms for the cognitive phenomenon in question, we need precise knowledge of what the system does under controlled experimental conditions. This means having both precise data about the system's behaviors and justifiable behavioral measures for the cognitive phenomenon being investigated. These are jobs for cognitive scientists and experimental psychologists, not electrophysiologists or molecular geneticists. We also need to know where to start inserting our cellular and molecular interventions. The "decomposition and localization" investigations of cognitive neuroscientists are crucial for this knowledge. We also need to know what types of neuronal activity to intervene into. Action-potential frequency? Action-potential dynamics? Field potentials? Something else entirely? The work of neurocomputational modelers and simulators is important here. Each of these neuronal activities has distinct molecular mechanisms, and so requires different molecular-biological intervention techniques. Molecular and cellular cognition needs a lot of higher level cognitive science and neuroscience to accomplish its potential reductions – and it now regularly draws upon such scientists to get these details right.

Molecular and cellular cognition clearly is a reductionistic field of current neuroscience. But that feature in no way precludes its use of higher level cognitive science and scientists.

Yet in the end, experiments that meet principles 2 and 3 cinch the empirical case for a proposed "mind-to-molecules link." These experiments certainly constitute the unique contributions of molecular and cellular cognition. The nature of real reductionism in genuinely reductionistic neuroscience therefore lies implicit in those two principles. Unlike classic intertheoretic reduction, experiments meeting those two principles neither require nor make use of explicit, complete sets of laws or explanatory generalizations that characterize the behaviors of reduced and reducing kinds in all contexts or circumstances. Real reduction is not a logical relationship between such laws or generalizations. Unlike functional reduction, real reductionism does not require the reduced concepts to be characterized exhaustively in terms of their causes and effects; nor are the nuances of its standard experimental practice of operationalizing cognitive concepts methodologically, in terms of behavioral measures and for the purposes of controlled experiments, even grossly characterized as "functionalizing" the concepts. (Freezing to the context 24 hours after having been shocked in it is not an *effect* of declarative memory consolidation; it is a measure of the occurrence of declarative memory consolidation, for the purpose of one particular experiment.) Instead of the logical derivation of theories, or the search for the actual mechanisms that approximate a functional analysis of a concept, real reductionism in genuinely reductionistic neuroscientific practice is a matter of

> *Intervening causally*, directly into processes at increasingly lower levels of biological organization (cellular, intra-cellular molecular, molecular genetic),

and then

> *Tracking* the effects of these interventions in living, behaving organisms, using a variety of measures widely accepted as indicative for the cognitive phenomenon being investigated.

(In Bickle [2006a], I offer an illustration of this new account of reductionism and contrast it with an illustration of the standard intertheoretic reduction account.)

When these interventions generate evidence for negative and positive alterations, against a background of evidence connecting the hypothesized cellular or molecular mechanism to the behaviors serving as measures for the cognitive phenomenon being investigated, a reduction is claimed as accomplished. The cognitive phenomenon reduces to the cellular or molecular mechanisms intervened into, within the anatomical circuits leading ultimately to the motor peripheries generating the measured behaviors. Molecular and cellular cognitivists then talk explicitly about having discovered "a molecular biology of cognition" (Bailey, Bartsch, and Kandel 1996: 13445), or of "providing an experimental framework for a molecular understanding" of a specific cognitive phenomenon (Abel et al. 1997: 623). From the perspective of molecular and cellular cognition, when all of the convergent four principles are met for some hypothesized mechanism and some methodologically operationalized cognitive phenomenon, higher level explanations of that phenomenon lose their status as causal-mechanistic – although such explanations still provide crucial empirical support for two of the four principles that our best causal-mechanistic explanation rests upon. This is the force of the direct "mind-to-molecules linkages" and their "relations to observable behavior" referred to in the passage from Kandel, Schwartz, and Jessell's (2001) textbook, with which this chapter began.

I close with a remark about the potential real reducibility of features of qualitative consciousness. The account of functional reduction is crucial to some of the strongest anti-reduction arguments about qualia. There are numerous thought experiments – about bats, zombies, color-deprived future neuroscientists, and more – designed to pump intuitions about unbridgeable differences between qualia and physical events. But additional premises are required to turn these pumped intuitions into *sound arguments* for the conclusion that qualia are not identical to brain states. Functional reduction serves this role. The pumped intuitions about qualia are interpreted to show that qualia can't be functionalized, and so the first stage of a (functional) reduction cannot be carried out. Qualia are thereby irreducible! But if we replace functional reduction with my scientifically plausible alternative, the intuitions about qualia pumped by the famous thought experiments lose their force. Real reductionism doesn't require functionalization of to-be-reduced concepts. Instead, it requires that these concepts be operationalized methodologically in terms of behavioral measures for the purposes of experimental investigation. Nothing revealed by the famous thought experiments rules out this requirement, and as a matter of fact there are now numerous measures being employed to investigate the molecular mechanisms of phenomenally rich features of conscious experience like awareness, arousal state, and anxiety levels. Investigations meeting the standard "intervene molecularly and track behaviorally" model of scientific reductionism have already borne fruit; agonistic activity at specific subunits of fast $GABA_A$ receptor proteins, a component of the most prominent inhibitory neurotransmitter system in the mammalian brain, are turning out to be crucial parts of the mechanisms of these "*P*-conscious" features. (See Bickle [2007] for some of these scientific details and an application of the account of reductionism sketched here.) If one argues that the famous qualia thought experiments show that any attempt to operationalize consciousness for the purposes of experimental test is doomed to fail, then this claim should be revealed for what it really amounts to: a blanket statement that a *science* of consciousness is ruled out from the start. There may be some in-your-face metaphysicians willing to swallow such an antiscientific claim; but I doubt that many readers of a companion to the philosophy of *psychology* will be so cavalier.

References

Abel, T., Nguyen, P., Barad, M., Deuel, T., Kandel, E. R., and Bourtchouladze, R. (1997) "Genetic Demonstration of a Role for PKA in the Late Phase of LTP and in Hippocampus-Based Long-Term Memory," *Cell* 88: 615–26.

Bailey, C. H., Bartsch, D., and Kandel, E. R. (1996) "Toward a Molecular Definition of Long-Term Memory Storage," *Proceedings of the National Academy of Sciences of the United States of America* 93: 13445–52.

Bickle, J. (1998) *Psychoneural Reduction: The New Wave*, Cambridge, MA: MIT Press.

—— (2003) *Philosophy and Neuroscience: A Ruthlessly Reductive Account*, Dordrecht: Kluwer.

—— (2006a) "Reducing Mind to Molecular Pathways: Explicating the Reductionism Implicit in Current Mainstream Neuroscience," *Synthese* 152: 411–34.

—— (2006b) "Ruthless Reductionism in Recent Neuroscience," *IEEE Transactions on Systems, Man, and Cybernetics* 36: 134–40.

—— (2007) "Who Says You Can't Do a Molecular Biology of Consciousness?" in M. Schouten and H. de Jong (eds), *Rethinking Reduction: Case Studies in the Philosophy of Mind and Brain*, London: Blackwell, pp. 175–97.

Kandel, E. R., Schwartz, J., and Jessell, T. (eds) (2001) *Principles of Neural Science*, New York: McGraw-Hill.

Kim, J. (2005) *Physicalism, or Something near Enough*, Princeton, NJ: Princeton University Press.

Han, J.-H., Kushner, S. A., Yiu, A. P., Cole, C. J., Matynia, A., Brown, R. A., Neve, R. L., Guzowski, J. F., Silva, A. J., and Josselyn, S. A. (2007) "Neuronal Competition and Selection During Memory Formation." *Science* 316: 457–460.

Levine, J. (1993) "On Leaving Out What It's Like," in M. Davies and G. Humphreys (eds), *Consciousness*, London: Blackwell, 121–36.

Nagel, E. (1961) *The Structure of Science*, New York: Harcourt, Brace, & World.

Penfield, W., and Perot, P. (1963) "The Brain's Record of Auditory and Visual Experience: A Final Summary and Discussion," *Brain* 83: 595–6.

Romo, R., Hernández, A., Zainos, A., and Salinas, E. (1998) "Somatosensory Discrimination Based on Microstimulation," *Nature* 392: 387–90.

Romo, R., Hernández, A., Zainos, A., Brody, C., and Lemus, L. (2000) "Sensing without Touching: Psychophysical Performance Based on Cortical Microstimulation," *Neuron* 26: 273–8.

Silva, A. J., and Bickle, J. (2009) "The science of research and the Search for Molecular Mechanisms of Cognitive Functions," in J. Bickle (ed.), *Oxford Handbook of Philosophy and Neuroscience*, Oxford: Oxford University Press (pp. 91–126).

Silva, A. J., Elgersma, Y., and Costa, R. M. (2000) "Molecular and Cellular Mechanisms of Cognitive Function: Implications for Psychiatric Disorders," *Biological Psychiatry* 47: 200–9.

Silva, A. J., Paylor, R., Wehmer, J. M., and Tonegawa, S. (1992) "Impaired Spatial Learning in α-Calcium-Calmodulin Kinase II Mutant Mice," *Science* 257: 206–11.

28
NETWORKS AND DYNAMICS: TWENTY-FIRST-CENTURY NEUROSCIENCE

William Bechtel

1 Introduction

Since the nineteenth century, brain research has focused on explaining the activities of the brain in terms of localized neuro-mechanisms. The quest for mechanistic explanations continues apace in the twenty-first century, but the range of explanatory tools neuroscientists invoke has expanded. I focus on two of these additional tools, network analysis and dynamical analysis. Mechanistic investigations adopt a reductionistic perspective, focusing on the contributions of component parts to the resulting phenomena. This reductionistic perspective has often attracted criticism from those who have insisted on the importance of understanding the whole integrated system within cells or organisms, but these holists have historically not offered a competing research program. Network and dynamical analyses provide strategies for characterizing and explaining behavior of whole systems. My aim is to show how these alternatives to traditional mechanistic approaches are being invoked in the neurosciences. For most researchers, these alternatives are intended not to supplant mechanistic approaches but to provide complementary perspectives that when combined with mechanistic approaches can result in an integrated reductionistic and holist understanding of the brain. After illustrating the mechanistic strategy in section 2, I will, in the following two sections, illustrate the strategies of network analysis and dynamic analysis. I will then conclude by briefly commenting on how these new approaches can figure in articulating a different view of the brain, one in which the brain is not, as has often been assumed, a reactive system, but an endogenously active system that initiates action on its own. Rather than activity beginning with a stimulus, stimuli serve to alter ongoing, endogenously generated, activity.

2 Twentieth-century neuroscience: identifying brain parts and localizing cognitive operations in them

Although the strategy of developing accounts of mechanisms to explain phenomena was widespread in biology, including in neuroscience,[1] since the seventeenth century, it was only at the end of the twentieth century that philosophers began to characterize mechanistic explanations (Bechtel & Richardson, 1993/2010; Glennan, 1996, 2002; Machamer, Darden, & Craver, 2000; Bechtel & Abrahamsen, 2005). While there are differences between these accounts, the key elements are shared: a mechanistic explanation links a phenomenon to be explained to a responsible mechanism; decomposes that mechanism into its parts and operations; and recomposes it to show how, when the parts are organized appropriately and the operations are orchestrated, the mechanism is able to generate the phenomenon. The application of this approach to the brain was rooted in the recognition that there are different types of mental activities (e.g. perceiving, inferring, remembering, deciding) and the determination that parts of the brain can be differentiated from one another. Gall's phrenological project provided an early, albeit contentious, exemplar of localizing different mental activities in different regions of the neo-cortex (Zawidzki & Bechtel, 2004). Beginning with the work of Broca (1861), researchers began to use tools such as deficit studies to characterize brain functions and link them to damaged areas of the brain. Through the nineteenth century, however, brain regions were generally differentiated in terms of the sulci and gyri resulting from the folding of the cortex, but these have turned out not to correspond in a productive way with psychological operations. Brodmann (1909/1994) was a pioneer in invoking cytoarchitectural criteria – the types of neurons, the distribution of neurons between cortical layers, etc. – to differentiate areas in neo-cortex. Although Brodmann anticipated that the areas he differentiated could be linked to psychological operations, actually doing so required techniques that he did not possess. In the twentieth century, however, a host of researchers further developed Broca's approach of analyzing the deficits resulting from lesions and deployed other methodologies, such as identifying the activities elicited by cortical stimulation and recording neural activity elicited by different stimuli. Although these approaches have been applied to the study of different mental activities, I will focus on the one that has yielded the greatest success, visual perception (for a more detailed analysis of research on visual processing and other mental mechanisms, see Bechtel, 2008).

Analyses of deficits in both human patients with brain damage and animals in which lesions were generated surgically, had, by the end of the nineteenth century, implicated the area at the rear of the cortex, which Brodmann would label Area 17, as the locus, or at least an important part of, the mechanism of visual perception. This localization was supported by the ability to map the inability of patients from the

Russo-Japanese War and World War I to see in particular parts of the visual field to damage in specific regions of Area 17 (Holmes, 1919). With the development of single-cell recording techniques, Hubel and Wiesel (1962, 1968) identified stimuli such as edges that elicited increased neural responses from cells in this region. But Hubel and Wiesel's research also made it clear that this area performed only an early stage in processing visual inputs. Researchers came to identify this region as visual area I (V1) and began the quest to identify other parts of the visual processing mechanism. Specifically, researchers moved forward in the brain, recording from other Brodmann areas and seeking stimuli that would elicit the most activity in these regions. For example, Zeki and his collaborators identified a region, V4, that registered color constancy (responded in the same manner to colors that appeared to perceivers as the same) and another, V5 or MT, that responded to motion. In the case of MT, single-cell recording studies were complemented by lesion studies on a patient who, as a result of damage to MT, could not perceive objects as moving, and stimulation studies in monkeys that showed that mild stimulation of MT that biased the response of these neurons could alter the animal's perception of motion (as registered in a behavior response) (Britten, Shadlen, Newsome, & Movshon, 1992).

By the 1980s the combined use of lesion, stimulation, and recording studies had identified more brain regions, including regions in the inferior temporal lobe (where Gross has found cells responsive to objects) and the parietal lobe (where regions involved in transformations between perceptually-based coordinates and motor-based coordinates were identified). Drawing upon the underlying neuroanatomy, including the projection patterns between neurons in different regions, Ungerleider and Mishkin (1982) advanced the proposal that there are two distinct processing pathways, both originating in V1 but in different populations of cells,[2] and that these processed different types of visual information. They proposed that the pathway leading to inferior temporal cortex serves to identify what object an organism is seeing while the one leading up to parietal cortex represents where the stimulus is located. Although questioning the strict division of pathways and characterizing these brain regions as constituting streams that sometimes intermingled, van Essen and Gallant (1994) advanced a detailed, integrated, account of processing starting in the retina and LGN. In their paper, they used icons to indicate the stimulus features to which cells in the different brain regions are responsive and lines of varying thickness to indicate the strengths of the connections between these regions.[3]

Van Essen and Gallant's account constitutes a macro-scale mechanistic analysis of visual perception, in which the parts are brain regions with distinctive neuroanatomy, the operations are the transformations of signals that are required to detect various features of stimuli, and the organization is provided by the connections between brain regions. The mechanistic strategy can be applied iteratively, treating the activity performed by a part as a phenomenon to be explained by the operations of the parts within it, and neuroscientists have pursued further mechanistic analyses at these lower levels. For neuroscientists interested in explaining cognitive activities, such analysis will typically bottom out at the level of cortical columns or individual neurons, although in some instances it might continue to an account in terms of the molecules within different parts of a neuron and the operations they perform. But even without engaging in further decomposition, van Essen and Gallant's account provides an exemplar of a mechanistic explanation that attempts to account for visual processing in terms of the parts and operations of a mechanism.

3 Twenty-first century neuroscience: from sequential components to networks

Mechanistic explanations have traditionally appealed to a relatively small number of parts organized in a sequential manner, with the result that researchers could mentally simulate the parts performing their operations to generate the phenomenon of interest. Constructing a diagram representing the parts and the operations they perform on each other often facilitates such mental simulation. A long as the operations are largely feedforward, as they are in van Essen and Gallant (1994), researchers can envision each operation as taking the product of the previous one and generating a further product. However, increasingly the idea of sequential operation is being recognized as a misleading idealization. Parts are connected to other parts in a wide variety of ways, and very often components thought to occur later have effects on those assumed to be earlier in a pathway. As a result, in many domains of biology, researchers are representing the systems they are investigating as networks of interacting components and attempting to understand their operation.

In fact, the visual processing areas included in van Essen and Gallant's processing diagram were already known by the investigators to involve both feedforward and recurrent connections. In a slightly earlier paper to the one previously discussed, Felleman and van Essen (1991) reported on the pattern of neural projections between visual processing areas in the macaque. One way they presented their findings was in a matrix.[4] In this matrix, the column on the left shows regions from which projections originate, and the row at the top shows those on which they terminate. A + in a box indicates that a projection from the specified source to the specified target had been identified in previous research (a large + indicates it was identified in a full research paper, a small + that it was reported in an abstract).[5] In the upper left corner of this matrix, +'s indicate a projection from V1 to V2 and from V2 to V1. As Felleman and van Essen discuss, the directionality of projections can be ascertained from the layers of cortex from which projections originate or which they target. In fact, most of the known projections from one area to another are complemented by projections in the opposite direction.

The matrix makes it clear that the system is a highly interactive one that cannot easily be understood by mentally simulating the operation of one brain region followed by that of the next. But there is also structure in the matrix – there are groups or clusters of regions that have a high number of connections running between them. These clusters somewhat correspond to the occipital, parietal, and temporal lobes. But note that parietal region PST receives and sends projections to many occipital regions. This is also true of temporal lobe regions MSTd, MSTl, PO, and PIP, although the location of these regions in the matrix makes it less obvious that they are part of a common cluster.

While a matrix provides one way to visualize the patterns of connectivity in a system, researchers often prefer network representations. A network representation employs nodes (often rectangles or ovals) for entities and edges (lines [or arrows if the researcher wants to show the directionality]) for relations. Felleman and van Essen also show the pattern of connectivity they identified in visual processing areas in a network representation, which leaves out some information.[6] In particular, since edges are shown as lines, not arrows, the network doesn't show the direction of projection (the authors simply note that most edges are bidirectional). Their network representation, however, also brings out a feature not captured in the matrix – the hierarchical nature of the whole network in which processing proceeds from the sensory periphery shown at the bottom (including parts of the retina and the lateral geniculate nucleus that are not included in the matrix) to the higher visual areas in temporal and parietal cortex shown at the top. Identifying a hierarchy was facilitated by the fact that forward, recurrent, and collateral projections differ in the cortical layers from which they originate and to which they project. Although from the perspective of how the brain arrives at identifications of, for example, objects, this is informative, from another perspective it is quite misleading as it suggests that the forward projections are more important in processing than the recurrent and collateral projections. Recurrent projections are often very important in determining how a given brain region will respond to a stimulus. Recognition of the prevalence of recurrent projections was a significant motivation for the development of the view that brains are largely engaged in prediction, with sensory input serving only as a corrective in cases of incorrect predictions (Clark, 2013).

Young (1993) extended the type of analysis offered by van Essen and Felleman to the whole macaque brain. Young also presented his results in a network diagram, in which the nodes for regions are positioned so as to best exhibit the pattern of connectivity in two dimensions.[7] Sporns and Zwi (2004) generated a matrix representation of Young's (1993) data.[8] In Felleman and van Essen's (1991) and Young's (1993) network representations, nodes are positioned either to exhibit a hierarchy or to maximally illustrate the pattern of connectivity. Another strategy is to position nodes in a fashion corresponding to the locations of the brain regions they represent. This approach is illustrated by Hagmann and colleagues (2008), whose network representation shows regions of the human brain laid out according to their location in either the left or right hemisphere or in a slice through the brain and the connections between them.[9] Sporns, Tononi, and Kötter (2005) introduced the term *connectome* for network representations of the human brain and initiated a research program intended to characterize the connectome in detail. (As the term connectome has been extended to other species, such as *Drosophila*, one should properly refer to the *human connectome*.) Hagmann and colleagues' (2008) network thus provides a representation of the human connectome.

Network diagrams provide a powerful visual representation of patterns of connections, but understanding the significance of what is presented in such diagrams requires analytic tools. The field of graph theory has provided a number of measures that characterize different types of networks. These serve not only to classify networks but also to offer understanding of how the physical systems that implement them will behave. Two of the most useful measures are the characteristic path length and the clustering coefficient. The characteristic path length is the number of edges that, on average, must be traversed to get from any node to a specific other node. Graph theorists in the twentieth century focused on network structures that featured either high clustering at the expense of having a long characteristic path length (randomly connected networks) or short characteristic path length with significant clustering (lattices or near-neighbor connected networks). Watts and Strogratz (1998) showed that by starting with a network with only near-neighbor connections (hence, exhibiting high clustering but long characteristic path length) and replacing a few near-neighbor connections with long distance connections, they greatly shortened the characteristic path length without significantly reducing the clustering coefficient. Watts and Strogatz termed such networks *small-world networks* and argued that they would be ideal candidates for processing information, presumably because the near-neighbor connections would allow connected units to work together in the achievement of tasks, while the long-range connections would allow for coordinated activity across the whole network.

In their paper, Watts and Strogatz argued that many real-world networks met the conditions of small-world networks. Their one neural example involved the neural network of the nematode, *Caenorhabditis elegans*, which had been mapped out by White, Southgate, Thomson, and Brenner (1986). Such an analysis of individual neurons was possible in C. *elegans* since it has only 302 neurons and somewhat more than 7,000 connections. This is not practical in the whole human brain with approximately 10^{11} neurons and 10^{15} connections. Instead, as van Essen did, researchers focus on brain areas. Sporns and Zwi (2004) analyzed the Felleman and van Essen data on the macaque visual system and Young's data on the whole macaque cortex as well as subsequent data collected by Young on the cat cortex (Scannell, Burns, Hilgetag, O'Neil, & Young, 1999). They compared the data with reference networks they generated assuming either random or nearest-neighbor connectivity, which provided benchmarks for characteristic path length and the clustering coefficient. Sporns and Zwi established that the networks of brain areas all had characteristic path lengths close to those for random networks and clustering coefficients close to those for near-neighbor networks, indicating the presence of small-world organization in each network.

The clustered units in a small-world network are frequently termed *modules*, but high-clustering alone reveals little about their organization. Shortly after Watts and Strogatz introduced small-world networks, Barabási and Bonabeau (2003) focused on a different measure of network organization, the distribution of node degree. The degree of a node is the number of edges linking it to others. Most previous analyses had assumed that node degree would be distributed in a Gaussian manner, but Barabási showed that in many real-world networks, degree is distributed according to a power law. In a power-law distribution most nodes have few connections to other nodes, but a few participate in a very large number of connections. Nodes within networks with especially high degree are characterized as *hubs*. Hub nodes are typically highly important for the functioning of the whole network since, if they are damaged, transmission through the network is substantially impaired. When hubs connect mostly to other nodes within a module, they constitute provincial hubs – when they are impaired, the ability of the module to function as a cohesive unit is jeopardized. When they are connected mostly to nodes in different modules, they are connector hubs (sometimes additional measures are invoked in identifying connector hubs such as short path length and high centrality). These serve as the primary integrators of activity through the whole system and when they are damaged, the overall functioning of the network is diminished.

Examining hubs provides a potent way of determining how activity will unfold in a network. An example of how this has proven useful in neuroscience is in the research on what is called the *rich-club* organization, in which brain regions that count as connector hubs are themselves highly interconnected with one another. Van den Heuvel and Sporns (2011) reconstructed whole-brain networks of 21 participants based on diffusion tensor imaging data and developed measures to identify regions in their brains that belonged to a rich-club structure. They identified 12 regions, each serving as a connector hub, that are highly connected: superior parietal area, precuneus, superior frontal cortex, putamen, hippocampus, and thalamus in both hemispheres.[10] These regions are even more interconnected than would be expected given their degree, suggesting that rich-club structure has additional significance for brain function than that bestowed by high-degree alone. Van den Heuvel and Sporns examined the effects of damage to the nodes of the rich-club network in computational simulations and showed that such damage is more likely to impair global communication in the brain than randomly distributed damage. They proposed that the generalized effects on cognition of diseases such as Alzheimer's and schizophrenia might stem from damage to nodes in the rich-club.

4 Twenty-first-century neuroscience: from feedforward processing to endogenous dynamics

The research on neural mechanisms discussed in section 2 assumed a feedforward conception of the mechanism, in accord with Machamer, Darden, and Craver's (2000) characterization of mechanisms as operating "from start or set-up to finish or termination conditions." In feedforward systems no complex dynamics occurs – the system simply generates a response. Assuming visual processing was primarily feedforward, the researchers discussed in part 2 typically presented a visual stimulus and recorded the response in the selected brain area. However, since the neuroanatomical investigations of Lorente de Nó (1938) and others, it has been known that recurrent projections outnumber forward projections. These recurrent connections figured prominently in the connection matrices described in the previous section. In their paper identifying small-world organization in cat and macaque brains, Sporns and Zwi (2004) included an analysis of cycles – feedback loops from one area to another viewed as earlier in the processing hierarchy. They found a much higher frequency of relatively short cycles in these actual networks than in corresponding random networks, suggesting that they are a distinctive feature of mammalian cortices.

The challenge has been to interpret the function of these recurrent and feedback connections since one cannot identify their operations by manipulating sensory inputs and recording the resulting activity. Even if one cannot readily identify the information flow through the network, however, one can consider the dynamics generated by feedback loops. One widely recognized role for feedback loops is to provide a mechanism for regulating an activity; for investigators such as Cannon (1929) this provided a model for how the autonomic nervous system regulated such physiological variables as body temperature. An ordinary thermostat provides an easily understood analogy. But a thermostat also points to another consequence of feedback loops – the generation of oscillations. With thermostats, temperature oscillates as first the heat source is activated and then it is shut off. The goal, for heating engineers, is to minimize the oscillations so as to maintain as close to a steady temperature as possible. But in many cases, oscillations can be put to productive use to do things such as orchestrate operations. In this section I will describe the recent discovery of very low-frequency oscillations (< 0.1 Hz) in the brain and research suggesting the sort of functionality it has.

Berger (1929) first identified oscillations of electrical activity when he developed the technique of *electroencephagraphy* (EEG), which involves recording from electrodes placed on the scalp. He detected low frequency (8–12 Hz), high amplitude oscillations, which he called *alpha waves*, when subjects were awake and quiet. He observed that these were replaced by higher-frequency (12–30 Hz), lower-amplitude oscillations, which he called *beta waves*, when subjects responded to a stimulus. Since they arise in the absence of activity, alpha waves reflect ongoing endogenous activity in the brain, a point to which I return later. Subsequently, oscillations at yet higher frequencies (gamma oscillations) and lower frequencies (delta and theta rhythms) have been detected with EEG. While sleep research drew directly on EEG results, EEG became a tool for cognitive research only when it was adapted to yield evoked response potentials (ERPs) that tied EEG activity to particular stimulus conditions, such as the mismatch between an expected and an actual stimulus (Kutas & Hillyard, 1980).

Beginning in the 1980s, researchers developed a different approach to measuring brain activity noninvasively, one with greater spatial but lesser temporal resolution. Instead of electrical potentials they measured blood flow, either through a radioactive tracer (positron emission tomography or PET) or through magnetic deflection (functional magnetic resonance images or fMRI). Blood flow is used as a proxy for neural activity (under the assumption that neural activity requires energy that is carried by the blood), and initially both PET and fMRI were used in studies designed to reveal changes in blood flow in response to stimuli. A standard approach involved subtracting the activity in a brain region during what was viewed as a baseline task from the activity detected during a task condition (Posner & Raichle, 1994). Regions that were more active when the individual was performing the task were inferred to play a central role in that task.

A different approach to analyzing fMRI data was developed in the mid-1990s after Raichle and his colleagues identified a number of brain regions that were *less* active in task conditions than during a condition in which no task was presented (a condition referred to as the *resting state*). In the resting state individuals lie in the scanner without being assigned any particular task. The idea is not that the brain is inactive during the resting state; rather, it is viewed as engaged in *mindwandering* – cognitive activity initiated endogenously by the subject. Raichle identified regions that are more active in the resting state and characterized them as constituting the *default mode network* (Raichle, MacLeod, Snyder, Powers, Gusnard, & Shulman, 2001). Subsequently, Raichle and other investigators applied to the analysis of the default mode network a technique for procuring time-series data from fMRI pioneered by Biswal, Yetkin, Haughton, and Hyde (1995). These researchers had identified low-frequency oscillations (< 0.1 Hz) that were synchronized across motor areas bilaterally. Greicius, Krasnow, Reiss, and Menon (2003) determined that regions in the default mode network oscillate in synchrony during the resting state. Synchronized activity across the default mode network indicates that the components of the network are functioning together in a coherent fashion. Mantini, Perrucci, Del Gratta, Romani, and Corbetta (2007) employed the same technique to reveal synchronized oscillations in the resting state between sets of brain areas that had been associated with specific types of tasks. Since the recordings were made in the resting state, the subject was not performing the tasks these brain regions were thought to subserve. Thus, what the results reveal is that not just the default mode network but other brain networks are active and synchronizing their activities when people are not explicitly asked to perform tasks.

One important consequence of synchronization of activity in brain areas is that neurons in an area are more likely to respond to stimuli from regions with which they are synchronized. This is because they do not remain at what is referred to as their resting potential but rather oscillate around it. These oscillations are in fact what is detected with EEG. When the electrical potential is less negative, it takes less input to drive the potential above the threshold so as to generate a spike than when it is more negative. Thus, when two neurons are synchronized, an action potential generated in one is more likely to generate an action potential in the neuron to which it projects.

The role synchronization can play in facilitating communication between brain regions is illustrated by Hasselmo, Bodelón, and Wyble's (2002) proposal for how information flow is regulated in the hippocampus. The role of the hippocampus in representing an animal's location in space has been extensively investigated since the pioneering research of O'Keefe (1976) revealed the presence of cells that generate spike trains when an animal is at a particular location in its enclosure. Within the hippocampus researchers have identified an ongoing theta rhythm and at least two different gamma oscillations. The interaction of these rhythms is proposed to regulate which of two pathways controls activity in the CA1 region of the hippocampus. The CA1 region receives input from both the CA3 region and the medial entorhinal cortex. The CA3 region receives its inputs from the medial entorhinal cortex via the dentate gyrus. Region CA3, which has a large number of recurrent connections, is thought to perform pattern completion on the sparse input signal it receives from the dentate gyrus – when the sensory input corresponds to information about a previous encoded location, a subpopulation of CA3 cells becomes highly active and activates the appropriate cells in CA1, thereby specifying the animal's location. This is facilitated by synchronizing CA1 cells to the slow gamma oscillations exhibited in CA3. When pattern completion fails, that indicates the animal is in a new location and needs to construct a new representation. It now synchronizes directly with the faster gamma oscillations of the medial entorhinal cortex and employs the learning process known as long-term potentiation to alter both CA3 and CA1 so that on subsequent occasions it reactivates this new response. It thus lays down a new spatial representation for that location.

The oscillations detected in the resting state are endogenously generated. But one might question whether they play a significant role in determining behavior. Fox, Snyder, Zacks, and Raichle (2006) provided evidence that they do. They took advantage of the fact that activity in the left and right somatosensory cortexes is synchronized. While scanning them, the researchers instructed participants to press a button with their right hand. This elicited additional activity in the left somatosensory cortex. The resulting activity in the left somatosensory cortex is quite variable, but the researchers showed that the endogenous oscillations recorded in the right somatosensory cortex (not involved in the task) accounted for much of this variability. In a further study, Fox, Snyder, Vincent, and Raichle (2007) determined that this variability also accounts for the variation in the force with which participants pressed the button.

So far I have focused on research that identifies endogenous activity in neural systems and showed how it appears to be synchronized across brain regions and to affect behavior. A further challenge is to explain how such endogenous activity arises in neural systems. This requires a significant extension of the strategies that figure in the research described in section 2, which advanced what I have called elsewhere *basic* mechanistic explanations (Bechtel, 2011). These proceed from start to termination conditions as characterized by Machamer, Darden, and Craver (2000). Although Machamer *et al.* allow for feedback within mechanisms, they do not consider such connections to raise any serious problems. Indeed, if the mechanism one envisioned had a single feedback loop, as in Figure 28.1, people can mentally rehearse its activity. Assume that the arrow indicates that X causes an increase in the concentration of Y; that the end-edged line indicates that, depending on its concentration Y inhibits the activity X; and the jagged arrow away from Y indicates that its concentration is gradually reduced. One can mentally rehearse the activity in such a system. If the concentration of Y is initially low, X causes it to increase. As the concentration of Y increases, it causes the action of X to decrease, stopping or reducing the increase in Y. But since the concentration of Y is being reduced, there is less of it to inhibit X, and X again causes the concentration of Y to increase. This provides an intuitive account of how negative feedback can generate oscillations. But the power of mental simulation soon reaches its limits. It cannot distinguish whether oscillation will continue indefinitely or reach a stable equilibrium at which the activity of X on Y is exactly balanced by the inhibition from Y, given the rate of decrease in Y's concentration.

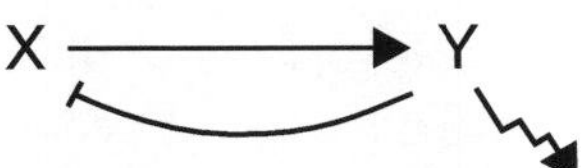

Figure 28.1 A simple feedback loop. See text for details.

To ascertain how a mechanism organized as that shown in Figure 28.1 will behave, researchers need to employ a different research strategy. They must represent the operations mathematically and either prove analytically what will happen or construct a computational simulation to exhibit the behavior. The need for such mathematical analysis becomes even more acute when the relations are such that they require nonlinear equations. It turns out, for example, that with purely linear relations negative feedback will reach equilibrium but that with appropriate nonlinear relations it can produce sustained oscillations.

A noteworthy feature of Figure 28.1 and of the mathematical representation developed from it is that they abstract from the details about the nature of the components and the specific nature of the relations between them. In the equations, the components are represented as variables and the relations characterized in terms of parameters on the mathematical operations relating the variables. This represents a significant departure from the approach of mechanistic explanation that focuses on the particular parts and operations into which a specific mechanism is decomposed. Emphasizing this difference, Craver (2007) has presented mathematical models as *how-possibly* models. He further maintains that in themselves the mathematical models do not explain. Only the detailed mechanism explains how the phenomenon is *actually* produced. However, the details of the mechanism themselves also fail to show how the phenomenon is brought about. Only when supplemented with a mental or computation simulation can one show that the mechanism is able to produce the phenomenon.

The strategies of decomposing a mechanism and modeling a mechanism are fundamentally different in many respects. Mathematical models share important similarities with deductive-nomological explanations, such as deriving phenomenon form laws or mathematical relations. Moreover, the people developing mathematical models are often distinct from those doing the mechanistic research, reflecting the difference in required skills (experimental manipulation versus mathematical analysis). Yet, the approaches can be integrated by relating the mathematical relations to the empirically established parts and operations. Abrahamsen and I refer to explanations that integrate information about parts and operations with computational models as *dynamic mechanistic explanations* (Bechtel & Abrahamsen, 2010) and have argued that they are needed to explain the endogenous dynamics exhibited by the brain (Abrahamsen & Bechtel, 2011).

5 Conclusion: from a reactive to an endogenously active conception of brains

The twentieth-century research on the brain mechanisms that figure in visual processing described in section 2 treated the brain as a reactive system. Stimuli were presented to the eyes and researchers traced the responses of different brain regions to determine what information they extracted. This research generated valuable knowledge about parts of the nervous system and some of the contributions they make to cognitive activities. Even this research could only identify how neurons in brain areas respond to stimuli on which they have been tested. Moreover, by not experimentally investigating other inputs, such as collateral and recurrent inputs, it at best provides a partial view of what operations a brain area performs. As Burnston (2016a, 2016b) has shown, as researchers become more creative in their experimental manipulations, they are coming not only to revise their initial assessment of what contributions a brain region makes but also to view its contributions as context sensitive.

Recognizing that the brain is an interactive network that exhibits endogenous activity requires not just a revision in some empirical results but a shift in perspective. This shift was already articulated by Thomas Graham Brown (1914) while working in the laboratory of Sherrington (1923), one of the early and forceful proponents of the reactive perspective. Based on his discovery that spinal cords isolated from cats continued to generate patterns of activity comparable to those produced in intact cats when executing motor, Brown argued for thinking of the brain as endogenously active. Rather than serving to initiate activity, on his view, stimuli perturbed ongoing activity. Except for research on central pattern generators, to which Brown's research was a predecessor, his perspective on the brain as endogenously active was largely neglected through the twentieth century (Llinás, 2001; Abrahamsen & Bechtel, 2011).

If the brain is endogenously active, and that activity affects how the brain responds to stimuli, an extremely important task is to characterize and explain the endogenous activity itself. The two tools I have discussed in sections 3 and 4, network analysis and dynamical analysis, provide avenues for doing so. Endogenous activity arises within systems of interconnected components – networks. Identifying and characterizing these networks mathematically is an important step to understanding how endogenous activity arises. Discovering and characterizing dynamical activity in these networks, such as ongoing oscillations and their synchronization, and then modeling them provides new ways to understand how brain mechanisms generate cognitive phenomena. The development and application of these tools is still in its infancy. Small worlds, for example, are broadly characterized as networks with short characteristic path lengths and high clustering. But presumably there are multiple types of small worlds that exhibit different behavior. Likewise, detecting neural oscillations and recognizing that they figure in coordinating brain activity between modules invites more detailed analyses of neural dynamics and the different roles they play in configuring the brain and affecting its responses to stimuli. Just recognizing endogenous activity is a start, but characterizing it more finely and showing how it is generated from an underlying mechanism is a task for the future.

Accomplishing these ends will likely require further development of network analyses and dynamical analyses. Neuroscience is rapidly moving beyond exclusive reliance on mechanistic approaches that emphasize decomposition of systems into their parts and operations. Mechanistic analysis of brains has yielded and continues to yield important knowledge about these parts and operations. But too often those pursuing mechanistic approaches have fallen short in the complementary activity of recomposing mechanisms. One reason for this is the tendency to think about mechanisms sequentially. Accordingly, mechanistic approaches need to be and are being supplemented with other approaches better suited to recognize the multiplicity of interactions and the complex dynamics that can arise in such mechanisms.

Notes

1. Applying the term *neuroscience* to brain research prior to the 1960s is anachronistic as the term was only invented to characterize the more integrated attempts to understand brain function that arose in that era, but no harm is done in applying it to the research on brain structure and function in earlier periods.
2. Other researchers traced the inputs to the different populations of V1 cells back to separate parts of the lateral geniculate nucleus of the thalamus and ultimately to different neurons in the retina.
3. The use of icons to represent types of processing performed by different brain regions and their organization into processing streams can be seen in Figure 2 of van Essen and Gallant (1994): https://doi.org/10.1016/0896-6273(94)90455-3.
4. The matrix being discussed is Table 3 in Felleman and van Essen (1991), which can be viewed here: https://doi.org/10.1093/cercor/1.1.1-a.
5. A dot indicates that researchers had looked for and failed to find a project. A blank box indicates the lack of any reports on the possible projection, and a question mark indicates a conflict between reports.
6. Felleman and van Essen's (1991) network representation is Figure 4 in their article, which can be viewed here: https://doi.org/10.1093/cercor/1.1.1-a.
7. This network diagram is Figure 3 in Young (1993), which can be viewed here: https://doi.org/10.1098/rspb.1993.0040.
8. Sporns and Zwi's (2004) matrix is Figure 1b. The paper can be viewed here: https://doi-org.www2.lib.ku.edu/10.1385/NI:2:2:145.
9. The network representation being discussed is Figure 3C in Hagmann et al. (2008), which can be viewed here: https://doi.org/10.1371/journal.pbio.0060159.
10. This rich-club network is shown as Figure 4D in van den Heuvel and Sporns (2011), which can be viewed here: https://doi.org/10.1523/JNEUROSCI.3539-11.2011.

References

Abrahamsen, A., & Bechtel, W. (2011). From reactive to endogenously active dynamical conceptions of the brain. In K. Plaisance & T. Reydon (Eds.), *Philosophy of behavioral biology* (pp. 329–66). New York: Springer.

Barabási, A.-L., & Bonabeau, E. (2003). Scale-free networks. *Scientific American*, 50–59.

Bechtel, W. (2008). *Mental mechanisms: Philosophical perspectives on cognitive neuroscience*. London: Routledge.

Bechtel, W. (2011). Mechanism and biological explanation. *Philosophy of Science*, *78*, 533–57.

Bechtel, W., & Abrahamsen, A. (2005). Explanation: A mechanist alternative. *Studies in History and Philosophy of Biological and Biomedical Sciences*, 36, 421–41.

Bechtel, W., & Abrahamsen, A. (2010). Dynamic mechanistic explanation: Computational modeling of circadian rhythms as an exemplar for cognitive science. *Studies in History and Philosophy of Science Part A*, *41*, 321–33.

Bechtel, W., & Richardson, R. C. (1993/2010). *Discovering complexity: Decomposition and localization as strategies in scientific research*. Cambridge, MA: MIT Press. 1993 edition published by Princeton University Press.

Berger, H. (1929). Über daas Elektrenkephalogramm des Menschen. *Archiv für Psychiatrie und Nervenkrankheiten*, *87*.

Biswal, B., Yetkin, F. Z., Haughton, V. M., & Hyde, J. S. (1995). Functional connectivity in the motor cortex of resting human brain using echo-planar MRI. *Magnetic Resonance in Medicine*, *34*, 537–41.

Britten, K. H., Shadlen, M. N., Newsome, W. T., & Movshon, J. A. (1992). The analysis of visual motion: A comparison of neuronal and psychophysical performance. *The Journal of Neuroscience*, *12*, 4745–65.

Broca, P. (1861). Remarques sur le siége de la faculté du langage articulé, suivies d'une observation d'aphemie (perte de la parole). *Bulletin de la Société Anatomique*, 6, 343–57.

Brodmann, K. (1909/1994). *Vergleichende Lokalisationslehre der Grosshirnrinde* (L. J. Garvey, Trans.). Leipzig: J. A. Barth.

Brown, T. G. (1914). On the nature of the fundamental activity of the nervous centres; together with an analysis of the conditioning of rhythmic activity in progression, and a theory of the evolution of function in the nervous system. *The Journal of Physiology*, *48*, 18–46.

Burnston, D. C. (2016a). A contextualist approach to functional localization in the brain. *Biology & Philosophy*, *31*(4), 527–50.

Burnston, D. C. (2016b). Computational neuroscience and localized neural function. *Synthese*, *193*(12), 3741–62.

Cannon, W. B. (1929). Organization of physiological homeostasis. *Physiological Reviews*, 9, 399–431.

Clark, A. (2013). Whatever next? Predictive brains, situated agents, and the future of cognitive science. *The Behavioral and Brain Sciences*, *36*, 181–204.

Craver, C. F. (2007). *Explaining the brain: Mechanisms and the mosaic unity of neuroscience*. New York: Oxford University Press.

Felleman, D. J., & van Essen, D. C. (1991). Distributed hierarchical processing in the primate cerebral cortex. *Cerebral Cortex*, *1*, 1–47.

Fox, M. D., Snyder, A. Z., Vincent, J. L., & Raichle, M. E. (2007). Intrinsic fluctuations within cortical systems account for intertrial variability in human behavior. *Neuron*, *56*, 171–84.

Fox, M. D., Snyder, A. Z., Zacks, J. M., & Raichle, M. E. (2006). Coherent spontaneous activity accounts for trial-to-trial variability in human evoked brain responses. *Nature Neuroscience*, 9, 23–25.

Glennan, S. (1996). Mechanisms and the nature of causation. *Erkenntnis*, *44*, 50–71.

Glennan, S. (2002). Rethinking mechanistic explanation. *Philosophy of Science*, *69*, S342–S353.

Greicius, M. D., Krasnow, B., Reiss, A. L., & Menon, V. (2003). Functional connectivity in the resting brain: A network analysis of the default mode hypothesis. *Proceedings of the National Academy of Sciences of the United States of America*, *100*, 253–58.

Hagmann, P., Cammoun, L., Gigandet, X., Meuli, R., Honey, C. J., Wedeen, V. J., & Sporns, O. (2008). Mapping the structural core of human cerebral cortex. *PLoS Biology*, 6, e159.

Hasselmo, M. E., Bodelón, C., & Wyble, B. P. (2002). A proposed function for hippocampal theta rhythm: Separate phases of encoding and retrieval enhance reversal of prior learning. *Neural Computation*, *14*, 793–817.

Holmes, G. M. (1919). Disturbances of visual spatial perception. *British Medical Journal*, *2*, 230–33.

Hubel, D. H., & Wiesel, T. N. (1962). Receptive fields, binocular interaction and functional architecture in the cat's visual cortex. *Journal of Physiology*, *160*, 106–54.

Hubel, D. H., & Wiesel, T. N. (1968). Receptive fields and functional architecture of monkey striate cortex. *Journal of Physiology*, *195*, 215–43.

Kutas, M., & Hillyard, S. A. (1980). Reading senseless sentences: Brain potentials reflect semantic incongruity. *Science*, *207*, 203–05.

Llinás, R. R. (2001). *I of the vortex: From neurons to self*. Cambridge, MA: MIT Press.

Lorente de Nó, R. (1938). The cerebral cortex: Architecture, intracortical connections and motor projections. In J. Fulton (Ed.), *Physiology of the nervous system* (pp. 291–301). Oxford: Oxford University Press.

Machamer, P., Darden, L., & Craver, C. F. (2000). Thinking about mechanisms. *Philosophy of Science*, *67*, 1–25.

Mantini, D., Perrucci, M. G., Del Gratta, C., Romani, G. L., & Corbetta, M. (2007). Electrophysiological signatures of resting state networks in the human brain. *Proceedings of the National Academy of Sciences*, *104*, 13170–75.

O'Keefe, J. A. (1976). Place units in the hippocampus of the freely moving rat. *Experimental Neurology*, *51*, 78–109.

Posner, M. I., & Raichle, M. E. (1994). *Images of mind*. San Francisco: Freeman.

Raichle, M. E., MacLeod, A. M., Snyder, A. Z., Powers, W. J., Gusnard, D. A., & Shulman, G. L. (2001). A default mode of brain function. *Proceedings of the National Academy of Sciences of the United States of America*, *98*, 676–82.

Scannell, J. W., Burns, G. A. P. C., Hilgetag, C. C., O'Neil, M. A., & Young, M. P. (1999). The connectional organization of the cortico-thalamic system of the cat. *Cerebral Cortex*, 9, 277–99.

Sherrington, C. S. (1923). *The integrative action of the nervous system*. New Haven: Yale University Press.

Sporns, O., Tononi, G., & Kötter, R. (2005). The human connectome: A structural description of the human brain. *PLoS Computational Biology*, *1*, e42.

Sporns, O., & Zwi, J. D. (2004). The small world of the cerebral cortex. *Neuroinformatics*, *2*, 145–62.

Ungerleider, L. G., & Mishkin, M. (1982). Two cortical visual systems. In D. J. Ingle, M. A. Goodale, & R. J. W. Mansfield (Eds.), *Analysis of visual behavior* (pp. 549–86). Cambridge, MA: MIT Press.

van den Heuvel, M. P., & Sporns, O. (2011). Rich-club organization of the human connectome. *The Journal of Neuroscience*, *31*, 15775–86.

van Essen, D. C., & Gallant, J. L. (1994). Neural mechanisms of form and motion processing in the primate visual system. *Neuron*, *13*, 1–10.

Watts, D., & Strogratz, S. (1998). Collective dynamics of small worlds. *Nature*, *393*, 440–42.

White, J. G., Southgate, E., Thomson, J. N., & Brenner, S. (1986). The structure of the nervous system of the nematode *Caenorhabditis elegans*. *Philosophical Transactions of the Royal Society of London, B, Biological Sciences*, *314*, 1–340.

Young, M. P. (1993). The organization of neural systems in the primate cerebral cortex. *Proceedings of the Royal Society of London, Series B: Biological Sciences*, *252*, 13–18.

Zawidzki, T. W., & Bechtel, W. (2004). Gall's legacy revisited: Decomposition and localization in cognitive neuroscience. In C. E. Erneling & D. M. Johnson (Eds.), *The mind as a scientific object*. Oxford: Oxford University Press.

29
EVOLUTIONARY MODELS IN PSYCHOLOGY

Michael Wheeler

Introduction

For anyone whose worldview is reliably informed by science, the idea that the complex organs of the human body should be explained scientifically as the product of evolution is, as they say, a no-brainer. And that includes the most complex organ of all, the human brain. But now what about the human mind? Is *that* to be explained scientifically as the product of evolution? Here it is worth beginning with what the psychologists Tooby and Cosmides (1992; more on them below) call the Standard Social Science Model (SSSM) of mind. According to the SSSM, the mind's innate evolutionary endowment (the cognitive elements with which we are born) is nigh on exhausted by our senses, some basic drives such as hunger and fear, and a capacity for general-purpose learning. In other words, knowledge-wise the mind at birth is pretty much what philosophers will recognize as a Lockean blank slate. What evolution has done is give that epistemically empty vessel the means to learn postnatally from its cultural environment. At root, then, it's culture, rather than evolution, that explains the character of the complex information-rich structure which that empty vessel becomes.

Now, Tooby and Cosmides are not just psychologists; they are *evolutionary* psychologists, and their understanding of what an evolutionary model in psychology ought to look like is very different indeed from the SSSM-generated picture. Here we need to get clear about some labels. In the current intellectual climate, the term "evolutionary psychology" is often used to identify not simply any psychological science that takes its cues from evolutionary biology, but rather a very specific, limelight-hogging, socially explosive, scientifically controversial, and philosophically intriguing stream of such work. The research in question is based on a number of conceptual and theoretical principles (to be discussed later) that are not merely antithetical to the SSSM model of mind; in addition, they are rejected by plenty of other psychological theorists who take their work to have robust evolutionary roots. The narrow use of the term "evolutionary psychology" is no doubt irksome to the latter group of thinkers, but (with suitable apologies) I shall adopt it in what follows. Moreover, given the fact that evolutionary psychology (narrowly conceived) has attracted a good deal of philosophical attention, both supportive and critical, I shall organize this entry around an attempt to lay bare exactly what the conceptual foundations of that specific paradigm are, plus a survey of some of the chief criticisms levelled against it. Certain other evolutionary models in psychology will make brief appearances as critical responses to evolutionary psychology, which is not to say that this exhausts the interest of those alternative models.

What is evolutionary psychology?

One might usefully think of evolutionary psychology as being defined by two baseline commitments and three big ideas. Let's start with the baseline commitments. These come to light once we try to be more specific about what might be meant by the terms "evolutionary" and "psychology" in the moniker "evolutionary psychology."

Natural selection occurs whenever one has heritable variation in fitness, where fitness is understood as a measure of the capacity of an organism to reproduce in some environment. Since organisms exhibiting fitter traits are, on average, more likely to reproduce, if the fitness-bestowing traits are heritable, if there is competition for resources, and if the environment is stable enough, those traits will, over time, tend to spread through the population. Sexual selection is a variant of natural selection in which certain phenotypic features of one sex in a species evolve because the other sex prefers to mate with individuals who have those features; canonical examples include the male peacock's tail and deep voices in male humans. Darwin identified both nonsexual natural selection and sexual selection as evolutionary processes, and henceforth I shall group them together under the banner of *Darwinian selection*. Darwinian selection is a mechanism that results in the phenomenon of adaptation. Adaptation is the calibration of organisms to their environments, and the calibrated traits are called adaptations. In principle of course there could be other explanations for adaptation (God could have designed organisms that way), but adaptationists in evolutionary biology take it that where one genuinely has an adaptation one is looking at a product of Darwinian selection. It seems to most biologists that however one cuts the evolutionary cake, Darwinian selection will be at the centre of our understanding of evolution. For the evolutionary psychologist, however, it often seems that evolution simply *is* Darwinian selection; so the term "evolutionary" in "evolutionary psychology" just means "explained by Darwinian selection." This is the first baseline commitment of evolutionary psychology.

So what precisely is the explanatory target of Darwinian theorizing here? In the intellectual arena within which evolutionary psychology has emerged, some thinkers have pursued the following thought: if differences in human social behaviour result in differences in fitness, and if those behaviours are heritable, then selection can favour the fitter behaviour. This is the classical form of the discipline known as *sociobiology* (Wilson 1975). Classical sociobiologists attempt to explain behaviours such as rape, incest avoidance, and male sexual promiscuity in terms of the fitness benefits that those behaviours might bestow under certain conditions. Thus Thornhill and Thornhill (1992) argue (controversially, as many critical responses at the time made clear) that rape by human males is an adaptation to sexual exclusion.

Ignoring empirical objections to particular models, is there anything wrong *in principle* with classical sociobiology? One big worry concerns the massive diversity of social behaviours that human beings perform – from culture to culture and from individual to individual. If human social behaviours are species-wide adaptations, the result of a long process of cumulative selection, one might expect those behaviours to be robust across different cultures. However, this is not the pattern we see in human cultural life. Human social behaviours seem extraordinarily sensitive to cultural factors, in a way that goes well beyond what could possibly be absorbed by the idea of adaptations that are expressed only in certain circumstances. And a similar point could be made about behavioural variations between individuals.

One response to this difficulty might be to run back into the arms of SSSM. But there is an alternative. Enter evolutionary psychology, which shifts the focus of Darwinian selective attention away from behaviours and on to the inner, neurally realized, psychological mechanisms that are the proximal causes of those behaviours. On this view, then, what gets selected for are not the behaviours themselves, but rather the psychological mechanisms that generate and control them. Just as there are anatomical adaptations (bodily structures shaped by natural selection to solve certain adaptive problems), there are psychological adaptations (cognitive structures shaped by natural selection to solve certain other adaptive problems). Thus, as Cosmides and Tooby (1987: 282) put it, "[the] *evolutionary function of the human brain is to process information in ways that lead to adaptive behavior*."

We have now unearthed our second baseline commitment of evolutionary psychology, which concerns the "psychology" part of the term. Evolutionary psychology is, as we have just seen, a species of *information-processing psychology*, a way of thinking about thinking inherited largely unmodified from mainstream cognitive science. Put a little crudely, on this view the brain is the hardware in which is instantiated a functionally specified (broadly) computational system of information retrieval and manipulation, geared towards generating behavioural outputs. That computational system is our cognitive architecture, which the evolutionary psychologist claims can be understood correctly only if one understands the adaptive problems that Darwinian selection has designed it to solve (more on this below). From this perspective, then, evolutionary psychology might be glossed as a way of Darwinizing cognitive science or, as Tooby and Cosmides (1998: 195) themselves put it, revealing their identification of evolution with Darwinian selection, of "evolutionizing the cognitive sciences."

Once selectionist thinking is applied to the mind-brain, rather than to behaviours directly, there emerges a compelling solution to the worry that human social behaviour displays too much cultural diversity to permit any kind of adaptationist explanation to get a grip. Broadly speaking, this solution has two dimensions. First, it is a mundane observation that almost any useful computer program, when triggered into action, may produce any one of a range of different outputs, depending on precisely which inputs it receives. So why shouldn't the same be true of our evolved psychological mechanisms? Here is the evolutionary-psychological picture: All developmentally normal human beings share a suite of innately specified psychological adaptations – selected-for internal information-processing mechanisms that are robust across cultures. Any (or perhaps most) of these evolved programs may produce any one of a range of behaviours by responding differentially to varying inputs. And do the relevant inputs vary? Yes they do. Variations in the social environments in which individuals (and thus their evolved brains) are embedded produce variations in the context-sensitive real-time informational inputs available to those mechanisms. Behavioural diversity is thus purchased using a currency of inner homogeneity plus input-sensitivity.

The second dimension of the evolutionary-psychological response to the worry about behavioural diversity appeals to a cluster of developmental issues. First we meet the developmental version of the position just described. The classic Chomskyan model of language learning posits the existence of an innately specified human-wide language acquisition device. However, as a result of that shared device being exposed to different developmental environments (different linguistic communities that provide different developmental inputs), different speakers learn and produce different languages. This model can be generalized to other innately specified psychological mechanisms. Second, evolutionary psychologists are not genetic determinists who think that innately coded-for adaptations will be present no matter what happens in the developmental environment. Whether or not a particular psychological adaptation is ultimately "wired up" properly in a specific individual will typically depend on the presence of certain environmental triggers that, under normal circumstances, occur reliably at critical stages during development. We are all familiar with the plight of children whose language learning is impaired by their exposure to a linguistically impoverished environment at critical stages of their development, but there will be less dramatic examples. Finally, there may be alternative psychological adaptations available to development, alternatives that are under the control of genetic switches that initiate different developmental trajectories. For example, evolutionary psychologists argue that men and women confront divergent, sex-relative adaptive problems when it comes to finding, holding on to, and reproducing with a mate. Thus men and women instantiate different, sex-relative psychological adaptations in the mating game (more on which below). Since sex determination is under the control of a genetic switch, so are these alternative psychological architectures. Behavioural diversity (e.g. different sex-relative mating strategies) results from such switching.

The focus on inner mechanisms as adaptations, plus an observation about the typically slow pace of evolutionary change, helps the evolutionary psychologist to head off another potential worry. Here's the worry: if our psychological mechanisms are adaptations, designed with fitness advantages in mind, how come many of the behaviours that modern human beings perform are so woefully maladaptive, or at best selectively neutral? Here are three well-worn examples: given the increasing prevalence of sperm banks, adult male humans could maximize their reproductive success through a policy of widespread sperm donation, but they don't adopt such a policy; given that overindulgence in the sugar-rich foods readily available in technologically advanced countries leads to unhealthy obesity, and thus, one might think, to a lessening of our survival and reproductive prospects, we should avoid such overindulgence, but we don't; empirical evidence confirms that human beings have a deep-seated fear of snakes, which makes no adaptive sense at all in modern urban environments. What all this tells us is that contemporary human behaviour is not always fitness maximizing, which brings us to the first of (what I am calling) evolutionary psychology's big ideas: the *environment of evolutionary adaptedness* (EEA).

To see how this works we can begin by noting the all-too-often elided but in truth crucial distinction between a trait being *adaptive* and it being an *adaptation*. A trait is adaptive if its possession by some individual would, on average, bestow a fitness advantage on that individual. By contrast, a trait is an adaptation if its possession by some individual now is explained by the fact that it bestowed a heritable fitness advantage in *ancestral* environments. These two notions can come apart. Any adaptation must have been adaptive at some time in the ancestral past, but it need not be adaptive now. Thus vestigial traits may be adaptations without being adaptive. Conversely, a trait that has entered the population only very recently, meaning that selection won't have had time to act, may be adaptive now without being an adaptation.

This distinction gives us the conceptual resources, where appropriate, to decouple the present performance of a psychological mechanism with regard to fitness from the evidence one would submit in connection with its status as an adaptation. In order to pursue the latter, one needs to make sure that one has in view the selection pressures that were operative in designing the trait in question. In other words, one needs to make sure that one has in view the "composite of environmental properties of the most recent segment of a species' evolution that encompasses the period during which its modern collection of adaptations assumed their present form" (Tooby and Cosmides 1990: 388). This is what evolutionary psychologists call the *environment of evolutionary adaptedness* (or EEA). Of course the relevant EEA may well not be the current environment in which a trait operates. Environments sometimes change, and especially in the case of complex traits (the human brain being the most complex trait around), evolution by cumulative Darwinian selection is typically a very slow process that may lag well behind. Indeed, evolutionary psychologists argue that the last time any significant modifications were made by Darwinian selection to the human brain's functional architecture was during the Pleistocene Epoch (approximately 2 million to 10 thousand years ago), when humans were hunter-gatherers. Thus the composite of selection pressures at work in the Pleistocene constitutes our EEA (see e.g. Crawford [1998] for discussion). These are the adaptive problems to which our modern brains, inherited essentially unchanged from our Pleistocene hunter-gatherer ancestors, constitute evolved solutions.

Working on the assumption that one can't hope to understand what the psychological adaptations here might look like unless one understands the problems to which they constitute evolved solutions, the evolutionary psychologist's first job is to specify the adaptive problems that were present in the human EEA. According to the evolutionary psychologists, these include things like how to select a mate (Buss 1992), how to speak and understand language (Pinker and Bloom 1990; Pinker 1994), how to engage in and reason about social exchange (Cosmides and Tooby 1992), and how to explain and predict each other's behaviour (Baron-Cohen 1999).

Now we can see how evolutionary psychologists will deal with the aforementioned troubling examples of adaptive shortfall. Two are examples of adaptations that are no longer adaptive due to environmental change. Our sweet tooth was adaptive in the nutritional challenges posed by the Pleistocene environment, but has since been rendered maladaptive by the mass availability of refined sugar. Unfortunately selection hasn't had the time to shift the trait. A fear of snakes was adaptive given the threat posed by such creatures in the Pleistocene environment but is now (presumably) selectively neutral, in that it is unlikely in the extreme that someone from, say, twenty-first-century Edinburgh, born with a "not-afraid-of-snakes" mutation, would do worse at survival and reproduction than her snake-fearing conspecifics. The final example is a case of a contemporary fitness-enhancing opportunity that fails to be grabbed because our psychological adaptations are meshed with our Pleistocene past: modern human males don't adopt a strategy of widespread sperm donation because our reproductive strategies are designed for Pleistocene conditions.

Evolutionary psychology's second big idea concerns the design of our evolved psychological architecture. Recall SSSM. According to that view the innate human cognitive architecture is essentially a *domain-general* learning and reasoning engine. By contrast, according to the evolutionary psychologists, the evolved human mind is (to use a now famous image) a kind of psychological Swiss army knife, in that it involves a large collection of specialized cognitive tools. As we have seen, evolutionary psychology is Darwinized information-processing psychology, so what we have here is a picture of mind as involving a *very large number* of *domain-specific information-processing mechanisms*, sometimes called *modules*, each of which (i) is triggered by informational inputs specific to a particular evolutionarily salient domain (e.g. choosing a mate, social exchange); and (ii) has access to internally stored information about that domain *alone*. Thus the Swiss army knife account of mind is sometimes glossed as the *massive modularity hypothesis* (Samuels 1998; Sperber 1996).

Evolutionary psychology's third big idea is that behind all that diversity in human social behaviour there lurks an *evolved universal human nature*. In a way this point is a repackaging of claims that we've met already, but it is worth pausing to note a certain slipperiness in what exactly that evolved universal human nature might be. This slipperiness is nicely isolated by Buller (2005). The most obvious candidate for an evolved universal human nature is the suite of Darwinian modules possessed by adult human beings, but, as we know, this suite is not strictly universal, due to the existence of different developmental trajectories. So what might be *strictly* universal? The answer is an evolved species-wide set of genetically specified developmental programs that control processes such as genetic switching and how the emerging human phenotype responds to critical environmental triggers. It's at that level that strict universality (allegedly) holds.

Now that we have a grip on the conceptual shape of evolutionary psychology, it is worth just mentioning some of the flagship empirical claims that the approach has generated. Cosmides and Tooby (1992) argue that human beings have an evolved cognitive module specialized for spotting cheats in social exchange. Symons (1979) and Buss (1994) argue that human beings have sex-relative domain-specific mechanisms of mate preference that result in males being attracted to females who exhibit certain signs of high reproductive potential, and females being attracted to males who exhibit certain signs of high status and resource possession. Daly and Wilson (1988) argue that children reared by substitute parents (especially genetically unrelated substitute parents) are more likely to be exploited and more at risk from abuse. And Miller (2000), in a treatment that stresses sexual rather than (strict) natural selection, argues that the products of contemporary human creative intelligence, such as novels, films, and jokes, need to be explained as human versions of the peacock's tail, in that they are elaborate ornaments that advertise the fitness of a potential mate precisely because they demonstrate that that individual has the spare capacity to use up resources on non-survival related projects.

Problems for evolutionary psychology

Both of evolutionary psychology's basic commitments and all three of its big ideas have been contested. In the rest of this entry I shall sample some of the lodged objections, *all* of which, I think, isolate open questions that are ripe for further research.

Ultra-Darwinism

Ultra-Darwinism is the view that almost all phenotypic traits in almost all populations of organisms are adaptations, that is, are the direct product of Darwinian selection. It does seem that evolutionary psychologists commit themselves to ultra-Darwinism about the mind, that is, to the claim that almost all features of the human cognitive architecture are psychological adaptations. Indeed, it seems to be a consequence of accepting that there is an evolutionary explanation for the human mind, and holding that evolution just means Darwinian selection (see above). So what is wrong with ultra-Darwinism? Gould (2000) argues (i) that ultra-Darwinism is on the retreat in evolutionary thinking generally; and (ii) that the human mind looks to be particularly resistant to any ultra-Darwinist treatment. The evidence for point (i) comes from (what Gould takes to be) an increasingly widespread recognition in biology that evolution is a mosaic of many different processes and phenomena, including not only Darwinian selection but also factors such as contingency, evolutionary spandrels (traits that are not themselves selected for, but rather are by-products of selection for other traits), and punctuated equilibria (according to which the emergence of new species is not a gradual process driven by natural selection acting on geographically isolated groups in different environments, but rather involves long periods of what is essentially stasis and then moments of abrupt change).

The notion of evolutionary spandrels is particularly salient here. Gould argues that since all organisms evolve as complex and interconnected wholes, selection-driven change to one feature will typically generate non-adaptive by-products. These by-products may later be co-opted by selection to perform some function, but the existence and structure of those by-products is not explained by selection. Given that the human brain is the most complex and internally interconnected organ around, it is very likely, as Gould puts it, to be "bursting with spandrels that establish central components of what we call human nature but that arose as non-adaptations, and therefore fall outside the compass of evolutionary psychology or any other ultra-Darwinian theory" (2000: 104). And that's the argument for point (ii).

Could evolutionary psychology divest itself of a perhaps indefensible ultra-Darwinism and yet remain true to its cause? I don't see why not. Indeed, evolutionary psychologists already make the point that *some* facets of our psychological profile will result from variation in selectively neutral features. Additionally conceding the existence of phenomena such as psychological spandrels would be a step towards adopting what Godfrey-Smith (2001) calls *explanatory adaptationism*, the view that while adaptation is not ubiquitous, adaptation, and especially complex adaptation, is the central problem in evolutionary biology, and to be explained by Darwinian selection. Wearing her explanatory adaptationist hat, the evolutionary psychologist could hold that psychological adaptation is the central problem in psychology, and that it is to be explained by Darwinian selection. Other aspects of the evolutionary-psychological picture (psychological adaptations as modules, the EEA) could stay in place.

Is the mind an information-processing system?

In considering this question it is worth noting that certain prominent evolutionary psychologists commit themselves to something more specific than just some broad view of cognition as information processing. Rather, they hold that the mind is a *classical* rather than a *connectionist* computational system. One crude but effective way to state the difference between classicism and connectionism in cognitive science is to say that whereas classicism uses the abstract structure of human language as a model for the nature of mind (and thus conceives the mind as a representational system with a combinatorial syntax and semantics), connectionism uses the abstract structure of the biological brain (and thus conceives the mind as being organized into a huge number of interconnected processing units that represent the world by entering into large-scale coalitions of activation). Evolutionary psychologists have often tended to pin their colours to the classical mast because they view connectionist research, which typically starts out with a knowledge-free network that is then tuned postnatally (as it were), using generic domain-general learning algorithms, as a return to the bad old ways of SSSM. However, this commitment to the classical framework does leave the evolutionary psychologist a hostage to the fortunes of that framework, which may not be a good thing if the ongoing debate between classicists and connectionists in cognitive science (see e.g., and famously, Fodor and Pylyshyn 1988) is ever resolved in favour of the latter. Entering that complex and thorny debate would take us too far afield, and in any case there seems to be no in-principle reason why one couldn't "pre-wire" domain specificity into a connectionist network to satisfy the evolutionary psychologist's conditions.

Specifying adaptive problems

The first job of the evolutionary psychologist is to specify the adaptive problems faced by our Pleistocene hunter-gatherer ancestors in the human EEA. However, some critics claim that hypotheses about how historically remote selective pressures shaped the design of minds in the distant past are hopelessly speculative, essentially untestable and thus scientifically empty (Smith et al. 2001). As Gould (2000) notes, the bands of ancient hunter-gatherers who are our target here did leave behind some tools and bones, meaning that paleoanthropologists have something to go on, but the detailed information concerning, for example, kinship relations, social structures, and the differences between the social activities of men and women that would be required to specify the relevant adaptive problems simply isn't available. Indeed, recall the claim that the human sweet tooth is an adaptation forged in the Pleistocene era. Gould (2000: 100) points to, among other things, the lack of any supporting paleontological data about ancestral feeding, as a way of dismissing that claim as "pure guesswork in the cocktail party mode." And even if one doesn't rule out such theorizing as overly speculative or unscientific, the fact is that paleoanthropologists and others have argued that the Pleistocene era was characterized by a highly variable set of environments and social systems, and, moreover, that some post-Pleistocene changes to the selective environment associated with the introduction of agriculture and urbanization have, in fact, left enough time for some more recent genetic evolution to have occurred (Smith et al. 2001). Serious worries, then, accompany the evolutionary psychologist's appeal to a human EEA.

Moreover, there is a deeper problem in the wings here, a conceptual worry about specifying adaptive problems that Sterelny and Griffiths (1999) dub the *grain problem*. Is, for example, choosing a mate a single adaptive problem, or is it a set of related problems, such as choosing someone of the opposite sex, someone who shows good reproductive prospects, and someone who shows signs of being a good parent? Or at a yet finer level of description, is the problem of choosing someone with good reproductive prospects a single problem or a set of related problems, such as choosing someone who is young, who is healthy, of high status, etc.? It seems there is no final answer to any of these questions, and thus that no particular level in a selective hierarchy – or, as one might say, no individual descriptive *grain* – takes explanatory precedence over any other. This does not augur well for the project of specifying the particular adaptive problems to which our brains are evolved solutions.

Sterelny and Griffiths go on to suggest that the grain problem may be solved where it is possible antecedently to identify a distinct cognitive device (the adapted trait) subserving a distinct type of behaviour. In other words, our all-important level-fixing decisions may be constrained by the prior identification of distinct cognitive devices. Unfortunately there is good reason to be suspicious of Sterelny and Griffiths' strategy, because the grain problem comes in not just one but two dimensions, the second of which concerns the cognitive devices themselves (Atkinson and Wheeler 2004). Thus, are the large-scale neural pathways in the human visual system distinct cognitive devices, or should we descend to a lower level of description and the thirty or so functionally distinct areas of visual cortex? Of course, if we knew what the adaptive problem was, we could determine the right architectural level, but that takes us back to the first dimension of the problem. Still, there might be a way out of the grain problem. Perhaps the evolutionary psychologist can avail herself of an established methodology already at work elsewhere in evolutionary theorizing about the mind/brain, a methodology that takes the grain problem on the chin by accepting that at least sometimes there will be equally good evolutionary stories to tell at different levels of organization, stories that must at least be compatible and ideally mutually supporting. (For more on how this story might go, see Atkinson and Wheeler [2004].)

Are there any good arguments for massive modularity?

In arguing for massive modularity, evolutionary psychologists sometimes develop in-principle arguments which aim to establish that domain-general mechanisms on their own, i.e. without assistance from domain-specific mechanisms, would not be able to solve the adaptive problems faced by our hunter-gatherer ancestors (see e.g. Tooby and Cosmides 1992: 102–12). Perhaps the most powerful of these arguments goes like this: In part, the domain generality of an inner mechanism would be guaranteed by that mechanism having free access to the overall stock of beliefs possessed by some system, such that it could operate in a large number of domains. However, before such a mechanism could determine a contextually appropriate response to some input, it would first need to consider all the beliefs to which it had access, in order to work out which of them were, in fact, relevant. (This will be familiar to some readers as the frame problem from artificial intelligence.) Tooby and Cosmides' point is that the number of beliefs that a domain-general mechanism would need to consider in this way would always be prohibitively large, leading to a crippling computational load and thus adaptive impotence. And as long as we preserve a commitment to domain-general mechanisms, this worry won't be deflected by some appeal to stored relevancy heuristics that determine which of the system's beliefs is relevant in any particular scenario, since this just ushers in another Herculean search problem – finding the right relevancy heuristic.

It is at least plausible that the massive modularity view avoids this difficulty. In any context of action, the domain-specific mechanism that is appropriately activated will (as a direct consequence of evolutionary design) have access to no more than a highly restricted subset of the system's entire range of beliefs. Moreover, that subset will include just those beliefs that are relevant to the adaptive scenario in which the system finds itself. Therefore the kind of unmanageable search space that stymies the progress of any domain-general mechanism is simply never established. Putting aside a nagging worry about just how the right module gets activated here (presumably not by some domain-general module-selection mechanism!), Tooby and Cosmides' argument in favour of domain specificity remains much too swift (Wheeler and Atkinson 2001; Mameli 2001; Atkinson and Wheeler 2004). That's because the deep reason why the modular architecture avoids the specified problem is that the body of information to which each module has access is restricted in adaptively useful ways. However, now consider an intrinsically domain-general psychological mechanism that, through the opportunistic process of design by selection, has been allowed access only to a restricted body of information. That mechanism would have the desired property too. If this is right, then the question of whether or not the mechanisms of mind are domain-specific or domain-general in character remains open.

Perhaps the case can be re-mounted as a matter of efficiency rather than all-or-nothing achievement. Thus Cosmides and Tooby claim that "domain-specific cognitive mechanisms … can be expected to systematically outperform (and hence preclude or replace) more general mechanisms" (1994: 89). The idea is that, in the human EEA, any domain-general mechanism in the population will typically have been systematically outperformed by any competing domain-specific mechanism. Thus it is the latter kind of mechanism that will have been selected for. However, Samuels (1998) points out that Cosmides and Tooby's arguments establish only that systems with domain-specific features of some kind, and that includes a domain-general mechanism with access to domain-specific information, will outperform competing systems without such features.

At this juncture it is worth noting two things. First, from the perspective of a broader evolutionarily-informed approach to psychology, the domain-specific versus domain-general issue has a life beyond the battle over massive modularity. Indeed, striking a balance *between* domain specificity and domain generality may itself be an adaptive problem that selection has solved. For example, Gigerenzer et al. (1999) defend the idea that human rationality is characterized largely by the deployment of *fast and frugal heuristics*, simple reasoning strategies that exploit the structure of environmental information to make adaptively beneficial decisions. Such heuristics are specific to particular information structures, but not so specific to particular environments that they don't generalize to previously unencountered environments, which indicates that some degree of domain generality is in play.

The second thing to note is that a more robust domain generality than this need not be anathema to evolutionary thinking in psychology. For example, drawing on Boyd and Richerson's (1985) dual inheritance model, which stresses cultural as well as genetic transmission in evolution, Coultas (2004) provides experimental evidence that individual human beings have an essentially domain-general tendency to conform in social groups, a tendency that can be adaptive for the individual when information gathering by that individual would be costly. And Tomasello (1999), in a treatment that also stresses dual inheritance, argues that evolution has endowed us with a set of basic cognitive capacities, including shared attention and the imitation of other humans' behaviours and intentions, that allow us to take developmental advantage of a kind of accumulated species-specific knowledge made available through human cultural environments. At the heart of this process, and the capacity that sets human beings apart from other species, is our ability to identify intentions in others. It's this uniquely human, essentially domain-general ability, argues Tomasello, that allows us to build on foundational capacities that we share with other animals (such as the capacities for tool use and for signalling), to become vastly more sophisticated thinkers in specific domains (e.g. vastly more sophisticated tool users and signallers) than have our evolutionary cousins. (For criticisms of this idea, see e.g. Hauser [2000].)

Is there an evolved human nature?

The evolutionary psychologist's notion of an evolved human nature is that of a species-wide set of genetically specified developmental programs that orchestrate the journey from genotype to phenotype. A maturing human being embedded in a normal developmental environment will thus end up with a particular, species-wide set of cognitive modules (allowing for some branching pathways, e.g. between the sexes). As Buller (2005) notes, this idea appears to depend on what Sober (1980) calls the natural state model in biology. With its roots in Aristotle, this model holds that diversity and variation among organisms of the same species are deviations from the species-relative natural state of those organisms, deviations caused by the operation of interfering forces, such as those in abnormal developmental environments. Thus the natural state model identifies the natural phenotype (e.g. the evolved human nature) by identifying a privileged developmental environment, the natural one. However, the natural state model, and thus (ironically) evolutionary psychology, is at root *in conflict with* contemporary neo-Darwinian evolutionary biology, which treats the biological realm as a place in which individual variation is conceived as the fundamental way of things, rather than as the product of interfering forces that deflect individuals from a path towards a state of species-wide uniformity. Thus contemporary evolutionary theory thinks in terms of norms of reaction (genotype-phenotype mappings in particular environments), with each phenotypic outcome, and thus each of the associated developmental environments, conceptualized as being *on an equal footing*.

The evolutionary psychologist, like any natural state theorist, needs to privilege one of the possible developmental environments as the "natural" one. It might seem that the EEA might be the ticket here – an environment that counts as privileged because it is the home of the adaptive problems to which our psychological adaptations constitute solutions, and which thus might be considered our natural environment. But this suggestion runs bang up against the aforementioned worry that the evolutionary psychologist mistakes Darwinian selection for the whole of evolution. As Buller (2005: 436) notes, "adaptation is just one process among many in evolution, and nothing in evolutionary theory privileges the process of adaptation over other processes [such as genetic drift or migration in and out of populations] by considering it more natural than other processes." In closing it is worth noting that this is a mistake that Darwin himself didn't make. So the much trumpeted Darwinization of psychology as championed by evolutionary psychology (narrowly conceived) may not be a genuine Darwinization at all. That would be achieved by a more pluralistic, multifaceted and correspondingly richer understanding of evolution, and thus of the evolved character of the human mind.

References

Atkinson, A., and Wheeler, M. (2004) "The Grain of Domains: The Evolutionary-Psychological Case against Domain-General Cognition," *Mind and Language* 19, no. 2: 147–76.

Baron-Cohen, S. (1999) "The Evolution of a Theory of Mind," in M. C. Corballis and S. E. G. Lea (eds), *The Descent of Mind: Psychological Perspectives on Hominid Evolution*, Oxford: Oxford University Press, pp. 261–77.

Boyd, R., and Richerson, P. J. (1985) *Culture and the Evolutionary Process*, Chicago: University of Chicago Press.

Buller, D. J. (2005) *Adapting Minds: Evolutionary Psychology and the Persistent Quest for Human Nature*, Cambridge, MA: MIT Press.

Buss, D. M. (1992) "Mate Preference Mechanisms: Consequences for Partner Choice and Intrasexual Competition," in J. H. Barkow, L. Cosmides, and J. Tooby (eds), *The Adapted Mind: Evolutionary Psychology and the Generation of Culture*, New York: Oxford University Press, pp. 249–66.

—— (1994) *The Evolution of Desire: Strategies of Human Mating*, New York: Basic Books.

Cosmides, L., and Tooby, J. (1987) "From Evolution to Behavior: Evolutionary Psychology as the Missing Link," in J. Dupre (ed.), *The Latest on the Best: Essays on Evolution and Optimality*, Cambridge, MA: MIT Press, pp. 227–306.

—— (1992) "Cognitive Adaptations for Social Exchange," in J. H. Barkow, L. Cosmides, and J. Tooby (eds), *The Adapted Mind: Evolutionary Psychology and the Generation of Culture*, New York: Oxford University Press, pp. 163–228.

—— (1994) "Origins of Domain Specificity: The Evolution of Functional Organization," in L. A. Hirschfeld and S. A. Gelman (eds), *Mapping the Mind: Domain Specificity in Cognition and Culture*, Cambridge and New York: Cambridge University Press, pp. 85–116.

Coultas, J. C. (2004) "When in Rome ... An Evolutionary Perspective on Conformity," *Group Processes and Intergroup Relations* 7, no. 4: 317–31.

Crawford, C. (1998) "Environments and Adaptations: Then and Now," in C. Crawford and D. L. Krebs (eds), *Handbook of Evolutionary Psychology: Ideas, Issues, and Applications*, Mahwah, NJ: Erlbaum, pp. 275–302.

Daly, M., and Wilson, M. (1988) *Homicide*, New York: Aldine de Gruyter.

Fodor, J. A., and Pylyshyn, Z. (1988) "Connectionism and Cognitive Architecture: A Critical Analysis," *Cognition* 28: 3–71.

Gigerenzer, G., Todd, P. M., and ABC Research Group (1999) *Simple Heuristics That Make Us Smart*, Oxford: Oxford University Press.

Godfrey-Smith, P. (2001) "Three Kinds of Adaptationism," in S. H. Orzack and E. Sober (eds), *Adaptationism and Optimality*, Cambridge: Cambridge University Press, pp. 335–57.

Gould, S. J. (2000) "More Things in Heaven and Earth," in H. Rose and S. Rose (eds) *Alas Poor Darwin: Arguments against Evolutionary Psychology*, New York: Harmony Books, pp. 101–26.

Hauser, M. D. (2000) "Et tu Homo sapiens?" (review of Tomasello 1999), *Science* 288, no. 5467: 816–17.

Mameli, M. (2001) "Modules and Mindreaders" (multiple book review), *Biology and Philosophy* 16: 377–93.

Miller, G. (2000) *The Mating Mind: How Sexual Choice Shaped the Evolution of Human Nature*, London: William Heinemann.

Pinker, S. (1994) *The Language Instinct*, London: Allen Lane-Penguin.

Pinker, S., and Bloom, P. (1990) "Natural Language and Natural Selection," *Behavioral and Brain Sciences* 13: 707–27.

Samuels, R. (1998) "Evolutionary Psychology and the Massive Modularity Hypothesis," *British Journal for the Philosophy of Science* 49: 575–602.

Smith, E. A., Borgerhoff Mulder, M., and Hill, J. (2001) "Controversies in the Evolutionary Social Sciences: A Guide for the Perplexed," *Trends in Ecology and Evolution* 16, no. 3: 128–35.

Sober, E. (1980) "Evolution, Population Thinking, and Essentialism," *Philosophy of Science* 47: 350–83.

Sperber, D. (1996) *Explaining Culture: A Naturalistic Approach*, Oxford: Basil Blackwell.

Sterelny, K., and Griffiths, P. E. (1999) *Sex and Death: An Introduction to Philosophy of Biology*, Chicago: University of Chicago Press.

Symons, D. (1979) *The Evolution of Human Sexuality*, Oxford: Oxford University Press.
Thornhill, R., and Thornhill, N. (1992) "The Evolutionary Psychology of Men's Coercive Sexuality," *Behavioral and Brain Sciences* 15: 363–421.
Tomasello, M. (1999) *The Cultural Origins of Human Cognition*, Cambridge, MA: Harvard University Press.
Tooby, J., and Cosmides, L. (1990) "The Past Explains the Present: Emotional Adaptations and the Structure of Ancestral Environments," *Ethology and Sociobiology* 11: 375–424.
—— (1992) "The Psychological Foundations of Culture," in J. H. Barkow, L. Cosmides, and J. Tooby (eds), *The Adapted Mind: Evolutionary Psychology and the Generation of Culture*, New York: Oxford University Press, pp. 19–136.
—— (1998) "Evolutionizing the Cognitive Sciences: A Reply to Shapiro and Epstein," *Mind and Language* 13: 195–204.
Wheeler, M., and Atkinson, A. (2001) "Domains, Brains and Evolution," in D. M. Walsh (ed.), *Naturalism, Evolution and Mind*, Cambridge: Cambridge University Press, pp. 239–66.
Wilson, E. (1975) *Sociobiology: The New Synthesis*, Cambridge, MA: Harvard University Press.

30
DEVELOPMENT AND LEARNING

Aarre Laakso

Introduction

Questions about learning and development are questions about the possibilities and limits of human nature – about the origins and prospects of our most basic abilities and our most unique traits. In addition to their intrinsic interest, these questions have important policy implications. Our theories about development and learning, whether they are informed or naïve, guide social policy in many areas, including medicine and education. Insofar as we know the means of cultivating the potential of our offspring, we will surely want to do so to the greatest extent possible. Hence, our understanding of development and learning shapes our individual and group practices of healthcare, child rearing, education and personal growth. Our theories about development and learning also guide our individual behavior toward children (and adults as well) as parents, relatives, neighbors, childcare providers, teachers, spouses, friends, colleagues, managers and mentors.

There is not enough space here to discuss every facet of development and learning. Learning is studied in many fields, including psychology, philosophy, mathematics, statistics, computer science, linguistics, neurophysiology, molecular biology and artificial intelligence. Each has its own methods, vocabulary and theories. The goal of this essay is to give the reader a sense of the diversity of theoretical issues about learning and development that may be of interest to philosophically inclined psychologists and psychologically inclined philosophers. Because this volume has separate entries on "Nativism" (Chapter 19) and "Evolutionary Models in Psychology" (Chapter 29) discussion of those issues is limited in this piece to the way they are treated in the developmental literature.

An uncontroversial but vague way of defining ***development*** is "the pattern of continuity and change in an entity over time." Philosophers of psychology are particularly concerned with the development of biological organisms, particularly human beings (human development). The interest is not limited to human beings, however. It extends to other organisms, especially animals, and to non-biological systems, including computers, robots and abstractions. Among both philosophers and psychologists, the interest in human development is most intense with regard to child development, because this is the period of most rapid and obvious transformation. The psychological study of human development, particularly child development, is known as "developmental psychology." It has three main branches: cognitive development, emotional development and social development. In recent years, a broader, more interdisciplinary field called "developmental science" has coalesced around studies of development more generally, in all species and across all periods of the life span.

It is more difficult to define *learning*, because one's definition of learning depends a great deal on one's theory of development. The distinction between learning and development is intimately tied up with questions about nativism. For the extreme empiricist, *all* mental development is learning. For the extreme nativist, learning is impossible and so does not exist. Another difficulty is that philosophers tend to take a narrower view of learning than psychologists do. On a standard psychological definition, "learning" refers to a change in behavior that results from interaction with the environment, excluding behavioral changes attributable to genetic factors, physiological influences (such as illness, fatigue, drugs or "blows to the head"), and maturation (e.g., Lewis et al. 1969). By contrast, an important philosophical definition of learning is "the acquisition of a form of knowledge or ability through the use of experience" (Hamlyn 1995: 496). Note the emphasis on *knowledge* or *ability* in contrast to *behavior*. Indeed, Hamlyn specifically denies that conditioning or imprinting are forms of learning, writing that "For learning to take place experience has to be *used* in some way, so that what results is in a genuine sense knowledge or is dependent on knowledge" (496). For present purposes, we may say that the term "development" refers to changes in an organism that tend to be broader, longer term, more biologically constrained, and more physical in nature than changes described as "learning."

From antiquity, three assumptions have framed philosophical debates about the nature of learning and development. The first is that the unit of analysis is the person (or, more generally, the whole organism), not some higher or lower level unit (such as the family or the cell). The second assumption is factors contributing to learning and development can be classified as either "innate" or "environmental." The final assumption is that there are two types of learning: (a) explicit learning of declarative, propositional knowledge to which the learner has conscious access; and (b) implicit learning of behavioral skills, to which the learner has no conscious access. Over the last 50 years, developments in psychology and other fields have challenged all three assumptions. The third section reviews the evidence that the individual organism is not always the appropriate unit of analysis. The fourth section reviews the conceptual difficulties with apportioning the causes of learning and development to the "genome" or the "environment." The fifth section reviews some of the wide variety of types and modes of learning that psychologists have discovered. First, however, we make a brief foray into history.

A brief history

As with most scientific concepts, the history of the concepts of development and learning is one of increasing differentiation and sophistication, driven by the goals of simultaneously encompassing all of the phenomena of interest while explaining each quantitatively and mechanistically. Developmental science, like all of the sciences, has its roots in philosophy (see the entries on the "Rationalist Roots of Modern Psychology" (Chapter 1), the "Empiricist Roots of Modern Psychology" (Chapter 2), and the "Early Experimental Psychology" (Chapter 3)). However, it also has a unique history that includes emphasis on certain works in the early canon over others as well as recent figures with distinct philosophical pedigrees.

Philosophers, starting with Plato, have traditionally distinguished just two modes of learning – "learning that" (explicit learning of propositional or declarative facts) and "learning how" (skill-based or implicit learning). Although Ryle (1949) coined the terms, the distinction is already captured in Meno's question to Socrates ("whether virtue is acquired by teaching or by practice"). In general, philosophers have tended to privilege propositional learning. Aristotle, for example, argued that "theoretical knowledge" was superior to "practical" or "productive" knowledge. However, a minority, notably Hubert Dreyfus (e.g., Dreyfus and Dreyfus 1986), have emphasized the priority of skill learning over propositional learning. (See also the entry on "Action and Mind" [Chapter 42].)

The first evidence collected about development and learning was primarily based on introspection. Augustine (1955 [397]), for example, claimed to remember in some detail his own acquisition of language. Systematic observation did not develop until the nineteenth century. Charles Darwin (1877) was an early practitioner of the "diary method" of developmental studies, whereby a caretaker keeps a careful record of the behaviors of his or her own child over time for use as scientific evidence. J. M. Baldwin (1906 [1895]) was the first to publish a report on a scientific experiment with a child (not coincidentally, his own daughter). He gave the account of child development in which mature cognitive capacities were hypothesized to develop out of simple infant behaviors in a series of qualitatively distinct stages. Although largely ignored in North America for most of the twentieth century, Baldwin's works had tremendous influence on developmental theory through Vygotsky and Piaget. G. Stanley Hall (1904) and his student Arnold Gesell (1925) compiled detailed normative information about everything from infants' motor achievements to adolescents' dreams. Freud's (1949 [1905]) psychosexual theory emphasized changes in the locus of sexual impulses during child development. Although it drew on his clinical experience with adults, Freud's theory was not based on direct studies of children and has largely fallen out of favor in studies of development. Russian psychologist Lev Vygotsky (1986 [1934]) emphasized the role of sociocultural influences in cognitive development, viewing learning as a process of interaction in social contexts that affects the relationship between people and their environment. Piaget developed his classic cognitive-developmental theory of child development in Switzerland starting in the 1930s. Baldwin's theory was a major influence on Piaget (1999 [1954]), and Piaget's is still the best-known stage theory. Piaget was not well known in North America until the 1960s, however, due to the dominance of behaviorism. Inspired by Pavlov's (1927) discovery of classical conditioning through studies of animal learning, as well as by an urge to rid psychology of the influence of psychoanalytic and metaphysical theorizing, Watson and Skinner emphasized the role of the environment in development and learning. Based primarily on animal studies, Skinner's (1935) theory of operant conditioning suggested that the frequency of a child's behavior could be increased by reinforcing it and decreased by punishing it through the application of external stimuli. Piaget's work came to be recognized in North America as part of the cognitive turn in psychology that started in the 1950s, and it still pervades much theorizing in developmental science.

Leading contemporary theories of learning and development are diverse; they include neo-behaviorist theories, such as Albert Bandura's (1986) "social cognitive theory"; neo-Piagetian or "constructivist" theories (e.g., Case 1992); information-processing and connectionist theories (e.g., MacWhinney et al. 1989); ethological and evolutionary theories, such as John Bowlby's (1982 [1969]) "attachment theory"; neo-Vygotskian theories, such as Barbara Rogoff's (2003) "sociocultural" theory; ecological systems theories, such as Urie Bronfenbrenner's "bioecological view" (Bronfenbrenner and Morris 2006); behavioral genetics theories (e.g., Plomin 1986); developmental systems theories (e.g., Gottlieb 2007); dynamic systems theories (Thelen and Smith 1994); and many others.

Units of analysis and levels of explanation

The "unit of analysis" is the class of entity that the theorist believes to develop or learn. In both psychology and philosophy, it has usually been assumed that the unit of analysis is the person or, more generally, the biological organism. The "level of explanation" is the class of entities used in the explanation. In the canonical case (see "What Is Psychological Explanation?" [Chapter 8]), the level of explanation is a sub-personal mechanism, typically a neural one (see "The Interface between Psychology and Neuroscience" [Chapter 11] and "Levels of Mechanisms" [Chapter 26]). Many contemporary theories of learning and development, however, depart from one or both of the canonical positions.

One reason to believe that the person (or child or organism) is not always the proper unit of analysis is the existence of abstract, formal learning theories developed in linguistics, mathematics, statistics and computer science, as well as in psychology. There are many different such theories, but all of them treat learning (to a greater or lesser degree) independently of human or even animal learning. These theories are relevant to developmental psychologists and philosophers of psychology because they attempt to develop quantitative models of learning that may be applicable to biological organisms.

Mathematical learning theory, as it was developed in psychology (Estes 1950), aims to predict biological behavior quantitatively – for example, to predict the frequency of behavioral responses as a function of stimulus features. In another sense, mathematical learning theory refers to "learning from data." There are a variety of approaches, but generally speaking they concern themselves with two primary problems. One is optimization – adaptation of the learner to maximize some measure of the quality of behavior. The second is complexity – the amount of (physical, spatial or temporal) resources required to implement a solution to the optimization problem.

One important variant of mathematical learning theory is Bayesian learning theory. In general, "Bayesian learning" refers to learning that uses methods based on the Bayesian interpretation of statistics (i.e., that probabilities represent a subjective degree of certainty as opposed to an objective relative frequency). In that wide sense, Bayesian learning applies to a variety of mathematical formalisms and techniques, including Bayes' theorem, and machine learning algorithms, such as expectation maximization (Russell and Norvig 2003).

The field known as statistical learning theory has concerned itself primarily with the optimization problem. Historically, the emphasis has been on learning solutions to regression and classification problems that minimize the error between known data points and the estimated solution. More recently, the emphasis has broadened to encompass not only minimizing error on known data but also generalizing well to new data (Vapnik 1999).

Algorithmic learning theory (sometimes also known as formal learning theory or the theory of inductive inference) is concerned specifically with the learnability in principle of languages (or theories), without consideration of the feasibility of learning under time and space constraints (Gold 1967).

Computational learning theory – sometimes referred to as probably approximately correct (PAC) learning – starts from the idea that learning is the "phenomenon of knowledge acquisition in the absence of explicit programming" (Valiant 1984: 1134) that is, "the process of deducing a program for performing a task" (1142). Learning is typically viewed as the application of an algorithm that, given some input, transforms the internal state of a computer to better predict future input. Computational learning theory is the study of mathematical models of machine learning, with a particular emphasis on "learnability" – on what sorts of resources (time, memory, computer architecture) would be required to learn certain kinds of things and, conversely, what kinds of things can be learned with a given set of resources. It therefore emphasizes issues of computational efficiency. The idea is to identify the contexts in which learning is computationally feasible, meaning that it can be performed in polynomial time.

Machine learning (Mitchell 1997) is the study of computer algorithms that automatically improve their performance, often by some form of induction. It has developed out of a confluence between computer science, particularly artificial intelligence, and statistics. The tasks considered in machine learning theory are typically classification tasks, regression tasks, sequential decision-making tasks or clustering tasks. Classification and regression tasks typically assume that the learning is "supervised," in the sense that the system is provided with a set of exemplar inputs with the "correct" outputs (a set of labeled training exemplars), and expected to learn from them the ability to generalize to new inputs. Sequential decision-making tasks usually assume a semi-supervised learning regime, in which decisions are rewarded or punished, in some cases only remotely (for example, by the outcome of a competition such as a chess game). Clustering tasks typically assume that the learning is "unsupervised," that is, that the system receives no feedback.

Unlike formal learning, biological learning (particularly the sort of learning one sees in human development) is ongoing and cumulative. Each learning accomplishment builds on what has been learned previously and sets the stage for what will be learned next. Often, "what will be learned next" is qualitatively different from what has come before. Moreover, this cumulative learning occurs on different time scales over the course of the lifespan – learning to tie one's shoes and learning to play master-level chess are good examples. By contrast, machine learning algorithms are typically designed to deal with a single kind of learning problem, and to stop when they have achieved a degree of correctness or generalization. Machine learning algorithms also typically do not take into account such factors as motivation, emotional state, multi-modal interactions, or limitations on memory.

However, studies in machine learning and studies in biological learning are converging. Although some types of neural networks (e.g., connectionist networks trained by backpropagation) are physiologically implausible, others approximate the actual behavior of biological neurons much better. Some of the formalisms and data structures developed in machine learning may have abstract correspondences to the activity of biological neurons, even if their mechanisms are quite different.

Besides the fact that learning is often studied in the abstract, there are more concrete indications that the individual organism is not always the most appropriate unit of analysis. There are many levels below the level of the organism that have been taken either as levels of explanation or units of analysis in theories of development and learning. These include the molecular level (DNA, RNA, polypeptides, proteins, neurotransmitters), the chemical level (methylation and acetylation, among others), the cellular level (cells, neurons), the inter-cellular level (e.g., synapses, neurotransmitters), and several distinct intra-cellular levels (in general, tissues and organs, and specifically in the nervous system: networks, circuits, functionally individuated volumes, anatomically individuated volumes, the neocortex, the brain as a whole, and the central nervous system in its entirety).

In neuroscience, learning is typically viewed at the synaptic level, as a biochemical process that has the effect of increasing or decreasing the firing rate of the downstream neuron. (See "Cellular and Subcellular Neuroscience" [Chapter 27].) Many neuroscientists agree that pairs of neurons connected by a synapse are capable of learning in a process similar to the one that Hebb (1949) suggested. Inter-cellular learning is typically explained in terms of long-term potentiation or long-term depression. In long-term potentiation (LTP), a synapse is altered by a stimulus (or series of stimuli) in such a way that subsequent activation at the presynaptic cell is more likely to elicit an action potential in the postsynaptic cell. In long-term depression (LTD), the synapse is altered in such a way that subsequent activation at the presynaptic cell is less likely to elicit an action potential in the postsynaptic cell. The exact mechanisms of LTP and LTD have been subject to intense scrutiny for some time but are not well understood and are non-uniform, differing by the organism, the brain region, the type of synapse, or the age (developmental maturity) of the organism (Malenka and Bear 2004).

Justifications for the claim that the appropriate level of explanation is sub-personal are complex and typically involve a combination of naive realism and naturalism. Both the process of learning and the result (the trace of what is learned) are taken to be situated in the mind (and therefore the brain) of the individual learner. That is, learning is a change of a property of a person, specifically a change in beliefs (the contents of an individual human mind). Jerry Fodor (1980) has defended this position on the grounds of what he calls "methodological solipsism," the view that the contents of thoughts are determined by the physical states of the individual having the thoughts. It is also a logical consequence of "psychophysical supervenience" (Kim 1982), the thesis that any psychological difference must have a corresponding physical difference. Cognitive psychologists, and many developmental scientists, often take this position, usually tacitly but sometimes explicitly.

Internal and external factors

The long debate about the respective roles of "nature" and "nurture" in development can be regarded as a debate about the respective roles of "internal" (sub-personal, genetic) and "external" (supra-personal, environmental) factors in development. In the contemporary debate, a common assumption is that variance across a population can be separated into independent genetic and environmental contributions to individual differences, plus statistical interactions of the two. As a consequence of this assumption, linear models (such as analysis of variance) have typically been used in attempts to demonstrate interactions between heredity and environment. However, pervasive evidence of gene-environment correlations and nonlinear interactions between genetic and environmental factors demonstrates that linear models are inadequate. The notion that genetic and environmental influences on development are strictly additive has given way recently to the recognition that development is shaped by frequent synergistic, non-additive interactions.

It is useful to distinguish two forms of interdependence between genotype and environment – genotype × environment interactions and genotype-environment correlations (Plomin et al. 1977). Genotype × environment interactions are the effects of environmental variation on gene expression, the reason that individuals with homogeneous genotypes respond differently to different environments. Genotype-environment correlations are genetic influences on individual variations in organisms' exposure to kinds of environments – the fact that different genotypes are selectively exposed to different environments. Parents create environments for their children that are influenced by their own heredity. For example, a parent who is a talented athlete may expose her own children to an "athletic environment" that is rich with sports gear and athletic competition. Although the child does not initially participate in creating this environment, he or she may have inherited some portion of the parent's athletic abilities. Hence, there may be a "passive correlation" between the environment and heredity. In addition, the child's behavior (which is influenced by the child's heredity) may evoke a behavioral response from the parent that in turn reinforces the child's behavior. These are known as "evocative correlations" between heredity and environment. Later in life, children can and do actively seek environments that complement their genetic tendencies, a process that has been called "niche picking" (Scarr and McCartney 1983).

What one considers "internal" or "external" depends upon what one takes the unit of analysis to be. Molecular biologists take the perspective that the genome is the appropriate unit of analysis. Relative to the genome, all else (including intra-cellular properties) constitutes the "environment." Even within the cell, many "external" factors regulate gene expression. Nearly every cell in the human body contains an identical copy of the person's DNA, which controls cellular construction and behavior. Yet, different cells are constructed and behave very differently depending on precisely where they are (what part of what tissue), what stage of development the person is at, and what is going on in the environment around the person. This is possible because the expression of protein-coding genes is modulated in response to external factors, during development and in differentiated cells.

It has become evident that causal role supposedly played by the so-called "gene" is not localizable to a stretch of DNA, but is shared by the DNA and a variety of other molecular resources. Because DNA is inert, genes depend on intracellular signals for initiating and terminating activity. Not only *when* the DNA activated but the *way* in which it is expressed depends on the nature of these intracellular signals, which vary across different cells and different phases of development. Some are naturally triggered by mechanisms outside the cell (for example, by hormones), often ultimately by influences outside the organism (for example, through grooming and other nurturing behaviors). A wide variety of normally occurring environmental and behavioral influences on gene activity have been documented in a range of species from nematodes to humans. The known environmental effects are implicated in normal variations, not just abnormalities, and collectively, they are convincing evidence that gene × environment interaction is not only possible but necessary for normal development. The causes of epigenesis are distributed among sequences of DNA, including regulatory sequences distributed throughout the genome, molecular factors extrinsic to the chromosome, their potential distal causes in the extra-cellular environment, and the contingent history of the cell. The sum of these ongoing, stochastic, bidirectional exchanges between external factors at many levels and heredity during the course of development has been called "probabilistic epigenesis" (Gottlieb 2007).

Many levels *above* the level of the organism have also been taken either as units of analysis or as levels of explanation in theories of development and learning. In roughly ascending order, these levels include the mother-child dyad; the home and nuclear family; the neighborhood (playground, friends and neighbors); the childcare, school or workplace; the community (including local services such as healthcare and children's services); the culture (including customs and values); the society (including laws and institutions); the climate; the historical timeframe; the environment; and the geological period.

There are a number of contemporary theories of learning and development that accept the classical assumption that the individual person (or organism) is the appropriate unit of analysis but reject the assumption that the appropriate level of explanation is exclusively sub-personal. On Bronfenbrenner's "bioecological model" (Bronfenbrenner and Morris 2006), for example, "proximal processes" (interactions with the immediate environment) are the "engines of development," and developmental outcomes (including learning) are joint functions of proximal processes, the characteristics of the person (in the relevant case, the learner), the environmental context both narrow and wide, and a time interval.

On a variety of "holistic" or "contextualist" theories of learning and development, the surrounding context is either or both: (a) necessary for understanding learning; or (b) part of the nature of learning and development itself. For example, Vygotsky argued that mind cannot be understood in isolation from society. Indeed, the view that the surrounding context is part of the nature of learning itself is a logical consequence of content externalism, as advocated, for example, by Hilary Putnam (1975). On these views, learning is learning a proposition or a practice (skill), either of which has meaning only in a rich socio-cultural context.

Entities larger than the individual also have lifetimes over which they may learn. The "situated cognition" movement has done productive research based on the assumption that entities such as ships and airplanes also learn (Hutchins 1995). Even if one does not want to go that far, it is common to acknowledge that learning is often distributed among group members, and it is the group that learns, not the individual.

In summary, development and learning usually result from nonlinear stochastic interactions between causes at multiple levels, both higher and lower. In particular, outcomes at the personal or organism level almost always result from a wide variety of sub-personal factors, including hereditary ones, interacting with a particular supra-personal milieu. As a consequence, outcomes are liable to change dramatically if either sub-personal or supra-personal factors change even slightly. The discovery of these facts has driven calls from various quarters for a range of changes to theory and practice. The most radical claim that sub-personal and supra-personal factors are "inseparable" and therefore urge abandoning all distinctions and embracing "postmodernism" wholeheartedly (e.g., Overton 2006). More reasonable proposals typically involve calls for a shift toward the practice of routinely using nonlinear statistical – or "systems" – models in developmental studies. As a result of these considerations, a consensus is converging that multilevel, nonlinear analyses and systems explanations are required in the developmental sciences (see the section, "Dynamic theories," below).

Modes and types of learning

As discussed in the second section, above, philosophers have traditionally emphasized just two modes of learning: explicit propositional or declarative learning ("knowing that"), and implicit practical, or skill learning ("knowing how"). The distinction between *implicit learning* and *explicit learning* has to do with whether the learner has conscious, reflective access to what has been learned. Knowledge that results from implicit learning is *tacit knowledge*, knowledge to which the learner does not have self-conscious access. They have also tended to privilege propositional learning over skill learning. Psychologists, on the other hand, distinguish many dozens of different forms of memory (Roediger et al. 2002), each one of which presumably involves a different kind of learning. Also, psychologists tend, if anything, to privilege implicit learning over explicit learning, as may be seen by the many studies of *priming* in the psychological literature.

The idea that learning is a change in behavior resulting from experience emphasizes the product of learning (the outcome, the change) as opposed to the process by which the product arises, chalked up blithely to "experience." Reliance on this conception of learning leads to a passive view of learning – that it is something that can be done for you or done to you, by a teacher for example. As many teachers know, this "commercial" view of learning (you can just go out and buy learning – it thereby becomes your rightful possession) is widespread among students and their parents. Another way of looking at learning is as a process, or better, an activity, something that a person *does* in order to understand the real world and bring meaning to life, as opposed to something that a person *has*. This view emphasizes the actions that a person takes, and the consequences they have, both internal and external, when learning takes place.

Habituation is a form of learning that results in a decrease of response to a repeated or continued stimulation. Habituation may be measured by looking time (decrease in looking time as a stimulus becomes more familiar), head turn (decrease in head orientation response as a stimulus becomes more familiar) or even heart rate (decrease in transitory heart-rate deceleration upon presentation as a stimulus becomes more familiar). Heart-rate measurements have even been used to measure habituation *in utero*.

Associative learning, broadly defined, is simply the learning of associations between one set of things and another. One of the reasons that associative learning is so popular in psychology is that, in certain forms, it can be described in strictly behavioral terms. Another is that it is consistent with the known neural mechanisms of learning. A third reason is that associative learning seems to be ubiquitous among animals.

Classical (or Pavlovian) conditioning starts with an "unconditioned" (previously associated) stimulus-response pairing, such as food and salivation. If a "conditioned" (not previously associated) stimulus, such as ringing a bell, is regularly paired with the unconditioned stimulus for a sufficient length of time, then the conditioned stimulus will become associated with the unconditioned response. The association (learning) may be demonstrated by presenting the conditioned stimulus alone (without the unconditioned stimulus) and observing that it elicits the same response as the unconditioned stimulus. Operant conditioning (or instrumental learning), by contrast, is concerned with associating new consequences (new postconditions) with preexisting, voluntary behavior in order to modify the frequency of the behavior. Rewards are, by definition, consequences that tend to increase the frequency of a behavior. Punishments are, likewise, consequences that tend to decrease the frequency of a behavior. The association (learning) is demonstrated in the change of frequency of the behavior.

In psychology, the term "statistical learning" may refer to learning based on statistical theory (including both associationism and Bayesian learning) or specifically to associative learning of the statistical relationships among items in experience. Usually, these are stimuli, but other items active in working memory (e.g., concepts retrieved from long-term memory) may also participate in statistical learning. Statistical learning has been demonstrated in nonhuman primates (cotton-top tamarins) and human adults, children and infants for a variety of types of stimuli, from sequential auditory patterns composed of either speech sounds or tones presented in rapid succession to shapes in a visual display (e.g., Saffran et al. 1999). Statistical learning of *nonadjacent* temporal dependencies (for example, among speech sounds generated by an artificial grammar, and among acoustic correlates of English phrases) has also been demonstrated in infants as young as eight months old, and on that basis, it has been hypothesized that statistical learning might play a critical role in acquiring syntax (Newport and Aslin 2004).

There is an important connection between a form of learning known in psychology as "perceptual learning" and the Churchlands' eliminative materialism. Eliminative materialism depends on the "plasticity of mind" because folk psychology can only be eliminated by inter-theoretic reduction if (1) it is a theory; (2) there is a better theory on offer; (3) the better theory on offer is reducible to a lower level theory; and (4) we can live without it. Because folk psychology is such a well-embedded part of our everyday experience, we can only live without it if we can change the way we experience everyday life. We can change the way that we experience everyday life only if the mind is sufficiently plastic that, in virtue of adopting a new theory, we can come to experience, or perceive, things differently. The Churchlands have argued forcefully from thought experiments and historical developments in science that the mind is sufficiently plastic that it is possible for us to come to perceive things differently. Perceptual learning just is the phenomenon of learning that changes the nature of our perceptions, and there is an impressive array of empirical evidence for perceptual learning (Goldstone 1998).

There are many other forms of learning. Clark Glymour, Alison Gopnik and their colleagues (Gopnik et al. 2004) have suggested that human learning of causal relationships (including the relationships between one's own actions and effects in the world) is a form of "Bayesian learning," that is, might be based on a mechanism that is capable of forming representations isomorphic to those formed in the "Bayes net" formalism for causal maps. Developmentalists agree that infants can learn by imitation (for example, to imitate facial expressions), although exactly how early they can do so remains a subject of debate. Humans often seem to learn a lot from a single example, particularly one accompanied by an explanation. This form of learning is often referred to as "learning by example." "Learning by analogy" is learning by using a mapping from one (known) domain to another (initially unknown) domain. "Imprinting" (for example in the way in which ducklings imprint on their mothers) is also often considered a form of learning in the psychological literature.

Methodological challenges

In addition to the general methodological issues in psychology at large (see "Conceptual Problems in Statistics, Testing and Experimentation" [Chapter 14]), there are several issues that are unique to developmental studies. There are many ethical and practical constraints on the study of learning and development, particularly in young human children. Because of these constraints, our knowledge about development and learning in children is on much shakier epistemological ground than is our knowledge about learning in adults, or even (in some respects) in nonhuman animals.

Although introspection is no longer widely used in psychology, self-reports (usually structured to some degree as clinical interviews or questionnaires) continue to be an important source of evidence in developmental science, particularly for older children and adolescents. Diary studies continue to be particularly important in the study of language acquisition, although they raise many important epistemological issues including investigator bias, sampling rate, and information about the context.

Systematic observation has also been widely used to study development and learning. Many developmentalists with a social orientation place particular emphasis on the importance of naturalistic observation. Thus, developmental studies become a kind of ethnography, sometimes to the degree that it is suggested that the only meaningful observations of development can happen when the child is completely unaware of the researcher. This is an interesting case of an argument against the use of experimental methods in science. One issue in any observational study is the choice of sampling strategy – whether to sample by time, or sample by event. It is virtually impossible to sample the child's environment continually, although new technologies are pushing the limits of what it is feasible (see below). The modality of sampling studies has changed with the times, from the handwritten records kept by Darwin and others through audio and video recording, with a transition to digital formats underway. Recordings are usually from the observer's point-of-view or some other ("third-person") point-of-view. Wireless lavaliere microphones are sometimes used to record a child's speech sounds more accurately.

Observational studies of all kinds are fraught with observer bias and observer influence. Both are exacerbated by the fact that the researcher is also the participant's mother or primary caretaker. If not, the caretaker is usually nearby and, naturally, wants to get involved or, intentionally or not, becomes the focus of attention. Because many observational studies also involve later coding or transcription from recorded media, a further opportunity for observer bias arises. This is usually quantified by statistical measures of agreement (e.g., Cohen's *kappa*), which can only measure the degree to which the two codings agree, not tell how much they might both be biased. In an ideal observation study, the data collection (the observations) and any further processing of the data, including coding and transcription, would all be performed by persons naïve to the purpose or hypothesis of the study. Such studies are rare, however.

Two main kinds of correlational studies are also widely used in research on development. One is cohort studies, in which groups that have something in common (for example, being in the same school district) at one point in time are studied longitudinally, and measures taken at later dates are correlated with measures taken at earlier dates. Among these, twin studies, which consist of studies of twins separated at birth, have been particularly important in attempts to untangle innate and environmental influences on development. The second kind of widely used correlational study is the corpus study. Particularly in the study of language acquisition, large corpora of observational data from many researchers have been collected and systematized (MacWhinney 2000). These corpora can then be searched for correlations, for example, between earlier parental behavior and later child behavior.

A wide variety of psychophysiological methods have been used in studies of development. Autonomic indicators such as heart rate, blood pressure, respiration, sucking rate, pupil dilation and electrical conductance of the skin are particularly useful in the youngest infants, because measurements are minimally invasive or disruptive. Indeed, heart rate is commonly used as a dependent measure in studies of *prenatal* development.

Measurements of brain activity are difficult with infants and young children, both because they find the procedures and equipment frightening and because they lack the capacity to voluntarily control their movement. Event-related potential (ERP) studies have been conducted even with neonates. However, the spatial resolution in these studies is generally lower than in adult studies. A state-of-the-art adult ERP system contains 256 electrodes, while those in common use contain 128 electrodes. Those used in infant studies typically contain a dozen or so electrodes, although infants as young as 5 months have been fitted with caps containing 128 electrodes (Reynolds and Richards 2005).

Functional magnetic resonance imaging (fMRI) is particularly challenging, because it requires the participant to remain motionless in a narrow, enclosed space for a long period, despite – among other challenges – an almost deafening roar from the equipment itself. This has limited the use of fMRI in younger children. Although sedation or general anesthesia is sometimes used for medical purposes, they are typically not justified for research and make behavioral experiments difficult or impossible. Researchers have worked around these problems by preparing children in a simulated scanner using a cover story (e.g., "we're going to ride on a spaceship") and behavioral training to reduce body motion (Kotsoni et al. 2006).

When interpreting the results of studies using psychophysiological methods, we must keep in mind that many factors influence physiological responses or their measurements, including hunger, boredom, arousal, fatigue and movement. Interpreting a physiological response requires inference. In particular, the fact that a stimulus produces a temporally or spatiotemporally consistent pattern of brain activation does not tell us how either the brain or the person processes the stimulus.

It is widely acknowledged that causal inferences are strongest when based on experimental studies, that is, on deliberate manipulations applied to individuals selected at random from a population. However, many experimental paradigms that have contributed to our current understanding of development and learning can only be used with animals. In some cases, this is because the manipulations are already ethically questionable when performed on immature nonhuman animals and would be abhorrent if performed on human children. These include a number of procedures that have yielded invaluable scientific information about learning and development. Among them are single-cell recording from awake, behaving animals (which typically requires open-scalp surgery) and a variety of environmental manipulations (including induced genetic abnormalities or complete deprivation of mobility or perceptual experience in one or more modalities until adulthood). In these cases, we must rely on inferences from the animal studies.

There are, of course, many experimental manipulations that can be performed at minimal risk to the well-being of the child. The younger the child is, however, the more difficult it is to design an experimental procedure, because the less ability infants have to communicate their experiences through coordinated movement. Early experimental studies of development, such as Piaget's, often relied on overt behavioral skills that required fine motor coordination (such as controlled reaching and searching). Many more recent procedures depend on measurements of looking time – the amount of time that an infant spends looking at one thing (or in one direction) rather than another. These include habituation and familiarization procedures, the "violation of expectancy" procedure, the "head-turn preference procedure" and the "intermodal preferential looking paradigm."

Habituation or familiarization to a repeated or continued stimulus may be measured by looking time, by head turn, by sucking rate, or even by heart rate. When a significant difference in one of these measures can be demonstrated, it is logical to conclude that the infant can discriminate the habituated stimulus from the novel one. On the other hand, when a significant difference in one of these measures is not demonstrated, it is not logical to conclude that the infant cannot discriminate the stimuli, for all the same reasons that we cannot generally draw conclusions from an experimental failure to find a significant effect. However, that conclusion is often drawn in the literature, and some important findings, such as estimates of infants' visual acuity, depend upon it.

Moreover, looking-time and head-turn measures are often interpreted as a "preference" for the stimulus toward which the eyes (or head) are directed longer or more frequently. Looking-time studies usually show a "preference" for novel stimuli. On the other hand, contingent sucking patterns (e.g., when an infant's sucking pattern determines which of two sounds an infant will hear) have often shown a "preference" for familiar stimuli, that is, a tendency to suck in the pattern that causes the familiar stimulus to continue.

The measurement in the violation of expectancy procedure is looking time. When an effect is found, it is a statistically significant difference between looking times in one condition (the "expectancy" condition) and another (the "violation" condition). In the head-turn preference procedure, an infant's attention to an auditory stimulus is examined by measuring the amount of time the infant's head orients toward the direction of the stimulus. This depends on the fact that infants tend to orient visually (and thus turn their heads) in the direction of a sound source. By being permitted to hear the sound only as long as the head turn is maintained, infants may be trained to maintain the response, increasing the sensitivity of the measure. In the intermodal preferential looking procedure, infants are simultaneously presented with a linguistic (or other auditory) stimulus and two video events, only one of which matches the linguistic stimulus.

In all of these procedures, interpreting a difference in looking time as something else (even as a violation of expectancy, a surprise or a preference, but especially as an indication of an inference, a belief or a theory) requires a sound argument connecting looking time with the language used in its interpretation. It is rare to see such an argument, but it is easy to slip into interpretations of looking-time differences as evidence for rich cognitive structures. Many published papers make such errors. Although a bias toward rich interpretations is enshrined in the very names of many of the procedures, it is very difficult to know whether a head-turn or looking-time measure is an indication of a "preference" for familiarity, a preference for novelty, a violation of expectancy, or any other mental state. Recently, Schöner and Thelen (2006) proposed a dynamic field theory (DFT) model that qualitatively fits many of the looking-time patterns reported in the literature based strictly on perceptual representations, without assuming any higher level cognitive states or processes. The model makes many simplifying assumptions and also leads to a number of empirical predictions that have yet to be tested, but it is suggestive.

Dynamic theories

Related to issues about units of analysis and levels of explanation are issues about the dynamics of learning, including time scales, continuity and stability. Focusing on the personal level, we tend to consider learning changes that occur on time scales from minutes to weeks and developmental changes that occur over the lifetime or within a life period measured in years. When we expand our focus to supra-personal levels, then we tend to consider longer time periods (decades for cultural and community developments, centuries for historical developments, and longer periods for evolutionary, climate and geological developments). Similarly, when we narrow our focus to sub-personal levels, then we tend to consider smaller time scales, from behaviors (head turns, looks) that may be measured in tenths of a second to broad changes in neural activity, which may be measured in 100ths of a second, down to milliseconds (action potentials).

One of the key theoretical issues in the study of development has been whether development is best regarded as a continuous process of quantitative change or whether it consists of discontinuous states that are qualitatively different. The classic stage theories posit sequences of qualitatively different periods in development. However, these theories have always been plagued by findings of vast individual differences. This is another force that has led toward the convergence on dynamical models of development – in a nonlinear system, qualitatively different behavior can arise from incremental, qualitative change.

A related issue is if it is appropriate to "discretize" time and other quantities in the study of development, a question that leads to debates about the nature of explanation and representation, levels of analysis and time scales. Information-processing theories of development and learning, including connectionist models, implicitly assume that there is no harm in considering only discrete intervals of time and other quantities (such as synaptic weighting and activation in connectionist models). Dynamical theories instead assume that time and other quantities are continuous, in the sense that an infinitesimally small difference in the state of the system could make a difference to its future behavior. This view receives some support from neuroscience, in that (continuous) spike-timing models of the neuron have been shown to be empirically more adequate than (discrete) firing-rate models, including in learning (spike-timing-dependent synaptic plasticity; Roberts and Bell 2002). However, it seems unlikely to make a difference in practice, given that digital computers built on top of analog circuits are used to model both discrete and continuous models of development and learning.

Another issue is whether developmental systems are inherently stable or dynamic. Information-processing models, including connectionism, take the natural state of the system to be "at rest." Input to the system is not destabilizing, but merely brings it directly to another stable state; nor is the lack of input destabilizing, but merely allows the system to continue in the current state. By contrast, dynamical models take the natural state of the system to be continuous change. Any apparent stability is hard won and precarious. Input to the system destabilizes it, and settling into a new equilibrium is an achievement. Information processing theorists generally interpret their models as abstractions of critical processes that are embedded in real organisms. They do not model the dynamics because they do not see the necessity of doing so for explaining the phenomena of interest. Detailed dynamical models of developmental phenomena (such as those built in the DFT framework), by contrast, model the dynamics themselves because the theorists who use them believe that they are relevant to the phenomena of interest. This may be part of the reason that DFT models have primarily been used for modeling motor behavior (such as reaching and perseveration) rather than for modeling higher level cognitive processes (such as decision-making and learning).

Embodiment

Does the body play a necessary role in learning, or merely an accidental one? The fact that there are so many formal theories of learning suggests that embodiment is not necessary in principle. However, abstract theories of learning may be parasitic on actual human learning. Indeed, the argument is well-known in philosophy that meaning depends on supra-personal states of affairs (Putnam 1975). It follows that learning the meaning of anything depends on those same states of affairs. One might argue that the sociocultural aspects of meaning depend on the capacity to participate in a society or culture, which in turn requires embodiment. If that were true, then learning the meaning of anything would require embodiment. It is not clear why that would have to be true, however. Certainly, there are many disembodied societies, including those involved in "massively multiplayer" online role-playing games and those involved in the bargaining negotiations conducted by software agents, although these may also be parasitic on real societies.

Even if embodiment is not necessary for learning in general, it may still be critical for actual human learning, in that learning mechanisms may be specialized for operating "within" a body. In a certain sense, that is trivially true, because the mechanisms that mediate learning among animals include nervous systems, which are parts of bodies. It may also be true in the more interesting sense that the neural mechanisms that mediate learning in different organisms may be specialized to the kinds of bodies they have. This is again true in a trivial sense – a nervous system is (directly) connected to sensory receptors and motor effectors in the body that it controls, not in any other body. But this latter trivial sense of embodiment also entails a deeper one – the modifications to the nervous system that comprise learning in any organism are specific to the environmental inputs and behavioral outputs that body is capable of receiving and performing. We know that we can adapt to changes to our bodies, including changes that happen during development, paralysis and the loss of limbs, as well as virtual reality environments and such things as remote piloting (Clark 2003). This may suggest that learning is disembodied – that what body you have doesn't make all that much of a difference – but it also suggests that the opportunities we have for learning are determined by the kinds of bodies we have, biological or otherwise.

The debate about embodiment has pragmatic implications. Distance learning, computer-based training, and "open education" in general depend upon the possibility of disembodied learning. The more effective forms tend to reduce the perceived distance between the learner's body and the educator's. This can happen by bringing the educator's body to the learner (for example, through multi-modal multimedia), by bringing the learner's body to the educator (for example, by providing the means for the learner to "raise his hand" and ask a question virtually), by turning the computer into the educator (for example, through interactive learning sessions that involve pressing keys or typing), or by turning the learner into the educator (for example, by motivating the learner to educate his or her self by finding meaning in what he or she learns). The most effective practices generally combine all four methods.

Looking forward

Because development and learning involve so many different phenomena, at different levels of explanation and different physical and temporal scales, with reciprocal influences within and between levels, interdisciplinary research is essential and is becoming more and more common. Both philosophical and psychological studies of development and learning suffer from an excessive reliance on research involving participants sampled from a small, culturally and socioeconomically homogenous, portion of the world's population. Broadening the pool of research participants to include a representative cross sample of the diverse world population is a major challenge that psychologists have only begun to tackle.

Cognitive developmental neuroscience (Nelson et al. 2006) is an emerging sub-discipline that uses primarily physiological methods to study cognitive development from before birth through adulthood. This field will continue to push the spatial and temporal limits of what we know about development and learning.

Adequately modeling nonlinear relationships, particularly among nested levels with reciprocal causation, requires sophisticated statistical techniques. To some extent, the techniques have already been developed (Goldstein 2003). However, many statistical software packages do not provide easy means of using the full range of hierarchical nonlinear models. Partially as a consequence of the limited availability of appropriate tools (but also partly as a consequence of limitations of training or habit), researchers tend to use linear models even in circumstances where they are clearly not appropriate. Researchers need to learn and teach their students the principles of multilevel nonlinear modeling, demand that providers of statistical software make them easy to use, and incorporate this knowledge and practice into the writing and review of research papers.

New technology is also enabling new forms of research. The recent widespread availability of high-quality digital audio- and video-recorders has vastly increased the amount of and dramatically changed the character of observational data that can be collected. Methods have been developed to perform relatively accurate eye-tracking, even with young infants (Aslin and McMurray 2004). A technique has recently been developed to mount a miniature video camera on a young child's head, providing a first-person point of view. And a study is underway at MIT (Roy et al. 2006) in which every room of a young child's home is video- and audio-recorded 16 hours a day!

References

Aslin, R. N., and McMurray, B. (2004) "Automated Corneal-Reflection Eye Tracking in Infancy: Methodological Developments and Applications to Cognition," *Infancy* 6: 155–63.

Augustine (1955 [397]) *Confessions*, Philadelphia: Westminster Press.

Baldwin, J. M. (1906 [1895]) *Mental Development in the Child and in the Race*, New York: Macmillan.

Bandura, A. (1986) *Social Foundations of Thought and Action*, Englewood Cliffs, NJ: Prentice-Hall.

Bowlby, J. (1982 [1969]) *Attachment and Loss*, vol. 1: *Attachment*, New York: Basic Books.

Bronfenbrenner, U., and Morris, P. A. (2006) "The Bioecological Model of Human Development," in R. M. Lerner (ed.), *Handbook of Child Psychology*, 6th edn, Hoboken, NJ: Wiley, pp. 793–828.

Case, R. (1992) *The Mind's Staircase*, Hillsdale, NJ: Erlbaum.

Clark, A. (2003) *Natural-Born Cyborgs*, Oxford: Oxford University Press.

Darwin, C. (1877) "A Biographical Sketch of an Infant," *Mind* 2: 285–94.

Dreyfus, H. L., and Dreyfus, S. E. (1986) *Mind over Machine*, New York: Free Press.

Estes, W. K. (1950) "Toward a Statistical Theory of Learning," *Psychological Review* 57: 94–107.

Fodor, J. A. (1980) "Methodological Solipsism Considered as a Research Strategy in Cognitive Psychology," *Behavioral and Brain Sciences* 3: 63–109.

Freud, S. (1949 [1905]) *Three Essays on the Theory of Sexuality*, London: Imago.

Gesell, A. (1925) *The Mental Growth of the Preschool Child*, New York: Macmillan.

Gold, E. M. (1967) "Language Identification in the Limit," *Information and Control* 10: 447–74.

Goldstein, H. (2003) *Multilevel Statistical Methods*, London: Hodder Arnold.

Goldstone, R. L. (1998) "Perceptual Learning," *Annual Review of Psychology* 49: 585–612.

Gopnik, A., Glymour, C., Sobel, D. M., Schulz, L. E., Kushnir, T., and Danks, D. (2004) "A Theory of Causal Learning in Children: Causal Maps and Bayes Nets," *Psychological Review* 111: 3–32.

Gottlieb, G. (2007) "Probabilistic Epigenesis," *Developmental Science* 10: 1–11.

Hall, G. S. (1904) *Adolescence*, New York: Appleton.

Hamlyn, D. W. (1995) "Learning," in T. Honderich (ed.), *The Oxford Companion to Philosophy*, New York: Oxford University Press, 496.

Hebb, D. O. (1949) *The Organization of Behavior: A Neuropsychological Theory*, New York: Wiley.

Hutchins, E. (1995) *Cognition in the Wild*, Cambridge, MA: MIT Press.

Kim, J. (1982) "Psychophysical Supervenience," *Philosophical Studies* 41: 51–70.

Kotsoni, E., Byrd, D., and Casey, B. J. (2006) "Special Considerations for Functional Magnetic Resonance Imaging of Pediatric Populations," *Journal of Magnetic Resonance Imaging* 23: 877–86.

Lerner, R. M. (ed.) (2006) *Handbook of Child Psychology*, vol. 1: *Theoretical Models of Human Development*, Hoboken, NJ: John Wiley & Sons.

Lewis, M., Goldberg, S., and Cambell, H. (1969) "A Developmental Study of Information Processing within the First Three Years of Life: Response Decrement to a Redundant Signal," *Monographs of the Society for Research in Child Development* 34, no. 9: 1–41.

MacWhinney, B. (2000) *The CHILDES Project: Tools for Analyzing Talk*, Mahwah, NJ: Erlbaum.

MacWhinney, B., Leinbach, J., Taraban, R. M., and McDonald, J. L. (1989) "Language Learning: Cues or Rules?" *Journal of Memory and Language* 28: 255–77.

Malenka, R. C., and Bear, M. F. (2004) "LTP and LTD: An Embarrassment of Riches," *Neuron* 44: 5–21.

Mitchell, T. M. (1997) *Machine Learning*, New York: McGraw-Hill.

Nelson, C. A., De Haan, M., and Thomas, K. M. (2006) *Neuroscience of Cognitive Development*, Hoboken, NJ: Wiley.

Newport, E. L., and Aslin, R. N. (2004) "Learning at a Distance," pt 1: "Statistical Learning of Non-Adjacent Dependencies," *Cognitive Psychology* 48: 127–62.

Overton, W. F. (2006) "Developmental Psychology: Philosophy, Concepts, Methodology," in R. M. Lerner (ed.), *Handbook of Child Psychology*, 6th edn, Hoboken, NJ: Wiley, 18–88.

Pavlov, I. P. (1927) *Conditioned Reflexes*, London: Oxford University Press.

Piaget, J. (1999 [1954]) *The Construction of Reality in the Child*, London: Routledge.

Plomin, R. (1986) *Development, Genetics, and Psychology*, Hillsdale, NJ: Erlbaum.

Plomin, R., Defries, J. C., and Loehlin, J. C. (1977) "Genotype-Environment Interaction and Correlation in the Analysis of Human Behavior," *Psychological Bulletin* 84: 309–22.

Putnam, H. (1975) "The Meaning of 'Meaning'," in K. Gunderson (ed.), *Language, Mind, and Knowledge*, Minnesota Studies in Philosophy of Science, vol. 7. Minneapolis: University of Minnesota Press, pp. 131–93.

Reynolds, G. D., and Richards, J. E. (2005) "Familiarization, Attention and Recognition Memory in Infancy: An Event-Related Potential and Cortical Source Localization Study," *Developmental Psychology* 41: 598–615.

Roberts, P. D., and Bell, C. C. (2002) "Spike-Timing Dependent Synaptic Plasticity in Biological Systems," *Biological Cybernetics* 87: 392–403.

Roediger, H. L., Marsh, E. J., and Lee, S. C. (2002) "Kinds of Memory," in H. Pashler and D. Medin (eds), *Steven's Handbook of Experimental Psychology*, 3rd edn, Hoboken, NJ: Wiley, pp. 1–41.

Rogoff, B. (2003) *The Cultural Nature of Human Development*, New York: Oxford University Press.

Roy, D., Patel, R., Decamp, P., Kubat, R., Fleischman, M., Roy, B., Mavridis, N., Tellex, S., Salata, A., Gunness, J., Levit, M., and Gorniak, P. (2006) "The Human Speechome Project," in R. Sun and N. Miyake (eds), *Proceedings of the Twenty-Eighth Annual Meeting of the Cognitive Science Society*, Mahwah, NJ: Erlbaum, pp. 192–6.

Russell, S., and Norvig, P. (2003) *Artificial Intelligence: A Modern Approach*, Englewood Cliffs, NJ: Prentice Hall.

Ryle, G. (1949) *The Concept of Mind*, New York: Barnes & Noble.

Saffran, J. R., Johnson, E. K., Aslin, R. N., and Newport, E. L. (1999) "Statistical Learning of Tone Sequences by Human Infants and Adults," *Cognition*, 70: 27–52.

Scarr, S., and McCartney, K. (1983) "How People Make Their Own Environments: A Theory of Genotype→Environment Effects," *Child Development* 54: 424–35.

Schöner, G., and Thelen, E. (2006) "Using Dynamic Field Theory to Rethink Infant Habituation," *Psychological Review* 113: 273–99.

Skinner, B. F. (1935) "Two Types of Conditioned Reflex and a Pseudo-Type," *Journal of General Psychology* 12: 66–77.

Thelen, E., and Smith, L. B. (1994) *A Dynamic Systems Approach to the Development of Cognition and Action*, Cambridge, MA: MIT Press.
Valiant, L. G. (1984) "A Theory of the Learnable," *Communications of the* ACM 27: 1134–42.
Vapnik, V. N. (1999) *The Nature of Statistical Learning Theory*, New York: Springer.
Vygotsky, L. S. (1986 [1934]) *Thought and Language*, Cambridge, MA: MIT Press.

31
UNDERSTANDING EMBODIED COGNITION THROUGH DYNAMICAL SYSTEMS THINKING

Gregor Schöner and Hendrik Reimann

Introduction

If we ask ourselves, what sets the human species apart in the animal kingdom, a variety of answers come to mind. The capacity to make skilful manipulatory movements – to direct action at objects, handle objects, assemble and reshape objects – is one of the possible answers. We are amazing movers, very good at dynamic actions as well, catching and throwing objects, anticipating requirements for upcoming movements. Some other species perform amazing specialized stunts, but none is as versatile and flexible as we are. Through our manipulatory skill we relate to the world in a highly differentiated way, transform some objects into tools, which we bind into our body scheme to bring about change in another object. "Homo Faber" is a very appropriate characterization of the human mind.

Examine a simple, daily-life example: Your toaster has stopped ejecting the slices of toast once done. In the hope of a cheap solution, you try to repair this defect by opening the toaster and searching for a dislocated spring. This will mean concretely that you will take the toaster toward a convenient workplace, the bench of your workshop if you are ambitious about such things. You will explore the toaster visually, turning it around while observing it to identify screws to undo, setting the toaster down, finding an appropriate screwdriver, loosening the screws, setting the toaster upright again, and carefully lifting up its cover. Some further examination leads you to, in fact, find a loose spring (your lucky day), which you attach back to the obvious hook on to which it fits. You refit the cover and find, insert, and turn each screw in succession. You carry the toaster back to the kitchen and test it out on an old piece of toast, and happily announce to all members of the household your heroic deed.

Now this action involves a lot of cognition. First, there is an indefinable amount of background knowledge (Searle 1983) that is used in multiple ways and at different levels during the repair. Knowing that a repair involves opening a device by taking off its cover and that screws need to be undone to that end are examples of high-level knowledge. Knowing what springs look like and that removing a screw means turning the screwdriver in counter-clockwise direction are examples of a lower level of knowledge, meaning knowledge more closely linked to the sensory or motor surfaces. Some of the background knowledge may have the discrete, categorical form of whether to turn a screwdriver to the left or to the right. Other background knowledge is more graded and fuzzy in nature, such as how much force to apply to a plastic vs. to a metallic part.

Visual cognition is required to detect the screws against the background and to categorize the screws so as to select the appropriate type of screwdriver. During active visual exploration, we may memorize where the screws are located, together with the pose and viewing angle of the toaster required to return to each screw, to work on it in the unscrewing phase.

At a more global level, we need to retain stably in our mind that we are trying to repair the toaster as we go about all these detailed actions and explorations. That overall goal was selected in light of predictions about its duration (e.g., short enough to make it to the cinema 30 minutes later), the worthiness of this project compared with alternatives, and the probability of success.

The whole project of repairing the toaster takes place in a concrete setting, which provides surfaces to work on, visual structure that helps orient, and mechanical structure that facilitates motor control by providing force feedback and stabilization through friction. Performing the action while situated in a structured and familiar environment alleviates some of the cognitive load of the task. For instance, working memory is less taxed, because the visual context provides cues to the screws' locations, or even just because they may always be found again by our re-exploring.

In addition to this sensory interaction, the task situation is central to the generation of movements as well. Sensorimotor coordination is required when turning the toaster around for one to be able to examine it from different angles and later to hold the toaster while attempting to loosen the screws. This entails generating just the right amount of torque so that the frictional force is overcome but slipping is avoided. That torque must continuously and rapidly be adjusted as the screw starts to turn and static friction is replaced by dynamic friction.

As we move ahead with the task, we need to smoothly switch from one motor state to another. For instance, while unscrewing a screw, we fixate the toaster with one hand and control the screwdriver with the other. Then we must release the toaster from fixation and move both hands into a coordinated grasp of the whole object as we reposition it, probably performing at the same time some finger acrobatics to hold on to the screwdriver.

This simple process of repairing a toaster clearly shows how a cognitive system can benefit from having a body and being in a specific situation. Compare the ease of performing this situated action with the much more challenging variant in which an engineer provides a robot with a sequence of detailed commands to achieve the same end.

But how central are the notions of embodiment and situatedness to understanding how cognitive tasks are achieved? Traditionally, it has been thought that the core of cognition forms around such things as language, thought, reasoning, or knowledge and is detached from the motor and sensory surfaces. This has given rise to the theoretical framework of information processing in which cognition is the manipulation of symbolic information. Instances of symbols represent states of affairs relatively independently of how these states were detected sensorially or how they are acted on by the motor system.

The stance of embodied and situated cognition (see other chapters in this book) postulates the opposite: All cognition is fundamentally embodied, that is, closely linked to the motor and sensory surfaces, strongly dependent on experience, on context, and on being immersed in rich and structured environments. Although there are moments when cognitive processes are decoupled from sensory and motor processes, the embodied stance emphasizes that whenever sensory information is available and while motoric action is going on, cognitive processes are maintaining continuous couplings to associated sensory and motor processes.

Arguments in favour of such an embodied and situated stance can take many forms (Thelen 1995; Thelen, Schöner et al. 2001; Riegler 2002). The line of thought that shall be described in the following is, in a half formal way, called dynamical systems thinking (DST). It focuses on the concepts of the stability of behavioural states, the spatiotemporal continuity of processes, and their capacity to update online at any time during processing (Erlhagen and Schöner 2002).

While symbolic information processing is about computing, receiving some form of input, and generating some form of output in response, DST is fundamentally about coupling and decoupling. Cognitive processes are tailored to the structure of the environment, so that they form stable relationships with sensed aspects of the environment or with motor systems. As a corollary, cognitive processes are not designed to deal with arbitrary inputs.

Both the embodied and situated stances and the theoretical framework of DST resonate with the renewed interest in understanding cognition and behaviour on a more explicitly neuronal basis. For a long time, a proposal made explicit by Marr (1982) had been the shared assumption across a broad range of sub-disciplines concerned with human cognition. The assumption was that we may study human perception, cognition, and motor planning at various levels of abstraction. The most abstract, purely computational level characterizes the nature of the problem solved by the nervous system. The second, algorithmic level consists of specific forms in which such abstract computations can be structured. Finally, the third level of neuronal implementation deals with how specific neuronal mechanisms may effectively implement algorithms. Although there are logical links between these levels, the research taking place at the different levels of description can, to some extent, be pursued independently of the other levels. In this conception, for instance, properties of the neuronal substrate are not relevant to the computational and algorithmic levels.

In contrast, the embodied stance emphasizes that the principles of neuronal function must be taken into account as fundamental constraints whenever models of neuronal function, of behaviour and cognition, are constructed. This does not mean that all models need to be neuronally detailed and realistic. Certain basic principles of neuronal function must not be violated, however. Among these are the continuous nature of neuronal processing, the potential to be continuously linked to sensory and motor surfaces, the notion that neurons are activated or deactivated, but do not transmit other specific messages (other than their activational state), and others, as we shall see below.

Being mindful of these properties has concrete implications for the kinds of theoretical frameworks that are compatible with the embodied stance. In particular, stability, continuous time, and graded states are necessary elements of any theoretical account of nervous function.

Finally, learning and development are sources of conceptual constraints for the embodied stance. At least since Piaget (1952), the sensorimotor basis of developmental processes has been in the foreground of developmental thinking. That development is largely learning and that cognition emerges from experience, building on sensorimotor skills, is not universally accepted. The embodied stance embraces this position and provides forceful arguments in its favour (Blumberg 2005). More generally, the openness to learning and adaptation is an important constraint for any theoretical framework that is compatible with neuronal principles. This requires, for instance, a substrate for cognition in which graded changes can occur, which is capable of keeping track of the slower time scale on which learning occurs, and which has sufficiently rich structure to enable the emergence of entirely new functions or the differentiation of skills and behaviours.

Dynamicism

Dynamicism or DST is a theoretical framework and language which enables understanding embodied and situated cognition. As a theoretical language DST makes it possible to talk about the continuous temporal evolution of processes, their mutual or unidirectional coupling and decoupling, and their coupling to sensory or motor processes. At the same time, DST provides an account for how discrete temporal events may emerge from such underlying temporal continuity (through instabilities). Relatedly, DST contains language elements to talk about graded states, but also to address the emergence of discrete categories (Figure 31.1).

The mathematical basis of DST is the mathematical theory of dynamical systems (Braun 1993; Perko 1991). That theory provides the language for much of what is quantitative in the sciences, for physics, chemical reaction kinetics, engineering, ecology, and much more. The mathematical concepts on which DST is based are much more specific, however, than this embedding in mathematical theory suggests. This section will introduce these main concepts now and provide the link to behaviour primarily by reference to sensory and motor processes and only the most modest forms of cognition.

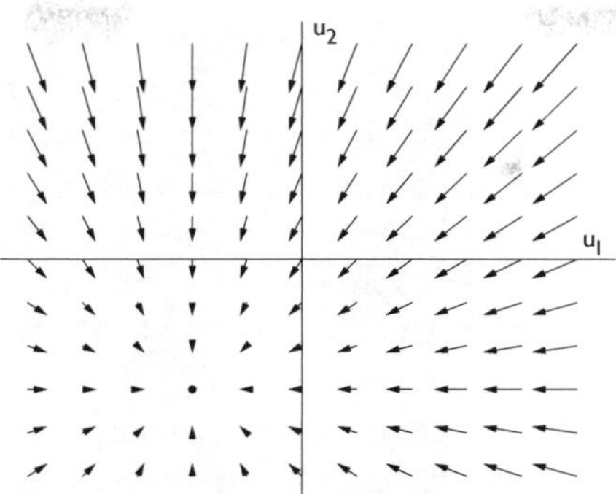

Figure 31.1 A two-dimensional vector field illustrating the rate of change of two activation variables u_1 and u_2 of a neural dynamics. For each value (u_1, u_2) of the state, the arrow indicates the direction and magnitude of the change the state variables will undergo in the immediate future. The dot in the lower left indicates a fixed-point attractor.

State spaces and rates of change

The central idea behind the mathematics of dynamical systems is that the temporal evolution of state variables is governed by a field of forces, the vector field, which specifies for every possible state of the system the direction and rate of change in the immediate future. Such a vector field is illustrated in Figure 31.1 for a system characterized by two variables, u_1 and u_2, which describe the state of the system.

To make things concrete, think of these variables as describing the level of activation of two neurons (or, more realistically, of two neuronal populations). Negative levels of activation indicate that the neurons are disengaged, unable to transmit information about their state on to other neurons. Positive levels of activation reflect an activated state, in which the neurons are capable of affecting neurons downstream in the nervous system (by emitting spikes which are transported along axons, but that mechanism will not be discussed here).

The vector field is a mapping in which each state of the variables is associated with the rate of change of the variables. These rates of change form vectors that can be visualized as arrows attached to each point in state space, as illustrated in Figure 31.1. In formal mathematical terms, then, a dynamical system is this mapping from a state space to the associated space of rates of change $u \rightarrow \frac{du}{dt} = f(u)$. For any vector u, here $u = (u_1, u_2)$, the mapping $f(u)$ is the vector field of forces acting upon the variable u in (that) specific state. The notation $\frac{du}{dt}$ indicates the temporal derivative of the activation variables, $\frac{du}{dt} = \left(\frac{du_1}{dt}, \frac{du_2}{dt}\right)$, so that the vector field and the state space have the same dimensionality.

Solutions of a dynamical system are time courses of the state variables, $u(t)$, that start from an initial state $u(0)$, where t indicates time. How the system evolves from any initial state is dictated by the forces acting upon the variables at each point in time, as indicated by the vector field. Starting from $u(0)$, the system evolves along a path determined by the vector field in a way that at each point in time, the path is tangent to the rate of change $f(u)$. The system state runs along these solution paths with a velocity that is set by the length of the arrows.

In Figure 31.1, all vectors point towards a point in the lower left quadrant of the space, marked by a small dot, at which the vector field converges and around which the length of the vectors becomes infinitesimally small. Once activation levels have reached this point, their rate of change is approximately zero, so the system will stay at those activation levels. This point in the state space is thus called a fixed point. Because the fixed point is automatically reached from anywhere around it, it is called an attractor.

Neural dynamics

Neuronal dynamics with attractors make it possible to understand how neural networks may be linked to sensory input. The attractor illustrated in Figure 31.1 lies in the lower left quadrant of the space of two activation variables: both neurons are at a low level of activation, not engaged in transmitting spikes to other neurons. This can be thought of as the resting state of the two neurons. An activating sensory input to both neurons can be thought of as an influence on the neurons that drives up their levels of activation.

In formal terms, this is written as $\left(\frac{du}{dt}\right) = f(u) + \text{in}(t)>$, where in$(t)$ is a time-varying input function that does not depend upon the state of u. Figure 31.2 illustrates the case in which only neuron 1 receives input (only the first component of the input vector is different from zero). This leads to an additional contribution to the vector field that points everywhere to the right. The resultant vector field, shown in Figure 31.3, is still convergent, but the attractor is shifted to the right, to positive levels, where the neuron u_1 has been activated, while u_2 remains at resting level.

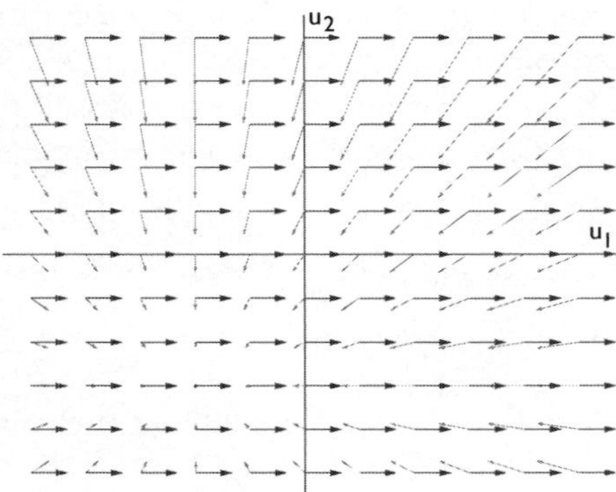

Figure 31.2 To the vector field of Figure 31.1 (redrawn here with thin arrows) is added an ensemble of vectors pointing to the right and representing constant input to u_1.

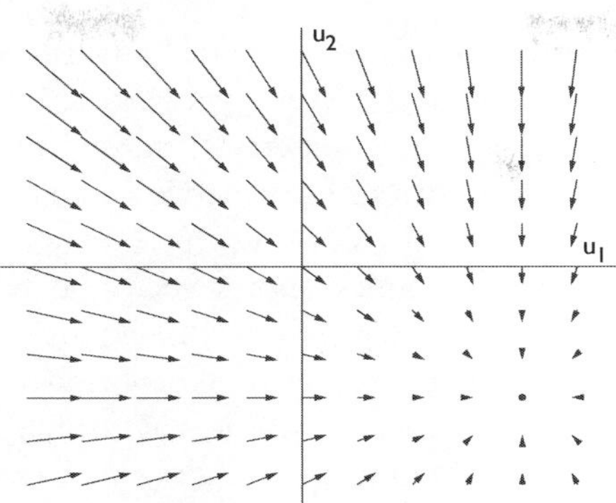

Figure 31.3 The sum of the two contributions to the vector field displayed in Figures 31.1 and 31.2 leads to the convergent vector field shown here. The attractor has been shifted to the right along the u_1 axis.

If the input is added when the system is in the previous attractor seen in Figure 31.1, with both neurons at resting level, the change of the system dynamics is followed by a change in the state variables. The rate of change at the previous fixed point is not zero anymore, but points to the right, towards the new fixed point. The system leaves the previously stable state, moving along a path dictated by the changed vector field, until it reaches the new fixed point attractor.

This illustrates the defining property of attractor states: attractors are (asymptotically) stable states, with the system dynamics working against all influences that may cause the state variables to deviate from the attractor, driving it back to the fixed point. In this instance, the recent history of activation is such an influence. If the added input in this example is removed after only a short period, it effectively becomes a transient perturbation. The system will return to the resting state, the original attractor in the lower-left quadrant. As neurons in the nervous system are richly connected, there are many potential sources for such transient perturbations. Any given neuronal state will persist long enough to have an effect on other neurons only if it is stabilized against the majority of such perturbative inputs.

A central concept of DST is that the dynamical systems which nervous systems form, together with their coupling to the sensory and motor systems, are best characterized by their attractor states. Dynamical systems with convergent vector fields that may form attractors represent a special class of dynamical systems, sometimes referred to as "dissipative" systems (Haken 1983). DST is thus postulating that the neuronal networks and their links to sensory and motor systems are all within this specific class of dynamical systems, so that the functional states of the nervous system may be attractor states. DST thus makes a much more specific proposal than merely saying that nervous systems can be modelled by differential equations.

What exactly is the neuronal basis of this postulate of DST? The first ingredient is the recognition that neurons are dissipative dynamical systems at the microscopic level, the biophysics of the neuronal membrane and the single cell. This has been known for a long time and is captured in a rich literature (Hoppensteadt and Izhikevich 1997; Wilson 1999; Deco and Schürmann 2000; Trappenberg 2002). The example of Figures 31.1 to 31.3 illustrates then how this property of individual neurons is bootstrapped up to the macroscopic level of entire neural networks and their linkages to sensory and motor systems (see Hock et al. 2003). If a base contribution, $f(u)$, generates a convergent vector field, then the more complex vector fields that are built by adding constant (or bounded) contributions also form convergent vector fields.

Thus, attractor states of neuronal networks take their origins in biophysical mechanisms, which are being propagated all the way to the macrostates that become behaviourally relevant. This does not mean that the entire nervous system is always in an attractor. As illustrated in Figures 31.1 to 31.3, transient sensory stimulation may quickly shift attractors around and the system may forever be chasing behind these moving attractors. The functional structure of macroscopic neural states is captured, however, by the layout of attractors and their dependence on sensory stimulation. In light of the strong interconnectedness of the central nervous system, only stable states will lead to robust function that resists change along the many directions along which other parts of the nervous system may pull at any time.

Stability works all the way through to the motor system. The muscle-joint system, for instance, the agent of elementary motor action, is characterized by an attractor dynamics that leads to a stable, mechanical state of the effector. There are contributions to this stable state from the passive elastic and viscous properties of muscles. Neuronal circuits support these properties and endow the system with flexibility so that it may shift the resulting attractor state (Latash 1993). Joint movement comes about by such a neuronally effected shift of the attractor of the muscle-joint system which then engages muscular activation through reflex loops.

Stability also provides an account for how organisms may couple their motor behaviour to sensory input derived from the world and thus, given the appropriate properties of the world, lock on to objects in their surroundings. A well-studied example at a very basic level is the tracking behaviour of the housefly (Reichardt and Poggio 1976). Flies are capable of locking their flight motor on to a visual object, simply a speck moving over their facet eye. They do this using basic motion detection circuitry and directly coupling the direction of detected motion into their motor system. The viscosity of the air helps stabilize the resultant tracking behaviour, which looks truly impressive when a male fly pursues a female one across complex evasive manoeuvres (the purpose is easily guessed).

This establishes the link to Cybernetics, a historical predecessor of DST. Cybernetics provided accounts for how organisms may couple motor systems to sensory input to bring about stable behavioural states. While very successful on its chosen terms, cybernetic thinking never really moved beyond the understanding of a single-purpose function, in which one particular perception-action linkage is at work. Stably linking, say, the flight motor output to the direction in which motion is sensed may lead to excellent pursuit behaviour. But how may the fly break out of it? And if it is able to break out of it, how does it initiate such a state, how does it select among other behaviours? How does it control which things to do in which circumstances?

Behavioural flexibility

How does DST overcome the well-known limitations of cybernetics? The kind of behavioural flexibility described requires that a state may be released from stability, the coupling may be broken, one behavioural pattern may become unstable while another pattern is stabilized. In other words, flexibility requires instability (Schöner and Kelso 1988).

To illustrate this idea we use the two dimensional dynamical system of (u_1, u_2) described above to model how a fly may track moving objects. The neurons could be linked to sensory input such as to respond to the visual motion of moving objects. One neuron would be tuned to become activated when a horizontally moving object is seen, the other when a vertically moving object is seen (in addition, the area in the visual array from which the neurons receive input may be limited to a receptive field, but we'll gloss over that for now).

Typically, only one moving object would be seen and its direction of motion would be registered by the appropriate neuron, which would be coupled appropriately to the wing motors, steering the fly into the appropriate direction to track the object. But now imagine that there were actually two flies in the scene, one moving upward, the other moving horizontally, both initially in the same region of the visual array. Both neurons would receive input. If they were both becoming activated, then the wing motors would receive both a command to track toward the right and upwards, leading to a flight manoeuvre into an oblique upward-rightward direction and missing both targets.

Instead of allowing both neurons to respond to their respective inputs, the fly's nervous system needs the neurons to make a selection decision, in which one neuron is activated so that only one type of motor command is sent to the wings. The other neuron, although it receives input, must be suppressed. This operation goes beyond a mere transformation of the pattern of sensory inputs (two motion signals in this case), requiring an active process of decision-making instead. The selection decision may depend on both the input and the current state of the neuronal dynamics itself. If the two neurons have previously settled on one particular motion direction, disregarding the other, that decision must be stabilized to prevent useless changes of strategy back and forth between the two possible choices.

The dependence of the rate of change of one state variable upon the value of another state variable is called coupling. For two neurons, such coupling may be brought about by direct synaptic connections between the neurons or, indirectly, by connections through one or multiple interneurons. A minimal solution is a inhibitory connection between the two neurons, u_1 and u_2. A contribution to the vector-field implementing such inhibitory coupling is illustrated in Figure 31.4. Only when a neuron is sufficiently activated does it contribute to neuronal coupling. This reflects that nature of synaptic transmission in which only sufficiently activated neurons emit spikes and affect the neurons with which they have synaptic connections. This dependence of neural coupling on the level of activation of a neuron is captured by a nonlinear, sigmoidal function. In Figure 31.4, for instance, inhibition of neuron u_1 by neuron u_2 is represented by vectors pointing into the negative direction along the u_1 axis, indicating negative rates of change of u_1. These vectors are present only, where

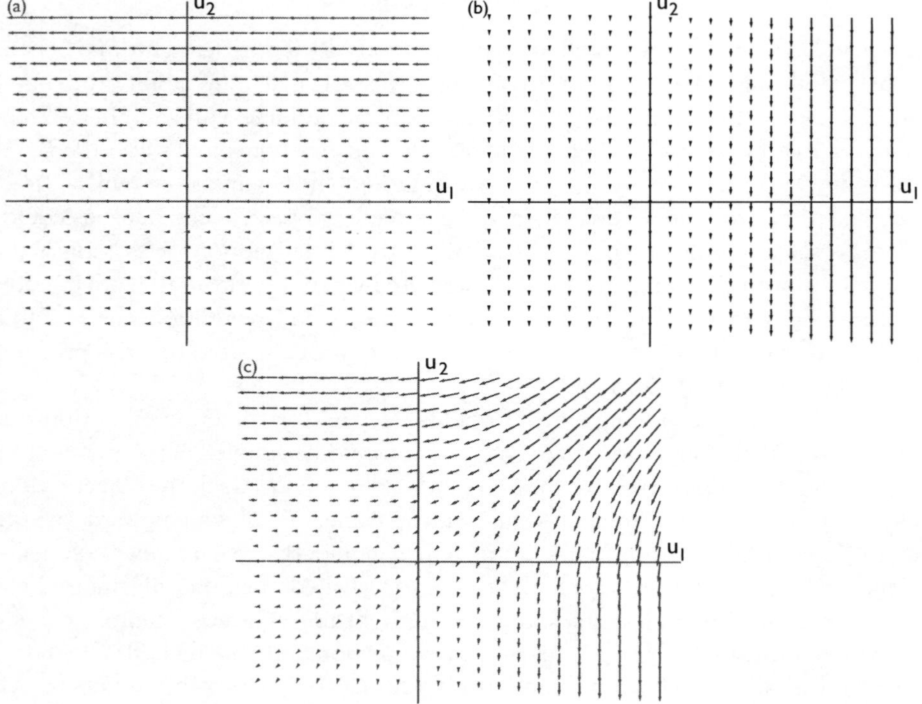

Figure 31.4 Contributions to the vector field that represent inhibitory coupling between two neurons, u_1 and u_2. (a) Neuron u_2 inhibits neuron u_1 through a negative contribution to the rate of change of neuron u_1 (arrows pointing left). This contribution is only present while u_2 is sufficiently activated (top). (b) The analogous contribution for how neuron u_1 inhibits neuron u_2. (c) Both contributions added up.

neuron u_2 has positive levels of activation (in the upper half of the plane). The length of these vectors reflects the sigmoid function. When the two inhibitory contributions in the two directions are overlaid, the vectors point away from the quadrant in which both neurons would be activated, promoting a splitting of the vector field into branches favouring either u_1 or u_2.

The effect of coupling can be examined by adding the inhibitory coupling contribution of Figure 31.4 to the convergent vector field representing the input-driven dynamics of Figure 31.3. As shown in Figure 31.5, this leads again to a convergent vector field. For weak inputs, this vector field has a single attractor, pushed towards weaker levels of activation by inhibitory coupling. For sufficiently strong inputs, this leads to two attractors. In one, neuron u_1 has positive activation, while neuron u_2 is suppressed to negative levels of activation in which it can transmit activation. In the other, the opposite is true. If input is gradually increased, the single attractor at symmetrical activation levels of both neurons becomes unstable, splitting in a bifurcation into two new asymmetrical attractors. In a variety of neuronal and behavioural

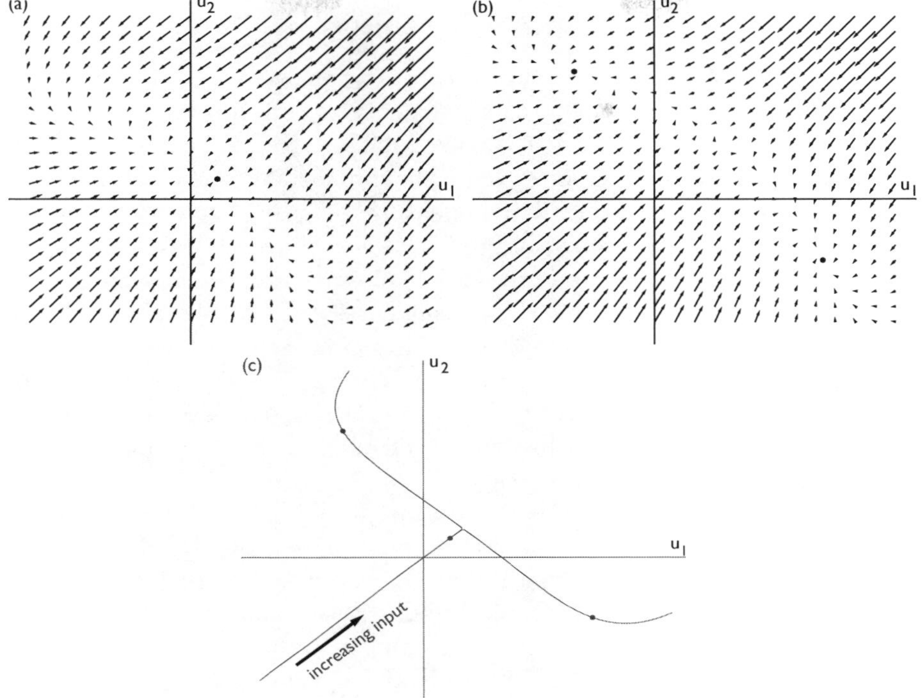

Figure 31.5 Vector fields for two neurons with mutually inhibitory interaction are shown when both neurons receive the same weak (a) or strong (b) input. (a) Weak input leads to a single attractor at small levels of activation. (b) Strong input leads to two attractors, one in which neuron 1 is activated, but not neuron 2 (bottom right), another in which the reverse is true (top left). (c) A schematic illustration of the location of the attractors in the space of the two state variables, u_1 and u_2, as a function of input strength shows the transition from a mono-stable state at weak input to a bi-stable state when increasing input starts to bring in inhibitory interaction.

systems, instabilities of this nature have been observed and identified as such (Schöner and Kelso 1988; Kelso 1995).

In the bi-stable regime, the dynamical neurons no longer just follow the input pattern. They actually decide something on their own: which neuron will become activated and thus, which moving target the fly will pursue. If inputs are symmetrical as in our illustrations, this decision may be driven by chance, a small fluctuation arising from noisy inputs. If one of the inputs is stronger (one of the objects provides a strong motion signal because it is closer, for instance), then the decision is biased toward that object. In either case, once a decision has been made by the neurons' activation levels relaxing to one of the two attractors, the neuronal dynamics stabilizes that decision. Even if inputs vary somewhat, the system will tend to stay in the attractor selected.

Dynamic field theory

The simple model of selecting one of two neurons we analyzed above incorporates two of the key elements of DST: stability and flexibility. By setting up appropriate couplings between different parts of a neuronal dynamics, stable states may be generated, shifted, made to appear or to disappear as the sensed environmental conditions change. This may happen without ever explicitly representing the goal of an action and how it changes under these changing conditions. There is no need, in this example, for an abstract, symbolic representation of the chosen movement target, an explicit computation of its velocity or position. The fly simply needs to couple its neural control system driving the wings to these dynamical neurons that receive sensory inputs about the presence of moving specks on the visual array. Given the capacity of these dynamical neurons to make sensorimotor decisions, this system is sufficient to achieve complex tracking behaviour, in which one fly chases another and is not distracted by other moving objects crossing its visual array.

But is this system truly free of representation? Would not the neurons themselves "represent" sensory stimuli, as well as the decisions made about them? In the present arrangement, such an interpretation is possible, but of limited power. For instance, although the neural dynamics can control tracking behaviour, it is unable to perform more abstract operations, such as flying into a direction that is a variable amount off the sensed movement direction (say 30° when one signal is given, 60° when another is given). This would seem to require a form of representation that has more flexibility and a stronger degree of independence of the particular, fixed coupling structure between sensory representation and motor system. Could other dynamical systems with more sophisticated coupling structure be devised that move beyond such limitations? Could neuronal dynamics be conceived that may generate stable states that represent something like a 30° turn from a sensory source, while still being continuously linked to sensory input, having stability properties and generating behaviour autonomously in real time?

Activation Fields

The key issue is to find a way that neural activation may represent metric information. The solutions are fields of neuronal activation that endow any dimension of metric information relevant to perception, action, or cognition with a continuous activation function. Each point along the dimension is assigned a particular level of activation. Such activation fields are spatially smooth and depend on time.

Metric information is then represented by patterns of activation with high activation levels around specific locations along the dimension (around 30° or 60° in the example) and low levels of activation elsewhere (Figure 31.6). Such localized peaks of activation are the units of representation in dynamic field theory. The amplitude of a peak indicates the presence or absence of information about the metric dimension, and modulates the extent to which that information is capable of impacting on other neuronal representations or directly on motor systems. The location of a peak encodes

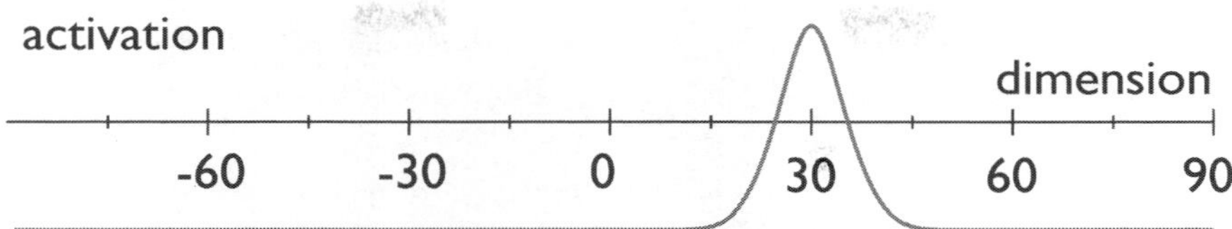

Figure 31.6 A localized peak of activation in an activation field defined over a metric dimension (here, heading direction) may represent both the presence of a visual or motor object (through its level of activation) and an estimate about this object (through the location of the peak along the metric dimension, here the heading direction of 30°).

the metric content of the representation, such as a sensory estimate, a motor plan, or metric working memory. The peak at 30° depicted in Figure 31.6, for instance, represents the task of turning by 30°. It may have arisen from sensory information or by computation within a neuronal dynamics. The peak may bring about the represented action by being coupled to the wing motors in ways that steer the fly in the indicated direction. The link of activation fields to sensory and motor surfaces, both through inputs and as targets of projection ensures that dynamical fields support embodied and situated cognitive processes, while the stability and autonomy of the peak solutions enable abstraction and operation on representations.

Field dynamics

To enable localized peaks to play this role of the units of representation in embodied cognition, they are made the attractor solutions of dynamical systems that describe the temporal evolution of activation fields. While inputs may drive activation to induced peaks, neuronal interaction among different field sites is responsible for stabilizing peak solutions against decay through local excitation and against diffusive spread through broader or global inhibition (Figure 31.7). Excitatory input into an activation field may come from any other part of a neuronal dynamical architecture, in particular, from sensor surfaces or other activation fields. Due to the broad connectivity in the central nervous system, such inputs typically contain random components modelled as Gaussian white noise. Interaction among field sites depends on the distance between any two sites, so that metrically close locations are mutually coupled excitatorily, while sites at larger distances are mutually coupled (potentially through interneurons) inhibitorily (Figure 31.7).

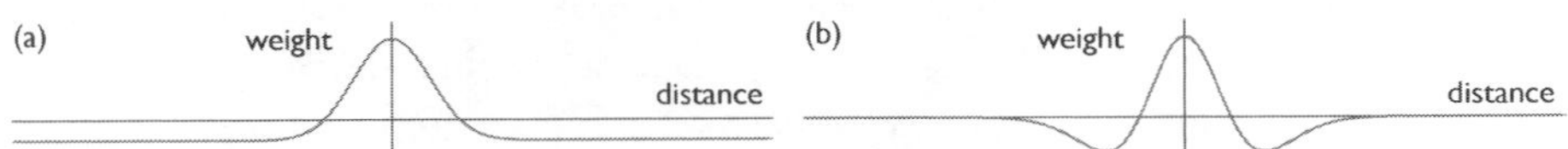

Figure 31.7 Two examples of interaction kernels: (a) Gaussian kernel with local excitation and global inhibition; (b) Mexican-hat-style kernel with local excitation, broader, but still having local inhibition and no global inhibition.

A generic mathematical formulation of the dynamics of activation fields that contain peaks as stable solutions was analyzed by (Amari 1977):

$$\tau \dot{u}(x,t) = -u(x,t) + h + \text{resting level} + \text{input} + \text{interaction}$$

The first three terms set up the linear dynamics of the activation level, $u(x, t)$, at any field site x in the manner of the vector fields examined earlier (Figures 31.2 and 31.3). In the absence of interaction, these terms lead to an attractor at an activation level matching the resting state plus any inputs provided at that field location, x.

Nonlinearity is introduced by the interaction between different field sites. The contribution of interaction to the rate of change of activation at a given field site, x, is a weighted sum over all other field sites x'. The weight, $w(x, x')$, determines both the sign and strength of the influence of activation at site x' on the rate of change of activation at site x. Positive values of $w(x, x')$ reflect excitatory coupling, negative values inhibitory coupling. The weight factor, also called coupling strength or interaction kernel depends only on the distance between x and x'. It is typically positive for small distances $x - x'$, and negative over larger distances to ensure the stability of localized peaks of activation (Figure 31.7).

Only sufficiently activated field sites contribute to interaction. This is formalized by multiplying each weight term with the current level of activation at site, x', which has passed through a sigmoidal threshold function, $\sigma(x')$. This nonlinear function is zero for sufficiently low levels of activation and one for sufficiently large levels of activation with a more or less step transition near the threshold level (conventionally chosen as the zero level of the activation variable). The generic dynamics of activation fields can thus be written in this form:

$$\tau \dot{u}(x,t) = -u(x,t) + h + \text{in}(x,t) + \int w(x-x')\sigma(x')dx'$$

where h is the resting level and $\text{in}(x, t)$ the sum of external inputs, which may vary in time.

Instabilities

Dynamical activation fields of this kind have two classes of attractor solutions. The first class consists of activation patterns that merely reflect the input to the field. In these solutions, interaction plays only a minor role, so that the activation pattern approximates the input pattern: $u(x, t) \approx \text{in}(x, t) + h$ (left panel of Figure 31.9). This is the dynamic regime in which most classical connectionist networks operate. The input function, $\text{in}(x, t)$, may link a sensory surface or another activation field characterized by another dimension, y, to the dimension x, represented by the activation field in question (Figure 31.8). These feed-forward links may implement feature extraction, mapping, or more complex operations such as association or correlation.

The input driven pattern of activation is stable only as long as activation is low enough so that interaction remains limited. Once the threshold of the sigmoidal

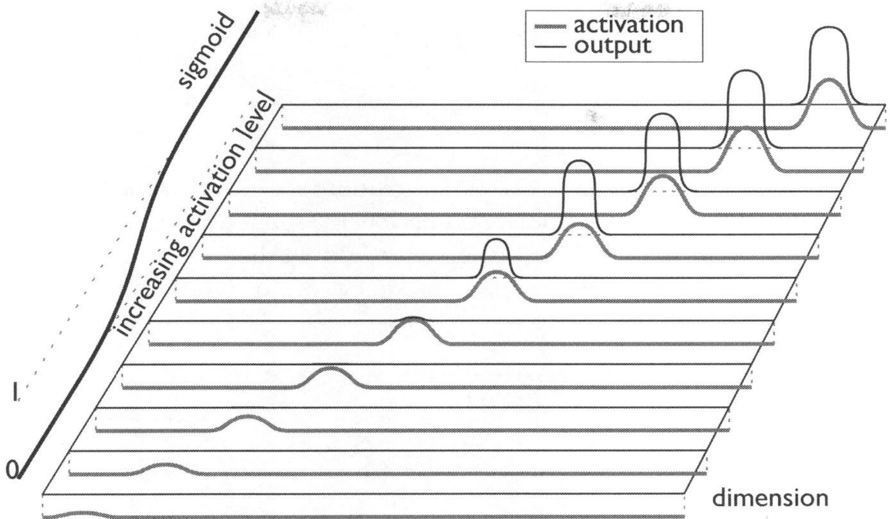

Figure 31.8 Multiple copies of an activation field over dimension *x* (horizontal axis) illustrate the effect of the sigmoidal nonlinearity. From front to back, a local peak of activation, with linearly increasing strength, is assumed (grey fat line). The amplitude of the sigmoidal activation (thin line) grows nonlinearly, being zero for small activation and reaching saturation for large activation levels, with a narrow transition regime. This amplitude is illustrated on the left, tracing the sigmoidal function itself as a function of the maximal level of activation in each copy of the field.

function is reached at any field site, local excitatory interaction kicks in. The input-driven solution becomes unstable. Activation continues to grow under the influence of local excitatory interaction. As a local peak grows, its outer rim moves away from the centre, ultimately coming within the distance from the centre at which interaction is predominantly inhibitory. This counteracts the growth that is driven by excitatory interaction, eventually reaching an equilibrium when the effect of local excitatory interaction and inhibition at the outer boundaries of the peak balance. The solution that emerges is an exemplar of the other category of attractor solutions, a localized, self-stabilized peak of activation (right panel of Figure 31.9).

The dynamic instability dividing these two types of attractor solutions, the largely sub-threshold activity mirroring the input and a supra-threshold self-stabilizing peak, is called the detection instability. It occurs, for instance, when the amplitude of a single localized input is increased gradually (Figure 31.10). At a critical point, the input-driven solution becomes unstable and a peak forms, "detecting" the input. When the input level is dropped again, local self-excitation supports the peak for a range of input strengths that previously were not sufficient to induce a peak from the input-driven regime. This bi-stable regime stabilizes the detection decision against fluctuating input.

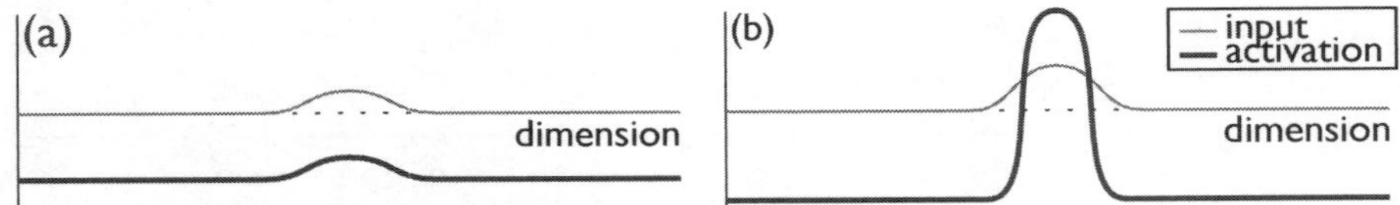

Figure 31.9 Two different types of attractor solutions for a dynamic field. (a) In the input-driven solution, the field activation mirrors the input pattern. (b) A localized, self-stabilized peak is induced by stronger inputs. Within the peak, activation exceeds input while elsewhere activation is suppressed below resting level.

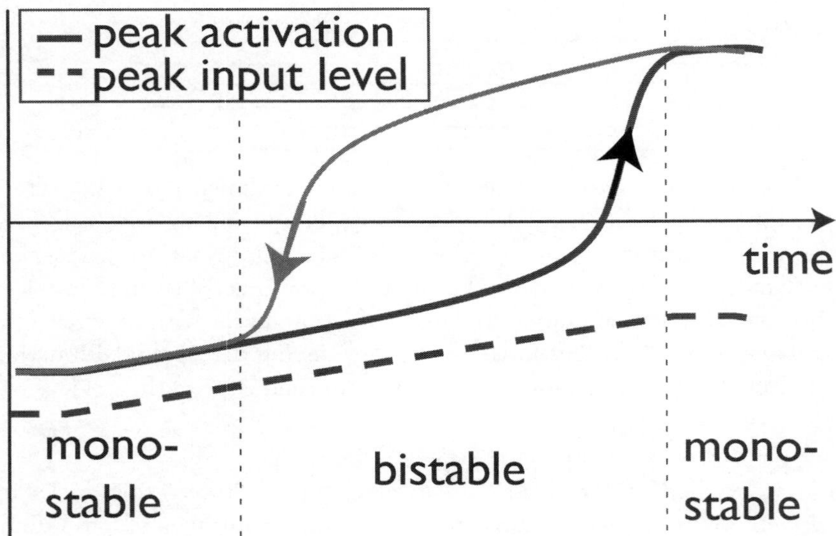

Figure 31.10 In this schematic illustration of the detection instability, the strength of a localized input is slowly increased in time, before reaching a plateau (dashed line) or, alternatively, decreased in time following the same trace. The induced activation pattern is illustrated by the peak activation level (bold with arrow pointing to the right for the increase; light grey with arrow pointing to the left for the decrease of input strength). This exposes the bistability of the input-driven and the self-stabilized solutions at intermediate levels of input strength, which leads to hysteresis for the detection decision. This regime is delimited by a mono-stable regime of the input-driven solution at low input levels and a mono-stable solution for the self-stabilized solution at high input levels.

Another fundamental instability is linked to the capacity to select among multiple inputs and is illustrated in Figure 31.11. When two localized inputs are provided to locations that are close to each other, a single self-stabilized peak may form over an averaged location. This is due to local excitatory interaction. If the distance between the two locations is increased, the single averaging solution becomes unstable,

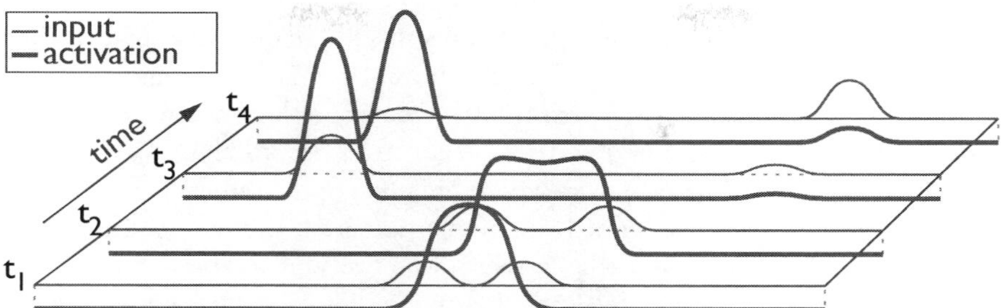

Figure 31.11 Two patterns of self-stabilized solutions of a dynamic field, the averaging and the selecting peak solutions, are separated by the selection instability. Input is given into a dynamic field at two different sites of varying distance. At first (point t_1 in time), the two input sites are close to each other and the field averages between these two locations forming one broad peak. As the input sites are moved further apart (t_2), the averaging peak solution becomes unstable. When the distance between input sites is further increased at t_3, the field selects the leftmost of the two sites with slightly larger input strength. This selection is maintained even after input strength at the right-most location becomes larger than at the left (t_4).

yielding to a bi-stable regime in which a peak may either be formed over one or over the other input location, but not over both at the same time. Which input is selected depends on which site receives larger input as well any fluctuations in the field. Once a peak has arisen over the site with stronger input, that selection decision is stabilized so that even when input over the alternate site becomes larger, the selected peak remains stable as illustrated in Figure 31.11.

Signatures of the selection instability can be observed in behavioural experiments. In general, tasks in which the correct response is not uniquely specified are experimentally problematic as participants tend to develop interpretations or strategies. One exception is the preparation and initiation of saccadic eye movements in response to visual stimuli, a process that is so highly automatic and fast, that cognitive strategies have limited impact. Participants who initially fixate a visual stimulus spontaneously make an abrupt eye movement or saccade when a new visual target is presented. If two targets are presented at the same time in two symmetrical visual locations (e.g., at the same distance at plus and minus 45° from the horizon), the saccade depends on the metrics of these targets. If the targets are metrically sufficiently close, so that both targets can be foveated at the same time, an averaging saccade is directed approximately to the centre of an imagined line that connects the two targets. If the targets are further apart, one of the two targets is selected (Ottes et al. 1984). Across multiple trials, this leads to a bimodal distribution with either target being selected on different trials.

In a dynamical field model of saccade preparation, the difference between these two regimes is accounted for in terms of the transition from averaging to selection (Kopecz and Schöner 1995). This transition occurs in an activation field that represents the saccadic endpoint in a manner that can be linked to the neuronal activation patterns observed in colliculus superior, as well as the frontal eye fields. A number of experimental features can be explained by the model. One example concerns the interaction between response probability and metrics. When trials in which the two targets are presented are intermixed with trials in which only one of the targets is shown, the rate at which either target is experienced can be manipulated. If one target appears more frequently than the other, then this leads to a metric bias in the averaging regime: the averaging saccade does not fall into the middle between the two targets, but on to a point closer to the more frequent target (Kowler 1990). In the bi-stable regime, in contrast, no such bias is observed. Saccades fall on to either target, although the less frequent target is selected less often. In the model, the probability of a target is acquired through a learning mechanism, which accumulates memory traces of prior activation patterns (Erlhagen and Schöner 2002). In the averaging mode, the peak is positioned such as to be sensitive to the asymmetrical total input, while in the selection mode, the peak is sensitive only to the local total input, which remains symmetric around either saccadic target (Figure 31.12).

This is only one of a range of experimental signatures through which the metrics (that is, where the saccades fall) and timing of the saccades (that is, when the saccades

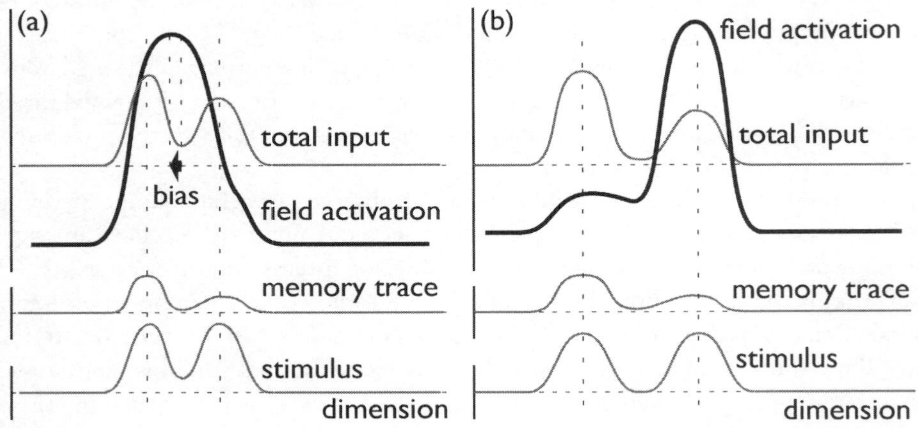

Figure 31.12 Dynamic activation fields defined over the dimension of saccadic endpoint (fat line) are shown together with stimulus input (bottom), the memory trace (middle), and their sum, the total input (thin line on top). (a) When the two targets are metrically close, the self-stabilized activation peak straddles the two locations and is sensitive to differences in total input due to a stronger pre-shape at the more frequent left-most than at the less frequent right-most target. This leads to a bias away from the arithmetic mean of the two target positions toward the more frequent target (arrow). (b) When the two targets are metrically sufficiently far, the self-stabilized activation peak is positioned over one of the two target locations, here the less frequent right-most one. Different strengths in memory trace do not affect the positioning of the peak.

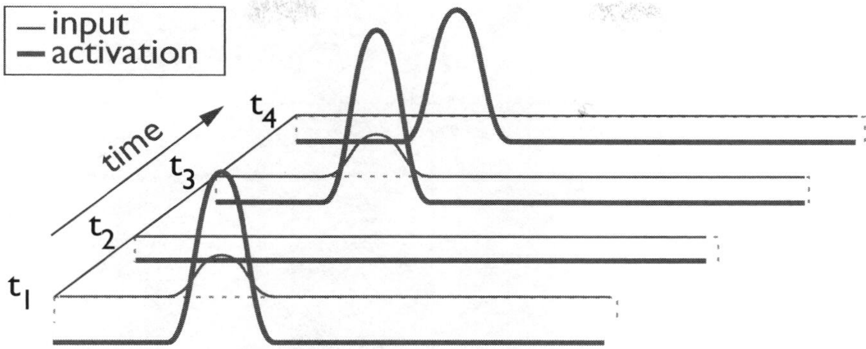

Figure 31.13 A self-stabilized peak of activation (fat line) induced by localized input (thin line) in the first frame (time t_1) does not persist when that input is removed (time t_2). The last two frames show how this is changed at a higher resting level or for a stronger interaction kernel. Now, an input induced self-stabilized peak (time t_3) is sustained when the localized input is removed (time t_4).

are initiated) reveal the underlying neural dynamic mechanisms (Kopecz and Schöner 1995; Trappenberg et al. 2001). Signatures of the detection instability can be found in how a self-stabilized peak is formed against the resistance of the fixation system (Wilimzig et al. 2006).

Finally, a third instability separates a regime in which self-stabilized peaks persist only in the presence of localized input from a regime, in which such peaks may be sustained in the absence of localized input. This is illustrated in Figure 31.13. The first two time-slices demonstrate a self-stabilized peak induced by localized input, which decays to a homogeneous pattern at the negative resting level when the localized input is removed at the second time frame. If the balance between input and interaction is shifted toward a stronger contribution of interaction (e.g., by increasing the resting level of the field; Amari 1977), then a self-stabilized peak induced by localized input at the third point in time remains stable, even when localized input is completely removed at the fourth point in time. This pattern of sustained activation has been invoked as a model of working memory in a variety of contexts (e.g., Amit 1994; Spencer and Schöner 2003). It becomes unstable in the memory instability, when the balance between input and interaction is shifted back toward a weaker interaction. A wide variety of behavioural and neuronal signatures of the memory instability and this particular mechanism for working memory exist (review in Johnson et al. [2008]). This includes the only other model system in which selection decisions can be reliably observed: having infants select a target for goal-directed reaching movements in Piaget's A-not-*B* paradigm. A dynamical-field account for the rich phenomenology of this paradigm postulates that infants may move through the memory instability during development, but also when environmental or task conditions are varied (Thelen et al. 2001; Schöner and Dineva 2006).

Finally, let us return to the question posed at the outset: How do self-stabilized peaks in dynamic activation fields enable operations to be performed on neuronally

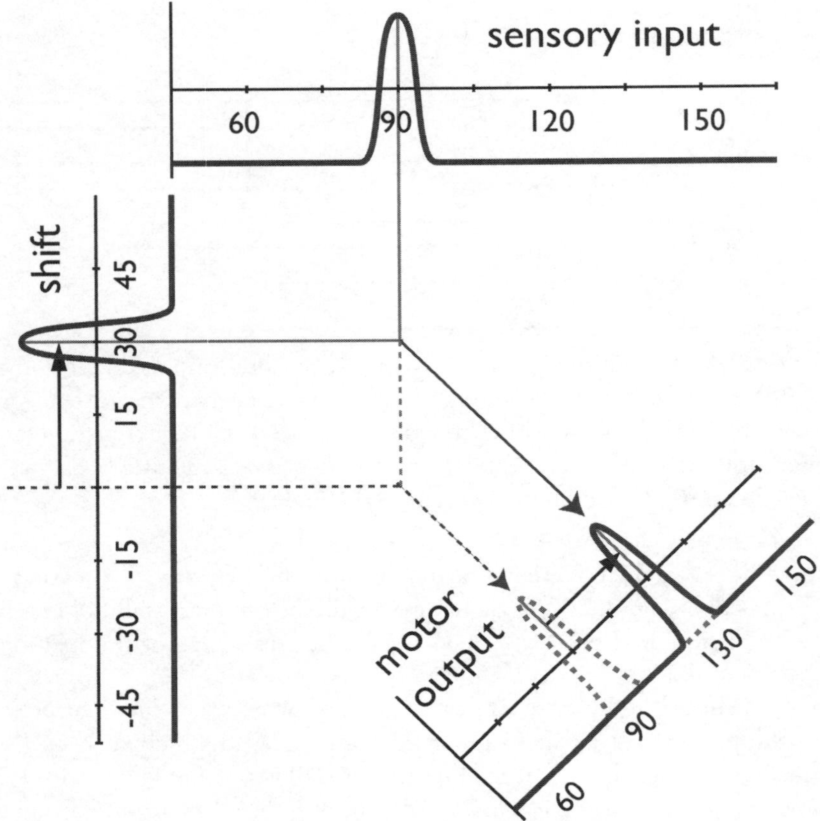

Figure 31.14 An architecture with three fields coupled systematically so that sensory information is transmitted to all locations in the output field, but modulated by the shift field. In this instance, activation in the sensory field at 90° is projected only to the 130° location in the motor field, because the associated shift of 30° is activated. All other projections from 90° in the sensory input are inactive, including the zero shift input indicated in dashed lines.

represented metric information? Figure 31.14 illustrates the operation invoked earlier: input from a sensory surface is to be shifted by 30° to generate a motor command that is at that angle to the source of sensory stimulation. That amount of shift is represented in a second activation field. The activation field receiving sensory input and this shift field project together on to a motor field (e.g., in additive form with a threshold or in a multiplicative "shunting" form). The geometry of this projection is illustrated by two neuronal couplings indicated in thin and dashed lines. The dashed line reflects the projection with zero shift, but is not effective here because no activation is present in the shift field at zero shift. The peak at a shift of 30° makes that this shifted projection is effective leading to the correct output peak.

Discussion

We have referred to self-stabilized peaks of activation arising from dynamic fields as units of representation. Do they satisfy typical criteria for representation? The authors are not trained philosophers, so our discussion of this issue, inspired by the list of such criteria presented in Rowlands (2006), is necessarily amateurish. Hopefully, readers will be able to transform this sketch into an acceptable argument.

The peaks definitely stand in relationship to something outside the nervous system. They are induced, for instance, by input that derives from sensory surfaces and reflects the structure of the environment. They may track such inputs and thus actively maintain this relationship. They may also be coupled to motor systems and bring about movement and thus change the state of the organism in the outer world. In fact, when that happens, the sensory information changes as well, in a way that reflects the structure of the world. The peaks continuously reflect how the system is embedded in its environment.

However, the peaks may also become decoupled from their initial sensory causes. This is obvious when peaks operate in the sustained regime, where no specific sensory information is needed to maintain the peaks. But this is also true, in a more subtle form, in the bi-stable regime around the detection instability, in which peaks stabilize a representation even as sensory information falls below an initial level of significance. Selection also reflects a partial decoupling, in which a peak no longer depends on sensory information concerning the suppressed alternative locations along the represented dimension. This capacity to stabilize selection decisions provides a form of robust estimation, that is, helps suppress outliers, maybe the most concrete and simple form of decoupling from sensory information. We illustrated, for instance, how in the selection regime the estimate of a metric dimension represented by a peak becomes insensitive to priors about that dimension. In this respect, dynamic fields go beyond the Bayesian framework, in which priors always play their role.

The peaks of activation are functional in that they support a particular mode of operation or of functioning, which is linked to a history of function. In fact, quite literally, the capacity to form peaks in a particular field is promoted by memory traces, which reflect that such peaks have been built before. In the dynamic field theory account of Piaget's infants, young infants are in an "out of sight, out of mind" mode, older infants are in a mode in which they are capable of stabilizing decisions against habits or distractors. Both modes are functional states that emerge at different points during development and are linked to the history of the nervous system. Infants may move from one to the other mode as they build up experience in a given context.

Peaks in dynamic fields are not merely dictated by sensory inputs, as happens in purely feed-forward neuronal networks. They may be generated and maintained through neuronal interaction within the field. This may lead to misrepresentation. For instance, a peak may be stabilized even though its inducing stimulus has actually moved to a new location if that shift occurred too fast or while sensory input strength was weak. In this case, the peak misrepresents a sensory estimate. Or a peak may be stabilized as a result of a selection decision although sensory evidence disfavours that decision. Perseveration, as observed in Piaget's *A*-not-*B* paradigm, is a form of misrepresentation.

Finally, peaks can be operated on and can be integrated into complex systems and interact in combination with other systems. We provided a very simple example of an operation above. For a demonstration of integration into a complex architecture see, for instance, Simmering et al. (2008) in the context of spatial working memory. It is the very stability of peak solutions that gives them the robustness required to link them into larger neuronal dynamics, so that they do not lose their identity and their link and linkability to sensory input. Stability is also critical for linking dynamic fields in closed loop to sensory-motor systems. Having said that, we recognize that we are only at the beginning of a fuller understanding of how the principles of dynamical field theory will impact on an ultimate account of complex, fully integrated cognition.

If we accept that dynamic fields with self-stabilized peaks deliver legitimate forms of representation, then we obtain the embodied and situated aspect of representation for free. We have emphasized how self-stabilized peaks may remain linked to the sensory and motor surfaces and have hinted at their neurophysiological foundation. A practical proof of embodiment comes from an ensemble of robotic implementations (e.g., Schöner et al. 1995; Bicho et al. 2000; Erlhagen and Bicho 2006; Faubel and Schöner, 2008). These demonstrate that using fairly simple sensory and motor systems, the dynamic field concepts are sufficient to endow autonomous robots with elementary forms of cognition. The situatedness of dynamic fields goes beyond the immediate coupling to the sensed environment. The mechanisms of pre-structuring activation fields through memory traces of activation patterns provides a form in which the structure of an environment may be acquired in a form that directly impacts on the units of representation and the associated behaviours.

One of the most conceptually challenging implications of DST is often perceived as a limitation: What is the ultimate account of cognition delivered by DST? Unlike classical, information-processing accounts of cognition, it is not plausible within DST, that a complete model would be that final product, a model whose modules would have fixed function, which would capture the complete range of behavioural functions. Instead, DST suggests a view in which an organism and its nervous system are immersed in complex structured environments, endowed with a history that has left its traces. Immersion and history together structure a huge, complex dynamical system. That system would not be arbitrarily shapeable by experience. It would be governed by constraints, such as the principle of stability, the need for instabilities to enable flexibility, the existences of different dynamic regimes that support identifiable functions. Dynamical systems theory would consist of identifying such principles.

In this conception, coupling is central rather than the forward flow of information processing. But uncovering the coupling structure of that big dynamical system does not subsume the role the concept of "architecture" plays in information-processing thinking. This is because any subsystem of the big dynamical system may undergo qualitative change, modifying its function and forming new substructures through coupling with other subsystems. Such change may be brought about by unspecific changes in the environment, in the system's own experience, or in its internal structure. Unspecific and graded changes may lead to the appearance of specific functions that were implicit in the neuronal dynamics and are lifted out of it as favourable conditions are created. These functions maybe created "on the spot," they do not necessarily reside somewhere waiting to be called up. They are, instead, potentialities of the nervous system that may "emerge" if conditions are right (Schöner and Dineva 2006). This also implies that there may be multiple causes for any particular function to arise and, conversely, that any individual subsystem may be involved in multiple functions. Again, understanding cognition then consists most likely of the understanding of general constraints, of limitations, symmetries, or modes of operation, rather than of an exhaustive account of cognitive function.

References

Amari, S. (1977) "Dynamics of Pattern Formation in Lateral-Inhibition Type Neural Fields," *Biological Cybernetics* 27: 77–87.

Amit, D. J. (1994) "The Hebbian Paradigm Reintegrated: Local Reverberations as Internal Representations," *Behavioral and Brain Sciences* 18, no. 4: 617–26.

Bicho, E., Mallet, P., and Schöner, G. (2000) "Target Representation on an Autonomous Vehicle with Low-Level Sensors," *International Journal of Robotics Research* 19: 424–47.

Blumberg, M. S. (2005) *Basic Instinct: The Genesis of Behaviour*, New York: Thunder's Mouth Press.

Braun, M. (1993) *Differential Equations and Their Applications*, 4 edn, New York: Springer-Verlag.

Deco, G., and Schürmann, B. (2000) *Information Dynamics: Foundations and Applications*, New York: Springer-Verlag.

Erlhagen, W., and Bicho, E. (2006) "The Dynamic Neural Field Approach to Cognitive Robotics," *Journal of Neural Engineering* 3, no. 3: R36–R54.

Erlhagen, W., and Schöner, G. (2002) "Dynamic Field Theory of Movement Preparation," *Psychological Review* 109: 545–72.

Faubel, C., and Schöner, G. (2008) "Learning to Recognize Objects on the Fly: A Neurally Based Dynamic Field Approach," *Neural Networks*, 21(4): 562–76.

Haken, H. (1983) *Synergetics – An Introduction*, 3 edn, Berlin: Springer-Verlag.

Hock, H. S., Schöner, G., and Giese, M. A. (2003) "The Dynamical Foundations of Motion Pattern Formation: Stability, Selective Adaptation, and Perceptual Continuity," *Perception and Psychophysics* 65: 429–57.

Hoppensteadt, F. C., and Izhikevich, E. M. (1997) *Weakly Connected Neural Networks*, New York: Springer-Verlag.

Johnson, J. S., Spencer, J. P., and Schöner, G. (2008) "Moving to Higher Ground: The Dynamic Field Theory and the Dynamics of Visual Cognition," *New Ideas in Psychology* 26, no. 2: 227–51.

Kelso, J. A. S. (1995) *Dynamic Patterns: The Self-Organization of Brain and Behavior*, Cambridge, MA: MIT Press.

Kopecz, K., and Schöner, G. (1995) "Saccadic Motor Planning by Integrating Visual Information and Pre-Information on Neural, Dynamic Fields," *Biological Cybernetics* 73: 49–60.

Kowler, E. (1990) "The Role of Visual and Cognitive Processes in the Control of Eye Movement," in E. Kowler (ed.), *Eye Movements and Their Role in Visual and Cognitive Processes*, Amsterdam: Elsevier, 1–70.

Latash, M. (1993) *Control of Human Movement*, Champaign, IL: Human Kinetics.

Marr, D. (1982) *Vision*, New York: W. H. Freeman & Co.

Ottes, F. P., Gisbergen, J. A. M. van, and Eggermont, J. J. (1984) "Metrics of Saccade Responses to Visual Double Stimuli: Two Different Modes," *Vision Research*, 24: 1169–79.

Perko, L. (1991) *Differential Equations and Dynamical Systems*, Berlin: Springer-Verlag.

Piaget, J. (1952) *The Origins of Intelligence in Children*, New York: International Universities Press.

Reichardt, W., and Poggio, T. (1976) "Visual Control of Orientation Behaviour in the Fly: I. A Quantitative Analysis," *Quarterly Reviews in Biophysics* 9: 311–75.

Riegler, A. (2002) "When Is a Cognitive System Embodied?" *Cognitive Systems Research* 3: 339–48.

Rowlands, M. (2006) *Body Language: Representation in Action*, Cambridge, MA: MIT Press.

Schöner, G., and Dineva, E. (2006) "Dynamic Instabilities as Mechanisms for Emergence," *Developmental Science* 10: 69–74.

Schöner, G., Dose, M., and Engels, C. (1995) "Dynamics of Behavior: Theory and Applications for Autonomous Robot Architectures," *Robotics and Autonomous Systems* 16: 213–45.

Schöner, G., and Kelso, J. A. S. (1988) "Dynamic Pattern Generation in Behavioral and Neural Systems," *Science* 239: 1513–20.

Searle, J. R. (1983) *Intentionality – An Essay in the Philosophy of Mind*, Cambridge University Press.

Simmering, V. R., Schutte, A. R., and Spencer, J. P. (2008) "Generalizing the Dynamic Field Theory of Spatial Cognition across Real and Developmental Time Scales," *Brain Research* 1202: 68–86.

Spencer, J. P., and Schöner, G. (2003) "Bridging the Representational Gap in the Dynamical Systems Approach to Development," *Developmental Science* 6: 392–412.

Thelen, E., Schöner, G., Scheier, C., and Smith, L. (2001) "The Dynamics of Embodiment: A Field Theory if Infant Perseverative Reaching," *Brain and Behavioral Sciences* 24: 1–33.

Thelen, E. (1995) "Time Scale Dynamics and the Development of an Embodied Cognition," in R. F. Port and T. van Gelder (eds), *Mind as Motion: Explorations in the Dynamics of Cognition*. Cambridge, MA: MIT Press, pp. 69–100.

Trappenberg, T. P. (2002) *Fundamentals of Computational Neuroscience*, Oxford: Oxford University Press.

Trappenberg, T. P., Dorris, M. C., Munoz, D. P., and Klein, R. M. (2001) "A Model of Saccade Initiation Based on the Competitive Integration of Exogenous and Endogenous Signals in the Superior Colliculus," *Journal of Cognitive Neuroscience* 13, no. 2: 256–71.

Wilimzig, C., Schneider, S., and Schöner, G. (2006) "The Time Course of Saccadic Decision Making: Dynamic Field Theory," *Neural Networks* 19: 1059–74.

Wilson, H. R. (1999) *Spikes, Decisions, and Actions: Dynamical Foundations of Neurosciences*, New York: Oxford University Press.

32
THE PHILOSOPHY OF PLANT NEUROBIOLOGY

Manuel Heras-Escribano and Paco Calvo

1 Introduction: plant neurobiology and its philosophy

The investigation of plant behavior and cognition has become a matter of interest in both biology and the philosophy of biology; in particular, in plant neurobiology (Baluška et al., 2004; Brenner et al., 2006) and the philosophy of plant neurobiology (Calvo, 2016). The target of plant neurobiology is plant intelligence; the underlying goal being to make sense of the way plants perceive and act in a purposeful manner.

To make sense of the way plants perceive and act, plant neurobiology helps itself to the resources of plant physiology, cell and molecular biology, biochemistry, evolutionary and developmental biology, and plant ecology. However, insofar as the target of plant neurobiology is plant behavior and cognition, its methodology cannot possibly reduce to the toolkit of the disciplines that constitute plant science. After all, its entry point is plant *behavior*. Plants are phenotypically plastic, and this allows them to manipulate the environment, enabling metabolic functioning. But no type of behavior brings cognition. It is *intelligent* plant behavior that plant neurobiology targets, in other words, the type of behavior that profits from experience during ontogeny. Today, we know that plants can alter their traits in the phenotype and select certain actions and not others, integrate informational sources, or anticipate the future, among a wider set of competencies (Calvo, 2018) that are currently being intensively researched.

From a (philosophy of) cognitive science perspective, we care about flexible and soft-wired responses, as opposed to rigid and hard-wired behavioral outputs. It is the increasing degree of flexibility reported in the behavioral repertoire of plants that allows plant neurobiology to ascribe intelligence (Trewavas, 2014). For this reason, resources from cognitive science and the philosophy of psychology are called for. In particular, we can locate the philosophy of plant neurobiology at the intersection of plant neurobiology and cognitive science. As such, the philosophy of plant neurobiology introduces new challenges and opens lines of research, furnishing plant neurobiology with an explanatory framework, together with guiding principles for the exploration of plant intelligence.

In this chapter, we first put plant neurobiology in perspective by briefly reviewing some of the pioneering botanical research of late nineteenth and early twentieth centuries. A representative subset of different aspects of plant behavior and cognition ranging from foraging to learning and even offline cognition will in turn be presented. We shall then "graft" on a number of post-cognitivist ways of studying behavior and cognition. In particular, predictive processing, enactivism, and ecological psychology will serve to contrast mainstream information-processing psychology with an embodied, situated, and distributed approach. Finally, we make explicit the role that a philosophy of plant neurobiology can play overall in the pursuit of plant intelligence.

2 Plant neurobiology in perspective

Plant neurobiology aims to honor the place of plants in nature. Unfortunately, we cannot help but approach plant life from a zoocentric standpoint. And yet, less than 1 percent of life on Earth is animal! This is a fact that Charles Darwin appreciated. According to him, botany should not be subordinate to zoology. In a sense, plant neurobiology aims to recover Darwin's agenda (Kutschera and Briggs, 2009). To do so, plant neurobiology (Brenner et al., 2006) studies the behavioral repertoire of plants and the types of cognitive processes that may underlie their overt adaptive responses. The objective is to unearth plant intelligence by combining results and resources from plant physiology, biochemistry, or cellular and molecular biology (among other plant science subdisciplines) with contemporary approaches to the study of behavior and cognition.

The scientific study of plant intelligence can be traced in history to the pioneering work of Charles Darwin, Wilhelm Pfeffer, Gottlieb Haberlandt, and Jagdish Chandra Bose, among others (Stahlberg, 2006; Baluška et al., 2009). These authors considered that plants like the Venus flytrap (*Dionea muscipula*) or the Sensitive plant (*Mimosa pudica*) shared a number of "animal features" (Darwin, 1875). These features were not just anatomical and functional but also behavioral and cognitive.

The mechanistic excitation of plant structures had been traditionally compared to that of animals (Cole and Curtis, 1938, 1939). This implied a functional significance for understanding the role of nervous excitation and action potentials (Gunar and Sinykhin, 1962, 1963; Pickard, 1973). As Bose argued in *The Nervous Mechanism of Plants*, there is no doubt about the "nervous character of the impulse transmitted to a distance" (1926). More importantly for our understanding of plant behavior and cognition, plants had the required *information-processing* machinery – in the jargon of the cognitive science of the past century: a system of nerves that constituted a single organized whole.

The development and profusion of empirical results and methodologies gave rise to the birth of the *Society for Plant Neurobiology* in 2005. Its goal is to promote further empirical research on cognitive phenomena in plants. In particular, in the last decade, the need of a unified account of integrated plant signaling with an eye to studying plant behavior and cognition has been stressed (Baluška et al., 2004). As a result, plant electrophysiology (Volkov, 2006), a traditionally neglected discipline in mainstream plant science, has been comprehensively linked to plant behavior. It describes the coordination of physiological needs and that integration of information signaling across the plant body is needed (Calvo, 2016). In this regard, the role of electrical signaling is pivotal.

One way or another, a number of analogies in the way sets of behaviors in animals and plants get organized is starting to be revealed. In the case of animals, their neural hardwiring was evolutionarily tailored for the sake of coordinating free-moving behavior. Of course, someone reluctant to pair the cognitive capacities of plants with those of animals could claim that motor functions are essential for differentiating between the two. It is true that there is a difference between the form of motor functions in animals and plants: animals, being heterotrophic, possess contractile muscles that allow them to acquire food and escape from threatening situations for surviving. On the contrary, plants, being autotrophic, were not required to evolve such adaptations. This, nonetheless, does not preclude plants from being motile.

For plants to meet the challenges they face, despite their apparent sessile nature, we must bear in mind that free-moving behavior can be recast under the lens of phenotypic plasticity (plants' form of movement). Once this is honored, the rationale behind the effort that plant neurobiology represents remains unchanged: the application of neurobiological principles to the study of the *sui generis* nature of plants.

In the light of the discovery of nervous-like structures with similar chemical and electric activity as those customarily resorted to in accounting for animal cognition (Baluška, 2010), contemporary plant neurobiologists envisage the existence of cognitive functions in plants. In fact, plant neurobiology studies a wide variety of neurobiology-based cognitive phenomena, such as movement (Sibaoka, 1969), communication (Baluška et al., 2005), memory (Bose and Karmakar, 2003), and decision-making (Li and Zhang, 2008).

3 Some aspects of plant behavior and cognition

Plant neurobiology offers a scientific understanding of plant sensing and responding, accounting for how metabolism and growth can be regulated by the endogenous integration of information signaling (Brenner et al., 2006). The discipline stresses nonprogrammed, soft-wired responses. In this way, plant cognition does not encompass just *any* form of behavior. Despite the lack of consistent definitions of what behavior and cognition are (Abramson and Calvo, 2018), we shall take plant cognition to encompass those patterns of behavior that are not only adaptive but also flexible, anticipatory, and goal directed (Calvo, 2018). In functional analogy with animal purposefulness and intentionality, we intend to identify those patterns of behavior that are, broadly speaking, systematic (Calvo et al., 2014).

To this end, a primary effort is directed toward discovering and understanding the action of systemic signals (Brenner et al., 2006). Today we know that plants are able to make decisions and solve highly complex problems; they learn and memorize (section 3.3), as in fact all eukaryotes do (Calvo and Baluška, 2015). Plants are territorial (Schenk et al., 1999) and can distinguish self from nonself. A further example to consider is root territoriality, where the geometric structure of the soil itself is exploited to the plant's benefit (Calvo and Keijzer, 2011).

Plants can anticipate competition (Novoplansky, 2016). Plants display a wide range of communication skills, too, being able to communicate with one another by means of airborne volatile organic compounds (VOCs) (Dicke et al., 2003; Baldwin et al., 2006). Plants can sense sounds and vibrations. A munching caterpillar triggers patterns of vibration that plants are able to detect. In response, they synthesize a number of toxins (Appel and Cocroft, 2014). The hair cells of some plants respond to mechanical stimulation, acting as "mechanical antennae" (Liu et al., 2017). Plants can in fact communicate not just with other plants but also with bacteria, fungi, and animals (Baluška, 2009).

In what follows, and before moving on to the type of cognitive architectures that might underlie such astonishing capacities, we shall review a subset of their astounding behavioral repertoire (for a full review, see Trewavas, 2014).

3.1 *Competition and foraging*

Plants actively forage for resources and are able to trigger behavioral changes on demand for the sake of securing a regular supply of energy. They actively forage for light, water, nitrates, phosphates, among other nourishment-providing substances (Trewavas, 2008). Given how heterogeneous their local environment can be, plants must be able to adapt on demand in the face of contingencies, selecting the most appropriate direction and rate of growth. Competition takes place both above and below ground, as the shoot and root apparatuses must adapt continuously in response to the dynamic distribution of resources. Decisions can involve a branch accelerating its rate of growth along a positive gradient of light. Shoots help themselves, for instance, to red:far-red light ratios, which provide valuable information as to how to grow out of shade (Ballaré and Pierik, 2017). Roots, in turn, can decelerate their rate of growth along a positive gradient of humidity or upon encountering a pocket of nutrients in a patchy area (Gundel et al., 2014).

Plants not only are sensitive to the magnitude and gradient of an environmental variable in question but are also able to detect how it changes over time and what sort of patterns or configurations can be formed by different meaningful variables (Silvertown and Gordon, 1989). Overall, flexible foraging behavior calls for a rather accurate set of structural changes, both reversible and irreversible, at all levels, from morphology to physiology and the phenotype.

Competition and foraging calls for signal integration with an eye to delivering a global response to environmental demands that is flexible enough and remains adaptive (De Kroon et al., 2009). In fact, plants are able to integrate a vast panoply of parameters, including not only abiotic signals such as humidity, light, gravity and temperature but also biotic ones, such as nutrient patches and microorganisms in the soil, as well as many more. The list (well over twenty different parameters) now includes proprioceptive and interoceptive cues (Bastien et al., 2013; Dumais, 2013). A highly sophisticated sensorimotor system underlies the sampling and integration of all such information (Hodge, 2009; Trewavas, 2009; Baluška and Mancuso, 2013). As a result, tropic (directional) responses (Gilroy, 2008) include positive (and negative) phototropic, hydrotropic, gravitropic, galvanotropic, oxytropic, and thigmotropism patterns of growth and movement, to name but a few (Barlow, 2010; Trewavas, 2003; Calvo and Keijzer, 2011). The same holds for nastic (nondirectional) responses, such as gravinastic or photonastic patterns of movement.

For the sake of illustration, consider the root apparatus. Roots are not just sensitive to water, minerals, and gravity. They also sense soil structure, allelopathy, herbivory, and neighbor competition (Calvo and Keijzer, 2011). This responsiveness to many different signals endows roots with a highly flexible behavior. While roots tend to grow downward, if they encounter obstacles they will develop horizontally even though they remain responsive to gravity (Massa and Gilroy, 2003). This shows a clear flexibility in the integration, processing, and responsiveness of many signals and environmental constraints.

Another example is the integration of salinity and gravity signals: while gravitropism is really important, an abnormal quantity of salinity triggers avoidance behavior in roots. The key point is that when both signals interact, roots integrate them and assess which is the best answer in order to optimize root growth (Li and Zhang, 2008).

These empirical results on root growth allow us to move from cognitive capacities like sensitivity and action to what are considered by many authors as "higher" cognitive capacities, such as decision-making and self-acquaintance (Baluška et al., 2010). This is related to the way in which plants compete for physical space and nutrients (McConnaughay and Bazzaz, 1991): plants tend to segregate their roots as much as possible with respect to the concentration of nutrients. Given a constant rate of nutrient addition, those plants that control more territory score higher in parameters such as growth and reproduction. The development of a root network depends on the available space and the concentration of nutrients. Tropisms show that roots, in addition to integrating signals, have to assess the pertinent strategy given the environmental conditions, which include competition with other plants.

3.2 *Decoupled offline behavior*

Decoupled offline behavior is one of the features that characterizes cognitive organisms. Although meant to untangle the conditions that can lead to a cognitive *robotics* and not plant science, this quote from Clark and Grush (1999) applies, *mutatis mutandis*, to plant neurobiology and the type of cognitive phenomena the discipline means to address:

> But what makes a phenomenon cognitive in the first place? We suggest that the truly cognitive phenomena are those that involve offline reasoning, vicarious environmental exploration, and the like. It is worth underlining the fact that this stance places us somewhat at odds with an increasingly influential view that either rejects the idea of a cognitive/non-cognitive divide altogether or (more commonly) expands the realm of the cognitive to include all kinds of adaptively valuable organism/environment coupling.
>
> (Clark and Grush, 1999, p. 12)

Offline processing appears to be pivotal for demarcating the cognitive from the non-cognitive, be the target discipline robotics or plant neurobiology. Furthermore, if online processes are dependent on looping dynamics in which the organism is engaged with its environment (Richardson et al., 2008; Barandiaran, 2016), the very possibility of offline processing is dependent on the capacity to manipulate representational resources (Clark and Toribio, 1994). Thus, a more demanding view of cognition is at stake. Could plants possess those allegedly required offline capacities? And if so, would this mean that plants are capable of manipulating representations?

In effect, some plants exhibit offline adaptive capabilities of the sort that have been exploited in past philosophical literature to demarcate between online routines and more sophisticated forms of behavior. Consider heliotropic nocturnal reorientation. Leaves of *Lavatera cretica* are able to reorient during the night and anticipate direction of sunrise. Heliotropic behavior constitutes a form of offline anticipatory behavior that goes a step beyond online phototropic behavior. Nocturnal reorientation permits plants to optimize light intake (Kreps and Kay, 1997) without entering into conflict with other metabolic processes that take place between nighttime and dawn.

The fact that *Lavatera cretica* leaves are able to reorient nocturnally and track the sun is congruent with the idea of some form of endogenous modeling. Environmental rhythms must somehow be incorporated into the plant's routines in order to perform nocturnal reorientation. Success appears to reside in the capacity of plants to generate reliable time-keeping oscillations that correspond, roughly, to the 24-hour cycle (García Rodríguez and Calvo Garzón, 2010). It should come as no surprise that plants can mimic biological rhythms and estimate time. Life on Earth has evolved adaptations to synchronize internal activity with planetary cycles, courtesy of circadian clocks. More interestingly, the molecular mechanisms that allow *Lavatera cretica* to reorient in the absence of a light source are similar to the molecular mechanisms that permit animals to tick in sync with the planetary clock. Oscillation-involving roles are similar across eukaryotes (Cashmore, 2003). Plants and animals appear to draw on the very same molecular networks when it comes to exploiting circadian clocks that give them an anticipatory edge.

It is noteworthy that nocturnal reorientation cannot be simply accounted for in terms of the previous sunrise. In the case of *Lavatera cretica*, the capacity to reorient in the absence of light cues at sunset or during daytime solar-tracking can be retained for a number of days (Schwartz and Koller, 1986).

Interestingly, and as a side note, it might be possible to posit an explanation of offline processes in *Lavatera cretica* by appealing to causal covariation rather than inner representations (García Rodríguez and Calvo Garzón, 2010). If so, the connection between offline processing and representations seems to be noncompulsory. The way in which offline processes work in plants (and in the rest of eukaryotes, for that matter) does not force us to accept a view based on representations. Other explanatory models, such as, say, those based on oscillators or dynamical systems, may likewise deliver the goods.

As the example of *Lavatera cretica* illustrates, some plants, insofar as they process information offline, could satisfy the demands for being categorized as cognitive. At the same time, the study of plant cognition opens the door to expanding and reconfiguring our understandings of widely accepted connections in the philosophy of psychology, such as those of representations and offline processing.

3.3 *Learning and memory*

If offline heliotropic behavior point toward some form of memory, the same holds with respect to plant learning. In fact, at a molecular level, learning processes are remarkably similar at least in terms of signal transduction in animals and plants (Trewavas, 1999, 2003). We may approach learning in terms of reinforcement: in the case of plants, it is nothing but the active maintenance of reciprocal channels of communication among different areas in the plant's organism and different environmental elements, understood as a trial-and-error mechanism. This trial-and-error strategy is consistent with plastic tropic responses (Calvo and Keijzer, 2011). However, the difference between animal and plant learning processes is related to a tissue factor: despite sharing the same information-processing mechanism, anatomical differences between animals and plants are reflected here:

> Just as the process of learning in a brain could be represented as a time series, a set of snapshots of developing brain connections, in plants, each snapshot may possibly be represented by developing plasmodesmatal connections or equally, successive new tissues. So, instead of changing dendrite connections, plants form new networks by creating new tissues, a series of developing brains as it were.
>
> (Trewavas, 2003, p. 14)

These new tissues, added on top of the former ones, include new networks that operate on their own as cells continue to divide during the organism's life. This means that it is not a matter of genetic pre-programming; on the contrary, phenotypic change lies at the very basis of memory processes in plants. There are different examples of these learning mechanisms in plants, such as optimization of stomatal aperture in water deficit situations, oscillations in gravitropic behavior, etc. (Trewavas, 2005).

As we could expect from the existence of learning processes, memory processes are also present in plants because of the same mechanisms of phenotypic plasticity, which include electrical and chemical changes. Take for example drought avoidance behavior, which results in a reduction of cell growth rate, which in turn implies certain chemical and electrical changes (Palmgren, 2001; Trewavas, 2003). This behavior and its underlying mechanism in plants are compared to those with typically minimal forms of cognition, such as *Aplysia*. In both cases there are a sufficient number of similarities (for example, changes in phosporylation and in Ca^{2+} channels) (Trewavas, 2003). Another example is that of carnivorous plants, such as *D. muscipula* and *A. vesiculosa*, where these short-term memory mechanisms are similar to those of bacteria (di Primio et al., 2000; Calvo and Keijzer, 2009, 2011), with similarly underlying action potentials.

Finally, under a neobehaviorist paradigm (Abramson and Chicas-Mosier, 2016), we may approach plant learning and memory from a comparative psychological perspective. In particular, we may pursue plant nonassociative and associative forms of learning, two forms of learning that have been reported to take place in plants (Gagliano et al., 2014, 2016). The former constitutes the simplest form of learning. Despite the fact that it can be distinguished from mere sensory adaptation, it is consistent with an instinctual interpretation of plant behavior. But plant associative learning is an entirely different matter. Intriguingly, Pavlovian classical conditioning has been documented in *Pisum sativum*, the garden pea (Gagliano et al., 2016). This lends support to the idea of more sophisticated forms of learning and memory.

4 Grafting onto different paradigms

Explaining plant intelligence suggests a question that is philosophical in its very nature: which theoretical framework should guide our research? Until recently, the default position was to endorse an information-processing paradigm (Calvo, 2007). If so, the mark of the cognitive would be demarcated by "all processes by which the sensory input is transformed, reduced, elaborated, stored, recovered, and used" (Neisser, 1967, p. 4). Plant cognition would thus amount to the sum of multiple subpersonal information-processing systems, provided that plants are seen as agents in the first place (Calvo, 2018). Plants ought to be able then to somehow construct internal representations of the outside world on which reasoning and decision-making can operate. Unearthing the type of mechanisms that allow plants to construct and make use of internal representations out of sensory data can be a daunting task, both empirically and conceptually, but it is not unlike the task of accounting for the cognitive abilities of nematodes and insects or even prokaryotic life forms (Ben-Jacob et al., 2004; Reading and Sperandio, 2006; van Duijn et al., 2006; Shapiro, 2007).

Alternatively, we may consider the structuring of flexible plant behavior noncomputationally, as the end result of the way endogenous and external factors couple together, as ecological psychology (among other approaches) holds (section 4.3).

Which framework should we use to explain cognition in plants? Answers can vary widely depending on whether a computational/representational framework is endorsed or not, and if so, depending on the type of computations and representations that we resort to. But we are not forced to choose between the two extremes. A number of intermediate positions are available in between a full-fledged computational/representational approach of the sort that mainstream cognitive psychology and artificial intelligence have dictated in the past and more radical neo-Gibsonian noncomputational/nonrepresentational approaches.

We may thus explore the guiding role that different models and theoretical frameworks may play. Given the manifest idiosyncrasies and constraints that plant anatomy and physiology highlight – to cut a long story short, plants are not only autotrophic but also "republican" (Calvo et al., 2017), that is, significantly more distributed and decentralized than "monarchic" animals. An embodied, "post-cognitivist" cognitive science (Gomila and Calvo, 2008) could furnish plant neurobiology with the natural contender to information-processing psychology.

Post-cognitivist approaches (Gibson, 1979; Beer, 1990; Varela et al., 1991) rely on different biologically inspired aspects, such as the embodiment or situatedness of cognitive processes. Intelligence is conceived not as a matter of subpersonal information-processing but as the sum of flexible capacities possessed by an organism for adapting as a whole to the specific circumstances of the environment. In this way, post-cognitivism understands intelligence in terms of the particular ways in which behavior remains adaptive. Overall, post-cognitivism does away with the idea of cognition as a centralized process. It is rather a distributed and self-organized process based on the mutual interaction of bodily, neural, and environmental factors. In principle, the same would hold when plants and not animals are our target. Plant cognition would be the end result of the interaction of their highly decentralized republican bodies with phyto-neural and environmental factors.

As we can see, the relation of influence between plant neurobiology and philosophy of psychology is bidirectional. While different psychological theories provide us with the conceptual tools and scientific methods that are necessary to look for specific experimental evidence, sometimes this evidence invites us to reconfigure our ideas of what to look for and where. For this reason, the emergence of plant neurobiology as a new field of study that can be approached from different psychological perspectives is key for the development of those very theories. In this sense, experimental evidence in plant neurobiology illuminates both the new possibilities and the limitations of the theoretical basis of each framework.

In this setting, we may approach plant intelligence from the standpoint of different schools. Without providing a defense of any school in particular, we consider next three highly influential formulae that have gained momentum in the last decade: predictive processing, enactivism, and ecological psychology. These are listed in increasing degree of detachment from their commitment to computationalism and/or representationalism.

4.1 Plant predictive processing

Anticipatory behavior constitutes a clear-cut mark of intelligence. Plausibly, only those systems that successfully predict the world and not merely react to it may survive (Clark, 2016). If so, and considering that plants exhibit not only flexible but also anticipatory behavior (Novoplansky, 2016), predictive processing – a particular application of the "free energy" principle (Friston, 2010, 2013; Kiefer and Hohwy, this volume) – could constitute a promising venue for exploration.

The main thesis of predictive processing is that anticipatory behavior relies on an estimation of the likelihood that a given state of sensory stimulation constitutes the *actual* source of energy impinging upon the periphery of the system. Plant perception would take place courtesy of some process whereby sensory signals are matched to the predictions being generated. This is what happens when the difference between an organism's model of the environment and actual sensorial states is minimized. Plants would maintain a model that generates predictions of future states of the causes of its sensory states. In turn, they would try to minimize prediction error with respect to this generative model. In this framework, the phenotype of plants constitutes the implicit expectations being held.

The capacity of plants to predict, update their expectations, and minimize error points toward a basic form of agency. Plants would be interpreted as pro-active agents that sample their local environment and estimate the likelihood that one external state of affairs and not another is the source of energy. In this way, plants would elicit information that has an adaptive value and that can be responded to accordingly.

For such a model to contribute to error minimization, plants must embody a model of the causes of the inputs and information must flow in a particular manner. Predictions of sensory signals are such that predicted inputs and actual inputs can be compared against each other. Whenever a prediction error is found, that is, a mismatch between the prediction generated and the incoming input signal, it is propagated upward. We may in this way speak of plant perception as the end result of a process whereby top-down predictions match the environmental input (Calvo et al., 2016).

Plants could minimize prediction error either by updating their expectations, by re-sampling via phenotypic plasticity, or by combining two forms of inference – "perceptual" and "active" (Calvo and Friston, 2017). In this way, plants may yield better predictions complementarily by (i) updating their expectations via the adjustment of their internal states ("perceptual inference") and (ii) being more selective in the way they sample their surroundings ("active inference"), making new samples better match their held expectations.

Although at present it remains an open empirical possibility whether plants can generate expectancies in line with a predictive-processing formulation, a number of experimental suggestions as to how to put the combination of plant perceptual and active inference to the test have been offered in recent years (Calvo et al., 2016). In particular, different aspects, both structural and functional, of plant systems fall within the explanatory scope of predictive processing. At the level of plant anatomy, the framework might help explain the type of hierarchical organization found in the vasculature of plants (Figure 32.1). Forward and backward connectivity among vascular bundles that encode expectations and prediction error would serve to implement predictive processing and error minimization. In a similar vein, predictive processing could shed light upon the role played by plant action potentials – as well as other electric signals identified by plant electrophysiology – in coding for surprising (unpredictable) stimuli. At the psychophysiological level, predictive processing may help unearth the behavioral correlates of physiological phenomena (Calvo and Friston, 2017).

Plant predictive processing constitutes but one approach. Having a sensorimotor organization that results in the manipulation of the environment allows for anticipatory functioning. Predictive processing relies upon the capacity of plants to endogenously model the environment – a way of making sense of plant behavior that remains computational and representational. In a sense, plants, under the free-energy formulation, would be seen as performing some form of Bayesian model selection, whereby they continuously change their internal representational states in order to infer what

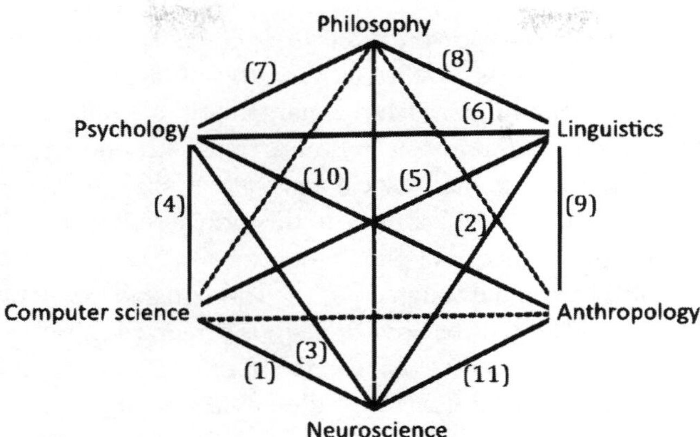

Figure 32.1 The "Cognitive Science hexagon" in 1978. Vertices represent contributing disciplines. Lines joining vertices represent the following interdisciplinary collaborations: (1) Cybernetics; (2) Neurolinguistics; (3) Neuropsychology; (4) Simulation of cognitive processes; (5) Computational linguistics; (6) Psycholinguistics; (7) Philosophy of psychology; (8) Philosophy of language; (9) Anthropological linguistics; (10) Cognitive anthropology; and (11) Evolution of brain. Continuous lines represent consolidated collaborations; unnumbered dotted lines, in-progress ties between philosophy and computer science, neuroscience and anthropology as of 1978 (adapted from the Sloan Report, pp. 3-ff.) (Calvo, 2016).

the world is like (Kiefer and Hohwy, this volume). However unorthodox such plant Bayesian modeling is viewed with respect to mainstream cognitivist approaches, it remains computational and representational at its core. We now turn to noncomputational/nonrepresentational post-cognitivist approaches.

4.2 Green sensorimotor contingencies

According to sensorimotor contingency theory (O'Regan and Noë, 2001), experiencing the external world is possible in the absence of mediating inner representations. Instead, sensorimotor contingency theory resorts to a type of active engagement with the environment:

> We shall say that perceivers have sensations in a particular sensemodality, when they exercise their mastery of the sensorimotor laws that govern the relation between possible actions and the resulting changes in incoming information in that sense modality.
>
> (O'Regan and Noë, 2001, p. 82)

Sensorimotor contingency theory is at the basis of different cognitive theories, mainly biologically oriented or autopoietic enactivism and perceptual or sensorimotor enactivism (Degenaar and O'Regan, 2015; Heras-Escribano et al., 2015). It has been applied to prokaryotic models of life (Barandiaran, 2016; Barandiaran and Egbert,

2014). Why then not to eukaryotic life forms like plants? An active process of engagement with the surroundings fits hand in glove with the idea of phenotypic plasticity enabling metabolic functioning through the manipulation of the environment. Under this light, plants could have sensory awareness of their surroundings via active exploration. Plants exploit, informationally speaking, the way changes are sensed as a result of the exploratory processes that takes place in the form of sensorimotor contingencies. Sensorimotor contingency theory, applied to plants, would predict that the structure of the environment is revealed through controlled growth and development. Behavior becomes adaptive provided that the environment is perceived throughout the particular sensorimotor contingencies that plants have mastered during ontogenic development. Plants perceive structural features of the environment with an adaptive value and modify their behavior accordingly.

Sensorimotor patterns work both online and offline, which allows for a sensorimotor organization of the organism that possesses these capacities. All these processes, online or offline, presuppose a relation between possible actions and the resulting changes in incoming information that can be related directly to the physical form and temporal scale of plants.

4.3 *An ecological approach to plant intelligence*

Another highly influential nonrepresentational, embodied, and situated approach to cognition is ecological psychology (Gibson, 1979; Lobo et al. 2018). According to the ecological approach, cognition is a matter of perceiving-acting through active exploration of the agent as a whole – a process that (dis)solves ambiguity. In a key contrast to predictive processing, it holds that environmental sources of stimulation are not seen as ambiguous. As a result, perception need not be mediated inferentially in the first place. Perception, if understood ecologically, can only be organized around actions. Generally speaking, organisms detect rich environmental information in the form of higher-order informational invariants that they actively pick up. Organisms are said to *resonate* with informational invariants, i.e. ecological information that specifies opportunities for interaction.

Ecological principles have been applied to many cognitive phenomena, such as vision (Gibson, 1979), learning (Jacobs and Michaels, 2007), or touch (Solomon and Turvey, 1988), and are a foundation for other scientific disciplines, such as robotics (Chemero and Turvey, 2007) or the development of sensory substitution devices (Lobo et al., 2014; Travieso et al., 2015). Exploration allows agents to perceive directly (that is to say, noninferentially) different *affordances* – opportunities for action – that they can take advantage of. If objects in the vicinity can present themselves as reachable, kickable, graspable, etc. to human and nonhuman animals, the same may be said of plants.

Can we then apply a set of ecological principles to the study of plant intelligence? In the same way that our environment is understood as an ecological informational scale whose elements are meaningful to us insofar as they relate to our abilities or capacities (Richardson et al., 2008; Heras-Escribano and Pinedo, 2016), attention could in principle be paid to the ecological scale at which interaction in between plants and their surroundings takes place.

And yet, Gibson himself turned a blind eye to this very idea. As he wrote at the very beginning of *The ecological approach to visual perception*:

> The environment of plants, organisms that lack sense organs and muscles, is not relevant in the study of perception and behavior. We shall treat the vegetation of the world as animals do, as if it were lumped together with the inorganic minerals of the world, with the physical, chemical, and geological environment. Plants in general are not animate; they do not move about, they do not behave, they lack a nervous system, and they do not have sensations. In these respects they are like the objects of physics, chemistry, and geology.
>
> (Gibson, 1979, p. 3)

Thus, Gibson rejected the possibility of talking of plant intelligence inasmuch as he considered that plants are not sensitive or motile, and they lack nervous systems. As he conceived of them, they were like inanimate objects rather than organisms, behaviorally speaking. Today, however, there is sufficient empirical data to reject Gibson's claims.

Ecologically-oriented psychologists and philosophers have in fact started to explore the idea that ecological principles could be extended to plants (Carello et al., 2012; Calvo et al., 2014; Fultot et al., 2016; Heras-Escribano, 2016).

We may consider the plant-environment system itself as the unit of ecological analysis in analogy with the case of animals. A climbing plant and its host, for instance, constitute a coupled system. As the vine circumnutates for the sake of exploration, it perceives its surroundings in terms of biologically relevant interactions. Plants, like animals, resonate to information that specifies ways of interaction. Rather than inferring the host's availability for twining, we may say that a climbing plant perceives *climbability* directly – the very possibility to interact with something that affords climbing.

To flesh out this ecological description, Calvo et al. (2017) have explored the possibility of understanding the guidance of circumnutation of climbing bean stems from a particular ecological perspective: "general *tau* theory" (Lee, 1998), a parsimonious and universal way to understand the natural regulation of goal-directed action across phyla (Lee, 2009). General tau theory aims to explain how agents guide goal-directed movements by using perceptual information – in this case, higher-order ecological invariants such as *tau* or time-to-contact. This framework illustrates how information directly available can specify unambiguously environmental properties and guide plant patterns of growth and movement. Although further research is needed, we believe the time is ripe to fully appreciate how general tau theory can deal with plants and their "power of movement" (Darwin, 1880; Lee and Calvo, in preparation). This is promising inasmuch as ecological psychology is starting to offer a consistent and unified cross-species informational framework for explaining agent-environment interaction from plants to humans – that is to say, without falling prey to anthropocentrism or to any other form of zoocentrism (Heras-Escribano, 2019: 163–70).

5 The role of philosophy in plant neurobiology

The philosophy of plant neurobiology provides a starting point for the scientific pursuit of (animal!) intelligence that is somewhat special. It furnishes a naturalistic explanation of the *emergence* of intelligence over the course of natural history in sharp contrast, phylogenetically and ontogenetically speaking, to the type of cognitive capacities customarily rehearsed in the case of adult human animals. Evolutionarily speaking, the mental realm was plausibly brought about by the hand of the increasing structural complexity that obtains as different subsystems played their partial causal roles in the integration of information (García Rodríguez and Calvo Garzón, 2010). This allows us to appraise the origins of intelligence irrespective of biological kingdoms or cladistic classifications.

To understand the particular role of philosophy, it is important to bear in mind that plant physiology, broadly speaking (see later in this section), despite its capacity to identify particular mechanisms at work, does not suffice to account for intelligence. If the foregoing considerations are on the right track, the behavior of plants cannot be equated with automatic physiological processes. Insofar as plant behavior escapes a reductionist physiological take, a different approach is needed altogether – an approach that can fill in something that pure physiological approaches miss by necessity. The philosophy of plant neurobiology tries to understand how plants are able to engage in *meaningful* ways with their local environment. In this respect, it defies a mechanistic reading.

The philosophy of plant neurobiology lays the stress upon systematic properties of the sort that can be found in the behavioral repertoire of the so-called "lower" organisms (Calvo et al., 2014). Put differently, insofar as those properties being targeted mark the borderline between patterns of behavior that are not automatic and those that are nonadaptive, the quest serves to shed light upon more sophisticated forms of behavior that are equally systematic. It is still a long way from plant behavior to full-fledged intentional action of the sort exhibited by human animals. But explaining the systematicity that we are able to appreciate in the behavioral repertoire of plants – courtesy, for example, of time-lapse techniques – may provide a less-biased basis for understanding the systematicity of animal behavior, including our own.

All in all, the philosophy of plant neurobiology aims to fill this gap by contributing its particular toolkit to the overall explanation of biological intelligence. In the last decade, plant neurobiology has consistently produced empirical data from different disciplines that hint at the existence of plant intelligence. Plant neurobiology, far from being relegated or excluded from the study of cognitive phenomena because of strict conceptual restrictions, has been developed and strengthened with the development of the cognitive sciences and the profusion of different theories for understanding what cognition is. This allows for increasing both the scope and the influence of plant neurobiology as an independent discipline in different aspects, both theoretical and experimental.

The interdisciplinary effort that plant neurobiology represents can be thought of in the very same way that gave rise to the consolidation of cognitive science. Cognitive science was developed as an interdisciplinary field of study that included several connections among the disciplines that shaped it (Figure 32.1). Such connections allowed for empirical and theoretical developments concerning the nature of the mind and a better understanding of the function of our cognitive capacities.

The philosophy of plant neurobiology emerges at the intersection of the philosophy of cognitive science and plant neurobiology. We can in fact identify an analogous structure and similar relationships between the subdisciplines that conform plant neurobiology (Figure 32.2) and those that conform the cognitive sciences.

For the sake of simplicity, only a handful of vertices appear in Figure 32.2. But the overall landscape is much more complex with many more vertices (and links) yet to be included. Comparative psychology and behavioral neuroscience, for instance, can contribute by highlighting respectively behavioral commonalities across phyla and the ways in which cognition and adaptive behavior at the organismic level and the underlying (phyto)-neural substrate constrain each other (Calvo, 2016). Cognitive ethology, bioinspired robotics, and artificial intelligence, among others, are disciplines that are likely to play a more active role in the future.

One way or another, disciplines such as physiological plant ecology ("ecophysiology" in Figure 32.1 – link #5) or evolutionary genetics (link #3) do not suffice by themselves to account for plant perception, learning, memory, attention, decision-making, and problem-solving. The problem is not that we are focusing on links #3 and #5 exclusively and not on, say, biochemical ecology (#1), molecular ecology, and ecological genetics (#2) or upon evolutionary ecology (#4). The problem is rather that the

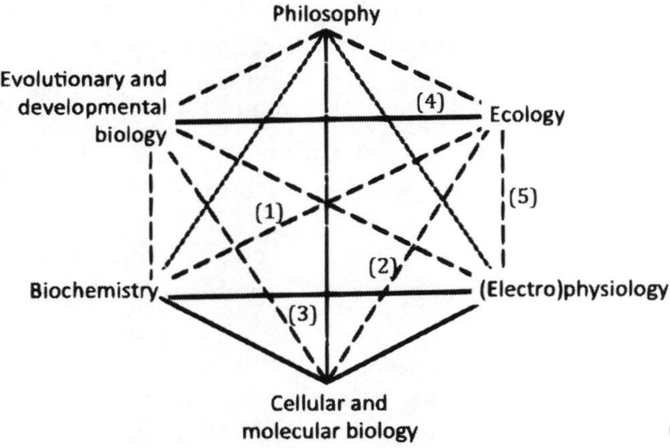

Figure 32.2 The hexagon of Plant Neurobiology in 2018. Vertices represent contributing disciplines. Lines joining vertices represent the following interdisciplinary collaborations (only a few are drawn): (1) Biochemical ecology; (2) Molecular ecology and ecological genetics; (3) Evolutionary genetics; (4) Evolutionary ecology; and (5) Ecophysiology. Continuous lines represent consolidated collaborations; dashed lines, in-progress ties; unnumbered dotted lines, areas necessitating more stable collaboration (Calvo, 2016).

exclusive focus upon plant science results in a form of tunnel vision that negatively impacts our comprehensive overall quest.

The naturalistic perspective that the philosophy of plant neurobiology represents can help consolidate plant neurobiology in a distinctive manner. Its particular methodology can contribute to making explicit how theoretical commitments bear upon our quest. If, say, a representational-computational model is favored, it can shed light upon the informational function that representations or computations may serve. Were representational models to be dispensed with altogether, as defended under some forms of enactivism and ecological psychology, it can contribute to the elaboration of a whole set of different empirical approaches.

Foundational issues of the sort philosophy of science has traditionally played can also contribute in a constructive manner, with a role akin to the role played in the cognitive sciences. In particular, it can do so by putting forward an integral framework at a more abstract level of analysis that defies a mechanistic, reductionist take, as pursued by plant science subdisciplines when taken in isolation.

Topics of interest in philosophy of psychology are likely to benefit from the particular approach proposed here. Think for instance of "domain-generality versus domain-specificity" discussions. Granting plants mental capacity for the sake of arguments, should we consider such capacity as domain-general or domain-specific?

Plant neurobiology does not attempt to reproduce systematic properties of an otherwise Fodorian architecture. It rather aims to explore alternative models of mind that do not focus on linguiform systematicity *exclusively* (Calvo et al., 2014). There is no reason to assume, for instance, that a syntactically and semantically combinatorial system of mental representations must be a condition on (plant) mindedness. Pictorial, vectorial, action-based, and other competing models must equally be considered. The philosophy of plant neurobiology insofar as it is freed from a logic-like inferential processing understanding of thought and related biases is able to explore alternative explanations more fully and without prejudice.

Overall, the philosophy of plant neurobiology has a guiding role to play that includes

(i) the analysis of the nature of the theories under consideration,
(ii) the identification of competing working hypotheses and the presentation of challenges in turn,
(iii) the sharpening of empirical hypotheses, and
(iv) the directing of novel lines of engagement with empirical investigation with an eye to the design of different experimental procedures and the generation of wider pools of testable predictions.

The contribution of philosophy should be evaluated as helping to consolidate plant neurobiology as "an interdisciplinary endeavor with a research agenda of its own" (Calvo, 2016) through the traditional tools of philosophy: mainly, conceptual analysis and the development of a consistent and unified theoretical framework that spells out how plant science subdisciplines relate to each other. This can help rephrase problems and guide research on plant intelligence, insofar as explanatory models transcend the nature of questions that have traditionally been posed from within each subfield. Integration of different levels of description and explanation is a necessary requirement. In this sense, it is urgent for philosophy to consolidate relations with disciplines, such as ecology and evolutionary biology, focusing on plants as both biological and cognitive agents. This collaboration would greatly benefit not only our understanding the nature of plant intelligence but also our understanding of the nature of cognition as a natural phenomenon of living beings. The better we understand plant intelligence, the better we will understand the natural origins of cognition.

Acknowledgments

This paper has been written thanks to a Contrato Puente Postdoctoral Research Fellowship funded by the Universidad de Granada, the research projects FFI2013–44836 and FFI2016–80088-P, a Juan de la Cierva-Formación postdoctoral Research Fellowship, The FiloLab Group of Excellence at the Universidad de Granada and a 2018 Leonardo Grant for Researchers and Cultural Creators, BBVA Foundation (The Foundation accepts no responsibility for the opinions, statements, and contents included in the project and/or the results thereof, which are entirely the responsibility of the authors) to MH-E. PC was supported by the US Office of Naval Research-Global through project 'Plant Intelligence for Robotics and AI'. Special thanks to František Baluška, Manuel de Pinedo, Adam Linson, Lorena Lobo, Stefano Mancuso, and Liz Van Volkenburgh for helpful comments and suggestions on a previous draft.

References

Abramson, C. I., & Calvo, P. (2018). General issues in the cognitive analysis of plant learning and intelligence. In M. Gagliano, F. Baluška, & G. Witzany (Eds.), *Memory and Learning in Plants*. Cham: Springer.

Abramson, C. I., & Chicas-Mosier, A. M. (2016). Learning in plants: Lessons from Mimosa pudica. *Frontiers in Psychology*, 7, 417.

Appel, H. M., & Cocroft, R. B. (2014). Plants respond to leaf vibrations caused by insect herbivore chewing. *Oecologia*, 175, 1257–66.

Baldwin, I. T., Halitschke, R., Paschold, A., von Dahl, C. C., & Preston, C. A. (2006). Volatile signaling in plant-plant interactions: "Talking trees" in the genomics era. *Science*, 311(5762), 812–15.

Ballaré, C. L., & Pierik, R. (2017). The shade-avoidance syndrome: Multiple signals and ecological consequences. *Plant, Cell and Environment*, 40(11), 2530–43.

Baluška, F., Mancuso, S., Volkmann, D., & Barlow, P. W. (2004). Root apices as plant command centres: The unique 'brain-like' status of the root apex transition zone. *Biologia*, 59, 7–19.

Baluška, F. (2009). Cell-cell channels, viruses, and evolution: Via infection, parasitism, and symbiosis toward higher levels of biological complexity. *Annals of the New York Academy of Sciences*, 1178, 106–19.

Baluška, F. (2010). Recent surprising similarities between plant cells and neurons. *Plant Signal Behavior*, 5(2), 87–89.

Baluška, F., & Mancuso, S. (2013). Ion channels in plants: From bio-electricity, via signaling, to behavioral actions. *Plant Signaling & Behavior*, 8, 23009.

Baluška, F., Mancuso, S., Volkmann, D., & Barlow, P. W. (2009). The "root-brain" hypothesis of Charles and Francis Darwin: Revival after more than 125 years. *Plant Signaling & Behavior*, 4, 1121–27. doi: 10.4161/psb.4.12.10574

Baluška, F., Mancuso, S., Volkmann, D., & Barlow, P. W. (2010). Root apex transition zone: A signalling-response nexus in the root. *Trends in Plant Science*, 15, 402–08.

Baluška, F., Volkmann, D., & Menzel, D. (2005). Plant synapses: Actin-based domains for cell-to-cell communications. *Trends in Plant Science*, 10(3), 106–11.

Barandiaran, X. E. (2016). Autonomy and enactivism: Towards a theory of sensorimotor autonomous agency. *Topoi*, in press.

Barandiaran, X. E., & Egbert, M. D. (2014). Norm-establishing and norm-following in autonomous agency. *Artificial Life*, 20(1), 5–28.

Barlow, P. W. (2010). Plastic, inquisitive roots & intelligent plants in the light of some new vistas in plant biology. *Plant Biosystems*, 144, 396–407.

Bastien, R., Bohr, T., Moulia, B., & Douady, S. (2013). Unifying model of shoot gravitropism reveals proprioception as a central feature of posture control in plants. *Proceedings of the National Academy of Sciences of the United States of America*, 110(2), 755–60.

Beer, R. D. (1990). *Intelligence as Adaptive Behavior: An Experiment in Computational Neuroethology*. Boston: Academic Press.

Ben-Jacob, E., Becker, I., Shapira, Y., & Levine, H. (2004). Bacterial linguistic communication and, social intelligence. *Trends in Microbiology*, 12, 366–72. doi: 10.1016/j.tim.2004.06.006

Bose, I., & Karmakar, R. (2003). Simple models of plant learning & memory. *Physica Scripta*, 106, 9–12.

Bose, J. C. (1926). *The Nervous Mechanism of Plants*. London: Longmans, Green and Co.

Brenner, E. D., Stahlberg, R., Mancuso, S., Vivanco, J. M., Baluška, F., & van Volkenburgh, E. (2006). Plant neurobiology: An integrated view of plant signaling. *Trends in Plant Science*, 11(8), 413–19.

Calvo, P. (2007). The quest for cognition in plant neurobiology. *Plant Signaling and Behavior*, 2(4), 208–11.

Calvo, P. (2016). The philosophy of plant neurobiology: A manifesto. *Synthese*, 193(5), 1323–43.

Calvo, P. (2018). Plantae. In J. Vonk & T. Shackelford (Eds.), *Encyclopedia of Animal Cognition and Behavior*. Cham: Springer.

Calvo, P., & Baluška, F. (2015). Conditions for minimal intelligence across Eukaryota: A cognitive science perspective. *Frontiers in Psychology*, 6, 1329. doi: 10.3389/fpsyg.2015.01329

Calvo, P., Baluška, F., & Sims, A. (2016). "Feature detection" versus "predictive coding" models of plant behavior. *Frontiers in Psychology*, 7, 1505.

Calvo, P., & Friston, K. (2017). Predicting green: Really radical (plant) predictive processing. *Journal of the Royal Society Interface*, 14, 20170096.

Calvo, P., & Keijzer, F. (2009). Cognition in plants. In F. Balusˇka (Ed.), *Plant-Environment Interactions: Signaling & Communication in Plants* (pp. 247–66). Berlin: Springer-Verlag.

Calvo, P., & Keijzer, F. (2011). Plants: Adaptive behavior, root brains and minimal cognition. *Adaptive Behavior*, 19(3), 155–71.

Calvo, P., Martín, E., & Symons, J. (2014). The emergence of systematicity in minimally cognitive agents. In P. Calvo & J. Symons (Eds.), *The Architecture of Cognition: Rethinking Fodor and Pylyshyn's Systematicity Challenge* (pp. 397–434). Cambridge, MA: MIT Press.

Calvo, P., Raja, V., & Lee, D. N. (2017). Guidance of circumnutation of climbing bean stems: An ecological exploration. *bioRxiv*. doi: 10.1101/122358

Calvo, P., Sahi, V. P., & Trewavas, A. (2017). Are plants sentient? *Plant, Cell & Environment*, 1–12.

Carello, C., Vaz, D., Blau, J. J. C., & Petrusz, S. C. (2012). Unnerving intelligence. *Ecological Psychology*, 24(3), 241–64.

Cashmore, A. R. (2003). Cryptochromes: Enabling plants & animals to determine circadian time. *Cell*, 114, 537–43.

Chemero, A., & Turvey, M. (2007). Gibsonian affordances for roboticists. *Adaptive Behavior*, 15, 473–80.

Clark, A. (2016). *Surfing Uncertainty: Prediction, Action, and the Embodied Mind*. Oxford: Oxford University Press.

Clark, A., & Grush, R. (1999). Towards a cognitive robotics. *Adaptive Behaviour*, 7(1), 5–16.

Clark, A., & Toribio, J. (1994). Doing without representing, *Synthese*, 101, 401–31.

Cole, K. S., & Curtis, H. J. (1938). Electric impedance of Nitella during activity. *The Journal of General Physiology*, 22, 37–64.

Cole, K. S., & Curtis, H. J. (1939). Electric impedance of the squid giant axon during activity. *The Journal of General Physiology*, 22, 649–70.

Darwin, C. (1875). *The Movements and Habits of Climbing Plants*. London, UK: John Murray.

Darwin, C. (1880). *The Power of Movement in Plants*. London, UK: John Murray.

Degenaar, J., & O'Regan, J. K. (2015). Sensorimotor theory and enactivism. *Topoi*, 1–15.

De Kroon, H., Visser, E. J. W., Huber, H., & Hutchings, M. J. (2009). A modular concept of plant foraging behaviour: The interplay between local responses and systemic control. *Plant, Cell & Environment*, 32, 704–12.

Dicke, M., Agrawal, A. A., & Bruin, J. (2003). Plants talk, but are they deaf? *Trends in Plant Science*, 8(9), 403–05.

di Primio, F., Muller, B. S., & Lengeler, J. W. (2000). Minimal cognition in unicellular organisms. In J. A. Meyer, A. Berthoz, D. Floreano, H. L. Roitblat, & S. W. Wilson (Eds.), *SAB2000 Proceedings Supplement, International Society of Adaptive Behavior* (pp. 3–12). Honolulu, Hawaii: International Society for Adaptive Behavior.

Dumais, J. (2013). Beyond the sine law of plant gravitropism. *Proceedings of the National Academy of Sciences of the United States of America*, 110(2), 391–92.

Friston, K. (2010). The free-energy principle: A unified brain theory? *Nature Reviews Neuroscience*, 11, 127–38.

Friston, K. (2013). Life as we know it. *Journal of the Royal Society Interface*, 10, 20130475.

Fultot, M. F., Nie, L., & Carello, C. (2016). Perception-action mutuality obviates mental construction. *Constructivist Foundations*, 11(2), 298–307.

Gagliano, M., Renton, M., Depczynski, M., & Mancuso, S. (2014). Experience teaches plants to learn faster and forget slower in environments where it matters. *Oecologia*, 175(1), 63–72.

Gagliano, M., Vyazovskiy, V. V., Borbély, A. A., Grimonprez, M., & Depczynski, M. (2016). Learning by association in plants. *Scientific Reports*, 6, 38427.

García Rodríguez, A., & Calvo, P. (2010). Is cognition a matter of representations? Emulation, teleology, and time-keeping in biological systems. *Adaptive Behavior*, 18(5), 400–15.

Gibson, J. J. (1979). *The Ecological Approach to Visual Perception*. Boston, MA: Houghton Mifflin.

Gilroy, S. (2008). Plant tropisms. *Current Biology*, 18, R275–R277.

Gomila, A., & Calvo, P. (2008). Directions for an embodied cognitive science: Toward an integrated approach. In P. Calvo & A. Gomila (Eds.), *Handbook of Cognitive Science: An Embodied Approach* (pp. 1–25). Amsterdam: Elsevier Science.

Gunar, I. I., & Sinykhin, A. M. (1962). A spreading wave of excitation in higher plants. *Proceedings of the Academy of Sciences of the USSR (Botany)*, 142, 214–15.

Gunar, I. I., & Sinykhin, A. M. (1963). Functional significance of action currents affecting the gas exchange of higher plants. *Soviet Plant Physiology*, 10, 219–26.

Gundel, P. E., Pierik, R., Mommer, L., & Ballaré, C. L. (2014). Competing neighbors: Light perception and root function. *Oecologia*, 176, 1–10.

Heras-Escribano, M. (2016). Embracing the environment: Ecological answers for enactive problems. *Constructivist Foundations*, 11(2), 309–12.

Heras-Escribano, M., Noble, J., & Pinedo, M. (2015). Enactivism, action and normativity: A Wittgensteinian analysis. *Adaptive Behavior*, 23(1), 20–33.

Heras-Escribano, M., & Pinedo, M. (2016). Are affordances normative? *Phenomenology and the Cognitive Sciences*, Online first: http://link.springer.com/article/10.1007/s11097-015-9440-0

Heras-Escribano, M. (2019). *The Philosophy of Affordances*. Cham: Palgrave Macmillan.

Hodge, A. (2009). Root decisions. *Plant, Cell & Environment*, 32(6), 628–40.

Jacobs, D. M., & Michaels, C. F. (2007). Direct learning. *Ecological Psychology*, 19, 321–49.

Kiefer, A., & Hohwy, J. (this volume). Representation in the prediction error minimization framework. In S. Robins, J. Symons, & P. Calvo (Eds.), *The Routledge Companion to Philosophy of Psychology*. Routledge.

Kreps, J. A., & Kay, S. A. (1997). Coordination of plant metabolism & development by the circadian clock. *Plant Cell*, 9, 1235–44.

Kutschera, U., & Briggs, W. R. (2009). From Charles Darwin's botanical country-house studies to modern plant biology. *Plant Biol*, 11, 785–95.

Lee, D. N. (1998). Guiding movement by coupling taus. *Ecological Psychology*, 10(3–4), 221–50.

Lee, D. N. (2009). General Tau theory: Evolution to date. *Perception*, 38(6), 837–50.

Lee, D. N., & Calvo, P. (in preparation). The neuro-power of movement in plants.

Li, X., & Zhang, W. S. (2008). Salt-avoidance tropism in Arabidopsis thalania. *Plant Signaling & Behavior*, 3, 351–53.

Liu, S., Jiao, J., Lu, T. J., Xu, F., Pickard, B. G., & Genin, G. M. (2017). Arabidopsis leaf trichomes as acoustic antennae. *Biophysical Journal*, 113, 2068–76.

Lobo, L., Travieso, D., Barrientos, A., & Jacobs, D. M. (2014). Stepping on obstacles with a sensory substitution device on the lower leg: Practice without vision is more beneficial than practice with vision. *PLoS One*, 9(6), e98801. doi: 10.1371/journal.pone.0098801

Lobo, L., Heras-Escribano, M., & Travieso, D. (2018). The history and philosophy of ecological psychology. *Frontiers in Psychology*, 9, 2228. doi:10.3389/fpsyg.2018.02228

Massa, G., & Gilroy, S. (2003). Touch modulates gravity sensing to regulate the growth of primary roots of Arabidopsis thaliana. *The Plant Journal*, 33, 435–45.

McConnaughay, K. D. M., & Bazzaz, F. A. (1991). Is physical space a soil resource? *Ecology*, 72, 94–103.

Neisser, U. (1967). *Cognitive Psychology*. New York: Appleton-Century Crofts.

Novoplansky, A. (2016). Future perception in plants. In M. Nadin (Ed.), *Anticipation across Disciplines* (pp. 57–70). Cham: Springer.

O'Regan, J. K., & Noë, A. (2001). A sensorimotor approach to vision and visual consciousness. *Behavioural and Brain Sciences*, 24(5), 939–73. *Behavioral and Brain Sciences*, 24(5), 883–917.

Palmgren, M. G. (2001). Plant plasma membrane H+ ATPases: Powerhouses for nutrient uptake. *Annual Review of Plant Physiology*, 52, 817–45.

Pickard, B. G. (1973). Action potentials in higher plants. *The Botanical Review*, 39(2), 172–201.

Reading, N. C., & Sperandio, V. (2006). Quorum sensing: The many languages of bacteria. *Federation of European Microbiological Societies Microbiology Letters*, January, 254(1), 1–11.

Richardson, M. J., Shockley, K., Fajen, B. R., Riley, M. A., & Turvey, M. (2008). Ecological psychology: Six principles for an embodied-embedded approach to behavior. In P. Calvo & A. Gomila (Eds.), *Handbook of Cognitive Science: An Embodied Approach* (pp. 161–90). Amsterdam: Elsevier Science.

Schenk, H. J., Callaway, R. M., & Mahall, B. E. (1999). Spatial root segregation: Are plants territorial? *Advances in Ecological Research*, 28, 145–80.

Schwartz, A., & Koller, D. (1986). Diurnal phototropism in solar tracking leaves of Lavatera cretica. *Plant Physiology*, 80, 778–81.

Shapiro, J. A. (2007). Bacteria are small but not stupid: Cognition, natural genetic engineering and socio-bacteriology. *Studies in History and Philosophy of Biological and Biomedical Sciences*, 38, 807–19. doi: 10.1016/j.shpsc.2007.09.010

Sibaoka, T. (1969). Physiology of rapid movements in higher plants. *Annual Review of Plant Physiology*, 20, 165–84.

Silvertown, J., & Gordon, G. M. (1989). A framework for plant behavior. *Annual Review of Ecology and Systematics*, 20, 349–66.

Solomon, H. Y., & Turvey, M. T. (1988). Haptically perceiving the distances reachable with hand-held objects. *Journal of Experimental Psychology: Human Perception and Performance*, 14(3), 404–27.

Stahlberg, R. (2006). Historical overview on plant neurobiology. *Plant Signaling & Behavior*, 1(1), 6–8.

Travieso, D., Gómez-Jordana, L., Díaz, A., Lobo, L., & Jacobs, D. (2015). Body-scaled affordances in sensory substitution. *Consciousness and Cognition*, 38, 130–38.

Trewavas, A. J. (1999). How plants learn. *Proceedings of the National Academy of Sciences USA*, 96, 4216–18.

Trewavas, A. J. (2003). Aspects of plant intelligence. *Annals of Botany*, 92, 1–20.

Trewavas, A. J. (2005). Plant intelligence. *Naturwissenschaften*, 92, 401–13.

Trewavas, A. J. (2008). Aspects of plant intelligence: Convergence & evolution. In Simon Conway Morris (Ed.), *The Deep Structure of Biology: Is Convergence Sufficiently Ubiquitous to Give a Directional Signal* (pp. 68–110). West Conshohocken, PA: Templeton Press.

Trewavas, A. J. (2009). What is plant behaviour? *Plant Cell and Environment*, 32, 606–16.

Trewavas, A. J. (2014). *Plant Behaviour and Intelligence*. Oxford: Oxford University Press.

van Duijn, M., Keijzer, F., & Franken, D. (2006). Principles of minimal cognition: Casting cognition as sensorimotor coordination. *Adaptive Behavior*, 14, 157–70.

Varela, F., Rosch, E., & Thompson, E. (1991). *The Embodied Mind*. Cambridge, MA: MIT Press.

Volkov, A. G. (Ed.). (2006). *Plant Electrophysiology*. Berlin: Springer.

Part V

Perceptual experience

33
CONSCIOUSNESS

Tim Bayne

After being sorely neglected for some time, consciousness is well and truly back on the philosophical and scientific agenda. This entry provides a whistle-stop tour of some recent debates surrounding consciousness, with a particular focus on issues relevant to the scientific study of consciousness. The first half of this entry (the first to fourth sections) focuses on clarifying the *explanandum* of a science of consciousness and identifying constraints on an adequate account of consciousness; the second half of this entry (the fifth to seventh sections) examines a number of the methodological challenges facing the science of consciousness.

The concept(s) of consciousness

Discussions of consciousness are plagued by disputes about how best to home in on the phenomenon in question. How can we pre-theoretically characterize the object of study? Indeed, is there but one object of study here, or do multiple types of states go under the label "consciousness"?

Let's start with an easy distinction – or at least, a distinction that should be easy. Sometimes people (or organisms more generally) are said to be conscious, at other times mental states are said to be conscious. This distinction has come to be known as the distinction between creature consciousness and state consciousness. But although widely invoked, the distinction between creature consciousness and state consciousness is not always employed in the same way. Some theorists take creature consciousness to be the property of being awake; on this view, creature consciousness is importantly distinct from state consciousness, and it is only state consciousness that is deeply puzzling. Other theorists see state consciousness and creature consciousness as intimately related to each other. According to one version of this view, creature consciousness is the determinable of which various states of consciousness are determinates: to say that a creature is conscious is to say that it is in some state of consciousness or other. This conception of creature consciousness allows that a creature could be conscious without being awake, for dream states qualify as states of consciousness. I will use "creature consciousness" in this latter sense, for it seems to me that to use "creature consciousness" to refer to the state of being awake merely fosters confusion.

Whether we are talking about conscious states or conscious creatures, we need a pre-theoretical gloss on consciousness if we are to get the project of theory-building off on the right foot. If there is any lesson to be learnt from the recent discussion of consciousness it is that any such gloss is very difficult to come by. Not only is there disagreement as to whether there is a single central form of consciousness. Those who hold that there is a single core notion of consciousness often have very different conceptions of what that core notion is. Here, as elsewhere in philosophy, it can be difficult to tell whether the disagreements are substantive or terminological or both. We can get a fix on some of the central disputes in this domain by considering three notions with which consciousness is often associated: qualia, subjectivity, and phenomenality.

Qualia

In its most neutral sense, the term "qualia" refers to the appearances of things. The look of a tomato, the sound of a trumpet, the taste of a cucumber all involve qualia to the extent that these states represent how objects appear. In this thin sense of the term, no one would deny that there are qualia. However, many theorists employ one or another of various theoretically loaded senses of "qualia" – senses in which the very existence of qualia is up for grabs. Block, for example, uses "qualia" to refer to the non-intentional features of conscious states. One could deny that Block-qualia exist without denying the existence of consciousness – indeed, many do. Dennett (1988) also uses "qualia" in a theoretically loaded sense. Dennett-qualia, if they existed, would be ineffable, intrinsic, private, and directly apprehensible properties of mental states. Again, one could deny that Dennett-qualia exist without denying the existence of consciousness, as Dennett himself does. Even the claim that qualia must be conscious is not universally endorsed, with some theorists arguing in defence of non-conscious qualia.

Qualia are often associated with the so-called secondary qualities (colours, tastes, smells, and so on), but it is clear that primary properties – such as spatial extension, solidity, motion – also appear to us in consciousness. Are there qualia for these properties? Some say "yes," some say "no." Such debates are most plausibly regarded as terminological squabbles about how "qualia" is to be used rather than substantive disagreements about the scope of consciousness. Although theorists often describe themselves (and more often their opponents) as qualiaphiles or -phobes, in the absence of an unequivocal notion of qualia these terms threatens to generate more heat than light.

Subjectivity

According to many the deepest problems of consciousness concern its supposed subjectivity (Levine 2001). Here too there is disagreement, both over what subjectivity itself involves and about how consciousness and subjectivity are related. A minimal conception of subjectivity identifies it with having a point of view. Most theorists regard consciousness as correlative with subjectivity in this minimal sense: to be conscious is to be a subject of experience, which in turn involves having a perspective on the world. A stronger conception of subjectivity ties the notion to self-consciousness, which is in turn unpacked in terms of having a conception of oneself as having a point of view or perspective. Just how this stronger notion of subjectivity might be related to consciousness is contentious. Some theorists would wish to sharply distinguish consciousness from strong subjectivity, holding that consciousness is one thing and self-consciousness is quite another. Other theorists argue that consciousness is constitutively dependent on strong subjectivity, and that one cannot be conscious without enjoying some form of self-consciousness.

Phenomenality

Arguably, the central notion of consciousness is that of phenomenality. Attempts to explicate the notion of phenomenality typically begin with examples: there is a distinctive phenomenal state associated with the taste of strawberries, there is another phenomenal state associated with the feeling of pain, and there is yet another phenomenal state associated with the smell of coffee. Each of these phenomenal states involves a distinctive phenomenal character – a distinctive "what-it's-likeness" (Nagel 1974). What it's like to taste strawberries differs from what it's like to experience pain, and both of these states differ in turn from what it's like to smell coffee. But insofar as each of these states is a phenomenal state it will possess the property of phenomenality: that is, there will be something it is like to instantiate it. Some theorists find what-it's-like talk illuminating, others find it less than helpful. The phrase is clearly not to be understood comparatively – for although there is something that is similar to the taste of strawberries, this is clearly not at issue – but alternative analyses of the phrase are not easily had. The fact that it is so difficult to explicate the notion of what-it's-likeness raises the question of whether theorists who disagree about how to explain phenomenal consciousness have a shared conception of the notion, or whether they might (to some degree at least) be offering accounts of different features or forms of consciousness.

The notion of phenomenal consciousness is arguably the central notion of consciousness; at any rate, it is the notion on which I will focus here. In part, this is because it is the form of consciousness on which most philosophical ink has been spilled, but it is also because it is the form of consciousness that appears to be most resistant to scientific investigation. We have good reason to think that phenomenality is grounded in neural processes, but we lack any clear conception of how it is that phenomenality might be so grounded.

The contents of consciousness

What kinds of states can be phenomenally conscious? Or, to put the question in another way, what kinds of contents are phenomenally admissible? This question has an important bearing on the science of consciousness, for we might learn something (indeed, a lot) about what consciousness is by learning what kinds of mental states can (and cannot) be phenomenally conscious. Let us examine three domains in which there is disagreement about the "reach" of phenomenality. In each domain, we can distinguish a conservative position from a more liberal one.

Consider first vision. According to an oft-told story, visual experience (that is, visual phenomenology) can represent objects as being variously shaped, coloured, and standing in certain spatial and temporal relations to each other, but it cannot represent objects as belonging to particular scientific categories, or as being particular individuals, as having dispositional properties, and so on. Liberals challenge this traditional picture, arguing that such "high-level" properties – such as being a tractor, being a pine tree, or being Mrs Rosenblatt – can enter into the content of visual phenomenology (see e.g. Siegel 2006).

A second locus of debate between conservatives and liberals concerns the phenomenology of agency (Bayne 2007; Horgan et al. 2003). The experience of being an agent is ubiquitous: we experience ourselves as engaged in both physical activity (opening doors; pulling ropes) and mental activity (deliberating about a career decision; trying to pay attention to a dull speaker). How should we conceptualize such experiences? Conservatives argue that agentive experience is thin and austere – that its content is limited to (say) the experience of effort. Liberals argue that agentive experience is rich with content – that its content includes not only the experience of effort but also experiences of freedom, deliberation, volition, and various kinds of causal relations. Of course, liberals will be quick to point out that just because we experience ourselves as (say) free or deliberating it does not follow that we are free or deliberating – in principle, for such experiences could be non-veridical.

From the perspective of the scientific study of consciousness, perhaps the most important domain in which the debate between conservatives and liberals is being played out concerns cognition. Is phenomenal consciousness restricted to perception, or does it permeate the cognitive realm? Liberals argue that there is a distinctive phenomenology associated with cognition (Pitt 2004; Siewert 1998; Strawson 1994). Some liberals hold only that the various propositional attitudes – intending, desiring, judging, and so on – have (or are associated with) proprietary phenomenal characters; others hold that particular propositional states, such as <intending to go to Paris> or <judging that camels have toes>, possess (or are associated with) distinctive phenomenal characters. Conservatives, by contrast, hold that phenomenality is the exclusive provenance of perception and sensation, and that there is no proprietary cognitive phenomenology no distinctive "what-it's-likeness" associated with either propositional attitudes or propositional attitude states (Carruthers 2005; Lormand 1996; Tye 1995). According to the conservative, what it's like to (say) judge that camels have toes is exhausted by whatever bodily, imagistic, or perceptual states happen to accompany such a judgment.

Arguments for cognitive phenomenology typically involve appeals to phenomenal contrasts (Kriegel 2007). What it is like to hear the sentence "Il fait froid" when one does not understand French differs from what it is like to hear the same sentence having learnt French. In a similar vein, what it is like to hear the sentence "Visiting relatives can be boring" depends on whether one takes the "boring" to qualify the relatives or the visiting. In response to such arguments, conservatives typically grant that the difference between the two scenarios does involve "what-it's-like" differences, but they insist that such differences can be fully accounted for in sensory or perceptual terms. Needless to say, proponents of cognitive phenomenology remain unconvinced by such claims. They allow that differences in understanding and interpretation might (typically) involve differences in sensory experience, but they deny that such differences exhaust the phenomenal contrasts present in such cases.

Leaving aside the apparent phenomenology of cognition proper, conservatives must also reckon with the phenomenal fringe. By this I mean such states as feelings of knowing, tip-of-the-tongue experiences, déjà vu and jamais vu experiences, and similar meta-cognitive states. Such states count as cognitive in some sense of the term, and thus put pressure on those forms of phenomenal conservatism that would restrict phenomenality to the purely sensory.

The debate between liberal and conservative conceptions of the scope of phenomenal consciousness is very puzzling. Why might it be so difficult to reach consensus on the reach of phenomenality? Leaving aside the possibility that conservatives and liberals are right about their own phenomenology but wrong only in generalizing from their own case to human phenomenology in general, there seem to be only two explanations of the debate: either introspection is leading one side of the debate seriously astray (Schwitzgebel 2008), or the debate is a terminological one, with conservatives and liberals talking past each other. Whichever of these diagnoses is right – and perhaps they both contribute to the confusion – it is clear that the science of consciousness cannot afford to set the debate between conservatives and liberals to one side.

Phenomenality and intentionality

One of the many fundamental issues in consciousness studies concerns the relationship between phenomenal character (or phenomenality more generally) and intentional content (or intentionality more generally). How are these two aspects of the mind related? Are they fundamentally distinct, or are they deeply related in some way?

Although classical discussions of the mind from the medieval period right up to the phenomenologists tended to approach consciousness and intentionality in tandem, modern philosophy of mind has been dominated by what Horgan and Tienson (2003) have dubbed "separatism." According to the separatist, there is no internal relationship between phenomenal properties and intentional properties. The widespread endorsement of separatism has led many to adopt a "divide-and-conquer" approach to the problems of phenomenality and intentionality: theorists have assumed that accounts of phenomenality place few (if any) constraints on accounts of intentionality, and vice versa. This assumption would need to be re-evaluated were separatism to be rejected.

Separatism has a number of motivations. Perhaps most fundamentally, intentionality and phenomenality have seemed to many to be very different types of things. The gap between physical/functional properties and phenomenal properties has seemed to many to be deeper and more daunting than the gap between physical/functional properties and intentional properties. In a similar vein, phenomenality generates a problem of other minds that seems not to apply quite so forcefully to intentionality. We have some grip on how intentionality might be grounded in the natural world, but phenomenality seems to float free of any attempt to naturalize it. Whereas intentionality raises *problems*, phenomenality raises *puzzles*.

A less abstract – but perhaps more influential – argument for separatism concerns the possibility of dissociations between intentionality and phenomenality. According to many, propositional-attitudes states such as judgments and intentions have intentional content – they are about states of affairs – but there is nothing it is like to be in them. Consider the fact that a person can be said to believe that anchovies are fish or desire to win the Indy 500, even while they are in a dreamless sleep. Just how compelling one finds this argument depends on one's views of cognitive phenomenology. Proponents of cognitive phenomenology might grant that propositional attitudes have no phenomenal character when understood as dispositions, but they will insist that such states have phenomenal character when occurrent.

A further argument for separatism derives from information-processing models of linguistics and psychology. These models posit multiple levels of content-bearing states, none of which seem to possess any iota of phenomenal character. In response to this challenge, some inseparatists attempt to restrict the connection between intentionality and phenomenality to personal-level intentional states; others argue that the content-bearing states posited by information-processing psychology enjoy only ersatz or "as-if" intentionality, and that states with real intentional content must possess phenomenal character. Neither of these responses is entirely unproblematic.

Can there be mental states that have phenomenality without intentionality? At one point in the not-so-distant past an affirmative answer to this question would have been uncontroversial, and the student of consciousness would have been told that pains, moods, and orgasms (for example) enjoy phenomenal character but lack intentional content. Times have changed, and representational (or intentional) analyses of such states is now commonplace if not orthodox. The phenomenal character of moods is said to represent the general state of the world; the phenomenal character of pains is said to represent the relevant body part as damaged in some way or other; and the phenomenal character of orgasm is taken to represent "a certain change down there as good." Needless to say, opinions vary widely on the plausibility of such analyses.

Whether or not all states with intentionality have phenomenality (and vice versa), we can ask how the intentional content is related to the phenomenal character of those states that do enjoy both intentional content and phenomenal character. Does the intentional content of a state exhaust its phenomenal character, or vice versa? Could the phenomenal character (intentional content) of a state vary independently of its intentional content (phenomenal character), or does fixing the one also fix the other? Certain reductive projects assume that phenomenal character (intentional content) cannot vary independently of intentional content (phenomenal character). In recent times, the most common reductive project in this vicinity has been to reduce phenomenal character to a certain kind of intentional content, but one might also attempt to reduce intentional content to a certain kind of phenomenal character.

Such reductive projects must reckon with inverted-spectrum (or inverted-qualia) scenarios. Some inverted-spectrum scenarios are designed to elicit the intuition that phenomenal character can vary independently of intentional content, whereas others are designed to elicit the intuition that intentional content can vary independently of phenomenal character. Inverted-spectra scenarios typically turn on the fact that intentional content seems to be "wide" – that is, dependent on the subject's environment and/or history – whereas phenomenal character seems to be "narrow," that is, independent of the subject's environment and/or history. The apparent wideness of intentional content allows it to vary independently of variations in phenomenal character.

Reductionists have three options open to them in responding to inverted-spectrum scenarios. Some theorists – "phenomenal externalists" – reject the assumption that phenomenal character is narrow. They hold that the phenomenal character of a state is determined by its environmental and historical relations. Other theorists reject the assumption that intentional content is wide. They hold that the intentional content of a state is determined by the intrinsic properties of the subject in question; indeed, perhaps those very same properties that determine the subject's phenomenal states A third group of theorists attempt to finesse the problem by distinguishing between narrow content, which is essentially tied to phenomenal character, and wide content, which is not. Each of these three positions has its advocates, and the precise relation between phenomenal character and intentional content is likely to remain on the philosophical agenda for some time (Chalmers 2004).

The structure of consciousness

At any one time, a subject's various experiences occur as parts (components, aspects) of a total phenomenal state. This state subsumes each of the experiences that the subject has at the time in question – it captures what it is like to be that subject. This is one fairly natural way to understand the claim that consciousness is unified (see also Dainton 2005; Hurley 1998; Tye 2003). Is consciousness *necessarily* unified, or is it possible for the unity of consciousness to break down under certain conditions? In other words, is it possible that a subject might have simultaneous experiences that are not subsumed by a single phenomenal state? The answer to this question bears on the scientific study of consciousness, for an account of consciousness ought to explain why consciousness is necessarily unified if it is, and it ought to explain why the unity of consciousness can break down if indeed it can.

Among the most striking of those conditions in which the unity of consciousness appears to break down is the commissurotomy (or "split-brain") syndrome. This syndrome results from a procedure in which the corpus callosum – the bundle of fibres that connect the two hemispheres of the brain – is severed in an effort to prevent epileptic seizures from migrating between hemispheres. Although split-brain patients show few signs of disunity in everyday life, under carefully controlled laboratory conditions they can be led to behave in ways that suggest that their consciousness is no longer unified. For example, if the word "key-ring" is presented so that the words "key" and "ring" fall within the patient's left and right visual hemi-fields respectively, the patient will say that she sees only the word "ring" when asked to report what she sees, yet she may select a picture of a key with her left hand while ignoring pictures of a ring and a key-ring.

According to many theorists, such behaviour indicates that split-brain patients have two streams of consciousness, one in each hemisphere. It is this duality of consciousness that is thought to explain (i) why the patient appears to have conscious representations of "key" and "ring" but no representation of "key-ring"; and (ii) why the patient's representations of "key" and "ring" are available to different consuming systems. Another model of the split-brain, suggested by Michael Lockwood (1989), takes split-brain patients to have a fragmented or partially unified stream of consciousness, with triplets of conscious states (e_1, e_2, and e_3) such that e_1 and e_2 are both unified with e_3 but not with each other.

Both the two-streams and partial-unity models entail that split-brain patients lack a unified consciousness. A third account of the split-brain – the switch model – holds that consciousness remains unified even in the split-brain. According to this model, the appearance of simultaneous but distinct streams of consciousness in the split-brain patient is an illusion generated by the fact that consciousness switches rapidly and seamlessly between the patient's two hemispheres; at no time does the patient have simultaneously conscious states that are not phenomenally unified (Bayne, forthcoming). The split-brain patient may have conscious representations of the word "key" and "ring," but these representations will be sequential rather than simultaneous.

The debate between these three accounts raises a number of interconnected issues. Two-streams accounts of the split-brain are well-equipped to explain the behavioural disunity that patients exhibit in laboratory conditions, but they struggle to account for the unity that patients exhibit in everyday situations. Lockwood's partial-unity model might do better at explaining the behaviour of split-brain patients in both everyday and experimental settings, but it is unclear whether consciousness can be partially unified. The switch model promises to explain the unity of the patient's behaviour and everyday life and the disunity of their laboratory behaviour, but faces the challenge of explaining why patients fail to realize that their stream of consciousness shuttles between hemispheres.

Whether or not the unity of consciousness might break down in the context of the split-brain syndrome (or other pathologies of consciousness), it is clearly unified in everyday life. Broadly speaking, there are two ways in which to conceptualise this unity: in terms of experiential building blocks or in terms of a unified phenomenal field (Searle 2000). The building-block approach regards consciousness as built up out of atomistic phenomenal states which are put together to form the subject's total phenomenal state. By contrast, the unified-field theorist regards consciousness as having a field-based structure, according to which subjects enjoy particular phenomenal states – the state of hearing a siren, having a headache, smelling strawberries – only in virtue of contents of the appropriate kind feeding into a phenomenal field. The unified-field approach to consciousness does not do away with the problem of accounting for the unity of consciousness, but it does perhaps make the problem more tractable.

There is some reason to prefer the unified-field model over the building-block model. If consciousness had a building-block structure, then we would expect there to be pathologies of consciousness in which consciousness would fragment into its constituent elements. However, there appear to be no such pathologies. To be sure, there are pathologies of consciousness in which the normal representational coherence and integration of consciousness is lost. For example, patients with visual agnosia can see the various parts of an object, but they cannot synthesize those components so as to form the representation of a unified object. But there is no reason to suppose that agnosics have visual experiences that fail to be phenomenally unified. Arguably, the pathology of consciousness in which the unity of consciousness seems most likely to break down is the split-brain syndrome, but we have seen that even here the case against the unity of consciousness is far from decisive. And even if consciousness is disunified in the split-brain, the units of consciousness that the split-brain patient enjoys are not plausibly regarded as the basic units of which a subject's total conscious state might normally be built.

Criteria for the ascription of consciousness

In order to study a phenomenon one needs to know which objects possess it and which objects do not. One need not be infallible when it comes to identifying the target property, but the poorer one's methods of detecting a property the harder it is to develop a theory of it. In light of this, the science of consciousness stands in need of criteria for the ascription of consciousness. We need decision-procedures by means of which we can tell whether very young human beings, the comatose, non-human animals and robots might be conscious.

Many scientists hold that the only reliable measure of consciousness is introspective report: to be justified in thinking that a subject was (or was not) conscious of a certain stimulus one must have elicited an appropriate introspective report from him or her. Accepting the introspective-report criterion has important ramifications for the scientific study of consciousness, for it radically curtails the subject pool from which such studies can draw. Young children, non-linguistic animals, and those in abnormal states of consciousness (such as delirium or hypnosis) are typically unable to produce introspective reports, yet it is often precisely such subjects that we wish to study (especially if we want to model non-standard forms of consciousness). The scientific study of consciousness would be that much more difficult were we to restrict ourselves to introspective reports.

Luckily, there is good reason not to restrict ourselves to introspective reports. Firstly, despite their official pronouncements, few studies of consciousness actually rely on introspective reports. Instead, studies typically ask subjects to report on the nature of their environment. Subjects are asked to respond whenever they (say) detect a red light, not whenever they detect an *experience* as of a red light. Of course, proponents of the introspective-report criterion might argue that environmental reports are operationally equivalent to introspective reports, at least where normal adult human beings are concerned. It is not obvious that this is so, but even if it is, most consciousness scientists are willing to accept the behavioural responses of creatures that are incapable of giving introspective reports. In their influential work using a binocular-rivalry paradigm in monkeys, Logothetis and colleagues trained monkeys to press levers depending on which of two pictures were presented to them (Logothetis and Schall 1989). Although I am inclined to grant that this behaviour can be used to track the conscious states of the monkeys, it is not even clear to me that the monkeys were producing reports of any kind, let alone introspective reports.

Before we turn to alternative criteria for the ascription of consciousness, it is worth asking why theorists emphasize the importance of introspective reports in studying consciousness. One motivation for the view may derive from the assumption that introspection is infallible, or at least highly reliable. In light of this, it is somewhat ironic that many of those who place most weight on the importance of introspective reports for the study of consciousness also hold that introspective judgments can be massively mistaken. They hold that we are subject to a "grand illusion" when it comes to perceptual consciousness – we ordinarily think (that is, believe) that we are conscious of much more than we are in fact conscious of. Evidence in favour of the grand illusion is controversial, but there is at least some reason to think that subjects' introspective judgments can be erroneous. For example, it is commonly believed that colour experience extends to the periphery of one's visual field, but it is at least arguable that we do not experience peripheral objects as coloured. But note that if we were serious about taking (sincere) introspective reports as the "gold standard" of consciousness, then we could never have good reason for thinking that introspection can lead subjects astray. Since we do have reason to think that introspection can lead subjects astray, we should refuse to take introspective reports as our sole criterion for the ascription of consciousness.

Another worry with relying on introspective reports to study consciousness is that subjects might fail to notice (and hence report) that they are in certain phenomenal states. The question of whether consciousness might outrun reportability is of more than merely theoretical interest. Consider the perceptual extinction paradigm, employed by Rees and colleagues for studying the neural correlates of visual consciousness (Rees et al. 2002). Perceptual extinction is a phenomenon in which stroke patients ignore stimuli presented in one visual field (typically the left) when such stimuli are presented together with stimuli in the other visual field. Rees and colleagues assume that patients are not conscious of the ignored (that is, unreported) stimuli, but one might argue that such stimuli are conscious but merely unnoticed.

Let us return to the question of what criteria we should adopt for the ascription of consciousness. One proposal worth serious consideration is that the capacity for intentional agency suffices to underwrite the ascription of consciousness. Consider the following functional magnetic resonance imaging study of a woman in a vegetative state (Owen et al. 2006). The patient was scanned while being asked to first imagine visiting the rooms in her house and then imagine playing tennis. The patterns of brain activation observed suggested that she had engaged in the appropriate mental imagery: the request to imagine visiting the rooms of her house generated activity in the parahippocampal gyrus, posterior parietal cortex, and lateral premotor cortex, whereas the request to imagine playing tennis generated activity in the supplementary motor areas that control motor responses. Does this activation provide good evidence that the patient was conscious? There is some temptation to think that it does. Arguably, the link between the neural activity observed here and the ascription of consciousness goes via the notion of intentional agency.

The criteria for the ascription of consciousness discussed thus far have been exclusively functional, but one might have reservations about purely functionalist approaches to the ascription of consciousness. For one thing, one might worry about zombies – that is, unconscious creatures whose functional profile mirrors our own. A purely functional approach to the problem of other minds would lead one to (falsely) regard one's zombie twin as conscious. Of course, it is controversial whether zombies are possible, but it's not obvious that they are impossible. Furthermore, even if *pure* zombies are impossible, partial zombies – that is, unconscious creatures that depart from our own functional profile in only minor ways – may well be possible, and a functionalist approach to the ascription of consciousness might lead one to regard one's partial-zombie twin as conscious.

Functional measures of consciousness also run the risk of excluding some of those who actually are conscious. Locked-in syndrome patients suffer from almost total paralysis and can communicate only by moving their eyes and/or blinking. Despite their behavioural incapacitation, locked-in patients are fully conscious; indeed, they can *tell* us that they are conscious. But now imagine a locked-in patient who loses even the ability to control the movements of his or her eyes but retains consciousness. A purely functional approach to the problem of other phenomenal minds might (falsely) pronounce such a person unconscious. Clearly we should be reluctant to employ any criteria for the ascription of consciousness that would lead us to regard a conscious human being as unconscious.

There is no straightforward solution to this problem. We could replace (or supplement) functional criteria for the ascription of consciousness with physical criteria. Perhaps the stuff of which an entity is made has a direct bearing – that is, a bearing independently of the functional roles that it realizes – on whether or not it is conscious. But this approach to the ascription of consciousness can easily be made to look unattractive. Suppose that you and I are made of different types of materials: I turn out to be carbon based whereas you turn out to be silicon based. Or suppose that we discover that I have only a left cerebral hemisphere whereas you have only a right cerebral hemisphere. Why should this (or similar) information have an impact on whether it is reasonable for me to regard you as conscious (or vice versa)? Surely it would be chauvinistic to suppose that an entity must be built out of the same stuff as us (or should I say "me"?) in order to be conscious.

In response to all of this, one might argue that even if our present methods for detecting consciousness are crude, confused, or just plain wrong, this state of affairs is not intractable: as our understanding of consciousness improves, so too will our ability to determine whether or not a creature is consciousness. We might be currently unsure as to how to weigh physical and functional properties in ascribing consciousness, but our difficulties here may be merely temporary (Block 2007).

But how exactly are we to develop scientifically grounded criteria for the ascription of consciousness? One strategy would be to start with paradigm cases of consciousness and take as one's criteria for consciousness whatever physical or functional properties apply in such cases. The problem with this approach is that only some of the physical and functional properties that apply in the paradigm cases will apply in the hard cases, and we will need to decide whether the similarities between the paradigm case and the hard case are strong enough to justify ascribing consciousness in the hard cases (Block 2002). In other words, the paradigm-case approach appears to be impotent exactly where it is most needed. An alternative strategy appeals to theories of consciousness. If we knew where in the architecture of cognition conscious states are generated, or on what kinds of physical or functional states consciousness supervenes, then we could tell what kinds of conscious states, if any, a target organism instantiates. The problem with this strategy is that in order to develop a theory of consciousness one needs to have criteria for the ascription of consciousness in place, and that is precisely what we don't have. Arguably, to develop rigorous criteria for the ascription of consciousness we would need to close – or at least narrow – the explanatory gap. It is only when we have a grasp of how functional and/or physical states realize or generate phenomenal states that we will be in a position to determine with any certainty whether or not organisms that differ radically from ourselves are conscious. There may be a degree of intractability about the distribution of consciousness if, as many suspect, the explanatory gap cannot be closed.

Content-based vs. creature-based methodologies

Let us leave to one side problems concerned with the ascription of consciousness and focus instead on how the science of consciousness might proceed. Two explanatory strategies can be discerned in current attempts to find the mechanisms underpinning consciousness. We might call these two approaches the "content-based approach" and the "creature-based approach." The content-based approach focuses on the mechanisms underlying specific contents of consciousness. The experimenter contrasts one type of conscious state with another and looks for the neural changes that are most closely correlated with changes in the contents of consciousness. A classic example of this paradigm can be found in the binocular-rivalry studies of Logothetis and colleagues, mentioned earlier. Binocular rivalry occurs when different stimuli are presented to the left and right eyes, as the subject's visual experience usually alternates between the two stimuli. Logothetis and colleagues trained monkeys to press a bar, depending on which of two visual stimuli they were seeing, and then recorded the neural responses of monkeys in this paradigm. They found that activity in the primary visual cortex correlated strongly with changes in stimuli but only weakly with changes in the monkeys' visual experience, whereas activity in later visual areas (such as inferior temporal cortex) correlated strongly with changes in visual experience.

Such findings tempt many to think of later visual areas as the neural correlates of visual consciousness.

What this view overlooks is the fact that activity in the later visual areas generates visual experiences only when various domain-general systems are active. Proponents of the creature-based approach to the study of consciousness focus on the search for these mechanisms. Adopting a creature-based methodology, Laureys and others have examined the neural mechanisms underlying the transition between the comatose state, in which the patient is assumed to be unconscious, and the minimally conscious state, in which the patient is assumed to go in and out of consciousness (Laureys 2005).

There is at present no consensus concerning which of these two methodologies ought to be adopted. Those who privilege the content-based approach to the study of consciousness don't deny that there are domain-general mechanisms of creature consciousness, but they tend to downplay their importance, referring to them as merely "enabling conditions." By contrast, those who privilege the creature-based approach tend to downplay the relevance of those mechanisms that serve to differentiate one state of consciousness from another in explaining consciousness. How, they ask, could studying the contrast between one state of consciousness and another shed light on consciousness itself? In part, the debate between these two methodologies turns on a more fundamental debate about the structure of consciousness. As discussed earlier, some theorists take consciousness to be built up out of phenomenal building blocks, whereas others hold that consciousness has a holistic, field-based structure. Proponents of the building-block conception of the structure of consciousness are likely to endorse the content-based methodology, for by looking at the neural mechanisms that are uniquely necessary for certain conscious states one might discover particular phenomenal building blocks. By contrast, proponents of the field-based view of consciousness are likely to be more sympathetic to the creature-based methodology, for the creature-based methodology would seem best-suited for identifying the mechanisms underlying the generation of the phenomenal field. However, there is some sense to be made of content-based methodology, even if consciousness has a field-like structure. Unlike the building-block theorist, the phenomenal-field theorist will be more interested in the domain-general mechanisms that are implicated in all conscious states than in the content-specific cortical nodes that underpin the contrast between one conscious state and another. The jury is still out on which of these two approaches to the study of consciousness ought to be pursued; arguably, both approaches have a place within the science of consciousness.

Functional reduction and levels of explanation

What – if any – kind of explanation of consciousness might we hope to discover? Arguably the deepest divide in this domain is between those who think that consciousness will succumb to a reductive analysis in much the way that other natural phenomena – such as life, photosynthesis, reproduction, and so on – have succumbed, and those who hold that consciousness will resist such an analysis.

Levine (1983), Chalmers (1996), and McGinn (1989), amongst others, argue that consciousness poses a unique explanatory gap, and that no amount of physical or functional knowledge would enable us to grasp how consciousness "arises out of" physical processes. Although these theorists deny that a deep or reductive explanation of consciousness will be found, they do not (or at least need not) deny that it might be possible to discover correlations between phenomenal and physical/functional properties. Finding these correlations and the mechanisms underlying them would provide us with an explanation of some kind, it's just that the explanation would leave something out.

The debate between these two camps has been waged on two fronts. One front concerns the prospects of an *a priori* functionalist analysis of phenomenal consciousness, and the implications that the failure of such an analysis might have for theories of consciousness. One line of thought runs as follows: To reduce a phenomenon one must first give an *a priori* functionalist analysis of it; since phenomenal consciousness cannot be so analysed it cannot be reduced. Some theorists take issue with the first claim, holding that phenomenal consciousness can be given an *a priori* functional analysis; others take issue with the second claim, arguing that a property can be reduced even if it cannot be given a functional analysis.

The second front in this debate has focused on why phenomenal consciousness seems to be uniquely resistant to scientific analysis. Whereas reductionists argue that phenomenal consciousness seems to be resistant because it is resistant, reductionists attempt to explain away that apparent refractoriness of consciousness to scientific explanation. A popular strategy here appeals to phenomenal concepts. Many of those who argue that consciousness can be given a reductive analysis argue that the appearance of a unique explanatory gap between phenomenal properties and physical/functional properties is generated by the fact that our perspective on our own phenomenal states is mediated by phenomenal concepts – concepts that can be deployed only from the first-person perspective. According to this line, the sense that there is an explanatory gap between phenomenal properties and physical/functional properties is a cognitive illusion, generated by the radical difference between first-person and third-person access to phenomenal properties (Tye 1999; Papineau 2002).

As we have seen, questions of whether the science of consciousness might be able to deliver a reductive explanation of consciousness quickly descend into complex debates concerning the nature of explanation and the relationship between concepts and properties. These issues stand at some distance from the science of consciousness itself. Of more concern to the science of consciousness are questions about the level at which an account of consciousness ought to be pitched. Of course, we should not assume that explanations of consciousness will be restricted to a single level of explanation, nonetheless, we can still usefully ask which explanatory level(s) will cast the most illumination on consciousness.

Some theorists appeal to the categories of folk psychology to explain consciousness. This is the approach that tends to be taken by proponents of higher-order theories of consciousness, who argue that a state is conscious in virtue of being the object of an appropriate higher-order thought or perception (Lycan 1996; Rosenthal 2004).

(Note that such accounts are not always advanced as accounts of phenomenal consciousness.) According to some versions of the higher-order approach, states are conscious in virtue of being the intentional object of another mental state; according to other versions of the approach, states are conscious in virtue of taking themselves as their own intentional objects (Kriegel and Williford 2006). Either way, the higher-order account of consciousness invokes only those states and relations recognized by folk psychology. Functionalist-cum-representational theories of consciousness typically employ folk-psychological categories in accounting for consciousness. For example, Tye (1995) holds that a mental state is conscious in virtue of being poised for employment by the subject's conceptual system. Common to all of these theories is the assumption that although scientific progress may be needed in order to fill in the details of how consciousness is implemented in a particular species, the heavy lifting in an account of consciousness is done by such folk-psychological categories as higher-order representation, availability to conceptual deployment, and the like.

Other theorists regard advances in psychology and neuroscience as indispensable for understanding consciousness. Typically, those who hold this view begin by identifying a functional role that is associated with consciousness, and then look for the cognitive and neural mechanisms which realize that role. The gamma oscillations account of consciousness provides a useful example of this approach (see e.g. Crick and Koch 1990). Proponents of this approach argue that consciousness involves gamma oscillations in the sensory cortices – so-called 40-hertz (Hz) oscillations – on the grounds that such oscillations are thought to play a role in dynamic feature binding, the process by means of which various perceptual features (representations of colour, shape, spatial location and orientation) – are bound together to form percepts of unified objects.

The 40-Hz proposal can be challenged on a number of grounds. Most fundamentally, it is unclear how robust the link between consciousness and feature binding is. What are the features that must be bound together in order to generate conscious moods, desires, intentions, and thoughts? Even where a mental state does require feature binding, it is not at all obvious that feature binding is sufficient for consciousness for there is some reason to think that binding can occur unconsciously. And even if one were to accept the connection between feature binding and consciousness, it is not obvious what implications that has for the connection between 40-Hz oscillations and consciousness. Proponents of the 40-Hz account of consciousness often suggest that consciousness might be *identified* with gamma oscillations but justifying an identity claim of this kind is problematic. Rather than identify consciousness with the mechanisms that realize feature binding in us, one could identify it with feature binding itself. Feature binding might be subserved by 40-Hz oscillations in humans but by an entirely different mechanism in other species. The contrast between these two positions has implications for the distribution of consciousness. Identifying consciousness itself with 40 Hz oscillations commits us to the view that there is nothing it is like to be a creature in which feature binding is realized by some other mechanism, whereas identifying consciousness with feature binding itself would allow us to regard such creatures as conscious.

It is now more common for cognitive neuroscientific accounts of consciousness to take global availability rather than feature binding as their starting point (Baars 1988; Dehaene and Naccache 2001). Global workspace accounts of consciousness identify consciousness with a domain-general working memory system, the contents of which are available to a wide range of the subject's consuming systems. On some versions of the account, the global workspace has a fixed neural architecture (typically thought to involve parietal and prefrontal networks); other versions allow that the global workspace might involve dynamic coalitions of widely distributed cortical areas.

Global workspace approaches to consciousness are well motivated, for the contents of consciousness are typically available to a wide range of consuming systems (verbal report, the voluntary allocation of attention, memory consolidation, belief formation, and so on). Nonetheless, the approach is vulnerable to a number of challenges. For one thing, it is debatable whether there is a single global workspace as opposed to a number of less-than-global workspaces. The fact that the contents of consciousness are typically available to a wide range of consuming systems might result from the operation of a number of domain-specific working memory systems rather than a single executive system. Further, it is not clear that all conscious contents make it into a working memory of any kind, let alone a domain-general one. One reason for distinguishing the contents of consciousness from those of working memory is that the two faculties appear to have different capacity constraints: on most accounts, working memory has at most a capacity of four items, whereas the capacity of phenomenal consciousness seems to be substantially larger. Arguably, many conscious states never make it from perceptual buffers into the global workspace (Block 2007).

Even if we were to associate consciousness with a global workspace, we would face the further question of whether to identify consciousness with the neural mechanisms that realize this workspace in us. Such a move would entail that creatures in which the global workspace is realized by some other neural or cognitive architecture would be unconscious, and it is by no means obvious that we ought to embrace this result. Understanding the mechanisms that allow the contents of our mental states to be globally available for cognitive and behavioural consumption will no doubt tell us something about consciousness, but it is unclear how much light it will shed on its essential nature.

Some theorists think that the fundamental explanation of consciousness will be found at the level of fundamental physics. Within this grouping some look to quantum theory; others, to some as-yet-undeveloped theory. Although theorists have various reasons for looking to physics for an account of consciousness, a common motivation for thinking that consciousness can be usefully tackled at a physical level involves the notion that phenomenal properties are not functional, and that it is only at the level of fundamental physics that we find non-functional properties. Many find this proposal implausible, for it appears to lead to some form of panpsychism: given that all objects presumably have these fundamental properties, it seems to follow from this view that all objects (and all parts of all objects!) are phenomenally conscious. Whatever attractions the physics-based approach might otherwise have, this implication alone suffices to rule it out of serious contention.

Conclusion

In *Empiricism and the Philosophy of Mind* Wilfrid Sellars distinguished two images of the world: the manifest image and the scientific image. Consciousness is a nonnegotiable component of the manifest image. From the first-person perspective, eliminativism is simply not an option. We cannot think phenomenality away, no matter how hard we try. But matters are very different from the third-person perspective of the scientific image. Consciousness is now taken as a serious subject of research within the cognitive sciences, but this should not obscure the fact that its scientific credentials are far from secure. It is, I think, very much an open question whether the sciences of the mind *need* to invoke consciousness, or whether they will get along just fine without it. It certainly cannot be said that consciousness has already earned its explanatory keep. The notion of consciousness may be one of the few notions that we retain not because it pays its way but because we are stuck with it.

References

Baars, B. J. (1988) *A Cognitive Theory of Consciousness*, Cambridge: Cambridge University Press.

Bayne, T. (2008) "The Phenomenology of Agency," *Philosophy Compass*, 3: 1–21.

Block, N. (2002) "The Harder Problem of Consciousness," *Journal of Philosophy* 99: 391–425.

—— (2007) "The Methodological Puzzle of Consciousness and the Mesh between Psychology and Neuroscience," *Behavioral and Brain Science* 30: 481–548.

Carruthers, P. (2005) "Conscious Experience versus Conscious Thought," in *Consciousness: Essays from a Higher-Order Perspective*, Oxford: Oxford University Press, pp. 134–56.

Chalmers, D. (1996) *The Conscious Mind*, Oxford: Oxford University Press.

—— (2004) "The Representational Character of Experience," in B. Leiter (ed.) *The Future for Philosophy*, Oxford: Oxford University Press, pp. 153–81.

Crick, F., and Koch, C. (1990) "Towards a Neurobiological Theory of Consciousness," *Seminars in the Neurosciences* 2: 263–75.

Dainton, B. (2005) *Stream of Consciousness*, 2nd edn, London: Routledge.

Dehaene, S., and Naccache, L. (2001) "Towards a Cognitive Neuroscience of Consciousness: Basic Evidence and a Workspace Framework," *Cognition* 79: 1–37.

Dennett, D. (1988) "Quining Qualia," in A. Marcel and E. Bisiach (eds), *Consciousness in Contemporary Science*, Oxford: Oxford University Press, pp. 42–77.

Dretske, F. (1995) *Naturalizing the Mind*, Cambridge, MA: MIT Press.

Horgan, T., and Tienson, J. (2002) "The Phenomenology of Intentionality and the Intentionality of Phenomenology," in D. Chalmers (ed.) *Philosophy of Mind: Classical and Contemporary Readings*, Oxford: Oxford University Press, pp. 520–33.

Horgan, T., Tienson, J., and Graham, G. (2003) "The Phenomenology of First-Person Agency," in S. Walter and H.-D. Heckmann (eds) *Physicalism and Mental Causation: The Metaphysics of Mind and Action*, Exeter, UK: Imprint Academic, pp. 323–40.

Hurley, S. (1998) *Consciousness in Action*, Cambridge, MA: Harvard University Press.

Kriegel, U. (2007) "The Phenomenologically Manifest," *Phenomenology and the Cognitive Sciences* 6: 115–36.

Kriegel, U., and Williford, K. (eds) (2006) *Self-Representational Approaches to Consciousness*, Cambridge, MA: MIT Press.
Laureys, S. (2005) "The Neural Correlate of (Un)Awareness: Lessons from the Vegetative State," *Trends in Cognitive Sciences* 9, no. 12: 556–9.
Levine, J. (1983) "Materialism and Qualia: The Explanatory Gap," *Pacific Philosophical Quarterly* 64: 354–61.
—— (2001) *Purple Haze*, Oxford: Oxford University Press.
Lockwood, M. (1989) *Mind, Brain and the Quantum*, Oxford: Blackwell.
Logothetis, N., and Schall, J. (1989) "Neuronal Correlates of Subjective Visual Perception," *Science* 245: 761–3.
Lormand, E. (1996) "Nonphenomenal Consciousness," *Nous* 30: 242–61.
Lycan, W. (1996) *Consciousness and Experience*, Cambridge, MA: MIT Press.
McGinn, C. (1989) "Can We Solve the Mind-Body Problem?" *Mind* 98, no. 391: 349–66.
Nagel, T. (1974) "What Is It Like to Be a Bat?" *Philosophical Review* 83: 435–50.
Owen, A. M., Coleman, M. R., Boly, M., Davis, M. H., Laureys, S., and Pickard, J. D. (2006) "Detecting Awareness in the Vegetative State," *Science* 313 (8 September): 1402.
Pitt, D. (2004) "The Phenomenology of Cognition *or* What Is It Like to Think That *P*?" *Philosophy and Phenomenological Research* 69: 1–36.
Papineau, D. (2002) *Thinking about Consciousness*, Oxford: Oxford University Press.
Rees, G., Kreiman, G., and Koch, C. (2002) "Neural Correlates of Conscious and Unconscious Vision in Parietal Extinction," *Neurocase* 8: 387–93.
Rosenthal, D. (2004) "Varieties of Higher-Order Theory," in R. Gennaro (ed.) *Higher-Order Theories of Consciousness*, Amsterdam and Philadelphia: John Benjamins, pp. 17–44.
Schwitzgebel, E. (2008) "The Unreliability of Naïve Introspection," *The Philosophical Review* 117, no. 2: 245–73.
Searle, J. (2000) "Consciousness," *Annual Review of Neuroscience* 23: 557–78.
Siegel, S. (2006) "Which Properties Are Represented in Perception?" in T. Gendler and J. Hawthorne (eds) *Perceptual Experience*, Oxford: Oxford University Press, pp. 481–503.
Siewert, C. (1998) *The Significance of Consciousness*, Princeton, NJ: Princeton University Press.
Strawson, G. (1994) *Mental Reality*, Cambridge, MA: MIT Press.
Tye, M. (1995) *Ten Problems of Consciousness*, Cambridge, MA: MIT Press.
—— (1999) "Phenomenal Consciousness: The Explanatory Gap as a Cognitive Illusion," *Mind* 108: 705–25.
—— (2003) *Consciousness and Persons*, Cambridge, MA: MIT Press.

34
ATTENTION

Christopher Mole

The first half of the twentieth century

Théodule Ribot's 1888 book, *The Psychology of Attention* (published in English in 1890), comes near the beginning of the historical sequence that leads up to our current psychological theories of attention. It provides a striking example of behaviourism *avant la lettre*:

> Are the movements of the face, the body, and the limbs and the respiratory modifications that accompany attention, simple effects, outward marks, as is usually supposed? Or are they, on the contrary, *the necessary conditions, the constituent elements, the indispensable factors of attention*? Without hesitation we accept the second thesis.
>
> (Ribot 1890: 25)

Despite the precedent that Ribot set, attention was rarely mentioned by the behaviourists, who dominated psychology in the first decades of the twentieth century (see Chapter 6 in this volume, by Braddon-Mitchell). This is because twentieth-century psychological behaviourism was committed to giving its theories as sets of rules governing the mapping from stimuli to behavioural responses. Attention can't be captured in a theory with that form (because the stimuli to which one can attend, and the responses that one can make attentively, are only slightly less diverse than one's entire perceptual and behavioural repertoire). Attention was among the phenomena that behaviourists wanted to leave out of their picture of the mind.

The suspicion that behaviourist science felt towards attention was also felt by many of the twentieth century's behaviouristically inclined philosophers. An example is Peter Geach, whose 1957 book, *Mental Acts*, mentions the mental act of attending only to ridicule its explanatory credentials. In discussing what's required for perceived things to become subjects of judgement Geach writes,

> So far as I can see, it is quite useless to say the relevant sense-perceptions must be attended to, either this does not give a sufficient condition, or else "attended to" is a mere word for the very relation of judgement to sense perception that requires analysis.
>
> (Geach 1957: 64)

The year after Geach's book, however, saw the publication of Donald Broadbent's *Perception and Communication*, and with it the establishment of attention as a respectable topic for enquiry in experimental psychology. Attention's return to the philosophical agenda came slightly later and, largely on account of the methodological idiosyncrasies of its advocates, it was much less successful. The treatment of attention given in Chapter 3 of Maurice Merleau-Ponty's *Phenomenology of Perception* (first translated into English in 1962) is so wedded to the methods of phenomenology, and the discussion of "heed concepts" in Alan White's *Attention* (1964) is so closely focused on natural language, that neither of these works succeeded in installing attention as a canonical topic for debate in mainstream philosophy of mind.

Broadbent succeeded in establishing attention as an agendum for experimental psychology by treating questions about attention in language "derived from communication theory." Broadbent thought about perception through the metaphor of the telephone exchange. Questions about attention entered this picture in the guise of questions about the *capacity* of the telephone exchange's channels. The notion of capacity was explained by Broadbent as

> the limiting quantity of information which can be transmitted through a given channel at a given time: if we send Morse code with a buzzer we cannot send a dot and a dash at the same time, but must send them successively [. . .] The fact that any given channel has a limit is a matter of central importance to communication engineers, and it is correspondingly forced on the attention of psychologists who use their terms.
>
> (Broadbent 1958: 5)

By using the language of communication engineering to give a theory of attention Broadbent inaugurated a research project that boomed (along with the information technology that provided its guiding metaphors) in the period between the late 1950s and the early 1990s, but it was a research project that subsequently fizzled out. Many of the philosophical questions about the psychology of attention as we have it today are questions about which features of our current theories are unwarranted inheritances from this tradition, and about how those unwarranted inheritances ought to be replaced.

The fate of Broadbent's project

Attention was, and remains, a paradigmatic *explanandum* for the version of cognitive science that was emerging when Broadbent wrote. From the perspective of Broadbent's cognitive science the following assumptions seemed natural: (1) attention was seen as the allocation of limited capacity processing resources; (2) the cognitive architecture of perception was seen as largely linear, so that it is the mechanisms responsible for the subject's awareness of simple perceivable features (such as shape and location) that provide the input for later mechanisms, responsible for the subject's awareness of more complex features (such as semantic content); and (3) conscious control was seen as being intimately related to the paying of attention, so that the processes not involving attention were regarded as "automatic," while those that *do* involve attention were thought of as proceeding in a way that is consciously overseen by the agent.

For the researchers who followed Broadbent in making these assumptions, a theory of attention was expected to take the form of an account of where in the linear perceptual processing stream the attention-managed limitations in the capacity for cognitive processing occur. The central question that was asked about attention was the question of whether attentional selection happens before or after the processing of complex and higher order properties (see Broadbent 1971).

There are two different ways of asking this question, both of which enjoyed currency. Sometimes the question was posed as a question about where the process of attention stands relative to other processes (Does attention occur early or late in the processing stream?), and sometimes it was posed as a question about where other processes stand relative to the process of attention (Which forms of processing "require attention," and which occur "preattentively"?).

Whichever way one asked it, the question seemed like a straightforward one to address empirically. All that needed to be done was to catalogue which sorts of features a subject can be aware of when he or she is not paying attention: one could then infer – it was supposed – that these features are processed preattentively. If there are few such features then attention must happen early in the stream. If there are many such features then attention must occur late. Faced with this seemingly tractable question the mood of researchers was optimistic. Posner and Marin's (1985) preface to the proceedings of the 11th meeting of the Attention and Performance Association began by saying that, "The meeting's topic was the quest for the mechanisms of attention." And went on to claim, a few pages later, that "there was a strong sense of common progress."

By the early 1990s, however, this "strong sense of common progress" in the "quest for the mechanisms of attention" had been replaced, in some quarters, with the sense that the quest had been a wild goose chase. What had appeared to be clear methods for addressing what had appeared to be clear questions delivered only patchy and conflicting results.

One body of results seemed to support an early-selection view of attention, according to which attention is the management of a bottleneck in our capacity to process all but the simplest of properties. It was found that one's awareness of the stimuli to which one is not attending is remarkably slight, being limited for the most part to the simple features of those stimuli. It was found that, when presented with more than one auditory stream, or with a crowded visual array, one is typically poor at answering questions about the stimuli to which one is not attending, and one is very slow and unreliable when asked to detect or locate occurrences of complex properties among them (Cherry 1953; Treisman 1988). The early-selectionists had a ready explanation for our lack of awareness of the complex properties of unattended stimuli: It could be explained as a consequence of our having insufficient processing capacity for the detection of those properties. Broadbent himself endorsed a view of this sort.

An additional body of data was soon gathered, however, that could not be accommodated by the early selectionist picture. These data seemed to show that, despite the subject's lack of awareness of the complex and higher order properties of unattended stimuli, those properties *are* processed and their presence *is* registered, but registered in ways of which the subject is unaware. This is particularly clear when the complex and higher order properties that are being ignored are semantic properties. It seems that semantic properties of unattended stimuli must be processed if we are to explain how it can be that an unattended stimulus can call attention to itself on account of its significance (a point that Deutsch and Deutsch [1963] emphasized in a much-cited discussion) – or if we are to explain why it is that the semantic properties of recently ignored stimuli take longer to detect when attention is subsequently paid to stimuli that instantiate those properties (Driver and Tipper 1989). It might also be, although this is more controversial, that unattended semantic properties can elicit a galvanic skin response in subjects who have been suitably conditioned (Corteen and Dunn 1974; Dawson and Schell 1982). Moreover, it seems that the attention-involving tasks that lead to a lack of awareness of the properties of unattended stimuli can be performed concurrently with other attention-involving tasks (Allport et al. 1972; Spelke et al. 1976) and so it seems that when attending to one task leads us to be unaware of the properties of unattended stimuli this cannot be because the attended task exhausts our capacity for processing.

Under the weight of these complications (and others that we shall see shortly) questions about the location of attentional selection ceased to generate productive experiments, and so lost their currency in the literature. At the meeting of the Attention and Performance Association in 1990 Alan Allport could claim, only somewhat controversially, that in the quest for the mechanisms of attention, we had been "asking the wrong questions":

> even a brief survey of the heterogeneity and functional separability of different components of spatial and non-spatial attentional control prompts the conclusion that, qua causal mechanism, *there can be no such thing as attention*. There is no *one* uniform computational function, or mental operation (in general no *one* causal mechanism) to which all so-called attentional phenomena can be attributed.
>
> (Allport 1993: 203)

The picture of the brain's information handling that was becoming established at the time of Allport's writing was a picture that included no processes that seemed fit to play the role that Broadbent had seen attention as playing. This was taken by some psychologists as showing that the post-behaviourist rehabilitation of attention had been misconceived, either because our concept of attention has something wrong with it, or else because there is no such thing as attention at all. Raja Parasuraman voiced these concerns in the introduction to his 1998 book, *The Attentive Brain:*

> When confronted with such a [diverse] list of putative functions [for attention], at least two reactions are possible. The first is to recognise the multifaceted nature of attention and to attempt to meet the challenge of understanding the similarities and differences between the varieties of attention. The second

> is to question the very concept of attention. If attention participates in all those functions, is it separate from each or is it an integral part of them? Or is attention epiphenomenal? Alternatively, if attention is not a single entity with a single definition, is it not an ill-conceived concept?
>
> Questions such as these have worried theorists and researchers for many years, as if the second of the two reactions to the diversity of attention were the stronger.
>
> (Parasuraman 1998: 3)

These worries about the concept of attention being "ill-conceived" or about attention being epiphenomenal were, as Parasuraman suggests, unfounded. What had become clear was that attention cannot be accounted for in the way envisioned by Broadbent, but the failure of a research programme does not show that its *explanandum* does not exist, nor that it is epiphenomenal. The early history of psychology is full of research programmes that failed, not because the things they attempted to explain turned out not to exist, but because they approached their *explananda* in the wrong way. (The failure of Francis Galton's attempt to give an account of intelligence as a simple property of the nervous system is a well-known example.) Broadbent's project failed, not because it lacked an *explanandum*, but because it carried commitments to certain false assumptions.

The recognition that Broadbent's project had failed was followed by a period in which, following several suggestions that Allport made in his influential "Attention and Performance" lecture (Allport 1993), the psychology of attention tried to free itself from unnoticed assumptions. This wariness of unnoticed assumptions was one of the factors that contributed to the popularity of research aimed at producing *computational models* of attention-involving phenomena. Implementing a computational model requires hidden assumptions to be made explicit, and, in a time of pessimism about the existing theories, model-building can be pursued somewhat independently from the project of giving an actual description of the mechanisms at work in the system being modelled. A considerable body of work continues to be aimed at the building of computational models of attention-involving phenomena, often focusing on a very restricted range of those phenomena, such as a certain sort of visual search (see Bundesen [2000] for a review). Here, as elsewhere, there are philosophical questions (discussion of which can be found in Downes [1992] and Godfrey-Smith [2006]) about how the attempt to produce a *model of* a phenomenon relates to the attempt to describe the *actual mechanisms* that are responsible for that phenomenon.

Rejecting the Broadbentian assumptions

Allport's 1993 paper suggested several ways in which the assumptions behind Broadbent's project might have gone wrong, but rejections of the Broadbentian approach in the psychological literature are usually made with a bare citation of Allport's paper. This has masked the fact that many psychologists disagree about where it was that Broadbent's approach fell into error. There are at least three points at which this disagreement is significant, corresponding to the three Broadbentian assumptions that were identified in the second section, above. The first point of disagreement concerns the extent to which Broadbent went wrong in taking perceptual processing to proceed in a linear fashion, and in taking attention to occur at a single locus in that line of processing. The second disagreement is about whether it was a mistake to treat the selectivity of attention as arising from a bottleneck in processing capacity. The third disagreement is about the intimacy of the relationship between attention and consciousness. We shall treat these in turn.

Linearity and uniqueness

One very widespread view of the failure of Broadbent's project is that the project went wrong in assuming that perceptual processing proceeds in a linear fashion. Those who followed Broadbent in asking whether the locus of attention is early or late were asking a question that makes sense only if attention occurs in a stream with earlier and later parts. And those who asked which processes come before attention, and which after, were asking a question that makes sense only if there is a linear sequence of processes in which attention has a place. But when we examine the neural architecture of the brain (see Chapters 26 and 27 in this volume, by Craver and Bickle), we find that the information passage between brain regions is almost always two-way, so that there is no one prevailing direction of information flow, and no sense, therefore, in calling one part of the stream earlier than another. We also find that many processes take place in parallel, and so cannot properly be said to stand to one another in the relation of earlier than or later than.

For many current psychologists the attempt to understand attention in Broadbent's terms was "classical work inspired by linear stage theory" (Prinz and Hommel 2002: 3). It is because they reject "linear stage theory" that these psychologists reject the Broadbentian project.

This is, perhaps, a little too quick. Although the processing responsible for perception is not now thought to be linear in the sense that Broadbent envisaged, it *is* often said to be *hierarchical* (see Kastner and Ungerleider 2000: 319). If the assumption of linearity were the only problem for Broadbent's project then the broad outlines of that project could, perhaps, be retained: Questions about whether attention is early or late in the processing sequence could be reformulated as questions about whether attention is high or low in the processing hierarchy. The falsity of the linearity assumption does require Broadbent's picture to be revised, but it is not sufficient by itself to justify the widespread view that the terms of Broadbent's project need to be rejected.

Linearity is not the only questionable assumption that must be made in order for there to be sense in asking Broadbent's questions about the early or late locus of attention, and it is not the only assumption that is now thought to have been mistaken. Another assumption required by the Broadbentian project is the assumption of uniqueness: as Allport pointed out, debates about *the locus* of attentional selection fail to make good sense if there are *many loci* of attentional selection.

Few, if any, psychologists would claim that either the uniqueness assumption or the linearity assumption should be retained in just the form in which Broadbent made them, but there is controversy about the extent to which current psychology has managed to, or needs to, free itself from these assumptions. In a paper from 2001 John Driver writes,

> This account [Broadbent's early selection account of attention] is still heavily influential today. The distinction between a parallel "preattentive" stage, encoding simple physical properties vs. a serial "attentive" stage encoding more abstract properties remains common in the current literature. Indeed, a dichotomous preattentive/attentive split is often assumed as given, perhaps too readily; likewise for the idea that selection may arise at just one particular point in processing.
>
> (Driver 2001: 56)

Driver clearly thinks that we need to distance ourselves further from Broadbent's assumptions, but his formulation of the assumption that he takes to be problematic is ambiguous and its ambiguity corresponds to a point about which current theorists disagree. There are two ways in which one might reject "the idea that selection may arise at just one particular point in processing," corresponding to the two ways in which one might interpret the scope of the quantifiers in the sentence: "All attentional selection takes place at some one point." One might reject the claim that whenever a subject attends there is a single point at which the thing to which he or she attends is selected (rejecting the claim in which the universal quantifier is given wide scope). One might, alternatively, accept that claim while rejecting the stronger claim that there is a single point such that, whenever the subject attends, the thing to which he or she attends is selected at that point (rejecting the claim in which the existential quantifier is given wide scope). It is unclear which of these Driver intends, and unclarity of this sort has made it difficult for psychologists to bring into focus their lack of agreement as to whether both of these claims need to be rejected, or whether, having rejected the stronger claim, we can retain the weaker one.

If one rejects both claims then one takes it that the fact that a particular stimulus is the one to which the subject is paying attention is not a matter of its having been selected by any *one* of these mechanisms but of its having done well in the variously selective environment of the brain. If, on the other hand, one rejects the stronger claim *while retaining the weaker one* then the resulting view is one according to which there is always *some locus or other* where stimuli are selected by attention, but no *one* locus where selection always happens. According to this view the mistake of twentieth-century research was to think that the bottleneck of limited capacity has a *stable* location: this view says that attentional selection is passage through a bottleneck but that the bottleneck is located in different places, depending on factors such as the demands of the subject's task.

The assumption about linearity and the assumptions about uniqueness are distinct. One can reject the strong uniqueness assumption, or reject only the weaker one, while holding a variety of views about the linearity assumption. One might nonetheless think that, having rejected the uniqueness assumption, one has no remaining motivation for the rejection of the linearity assumption, or that having rejected the linearity assumption, one has no remaining motivation for rejecting the assumption about uniqueness. Those psychologists who take issue with the uniqueness assumption often do seem to reason in this way. They treat the Broadbentian assumptions as credible until proven false, and so take their rejection of the uniqueness assumption as enabling them to retain talk of early and late instances of attention. They thereby incur a commitment to the assumptions about linearity that such talk requires. Nilli Lavie, the most prominent defender of a moving-bottleneck view of attention, takes a view along these lines. She claims that:

> early selection is both the inevitable outcome of allocating attention from a limited pool . . . and impossible to achieve when capacity is not exceeded . . . This view proposes a compromise between early and late selection approaches.
>
> (Lavie 1995: 452)

Lavie rejects the strong uniqueness assumption (that the attentional bottleneck has a stable location), but retains the claim that there is such a thing as early selection (in circumstances where perceptual load is high). This, as we have said, is a way of speaking that makes sense only if instances of attention occur at a place in a processing stream with earlier and later parts. A 2004 paper by Lavie et al. is explicit in its intention to retain the spirit of Broadbent's linearity assumption, claiming that once the uniqueness assumption has been recognized as faulty, the rejection of the linearity assumption can be seen to have been premature:

> The existence of discrepant evidence even within the same task has led some to doubt that the early and late selection debate can ever be resolved . . . However, Lavie . . . has recently suggested that a resolution to the early and late selection debate may be found if a hybrid model of attention that combines aspects from both views is considered.
>
> (Lavie et al. 2004: 340)

Lavie's view of attention is not the only current view that retains the vocabulary of early and late selection, and thereby retains a commitment about linearity. Irwin Mack and Arian Rock's 1998 book, *Inattentional Blindness*, is wedded to the linearity view to such an extent that they take any alternative to be in principle impossible. In the concluding chapter of their book, they write:

> An obvious next question is when in the sequence of events leading to conscious perception is attention likely to be captured . . . In principle, there seem to be three possible answers . . . Either attention is captured early by the products of a low-level analysis of the input . . ., later, after some or all of the processing is complete . . . or attention is captured either at an early or late stage of processing, depending on some specifiable other factor(s) . . .
>
> (Mack and Rock 1988: 229)

In these examples we see that talk of attention as occurring early or late continues to be used, despite the widespread view that the cognitive architecture of perception is parallel and two-way to an extent that appears to undermine the meaningfulness of such talk. A combination of empirical and philosophical work is needed if we are to be sure that this talk of early/late selection does not lapse into meaninglessness. It is a philosophical task to limn the extent of the commitments that the use of early/late vocabulary incurs: does this talk require a feed-forward, serial architecture, or is there an interpretation on which it can be applied to hierarchical system? And it is an empirical task to marshal the data (only part of which will be drawn from studies of attention) to show whether these commitments are met.

The origins of selectivity and the function of attention

Another dispute among current psychologists, and one that has been rather poorly articulated in the literature, is over the question of whether we should give up Broadbent's idea that the selectivity of attention is to be understood as selectivity of the sort that arises from the management of a limitation in information-processing capacity.

Many researchers treat this as if it were not controvertible. Although they might give up the idea that attention corresponds to a single bottleneck in processing capacity, they continue to take it to be axiomatic that limitations in processing capacity are the reason for the selectivity of attention, and they write as if it would be a change of topic to talk about anything other than capacity limitations when discussing attention. Bricolo et al., for example, write that:

> In general set-size effects are taken to indicate that processing of the array of elements depends on limited capacity resources, *that is, it involves attention*.
> (2002: 980; emphasis added)

This is too quick: a dependence on limited-capacity processing resources is *not* the only reason why an effect might be attention involving. It could be that, instead of managing a limitation of processing capacity, the function of attention is to impose constraints of coherence and appropriateness on a system of processing that has the capacity to handle far more stimuli than those pertaining to the subject's current task. It is because we *can* process these stimuli that we can be distracted by them, and it is because we can be distracted by them, not because we can't process them, that we need mechanisms of attention to provide selectivity and focus.

The idea that attentional selectivity might serve the function of *over*-capacity management can be found in work by Odmar Neumann, and in work by Alan Allport, each writing in 1987. In its original form the idea took the form of the "selection-for-action hypothesis" and it was not properly distinguished from a version of the late-selection view in which attention is the management of a bottleneck in the capacity for the performance of actions, rather than for the processing of stimuli. As an hypothesis about the locus of the attentional bottleneck the selection-for-action view was deservedly unpopular, but the view is better understood, not as a theory about the locus of attentional selection, but as one about the nature and function of that selection. The view helped to establish the idea that there are functions for attentional selectivity, even in a cognitive architecture that doesn't have a bottleneck in perceptual-processing capacity, functions including "conflict-monitoring," the suppression of "crosstalk interference between parallel processes" (see Botvinick et al. 2001) and the imposition of constraints of coherence and appropriateness.

In addition to the psychological research indicating several possible functions for attentional selectivity other than the function of limitation management, a strand of more purely philosophical thinking has developed that suggests a more crucial role for attention in perception. This line of philosophical thinking has a long history (beginning with Kant, and proceeding via P.F. Strawson, Gareth Evans, and John McDowell, among others), and it is a difficult one to summarize concisely. The central thought is that for perception to put us in touch with an independent world it must be that the content of our experience is *conceptualized* in something like the way that our beliefs are. This conceptualization of experience typically involves thinking of the things perceived under a demonstrative concept (that is, thinking of them as "*that* thing"). And the application of these demonstrative concepts to a thing seems, at least in many cases, to involve the focusing of attention on that thing. According to this line of thinking, then, it is only because we can attend to the things we perceive that our perception can provide us with reasons to believe in the independent existence of those things. The most explicit statement of this thought is given in an essay by Naomi Eilan from 1998, and it has a central role in recent work by John Campbell (2002).

Although the philosophical arguments here are made on *a priori* epistemological grounds it is natural to see recent empirical work into "inattentional blindness" as a counterpart to the philosophical thought that unattended, unconceptualized experience cannot provide reasons for belief. In inattentional blindness experiments (such as those of Simons and Chabris 1999) subjects who take themselves to be having an experience of a scene turn out to know remarkably little about the unattended parts of that scene. The convergence of these two very different research programmes is something that has yet to be explored, and it may prove to be a promising direction for future research.

However the relation of perception to attention needs, in the final analysis, to be understood, it is at least clear that there is room for a function for attention other than the management of limitations in processing capacity, and with this it becomes clear that bottlenecks of processing capacity are not the only sort of *mechanism* that could implement attentional selectivity. Allport and Neumann introduced the selection-for-action theory at a time of enormous progress in the use of connectionist networks to model cognitive processes (see Chapter 12 in this volume, by Sharkey and Sharkey). A ubiquitous feature of such models is the use of competition to effect a selection between two competing possible outputs (Navon and Miller 1987; Mozer 1991; Mozer and Sitton 1998). It was natural to suggest, therefore, that the mechanisms responsible for the selectivity of attention are competitive mechanisms, and not bottlenecks.

It is rarely realized that the selectivity of a bottleneck and the selectivity of a competitive mechanism are quite different. In a paper from 2000, John Reynolds and Robert Desimone begin their discussion of competitive mechanisms of attention with the thoroughly Broadbentian remark that

> The visual system is limited in its capacity to process information. However, it is equipped to overcome this constraint because it can direct this limited-capacity channel to locations or objects of interest.
>
> (Reynolds and Desimone 2001: 233)

But the mechanisms that Reynolds and Desimone go on to describe are *competitive* ones and the selectivity of these mechanisms has nothing to do with limitations in the information carrying capacity of a channel. Competitive mechanisms are *always* selective, in ways that have nothing to do with the capacity limitations of the processes that compete, in just the same way that a tournament or a league necessarily selects one winning team, however many teams compete and however large and skilful each team is. The selectivity of a competition is not the selectivity of a limitation in processing capacity and Reynolds' and Desimone's competitive view of attention is a much more radical break with Broadbentian thinking than is suggested by the way in which they introduce that view.

Unlike the rejection of the assumptions about linearity and uniqueness, the rejection of the assumption about attentional selectivity being the selectivity of a bottleneck is *not* easily compatible with the retention of the other aspects of the Broadbentian picture. To reject the idea that there is a bottleneck of attention, is, *a fortiori*, to reject the idea there is a single bottleneck, or a bottleneck with a stable location. We could try to retain the spirit of these assumptions by giving a theory in which there is a single, stable locus at which the attentional competition occurs, but nobody has tried to give such a theory and there are excellent empirical reasons for thinking that it would be a mistake to do so. Reynolds and Desimone's work on a competition-based view of attentional selection has provided the theoretical basis for a number of studies using cell-recording and functional brain imaging techniques. These suggest that competition between stimuli occurs throughout the sensory cortex, that a distributed network of loci contribute to the outcome of these competitions, and that all of this competition is involved in attention. (See Kastner and Ungerleider [2000] for review.)

Attention and consciousness

A third point of contention in current thinking about attention is rather different from the previous two, and concerns the relationship between attention and consciousness. It would seem, from the point of view of commonsense psychology, that one cannot have one's attention directed on something unless one is consciously aware of that thing, and it therefore seems that attention is sufficient for consciousness. Commonsense psychology also suggests that, for many stimuli, attention is necessary for conscious awareness: We often explain our lack of conscious awareness of something by saying that we weren't paying attention. It is natural, therefore, to think that attention and consciousness are intimately related. But it is much less natural to think that attention is *always* necessary for consciousness. This is less natural because commonsense allows for our consciousness to include a background of things that we are dimly aware of, and to which we could switch our attention, but which are currently receiving no attention at all.

Broadbent and his contemporaries followed the lead of commonsense on these points, taking all attention to be conscious attention, but not taking it that one is conscious of only those things to which one attends.

Current thinking among psychologists suggests that at least the second of these points is mistaken, and maybe the first too. Evidence suggesting that attention might always be necessary for consciousness comes from a memorable range of experiments in which people show no awareness of stimuli that are not relevant to the task at hand, even when these stimuli are salient and centrally located. A well-known example is the demonstration by Simons and Chabris (1999) that a surprisingly large number of subjects (about one in three) fail to notice when a man in a gorilla suit appears in the middle of a basketball game to which they are closely attending. In tasks using stimuli that are presented much more briefly the proportion of subjects who fail to notice unattended stimuli is much higher (Mack and Rock 1998). Commonsense psychology allows that inattention can *sometimes* explain a lack of conscious awareness; experiments such as these have been taken to suggest that inattention *invariably* leads to a lack of conscious awareness (although work by Valerie Grey Hardcastle [2003] offers a different interpretation of these results).

If the result that inattention invariably leads to a lack of conscious awareness could be established, it would be particularly welcome news for psychologists with ambitions to explain consciousness. If attention could be shown to be necessary for consciousness then, if we could retain the commonsense view that consciousness is necessary for attention, we could conclude that attention and consciousness are exactly coextensive, and so our best theories of attention could be traded in, at no extra cost, for theories about the psychological basis of consciousness.

For some psychologists this prospect of using theories of attention to explain consciousness seems always to have been in view, "attention" having been adopted as a convenient cover to avoid the philosophical contention that inevitably accompanies claims about consciousness. William James switched freely between asking "To How Many Things Can We Attend at Once?" and "The question of *the span of consciousness*" (James 1983 [1890]: 405; italics in original), and in 1980 Alan Allport wrote that "Ninety years later [after James] the word ["Attention"] is still used, by otherwise hard-nosed information-processing psychologists, as a code name for consciousness" (113).

One bar to the attempt to turn theories of attention into theories of consciousness is the finding that while inattentional blindness effects suggest that attention might, surprisingly, be necessary for consciousness, attention-like effects in blindsight patients suggest that, again surprisingly, it might not be sufficient (Kentridge et al. 2004; Kentridge and Heywood 2001).

Those who want to claim that attention and consciousness are coextensive might be tempted to rule out Kentridge and Heywood's findings of unconscious attention on conceptual grounds, arguing that no *unconscious* cueing and priming effects can *possibly* count as instances of attention. Such an argument would need to avoid trading on intuitions of a sort that we ought to regard as unreliable, given the evidence for the counterintuitive conclusion that attention is necessary for consciousness.

It may be, however, that even without an argument to rule out cases of unconscious attention, we can establish the desired conclusion that our discoveries about the psychology of attention reveal features of the psychological underpinnings of consciousness. Researchers into attention have typically used the subjects' conscious awareness of stimuli as a criterion for identifying whether or not they are attentive. It is plausible, therefore, that, even if attention can occur without consciousness, the phenomenon studied by psychologists under the rubric of attention is one that only occurs for those stimuli of which the subject is conscious. That, combined with inattentional blindness research, may justify some of the current optimism about using the information gathered in the study of attention to tell us about the cognitive goings on that play a role in making us conscious.

References

Allport, A. (1980) "Attention and Performance," in Guy Claxton (ed.), *Cognitive Psychology: New directions*, London: Routledge & Kegan Paul, pp. 112–53.

—— (1987) "Selection for Action: Some Behaviorial and Neurophysiological Considerations of Attention and Action," in Andries Sanders and Herbert Heuer (eds), *Perspectives on Perception and Action*, Hillsdale, NJ: Erlbaum, pp. 395–419.

—— (1993) "Attention and Control: Have We Been Asking the Wrong Questions? A Critical Review of Twenty-Five Years," in Sylvan Kornblum and David Meyer (eds), *Attention and Performance*, 14: *Synergies in Experimental Psychology, Artificial Intelligence, and Cognitive Neuroscience*, Cambridge, MA: MIT Press, pp. 183–218.

Allport, A., Antonis, B., and Reynolds, P. (1972) "On the Division of Attention: A Disproof of the Single Channel Hypothesis," *Quarterly Journal of Experimental Psychology* 24, no. 2: 225–35.

Botvinick, M., Braver, T., Barch, D., Carter, C., and Cohen J. (2001) "Conflict Monitoring and Cognitive Control," *Psychological Review* 108, no. 3: 624–52.

Bricolo, E., Gianesini, T., Fanini, A., Bundesen, C., and Chelazzi, L. (2002) "Serial Attention Mechanisms in Visual Search: A Direct Behavioural Demonstration," *Journal of Cognitive Neuroscience* 14, no. 7: 980–93.

Broadbent, D. (1958) *Perception and Communication*, London: Pergamon.

—— (1971) *Decision and Stress*, Oxford: Academic Press.

Bundesen, C. (2000) "Attention: Models of Attention," in Alan Kazdin (ed.), *Encyclopedia of Psychology*, vol. 1, Washington, DC: American Psychological Association, pp. 295–99.

Campbell, J. (2002) *Reference and Consciousness*, Oxford: Oxford University Press.

Cherry, C. (1953) "Some Experiments on the Recognition of Speech, with One and with Two Ears," *Journal of the Acoustical Society of America* 25: 975–9.

Corteen R. S., and Dunn D. (1974) "Shock Associated Words in a Nonattended Message: A Test for Momentary Awareness," *Journal of Experimental Psychology* 102, no. 6: 1143–4.

Dawson, M. E., and Schell, A. M. (1982) "Electrodermal Responses to Attended and Nonattended Significant Stimuli during Dichotic Listening," *Journal of Experimental Psychology: Human Perception and Performance* 8, no. 2: 315–24.

Deutsch, J. A., and Deutsch, D. (1963) "Attention: Some Theoretical Considerations," *Psychological Review* 70: 80–90.

Downes, S. (1992) "The Importance of Models in Theorizing: A Deflationary Semantic View," *PSA: Proceedings of the Biennial Meeting of the Philosophy of Science Association* 1: 142–53.

Driver, J. (2001) "A Selective Review of Selective Attention Research from the Past Century," *British Journal of Psychology* 92, no. 1: 53–78.

Driver, J., and Tipper, S. P. (1989) "On the Nonselectivity of 'Selective' Seeing: Contrasts between Interference and Priming in Selective Attention," *Journal of Experimental Psychology: Human Perception and Performance* 15: 304–14.

Eilan, N. (1998) "Perceptual Intentionality, Attention and Consciousness," in Anthony O'Hear (ed.), *Current Issues in Philosophy of Mind*, Royal Institute of Philosophy Supplement 43, Cambridge: Cambridge University Press, pp. 181–202.

Geach, P. (1957) *Mental Acts*, London: Routledge & Kegan Paul.

Godfrey-Smith, P. (2006) "The Strategy of Model-Based Science," *Biology and Philosophy* 21: 725–40.

Hardcastle, V. (2003) "Attention versus Consciousness: A Distinction with a Difference," in Naoyuki Osaka (ed.) *Neural Basis of Consciousness*, Amsterdam: John Benjamins, pp. 105–20.

James, W. (1983 [1890]) *The Principles of Psychology*, Cambridge, MA: Harvard University Press.

Kastner, S., and Ungerleider, L. G. (2000) "Mechanisms of Visual Attention in the Human Cortex," *Annual Review of Neuroscience* 23: 315–41.

Kentridge, R., and Heywood, C. (2001) "Attention and Alerting: Cognitive Processes Spared in Blindsight," in Beatrice De Gelder, Edward De Haan, and Charles Heywood (eds), *Out of Mind: Varieties of Unconscious Processes*, New York: Oxford University Press, pp. 163–81.

Kentridge, R., Heywood, C., and Weiskrantz, L. (2004) "Spatial Attention Speeds Discrimination without Awareness in Blindsight," *Neuropsychologia* 42, no. 6: 831–5.

Lavie, N. (1995) "Perceptual Load as a Necessary Condition for Selective Attention," *Journal of Experimental Psychology: Human Perception and Performance* 21, no. 3: 451–68.

Lavie, N., Hirst, A., de Fockert, J., and Viding, E. (2004) "Load Theory of Selective Attention and Cognitive Control," *Journal of Experimental Psychology: General* 133, no. 3: 339–54.

Mack, A., and Rock, I. (1998) *Inattentional Blindness*, Cambridge MA: MIT Press.

Merleau-Ponty, M. (1962) *Phenomenology of Perception*, London: Routledge & Kegan Paul.

Mozer, M. (1991) *The Perception of Multiple Objects: A Connectionist Approach*, Cambridge, MA: MIT Press.

Mozer, M., and Sitton, M. (1998) "Computational Modeling of Spatial Attention," in Harold Pashler (ed.), *Attention*, Hove, UK: Psychology Press, 341–93.

Navon, D., and Miller, J. (1987) "Role of Outcome Conflict in Dual-Task Interference," *Journal of Experimental Psychology: Human Perception and Performance* 13, no. 3: 435–48.

Neumann, O. (1987) "Beyond Capacity: A Functional View of Attention," in Andries Sanders and Herbert Heuer (eds), *Perspectives on Perception and Action*, Hillsdale, NJ: Erlbaum, pp. 361–94.

Parasuraman, R. (1998) *The Attentive Brain*, Cambridge MA: MIT Press.

Posner, M., and Marin, O. (1985) Preface to *Attention and Performance*, vol. 11, ed. Oscar S. M. Marin and Michael I. Posner, Hillsdale, NJ: Erlbaum, pp. xxi–xxiii.

Prinz, W., and Hommel, B. (2002) *Attention and Performance*, vol. 19: *Common Mechanisms of Perception and Action*, Oxford: Oxford University Press.

Reynolds, J., and Desimone, R. (2000) "Competitive Mechanisms Subserve Selective Visual Attention," in Alec Marantz, Yasushi Miyashita, and Wayne O'Neil (eds), *Image, Language, Brain: Papers from the First Mind Articulation Project Symposium*, Cambridge, MA: MIT Press, pp. 233–47.

Ribot, T. (1890) *The Psychology of Attention*, Chicago: Open Court.

Simons, D. J., and Chabris, C. F. (1999) "Gorillas in Our Midst: Sustained Inattentional Blindness for Dynamic Events," *Perception* 28: 1059–74.

Spelke, E., Hirst, W., and Neisser, U. (1976) "Skills of Divided Attention," *Cognition* 4, no. 3: 215–30.

Treisman A. (1988) "Features and Objects: The Fourteenth Bartlett Memorial Lecture," *The Quarterly Journal of Experimental Psychology A: Human Experimental Psychology* 40A, no. 2: 201–37

White, A. R. (1964) *Attention*, Oxford: Basil Blackwell.

35
INTROSPECTION

Jordi Fernández

Introspection: philosophy and psychology

Introspection is the subject of investigations in both philosophy and psychology.[1] Philosophers are often concerned with the seemingly privileged status of those beliefs formed through introspection and the metaphysical import of the views that try to account for it. By contrast, psychologists seem to be more concerned with the reliability of introspection as well as its scope. There seem to be some connections between these issues, but it is not clear how exactly philosophical research and psychological research on introspection relate to each other. How do philosophical theories of introspection constrain the empirical research carried out by psychologists? How do psychological data inform the conceptual work being done by philosophers?

In what follows, I will assume a particular picture of the relation between philosophical work and psychological work on introspection. I will sketch this picture in what remains of this section. Next, I will turn my attention to two disorders of introspection. This will occupy our discussion during the second to seventh sections. I will then draw some philosophical implications from this psychological research in the eighth section. And, finally, I will return to the general picture about the relation between philosophy and psychology.

Here is an outline of a certain framework wherein we can understand the interaction of philosophical and psychological research on introspection.[2] We can view the notion of introspection as the concept of a theoretical entity. As such, it can be seen as a concept whose content is determined by the role that it plays within a particular theory. In the case of introspection, that theory is folk psychology. We can think of folk psychology as the collection of claims that describe the typical causal relations that hold between our perceptual *stimuli*, our behavioral responses, and the different kinds of mental states that we occupy. Folk psychology is common knowledge to us in that we have implicit knowledge of those claims. Thus, in order to spell out the claims that jointly constitute our characterization of introspection, we can simply reflect on our intuitive concept of introspection and analyze it. I propose to view this "analysis" aspect of an investigation of introspection as, mainly, the philosopher's job. Nonetheless, psychology can contribute to this kind of enquiry in an important way. Let me explain.

When it comes to investigating introspection, the philosopher will deal with questions such as the following: Is introspection a faculty that gives us *a priori* knowledge? Is it inferential? Does introspection give us knowledge about our own minds? Our answers to questions of these kinds will tell us what it takes for a certain property, process or mechanism to count as introspective. Basically, they draw the line between what we count as introspection and what we count as something else. Now, how do we go about answering these questions? Typically, the philosopher will proceed by way of thought experiments. The philosopher will entertain situations where a certain knowledge-acquisition process that resembles introspection will occur under circumstances that differ from the actual ones. (For instance, we may be asked to imagine a faculty that gives us non-inferential, *a priori* knowledge of other people's minds.) We will then be asked whether, intuitively, we would count those processes as introspective. Our answers to such questions are meant to reveal what our notion of introspection is like.

However, this kind of methodology is not effective unless we are confronted with clear cases, which is why psychological research can make a crucial contribution to it. If we are asked to consider cases of subjects who seem to gain knowledge through processes that resemble introspection and, then, we need to decide whether those processes should indeed count as introspective, our intuitions will not be robust enough unless those cases are clearly described. And psychological research can provide us with clear, precise descriptions of interesting cases for those purposes. There are various disorders of thought, especially in schizophrenia, that constitute very effective tests for our intuitions with regards to some of the questions that the philosopher asks about introspection.

Furthermore, there is a different contribution that psychology makes to the study of introspection. This is the identification of the property, process, or mechanism that, in humans, constitutes introspection. Even if we spell out all the features that a certain mechanism must have in order to qualify as introspection in us, we are still left with the question of which mechanism actually has all of those features. As I see it, this "identification" aspect of an investigation of introspection is an empirical project, and pursuing it is the psychologist's job. Notice that, in different senses, both the project of analysis and the project of identification attempt to answer the question, "What is introspection?" The philosopher will pursue an answer of the kind "It is whatever mechanism meets such-and-such conditions." By contrast, the psychologist will answer the question by locating the mechanism that actually meets those conditions.

To illustrate this picture, I will be discussing two disorders of introspection, namely, thought insertion and thought broadcast. I will first consider several approaches to these two disorders. The discussion of those different approaches will lead us to briefly consider two other pathologies of introspection, that is, multiple-personality disorder (MPD, hereafter) and thought control. Then, I will identify some philosophical questions about introspection for which thought insertion and thought broadcast seem particularly relevant. The discussion of those questions will get us back to the issue of how psychology contributes to the project of analysis and, therefore, how psychological data bears on the philosophical research on introspection.

Thought insertion and thought broadcast

Thought insertion is a disorder wherein the subject is under the impression that certain thoughts that she has are not her own thoughts. In fact, subjects who experience thought insertion often report that other people's thoughts are happening in their own minds. The following is a report from a patient with thought insertion (Mellor 1970: 17):

> I look at the window and I think that the garden looks nice and the grass look cool, but the thoughts of Eamonn Andrews come into my mind. There are no other thoughts there, only his ... He treats my mind like a screen and flashes thoughts onto it like you flash a picture.

By contrast, thought broadcast is a disorder wherein the subject is under the impression that certain thoughts that she has escape her own mind. In fact, subjects who experience thought broadcast often report that other people can have access to those thoughts. According to Koehler (1979: 239), in thought broadcast the subject "is quite certain of 'negatively' being aware that he has lost HIS OWN thoughts, feelings and so on because in some way they passively diffuse into or are lost to the outside world against his will." The following is a report from a patient with thought broadcast (Mellor 1970):

> As I think, my thoughts leave my head on a type of mental ticker-tape. Everyone around has only to pass the tape through their mind and they know my thought.

There are two interesting questions that one might raise about these disorders. We could call them the "what-question" and the "why-question."[3] The what-question is, What are these subjects experiencing when they make reports such as the two reports above? What are they trying to express exactly? Subjects who suffer these two disorders seem to be having some odd experiences that they cannot quite put into words. One would want to know what subjects with thought insertion and thought broadcast are trying to get at when they describe the way in which they experience their relation to their own thoughts. By contrast, the why-question is, Why do these subjects have the strange sort of experience that leads them to make reports of that kind? Why does such an odd type of experience arise in these subjects?

Here is one way of looking at the contrast between the two questions. When one asks the what-questions about thought insertion and thought broadcast, one is enquiring about how subjects with those disorders represent the world and their own minds, whereas when one asks the why-questions, one is enquiring about the causes that made those subjects represent things in that way. There is a sense in which the what-questions about thought insertion and thought broadcast are therefore more basic than their corresponding why-questions: answers to each why-question will presuppose answers to their corresponding what-questions. Basically, we cannot begin to discern why a subject with, let us say, thought insertion has the kind of experience that she tries to express by saying things such as "I have such-and-such thought, but it is not my thought" until we have a certain grasp of what that experience could be like. Thus, in the following five sections, I will concentrate on some possible answers to the what-questions about thought insertion and thought broadcast, and I will leave the corresponding why-questions aside.

Thought insertion: displacement and MPD

One possible answer to the what-question about thought insertion is the following: The subject is misrepresenting the boundaries of her ego. In fact, she is under the impression that such boundaries are narrower than they really are. Therefore, she takes certain states of her own mind to be states of other entities out there, in the world (Sims 1995: 152):

> In thought insertion, [the subject] experiences thoughts that do not have the feeling of being his own, but he feels that they have been put in his mind without his volition, from the outside. As in thought withdrawal, there is clearly a disturbance of self-image, and especially in the boundary between what is self and what is not.

Basically, the idea is that the subject with thought insertion attributes some of her thoughts to other people's minds because she is wrong about where the boundaries that separate her own mind from others stand. Thus, according to this answer to the what-question about thought insertion, subjects who suffer this disorder essentially feel as if they had access to other people's minds. We may call this model of thought insertion, the "displacement model."[4]

Notice that, within the displacement model, part of the report that a subject with thought insertion typically makes is taken at face value, but part of it is not. Consider a report of the form "I believe that *P* but that is not my thought." When a subject with thought insertion claims "that is not my thought," the displacement theorist takes this part of the report at face value: The theorist assumes that the thought that the subject is being aware of is indeed not experienced by her as being her own thought. However, when the subject claims "I believe that *P*," the theorist takes the subject to mean something slightly (but importantly) different: the displacement theorist reads the subject as saying that she is aware that the fact that *P* is being believed.

This feature of the displacement model has brought it under attack. Thus, Graham and Stephens (2000: 126) complain that in the examples of thought insertion in the clinical literature, "patients are well aware of the subjectivity of their thoughts: of where they occur. They regard them as occurring within their ego boundaries."[5] The objection against the displacement model is therefore that the subject with thought insertion does not seem to be confused about where the thought is taking place. It seems to be relatively clear that she takes the thought to be occurring in her own mind.[6] One way of motivating the objection further is to consider other disorders that, intuitively, seem to be accurately described by the displacement model, and consider whether thought insertion is sufficiently analogous to those disorders or not.

Subjects who suffer from MPD have two or more personality states, or "alters." Each of these alters has a specific set of mental states, such as beliefs, desires, emotions, and memories, and they take turns controlling the subject's behavior. For the purposes of studying introspection, the following fact is particularly interesting about MPD: Usually, when a particular alter is controlling the MPD subject's behavior, that alter only has introspective access to her own mental states. Occasionally, though, an alter may be aware of what other alters think, what they intend to do or how they feel about a certain person or situation. One such case was well documented at the beginning of the twentieth century. This is the case of Doris Fischer.[7] Some of Fischer's alters claimed to have access to some of her other alters' mental states. Thus, one of Fischer's alters, "Sleeping Margaret," narrated the following. Initials stand for her other alters "Margaret," "Sick Doris" and "Real Doris" (Prince 1916: 109):

> S.D. [Sick Doris] watched when R.D. [Real Doris] was out. There would be three of us watching her, each with thoughts of her own. S.D. watched R.D.'s mind, M. [Margaret] watched S.D.'s thoughts of R.D., and I watched all three. Sometimes we had disagreements. Sometimes a jealous thought would flit through S.D.'s mind – she would think for a moment that if R.D. would not come out any more M. might not like her as well as R.D.

The displacement model seems to capture what Sleeping Margaret's experience might have been like when Real Doris was "out" (in control of Fisher's body). Sleeping Margaret claims to be aware of Sick Doris's thoughts in that situation. So it seems that, when Real Doris is out, we have a case of a subject (Sleeping Margaret) who is aware of certain mental states that are not presented to her as being her own. Notice that this point is independent of our position with regards to the veridicality of such an experience. With regards to that issue, we have of course two options. Either we take each personality to constitute a person, or we decide that there is only one person here, namely, Fisher. In the former case, Sleeping Margaret is aware of a mental state that is not her own, since she is not the same person as Sick Doris. Interestingly, this commits us to the view that there are actual cases of telepathy. In the latter case, Sleeping Margaret (or Fisher, since they are one and the same person in this scenario) is under the wrong impression that certain mental states that she has are not her own. Either way, we have a case of a subject who has introspective access to mental states that do not appear to her as being her own. Thus, the displacement model seems to be particularly well suited to capture what goes on in some cases of MPD.

The question is now whether thought insertion is analogous to MPD. It does not seem to be. What differentiates the two pathologies is, basically, Graham and Stephens's point. Sleeping Margaret talks about "watching" someone else's mind and thoughts, whereas the patient who is concerned with Eamonn Andrews does not claim to be aware of Andrews's thoughts. It does not seem that, from this patient's point of view, the thought that the garden is nice appears to take place in Andrews's mind. She seems to think that it occurs in her own mind, that is, she seems to think that the property of thinking that the garden looks nice is a property that she has. Thus, it seems that the displacement model is more adequate to approach MPD than thought insertion.

Thought insertion: agency and thought control

A different approach to the what-question about thought insertion treats thinking as a kind of action. Within the "action" model of thought insertion, having a thought is something that we do, just as, let us say, raising an arm is something that we do. Now, notice that there are circumstances in which it makes sense that my arm went up, even though I did not raise my arm. (Someone may have kicked my arm, for instance.) In certain circumstances, that movement may have occurred in my body, even though I was not the agent of it. It is not something that I did. If we construe thinking as a kind of action, we may similarly distinguish two senses in which a certain thought can be mine. In one sense, the thought is mine if it occurs in my mind, that is, if the property of having the thought is instantiated in me. In a different sense, the thought is mine if I am the person doing the thinking. The crucial point for the purposes of answering the what-question about thought insertion is that the two senses may come apart. Harry Frankfurt makes the point nicely (1988: 59):

> The verb "to think" can connote an activity – as in "I am thinking carefully about what you said" – and with regard to this aspect of its meaning, we cannot suppose that thoughts are necessarily accompanied by thinking. It is not incoherent, despite the air of paradox, to say that a thought that occurs in my mind may or may not be something that *I think*.

Now, this point has been used to answer the what-question about thought insertion. Basically, the idea is that the subject with thought insertion experiences that some thought occurring in her own mind is carried out by someone else (Graham and Stephens 2000: 154). She acknowledges that she is the subject in whom the thought occurs, but she does not have the sense that she is doing the thinking. But this answer to the what-question about thought insertion appears to have a problem. The problem is that the agency model seems to conflate thought insertion with a different disorder, which we may call "thought control."

Subjects who suffer thought control claim that some of their thoughts have emerged as a result of the influence of an external agent. In other words, they claim that they have been made to think certain things (Hamilton 1984: 48–9).[8] In the clinical literature, it is often pointed out that thought control is different from thought insertion. In the former case, the subject is meant to own the thought, whereas in the latter case the subject is supposed to disown it. Thus, the standard view is that subjects with thought insertion do not thereby suffer from thought control (Fulford 1989; Taylor and Heiser 1971; Koehler 1979). Conversely, it is often claimed that subjects with thought control do not thereby suffer from thought insertion (Mullins and Spence 2003: 295). The problem for the action model of thought insertion is that, if it is correct, then all cases of thought insertion are cases of thought control, and *vice versa*. This criticism rests on two points.

The first point concerns the "control" aspect of thought control. The point is that, in the robust sense of "action" used within the agency model, one cannot be made to perform a certain action. Admittedly, some physical movements can be forced on us. Surely somebody could grab my hand, put a pen in it, and move it in such a way that my name is written on a piece of paper. But notice that this would not be a case where somebody has made me sign my name. My bodily movement does not seem to amount to an action. Basically, it seems that for a certain event to count as an action of mine, it must be up to me whether the event happens or not. If it is not within my control to make it happen, then it is hard to see that event as an action that I perform. Now, if we take thinking to be a kind of action, then this means that, arguably, it is not possible to be forced to think anything. To the extent that the thought is forced on one by some external influence, one is not doing the thinking. The upshot is that, if thinking is an action, then subjects who suffer thought control cannot be experiencing their process of thinking as being controlled from outside. The agency theorist is committed to the view that if the thinking process is controlled from outside, then that thinking process is not up to those subjects and, therefore, it is not their own thinking.

The second point concerns the "insertion" aspect of thought insertion. Subjects with thought insertion do not only claim that somebody else is thinking the thoughts that occur in their minds. They also claim that those thoughts have been inserted in their minds.[9] Which suggests that they are under the impression that those thoughts occur in their minds because somebody else is thinking them. Thus, it is not enough for the action theorist to describe the experience of thought insertion as the experience that a certain thought occurs in oneself while somebody else is thinking it. The best version of the agency model seems to be that the experience in question is the experience that a certain thought occurs in oneself because somebody else is thinking it.

We can now see that thought control and thought insertion conflate if we take thinking to be a kind of action. All cases of thought insertion will be cases of thought control, and all cases of thought control will be cases of thought insertion. Since the reasons for both claims are analogous, I will elaborate on the first claim only: Suppose that thinking is a kind of action. Consider a given event *E* that is a case of thought insertion. Given the second point above, cases of thought insertion should be construed by the action theorist as cases where the subject experiences a thought occurring in her mind because somebody else is thinking it. Thus, *E* should be construed as a case where the subject has the sense that a thought occurs in her mind because somebody else is thinking it. Does *E* count as a case of thought control, then? One might think that it does not, since the subject is supposed to own her thought in cases of thought control. However, the first point above is that the action theorist cannot describe the experience of thought control as the experience of being the thinker of a thought resulting from external influences. If we construe thinking as a kind of action, then one cannot be the agent of a certain thought that has been forced upon oneself. This means that no characterization of thought control allowing the subject to own the "controlled" thought is available to the agency theorist. So it is hard to see why *E* should not count as a case of thought control. There is considerable pressure, then, for the agency theorist to take any case of thought insertion to be a case of thought control. Parallel reasons suggest that all cases of thought control will count as cases of thought insertion as well.

Introspective phenomenology: participation and intrusion

An interesting outcome of this discussion is that thought insertion suggests the possibility of two peculiar introspective experiences. One of them is the experience of having access to a thought that occurs in somebody else's mind. We could call this the experience of "intrusion." The other is the experience of having access to a thought that somebody else thinks in one's own mind. We could call this the experience of "participation."

The displacement model of thought insertion attributes experiences of intrusion to subjects with thought insertion. According to this model, what they experience is, basically, the exercise of telepathy. By contrast, the action model of thought insertion attributes experiences of participation to subjects with thought insertion. The idea is that those subjects experience being the host of a thought that somebody else is thinking. In that sense, they experience participating in that thought with somebody else.

There is a sense in which both types of experience have a kind of direction. In both cases, we can think of a sort of "mirror image" experience. For instance, if we accept that some subjects do have the experience of having access to a thought that occurs in somebody else's mind, then we might wonder if it is also possible to experience that somebody else is having access to a thought that occurs in one's own mind. Likewise, if we accept that some subjects do experience having access to a thought that somebody else is thinking in their own minds, then we could ask if it is possible to experience having access to a thought that one is thinking in somebody else's mind. The former kind of experience would be the counterpart of the experience of intrusion whereas the latter kind would be the counterpart of the experience of participation. Interestingly, some definitions of thought broadcast seem to rely on attributing, roughly, these "counterpart" experiences to the relevant subjects.

Thought broadcast: the audition model

Thought broadcast has been characterized in different ways by different authors, and some of those characterizations seem to mirror the attributions of experiences of participation and intrusion that take place in models of thought insertion. One popular characterization of thought broadcast links this disorder to a certain auditory hallucination. According to this characterization, subjects with thought broadcast experience that their own thoughts are being spoken aloud. For instance, a contemporary psychiatric textbook claims that these subjects "believe that their thoughts can be heard by other people" (Gelder et al. 1996: 14). This idea provides us with a straightforward answer to the what-question about thought broadcast: what subjects with thought broadcast experience is that their thoughts are made public, that is, they experience that other subjects are aware of those thoughts.

Interestingly, this way of answering the what-question about thought broadcast mirrors the answer to the what-question about thought insertion that the displacement theorist advocates. The displacement theorist claims that in thought insertion, the subject experiences that she is aware of other people's thoughts. Analogously, the audition theorist claims that, in thought broadcast, the subject experiences that other people are aware of her own thoughts. An experience of the intrusion type is attributed to the relevant subject in each case. The displacement theorist attributes the experience of intruding into other people's minds to the subject with thought insertion, whereas the audition theorist attributes the experience of being intruded upon to the subject with thought broadcast.

This comparison raises a rather natural question: Is there an answer to the what-question about thought broadcast that relies on an experience of the participation type, just like the action model of thought insertion resorts to experiences of that type to answer the corresponding question? It is quite interesting to notice that there is indeed such a way of understanding thought broadcast.

Thought broadcast: the diffusion model

Thought broadcast is often discussed in connection with Schneider's first-rank symptoms of schizophrenia. Schneider himself addresses thought broadcast, but he calls it "thought diffusion" (Schneider 1959: 100):

> Equally important are the thoughts which are no longer private but shared by others, the whole town or the whole world. To this symptom, the direct participation of others in the patient's thoughts, we have given the title "expropriation of thoughts" or "diffusion of thoughts."

Notice that Schneider does not mention the impression that one's thoughts are spoken aloud. The idea is rather that the subject is under the impression that other people are able to participate in her thought, or "share in their agency" (Pawar and Spence 2003: 288). As Fish puts it, the subject with thought broadcast "knows that as he is thinking everyone else is thinking in unison with him" (Fish 1967: 39).

The kind of experience that Fish and Schneider attribute to the subject with thought broadcast is therefore quite similar to the experience that the agency theorists attribute to the subject with thought insertion. In fact, it is easy to see the former experience as the mirror image of the latter one. According to the agency theorists, in thought insertion the subject experiences that a thought which others are thinking occurs in oneself.[10] By contrast, the experience that the diffusion theorists posit in thought broadcast seems to be the experience that a certain thought, which one is thinking, occurs in other people's minds as well.

What pathology teaches us about introspection

Suppose that the diffusion theorist is right. We might then wonder whether we should view the faculty that a subject with thought broadcast thinks that she is using as introspection. Similarly, it would be interesting to consider whether the faculty that the subject in question thinks that she is using should qualify as introspection if the audition theorist is right. Parallel questions suggest themselves about thought insertion: Suppose that the displacement theorist about thought insertion is right. Will we then be inclined to call the faculty that the subject with thought insertion thinks that she is using "introspection"? Would we be so inclined if the agency theorist were right?

The importance of these questions is the following. In some cases, we may be inclined to agree that the kind of faculty that the subject with one of the two disorders thinks that she is using when she has access to her thoughts is indeed introspection. In other cases, though, our reaction may be that no faculty matching the patient's characterization could be introspection. These results allow us to sharpen our own concept of introspection. Thus, enquiring about our intuitions with regards to the faculty that the subject with either thought insertion or thought broadcast thinks that she is using helps us to spell out our own intuitive notion of introspection.

Let *S* stand for a subject, and let *T* stand for a thought. Consider the following four conditional claims about introspection:

(i) If *S* can introspectively know that *T* occurs in someone, then *T* occurs in *S*.
(ii) If *S* can introspectively know that someone is the thinker of *T*, then *S* is the thinker of *T*.
(iii) If *T* occurs in *S*, then only *S* can introspectively know that it does.
(iv) If *S* is the thinker of *T*, then only *S* can introspectively know that she is the thinker of *T*.

Should these claims be part of the collection of those characterizing introspection? Should they belong to the set of claims determining the place of the concept of introspection within folk psychology? The various theories of thought insertion and thought broadcast may help us make up our minds about this issue.

Consider claim (i). According to the displacement theorist of thought insertion, the subject with thought insertion is committed to (i) being false. After all, she is meant to be under the impression that she has access to other people's thoughts. We can ask ourselves whether we should, strictly speaking, call the faculty that this subject thinks that she is using "introspection." If our intuition is that we should, then this counts as evidence in support of the view that (i) is spelling out (part of) our concept of introspection. If our intuition is that we should not, then this counts as evidence in support of the view that (i) should not be part of our characterization of introspection.

Consider (ii) next. According to the agency theorist of thought insertion, the subject with thought insertion is committed to (ii) being false. After all, such a subject is supposed to be under the impression that she is the host of certain thoughts that she herself is not thinking. We may wonder whether we should call the faculty that this subject thinks that she is using "introspection." Our intuitions on this issue will inform us of whether we should make (ii) part of our characterization of introspection as well.

What about claim (iii)? According to the diffusion theorist of thought broadcast, the subject with thought broadcast will view (iii) as false. After all, that subject is meant to be under the impression that other people participate in her thoughts. And she thinks that those people are not the only subjects who are aware of having those thoughts. (She thinks she is aware of the fact that they are having them.) Once again, we can ask ourselves whether the faculty that would be used in the situation that this subject has in mind qualifies as introspection. Our position with regards to that issue will tell us something about our notion of introspection. It will tell us whether (iii) is part of that notion or not.

One might think that the audition model of thought broadcast should similarly help us with regards to (iv). Unfortunately, things are a bit more complicated in this case. The audition model of thought broadcast is that the subject is under the impression that other people "hear" her thoughts. If we take this literally, then she obviously does not think that other people know her thoughts introspectively. (They know them through their perceptual faculties.) So it is not clear that the audition model of thought broadcast will help us decide whether we should include (iv) in our characterization of introspection after all.[11]

Let us take stock. We started with a certain picture of the relation between philosophical and psychological research on introspection. The basic idea was that, in the first instance, we need to describe the characteristic features that introspection has. And, then, we need to identify the cognitive mechanism that actually has those features. I proposed that the former task (the task of analysis) is the main role of the philosophy of introspection whereas the latter task (the task of identification) is the main role of the psychology of introspection. However, I argued that psychology provides us with clear cases that test our sense of which faculties we would intuitively count as introspection, thus contributing to the first task. Next, we examined several theories of two disorders of introspection, namely, thought insertion and thought broadcast. We have seen that these theories attribute different experiences to the subjects who have those two disorders. We have also seen that, consequently, these theories implicitly attribute different beliefs about introspection to those subjects as well. This point finally gave us the opportunity to evaluate our intuitions about what kind of faculties we would count as introspection. The idea is that this exercise will help us with the task of analysis in our investigation of introspection.

Our discussions of thought insertion and thought broadcast are meant to be case studies of this picture about the relation between the philosophy of introspection and the psychology of introspection. Where should we go from here? To broaden this investigation, we should consider other disorders of introspection next. Psychology can provide philosophers with accurate descriptions of disorders where subjects are unaware of actions that they are performing or perceptual experiences that they are having. Phenomena such as blindsight and anosognosia, for instance, should now be factored into our investigation. The hope is that the philosophers of introspection will eventually be able to use this kind of input from psychology to clarify what counts as introspection. And the relevant list of criteria will be precise enough for the psychologists to identify the relevant mechanism and, thus, finally tell us what introspection is.

This research was supported by grants from the Spanish Ministry of Science and Technology for the projects HUM2007-61108 and HUM2006-09923.

Notes

1. For an example of a psychological investigation; see Wilson (2002). See the essays in Cassam (1996) for examples of philosophical discussions.
2. The following is meant to be a very rough description of, basically, David Chalmers's 'functional reduction' framework in (1995). I take it that one of the sources of this framework is David Lewis's work on theoretical entities in (1972).
3. The point that there are different kinds of explanations that one may seek about thought disorders is not new. See Jaspers (1963) for a similar idea.
4. This model has a long history. It can arguably be attributed to Sigmund Freud, for instance, when he claims that pathology "has made us acquainted with a great number of states in which the boundary lines between the ego and the external world become uncertain or in which they are actually drawn incorrectly. There are cases in which parts of a person's own body, even portions of his own mental life – his perceptions, thoughts and feelings – appear alien to him and not belonging to his own ego" (Freud 1975: 3).
5. I am sympathetic to Graham and Stephens's take on this model of thought insertion. For a more detailed discussion of all the material in this section, including multiple personality disorder, see Chapter 6 in their 2000.
6. This kind of talk is metaphorical, since thoughts have no spatial location. However, we can think of something like the location of a thought along the following lines. The property of having a certain thought can be instantiated in different subjects or in the same subject at different times. We could then take the location of a thought (token, that is) to be the location of the subject who instantiates the property of having that thought.
7. See Prince (1916).
8. In some cases, the control of the relevant thought is attributed to a machine. In the literature on schizophrenia, it is possible to find reports of "air-loom machines" (Porter 1991), as well as "electrical machines" (Tausk 1988), controlling thought.
9. Some are even ready to locate the point of entry into their heads (Cahill and Frith 1996).
10. I have argued that agency theorists should add "because others are thinking it" to this description of the experience. In so far as this point is correct, the parallel between the two experiences is not exact. The reason is that diffusion theorists do not claim that the subject with thought broadcast has the experience of *making* other people think with him.
11. Arguably, the agency model of thought insertion provides us with a better test for our intuitions on that matter. If the agency theorist is right, the subject with thought insertion will take (iv) to be false, as well as (ii).

References

Cahill, C., and Frith, C. (1996) "False Perceptions or False Beliefs? Hallucinations and Delusions in Schizophrenia," in P. W. Halligan and J. C. Marshall (eds) *Method in Madness: Case Studies in Cognitive Neuropsychiatry*, Hove: Psychology Press, pp. 267–91.

Cassam, Q. (ed.) (1996) *Self-Knowledge*, Oxford: Oxford University Press.

Chalmers, D. (1995) *The Conscious Mind*, Oxford: Oxford University Press.

Fish, F. (1967) *Clinical Psychopathology: Signs and Symptoms in Psychiatry*, Bristol: J. Wright & Sons.
Frankfurt, H. G. (1988) *The Importance of What We Care About: Philosophical Essays*, Cambridge: Cambridge University Press.
Freud, S. (1975) *Civilization and Its Discontents*, London: Hogarth Press.
Fulford, K. W. M. (1989) *Moral Theory and Medical Practice*, Cambridge: Cambridge University Press.
Gelder, M., Gath D., Mayou, R., and Cohen, P. (1996) *Oxford Textbook of Psychiatry*, Oxford: Oxford University Press.
Graham, G., and Stephens, G. L. (2000) *When Self-Consciousness Breaks: Alien Voices and Inserted Thoughts*, Cambridge MA: MIT Press.
Hamilton, M. (ed.) (1984) *Fish's Schizophrenia*, London: Wright PSG.
Jaspers, K. (1963) *General Psychopathology*, Manchester: Manchester University Press.
Koehler, K. (1979) "First Rank Symptoms of Schizophrenia: Questions Concerning Clinical Boundaries," *British Journal of Psychiatry* 134: 236–48.
Lewis, D. (1972) "Psychophysical and Theoretical Identifications," *Australasian Journal of Philosophy* 50: 249–58.
Mellor, C. S. (1970) "First Rank Symptoms of Schizophrenia," pt 1: "The Frequency of Schizophrenics on Admission to Hospital," and pt 2: "Differences between Individual First Rank Symptoms," *British Journal of Psychiatry* 117: 15–23.
Mullins, S., and Spence, S. (2003) "Re-examining Thought Insertion: Semi-structured Literature Review and Conceptual Analysis," *British Journal of Psychiatry* 182: 293–8.
Pawar, A. V., and Spence, S. A. (2003) "Defining Thought Broadcast: Semi-structured Literature Review," *British Journal of Psychiatry* 183: 287–91.
Porter, R. (1991) *The Faber Book of Madness*, London: Faber & Faber.
Prince, W. F. (1916) "The Doris Case of Quintuple Personality," *Journal of Abnormal Psychology* 11: 73–122.
Schneider, K. (1959) *Clinical Psychopathology*, New York: Grune & Stratton.
Sims, A. (1995) *Symptoms in the Mind: An Introduction to Descriptive Phenomenology*, London: Saunders.
Tausk, V. (1988) "On the Origin of the 'Influencing Machine' in Schizophrenia," in P. Buckley (ed.), *Essential Papers on Psychosis*, New York: New York University Press, pp. 49–75.
Taylor, M. A., and Heiser, J. F. (1971) "Phenomenology: An Alternative Approach to Diagnosis of Mental Disease," *Comprehensive Psychiatry* 12: 480–6.
Wilson, T. D. (2002) *Strangers to Ourselves: Discovering the Adaptive Unconscious*, Cambridge MA: Belknap Press.

36
DREAMING

John Sutton

Introduction

As a topic in the philosophy of psychology, dreaming is a fascinating, diverse, and severely underdeveloped area of study. The topic excites intense public interest in its own right, while also challenging our confidence that we know what the words "conscious" and "consciousness" mean. So dreaming should be at the forefront of our interdisciplinary investigations: theories of mind which fail to address the topic are incomplete. Students can be motivated to think hard about dreaming, so the subject has definite pedagogical utility as entry into a surprising range of philosophical topics. Learning even a little about the sciences of sleep and dreaming, and about the many ingenious experiments designed by dream psychologists, is an excellent way into thinking about relations between phenomenology and physiology, and between empirical and conceptual strands in the study of mind. Students and researchers seeking complex and multifaceted intellectual challenges will increasingly be drawn to explore resources for the study of dreams.

But despite the fascination of dreams for modern Western culture, the story of the discovery of REM (rapid eye movement) sleep and the subsequent exploration of the psychophysiology of dreaming, which was among the great adventures of twentieth-century science (Hobson 1988: Ch. 6; Aserinsky 1996; Foulkes 1996; Kroker 2007), has barely influenced the active self-image of mainstream philosophy of mind. Although epistemologists still use dreaming to focus concerns about scepticism, the *psychology* of dreams remained until recently a marginal subject in philosophy and the cognitive sciences alike. There are no references to sleep or dreams in Blackwell's 1998 *Companion to Cognitive Science*; only short single entries in the substantial encyclopaedias of cognitive science published by MIT and by the Nature Publishing Group, and both by the same author (Hobson 1999a, 2003); and at the time of writing no entry on dreaming is listed in the projected contents of the online *Stanford Encyclopedia of Philosophy*. Yet this chapter can now draw on a small but increasing wave of recent work on dreams which takes a naturalistic and integrative attitude to philosophy of psychology, foreshadowed by Daniel Dennett (1976) and Patricia Churchland (1988), and exemplified by Owen Flanagan's *Dreaming Souls* (2000).

The previous significant philosophical monograph on the subject, written in a very different intellectual climate, was Norman Malcolm's controversial *Dreaming* (1959), which dramatically amplified some scattered and cryptic remarks of Wittgenstein's. Malcolm started from what he saw as the analytic claim that no judgements can possibly be made in sleep – whether that I am asleep, or that I am seeing and experiencing various things. Noting that the criterion for ascribing a dream is the dreamer's later report, Malcolm argued that there can be no other criteria – such as physiological criteria – because they could only be established and maintained by reference to the primary criterion of waking testimony. Malcolm claimed that reports of mental phenomena in dreams do not report reasoning, remembering, or imagining in the same sense as while waking: "if a man had certain thoughts and feelings in a dream it no more follows that he had those thoughts and feelings while asleep, than it follows from his having climbed a mountain in a dream that he climbed a mountain while asleep" (1959: 51–2; see also McGinn 2004: 96–112; Sosa 2005). Malcolm did not *identify* dreams with waking reports or impressions (1959: 59), but he has consistently been read as simply denying that dreams are experiences we have during sleep. This bewildering view, which seems to fly in the face of subjective, conceptual, and scientific evidence alike, has prompted in response some of the best philosophical work on dreams (Putnam 1975 [1962]; Dennett 1976; Revonsuo 1995, 2005; Windt and Metzinger 2007), but may also have had a more generally "dispiriting" effect on the field (Dreisbach 2000: 37).

There are other plausible and compatible explanations for the longstanding neglect of dreaming in philosophy of psychology: widespread suspicion of Freud, ongoing obsessions with Cartesian doubt, the fragmentation and swift professionalization of the sciences of sleep physiology, which encouraged their divorce from the psychology of dreaming (Foulkes 1996), and the uneasiness about consciousness which long characterized the cognitive sciences (Foulkes 1990: 46). But perhaps behind all these diagnoses lies the sheer difficulty of the enterprise. Integrated, multilevel theories of dreaming are unusually hard to develop because our access to the phenomena is unusually indirect, so that it is unusually difficult to manipulate postulated mechanisms and identify the causally relevant components of the dreaming mind/brain system.

While researchers seek both conceptual and empirical ways to address these difficulties, it is unsurprising that theories of dreams lag behind work on memory, imagery, colour vision, or emotion (say) in the identification of robust, independent but converging lines of evidence for the entities and activities postulated in any inchoate model. Higher level synthetic and conceptual work is vital, especially given recent signs of new momentum in the field. Alongside the sudden emergence of "consciousness studies" in the last 15 years, we can point to the strength of the pluralistic organization IASD (the International Association for the Study of Dreams) and its excellent journal *Dreaming*, published since 1991; to a remarkably rich special issue of *Behavioral and Brain Sciences* in 2000, with six target articles and 76 commentaries (republished in book form as Pace-Schott et al. 2003); and to the promise of improved neurocognitive techniques, such as the better temporal resolution in newer neuroimaging technologies. Naturalistically oriented philosophers can realistically hope to help when, as now, rapid increase in experimental data has not been matched by new maturity in theories.

This chapter illustrates the tight links between conceptual and empirical issues by highlighting surprisingly deep disagreements among leading dream scientists over what might seem basic aspects of their topic. Philosophers who discuss dream science have in the main taken their picture of the field from the impressive and ambitious work of J. Allan Hobson and his team at Harvard Medical School (Hobson 1988, 2002; Flanagan 2000; Metzinger 2004; Clark 2005; but see Kitcher [1992: 141–9] for a more cautious approach), so we start by sketching his account. Hobson is the pre-eminent dream scientist of the last 30 years, but his views are far from uncontroversial. We then analyse the conceptual significance of some important but (as yet) less influential alternatives, focusing on research by Mark Solms, David Foulkes, and G. William Domhoff, which remains unjustly neglected by philosophers: it's surprising, for example, that all three authors are omitted from Windt and Metzinger's impressive survey of the philosophy of dreaming and self-consciousness (2007).

In focusing closely on the sciences of dreaming in this way, this chapter omits discussion of dreaming in the history of philosophy (see Hacking 2002; Holowchak 2002), history of science (Lavie and Hobson 1986; Ford 1998; Dacome 2004), philosophy of psychoanalysis (Kitcher 1992; Blechner 2001), and the social sciences (D'Andrade 1961; Burke 1997; Stansell 2006). This is emphatically not to see such enquiries as entirely disconnected from psychology, which as we'll see could benefit greatly from closer integration with historical and cultural investigations of practical attitudes to dreaming. Among the intriguing live questions in the psychology of dreaming which we also don't discuss are issues about the relation between dreaming and attitude to dreams (Wolcott and Strapp 2002; Beaulieu-Prévost and Zadra 2005), and about the methods for and results of systematic content analysis of dream reports (van de Castle 1994: 291–358; Strauch and Meier 1996; Domhoff 2003: 67–134). However, the best initial view of the fertile philosophical territory can perhaps be gained from within the rich core scientific debates about how to overcome the difficulty of access to the mind in sleep.

Phenomenology and physiology: the cognitive neuroscience of dreaming

David Foulkes, a cognitive psychologist whose positive views on dreaming we examine below, offers a relatively neutral characterization of the phenomena in question: dreaming is "the awareness of being in an imagined world in which things happen" (Foulkes 1999: 9). This contrasts dramatically with the description of dreaming preferred by Hobson's team. For them, it is

> [m]ental activity occurring in sleep characterized by vivid sensorimotor imagery that is experienced as waking reality despite such distinctive cognitive features as impossibility or improbability of time, place, person and actions; emotions, especially fear, elation, and anger predominate over sadness, shame and guilt and sometimes reach sufficient strength to cause awakening; memory

> for even very vivid dreams is evanescent and tends to fade quickly upon awakening unless special steps are taken to retain it.
>
> (Hobson, Pace-Schott, and Stickgold 2000a: 795)

Although Hobson suggests that this "highly specified definition" serves folk psychology well by capturing "what most people mean when they talk about dreams," it is also clearly intended to build in some substantial assumptions, and to encapsulate the key *explananda* of a particular neurocognitive theory. The theory in question has evolved from an "activation-synthesis model" (Hobson and McCarley 1977) to the current activation-input-modulation (AIM) model (Hobson, Pace-Schott, and Stickgold 2000a; Hobson and Pace-Schott 2002), through the incorporation of vast arrays of additional data (especially in neurochemistry) in an admirably ambitious multileveled research program. The common thread has been to emphasize "such aspects of the form of dreams which might be expected to have their roots traced to isomorphic forms of brain activity" (Hobson, Pace-Schott, and Stickgold 2000a: 823). We can examine the ensuing picture of dream phenomenology and physiology in turn.

While Hobson acknowledges a range of other kinds of mentation in sleep, he takes the following features to be paradigmatic of core cases of dreaming. Expanding on the above definition in ways which (as he notes) match widely shared assumptions, Hobson argues that consistently in dreaming we experience "hallucinatory perceptions," especially visual and motoric; our imagery "can change rapidly, and is often bizarre"; the content lacks "orientational stability," in that persons, times, and places are "plastic, incongruous and discontinuous"; story-lines emerge to "explain and integrate all the dream elements in a single confabulatory narrative"; we have "increased and intensified emotions" in dreams, but usually our volitional control is severely diminished and our reflective and metacognitive capacities reduced (Hobson, Pace-Schott, and Stickgold 2000a: 799); we have little access in dreaming to coherent narrative units of our episodic memories (Fosse, Fosse, Hobson, and Stickgold 2003), and in turn have very poor recall for dream content. Most of us recognize this description of dreaming, for Hobson, not because these are features of a few, atypically memorable dreams, but because this kind of intense "dreaminess" is indeed typical of mentation in key forms of sleep.

After the discovery of REM sleep, the initial hope was that, not only such general formal features of dreaming, but also specific dream contents could be mapped on to and explained by reference to particular features of the unique neurophysiology of this stage of sleep. In sharp contrast to the various "deeper" stages of sleep (collectively labelled non-REM, or NREM), in REM sleep (in addition to the unusual clusters of eye movements) muscle tone is exceptionally low, and brain activity is wake-like, though heavily influenced by phasic activation from the brainstem in the form of irregular PGO (ponto-geniculo-occipital) waves. From the start of the experimental studies of REM-dream correlations, people woken from REM sleep reported dreams much more frequently than when woken from NREM. Although by the early 1960s it was clear that NREM sleep can also produce dream reports, NREM dreams are in general less intense and more "thought-like." There are ongoing controversies about relations between REM sleep and dreaming, to which we return in the third section, below, but Hobson's assessment of this substantial body of research is that it has established "clear-cut and major" differences in phenomenology between "the states of waking, sleeping (NREM), and dreaming (REM)," and that all of the peculiar phenomenological features of REM dreams, as listed above, "will eventually be explainable in terms of the distinctive physiology of REM sleep" (Hobson, Pace-Schott, and Stickgold 2000a: 799).

The AIM (activation-input-modulation) model offers a three-dimensional-state space, which allows for intermediate states and for gradual, as well as discontinuous, transitions between states. The three factors together should explain the loss of volition and executive control in dreams as we swing from directed waking thought to hallucinatory activity (Fosse et al. 2001). While general brain-activation levels in REM sleep show significant similarities with waking, imaging and other recent studies identify a range of finer grained differences, notably in the deactivation of the prefrontal cortex in REM. The information sources for waking cognition are often dominated by external inputs from the world, as our perceptual systems register our surroundings and we in turn act on our environment: in normal REM, the dreamer is cut off from the world, with sensory input all but eliminated and motor output inhibited, so that only internal information sources are available. Finally, the neurochemical modulation characterizing REM is, roughly, a switch in the neurotransmitter balance, from aminergic predominance (noradrenaline and serotonin) in waking to significant cholinergic influence (acetylcholine) in REM, with intermediate chemical modulation in deep NREM. These three neurobiological dimensions are intended also to have psychological referents, to be established empirically (Hobson, Pace-Schott, and Stickgold 2000a: 794). This is a tough long-term project, in which much of the burden of explaining the unique features of REM dreaming will fall to correlations between altered neuromodulation and alterations in "the way in which the information in the system is processed (mode)" (794).

Hobson's reductionism is admirably forthright, and as an integrative ideal is clearly and correctly distinguished from eliminative materialism (Hobson, Pace-Schott, and Stickgold 2000b: 1030). The positive metaphysics of his "brain-mind isomorphism" are harder to pin down. Sometimes the view is expressed oddly, as if the brain is itself the object of dreaming cognition – "dreaming is the conscious experience of hyper-associative brain activation that is maximal in REM sleep" (Hobson and Pace-Schott 2002: 691) – but usually the kind of "isomorphism" in question seems to be some kind of identity, in which subcortical stimuli are themselves informational. So, for example, dreams of flying are a "logical, direct, and unsymbolic way of synthesizing information generated endogenously by the vestibular system" (Hobson and McCarley 1977: 1339). In this earlier work, the picture was that strong, irregular, and unstable input from the brainstem is synthesized into bizarre narrative form by forebrain systems (Hobson 1988): "in dream bizarreness we see a mental readout of the chaotic brainstem activity of REM sleep" (Hobson and Stickgold 1994: 10–11). There was no particular theory of mental representation, or of the nature of computation, invoked to support this direct mapping between physiological chaos and cognitive chaos. Even

Michel Jouvet, on whose pioneering studies of this brainstem activity Hobson relies, could see the difficulty in interpreting PGO waves in informational terms: "the almost random volleys of PGO activity are hardly compatible with any attempt at semantics" (Jouvet 1999: 87).

Hobson's more recent model offers much more fineness of detail on both physiological and psychological dimensions, with rich extensions into many related areas of sleep science, learning and memory, and neurochemistry: it must remain the starting point for any empirically informed philosophy of dreams. But the model has not obviously yet incorporated the requisite conceptual advances to explain the implications for dream science of the broad claim that "every form of mental activity has a similar form of brain activity" (Hobson 2002: 33). Hobson intends this to be much more than correlation, and to amount to something more specific than the general materialist commitment that features of dreaming are in some general way "brain-based" (Hobson and Pace-Schott 2002: 686): we should interpret talk of phenomenology "reflecting" changes in the brain (Hobson, Pace-Schott, and Stickgold 2000a: 812) as a quite specific "readout," as particular "formal psychological features of dreaming are determined by the specific regional activation patterns and neurochemistry of sleep" (Hobson and Stickgold 2002: 691). In other words, there are direct isomorphisms between *particular* properties represented in dream content and *particular* properties of the representing vehicles of that content.

A challenge for Hobson-style theories, then, is to defend such direct isomorphisms for the case of dreaming against the general charge that they unnecessarily conflate properties of representings with properties of representeds (Dennett 1991; Hurley 1998). Just as "there are gigantic pictures of microscopic objects," so any candidate neural code can in principle represent any perceptual dimension (Dennett 1991: 147), and so the representing vehicle of dream bizarreness need not itself be particularly bizarre or chaotic. Of course, a case may be made for the significance of more complex forms of resemblance or isomorphism between vehicle and content (O'Brien and Opie 2004). But Hobson sees no need to make this case, because he allows no theoretical space for any materialist theory which distinguishes vehicles from contents in the ways Dennett and Hurley recommend. This is apparent in the charge that psychologists like Foulkes who reject such direct isomorphisms are treating cognitive activation as entirely "independent of brain activation," or reaching "the absurd and unacceptable conclusion that brain and mind have nothing to do with each other" (Hobson, Pace-Schott, and Stickgold 2000a: 804). In examining some alternative views below, I'll suggest that this charge does not stick, and that there is room for genuinely cognitive or representational levels of analysis between phenomenology and physiology, through which claims of isomorphism need to be mediated.

Neuropsychology and dream bizarreness

Some philosophical attention has focused on recent debates between Hobson and the "neuropsychoanalytic" views of clinical neuroanatomist Mark Solms, including their "dream debate" at the 2006 Tucson consciousness conference (Faw 2006: 87–9;

Hobson 1999b, 2005, 2006; Solms 1995, 1999, 2006). This section describes the basis of their disagreements over dream science, bypassing for present purposes the radically different attitudes to Freud which animate their work, but then (following Domhoff [2005]) argues that these real disagreements coexist with, and tend to mask, substantial shared assumptions on some other key issues.

Hobson, as we've seen, ascribes the neural origins of dreaming to noisy, disordered PGO waves from the brainstem, or to the cholinergic neuromodulation which, in dominating aminergic influence during REM, "underlies the similar modal shifts in information processing" (Hobson, Pace-Schott, and Stickgold 2000a: 833). In other words, the same processes underlie both REM sleep and dreaming: indeed, Hobson approves of the idea that dreamlike mentation in NREM sleep too could be ascribed to ongoing stimulation from the brainstem in "covert REM sleep" (Nielsen 2000), arguing that "all sleep is REM sleep (more or less)" (Hobson 2000: 952). For Solms, in contrast, the complex mechanisms driving REM sleep are in principle entirely independent of the mechanisms of dreaming. Even if there is a well-defined cholinergic "REM-on" brainstem system, he argues that the chemistry of the "dream-on" system is "controlled by dopaminergic forebrain mechanisms," those which in waking support goal-seeking behaviour and appetitive interaction with the world (Solms 2000: 843–6).

Solms makes these claims on the basis of groundbreaking detective work, both "clinico-anatomical" and historical, into the neuropsychology of dreams (Solms 1997). Firstly, although evidence is sketchy, large-scale lesions of the pontine brainstem which eliminate REM do not seem necessarily to eliminate dreaming. More significantly, Solms found a large range of cases in which dreaming is eliminated or dramatically altered by forebrain lesions which completely spare the brain stem. Solms reanalysed nineteenth-century case studies by Charcot and others, and psychosurgical reports of the prefrontal leukotomies carried out on many human subjects in the mid-twentieth century, and gathered information on the dreaming of 361 neurological and neurosurgical patients and controls of his own. Most of these patients reported no changes in dreaming, indicating that their lesions were in brain areas which do not have substantial roles to play in dreaming. But the key results included two large groups of patients who reported global cessation of dreaming after their lesion, despite the absence of damage to the brainstem and despite the continuation of ordinary REM sleep. In one group, lesions were in the region of the parieto-temporal-occipital junction, which supports various cognitive functions related to mental imagery and spatial representation; in the other group, which included the leukotomized subjects, lesions were in the ventromesial quadrant of the frontal lobes, in the dopaminergic appetitive circuit mentioned above (Solms 1997, 2000). Other notable results concern the bases of sensory imagery in dreaming: visual imagery in dreams was intact after lesions to primary visual cortex (as it is in people who go blind after the age of 5–7 or so [Kerr and Domhoff 2004]), but significantly affected in two patients with damage to the occipito-temporal region of their visual association cortex, to the extent that their dreams became "nonvisual" (Solms 1997: 93–106). These last points, and related evidence for other sensory modalities, are important because they show that "perceptual and motor dream imagery does not isomorphically reflect the simple activation of perceptual and motor cortex during sleep," but that such imagery is "actively constructed through complex cognitive processes" as in waking imagery (Solms 2000: 848).

On the one hand, Solms takes these results to demonstrate a double dissociation between dreaming and REM sleep. There are dreams with no REM, as well as genuine and distinctive NREM dreams; and there is cessation of dreaming with REM preserved. On the other hand, in constructive mode Solms suggests that a complex, highly specific network of forebrain mechanisms acts as the generator of dreams, in the wider cerebral context of a basic level of arousal or activation which is usually (but not essentially) provided by the REM state through a quite distinct mechanism (Solms 2000; Domhoff 2001, 2003: 9–18). This network, which must take some time to emerge over the course of neurocognitive development, includes a "seeking" system which taps our interests and goals: this leaves room for Solms to build both cognitive and motivational factors into the heart of the model of dreaming, thus driving a broader defence of certain aspects of psychoanalytic theory (Solms 2006), and the resulting standoff with the Hobson camp.

Yet Solms's defence of the "meaningfulness" and symbolic nature of dreams is still conducted wholly at a neurobiological level: he invokes neither a particular cognitive or representational theory, nor any detailed and systematic analysis of dream contents. Like Hobson, he sees questions of dream psychology as needing to be settled only by the neurobiology of dreaming. The concern here, again, is not about reductionism *per se*, but about over-hasty versions, which jump levels too fast in bypassing representation and content. Better forms of reductionism for dream science, one might think, would not only "be compatible with great explanatory pluralism" (Murphy 2006), but in suggesting multilevel experimental strategies would also look for evidence directly at the cognitive level.

The appropriate use of imaging studies is also at stake here: because some imaging studies have simply identified dream sleep with REM sleep (thus always finding that the pontine brain stem is involved in dream sleep), they do not independently compare dreaming with nondreaming NREM epochs, to try to discover just what's in common across all episodes of dreaming (Solms 2000: 848). Ideas about better imaging methods have been suggested recently by Sophie Schwartz and colleagues. They suggest, firstly, comparing bizarre but common features of dreams with similar but independently verified neuropsychological syndromes: for example, the common mismatch in dreams between a character's appearance and identity ("she looked like X, but I knew she was really Y") is compared with the related waking delusional misidentification condition called Frégoli syndrome (Schwartz et al. 2005: 434–5). The point is that such comparisons should generate predictions about the underlying transient neuropsychology of dreaming, which could then in principle be tested in neuroimaging studies (see also Dang-Vu et al. 2005).

A further point of contact between Hobson and Solms is that, despite their very different explanations, Solms's view of the formal characteristics of dreams – "hallucination, delusion, disorientation, negative affect, attenuated volition, and confabulatory paramnesia" (Solms 2000: 848) – is close to Hobson's account of dreams as essentially bizarre, and dream narratives as paradigmatically implausible. Where for Solms dreams are bizarre because they are disguised wishes, dreaming for Hobson is a form of psychosis or delirium: "the mind becomes formally psychotic. Wild and bizarre delusions are fed by visual and auditory hallucinations ... The mind becomes hyper-emotional, alternately terrified and ecstatic. Profound anxiety alternates with a sense of omnipotent grandiosity" (Stickgold and Hobson 1994: 141–2). Hobson's team has sought to discover just how bizarre dreams really are, working from a classification of types of bizarreness into incongruity, uncertainty, and discontinuity: but casual readers of their work or that of philosophers reliant on it (Flanagan 2000: 147–8) would not realize just how difficult it is to find agreement on methods and results concerning dream bizarreness (Colace 2003).

One early sleep lab study of 635 REM dream reports assessed bizarreness as "the extent to which the described events were outside the conceivable expectations of everyday life; to put it bluntly: the craziness of the dream" (Snyder 1970: 146). Fewer than 10 percent were scored as highly bizarre, while 75 percent contained little or no drama. Subsequent studies both in sleep labs and in home settings use many different measures of both bizarreness and emotion. In general, studies find that many dreams have no emotional content at all, and only 20–30 percent are highly emotional: most emotions in dreams are appropriate to the dream context, save for the occasional absence of emotions which would be normal in waking life. Part of the difficulty with measuring dream bizarreness is that in many studies (like Snyder's) it is judged by comparison with waking real-life events, whereas there is some reason to think it would be more accurate to compare dreaming to waking mental life. A sequence of events might be implausible in external reality, but as easy and natural to imagine as to dream. The suspicion is that only a broadly perceptual or hallucinatory model of dreaming makes this comparison of the dream world to the (perceived) external world, rather than to an imagined world, seem obvious. But systematic comparisons of dreaming with imagination, narrative, and fantasy, rather than with "everyday life," might reveal, as Domhoff suggests, that "there is far more discontinuity, drift, and inattention in waking thought than is implied by the claim that changes in dream scenes or settings are inherently bizarre" (Domhoff 2003: 153; see also Flanagan 2000: 58–61).

Having noted these points of contact between Hobson and Solms in relation both to the relation between levels of explanation, and to the characterization of the phenomenological data, we can now examine an alternative theoretical perspective in which dreams are a more sophisticated cognitive achievement, and are typically not so bizarre or fraught with emotion. The best way into this is through a discussion of children's dreams.

Children's dreams and dreaming as a cognitive achievement

In remarkable longitudinal and cross-sectional studies from the late 1960s to the 1980s, David Foulkes and his co-workers investigated the frequency of dream recall and the content of dream reports in children from age 3 to age 15. The results were surprising, and conflict with assumptions about dreaming in both folk and scientific psychology: but even after Foulkes presented them in more accessible form in *Children's Dreaming and the Development of Consciousness* (1999; see also the more technical account in Foulkes 1982), they remain strangely little known outside the dream-research community (see Domhoff 2003: 18–25).

The first, longitudinal, study began in Laramie, Wyoming in June 1968. Foulkes tracked two groups of children over 5 years: one group from age 3 or 4 to age 8 or 9, the other from age 9 or 10 to age 14 or 15. In each group, 7 or 8 boys and 7 or 8 girls slept in the lab for nine nights each in the first, third, and fifth years of the study. More children joined the study in the third and fifth years, to check on any effect of participation. Only four of the older children, whose families left town, did not participate through the full study. Foulkes himself woke each child three times a night from either REM or NREM sleep, a total of 2711 awakenings. In the second and fourth years, children had their dream reports collected after uninterrupted nights of sleep at home, and took part in a range of other cognitive and personality tests. Core results of this longitudinal study from a small town were later replicated in a cross-sectional study of 80 children between the ages of 5 and 8 in metropolitan Atlanta.

Before sketching some of Foulkes's specific results, we can highlight the common assumptions about children's dreaming which he thinks they challenge. On the basis of his studies, Foulkes rejects the idea that dreaming "has always been there, even in infancy, in pretty much the form that we know it now" (1999: 6). He suggests, plausibly, that many people – including scientists – interpreted the discoveries that infants have more REM than adults as suggesting "a rich infantile dream life"; and that in the broader Western culture at least, "there is an expectation that children's dreams will be dripping with feelings, mostly unpleasant ones at that" (1999: 7, 68). He links these assumptions, plausibly, to "an implicit equation of dreaming with perception" (1999: 11), by which the dreamer, whether adult, child, or nonhuman animal, is quasi-perceptually registering what happens in the absent or virtual dreamed world when they have vivid, hallucinatory, self-involving, emotional oneiric experiences.

But in Foulkes's studies, the younger children (ages 3–5) dreamed very little: no NREM awakenings, and only around 15 percent of REM awakenings elicited dream reports, and those reports were "very brief and insubstantial" – one boy's only two dream reports from 15 REM awakenings in the year from 4 years 8 months were "I was asleep and in the bathtub" and "I was sleeping at a co-co stand, where you get Coke from" (1999: 56, 159). Right up to ages 9–11, only about 30 percent of REM awakenings produced dream reports; but from that age, frequency increased substantially and swiftly to typical adult rates of around 80 percent.

A natural response is that Foulkes has only measured children's verbal skills, or their memory: isn't it just that such young children are unable to report their rich and vivid dream life? This is certainly the view of the Hobson team, who "specifically suggest that the human neonate, spending as it does more than 50% of its time in REM sleep, is having indescribable but nevertheless real oneiric experiences" (Hobson et al. 2000a, p. 803). But although Foulkes acknowledges that the results with very young children are harder to interpret, he defends confidently his claim of the paucity of dreams from ages 5 to 9: what's striking here is that there are no correlations between dream frequency and richness, on the one hand, and verbal skills or memory development on the other hand, right through the age groups. Children whose general verbal skills were relatively poor were just as likely to report more vivid dreams, and those who had the best linguistic abilities were just as likely to report few and bland dreams. The variable from waking cognitive life which correlated most with dreaming was the child's visual-spatial skill, as tested on tasks involving visual imagery and spatial imagination. Significantly, two children who joined the study at ages 11 and 12 had typical verbal, memory, and general cognitive skills for their age, but visual-spatial skills comparable only to those of 5–7 year olds: they also had extremely low dream recall, also like the younger age group. So, Foulkes argues, it's not likely that either these two or the younger children were having rich dreams but failing to remember or describe them well. Instead, along with the development of narrative memory and theory-of-mind capacities, the gradual development of a rich visual-spatial imagination may be among the key cognitive prerequisites for a fuller dream life.

Since early dreams are thus (in general) relatively static and bland, they have weak narratives: further, before the age of 7 or so the self is rarely an active participant, and there are few complex social situations. And in the relatively rare case in which dream reports are emotional or stressful, they still show lower levels than older children and adults of aggression, misfortune, and negative emotion. No significant gender or personality differences emerge in the content of typical dreams until adolescence. Dreaming, Foulkes concludes, is an organizing, constructive process which requires cognitive sophistication, and is continuous with waking cognitive and emotional life. It is less like perceiving than other forms of thinking about or imagining what is absent (see also McGinn 2004: 74–95; Sosa 2005), so is much harder before the development of fuller representational and narrative capacities.

The prevailing view that even very young infants must have vivid dreams, suggests Foulkes, is supported primarily by the pervasive assumption of identity or correlation between dreaming and REM sleep, by adults' memories of a few atypical bizarre dreams in their childhood, and by the striking nature of their own children's reactions to rare powerful dreams or night terrors (which in fact are not part of ongoing dreams, but arise in deep and dreamless sleep). A distinct account of the nature of adult dreaming also emerges: instead of the stress on bizarre hallucination, Foulkes argues that dreaming is at heart an organizing process, a high-level symbolic skill, and a form of intelligent behaviour with cognitive prerequisites (Foulkes 1990, 1999). The virtual world we inhabit in dreams is one which we have constructed, though usually without either voluntary control or current sensory input.

There are, of course, a host of further methodological questions about these studies. There are difficult issues about differences between dream reports collected in the sleep lab and the home environment, and by experimenter and parent. Critics have not always accepted Foulkes's claims that the children's home dreams in his study did not differ significantly from those collected in controlled conditions, or that any of the dreams collected by an experimenter is representative. It's also worth noting that one study by Hobson's team, in which parents asked about their children's dreams on waking at home in the morning, did find children giving "long, detailed reports of their dreams which share many formal characteristics with adult dream reports" (Resnick et al. [1994], followed by Flanagan [2000: 146–7]). While parents were asked not to pressure their children, on some of the nights the children had to repeat "I will remember my dreams" three times out loud before going to sleep, and parents were "explicitly instructed to elicit as much detail as possible by guiding their children." Rather than addressing further details of the consequent disputes about method (see Foulkes 1999: 18–39; Domhoff 2003: 39–66), here we can focus the difference between Hobson's and Foulkes's picture in one last way which also returns us to the philosophical literature. In Part II of the *Philosophical Investigations*, Wittgenstein described

> People who on waking tell us certain incidents (that they have been in such-and-such places, etc.). Then we teach them the expression "I dreamt," which precedes the narrative. Afterwards I sometimes ask them "did you dream anything last night?" and am answered yes or no, sometimes with an account of a dream, sometimes not. That is the language game.
>
> (Wittgenstein 1953: 184)

Foulkes is not quite suggesting that children have to learn to dream, but the idea is at least thinkable in the context of his theory, whereas for Hobson it is absurd, because the hallucinosis and emotionality of dreaming is a basic neurobiological given. Despite his notorious reluctance to ask what dreaming really is (Malcolm 1959: 59, 83), Norman Malcolm, in Wittgenstein's wake, offers a rather careful discussion of the senses in which this language game is and isn't learned. In my own case, Malcolm acknowledges, I don't rely on my own waking report to know that I have dreamt: rather, I wake with certain impressions and infer that "I dreamt so and so" (1959: 64–5). This "raw material," these "impressions" which form the basis for the language game of telling dreams, are not learned but are given, "a part of the natural history of man" (1959: 87–9). What we *do* learn is not just the inessential language of telling dreams, but most importantly, how "to *take* an after-sleep narration in a certain way," distinguishing it from a true or false recollection of events that occurred before or during sleep, and "not questioning the accuracy of the impression but accepting the narrative on the speaker's say-so" (1959: 88). The practical meaning of the dream impressions, in contrast to other impressions, lies in the practical significance we learn to attribute to them (Schroeder 1997: 32; Child 2007). Even in cultural contexts in which enormous significance is attributed to dreams, in the diverse ways anthropologists have shown (von Grunebaum and Caillois 1966; Tedlock 1991), they are not connected to the rest of experience or owned *in the same way* as autobiographical memories, thoughts, and so on. Our norms for remembering, for example, are quite differently connected to many diverse practical activities and negotiations.

But Foulkes's account of dreaming as a cognitive achievement suggests a compatible and stronger role for learning and development. As well as learning the peculiar relation of dreams to the rest of practical life, children have to learn quite complex understandings of what dreams are, and of their relation to imagination, pretence, memory, and so on. On top of learning basic differences between the real and the imaginary, this involves acquiring more sophisticated beliefs about the origins and controllability of dreams, beliefs which remain open to some individual and cultural variation into later life (Woolley and Boerger 2002).

For Foulkes, the offline visual-spatial imagining of worlds in which a represented self can act in complex social contexts amidst rich kinaesthetic and sensory imagery requires a whole raft of complex cognitive capacities, as the putative neural network for dreaming comes into operation. One further example of the lines of research this suggests is the following. If early visual-spatial skills, rather than verbal skills, drive frequent and richer early dreaming, then autistic children (who score relatively highly on tests of visual-spatial capacity) should have relatively early and rich dreams; but then, if the fuller temporal organization of narrative thought is required to build richer dreams from early adolescence onwards, autistic children might be left with more disconnected or fragmentary imagistic dream experience. Foulkes (1999: 153–5) notes the paucity of evidence about such aspects of autistic experience, but there is just a little work on both episodic memory and dreaming (Godbout et al. 1998; Boucher 2001; Boucher and Bowler 2008) which might suggest more about the relative roles of narrative and spatial thinking at different stages of development.

The phenomenology of dreaming

Sticking close to the sciences of dreaming, as we've seen, immediately raises questions of obvious philosophical interest. What are the best metaphysical and methodological approaches to understanding relations between the phenomenology and the neurophysiology of dreams? What room is there for an integrated cognitive level of analysis through which accounts of representation and computation can interlock with more general theories in cognitive science? What are the theoretically and empirically plausible roles of motivation, emotion, imagination, and memory in dreaming? Are there conceptual suggestions that might help clarify or resolve the scientific disagreements over the extent and nature of bizarre mentation in dreaming, and over children's dreaming? Do individually and culturally variable beliefs about dreaming only influence dream reports, or is the form of dreams themselves in certain respects also malleable? Most broadly, is dreaming a quasi-perceptual hallucination or an imaginative construct?

One natural reaction to this plethora of unresolved questions is bewilderment. Can't we just solve – or dissolve – at least some of these debates by combining the psychological results with some better, careful introspective reflection on our own dream experience? This is certainly a common reaction to the antirealism about dreaming commonly ascribed to Wittgenstein and Malcolm. For example, Windt and Metzinger (2007: 194) answer Malcolm with a detailed phenomenological account of "the subjective quality of the dream experience," as "the appearance of an integrated, global model of reality within a virtual window of presence." But how clear a consensus can we obtain about the details of the phenomenology of dreaming? How good is our access to our own experience?

This chapter concludes by examining one pessimistic answer to these questions from the recent work of philosopher Eric Schwitzgebel. But first, in a spirit of further proliferation of paths for interdisciplinary research, we sketch two more distinct aspects of the phenomenology of dreaming, which can both be used as test cases in assessing those general issues, and which both intersect in their own right with broader questions in philosophy and psychology. In turn we briefly examine perspective and vantage-point in dreams, and the nature and implications of lucid dreaming.

In his work on children's dreams, Foulkes suggested a connection between dreaming and skills in the mental imagining and manipulation of figures or patterns. One thought is that perhaps visual-spatial capacities somehow help to generate the continuous kinematic imagery typical of richer dreams: very young children's dreams are relatively static. But Foulkes also links "the sustained production of involuntary kinematic imagery" with another aspect of imagery. In a further sleep lab study with young adults, Foulkes and Kerr (1994) asked subjects who reported preawakening visual imagery, whether they could see themselves the way another person might, or whether they were seeing through their own eyes. They found that only a small number of dreams were experienced in what they called "the see-oneself mode," and that in the "see-oneself" reports there was a dramatically smaller amount of kinematic imagery: in contrast, in the larger number of "own-eyes" reports, most experience is kinematic.

These ideas about point of view, perspective, or vantage point in dreaming are connected to related work on autobiographical memory. Sometimes I remember events in my personal past from the inside, experiencing the scene from my own past perspective; sometimes, in contrast, I see myself in the remembered scene. Psychologists call the former "field memories" and the latter "observer memories" (Nigro and Neisser 1983), and have found that field memories are more common and generally contain more information on emotional and other subjective states than observer memories (Berntsen and Rubin 2006). The field-observer distinction also has under-explored philosophical implications (but see Debus [2007]). Although it might seem that the "own-eyes" or "field" perspective is the default vantage point, Foulkes and Kerr make the bold case that young children find it relatively more difficult "to adopt the own-eyes perspective as an actively participating character in their own dream scenarios," and thus don't so easily engage in the involuntary elaborations associated with dreaming (1994: 360).

Studies which explicitly ask subjects to specify one of two possible perspectives of their dream or memory experience are not the ideal option in this fascinating domain: many people spontaneously flip or switch between the perspectives, and confidence in retrospective judgements of dream or memory perspective is not always high. It should be possible to examine dream reports collected without such explicit enquiry, to look for references to the self as an observed character, and to assess the speculation offered by Foulkes and Kerr that observer perspectives may be linked with reduced movement and kinematic imagery in dreams, and with less active self-participation. Such a project might add detail to our understanding of complexity of self-representation and emotion in dreams.

So far, more work has focused on links between perspective and lucid dreaming: there is some evidence, for example, that those who report more lucid dreaming are also more easily able to switch between viewpoints in waking mental life (Blackmore 1988: 385–6). A lucid dream is one in which I become aware that I am dreaming. As Metzinger puts it, "the lucid dreamer is fully aware of the fact that her current phenomenal world does not, in its content, covary with external physical reality": in the extreme, the lucid dreamer also recovers full access to memory, and regains at least aspects of the phenomenology of agency (Metzinger 2004: 530–1). There is good psychophysiological evidence for lucid dreaming through indications from experienced lucid dreamers in the form of agreed eye movement signals while clearly in REM sleep (LaBerge 1988), in a striking form of "trans-reality communication" (Metzinger 2004: 536). We also have careful delineations of "the variety of lucid dreaming experience" (LaBerge and DeGracia 2000). It's clear that certain forms of training can enhance the capacity for lucid dreaming: recent social movements in which people seek new forms of consciousness have promoted the urge to achieve control and awareness within what is otherwise an involuntary and entirely immersed part of our mental life.

The philosophical significance of lucid dreaming is only beginning to be explored. Revonsuo (1995, 2005) and Metzinger (2004; Windt and Metzinger 2007) highlight lucid dreaming as a distinctive and instructive form of consciousness, in which a full phenomenal world is inhabited without "the all-pervading naïve realism – which also characterizes ordinary waking states" (Metzinger 2004: 537). The virtual nature of the world created by the lucid dreamer's consciousness is available as such to the dreamer, who understands (and acts on the basis of) the simulational or misrepresentational character of the experiential process. This may drive a particularly strong form of indirect realism: the idea is that in lucid dreaming the brain, so to speak, *realizes* that it's in a vat. For Revonsuo, for example, our understanding of ordinary experience should be modelled on dreams, because dreaming and especially lucid dreaming show us that "we are not *really* out of our brains in our experiences" (1995: 51): waking experience too is experience of a brain-generated model or a virtual world which just happens to be more constrained, a dream guided by the senses (Revonsuo 1995: 47, quoting Llinás and Paré 1991: 525).

Such views offer a challenge to theories of mind which stress the extended or situated nature of cognitive processes and states. The immediate line of enquiry required before returning to the classic epistemological issue is to investigate whether even lucid dream experience is indeed as realistic as ordinary perceptual experience, and in relevant similar ways. On a contrary view, based for example on privileging the analogy between dreaming and imagining over the analogy between dreaming and perceiving, it is even more gappy and fragmentary than perceptual experience: just because the mind can draw neither on sensorimotor access to the world nor the usual interpersonal support, the thought is, "consciousness appears severely reduced and in a shrunken state in nocturnal life" (Halbwachs 1992 [1925]: 42). The fact that the experiential world of the lucid dream *seems* to be rich, full, and detailed does not of itself demonstrate that it is so. At present, this is a standoff, so systematic work with experienced lucid dreamers needs significant conceptual development to inform the philosophical debate.

This, then, is another instance of the line of thought with which this section began, that consensus about the phenomenology of dreaming is hard to find. We conclude by examining one further argument for caution. Eric Schwitzgebel (2002, 2003, 2006) has examined the case of dreaming as part of a general argument "that we are pervasively and grossly mistaken about our own conscious experience" (2002: 658). Combining historical, psychological, and philosophical analysis, Schwitzgebel examines references to colour in dreams over a long historical period. While writers on dreams had previously often referred to colour in dreams, suddenly in the 1940s and 1950s psychologists, and the people they surveyed, came to "the opinion that dreaming is predominantly a black and white phenomenon," with (in a typical study) 40 percent of people claiming never to see colour in dreams; and 31 percent, that they do so only rarely (Schwitzgebel 2002: 650). More recent popular and scientific opinion, though, as confirmed by Schwitzgebel's own (2003) attempt to replicate that particular study, has entirely reverted to the view that in general there are colours in most dreams.

What could explain the sudden rise and fall of the opinion that dreams are a black-and-white phenomenon? Schwitzgebel considers four options. Least likely, in his view, is the possibility – intriguing speculation though it is – that the rapid spread of black and white media technology actually caused our dreams to change. If, instead, it was the reporting of dreams that changed (rather than their content), then in at least one period the majority of scientists and people "must have seriously misdescribed the experience of dreaming" (2002: 654), even though most show considerable confidence in their own answers to such questions. Either the mid-twentieth-century view was correct and everyone else has been wrong, or – more likely – dreams really are predominantly in colour and the 1950s view was wrong, with the reports of that time being tainted by the media with which subjects then compared their dreams. This last view seems plausible: but Schwitzgebel is equally attracted to a fourth possibility – "that dreams are *neither* coloured nor black and white, that applying either of these categories is misleading" (2002: 655). Novels are neither in colour nor in black and white, although particular fictional objects can be coloured: perhaps the same holds for dreams, with most elements in dreams being of indeterminate colour.

How then should we decide between these last two possibilities – are dreams really in colour, or do most objects in dreams have no determinate colour? Surely, Schwitzgebel suggests, the subjective experience would be quite different in the two cases, so that we should be able simply to reflect on the phenomenology of dreaming to decide the question. Yet here he finds himself "quite thick," as "incompetent," as at least some of the historical respondents must have been: so he concludes by suggesting "that people's self-confidence in this matter is misplaced. We don't know the phenomenology of dreaming nearly as well as we think we do" (Schwitzgebel 2002: 657).

This may seem a pessimistic way in which to wind up a survey of the current state of the interdisciplinary study of dreaming. It does underline the point that we are far less advanced in drawing convincing connections between phenomenology, psychology, and physiology in the case of dreams than for memory, colour, or emotion. But this pre-paradigmatic situation offers many opportunities, not only to watch the relevant scientific communities in the heat of action, but to contribute directly to the required interdisciplinary projects. Perhaps the gulf between dreaming and the evidence which we can access for it can be gradually overcome. This will involve – among other things – improved methods of collecting and analysing dream reports, more subtle interlevel experiments linking neural processes with experience, systematic attempts to identify those aspects of dreaming which are influenced by beliefs and attitudes and those which are not, and neurocognitive theories which are more thoroughly integrated with our best accounts of other psychological domains. The future of dreaming in both science and culture is at present intriguingly unpredictable.

Acknowledgements

Thanks to Tim Bayne, John Buckmaster, Claudio Colace, Caroline Horton, Doris McIlwain, Richard Menary, Gerry Nolan, Gerard O'Brien, Jon Opie, Perminder Sachdev, Mike Salzberg, Maria Trochatos, to the audience at the joint meeting of the Society for Philosophy and Psychology and the European Society for Philosophy and Psychology in Barcelona in 2004, to my students in Phil 363 at Macquarie University, and to the editors.

References

Aserinsky, Eugene (1996) "The Discovery of REM Sleep," *Journal of the History of the Neurosciences* 5: 213–27.

Barrett, Deirdre, and McNamara, Patrick (eds) (2007) *The New Science of Dreaming*, 3 vols, Westport, CT: Praeger-Greenwood.

Beaulieu-Prévost, Dominic, and Zadra, Antonio (2005) "Dream Recall Frequency and Attitude towards Dreams: A Reinterpretation of the Relation," *Personality and Individual Differences* 38: 919–27.

Berntsen, Dorthe, and Rubin, David C. (2006) "Emotion and Vantage Point in Autobiographical Memory," *Cognition and Emotion* 20: 1193–1215.

Blackmore, Sue (1988) "A Theory of Lucid Dreams and OBEs," J. Gackenbach and S. LaBerge (eds), *Conscious Mind, Sleeping Brain: Perspectives on Lucid Dreaming*, New York: Plenum Press, pp. 373–87.

Blechner, Mark J. (2001) *The Dream Frontier*, Hillsdale, NJ: Analytic Press.

Boucher, Jill (2001) "'Lost in a Sea of Time': Time-Parsing and Autism," in C. Hoerl and T. McCormack (eds), *Time and Memory: Philosophical and Psychological Perspectives*, Oxford: Oxford University Press, pp. 111–35.

Boucher, Jill and Bowler, Dermot (eds) (2008) *Memory in Autism: Theory and Evidence*. Cambridge: Cambridge University Press.

Burke, Peter (1997) "The Cultural History of Dreams," in *Varieties of Cultural History*, Ithaca, NY: Cornell University Press, pp. 23–42.

Child, William (2007) "Dreaming, Calculating, Thinking: Wittgenstein and Anti-Realism about the Past," *Philosophical Quarterly* 57: 252–72.

Churchland, Patricia Smith (1988) "Reduction and the Neurobiological Basis of Consciousness," in A. J. Marcel and E. J. Bisiach (eds), *Consciousness in Contemporary Science*, Oxford: Oxford University Press, pp. 273–304.

Clark, Andy (2005) "The Twisted Matrix: Dream, Simulation, or Hybrid?" in C. Grau (ed.), *Philosophers Explore* The Matrix, Oxford: Oxford University Press, pp. 177–97.

Coe, Jonathan (1998) *The House of Sleep*, London: Penguin.

Colace, Claudio (2003) "Dream Bizarreness Reconsidered" (editorial), *Sleep and Hypnosis* 5: 105–27.

Crick, Francis, and Mitchison, Graeme (1986) "REM Sleep and Neural Nets," *Journal of Mind and Behavior* 7: 229–50.

D'Andrade, Roy (1961) "Anthropological Studies of Dreams," in F. K. Hsu (ed.), *Psychological Anthropology*, Homewood, IL: Dorsey Press.

Dacome, Lucia (2004) "'To what purpose does it think?': Dreams, Sick Bodies, and Confused Minds in the Age of Reason," *History of Psychiatry* 15: 395–416.

Dang-Vu, T. T., Desseilles, M., Albouy, G., Darsaud, A., Gais, S., Rauchs, G., Schabus, M., Sterpenich, V., Vandewalle, G., Schwartz, S., and Maquet, P. (2005) "Dreaming: A Neuroimaging View," *Schweizer Archiv für Neurologie und Psychiatrie* 156: 415–25.

Debus, Dorothea (2007) "Perspectives on the Past: A Study of the Spatial Perspectival Characteristics of Recollective Memories," *Mind and Language* 22, 173–206.

Dennett, Daniel C. (1976) "Are Dreams Experiences?" *Philosophical Review* 73: 151–71.

—— (1991) *Consciousness Explained*, New York: Little, Brown.

Domhoff, G. William (2001) "A New Neurocognitive Theory of Dreams," *Dreaming* 11: 13–33.

—— (2003) *The Scientific Study of Dreams: Neural Networks, Cognitive Development, and Content Analysis*, Washington, DC: American Psychological Association.

—— (2005) "Refocusing the Neurocognitive Approach to Dreams: A Critique of the Hobson versus Solms Debate," *Dreaming* 15: 3–20.

Dreisbach, Christopher (2000) "Dreams in the History of Philosophy," *Dreaming* 10: 31–41.

Faw, Bill (2006) "Are We Studying Consciousness Yet?" (Towards a Science of Consciousness, Tucson Conference, April 4–5), *Journal of Consciousness Studies* 13: 81–99.

Flanagan, Owen (2000) *Dreaming Souls: Sleep, Dreams, and the Evolution of the Conscious Mind*, Oxford: Oxford University Press.

Ford, Jennifer (1998) *Coleridge on Dreaming: Romanticism, Dreams, and the Medical Imagination*, Cambridge: Cambridge University Press.

Fosse, Magdalena J., Fosse, Roar, Hobson, J. Allan, and Stickgold, Robert J. (2003) "Dreaming and Episodic Memory: A Functional Dissociation?" *Journal of Cognitive Neuroscience* 15: 1–9.

Fosse, Roar, Stickgold, Robert, and Hobson, J. Allan (2001) "Brain-Mind States: Reciprocal Variation in Thoughts and Hallucinations," *Psychological Science* 12: 30–6.

Foulkes, David (1982) *Children's Dreams: Longitudinal Studies*, New York: Wiley.

—— (1990) "Dreaming and Consciousness," *European Journal of Cognitive Psychology* 2: 39–55.

—— (1996) "Dream Research: 1953–1993," *Sleep* 19: 609–24.

—— (1999) *Children's Dreaming and the Development of Consciousness*, Cambridge, MA: Harvard University Press.

Foulkes, David, and Kerr, Nancy H. (1994) "Point of View in Nocturnal Dreaming," *Perceptual and Motor Skills* 78: 690.

Godbout, Roger, Bergeron, Cybèle, Stip, Emmanuel, and Mottron, Laurent (1998) "A Laboratory Study of Sleep and Dreaming in a Case of Asperger's Syndrome," *Dreaming* 8: 75–88.

Hacking, Ian (2002) "Dreams in place," in *Historical Ontology*, Cambridge, MA: Harvard University Press, pp. 227–54.

Halbwachs, Maurice (1992 [1925]) "The Social Frameworks of Memory," in L. Coser (ed.), *On Collective Memory*, Chicago: University of Chicago Press.

Hobson, J. Allan (1988) *The Dreaming Brain*, New York: Basic Books.

—— (1999a) "Dreaming," in R. A. Wilson and F. C. Keil (eds), *The MIT Encyclopedia of the Cognitive Sciences*, Cambridge, MA: MIT Press, pp. 242–4.

—— (1999b) "The New Neuropsychology of Sleep: Implications for Psychoanalysis," *Neuro-Psychoanalysis* 1: 157–83.

—— (2000) "The Ghost of Sigmund Freud Haunts Mark Solms's Dream Theory," *Behavioral and Brain Sciences* 23: 951–2.

—— (2002) *Dreaming: An Introduction to the Science of Sleep*, Oxford: Oxford University Press.

—— (2003) "Sleep and Dreaming," in L. Nadel (ed.), *Encyclopedia of Cognitive Science*, London: Nature Publishing Group, vol. 4, pp. 46–52.

—— (2005) "In Bed with Mark Solms? What a Nightmare! Reply to Domhoff (2005)," *Dreaming* 15: 21–9.

—— (2006) "Freud Returns? Like a Bad Dream," *Scientific American Mind* 17, no. 2: 35.

Hobson, J. Allan, and McCarley, R. (1977) "The Brain as a Dream-State Generator: An Activation-Synthesis Hypothesis of the Dream Process," *American Journal of Psychiatry* 134: 1335–48.

Hobson, J. Allan, and Stickgold, Robert (1994) "Dreaming: A Neurocognitive Approach," *Consciousness and Cognition* 3: 1–15.

Hobson, J. Allan, and Pace-Schott, Edward F. (2002) "The Cognitive Neuroscience of Sleep: Neuronal Systems, Consciousness and Learning," *Nature Reviews Neuroscience* 3: 679–93.

Hobson, J. Allan, Pace-Schott, Edward F., and Stickgold, Robert (2000a) "Dreaming and the Brain: Toward a Cognitive Neuroscience of Conscious States," *Behavioral and Brain Sciences* 23: 793–842.

—— (2000b) "Dream Science 2000: A Response to Commentaries on 'Dreaming and the Brain'," *Behavioral and Brain Sciences* 23: 1019–35.

Holowchak, M. Andrew (2002) *Ancient Science and Dreams: Oneirology in Greco-Roman Antiquity*, Lanham, MD: University Press of America.

Hurley, Susan (1998) "Vehicles, Contents, Conceptual Structure, and Externalism," *Analysis* 58: 1–6.

Jouvet, Michel (1999) *The Paradox of Sleep: The Story of Dreaming*, Cambridge, MA: MIT Press.

Kerr, Nancy H., and Domhoff, G. William (2004) "Do the Blind Literally 'See' in Their Dreams? A Critique of a Recent Claim That They Do," *Dreaming* 14: 230–3.

Kitcher, Patricia (1992) *Freud's Dream: A Complete Interdisciplinary Science of Mind*, Cambridge, MA: MIT Press.

Kroker, Kenton (2007) *The Sleep of Others and the Transformations of Sleep Research*, Toronto: University of Toronto Press.

LaBerge, Stephen (1988) "The Psychophysiology of Lucid Dreaming," in J. Gackenbach and S. LaBerge (eds), *Conscious Mind, Sleeping Brain: Perspectives on Lucid Dreaming*, New York: Plenum Press, pp. 135–53.

LaBerge, Stephen, and DeGracia, Donald J. (2000) "Varieties of Lucid Dreaming Experience," in R. G. Kunzendorf and B. Wallace (eds), *Individual Differences in Conscious Experience*, Amsterdam: John Benjamins, pp. 269–307.

Lavie, Peretz, and Hobson, J. Allan (1986) "Origin of Dreams: Anticipation of Modern Theories in the Philosophy and Physiology of the 18th and 19th Centuries," *Psychological Bulletin* 100: 229–40.

Llinás, Rodolfo R., and Paré, D. (1991) "Of Dreaming and Wakefulness," *Neuroscience* 44: 521–35.

Malcolm, Norman (1959) *Dreaming*, London: Routledge & Kegan Paul.

McGinn, Colin (2004) *Mindsight: Image, Dream, Meaning*, Cambridge, MA: Harvard University Press.

Metzinger, Thomas (2004) *Being No-one: The Self-Model Theory of Subjectivity*, Cambridge, MA: MIT Press.

Murphy, Dominic (2006) *Psychiatry in the Scientific Image*, Cambridge, MA: MIT Press.

Nielsen, Tore A. (2000) "A Review of Mentation in REM and NREM Sleep: 'Covert' REM Sleep as a Possible Reconciliation of Two Opposing Models," *Behavioral and Brain Sciences* 23: 851–66.

Nigro, Georgia, and Neisser, Ulric (1983) "Point of View in Personal Memories," *Cognitive Psychology* 15: 467–82.

O'Brien, Gerard, and Opie, Jon (2004) "Notes Towards a Structuralist Theory of Mental Representation," in H. Clapin, P. Staines, and P. Slezak (eds), *Representation in Mind*, Amsterdam: Elsevier, pp. 1–20.

O'Shaughnessy, Brian (2002) "Dreaming," *Inquiry* 45: 399–432.

Pace-Schott, Edward F., Solms, Mark, Blagrove, Mark, and Harnad, Stevan (2003) *Sleep and Dreaming: Scientific Advances and Reconsiderations*, Cambridge: Cambridge University Press; updated repr. of a special issue of *Behavioral and Brain Sciences*.

Putnam, Hilary (1975 [1962]) "Dreaming and 'Depth Grammar'," in *Mind, Language, and Reality: Philosophical Papers*, vol. 2, Cambridge: Cambridge University Press, pp. 304–24.

Resnick, Jody, Stickgold, Robert, Rittenhouse, Cynthia D., and Hobson, J. Allan (1994) "Self-representation and Bizarreness in Children's Dream Reports Collected in the Home Setting," *Consciousness and Cognition* 3: 30–45.

Revonsuo, Antti (1995) "Consciousness, Dreams, and Virtual Realities," *Philosophical Psychology* 8: 35–58.

—— (2005) *Inner Presence: Consciousness as a Biological Phenomenon*, Cambridge, MA: MIT Press.

Schönhammer, Rainer (2005) "'Typical Dreams': Reflections of Arousal," *Journal of Consciousness Studies* 12: 18–37.

Schroeder, Severin (1997) "The Concept of Dreaming: On Three Theses by Malcolm," *Philosophical Investigations* 20: 15–38.

Schwartz, S., Dang-Vu, T.T., Ponz, A., Duhoux, S., and Maquet, P. (2005) "Dreaming: A Neuropsychological View," *Schweizer Archiv für Neurologie und Psychiatrie* 156: 426–39.

Schwitzgebel, Eric (2002) "Why Did We Think We Dreamed in Black and White?" *Studies in History and Philosophy of Science* 33: 649–60.

—— (2003) "Do People Still Report Dreaming in Black and White? An Attempt to Replicate a Question from 1942," *Perceptual and Motor Skills* 96: 25–9.

—— (2006) "Do We Dream in Color? Cultural Variations and Scepticism," *Dreaming* 16: 36–42.

Snyder, Frederick (1970) "The Phenomenology of Dreaming," in L. Madow and L. H. Snow (eds), *The Psychodynamic Implications of the Physiological Studies on Dreams*, Springfield, IL: Charles C. Thomas, pp. 124–51.

Solms, Mark (1995) "New Findings on the Neurological Organization of Dreams: Implications for Psychoanalysis," *Psychoanalytic Quarterly* 44: 45–67.

—— (1997) *The Neuropsychology of Dreams: A Clinico-Anatomical Study*, Hillsdale, NJ: Erlbaum.

—— (1999) "The New Neuropsychology of Sleep: Commentary by Mark Solms," *Neuro-Psychoanalysis* 1: 183–95.

—— (2000) "Dreaming and REM Sleep Are Controlled by Different Brain Mechanisms," *Behavioral and Brain Sciences* 23: 843–50.

—— (2006) "Freud Returns," *Scientific American Mind* 17, no. 2: 28–35.

Sosa, Ernest (2005) "Dreams and Philosophy," *Proceedings and Addresses of the American Philosophical Association* 79, no. 2: 7–18.

Stansell, Christine (2006) "Dreams," *History Workshop Journal* 61, no. 1: 241–52.

Stickgold, Robert, and Hobson, J. Allan (1994) "Home Monitoring of Sleep Onset and Sleep-Onset Mentation Using the Nightcap," in R. D. Ogilvie and J. R. Harsh (eds), *Sleep Onset: Normal and Abnormal Processes*, Washington, DC: American Psychological Association, pp. 141–60.

Strauch, Inge, and Meier, Barbara (1996) *In Search of Dreams: Results of Experimental Dream Research*, New York: State University of New York Press.

Tedlock, Barbara (1991) "The New Anthropology of Dreaming," *Dreaming* 1: 161–78.

van de Castle, Robert L. (1994) *Our Dreaming Mind*, New York: Ballantine.

von Grunebaum, Gustav, and Caillois, Roger (eds) (1966) *The Dream and Human Societies*, Berkeley, CA: University of California Press.

Windt, Jennifer M., and Metzinger, Thomas (2007) "The Philosophy of Dreaming and Self-Consciousness: What Happens to the Experiential Subject During the Dream State?" in D. Barrett and P. McNamara (eds), *The New Science of Dreaming*, vol. 3: *Cultural and Theoretical Perspectives*, Westport, CT: Praeger-Greenwood, pp. 193–247.

Wittgenstein, Ludwig (1953) *Philosophical Investigations*, Oxford: Blackwell.

Wolcott, Sommer, and Strapp, Chehalis M. (2002) "Dream Recall Frequency and Dream Detail as Mediated by Personality, Behaviour, and Attitude," *Dreaming* 12: 27–44.

Woolley, Jacqueline D., and Boerger, Elizabeth A. (2002) "Development of Beliefs about the Origins and Controllability of Dreams," *Developmental Psychology* 38: 24–41.

Further reading

An excellent and philosophically rich entry into the field is Owen Flanagan, *Dreaming Souls: Sleep, Dreams, and the Evolution of the Conscious Mind* (Oxford: Oxford University Press, 2000). For a more popular and a more technical first read, try A. Alvarez, *Night: Night Life, Night Language, Sleep, and Dream* (New York: W. W. Norton, 1994) and William G. Domhoff, *The Scientific Study of Dreams: Neural Networks, Cognitive Development, and Content Analysis* (Washington, DC: American Psychological Association, 2003), respectively. Other accessible introductions to the field as a whole are Robert L. van de Castle, *Our Dreaming Mind* (New York: Ballantine, 1994) and Kelly Bulkeley, *An Introduction to the Psychology of Dreaming* (Westport, CT: Praeger, 1997). Among the great philosophers, Aristotle (David Gallop, *Aristotle on Sleep and Dreams* [Peterborough, Canada: Broadview Press, 1990]) and David Hartley, *Observations on Man, His Frame, His Duty, and His Expectations* (New York: Garland, 1971 [1749], Bk I, pt 3, sec. 5), offered particularly impressive theories of dreaming. For modern theories, the work of J. Allan Hobson is essential: *The Dreaming Brain* (New York: Basic Books, 1988) is an extraordinarily detailed historico-scientific *tour de force*, while *Dreaming: An Introduction to the Science of Sleep* (Oxford: Oxford University Press, 2002) offers a shorter but unreferenced update. Norman Malcolm, *Dreaming* (London: Routledge & Kegan Paul, 1959) remains a worthwhile provocation, while the more recent interdisciplinary philosophy books by Thomas Metzinger, *Being No-one: The Self-Model Theory of Subjectivity* (Cambridge, MA: MIT Press, 2004) and Antti Revonsuo, *Inner Presence: Consciousness as a Biological Phenomenon* (Cambridge, MA: MIT Press, 2005) include substantial self-contained sections on dreams. For other scientists discussed in this chapter, start with Mark Solms, *The Neuropsychology of Dreams: A Clinico-Anatomical Study* (Hillsdale, NJ: Erlbaum, 1997) and David Foulkes, *Children's Dreaming and the Development of Consciousness* (Cambridge, MA: Harvard University Press, 1999), respectively. Favourite philosophical papers on dreams include Daniel C. Dennett, "Are Dreams Experiences?" *Philosophical Review* 73 (1976): 151–71; Antti Revonsuo, "Consciousness, Dreams, and Virtual Realities," *Philosophical Psychology* 8 (1995): 35–58; Ian Hacking, "Dreams in Place," in *Historical Ontology* (Cambridge, MA: Harvard University Press, 2002), pp. 227–54; Brian O'Shaughnessy, "Dreaming," *Inquiry* 45 (2002): 399–432; and Eric Schwitzgebel, "Why Did We Think We Dreamed in Black and White?" *Studies in History and Philosophy of Science* 33 (2002): 649–60. A major three-volume collection *The New Science of Dreaming* edited by Deirdre Barrett and Patrick McNamara appeared in 2007 (Westport, CT: Praeger-Greenwood), with new papers by many of the leading researchers across the disciplines of dreaming. Membership of the International Association for the Study of Dreams (http://www.asdreams.org/) is open to all, and includes a subscription to the journal *Dreaming*. Finally, Jonathan Coe's *The House of Sleep* (London: Penguin, 1998) is a glorious serio-comic novel substantially inspired by the sciences of sleep and dreams.

The highlight of recent philosophical work on dreaming is Jennifer M. Windt's indispensable and hugely impressive book *Dreaming: A Conceptual Framework for Philosophy of Mind and Empirical Research* (Cambridge, MA: MIT Press, 2015). A solid update on scientific research can be found in Michael Schredl, *Researching Dreams: The Fundamentals* (London: Palgrave Macmillan, 2018). Questions about method and the reliability of dream reports are discussed in Melanie G. Rosen, "What I make up when I wake up: anti-experience views and narrative fabrication of dreams," *Frontiers in Psychology* 4 (2013), 514. Thomas K. Metzinger sets out an important agenda for philosophical work in "Why are dreams interesting for philosophers? The example of minimal phenomenal selfhood, plus an agenda for future research," *Frontiers in Psychology* 4 (2013), 746. New research has highlighted four fascinating areas for ongoing investigation, each of which needs more attention from philosophers: advances in studies of lucid dreams are reviewed in Kristoffer Appel, Gordon Pipa, & Martin Dresler, "Investigating consciousness in the sleep laboratory: an interdisciplinary perspective on lucid dreaming," *Interdisciplinary Science Reviews* 43 (2018), 192–207; questions about visuospatial perspective in dreams are discussed in Melanie G. Rosen and John Sutton, "Self-Representation and Perspectives in Dreams," *Philosophy Compass* 8 (2013), 1041–53; similarities and differences between dreaming and mind-wandering are the starting point for G. William Domhoff's book *The Emergence of Dreaming: Mind-Wandering, Embodied Simulation, and the Default Network* (Oxford: Oxford University Press, 2017); and Jennifer Windt offers a significant account of dreaming in light of current ideas about predictive processing and active inference in "Predictive brains, dreaming selves, sleeping bodies: how the analysis of dream movement can inform a theory of self-and world-simulation in dreams," *Synthese* 195 (2018): 2577–625.

37
EMOTION

Anthony P. Atkinson

Emotions are central to human existence. Emotions colour our lives, to use a hackneyed phrase; without them life would at best be dull, but even dull experiences are arguably emotional, which makes it hard to imagine what living a truly non-emotional life would be like. In fact, human life (and the life of many other animals) would not be possible without emotions; they help us avoid dangers and take advantage of opportunities, to form and manage social relations, in ways that can make a difference to survival and reproductive success. Emotions are also intimately bound up with memory and learning and likely ground our everyday reasoning and decision-making, our values and morality. The study of emotions is therefore central to the psychological sciences and thus to the philosophy of psychology. What follows is a brief tour of the main contemporary positions on the nature of emotions.

Emotions as social constructions

The idea that emotions are socially constructed is the idea that they are embedded in and defined or even constituted by cultural practices, and thus that the study of emotions requires examination of the cultural context in which emotions are experienced, displayed and discussed. Emotions are thus culturally relative. A strong reading of this cultural-relativity thesis is that, in addition to culturally shared emotions, which may differ with respect to such things as their display rules and the terms used to refer to them, there will be some emotions that are culturally specific. One alleged example of such a culturally specific emotion is the Japanese *amae*, which denotes generally positive feelings of attachment and dependency on a person or institution, incorporating a desire to be loved. However, it is arguable that *amae* is not uniquely Japanese, but rather a complex of feelings and thoughts found in all cultures, unified under a single concept in Japanese culture because of its importance in Japanese interaction and customs. Accepting that, however, is not necessarily to deny that *amae* is an example of a socially constructed emotion.

A well-worked out example of a social constructivist theory of emotion is Averill's (1980) proposal that emotions are transitory social roles. Emotional roles are prescribed within particular societies or social groups, much as the familiar social roles of parent, spouse, waiter, and candlestick maker are; indeed, emotional roles and wider social roles are intertwined, with the latter specifying which of the former ought to be enacted and how. Individuals "improvise" these socially defined emotional roles insofar as their behaviour and feelings are based upon and guided by these emotional and social norms. Those emotional and social norms are internalized in the form of cognitive structures or schemata, or according to an alternative reading of the social role model, are embodied in social practices in such a way as to reinforce socially appropriate emotional responses. On Averill's view, improvised enactments of emotions *qua* transitory social roles require the individual to interpret the roles (usually unconsciously) within their current contexts and in relation to the object of the emotion. Such appraisals of emotional objects in part distinguish amongst specific emotions; what else helps distinguish one emotion from another is the socially defined meaning of the emotional concept.

A social constructivist thesis does not necessarily deny that emotions have an underlying physiological basis, or that certain emotional responses may have an evolutionary history, but these biological aspects are seen more as the background enabling conditions for the emotional behaviours and experience of social beings, aspects that do not capture what emotions are and that are unable to delineate and fully characterize individual emotions. Social constructivists usually distinguish between emotions that have analogues in neonates and nonhuman animals, such as fear, joy and sadness, and those that do not have natural analogues, such as anger, shame, contempt, and romantic love. The latter presuppose social concepts; for example, anger presupposes a personal transgression, shame an ethical notion of right and wrong. But even those emotions that non-human animals and neonates are capable of experiencing are shaped by social forces when experienced by mature humans, and are also often mediated by social norms and concepts and their interpretations. This distinction between two classes of emotion might seem at first glance to be akin to the distinction between basic emotions and more complex emotions that are compounds of basic ones (see below). However, this latter distinction is not part of and is not tenable from the social constructivist perspective, according to which no emotion is fully delineable in biological terms and thus no emotion can be biologically basic; all emotions, on this view, include both biological and socio-cultural elements to varying degrees.

A more extreme social constructionist critique of biological theories of emotion holds that such theories mistakenly reify many or even all emotions, a post-modernist view encapsulated in Harré's (1986: 4) claim that, "Psychologists have always had to struggle against a persistent illusion that in such studies as those of the emotions, there is something *there*, the emotion, of which the emotion word is a representation." Harré's view is that we emote rather than have emotions, and that the proper subject matter for students of emotion is the process of emoting rather than emotions as objects.

A common strategy for social constructionists is to highlight cross-cultural differences and within-cultural similarities in emotion concepts, expressions, and behaviour. Yet the assumption that cross-cultural variation in a psychological trait necessarily precludes an evolutionary or otherwise naturalistic account of that trait is mistaken (as we shall see in the next section). Moreover, many of the social constructionist arguments are built on cross-cultural differences in the typical specific causes of a given emotion, whereas most naturalistic theories of emotion are accounts of specific effects, rather than of specific causes. Claims of universality or panculturalism about emotions (see below) are claims about physiological and behavioural responses; to the extent that naturalistic theories make claims about causes of emotions, those claims are couched in very general terms, so as to capture a wide range of actually instantiated causes (e.g., whatever happens to constitute a threat or a noxious substance in a particular environment). Many naturalists about the emotions accept that a social constructionist perspective can and does provide useful insights into the nature of emotions, although there is some disagreement among such naturalists as to just how far a social constructionist perspective can be integrated with a naturalistic or biological one (see especially Prinz [2004], who goes quite far, and Griffiths [1997, 2008], who in the latter publication argues that Prinz goes too far).

Emotions as biological phenomena

In his seminal book, *The Expression of Emotions in Man and Animals*, Darwin (1998 [1872]) argued for a degree of phylogenetic continuity between humans and other animals with respect to emotions and their expression. Some human expressions, he argued, originated in movements or habits useful to our ancestors, insofar as they had some fitness value to the organism in the types of situation that elicit the emotion. Contemporary biological theories of emotion tend to agree with Darwin that certain emotional expressions are vestiges of adaptive responses in ancestral species, but they also consider (as, arguably, did Darwin) that these expressions were subsequently selected for their communicative value. On this view, if certain patterns of response in others (postures and movements of the face and body, vocal sounds and inflections) reliably indicate specific reactions to particular threats or opportunities in the physical and social environment, reactions that can initiate or inform one's own response, then the ability to perceive emotions expressed by others and the concomitant ability to signal one's own emotional states to others will themselves have adaptive value.

A central bone of contention between promoters of such a biological perspective on emotional expressions and its detractors has been whether there are any culturally universal signals of emotion, and if so, which ones. As Griffiths (1997) points out, it is important to distinguish between two senses of a trait's being universal: a monomorphic trait is one that exists in the very same form in every normal human being, whereas a pancultural trait is simply one that exists in all or most cultures, even if there are people in those cultures who do not manifest that trait. Most cross-cultural studies of emotion perception and production aim to test whether certain emotions are pancultural, not whether they are monomorphic. Those studies have shown that facial expressions of at least the basic emotions are recognizable at above-chance levels across cultures, and with a good deal of cross-cultural agreement. Debate continues as to the extent of cultural variation in emotion recognition accuracy, whether such variation falls along the lines of specific emotion categories or broader dimensions such as valence and arousal, what theoretical and methodological reasons might account for such variation, and what influence culture plays in the display of emotions.

Contemporary biological theorists of emotion have extended Darwin's ideas to develop theories of emotions in the round. Prominent theorists in this tradition include Ekman (1992, 1999), Izard (1971), Plutchik (1980), and Panksepp (1998). In broad outline, emotions are regarded as preparatory adaptive responses, that is, coordinated systems of response shaped by natural selection to enable animals to cope with threats and opportunities presented to them by their physical and social environments. Obvious environmental challenges include avoiding physical harm (fear) and contaminants (disgust); somewhat more controversially, some of the more complex social emotions, such as jealousy, guilt, and embarrassment, can be analyzed this way also. Amongst the coordinated systems of response are changes in internal body state (autonomic, visceral, hormonal), musculoskeletal changes (e.g., retching, flinching) and changes in posture and movement of the face and body, which together prepare and implement adaptively appropriate actions, such as fleeing or fighting. Emotion-related responses also include cognitive phenomena such as changes in the direction and focus of attention, as well as emotional feelings.

It is obvious that most (arguably all) emotions involve changes in bodily state, from literally hair-raising experiences to episodes of clammy palms and shaking arms, and much else besides. What theorists disagree about is the centrality of physiological responses to defining what emotions are and to delineating one emotion from another. In the late nineteenth century, William James and Karl Lange developed independently a theory based on the idea that emotions are bound up with changes in bodily states. According to the James-Lange theory, our emotions – and in particular, emotional feelings – are the sensations of bodily changes triggered by our perceptions of objects and events. This theory turned on its head a commonsense view of emotions, that bodily changes occur as a consequence of changes in emotional state. I become disgusted because of the churning in my gut and my convulsive retching consequent upon my viewing and smelling vomit, not because viewing and smelling vomit causes me to feel disgusted which then leads me to feel nauseous and retch. Such somatic theories have been controversial, and their popularity has waned more than waxed over the years, resulting in the body taking a backseat in many alternative theories. More recently, however, a growing interest in the study of emotion by neuroscientists, at the centre of which was the brain's control over bodily functions and its representation of changes in bodily states, spearheaded a resurgence of interest in the James-Lange theory (to be discussed in more detail in the fourth section, "Emotions as embodied appraisals").

Consonant with the view that emotions are preparatory adaptive responses is an expectation that the underlying neural systems will be organized in a modular fashion to some degree (see Gottschling's entry, "Modularity" [Chapter 18]). Both the requirement for speed and the need to trigger a particular class of behaviours may make specialized systems advantageous, and may have resulted in neural mechanisms that are relatively specialized to process certain emotionally relevant information. Some biological theories of emotion, notably Panksepp's (1998), in fact categorize emotions according to the neural systems that implement ecological packages of behavioural mechanisms. The main purpose of this initial processing is to provide a crude assessment of the value of the stimulus (good or bad, harmful or pleasant) and thus to motivate behaviour (e.g., approach or avoid). In addition to this very fast, automatic, and coarse processing, the presentation of an emotional stimulus will also typically initiate more detailed perceptual and recognition processing, which is likely to be less classically modular (e.g., slower, less automatic and encapsulated), and can include more complex attributions and rationalizations of the causes of an emotion, and regulation of its expression.

Biological theories of emotion are often associated and sometimes even synonymous with the so-called basic emotion view. Yet the term basic emotion is used in at least three different (albeit not mutually exclusive) ways. On one interpretation, "basic" refers simply to the idea that emotions serve fundamental life events, that is, that they evolved as adaptive responses to threats and opportunities. The term basic can also refer to the idea that some emotions are more basic or fundamental than others. Closely related to this interpretation is the idea that basic emotions are the building blocks of more complex emotions. While the idea that *all* emotions are either basic or blends of two or more basic ones has been largely discredited, there is nevertheless a case to be made that some complex emotions are blends of more basic ones: contempt as a blend of disgust and anger, for example. There is also a promising variant of the basic emotions-as-building-blocks view, which combines the blending metaphor with – or eschews it altogether in favour of – the idea that complex emotions are cognitive elaborations of basic ones – basic emotions with bells on.

Not all biological theories of emotion succeed in avoiding the dangers associated with adaptive explanations (see Wheeler's entry, "Evolutionary Models in Psychology" [Chapter 26]), including that of post-hoc "just-so" adaptive story telling. Plutchik's (1980) theory suffers particularly from such ills. Adaptive explanations need to be constrained in several ways: *inter alia*, they must be coherent with one another, have a plausible mechanistic implementation whose account specifies how those individual phenotypic features function as well-engineered adaptive devices, and must survive rigorous testing using the comparative method (analyses of the historical development of the traits across related species) and co-evolutionary studies (analyses of the congruency of traits between interacting species).

A criticism that has been levied at biological theories of emotion is that a programme of identifying emotions with any one particular response type, such as distinct facial expressions, patterns of autonomic response, or distinct neural activity, is untenable, because such responses are neither necessary nor sufficient for a state's being an emotion. Counterexamples suggest that a given expression or bodily response is sometimes associated with states that on other criteria would be classified as distinct emotions, or that such responses occur in the absence of all the other markers of emotional states, or that some emotions do not involve bodily changes at all. One response to this line of criticism is to argue that emotions can be individuated according to some combination of response types. Ekman, for example, in his more recent writings, argues that distinctive facial expressions are characteristic of, but neither necessary nor sufficient for, an emotion's being basic. Basic emotions are to be defined by distinctive sets of correlated response patterns, not by a single response type. Yet it is still arguable that the weight of evidence does not warrant even this more relaxed method for individuating emotions; Barrett (2006), for example, points out that strong correlations rarely exist among self-report, behavioural, and physiological measures of emotion.

Perhaps the net for individuating emotions needs to be cast wider than response types. Biological theorists have more recently been emphasizing ideas central to cognitive theories, suggesting, for example, that basic emotions involve processes of automatic appraisal tuned to recurring environmental conditions relevant to adaptive success. Thus emotions might be jointly individuated not only by physiology and behaviour, but also by their eliciting conditions and some appraisal or cognitive interpretation.

Emotions as cognitions

According to cognitive theories of emotion, an essential property of emotions is that they are intentional states, typically either a belief or judgement, which entails that they are about or directed at something or someone. Emotions are about things or have objects in two senses: they have formal objects (e.g., fears are about dangers) and particular objects (e.g., each particular fear is about a particular danger). Emotion types (e.g., anger, fear) are delineated by the fact that every instance of a given type shares the same or similar formal object. Furthermore, the cognitive states at issue are a particular class of intentional states insofar as they are (usually unconscious) judgements as to the value of events to one's welfare and interests; their formal and particular objects pertain to how states of affairs in the world will affect or are affecting one's wellbeing.

One apparent problem with this view is that, if emotions are intentional states and intentional states are attitudes towards propositions, that is, states whose content is represented as a proposition, a linguistic property, then on the face of it the cognitivist is obliged to deny emotions to non-linguistic beings (nonhuman animals, pre-linguistic infants). Cognitive theorists need not live with this outcome, however, as it is possible to hold that emotions essentially involve judgements or appraisals, and are thus about states of affairs related to wellbeing, without also holding that they essentially involve propositional contents.

Griffiths (2004a, b) has argued that cognitive theories of emotion that restrict themselves to theories of content fall short of being *psychological* theories because they have nothing to say about mechanisms. Regardless of whether one agrees with Griffiths that for a theory to count as psychological it must be about both content and mechanisms, one can surely agree that a full understanding of what emotions are will require theories about both. What, then, might a theory that combined emotional appraisals with emotion mechanisms look like? We can see the beginnings of such theories in attempts to extend the notion of appraisals beyond "high-level" cognitive evaluations, to include "low-level," fast and fairly crude evaluations of stimuli or events, evaluations of situations in terms of a small number of simple categories (e.g., good/bad). Theories of low-level emotional appraisals have mostly consisted in theories of the neural and information-processing mechanisms that instantiate them, such as those proposed by LeDoux (1998), Rolls (2005), and Panksepp (1998). However, there is disagreement over whether such low-level appraisals really count as appraisals *qua* evaluative judgements. Griffiths (2004a), for example, argues that, because of their response-specific nature and associated narrow inferential role in the cognitive economy, it is misleading to state or imply that low-level appraisals are evaluative judgements in the sense that they pertain to the person's goals and plans.

Emotions as embodied appraisals

Neurobiological theorists, including those mentioned in the previous paragraph, have also provided mechanistic accounts of higher level emotional appraisals. One of the most influential is Damasio's (1994, 1999, 2003) "somatic-marker" hypothesis. Somatic markers are representations of bodily responses associated with previously experienced emotionally salient events that are reactivated by current events and which thus influence or guide responses to those current events. These somatic markers influence processes at multiple levels of organization, including higher level processes involved in decision-making about the potential future outcomes of choices. Thus Damasio has answered an alleged failing of the James-Lange somatic theory of emotion, namely, that emotions are about the significance or value of events encountered in our engagements with the world, not about our bodily responses to those events; they represent affairs of the heart, gut, and gonads, not the operation or state of those organs. Damasio's response is to propose that emotions are sensations of bodily changes *coupled with* cognitive evaluations. Taking up the mantle of a somatic approach to emotion, but disagreeing with Damasio on this point, Prinz (2004) argues that the content of emotional states – what they are appraisals of – is provided first and foremost by the bodily perceptions. On Prinz's theory, emotions are embodied appraisals. Emotions are "embodied" insofar as they are states reliably caused by bodily changes (or by simulations of bodily changes), and that these changes in the states of the autonomic nervous system, viscera, and the like, are tracked by – indeed, represented in – certain brain systems, especially somatosensory-related cortices. Emotions are "appraisals" in the general sense described above, that is, judgements as to the value of events to one's welfare and interests. Yet furthermore, the contents of those representations comprise "core relational themes," a term Prinz borrows from Lazarus (1991). Core relational themes are the essence of the adaptive problems for which emotions evolved as solutions. So, for example, fear represents imminent danger, sadness represents an irrevocable loss, and anger a personal transgression. Thus, on Prinz's theory, emotions represent core relational themes *and* bodily changes. How is that possible? Prinz's answer hinges on a distinction between "real" and "nominal" representational contents. The real content of concepts refers to their essences, which are often not directly perceivable when we are presented with exemplars of those concepts. For example, the ancestry and genetic makeup of cats plausibly constitutes the essence of cat-hood (and thus the real content of the concept "cat"), but neither is directly perceivable when we see an individual cat. The nominal content of a concept captures the perceptible appearances of its exemplars (e.g., how cats look, sound, smell, and behave). Nominal and real contents are normally kept in step because a particular essence reliably co-occurs with a particular cluster of perceptible features (in the case of organisms, thanks to a reliable mapping between genotype and phenotype secured during the developmental process). Prinz's proposal is that emotions have as their real contents core relational themes, but their nominal contents are bodily changes.

A criticism levied at biological theories is that they do not or are unable to distinguish emotions from motivations (including certain desires). If the distal function of emotions is the facilitation of solutions to certain classes of adaptive problem, solutions that are implemented by the more proximal function of motivating behaviour, then how are emotions to be distinguished from motivational states such as hunger, thirst, and sex drive, which also fulfil such functions, and which also involve bodily states of affairs and representations thereof? A criticism levied at cognitive theories is that they do not or are unable to account for the motivating functions of emotions. On one level, the criticism amounts to saying that appraisals are exemplars of "cold" cognition and are thus no more motivating than any other cognitive state, such as thoughts or beliefs. On another level, the problem is that while appraisals are judgements about the significance of events in relation to our wellbeing, they do not represent those events *as* bearing on wellbeing. So how can hybrid cognitive-biological theories of the sort discussed above overcome these shortcomings of their component approaches? Prinz's (2004) solution is to argue that emotions are valenced embodied appraisals. Thus emotional or "hot" appraisals are distinguished from non-emotional or "cold" appraisals insofar as the former represent not only those things that matter to us, but also the fact *that* they matter. In other words, valence is the motivating element of emotions; it is what gives them their oomph. And emotions are distinguished from motivations insofar as the latter are valenced imperatives to act (Eat! Drink! Make love! You'll feel better if you do.), rather than valenced appraisals, and so press action more urgently than emotions.

Are emotions natural kinds?

When we manage to carve nature accurately at its joints, will the emotions form one of those joints? That is, do the emotions correspond to a real distinction in nature, such that there is a class of properties essential to something's being an emotion that is bound by the laws and law-like generalizations of nature? This is the issue of whether the emotions constitute a unified set of phenomena, not in everyday discourse but as a scientific category. There is a further question or set of questions, not always clearly distinguished from the first, of whether a given individual emotion conceptualized within everyday language and thought – anger, fear, or jealousy, for example – constitutes a natural kind. The dangers in conflating these two questions are twofold: even if several vernacular emotions are successfully captured within a scientific theory (even if slightly altered) it is still quite possible that the emotions per se will not constitute a single natural kind, yet successful scientific theories of a given individual emotion or class of emotions should not be rejected simply because the emotions cannot all be brought under a single theory.

A number of emotion theorists have voiced a negative answer to the question of whether emotions constitute a natural kind. Griffiths (1997) provides a sustained defence of this position, while at the same time clearly distinguishing this issue from the issue of whether any given emotion or class of emotions might constitute a natural kind. With respect to emotion, Griffiths is an eliminativist: the concept will have no use in a fully fledged scientific psychology. In this scientific psychology, the specific emotions identified in our everyday discourse, such as anger, fear, love, and guilt, or classes of them, will be subsumed under different theories, if they feature in science at all. It might turn out that subsets of the phenomena formerly known as emotions form natural kinds, such as "affect programs," but emotion per se will not do so. Griffiths bases his argument on two subsidiary arguments: (1) that basic and non-basic or complex emotions are two different classes of phenomena, and more specifically, the complex emotions are unlikely to be reduced to or subsumed by basic emotions; and (2) that any theory of emotion in general would not uncover a set of behaviour-producing mechanisms with common ancestral forms (i.e., any such theory would not admit of homologues, only analogies – features that are adapted for the same function but are unrelated).

Prinz (2004) provides a spirited defence of the claim that emotions are a natural kind. As we have seen, Prinz regards emotions as valenced embodied appraisals: "gut reactions." This characterization is epitomized by the basic emotions, such as fear and disgust, but extends to the more complex emotions as well. Complex emotions are either blends of basic emotions or cognitively elaborated basic emotions. Thus emotions have an essence, on Prinz's view, which is derived from their basic emotional core: they involve representations of bodily states that also represent worldly states of affairs as bearing on wellbeing, and thus push or pull behaviour in certain directions to maintain or increase that wellbeing. The basic emotional core of emotions is like the alcohol in an alcoholic beverage, to use Prinz's metaphor, which might be shots of a single type of liquor or mixtures of two or more types. While different liquors have a common effect (intoxication), they differ in flavour; mixing a drink by adding additional liquors or non-alcoholic mixers (cognitive evaluations) changes the flavour.

The disagreement between Griffiths and Prinz on this issue turns on what constitutes a natural kind. Prinz's argument that emotions are natural kinds is based on the idea that natural kinds are delineated by essences. On Griffiths' view, essences are not necessary or even desirable features of natural kinds; rather, instances of natural kinds are embedded in theoretically fruitful research programmes and have a rich set of properties that license inductive inferences, that is, properties that apply to and thus enable reliable delineation of other instances of that category. Such "projectable properties" will include outwardly observable features and effects as well as underlying causal mechanisms.

Barrett (2006) has argued against any natural-kind view of emotions, on the basis that the weight of empirical evidence strongly indicates that no class of emotions, not even the basic emotions or a subset of them, have a common set of projectable properties, either in terms of correlated response patterns or with respect to causal mechanisms. Barrett advances some ideas for a replacement to the natural-kind paradigm, drawing upon models that assume that the observable manifestations of the emotions emerge from interactions of more fundamental psychological processes, one of which might be "core affect" or some similar general affect system. The notion of core affect, as developed by Russell and Barrett (Russell and Barrett 1999; Russell 2003), refers to continuously experienced, elemental, consciously accessible feelings and their neurophysiological substrates that indicate the value of events or objects with respect to two basic dimensions, hedonic tone or valence (good-bad or pleasure-displeasure) and arousal (activated-deactivated). As Barrett (2006: 48) captures the idea, "core affect is a neurophysiological barometer of the individual's relation to an environment at a given point in time, and self-reported feelings are the barometer readings." Thus core affect is not unlike the liquor of Prinz's valenced embodied appraisals. Actually, core affect is more like ethanol, the underlying chemical compound of alcoholic beverages. Discrete emotional states occur when perceptual and conceptual knowledge (including knowledge of antecedent events, past experiences, and social norms, as well as cognitive evaluations) are applied to momentary states of core affect, resulting in the categorization of that affect in thought, language, and behaviour.

Situated emotions

A new and promising perspective on emotions is emerging that parallels the situated cognition movement [see Aizawa and Adams' entry, "Embodied Cognition and the Extended Mind" [Chapter 13]), and which has roots in the social transactionist and behavioural ecology approaches to emotion proposed by Fridlund (1991) and Parkinson et al. (2005), amongst others. It also has elements of a Gibsonian view of social perception (McArthur and Baron 1983) and shares some ideas with phenomenological approaches to social perception and cognition (Gallagher 2004, 2005; Ratcliffe 2007). This situated perspective on emotions (Griffiths and Scarantino, 2008) does not in principle oppose the cognitive and biological theories of emotion, and indeed can be taken to complement them. In cognitive and biological theories, the role of the environment is typically limited to providing stimuli and receiving actions. A situated perspective on emotion accords the environment a more active role in the production and development of emotional states. Emotions are regarded as forms of skilful engagement with the world; the environment affords certain actions, and since much of that world is social, many emotions involve the deployment of social skills. The environment enables and structures emotional engagements with the world in two respects: by providing a repertoire of emotional abilities (such as those specified by social roles and cultural norms) and by supporting individual deployments of those abilities (the particularities of a given social context). The situated perspective on emotions also recognizes that there is a dynamic coupling between the social context and its participants: emotional episodes are shaped by the social context in which they develop and those social contexts are in turn shaped by the evolving emotional episodes. Thus the situated perspective on emotions also has affinities with social constructionist ideas. From the situated perspective, emotional expressions not only signal to others whether some object or event is good or bad, harmful or beneficial, they can also signal reactions to and appraisals of the signallers and their actions, and thus have a crucial role in regulating social relations. An expression of anger, for example, may be a threat of retaliation to a personal transgression, thus promoting restitution or a reduction in recidivism, an expression of sadness may promote compassion and comfort from others, and smiles may act as affiliative gestures. That is, emotional expressions are regarded as key elements in social transactions, not (or at any rate, not solely or not always) as reflexive displays of internal states. Finally, a core idea emphasized by the situated perspective is that psychological phenomena are inherently temporal. Whereas cognitive and biological approaches conceive of emotions as transitory states and study them in isolation, a situated perspective emphasizes the evolution of those states across time within and between individuals; to understand emotions and other psychological states, one needs to understand modes and rates of time-dependent change, not merely, say, the content of essentially atemporal states.

References

Averill, J. R. (1980) "A Constructivist View of Emotion," in R. Plutchik and H. Kellerman (eds), *Emotion: Theory, Research, and Experience*, New York: Academic Press, pp. 305–39.

Barrett, L. F. (2006) "Are Emotions Natural Kinds?" *Perspectives on Psychological Science*, 1: 28–58.

Damasio, A. R. (1994) *Descartes' Error: Emotion, Reason and the Human Brain*, New York: Putnam.

—— (1999) *The Feeling of What Happens: Body and Emotion in the Making of Consciousness*, New York: Harcourt Brace.

—— (2003) *Looking for Spinoza: Joy, Sorrow, and the Feeling Brain*, San Diego: Harcourt.

Darwin, C. (1998 [1872]) *The Expression of the Emotions in Man and Animals*, 3rd edn, ed. P. Ekman, London: Harper Collins.

Ekman, P. (1992) "An Argument for Basic Emotions," *Cognition and Emotion*, 6, 169–200.

—— (1999) "Basic Emotions," in T. Dalgleish and T. Power (eds), *The Handbook of Cognition and Emotion*, New York: Wiley, pp. 45–60.

Fridlund, A. J. (1991) "Evolution and Facial Action in Reflex, Social Motive, and Paralanguage," *Biological Psychology*, 32: 3–100.

Gallagher, S. (2004) "Understanding Interpersonal Problems in Autism: Interaction Theory as an Alternative to Theory of Mind," *Philosophy, Psychiatry, and Psychology* 11: 199–217.

—— (2005) "Phenomenological Contributions to a Theory of Social Cognition," *Husserl Studies* 21: 95–110.

Griffiths, P. E. (1997) *What Emotions Really Are: The Problem of Psychological Categories*, Chicago: University of Chicago Press.

Griffiths, P. E. (2004a) "Is Emotion a Natural Kind?" in R. C. Solomon (ed.), *Thinking about Feeling: Contemporary Philosophers on Emotion*, Oxford: Oxford University Press, pp. 233–49.

—— (2004b) "Towards a Machiavellian Theory of Emotional Appraisal," in P. Cruse and D. Evans (eds), *Emotion, Evolution and Rationality*, Oxford: Oxford University Press, pp. 89–105.

—— (2008) Review of *Gut Reactions: A Perceptual Theory of Emotion*, by Jesse Prinz, *British Journal for the Philosophy of Science* 59: 559–67.

Griffiths, P. E., and Scarantino, A. (2008) "Emotions in the Wild: The Situated Perspective on Emotion," in P. Robbins and M. Aydede (eds), *Cambridge Handbook of Situated Cognition*, Cambridge: Cambridge University Press.

Harré, R. (1986) *The Social Construction of the Emotions*, Oxford: Oxford University Press.

Izard, C. E. (1971) *The Face of Emotion*, New York: Appleton-Century-Crofts.

Lazarus, R. S. (1991) *Emotion and Adaptation*, New York: Oxford University Press.

LeDoux, J. (1998) *The Emotional Brain: The Mysterious Underpinnings of Emotional Life*, New York: Simon & Schuster.

McArthur, L. Z., and Baron, R. M. (1983) "Toward an Ecological Theory of Social Perception," *Psychological Review*, 90: 215–38.

Panksepp, J. (1998) *Affective Neuroscience: The Foundations of Human and Animal Emotions*, New York: Oxford University Press.

Parkinson, B., Fischer, A. H., and Manstead, A. S. R. (2005) *Emotions in Social Relations: Cultural, Group and Interpersonal Processes*, New York: Psychology Press.

Plutchik, R. (1980) *Emotion: A Psychoevolutionary Synthesis*, New York: Harper & Row.

Prinz, J. J. (2004) *Gut Reactions: A Perceptual Theory of Emotion*, New York: Oxford University Press.

Ratcliffe, M. (2007) *Rethinking Commonsense Psychology: A Critique of Folk Psychology, Theory of Mind and Simulation*, Basingstoke: Palgrave Macmillan.

Rolls, E. (2005) *Emotion Explained*, Oxford: Oxford University Press.

Russell, J. A. (2003) Core Affect and the Psychological Construction of Emotion, *Psychological Review* 110: 145–72.

Russell, J. A., and Barrett, L. F. (1999) "Core Affect, Prototypical Emotional Episodes, and Other Things Called Emotion: Dissecting the Elephant," *Journal of Personality and Social Psychology* 76: 805–19.

Further reading

A collection of chapters by leading psychologists, neuroscientists, and philosophers on the conscious and unconscious processes involved in emotion, is L. F. Barrett, P. M. Niedenthal, and P. Winkielman (eds) *Emotion and Consciousness* (New York: Guilford Press, 2005). The chapters summarize state-of-the-science research and theorizing on emotion and its relationship to consciousness, and articulate and interrogate key assumptions in the field. *Descartes' Error: Emotion, Reason and the Human Brain* (New York: Putnam, 1994) is A. R. Damasio's first book-length treatment of the emotions from a neuroscientific perspective, in which he presents his influential somatic theory of emotion, a theory that he extended and refined in two subsequent books. Read all three books if you can. P. Ekman and R. J. Davidson (eds) *The Nature of Emotion: Fundamental Questions* (Oxford: Oxford University Press, 1994) is a useful, if in parts outdated, *vade mecum* for students of the emotions, in which leading psychologists and neuroscientists of emotion present their answers to fundamental questions about the nature of emotions and about how the emotions are related to other psychological phenomena. Each question is addressed by several different authors, providing the reader with succinct overviews of different perspectives and thus of areas of agreement and disagreement. An updated edition would be welcome. P. Goldie, *The Emotions: A Philosophical Exploration* (Oxford: Clarendon Press, 2002) is an interesting philosophical treatise on the emotions that draws upon literature, as well as science. Central to Goldie's argument is the idea of a personal perspective or point of view, in contrast to the impersonal stance of the sciences. He argues that personal narratives are what bind the various elements of emotional experience together (feeling, thoughts, expressions, bodily changes) and allow us to make sense of our own and others' emotional lives. P. E. Griffiths, *What Emotions Really Are: The Problem of Psychological Categories* (Chicago: University of Chicago Press, 1997), first argues against a philosophy of the emotions, based on formalized versions of folk psychology, and goes on to integrate theory and evidence from psychology, ethology, evolutionary biology, anthropology, neuroscience, and philosophy to suggest that there are at least three main classes of emotion. He then argues that, because the three kinds of emotion have so little in common, "emotion" is not a natural kind, and so there can be no useful science of emotion *per se*. R. C. Solomon (ed.) *Thinking about Feeling: Contemporary Philosophers on Emotion* (Oxford: Oxford University Press, 2004) presents essays from some of the best Anglo-American philosophers now writing on the philosophy of emotion, with each author neatly summarizing his or her own theoretical position. Topics examined include the nature of emotions and the relationships between emotion and cognition, knowledge, rationality, freedom, value, desire, and action. J. J. Prinz, *Gut Reactions: A Perceptual Theory of Emotion* (New York: Oxford University Press, 2004), brings to light the philosophical commitments that underlie somatic theories of emotion, while at the same time defending such theories against criticisms and alternative proposals, and distilling his own theory. He argues that emotions represent both our external (physical and social) and internal (bodily) milieu, and that the latter enables the former.

38
VISION

Valtteri Arstila

Introduction

Vision is often described as a sensory system that provides us with information about three-dimensional objects, based on their two-dimensional retinal projection. Presumably it has been evolutionarily advantageous to have this kind of a sensory system that functions without an active encounter with seen things. Unlike touch, for example, vision does not place us in too close proximity with predators or other threats, but provides us with information about things of various sizes, colors, and shapes even at great distance. Vision appears to succeed in its task with an apparent ease, but accomplishing the task requires a number of resources and a great deal of complex processing. Indeed it is estimated that from one-third to a half of the cortex is employed in processing visual information. Emphasizing the importance of vision, which is possibly our most important sensory system, a major part of neuroscientific research has focused on discovering the processing that occurs in these areas. Fortunately it can be said that the interdisciplinary field of vision science has been one of the most successful branches of cognitive science, with the result that a great deal of the anatomical and organizational basis of this processing is nowadays relatively well known. A very short introduction to this empirical knowledge of vision is given in the first section. This research has been guided by various theoretical approaches to vision. These and the challenges facing the predominant theory of vision are then described in the following two sections. The last section deals with the issues related to unconscious and conscious vision.

Anatomical and organizational basis of vision

In order for us to see, the light reflected from objects needs to be registered. This happens in the retina, in the bottom of the eyes, where two types of photoreceptors lie. *Rods* are used in dim light, whereas three types of *cones* are used in normal trichromate color vision under normal lighting conditions. These photoreceptors basically work in the same way by absorbing the light scattered to eyes and transmitting the information about this event to other cells in the retina, namely to bipolar cells and retinal ganglion cells.

The retinal ganglion cells send the information to the visual cortex via the lateral geniculate nucleus (LGN) in three separate pathways. These pathways originate from different types of ganglion cells, and they can be separated on the basis of their physiological characteristics and the type of information they carry. The nerves in the *magnocellular* pathway are the fastest and carry information about motion and achromatic low contrasts. The nerves in the *parvocellular* pathway in turn are slower and provide the bases for color and form perception. The parvocellular pathway also mediates visual acuity. Less is known about the third pathway, the *koniocellular* pathway, although evidence is emerging that it is (partly) sensitive to yellow and blue stimuli.

All these pathways synapse on different layers of the primary visual cortex, V_1, at the back of the head, which is thus the first (and also largest) area of the cortex that codes visual information. Together with the next area, V_2, it distributes the information related to different visual features to different areas of cortex that are specialized in processing that information. Often-referred-to exemplar areas are V_4, which is thought to process color-related information, and V_5, in which motion perception is processed. Thus the distinctness of the information conveyed by magnocellular and parvocellular pathways is essentially maintained also in the visual cortex. Here too the anatomical structures and the function they serve appear to be thus intimately tied together, and different visual features are processed *mostly in parallel* and *independent* of each other. Another important feature of these first areas of the visual cortex is that they are *retinotopically organized*, meaning that the neurons representing adjacent places in space are adjacent to each other (in all layers).

The processing of visual information is thought to be hierarchical, in the sense that the results of the previous processes are employed by the processes in the later stages of visual processing. Steps in the processing increase the complexity of the processed stimuli. Hence in the first step, visual features of the stimulus are processed separately, and then for example they are projected to inferotemporal cortex, where they are processed together in processes related to object recognition. It should be noted that in addition to picturing visual processing often occurring in a stimulus-driven or bottom-up fashion, it is well known that all areas of the visual cortex (and even LGN) also receive feedback from the areas of the visual cortex where "higher order" processing takes place.

The above described processing from V_1 and V_2 to inferotemporal lobe through V_4 (from the back of the head to the front via the bottom and sides of the brain) forms the *ventral pathway*. In addition to this processing stream in the visual cortex, there is another one called the *dorsal pathway*, which proceeds from V_1 and V_2 to the front via the top of the brain. David Milner and Melvyn A. Goodale (1995) argue that these two processing streams can be distinguished in terms of the use of the processed information; while the ventral pathway is used for conscious perception (as in above), the dorsal pathway is used for action. The ventral pathway is also slower and sharpest in the fovea, whereas the dorsal pathway is fast and equally sharp through most of the visual field. Goodale and Milner base their claim on patient D.F., whose visual perception does not allow her to determine features of objects, such as their shape and distances. Yet she can, for example, pick up the object without substantial difficulty. In other words, without a perception of the object, D.F. can still process the information needed to conduct successful action that requires her to reach out in the right direction and distance and then adjust her grip correctly. The justification for the separation of these two pathways receives complementary support from the existence of a disorder known as optic ataxia, where the deficit is reversed (see, for example, Perenin 1997): patients perceive the object, but they are impaired in their actions toward it (for example, reaching for it).

Psychological theories of vision

The main objective of the psychological theories of vision is to explain how we achieve knowledge of the seen objects, based on the light they reflect or emit. In specific their aim can be understood to provide an answer to the question how the pattern of stimulation in the retina gives rise to our perceptions. This problem, which is sometimes called *the inverse problem*, is challenging because our three-dimensional perceptions are based on the two-dimensional retinal images. Since countless different kinds of three-dimensional worlds can create the same kind of two-dimensional retinal images, logically there is no solution for the inverse problem. Yet, somehow our vision succeeds in its task and the psychological theories of vision try to explain how it happens.

These theories should be distinguished from the philosophical theories and questions of vision. For example, while philosophers are often perplexed by issues such as the qualitativeness of visual experiences (qualia), sense-data, nature of causality in perception, and so forth, psychological theories of vision do not tackle those issues. Similarly illusions arouse the interest of psychologists due to the fact that they shed light on how vision functions not because they pose us the challenge of skepticism. Psychological theories of vision should also be separated from neurophysiological theories, which are more engaged in how vision is implemented on the neuronal level and often focus on more detailed questions.

Until the Gestalt psychology movement in Germany in the 1920s and 1930s, the received view was that visual experience of a given region of the visual field was a result of the activity of a photoreceptor corresponding to that region. Gestalt psychology, partly rising as a reaction to this kind of structuralism, maintains instead that visual perceptions cannot be analyzed in this fashion by reducing entities to their simple components. Rather, as the name of the movement already indicates, the perception should be understood as a holistic process; objects are automatically arranged into wholes. For example, four dots that are close to each other are usually perceived as a group of dots not as four individual dots.

Gestalt psychologists maintain that these modes of organization are not determined arbitrarily. Consequently they put much effort and time to understand and describe the factors influencing the ways in which objects are perceived as wholes. These principles, including say proximity and similarity, are nowadays called Gestalt laws or Gestalt principles. Gestalt psychologists thought that the principles reflect the brain states underlying the visual experiences and thus they maintained an isomorphism between brain states and visual experiences. Furthermore, Gestalt psychologists argue that these principles function automatically before conscious perception. Hence, even though the way in which objects are grouped depends on the way in which our vision functions, the perception of those objects is direct, in the sense that the way in which objects are grouped and perceived does not depend on any mental processes.

After the Gestalt movement ended, partly due to the Second World War, the next significant theory was James Gibson's ecological optics (1966, 1979). While Gestalt psychologists argued that perceptual theory should be based on our visual system, since that is what the Gestalt laws mirror, Gibson argues that the best way to understand visual perception is by analyzing its informational basis – the organism's environment and stimuli it provides.

Gibson argues that stimuli provide much more information than had been previously postulated. The reason for this mistake was, according to Gibson, that stimuli were taken to be comprised of a series of still images. Instead of considering stimuli as single frames in movie films, he argues that the central part of the visual perception is the flow of information in the patterns of light reaching the eye – not what is available at the retina at one particular moment. In this flow of information certain invariants that structure the patterns of light in law-like ways are crucial. Furthermore, extracting these invariants requires movement on the part of the perceiver, such as eye or body movements. To give an example of the process, when walking towards an open doorway, the order of the sides of the doorframe remains the same and all parts appear to drift apart in a regular way.

The optic flow in the retina does not therefore include stationary objects but the implicit information of changes and constancies in the patterns of light reaching the eye. These invariant structures were thought to provide unambiguous information about the spatial layout of objects. Furthermore, Gibson argues that our vision is sensitive to or resonates with these invariants. Hence our vision is able to solve the inverse problem. Gibson, in fact, thought that the constancies in perspective information in motion are already enough for solving the inverse problem, as they change in accordance with the movement of the perceiver. This emphasis on motion illustrates that ecological optics is a theory in which perceiving is understood as an active exploration of the world.

Considering how the patterns of light change over time (motion), the stimulus provides us with a rich source of information only if the whole pattern is taken into account. Hence although Gibson was not a successor of the Gestalt movement, he shares with it the conviction that visual perception cannot be understood as a simple correspondence between a region in the retina and a region in the visual field.

Another common feature in these two theories is that Gibson strongly believed that visual perception is direct. Because vision resonates with the constancies in the world, it does not need to be represented internally by the means of representations that are somehow separate from the stimulus. Hence the perception is not mediated or intertwined with psychological or mental processes.

Though Gibson's ideas have been influential and inspired a great deal of research, it should be noted that taking invariants in the retinal flow when the perceiver is moving does not solve the inverse problem. Instead, it simply brings along one more dimension. That is, when the "original" inverse problem was how to calculate three-dimensional perceptions based on two-dimensional stimuli, Gibson is now faced with solving how the two-dimensional spatial information that changes over time provides us with perception that is three dimensional and changes over time. There are other reasons to criticize ecological optics too, such as the notion of being sensitive to constancies or invariants of optic flow, or the notion of direct perception. Yet, the main reason why Gibson's ecological optics went out of fashion is the emergence of computational theories of perception.

The computational theory of vision has been the predominant approach to vision since the publication of David Marr's *Vision* (1982), where he argues that vision is a "process of discovering from images what is present in the world, and where it is." Marr's main complaint against ecological optics, which he considers coming relatively close to computational theory of vision, is that Gibson belittles the complexity of vision. To properly understand vision, Marr argues, requires understanding vision as an information-processing task and it cannot be restricted to scrutinizing the information in the optic flow. Instead the objective of theories of vision should be to describe how the entities of the external world are represented by vision and describe processes that operate on these representations. Hence, the study of vision is an inquiry into the nature of the processes involved and the nature of representations that are inputs and outputs of those processes. This necessitates that vision must be tackled on three different explanatory levels.

The most abstract level is *the computational level* that characterizes the functions an organism needs to compute. This level provides an abstract description of the computational problem – what the organism computes and what the goals of these computations are. The next level is *the algorithm level*. This one characterizes the algorithms used for computing and the nature of representations for the input and output of those algorithms. The algorithm level thus specifies which rules solve the computations. Finally, *the implementation level* describes how the algorithms and the representations they manipulate are physically realized in our brains. Marr emphasizes the importance of the computational level because he thinks that algorithms and representations they operate with are more easily understood if we know what computations need to be done instead of merely studying their neurophysiological implementation.

Marr argues that these three levels are autonomous levels of explanation and largely independent of each other. A computation, for example, can be solved with the various kinds of algorithms and an algorithm can be used as a part of various computations. Likewise, an algorithm can be implemented in countless different ways, and a mechanism can be part of different algorithms. This does not mean, however, that these levels are fully independent, since "the choice of an algorithm is influenced for example, by what it has to do and by the hardware in which it must run."

In addition to describing the program for the computational theory of vision, Marr presents an influential account on how vision solves the inversion problem – what the computational steps that vision takes to compute three-dimensional representation of the world based on two-dimensional retinal images are. In his theory this requires three different types of representation, each of which take the outputs of previous stages of processing as their input and make implicit information in them explicit.

The first level of representation is *the primal sketch*. It takes the two-dimensional image on the retina as its input with the purpose of making explicit the local geometry information about the intensity changes of light in this image. This is done with the primitive representations that include edges, lines, blobs, and terminations and discontinuities. The full primal sketch includes also boundaries and segmented groups.

The primal sketch makes explicit the information that is required for processing of *the 2.5-D sketch*, which is the second type of representation. This representation is between the two-dimensional level of the primal sketch and full-blown three-dimensional representations of objects. It is a viewer-centered representation that makes explicit the (spatial) features of visible surfaces – their depth, orientation, distance from viewer and so forth. Here the results of the processes related to the primal sketch are combined.

The final representation is *the 3-D model*. As the primal sketch makes explicit the two-dimensional geometry by the means of two-dimensional primitives, the 3-D model makes explicit the three-dimensional space that an object occupies by the means of three-dimensional primitives. These primitives come in various shapes and sizes, and they are structurally organized.

There are a number of features in Marr's theory that are worth noting. *First*, this theory is clearly a bottom-up or data-driven theory. It takes retinal images as the input, and the processing advances hierarchically. *Second*, Marr regards vision as essentially passive. In Gibson's ecological optics perceivers are considered active explorers and the motion of the perceiver is built into the theory. For Marr, in contrast, vision does not require this kind of active exploration. This conclusion is emphasized by the fact that the questions how we see and what vision is used for are separate questions for him. *Third*, Marr's vision is largely modular – processes related to extracting information to any given representation within one level run independently of other processes and they can be explained independently of other modules. *Fourth*, Marr's theory is not aimed at describing higher-level visual processing, such as categorization of objects. Rather, his theory is basically restricted to processing in retinotopically indexed cortical areas. *Fifth*, because Marr's theory postulates internal representations and assumptions on what type of information should be extracted from retinal images, the information in stimuli alone does not determine our visual perceptions. Accordingly Marr's theory is a version of indirect perception.

In general Marr's theory fits well with the functional organization of vision discussed above, especially regarding the parallel processing and how vision is thought to proceed from a two-dimensional image-based stage to a three-dimensional object-based stage through a 2.5-dimensional surface-based stage. The details of his ideas, however, have later been challenged. These include, say, the independency of the levels of explanation, the nature of some of the primitives in the primal sketch and how the slightly different projections an object provides on the two retinas are used in the perception of depth. Nevertheless Marr's theory made lasting impact on the theories of vision and despite the considerable disagreement on the details, the currently prevalent theories of vision are mainly in line with Marr.

The above does not imply that older theories would not have their place either. This influence is limited though. The Gestalt movement has regained interest again, especially due to Gestalt principles because those appear to play a significant role in segmenting the visual field into meaningful wholes. Likewise, Gibson's influence can be seen in the practice of many computational vision scientists who focus on the information present in the environment and compare distal stimuli to proximal stimuli.

Recent challenges for the theories of vision

As mentioned above, our increasing knowledge of vision has made current theorists challenge many of the details of Marr's theory. This increased knowledge has also amounted to more theoretical work and adding possible computations and processes on various levels. This holds especially for the higher order states because Marr did not pay much attention to them. Yet this does not mean that our new knowledge has an effect on how we perceive the world and especially how the inverse problem is solved. Many empirical studies suggest, however, that higher order states do have the effect, and thus computationalists need to describe not only the computations required for them but also how their output can influence the way we perceive the world.

To give a few examples, it has been shown that when the object is recognized, it can influence the ways in which it is perceived. For instance, the familiarity of an object is thought to play a prominent role in size perception (Hershenson, 1999). When we perceive some familiar object, we "remember" its size, which in turn influences the way in which we perceive its size. Likewise, our memory of a stereotypical color of an object has an effect on the perceived color of the object, which explains why a banana is often perceived as more yellow than another object with identical surface properties (Hansen et al. 2006). Two aspects make this kind of influence significant for the discussion at hand. First, it can only happen when vision has already formed a representation of the object, recognized it, and accessed our (implicit) knowledge of objects of that kind. Second, this information needs to be transmitted back to areas that supposedly compute the perceived size and colors.

Another example relates to the advantageousness of data-driven processing compared with top-down processing. The idea that speaks for the former is that it is usually thought to be faster because of fast modular processing and because then vision need not take time to access high-level knowledge to occur. The downside of this type of processing is that it requires much resource. However, were the processing guided by initial guesses of what kind of an object we perceive, the computational demands would be greatly facilitated. Indeed, Moshe Bar (2003) argues that this is how things appear to happen in vision: parts of the retinal image are directly projected to the prefrontal cortex, from which the initial guesses of the correct category (dog or cat, for instance) are then back-projected to inferotemporal cortex to facilitate the processing required for object recognition.

These cases challenge at least two features of Marr's theory. The most obvious one is the assumption that processing advances from the processing of simple features to more complex ones. In contrast, it seems that solving the inverse problem may require taking into account also the top-down influences. Another challenged feature is the modularity of processing because our knowledge does influence their functioning. These challenges can be met by a computationalist, however, because there is nothing in their theory that prevents them loosening the notion of modularity and incorporating top-down influence into it. Hence these challenges do not question the computational theory of vision *per se*, but illustrate new theoretical and conceptual issues that need to be and increasingly are addressed. At the same time, it should be said that these changes are significant and presumably change the computational needs of the vision, as Bar's (2003) study illustrates.

Recent years have brought up possibly a more serious challenge, however, with the idea of enactive or embodied vision gaining prominence as a result of work done by, for example, Andy Clark, Alva Noë, and Evan Thompson. Although there are differences between these theorists, they share the common objection against Marr's theory and its legacy that vision cannot be understood separately from the uses it is put to. Instead, vision must be understood in relation to action and embodiment. Hence, this objection has its intellectual basis in Gibson's ecological optics.

This objection is justified at least to some extent because a proper theory of vision must take into account, for example, eye and head movements, as well as the information received from other sensory systems. Yet this much computationalists can admit too. More crucially, however, this objection challenges the core idea of their theory that the brain is enough for vision. In Marr's theory it is the brain that manipulates various types of representations and gives rise to visual experiences. Now if visual experiences can only be understood in the context of embodiment, as above-mentioned theorists claim, then, the body and action become part of vision. That is, the activity of the body itself forms a part of the visual experiences.

This idea, it is safe to say, has been received with suspicion and many problems in it have been pointed out. To name a few, in his thorough review of Noë's book (2004) *Action in Perception*, Ned Block (2005) has forcefully argued that Noë succeeds only in demonstrating that behavioral context has a causal influence on what we perceive (which computationalists can happily accept) not that the activity of body constitutes part of the content of visual perception. Commenting on the same book, Pierre Jacob (2006), in turn, points out that Noë simply dismisses the idea of two separate pathways for perception and action, even though it would deserve attention since it may not be compatible with Noë's enactive theory. Partly due to these reasons, the impact of enactive theories of vision on psychological theories of vision has remained limited. This may change though since many versions of enactive theories of vision have been formulated only recently.

Conscious and unconscious visual perception

The discussion and main bulk of theoretical interest in vision has thus far focused on solving the inverse problem. The solution requires an account of complex processing, a great deal of which occurs unconsciously. For example, it is plausible to think that we are never directly aware of, say, the states of opponent processes in LGN, and there has been a considerable discussion whether we are aware of the processes occurring in V_1.

The unconscious processing is in no sense trivial, as it enables us to do a great many things. A prime example is Goodale and Milner's patient D.F., who was able to grasp objects and to avoid obstacles without conscious experiences of those objects and obstacles. Given that in some cases we might not be aware of the stimulus, but can still react to it properly, a number of theoretically interesting questions arise. These include the following two, discussed further below: what is required in order for the content or processes to become conscious, and in what ways do conscious and unconscious (but almost conscious) visual states differ?

Especially the first question has also been discussed under the topics of consciousness and attention. It is worthwhile summarizing briefly the current view on that here as well, because, after all, most of the research done on it is visual in nature and thus sheds light on how vision functions. Moreover, some of the proposed answers to this question, such as that consciousness is needed for rational reasoning, do not involve vision and thus do not refer to vision-specific questions.

In short, the converging evidence suggests that what is required for a visual mental state to become conscious is that one should pay attention to it. In addition to everyday observations, normal subjects illustrate this also when experiencing a phenomenon called *inattentional blindness* in which subjects are not conscious of stimuli they do not attend to. Simons and Chabris (1999) famously illustrated this by showing a video of two teams passing a basketball to their team members. The task of the subjects was to count how many times the white team passes the ball. This proved to be so demanding that many subjects failed to notice a person in a gorilla suit walking through the video and even stopping in the middle.

The idea that attention is needed for a mental state to become conscious receives support also from neglect-syndrome patients who fail to react to a stimulus or part of it, although their eyes and primary visual cortex are intact (for an excellent sourcebook for neglect syndrome, see Karnath et al. 2002). Because this is not a deficit in seeing as such (neglect syndrome occurs in all sense modalities), this is considered to be a deficit of attention. Typical situations with neglect patients are those in which the patients eat only food from the right side of the plate or when they are asked to copy a picture, they copy only half of it. At the same time, a great deal of this information that they fail to become aware of must be processed, because neglect patients are still able to react to the unconscious stimuli in a goal-directed way. For example, when neglect patients are asked in which one of the two houses, whose pictures they are shown, they want to live, they pick the one that is not on fire, although they report that the two pictures look identical to them.

It appears therefore that attention is required for a stimulus to become conscious. It is not enough, however, as studies with *blindsight* patients demonstrate (see Weiskrantz 1986, 1997). This paradoxical term refers to a phenomenon in which patients with damaged V_1 can respond appropriately with greater than chance probability to stimuli that they report having no visual experiences of. For example, blindsight patients can be asked to say whether there is a letter X or a letter O on the blind part of their visual field. Although these patients are reluctant to answer, because they think that they are merely guessing, when they are forced to answer they are correct almost every time. More strikingly, if possible, blindsight patients have also been shown to demonstrate attentional selection towards a stimulus they report not seeing. Hence, although attention might be a necessary condition for a stimulus to become conscious, it is not sufficient (Kentridge et al. 1999).

Above-discussed blindsight patients, neglect patients, and patient D.F. also suggest a preliminary answer to the question in what ways do conscious and unconscious visual states differ: patients without conscious perception are limited to choosing between predetermined alternatives at forced-choice tasks. What they appear to lack is the ability to have stimulus-driven knowledge of the external world, and it appears that they cannot self-initiate actions towards a stimulus.

While this answer is justified in the light of the previous discussion, it assumes a notion of unconscious perception that has been questioned in the debate over subliminal perception. This term refers to a perception of a stimulus without conscious awareness of the stimuli. Within this debate and relating to the issue at hand, the question what is the right criterion for distinguishing unconscious from conscious perception has received a considerable amount of interest in recent decades, and many of the studies are done with vision. For this, three different types of criteria have been proposed.

The first one, the subjective criterion, is based on subjective reports (Cheesman and Merikle 1986) – here subjects are thought to be unconscious of the stimulus if they say so. According to this criterion, the previous answer to the second question was right.

The second, the objective, criterion is based on subjects' ability to discriminate between alternative stimulus states, such as their presence and absence (Eriksen 1960; Holender 1986). This is an indirect criterion in a sense that only the presence of stimulus needs to be reportable not what is perceived. This criterion in turn makes blindsight patients conscious of their states since they are able to discriminate between the presences of stimuli. In the same place, it should be noted, though, that since conscious states are here defined as those that provide such minimal behavioral effects, the existence of unconscious perception is in effect rejected.

The last criterion is based on the qualitative differences between the consequences of conscious and unconscious perception. To put this somewhat differently, both the existence of unconscious perception and the dissimilarity between conscious and unconscious perception is already assumed (Merikle 1992; Merikle and Joordens 1997). Although this fails to take a clear stand on whether blindsight patients are conscious or unconscious of a stimulus they can respond to, patient D.F. clearly exhibits unconscious perception, according to this criterion.

Since the second criterion basically denies the existence of unconscious perception and the third criterion takes the difference between conscious and unconscious states as given, the first criterion is assumed below. With this provision, and given the answer to the first question, the question in what ways do conscious and unconscious visual states differ can be understood as the question whether there is a principled difference between pre-attentive and attended-to visual states.

According to a long-standing answer there is a difference because attention binds the various visual features together into a proper representation of an object. As already mentioned, the various features of objects (color, form, motion, size, and so forth) are processed in physically distinct areas of the brain. This also means that information about the features of an object is located in physically separate areas of the brain. Given that we perceive the world and its objects as unified wholes, these features are somehow bound together in our experiences. The question is, how?

This is a real question, known as the binding problem, since on some occasions the features of objects are mixed; for example, when being shown a red ball and a blue triangle, one may perceive a blue ball and a red triangle. The answer to it provided by Anne Treisman's (Treisman 1996; Treisman and Gelade 1980) feature-integration theory is that, by attending to a location, we take the visual features of that location into a further processing, and in this process they become bound together.

If attention makes us conscious of a stimulus and simultaneously binds its features together, then unconscious mental states are unbound. Hence, if Treisman's theory is true, it also answers our main question: there is a principled difference between conscious and unconscious visual states, as only in the former ones do we have a representation of an object in which its features are bound.

However, the feature-integration theory has been reformulated many times to accommodate new findings, such as the existence of implicit binding, with the effect of making pre-attentive states more similar to attended-to conscious stimuli. This does not mean that the similarity would extend all the way, though. Indeed, according to Jeremy M. Wolfe and Sara C. Bennett (1997), although features of objects are bound together pre-attentively, the overall shape of these bundles (often called proto-objects) is not processed without attention. To give an example, according to Wolfe the feature bundles of a "plus" sign and a square are the same, since both are comprised of four straight lines and four corners. What separates them, obviously, is their overall shape – how these features are put together. Yet this information is processed only with attention.

Even this difference between conscious and unconscious states can be questioned though: how come neglect patients can attend to only half of the objects? To draw the right side of an object, for example, the overall shape must be already settled contrary to Wolfe and Bennett's results. This is also in accordance with the results that object surfaces are created pre-attentively (Mattingley et al. 1997). However, if we assume that attention does organize bundled features to the overall shape of an object, but that this does not yet make the object conscious, even with intact V_1, then we are contradicting our response to the first question – that is, the assumption on which this discussion was based. One possible way to resolve this inconsistency would be to argue that the characteristics of pre-attentive states differ depending on task. Then they could be anything from unbound features to shapeless bundles of features, and even have the overall shape processed in special cases. Whether this is a feasible way to proceed remains an open theoretical question requiring more research.

References

Bar, M. (2003) "A Cortical Mechanism for Triggering Top-Down Facilitation in Visual Object Recognition," *Journal of Cognitive Neuroscience*, 15, no. 4: 600–9.

Block, N. (2005) Review of *Action in Perception*, by Alva Noë, *The Journal of Philosophy*, 102, no. 5: 259–72.

Cheesman, J., and Merikle, P. M. (1986) "Distinguishing Conscious from Unconscious Perceptual Processes," *Canadian Journal of Psychology*, 40: 343–67.

Eriksen, C. W. (1960) "Discrimination and Learning without Awareness: A Methodological Survey and Evaluation," *Psychological Review*, 67: 279–300.

Gibson, J. (1966) *The Senses Considered as Perceptual Systems*, Boston: Houghton Mifflin.

—— (1979) *The Ecological Approach to Visual Perception*, Boston: Houghton Mifflin.

Hansen, T., Olkkonen, M., Walter, S., and Gegenfurtner, K. R. (2006) "Memory Modulates Color Appearance," *Nature Neuroscience* 9, no. 11: 1367–8.

Hershenson, M. (1999) *Visual Space Perception: A Primer*, Cambridge, MA: MIT Press.

Holender, D. (1986) "Semantic Activation without Conscious Identification in Dichotic Listening, Parafoveal Vision, and Visual Masking: A Survey and Appraisal," *Behavioral and Brain Sciences* 9: 1–23.

Jacob, P. (2006) "Why Visual Experience Is Likely to Resist Being Enacted," *Psyche* 12, no. 1: 1–12.

Karnath, H. O., Milner, D. A., and Vallar, G. (eds) (2002) *The Cognitive and Neural Bases of Spatial Neglect*, Oxford: Oxford University Press.

Kentridge, R. W., Heywood, C. A., and Weiskrantz, L. (1999) "Attention without Awareness in Blindsight," *Proceedings of the Royal Society of London, Series B* 266, no. 1430: 1805–11.

Marr, D. (1982) *Vision*, San Francisco: W. H. Freeman & Co.

Mattingley, J. B., Davis, G., and Driver, J. (1997) "Preattentive Filling-in of Visual Surfaces in Parietal Extinction," *Science* 275: 671–4.

Merikle, P. M. (1992) "Perception without Awareness: Critical Issues," *American Psychologist* 47: 792–5.

Merikle, P. M., and Joordens, S. (1997) "Parallels between Perception without Attention and Perception without Awareness," *Consciousness and Cognition* 6: 219–36.

Milner, D., and Goodale, M. A. (1995) *The Visual Brain in Action*, Cambridge, MA: MIT Press.

Noë, A. (2004) *Action in Perception*, Cambridge, MA: MIT Press.

Perenin, M.-T. (1997) "Optic Ataxia and Unilateral Neglect: Clinical Evidence for Dissociable Spatial Functions in Posterior Parietal Cortex," in H.-O. Karnath and P. Thier (eds), *Parietal Lobe Contributions to Orientation in 3D Space*, Berlin: Springer, pp. 289–308.

Simons, D. J., and Chabris, C. F. (1999) "Gorillas in Our Midst: Sustained Inattentional Blindness for Dynamic Events," *Perception* 28: 1059–74.

Treisman, A. (1996) "The Binding Problem," *Current Opinion in Neurobiology* 6: 171–8.

Treisman, A., and Gelade, G. (1980) "A Feature-Integration Theory of Attention," *Cognitive Psychology* 12, no. 1: 97–136.

Weiskrantz, L. (1986) *Blindsight: A Case Study and Its Implications*, Oxford: Oxford University Press.

—— (1997) *Consciousness Lost and Found: A Neuropsychological Exploration*, Oxford: Oxford University Press.

Wolfe, J. M., and Bennett, S. C. (1997) "Preattentive Object Files: Shapeless Bundles of Basic Features," *Vision Research* 37, no. 1: 25–43.

39
COLOR

Jonathan Cohen

Color ontology and its significance

Questions about the ontology of color matter because colors matter. Colors are (or, at least, appear to be) extremely pervasive and salient features of the world. Moreover, people care about the distribution of these features: they expend money and effort to paint their houses, cars, and other possessions, and their clear preference for polychromatic over monochromatic televisions and computer monitors have consigned monochromatic models to the status of rare antiques. The apparent ubiquity of colors and their importance to our lives makes them a ripe target for ontological questions such as the following:

- What is the nature of colors?
- Are they, as they seem to be, properties of objects?
- Or are they, as many have claimed, illusory inexistents erroneously projected on to objects by our minds?

Such questions can seem even more pressing in light of the difficulty of locating colors within our best fundamental theories of the furniture of the world. These theories include properties like *mass*, *charge*, and *spin-up* in their inventories, but they seem not to mention properties like *red* and *blue* at all. This fact has led some to conclude that there are no colors after all. But it has led others to the conclusion that the inventories of our best fundamental physical theories don't exhaust the properties of the world. Indeed, this line of thought has even led some to hope that reflection on the nature of color might provide lessons about how to reconcile our best physical theories with other kinds of properties that don't appear in physical inventories, such as *value*, *moral goodness*, *beauty* (see Hume 1978 [1739]: Bk 3, pt 1, sec. 1). Thus, reflection on colors also leads to these questions:

- What is the relationship of colors to the properties recognized by our best physical theories?
- What is the relationship of colors to properties apparently *not* recognized (*per se*) by our best physical theories, but which many philosophers have wanted to admit into their ontologies?

Importantly, when they are asked about colors, these ontological questions are directed on a domain that has been the object of longstanding scientific research which can itself be drawn upon in providing philosophical answers. Indeed, many of the great historical philosophers writing on these matters – e.g., Aristotle, Galileo, Locke – have explicitly drawn on the best contemporary color science to provide constraints on their ontological theorizing. While this interplay between color ontology and color science may have been less robust during much of the twentieth century, it is once again the rule rather than the exception that writings on color ontology make extensive and crucial use of empirical results in color science. This fact has a special importance in light of the aforementioned possible analogies between colors and other properties not listed in inventories of the physical. For while several of the ontological questions listed above could be asked about properties other than colors (e.g., with respect to aesthetic or moral properties), many have thought that they can be pursued more fruitfully (at least for now) with respect to color, precisely because there is, in that domain, a vast body of empirical results that can constrain philosophical inquiry. If so, then, even philosophers whose main interests lie in aesthetics and meta-ethics, for example, have a stake in matters of color ontology.

Theories of color

In this section I'll describe critically some of the most popular views about the nature of color. This discussion is not meant to be exhaustive, but only to present some of the most popular views in current philosophical discussion, and to lay out some of the most important advantages and disadvantages of these views.

Eliminativism

Color eliminativists believe that, strictly speaking, nothing in the actual world is colored: ripe lemons are not yellow, traffic stoplights are not red, and so on. Of course, eliminativists allow that these objects are perceptually represented as bearing colors: ripe lemons look yellow, traffic stoplights look red, and the like. It is just that, in their view, these perceptual representations are erroneous.

Philosophers have offered several reasons for endorsing color eliminativism. First, one might reject the existence of all properties, and regard color eliminativism as a special case of a more thoroughgoing nominalism (Goodman and van Orman Quine 1947; Goodman 1951). Second, one might accept color eliminativism because it is entailed by the claims that (i) colors are not found among the properties listed by the inventories of the basic physical sciences; and (ii) the only properties we should posit are those that are found among the inventories of the basic physical sciences (Aune 1967: 172). Third, some eliminativists (Hardin 1988; Maund 1995; Pautz unpublished manuscript) have argued that no realist/non-eliminativist account of color properties can both avoid internal difficulties and satisfy certain intuitively and empirically motivated constraints about what colors must be.

Eliminativism is sometimes associated with the mentalist view that internal mental items (e.g., sense-data), rather than ordinary fruit, lights, and the like, are the true bearers of colors. Although it is true that mentalism and eliminativism are in some ways alike (e.g., they agree in treating the ordinary perceptual representation of colors of external objects as erroneous projections), they are in fact incompatible (at least as formulated above), given the assumption that the mental items the mentalist takes to exemplify colors are actual. For if so, then the mentalist is committed to saying that the colors are exemplified by actual individuals, thereby denying eliminativism.

(It should also be noted that, on the above formulation, eliminativism about color leaves open that colors are exemplified by non-actual objects. Eliminativists who adopt this line will claim that colors are *bona fide* properties that are not exemplified, but might have been.)

The most pressing objection against color eliminativism, to my mind, is that it convicts ordinary perception of an extremely widespread error, and so is obviously a deeply revisionary view. Now, eliminativists might respond to this objection by noting that deep revisions are sometimes appropriate – especially if, as eliminativists maintain, what initially seemed to be less revisionary alternatives turn out, on inspection, to have exorbitant costs of their own. However, it seems to me that this strategy of response, while reasonable as far as it goes, leaves the wouldbe eliminativist in a fairly weak dialectical position. For it amounts to admitting that eliminativism should only be adopted at such time as all other alternatives are decisively shown to be unacceptable – it makes eliminativism a position of last resort. And since refutations in philosophy are almost never decisive, this means that we may have to wait an awfully long time to be in a position to accept eliminativism.

Dispositionalism

Dispositionalism is a family of views of color ontology according to which colors are dispositions to have certain effects on the visual systems of certain perceivers in certain conditions. This core claim, however, requires considerable clarification: to fill out her view, the dispositionalist needs to say more about which perceivers, which circumstances, and exactly which effects in those perceivers in those circumstances, she has in mind. The many species of dispositionalism can be distinguished by the ways they fill in those blanks. For example, one canonical form of dispositionalism holds that red is the disposition to cause red sensations (/to look red) to normal observers in normal circumstances. Versions of dispositionalism have been ascribed (controversially) to modern philosophers such as Galileo, Boyle, Newton, and Locke. More recent defenders of dispositionalism include McGinn (1983); Peacocke (1984); Johnston (1992).[1]

One reason for taking dispositionalism seriously as a color ontology comes from the observation that the objects we take to exemplify colors do, uncontroversially, exemplify dispositions to look colored to perceivers – e.g., red ripe tomatoes are uncontroversial bearers of the disposition to look red to normal trichromatic observers (say, under uniform daylight illumination and viewed at a distance of one meter).

One particularly simple and attractive way of explaining the extensional overlap of colors and dispositions to look colored is to identify the two, thereby endorsing dispositionalism.

A second motivation for dispositionalism is that the view is well-suited to explain interpersonal and intrapersonal perceptual variation in respect of color, which turns out to be widespread (this motivation can be found in the writings of Galileo and Boyle, among others; for more recent versions, see McGinn (1983); Cohen (2004)). For instance, consider that an unilluminated region of the television looks greyish when the television is off, but dark black (even though illuminated in exactly the same way) when it falls within the part of the screen on which the villain's hat is represented. This single region of the screen, though locally qualitatively identical in the two viewing conditions, looks grey in one viewing condition and black in another. Partly because neither of these viewing conditions has a plausible claim to be more naturalistic than the other, it has seemed to some that there is no principled reason for claiming that the way it looks in either viewing condition is a veridical representation of its color at the expense of the other. One could instead claim that *neither* representation is veridical; but this strategy, suitably generalized to cover all cases of perceptual variation, would entail the counterintuitive eliminativist conclusion that no objects bear the colors they look to have. But if it is implausible both to side with one representation at the expense of the other and to reject both of them, then the only option left is to claim that both are correct – that the television region has one color in one circumstance, and a different color in a different circumstance.

There are analogous cases of perceptual variation that turn on variation between perceivers. Thus, consider that a chip can look blue without looking at all greenish to one observer but bluish green to another, even if both observers pass all the standard psychophysical tests for normal color vision. As before, rejecting both representations of the chip's color leads quickly to eliminativism, while there don't seem to be principled, nonarbitrary reasons for favoring one representation at the expense of the other. Consequently, many have thought, the best theory of color should sustain the verdict that *both* representations are veridical.

These considerations motivate dispositionalism because that theory (or some forms of it) can indeed secure the verdict that both representations are veridical. For example, a dispositionalist can say that the region R of the television screen is grey to a perceiver S_1 in perceptual circumstance C_1 by virtue of being disposed to look grey to S_1 in C_1, and compatibly that it is black to perceiver S_2 in circumstance C_2 by virtue of being disposed to look black to S_2 in C_2. Likewise the problematic chip can bear the disposition to look blue but not greenish to S_1 in C_1 while simultaneously and compatibly exemplifying the disposition to look bluish green to S_2 in C_2; consequently, if these dispositions are identical to (distinct) colors, as per dispositionalism, then the chip can exemplify both of them simultaneously, and thereby make true both of the representations of its color (viz., the way the chip looks to S_1, the way it looks to S_2).

Notwithstanding its advantages, dispositionalism faces a number of challenges.

A first difficulty is aimed at only some forms of the view – those that invoke the notion of a normal/standard observer or a normal/standard circumstance in filling out the core dispositionalist claim given above. The problem here is that there do not appear to be anything like principled specifications of normal/standard observers or circumstances (Hardin 1988); in particular, the various standards in psychophysics and industrial applications (presumably our best motivated candidates) seem to have been chosen for mathematical convenience or industrial standardization, but are (from a metaphysical point of view) arbitrary. But without a principled way of unpacking the notions of normal/standard observer and normal/standard circumstance, it would seem hard to understand forms of dispositionalism that invoke these notions as making any substantive claim at all.

A second difficulty for dispositionalism is that it threatens to preclude distinct individuals (or even time slices of one individual) from ascribing the same color to an object. For example, suppose that the chip looks blue but not greenish to you in C_1, but my visual system attributes to the chip a color of the form *c* to me in C_2. Unless me = you and $C_1 = C_2$, it would seem that the colors attributed on these two occasions will be necessarily distinct, and thereby prevents distinct individuals (/time slices of one individual) from perceiving the single color. It also clearly threatens the possibility of our agreeing about the colors of objects (compare the following: if you are in Vancouver and I am in New York, then even if we both utter the sentence "it is raining here," we are not agreeing about the weather in any place). It also threatens the possibility of our disagreeing about colors, since it seems to be a presupposition of such disagreement that the property you ascribe is incompatible with that I ascribe (compare the following: if you utter "it is raining here" while in Vancouver and I utter "it is not raining here" while in New York, we do not thereby manifest disagreement about the weather in any place). A related difficulty concerns the dispositionalist's treatment of errors of color perception; briefly, the worry is that the very inclusiveness that undergirds the dispositionalist's response to perceptual variation will prevent her from saying that any representation of *x*'s color is erroneous (on this topic, see Cohen 2007).

A third objection against dispositionalism involves the accusation that the view is, when combined with popular views about sensory experience, viciously circular. Recall that, for dispositionalists, the definiens used to understand color properties include mention of color experiences; thus, *red* is identified with (as it might be) the disposition to look red to normal observers in normal conditions of observation. How should we understand the expression "looks red" that occurs on the right hand side here? One response, advocated by Peacocke (1984), is to deny that "red" is a semantically significant constituent of that expression (thereby avoiding regress), and instead to maintain that the expression "looks red" picks out a state of undergoing a particular kind of sense-datum. Many philosophers, however, reject a sense-datum understanding of visual experience, and instead favor the so-called intentionalist/representationalist view that something's looking red just is that thing's being visually represented as red (Harman 1990; Tye 1995; Dretske 1995). But this treatment has the consequence that "red" occurs in an unreduced form on the right hand side of the dispositionalist's account of *red*. And many have claimed that this regress is a fatal flaw of dispositionalism (see Boghossian and Velleman [1989]; for responses, see Lewis 1997; McLaughlin 2003).

A final objection against dispositionalism urges that the view does violence to ordinary color phenomenology – that colors just do not look to be relational/dispositional (Boghossian and Velleman 1989; McGinn 1996). In response, dispositionalists have sometimes maintained that colors do in fact look to be dispositional – given an appropriate understanding of what it would mean for a property to look dispositional (McDowell 1985; Levin 2000).

Physicalism

Color physicalism is best understood as a kind of identity theory of color analogous to identity theories familiar from philosophy of mind; it says that colors are identical to particular (physically or functionally specifiable) kinds.[2] Although earlier physicalists tended to identify colors with microphysical constitutions (Armstrong 1968; Smart 1975), more recent physicalists have tended to prefer to identify colors with (classes of) reflectance functions – i.e., functions that represent surfaces' dispositions to reflect differing percentages of the incident light of different wavelengths. The older sort of color physicalism can be thought of as a form of type-physicalism (/type-identity theory) about color, while the newer sort can be regarded as a form of token-physicalism (/token-identity theory) about color.[3]

Proponents of color physicalism sometimes motivate the view by pointing to its consonance with the broadly physicalist and reductionist ideas in the current philosophical zeitgeist. Whether one finds this motivation compelling will depend not only on one's sympathy for the zeitgeist but also on one's view of how competing views fare on this dimension (see note 2). A more specific consideration adduced on behalf of physicalism concerns the phenomenon of color constancy, which we might characterize this way: subjects will characterize a ripe tomato as red when viewed under a variety of illuminants (say, under direct noontime sunlight and under indoor fluorescent light), although the character of the light reaching their eyes from that tomato is markedly different in the two conditions. Color physicalists often take this and similar cases as justifying the claim that objects (appear to) maintain their colors under different illuminants, and therefore that we should prefer a theory, such as color physicalism, that vindicates this claim by making colors observer-independent, conditions-independent properties of objects (see, for example, Tye 2000: 147– 8; Hilbert 1987: 65; Byrne and Hilbert 2003: 9; but see Cohen 2007; Thompson 2006).

Color physicalism has been criticized for failing to do justice to the facts about perceptual variation discussed the section "Dispositionalism," above. Consider again the chip that looks blue but not greenish to you, while looking bluish green to me. If its color is, as per physicalism, determined by which observer-independent, circumstance-independent physical kind the chip exemplifies, then it would seem to follow that at most one of the competing representations of its colors (that in your head, that in mine) is veridical. But what could make it the case that one of them is veridical rather than the other?

Color physicalists have sometimes answered: what makes one (yours, say) veridical at the expense of another (mine, say) is that yours represents the chip as being blue but not greenish *and the chip is blue but not greenish*, whereas mine represents the chip as being bluish green *and the chip is not bluish green* (Byrne and Hilbert 2003: 17; Byrne and Tye 2006: 11; Tye 2006: 3). In support of this answer, physicalists sometimes offer an analogy concerning representational variation with respect to shape. Thus, although a figure might look circular when viewed from angle θ_1 and elliptical when viewed from angle θ_2, at most one of these visual representations is veridical: the representation in θ_1 is veridical (say) insofar as it represents the figure as being circular, *and the figure is circular*.

But this response is unconvincing. It is of course correct that what *would* make one representation *R* of the chip veridical at the expense of others would be that (i) *R* represents the chip as being some particular color that the others do not; and (ii) that the chip in fact exemplifies the color that *R* represents it as having but does not exemplify the color that the others represent it as having – that two-part condition correctly unpacks what it is for a representation to be veridical at the expense of other representations. But laying out this condition does not answer the question asked; instead it pushes that question back a step. For in asking what makes it the case that one representation is veridical at the expense of the others, the critic is precisely asking what makes it the case that that two-part condition is satisfied by at most one representation, as the physicalist maintains. And the response we are considering does nothing to answer that question. Moreover, the analogy with shape properties is questionable (indeed, it seems to presuppose something like a physicalist understanding of color). A reason for doubting that analogy is that, in the shape case, the properties at issue have (abstract) essences – essences that comprise the subject matter of plane geometry – that serve as a representation independent standard for veridicality of particular representations. In contrast, in the color case, we seem not to be committed to the existence of an (abstract or natural) essence that would adjudicate between competing representations of objects' colors. (This explains why, among other things, the range of inductive causal generalizations we are willing to make about red things seems far smaller than the corresponding range for circular things.)

In short, the physicalist's commitment to a single, uniquely veridical variant in all cases of perceptual variation with respect to color is hard to accept, and physicalists' attempts to make this commitment seem more palatable have been (in my view) unpersuasive.

A second objection to color physicalism, due originally to Hardin (1988), concerns its ability to respect certain structural features of the colors. For example, the colors stand in certain similarity and exclusion relations (red is more similar to orange than it is to green, no shade of blue is a shade of yellow). Moreover, there are exactly four chromatic colors (yellow, blue, red, green) that have shades that seem to be perceptually unmixed, or "unique," while the shades of all other colors are such that they appear perceptually mixed, or "binary" (every shade of orange looks reddish and yellowish, every shade of purple looks reddish and bluish, etc.). The objection we are now considering holds that, as the physicalist construes them, there is no obvious explanation for these structural properties of the colors: for example, there is no obvious similarity metric defined over classes of reflectance functions that would make the class the physicalist identifies with red more proximate to that associated with orange than it is to that associated with green (for responses and evaluation of this argument, see Cohen 2003; Byrne 2003; Pautz 2006).

Primitivism

Color primitivism amounts to a kind of quietism about color. The primitivist maintains that colors are irreducible in the sense that there are no true and informative type-identities of the form $\ulcorner C = P \urcorner$, where $\ulcorner C \urcorner$ is the name of a color and $\ulcorner P \urcorner$ picks out a property in terms that don't include color vocabulary (but might include physical, functional, phenomenal, or intentional vocabulary). Primitivists think that colors are genuine properties, but that the irreducibility of these properties makes them primitive, or *sui generis*. In recent years, color primitivism has grown in popularity; some form of the view is endorsed by Westphal (1987, 2005), Campbell (1993), Yablo (1995), McGinn (1996), Watkins (2002, 2005), Johnston (forthcoming), and (arguably) Stroud (2000). Primitivism is ordinarily counted a form of realism about color, but it need not be. For, just as there can be eliminativists who think that colors are, say, physical types that might be but are not in fact exemplified, there can be eliminativists who think that colors are primitive properties that might be but are not in fact exemplified.

Of course, primitivists deny that colors are identical to the physical types and dispositions with which physicalists and dispositionalists claim they are identical; but the primitivist is free to hold that colors are universally correlated with these sorts of properties. Color primitivists who think there is such a correlation, then, are not denying the existence or exemplification of the physical types or dispositions that their opponents take to be identical to colors. Rather, they are convinced (perhaps by some of the objections given above against these views) that such properties cannot be identified with the colors, and therefore that the colors must be distinct (even if universally correlated). The most frequently invoked motivation offered in support of color primitivism is an argument from the failure of other views. After showing the problems with these other views, primitivism is then held out as a way of endorsing realism about color (but see above) without falling victim to the faults that plague other theories.

Unfortunately, like the corresponding argument offered in support of eliminativism (see the section on "Eliminativism," above), the argument for primitivism from the failure of alternatives leaves the primitivist in a relatively weak dialectical position, for it essentially begins by conceding that primitivism is a position of last resort. Moreover, like all arguments by elimination, this argument is only as good as the weakest of the refutations of which it makes use. As before, this is a serious dialectical weakness, given the non-decisive quality of philosophical argumentation.

Moreover, critics have objected that primitivism is *ad hoc*. For, while primitivism's *sui generis* colors are surely coherent, it is suspiciously easy (i.e., unconstrained) to construe some property/properties as *sui generis* when we are otherwise unable to understand them. For example, this strategy seems no less applicable to such properties as *witch* or *phlogiston* (about which, presumably, eliminativism is a more appropriate response) or for that matter heat at a time prior to the emergence of thermodynamics (about which the correct response, though unknown at the time, turned out to be some kind of reductive physicalism). But if primitivism would have led to erroneous ontological verdicts in these cases, we should be wary of embracing it in the case of color.

Finally, Byrne and Hilbert (2006) have objected to color primitivism on the basis of considerations about color vision in nonhuman animals. Their objection builds on the observation that goldfish can discriminate surfaces that human beings fail to discriminate based on differences in those surfaces' dispositions to reflect light in the near ultraviolet range (this light falls out of the range to which human cones are sensitive). The natural (and common in comparative color science) description of the situation is that, in so discriminating, goldfish are responding to the surfaces' colors. For primitivism makes no room for any (reductive) explanation of what counts as a color, but can only rely on the discriminations of human subjects (with respect to which the surfaces are exactly alike). Thus, Byrne and Hilbert allege, color primitivism makes unavailable the best descriptions of the visual behavior of nonhuman animals.

Conclusion

Color has attracted significant and growing attention from philosophers in recent years. Moreover, the empirical and philosophical sophistication of work in this area has increased rapidly in recent years. While the present essay comes nowhere near exhausting the territory, I hope it provides a useful point of entry into philosophical controversies about color.

Notes

1. In recent years several philosophers have attempted, in different ways, to retain some of the advantages of dispositionalism, while rejecting (or at least remaining agnostic about) the specific claim that colors are identical to dispositions to affect perceivers. See, for example, Jackson and Pargetter (1987), Lewis (1997), McLaughlin (2003), Cohen (2004), and Matthen (2005).
2. It should be noted that there is nothing particularly more or less physicalist about color physicalism than other views; dispositionalism and primitivism, for example, are straightforwardly compatible with the claim that colors are physical (they can be regarded as token-identity theories of color), and even an eliminativist could maintain that colors are physical but uninstantiated by actual objects. Moreover, one who held that colors are type-identical with nonphysical kinds might reasonably be thought of as sharing the most important theoretical commitments with some color physicalists (whether or not to apply this label to such a view strikes me as more or less an unimportant terminological matter). The label "physicalism," then, is unfortunate and potentially misleading, but by now (lamentably) well-entrenched.
3. Here I adopt the usual assumption that functional types are not physical types.

References

Armstrong, D. (1968) *A Materialist Theory of the Mind*, London: Routledge.

Aune, B. (1967) *Knowledge, Mind, and Nature*, New York: Random House.

Backhaus, W. G. K., Gliegl, R., and Werner, J. S. (eds) (1998) *Color Vision: Perspectives from Different Disciplines*, Berlin: Walter de Gruyter.

Boghossian, P. A., and Velleman, J. D. (1989) "Colour as a Secondary Quality," *Mind* 98: 81–103; repr. Byrne and Hilbert (1997b): 81–103.

—— (1991) "Physicalist Theories of Color," *Philosophical Review* 100: 67–106.

Byrne, A. (2003) "Color and Similarity," *Philosophy and Phenomenological Research* 66: 641–65.

Byrne, A., and Hilbert, D. R. (1997a) "Colors and Reflectances," in A. Byrne and D. R. Hilbert (eds), *Readings on Color*, vol. 1: *The Philosophy of Color*, Cambridge, MA: MIT Press, pp. 263–88.

—— (eds) (1997b) *Readings on Color*, vol. 1: *The Philosophy of Color*, Cambridge, MA: MIT Press.

—— (1997c) *Readings on Color*, vol. 2: *The Science of Color*, Cambridge, MA: MIT Press.

—— (2003) "Color Realism and Color Science," *Behavioral and Brain Sciences* 26, no. 1: 3–64.

—— (2006) "Color Primitivism," in R. Schumacher (ed.), *Perception and Status of Secondary Qualities*, Dordrecht: Kluwer.

Byrne, A., and Tye, M. (2006) "Qualia Ain't in the Head," *Nous* 40: 241–55.

Campbell, J. (1993) "A Simple View of Color," in J. Haldane and C. Wright (eds), *Reality, Representation, and Projection*, New York: Oxford University Press; repr. Byrne and Hilbert (1997b): 177–90.

Cohen, J. (2003) "On the Structural Properties of the Colors," *Australasian Journal of Philosophy* 81, no. 1: 78–95.

—— (2004) "Color Properties and Color Ascriptions: A Relationalist Manifesto," *Philosophical Review* 113, no. 4: 451–506.

—— (2007) "A Relationalist's Guide to Error about Color Perception," *Nous* 41: 335–53.

—— (2008) "Color Constancy as Counterfactual," *Australasian Journal of Philosophy* 86: 61–92.

Dretske, F. (1995) *Naturalizing the Mind*, Cambridge, MA: MIT Press; originally delivered as the 1994 Jean Nicod Lectures.

Gegenfurtner, K. R., and Sharpe, L. T. (eds) (1999) *Color Vision: From Genes to Perception*, Cambridge: Cambridge University Press.

Goodman, N. (1951) *The Structure of Appearance*, Cambridge, MA: Harvard University Press.

Goodman, N., and van Orman Quine, W. (1947) "Steps toward a Constructive Nominalism," *Journal of Symbolic Logic* 12: 105–122.

Hardin, C. L. (1988) *Color for Philosophers: Unweaving the Rainbow*, Indianapolis: Hackett.

Harman, G. (1990) *The Intrinsic Quality of Experience*, Atascerdo, CA: Ridgeview Publishing, vol. 4: 31–52.

Hilbert, D. R. (1987) *Color and Color Perception: A Study in Anthropocentric Realism*, Stanford, CA: Center for the Study of Language and Information.

Hume, D. (1978 [1739]) *A Treatise of Human Nature*, ed. L. A. Selby-Bigge, Oxford: Clarendon Press.

Jackson, F., and Pargetter, R. (1987) "An Objectivist's Guide to Subjectivism about Color," *Revue Internationale de Philosophie* 160: 127–41; repr. Byrne and Hilbert (1997b): 67–79.

Johnston, M. (1992) "How to Speak of the Colors," *Philosophical Studies* 68: 221–63; repr. Byrne and Hilbert (1997b): 137–76.

—— (forthcoming) *The Manifest*, manuscript, Princeton University.

Levin, J. (2000) "Dispositional Theories of Color and the Claims of Common Sense," *Philosophical Studies* 100: 151–74.

Lewis, D. (1997) "Naming the Colors," *Australasian Journal of Philosophy* 75, no. 3: 325–42.

Matthen, M. (2005) *Seeing, Doing, and Knowing: A Philosophical Theory of Sense Perception*, Oxford: Oxford University Press.

Maund, B. (1995) *Colours: Their Nature and Representation*, New York: Cambridge University Press.

McDowell, J. (1985) "Values and Secondary Qualities," T. Honderich (ed.), *Morality and Objectivity: A Tribute to J. L. Mackie*, London: Routledge & Kegan Paul, pp. 110–29.

McGinn, C. (1983) *The Subjective View: Secondary Qualities and Indexical Thoughts*, Oxford: Oxford University Press.

—— (1996) "Another Look at Color," *Journal of Philosophy* 93, no. 11: 537–53.
McLaughlin, B. (2003) "The Place of Color in Nature," in R. Mausfeld and D. Heyer (eds) *Colour Perception: Mind and the Physical World*, New York: Oxford University Press, pp. 475–502.
Pautz, A. (2006). "Can the Physicalist Explain Colour Structure in terms of Colour Experience?" *Australasian Journal of Philosophy* 84: 535–64.
—— Pautz, A. "Colour Eliminativism," Unpublished Manuscript.
Peacocke, C. (1984) "Colour Concepts and Colour Experiences," *Synthese* 58, no. 3: 365–81; repr. Rosenthal (1991): 408–16.
Rosenthal, D. (1991) *The Nature of Mind*, New York: Oxford University Press.
Smart, J. J. C. (1975) "On Some Criticisms of a Physicalist Theory of Colors," in C. Cheng (ed.), *Philosophical Aspects of the Mind-Body Problem*, Honolulu: University Press of Hawaii; repr. Byrne and Hilbert (1997b): 1–10.
Stroud, B. (2000) *The Quest for Reality: Subjectivism and the Metaphysics of Colour*, New York: Oxford University Press.
Thompson, B. (2006) "Colour Constancy and Russellian Representationalism," *Australasian Journal of Philosophy* 84, no. 1: 75–94.
Tye, M. (1995) *Ten Problems of Consciousness: A Representational Theory of the Phenomenal Mind*, Cambridge, MA: MIT Press.
—— (2000) *Consciousness, Color, and Content*, Cambridge, MA: MIT Press.
—— (2006) "The Puzzle of True Blue," *Analysis* 66: 173–8.
Watkins, M. (2002) *Rediscovering Colors: A Study in Pollyanna Realism*, Boston: Dordrecht.
Watkins, M. (2005) "Seeing Red: The Metaphysics of Colour without the Physics," *Australasian Journal of Philosophy* 83, no. 1: 33–52.
Westphal, J. (1987) *Colour: Some Philosophical Problems from Wittgenstein*, Oxford: Blackwell.
—— (2005) "Conflicting Appearances, Necessity and the Irreducibility of Propositions about Colours," *Proceedings of the Aristotelian Society* 105, no. 2: 235–51.
Yablo, S. (1995) "Singling Out Properties," *Philosophical Perspectives* 9: 477–502.

Further reading

While there are many useful works that might be consulted by interested readers, here I list a few useful resources for further reading: C. L. Hardin, *Color for Philosophers: Unweaving the Rainbow* (Indianapolis: Hackett, 1988) is often credited with reigniting philosophical interest in color, partly by showing how empirical color science could usefully constrain debates about the nature of color. Three other general works on color and perception are A. Byrne and D. R. Hilbert, "Color Realism and Color Science," *Behavioral and Brain Sciences* 26, no. 1 (2003): 3–64; Evan Thompson's *Colour Vision: A Study in Cognitive Science and the Philosophy of Science* (London: Routledge, 1995); and M. Matthen, *Seeing, Doing, and Knowing: A Philosophical Theory of Sense Perception* (Oxford: Oxford University Press, 2005).

Byrne and Hilbert's two-volume *Readings on Color* (Cambridge, MA: MIT Press, 1997) anthologizes some of the classic philosophical and scientific work on color that had appeared prior to its publication. Their introductions to the volumes are especially useful in setting out the terms of debate and explaining the relationships between issues. Other excellent and reasonably recent anthologies on color science include W. G. K. Backhaus, R. Gliegl, and J. S. Werner (eds) *Color Vision: Perspectives from Different Disciplines* (Berlin: Walter de Gruyter, 1998), and K. R. Gegenfurtner and L. T. Sharpe (eds) *Color Vision: From Genes to Perception* (Cambridge: Cambridge University Press, 1999).

40
AUDITION

Casey O'Callaghan

Introduction

Vision dominates philosophical theorizing about perception, experience, and the mind. The psychology and cognitive science of vision have captivated philosophers, and other modalities of sensation and perception have received little consideration. Increasingly, however, philosophers recognize the drawbacks of this unbalanced approach, and interest recently has grown in providing an account of audition and its objects. The philosophical study of audition promises to enrich work on the nature and character of perceptual experience since hearing provides a distinctive variety of awareness whose features distinguish it from vision. Hearing poses challenging puzzles for any comprehensive, general theory of perception. In addition, a fertile and growing empirical literature exists to inform philosophical work. Attention to theoretical issues and experimental results in the psychology of audition raises fresh questions about the nature of sounds, and hearing and impacts longstanding philosophical debates about perceptual experience. I wish in this essay to provide the theoretical and psychological framework to the philosophy of sounds and audition. Four fruitful areas deserve attention: auditory scene analysis and the nature of sounds; spatial hearing; the audible qualities; and cross-modal interactions.

Auditory scene analysis

We hear many things. When walking the dog, you might hear the sounds of cars passing, a plane overhead, your own footsteps, and the rattle of metal tags. Among the things we hear are sounds. Sounds are the immediate objects of auditory perception in the harmless sense that whatever else you hear, you hear it in virtue of hearing a sound. Though you might hear an ambulance or a collision, you hear it by or in hearing its sound. Naturally, the philosophical investigation of audition largely concerns the perception of sounds. What, then, are the natures of the sounds we hear?

Consider the central task of audition. From complex patterns of pressure variation at your two eardrums, you are able to discern and listen to a variety of sounds in your environment. I now hear the sound of an unmuffled truck passing on the street behind me, the sound of music from speakers on my bookshelf, a voice calling from down the hall, and the sound of a vacuum running next door. Hearing furnishes information about what is around you, where it is located, what is happening, and how long it lasts (see Gaver 1993). It does so through your awareness of numerically distinct sounds that unfold over time. The proximal stimulus to audition, however, involves oscillations of two membranes within your ears. The mechanical vibrations of the eardrums hold complex information about your surroundings. Bregman (1990) likens the problem of extracting information about the sounds one's environment contains from wave oscillations, which he calls the problem of *auditory scene analysis*, to determining the number, type, and location of boats on a lake just by observing the motions of two handkerchiefs suspended into narrow channels dug at the lake's edge. The central problem of auditory perception involves the auditory system's capacity to discern from complex wave information the number, qualities, location, and duration of sounds and sources in one's environment. On the basis of pressure variations at your ears, you gain access to an abundantly detailed world of sounds, things, and happenings.

How audition carves a pattern of pressure variations into auditory objects, streams, or percepts is a question for empirical psychology. Criteria proposed include temporal and qualitative continuity, temporal and qualitative proximity, and coincident patterns of change through time (see Bregman 1990). Whatever the details of the mechanisms by which audition organizes the perceptual scene, features of auditory percepts bear upon philosophical characterizations of audition's content and of sounds. Auditory scene analysis constrains a theory of sounds under the assumption that sounds are represented in audition without wholesale illusion.

Philosophy traditionally has counted the sounds, along with the colors, tastes, and smells, among the sensible properties or secondary qualities. Locke, for instance, claims in his *Essay* that sounds, like colors, smells, and tastes, are powers of objects to produce experiences in sensing subjects (Bk 2, ch. 8, sec. 14). Sounds, on this historically prevalent understanding, are *properties* or attributes either of sounding bodies or of a medium such as air, water, or helium. Pasnau (1999) revives an account according to which sounds are properties. Pasnau argues that sounds are identical with or supervene upon the physical vibrations of objects and bodies. Pasnau ascribes sounds to what we ordinarily count as the sources of sounds. As such, Pasnau's property view differs from the commonplace view that sounds exist within a medium in wave-like motion.

Perhaps the most important constraint on a theory of sounds stems from the fact that auditory scene analysis is the task of segregating sensory information into discrete, coherent auditory *streams* (see Bregman 1990). The immediate objects of auditory experience are dynamic streams that have duration and extend through time. The need to accommodate the temporal characteristics of auditory streams poses problems for those who identify sounds with properties of either the source or the medium.

Auditory streams are characterized by audible qualities such as pitch, timbre, and loudness, and may change a great deal over time while remaining the numerically same stream. Sounds are treated in audition as the bearers of audible qualities – as the particulars that ground audible quality grouping and binding. If sounds are the primary particulars audition tracks, and are characterized in terms of their own range of attributes, sounds themselves are not mere dimensions of similarity among other particulars. Sounds, then, are not properties. Furthermore, since a sound might start out loud and high-pitched and end up soft and low-pitched, sounds persist through changes to their audible attributes through time. Qualities, however, do not survive change in this way. The color of the wall does not survive the painting. The circularity does not survive the squaring. The sweet smell of apples does not survive the rotting. Auditory scene analysis supports the view that sounds are particulars that bear pitch, timbre, and loudness and survive qualitative change.

The predominant, science-inspired conception of sounds nonetheless holds that sounds are traveling waves. Sounds, that is, are, or depend upon, longitudinal pressure waves that propagate through the medium surrounding a vibrating object or interacting bodies (see, e.g., Perkins 1983; Armstrong 1961: 147–8). Sounds, according to a wave-based theory, travel at speeds determined by the density and elasticity of the medium from their sources outward toward perceiving subjects.

What is entailed by saying that audition represents waves is somewhat obscure, and there are several interpretations of what one is committed to in saying that sounds are identical with or depend upon waves. One view of sounds construed as waves holds that sounds are properties or attributes of the medium. Such a view suffers from the weaknesses of other property views. A psychologically plausible wave-based conception requires that sounds are particulars that survive change and bear audible qualities.

Perhaps surprisingly, some plausibility attends thinking that sounds are object-like particulars. The wave bundles salient to auditory perception have spatial boundaries, travel through the medium from source to subject, and are characterized by physical properties, such as frequency and amplitude, that determine pitch, timbre, loudness, and other audible qualities. Such object-like particulars might therefore bear audible qualities, survive change, stand in causal relationships to sound sources, and exist in space and time. Nonetheless, sounds do not inhabit time in the way that objects do. Sounds survive changes to their attributes as objects do, but also possess duration essentially. Sounds do not merely last through time; sounds are creatures of time. The identities of many common sounds, such as spoken words and birds' calls are tied to a pattern of changes through time. In contrast to objects, which intuitively are wholly present at each moment at which they exist, a sound must unfold over time. Hearing one syllable does not suffice to hear the sound of the word. A momentary sound is as intelligible as a point-sized plaid particular.

Some suggest, therefore, that sounds are best understood as event-like particulars (Casati and Dokic 1994, 2005; Scruton 1997, 2009; O'Callaghan 2007). Sounds *happen*, *occur*, or *take place* in an environment populated with everyday objects and events. Sounds occupy time and have durations. Sounds figure in causal transactions. Construing sounds as events caused by but independent from their sources meets the constraints upon a theory of sounds and their perception that are imposed by auditory scene analysis.

Spatial hearing

Hearing provides information not just about the identities and characteristics of sounds and sources in your environment, but also about their locations. When you listen to the sounds around you, you learn something about where those sounds and their sources stand in relation to yourself. You learn whether the unmuffled truck travels from left to right or from right to left. You learn which speaker has ceased to produce sound, and whether the voice comes from up or downstairs. Audition, like vision, but probably unlike olfaction and gustation, is a spatial perceptual modality. Audible location is one key criterion for segregating sounds during auditory scene analysis (see Bregman 1990; Blauert 1997; Best et al. 2006).

The spatial resolution limit of audition, however, lags that of vision by nearly two orders of magnitude. Though vision's directional accuracy approaches less than 1′ (minute) of arc, hearing is nevertheless capable of discriminating directional changes of roughly 1° of arc (Blauert 1997: 38–9). Hearing provides strikingly useful information about the direction of audible events on the basis of binaural cues that stem primarily from differences in wave onset time, amplitude, and phase (see Blauert 1997; Colburn et al. 2006).

Locational information furnished in audition is not limited to direction. Hearing also represents distance to sounds and sources in one's surroundings (see Blauert 1997). Thanks to auditory cues that include amplitude, timing of secondary reverberations, and transformations (*head-related transfer functions*, or HRTFs), due to the asymmetries of the head and pinnae (outer ears), you are able to discern in hearing whether the truck is nearby or far away, and whether the voice comes from the next room or down the hall. Sounds seem in ordinary hearing to come from outside the head, or to be *externalized* (see Hartmann and Wittenberg 1996). Headphone listening, in contrast, involves hearing sounds that seem to come from somewhere between the two ears. Hearing, in a wide range of common circumstances, therefore represents location in three-dimensional egocentric space.

Strong indications suggest that spatial audition presents sounds not as traveling or propagating through the environment as do sound waves, but as having stationary, distal locations. Though a sound might seem more diffuse in one's surroundings than its source appears, and though under certain conditions sounds seem to come from all around, as in night clubs with loud bass, a sound seems to travel toward you only when its source does. Consider how odd it would be to hear a sound to emerge from its source and then speed through the air toward your head as if it were an auditory missile. It would be equally odd to hear a sound emerge from its source like a water wave and subsequently wash through the air, into your ears, around your head, and past you. The point is that sounds do not, auditorily, seem to be located where the waves are. The locations of sounds you hear are connected with the locations of their sources in the environment. Since you hear sound sources only in virtue of hearing their sounds, hearing the location of a sound source depends upon locational information about the sound.

If this phenomenological claim about the audible locations of sounds is correct, then views according to which sounds are identical with, or supervene upon, sound waves must attribute systematic and pervasive illusion with respect to the experienced locations of sounds. Furthermore, if sounds indeed travel as do pressure waves, the apparent *temporal* characteristics that one experiences sounds to possess, including duration and patterns of change through time, are mere projections of temporal aspects of one's experience of the *spatially* extended wave bundle that passes. If sounds are waves, sounds themselves lack the durations we experience them to possess. A desire to capture the phenomenology of spatial audition, as well as its roles in acting upon and forming beliefs about the locations of things and events in one's environment, motivates several philosophers to propose that sounds are in fact located at or near their sources (Pasnau 1999; Casati and Dokic 2005; O'Callaghan 2007).

Philosophers on the whole, nonetheless, have been skeptical about the spatial characteristics of audition. Malpas (1965) claims that one could not, strictly speaking, discover the location of a sound, because sounds have no places. Nudds (2001, 2009) argues that sounds are not experienced as standing in any relation to the space they may in fact occupy. O'Shaughnessy (2002) argues that sounds never are heard to be at any place. In perhaps the most famous philosophical discussion of sounds, P. F. Strawson (1959: Ch. 2) claims that an exclusively auditory experience, unlike an analogous visual experience, would be entirely non-spatial. Hearing, he claims, unlike vision and tactile-kinesthetic experience, is not an intrinsically spatial perceptual modality.

The results of empirical research make such skepticism surprising. But Strawson, at least, does not wish to deny that under ordinary circumstances one might hear the locations of things, or even the locations of sounds, on the strength of audition. Rather, he claims, audition's spatial content depends upon that of another intrinsically spatial modality, such as vision or tactile-kinesthetic experience. Audition on its own would lack the resources to represent space. But the phrase "intrinsically spatial" is tendentious, and it is not clear that the exclusively auditory experience can be understood in a way that distinguishes audition from vision with respect to the capacity for spatial experience.

Suppose Strawson's claim is that a subject who enjoyed only auditory experiences without visual or tactile-kinesthetic ones would fail to experience space, while a subject who enjoyed only visual or tactile-kinesthetic experiences would experience space. That appears false. Even the most rudimentary auditory experiences furnish the materials for an experience with spatial attributes. Consider hearing sounds alternate between two earphones, or sounds projected from random directions, or a sound that changes direction. Research on neurophysiological representation of space supports the view that auditory spatial experience develops even in absence of vision (see Carr 2002). Perhaps no single perceptual modality on its own could provide an experience of space (see, e.g., Evans 1982; Noë 2004), but that strike is not exclusive to audition.

One could, however, enjoy a minimal or rudimentary experience that counts as auditory, but which is not clearly spatial. This seems possible. Suppose you hear a qualitatively uniform field in which sound seems to be all around. Imagine hearing just an invariant sinusoidal tone presented with no binaural directional or distance cues.

Such an experience, perhaps, would not provide the materials for spatial concepts. But, plausibly, the same holds for visual and tactile-kinesthetic experience. Consider the visual experience of a uniform gray Ganzfeld, or the tactile experience of being immersed in the warm bath of a buoyancy-neutral sensory deprivation tank. Such experiences certainly count as minimal visual, tactile, and kinesthetic experiences, but, just as plausibly, do not count as spatial experiences.

Strawson's contention might amount simply to the claim that sounds themselves are not intrinsically spatial, or have no spatial characteristics intrinsically (see Nudds [2001] for discussion). Perhaps one could not enjoy a spatial but exclusively auditory experience because the proper objects of audition, sounds, have no intrinsic features that involve space. The objects of vision – colors and shapes – nonetheless are intrinsically spatial.

Perhaps the audible qualities of sounds, in contrast to the visual qualities of color and shape, or the tactile and kinesthetic qualities of texture, solidity, and bodily arrangement, are not intrinsically spatial qualities. Even if one might conceive of pitch and loudness without deploying spatial notions, perhaps one could not do the same for color or texture. One certainly could not do so for shape or arrangement. Though plausible, this does not debunk the idea that audition, even in isolation, is spatial. Unless pitch, loudness, and timbre exhaust the intrinsic qualities of sounds and are the sole objects of audition, it implies neither that sounds are not intrinsically spatial nor that one could hear a sound without experiencing space.

The truth in Strawson's observation is that sounds do not auditorily appear with detailed internal spatial characteristics, such as shapes or three-dimensional contours. Since sounds may seem to occupy greater or smaller portions of surrounding space, and some sounds seem point-like and others diffuse, this is best taken as an upshot of audition's resolution or grain.

Severe skepticism, then, appears unwarranted. Auditory perceptual experience constitutes a valuable source of spatial information about one's environment. The vast majority of commonplace auditory experiences are richly spatial, and audition's spatial content does not differ from vision's in requiring spatial experience in another modality. It therefore is plausible to hold that we learn about the spatial arrangement of sound sources by hearing sounds and their audible qualities as located in our surroundings. Sounds might even be intrinsically spatial if the natures of pitch, timbre, and loudness are not exhaustively manifested in experience or if sounds possess further attributes. Skepticism about the spatial characteristics of sounds and audition appears to trade on a particularly insidious form of visuocentrism. It mistakes reduced acuity in a particular modality either for parasitism or for outright incapacity.

Audible qualities

Sounds appear to have pitch, timbre, and loudness. The pitch of a piccolo's notes generally is higher than those from a tuba. Pitch comprises a dimension along which tones fall in a linear ordering according to height. The sound of a cannon generally is louder than that of a dog's bark. Loudness might be described as the volume, quantity, or intensity of a sound. Characterizing timbre is more difficult. Timbre is that attribute in virtue of which sounds that share pitch and loudness might differ in quality or "tone color." Thus, a clarinet and a saxophone playing the same note differ in timbre. Timbre has been described as "the psychoacoustician's multidimensional wastebasket category" (McAdams and Bregman 1979).

Though sounds are not best understood on the model of secondary or sensible qualities, audible attributes of sounds stand as correlates to the hues, tastes, and olfactory qualities. This suggests that familiar accounts of colors and other sensible attributes extend to the audible qualities (see Cohen, "Color," this volume). Pitch, for instance, might be a simple, unanalyzable, primitive property, a disposition to produce certain auditory experiences, or a physical attribute of sounds. What, then, are the constraints on an account of the audible qualities?

Physical science and psychoacoustics have taught that frequency, amplitude, and wave shape determine the audible qualities of a sound (see, e.g., Gelfand 2004). I will focus primarily on pitch since it often is compared with color (but see Handel and Erickson 2003). Though not all sounds have pitch, some pitched sounds have a simple, sinusoidal frequency, and some are complex with sinusoidal constituents at multiple frequencies. Nonetheless, the pitched sounds are those whose sinusoidal constituents, or partials, all are integer multiples of some common *fundamental* frequency. The pitched sounds, that is, all comprise periodic pressure variations that repeat some common motion at a regular interval whose inverse is the fundamental frequency. Thus simple sinusoids and complex waveforms that share fundamental frequency might match in pitch, though they differ in timbre. The phenomenon of the *missing fundamental* demonstrates that a sinusoidal constituent at the fundamental frequency need not be present for a complex sound to match the pitch of another sound, simple or complex, whose fundamental frequency it shares (Helmholtz 1954 [1877]; Schouten 1940).

A philosophical theory of pitch involves an account of the relationship between such physical properties as periodicity or frequency and the pitches of sounds.

A straightforward account is that the pitch of a sound is identical with its periodicity, a physical property we might characterize in terms of fundamental frequency. This account captures much of what we want from a theory of pitch. It explains the linear ordering of pitches. In addition, it captures the musical intervals and relations, including the *octave*, *fifth*, *fourth*, and so on. The musical intervals are pitch relations among periodic tones and amount to small integer ratios between fundamental frequencies. Thus, octave-related tones are those whose fundamental frequencies stand in 1:2 ratios. The fifth is a 2:3 relationship, the fourth, 3:4, and so on. Such ratios figure in adapting the pitch ordering to accommodate the sense in which octave-related tones are *the same* in pitch. Consider twisting the line into a helix, with successive octave-related tones falling at the same angular position. One gets the very strong sense that the natures of the musical relations are revealed by this discovery.

Some suggest that what we say about visible color holds for other sensible attributes such as audible and olfactory qualities (see, e.g., Byrne and Hilbert 2003). Physicalism, dispositionalism, or primitivism about sensible qualities, on such a view, transposes across the senses. I wish here to draw attention to two noteworthy places where arguments against a physical theory of color fail to transpose neatly to the case of pitch, and to two places where pitches raise difficulties similar to colors. The lesson is that we should not just assume that arguments effective in the case of color have equal force applied to other sensible qualities. Color, perhaps, is a uniquely difficult case, and theories of sensible qualities may not intuitively translate across the senses. At the least, we should take care to be clear upon which key points such theories turn.

Consider the following two counts on which a physicalist account of pitch fares better than color. First, consider the phenomenological distinction between unique and binary hues. Some colors appear to be a mixture of other colors, and some do not. Furthermore, this fact seems essential to any given hue. Hardin (1993) issues a challenge to physicalist theories to explain the distinction in terms that do not essentially invoke the visual experiences of subjects. It is difficult, for instance, to see how "unique" reflectance classes differ from "binary" ones (see the section entitled, "Physicalism," in Cohen, this volume). But consider an analogous issue for pitch. Some pitched sounds seem simple, and others are comprised of discernible components. The difference, however, is captured by the simplicity or complexity of a sound's partials. Nonetheless, unlike the case of color, no pitch that is essentially a mixture of other pitches uniquely occupies a place in pitch space.

Second, no worry analogous to metamerism exists for pitch. Metamerism, or color matching among surfaces with very different surface reflectance properties, poses a problem for physicalist accounts of color because metamerically matching pairs share no obvious physical property. The worry is that no natural physical property exists that could count as the color. Consider pitch. Pitch matching does exist among sounds with very different spectral frequency profiles. For instance, a simple sinusoid matches pitch with each of the many complex sounds whose fundamental frequency it shares. For pitch, however, a single natural physical property exists which unifies the class. Each tone shares a fundamental frequency. Notwithstanding suspicion that physicalism for all sensible qualities stands or falls with the colors, pitch may prove fertile territory for a defense of a variety of physicalism for at least certain sensible qualities.

Philosophers must, however, deal with arguments concerning the viability of *any* physicalist or objectivist theory of pitch. Some such arguments are equally pressing in the case of pitch. First, substantial variation in frequency sensitivity exists among perceivers and is manifested, for example, in which frequency a subject identifies as *middle* C. More dramatically, an actual case of spectral shift, sometimes pronounced, exists for audible qualities in the form of pitch shifts commonly experienced by cochlear implant recipients. Perhaps it is more plausible that an objective standard exists for *middle* C than for *red*, but it is difficult to see how any given pitch experience holds definitive normative significance (see the section, "Physicalism," in Cohen, this volume).

In addition to confronting such familiar concerns, philosophers of audition, like philosophers of color, must contend with a controversy among psychologists and empirical researchers. The worry concerns the phenomenological adequacy of the periodicity theory of pitch and the threat of an error theory or eliminativism about pitch. Consider two sorts of psychophysical experiments. During *fractionalization* tasks, subjects are instructed to adjust a test tone until its pitch is half that of a reference tone. During *equisection* tasks, subjects are instructed to adjust several tones until they are separated by equal pitch intervals. In a series of classic psychophysics papers, S. S. Stevens argues on the basis of the results that pitch is not frequency (Stevens et al. 1937; Stevens and Volkmann 1940). Such experiments appear to show that equal pitch intervals do not correspond to equal frequency intervals. For example, according to these well-known results, doubling frequency does not uniformly affect perceived pitch. The frequency of a 1,000-hertz tone must be tripled in order to affect the same increase in pitch as quadrupling the frequency of a 2,000-hertz tone. The relationship is neither linear nor logarithmic. Fractionalization, equisection, and subsequent experiments reveal a scaling according to which pitch is a relatively complex function of frequency (see Stevens and Davis 1937: Ch. 3; Houtsma 1995; Hartmann 1997: Ch. 12; Gelfand 2004: Ch. 12; Zwicker and Fastl 2006: Ch. 5).

The pitch scale derived from such psychoacoustic data assigns to equal pitch intervals equal magnitudes measured in units called *mels*. The mel scale of pitch therefore is an *extensive* or *numerical* pitch scale, in contrast to the *intensive* frequency scale for pitch. The former, but not the latter, preserves ratios among quantities. The more recent *bark* scale, which is derived from features of the auditory system and not directly from psychophysical data, is a similar extensive pitch scale that closely resembles the mel scale (Zwicker 1961; Zwicker and Terhardt 1980).

Psychoacousticians, in response to such results, reject the identification of pitch with frequency or periodicity. The accepted view among auditory researchers is that pitch is a *subjective* or *psychological* quality merely correlated with frequency (see, e.g., Gelfand 2004; Houtsma 1995). Pitch, that is, strictly belongs only to experiences. The standard view of pitch thus is a form of error theory according to which pitch experience involves a radical projective illusion.

One might challenge the psychophysical results. Warren (1999), for instance, argues that subjects who attempt to estimate sensory magnitude instead appeal to some independent physical scale because "there is an obligatory interpretation of sensory input in terms of conditions and events responsible for stimulation" (111). This perhaps explains why musically initiated subjects frequently perform differently in fractionalization and equisection tasks. Laming (1997) objects to the claim that there is any such thing as a sensation to be measured, since to the subject "the stimulus is perceived as 'out there', not as an internal sensation (internal stimuli such as pain and tickle excepted)" (205). But even if we accept that subjects do not measure sensations, their patterns of judgment require explanation. It is natural to suppose that subjects respond based upon how they experience pitch. If relationships among experienced pitches differ from those among frequencies, then subjects misperceive relations that hold in virtue of pitch or else pitch is not frequency.[1]

Accepting that the mel scale is a well-founded measure that depends upon a genuine dimension of the experience of pitch need not, however, compel us to accept an error theory.[2] Several philosophical alternatives exist. One might accept either that pitches are dispositions to produce psychological states or that pitches are primitive properties of sounds. But one also might either retain the periodicity theory and explain experimental results in terms of pitch experiences, or seek a more adequate physical candidate for pitch. Empirical work on *critical frequency bands* (see, e.g., Zwicker and Fastl 2006), for instance, provides the materials either for an account of experiential discrepancies between pitch and frequency ranges or for an account according to which pitches are complex physical properties of solely anthropocentric interest (O'Callaghan 2002). What seems clear is that considering in detail the nature and experience of audible qualities promises insights into traditional debates concerning color and the sensible qualities.

Cross-modal interactions

The most fertile ground for future research on the nature, character, and function of perception does not concern experiences that take place within a given modality, but deals with interactions that take place among sensory modalities. A prominent empiricist understanding of sense perception assumes that one's overall perceptual experience amounts to the sum or compilation of experiences stemming from separate modalities of awareness, and that experiences of items and qualities that occur through different modalities exhibit distinctive characteristics.[3] Recent empirical work throws into doubt this traditional understanding of experience. Emerging evidence challenges the assumption that the senses function as independent systems and furnish encapsulated channels of awareness. Perceiving involves extensively comparing, weighing, reconciling, adjusting, and integrating the evidence of the senses. Experience is shaped by robust cross-modal interactions.

Consider ventriloquism. This well-established perceptual illusion, which need not involve speech, occurs when the visible location of a sound source affects the auditory experience of location (Howard and Templeton 1966; Bertelson 1999; Vroomen et al. 2001). The fascinating McGurk effect upon perceiving speech sounds involves a change to the phoneme one hears that results from watching the lips of a speaker pronounce a different phoneme (McGurk and Macdonald 1976).

Cross-modal illusions and interactions, however, are not limited to visual dominance. The recently discovered *sound-induced flash illusion* is a visual illusion induced by sound. Subjects shown a single visual flash with two audible beeps experience *two visual flashes* (Shams et al. 2000, 2002). Shams et al. claim that the effect is neither cognitive nor based on a strategy for responding to ambiguous stimuli. Rather, it is a persistent phenomenological change to perceptual experience. These and other cross- and inter-modal illusions, in which one perceptual modality impacts experience in another, call out for explanation (see Spence and Driver [2004] and Bertelson and de Gelder [2004] for further examples). The simple model of the senses as separate systems and atomistic modes of awareness requires revision. Conceiving of the senses as autonomous domains of philosophical inquiry has reached its limits.

I have proposed that to explain the adaptive significance of cross-modal illusions requires positing a dimension of perceptual content that is shared across modalities

(O'Callaghan 2007). Such effects demonstrate a form of perceptual traction upon salient environmental sources of sensory stimulation. The mechanisms by which sensory information acquired through different modalities is reconciled otherwise remain unintelligible. Only under the perceptual assumption that auditory and visual stimulation, or visual and tactile stimulation, stem from a common environmental source do the cross-modal interactions that lead to illusion make sense as strategies for dealing with one's environment (Welch and Warren 1980). The principles by which stimuli are organized, adjusted, or reconciled must, moreover, construe significant environmental sources of stimulation in multi-modal or modality-independent terms, but not in terms specific to a single perceptual modality. Cross-modal illusions provide strong reasons to believe in certain unifying contents shared across perceptual modalities. Thus audition might furnish awareness as of things and happenings common to vision.

Traditional doubts concerning our capacity for perceptual awareness of particulars beyond sensible qualities perhaps, therefore, trade on an understanding of perceptual phenomenology grounded in an outmoded conception of the senses as discrete avenues of experience (see Russell 1912; cf. Lewis 1966). What is most striking about the perceptual modalities, including vision and audition, may be not the features distinctive to a particular mode of experience, but rather the ways in which they cooperate and interact to reveal a world of objects and events. Only attention to non-visual modalities makes this apparent.

Notes

1. This kind of issue, it warrants mentioning, is utterly common among sensory qualities. Brightness, loudness, and other intensities vary logarithmically with simple physical quantities.
2. The mel scale is not accepted as such by all. See Siegel (1965) and Greenwood (1997) for further empirical criticisms. But see Yost and Watson (1987), Bregman (1990), Houtsma (1995), Gelfand (2004), and Zwicker and Fastl (2006) for assent.
3. Thus many empiricists have resisted answering affirmatively Molyneux's question whether an individual born blind could, upon gaining sight, visually identify a shape formerly only felt. See discussions of the Molyneux question in Evans (1985), Campbell (1996), and Loar (1996).

References

Armstrong, D. M. (1961) *Perception and the Physical World*, London: Routledge & Kegan Paul.

Bertelson, P. (1999) "Ventriloquism: A Case of Cross-Modal Perceptual Grouping," in G. Aschersleben, T. Bachmann, and J. Müsseler (eds), *Cognitive Contributions to the Perception of Spatial and Temporal Events*, Amsterdam: Elsevier, pp. 347–62.

Bertelson, P., and de Gelder, B. (2004) "The Psychology of Multimodal Perception," in Spence and Driver (2004): 141–77.

Best, V., Gallun, F. J., Ihlefeld, A., and Shinn-Cunningham, B. G. (2006) "The Influence of Spatial Separation on Divided Listening," *Journal of the Acoustical Society of America* 120, no. 3: 1506–16.

Blauert, J. (1997) *Spatial Hearing: The Psychophysics of Human Sound Localization*, Cambridge, MA: MIT Press.

Bregman, A. S. (1990) *Auditory Scene Analysis: The Perceptual Organization of Sound*, Cambridge, MA: MIT Press.

Byrne, A., and Hilbert, D. (2003) "Color Realism and Color Science," *Behavioral and Brain Sciences* 26: 3–21.

Campbell, J. (1996) "Molyneux's question," in Villanueva (1996), pp. 301–18.

Carr, C. (2002) "Sounds, Signals, and Space Maps," *Nature* 415: 29–31.

Casati, R., and Dokic, J. (1994) *La philosophie du son*, Nîmes: Éditions Jacqueline Chambon.

—— (2005) "Sounds," in Edward N. Zalta (ed.) *The Stanford Encyclopedia of Philosophy*, Stanford, CA: Stanford University Press.

Colburn, H. S., Shinn-Cunningham, B., Kidd, G., and Durlach, N. (2006) "The Perceptual Consequences of Binaural Hearing," *International Journal of Audiology* 45: S34–S44.

Evans, G. (1982) *The Varieties of Reference*, Oxford: Oxford University Press.

—— (1985) "Molyneux's question," in *Collected Papers*, Oxford: Oxford University Press, pp. 364–99.

Gaver, W. W. (1993) "What in the World Do We Hear?: An Ecological Approach to Auditory Event Perception," *Ecological Psychology*, 5: 1–29.

Gelfand, S. A. (2004) *Hearing: An Introduction to Psychological and Physiological Acoustics*, 4th edn, New York: Marcel Dekker.

Greenwood, D. D. (1997) "The Mel Scale's Disqualifying Bias and a Consistency of Pitch-Difference Equisections in 1956 with Equal Cochlear Distances *and* Equal Frequency Ratios," *Hearing Research* 103: 199–224.

Handel, S., and Erickson, M. L. (2003) "Parallels between Hearing and Seeing Support Physicalism," *Behavioral and Brain Sciences* 26: 31–2.

Hardin, C. L. (1993) *Color for Philosophers*, exp. edn, Indianapolis, IN: Hackett.

Hartmann, W. M. (1997) *Signals, Sound, and Sensation*, New York: Springer.

Hartmann, W. M., and Wittenberg, A. (1996) "On the Externalization of Sound Images," *Journal of the Acoustical Society of America* 99, no. 6: 3678–88.

Helmholtz, H. (1954 [1877]) *On the Sensations of Tone*, 4th edn, New York, Dover.

Houtsma, A. J. M. (1995) "Pitch Perception," in B. C. J. Moore (ed.), *Hearing*, New York: Academic Press, pp. 267–91.

Howard, I. P., and Templeton, W. B. (1966) *Human Spatial Orientation*, London: Wiley.

Laming, D. (1997) *The Measurement of Sensation*, Oxford: Oxford University Press.

Lewis, D. (1966) "Percepts and Color Mosaics in Visual Experience," *The Philosophical Review* 75: 357–68.

Loar, B. (1996) "Comments on John Campbell, 'Molyneux's Question'," in Villanueva (1996), pp. 319–24.

Malpas, R. M. P. (1965) "The Location of Sound," in R. J. Butler (ed.), *Analytical Philosophy*, 2nd series, Oxford: Basil Blackwell, pp. 131–44.

McAdams, S., and Bregman, A. S. (1979) "Hearing Musical Streams," *Computer Music Journal* 3, no. 4: 26–43.

McGurk, H., and MacDonald, J. (1976) "Hearing Lips and Seeing Voices," *Nature* 264: 746–8.

Noë, A. (2004) *Action in Perception*, Cambridge, MA: MIT Press.

Nudds, M. (2001) "Experiencing the Production of Sounds," *European Journal of Philosophy* 9: 210–29.

—— (2009) "Sounds and Space" in M. Nudds and C. O'Callaghan (eds.), *Sounds and Perception: New Philosophical Essays*, Oxford: Oxford University Press.

Nudds, M., and O'Callaghan, C. (eds) (forthcoming) *Sounds and Perception: New Philosophical Essays*, Oxford: Oxford University Press.

O'Callaghan, C. (2002), *Sounds*, PhD thesis, Princeton University.

—— (2007) *Sounds: A Philosophical Theory*, Oxford: Oxford University Press.

O'Shaughnessy, B. (2002) *Consciousness and the World*, Oxford: Oxford University Press.

Pasnau, R. (1999) "What Is Sound?" *Philosophical Quarterly* 49: 309–24.

Perkins, M. (1983) *Sensing the World*, Indianapolis, IN: Hackett.

Russell, B. (1912) *The Problems of Philosophy*, Oxford: Oxford University Press.

Schouten, J. F. (1940) "The Residue, a New Concept in Subjective Sound Analysis," *Proceedings of the Koninklijke Nederlandse Akademie*, 43: 356–65.

Scruton, R. (1997) *The Aesthetics of Music*, Oxford: Oxford University Press.

—— (2009) "Sounds as Secondary Objects and Pure Events" in M. Nudds and C. O'Callaghan (eds.), *Sounds and Perception: New Philosophical Essays*, Oxford: Oxford University Press.

Shams, L., Kamitani, Y., and Shimojo, S. (2000) "What You See Is What You Hear," *Nature*, 408: 788.
—— (2002) "Visual Illusion Induced by Sound," *Cognitive Brain Research* 14: 147–52.
Siegel, R. J. (1965) "A Replication of the Mel Scale of Pitch," *American Journal of Psychology* 78, no. 4: 615–20.
Spence, C., and Driver, J. (eds) (2004) *Crossmodal Space and Crossmodal Attention*, Oxford: Oxford University Press.
Stevens, S., and Volkmann, J. (1940) "The Relation of Pitch to Frequency: A Revised Scale," *American Journal of Psychology* 53: 329–53.
Stevens, S., Volkmann, J., and Newman, E. (1937) "A Scale for the Measurement of the Psychological Magnitude Pitch," *Journal of the Acoustical Society of America* 8, no. 3: 185–90.
Strawson, P. F. (1959) *Individuals*, New York: Routledge.
Villanueva, E. (ed.) (1996) *Perception*, vol. 7 of *Philosophical Issues*, Atascadero, CA: Ridgeview.
Vroomen, J., Bertelson, P., and de Gelder, B. (2001) "Auditory-Visual Spatial Interactions: Automatic Versus Intentional Components," in B. de Gelder, E. de Haan, and C. Heywood (eds), *Out of Mind*, Oxford: Oxford University Press, pp. 140–50.
Warren, R. M. (1999) *Auditory Perception: A New Analysis and Synthesis*. Cambridge: Cambridge University Press.
Welch, R. B., and Warren, D. H. (1980) "Immediate Perceptual Response to Intersensory Discrepancy," *Psychological Bulletin* 88, no. 3: 638–67.
Yost, W. A., and Watson, C. S. (eds) (1987) *Auditory Processing of Complex Sounds*, Hillsdale, NJ: Erlbaum.
Zwicker, E. (1961) "Subdivision of the Audible Frequency Range into Critical Bands (*Frequenzgruppen*)," *Journal of the Acoustical Society of America* 33: 248.
Zwicker, E., and Fastl, H. (2006) *Psychoacoustics: Facts and Models*, 3rd edn, New York: Springer.
Zwicker, E., and Terhardt, E. (1980) "Analytical Expressions for Critical-Band Rate and Critical Bandwidth as a Function of Frequency," *Journal of the Acoustical Society of America* 68: 1523–5.

41
SOME RECENT DIRECTIONS IN THE PHILOSOPHY AND PSYCHOLOGY OF THE TEMPORAL CONTENT OF PERCEPTUAL EXPERIENCE

Rick Grush

Introduction

While the temporal content of experience and perception has historically been an important topic in philosophy and psychology, the amount of attention devoted to it waned somewhat in the latter half of the twentieth century. This trend reversed in the '90s, however, and the issues are seeing a marked increase of interest among psychologists, neuroscientists, and philosophers. In this paper I will outline a few of the major issues, and indicate some approaches that I think hold promise.

Historical remarks

The topic of this paper is recent directions in the study of temporal content. But the main ideas that inform these directions are not new. Rather, the heyday was mostly in the 1800s, reaching a sort of historical touchstone in the work of William James (1890) and Edmund Husserl (1966). I will focus on two areas of brewing ideas.

The first is experimental. The rise of experimental psychology in Germany in the 1800s had as one of its primary paradigms of investigation the nature of temporal perception. This research was often framed as an investigation of the time sense, and by this, researchers typically meant that they understood the temporal content of perception to be analogous to the spatial content of (visual) perception. So just as vision, as was the standard view at the time, gives us immediate access to a two-dimensional spatial extent, so too we have a 'time sense' that gives us access to a span of temporal content. The analogy was first explicitly stated and explored by Thomas Reid in his essay, "Memory," in *Essays on the Intellectual Powers of Man* (1785). The analogy suggests two avenues of exploration. First, there is a limit to visual acuity, meaning that as two stimuli get closer, there is a point at which one will no longer be able to discern whether they are at distinct locations or the same location. And so by analogy, the time sense should also have an acuity limit, a temporal interval such that one is no longer able to reliably tell if the stimuli were simultaneous or successive. Second, there is an expanse of the visual field, a maximal magnitude of what can be taken in at once – while I can see all of my computer screen as I type, I cannot see all of my study, but must move my head and eyes around to take it in, in a number of chunks.

Both of these avenues were staples of early experimental psychology research (for a good account, see Boring 1942). Ernst Mach undertook some of the earliest well-conceived experiments, and one of his earliest experiments was, interestingly, essentially one Reid himself had implemented and described in Reid (1785). It involved investigating the accuracy with which subjects can reproduce beats of short or long duration. A number of investigations following Mach's (including those by a number of researchers involved in Wundt's laboratory) seemed to converge upon a duration that was most accurately reproducible, in that shorter or longer intervals would be reproduced with greater error. This privileged interval was taken to be something of a psychological temporal unit, analogous to the foveal area of vision. Wundt's own studies on rhythm (1874) were aimed at finding the largest temporal "object," in this case patterns of beats, that could be taken in at once, and capacity to reproduce with accuracy was taken as evidence that an object was taken in at once.

Different studies attempted to discern the maximal temporal acuity. Exner (1875) used an apparatus that could produce sparks at spatial and temporal intervals that could be very carefully controlled, and studied both the minimal spatial and temporal intervals that could be discerned. And interestingly, Exner investigated how these intervals influenced motion perception, what would later come to be called apparent motion, where two briefly presented stimuli in close spatial and temporal proximity appear to the subject to be motion from the location of the first stimulus to that of the second.

Parallel to this trend in experimental psychology, a brew of ideas was fermenting in philosophical circles. Also inspired by Reid, a diachronic debate began, initially confined to philosophers at Edinburgh, including Reid, Dugald Stewart, Thomas Brown, William Hamilton, but eventually taken up by E. Robert Kelly (Anonymous 1882) and Shadworth Hodgson (1865, 1878, 1898, 1900). The issue was the temporality of perception, and in particular was an attempt to work out why it seems to us as though we have perceptual access to temporal magnitudes in a way that seems to be more like perception than memory.

Reid's own position was that the psychological faculty that provided the mind with access to temporal durations was memory; perception was limited to temporally punctate snapshots of the knife-edged *now*, and provided access to, *inter alia*, spatial, but not temporal, magnitudes. There was for Reid a strong dichotomy in the kinds of content made available by the different psychological faculties. Reid's successors at Edinburgh, especially Dugald Stewart, Thomas Brown, and William Hamilton, all addressed the topic of the temporal content of perception, driven by the implausibility of Reid's dichotomy.

This line of debate had culminations in two notable figures. First, E. Robert Kelly, who in his anonymously published *The Alternative* (Anonymous, 1882) explicitly stated a doctrine according to which the contents of perceptual experience were not limited to a punctate instant, but spanned a temporal interval. Kelly coined the expression "specious present" for this interval, the "present" that was apparent to consciousness. However, before Kelly, Shadworth Hodgson (1878) also developed essentially the same doctrine, though he named it *the empirical present*. William James was strongly influenced by both Kelly (whom he pseudonymously cites as "E. R. Clay") and Hodgson in his work on time consciousness.

Later in the 1880s and 1890s, Hodgson (1898, 1900) developed a much more nuanced theory of time consciousness, one that went beyond the empirical-present doctrine of his earlier work, and developed a number of doctrines now almost universally credited to Husserl, such as the notion of *retention* as a specific aspect of temporal awareness. And in the early 1900s, Husserl began what remain some of the most detailed investigations of time consciousness (Husserl 1966), and while many of the doctrines Husserl discusses were first developed by Hodgson, many others were original developments of Husserl.

There is much more of historical interest, but it is beyond the scope of this paper. For much more detail on Reid, Reid's Edinburgh successors, Kelly, and especially Hodgson and Hodgson's likely strong, but almost unknown, influence on Husserl, see Andersen and Grush (2009). Gallagher (1998) has a good discussion of different aspects of this history.

The empirical present: the experience of temporal intervals

There is a standard way in which the temporality of perception is conceived. I will call it the mirror model. There are two features that define the mirror model. First it maintains that the temporal content of a given perceptual episode is temporally punctate. This might be put by saying that at any time, what is perceived is the state of the environment at that time. And in the limit, what is perceived during any instant is the state of the environment as it is at that corresponding instant. Second, the temporal content of perception is derived entirely from the temporal features of the perceptual episodes themselves. That is, for perceptual processes anyway, the temporal content of a perception is determined by the time at which that perceptual state is produced. One can perceive a succession only by having a succession of perceptions, for example.

These two assumptions – the content of perceptual states is temporally punctate, and that time is its own representation – derive support from the fact that at large time scales they clearly hold in all but pathological cases, and that there is not any blatantly obvious reason to think that they won't continue to hold as the time scales are reduced (though as I shall argue later, there are good, but non-obvious reasons). My belief that the rock was on the cliff before the rock was on the beach – a single representational state whose content is about a succession – is largely based upon the fact that I perceived it on the cliff yesterday, and I can perceive it on the beach today – a succession of representational states each of which has for its content what is essentially a specification of a static state. In motto form, a representation of succession is based upon a succession of representations. And similar remarks hold of my belief that the rock was on the cliff before it was on the beach if we shorten the time frame to hours, or even minutes. And so it can seem as though it holds at all time scales, including the millisecond scale. There is thus a pull to see all perceptually based representations about succession as deriving from a succession of states whose contents are themselves punctate. And the view of the content of perception that one gets from this shrinking of time scales is further emboldened by the fact that it is consistent with another folk view of perception as essentially a matter of mirroring the environment. The image in the mirror at any instant is a snapshot; and the mirror reflects motion only by reflecting a continuous sequence or series of images, whose individual contents are state contents, and whose succession *mirrors* the succession of states in the environment.

I will try to produce some considerations that put both assumptions of the mirror model into question. First, in this section, I will discuss what it might mean to claim that the content of perception is, at any time, not a corresponding instant, but rather a temporal interval. This is essentially Hodgson's (and later, Kelly's, James', and Husserl's) contention. In the next section I will try to argue that the specific temporal content of this interval is not a passive reflection of the temporal features of the perceived events, but is rather an active interpretation. But for now, to the temporal interval content of perception.

There are two related but distinct senses (perhaps more, but I will focus on two) in which temporal intervals can figure in perceptual content. First, we often perceive something that is part of a temporally extended whole and we perceive it *as* part of that whole. A favorite example is notes as parts of melodies. When one who is familiar with Beethoven's Ninth Symphony hears the fifth note of the main theme, that very note has a phenomenal character to it that is not exhausted by the note itself, but is in part colored by the surrounding temporal context, including prior notes that are no longer being heard. While Husserl (1966) is not nearly as clear in this topic as one would like, it seems likely that this element of temporal content of perception is the one he is most centrally addressing. The centerpiece of his analysis is the tripartite structure of time consciousness, according to which the contents of consciousness include not only a "primal impression" given as new and now, but also "retentions" of previous phases of the perceived temporal object, and protentions of imminent phases. It is because of this that, for instance, we hear the currently sounding note as one part of a melody, the other parts of which, while not currently manifest in consciousness in the same way as the currently sounding note, are nevertheless still in consciousness in these temporally modified ways (see Brough 1989 for a good discussion of Husserl's views).

A second sense in which temporal intervals can figure in the content of temporal experience is that, perhaps, what is directly given in perception *at any time* (this expression will need to be explored) is not a temporally punctate snapshot, but is rather a temporally extended interval. One motivation for this idea is our capacity to perceive motion. Since motion necessarily takes time to manifest – that is, must be extended over a temporal interval – then the content of perception must include a non-zero temporal interval if we can directly perceive motion. Of course this interval might be rather brief, much briefer than the sort of intervals arguably in play in the music appreciation phenomenon discussed in the previous paragraph. The relevant temporal context for hearing a note as part of a melody can be on the order of seconds or perhaps even minutes. But when note 36 is playing in a melody, there is no sense to be made that note 1 that sounded, say, 4 seconds ago, is perceptually present in the same way that the currently sounding note 36 is, even if in some sense note 1 is providing something like a temporal context within which note 36 is aesthetically appreciated.

By contrast, consider a bowling ball speeding down the lane, and in particular a small interval of its motion over the half a meter just before it strikes the first pin, a distance the ball traverses in about 50 milliseconds (ms). It is not clear that the same sort of intuitions that allowed us to confidently say that at the time of note 36, note 1 was no longer being perceived, will allow us to say that the entire interval of the ball's motion over that 50 ms is not present to perceptual awareness.

Now this doctrine is sometimes misunderstood as a doctrine according to which the content of perceptual experience is something like a time-lapse photograph. And in the early part of the twentieth-century objections were raised to the "specious-present" doctrine that were objections to the idea that experience as a time-lapse photograph could explain the perception of motion. Of course this is right: if the *explanandum* is our ability to perceive motion, then crediting perception with a capacity to form time-lapse images isn't a sufficient *explanans*. But the doctrine is not that perception works like a time-lapse photograph. Rather, the proposal is that the content of perception, *at any instant* (see below for what this means), is a temporal interval *as such*, it is an interval that represents events as being temporally ordered, with succession, duration, simultaneity, and so forth.

I will use Hodgson's expression *empirical present* to refer to the temporal interval that is presented manifest in perceptual awareness in this way, if there is such. (Kelly's term *specious present* is much better known, but also has over a century of theoretical baggage associated with it.) I have so far provided two motivations for the empirical present doctrine. First, we seem to be able to perceive motion, and motion necessarily occurs only over a temporal interval, therefore it seems that we have available to us in perception contents whose temporal aspect spans some interval. This sort of argument has been central among proponents of the specious-present doctrine, including Kelly, and C. D. Broad (1923). A second consideration is the sort of introspective phenomenological suggestion about the difference between (i) the two notes separated by four seconds; and (ii) the bowling ball's being at two locations separated by 50 ms. While neither of these considerations is scientifically compelling, they are at least consistent. But I think that an argument that has some force can be constructed by bringing in considerations aimed at the second assumption of the mirror model. This is the topic of the next section.

But before moving on, a brief word of clarification. I characterized the empirical present doctrine as one which maintains that at any instant, the content of perceptual experience comprehends a temporal interval. This might reasonably be objected to on the ground that, given the way neurally implemented perceptual systems operate, it is not clear that it makes sense to credit the perceptual systems with doing anything at a strictly instantaneous time-slice. This observation is right. I'm not sure what the smallest time frame is over which it makes sense to credit the perceptual system with producing and maintaining some perceptual content, but I'm prepared to admit that making reference to a strict instant is an idealization. So let me rephrase the doctrine more carefully. It is that there is some temporal interval *I* such that a perceptual state that manifests over that interval has, as its content, a temporal interval of magnitude C, where C is significantly greater than *I*. And in fact I will be more specific in that I think a case can be made that *I* lies entirely within C. Furthermore, though *I* is temporally extended, its temporal extent is not, on the model I will suggest, used to represent time. It is not the case that earlier phases of *I* are representing earlier phases of C, for example.

There is another understanding of the specious-present doctrine that hinges on the idea behind the objection discussed in the last paragraph, an understanding first voiced by Stern (1897), and more recently by Dainton (2000). This understanding, which I shall call the *extended-act view*, is that the content of perceptual experience comprehends temporal intervals exactly because perceptual processes themselves are extended in time over those intervals, and that it is the time of the extended perceptual act that represents the temporality of the perceived events. I will return to this *extended-act* view in the next section.

The construction of temporality

In this section I examine the other component of the mirror model: the idea that the temporal content of perception is a passive reflection of the temporality of the events perceived. Before moving on to treating this topic specifically, let me remark that a general trend in understanding the processes of perception has been understanding them as essentially interpretive and infused by theory and expectation, as opposed to understanding them as passively registering what is there to be perceived. One standard tool for investigating the extent and nature of this interpretive aspect of perception is the perceptual illusion. Consider Figure 41.1. When subjects see a scene such as A, they interpret it as a circle partially occluding a bar, even though this goes beyond what is given in the sensory information itself. And in fact, the

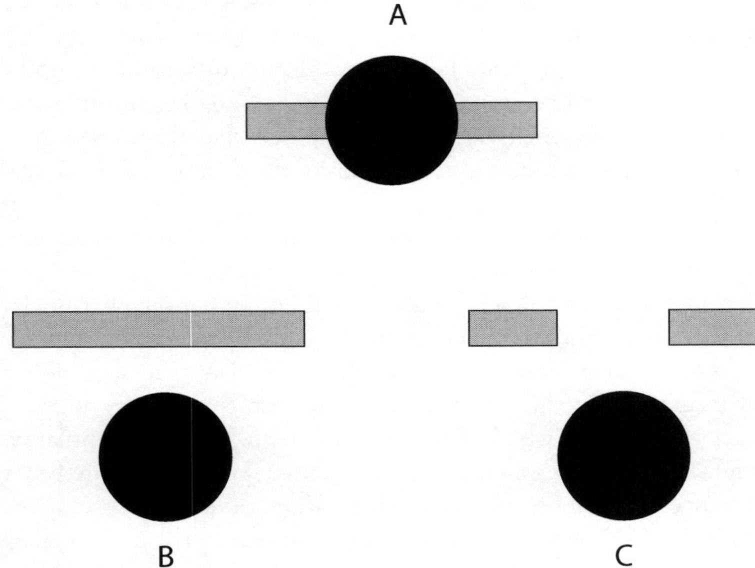

Figure 41.1 The interpretive aspect of perception.

surprising result would be if the scene turns out to be exactly what is shown: a circle flanked by two short but aligned bar segments (as in 1C)! From phenomena such as this, we can reasonably conclude that the perceptual system has a tendency to prefer certain kinds of regular shapes, continuity, and so forth, and within limits is prepared to let these top-down expectations trump what is present in the sensory signal itself when it produces an interpretation of what is there in the perceived environment.

The same general pattern of inference is valid when we turn from non-temporal to temporal features of perceptual content. There is no obvious reason to suppose that the factors that motivate top-down interpretive influence in non-temporal cases (the imperfect operation of sensation, including but by no means limited to its inability to "see through" opaque objects) are absent in the case of temporal features. Nor is there reason to suppose that the assignation of temporal content, at least at short time scales, is not among the degrees of interpretive freedom available to the perceptual system. Now to details.

There appear to be situations, *temporal illusions*, where though there is reason to think that the subject perceived *Q* before they perceived *P*, they nevertheless perceive *P* to have preceded *Q*. Consider the apparent motion phenomenon (see MacKay 1958; Kolers 1972; Williams et al., submitted; Ramachandran and Anstis 1983). As Dennett and Kinsbourne (1992) pointed out, there is a temporal element to this illusion. To perceive a dot as moving from A to C is to perceive it as being at A, and then subsequently at *B*, and subsequently at C. While the motion may be continuous, I am merely drawing attention to three points along the continuous line of motion. If the dot were perceived as being at A, then C and then *B*, this would perhaps be some sort of motion, but it wouldn't be motion from A through *B* to C. I take it that this is unobjectionable.

Apparent motion is an example (though there are others: see Dennett and Kinsbourne 1992; Grush 2005a, b). When the dot flashes at A, and then 100 ms later at C, the subject sees the dot as moving from A to C, and this motion is seen as traversing intermediate locations such as *B* before the motion's termination at C. But there is a paradox here. Until the subject sees the second light flash at C, the subject has no idea that there would be a second flash, nor in what direction it would be if there is one. This is known because trials can be randomized and controlled and the result is the same. So the subject, in order to perceive the motion from A through *B* to C must perceive that it was at *B* before it was at C. But we know that the subject must have perceived the flash as being at C before perceiving it at *B*, since perceiving the flash at C is a precondition for seeing it at *B*.

It will help to be more clear about what is going on, and the timing. What we know for sure is that subjects will report, when asked, seeing the motion from A through *B* and to C. And they can be shown to be sensitive to that content even if not reporting it. But these tests for what was perceived are all after the fact, that is, after C has flashed, typically several hundred milliseconds or more after C has flashed.

We can all agree that the motion, and in particular the location of the dot at location *B*, is not in the stimulus but is in one way or another supplied by the perceptual system. And we can all also agree that the perceptual system can't know that it has to supply motion, or an apparent dot passing through *B*, until after it gets information about the flash at C. And I assume we can all agree that, to a first approximation, the perceptual system does this because, so to speak, it is trying to accurately represent events, and it takes it that an imperfectly perceived continuous rectilinear motion from A to C is, in the sort of situation described, involving small temporal and spatial intervals, much more likely than two distinct stimuli that have been accurately sensed in close spatial and temporal proximity.

There are a number of potential ways this apparent paradox could be explained. I will mention three. The first option, which nobody takes seriously, is that the perceptual system can somehow look ahead in time to see that there will be a flash at C at $t = 3$, so that at $t = 2$, it can fill in the dot at *B*. Call this the *prescience model*.

A second possibility is that perception is subject to a continual and purposeful delay, say of about 100 ms. (This is the view of Eagleman and Sejnowski [2000] and Rao et al. [2001].) On this view, while the perceptual system collects information as it comes in, it holds off on making any perceptual interpretation for 100 ms. The reason for this is that greater perceptual accuracy can be achieved when one has more data to go on, and data about what happens in later stages of a process can be tremendously helpful in deciding what happened in earlier stages. The reason for thinking that the delay might be about 100 ms is that this seems to be about the longest temporal delay over which one can induce illusions of this sort. When data are sensed that could bear on the interpretation of a prior event but they are picked up more than 100 or so ms after that event, they do not result in this sort of illusion. I will follow Rao et al. and call this the *smoothing model*.

A third possibility is that at $t = 2$ there is a perceptual state to the effect that nothing is at B. But later, this is misremembered as there being a perception of the dot at B at $t = 2$. On this account there is no tinkering with time as in option 1, and no delay in perceptual processing as in the smoothing model. While this seems to have a certain kind of theoretical parsimony, it seems to throw the baby out in its quest for simplicity. Why, indeed, posit a process called "perception" at all if what subjects claim to perceive, even at time scales of a fraction of a second, are subject to reinterpretation as the operation of memory?

I won't continue to argue against this third option, directly, since I think a fourth possibility captures what is right in the third option in such a way that those who were inclined to embrace the third will jump ship to the fourth. And ditto for proponents of the smoothing model. Proponents of perceptual prescience are beyond redemption.

The fourth model I have called the *trajectory estimation model*. I will here provide only a qualitative description of this model, but readers interested in some detailed neural information-processing implementation should consult Grush (2005a, 2005b, 2007). On this model, the perceptual system interprets the represented system in terms of trajectories and processes. These form, so to speak, the basic vocabulary of the perceptual system. Of course there are degenerate processes, such as something that remains static over some temporal interval. And there can be events such as the instantaneous appearance and disappearance of some stimulus. What makes this qualify as a process is that it is one aspect of a temporally extended event which includes some span of time before the appearance of the stimulus and a span of time after its disappearance. But these are special degenerate cases.

The important point about the trajectory estimation model is that at any time t (recall, though I am treating t as an instant, it might in fact be a small temporal span), it produces as its representation an estimate of the evolution of the perceived event over the interval $[t - l, t + k]$ for some small lag l and some small reach k. There is reason to think that l and k are both on the order of about 100 ms, making the entire estimated interval about 200 ms. The estimate produced at t takes into account all sensory input collected up to and including t, and using that data produces the best estimate it can of the evolution of the process, not only up to time t, but also a prediction of how that process will continue into the very near future.

At time t' (to get some numbers for the sake of example, perhaps 10 ms after t) a new estimate is produced that takes into account all data received up to t'. But though the interval estimated at t' overlaps the interval estimated at t by 190 ms, the estimate produced at t' might differ significantly from the one produced at t. The sensory data that were collected during the 10 ms since t might suggest that what unfolded during the 90 ms prior was different from what was suggested by the data received prior to that. In such a case, the prior estimate is wiped, and typically the subject will have no explicit memory of ever having that perceptual content.

This is exemplified by the temporal illusions. Let's suppose that t is just before the second dot flashes. At this point, the trajectory estimate of what has happened is that there was one flash at A, say 50 ms ago, followed by nothing, including nothing at B 20 ms ago. But at t' sensory information about a stimulus at C comes in. The new

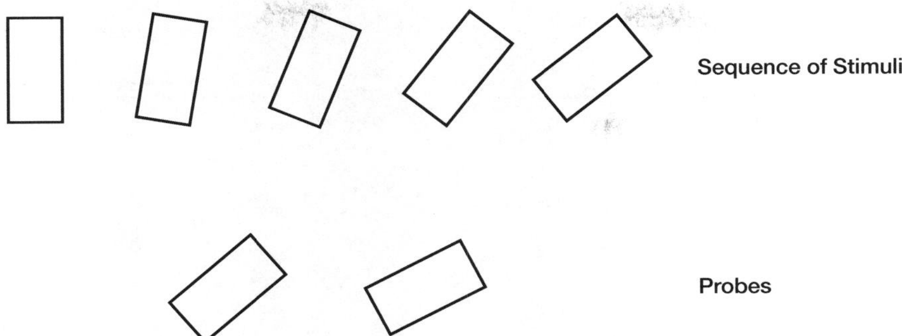

Figure 41.2 Representational momentum.

trajectory estimate produced at *t′* now differs from that produced at *t*, notably with respect to what is taken to have happened after the flash at A. Now, the estimate is that there was motion from A through *B*, terminating at C. The prior estimate from *t* had nothing happening at *B* 30 ms after the flash at A, but the estimate produced at *t′* has a stimulus at *B* 30 ms after the flash at A. The prior estimate is washed, as is evident from the fact that subjects don't report the apparent motion situations as seeing a flash followed by nothing, and then having a contradictory perceptual experience to the effect that there was motion. What they report is simply the most recent non-overwritten estimate.

I will compare the trajectory estimation model to the other proposals, but first I need to bring attention to one more perceptual phenomenon, *representational momentum* (Freyd and Finke 1984; Thornton and Hubbard 2002). This is illustrated in Figure 41.2. Subjects are presented with a sequence of images implying motion (and in some cases actual motion) until the scene goes black. They are then tested to ascertain what the final state was that they perceived. The result is that subjects overshoot, claiming that they saw the motion continue to a point that was farther along the clearly implied trajectory than in fact it was.

The representational-momentum effect is robust, but is also sensitive to a number of variables, including how long after the cessation of motion the subject's responses are probed. The details are beyond the scope of this paper. The take-home point is that it appears that the perceptual system is actively constructing representations that anticipate motion that it has not in fact received direct sensory information about. And the amount of time that is involved in this prediction – the amount of time that the displayed motion would have had to actually continue in order to reach the stage that subjects claimed it reached – is on the order of a hundred milliseconds to a few hundred milliseconds.

I will now turn to a comparison of the four models (I am discounting the perceptual prescience model). For convenience I diagram them in Figure 41.3. The mirror model and the smoothing model are not well suited to addressing the capacity to perceive motion. While this is not the most significant consideration, the extended-act model and the trajectory estimation model seem to be consistent with the phenomenology

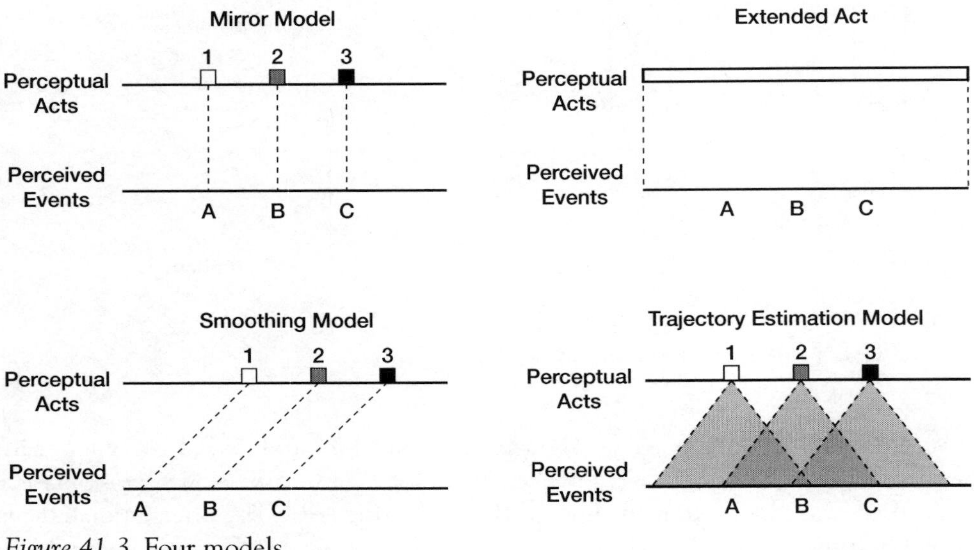

Figure 41.3 Four models.

of the perception of motion over small temporal intervals. But great weight should perhaps not be placed on this sort of consideration.

The mirror model and the extended-act model are unable to accommodate temporal illusions, as both let time represent time. The best that they can do is to claim that they are misrememberings. When the time scales involved are tenths of a second, shunting the phenomenon off to memory seems heavy handed at best. For a critique of this move see Dennett and Kinsbourne (1992).

The smoothing model is able to accommodate temporal illusions. Since it claims that perceptual interpretations are delayed for 100 ms to allow more sensory data to be collected, it is able to explain how things that occur after some event are able to influence how that event is perceived. However, the smoothing model posits a costly delay in perceptual processing. If one thing is clear it is that timely processing of perceptual information is important for sensorimotor control, and adaptiveness generally. Delaying perceptual processing by 100 ms seems a high price to pay for greater accuracy in some pathological cases. Note that the proponent of this view cannot, without falling into the prescience model, claim that perceptual processing is only sometimes delayed. Whether a given perceptual interpretation will benefit from being delayed cannot be known until the sensory information that would induce a reinterpretation is received. The perceptual system would have to know that, say, a 100 ms in the future a crucial piece of information will be received, and on that basis delay its perceptual processing just in those cases. And it can't be random, since the apparent motion effect is robust.

Not only does the trajectory estimation model not posit a delay, it credits the perceptual system with anticipatory representations, such as those apparently involved in the representational-momentum effect – and does so while being able to accommodate the phenomenon that the smoothing model is tuned to accommodate. If new sensory information comes in to suggest a very different interpretation of a very recent event, then a new estimate is produced and the old one wiped.

In sum, the trajectory estimation model seems to have strong advantages over the obvious competitors, and no obvious disadvantages. It accommodates the phenomenal intuition that we can directly perceive motion, it can handle temporal illusions, and it has something to say about perceptual systems being geared to anticipation as well as accuracy, providing a unified account for understanding prediction as well as retrodiction. (For more on the trajectory estimation model, see Grush [2005a, 2007].)

Timing and agency

All of the discussion so far has been directed at the temporal content of perception, where "perception" has been understood to be a matter of access to external happenings, prototypically in the environment. But there are also issues of interest in what might be called *internal* temporal content, our sense of the temporal features of our mental states. Libet's protocol exhibits the phenomenon: subjects are asked to push a button whenever they feel like it (within limits, see Libet et al. [1983]; for extended discussion, see the special issue introduced by Banks [2002]). What subjects are here asked to be sensitive to are their own mental states, and in particular the timing of those states. While the methodology has been challenged, the fact remains that subjects seem to have no problem interpreting the instructions and giving an answer.

A lot of questions have been raised about Libet's studies, and among them are questions about exactly what it is that subjects are reporting on when they are asked to introspect for their volitions. But one aspect that has not been questioned is the veracity of the timing of whatever it is they claim to be reporting on. The timing is carefully examined, and corrections are made for reaction times and such.

But another possibility is open. It might be that subjects are in fact correctly sensing an inner mental event that is something like a volition, and this volition precedes or is simultaneous with the detected neural events. But for some reason they are systematically assigning incorrect temporal content to this event.

Before exploring this more, consider the unbeatable rock-paper-scissors machine (RPS) (Jacobson 2005). There are two phases to the experiment. First, in the training phase, subjects play RPS with a computer: upon the completion of a numerical countdown, subjects press one of three buttons corresponding to rock, paper, or scissors, and the subject's choice is displayed on the monitor. At the same time, the computer produces, randomly, rock, paper or scissors, and this is also displayed on the monitor at about the same time as the subject's choice (depending on how quickly the subject presses the button, the subject's choice may be slightly ahead of, or behind, the computer's). Subjects are told that during this phase, the computer is learning the subject's tendencies. Really, though, the program is slowly introducing a delay between when the subject presses the button and when the subject's choice is displayed on the screen. At the end of the "training" period a delay of about 100 ms is introduced without the subject noticing. Then subjects are told that the real game is beginning. A countdown appears on the screen, and subjects press one of three buttons; the computer then determines which choice will defeat the subject's choice, and displays this choice on the screen; then just a few tens of milliseconds later, the subject's choice is displayed on the screen. As described it is no mystery why the computer can always win. Anyone allowed to see an opponent's choice before choosing will always be able to win. But, to the subject it looks as though the computer makes its choice before the subject does. When the countdown reaches zero, it seems to the subject that the subject begins pressing one of the buttons, the computer's choice then appears before the subject's button press, but too late for the subject to change which button he is about to press, and then the subject's choice appears on the screen. That is, even though in fact the subject presses the button before the computer makes and displays its choice, it seems to the subject as though the computer's choice is on the screen just before her own button press!

There are a number of things going on with this phenomenon, and a full discussion is beyond the scope of this paper. But one thing that seems to be happening is a misestimation, on the parts of the subjects, of the timing of their own agentive action. For further discussion along these lines, directed towards Libet phenomena as opposed to Jacobson's, see Lau et al. 2006, and Eagleman 2004 (interestingly, Eagleman suggests that the operation of emulation mechanisms (see Grush, 2004) may play a crucial role in self-timing of the psychological intentions that precede movements).

The tentative upshot of this discussion is that the trajectory estimation model may apply not only to the perception of external events, but also to aspects of the introspection of internal psychological events.

Conclusion

The temporal content of perception, including introspection, are topics that are attracting increasing interest among philosophers, psychologists and neuroscientists. Getting the story right is not only a desirable end in itself, but it has ramifications for other areas of the study of human mentality. The Libet phenomenon is a case in point. Subjective reports of temporality have been used in scientific contexts, and conclusions drawn in part on their basis. Understanding better the mechanisms of how perceptual and introspective systems assign the temporal contents that, among other things, form the basis of subjective reports will contribute positively to this topic. And subjective reports of temporality have also formed premises in philosophical arguments about the metaphysical nature of time (McTaggert 1908; Butterfield 1984). An increasing amount of work in linguistic semantics is turning to the representation of time, both at the cognitive level as well as how this is coded linguistically (Langacker 1991; Núñez et al. 2006).

In this paper I have only sketched a few of what strike me as the most foundational topics, and made some suggestions about how to understand the temporal content of perceptual experience – suggestions that run counter to commonsense views of temporal perception, but nevertheless have significant considerations speaking in their favor. But this sketch and these suggestions should be taken as just that: a sketch and some suggestions. The issues here are deep and subtle, and a good deal of work remains to be done.

References

Andersen, Holly, and Rick Grush (2009) "A Brief History of Time-Consciousness: Historical Precursors to James and Husserl," *Journal of the History of Philosophy* 47: 277–307.

Anonymous [E. Robert Kelly; aka E.R. Clay] (1882) *The Alternative: A Study in Psychology*, London: Macmillan & Co.

Banks, William (2002) "On Timing Relations between Brain and World," *Consciousness and Cognition* 11: 141–3.

Boring, Edwin G. (1942) *Sensation and Perception in the History of Experimental Psychology*, New York: Appleton-Century-Crofts.

Broad, C. D. (1923) *Scientific Thought*, New York: Harcourt, Brace & Co.

Brough, John (1989) "Husserl's Phenomenology of Time Consciousness," in J. N. Mohanty and William R. McKenna, *Husserl's Phenomenology: A Textbook*, Landham, MD: University Press of America.

Butterfield, J. (1984) "Seeing the Present," *Mind* 93, no. 370: 161–76.

Dainton, Barry (2000) *Stream of Consciousness: Unity and Continuity in Conscious Experience*, New York: Routledge.

Dennett, D. C., and Kinsbourne, M. (1992) "Time and the Observer: The Where and When of Consciousness in the Brain," *Behavioral and Brain Sciences* 15, no. 2: 183–247.

Eagleman, D. M. (2004) "The Where and When of Intention," *Science* 303: 1144–6.

Eagleman, D. M., and Sejnowski, T. J. (2000) "Motion Integration and Postdiction in Visual Awareness," *Science* 287: 2036–8.

Exner, S. (1875) "Über das Sehen von Bewegungen und die Theorie des zusammengezetzen Auges" [On motion perception and the theory of compound eyes], *Sitzungberichte Academie Wissenschaft Wien* 72: 156–90.

Freyd, J. J., and Finke, R. A. (1984) "Representational Momentum," *Journal of Experimental Psychology* 10: 126–32.

Gallagher, Shaun (1998) *The Inordinance of Time*, Evanston, IL: Northwestern University Press.

Grush, Rick (2004) "The Emulation Theory of Representation: Motor Control, Imagery, and Perception," *Behavioral and Brain Sciences* 27, no. 3: 377–442.

—— (2005a) "Internal Models and the Construction of Time: Generalizing from *State* Estimation to *Trajectory* Estimation to Address Temporal Features of Perception, Including Temporal Illusions," *Journal of Neural Engineering* 2, no. 3: S209–S218.

—— (2005b) "Brain Time and Phenomenological Time," in A. Brook and K. Akins (eds) *Cognition and the Brain: The Philosophy and Neuroscience Movement*, Cambridge: Cambridge University Press, pp. 160–207.

—— (2007) "Space, Time and Objects," in John Bickel (ed.), *The Oxford Handbook of Philosophy and Neuroscience*, New York: Oxford University Press.

Hodgson, Shadworth Hollway (1865) *Time and Space*, London: Longman, Green, Longman, Roberts, & Green.

—— (1878) *Philosophy of Reflection*, 2 vols., London: Longmans, Green, & Co.

—— (1898) *Metaphysic of Experience*, 4 vols., London: Longman, Green, & Co.; repr. (1980) Garland Publishing, New York.

—— (1900) "Perception of Change and Duration – A Reply," *Mind* 9, no. 34: 240–3.

Husserl, Edmund (1966) *Zur Phaenomenologie des inneren Zeitbewusstseins (1893–1917)*, ed. Rudolf Boehm, Husserliana X, The Hague: Kluwer.

Jacobson, John (2005) "Undefeatable Rock, Paper, Scissors," demonstration at Vision Sciences Symposium, Sarasota FL, May.

James, William (1890) *Principles of Psychology*, New York: Henry Holt.

Kolers, P. A. (1972) *Aspects of Motion Perception*, London: Pergamon Press.

Langacker, Ronald (1991) "The English Passive," in Ronald Langacker, *Concept, Image, and Symbol*, Berlin: Mouton de Gruyter.

Lau, Hakwan C., Rogers, Robert D., and Passingham, Richard E. (2006) "On Measuring the Perceived Onsets of Spontaneous Actions," *The Journal of Neuroscience* 26, no. 27: 7265–71.

Libet, B., Gleason, C. A., Wright, E. W., and Pearl, D. K. (1983) "Time of Conscious Intention to Act in Relation to Onset of Cerebral Activity (Readiness Potential): The Unconscious Initiation of a Freely Voluntary Act," *Brain* 106: 623–42.

MacKay, D. M. (1958) "Perceptual Stability of a Stroboscopically Lit Visual Field Containing Self-Luminous Objects," *Nature* 181: 507–8.

McTaggart, J. E. (1908) "The Unreality of Time," *Mind* 17: 456–73.

Núñez, R., Motz, B., and Teuscher, U. (2006) "Time after Time: The Psychological Reality of the Ego- and Time-Reference-Point Distinction in Metaphorical Construals of Time," *Metaphor and Symbol* 21: 133–146.

Ramachandran, V. S., and Anstis, S. A. (1983) "Extrapolation of Motion Path in Human Visual Perception," *Vision Research* 23: 83–5.

Rao, Rajesh, Eagleman, David, and Sejnowski, Terrence (2001) "Optimal Smoothing in Visual Motion Perception," *Neural Computation* 13: 1243–53.

Reid, Thomas (1785) *Essays on the Intellectual Powers of Man*, Menston: Scolar Press; repr. of Edinburgh original.

Stern, William (1897) "Psychische Präsenzzeit," *Zeitschrift für Psychologie und Physiologie der Sinnesorgane* 13: 325–49.

Thornton, Ian M., and Hubbard, Timothy L. (2002) "Representational Momentum: New findings, new directions," *Visual Cognition* 9, no. 1–2: 1–7.

Williams, L. E., Hubbard, E. M., and Ramachandran, V. S (submitted) "Retrodiction in Apparent Motion."

Wundt, Wilhelm (1874) *Grundzüge der physiologischen Psychologie*, Leipzig: Engelmann.

Part VI

Personhood

42
ACTION AND MIND

Alfred R. Mele

Two questions lie at the heart of the philosophy of action: What is an action? And how are actions to be explained? The first question directly raises two others: How do actions differ from nonactions? And how do actions differ from one another? A theorist who asks the question about explanation may be looking for a theory about how to explain why agents perform the actions they perform, a theory about *how* actions are produced, or both. These questions guide this article. Important work on them in philosophy and the human sciences is discussed.

Actions and other events

According to a popular answer to the question how actions differ from nonactions, actions are like sunburns in an important respect. The burn on Al's back is a sunburn partly in virtue of its having been caused by exposure to the sun's rays; a burn that looks and feels just the same is not a sunburn if it was caused by a heat lamp. Similarly, a certain event is Al's raising his right hand – an action – partly in virtue of its having been appropriately caused by mental items (or their neural correlates). An influential version of this view claims that reasons, understood as combinations of beliefs and desires, are causes of actions and that an event counts as an action partly in virtue of its having been suitably caused by a reason. Alternative conceptions of actions include an internalist view according to which actions differ experientially from other events in a way that is essentially independent of how, or whether, they are caused; a conception of actions as composites of nonactional mental events or states (e.g., intentions) and pertinent nonactional effects (e.g., an arm's rising); and views identifying an action with the causing of a suitable nonactional product by appropriate nonactional mental events or states – or, instead, by an agent.

There are three main theories about how actions differ from one another: a fine-grained theory, a coarse-grained theory, and a componential theory. According to the fine-grained theory, *A* and *B* are different actions if, in performing them, the agent exemplifies different act-properties. For example, if Ann starts her car by turning a key, her starting the car and her turning the key are two different actions, since the act properties at issue are distinct: one can start a car without turning a key and turn a key without starting a car. The coarse-grained theory asserts that Ann's turning the key and her starting the car are the same action described in two different ways. The componential theory claims that Ann's starting her car is an action having various components, including (but not limited to) her moving her arm, her turning the key, and the car's starting. Where the first two theories claim to find, alternatively, a collection of related actions, or a single action under different descriptions, component theories assert that there is a larger action having smaller actions among its parts.

Most philosophers agree that at least a sketch of an explanation of an intentional action can be provided by identifying the reasons for which the agent performed it. Some philosophers regard reasons as mental states, and some do not. Whether reasons – or their neural correlates, if reasons are mental states – can have a place in *causal* explanations of actions is controversial. In a landmark article, Donald Davidson (1963) challenged anti-causalists about "reasons-explanations" to provide an account of the reasons for which we act that does not treat those reasons as causes of relevant actions. Imagine that Al has a pair of reasons for using his leaf blower this morning, one having to do with convenience and the other with revenge. Al wants to clear the leaves from his lawn today, and he regards this morning as a very convenient time. But he also has a desire to repay his neighbors for awakening him yesterday with their noisy leaf blower, and he believes that blowing the leaves off of his lawn this morning would accomplish that. As it happens, Al uses his leaf blower this morning only for one of these reasons. In virtue of what is it true that he uses it for this reason, and not for the other, if not that this reason, and not the other, makes an appropriate causal contribution to his using it? Detailed attempts to meet Davidson's challenge have been revealingly problematic (see Mele 2003: Ch. 2).

In contemporary philosophy, a causal view of the nature and explanation of actions typically is embraced as part of a naturalistic stand on agency according to which mental items that help to explain actions are in some way dependent on or realized in physical states and events. A variety of options are open, and any viable solution to the mind-body problem that supports the idea that mental terms can legitimately be used in causal explanations of actions can, in principle, be welcomed by many proponents of the view.

Intentions and action production

Owing partly to the close connection in ordinary thought and language between intentions and actions, intentions have received a lot of attention not only in the philosophy of action but also in work on action in neuroscience, psychology, and legal theory. It should not be assumed that the term "intention" is understood in the same way in all of these fields. Nor should it be assumed that there is a uniform understanding of the term within each field.

Here is a representative account of intention from the neuroscience literature:

> Intention is an early plan for a movement. It specifies the goal of a movement and the type of movement ... We can have intentions without actually acting upon them. Moreover, a neural correlate of intention does not neces-

> sarily contain information about the details of a movement, for instance the joint angles, torques, and muscle activations required to make a movement ... Intentions are initially coded in visual coordinates in at least some of the cortical areas within the [posterior parietal cortex]. This encoding is consistent with a more cognitive representation of intentions, specifying the goals of movements rather than the exact muscle activations required to execute the movement.
>
> (Andersen and Buneo 2002: 191)

This account is similar in some respects to my own account of intentions as executive attitudes toward plans (Mele 1992). Intentions, like many psychological states, have both a representational and an attitudinal dimension. The representational content of an intention may be understood as a *plan*. The intending *attitude* toward plans may be termed an *executive* attitude. Plans, on one conception, are purely representational and have no motivational power of their own. People may have any number of attitudes toward plans, in this sense. They may believe that a plan is elegant, admire it, hope that it is never executed, and so on.

To understand the executive dimension of intention, compare an intention to attend Joe's party with a *desire* to attend the party. Both encompass motivation to attend the party, and the content of each is or includes a representation of the prospective course of action. But although one can have a desire to attend a party without being at all *settled* on doing so, intending to attend a party is partially constituted by being settled on so doing. This is compatible with intentions' being revocable and revisable. Though Ann is now settled on attending Joe's party, she would change her plans were a pressing problem to arise at home.

An important motivational difference between desires and intentions may lie in their access to the mechanisms of intentional action. This difference coheres with the claim that intending to A entails being settled on A-ing, while desiring to A does not. Whereas our becoming settled on A-ing straightaway is normally sufficient to initiate an A-ing at once, this is false of the acquisition of desires to A straightaway. To be sure, someone's being settled now on A-ing later normally will not initiate an A-ing now. But if the intention is still present at the later time and the agent recognizes that the designated time has arrived, an attempt at A-ing will normally be immediately forthcoming. This is not true of someone who still has a mere desire at the later time to A. Such a person may choose not to A and behave accordingly. Perhaps the person has a stronger desire to do something else or deems some other course of action better.

If intentions initiate actions, it is *proximal* intentions that do so – roughly, intentions to do something straightaway, as opposed to *distal* intentions (intentions for the nonimmediate future). More precisely, it is the *acquisition* of a proximal intention that plays this role.[1] But why do acquisitions of proximal intentions initiate the actions they do? Why, for example, does the acquisition of a proximal intention to turn a key tend to initiate one's turning a key rather than one's flipping a switch or ordering a pizza? Return to the representational side of intentions. An intention to A incorporates a plan for A-ing, and *which* intentional action or actions an intention generates is a partial function of the intention-embedded plan. In the limiting case, A-ing is a basic action (e.g. my raising my right arm) and the plan is a simple prospective representation of one's A-ing. Often, intention-embedded plans are more complex. For example, Ann's intention to check the oil in her car incorporates a plan that includes her first unlatching the hood, then opening the hood, then unscrewing the oil cap, and so on. An agent who successfully executes an intention is *guided* by the intention-embedded plan.

An intention-embedded plan identifies a goal and (in non-limiting cases) provides action-directions, as it were. Exactly how deep the representational content of intentions runs is an interesting question. Even when what is intended is routine and very simple behavior for the agent – a doctor's signing a prescription, for example – much is going on representationally. Some psychologists take the representational content of motor schemata to run deep, suggesting, for example, that motor schemata involved in handwriting include representations of the neuromuscular activity required to achieve the movement represented by their higher level components. Standard philosophical conceptions of intention seem not to countenance such representations as parts of the representational content of normal agents' intentions to write their names, probably because of the apparent inaccessibility of these representations to consciousness. On standard conceptions, however, intentions guide actions in ways that depend on their representational content. If plans embedded in standard writing intentions do not incorporate representations of low-level neuromuscular activity, they can provide guidance at a higher level, with the assistance of motor schemata that are external to intentions.

Action science and free will

Neurobiologist Benjamin Libet and psychologist Daniel Wegner have defended some striking theses about intentions and actions based on empirical studies. A 1983 article by Libet and colleagues (Libet et al. 1983) has been described as "one of the most philosophically challenging papers in modern scientific psychology" (Haggard et al. 1999: 291). A striking thesis of that 1983 article is that "the brain … 'decides' to initiate or, at the least, [to] prepare to initiate [certain actions] at a time before there is any reportable subjective awareness that such a decision has taken place" (640). In a recent article, Libet pointedly asserts, "If the 'act now' process is initiated unconsciously, then conscious free will is not doing it" (2001: 62).

Wegner argues that "conscious will is an illusion … in the sense that *the experience of consciously willing an action is not a direct indication that the conscious thought has caused the action*" (2002: 2). He contends that "The experience of will is merely a feeling that occurs to a person" (14). More specifically, "conscious will … is a feeling of doing" (325). Wegner writes, "The new idea introduced here is the possibility that the experience of acting develops when the person infers that his or her own *thought* (read intention, but belief and desire are also important) was the cause of the action" (66). Collectively, these last three quotations suggest that his claim about illusion may be understood as follows: the feeling of doing "an action is not a direct indication that the conscious [intention to perform the action] has caused the action."

Obviously, how this claim is to be interpreted depends partly on what Wegner means by "conscious intention." He writes, "*Intention* is normally understood as an idea of what one is going to do that appears in consciousness just before one does it" (2002: 18). This assertion does not apply to *distal* intentions (again, intentions for the nonimmediate future). Nor does it identify a sufficient condition for something's being an intention. As you are driving, another driver cuts you off. The following idea of what you are "going to do ... appears in consciousness just before" you hit his car: "Oh no! I'm going to hit that car." The idea expresses a prediction, not an intention; and "intention" definitely is not normally understood in such a way that this idea is an intention.

Perhaps what Wegner means is that proximal intentions, as normally understood, are ideas of what one is *intentionally* "going to do" that appear "in consciousness just before one does it" (in those cases in which one succeeds in doing what one proximally intends). Readers who do not *identify* proximal intentions with such ideas have some options about how to read Wegner's expression "conscious intention." They may read it as referring to an intention that appears in consciousness *as an intention* or instead as referring to an intention some aspect of which appears in consciousness. On the second reading, the aspect would apparently be some "idea of what one is going to do." Because the second reading is more modest, it is more charitable. One who thinks of intentions as executive attitudes toward plans may regard the "idea of what one is going to do" that is supposed to appear in consciousness as the plan component of a proximal intention or some aspect of that plan.

Among the work to which Wegner appeals in defending his thesis about illusion is Libet's. In Libet's (1985) main experiment, subjects are instructed to flex their right wrists or the fingers of their right hands whenever they wish. Electrical readings from the scalp – averaged over at least 40 flexings for each subject – show a shift in "readiness potentials" beginning about 550 milliseconds (ms) before the time at which an electromyogram shows relevant muscular motion to begin. Subjects are also instructed to "recall ... the spatial clock position of a revolving spot at the time of [their] initial awareness" (529) of something, *x*, that Libet variously describes as an "intention," "urge," "wanting," "decision," "will," or "wish" to move.[2] On average, "RP onset" preceded what the subjects reported to be the time of their initial awareness of *x* (time W) by 350 ms. Time W, then, preceded the beginning of muscle motion by about 200 ms. These results are represented in the following table:

Libet's results		
–550 ms	–200 ms	0 ms
RP onset	Time W	Muscle begins to move

(Libet finds independent evidence of a slight error in subjects' recall of the times at which they first become aware of sensations. Correcting for that error, time W is –150 ms.)

Wegner writes,

> The position of conscious will in the time line suggests perhaps that the experience of will is a link in a causal chain leading to action, but in fact it might not even be that. It might just be a loose end – one of those things, like the action, that is caused by prior brain and mental events.
>
> (2002: 55)

By "the experience of will" here, Wegner means "the experience of wanting to move" (55). He is suggesting that this is not a cause of the flexing. Here one must be careful. Consider Ann, an arbitrarily selected subject. Her wanting to flex soon and her experience of wanting to flex soon are not identical. So to grant that Ann's experience of wanting to flex soon is not a cause of her flexing is not to grant that her wanting to flex soon also is not a cause of her flexing.

Move from wanting to intending. An intention to flex straightaway is a proximal intention. Suppose that Libet's subjects have many conscious intentions of this kind during the course of an experiment. Suppose also that neither their *experiences* of proximally intending to flex nor the neural correlates of those experiences are causes of their flexing actions. These suppositions leave it open that the subjects' proximal intentions or their neural correlates are causes of these actions; for their experiences of their proximal intentions are not identical with the intentions themselves.

Partly because they are told that they need to "recall ... the spatial clock position of a revolving spot at the time of [their] initial awareness" of their urges (or wishes, intentions, etc.) to flex (Libet 1985: 529), Libet's subjects may interpret their instructions as calling for them to wait until they feel – that is, experience – an urge to flex before flexing and to flex in response to that feeling. If they comply with the instructions, so understood, the feelings are among the causes of the flexings: the feelings serve as cues to begin flexing. This obvious point is a problem for Wegner's *statement* of his position – specifically, for his claim that "the experience of wanting to move" in Libet's subjects is not "a link in a causal chain leading to action" (2002: 55). However, Wegner's actual position is more subtle. It is that the basic causal process that leads to flexing in these subjects does not depend on consciousness of – that is, feeling – an urge to flex. The idea is that even if the subjects were not waiting to feel an urge as a cue for flexing – even if, as one might put it, they did not interpret an instruction to flex whenever they *feel* like it in a phenomenological way – flexing would be produced in the same basic way: the consciousness of the urge is "just ... a loose end" in this process (Wegner 2002: 55), and the same is true of the consciousness aspect of any conscious proximal intention to flex that may emerge.

Suppose that Wegner is right about this. What would the upshot be? If, as Anthony Marcel (2003) maintains, non-conscious proximal intentions can produce corresponding intentional actions, an agent's conscious proximal intention to flex may produce a flexing action in a way that does not depend on the intention's consciousness aspect. If many proximal intentions produce actions without the intentions showing up in consciousness, this is not a terribly surprising result. When you signal for turns you make in your car, do you *consciously* intend to signal? Probably not, in normal circumstances. Even so, it is arguable that you do intend to signal and that your intentions (or their neural correlates) help to produce your signaling actions.

But *is* Wegner right? Is Libet right? There are significant grounds for doubting that the RPs observed in Libet's main experiment – type-II RPs – are correlated specifically with proximal decisions or intentions to flex as opposed to a variety of other things: for example, (roughly) proximal unconscious urges to flex, brain events that are pretty reliable relatively proximal causal contributors to (roughly) proximal urges to flex, relevant motor preparedness, and even imagining or anticipating flexing very soon ("the pattern of brain activity associated with imagining making a movement is very similar to the pattern of activity associated with preparing to make a movement" [Spence and Frith 1999]). It will be useful to have a name for this collection of alternative possibilities. I call it the *ALT collection*.

If makings of proximal decisions to flex or acquisitions of proximal intentions to flex (or the neural correlates of these things) cause muscle motion, how long does it take them to do that? Does it take about 550 ms? Might reaction time experiments show that 550 ms is too long a time for this?

In typical reaction time experiments, subjects have decided in advance to perform an assigned task – to A, for short – whenever they detect the relevant signal. When they detect the signal, there is no need for a proximal *decision* to A. But it is plausible that after they detect the signal, they acquire a proximal *intention* to A. That is, it is plausible that the combination of their conditional intention to A when they detect the signal (or the neural correlate of that intention) and their detection of the signal (or the neural correlate of that detection) produces a proximal intention to A. The acquisition of this intention (or the neural correlate of that event) would then initiate the A-ing.[3] And in a reaction time experiment (described shortly) that is very similar to Libet's main experiment, the time between the "go" signal and the onset of muscle motion is much shorter than 550 ms. This is evidence that proximal intentions to flex – as opposed to items in the ALT collection – emerge much closer to the time of the onset of muscle motion than 550 ms. There is no reason, in principle, that it should take people any longer to start flexing their wrists when executing a proximal intention to flex in Libet's studies than it takes them to do this when executing such an intention in a reaction time study. More precisely, there is no reason, in principle, that the interval between proximal intention acquisition and the beginning of muscle motion should be significantly different in the two scenarios.[4]

The line of reasoning just sketched depends on the assumption that, in reaction time studies, proximal intentions to A are at work. An alternative possibility is that the combination of subjects' conditional intentions to A when they detect the signal and their detection of the signal initiates the A-ing without there being any proximal intention to A. Of course, there is a parallel possibility in the case of Libet's subjects. Perhaps the combination of their conditional intentions to flex when they next feel like it – conscious intentions, presumably – together with relevant feelings (namely, conscious proximal urges to flex) initiates a flexing without there being any proximal intentions to flex. (They may treat their initial consciousness of the urge as a "go" signal, as suggested in Keller and Heckhausen [1990: 352].) If that possibility is an actuality, then Libet's thesis is false, of course: there is no intention to flex "now" in his subjects and, therefore, no such intention is produced by the brain before the mind is aware of it.

The reaction-time study I mentioned is reported in Haggard and Magno (1999):

> Subjects sat at a computer watching a clock hand … whose rotation period was 2.56 s … After an unpredictable delay, varying from 2.56 to 8 s, a high-frequency tone … was played over a loudspeaker. This served as a warning stimulus for the subsequent reaction. 900 ms after the warning stimulus onset, a second tone … was played. [It] served as the go signal. Subjects were instructed to respond as rapidly as possible to the go signal with a right-key press on a computer mouse button. Subjects were instructed not to anticipate the go stimulus and were reprimanded if they responded on catch trials. (103)

"Reaction times were calculated by examining the EMG [electromyogram] signal for the onset of the first sustained burst of muscle activity occurring after the go signal" (p. 104). "Reaction time" here, then, starts *before* any intention to press "now" is acquired: obviously, detecting the signal takes time; and if detection of the signal helps to produce a proximal intention, that takes time too. The mean of the subjects' median reaction times in the control trials was 231 ms. If a proximal intention to press was acquired, that happened nearer to the time of muscle motion than 231 ms and, therefore, much nearer than the 550 ms that Libet claims is the time proximal intentions to flex are unconsciously acquired in his studies. And notice how close we are getting to Libet's time W, his subjects' reported time of their initial awareness of something he variously describes as an "intention," "urge," "wanting," "decision," or "wish" to move (–200 to –150 ms). If proximal intentions to flex are acquired in Libet's studies, Haggard and Magno's results make it look like a better bet that they are acquired around time W than that they are acquired around –550 ms.[5] How seriously we should take his subjects' reports of the time of their initial awareness of the urge, intention, or whatever, is a controversial question that I leave open here.

When Libet's work is applied to the theoretically subtle and complicated issue of free will, things can quickly get out of hand. The abstract of Haggard and Libet (2001) opens as follows:

> The problem of free will lies at the heart of modern scientific studies of consciousness. An influential series of experiments by Libet has suggested that conscious intentions arise as a result of brain activity. This contrasts with traditional concepts of free will, in which the mind controls the body. (47)

Now, only a certain kind of mind-body dualist would hold that conscious intentions do *not* "arise as a result of brain activity." And such dualist views are rarely advocated in contemporary philosophical publications on free will. Moreover, contemporary philosophers who argue for the existence of free will typically shun substance dualism. If Libet's work is of general interest to philosophers working on free will, the source of the interest lies elsewhere than the theoretical location specified in this passage (see Mele 2006: Ch. 2, or 2009: Ch. 4).

In a recent article, Libet writes, "it is only the final 'act now' process that produces the voluntary *act*. That 'act now' process begins in the brain about 550 msec [ms] before the act, and it begins unconsciously" (2001: 61). "There is," he says, "an unconscious gap of about 400 msec between the onset of the cerebral process and when the person becomes consciously aware of his/her decision or wish or intention to act." (A page later, he identifies what the agent becomes aware of as "the intention/wish/urge to act" [62].) Libet adds, "If the 'act now' process is initiated unconsciously, then conscious free will is not doing it."

I have already explained that Libet has not shown that a decision to flex is made or an intention to flex acquired at –550 ms. But even if the intention emerges much later, that is compatible with an 'act now' process having begun at –550 ms. One might say that "the 'act now' process" in Libet's spontaneous subjects begins with the formation or acquisition of a proximal intention to flex, much closer to the onset of muscle motion than –550 ms, or that it begins earlier, with the beginning of a process that issues in the intention. I will not argue about that. Suppose we say that "the 'act now' process" begins with the unconscious emergence of a (roughly) proximal urge to flex – or with a pretty reliable relatively proximal causal contributor to a (roughly) proximal urge to flex – at about –550 ms, and that the urge plays a significant role in producing a proximal intention to flex many milliseconds later. We can then agree with Libet that, given that the "process is initiated unconsciously … conscious free will is not doing it" – that is, is not initiating "the 'act now' process." But who would have thought that free will has the job of producing urges (or causal contributors to urges)? In the philosophical literature, free will's primary locus of operation is typically identified as deciding (or choosing), and for all Libet has shown, his subjects make their decisions (or choices) consciously.

Libet asks (2001: 62), "How would the 'conscious self' initiate a voluntary act if, factually, the process to 'act now' is initiated unconsciously?" In this paragraph, I offer an answer. One significant piece of background is that an "'act now' process" that is initiated unconsciously may be aborted by the agent; that apparently is what happens in instances of spontaneous vetoing that Libet discusses, if "'act now' processes" start when Libet says they do.[6] Now, processes have parts, and the various parts of a process may have more and less proximal initiators. A process that is initiated by something in the ALT collection may have a subsequent part that is directly initiated by the conscious formation or acquisition of an intention. The "conscious self" – which need not be understood as something mysterious – might more proximally initiate a voluntary act that is less proximally initiated by something in the ALT collection. (Readers who, like me, prefer to use "self" only as an affix may prefer to say that the acquisition or formation of a relevant proximal intention, which intention is consciously acquired or formed, might more proximally initiate an intentional action that is less proximally initiated by something else.)

Libet himself says that "conscious volitional control may operate … to select and control ["the volitional process"], either by permitting or triggering the final motor outcome of the unconsciously initiated process or by vetoing the progression to actual motor activation" (1985: 529). "Triggering" is a kind of initiating. In "triggering the final motor outcome," the acquisition of a proximal intention would be initiating an action in a more direct way than does whatever initiated a process that issued in the intention. According to one view of things, when proximal action-desires help to initiate overt actions they do so by helping to produce pertinent proximal intentions the formation or acquisition of which directly initiates actions (Mele 1992). What Libet says about triggering here coheres with this.

In an exchange with Libet, Patrick Haggard remarks that "conceptual analysis could help" (Haggard and Libet 2001: 62). I agree. Attention not only to the data but also to the concepts in terms of which the data are analyzed makes it clear that Libet's striking claims about decisions, intentions, and free will are not justified by his results. Libet asserts that his "discovery that the brain unconsciously initiates the volitional process well before the person becomes aware of an intention or wish to act voluntarily ... clearly has a profound impact on how we view the nature of free will" (2004: 201). Not so. That, in certain settings, (roughly) proximal urges to do things arise unconsciously or issue partly from causes of which the agent is not conscious – urges on which the agent may or may not subsequently act – is a cause neither for worry nor for enthusiasm about free will.

Despite the reservations I have voiced about Libet's work, it is interesting and important. For one thing, the data give us a sense of how much time might elapse between the acquisition of a conscious proximal urge to A – even one that is stronger than any competing desire – and an A-ing motivated by that urge. Perhaps, in some cases in which such urges conflict with what the agents consciously believe it would be best to do, there is time enough for them to reverse the balance of their motivation, thereby deflecting themselves away from a course of action that is contrary to their better judgment. If so, Libet's work provides fertile ground for reflection on some issues central to the interrelated topics of weakness of will (akrasia) and self-control (see Mele 1997, 2003: Ch. 8). A defining feature of akratic action, on a traditional conception, is that it is *freely* performed contrary to the agent's better judgment.[7] Libet's data have some bearing on free will by way of their bearing on the conceivability of situations in which agents' strongest (roughly) proximal desires are at odds with their conscious beliefs about what it would be best to do and both akratic action and its contrary are real possibilities.

The Future

Some work in the philosophy of action is deeply engaged with scientific work on action. Indeed, there is a trend in that direction, and I predict that it will become stronger. Philosophers of action can learn much from action science, and conceptual work in the philosophy of action can assist in the formulation of interesting testable hypotheses about action and in the evaluation of data.

Notes

1. Sometimes, for stylistic reasons, I will omit reference to acquisition events in discussing action initiation.
2. Libet et al. report that "the subject was asked to note and later report the time of appearance of his conscious awareness of 'wanting' to perform a given self-initiated movement. The experience was also described as an 'urge' or 'intention' or 'decision' to move, though subjects usually settled for the words 'wanting' or 'urge'" (1983: 627).
3. Hereafter, the parenthetical clauses should be supplied by the reader.
4. Notice that the interval at issue is distinct from intervals between the time of the occurrence of events that cause proximal intentions and the time of intention acquisition.
5. In a study by Day et al. of eight subjects instructed to flex a wrist when they hear a tone, mean reaction time was 125 ms (1989: 653). In their study of five subjects instructed to flex both wrists when they hear a tone, mean reaction time was 93 ms (658). The mean reaction times of both groups of subjects – defined as "the interval from auditory tone to onset of the first antagonist EMG burst" (651) – were much shorter than those of Haggard and Magno's subjects. Day's subjects, unlike Haggard and Magno's (and Libet's), were not watching a clock.
6. Subjects encouraged to flex spontaneously "reported that during some of the trials a recallable conscious urge to act appeared but was 'aborted' or somehow suppressed before any actual movement occurred; in such cases the subject simply waited for another urge to appear, which, when consummated, constituted the actual event whose RP was recorded" (Libet 1985: 538). Notice that it is *urges* – not decisions or intentions – that these subjects are said to report and abort or suppress. In addition to vetoing urges for actions that are not yet in progress, agents can abort attempts, including attempts at relatively temporally short actions. When batting, baseball players often successfully halt the motion of their arms while a swing is in progress. Presumably, they acquire or form an intention to stop swinging while they are in the process of executing an intention to swing.
7. Agents who manifest weakness of will in acting contrary to what they judge best are distinguished, for example, from (actual or hypothetical) addicts who, owing to compulsions, unfreely do something that they judge it best not to do.

References

Andersen, R., and Buneo, C. (2002) "Intentional Maps in Posterior Parietal Cortex," *Annual Review of Neuroscience* 25: 189–220.

Davidson, D. (1963) "Actions, Reasons, and Causes," *Journal of Philosophy* 60: 685–700.

Day, B., Rothwell, J., Thompson, P., Maertens de Noordhout, A., Nakashima, K., Shannon, K., and Marsden, C. (1989) "Delay in the Execution of Voluntary Movement by Electrical or Magnetic Brain Stimulation in Intact Man," *Brain* 112: 649–63.

Haggard, P., and Libet, B. (2001) "Conscious Intention and Brain Activity," *Journal of Consciousness Studies* 8: 47–63.

Haggard, P., and Magno, E. (1999) "Localising Awareness of Action with Transcranial Magnetic Stimulation," *Experimental Brain Research* 127: 102–7.

Haggard, P., Newman, C., and Magno, E. (1999) "On the Perceived Time of Voluntary Actions," *British Journal of Psychology* 90: 291–303.

Keller, J., and Heckhausen, H. (1990) "Readiness Potentials Preceding Spontaneous Motor Acts: Voluntary vs. Involuntary Control." *Electroencephalography and Clinical Neuropsychology* 76: 351–61.

Libet, B. (1985) "Unconscious Cerebral Initiative and the Role of Conscious Will in Voluntary Action," *Behavioral and Brain Sciences* 8: 529–66.

—— (2001) "Consciousness, Free Action and the Brain," *Journal of Consciousness Studies* 8: 59–65.

—— (2004) *Mind Time*, Cambridge, MA: Harvard University Press.

Libet, B., Gleason, C., Wright, E., and Pearl, D. (1983) "Time of Unconscious Intention to Act in Relation to Onset of Cerebral Activity (Readiness-Potential)," *Brain* 106: 623–42.

Marcel, A. (2003) "The Sense of Agency: Awareness and Ownership of Action," in J. Roessler and N. Eilan (eds) *Agency and Self-Awareness*, Oxford: Clarendon Press.
Mele, A. (1992) *Springs of Action: Understanding Intentional Behavior*, New York: Oxford University Press.
—— (1997) "Strength of Motivation and Being in Control: Learning from Libet," *American Philosophical Quarterly* 34: 319–33.
—— (2003) *Motivation and Agency*, New York: Oxford University Press.
—— (2006) *Free Will and Luck*, New York: Oxford University Press.
—— (2009) *Effective Intentions: The Power of Conscious Will*, New York: Oxford University Press.
Spence, S., and Frith, C. (1999) "Towards a Functional Anatomy of Volition," *Journal of Consciousness Studies* 6: 11–29.
Wegner, D. (2002) *The Illusion of Conscious Will*, Cambridge, MA: MIT Press.

43
MORAL JUDGMENT

Jennifer Nado, Daniel Kelly, and Stephen Stich

Introduction

Questions regarding the nature of moral judgment loom large in moral philosophy. Perhaps the most basic of these questions asks how, exactly, moral judgments and moral rules are to be defined. What features distinguish them from other sorts of rules and judgments? A related question concerns the extent to which emotion and reason guide moral judgment. Are moral judgments made mainly on the basis of reason, or are they primarily the products of emotion? As an example of the former view, Kant held that all moral requirements are ultimately grounded in rationality, and could be derived from the categorical imperative. As an example of the latter, Hume famously claimed that reason is "the slave of the passions" and that moral judgments stem from the moral emotions.

When addressing these issues, philosophers have largely relied on the traditional tools of philosophical analysis, along with introspection, anecdotal evidence and armchair speculation. In recent years, however, a rich body of experimental psychology has emerged which, in the view of a growing number of philosophers, casts important new light on these venerable questions. Our aim in this chapter is to illustrate how empirical methods can help move traditional philosophical debates forward in interesting and important ways. Since space does not permit an exhaustive survey of the relevant experimental work, we will focus on a few of the most compelling examples.[1]

The definition of morality

In 1957, Alasdair MacIntyre wrote, "The central task to which contemporary moral philosophers have addressed themselves is that of listing the distinctive characteristics of moral utterances" (MacIntyre 1957: 325). Thirteen years later, MacIntyre's article was reprinted in an anthology called *The Definition of Morality* (Wallace and Walker 1970), which also included papers by such leading figures as Elizabeth Anscombe, Kurt Baier, Philippa Foot, William Frankena, and Peter Strawson. All of these, in one way or another, tackled the question of how "morality" is best defined. As one might expect from this distinguished list of authors, many of the arguments developed in the book are subtle and sophisticated. And as one might expect in just about any group of thirteen philosophers, no consensus was reached. In addition to debate about how the notions of moral utterance, moral rule and moral norm are to be defined, many of the contributors to the volume also discuss a cluster of meta-philosophical questions, such as "What is a definition of morality supposed to do?" and "What counts as getting the definition right?" Here again, no consensus was reached.

A few years later, Paul Taylor published a long paper whose goal was to elaborate and defend an account of what it is for a norm to be a *moral* norm for a group of people (Taylor 1978). Taylor also provides a useful taxonomy of various positions one might take on the meta-philosophical issue. What, Taylor asks, might philosophers be trying to do when they offer a definition of "morality" or "moral rule"? One option is that they are offering a *linguistic analysis* which tries to capture how the word "moral," or phrases like "moral rule" and "moral norm" are used by English speakers. A second, closely related possibility is that they are proposing a *conceptual analysis*, aimed at making explicit the concept of morality held by people in our society. A third, quite different alternative is that philosophers are trying to specify the *essence* of morality. Philosophers pursuing this project would maintain that moral rules or norms constitute a *natural kind* whose members all share some essential property or set of properties. The goal of the project is to discover what those essential properties are. Taylor suggests that this is a misguided project, since he believes that "there is no such essence" (52), though he recognizes that others might disagree with this assessment.[2]

At about the same time, a group of developmental psychologists who had been influenced by some of the philosophical literature aimed at defining morality began developing and defending their own definition. On one interpretation of their work, these psychologists were demonstrating that Taylor was wrong: morality *is* a natural kind, and via their experiments they were beginning to discover what the essential properties of moral rules are. For about two decades, this work was all but unknown to philosophers. But as the twentieth century drew to a close, interest in the empirical study of morality increased dramatically among philosophers, and this work became increasingly influential.

The central figure in this research tradition is Elliot Turiel, who proposed a definition of "moral rule" together with a definition of "conventional rule" – another notion on which philosophers like David Lewis had recently lavished a fair amount of attention. Turiel did not defend his definitions using abstract philosophical arguments, however, nor did he make claims about how the words "moral" and "conventional" are used. Rather, he used his definitions to design psychological experiments, and those experiments produced some very extraordinary findings on moral judgment (Turiel 1979, 1983).

The core ideas in the definitions that Turiel and his followers have offered are as follows:

(i) Moral rules are held to have an objective, prescriptive force; they are not dependent on the authority of any individual or institution.
(ii) Moral rules are taken to hold generally, not just locally; they not only proscribe

behavior here and now, but also in other countries and at other times in history.

(iii) Violations of moral rules involve a victim who has been harmed, whose rights have been violated, or who has been subject to an injustice.

(iv) Violations of moral rules are typically more serious than violations of conventional rules.

Conventional rules, on Turiel's account, have just the opposite cluster of properties. They do not have objective, prescriptive force; rather they are viewed as arbitrary or situation dependent, and can be suspended or changed by an appropriate authoritative individual or institution. Conventional rules are often geographically and temporally local; those applicable in one community often will not apply in other communities or at other times in history. Violations of conventional rules do not involve a victim who has been harmed, whose rights have been violated, or who has been subject to an injustice, and these violations are typically less serious than violations of moral rule.

Guided by these definitions, Turiel and his associates developed an experimental paradigm that has become known as the *moral/conventional task*. In this task, participants are presented with examples of transgressions of prototypical moral rules and prototypical conventional rules, and are asked series of probe questions. Some of the questions are designed to determine whether the participants consider the action to be wrong, and if so, how serious it is. Other questions explore whether participants think that the wrongness of the transgression is "authority dependent." For example, a participant who has said that a specific rule-violating act is wrong might be asked, "What if the teacher said there is no rule in this school about [that sort of rule violating act], would it be right to do it then?" A third group of questions aim to determine whether participants think the rule is general in scope. Is it applicable to everyone, everywhere, or just to a limited range of people, in a restricted set of circumstances? Finally, participants are asked how they would justify the rule – do they invoke harm, justice or rights, or do they invoke other factors?

Early results suggested that the categories of moral and conventional rules, as defined by Turiel, are robustly psychologically significant. In experiments in which they were asked about both prototypical moral transgressions and prototypical conventional transgressions, participants' responses to the two sorts of transgression differed *systematically*, and in just the way suggested by Turiel's characterization of the distinction. Transgressions of prototypical moral rules almost always involved a victim who was clearly harmed; common examples included one child hitting another, or one child pushing another child off a swing. As Turiel's account predicted, these were judged to be more serious than transgressions of prototypical conventional rules, the wrongness of the transgression was judged not to be authority dependent, the violated rule was judged to be general in scope, and judgments were justified by appeal to the harm they caused. By contrast, transgressions of prototypical conventional rules, such as a child talking in class when she has not been called on by the teacher, or a boy wearing a dress to school, were judged to be less serious, the rules were judged to be authority dependent and not general in scope, and judgments were not justified by appeal to harm. In the three decades after the moral/conventional task was first introduced, this pattern of results has been found in an impressively diverse range of participants differing in religion, nationality, culture and age – from 3.5 years to adulthood (see Nucci [2001] for a recent overview).

What conclusions can be drawn from these results? It is not entirely clear how Turiel and his associates would answer this question, since much of their own discussion is couched in the philosophically tendentious and less than perspicuous terminology that grows out of the Piagetian tradition. Rather than getting bogged down in textual exegesis, we'll set out some conclusions that are plausible to draw from these findings, conclusions which many philosophers impressed by the results appear to accept. Since we'll have occasion to refer back to these conclusions, it will be useful to give them numbers.

(1) Participants in moral/conventional task experiments will typically display one of the two *signature response patterns* described in the previous paragraph. Moreover, these response patterns are *nomological clusters* – there is a strong ("lawlike") tendency for the members of the cluster to occur together.
(2) Each of these signature response patterns is associated with a certain type of transgression. (2a) The "moral" signature response pattern is evoked by transgressions involving harm, justice, welfare or rights; (2b) the "conventional" signature response pattern is evoked by transgressions that *do not* involve harm, justice, welfare, or rights.
(3) The regularities described in (1) and (2) are pan-cultural, and they emerge quite early in development.

Since nomological clusters like those noted in (1), and generalizations like those noted in (2a) and (2b), are central in philosophical accounts of natural kinds (Boyd 2002), it is plausible to draw the further conclusion that both moral rules and conventional rules are indeed *natural kinds*, and that the essential features of the kinds are just those specified in Turiel's definitions.

It is not surprising that as the results of experiments using the moral/conventional task became more widely known, this work began to make an impact on naturalistically inclined philosophers interested in moral psychology. For, if true, the conclusion that both moral rules and conventional rules are natural kinds is profoundly important. There are, however, a growing number of empirically informed skeptics who doubt that conclusion is warranted. For the most part, the skeptics have focused on evidence that challenges (2b). There are many societies, the skeptics maintain, in which transgressions that do *not* involve harm, justice, welfare and rights fail to evoke the full "conventional" response pattern. Rather, these transgressions evoke one or more of the signature "moral" responses. Perhaps the best known study illustrating this phenomenon was conducted by Jonathan Haidt and colleagues, who explored people's judgments about a variety of transgressions, including the following memorable example:

> A man goes to the supermarket once a week and buys a dead chicken. But before cooking the chicken, he has sexual intercourse with it. Then he cooks it and eats it.
>
> (Haidt et al. 1993: 617)

Haidt and colleagues found that low socioeconomic status participants in both Brazil and the United States judged this, and a variety of other disgusting, but not harmful, transgressions to be authority *in*dependent and generally applicable, both of which are features of the signature moral response pattern. In a more recent study, Nichols (2002, 2004) explored participants' reactions to violations of etiquette norms, comparing rules that prohibit disgusting behavior – for example, a dinner guest snorting into his water glass then taking a drink – with rules that prohibit behavior that is not disgusting, like a dinner guest drinking tomato soup out of a bowl. Nichols found that in children the disgusting etiquette transgressions evoked three of the signature "moral" responses – they were more serious than the conventional transgression, not authority dependent and generalizable to other groups – while the non-disgusting transgressions evoked all of the signature "conventional" responses. With adults, the disgusting transgressions evoked two of the signature "moral" responses – they were more serious and not authority dependent, but they did *not* generalize to other groups. In addition to challenging (2b), Nichols' results pose a particularly clear challenge to the claim that the signature response patterns are nomological clusters, since he finds that for etiquette rules the signature "conventional" response pattern comes apart in three different ways!

These are not the only studies that raise problems for (2b).[3] However, we suspect that the published studies challenging (2b) may only be the tip of the iceberg. For a variety of reasons, researchers using the moral/conventional task have focused on a very narrow range of "conventional" transgressions, restricted almost entirely to those that would be readily understood by children. As a wider range of "conventional" transgressions is explored, we expect there will be many more cases that fail to support (2b). The emphasis on "schoolyard" transgressions in the literature is even more pronounced in the case of "moral" transgressions. Indeed, as this is being written (in 2006), there is only one study that explores a substantial range of harmful moral transgressions of the sort that would not be familiar to young children. In this study, Kelly et al. (2007) used probes like the following:

> (A) Three hundred years ago, whipping was a common practice in most navies and on cargo ships. There were no laws against it, and almost everyone thought that whipping was an appropriate way to discipline sailors who disobeyed orders or were drunk on duty.
>
> Mr Williams was an officer on a cargo ship 300 years ago. One night, while at sea, he found a sailor drunk at a time when the sailor should have been on watch. After the sailor sobered up, Williams punished the sailor by giving him five lashes with a whip.

Is it OK for Mr Williams to whip the sailor?

YES NO

On a scale from 0 to 9, how would you rate Mr Williams' behavior?

(B) Mr Adams is an officer on a large modern American cargo ship in 2004. One night, while at sea, he finds a sailor drunk at a time when the sailor should have been monitoring the radar screen. After the sailor sobers up, Adams punishes the sailor by giving him five lashes with a whip.

Is it OK for Mr Adams to whip the sailor?

YES NO

On a scale from 0 to 9, how would you rate Mr Adams' behavior?

The results were quite dramatic. In this case, 52 percent of participants said it was OK to whip the sailor 300 years ago, but only 6 percent said it was OK to do it in 2004. This suggests that the participants in this study did *not* judge the rule prohibiting whipping in the contemporary world to be applicable at other times in history. The results on other probes used by Kelly et al. were similar. This is just one study, of course, and more work is needed before we can draw any definitive conclusion about whether Turiel and his followers have discovered the essential properties of moral and conventional rules. But we think it is already abundantly clear that experimental work of the sort we have recounted in this section provides a new and important tool for exploring a central question in moral philosophy.

Reason and emotion in moral judgment

As noted in the introduction, another venerable issue in philosophical debates about moral judgment centers on whether emotion or reason plays the more important role. In the psychological literature, where the theories of Jean Piaget and of Lawrence Kohlberg enjoyed wide influence, the prevailing view for much of the twentieth century favored reason. Though they differ over many important details, both Piaget and Kohlberg claim that children progress through different stages in their ability to make moral judgments, with each stage employing more sophisticated and complex moral reasoning than the last. Recently, however, a number of psychologists have offered accounts of moral judgment in which emotion has the upper hand.

One of the most radical and provocative of these accounts was proposed by Jonathan Haidt. According to Haidt's "social intuitionist" model, emotional capacities involving affect and intuition do almost all of the work in generating moral judgments (Haidt 2001). Reason, on the other hand, is relegated to the role of a lawyer or public relations agent, whose job it is to offer public, *post-hoc* justifications for judgments after

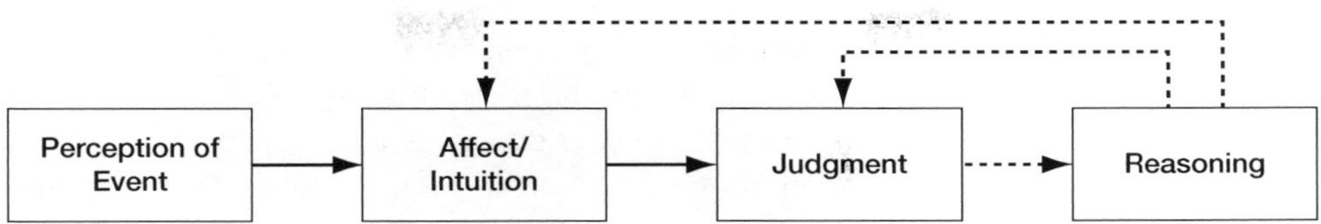

Figure 43.1 Haidt's social intuitionist model.

they have been made. Figure 43.1 is a simplified depiction of the model Haidt defends. The first step in the process leading to moral judgment, in this model, is the perception of a morally relevant event. The second box represents "moral intuitions," which rapidly and spontaneously appear in consciousness in response to the witnessed moral situation. The person experiencing these intuitions normally lacks any awareness of having gone through a process of reasoning to arrive at them. Rather, Haidt characterizes these intuitions, which he holds to be the fundamental determinants of moral judgment, as affective reactions – quick flashes of disgust or anger, for instance. Often, the entire process stops once the intuition gives rise to a judgment. However, when circumstances require the person to justify her judgment, she will engage in conscious reasoning in order to produce a justification. This *post-hoc* reasoning process usually supports the affective intuition, but will occasionally override the initial affective judgment – and it may even occasionally affect the system responsible for affective intuitions. Since neither reasoning nor the downstream effects of reasoning need always occur, we've represented them with dashed arrows in Figure 43.1.

In support of this model, Haidt offers an extensive array of empirical findings. Among the most striking of these is a study in which participants were presented with vignettes, like the one that follows, which engender substantial affect but which are carefully designed to rule out most of the justifications that participants are likely to come up with.

> Julie and Mark are brother and sister. They are traveling together in France on summer vacation from college. One night they are staying alone in a cabin near the beach. They decide that it would be interesting and fun if they tried making love. At the very least, it would be a new experience for each of them. Julie was already taking birth control pills, but Mark uses a condom too, just to be safe. They both enjoy making love, but they decide not to do it again. They keep that night as a special secret, which makes them feel even closer to each other. What do you think about that? Was it okay for them to make love?
>
> (Haidt 2001: 814)

Haidt found that participants typically answer "immediately," insisting that the behavior was wrong. When asked why, they begin "searching for reasons" (814). But the most obvious reasons to oppose incest, like the risk of pregnancy, the higher probability of having a child with birth defects, or acquiring an unsavory reputation, do not apply in this case. When the experimenter, playing the devil's advocate, points this out, the typical participant will readily acknowledge the point, but will still not withdraw his initial judgment. Rather, he will insist that his judgment is correct even though he cannot offer any reasons in support of that judgment. The conclusion that Haidt draws from this phenomenon, which he calls "moral dumbfounding," is that reasoning typically plays no role in the production of moral judgment.

In another important experiment, Wheatley and Haidt (2005) hypnotized participants and told them to feel disgust when they encountered the emotionally neutral words "take" or "often." Participants were then asked to judge vignettes in which people behaved in morally problematic ways or in entirely unproblematic ways. Half of the participants were given versions of the vignettes with the hypnotic cue word included, while the other half received nearly identical versions of the vignettes with the hypnotic cue word omitted. This is one of the morally problematic vignettes:

> Congressman Arnold Paxton frequently gives speeches condemning corruption and arguing for campaign finance reform. But he is just trying to cover up the fact that he himself [will take bribes from / is often bribed by] the tobacco lobby, and other special interests, to promote their legislation.
>
> (781)

And this is the morally neutral one:

> Dan is a student council representative at his school. This semester he is in charge of scheduling discussions about academic issues. He [tries to take / often picks] topics that appeal to both professors and students in order to stimulate discussion.
>
> (782)

The presence of the hypnotic cue word in the morally problematic scenarios led the participants to assess the transgressions significantly more harshly. In the morally neutral scenarios, the presence of the cue word led a significant number of participants to judge that the agent's actions were morally questionable! Participants were asked for comments at the end of the study and, Wheatley and Haidt report, "the post hoc nature of moral reasoning was most dramatically illustrated by the Student Council story. Rather than overrule their feelings about Dan, some participants launched an even more desperate search for external justification. One participant wrote: 'It just seems like he's up to something'. " (783)

Another account of moral judgment in which emotion plays a major role has been proposed by Joshua Greene. However, on Greene's account, reasoning also plays a role in the production of moral judgment in an important class of cases. Greene et al. (2001) administered functional magnetic resonance imaging (fMRI) scans to participants while they made judgments about how people should behave when confronting a number of moral dilemmas. The dilemmas were divided into two groups. The first group involved "impersonal" moral situations like the classic "trolley problem," where one must choose whether to flip a switch to divert a runaway trolley from a track on which it will run over five individuals to a track on which it will only kill one. The second group of dilemmas, the "personal" moral situations, included cases like the

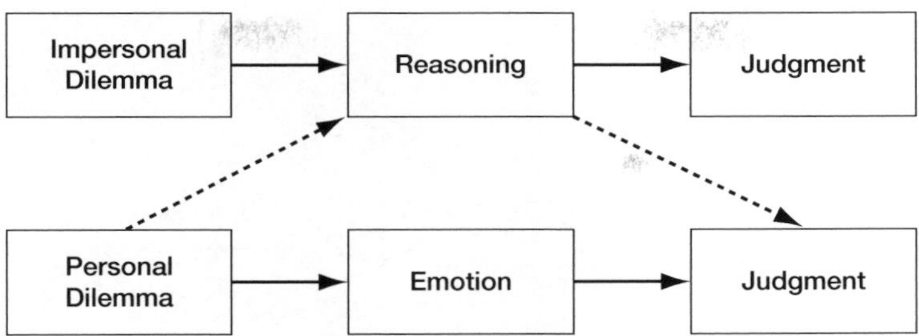

Figure 43.2 Greene's model of the processes underlying moral judgment.

"footbridge problem" – a variation on the trolley problem where, rather than flipping a switch, one must decide whether to push an overweight man off a footbridge to block a trolley that will kill five people if it is not stopped. The fMRI scans revealed that brain areas associated with emotion were much more active during contemplation of the personal moral dilemmas. In addition, most people judged the actions described in the personal moral dilemmas to be less permissible, and those who did judge them to be permissible took longer to make their judgments. Greene et al. believe this last finding to be a type of interference effect, where participants must suppress their tendency to judge the action impermissible.

Though Greene does not offer an explicit psychological model, his interpretation of these data suggests a model that would look something like Figure 43.2. In this model, personal moral dilemmas trigger emotion systems, which then play a major causal role in producing a moral judgment. Impersonal moral dilemmas, however, leave the judgment to reasoning systems. The role of reasoning in personal dilemmas is either diminished or entirely absent – the dotted lines in Figure 43.2 represent the claim that reasoning can play a minor role in personal moral dilemmas. Although Greene's model accords reasoning a more substantial role than Haidt's, a central feature of both models is the heavy emphasis on the causal efficacy of emotion in the production of moral judgments. (For some discussion of issues on which Haidt and Greene agree, see Greene and Haidt 2002.)

Despite the findings of Greene and Haidt, many reject the idea that reasoning processes should be given second billing. Marc Hauser has recently argued that emotional response cannot be the primary means by which we produce our moral judgments. His own proposal is that we possess an innate, tacit capacity for moral judgment that is in many ways parallel to our capacity for language.

Hauser argues that humans are endowed with an innate "moral grammar," akin to the linguistic universal grammar posited by Chomsky and his followers (Hauser 2006; Samuels, this volume). As in language development, this innate moral grammar provides information regarding core principles common to all moral systems. That information enables children to use cues from their environment to extract and internalize the specific moral rules present in whatever culture they are born into, even in the face of impoverished stimuli. In addition, like the linguistic faculty, the innate moral faculty operates unconsciously, quickly, and automatically. Thus, as in Haidt's

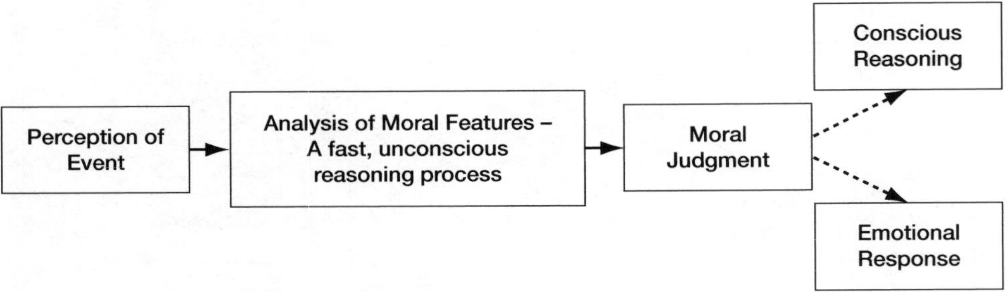

Figure 43.3 Hauser's "Rawlsian" model of moral judgment.

account, moral judgment is primarily intuition based. However, Hauser denies that these intuitions are *affective*.

Hauser's view is inspired by a passage in *A Theory of Justice* in which John Rawls suggests the use of a linguistic analogy for morality (Rawls 1971: 64). Hauser proposes that humans are "Rawlsian creatures" who produce moral judgments in the following manner. First, the perception of a morally significant event triggers an analysis of the actions involved. That analysis, though fast and unconscious, is a complex cognitive process in which many factors must be considered. In an important sense, it is a *reasoning* process – albeit not a conscious one. The analysis, in turn, is used to form a permissibility judgment. Emotions are triggered only after this judgment has occurred, and are relevant mainly for controlling our behavioral response to the perceived act. As in Haidt's model, *conscious* reasoning may also come in after the initial intuitive judgment. Figure 43.3 lays out the central features of Hauser's view. Hauser contrasts the Rawlsian position with the position of those, like Haidt, who portray humans as "Humean creatures" whose emotions play a causal role in the production of moral judgments and whose reasoning capacity comes in only after the fact, and also with those, like Piaget and Kohlberg, who suggest that humans are "Kantian creatures" whose moral judgments are largely or entirely subserved by conscious reasoning.

In arguing against the Humean creature view, Hauser notes that "neither we nor any other feeling creature can just *have* an emotion. Something in the brain must recognize – quickly or slowly – that this is an emotion-worthy situation" (Hauser 2006: 8). Before emotions can play any role, Hauser argues, a complex analysis of the relevant event must occur that scrutinizes the consequences, intentions, and participants involved. We must determine who did what, and why. Only then will we be equipped to make the remarkably fine-grained moral discriminations that we make.

One piece of evidence that Hauser invokes in support of his view is the fact that very slight alterations to a given situation can result in a sharp shift in permissibility judgments. Importantly, it is often difficult to account for such shifts by appeal to differences in emotional response. Hauser cites a set of trolley-problem cases developed by John Mikhail that demonstrate this phenomenon (Mikhail 2000; Mikhail et al. 2002). Recall that Greene found the emotion centers of the brain are activated during contemplation of the footbridge variant of the trolley problem. Greene hypothesized that this increased emotional reaction is responsible for our judgment that pushing the man is impermissible. Mikhail and Hauser, on the other hand, hypothesize that our innate moral grammar encodes a rule to the effect that using someone as a means to an end is wrong. Thus, pushing the man off the footbridge is impermissible because it wrongly uses the man as a means, while flipping the switch in the standard trolley case is permissible because the death of the person on the other track is a mere side effect of the intended act of saving the five.

Mikhail presented participants with two ingenious variations on the footbridge case intended to test this hypothesis. In one case, Ned has the option of flipping a switch to divert a trolley from a track with five hikers to a looping side track containing one overweight man. If the overweight man were not present, the trolley would loop back around to the initial track and kill the five, but the overweight man is heavy enough to stop the trolley before this occurs. Thus, the overweight man is a means to saving the five. In the second case, Oscar faces a situation which is identical, except that instead of an overweight man the looping side track contains both a heavy weight and a single slim hiker. The hiker is not heavy enough to stop the trolley, but the weight is; the hiker is simply in the wrong place at the wrong time, and his death will be a side effect of (rather than a means to) saving the five.

If the footbridge case is impermissible not because of its "personal" nature but because someone is used as a means, participants should judge Ned's flipping the switch to hit the overweight man impermissible as well. This is in fact what Mikhail's study found. In a separate study, Hauser found that, while about 90 percent of his participants considered deflecting the trolley in the standard trolley case to be permissible, only 50 percent found it permissible in Ned's case (Hauser 2006: 128). This poses a problem for purely emotion-driven accounts: why should flipping a switch to hit an overweight man on a looped track be more emotion-triggering than flipping a switch to hit a thin man on a looped track?

Though Hauser found an impressive difference between these two cases, the response on the Ned case is still quite a far cry from the response on the standard footbridge case, where only 10 percent deemed pushing the man off the footbridge to be permissible. However, this does not necessarily undermine Hauser's hypothesis that emotional activation plays no causal role in permissibility judgments. Hauser notes that up-close and personal moral dilemmas may trigger our moral faculty differently than action-at-a-distance cases. Consider two cases due to Peter Unger (1996). Most people judge it impermissible to leave a bleeding man lying on the side of the road even though taking him to the hospital would cause $200 worth of damage to your car's upholstery. However, few people consider it obligatory to donate $50 to UNICEF, even if doing so would save twenty-five children's lives. Hauser argues that we sense a moral difference in these two cases because "in our [evolutionary] past, we were only presented with opportunities to help those in our immediate path … The psychology of altruism evolved to handle nearby opportunities, within arm's reach" (Hauser 2006: 10). A similar explanation may apply to the difference between Ned's case and the footbridge dilemma.

We are inclined to think that Hauser has marshaled a persuasive defense for the claim that much complex cognitive analysis of the situation must take place prior to making the subtle and fine grained moral discrimination that people actually make. Moreover, since these discriminations are made quickly and people typically cannot give a convincing account of the considerations involved, most of the mental processing involved must be unconscious, much as it is when we make grammatical judgments. We are, however, not persuaded by Hauser's contention that emotions enter the process only *after* moral judgments are made. The argument that Hauser offers for this aspect of his theory is indirect and far from conclusive, and the Wheatley and Haidt experiment provides some impressive evidence that, sometimes at least, emotions come first and moral judgments follow.

Conclusion

The use of empirical methods to explore traditional questions in moral theory is still very much in its infancy, and there is a great deal yet to be learned. In this article we have reviewed just a small sampling of work in this area. Our aim was to illustrate how this work can shed important light on areas of inquiry traditionally of interest to philosophers. At the very least, we hope we have said enough to convince you that it would be intellectually irresponsible for philosophers interested in these issues to ignore the burgeoning, and fascinating, empirical literature in moral psychology.

Notes

1. For more extensive reviews of the literature, see Doris and Stich (2005, 2006).
2. Philosophical discussion of the definition of morality has continued into the new millennium. See, for example, Gert (2005).
3. For a more detailed survey, see Kelly and Stich (2007).

References

Boyd, R. (2002) "Scientific Realism," in Edward N. Zalta (ed.), *The Stanford Encyclopedia of Philosophy* (Summer edn); available: http://plato.stanford.edu/archives/sum2002/entries/scientific-realism/

Doris, J., and Stich, S. (2005) "As a Matter of Fact: Empirical Perspectives on Ethics," in F. Jackson and M. Smith (eds) *The Oxford Handbook of Contemporary Philosophy*, Oxford: Oxford University Press, 114–52.

—— (2006) "Moral Psychology: Empirical Approaches," in Edward N. Zalta (ed.), *The Stanford Encyclopedia of Philosophy* (Summer edn); *available:* http://plato.stanford.edu/archives/sum2006/entries/moral-psych-emp/

Gert, B. (2005) "The Definition of Morality," in Edward N. Zalta (ed.), *The Stanford Encyclopedia of Philosophy* (Fall edn); available: http://plato.stanford.edu/archives/fall2005/entries/morality-definition/

Greene, J. D., and Haidt, J. (2002) "How (and Where) Does Moral Judgment Work?" *Trends in Cognitive Science* 6: 517–23.

Greene, J., Sommerville, R., Nystrom, L., Darley, J., and Cohen, J. (2001) "An fMRI Investigation of Emotional Engagement in Moral Judgment," *Science* 293 (14 September): 2105–8.

Haidt, J. (2001) "The Emotional Dog and Its Rational Tail: A Social Intuitionist Approach to Moral Judgment," *Psychological Review* 108: 814–34.

Haidt, J., Koller, S., and Dias, M. (1993) "Affect, Culture, and Morality, or Is It Wrong to Eat Your Dog?" *Journal of Personality and Social Psychology* 65: 613–28.

Hauser, M. (2006) *Moral Minds: How Nature Designed Our Universal Sense of Right and Wrong*, New York: HarperCollins.

Kelly, D., and Stich, S. (2007) "Two Theories about the Cognitive Architecture Underlying Morality," in P. Carruthers, S. Laurence, and S. Stich (eds) *Innateness and the Structure of the Mind*, vol. 3: *Foundations and the Future*, New York: Oxford University Press, 348–66.

Kelly, D., Stich, S. Haley, K., Eng, S., and Fessler, D. (2007) "Harm, Affect and the Moral/Conventional Distinction," *Mind and Language* 22 (2): 117–31.

MacIntyre, A. (1957) "What Morality Is Not," *Philosophy* 32: 325–35.

Mikhail, J. (2000) "Rawls' Linguistic Analogy: A Study of the 'Generative Grammar' Model of Moral Theory Described by John Rawls in 'A Theory of Justice'," PhD thesis, Cornell University.

Mikhail, J, Sorrentino, C., and Spelke, E. (2002) *Aspects of the Theory of Moral Cognition: Investigating Intuitive Knowledge of the Prohibition of Intentional Battery, the Rescue Principle, the First Principle of Practical Reason, and the Principle of Double Effect*, unpublished manuscript, Stanford, CA.

Nichols, S. (2002) "Norms with Feeling: Toward a Psychological Account of Moral Judgment," *Cognition* 84: 223–36.

—— (2004) *Sentimental Rules: On the Natural Foundations of Moral Judgment*, Oxford: Oxford University Press.

Nucci, L. (2001) *Education in the Moral Domain*, Cambridge: Cambridge University Press.

Rawls, J. (1971) *A Theory of Justice*, Cambridge, MA: Harvard University Press.

Taylor, P. (1978) "On Taking the Moral Point of View," in P. A. French, T. E. Uehling, and H. K. Wettstein (eds), *Studies in Ethical Theory*, Midwest Studies in Philosophy, vol. 3, Minneapolis: University of Minnesota Press, pp. 35–61.

Turiel, E. (1979) "Distinct Conceptual and Developmental Domains: Social Convention and Morality," in H. Howe and C. Keasey (eds), *Nebraska Symposium on Motivation, 1977*, Social Cognitive Development 25, Lincoln: University of Nebraska Press, 77–116.

—— (1983) *The Development of Social Knowledge*, Cambridge: Cambridge University Press.

Unger, P. (1996) *Living High and Letting Die*, New York: Oxford University Press.

Wallace, G., and Walker, A. (eds) (1970) *The Definition of Morality*, London: Methuen and Co.

Wheatley, T., and Haidt, J. (2005) "Hypnotically Induced Disgust Makes Moral Judgments More Severe," *Psychological Science* 16, 780–4.

Further reading

An overview of recent empirical literature, with important implications for debates in moral theory, is given by J. Doris and S. Stich, "As a Matter of Fact: Empirical Perspectives on Ethics," in F. Jackson and M. Smith (eds), *The Oxford Handbook of Contemporary Philosophy* (Oxford: Oxford University Press, 2005), pp. 114–52. J. Haidt, "The Emotional Dog and Its Rational Tail: A Social Intuitionist Approach to Moral Judgment," *Psychological Review* 108 (2005): 814–34, gives a detailed exposition and defense of Haidt's model of moral judgment; and M. Hauser, *Moral Minds: How Nature Designed Our Universal Sense of Right and Wrong* (New York: HarperCollins, 2006), offers a detailed exposition and defense of Hauser's "Rawlsian" model of moral judgment. An influential volume, setting out original views on a range of issues in moral psychology, is S. Nichols, *Sentimental Rules: On the Natural Foundations of Moral Judgment* (Oxford: Oxford University Press, 2004). A model of moral judgment supported by a range of evidence in anthropology, psychology, neuroscience, and experimental economics is C. Sripada and S. Stich, "A Framework for the Psychology of Norms," in P. Carruthers, S. Laurence, and S. Stich (eds), *The Innate Mind: Culture and Cognition* (Oxford: Oxford University Press, 2007), pp. 280–301.

44
PERSONAL IDENTITY

Marya Schechtman

Imagine the following scenario: I am supposed to meet my friend Mary for lunch in a crowded restaurant. Arriving twenty minutes late, I wonder if she will still be there. She hates to be kept waiting, and told me that she will leave after waiting ten minutes. With some relief I hear her calling my name from a table across the room. "I should have left like I threatened," she says, "but I was too hungry."

There is nothing remarkable in this story, least of all the fact that I am able to tell that the person with whom I finally sit down to eat is my friend, Mary. Many of our everyday activities involve re-identifying other people. Without the capacity to make quick and (usually) accurate judgments about when we are dealing with the same person at two different times, we could not do much of what we do. When we stop to ask what it is that actually *makes* someone the same person at two different times, however, it is surprisingly difficult to find a satisfying answer.

In the story described above various cues indicate that the person with whom I am lunching is the friend with whom I made the plan to lunch. Some of these have to do with evidence that the human being at the table is the same human being with whom I made the plan – her voice sounds like Mary's and she looks like Mary. Other cues have more to do with evidence that the person in the restaurant is psychologically continuous with my friend – this person obviously remembers making a lunch date with me and threatening to leave if I was late; I will undoubtedly also find that she remembers a great deal of Mary's past and in other ways demonstrates a psychological life continuous with the person with whom I made my plans. All of these factors taken together present me with such strong reasons to believe that this is Mary that it is almost misleading to say that I *judge* this person to be Mary; it will almost certainly never enter my mind that she might not be.

But what if we imagine circumstances in which the various features that reveal this person to be Mary diverge? Suppose, for instance, that upon entering the restaurant I hear Mary's voice, and look over to the table where I see someone I recognize as Mary. When I go over to join her however, she has no idea who I am. Seeing her up-close and getting a good look at the distinctive birthmark on her hand, I am convinced that this human being is the same human being I have known as my friend Mary. But she denies having ever seen me before and acts nothing like Mary.

My immediate reaction would likely be to assume that the individual sitting at the table is Mary, suffering from some terrible psychological disorder. Suppose further, however, that when I leave the restaurant, wondering how to find help for my friend, someone I have never seen before rushes up to me in a panic. She insists that she is Mary and that she and the person now in her body were kidnapped by an evil philosopher-neurosurgeon who subjected them to an experimental brain transplant procedure. Mary's brain was transplanted to the body now speaking to me, while the brain taken from that body was placed in Mary's old body, the one now sitting in the restaurant. Were it not for the strange experience in the restaurant, I would probably dismiss these claims as insane. But the behavior of the person in the restaurant makes me wonder, so I talk to this "stranger" a bit longer and find that she reacts to things just as Mary would, remembers parts of our history that only Mary and I know about, and otherwise convinces me that her inner life is indeed continuous with Mary's. I therefore come to believe that this incredible story is true, and that Mary's psychological life has become decoupled from her body.

This case is highly fanciful and probably impossible. Still, it does seem to reveal something important. It demonstrates the need to distinguish between the criteria we use to *determine* when we are dealing with the same person (*epistemic* criteria of identity) and what actually *makes* the person the same person we encountered before (*metaphysical* criteria of identity). In everyday life the continuation of a single human being and of a psychological life usually coincide. Where we find one we typically find the other, and so we use both (or either) to make our judgments of identity. This leaves it unclear which of these types of continuity is mere evidence of sameness of person and which (if either) is what actually constitutes this sameness.

Hypothetical cases of the sort I have described, where the continuities that usually occur together come apart, can serve as thought experiments to help determine which (if any) of the many kinds of continuity we use to make judgments of personal identity can provide a metaphysical identity criterion. The two most salient possibilities are those mentioned above – psychological continuity and biological continuity. Much of the philosophical discussion of personal identity is thus devoted to investigating these two types of continuity and arguing about which is the relation that constitutes personal identity.

Psychological continuity theories

It is generally (but not universally) agreed that hypothetical cases like the scenario described above provide good evidence that it is psychological and not biological continuity that constitutes personal identity. It is natural to describe such a case as one in which Mary and another person have switched bodies. If my friendship with Mary continues it will continue with the person in the unfamiliar body. It seems fair that this is the person who should have access to Mary's hard-earned savings, live in the house she paid for, and continue in her job. If, after explaining the brain transplant, the evil philosopher-neurosurgeon tells his captives that one of them will be set free and the other kept for further experimentation, Mary will have reason to hope (from a self-interested perspective) that the person with her psychological life and the other woman's body is the person who is released. All in all, then, when biological and psychological continuity diverge in Mary's case, it seems that *Mary* goes with the psychological and not the biological life.

Psychological continuity theories have been the most widely defended theories of this topic, through much of the modern discussion of personal identity, and they are frequently defended using cases such as the one I described. It is important to be clear at the outset, however, that the psychological continuity theory is *not* the view that persons are immaterial souls or that the persistence of a person depends upon the continuation of a single soul. Although historically several philosophers have defined personal identity in terms of sameness of soul, there are few philosophers writing today who defend such a view. One of the reasons for this is that sameness of soul does not seem to guarantee the kind of psychological continuity we are looking for. John Locke (1975), who is taken by most to be the progenitor of modern psychological continuity theories, uses hypothetical cases to reveal that psychological continuity can diverge from sameness of soul as well as from sameness of human body. The soul as it is understood in this context is an immaterial substratum that is the locus of thought and experience. Each experience is the experience of some soul, but as far as we know there is nothing that necessitates that what is experienced as a single stream of consciousness implies the involvement of one and only one soul. The soul that starts a thought might be replaced midway through with another soul who has a memory of the beginning of the thought and goes on to complete it. There would be no way to detect such a change, and for all we know it is happening constantly in what we introspectively experience as a single stream of consciousness. On the other hand, a person's current soul may once have supported a completely different stream of consciousness to which he currently has no access at all – it might, to use Locke's example, have been the soul of Nestor or Thersites at the siege of Troy without him having any consciousness of either of their actions. Psychological continuity is no more clearly coextensive with sameness of soul than it is with sameness of human being.

Psychological continuity theorists thus seek to define personal identity not in terms of the continuity of an immaterial substance, but directly in terms of psychological relations. Those who defend these views thus need to describe in more detail the kinds of psychological relations that constitute personal identity. A natural starting point for this endeavor is Locke's view. Locke says that it is sameness of consciousness that makes a person at one time the same person as a person at another time. It is generally believed that what he has in mind when he talks about "sameness of consciousness" is the kind of connection built by autobiographical memories. The view, interpreted this way, thus says that it is my remembering past experiences that makes them part of my consciousness and so makes me the person who had those experiences.

It is not entirely clear that this is exactly what Locke meant. What is clear, however, is that a simple memory theory is vulnerable to serious objections that prevent it from providing a viable account of personal identity. One important objection (attributed to Joseph Butler [1975]) charges the memory theory with circularity. This objection points out that the memory theory cannot very well claim that every experience I *think* I remember is my experience. Someone who is delusional might think that she remembers the experiences of Joan of Arc, but she would be mistaken. The memory theory is not even remotely plausible unless it says that in order for a past experience to be mine I must genuinely remember it, and not just have an experience that is phenomenologically *like* a memory. The problem is that the distinction between a genuine memory and a delusional memory-like experience seems to be that in the former case the experience remembered is one I actually experienced and in the latter it is one I wrongly believe myself to have experienced. This means that genuine memory is defined in terms of personal identity, and defining identity in terms of genuine memory is viciously circular.

A second significant objection (attributed to Thomas Reid 1975) is that the memory theory leads to absurdities. This is because we can forget what we once knew. At age thirty, a man may remember well something that he did when he was ten. At age fifty, he may remember well what he did at thirty, but have no recollection whatsoever of what he did at age ten. According to the memory theory, the thirty-year-old's memories of the ten-year-old's experiences make them the same person, and the fifty-year-old's memories of the thirty-year-old's experiences make them the same person. By the transitivity of identity (the rule that if A is identical to B, and B is identical to C, A must be identical to C), this means that the fifty-year-old and the ten-year-old are the same person. But the fifty-year-old does not remember any of the experiences of the ten-year-old, so the memory theory also says they are not the same person. Since the fifty-year-old and ten-year-old cannot both be and not be the same person, the memory theory is absurd.

These two objections, among others, are generally taken to be deadly to the memory theory. In the last several decades, however, philosophers convinced by the arguments in favor of a psychological account of identity have attempted to rehabilitate the basic Lockean insights into a more plausible view. To answer Butler's circularity objection, these theorists define a notion of "quasi-memory." Someone has a quasi-memory of a past event if (1) she has a memory-like experience of the event; and (2) the memory-like experience is caused in the right kind of way by the event remembered. The "right kind of cause" is usually defined in terms of the ordinary physical mechanism for laying down memories. All genuine memories are quasi-memories. In principle, however, someone could have a quasi-memory of an experience that was not her own, yet is nonetheless (because of its causal link to the original event) not delusional (e.g. if a neurosurgeon could transplant a single memory trace into another brain, giving the recipient a quasi-memory of someone else's experience). Psychological continuity theorists then define identity in terms of quasi-memories rather than genuine memories, thereby avoiding circularity.

To answer Reid's objection, psychological theorists define identity in terms of overlapping chains of direct memory connections rather than direct connections alone. For a person at time t_2 to be the same person as a person at time t_1 she need not directly remember any experiences of the person at t_1 but only directly remember experiences of a person who directly remembers experiences of a person, etc., who directly remembers experiences of the person at t_1.

Psychological theorists also question why memory should be the only psychological connection relevant to constituting personal identity. Other kinds of connections, they argue, can also contribute to personal identity. Their criteria thus define identity in terms of (quasi) memory connections, but also in terms of connections between intentions and the actions that carry them out and between the different moments of a continuing belief, desire, or trait. In its most general form the psychological continuity theory says that a person at time t_2 is the same person as a person at time t_1 just in case there exists between them an overlapping chain of appropriately caused psychological connections.

Objections to psychological continuity theories

While psychological continuity theories do, for the most part, avoid the objections that lead to the rejection of the memory theory, they have been subject to serious objections of their own. There are two in particular that have been especially significant.

Fission cases

Hypothetical cases can be used not only to support psychological continuity theories but also to reveal difficulties within them. One case that has been especially challenging is the "fission" case, in which a person splits into two psychological continuants, each psychologically continuous with the person at the moment of splitting. Consider Derek Parfit's (1984) version of this case. We are to imagine someone with complete redundancy between the two hemispheres of his brain, so that all of his memories and psychological attributes are stored twice, once in each half of his brain. We are to imagine also that this man is one of a set of triplets. Speaking from the point of view of this person, Parfit offers the following case:

> My body is fatally injured, as are the brains of my two brothers. My brain is divided, and each half is successfully transplanted into the body of one of my brothers. Each of the resulting people believes that he is me, seems to remember living my life, has my character, and is in every other way psychologically continuous with me.
>
> (Parfit 1986: 254–5)

The question Parfit raises is what we are to say about the identity of the original person with the two resulting people.

Call the triplet who receives the left half of the brain "Lefty," the person who receives the right half of the brain "Righty," and the original person "Donor." There seem only four possible claims to make about identity in this case: (1) Donor is identical to both Lefty and Righty; (2) Donor is identical to Righty but not Lefty; (3) Donor is identical to Lefty but not Righty; and (4) Donor is identical to neither Lefty nor Righty. The first possibility seems ruled out by the transitivity of identity. It is difficult to make a plausible case that Lefty and Righty are identical to one another.

They lead separate lives and might not even know of each other's existence. If Lefty and Righty are not identical to each other, however, transitivity prohibits them from both being identical to Donor.

Options (2) and (3) are implausible because Lefty and Righty each have exactly the same relation to the original person, and it is hard to justify the claim that one but not the other might be identical to him. Option (4) is problematic because each of Righty and Lefty bears the relation to Donor that the psychological continuity theory says constitutes identity. If only one hemisphere were transplanted resulting in only one psychological continuer, the psychological continuity theory would say unequivocally that that continuer was identical to Donor. Since Righty and Lefty each have everything necessary to be identical to Donor, how could neither be?

There are two major strategies psychological theorists have used to respond to the fission case. One is to take a four-dimensionalist approach to identity. Four-dimensionalists see continuing objects as spread out over time in much the same way they are spread out over space. Just as a three-dimensional object is not wholly present at any one point in space, but only over the totality of the space it covers, so a four-dimensional object is not wholly present at any point in its history, but only over the whole of the time it occupies. What is present at a point in space is a spatial part of the spatially extended object, and what is present at a point in time is a temporal part of the temporally extended object. On the four-dimensional view of persons a person at time t_1 is never, strictly speaking, *identical* to a person at time t_2. At most a person time-slice at t_1 and a person time-slice at t_2 can be time-slices of the same extended person. The four-dimensionalist can thus analyze the fission case as one in which two distinct temporally extended persons overlap for a time, sharing a number of time-slices.

If Figure 44.1 represents the fissioning of Donor into Righty and Lefty, the four-dimensionalist will view the entire span from A to B as one person, and the entire span from A to C as a distinct person. AB and AC share a segment, but they are different people, each numerically identical to itself and numerically distinct from the other. Just as two roads may overlap, sharing a bit of pavement for a while before they diverge, so two people may share a stretch of person-stages and then diverge. For

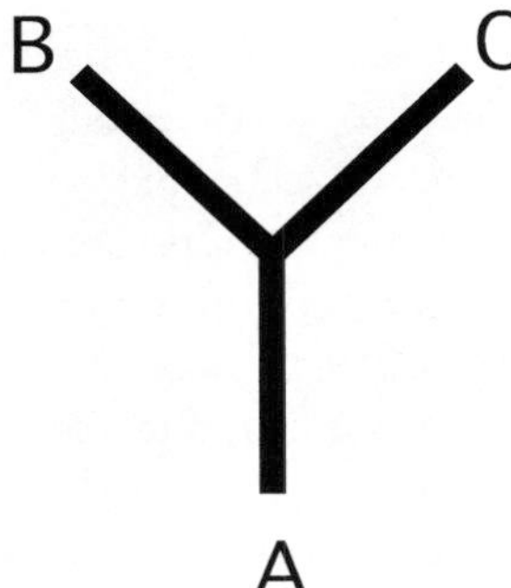

Figure 44.1 Donor's fission.

the four-dimensionalist the fission case describes two temporally extended people who share a segment, and there is no transitivity problem.

The four-dimensionalist approach does provide a technically viable solution to the problem raised by fission, but this solution comes at a cost. This response implies, among other counterintuitive consequences, that any human person one encounters might in fact be (or, more precisely, be a segment of) more than one person. Whether this is the case will depend upon what happens later. If there is no fission in the future then there is (a segment of) only one person. If there is fission later on then there is, even pre-fission, (a segment of) more than one. This makes it awkward, for instance, to enforce bigamy laws, or to know how many votes a given person-stage should be allowed. Philosophers differ on how serious the objections to four-dimensionalism are in the end, and the debate between three-dimensionalist and four-dimensionalist accounts of personal identity continues, as do larger metaphysical disputes about whether objects in general should be thought of as three- or four-dimensional.

Parfit (1984) offers a different and quite radical proposal in response to the fission case. What the fission case tells us, he says, is that "identity is not what matters in survival." He comes to this conclusion because he believes that the only coherent description of what happens in the fission case is to say that neither of the post-fission individuals is the same person as the pre-fission individual. In other words, the pre-fission individual goes out of existence when he divides, and is replaced by two other people, each of whom is psychologically continuous with him but neither of whom is identical to him. To make this result compatible with the psychological continuity theory, a non-branching clause must be added to that view. Instead of saying simply that personal identity consists in psychological continuity, the view must say that a person at time t_2 is the same person as a person at earlier time t_1 provided that the person at t_2 is psychologically continuous in the right way with the person at t_1 *and no one else is psychologically continuous with that person*. The person who undergoes fission thus ceases to exist through a failure of uniqueness.

It is obvious, however, that there is a vast difference between going out of existence by having *no one* in the future psychologically continuous with oneself, as happens in ordinary death, and going out of existence by having *more than one* person in the future psychologically continuous with oneself. Whatever practical complications having a double might engender, it is not the same as dying. Each of the continuers in the fission case contains all of what the psychological account deems necessary for survival, so it seems problematic to say that doubling constitutes the end of one's existence. It is for this reason that Parfit concludes that identity is not what matters in survival. What we care about, says Parfit, is psychological continuity. Since identity is a form of psychological continuity (continuity that is non-branching), identity is important to us. But it is not important to us *because* it is unique, and so not *because* it is identity. Since fission does not occur in our world, all instances of psychological continuity are also instances of identity, and so it is not surprising that we mistakenly attribute this importance directly to identity. Thinking about a hypothetical world that includes fission, however, helps us to see the deeper source of identity's importance in our world. This analysis has been extremely influential, and many philosophers have turned their attention from the project of defining personal identity *per se* to the project of defining the relation that provides what matters in survival.

The extreme claim

Another objection to the psychological approach that has had a significant impact is the claim that psychological continuity theories cannot explain the immense practical importance of personal identity. This may seem a strange challenge, given that the original impetus for these theories is the recognition that practical judgments of identity follow psychological rather than biological continuity. The objection holds, however, that when these views are fully developed it is obvious that the relation in terms of which they define identity is not strong enough to do the job for which it is intended.

The most standard versions of this objection, which Parfit names "the extreme claim," focus on egoistic self-concern. There is a certain kind of concern that I have for only my own future. Although I may care *more* about the well-being of those I love than I do about my own, the concern will be different in kind. It is a different thing to know that someone one cares about will suffer than to know that one will suffer oneself. Taking on a small amount of pain to prevent someone else from experiencing a much larger amount is loving or altruistic; taking on a small amount of pain now so that I can avoid experiencing a much larger amount later is simply rational. The difference depends upon the fact that I (rationally) anticipate my own experiences and not the experiences of others. Even if I care more about the suffering of my children than of my self, I will directly experience only my own suffering, and this makes the character of the concern different.

The extreme claim argues that the relation that constitutes personal identity according to psychological continuity theorists makes us psychologically *like* our future selves, but does not give us reason to anticipate their experiences. This means that one's relation to one's future self is not different in kind from one's relation to others, and so that there is no rational basis for egoistic concern. This is not the same as the argument that identity is not what matters in survival. The argument here is not about identity *per se*, but about psychological continuity more broadly, and stems from the fact that this continuity is defined in terms of psychological *contents*. The overlapping chain of direct connections in terms of which the psychological continuity theory defines identity ultimately provides only similarity of psychological make up between distinct person-stages, and this does not seem to provide a basis for anticipation of future experiences, and hence for egoistic concern. Since we do believe that our special kind of concern for our own futures is rationally justified, it seems that such overlapping chains cannot really describe the relation that constitutes personal identity.

This objection to psychological continuity theories has been taken very seriously, and a wide variety of responses have been offered. One reply is to argue that our special concern for our own futures rests on our interest in seeing our plans and projects carried out rather than on anticipation. John Perry (1976) uses this strategy, arguing that on the psychological approach our future selves are more like us than anyone else, and so are most likely to carry out our plans. Other philosophers have used similar analysis to argue that identity should not be defined in terms of continuity of psychological subject, but rather in terms of the unity of a rational or moral agent. Agential unity, it is argued, automatically provides a reason to care about one's future self because the unity of an agent depends upon having reasons that extend into the future. Another strategy for responding to the extreme claim involves trying to provide an account of psychological continuity that is richer or deeper than that provided in the traditional psychological continuity theories and arguing that this richer notion can explain our special concern for our futures. There are a variety of different versions of this approach, but most rely on the idea that our psychological lives are narrative in form, and/or on the idea that our identification with our past and future selves is a crucial element of the psychological continuity that defines our persistence.

A final response to this challenge is the one offered by Parfit (1986), who again takes a radical approach. Rather than trying to overcome the fact that the psychological continuity theory cannot explain the rationality of egoistic concern, Parfit embraces this result. Since we know on independent metaphysical grounds that the psychological continuity theory is correct, he says, and since we see that it cannot justify egoistic concern, we must conclude that this concern is unjustified. Our relation to other parts of our own lives is not, as we thought, fundamentally different in kind from our relation to other people. While Parfit acknowledges that this result is deeply counterintuitive, he also believes that it is not entirely negative. Recognizing this fact can be both comforting and enlightening. More important yet, he believes that understanding the superficiality of the unity of persons has important ethical consequences. Once we recognize how loose the bonds within a life really are, he says, we will see that objections to consequentialist ethics based on considerations of distributive justice no longer apply. The difference between bearing a burden for someone else's sake and bearing a burden for the sake of one's own future well-being is no longer a significant difference, and this means that the most rational thing to do is to maximize well-being overall, without regard to whose well-being it is.

The biological approach

The psychological approach is not, of course, the only possible approach to questions of personal identity. In everyday life we rely upon both biological and psychological continuity to make judgments of personal identity. Despite the dominance of the psychological approach, there have always been some who have defended the view that it is biological rather than psychological continuity that actually constitutes personal identity.

Early versions of this approach tend to argue that personal identity consists in sameness of *body*. For a variety of reasons, including the difficulty of providing a precise definition of what a body is and of what makes for sameness of body, more recent instances tend to place identity in *biological* rather than *physical* continuity. This means that instead of saying that identity depends upon the continuity of a physical body, these views hold that it consists in the continuity of a single organic life, that "one survives just in case one's purely biological functions – metabolism, the capacity to breath and to circulate one's blood, and the like – continue " (Olson 1997: 16).

Arguments for the biological approach generally focus on the difficulty psychological theories have explaining the relation between persons and human animals. All of the uncontroversial examples of persons are human persons like us, and so biological theorists focus on persons who are also humans. Since the psychological approach tells us that persons and human animals have different persistence conditions, it follows that persons and human animals must be distinct entities; no person can be identical to any human animal. If this is the case, biological theorists say, defenders of psychological views owe us an explanation of exactly what relation a person has to the human animal with which he is associated. When I converse with a human person, who is talking, the animal or the person? If it is the person, something more must be said about how it is that the animal fails to speak when its vocal cords vibrate and air is moving through its lungs. Psychological theories have similar difficulties unpacking such ordinary sentences as "I am 5′ 7″ tall" or "I am an animal," or "I was once a fetus." If the person is not identical to the human animal these sentences must be false, but it seems obvious that they are true.

Eric Olson (1997), one of the foremost defenders of the biological approach, argues that psychological continuity theories fall into these difficulties because they confuse metaphysical and practical questions of personal identity. Hypothetical cases like the brain transplant case do show that moral responsibility, egoistic concern, and other practical matters are associated with psychological rather than biological continuity, but this does not show that *identity* must be associated with psychological continuity. Olson argues that there is no reason to assume that the relation that defines our literal persistence should also be the relation that we find most practically important. If we look at the question of what constitutes the continuity of a human person in purely metaphysical terms, Olson says, the biological view is far more compelling than the psychological view. Not only does the biological view avoid the difficulties the psychological approach encounters, it makes our persistence conditions like those of other animals, and accurately reflects our place in the natural order.

Olson is, however, committed to showing how the intuitions behind the psychological approach can be accommodated within the biological theory. To do this, he makes use of the distinction between "phase sortals" and "substance concepts." A substance concept is, roughly, the description of a concrete particular that must continue to apply if that particular is to continue at all; phase sortals are descriptions that apply during some phase in the existence of a particular continuing substance. Phase sortals include things like "athlete," "mother," "student," and "child." We believe that a single individual can be at one time an athlete, mother, student, or child, and at another time fail to be any of these things, while remaining the same entity. Things are otherwise with substance concepts. To borrow an example from P. F. Snowdon (1990), the Monty Python skit in which something is introduced as an "ex-parrot" is comical precisely because we do not believe that something that is a parrot can cease to be a parrot without ceasing to exist. "Parrot" is a substance concept.

The real metaphysical question about our identity, according to Olson, is whether our substance concept is "person" or "human animal." Reflection shows that the former is problematic when taken as a substance concept, and the latter far more viable. The insights generated by the hypothetical cases that support the psychological approach can be respected, however, if we recognize that "personhood," defined in terms of higher order psychological capacities, is a phase sortal of human animals. Most humans enjoy this phase for most of their lives, but some do not. Someone who falls into an irreversible vegetative state, for instance, loses consciousness forever, and so ceases to be a person. Since the basic metabolic functions continue in such a state the human animal continues but is no longer a person, something whose coherence the psychological approach must deny. Calling the question with which we start the "problem of personal identity" is misleading, according to Olson, since this implies that it is the question of what is required for a person at one time to be identical to a *person* at another time. The more interesting metaphysical question is the question of what is required for someone who is a person at one time to be identical to *anything* at another time. "Personal identity" is no more a metaphysical question than "athlete identity" or "president identity"; the question is the question of *our* identity, and this is best answered in biological terms.

Biological views are, naturally, subject to many challenges and objections. Since this approach has only recently come to be widely discussed, the objections and replies are not as systematically developed as in the case of the psychological approach. Nonetheless they are very instructive. Some objections to the biological account are internal to the view. When biological continuity or the persistence conditions for human animals are spelled out in detail biological views have implications which may be just as counterintuitive as those of psychological views. Other responses to the biological approach reject its claim that psychological views are implausible, arguing, for instance, that psychological theorists can provide a perfectly coherent account of the relation between persons and humans by saying that persons are *constituted* by human animals in something very like the way statues are constituted by the marble out of which they are sculpted. Finally, the biological approach depends upon a number of controversial metaphysical positions, including the rejection of four-dimensionalism and the assumption that each concrete particular has exactly one set of persistence conditions. The view can thus be criticized by attacking these presuppositions.

The debate between biological and psychological theorists is likely to continue for some time. The emergence of the biological approach as a powerful competitor to psychological views has, however, added an important dimension to the current debate on personal identity, raising fruitful questions that have been largely neglected in recent years.

There are many aspects of the personal identity debate that crisscross the issues described here. Questions arise, for instance, about what role social and environmental factors play in determining facts about personal identity. Theorists of practical identity engage in discussions of personal identity and its relation to autonomy in work on practical reasoning. These discussions do not claim to be about metaphysical problems of identity, but they do intersect metaphysical concerns at several points, and it is important to gain more clarity about how these two investigations of identity are related.

One theme that runs through almost every aspect of work on personal identity is the need to understand the connection between practical and metaphysical questions of personal identity. As we have seen, some theorists presume that we must start with the practical facts and use them as data against which to test proposed metaphysical accounts. Others argue that the metaphysical question should be settled on its own terms, and that practice must conform to our metaphysical conclusions if it is to be rational. Still others see the practical and metaphysical questions as entirely independent issues which are often confused and must be sharply separated. The challenge from the biological approach to identity has helped to push these issues to the fore, and it is to be expected that an increasing amount of work will focus directly on questions about how metaphysical and practical concerns about identity should interact. The problem of personal identity is so compelling, and so complicated, because judgments of identity play such an important role in everyday life. Understanding this importance and its role in defining identity will undoubtedly be a central part of the ongoing philosophical investigation of personal identity.

References

Butler, J. (1975) "Of Personal Identity," in J. Perry (ed.) *Personal Identity*, Berkeley: University of California Press, pp. 99–106.

Locke, J. (1975) *An Essay Concerning Human Understanding*, ed. P. Nidditch, Oxford: Clarendon Press.

Olson, E. (1997) *The Human Animal: Personal Identity without Psychology*, New York: Oxford University Press.

Parfit, D. (1984) *Reasons and Persons*, Oxford: Clarendon Press.

Perry, J. (1976) "The Importance of Being Identical," in A. Rorty, ed., *The Identities of Persons*, Berkeley and Los Angeles: University of California Press, pp. 67–90.

Reid, T. (1975) "Of Mr. Locke's Account of Our Personal Identity," in J. Perry (ed.), *Personal Identity*, Berkeley: University of California Press, pp. 113–18.

Snowdon, P. F. (1990) "Person, Animals, and Ourselves," in C. Gill (ed.), *The Person and the Human Mind: Issues in Ancient and Modern Philosophy*, Oxford: Clarendon Press, pp. 83–107.

Further reading

An argument for a psychological approach to identity, involving the development of a constitution model of the relation between persons and human animals is provided by L. Baker, *Persons and Bodies: A Constitution View* (Cambridge: Cambridge University Press, 2000). The work by D. DeGrazia, *Human Identity and Bioethics* (Cambridge: Cambridge University Press, 2005), develops a two-part theory of identity that involves both numerical identity and narrative identity, and applies this theory to outstanding problems in bioethics. A collection of papers on personal identity in both ancient and modern philosophy is offered by C. Gill (ed.) *The Person and the Human Mind: Issues in Ancient and Modern Philosophy* (Oxford: Clarendon Press 1970). *A Treatise of Human Nature*, ed. L. A. Selby-Bigge (Oxford: Clarendon Press, 1979; original work published in 1739), includes Hume's famous argument that a person is nothing more than a bundle of perceptions.

The famous arguments of David Lewis for a psychological account of personal identity and his reaction to the fission case are included in *Philosophical Papers*, 2 vols (New York: Oxford University Press, 1986). J. Locke, *An Essay Concerning Human Understanding*, ed. P. Nidditch (Oxford: Clarendon Press, 1975; original work published in 1690), includes Locke's seminal development of a relational account of personal identity. A phenomenological study of survival and identity is found in R. Martin, *Self-Concern: An Experiential Approach to What Matters in Survival* (Cambridge: Cambridge University Press, 1998), and R. Martin and J. Barresi, *Naturalization of the Soul: Self and Personal Identity in the Eighteenth Century* (London: Routledge), give an account of how the notion of self became naturalized in the eighteenth century. Their edited, *Personal Identity* (Malden, MA: Blackwell, 2003), is a collection of some of the most important papers on personal identity in the last few decades.

A critical reflection on existing theories of personal identity and the application of an alternative theory to ethical questions having to do with the endpoints of life is J. McMahan, *The Ethics of Killing: Problems at the Margins of Life* (Oxford: Oxford University Press, 2002). D. Meyers (ed.) *Feminists Rethink the Self* (Boulder, CO: Westview, 1997) contains essays by leading feminist thinkers on self and identity, and H. Noonan, *Personal Identity* (London: Routledge 1989), offers a critical account of the major positions on personal identity; E. Olson, *The Human Animal: Personal Identity without Psychology* (New York: Oxford University Press, 1997), a defense of a biological approach to personal identity; and Derek Parfit, *Reasons and Persons* (Oxford: Clarendon Press, 1984), a watershed discussion and defense of the psychological continuity theory of personal identity and its relation to ethics. J. Perry (ed.) *Personal Identity* (Berkeley: University of California Press, 1975) contains important essays on personal identity, both historical and contemporary; and his *A Dialogue on Personal Identity and Immortality* (Indianapolis: Hackett, 1978) gives an introduction to the major positions in the philosophy of personal identity in dialogue form. A collection of essays about both metaphysical and ethical questions of personal identity is A. Rorty, *The Identities of Persons* (Berkeley: University of California Press, 1976).

An argument for an account of personal identity in terms of the unity of practical agents is found in C. Rovane, *The Bounds of Agency: An Essay in Revisionary Metaphysics* (Princeton: Princeton University Press, 1998), and M. Schechtman, *The Constitution of Selves* (Ithaca: Cornell University Press, 1996) offers a critical account of the state of the personal identity debate and an argument for a narrative account of personal identity. S. Shoemaker, *Identity, Cause and Mind: Philosophical Essays* (Cambridge: Cambridge University Press, 1984) contains essays on personal identity and its relation to issues in the philosophy of mind. His and Richard Swinburne's *Personal Identity* (Oxford: Blackwell, 1984) contains a debate between materialist and immaterialist views of personal identity. *The Diachronic Mind: An Essay on Personal Identity, Psychological Continuity, and the Mind-Body Problem* (Dordrecht: Kluwer, 2001), by M. Slors, gives us a narrative account of personal identity that incorporates insights from the philosophy of mind. P. Unger, *Identity, Consciousness, and Value* (New York: Oxford University Press, 1990), offers an argument for an account of personal identity in terms of continuity of core psychology and an investigation of the relation between identity and what matters.

The classic, David Wiggins, *Sameness and Substance* (Cambridge, MA: Harvard University Press, 1980), examines the logic of identity and its implications for personal identity, whereas K. Wilkes, *Real People: Personal Identity without Thought Experiments* (Oxford: Clarendon Press, 1988), criticizes the use of science-fiction cases in the philosophy of personal identity and reflects upon real-life cases that raise identity questions. A collection of papers, B. Williams, *Problems of the Self: Philosophical Papers 1956–1972* (Cambridge: Cambridge University Press, 1973), considers various problems of self and identity and their relation to practical questions; and Richard Wollheim, *The Thread of Life* (Cambridge: Cambridge University Press, 1984), offers a psychologically rich investigation about the relations that make up identity in an actual human life.

45
THE NAME AND NATURE OF CONFABULATION

William Hirstein

Making a sincere claim to someone, especially in response to a specific request, is similar in many ways to giving someone a present. We tell people things because we care about them. The present may be small or large, expected or a complete surprise, and it may be of great value, or worthless. False claims make bad presents; their normal value is nothing. Or worse than nothing, we may still waste time and energy because we believed the claim. Our minds track the value of these presents with great accuracy, especially when we are considering offering one. We do not give away valuable information to just anyone. We also do not give worthless items to someone for no reason. We do not deliberately make false claims to our friends, and lying to random strangers is considered pathological. To care about someone is to care about what you say to her. Confabulators fail exactly here; they dispense worthless claims sincerely, while not seeming to care that they are disbelieved. Their claims seem valuable to them, but they are actually worthless because they were generated by malfunctioning brain processes.

"Confabulation" was first applied as a technical term by the neurologists Bonhoeffer, Pick, and Wernicke in the early 1900s to false memory reports made by their patients, who suffered from an amnesic syndrome that later came to be known as Korsakoff's amnesia. When asked what they did yesterday, these patients do not remember, but will report events that either did not happen, or happened long ago. During the remainder of the twentieth century, however, the use of "confabulation" was gradually expanded to cover claims made by other types of patients, many of whom had no obvious memory disorder. This list grew to include patients who deny that they are injured, paralyzed, or blind; split-brain patients; patients with misidentification disorders (i.e., they make false claims about the identities of people they know); and patients with schizophrenia, as well as normal people, and children. Thus there are currently two schools of thought on the proper scope of the concept of confabulation, those who remain true to the original sense and so believe that the term should only be applied to false memory reports, and a growing number of those who believe that the term can be usefully applied to a broader range of disorders.

It is widely accepted that confabulation comes in more and less severe forms. Historically, a division has been made between a milder version that includes the above examples, and a more severe and rare version in which the patient invents fantastic or absurd stories. The milder version was initially referred to as "momentary confabulation" by Bonhoeffer in his writings on Korsakoff's patients (Bonhoeffer 1901, 1904). He also called these "confabulations of embarrassment," and speculated that they are created in order to fill in gaps in memory. Alternatively, what Bonhoeffer referred to as "fantastic confabulations" tend to be implausible and overlap heavily with things people who are under the influence of delusions say. Kopelman (1987) argued convincingly that the momentary/fantastic distinction "confounds a number of factors, which are not necessarily correlated" and urged instead the distinction between provoked and spontaneous confabulations. Provoked confabulation is produced in response to a question, while spontaneous confabulators produce their confabulations without being asked. Kopelman's provoked/spontaneous dichotomy has gained some acceptance, and there is a body of recent research that makes use of those concepts, for instance, in discussing whether they involve separate sites of damage (see, e.g., Schnider et al. 1996). DeLuca and Cicerone (1991) resist Berlyne's claim that "fantastic confabulation seems to be a distinct entity having nothing in common with momentary confabulation" (1972), arguing that the two types exist on a continuum. Most recent study has focused on the milder form of confabulation, as study of the more severe form is usually done under the rubric of the effort to understand schizophrenia.

The original definition of "confabulation" contains three criteria: 1) confabulations are false; 2) confabulations are reports; and 3) confabulations are about memories. There are significant problems with each of the three, however. First, relying on falsity alone to characterize the problem in confabulation can produce arbitrary results. If a Korsakoff's patient is asked what day of the week it is and happens to state correctly that it is Tuesday, we may still want to consider this a confabulation, since he has e.g., been wrong the previous four times he answered this question. Second, the idea that confabulations are reports, or stories, implies that confabulations must be in a linguistic form, yet several researchers have categorized nonlinguistic responses as confabulations. One group had patients (undergoing Wada testing, in which one hemisphere is temporarily disabled) point to fabric samples with one hand to indicate which texture of fabric they had been stimulated with on the other hand. Another research group had patients reproduce from memory certain drawings they had seen, and referred to cases in which the patients added extra features to the drawings which were not actually present as confabulations. Other researchers applied the term "confabulation" to the behavior of patients who produced meaningless drawings as if they were correctly reproducing designs seen earlier. Finally, the problem with calling confabulations *memory* reports at all is that even in Korsakoff's syndrome, many confabulations are simply made up on the spot, and not traceable to any actual memories.

An examination of the etymology of the term "confabulation" itself turns out not to be terribly helpful. The Latin root "con" means with, while "fabulari" means to talk or converse, so that its original meaning was simply, to talk with. The word "confab," used today to refer to an occasion when a group of people get together to talk about an issue, is truer to these roots. When the German neurologists at the turn of the twentieth century began using *Konfabulation*, they probably meant that their memory patients were creating fables when asked about their pasts. The patients were fabulists – fable tellers.

Those using "confabulation" in the broader sense simply ignore the memory criterion, assuming something else to be the core feature of confabulation. Neurologist Norman Geschwind's classic pair of articles entitled, "Disconnexion Syndromes in Animals and Man," published in the journal *Brain* in 1965, no doubt played a role in popularizing the broader sense of "confabulation." Geschwind used the word in a natural-sounding way that had nothing to do with memory, speaking for instance of a patient who "gave confabulatory responses to visual field testing when there was no stimulus in the field" (1965: 597). "I have seen a confused patient," he says, "who gave confabulatory responses when asked to name objects held in his hand" (597). Similarly, patients who deny that they are paralyzed have been claimed to confabulate when they provide reasons for why they cannot move ("My arthritis is bothering me," "I'm tired of following your commands"). Another type of patient will deny blindness and attempt to answer questions about what he sees, producing what have been called confabulations. Misidentification patients have been said to confabulate when asked what the motives of the "impostor" are, or why someone would go through the trouble to impersonate someone else ("Perhaps my father paid him to take care of me"). Similarly, when the left hemispheres of split-brain patients attempt unsuccessfully to answer questions without the necessary information (which is contained in their right hemispheres), this has also been called a confabulation.

Types of confabulations

Researchers have recorded confabulation in the following cases.

Memory confabulations

These are a defining characteristic of Korsakoff's syndrome and a near relation caused by aneurysm of the anterior communicating artery. Alzheimer's patients will often produce memory confabulations, and children up to a certain age are also prone to report false memories, apparently because their brain's prefrontal areas have not yet fully developed. All of these confabulators have an initial memory retrieval problem, coupled with a failure to check and correct their false "memories." In contrast, there exist many memory patients with only damage to the memory system itself (e.g., to the hippocampus) who freely admit that they cannot remember, and are not prone to producing confabulations.

Perceptual confabulations

These are issued by patients suffering from the misidentification syndromes (especially Capgras' syndrome). These syndromes may be caused by a deficit in representing the mind of the person who is misidentified (Hirstein, 2009), coupled with an inability to realize the implausibility of the impostor claim. The patients who deny paralysis have a condition referred to as *anosognosia*, meaning unawareness of illness. They typically have a loss of one or more somatosensory systems for the affected limb. Apparently, certain types of damage (e.g., to the right inferior parietal lobe) can cause both the somatosensory problem, and at least temporarily affect prefrontal functioning enough to cause the confabulated denials of illness (Berti et al. 2005). Anton's syndrome patients are at least partially blind, but insist that they can see. Their posterior damage typically involves bilateral lesions to the occipital cortex, causing the blindness, coupled with prefrontal damage, causing the inability to become aware of the blindness.

Confabulations about intentions

Patients who have undergone a split-brain operation will tend to confabulate about actions performed by the right hemisphere. In a typical experiment, commands are sent to the right hemisphere only, but the left hemisphere, unaware of this, confabulates a reason for why the left hand obeyed the command. Similar sorts of confabulations can be elicited by brain stimulation. For example, the patient's cortex is stimulated, causing her arm to move. When asked why the arm moved, the patient claims she felt like stretching her arm. Hypnotized people may also confabulate, e.g., the subject is given a hypnotic suggestion to perform a certain action, but then confabulates a different reason for it when asked.

Confabulations about emotions

False attributions of emotions can count as confabulations. For example, in one experiment, people were given adrenaline without their knowledge, but attributed their inability to sleep to, e.g., nervousness about what they had to do the next day. We may all be guilty of confabulating about our emotions on occasion, perhaps due to the combination of our feeling responsible for giving coherent accounts of our emotions and the opacity of our emotions to cognition.

Apparently there are confabulations about every type of intentional state, that is, every type of mental state with representational content. Even the emotions that we confabulate about at least present themselves as having a specific representational content, e.g., I am anxious *about my upcoming exam*. In theory, given the brain's large number of knowledge sources, there are many more confabulation syndromes than those listed here, but they should all follow the same pattern, damage to a posterior knowledge system (either perceptual or mnemonic), coupled with damage to prefrontal executive processes responsible for monitoring and correcting the representations delivered by that epistemic system.

An epistemic theory of confabulation

If the original definition of "confabulation" is problematic, that may be one reason why it was ignored by those who later described claims made by other, non-memory, patients. It seems that confabulations need not be false, need not be reports, and need not be about memories, if we allow these later uses. But then what is the definition of "confabulation"? Because of this recent proliferation of confabulation syndromes, contemporary writers attempting to construct a definition of "confabulation" have despaired of the fact that some of these syndromes involve memory disorders (Korsakoff's and aneurysm of the anterior communicating artery), whereas others involve perception (denial of paralysis or blindness, split-brain syndrome, misidentification disorders) (e.g., Johnson, 2000). Since both memory and perception are knowledge domains, however, this perhaps indicates that there is a broader sense of "confabulation" that has to do with knowledge itself, or more specifically, the making of claims based on one's perception or memory. According to this approach, to confabulate is to unintentionally make an ill-grounded (and hence probably false) claim that one should know is ill-grounded (Hirstein 2005).

Confabulations are the result of two different phases of error. The first occurs in one of the brain's epistemic systems, either mnemonic or perceptual. This produces a flawed memory or perception. These perceptual or mnemonic processes tend to be located in the back half of the brain, in the temporal or parietal lobes. Second, even with plenty of time to examine the situation and with urging from doctors and relatives, the patient fails to realize that the response is flawed, due to a second malfunction of executive processes based in the prefrontal lobes. Our brains create flawed responses all the time, but we are able to correct them, using different prefrontal processes. If I ask you whether you have ever been inside the head of the Statue of Liberty, for instance, your brain is happy to provide an image of a view from inside, even if you've never been near the statue. But you are able to reject this as a real memory. You catch the mistake at the second phase. Thus the typical etiology of confabulation involves damage in the posterior of the brain to some perceptual or mnemonic process, causing the first error stage, coupled with damage to the relevant prefrontal process, causing the second error stage.

Once we understand confabulation as a fundamentally epistemic problem, the confabulation syndromes can be categorized as disorders of the brain's knowledge domains:

1 Knowledge of the body and its surroundings (denial of paralysis)
2 Knowledge of recent events involving oneself, i.e., autobiographical memories (Korsakoff's syndrome; anterior communicating artery syndrome)
3 Knowledge of other people (the misidentification syndromes)
4 Knowledge of our minds (split-brain syndrome)
5 Knowledge derived from visual perception (Anton's syndrome).

Stated in terms of individually testable criteria, the definition of "confabulation" proposed here is: S confabulates (that *P*) if and only if 1) *S* claims that *P*; 2) *S* believes that *P*; 3) *S*'s thought that *P* is ill-grounded; 4) *S* does not know that her thought is ill-grounded; 5) S should know that her thought is ill-grounded; and 6) *S* is confident that *P*. "Claiming" is broad enough to cover a wide variety of responses by subjects, including drawing and pointing. The second criterion captures the sincerity of confabulators. The third criterion refers to the problem that caused the flawed response to be generated: processes within the relevant knowledge domain were not acting optimally. The fourth criterion refers to a cognitive failure at a second phase, the failure of the relevant executive process to check and reject the flawed response. The fifth criterion captures the normative element in our concept of confabulation: If the confabulator's brain were functioning properly, she would know that the claim is ill-grounded, and not make it; the claims made are about things that any normal person would easily get right. The sixth and last criterion refers to another important aspect of confabulators observed in the clinic, the serene certainty they have in their communications, often in the face of obvious disbelief by their listeners. Defining "confabulation" in this way eliminates a problem with the falsity criterion in the original definition according to which confabulations are false memory reports: A patient might answer correctly out of luck. The problem is not so much the falsity of the patients' claims but rather their overall ill-groundedness and consequent unreliability.

Any insights the study of confabulation has to offer contemporary epistemology depend on the possibility of what Quine called naturalized epistemology. In this conception, epistemology, normally a solely philosophical, *a priori*, endeavor, becomes something studied by scientists. The use that confabulation has for epistemologists has more to do with the insights it might offer into what sort of epistemic system we do employ, rather than normative questions about what we should employ. Epistemology is also about standards, but so is engineering. We can imagine organisms with fewer epistemic flaws than we have, organisms with better epistemic engineering, more sensitive perceptual organs, less interference due to emotions, and so on.

Philosophical connections

The study of confabulation can reveal important facts about the structure of our minds, our communications, and our basic nature. This section contains brief descriptions of several cases in which the phenomena of confabulation can help shed light on a classical philosophical question.

Confabulation and self-deception

Confabulation arises when a malfunctioning perceptual or mnemonic process creates a flawed mental representation that a malfunctioning prefrontal process is unable to correct. This basic pattern of malfunction may also occur when normal people succeed in deceiving themselves. The person's brain creates a flawed, often wishful, thought that the person's prefrontal executive processes fail to correct. There is a crucial difference: In confabulatory neurological patients, the prefrontal checking processes themselves are damaged, or in some more permanent and concrete way kept from checking the candidate belief. Self-deception may include cases such as these where the prefrontal processes are destroyed or disabled by brain lesion, but it also seems to include a wide variety of cases where the prefrontal processes are simply not employed, distracted, discounted, or simply selectively not used. We also may want to consider a person self-deceived who *should* have developed executive processes capable of rejecting his happy belief, but hasn't, due to events within his power.

In the mind of the self-deceived person, the misuse or non-use of executive processes conspires together with inaccurate, wishful, inadequate, degraded, or otherwise ill-grounded memories or perceptions to produce the desired result. In the case of self-deception, some process is capable of keeping the checking processes away from the thought that needs to be checked. Stone and Young (1997) point out that we sometimes temporarily protect a thought from dismissal, if we have special reason to, perhaps just because accepting it would require changing huge numbers of our existing beliefs. If this is correct, it also indicates that we possess processes capable of protecting thoughts from being corrected or checked by the prefrontal processes. One can then frame the classic question of whether self-deception is intentional in terms of whether the agent has voluntary control over these prefrontal processes. There are two places where voluntary control might operate: Either the thought needs to be kept away from any checking processes, or the checking processes need to be kept away from the thought. It is possible that both of these can be done either intentionally, or non-intentionally.

Another connection between the two phenomena is that some types of confabulation might be seen as arising from an extreme form of self-deception. The best sorts of examples for this hypothesis are the confabulations of patients with denial of hemiplegia. Their claims to be of sound body seem to be an attempt to hide their dire situation from themselves. Often when patients are asked about their denials once they have come to accept the paralysis, they say things that support this hypothesis. When one woman was asked why she had denied paralysis a few days before, she replied, "Maybe I didn't want to look crippled." Split-brain patients also fit this hypothesis: They (or their left hemispheres) insist on answering even without evidence, because they are so loathe to admit that they do not know something they should know. This admission is tantamount to an admission of abnormality, something most of us would do only grudgingly.

Confabulation and sociopathy

Sociopaths might as a group be considered confabulatory, on the wider sense of "confabulation" I am urging. Sociopaths are known for confidently making claims that they either know are false or do not have evidence for. Typically, sociopaths know their claims are ill-grounded because they know they just made them up. Often they know, or have reason to believe, that their claims are false. If you do not have evidence for a claim when you make that claim, are you lying? Context is crucial here. In situations where knowledge is demanded there is a tacit understanding that people know what they claim. The claimant can use a number of established techniques for revoking this understanding, including saying such things as, "I'm not sure about that," or, "That's just a guess, though," and so on. So claiming something in a situation in which you have no evidence gets closer to lying.

Several recent works have described the continuing decline in the value of communications we offer each other. Philosopher Harry Frankfurt's surprise bestseller, *On Bullshit*, contains a detailed analysis of that concept. Bullshitting seems to fall between confabulating and lying on a continuum of how aware the speaker is that what he is saying is false. The liar knows that what he is saying is false, whereas the confabulator believes what he is saying. The bullshitter falls somewhere in between. Within the past few years, confirmation has been found for the hypothesis that sociopaths are not perceiving and representing other people in the normal way. Sociopaths may well not care about the people they tell things to. That would explain why they lie so easily. Many criminal sociopaths seem to view people the way that safecrackers might view safes: just use the right codes, the right tricks, and this thing will open up and give you what you want.

Confabulation and epistemology

The phenomena of confabulation can tell us a great deal about the human experiences of certainty and doubt. In cases where self-deceived people possess evidence against their self-deceptive belief that they are not able to fully suppress, the person can experience doubt, anxiety, or what I will just call tension. Confabulators experience no tension at all, due to their brain damage, even when confronted with contradictions in their claims. Sociopaths fall between confabulators and self-deceived normal people. If they possess these checking processes, the processes seem to lack the emotional force needed to inhibit unwise or hurtful actions. People with obsessive-compulsive disorder (OCD) fall at the far other end: In their minds, the thought that I need to wash my hands for instance, is powerful enough to interrupt the flow of thought and force the person to go wash her hands. Their tension level is high, because of the high activity of the frontal checking processes and their autonomic connections, on this view. All of this suggests a continuum on which these different types can be placed:

Clinical confabulator
Sociopath
Self-deceived normal person without tension
Normal confabulator
Neutral normal person
Self-deceived normal person with tension
Lying normal person
Obsessive-compulsive normal person
Clinical OCD sufferer

At the top, confabulators experience no tension at all when they make their ill-grounded claims. Tension steadily increases as we go down, peaking in the case of the person with severe OCD and unbearable tension. This continuum can also be understood epistemically; we might also describe it as running from extreme certainty at the top to extreme doubt at the bottom. Is this hypothesis correct? Is there a psychological continuum, from pathological certainty to pathological doubt? Is confabulation caused by an inability to doubt? Is it the opposite of OCD, since people who suffer with this disorder can be plagued by doubt? In this view, doubt and certainty are understood more as biological phenomena in us than as idealized semantic functions.

Confabulations about actions and freedom of the will

The confabulations that split-brain patients produce belong to a larger family of confabulations made by patients about why they did something. When Wilder Penfield electrically stimulated people's brains in the 1950s, he was able to cause them to make movements or make sounds. Sometimes the patients claimed that Penfield was the cause of their action, making remarks such as, "I didn't do that. You did," or, "I didn't make that sound. You pulled it out of me" (1975: 76). In a middle case, Hecaen et al. (1949) electrically stimulated a different part of the brain, which caused the patients' fists to clench and unclench, or make "pill rolling" motions. The patients claimed that they had done this intentionally, but were unable to offer a reason for the action. Finally, Delgado's brain stimulation patients also claimed they had performed the actions voluntarily, but produced confabulated reasons why. When Delgado's patients were asked why they engaged in those actions, genuine confabulations seemed to result: "The interesting fact was that the patient considered the evoked activity spontaneous and always offered a reasonable explanation for it. When asked 'What are you doing?' the answers were, 'I am looking for my slippers', 'I heard a noise', 'I am restless', and 'I was looking under the bed'" (1969: 115–16).

These sorts of cases, together with others (Libet 1996) have encouraged several writers to argue that most or all of our explanations for actions and avowals of intention are confabulations. Magicians can trick us, but that does not mean that the vast majority of our perceptions are not accurate. Both our senses and our thought processes themselves are specially adapted, constructed, and tuned to think about a rather narrow range of things, especially other people and things of value that are close to us in space. We aren't very good at thinking about certain questions, for instance, how did the universe begin, i.e., how did something come from nothing, what does it mean for something to be infinite?, how can the mind be physical?, and so on. This list will coincide at many points with the list of philosophical questions. Psychologists are good at finding the chinks in our epistemic armor, but every physical process has its weaknesses. These are typically places where the physical nature of the process forces design (i.e., evolution) into a situation that is less than ideal from an epistemic point of view. But those who are so negative about our capacities to know and the power of our wills are forgetting about all the times we succeed in finding our cars in the parking lot, flipping the light switch and grasping our coffee cups, and all the appointments and promises we keep. Focusing on the borderline cases is of great use for exploring the nature of our minds, but not good for judging how well a concept applies overall.

Confabulation and the self

Is the person that we present to others as ourselves in some way a product of confabulation? Some writers see confabulation as a self-creating activity (Dennett 1991). Our confabulations tend to depict us in favorable ways, and taken together they constitute a sort of story we create and tell to others, about the sort of person we are. Typically these stories depict us as intelligent, in command of the situation and its relevant facts, and fully aware of the reasons and intentions behind our actions. Are all such self-presenting claims actually confabulations? Another way to pose the question would involve collecting all of the instances in which a person used the word "I," and attempting to determine if any self-like brain process plays the proper role in the causal history of such I-claims. Our I-reports might be generated by several different processes, however, which share nothing significant, and this can begin to make any notion of the self based on these I-claims look like a motley collection of processes, cobbled together for various motives and conveniences. This virtual self is then presented to others, and protected by confabulation.

Confabulation and mind reading

The insensitivity of confabulators to the reactions of their listeners should intrigue us. Patients who deny paralysis seem especially insensitive, refusing to acknowledge the concerns of their loved ones as they blithely claim to be just fine. A normal person who produced false answers at the rate that split-brain patients do in some situations would be taken to be joking, or a pathological liar. Offering false answers to people who have asked questions in earnest is impolite, if not unethical. Some of the brain areas damaged in confabulators overlap with or are near brain areas thought to be involved in understanding the minds of others, such as the right inferior parietal cortex, and the orbitofrontal cortex. Perhaps this mind reading problem is something all confabulators have. It would explain some of the things other confabulation syndrome patients do.

Sometimes failure to correct a confabulation is due to what we might describe as an inability to let another person play the role that should be played by one's prefrontal executive processes, and to correct one's belief, based on the other's reaction to the confabulation. Why not take a neurologist's word for it when he tells you that your arm is paralyzed?

Confabulation and consciousness

One message carried by the phenomena one encounters in a study of confabulation is that consciousness does not contain labels saying, *An adequate representation of your left arm is missing* (denial); *There is a gap in your memory here* (memory syndromes); *You have no information about why your left arm just pointed at a picture of a cat* (split-brain syndrome); or *Your representation of your father's mind is missing* (Capgras' syndrome). Both the data and the checker of the data are flawed. There is no reason to think that an executive process that operates on representations of type *x* should be able to "know" when there are no representations of that type available when there should be. The checking processes can check, but they can't object when there is nothing to work on. If they did, this would interfere with a function of consciousness.

Is confabulation then a type of filling-in? It might be considered filling in at a higher, social level. It fills in social gaps in information. What fills in the gap in memory is a memory illusion. When it becomes the basis of a claim, that claim is a confabulation. There may also be information here relevant to another question in philosophy and the cognitive sciences: What is the function of consciousness? The existence of confabulation may show that consciousness functions as a testing ground, where thoughts and ideas can be checked.

Confabulation and human rationality

Are confabulatory neurological patients irrational? Human rationality depends on a system of the type we exemplify operating correctly. The design of our brain acknowledges that perceptions and memories are fallible by building in a second layer, the system of executive processes, designed to check and correct them. The specificity of the patients' problem thus makes them good objects of study, but it creates another problem. To state, as many clinicians do, that these patients are otherwise rational, is to beg the question against holistic theories of rationality, according to which isolated islands of irrationality are impossible. Our beliefs are so thoroughly and densely interconnected that any irrational beliefs would immediately infect huge numbers of other beliefs with their irrationality, according to the holist. Quine called it the web of belief; one cannot pull on one part of a spider web without bringing the rest of the web along. Some of the beliefs in the web, those toward the center are more basic and foundational than the others. They are less likely to be changed by experience, but Quine insisted that experiences could still come along that would change them. These holists agree, however, that changing the more basic beliefs should force greater changes in the entire web. Yet somehow these patients accomplish this odd specificity. The data from confabulating patients seem to indicate that our set of beliefs is not homogeneous, and may be partitioned into separate domains. The patient is not concerned when confronted with patent contradictions between the delusional belief and other firmly held beliefs. The patients' ability to think and reason runs into a firmly held but irrational belief, and the reasoning system meekly defers to the irrational belief. A study of them might reveal hidden features of our rationality.

Do normal people confabulate? If so, in what ways? Are human beings fundamentally a confabulatory species? If so, why? We certainly consider language use to be one of our defining characteristics. What about overconfident, inflationary language use? If we engage in a large amount of less than sincere speech nowadays, were we always this way? There have always been clichés about certain peoples' being long winded, or tight-lipped, clear or vexatious, veracious or fabulatory. Or is confabulation merely an odd byproduct of injury to a cognitive system with a certain structure? Or does confabulation sink deeper into our nature than this? If knowledge is power, then ignorance is impotence. Among ancient peoples, the answers to certain questions were badly needed. What will the weather be like? What causes lightning, drought, flood, rain, pestilence, hurricanes, etc.? What will the future bring for me? How can I achieve success? Some people claimed to have answers, usually for a price. This may be the beginnings of confabulation – it is a type of linguistic inflation caused by the desire to obtain the benefits of being the one who knows the answers to life's important questions. To confabulate is to speak from ignorance, as opposed to speaking from knowledge. Confabulation is ignorant, but confident communication, according to the epistemic approach.

References

Berti, A., Bottini, G., Gandola, M., Pia, L., Smania, N., Stracciari, A., Castiglioni, I., Vallar, G., and Paulesu, E. (2005) "Shared Cortical Anatomy for Motor Awareness and Motor Control," *Science* 309, no. 5733: 488–91.

Delgado, J. M. R. (1969) *Physical Control of the Mind: Toward a Psychocivilized Society*, New York: Harper & Row.

DeLuca, J., and Cicerone, K. D. (1991) "Confabulation Following Aneurysm of the Anterior Communicating Artery," *Cortex* 27: 417–23.

Dennett, D. (1991) *Consciousness Explained*, Boston: Little, Brown & Co.

Geschwind, N. (1965) "Disconnexion Syndromes in Animals and Man," *Brain* 88: 237–644.

Hirstein, W. (2005) *Brain Fiction: Self-Deception and the Riddle of Confabulation*, Cambridge, MA: MIT Press.

—— (2009) "Confabulations about People and Their Limbs, Present and Absent," in J. Bickle (ed.), *The Oxford Handbook of Philosophy and Neuroscience*, Oxford: Oxford University Press (pp. 473–512).

Libet, B. (1996) "Neural Processes in the Production of Conscious Experience," in M. Velmans (ed.), *The Science of Consciousness*, London: Routledge, 96–117.

Kopelman, M. D. (1987) "Two Types of Confabulation," *Journal of Neurology, Neurosurgery, and Psychiatry* 50: 1482–7.

Penfield, W. (1975) *The Mystery of the Mind*, Princeton, NJ: Princeton University Press.

Schnider, A. (2001) "Spontaneous Confabulation, Reality Monitoring, and the Limbic System: A Review," *Brain Research Reviews* 36: 150–60.

Stone T., and Young, A. W. (1997) "Delusions and Brain Injury: The Philosophy and Psychology of Belief," *Mind and Language* 12: 327–64.

Further reading

Further readings on this topic are the following: Donald Davidson, "Deception and Division," in J. Elster (ed.) *The Multiple Self* (Cambridge: Cambridge University Press, 1985), pp. 199–212; D. M. Wegner, *The Illusion of Conscious Will* (Cambridge, MA: MIT Press, 1982); and Ludwig Wittgenstein, *On Certainty* (Oxford: Basil Blackwell, 1969).

46

BUDDHIST PERSONS AND *EUDAIMONIA*[BUDDHA]

Owen Flanagan

Eudaimonia[Buddha]

A philosophical psychology ought to answer questions such as these:

- What, if anything, are humans like deep down inside, beneath the clothes of culture?
- What, if any, features of mind-world interaction, and thus of the human predicament, are universal?
- Is there any end state or goal (*telos*) that all humans seek because it is worthy, or what is different, ought to seek because it is worthy?
- Assuming that there is such an end state, one that is universal, and that is defensible as very good or the best, which natural traits ought to be nourished and grown to achieve it and which ones ought to be weeded out, possibly eliminated insofar as they are obstacles to that end state?

Here I discuss the Buddhist answers to these questions. Buddhist philosophical psychology is especially interesting to Westerners because Buddhists deny (or, so it is said) that there are any such things as persons or selves (*atman*) while offering advice, philosophical therapy, about how best to live a good and meaningful life as a person. How a non-person without a self lives a good human life, how a non-person with no self lives morally and meaningfully and achieves enlightenment or awakening, is deliciously puzzling. I'll explain how non-persons flourish, and achieve, or might achieve, a stable state of what I call *eudaimonia*[Buddha].

My interpretive strategy assumes this: Aristotle was right that all people at all times seek to flourish, to find fulfillment, to achieve eudaimonia, but that people disagree about what it is. When Aristotle said this he had in mind disagreements internal to the Greek situation about whether pleasure, money, reputation, contemplation, or virtue bring eudaimonia. And he thought that he could give an argument internal to the logic of his tradition that favored the last answer. The problem repeats, however, across traditions. Thus I use – and recommend that others doing comparative work use – a superscripting strategy, eudaimonia^{Buddha}, eudaimonia^{Aristotle}, eudaimonia^{Hedonist}, to distinguish between conceptions of the good life. Whether there are ways to critically compare these different views according to some shared logic is something I offer no opinion about here (Flanagan 2007). The superscripting strategy allows us to draw distinctions or contrasts between conceptions of eudaimonia such as this:

- Eudaimonia^{Aristotle} = an active life of reason and virtue where the major virtues are courage, justice, temperance, wisdom, generosity, wit, friendliness, truthfulness magnificence (lavish philanthropy), and greatness of soul (believing that one is deserving of honor *if* one really is deserving of honor).
- Eudaimonia^{Buddha} = a stable sense of serenity and contentment (not the sort of happy-happy/joy-joy/click-your-heels feeling state that is widely sought and promoted in the West as the best kind of happiness) where this serene and contented state is caused or constituted by enlightenment (*bodhi*)/wisdom (*prajna*) and virtue (*sila*), where the major virtues are these four conventional ones: right resolve (aiming to accomplish what is good without lust, avarice, and ill-will), right livelihood (work that does not harm sentient beings, directly or indirectly), right speech (truth-telling and no gossiping), right action (no killing, no sexual misconduct, no intoxicants), as well as these four exceptional virtues: compassion, loving-kindness, sympathetic joy, and equanimity.

Atman and anatman

Before I proceed I better explain what a person^{Buddha} is, and is not. Although Buddhists are said to deny that there are persons and selves or persons with selves, this is not really so. Some kinds of persons, eternal persons, and some kinds of selves, indestructible transcendental egos or immortal souls, do not exist, but Heraclitean selves do exist. Heraclitean selves are like Herclitean rivers where both subsist in a Heraclitean universe. We are Heraclitean selves (or, as I will now say, Lockean selves) living in a Heraclitean universe.

Person^{Buddha} (*pudgala*) is close to person^{Locke} and far from person^{Reid} or person^{Butler} (Perry 1975). I say "close to" or "far from" because part of the Buddhist insight is that no two things, events, processes, or concepts are or can be exactly the same. Buddhist metaphysics privileges processes and events. Perhaps it does more even than privilege processes and events: What there is, and all there is, is an unfolding (the overarching process, the mother of all processes) in which we participate. What we call and conceive as "things" are relatively stable processes or events inside the mother of all unfoldings. The picture here is familiar from contemporary physics (which is why A. N. Whitehead at the dawn of elementary particle physics endorsed "process philosophy"). Person^{Reid} or person^{Butler} is the view that what makes an individual the same person over time is each individual's possession of an immutable, indestructible essence (= *atman*). Person^{Locke} is the view that a person is an unfolding that has stability in virtue of possessing certain kinds of psychological continuity and connectedness, e.g., first-personal memory connectedness (= *anatman*).

Buddhism is sometimes said to be incoherent because it gives advice on how to live a good life as a good person, while denying that there are persons. But Buddhism does not deny that there are persons^Buddha^ who live lives. It denies that a person – any person – is an eternal self-same thing, or possesses an immutable, indestructible essence which is its self (*atman*). If you think you are or possess some such thing, you are mistaken. If you don't think this, then you are not making a common and morally consequential metaphysical mistake. The consequential moral problem is that selfishness or egoism despite being a commonly adopted strategy for living does not bring eudaimonia^Buddha^. If I don't conceive of myself as a metaphysically permanent ego, as *atman* (which is a mistake since I am *anatman*), I am better positioned to adjust how I live – specifically less egoistically – so that I have a chance to achieve eudaimonia^Buddha^.

I think of the connection between metaphysics and morals as understood by Buddhists as similar to Bishop Berkeley's insight that metaphysical materialism and ethical materialism go together. They don't, in either case, logically necessitate the other, but they mutually reinforce each other psychologically. If what there is, and all there is, is material stuff, then what else am I to do than to try to get as much of that stuff (the only stuff that there is and thus that matters) for myself as I can?

Human nature and the human predicament

Eudaimonia^Buddha^ is the highest good, the *summum bonum* for sentient human beings in time.[1] We are not there yet. What route or path (*dharma* or *dao*) should we take to get from here to there? To answer we need to know our starting point. What is our nature, what is our predicament?

The Buddhist answer is this: Humans are beings in time who are thrust into a world in which the first universal feature of being in time in the world is that you are an unfolding, not a thing in an unfolding, but an unfolding that is part of a greater unfolding, the mother of all unfoldings. At each moment that you are unfolding or becoming in the greater unfolding, which is the sum of all unfoldings, you considered as a series of connected and continuous events – as *anatman* – have desires that you want satisfied. But your desires cannot be satisfied. There are several reasons: sometimes (actually often) one's wanting nature overreaches and asks for more than the world can give. Other times, one changes enough that if and when one gets what one wants, one (actually one's successor self) no longer wants it. Still other times, one makes mistakes about what one wants and about what getting what one thinks one wants will do for oneself, e.g., make one happy. Then there is the fact that even when one gets what one wants one doesn't get to keep it for very long or, what is different, there isn't enough of it.

The first of the "four noble truths" of Buddhism says that there is *dukkha*. Some say *dukkha* means that always and everywhere all there is for humans (and other sentient beings) is suffering. A more plausible (charitable) interpretation is this: The world in which we are thrust, and in which we live, is one in which the supply of things that can satisfy our desires is outstripped by our desiring nature. This interpretation is reinforced by the second and third noble truths, which spell out the causes of suffering as follows: Sometimes there is not enough objectively as in the case of shortages or scarcity of material resources. Other times, we want more than is sensible or sufficient, as in the case of having a satisfactory car but wanting the finest that there is, or in cases where there is love and one wishes never for the bloom to fade or even more unrealistically for the beloved (or oneself) never ever to die. And then there is the fact that we are prone to making mistakes and repeating them. Most people, even those with lots of experience on the hedonic treadmill, and who know that accumulating more wealth or stuff never brings stability and serenity, nonetheless keep seeking more and more.

The first noble truth of *dukkha* says then that humans are desiring beings who want their desires satisfied. Our desires are sometimes satisfied short term. But long term, no one gets everything she wants (the picture is familiar from Freud and Mick Jagger). Things are unsatisfactory in a literal sense: desires are unsatisfied.

What to do? We can't do much about the features of the world that don't deliver what we want (at least not individually and not immediately), but we can do a lot about the features of ourselves that grasp ego-maniacally, that continually overreach, that cause us to think (mistakenly) that we need what in fact we don't need, and that cause us to become angry and frustrated when our consumptive ego doesn't get what it wants.

To overcome our consumptive ego, insofar as it engenders its own dissatisfaction, it makes sense to follow the "noble eightfold path." The noble eightfold path (see Rahula 1974 [1954]) is the solution, insofar as one is possible, to the problem of *dukkha*. The eightfold path contains the sort of information that one could carry on a card in one's wallet, but its bulleted form is misleading. The eightfold path is actually the entry ticket to an elaborate and complex form of life, to a long and winding road (*dharma* or *dao*) that one will need to follow if one has any hope of attaining eudaimonia^{Buddha}.

Briefly the project as laid out by the noble eightfold path is to practice four conventional virtues (*sila*) listed above in the schema for eudaimonia^{Buddha}: right resolve (aiming to accomplish what is good without lust, avarice and ill-will), right livelihood (work should not harm sentient beings, directly or indirectly), right speech (truth-telling and no gossiping), right action (no killing, no sexual misconduct, no intoxicants).

The noble eightfold path contains then the blueprint for the project of moderating desires, tuning desires to be less acquisitive, less avaricious, and less insatiably consumptive, so that the inevitable shortage of satisfactions causes as little pain and suffering as possible.

But practicing the four conventional virtues is not sufficient to tune down destructive desires and to achieve eudaimonia^{Buddha}. In addition one needs to attain wisdom (*prajna*) about such matters as the fact that everything is impermanent and that the self is one of the impermanent things (*anatman*). Gaining metaphysical wisdom supports the worthy aim of seeing reality as it is, as well as the aim of developing strategies and techniques for moderating and modifying (possibly eliminating) destructive states of mind that interfere with the project of achieving eudaimonia^{Buddha} (Flanagan 2000; Goleman 2003a, b). Buddhist ethics is metaphysically rich and is in that sense *cognitivist*, or, to put it another way, being morally excellent, as conceived by Buddhism, requires seeing things truthfully without delusion or wishful thinking.[2] A morally very good person does not achieve eudaimonia^{Buddha} unless she also knows a fair amount of Buddhist metaphysics, *prajna*.

In addition to practicing the conventional virtues listed and gaining the requisite metaphysical insight into the ubiquity of impermanent processes, the eightfold path also requires the practice of mindfulness and concentration.[3] Mindfulness and concentration will be most familiar to Westerners as meditation.

Three Poisons

Original sin, Buddhist style, consists of the three poisons of delusion (*moha*), avaricious, greedy desire (*lobha*), and hatred (*dosa*). The poisons obstruct gaining eudaimonia^{Buddha}, and they come with being a human.[4] It would be good to learn to moderate, modify, or eliminate the poisons. Luckily the universe unfolds (Buddhism is fine with there being no overarching reason for things unfolding as they do), so that we are positioned to see that our desiring nature overreaches and in particular that it contains the *three poisons* of delusion (*moha*), avaricious, greedy desire (*lobha*), and hatred (*dosa*).[5] *Moha* causes us to think we need things we don't need (things that will not make us happy but that will make us suffer instead). *Lobha* causes us to throw caution to the wind as we seek to acquire and hoard as much of the stuff we think (incorrectly) we want, as quickly as possible. *Dosa* makes us hate, despise, and wish to crush whatever and whoever gets in the way of our acquiring what we (mistakenly) think we want in order to be happy.

Think of the three poisons, as deadly weeds or the seeds for poisonous weeds, for *kudzu*. The project is to keep these poisonous weeds from overtaking the garden, from sucking the life out of the good seeds or beautiful plants, or from pulling all the nutrients from the soil. If we can do this, stop or control the poison, then we have a chance (a) to not suffer; and (b) to achieve a modicum of happiness (*sukkha*), or better, eudaimonia^{Buddha}.

Wisdom (*prajna*) and virtue (*sila*) go some distance towards keeping the poisons under control and thus increase our chances of achieving eudaimonia^{Buddha} . But there are other tools required, specifically concentration and mindfulness, or what we often simply call, "meditation." We can understand what meditation is supposed to do if we look closely at the intricate analysis of mental life provided by the first great psychology text in any tradition, the Buddhist *Abhidhamma* (Pali) (*Abhidharma*, Sanskrit) (Bhikkhu Bodhi 1993).

Meditation and the therapy of desire

Abhidhamma is part of the original three baskets of the Pali canon (compiled between 200 BCE and CE 400), and contains the earliest compendia of Buddhist metaphysics. Understanding the nature of things – space, time, causation, impermanence, the non-self (*anatman*), emptiness (*sunyata*), and the like, is the basis of wisdom (*prajna*), which, along with virtue (*sila*), is a necessary condition for eudaimonia^{Buddha}. But wisdom and virtue are not sufficient to produce eudaimonia^{Buddha}. In addition to wisdom and virtue there is a third element required: concentration and mindfulness. Concentration and mindfulness are techniques for mental and moral discipline, what Foucault called "technique de soi."

A brief tour of the *Abhidhamma* reveals why "concentration," understood as acute sensitivity to the patterns that mental states abide as they unfold, and "mindfulness" understood as *technique de soi*, are necessary if eudaimonia^{Buddha} is to be attained.

The first thing that will strike the Western reader who has taken Psychology 101 (thus everyone) is that the *Abhidhamma* taxonomizes mental states into *wholesome* and *unwholesome* and, to a lesser extent, *neutral* kinds. This can generate the observation (really it's an objection) that "this is ethics *not* psychology." And indeed it is. Or better: it is both. The current 14th Dalai Lama writes,

> The principal aim of Buddhist psychology is not to catalog the mind's makeup or even to describe how the mind functions; rather its fundamental concern is to overcome suffering, especially psychological and emotional afflictions, and to clear those afflictions.
>
> (2005: 165–6)

So Buddhist psychology is overtly normative or, to put it more precisely, ethics and psychology interpenetrate. But if this is right as regards the ultimate concern of Buddhist psychology – and it is – then positivist reactions will surface and we will hear not only that this isn't psychology but also that it is shockingly irresponsible to mix scientific psychology with ethics.

There is a principled reply that can work to deflate the objection: Think of psychiatry and abnormal psychology texts, or of anatomy and physiology texts, or of surgical manuals. All these bleed normativity. Is that an objection to these texts and the fields they represent? Even engineering is normative. The principles of structural engineering enable us to build bridges and skyscrapers that last. That is what structural engineering is for. The fact that engineering is normative is not an objection to its status as science. Indeed, we like it that engineers operate with good design ends in mind. Thus the fact that the mental and moral sciences are normative, as is engineering, is not an objection in and of itself. One can, of course, criticize a physiology, psychiatry, or engineering text if it gets the facts wrong or if it imports controversial or unwarranted norms without marking this; otherwise not. The fact that the *Abhidhamma* combines descriptive, as well as normative, insights gathered from the Buddha's teachings is not an objection of any sort, so long as the norms can be supported by evidence that embracing them captures worthy aims, and that abiding them increases the chances of achieving whatever good it is that the norms aim at, namely, eudaimonia^{Buddha}.

The *Abhidhamma* is a masterpiece of phenomenology, an early exercise in what I call, analytic existentialism (which is, I think, one reason it appeals to both analytic philosophers and to phenomenologists and existentialists). And despite what the 14th Dalai Lama says about not being concerned with taxonomy, the *Abhidhamma* remains arguably the best taxonomy of conscious-mental-state types ever produced. In that sense it is analytic with a vengeance.

The book begins with a decomposition of consciousness (*Citta*) into conscious-mental-state types. These number eighty-nine initially, and reach one hundred twenty-one after some adjustments. Each type is characterized in terms of the sort of object it takes in (so visual and auditory consciousness differ in an obvious way); its phenomenal feel (e.g., sad or happy); its proximate cause or root (e.g., there is greed-rooted and hatred-rooted consciousness – I have your money and I am happy; this might be so because I hate you, or I might like you but want your money); and its function or purpose (scientific consciousness seeks [sometimes] to uncover the nature of things by decomposing them into elements [possibly *ad infinitum*], whereas musical consciousness functions to reveal or create patterns or relations among sounds).[6]

Most important for our purposes is the elaborate analysis of the hidden, deep structure of the three poisons. The three poisons are first elaborated as giving rise to "the Six Main Mental Afflictions," attachment or craving, anger (including hostility and hatred), pridefulness, ignorance and delusion, afflictive doubt, and afflictive views. These in turn are roots for the "the Twenty Derivative Mental Afflictions," anger, which comes in five types (wrath, resentment, spite, envy/jealousy, cruelty); attachment, which also comes in five types (avarice, inflated self-esteem, excitation, concealment of one's own vices, dullness); and four kinds of ignorance (blind faith, spiritual sloth, forgetfulness, and lack of introspective attentiveness). Finally, there are six types caused by ignorance + attachment: pretension, deception, shamelessness, inconsideration of others, unconscientiousness, and distraction.

The decomposition reveals how the poisons ramify, how they mutate into, and germinate and generate, new poisonous offspring, which create ever-new obstacles to eudaimonia^Buddha. How does all this taxonomizing and decomposition relate to concentration and mindfulness, to what we call meditation? The answer, I hope, is obvious. If you know how the mind works you are positioned to control it. This would be good, because we know (thanks to the four noble truths) that you can't (normally) control the suffering that the world summons up on your behalf (the tsunami hits), but that you can control the contribution you (as *anatman*) make to your own *dukkha* and to the *dukkha* of those with whom you interact.

When we follow the trail of the three poisons, we see that there are many, many psychological ways by which we undermine our quest for eudaimonia^Buddha. We will need multifarious mind control techniques suited for different kinds of mistakes and missteps. This is the work of meditation.

Some meditation techniques are suited for everyday problems, so the antidote for lust involves imaging the object of lust old and decrepit or, as necessary, dead and decomposing. Nonjudgmental detached thought acknowledges that normal folk might have occasional homicidal thoughts about other drivers or rude telephone solicitors and recommends that one notice such thoughts, but allow them to pass through one's mind without judgment (and of course without action).

There are many other kinds of mental disciple or meditation. The familiar practice of concentrating on the breath (for hours) is for what? A standard view is that it is for people who perseverate on things not worth thinking about. Another idea is that it is for training in attention itself, which will come in very handy when one needs to figure out what state one is in and why, this being necessary if one is to effectively control negative states. Then there are trance-like techniques whose function is practice in learning about impermanence or emptiness by analyzing and decomposing some "thing" in thought. Finally, there is specifically moral meditation. *Metta* meditation (loving kindness), for example, involves guided thought experimentation, pitting one's selfish side against one's compassionate, loving side. Normally, when *metta* goes as planned, one will find oneself identifying with one's loving self and not with one's inner selfish creep. And this will help strengthen that positive and (now) reflectively endorsed identification.

Overall the Buddhist *techniques de soi* are similar to some techniques of cognitive-behavioral therapy, but with a depth psychological twist, since the three poisons create mischief in multifarious, often sneaky ways. Whether meditation be focused on the breath, or whether it involves relaxation exercises, or the antidotes for lust and anger, or physical techniques such as yogic exercises, the aim of meditation is to amplify wholesome ways of feeling, thinking, and being and to reduce, ideally, to eliminate, the afflictions of the mind.

The Bodhisattva's Psyche

The final piece of business is to speak about the four exceptional virtues required for eudaimonia^{Buddha}:

- Compassion (*karuna*)
- Loving kindness (*metta*)
- Appreciative joy (*mudita*)
- Equanimity (*upekkha*).

Any person who cultivates these four exceptional virtues is a *bodhisattva*, a Buddhist saint, or better perhaps, she has entered the bodhisattva's path. These four virtues are the "Four Divine Abodes" (*brahmaviharas*) – "illimitables" or "immeasurables" (*appamanna*).[7]

The divine abodes are states of mind of the individual who has them, and they have unique first-personal phenomenological feel for that person. Each abode also necessarily involves a distinctive state of mind towards others.

The aim of compassion (*karuna*) is [to end the suffering of others]. The aim of loving kindness (*metta*) is [to bring happiness to others in the place of suffering].[8] Sympathetic joy (*mudita*) is [joy at the success of, or, what is different, the good fortune of others]. Sympathetic joy is appropriate even in zero-sum games, where the one who I am happy for has just beaten me fair and square.[9] Even equanimity (*upekkha*) has the good of another as its object, which shows that the translation of *upekkha* as equanimity is not perfect. In English, "equanimity" can refer to a narrow state of my heart-mind which has nothing to do with anyone else's welfare, and which is not directed at, for, or towards anything outside me. My being calm and serene might make me more pleasant to be around, or more caring towards others, but it is not constitutive of equanimity, as we English speakers understand the state, that it has this aim or quality.

This is not how Buddhists understand equanimity. Equanimity (*upekkha*) means more than personal serenity. It is constitutive of *upekkha* that I feel impartially about the wellbeing of others. If I am in the state of equanimity, interpreted as *upekkha*, I am in a state that involves, as an essential component, equal care and concern for all sentient beings. We might translate *upekkha* as equanimity in community, if it helps avoid confusion with our understanding of equanimity as a purely self-regarding state of mind.

The four divine virtues complete the picture of eudaimonia^{Buddha}. Perhaps with the description in place we can feel our way into what it would be like to achieve eudaimonia^{Buddha}, as opposed to what it would be like to achieve eudaimonia^{Aristotle}, or even some more familiar conception such as eudaimonia$^{\text{North Atlantic Liberal Early Twenty-First Century}}$. Each conception of the good life both presupposes and requires a certain psychological configuration. Buddhism is better than most other traditions in spelling out the psychology and explaining how to attain it. That said, a Westerner might wonder this: what "reasoning" (deep throat) could lead a tradition to develop a theory of eudaimonia that entails that the best life for a human is a life of maximal service to others?

The Buddhist answer is this: Our epistemology values experience first and foremost. When experience is not transparently conclusive about some matter of importance we try to reason our way to a conclusion. Our wisdom literature is a compendium of past observation and reasoning. It is not the word of any god (we don't have gods), so we do not normally go to that literature for the truth. Instead we send truths we discover by observation and reason to that literature. Our wisdom literature contains the (fallible) conclusions we have reached based on past experience. It does not tell us what is true *a priori*. The answer, therefore, as to why eudaimonia^{Buddha} has the character it has, and why, in particular, it claims that a life of maximal devotion to others is the only kind of life that has meaning and significance, and that might bring happiness (*sukkha*) to the person who lives this way, is because it is true. And it is true because we have watched many experiments in living, many different strategies for attaining eudaimonia, and eudaimonia^{Buddha} is the only form of life, the only way of living, that works consistently to produce eudaimonia.[10]

Experiments in *eudaimonics*

This claim – that among all known experiments in living, only eudaimonia^{Buddha} produces "true happiness" – appears to be empirical. It would be nice to know if it were true. *Eudaimonics* is the scientific study of eudaimonia. But studying eudaimonia empirically has proven exceedingly difficult. I do not think the reason has to do with the fact that eudaimonia is an inherently mysterious phenomenon. But studying various conceptions of eudaimonia requires considerably more delicacy than investigators have thus far shown. Indeed, I became convinced of the merits of the superscripting strategy because of a certain amount of loose talk on the alleged connection between happiness, and other good states of the mind and the body, and Buddhism. Let me explain.

At the beginning of the twenty-first century, and thanks largely to the 14th Dalai Lama's (2005) collaboration with Western philosophers and scientists over the course of the previous thirteen years, research exploring, and also often claiming, a link between Buddhism and happiness began to appear (see Davidson, 2000, 2003, 2004; Davidson and Irwin 1999; Davidson et al. 2003; Flanagan 2000, 2002, 2003; Goleman 2003a, b; Gyatso 2003a, b).

In the 1970s, credible work had been published claiming that certain kinds of meditation are useful in relaxing high-strung folk, and in that way leading to better cardiovascular health. But the turn of the century work was overtly eudaimonistic – it claimed that there was an unusual link between Buddhism and happiness (Harrington 2008). In my experience, the hypothesis that Buddhism leads to happiness, or that Buddhists are very happy, is thought to have been confirmed (at least this is so among people I speak with who have any opinion at all on the matter) and not merely advertised by Buddhists to have this effect. But that is not so. And what I have said so far explains, at least to a point, why it has not been confirmed. But there is more:

- First, the research on happiness depended on prior findings that show leftward activity in prefrontal cortex (LPFC) among (mostly) American students who report being in a good mood. But we do not know whether and, if so, how, being-in-a-good-mood^{American} is related to, e.g., being-in-a-good-mood^{Tanzanian} or how being in a good mood relates to such concepts as happiness, fulfillment, and eudaimonia. But suppose (incredibly) that being in a good mood = eudaimonia.
- Second, suppose that (a) being in a good mood = eudaimonia across all countries, cultures, traditions; and that (b) being in a good mood = eudaimonia lines up perfectly with LPFC activity. If (a) and (b) were true, then we would have learned that LPFC isn't all that illuminating, since we know in advance that different conceptions of eudaimonia are different. There is, e.g., eudaimonia^{Buddha} and eudaimonia^{Aristotle}, and these ought not to reveal themselves in exactly the same way in the folk who realize the relevant conception.
- Third, the research on Buddhism and happiness is almost always on whether Buddhist-inspired *meditation* (but not, e.g., Buddhist robes or Buddhist haircuts or even Buddhist ethics) produces good effects. But the good effects of meditation that are studied are about much more than anything that could be described as happiness$^{\text{Standard American}}$ let alone as eudaimonia^{Buddha}. There is research on ADD, on the number of influenza antibodies after flu shots with and without meditation, on arthritis pain, and much else.
- Fourth, much of the neuro-journalism that claims to be reporting what good effects of Buddhist practice have been *confirmed*, actually reports what studies (often pilot studies) are being undertaken or, again – and even worse – what Buddhists say

about what Buddhism delivers (see Stroud [2008], for an egregious example of both the latter tricks).

- Fifth, the only meta-analysis that has been done so far on the good effects of Buddhist meditation on mental and physical health over the last fifty years (through 2002) by Ospina et al. (2007) for the US Department of Health and Human Services claims that the results are inconclusive.
- Finally, we have seen how we might proceed: (1) get clear on what conception of eudaimonia is being studied, i.e., eudaimonia^{Buddha}, eudaimonia^{Aristotle}, eudaimonia^{Hedonist}; (2) because each kind of eudaimonia (is said) to differ in terms of the mental states that cause and constitute it, expect these differences to show up when you look at the brains of those who (are thought to embody) the relevant kind of eudaimonia (e.g., serenity and equanimity are part of eudaimonia^{Buddha} but not part of eudaimonia^{Aristotle}, and if eudaimonia^{Buddha} and eudaimonia^{Aristotle} are realized in actual people, in the advocates of each form of life, then the brains of practitioners should light up in different ways, not in the *same* way, as most of the research so far assumes); and (3) if the researchers are assuming that there *is* a state of the mind-brain that is the essence, or kernel, of "true happiness," then they need to explain what this essence is, and why we should believe there is such a thing.

Eudaimonics can and should proceed, but only if there is a clear understanding that the question of what eudaimonia is, where (if anywhere) it is located, and which conception of eudaimonia is the best, the real deal, is not a question that falls within the domain of brain science. It is a wide normative question about mind-world-norms-ends fit. Eudaimonia^{Buddha} and eudaimonia^{Aristotle} are only two from among several credible conceptions of the good life and both are defined as syndromes, ways of being and living with distinctive causes and components. Whatever it means to be eudaimon^{Buddha} or eudaimon^{Aristotle} it involves a great deal more than what goes on between the ears.

This is a good way to end. It leaves the philosopher with this delicious question: Is eudaimonia^{Buddha} a good way to live and be only for Buddhists, or does it depict a way of living that is *the* best, or at least better than other contender conceptions of eudaimonia? As the teacher says, Why? Why not? What would Plato, Aristotle, Confucius, Jesus, Mohammed, Hobbes, Kant, and Mill say about the picture of eudaimonia^{Buddha} and the defense of it? Explain and defend your answer.

Notes

1. I leave aside the question whether eudaimonia^{Buddha}, the highest state that sentient beings can attain, is the very best, the highest state of all. Many Buddhists will say the highest state of all is attainment of *nirvana*, at which point one ceases to exist as a desirer and the flame that one was is extinguished forever. This however is a matter of controversy. Both ancient Theravada Buddhism and contemporary secular Western varieties go light on some of the more familiar Buddhist metaphysical exotica of rebirth, *nirvana*, what I call *karma*^{untame} (2007), and the like.
2. Some, possibly many, Buddhists believe in rebirth. The idea that there is or could be rebirth is unstable in relation to the idea of *anatman* (that is, if there is no *atman* to be reborn?) and in addition

looks suspiciously like a piece of consoling delusion. In 2005 the Dalai Lama said that the doctrine of rebirth should yield, if we can make no sense of it scientifically (see Flanagan 2007).

3. When a Buddhist says she is "practicing" she means she is doing some form of meditation regularly, alone or with others in silence.
4. In virtue of the doctrine of *anatman* Buddhism can seem anti-essentialist. But despite the fact that the poisons are sensitive to local ecology, so that, for example, thirst for a fancy car occurs only after 1900 when fancy cars appeared, the poisons are natural dispositions, part of human nature, that come with the equipment. A Buddhist friendly to Darwinism (most sensible contemporary Buddhists) can explain why.
5. *Karma* provides some structure to the apparently senseless trajectory of the universe once sentient beings happen along. Familiarly, a karmic eschatology is one in which good actions pay and bad actions cost.
6. *Buddhist Intentionality*: *Citta* = consciousness, and the *cittas* = types of consciousness, e.g., consciousness in each sensory modality. The *citta*, for example, of olfactory consciousness is different from the *citta* of visual consciousness, and the *cittas* can be analytically distinguished from the mental factors (*citasekas*) that they, as it were, can contain. Buddhist intentionality is pretty much the same as Aquinas- and Brentano-style intentionality. So, olfactory consciousness might contain the smell [of coffee] or [of roses]. In some cases, e.g., joy consciousness about births in my family, where I am joyful that [sister Nancy had a baby] and that [sister Kathleen had a baby], the feeling may be the same, while the intentional content, marked off by brackets, differs.
7. Strictly speaking a bodhisattva has a constant and spontaneous desire to liberate all sentient beings.
8. Not suffering ≠ being happy. Anti-depressants make people suffer less. But even if they eliminate suffering, they do not also by themselves bring happiness.
9. Several years ago, 2003 I think, Luol Deng, now a professional basketball player, returned to Duke after losing an important NCAA game to the University of Connecticut. He thanked his teachers (my colleague David Wong and I) and his classmates (Comparative Ethics) for their support, and explained his admiration and happiness for Emeka Okafor and Ben Gordon, two excellent players on the victorious University of Connecticut team. That's *mudita*. *Mudita* is the opposite of *Schadenfreude*.
10. Donald Lopez reminds me that there is an (over-) simplification in the last few paragraphs. In Theravada, "equanimity" is sometimes described as a state of an individual heart-mind, not as inherently social or moral. Relatedly, the *arhat* of the earlier tradition, unlike the bodhisattva of the Mahayana tradition, achieves nirvana without necessarily living a life of maximal devotion to others.

Acknowledgements

I am grateful to Donald Lopez for very helpful comments.

References

Buddhist sources

Bhikkhu Bodhi (ed.) (1993) *A Comprehensive Manual of Abhidhamma*, Sri Lanka: Buddhist Publication Society.

Other texts cited

Dalai Lama (2005) *The Universe in a Single Atom: The Convergence of Science and Spirituality*, New York: Morgan Road Books.

Davidson, R. J. (2000) "Affective Style, Psychopathology and Resilience: Brain Mechanisms and Plasticity," *American Psychologist* 55: 1196–1214.

—— (2003) "Affective Neuroscience and Psychophysiology: Toward a Synthesis," *Psychophysiology* 40: 655–65.

—— (2004) "Well-being and Affective Style: Neural Substrates and Biobehavioral Correlates," *Philosophical Transactions of the Royal Society of London B*, 359: 1395–1411.

Davidson, R. J., and Irwin, W. (1999) "The Functional Neuroanatomy of Emotion and Affective Style," *Trends in Cognitive Sciences* 3, no. 1 (January): 11–21.

Davidson, R. J., Kabat-Zinn, J., Schumacher, J., Rosenkrantz, M., Muller, D., Santorelli, S. F. et al. (2003) "Alterations in Brain and Immune Function Produced by Mindfulness Meditation," *Psychosomatic Medicine* 65: 564–70.

Flanagan, Owen (2000) "Destructive Emotions," *Consciousness and Emotions* 1, no. 2: 259–81.

—— (2002) *The Problem of the Soul: Two Visions of Mind and How to Reconcile Them*, New York: Basic Books.

—— (2003) "The Colour of Happiness," *The New Scientist*, 24 May.

—— (2007) *The Really Hard Problem: Meaning in a Material World*, Cambridge, MA: MIT Press.

Goleman, Daniel (2003a) *Destructive Emotions: How Can We Overcome Them?* New York: Bantam Books.

—— (2003b) "Finding Happiness: Cajole Your Brain to Lean Left," *The New York Times*, 4 February.

Gyatso, Tenzin (2003a) "The Monk in the Lab," *The New York Times*, 26 April.

—— (2003b) "On the Luminosity of Being," *The New Scientist*, 24 May.

Harrington, Anne (2008) *The Cure Within: A History of Mind-Body Medicine*, New York, Norton.

Harvey, Peter (2003) *Dictionary of Buddhism*, Oxford: Oxford University Press.

Ospina, M.B., Bond, T.K., Karkhaneh, M., Tjosvold, L., Vandermeer, B., Liang, Y., Bialy, L., Hooton, N., Buscemi, N., Dryden, D.M., and Klassen T.P. (2007) *Meditation Practices for Health: State of the Research*, Rockdale, MD: Agency for Healthcare Research and Quality-US Department of Health and Human Services (contract 290-0200023).

Perry, John (ed.) (1975) *Personal Identity*, Berkeley: University of California Press.

Rahula, Sri Walpola (1974 [1954]). *What the Buddha Taught*, rev. edn, New York: Grove.

Siderits, Mark (2007) *Buddhism as Philosophy*, Indianapolis: Hackett.

Stroud, M. (2008) "Mindfulness of Mind," *Shambala Sun*, March.

Further reading

Steven Collins, *Selfless Persons* (Cambridge: Cambridge University Press, 1982) is a modern classic on the doctrine of no-self: great reading for analytic philosophers. Edward Conze, *Buddhism: Its Essence and Development* (New York: Dover, 2003 [1951]) is an authoritative classic. See Owen Flanagan, "The Bodhisattva's Brain: Neuroscience and Happiness," in D. K. Nauriyal, M. Drummond and Y. B. Lal (eds), *Buddhist Thought and Applied Psychological Research* (London: Routledge, 2006), pp. 149–74, for Buddhist ethics and its possible connection with happiness; and 2009 "Neuro-Eudaimonics or Buddhists Lead Neuroscientists to the Seat of Happiness," in John Bickle (ed.), *Oxford Handbook of Philosophy and Neuroscience* (New York: Oxford University Press, 2009), for Buddhism and the neurophenomenology of happiness. Peter Harvey, *An Introduction to Buddhist Ethics* (Cambridge: Cambridge University Press, 2000) is an excellent introduction for philosophers. For Buddhism as a kind of virtue ethics, see Damien Keown, *The Nature of Buddhist Ethics* (Hampshire, UK: Palgrave, 2001 [1992]). Mark Siderits, *Personal Identity and Buddhist Philosophy* (Aldershot, UK: Ashgate, 2003) offers analytic philosophy of persons and Buddhist reductionism – deep and difficult.

47
THE PSYCHOLOGY OF EPISTEMIC JUDGEMENT

Jennifer Nagel and Jessica Wright

1 Introduction: evaluations of knowledge, belief, and justification

Human social intelligence includes a remarkable power to evaluate what people know and believe and to assess the quality of well- or ill-formed beliefs. Epistemic evaluations emerge in a great variety of contexts, from moments of deliberate private reflection on tough theoretical questions to casual social observations about what other people know and think. We seem to be able to draw systematic lines between knowledge and mere belief, to distinguish justified and unjustified beliefs, and to recognize some beliefs as delusional or irrational. This chapter outlines the main types of epistemic evaluations and examines how our capacities to perform these evaluations develop, how they function at maturity, and how they are deployed in the vital task of sorting out when to believe what others say.

1.1 Knowledge and belief attribution

At a formal dinner party, your hand slips and you knock over a full glass of red wine. Silence falls. Your sense of awkwardness is immediate and very different in character from the feeling you'd get from a similar moment of clumsiness while home alone: your embarrassment in the social setting is made possible in part by your instant capacity to register that others know that you were the one who did this. Human beings are naturally alert not only to what others know but also to what they think: in a variation of our scenario, imagine a situation in which the other guests are distracted at the moment when your neighbor hits your wine glass, and then they all look over at you, wrongly believing that you are the culprit behind the spreading stain on the tablecloth. Here again you'll have an instant emotional reaction as you register their misunderstanding. But how could you detect so swiftly what your dining companions knew or wrongly thought to be the case, even before any of them had the chance to speak? How could you read their minds?

By reviewing some basic structural features of the states of knowing and of thinking that something is the case, we can start to make sense of the human capacity to register these states. Epistemologists disagree about the finer details, but certain core features of the relationship between knowing and believing are widely recognized. It is widely agreed that both knowledge and belief are states that link an agent to a proposition (the verbs "know" and "believe" have other senses as well, but here we'll focus on propositional knowledge and belief). Read broadly, the term "agent" includes anything that can act, including groups and nonhuman animals; for simplicity in what follows, our main examples of knowing and believing agents will be individual human beings. Propositions are commonly understood to be packages of information, packages like the meanings of natural language sentences, which serve as "the primary bearers of truth and falsity" (King et al., 2014, p. 5). Propositions can be expressed directly in natural language, using "that-" clauses ("the host thinks that I broke the wine glass"; "my friend knows that I am seated on his left"). They can also be expressed indirectly, as embedded questions or "wh-" clauses: ("the host knows what was in the glass"; "my friend knows where the glass fell"). The proposition that is known here is the true answer to the embedded question ("there was pinot noir in the glass"; "the glass fell beside his plate"), whatever that answer might be (Karttunen, 1977). Our ability to use embedded questions to express a proposition indirectly enables us to characterize others as knowing things that we don't know ourselves. For example, you can say or judge, "This tall man knows what is on the far side of this wall," where the proposition "the goat is on the far side of this wall" is the thing he knows and you don't. We can keep track of whether others share our knowledge or know more or less than we do; we can also keep track of what they believe, whether it is true or false.

One major point of contrast between knowledge and belief concerns the range of truth values available for believed and known propositions: philosophers since Plato (369 bce / 1990) have accepted that what is believed can be true or false, but what is known can only be true (or factual). The other dinner guests can believe that you knocked over the wine glass when you didn't, but they cannot know something that was not in fact the case. Of course, we sometimes mistakenly take someone to know something that later turns out to be false, but as soon as we discover the falsity, we have to retract the judgment that the agent knew it to be the case.

Knowledge attributions are expressed in language not only with the use of the verb "to know" but also with a broader family of related verbs. Attitude verbs like "to know" that can take only true complements are called "factive" verbs: other factives include "realize that," "notice that," "see that," and "be aware that" (Kiparsky and Kiparsky, 1970). Nonfactives like "believe that," "think that," "hope that," and "doubt that" can take both true and false complement clauses. The line between factives and nonfactives seems to be drawn in all languages, with significant characteristics of this distinction appearing cross-linguistically (Egre, 2008; Lahiri, 2002).

Extending the terminology of linguistics into epistemology, attitudes that can be held only to truths are called factive attitudes; some of these attitudes (like knowing) constitute states, where others (like learning or forgetting) constitute events or processes. According to one influential account of knowledge, knowledge is the most general factive mental state: on this account, realizing, noticing, perceiving, being aware, or seeing that *p* is the case all entail knowing that *p* (Williamson, 2000). There is some controversy about this account of knowledge: some deny that knowledge is best characterized as a mental state (e.g. Fricker, 2009), and others raise doubts about whether *all* factives entail knowing, particularly emotive factives such as "is happy that" (Fantl, 2015). But it is broadly agreed that the verb "to know" is not the only verb denoting the possession of knowledge and that factives like "is aware that" and "recognizes that" also function to attribute knowledge. It is also widely agreed that it is essential to the state of knowledge that the knower is getting things right.

It is clearly possible to believe without knowing, notably in cases where one's belief is false. But is it possible to know without believing? Most contemporary epistemologists take knowledge to entail belief: if Jones knows that the meeting is canceled, it follows automatically that Jones believes that the meeting is canceled (Steup and Ichikawa, 2008). This entailment thesis is sometimes challenged. Colin Radford (1966) introduced an intuitive example involving a hesitant student being quizzed on historical facts. When asked for the date of Queen Elizabeth the First's death, the student very hesitantly answers "1603." The student reports that he feels he is just guessing, has no clear sense of which of his answers are likely to be right, but produces a reasonable number of accurate answers, which Radford argues he must be remembering and therefore must know. On the basis of several such examples, Radford ultimately concludes that knowledge requires neither confidence nor even belief. Radford's examples did not originally win a warm reception: philosophers have suggested that these cases do actually manifest belief or that they fail to manifest knowledge or have argued that they are equally dubious or borderline examples of both knowledge and belief (e.g. Armstrong, 1969; Lehrer, 1968).

Radford's challenge has been revived in recent years, as experimental philosophers have used more systematic methods to test attributions of knowledge and belief. In a between-subjects design, Blake Myers-Schulz and Eric Schwitzgebel (2013) probed responses to a case directly modeled on Radford's and to other cases involving ambivalent, distracted, and self-deceived agents, generally agents who are now failing to act on the basis of what they have at some point learned. Participants read these cases and were asked either a question of the form "does [name] know that [key proposition]?" or "does [name] believe/think that [key proposition]?" In all of the five cases they tested, the group asked about knowledge was more willing to attribute it than the group asked about belief. The between-subjects design made it hard to measure compliance to the thesis that knowledge entails belief, but the authors extrapolated that only about half of their participants made judgments in line with that principle for these cases.

There are several ways to respond to these results: one possible response is to insist that the state of knowledge actually does entail belief, while seeing experimental participants' intuitive responses as compromised or distorted in these interesting and complex cases. Perhaps participants are more cautious or thoughtful when asked what ambivalent characters believe or think than when asked what they know, and these borderline cases show something about our variable epistemic sensitivities rather than the nature of knowledge and belief. It is also possible to argue that lay epistemic judgments do generally reflect the principle that knowledge entails belief and instead criticize the methods that have produced apparently contrary evidence. Perhaps there are several senses of "believe," and if we direct attention to the right sense of the word, we'll see results more in line with the traditional view that knowing entails believing. One hint that there may be some ambiguity in "believe," which is activated in these cases, is that Myers-Schulz and Schwitzgebel got markedly different responses to some of their cases when they used the verb "think" as opposed to "believe." In the sense that takes a propositional complement, these verbs are typically interchangeable in English: "John thinks that the ball is in the box" and "John believes that the ball is in the box" usually register as equally true (or false). But especially in contexts where people are feeling torn about what to say or do, the verb "believe" may have more vivid connotations of what is currently in mind. For Myers-Schulz and Schwitzgebel's case involving a self-deceived husband whose wife was cheating on him and for their more dramatic version of Radford's student case, in which the student (Kate) was extremely stressed under time pressure and found her mind blank, participants were especially reluctant to describe the agent as believing that the key proposition was true, although a clear majority was willing to describe the agent as thinking it was so and as knowing it was so.

According to David Rose and Jonathan Schaffer (2013), the sense of "believe" that matters for epistemology is a dispositional rather than an occurrent (activated) sense: just as you can have standing knowledge on a point not currently in mind, you can have a standing belief that isn't conscious at this moment. They retested the Myers-Schulz cases with questions designed to elicit that sense of "believe"; for example, "Did Kate still believe (in the sense that she still held the information in her mind even if she could not access it) that Queen Elizabeth died in 1603?" When prompted in this manner, most participants reverted to complying with the principle that knowledge entails belief. In a somewhat similar spirit, Wesley Buckwalter and colleagues (Buckwalter et al., 2015) distinguished a thin and a thick sense of "believe," where the thin sense requires only the storage of information and the thick sense involves active endorsement and the control of action. Generally, these two senses are aligned, but in special cases, like the ambivalent cases probed by Myers-Schulz, they can come apart. Buckwalter and colleagues elicited attributions of "thin" belief by asking questions of the form "at least on some level, does [agent] think that [key proposition]?" Similar probes tested for thin knowledge attributions. Under these conditions, an overwhelming majority of participants showed intuitions complying to the principle that knowledge entails belief.

To accommodate those who worry that delicate scenarios of ambivalence and self-deception may constitute exceptions to the general rule that knowledge entails belief, we'll set those aside and focus on simpler core cases, where what is known is also believed. We have observed that what is known must be true, but not every true belief constitutes knowledge: lucky guesses and wishful-thinking can be true while falling short of knowledge. Knowledge requires some sort of "good basis," and cannot be arbitrary and unjustified. It remains controversial in epistemology exactly what kind of justification or basis is required for knowledge, but we can start by examining our natural resources for making basic judgments about evidence, justification, and the quality of judgments.

1.2 Justification and evidence collection

Some judgments are careful, patient, and well considered; others are hasty and confused. Epistemologists' stock examples of justified beliefs include perceptual judgments in favorable circumstances, sound inferences, and responsible learning from testimony; stock examples of unjustified belief include wishful-thinking and hasty generalization. There is evidence that laypeople agree with epistemologists about stock examples of justified and unjustified beliefs and also agree that some false judgments can nevertheless be justified – for example, where agents judge carefully on the basis of extensive but misleading evidence (Nagel et al., 2013). There are various theories of how we evaluate the judgments of others as justified or unjustified. One prominent theory suggests that we do so by comparing these judgments to learned stereotypes of reliable and unreliable belief formation (Goldman, 1994); others have argued that we ultimately evaluate not in terms of reliability but in terms of some other factor, such as ability (Turri, 2016).

Justification comes in degrees, and the question of what constitutes a good enough basis for a belief to count as adequately justified is a difficult one. Rival theories generally agree that having more evidence for a proposition tends to improve one's level of justification, but how much evidence does one need to collect before one is justified enough to count as knowing? If you are wondering whether your bank will be open this Saturday, is it enough to remember a Saturday visit at some point in the past, or do you have to double-check the website or visit the branch to make sure? We have some reason to expect variation here, depending on the circumstances of the person making a judgment. Work on adaptive decision-making has shown that when stakes are high we instinctively collect more information before making up our minds, and we also expect others to do the same (see Nagel, 2010a, for a review). We also adapt our methods of inquiry, switching from more automatic, intuitive ways of making judgments to more reflective and deliberate ways. We search for less information in easy evidential climates, where we learn that we can get the right answer by looking at a few cues, and we search much more extensively in climates where we discover that initial impressions can be misleading (Lee et al., 2014). If we are evaluating the epistemic states of someone in a high-stakes situation, we will naturally expect them to be more cautious, and we will collect more evidence than we would for its low-stakes counterpart before arriving at a firm belief. Given our current working assumption that belief is one of the necessary conditions for knowledge, we will expect high-stakes thinkers to work harder than their low-stakes counterparts to achieve a state that we count as knowledge.

1.3 The social neuroscience of epistemic judgments

Judging whether someone knows or believes something can involve a great range of cognitive functions: we take in various perceptual cues; we calculate the visual perspectives of others; we process language, either in a story about the agent or in listening to what the agent is saying; we draw on background information about the world in general and social scripts in particular; and we make various types of explicit and implicit inferences (for a review, see Apperly, 2011). With such a diverse array of mental functions feeding into the attribution of knowledge and belief, there is nevertheless a surprisingly high level of specialization in the brain for the attribution of these epistemic states.

Functional neuroimaging has extracted an increasingly sharp picture of the brain regions implicated in epistemic evaluations by matching epistemic judgment tasks against control tasks closely matched for their demands on language, perspective-taking, and other dimensions of appraisal. Within the range of brain regions involved in social cognition (including perception of agency and emotion), several regions seem especially significant for epistemic evaluation, most notably the medial prefrontal cortex (mPFC) and the bilateral temporo-parietal junction (TPJ). The mPFC is thought to be activated in a wide range of social cognition, including thoughts about human appearances, traits, sensations, and personalities (Saxe and Powell, 2006); it also seems to play a significant role in keeping track of the reliability or "social value" of others – for example. in playing strategic games with partners over time (Behrens et al., 2008). While the mPFC was once thought to serve as the "decoupling mechanism" for separating representations from reality in our evaluations of others, enabling the representation of misconceptions (Frith and Frith, 2003), there is increasing evidence that this function is handled instead by the TPJ, together with reasoning about knowledge or true belief (Aichhorn et al., 2009). Across fMRI studies, the TPJ is consistently activated in reasoning about the knowledge and beliefs of others (Schurz et al., 2014); sharp deficits in epistemic state reasoning are produced when this region is temporarily impaired through transcranial magnetic stimulation (Young et al., 2010) or more permanently impaired following a stroke or injury (Apperly et al., 2004).

Researchers probing the nature of epistemic evaluations have a number of tools at their disposal. For example, we can make epistemic evaluations either in the course of verbal tasks, such as reading hypothetical stories about agents, or in nonverbal tasks, such as watching silent films or playing strategic games with live partners. Interestingly, it does not seem to matter whether we are cued by linguistic or nonlinguistic stimuli: a comprehensive meta-analysis of imagining studies found no significant differences in activation between verbal and nonverbal "theory of mind" tasks (Carrington and Bailey, 2009). This result matters to epistemologists who may be wondering whether evaluations of narrative thought experiments – like the Gettier case scenarios discussed in section 3 – are managed differently from epistemic evaluations in the wild. Physiologically, these evaluations seem to work at least roughly the same way.

There is nevertheless a complex relationship between language and epistemic evaluation. Children's linguistic abilities are highly correlated with their ability to pass tests of explicit false belief attribution, with early linguistic ability an even stronger predictor of early mindreading ability than the converse (Milligan et al., 2007). The causal dependencies here are hard to calculate, however, not least because explicit false belief tests place significant demands on linguistic competence, including managing the odd pragmatics of being asked a question about belief by someone who already knows the answer (Helming et al., 2014). Interestingly, adults with severely impaired syntax are able to perform very well on first- and second-order mental state attribution tasks presented pictorially (Apperly et al., 2006; Varley et al., 2001). Adults can make intelligent judgments about others' knowledge, beliefs, and even others' false beliefs about the false beliefs of third parties, despite an inability to understand spoken that-clauses or to distinguish between the sentences "the fish was eaten by the cat" and "the fish ate the cat." Even if language plays a key role in the development of our capacity for epistemic evaluations, and even if adults in the nonclinical population often use language to express their epistemic evaluations, competence in epistemic evaluation is interestingly independent of competence in grasping the syntactic structure of language.

Some epistemic evaluations are executed deliberately: for example, members of a jury may be instructed to reflect on the question of whether the defendant suspected or knew that the gun was loaded. Epistemic evaluations are also performed without specific instruction, and there is a lively debate about the extent to which we make such evaluations automatically or spontaneously. Are we invariably and involuntarily triggered to track what others around us see, know, and believe? Researchers have probed this question in a number of ways. In the dot perspective task, participants need to count the number of dots presented in a virtual room on a screen in front of them: sometimes they see an image of a person standing in the middle of the virtual room looking at the dots on one side of the room, with his back to either more dots or a blank wall behind him. Participants are asked how many dots they themselves can see and respond more swiftly if the on-screen avatar can see that same number of dots; when the image of a person is replaced with an image of a similarly sized column, the effect vanishes (Samson et al., 2010). This and various other effects of interference from the perspectives of others have led some researchers to believe that we automatically devote mental resources to computing what others can see, even when this is not relevant to our current task. Not all researchers are persuaded: some have argued that the effect has more to do with domain-general direction of attention, discovering that the "perspective interference" effect appears again if we replace the virtual person with a directional arrow rather than a column (Santiesteban et al., 2014). However, there is continuing controversy over whether the underlying basis of our response to what others can see is different in extent or kind when compared to well-matched control conditions (Catmur et al., 2016; Schurz et al., 2015). In any event, whether or not we have a special domain-specific response to the minds of others that is invariably triggered by witnessing other agents, it is widely agreed that epistemic evaluations of one kind or another are performed very frequently and rapidly in ordinary social navigation and conversational exchanges.

2 The development of knowledge and belief attribution

2.1 Developing a capacity for explicit epistemic evaluations

When and how do human beings gain the ability to evaluate epistemic states? To answer this question, researchers have studied children's competence in answering explicit questions about knowledge and belief, and questions about how agents with different epistemic positions will act; they have also looked at spontaneous use of mental state terms and at subtler patterns of anticipatory looking and surprise in reaction to agents who are seen to either witness or fail to witness changes in the world that are relevant to the actions they are about to perform.

One of the most clearly established findings concerns the emergence of an ability to pass the explicit false belief test, usually between ages 4 and 5 (Wimmer and Perner, 1983). In this test, the child sees an agent placing an object (such as a bar of chocolate) in a certain location (say, a cupboard); the agent then briefly leaves the scene. During her absence, the chocolate is moved (say, to a drawer) as the child watches. The child is asked where the agent will look for the chocolate when she returns. Around the time that they turn 3, children typically fail this task: a large-scale meta-analysis found roughly two-thirds of 36-month-olds saying that the agent will look in the closed drawer, where the chocolate is now located; by 44 months about half are answering correctly, expecting the agent to look in the cupboard where she last saw the chocolate; and a year later about three-fourths produce the right answer (Wellman et al., 2001). Similar progressions are seen in children from different cultures and appear whether the task is presented with live actors, puppets, or videos.

One way of understanding the switch from failing to passing the false belief test is to say that it is only in the fourth year of life that children develop the concept of belief (Rakoczy, 2015; Perner, 1991). Before this age, children can see agents as having some mental states – notably goals, such as the goal of getting the chocolate – but they seem to be unable to represent agents as having states of mind that may be out of line with reality. Children are sometimes described as having a natural bias toward egocentrism in their epistemic evaluations: they find it hard not to project their own knowledge onto others, a tendency that also appears, in subtler ways, in the epistemic evaluations of adults (Birch and Bloom, 2004; Keysar et al., 2003).

Interestingly, the capacity to attribute knowledge, a state that is always in line with reality, seems to emerge before the capacity to attribute belief. Children can explicitly attribute knowledge and ignorance by the age of 3 (Pratt and Bryant, 1990). Across cultures, children use words meaning "know" earlier and more often than they use words meaning "believe" (Tardif and Wellman, 2000; Shatz et al., 1983; Pascual et al., 2008). Some researchers had been inclined to dismiss children's very early talk of knowledge – especially their use of "I don't know" (or "I dunno") – as merely formulaic, but more recent cross-cultural research has supported the idea that by the age of 2 children speak of knowledge in a way that is sensitive to what is known and show similar patterns in describing their own lack of knowledge and in asking others what they know (Harris et al., 2017). Describing the knowledge that agents possess or lack is in one important way simpler than describing the beliefs that they have: the natural domain of what can be known is reality, where the natural domain of what is believed is much wider because people can believe virtually any imaginable truth or falsehood. If knowledge is a window into reality (which may be blocked in cases of ignorance), belief is a depiction of something that may be reality-independent; in order to track the false beliefs of others, one must devote some cognitive resources to representing those belief contents, decoupled from reality and tied to the relevant agents, alongside a rival representation of reality itself. As adults we find it easy to notice and report the misconceptions of others; by reviewing the difficulties that young children seem to have on this frontier, we can come to appreciate how difficult it is to perform explicit epistemic evaluations of mistaken agents. At present, the capacity to track false beliefs appears to be uniquely human: while nonhuman primates show some capacity to track whether other members of their species have knowledge, they have not shown any ability to represent false belief (Kaminski et al., 2008; Marticorena et al., 2011).

2.2 Implicit epistemic evaluations

Well before they can give accurate explicit answers to questions about knowledge and belief, infants and children show subtler signs of tracking epistemic states. Three-year-olds who give the wrong answer to the explicit false belief test nevertheless consistently look at the right location as they anticipate the returning agent's search for the chocolate (Clements and Perner, 1994). Researchers have suggested that even younger children show signs of implicit belief attribution: in a "violation of expectancy" paradigm, 15-month-olds are reported to look longer, as if in surprise, at returning agents who search for an object at its new and actual location rather than at the last place the agent saw it (Onishi and Baillargeon, 2005). Implicit false belief attribution is gauged not only by means of anticipatory looking direction and looking time but also in helping tasks, where it seems 18-month-old toddlers can modify their behavior to help agents who may have false beliefs (Buttelmann et al., 2009). Findings for knowledge are even more striking: looking time measures have also been taken to show that infants seem to be able to track the difference between other agents' knowledge and ignorance as early as 12.5 months (Luo and Baillargeon, 2007).

Various rival theories attempt to explain the early infant findings and the reasons why explicit false belief attribution apparently lags early sensitivity to false belief. Some have argued that the infant results should be understood not as signs of genuine epistemic evaluation but as low-level responses to perceptual patterns in the stimuli (Heyes, 2014) or as the products of domain-general statistical learning processes, guided by infant biases to attend to human faces and actions (Ruffman, 2014). Others argue that infants really do see others as knowing and believing, possessing a repertoire of innate or early-developing mental state concepts whose expression is initially blocked in explicit tasks for reasons having to do with factors such as processing load or the difficult pragmatics of responding to questions about false beliefs (Carruthers, 2016; Helming et al., 2014). Some see children as progressing from a stage at which they use a more basic subsystem to attribute goals and knowledge to a later stage at which a distinct subsystem makes belief attribution possible, first implicitly and then explicitly (Baillargeon et al., 2010). Others have a more radical two-systems view, in which infants initially track something more basic than full-blown propositional attitudes: perhaps infants first encode just relationships between agents, objects, and locations (Butterfill and Apperly, 2013) or records of the objects and events associated with the agent (Perner and Roessler, 2012); only much later do they become capable of the flexible and inferentially rich theory of mind that propositional attitude attribution makes possible. Advocates of the two-system view argue that the more basic infant system is retained in adults and used for rapid judgments in daily social navigation. Meanwhile, other researchers have raised doubts about the replicability and convergent validity of non-verbal measures of mental state attribution in infants (Dörrenberg et al., 2018).

Whether genuine epistemic evaluations are ultimately established to be early- or late-developing, all researchers face the challenge of explaining how it is that we come to be able to compute the contents of the knowledge and beliefs of other agents. There is a general consensus that our grasp of these contents begins with our ability to detect others' perceptual access to reality, but there is ongoing controversy about how we move from seeing others as knowing about certain aspects of reality to seeing them as having potentially false beliefs about various other ways the world might be. Ongoing research into the emergence of our capacities to attribute knowledge and belief promises to shed further light on the nature of these capacities and the relationship between these epistemic states themselves.

3 Mature epistemic evaluations: biases and paradoxical patterns

3.1 *Shifting intuitions about knowledge*

Some patterns of instinctive epistemic evaluation are surprising, counter-intuitive, and even paradoxical. One of the most striking such patterns is associated with skepticism. We are ordinarily quite liberal in our positive attributions of knowledge: "know" is one of the ten most-common verbs in English (Davies and Gardner, 2010), and a quick corpus search of spontaneous use of this verb in conversation and writing shows that it most commonly appears without negation. Reading a story about an ordinary man in a furniture store looking at a bright red table and asking his wife whether she likes this red table, you wouldn't ordinarily hesitate to say that he knows that the table is red; indeed, this looks like a paradigm case of knowing. Still, there are ways of getting people to hesitate to attribute knowledge here. You could, for example, mention that a white table under a bright red spotlight would look exactly the same to this shopper, and he hasn't checked whether the lighting is normal. Even if you make it clear to the reader that the lighting is normal and the table is red, knowledge attribution rates plummet as that problematic hypothetical possibility is mentioned, with only a minority still seeing the shopper as knowing (Nagel et al., 2013).

Virtually any case of ordinary empirical knowledge can be rewritten as a "skeptical pressure" case by mentioning some problematic possibility. Does a woman who glances at a working clock know what time it is? Of course. But if we emphasize that although this particular clock is working, sometimes clocks are broken, and that our woman doesn't look at the clock for long enough to be sure that it is operating correctly, there is considerable reluctance to see her as really knowing what time it is on the basis of her glance at the clock. What is interesting about the shifts in these cases is that they simply highlight something we in some sense knew all along (such as the fact that clocks are sometimes broken). When attention is directed to this fact, the case no longer registers as a very good intuitive case of knowledge.

By describing a situation in slightly different ways, we can manipulate whether it seems like a case of knowledge or ignorance. We can also shift ourselves from thinking to doubting that we know anything at all about our environment by focusing on problematic possibilities concerning large-scale deceptive scenarios (could I be a brain in a vat?). Some philosophers have proposed subtle theories about the semantics of "knows" to explain these shifts; others have argued that knowledge itself is more complex than it might appear or that something is going wrong in our intuitive impressions of knowledge in these cases, just as something goes wrong in our intuitive impressions of the length of lines in the Müller-Lyer illusion.

The dominant semantic theory is known as contextualism. According to contextualists, "know(s)" is a context-sensitive term, like "here," "tomorrow," or "tall" (DeRose, 2009). There is no fixed height that makes something count as tall: what it takes to be tall for a rose bush is rather different from what it takes to be tall for a redwood. Implicit comparison classes seem to be called into play, with "tall" always meaning something like "relatively great in vertical magnitude compared with things of its class." The same thing can be judged different ways in comparison to two classes of which it is a member: a man can be tall for an American but not tall for a basketball player. Applied in the epistemic realm, contextualists say that we have variable epistemic standards: someone can count as knowing by the standards of the casual bus stop conversation without counting as knowing by the standards prevailing in a court of law (Stine, 1976). There are various theories of how these shifting standards function: some argue that what shifts is how much evidence we need (Cohen, 1999), while others argue that what shifts is how large a range of possibilities of error we need to eliminate (Lewis, 1996). However standards are operationalized, contextualists typically hold that the average John Doe can be speaking truly when he says, in a causal context, "I know that there is beer in my fridge," while the skeptic who looks down on John Doe from a discussion about brains in vats can also be speaking truly when he says, "John Doe does not know that there is beer in his fridge." These two speakers are not contradicting each other, according to contextualism, because they are not latching onto the same thing with their use of the word "know."

Contextualism faces a number of challenges. For ordinary context-sensitive terms like "tomorrow," there is a relatively simple and easily learned recipe for calculating the content expressed by the term in any given context of use. If "knows" is context-sensitive, it is not so obvious how this sensitivity works; critics of contextualism have argued that it does not exactly fit the pattern of gradable adjectives like "tall" (Stanley, 2005), while defenders have suggested that "know(s)" must have its own distinctive type of context-sensitivity (DeRose, 2009). To date, contextualists have provided only partial accounts of the circumstances under which epistemic standards shift one way or another, and the search for alternate explanations continues.

One rival explanation of shifts in knowledge attribution focuses not on the attributor of knowledge but on the knowing subject. Some of the most-discussed cases of apparently shifting standards for knowledge concern shifts from low- to high-stakes situations. For example, a person with casual curiosity about whether a flight will have a layover in Chicago could seem to know that it will stop there after a quick glance at a schedule, while a person for whom the location of the layover is a life-and-death matter would need to do more research in order to come across as knowing (Cohen, 1999). According to the position now known as "interest-relative invariantism" (IRI), the verb "know(s)" always denotes the same relation between an agent and a proposition, but it is a relation in which stakes matter directly as a factor in whether someone has knowledge (Stanley, 2005). Advocates of this view have aimed to support it by appealing to patterns of intuitive epistemic evaluation and also by appeal to more abstract principles about the relationship between knowledge and action. Meanwhile, critics of IRI have offered alternative accounts of the relationship between stakes and knowledge; for example, focusing on the impact that stakes have on confidence (Weatherson, 2005; Bach, 2005; Nagel, 2010a). Critics of IRI have also noted that the theory does not seem to explain superficially similar shifts in apparent knowledge, like those occurring in the clock case, where nothing much needs to be at stake in order to produce the skeptical impression that the person glancing at the clock fails to have knowledge.

Another strategy to handle conflicting or paradoxical patterns of epistemic intuition is to argue that some intuitions are the products of illusion or bias. Some philosophers have argued that rising stakes switch our attention from ordinary ground-level questions of what is known up to higher-level questions concerning iterations of knowledge (do I know that I know this?), distracting us from what is really at issue (Williamson, 2005). Others have argued that by mentioning hypothetical possibilities of error we bias the focus of epistemic evaluation in a distorting fashion in one way or another (Gerken, 2013; Nagel, 2010b). Shifting patterns of epistemic evaluation remain an open source of controversy in epistemology, philosophy of language, and philosophy of mind.

3.2 Gettier cases

The person who looks at a broken clock doesn't often come away knowing what time it is. But imagine someone who looks at a stopped clock at just the right moment to form a true belief. Does she know, as she looks at the hands of the broken clock pointing to 3:15, that it is now 3:15? Notice that this is not only a true belief but a justified true belief in some sense of "justified." The person who looks at a clock in order to tell the time is behaving responsibly and collecting evidence relevant to the question she is settling (and indeed in luckier circumstances, with a functioning clock, we'd be happy to count her as knowing the time).

The case of the accurate broken clock is generally seen as a case of justified true belief without knowledge, a type of scenario known in the literature as a "Gettier case," after Edmund Gettier, who included several such cases in a short paper arguing against the idea that knowledge could be analyzed as justified true belief (Gettier, 1963). Gettier's counterexamples spurred the development of a series of more elaborate theories of knowledge, in which additional conditions were added to justified true belief, as well as fresh analyses of knowledge in terms of causal and counterfactual conditions (Shope, 1983). To date no proposed analysis of knowledge has won very widespread acceptance among epistemologists, and some now argue that it is unlikely to be possible to analyze knowledge into true belief plus nonepistemic factors (Williamson, 2000).

Whether they are trying to forge a new analysis of knowledge or trying to show that no such analysis will be satisfactory, epistemologists often rely on intuitive assessments of particular cases like the stopped clock case as evidence about the nature of knowledge. Concerns are sometimes raised about these subtle epistemic evaluations. In one heavily cited paper from 2001, three critics of intuition-driven philosophy argued that epistemic evaluations of Gettier cases might show more about local cultural practices than about the nature of knowledge itself (Weinberg et al., 2001). On the basis of a small-scale study of American undergraduates of different ethnic backgrounds, they concluded that Gettier case evaluations differed by cultural group, with East and South Asian participants attributing knowledge where Western participants saw true belief. These conclusions were based on responses to the following case:

> Bob has a friend, Jill, who has driven a Buick for many years. Bob therefore thinks that Jill drives an American car. He is not aware, however, that her Buick has recently been stolen, and he is also not aware that Jill has replaced it with a Pontiac, which is a different kind of American car. Does Bob really know that Jill drives an American car, or does he only believe it?
>
> REALLY KNOWS ONLY BELIEVES

Subsequent researchers failed to replicate the original findings of cultural variation for this case, finding instead that most respondents across different cultural backgrounds evaluated it as a case of mere belief, in line with the traditional philosophical view that cases like these show justified true belief without knowledge (Kim and Yuan, 2015; Seyedsayamdost, 2015; Nagel et al., 2013). A much larger study of participants in Brazil, India, Japan, and the USA found similar responses to a variety of Gettier cases across all of these cultures, prompting the conclusion that these responses are part of an innate and universal "core folk epistemology" (Machery et al., 2015). The extent to which intuitions about knowledge are shared across cultures and the ultimate basis of these intuitions are questions for further research.

4 Epistemic vigilance

Much of what we learn from the world comes from what others tell us. Hand in hand with this fact, however, comes a hard truth – for a variety of reasons, what others tell us is not always going to be true. In response to this social reality, we have various mechanisms for "epistemic vigilance" – sorting good from bad information (Sperber et al., 2010). Research on epistemic vigilance has both descriptive and normative dimensions. The descriptive side concerns what cognitive mechanisms, if any, we use for epistemic vigilance. The normative side concerns how these mechanisms are evaluable by epistemic standards like knowledge and moral standards like justice. Both descriptive and normative issues arise on two different fronts: vigilance toward the *informant* and vigilance toward the *information* communicated.

4.1 Vigilance toward the informant

Imagine that you are at an art museum and a very young child approaches you and tells you, with great sincerity, that the museum has made a mistake in taking Picasso to have painted the work of art you are looking at. If your reaction is to express surprise or doubt in response to this statement because of her age – as it likely would be – this is an instance of you exhibiting vigilance toward the *source*.

Vigilance toward the source of testimony is perhaps the most obvious type of epistemic vigilance. Vigilance toward the source can manifest itself in a number of different ways. We can doubt that the person *knows* or is competent to know (even if she thinks she knows), we can doubt that the person is being sincere, and we can judge the informant on the basis of generalized heuristics, like a sense of trustworthiness. One of the ways that we manifest this tendency is in thinking of an informant as *trustworthy* or *untrustworthy*, *credible* or *not credible*. Such judgments can be made very quickly. In a study probing the evaluation and attribution of traits like trustworthiness and competence, researchers found that after a glimpsing a face for just one tenth of a second, participants were able to form judgments of trustworthiness that correlated very closely with judgments of trustworthiness made without time pressure, and more closely than corresponding judgments of attractiveness (Willis and Todorov, 2006). Young children already exhibit source-directed vigilance. In particular, like adults, young children see informants as having traits such as trustworthiness, competence, and accuracy (Cogsdill et al., 2014; Kuhlmeier et al., 2003).

In attributions of trustworthiness or credibility as a trait to the source, one is judging not the quality of the *information* transmitted but rather the quality of the *informant*. This move of attributing a trait to an informant may be problematic if it is an instance of the "fundamental attribution error"(Ross, 1977), where agents downplay situational factors and overestimate the contribution of personality and dispositional traits to an agent's behaviour (O'Sullivan, 2003; Gilbert and Malone, 1995). Even more problematically, judgments of trustworthiness, competence, and credibility may be based on things that are not epistemically relevant, like the shape of a face (Zebrowitz et al., 1996).

When it is not too costly to do so, agents will exert other kinds of source-centered vigilance. Vigilance toward the source requires that we be aware of not only the agent's explicit interests and motivations but also who she is in relation to the information that is being communicated to us and in relation to us. In particular, vigilant agents need to know if the source is competent (i.e., does she know or have reason to believe the information?) and if the source is warm or benevolent (i.e., is she well intentioned toward you?). Across cultures, evaluations of competence and warmth play a leading role in the interpretation of social behavior (Fiske et al., 2006).

Whatever situation-based or trait-based mechanisms we use in ordinary social navigation, they are hard-pressed to detect deliberate deception. Studies have shown that people, even those trained to detect lies, are remarkably bad at telling when someone is lying (Ekman and O'Sullivan, 1991; Bond and DePaulo, 2006). The verbal and nonverbal cues most often read as markers of lying (such as avoidance of eye contact) are not generally valid signs of deception (Sporer and Schwandt, 2007; Sporer and Schwandt, 2006).

These considerations together paint a dim picture of source-directed epistemic vigilance. However, research on our limitations needs to be balanced against research on our strengths in source-centered vigilance. The more successful side of our basic capacities for epistemic vigilance has been explored most extensively in research on children's learning. It was once thought that children under a certain age are naive epistemic agents – that they will believe anything an informant tells them. Recent work on the topic, however, shows that children are surprisingly discerning in their epistemic evaluations (Woolley and Ghossainy, 2013; Vanderbilt et al., 2014; Clément, 2010). By the age of 2, children prefer to learn from informants who were previously accurate (Clément et al., 2004; Koenig and Harris, 2005; Koenig and Woodward, 2010); by 4, children will be vigilant toward informants on the basis of probabilistic evidence (Pasquini et al., 2007). Young children will also take into account how knowledgeable their source is (Sabbagh and Baldwin, 2001; Sobel and Kushnir, 2013; Tummeltshammer et al., 2014; Stephens et al., 2015). Many psychologists now think that children, rather than being gullible, are in fact quite intelligently vigilant toward sources of testimony.

4.2 Vigilance toward the information: coherence

Agents also exhibit epistemic vigilance in relation to the information transmitted to them. The main criterion for vigilance relative to the information itself is whether the information is *coherent* with one's other beliefs. Developmental psychologists have found sophisticated coherence-checking behaviors in children, looking at their responses to labeling errors, inaccuracy, grammatical errors, and inconsistent, illogical, and improbable statements (Stephens et al., 2015). Eight-month-old infants already prefer to follow the gaze of a reliable looker – one who consistently looks at objects on a screen, as opposed to someone who inconsistently does so (Chow et al., 2008; Tummeltshammer et al., 2014). This is thought to show that infants track coherence (Stephens et al., 2015). Adults also track the coherence of what they are being told, perhaps in part by means of an intuitive sense of how fluently new information can be processed (Reber and Unkelbach, 2010).

4.3 Epistemic injustice

After examining the mechanisms behind epistemic vigilance, we can wonder whether these social mechanisms are operating in the way that they ought to. For example, mechanisms for social vigilance are open to socially learned generalizations and associations that may compromise our epistemic evaluations either epistemically or morally in various forms of "epistemic injustice" (Fricker, 2007).

Gender is one representative area of concern. Studies on the credibility of expert witnesses are potentially illuminating here. In courtroom decisions, juries may be swayed by gender stereotypes in assessing the credibility of male and female expert witnesses.

For example, one team of researchers studied responses to transcripts of a price-fixing case set in a domain that was traditionally either male (automotive services) or female (cosmetics), with key testimony in otherwise identical cases ascribed to male and female expert witnesses; they found higher evaluations of the expert witnesses who were testifying in their gender stereotype-congruent domains, and in the traditionally female domain, higher damages were awarded to the side represented by the female expert witness (McKimmie et al., 2004). These studies do not show a clear-cut ranking in the perceived credibility of female and male expert witnesses; indeed, other studies have found results cutting against the stereotype-congruity findings (Couch and Sigler, 2002). The credibility of male and female expert witnesses depends on a number of different situational factors, including the domain of the case, the complexity of the testimony, and the extent of deliberation (Neal, 2014).

If an expert's actual knowledge or objective credibility on a subject has very little to do with his or her gender and the congruency of his or her gender with the expert's field, instinctive mechanisms for epistemic vigilance can lead us to make epistemically defective or morally problematic judgments about our informants. The kinds of problematic generalizations that matter are ones like "car mechanics tend to be men." When faced with a woman who is testifying about car repair issues, we may dismiss her as a credible source on the basis that she doesn't fit into our stereotype of "car mechanic." This dismissal may be more or less conscious or controllable (Levy, 2015).

One question is what kind of a mistake people are making when they rely on these kinds of cues, consciously or unconsciously. It is not obvious how individuals can resist the pervasive influence of cultural stereotypes, especially if stereotypes are generally inculcated by statistical learning processes that often result in true beliefs (Begby, 2013; Gendler, 2011; Egan, 2011). In some cases, skewed media presentations of a group may inculcate stereotypes that are frankly inaccurate; for example, associating black Americans with guns when white Americans are 50% more likely than blacks to report that they are gun owners (Parker, 2017, p. 7). But even in cases where the stereotype is accurate – assume, for the sake of argument, that women know less about cars than men do – discounting the testimony of an individual female car mechanic on the basis of such a stereotype seems morally problematic. Epistemic evaluations are deeply linked to relationships of social trust and have broad implications for how we treat others and learn from them. Closer psychological and philosophical examination of the nature of these evaluations can help us to appreciate their power, understand their shortcomings, and search for ways to correct them.

Bibliography

Aichhorn, M., Perner, J., Weiss, B., Kronbichler, M., Staffen, W. & Ladurner, G. (2009). Temporo-Parietal Junction Activity in Theory-of-Mind Tasks: Falseness, Beliefs, or Attention. *Journal of Cognitive Neuroscience*, 21(6), pp. 1179–92.

Apperly, I. A. (2011). *Mindreaders: The Cognitive Basis of "Theory of Mind"*, Hove and New York: Psychology Press.

Apperly, I. A., Samson, D., Carroll, N., Hussain, S. & Humphreys, G. W. (2006). Intact First- and Second-Order False Belief Reasoning in a Patient with Severely Impaired Grammar. *Social Neuroscience*, 1(3–4), pp. 334–48.

Apperly, I. A., Samson, D., Chiavarino, C. & Humphreys, G. W. (2004). Frontal and Temporo-Parietal Lobe Contributions to Theory of Mind: Neuropsychological Evidence from a False-Belief Task with Reduced Language and Executive Demands. *Journal of Cognitive Neuroscience*, 16(10), pp. 1773–84.

Armstrong, D. (1969). Does Knowledge Entail Belief? *Proceedings of the Aristotelian Society*, 70, pp. 21–36.

Bach, K. (2005). The Emperor's New "Knows". In G. Preyer & G. Peter, eds. *Contextualism in Philosophy: Knowledge, Meaning, and Truth*, New York: Oxford University Press, pp. 51–89.

Baillargeon, R., Scott, R. M. & He, Z. (2010). False-Belief Understanding in Infants. *Trends in Cognitive Sciences*, 14(3), pp. 110–18.

Begby, E. (2013). The Epistemology of Prejudice. *Thought: A Journal of Philosophy*, 2(2), pp. 90–99.

Behrens, T. E. J., Hunt, L. T., Woolrich, M. W. & Rushworth, M. F. (2008). Associative Learning of Social Value. *Nature*, 456(7219), pp. 245–50.

Birch, S. & Bloom, P. (2004). Understanding Children's and Adults' Limitations in Mental State Reasoning. *Trends in Cognitive Sciences*, 8(6), pp. 255–60.

Bond, C. F. & DePaulo, B. M. (2006). Accuracy of Deception Judgments. *Personality and Social Psychology Review*, 10(3), pp. 214–34.

Buckwalter, W., Rose, D. & Turri, J. (2015). Belief through Thick and Thin. *Noûs*, 49(4), pp. 748–75.

Buttelmann, D., Carpenter, M. & Tomasello, M. (2009). Eighteen-Month-Old Infants Show False Belief Understanding in an Active Helping Paradigm. *Cognition*, 112(2), pp. 337–42.

Butterfill, S. A. & Apperly, I. A. (2013). How to Construct a Minimal Theory of Mind. *Mind & Language*, 28(5), pp. 606–37.

Carrington, S. J. & Bailey, A. J. (2009). Are There Theory of Mind Regions in the Brain? A Review of the Neuroimaging Literature. *Human Brain Mapping*, 30(8), pp. 2313–35.

Carruthers, P. (2016). Two Systems for Mindreading? *Review of Philosophy and Psychology*, 7(1), pp. 141–62.

Catmur, C., Santiesteban, I., Conway, J. R., Heyes, C. & Bird, G. (2016). Avatars and Arrows in the Brain. *NeuroImage*, 132, pp. 8–10.

Chow, V., Poulin-Dubois, D. & Lewis, J. (2008). To See or Not to See: Infants Prefer to Follow the Gaze of a Reliable Looker. *Developmental Science*, 11(5), pp. 761–70.

Clément, F. (2010). To Trust or Not to Trust? Children's Social Epistemology. *Review of Philosophical Psychology*, 1, pp. 531–49.

Clément, F., Koenig, M. A. & Harris, P. (2004). The Ontogenesis of Trust. *Mind & Language*, 19(4), pp. 360–79.

Clements, W. A. & Perner, J. (1994). Implicit Understanding of Belief. *Cognitive Development*, 9(4), pp. 377–95.

Cogsdill, E. J., Todorov, A., Spelke, E. & Banaji, M. (2014). Inferring Character from Faces: A Developmental Study. *Psychological Science*, 25(5), pp. 1132–39.

Cohen, S. (1999). Contextualism, Skepticism, and the Structure of Reasons. *Philosophical Perspectives*, 13(s13), pp. 57–89.

Couch, J. V. & Sigler, J. N. (2002). Gender of an Expert Witness and the Jury Verdict. *The Psychological Record*, 52, pp. 281–87.

Davies, M. & Gardner, D. (2010). *Frequency Dictionary of American English*, New York: Routledge.

DeRose, K. (2009). *The Case for Contextualism: Knowledge, Skepticism, and Context*, Volume 1, New York: Oxford University Press.

Dörrenberg, S., Rakoczy, H. & Liszkowski, U. (2018). How (Not) to Measure Infant Theory of Mind: Testing the Replicability and Validity of Four Non-Verbal Measures. *Cognitive Development*, 46, 12–30.

Egan, A. (2011). Comments on Gendler's "the Epistemic Costs of Implicit Bias". *Philosophical Studies*, 156(1), pp. 65–79.

Egre, P. (2008). Question-Embedding and Factivity. *Grazer Philosophische Studien*, 77(1), pp. 85–125.

Ekman, P. & O'Sullivan, M. (1991). Who Can Catch a Liar? *American Psychologist*, 46(9), pp. 913–20.

Fantl, J. (2015). What Is It to Be Happy That P? *Ergo, an Open Access Journal of Philosophy*, 2.

Fiske, S. T., Cuddy, A. J. C. & Glick, P. (2006). Universal Dimensions of Social Cognition: Warmth and Competence. *Trends in Cognitive Sciences*, 11(2), pp. 77–83.

Fricker, M. (2007). *Epistemic Injustice: Power and the Ethics of Knowing*, Oxford: Oxford University Press.

Fricker, E. (2009). Is Knowing a State of Mind? The Case against. In P. Greenough & D. Pritchard, eds. *Williamson on Knowledge*, New York: Oxford University Press, pp. 31–60.

Frith, U. & Frith, C. D. (2003). Development and Neurophysiology of Mentalizing. *Philosophical Transactions of the Royal Society of London. Series B, Biological Sciences*, 358(1431), pp. 459–73.

Gendler, T. S. (2011). On the Epistemic Costs of Implicit Bias. *Philosophical Studies*, 156(1), pp. 33–63.

Gerken, M. (2013). Epistemic Focal Bias. *Australasian Journal of Philosophy*, 91(1), pp. 41–61.

Gettier, E. L. (1963). Is Justified True Belief Knowledge? *Analysis*, 23(6), pp. 121–23.

Gilbert, D. T. & Malone, P. S. (1995). The Correspondence Bias. *Psychological Bulletin*, 117(1), pp. 21–38.

Goldman, A. (1994). Naturalistic Epistemology and Reliabilism. *Midwest Studies in Philosophy*, 19(1), pp. 301–20.

Harris, P. L., Yang, B. & Cui, Y. (2017). "I Don't Know": Children's Early Talk about Knowledge. *Mind & Language*, 32(3), pp. 283–307.

Helming, K. A., Strickland, B. & Jacob, P. (2014). Making Sense of Early False-Belief Understanding. *Trends in Cognitive Sciences*, 18(4), pp. 167–70.

Heyes, C. (2014). False Belief in Infancy: A Fresh Look. *Developmental Science*, 17(5), pp. 647–59.

Kaminski, J., Call, J. & Tomasello, M. (2008). Chimpanzees Know What Others Know, But Not What They Believe. *Cognition*, 109(2), pp. 224–34.

Karttunen, L. (1977). Syntax and Semantics of Questions. *Linguistics and Philosophy*, 1(1), pp. 3–44.

Keysar, B., Lin, S. & Barr, D. J. (2003). Limits on Theory of Mind Use in Adults. *Cognition*, 89(1), pp. 25–41.

Kim, M. & Yuan, Y. (2015). No Cross-Cultural Differences in Getter Car Case Intuition: A Replication Study of Weinberg et al. 2001. *Episteme*, 12(3), pp. 355–61.

King, J. C., Soames, S. & Speaks, J. (2014). *New Thinking about Propositions*, Oxford: Oxford University Press.

Kiparsky, P. & Kiparsky, C. (1970). Fact. In M. Bierwisch & K. E. Heidolph, eds. *Progress in Linguistics*, The Hague: Mouton, pp. 143–73.

Koenig, M. A. & Harris, P. L. (2005). Preschoolers Mistrust Ignorant and Inaccurate Speakers. *Child Development*, 76(6), pp. 1261–77.

Koenig, M. A. & Woodward, A. L. (2010). Sensitivity of 24-Month-Olds to the Prior Inaccuracy of the Source: Possible Mechanisms. *Developmental Psychology*, 46(4), pp. 815–26.

Kuhlmeier, V., Wynn, K. & Bloom, P. (2003). Attribution of Dispositional States by 12-Month-Olds. *Psychological Science*, 14(5), pp. 402–08.

Lahiri, U. (2002). *Questions and Answers in Embedded Contexts*, Oxford: Oxford University Press.

Lee, M. D., Newell, B. R. & Vandekerckhove, J. (2014). Modeling the Adaptation of Search Termination in Human Decision Making. *Decision*, 1(4), pp. 223–51. Available at: http://doi.apa.org/getdoi.cfm?doi=10.1037/dec0000019.

Lehrer, K. (1968). Belief and Knowledge. *The Philosophical Review*, 77(4), p. 491.

Levy, N. (2015). Neither Fish Nor Fowl: Implicit Attitudes as Patchy Endorsements. *Noûs*, 49(4), pp. 800–23.

Lewis, D. (1996). Elusive Knowledge. *Australasian Journal of Philosophy*, 74(4), pp. 549–67.

Luo, Y. & Baillargeon, R. (2007). Do 12.5-Month-Old Infants Consider What Objects Others Can See When Interpreting Their Actions? *Cognition*, 105(3), pp. 489–512.

Machery, E., Stich, S., Rose, D., Chatterjee, A., Karasawa, K., Struchiner, N., Sirker, S., Usui, N. & Hashimoto, T. (2015). Gettier across Cultures. *Noûs*, 51, pp. 645–64.

Marticorena, D. C. W., Ruiz, H. M., Mukerji, C., Goddu, A. & Santos, L. R. (2011). Monkeys Represent Others' Knowledge But Not Their Beliefs. *Developmental Science*, 14(6), pp. 1406–16.

McKimmie, B. M., Newton, C. J., Terry, D. J., & Schuller, R. A. (2004). Jurors' Responses to Expert Witness Testimony: The Effects of Gender Stereotypes. *Group Processes & Intergroup Relations*, 7(2), pp. 131–43.

Milligan, K., Astington, J. W. & Dack, L. A. (2007). Language and Theory of Mind: Meta-Analysis of the Relation between Language Ability and False-Belief Understanding. *Child Development*, 78(2), pp. 622–46.

Myers Schulz, B. & Schwitzgebel, E. (2013). Knowing That P without Believing That P. *Nous*, 47(2), pp. 371–84.

Nagel, J. (2010a). Epistemic Anxiety and Adaptive Invariantism. *Philosophical Perspectives*, 24, pp. 407–35.

Nagel, J. (2010b). Knowledge Ascriptions and the Psychological Consequences of Thinking about Error. *Philosophical Quarterly*, 60(239), pp. 286–306.

Nagel, J., Juan, V. S. & Mar, R. A. (2013). Lay Denial of Knowledge for Justified True Beliefs. *Cognition*, 129(3), pp. 652–61.

Neal, T. M. S. (2014). Women as Expert Witnesses: A Review of the Literature. *Behavioral Sciences & the Law*, 32, pp. 164–79.

Onishi, K. H. & Baillargeon, R. (2005). Do 15-Month-Old Infants Understand False Beliefs? *Science*, 308(5719), p. 255.

O'Sullivan, M. (2003). The Fundamental Attribution Error in Detecting Deception: The Boy-Who-Cried-Wolf Effect. *Personality and Social Psychology Bulletin*, 29(10), pp. 1316–27.

Pascual, B., Aguardo, G., Sotillo, M., & Masdeu, J. C. (2008). Acquisition of Mental State Language in Spanish Children: A Longitudinal Study of the Relationship between the Production of Mental Verbs and Linguistic Development. *Developmental Science*, 11(4), pp. 454–66.

Pasquini, E. S., Corriveau, A. H., Koenig, M., & Harris, P. L. (2007). Preschoolers Monitor the Relative Accuracy of Informants. *Developmental Psychology*, 43(5), pp. 1216–26.

Perner, J. (1991). *Understanding the Representational Mind*, Cambridge, MA: MIT Press.

Perner, J. & Roessler, J. (2012). From Infants' to Children's Appreciation of Belief. *Trends in Cognitive Sciences*, 16(10), pp. 519–25.

Parker, K., Horowitz, J., Igielnik, R., Oliphant, B., & Brown, A. (2017). *America's complex relationship with guns: An in-depth look at the attitudes and experiences of US adults*. Washington, DC: Pew Research Center.

Plato. (1990). *The Theaetetus of Plato*, Indianapolis: Hackett.

Pratt, C. & Bryant, P. (1990). Young Children Understand That Looking Leads to Knowing (So Long as They Are Looking into a Single Barrel). *Child Development*, 61(4), pp. 973–82.

Radford, C. (1966). Knowledge: By Examples. *Analysis*, 27(1), pp. 1–11.

Rakoczy, H. (2015). In Defense of a Developmental Dogma: Children Acquire Propositional Attitude Folk Psychology around Age 4. *Synthese*, pp. 1–19.

Reber, R. & Unkelbach, C. (2010). The Epistemic Status of Processing Fluency as Source for Judgments of Truth. *Review of Philosophy and Psychology*, pp. 1–19.

Rose, D. & Schaffer, J. (2013). Knowledge Entails Dispositional Belief. *Philosophical Studies*, 166(Suppl 1), pp. 19–50.

Ross, L. (1977). The Intuitive Psychologist and His Shortcomings: Distortions in the Attribution Process. *Advances in Experimental Social Psychology*, 10, pp. 173–220.

Ruffman, T. (2014). To Belief or Not Belief: Children's Theory of Mind. *Developmental Review*, 34(3), pp. 265–93.

Sabbagh, M. A. & Baldwin, D. A. (2001). Learning Words from Knowledgeable versus Ignorant Speakers: Links between Preschoolers' Theory of Mind and Semantic Development. *Child Development*, 72(4), pp. 1054–70.

Samson, D., Apperly, I. A., Braithwhite, J. J., Andrews, B. J. & Bodley Scott, S. E. (2010). Seeing It Their Way. *Journal of Experimental Psychology-Human Perception and Performance*, 36(5), pp. 1255–66.

Santiesteban, I., Catmur, C., Coughlin Hopkins, S., Bird, G., & Heyes, C. (2014). Avatars and Arrows: Implicit Mentalizing or Domain-General Processing? *Journal of Experimental Psychology: Human Perception and Performance*, 40(3), p. 929.

Saxe, R. & Powell, L. J. (2006). It's the Thought That Counts: Specific Brain Regions for One Component of Theory of Mind. *Psychological Science*, 17(8), pp. 692–99.

Schurz, M., Kronbichler, M., Weissengruber, S., Surtees, A., Samson, D. & Perner, J. (2015). Clarifying the Role of Theory of Mind Areas during Visual Perspective Taking: Issues of Spontaneity and Domain-Specificity. *NeuroImage*, 117, pp. 386–96.

Schurz, M., Radua, J., Aichhorn, M., Richlan, F., & Perner, J. (2014). Fractionating Theory of Mind: A Meta-Analysis of Functional Brain Imaging Studies. *Neuroscience & Biobehavioral Reviews*, 42, pp. 9–34.

Seyedsayamdost, H. (2015). On Normativity and Epistemic Intuitions: Failure to Detect Differences between Ethnic Groups. *Episteme*, 12(1), pp. 95–116.

Shatz, M., Wellman, H. M. & Silber, S. (1983). The Acquisition of Mental Verbs: A Systematic Investigation of the First Reference to Mental State. *Cognition*, 14(3), pp. 301–21.

Shope, R. K. (1983). *The Analysis of Knowing: A Decade of Research*, Princeton: Princeton University Press.

Sobel, D. M. & Kushnir, T. (2013). Knowledge Matters: How Children Evaluate the Reliability of Testimony as a Process of Rational Inference. *Psychological Review*, 120(4), pp. 1–19.

Sperber, D., Clement, F., Heintz, C., Mascaro, O., Mercier, H., Origgi, G. & Wilson, D. (2010). Epistemic Vigilance. *Mind & Language*, 25(4), pp. 359–93.

Sporer, S. L. & Schwandt, B. (2006). Paraverbal Indicators of Deception: A Meta-Analytic Synthesis. *Applied Cognitive Psychology*, 20, pp. 421–46.

Sporer, S. L. & Schwandt, B. (2007). Moderators of Nonverbal Indicators of Deception: A Meta-Analytic Synthesis. *Psychology, Public Policy, and Law*, 13(1), pp. 1–34.

Stanley, J. (2005). *Knowledge and Practical Interests*, Oxford: Oxford University Press.

Stephens, E., Suarez, S. & Koenig, M. (2015). Early Testimonial Learning: Monitoring Speech Acts and Speakers. *Advances in Child Development and Behavior*, 40, pp. 151–83.

Steup, M. & Ichikawa, J. (2008). The Analysis of Knowledge. *Stanford Encyclopedia of Philosophy*. Available at: http://pla.

Stine, G. C. (1976). Skepticism, Relevant Alternatives, and Deductive Closure. *Philosophical Studies*, 29(4), pp. 249–61.

Tardif, T. & Wellman, H. M. (2000). Acquisition of Mental State Language in Mandarin- and Cantonese-Speaking Children. *Developmental Psychology*, 36(1), p. 25.

Tummeltshammer, K. S., Wu, S., Sobel, D. M., & Kirkham, N. Z. (2014). Infants Track the Reliability of Potential Informants. *Psychological Science*, 25(9), pp. 1730–38.

Turri, J. (2016). A New Paradigm for Epistemology: From Reliabilism to Abilism. *Ergo*, 3(8), pp. 189–231.

Vanderbilt, K. E., Heyman, G. D. & Liu, D. (2014). In the Absence of Conflicting Testimony Young Children Trust Inaccurate Informants. *Developmental Science*, 17(3), pp. 443–51.

Varley, R., Siegal, M. & Want, S. C. (2001). Severe Impairment in Grammar Does Not Preclude Theory of Mind. *Neurocase*, 7(6), pp. 489–93.

Weatherson, B. (2005). Can We Do without Pragmatic Encroachment? *Philosophical Perspectives*, 19(1), pp. 417–43.

Weinberg, J., Nichols, S. & Stich, S. (2001). Normativity and Epistemic Intuitions. *Philosophical Topics*, 29(1), pp. 429–60.

Wellman, H. M., Cross, D. & Watson, J. (2001). Meta Analysis of Theory of Mind Development: The Truth about False Belief. *Child Development*, 72(3), pp. 655–84.

Williamson, T. (2000). *Knowledge and Its Limits*, New York: Oxford University Press.

Williamson, T. (2005). Contextualism, Subject-Sensitive Invariantism and Knowledge of Knowledge. *Philosophical Quarterly*, 55(219), pp. 213–35.

Willis, J. & Todorov, A. (2006). First Impressions: Making Up Your Mind after a 100-Ms Exposure to a Face. *Psychological Science*, 17(7), pp. 592–98.

Wimmer, H. & Perner, J. (1983). Beliefs about Beliefs: Representation and Constraining Function of Wrong Beliefs in Young Children's Understanding of Deception. *Cognition*, 13(1), pp. 103–28.

Woolley, J. D. & Ghossainy, M. E. (2013). Revisiting the Fantasy-Reality Distinction: Children as Naïve Skeptics. *Child Development*, 84(5), pp. 1496–510.

Young, L., Camprodon, J. A., Hauser, M., Pascual-Leone, A., & Saxe, R. (2010). Disruption of the Right Temporoparietal Junction with Transcranial Magnetic Stimulation Reduces the Role of Beliefs in Moral Judgments. *Proceedings of the National Academy of Sciences*, 107(15), pp. 6753–58.

Zebrowitz, L. A., Voinescu, L. & Collins, M. A. (1996). "Wide-Eyed" and "Crooked-Faced": Determinants of Perceived and Real Honesty across the Lifespan. *Personality and Social Psychology Bulletin*, 22(12), pp. 1258–69.

48
GROUP COGNITION

Deborah Tollefsen and Kevin Ryan

1 Introduction

In this chapter, we offer an overview of contemporary theoretical debates about group cognition. As with most debates, it is equally important to understand the history of the concept and ideas as well as the current stakes and issues. In section 2, we explore some history of group cognition, focusing in particular on nineteenth- and twentieth-century debates in collective psychology and the super-organism tradition. In section 3, we consider philosophical developments in the twentieth century that have led to the revival of the idea of group cognition in the early twenty-first century. Section 4 introduces several positive accounts in the contemporary literature, while section 5 is focused on criticisms of group cognition, as well as possible responses to these worries.

2 History of the idea of group cognition/group mind

The idea of group cognition, or group minds, is not new. The origins of the idea can be traced back to ancient times. The ancient Romans, for instance, built their law around the idea of corporate responsibility, speaking of organized collectives that were referred to by terms such as *universitas*, *corporation*, and *colleguium*. A corporate group was contrasted with *societas*, a collection of individuals that interacted but were less tightly connected and did not form a persona capable of action and capable of making promises. For the Romans, the capacity for intentionality and responsibility determined whether a group of people formed a corporate person. Though contemporary thinkers are likely to make a distinction between persons and minds, the ancients' attempt to identify the "mark" of personhood is similar to recent attempts to identify the "mark" of cognition – a definitive property that can be used to distinguish between *real* cognition and *as if* cognition. As we shall see, how one defines the "mind" and what one identifies as the distinguishing feature of cognition plays a crucial role in debates about group cognition.

The most sustained development of group cognition, however, arose in the nineteenth and early twentieth centuries. Nineteenth-century political theory struggled with the questions with the relationship between the individual and society. This gave rise to various theories often associated with the idea of group minds. Hegel's idea of a group spirit or consciousness is often appealed to as the paradigm theory of group minds. The rise of the biological sciences in the late nineteenth century introduced the idea of the hive mind. Alfred Espinas's (1844–1922) work on bee colonies gave credibility to the idea that groups of individuals could organize to form a whole that exhibits its own consciousness. Espinas thought that not only bees but also other animals and humans could form unities that exhibited collective consciousness. W. M. Wheeler (1865–1937), a Harvard entomologist, compared human civilization itself to an ant colony.

Emile Durkheim (1858–1917) is credited with being a founder of modern sociology and is often associated with the idea that groups have minds. His theory of collective representations and collective consciousness was criticized for reifying the group. Durkheim had in mind forms of individual thought that were determined by one's social milieu. Language, for instance, was a shared set of representations that shaped human thought. On this understanding of Durkheim's work, the representations were had by individual minds. Although he is often associated with the idea of group minds, it isn't clear that Durkheim thought that the group itself was capable of having representations. Rather, he seemed to be interested in the ways that one's social context shaped and informed the individual mind.

While Durkheim was interested in classes or large social groups, there were other theorists who were focused on a new sort of phenomenon – the mob or crowd. Various historical events during the latter part of the nineteenth century, including the Paris Commune, the rise of George Ernest Boulanger, and the Dreyfus Affair, contributed to an interest in understanding how the mob functioned and gave rise to a psychology of the mob. Gustave LeBon (1841–1931), George Simmel (1858–1918), and Gabriel Tarde (1843–1904) all attempted to provide theories of the behavior of crowds. In *The Crowd: A Study of the Popular Mind* (1895/2008), LeBon argues that there is a special power that the crowd exerts on its members. The psychology of the individual is influenced by the psychology of the crowd. The emphasis in their work was in explaining how the individual loses control within the mob and how rational people can be overcome by the "mob mentality."

William McDougall (1871–1938) pioneered the field of social psychology. In 1920 he published *The Group Mind*. Unlike LeBon and others focused on the psychology of the mob, McDougall was interested in large groups – societies and nations. This is the first sustained attempt to draw the analogies between the individual mind and the group mind. McDougall defines the mind as an organized system of mental or purposive forces. He provides a functionalist account of the mind and extends it to groups. As we will see, this approach has been resurrected in contemporary debates.

3 Resurrection of the idea

In part because of Karl Popper's staunch defense of individualism and criticisms that collectivism leads to ontological excess, group minds fell out of favor until the end of the twentieth century. The idea has since arisen in a variety of different areas of philosophy.

In the philosophy of biology, the concept of group selection – where evolution selects group-level adaptations – introduced the idea of group cognition. David Sloan

(Wilson (1997a, 1997b; Wilson et al. 2000) argues that we should think of group cognition as the result of group-level selection. In the philosophy of mind, as functionalism gained traction as a theory of mind in the late 1960s (Putnam 1960, 1967), '70s, and '80s, a few philosophers suggested an obvious extension to groups. Ned Block (1978) and John Biro (1981) were some of the first contemporary philosophers to suggest that homuncular functionalism can be flipped on its head. The former used the idea to criticize functionalism in his famous "Chinese Nation" thought experiment; the latter, to support the idea of group mind. According to Biro, just as the individual mind is a collection of discrete interacting systems, so too is the corporation a collection of discrete, interacting units. In social philosophy, Peter French's work on corporate agency (1987) and corporate responsibility introduced the notion of a corporate decision-making structure. Though French doesn't specifically develop a theory of corporate *cognition*, his defense of group agency and personhood reintroduced the analogy between individual minds and group minds.

In 1989 Margaret Gilbert published *On Social Facts*. In it, she resurrects debates in the philosophy of social science by reintroducing concepts such as group belief and group intention. According to Gilbert, individuals can fuse together to form a *plural subject*. Joint commitments are the binding agent. Joint commitments occur when individuals express their willingness to do things as a body with others, including believing as a body. Gilbert's work and the work of philosophers such as Raimo Tuomela (1995) gave rise to a new field of research called *collective intentionality*. Although many of the accounts of group belief and group intention reduce them to individual intentional states that are interrelated (Bratman 1993; Searle 1990, 1995), some have argued that groups themselves are agents and can be held morally responsible (List & Pettit 2014; Tollefsen 2002, 2015). Discussions of group intention and group belief within collective intentionality have also contributed to consideration of the ways in which groups might realize cognitive states.

Philosophical discussions of group cognition since the 1990s have been influenced by the work of Edwin Hutchins. In 1995, Hutchins published *Cognition in the Wild*, a detailed study of navigation on a naval vessel. By providing an ethnographic account of how cognition is distributed across both people and instruments onboard a naval vessel, Hutchins made the case that the act of navigation, a cognitive task, was not located in the heads of individual agents, not even that of the captain. Hutchins's work extends cognitive models such as constraint satisfaction models to groups and has been instrumental in developing the field of distributive cognition. At about the same time, philosophers Andy Clark and David Chalmers published their article "Extended Mind" (1998), which built on work in cognitive science and psychology on external representations (Kirsh 2006; Kirsh & Maglio 1994; Zhang & Norman 1994) and provided a philosophical argument for the idea that the mind is not bounded by skin and bones but extends to encompass aspects of the environment. Clark and Chalmers introduce the *parity principle*:

> If, as we confront some task, a part of the world functions as a process which, were it done in the head, we would have no hesitation in recognizing as part

> of the cognitive process, then that part of the world (so we claim) is part of the cognitive process.
>
> (1998, p. 8)

Although Clark and Chalmers focus on the extension of mind to artifacts such as smart phones, these discussions contributed to a rethinking of the possibility of group minds and group cognition.

It is worth pausing to clarify some terminology here. Extended cognition refers to the possibility of cognitive processes and states extending beyond the boundaries of skin and bones. Clark and Chalmers's original thought experiment involved Inga, a healthy person with fully functioning memory capacities, and Otto, an individual suffering from memory loss, who relies on his notebook in a substantive way to live in the world. Clark and Chalmers argued that Otto's notebook is an extension of his biological memory because it plays the same functional role. In this example, the mind extends to a single artifact. Distributed cognition, as developed by Hutchins, involves a distribution of cognition across artifacts, environments, and people. Distributed cognition tends to indicate a more systematic and encompassing form of extension. The literature uses these two terms – distributed cognition and extended cognition – interchangeably. To mark that extension involves people and social institutions, some authors have adopted the phrase *socially extended cognition* to mark that extension goes beyond mere artifacts. As it is a new field, its terminology is continuing to evolve and be refined.

We think the idea of group cognition is clearly related to, but distinct from, extension and distribution. Group cognition refers to the capacity of a group *itself* to form a cognitive system – a system that undergoes cognitive processes. To say that cognitive processes are distributed across a number of different people is not yet to say that the group of people forms a distinct cognitive system with cognitive properties unique to it. One might have distribution of cognition and agency without thereby forming a single cognitive agent.[1] Although the concept of a mind is by no means clearly defined, to ask whether a group can undergo cognition is to ask whether groups have minds.

4 Recent accounts

4.1 Extending the extended mind

As we noted earlier, the extended mind thesis has played a role in resurrecting the idea of group minds/cognition. Clark and Chalmers focus on what Deborah Tollefsen (2006) calls "solipsistic systems" (single agent coupled with artifacts and environments), but things get more complicated and more interesting when we consider what Tollefsen calls "collective systems," those involving multiple agents who mutually interact to bring about change in their environment. The application of Clark and Chalmers's "parity principle" to social contexts allows one to move from the idea of extended minds to group minds.

Building on thought experiments introduced by Clark and Chalmers (1998), Tollefsen (2006) offers a thought experiment in defense of group cognition. Instead of Otto and Inga, Tollefsen considers the case of absent-minded philosophy professor Olaf and his partner, Inga. Olaf often relies on Inga for a variety of cognitive tasks, such as remembering his meeting schedule or travel directions, much akin to how Otto uses his notebook. The interaction between Olaf and Inga is also guided in a closely analogous way to the situation between Otto and his notebook, including Olaf's trust in the information Inga provides and the fact that he often defers to her for help throughout the day. As a result, Tollefsen suggests that "if C and C are correct, the mind not only extended to encompass non-biological artifacts . . . but it also occasionally forms collective systems that support cognition and belief" (2006, p. 143). Some have read Tollefsen's extension of the extended mind to group cognition as proposing a social parity principle (Theiner 2008; Ludwig 2015). According to this principle, "If, in confronting some task, a group collectively functions in a process which, were it done in the head, would be accepted as a cognitive process, then that group is performing that cognitive process" (Ludwig 2015, p. 197).

Importantly, Tollefsen points out that the possibility of group cognition rests on substantive two-way interaction between individuals. Without such interaction, Olaf's mind merely extends to Inga's. This two-way interaction provides for cognitive integration, an interdependence of cognitive functions and the basis for thinking of the group as a system in itself rather than simply a collection of individual cognitive systems. Tollefsen further develops her example of Olaf and Inga by considering cases where their cognitive systems are interdependent and integrated. She appeals to research on transactive memory systems (TMS) (Wegner 1987; Wegner et al. 1991; Sutton 2006; Sutton et al. 2010) as an example of substantive interaction between individuals.

In "transactive memory," one individual's memory is shown to function alongside that of another person's or persons' as a kind of socially extended memory system (e.g., Wegner 1987; see also recently Woolley et al. 2007). A transactive memory system involves the complex interaction of individual memory systems. These individual memory systems are not merely external storage devices – both the process of remembering and storage of memories are done in an interactive and dialogical manner. Unlike a notebook, which does not itself have the characteristic of memory identified by mainstream memory research (learning time and access time),[2] a group of individual memory systems can, it seems, become unified and produce a memory product (recall an event, say) that is richer than that recalled by an individual.

Transactive memory systems as described by Wegner go through the same stages that occur at the individual level: encoding, storage, and retrieval. Encoding at the collective level occurs when members discuss information and determine the location and form in which it will be stored within the group. Storage can occur when individuals remembering specific information, in part or as a whole, or when information is stored on external devices, such as notepads, computers, or meeting minutes. Retrieval involves identification of the location of the information. Retrieval is transactive when the person holding an item internally is not the person who asked to retrieve it. In our case above, a faculty member may have promoted retrieval of information from another faculty member by asking questions and offering alternative hypotheses that the committee member needed to consider.

Consider the case of a department subcommittee charged with revising the department's policies and procedures. Faculty member A, the default historian of the department, might remember the origin of and rationale for certain policies; faculty member B might offer information about what the department chair requires of the committee as she was tasked with meeting with the chair prior to the committee meeting; and faculty member C might remember something said by the provost regarding policy-making as he was tasked with going to the provost's meeting on policies and procedures. As a result, the committee might recall a great deal more information relevant to their task than any individual alone, and we can imagine that such recall is done in a collaborative and dialogical process, through conversation in which individual memories are cued by the input of other participants. The committee might decide to store the information that they have collaboratively produced in the form of "minutes" which can be accessed by other faculty and the chair.

Tollefsen argues that the extended mind hypothesis is much more plausible when it comes to social coupled systems (involving other cognitive agents) than when it simply involves artifacts. Research on alignment in conversation and social interaction (Tollefsen et al. 2013) suggests that we were built to couple with others cognitively and not with artifacts like notebooks. The synergy, mutual adaptation, and ongoing interaction that are required for systems are more plausibly found in transactive memory systems than between Otto and his notebook.

4.2 Functionalism revisited

In *Macrocognition: A Theory of Distributed Minds and Collective Intentionality* (2014), Bryce Huebner argues that a successful account of group cognition should combine intentional systems theory with a cognitive architecture of a particular kind (p. 96). The type of cognitive architecture he proposes is a functionally decomposable system, wherein a variety of integrated subsystems run various computations, usually in a highly distributed manner and over multiple representational formats. This architecture, in turn, allows a system to carry out tasks necessary for its survival, including many fluid and flexible interactions with its surrounding environment. He moreover discusses several potential cases of group minds – from beehives and stock markets to TMS and research in high energy physics. Huebner offers a scale to situate these different putative cases from not yet minimally minded to maximally minded entities.

Huebner (2014) offers three principles that must be maintained in any account of group cognition:

Principle 1: Do not posit collective mentality where collective behavior results from an organizational structure set up to achieve the goals or realize the intentions of a few powerful and/or intelligent people (p. 21).

Principle 2: Do not posit collective mental states or processes where collective behavior bubbles up from simple rules governing the behavior of individuals;

intentional states, decisions, or purposes cannot legitimately be ascribed to such collectives (p. 23).

Principle 3: Do not posit collective mental states where the capacities of the components belong to the same intentional kind as the capacity that is being ascribed to the collectivity and where the collective computations are no more sophisticated than the computations that are being carried out by the individuals who compose the collectivity (p. 72).

Each of these principles is paired with an example of the mistakes that may befall someone who fails to follow them.

For principle 1, Huebner considers the case of Oak Ridge National Lab (ORNL). This lab was a massive and secret undertaking to enrich uranium during WWII in America. For reasons of secrecy, work was heavily compartmentalized and results were kept isolated. As a result, it was often the case that no individual scientist, engineer, or worker associated with the project knew that he or she was, in fact, working to enrich uranium. As such, some may suggest that the only way to understand this situation – i.e., cases where no individual in the group has any knowledge of the group activity or output – is to posit some cognitive processes at the group level.

The problem with assuming ORNL or similar entities are relevantly minded, suggests Huebner, is that the purpose for impoverished understandings at the individual level was largely the byproduct of information control from those who knew what was going on. While the ORNL was a case of a massively distributed cognitive system and even if the results from the work could not have been carried out by any single individual or small group, the entity should not be considered minded in any meaningful sense since it was simply a tool being used by individuals who controlled the project and, as individuals, knew what was happening.

For principle 2, Huebner examines the case of termite nest construction. Termite nests are large, intricate, and emergent structures. This fact notwithstanding, a proper explanation of how termite nests are formed can be exhaustively explained by understanding facts about the constitution of individual ants and how their actions are aggregated based on certain rules and responses to environmental stimuli. In this case, there is no real reason to postulate any *collective* representations or related cognitive process.

Finally, for principle 3, Huebner considers the case of how the stock market responded to the Challenger explosion. Four companies were largely responsible for various parts of the spacecraft and launch process, yet only one (Morton Thiokol) had stocks that dropped faster and continued dropping much lower than those of the other three companies. As a result, some people have suggested that the stock market itself *decided* to blame Morton Thiokol for the disaster. In this case, however, the actual mental states responsible for action were happening at the level of the traders themselves. Group cognition seems to be explanatorily superfluous.

Huebner's positive theory combines the intentional stance (Dennett 1987) with a specific type of cognitive architecture. According to Huebner, the intentional stance opens up the possibility that some collectives may have cognitive states. Unfortunately, the intentional stance alone doesn't allow us to distinguish between the cases mentioned earlier and genuine group cognition. What is needed is a specification of the mechanisms that produce the complex behavior that is interpretable from the intentional stance. Huebner argues that cognitive architecture distinguishes real minds from *ersatz* minds.

According to Huebner, the architecture that will most likely allow for genuine group minds and group cognition takes place in parallel processing systems, wherein local computations and processes act as constraints that, in turn, bring together different, discrete subsystems into active coordination. As a result, Huebner argues that "we should only posit mentality where interfaced networks of computational systems are jointly responsible for the production of systems-level behavior" (p. 13). While this point is particularly apt for individuating and examining group minds, it is important to note that macrocognition is also the norm for individual organisms; human cognition, after all, operates by drawing on discrete subsystems in the brain and perhaps elsewhere in the body or world and combining them in coordinated ways to flexibly act in their environment.

Huebner provides examples of several groups that are close to realizing this architecture and that seem to be candidates for mindedness, though he admits that in some cases they will realize only a minimal mind. Crime scene investigation teams appear to implement an architecture that is widely distributed and involves the compartmentalization of individuals with specific tasks and specializations. These different individuals and subgroups produce representations that are then used to produce more complex representations in the form of narratives and "trading languages" between different specialists. Research in high energy physics (HEP) is done by large research groups, and Huebner tentatively suggests that these groups might approach maximal minds. The distribution of cognitive labor in these groups results in representations that are transferred through various media to form collective representations that function to adjust the system's behavior (2014, p. 254). Further, these groups seem capable in some cases of misrepresenting the world and have various ways of preventing misrepresentation. They seem to respond to the norms of experimentation established within their community and thus appear to be reasons responsive.

4.3 Emergence

Georg Theiner and colleagues (Theiner et al. 2010; Theiner & O'Connor 2010; Theiner 2014) have developed a case for group cognition that combines the extended mind hypothesis with a particular account of emergent group-level properties. In doing so, Theiner *et al.* suggest it is possible to posit group cognition that is neither reducible to an individual or subset of individuals nor "spooky" in the manner that plagued most metaphysical and scientific accounts of group minds in the early twentieth century. In order to understand the main upshot of this account, there are two additional conceptual components that must be introduced in detail. First, the specific nature of emergence in question must be fleshed out. Second, the concept of "demergence" (Theiner et al. 2010) must be explained vis-à-vis emergence.

Following Wimsatt (1986), Theiner and colleagues suggest three different components of emergence that are potentially important for group cognition. First, (E1) concerns a failure of aggregativity; second, (E2) there may be cases where the pooling together of individual actions has opposite an effect at the individual and group levels; and third, (E3) there are reasons to support a functionalist account of mental states. E1, E2, and E3 can also be understood in terms of organization-independence, the absence of intentional design, and multiple realizability, respectively (cf. Theiner & O'Connor 2010).

Theiner et al. (2010) have suggested that in addition to defining emergence we need to consider the inverse concept of "group-level anti-demergentism" (GLAD). Demergence is, in their words, "The situation where larger scale structures not only lack the properties that their components have, but are somehow constitutionally incapable of having those properties" (p. 383). The example they give of demergence is the traditional view of consciousness. For a defender of the traditional account, consciousness can only be found at the level of individual biological organisms and "disappears from higher levels of organization except insofar as it is found in the parts" (p. 383).

Like Huebner, Theiner *et al.* use examples to motivate the existence of genuine group-level cognition. Consider stigmergic path formation (Theiner et al. 2010, p. 385). Stigmergic path formation occurs when a group figures out the optimal set of trails for the individuals traversing them, even though the individuals who make up the group don't intend to do so. Specific examples include ant trails for more efficient foraging and the creation of interconnected trails among university buildings. As a result, Theiner *et al.* suggest that the group is capable of solving problems that individuals are not. Moreover, since the solutions are not entertained by individual members, "Path systems are solutions to a problem for the group, not the individuals" (2010, p. 385). The final paths are a combination of individual agents, existent paths, and decay rates of those paths. One of the main upshots of this example is the relation to the importance of GLAD. On this account, the postulation of psychological states and explanatory tools offers predictive and explanatory benefits. Indeed, the group may be operating in a fashion much akin to the structure of neural processing in individual agents.

Theiner *et al.* also appeal to transactive memory (TMS) as a case of group cognition. A TMS can be broken down into two components: one representational and one procedural (Theiner et al. 2010, p. 388). The representational component is the combination of individual memories and higher-order memories concerning the location of knowledge within the group. The procedural component concerns any and all communications, or "transactions," between individuals that facilitate the creation, maintenance, and retrieval of various relevant memories.

Moving from these case studies, Theiner *et al.* suggest three important upshots to consider. First, examining the group focuses our attention on the fact that group-level phenomena are essentially embedded and enabled within specific, environmentally situated interactions between people. Second, groups may address problems that are not entertained at the level of the individuals making up the group. Third, the cases of group problem-solving canvased earlier are not simply an aggregation or composite of individual decision-making processes. They are distinct processes of group cognition that should be studied as such.

5 Objections

There has been a variety of objections to group cognition. We can't canvas them all here, but the following seem to represent some major challenges.

5.1 *The "mark" of the cognitive*

The have been a number of attempts by critics of the group cognition to identify the "mark" of cognition and show that putative cases of group cognition lack it. One primary example involves arguing that cognition requires consciousness. In Ned Block's "Trouble with Functionalism" (1978), he develops a thought experiment involving the nation of China. If the nation of China was organized in such a way as to mimic the functional organization of the human mind, would it have a mind? According to Block and many others who rejected functionalist account of mind, the answer is obviously "no." The nation of China, however expertly organized, would never be conscious, and consciousness is required for mind and mentality.[3] The objection from consciousness rests on the intuition that cognitive states essentially involve some sort of consciousness. According to John Searle, for instance, mentality has a distinctive aspectual shape (1992). This shape entails that all genuine mental activities must be viewed from a particular point of view – a first-person phenomenological point of view. Other philosophers have argued that cognitive states such as belief and intention involve a distinct phenomenology Horgan and Tienson (2002). Geirsson (2004) has adopted this "mark of cognition" and uses it to argue against the idea that groups have beliefs and intentions or realize cognitive processes such as memory. Though Tollefsen (2015) and others (Rovane 1998) have argued that certain groups might achieve a unified perspective, it is implausible to think that it would be a conscious one capable of experiences over and above those experienced by the individuals that compose it. If consciousness is the "mark" of cognition, group cognition will be difficult to establish.

Another attempt to discount the idea of group cognition can be found in arguments against extended mind. Adams and Aizawa (2008) argue against the extended mind hypothesis developed by Clark and Chalmers (1998) on the grounds that cognition involves underived intentionality. Intentionality is the ability of something to be "about" something else or to represent something else. Adams and Aizawa argue that mental states represent in virtue of underived content. Intrinsic content is, according to Adams and Aizawa, *the* "mark" of cognition. A book has meaning (it is about something), but its content (or meaning) is derived from the author. Thus, a book has derived intentionality. Cognition, according to Adams and Aizawa, occurs only over representations with underived content. The smartphone that contains the addresses of family members cannot be part of an individual's memory, because its content is derived. Kirk Ludwig (2015) has extended this line of argument against group cognition. According to Ludwig, in order for group level cognitive processes to be anything more than Pickwickian, they must involve a transition in cognitive states that have "original" and not derived content (2015, p. 204). Those who argue for group cognition seem to want to extend our ordinary notion of cognition and cognitive processes to groups, and yet, according to Ludwig, our ordinary notions don't easily extend to groups.

In response to the intentionality objection, Huebner suggests that focusing solely on the first-person level of full-blown beliefs and desires will miss the fact that the subpersonal processes realizing person-level states may not operate with the same representational formats (2014, pp. 119–23). Considering that cognition over different representational formats may be the norm for individual human agents, a similar point can be made about the sorts of representations relevant for group cognition. The cognition that occurs at the level of groups may not involve full-blown beliefs and intentions but rather more simple representations, which could operate without the need for full-blown intentionality.

In responding to objections based on consciousness, (Tollefsen 2015) has argued that to tie cognition and propositional attitudes to consciousness so tightly removes the possibility of artificial intelligence and a variety of explanatory projects in cognitive science that aim to isolate and model aspects of cognition. The defender of group cognition can readily admit that group cognition is different from human cognition but will urge that the difference is a matter of degree and not kind. There are all kinds of minds – human, animal, artificial, and group. This has seemed to critics like Ludwig as an admission that group cognition is merely *as if* cognition.

5.2 *Causal not constitutive objection*

One of the major objections to extended mind was the charge that the theory confused causal contribution with constitutiveness. Otto's notebook causally contributes to his remembering where a certain place is, but the mere fact that something causally contributes to cognition does not mean that it constitutes the cognitive process. Oxygen causally contributes to our being able to solve problems and various other cognitive processes and states, but we would not want to say that oxygen is part of every cognitive process. This is called the causal constitution fallacy (Adam & Aizawa 2008). If the extended mind thesis can't clearly distinguish between elements of the environment that merely causally contribute and those that constitute cognitive processes, they run the risk of "cognitive bloat," where everything becomes part of the mind. Clark (2007) has responded to the causal constitution fallacy and the problem of cognitive bloat in a variety of ways. We won't attempt to cover these responses here as our focus is on group cognition. But a similar challenge has been raised for defenders of group cognition. The fact that individual cognition often takes place in a group and involves substantive interaction between individual members does not yet mean that such processes constitute a cognitive process in their own right.

Rob Wilson (2005) argues that defenders of group cognition often conflate group cognition with cognition that is conducted by individuals in certain social situations. The phenomenon that advocates of group cognition point to is, according to Wilson, better explained by appeal to the *social manifestation thesis*, where individual cognition *manifests* itself in unique ways in certain social/causal conditions. Defenders of group cognition need to be able to distinguish mere causal contribution to individual cognition (when a colleague raises an objection to your view and you think through possible replies and incorporate them into your work) and genuine group cognition (when you and your colleague collaborate, develop a thesis together, and jointly author a work). One way advocates have tried to do this is by focusing on the idea of cognitive integration and systematicity. We have more to say about this later when considering the system's objection.

5.3 Explanatory superfluity objection

In a recent series of articles and a manuscript (2005, 2009), Rob Rupert has raised the criticism of explanatory superfluity. In short, if the group minds hypothesis is to carry theoretical weight, it must provide a causal-explanatory story above and beyond that already captured by individual-level, nongroup mind explanations of the same phenomenon. While open to the possibility that this criterion may be reached in principle, Rupert contends that it has not been achieved yet in practice.

For example, consider the case of Microsoft *intending* to develop an operating system (Rupert 2014, Section I). Does attributing this intention to Microsoft offer any causal explanation of the data? Perhaps it explains the company's decision to hire new employees in terms of expertise or reformulate company policy for a new hiring practice. Yet, upon closer examination, it seems that the real causal work for such decisions and actions comes on the communication between individuals within the company, the cognitive activity of these individuals, and actions of individuals. The literal attribution of cognitive activity at the level of Microsoft taken as an entity over and above these individuals does not capture any of the causal workings underlying Microsoft's cognitive processing. It is entirely superfluous in any explanation.

In addition to charges of explanatory superfluity, Rupert has raised considerations about the nature of inter-level relations. There is an inter-level relation between the personal and subpersonal levels within an individual. The personal level includes consciousness and many different features of intentional states. In Microsoft, we find an inter-level relation between the individual employees and the company as a whole. Rupert suggests that while similar insofar as both being cases of "inter-level" relations, there are important disanalogies between individual minds and putative group minds. The differences are most clearly noticeable in relation to the structure of psychological laws and explanations for the physical realizers of mental states. In individual minds, we have, at most, a vague understanding of how the physical basis of mental states connects with any token mental state. In contrast, we have a clear case for understanding how to reduce group cognition to the case of individual cognition. While this relationship may be more complex than mere aggregation of individuals, the general structure of individual mental states underlying group cognitive activities is clearly understood (2005, p. 180).

Defenders of group cognition have attempted to provide responses to these concerns, such as making distinctions between different sorts of causal explanations (List & Pettit 2014). It may also be a mistake to assume that reduction is easier in the group case than in the individual case. Just as individual human behavior exhibits "real patterns" (Dennett 1987) that can be usefully explained by appeal to folk psychology, group behavior exhibits "real patterns" that are usefully explained by appeal to concepts such as group intention, belief, and cognition (Tollefsen 2015). Finally, if Theiner and colleagues are correct and certain group-level properties are emergent, we don't, as Rupert suggests, have a clear conception of how to reduce group cognition to individual cognition.

Responses to explanatory superfluity also highlight a more pragmatic and ecumenical approach. For instance, Huebner suggests a pragmatist's gambit that entails a

> moderate but important reconceptualization of the foundational assumptions of the cognitive sciences . . . [which] means that a plausible account of mentality must reject the far too common Cartesian presumption that there can be at most one mind for each body, and at most one body for each mind.
>
> (164)

If this gambit is accepted, the oft-stated assumption of methodological individualism must be defended instead of simply asserted. Moreover, as we find in both Rupert and Wilson, some of the main criticisms of group cognition contain an implicit assumption that if there is cognition happening at the level of individual minds, there cannot be cognition occurring at the level of a group mind. Accepting the gambit fundamentally opens up the possibility for including a variety of other systems operating at multiple levels of explanation that can be studied by cognitive science.

5.4 Systems objection

Whether a group has cognitive processes and cognitive states depends in part on whether it forms the sort of thing that could sustain such things. This point is made by Huebner (2014), who argues that group cognition is possible only if the group is able to realize a certain type of cognitive architecture. The idea that, in order for processes and states to count as cognitive, they must be integrated into a system or structure has been developed by Rupert in response to the extended mind thesis. His arguments extend easily to the idea of group cognition. In *Cognitive Systems and the Extended Mind* (2009) and in more recent articles (e.g., Rupert 2011), Rupert defines a cognitive state in terms of its role in a larger system, such that a state is cognitive if and only if

> it is the state of one or more of an integrated set of mechanisms that contribute distinctively (i.e. not as background conditions) to the production of a wide range of cognitive phenomena, across a variety of conditions, working together in overlapping subsets.
>
> (2011, p. 637)

In short, a state is cognitive if it functions within a cognitive system, where a cognitive system involves various mechanisms and processes that "contribute causally to the production of a wide range of cognitive phenomena, across a variety of conditions, working together in an overlapping way with a variety of other mechanisms of similar standing" (2009, p. 41).

Cognitive systems are persistent and display a set of capacities that persist across different contexts. This persistence is best explained, according to Rupert, by the fact that they are realized in a physically bounded organism:

> There is a natural explanation of the persistence of the relevant capacities; they are physically realized, and the persisting organism provides their integrated, physical substrate; the organism as an integrated physical entity appears in the various circumstances of interest, and its persistence explains the persistent appearance of the integrated set of cognitive capacities realized by the organism.
>
> (2009, p. 40)

This systems-based approach is then used by Rupert to rule out (or at least cast serious doubt on) artifacts like cellphones or calculators as part of the cognitive system and activities involving these artifacts as cognitive processes because such things are not integrated in the ways that, say, vision, linguistic processes, and short-term memory are typically integrated. The systems objection can be used to rule out group cognition as well since group cognition is often context-dependent, intermittent, and transitory.

Tollefsen et al. (2013) have argued that the conditions for an integrated system could be met by small task groups, particularly those that work together over time. They appeal to empirical studies on alignment in conversational contexts as a case of physical integration. They also argue that various cognitive architectures are being used to explore group-level phenomenon, including constraint satisfaction networks (Hutchins 1995); to rule these out as genuine cognitive phenomenon seems *ad hoc*.

6 Future directions

Those that object to extended cognition and its social counterpart – group cognition – often appeal to the fact that these phenomena are not *really* cognitive. They do so by identifying *the* mark of the cognitive (underived content, consciousness, systematicity, explanatory power) and showing that groups or explanations in terms of group cognition lack this feature. This has led to a bit of a stalemate, with one side insisting the groups *really* can cognize and the other saying it all depends on what you mean by *cognition*.

Recent approaches to understanding group dynamics and social interaction have adopted a dynamical systems approach. These approaches differ from those highlighted in section 4 because they are not engaged in arguing for the view that group cognition is *really* cognition. A dynamical system is not a cognitive architecture or a theory of mind. It is, rather, a framework for studying systems with multiple parts that change over time. Rooted in mathematics, the principles of dynamical systems apply across disciplines as diverse as biology, physics, and economics. The dynamical systems approach has become increasingly popular in cognitive science (Chemero 2009; Port & Van Gelder 1995; Richardson et al. 2014; Spivey 2007; Thelen & Smith 1994;

Turvey 1990; Beer & Williams 2015). Systems theory takes in to account the dynamic interactions of all the factors contributing to a particular phenomenon. These factors may balance one another in order to attain stability within the system, or in some cases there will be a factor that destabilizes the system, and this leads to a new stable state. Dale et al. (2014) have argued persuasively that the framework of dynamical systems can help to integrate a variety of different approaches to understanding social interaction and that coupling dynamical systems with computational approaches to cognition might yield an approach that integrates the unique aspects of cognition within an individual and the dynamics processes that occur between individuals in social interaction.

Viewing groups as dynamical systems is less provocative than viewing them as *cognitive* systems or collective *minds*. It may seem to some that such an approach concedes too much to the critics of group cognition by focusing on dynamical interactions between individuals and avoiding talk of group belief, group intention, and group cognition. For some, however, the dynamic systems approach offers an opportunity to escape what appears to be purely philosophical and semantic disputes about the terms "mind" and "cognition" and promises to open up new avenues of research for those interested in group-level phenomena.

Notes

1. Ronald Giere makes a similar point in 2007.
2. A recent article by Robert Rupert (2004) argues the extended mind hypothesis is wrong to think of external aids (notebook) as part of the cognitive system because external memory differs radically from internal memory. We don't think those objections apply to the case of transactive memory as the transactive memory system is a meshing of traditionally conceived of individual memory systems. See Tollefsen (2005) for a similar response to worries about memory and collective cognition.
3. However, for a positive account of group consciousness, see Mathiesen (2005).

References

Adams, F. & Aizawa, K. (2008). *The Bounds of Cognition*. Oxford, UK: Blackwell Publishing.

Beer, R. & Williams, P. L. (2015). "Information Processing and Dynamics in Minimally Cognitive Agents." *Cognitive Science*, 39: 1–38.

Biro, J. (1981). "Persons as Corporate Entities and Corporations as Persons." *Nature and System*, 3: 173–80.

Block, N. (1978). "Troubles with Functionalism." *Minnesota Studies in the Philosophy of Science*, 9: 261–325.

Bratman, M. (1993). "Shared Intention." *Ethics*, 104: 97–113.

Chemero, A. (2009). *Radical Embodied Cognitive Science*. Cambridge, MA: MIT Press.

Clark, A. (2007). "Curing Cognitive Hiccups: A Defense of the Extended Mind." *The Journal of Philosophy*, 104: 163–92.

Clark, A. & Chalmers, D. (1998). "The Extended Mind." *Analysis*, 58: 10–23.

Dale, R., Fusaroli, R., Duran, N. D. & Richardson, D. C. (2014). "The Self-Organization of Human Interaction." In B. Ross (Ed.), *Psychology of Learning and Motivation* (pp. 43–95). Waltham, MA: Academic Press.

Dennett, D. (1987). *The Intentional Stance*. Cambridge, MA: MIT Press.

French, P. (1987). "Collective and Corporate Responsibility." *Philosophical Review*, 96: 117–19.

Geirsson, H. (2004). "Contra Collective Epistemic Agency." *Southwest Philosophy Review*, 20: 163–66.

Giere, R. N. (2007). "Distributed Cognition without Distributed Knowing." *Social Epistemology*, 21: 313–20.

Gilbert, M. (1989). *On Social Facts*. New York, NY: Routledge.

Horgan, T. & Tienson, J. (2002). "The Intentionality of Phenomenology and thePhenomenology of Intentionality." In D. J. Chalmers (Ed.), *Philosophy of Mind: Classicaland Contemporary Readings* (pp. 530–33). Oxford, UK: Oxford University Press.

Huebner, B. (2014). *Macrocognition: A Theory of Distributed Minds and Collective Intentionality*. Oxford, UK: Oxford University Press.

Hutchins, E. (1995). *Cognition in the Wild*. Cambridge, MA: MIT Press.

Kirsh, D. (2006). "Distributed Cognition: A Methodological Note." *Pragmatics & Cognition*, 14: 249–62.

Kirsh, D. & Maglio, P. (1994). "On Distinguishing Epistemic from Pragmatic Action." *Cognitive Science*, 18: 513–49.

LeBon, G. (1895). "The Crowd: A Study of the Popular Mind." *Project Guttenburg eText*. Accessed at www.gutenberg.org/cache/epub/445/pg445-images.html

List, C. & Pettit, P. (2014). *Group Agency: The Possibility, Design, and Status of Corporate Agents*. Oxford, UK: Oxford University Press.

Ludwig, K. (2015). "Is Distributed Cognition Group Level Cognition." *Journal of Social Ontology*, 1: 189–224.

Mathiesen, K. (2005). "Collective Consciousness." In D. W. Smith & A. L. Thomasson (Eds.), *Phenomenology and Philosophy of Mind* (pp. 235–52). Oxford, UK: Clarendon Press.

McDougall, W. (1920). *The Group Mind*. Project Guttenburg eText. Accessed at www.gutenberg.org/files/40826/40826-h/40826-h.htm

Port, R. & Van Gelder, T. (Eds.). (1995). *Mind as Motion: Explorations in the Dynamics of Cognition*. Cambridge, MA: MIT Press.

Putnam, H. (1960). "Minds and Machines." In S. Hook (Ed.), *Journal of Symbolic Logic* (pp. 57–80). New York: New York University Press.

Putnam, H. (1967). "The Nature of Mental States." In W. H. Capitan & D. D. Merrill (Eds.), *Art, Mind, and Religion* (pp. 1–23). Pittsburgh, PA: Pittsburgh University Press.

Richardson, M. J., Dale, R. & Marsh, K. L. (2014). "Complex Dynamical Systems in Social and Personality Psychology: Theory, Modeling and Analysis." In H. T. Reis & C. M. Judd. (Eds.), *Handbook of Research Methods in Social and Personality Psychology* (2nd Ed., pp. 253–82). New York: Cambridge University Press.

Rovane, C. (1998). *The Bounds of Agency: An Essay in Revisionary Metaphysics*, Princeton, NJ: Princeton University Press.

Rupert, R. D. (2004). "Challenges to the Hypothesis of Extended Cognition." *Journal of Philosophy*, 101: 389–428.

Rupert, R. D. (2005). "Minding One's Own Cognitive System: When Does a Group of Minds Constitute a Single Cognitive Unit?" *Episteme*, 1: 177–88.

Rupert, R. D. (2009). *Cognitive Systems and the Extended Mind*. Oxford, UK: Oxford University Press.

Rupert, R. D. (2011). "Empirical Arguments for Group Minds: A Critical Appraisal." *Philosophy Compass*, 6, 9: 630–39.

Rupert, R. D. (2014). "Against Group Cognitive States." In S. Chant, F. Hindriks & G. Preyer (Eds.), *From Individual to Collective Intentionality: New Essays*. Oxford, UK: Oxford University Press.

Searle, J. R. (1990). "Collective Intentions and Actions." In P. Cohen, J. Morgan & M. E. Pollack (Eds.), *Intentions in Communication* (pp. 401–16). Cambridge, MA: Bradford Books & MIT press.

Searle, J. R. (1992). *The Rediscovery of the Mind*. Cambridge, MA: MIT Press.

Searle, J. R. (1995). *The Construction of Social Reality*. New York, NY: Free Press.

Spivey, M. (2007). *The Continuity of Mind*. Oxford, UK: Oxford University Press.

Sutton, J. (2006). "Distributed Cognition: Domains and Dimensions." *Pragmatics and Cognition*, 14: 235–47.

Sutton, J., Harris, C. B., Keil, P. G. & Barnier, A. J. (2010). "The Psychology of Memory, Extended Cognition, and Socially Distributed Remembering." *Phenomenology and the Cognitive Sciences*, 9: 521–60.

Theiner, G. (2008). *From Extended Minds to Group Minds: Rethinking the Boundaries of the Mental*. Doctoral dissertation, Department of Philosophy & Cognitive Science Program, Indiana University, Bloomington.

Theiner, G. (2014). "A Beginner's Guide to Group Minds." In J. Kallestrup & M. Sprevak (Eds.), *New Waves in Philosophy of Mind* (pp. 301–22). Basingstoke, UK: Palgrave Macmillan.

Theiner, G., Allen, C. & Goldstone, R. L. (2010). "Recognizing Group Cognition." *Cognitive Systems Research*, 11: 378–95.

Theiner, G. & O'Connor, T. (2010). "The Emergence of Group Cognition." In A. Corradini & T. Connor (Eds.), *Emergence in Science and Philosophy* (pp. 78–117). New York: Routledge.

Thelen, E. & Smith, L. B. (1994). *A Dynamic Systems Approach to the Development of Cognition and Action*. Cambridge, MA: MIT Press.

Tollefsen, D. (2002). "Organizations as True Believers." *Journal of Social Philosophy*, 33: 395–411.

Tollefsen, D. (2005). "Let's Pretend!: Children and Joint Action." *Philosophy of the Social Sciences*, 35: 75–97.

Tollefsen, D. (2006). "From Extended Mind to Collective Mind." *Cognitive Systems Research*, 7: 140–50.

Tollefsen, D. (2015). *Groups as Agents*. Cambridge, UK: Polity Press.

Tollefsen, D., Dale, R. & Paxton, A. (2013). "Alignment, Transactive Memory, and Collective Cognitive Systems." *Review of Philosophy and Psychology*, 4: 49–64.

Tuomela, R. (1995). *The Importance of Us*. Stanford, CA: Stanford University Press.

Turvey, M. T. (1990). "Coordination." *American Psychologist*, 45: 938–53.

Wegner, D. M. (1987). "Transactive Memory: A Contemporary Analysis of the Group Mind." In B. Mullen & G. R. Goethals (Eds.), *Theories of Group Behavior* (pp. 185–208). New York: Springer.

Wegner, D. M., Erber, R. & Raymond, P. (1991). "Transactive Memory in Close Relationships." *Journal of Personality and Social Psychology*, 61: 923–29.

Wilson, D. S. (1997a). "Altruism and Organism: Disentangling the Themes of Multi-Level Selection Theory." *American Naturalist*, 150 (Supplement): S122–S134.

Wilson, D. S. (1997b). "Incorporating Group Selection into the Adaptionist Program: A Case Study Involving Human Decision Making." In J. Simpson & D. Kendrick (Eds.), *Evolutionary Social Psychology* (pp. 345–86). Hillsdale, NJ: Earlbaum.

Wilson, D. S., Wilczynski, C., Wells, A. & Weiser, L. (2000). "Gossip and Other Aspects of Language as Group-Level Adaptations." In C. Heyes & L. Huber (Eds.), *Evolution and Cognition* (pp. 347–65). Cambridge, MA: MIT Press.

Wilson, R. A. (2005). *The Boundaries of the Mind: The Individual in the Fragile Sciences*. Cambridge, UK: Cambridge University Press.

Wimsatt, W. C. (1986). "Forms of Aggregativity." In M. G. Grene, A. Donagan, A. N. Perovich & M. V. Wedin (Eds.), *Human Nature and Natural Knowledge* (pp. 259–91). Dordrecht: Reidel.

Woolley, A. W., Hackman, J. R., Jerde, T. E., Chabris, C. F., Bennett, S. L. & Kosslyn, S. M. (2007). "Using Brain-Based Measures to Compose Teams: How Individual Capabilities and Team Collaboration Strategies Jointly Shape Performance." *Social Neuroscience*, 2: 96–105.

Zhang, J. & Norman, D. A. (1994). "Representations in Distributed Cognitive Tasks." *Cognitive Science*, 18: 87–122.

INDEX

Note: Page numbers in *italic* indicate a figure on the corresponding page.